TRANSNATIONAL COMMERCIAL LAW

Text, Cases, and Materials

ROY GOODE

*Emeritus Professor of Law in the University of Oxford and
Emeritus Fellow of St John's College, Oxford*

HERBERT KRONKE

*Secretary-General UNIDROIT, Rome, and
Professor of Law at the University of Heidelberg*

EWAN MCKENDRICK

*Herbert Smith Professor of English Private Law and Pro-Vice-Chancellor
University of Oxford; Fellow of Lady Margaret Hall*

Consultant on International Commercial Law and Practice

JEFFREY WOOL

*Freshfields Bruckhaus Deringer, London,
and Secretary, Aviation Working Group*

OXFORD

UNIVERSITY PRESS

OXFORD
UNIVERSITY PRESS

Great Clarendon Street, Oxford OX2 6DP

Oxford University Press is a department of the University of Oxford.
It furthers the University's objective of excellence in research, scholarship,
and education by publishing worldwide in

Oxford New York

Auckland Cape Town Dar es Salaam Hong Kong Karachi
Kuala Lumpur Madrid Melbourne Mexico City Nairobi
New Delhi Shanghai Taipei Toronto

With offices in

Argentina Austria Brazil Chile Czech Republic France Greece
Guatemala Hungary Italy Japan Poland Portugal Singapore
South Korea Switzerland Thailand Turkey Ukraine Vietnam

Oxford is a registered trade mark of Oxford University Press
in the UK and in certain other countries

Published in the United States
by Oxford University Press Inc., New York

British Library Cataloguing in Publication Data
Data available

Library of Congress Cataloging in Publication Data
Data available

Typeset by Newgen Imaging Systems (P) Ltd, Chennai, India
Printed in Great Britain
on acid-free paper by
Ashford Colour Press Ltd, Gosport, Hampshire

ISBN 978–0–19–925166–7

7 9 10 8 6

1006075482

PREFACE

This book has its origins in a postgraduate course which has for many years been taught in the Oxford University BCL/MJur programme and has proved very popular with students, whether from common law, civil law, or other jurisdictions. Its primary aim is to place transnational commercial law firmly on the academic map in much the same way as other pioneering works have done for subjects such as international economic law and corporate insolvency law. A key characteristic of the subject is that it is not based on national law but is supranational in its approach. This means that this work can be used as a coursebook in all countries where the students have a reasonable command of English. Indeed, our hope is that it will encourage the development of parallel courses around the world and that the teachers will interact with each other, comparing notes, sharing experiences, and offering suggestions for improvement. We might in due course envisage an annual gathering of teachers of transnational commercial law to discuss emerging issues.

The book seeks to provide the student with an insight into the way in which uniform laws governing cross-border commercial transactions have developed, the sources of transnational commercial law, and the instruments and institutions which have helped to fashion it. Its focus is on international instruments sponsored by four organizations in particular: the International Institute for the Unification of Private Law (UNIDROIT); the United Nations and its specialist agency, the United Nations Commission on International Trade Law (UNCITRAL); the Hague Conference on Private International Law; and the International Chamber of Commerce (ICC). But we have also included instruments produced by regional organizations, notably the European Community, the Organization of American States (OAS) and Mercosur. In order to make the work as easy to use as possible, summary and full tables of contents, tables of conventions, model laws, uniform rules, codes and the like, and a very detailed index have been prepared by the publishers, Oxford University Press.

Transnational commercial law raises issues of intense theoretical as well as practical interest. But the theory can be understood only in the context of the business background, and in the second part of this work we have selected a range of typical cross-border transactions—sale, agency, banking, secured transactions, and the like—to illustrate the problems and policy issues which international lawmakers have to confront, the techniques used to surmount impediments to business, and the various ways of accommodating competing interests. We have not confined ourselves to hard law, such as international conventions, model laws, and regulations. There has been a growing appreciation of the value of soft law, for example, uniform trade rules and contract terms, and scholarly restatements of contract law such as the UNIDROIT Principles of International Commercial Contracts and their European counterpart, the Principles of European Contract Law, prepared by the Commission on European Contract Law. We hope the student will find the study of transnational commercial law as exciting and challenging as we ourselves have done.

In the preparation of this work we are indebted to a number of people. First and foremost is Jeffrey Wool, Head of Aerospace Law and Policy at Freshfields Bruckhaus Deringer and secretary and general counsel of the Aviation Working Group, the industry body for aviation finance and regulation. Jeffrey had originally been a co-author of this volume, contributing greatly to the early stages of its development, but the pressures of a busy international practice made it impossible for him to continue in that capacity. Happily we have continued to enjoy his services as a consultant on international commercial law and practice, and hope he will find the time to join in teaching courses based on this volume. He is also co-author of the companion volume to this work, *Transnational Commercial Law: Primary Materials*, produced with the present authors.

Others who helped us greatly are: Professor Alan Boyle, of Edinburgh University, who kindly read the chapter on international law and saved us from a number of errors; Professor Basil Markesinis, formerly of University College, London, and Oxford University, who provided a like service in relation to the chapter on comparative law and gave us insights into new approaches; Professor Dan Sarooshi, of Queen's College, Oxford, who gave us illumination on the rights of non-State parties affected by a State's breach of its obligations under an international convention; Professor Reinhard Zimmermann, of the Max-Planck Institute for Comparative and International Private Law, who kindly made available prior to publication an electronic copy of *The Oxford Handbook of Comparative Law*, edited by him and Professor Mathias Reimann; Luke Adams, of Edward Elgar Publishing, who was equally helpful in providing us with an advance electronic copy of the *Elgar Encyclopaedia of Comparative Law*, edited by Professor Jan Smits; Adam Kramer, Catherine Lee, and Paul-John Loewenthal, who were at different times research assistants for the project and who helped us greatly with literature searches and proofreading; and the British Academy, which generously provided us with a grant for research assistance.

Last but not least, we owe a considerable debt to Oxford University Press for steering this work through to publication. We should particularly like to thank Rachel Mullaly, senior commissioning editor; Rebecca Howes, assistant commissioning editor; Darcy Ahl, production editor; Faye Judges, commissioning assistant; John Ralph, copy-editor; Margaret Hibbert, who prepared the tables; Kim Harris, the indexer; Tony Williams, the proofreader, and Newgen Imaging Systems, the type-setters. To all of them we express our gratitude.

Roy Goode
Herbert Kronke
Ewan McKendrick

26 April 2007

ACKNOWLEDGEMENTS

Grateful acknowledgement is made to the following authors and publishers for their kind permission to reprint the copyright material which appears in this book:

Ashgate Publishing Limited

American Bar Association

American Law Institute

The British Institute of International and Comparative Law

Brill

Brooklyn Journal of International Law

Bruylant

Cambridge University Press

Centre for Commercial Law Studies Queen Mary, University of London

Dickinson School of Law

Duke University School of Law

Edward Elgar Publishing

European Journal of Law Reform

FindLaw

Hachette Livre

Hart Publishing

Helbing & Lichtenhahn

Professor Norbert Horn

Informa Law

Institute of International Banking Law & Practice

International Chamber of Commerce (ICC)

International Institute for the Unification of Private Law (UNIDROIT)

Israel Law Review Association

Iustus Vorlag

Lawyer's Co-operative Publishing

Lexis Nexis Butterworths

Louisiana Law Review

Loyola Law Review

Lustus Forlag

Michigan Journal of International Law

Michigan Law Review

Mohr Siebeck

Netherlands Law Review

Northwestern School of Law

Office for Official Publications of the European Communities

Pace University School of Law

Penguin Books

Princeton University Press

Sellier European Law Publishers

Singapore Academy of Law

Professor Rolf Sturner

Sweet & Maxwell

Texas International Law Journal

T.M.C. Asser Press

Tulane Law Review

Professor Frederick Tung

UCLA School of Law

United Nations Commission on International Trade Law (UNCITRAL)

University of Pittsburgh School of Law

University Press of Virginia & Scottish Academic Press

Professor Catherine Walsh

Wolters Kluwer

CONTENTS—SUMMARY

Table of Cases	xxix
Table of Statutes and Statutory Instruments	xxxiii
Table of Codes	xxxv
Table of International Conventions and Model Laws	xxxvii
Table of EC Treaties and Legislation	xlvii
Table of Uniform Rules, Uniform Trade Terms, Restatements and Model Forms	xlix
Table of Other Documents	liii
Table of Abbreviations	lv
Introduction	lix
Introductory Reading	lxi

I GENERAL PRINCIPLES

1. The Nature, History and Sources of Commercial Law	3
2. The Conflict of Laws in Commercial Transactions	57
3. International Law as It Affects Private Law Conventions Governing Cross-border Commercial Transactions	89
4. Comparative Law and Its Relevance to Transnational Commercial Law	133
5. The Harmonization of Commercial Law: Instruments and Institutions	191
6. The Harmonization Process	215

II A VIEW THROUGH ILLUSTRATIVE CONTRACTS AND HARMONIZING INSTRUMENTS

7. International Sales and the Vienna Sales Convention	255
8. Agency and Distribution	317
9. International Bank Payment Undertakings	347
10. Financial Leasing: the 1988 UNIDROIT Convention and the UNIDROIT Draft Model Law	389

11. Receivables Financing: the UNIDROIT Convention on
    International Factoring and the United Nations Convention
    on the Assignment of Receivables in International Trade   405

12. International Interests in Mobile Equipment and the Cape Town
    Convention and Aircraft Protocol: Adding a New Dimension
    to International Law-making   433

13. Transactions in Securities   471

III HARMONIZATION OF GENERAL CONTRACT LAW

14. Restatements of Contract Law   505

IV TRANSNATIONAL INSOLVENCY

15. Harmonization and Co-operation in Cross-border Insolvency   541

V INTERNATIONAL DISPUTE RESOLUTION

16. International Civil Procedure   581

17. International Commercial Arbitration   621

VI RECURRENT ISSUES OF HARMONIZATION

18. The Sphere of Application of a Convention; the Role of the Conflict
    of Laws; Determining the Connecting Factor; Co-existence and
    Conflicts of Instruments   687

19. Uniformity in Transnational Commercial Law   701

20. Getting to Yes: Practical and Political Problems of Harmonization   729

Index   741

CONTENTS

Table of Cases	xxix
Table of Statutes and Statutory Instruments	xxxiii
Table of Codes	xxxv
Table of International Conventions and Model Laws	xxxvii
Table of EC Treaties and Legislation	xlvii
Table of Uniform Rules, Uniform Trade Terms, Restatements and Model Forms	xlix
Table of Other Documents	liii
Table of Abbreviations	lv
Introduction	lix
Introductory Reading	lxi

I GENERAL PRINCIPLES

1. The Nature, History and Sources of Commercial Law

A. The Nature of Commercial Law

Three definitions	1.01
Commercial law	1.02
Transnational commercial law	1.03
Lex mercatoria	1.04
What drives commercial law?	1.05
A medieval example	1.06
A later example	1.07
A modern example	1.08
Commercial law and civil law	1.10
The transition from planned economies to market economies	1.14

B. The History of Commercial Law

The early and medieval codes	1.15
Characteristics of the medieval law merchant	1.20
The nationalization of commercial law	1.24
The return to internationalism and the growth of transnational commercial law	1.25
The growth of regionalism	1.31

C. The Sources of National Commercial Law | 1.32

Contract	1.33

Usage	1.34
Suppletive rules of common law	1.35
Domestic legislation	1.36
D. The Nature and Sources of Transnational Commercial Law	1.37
Is there an autonomous transnational commercial law?	1.38
The *lex mercatoria* and the conflict of laws	1.39
External validation by a court or tribunal	1.45
Determination in accordance with law	1.47
The sources of transnational commercial law	1.52
Lex mercatoria	1.53
International and regional instruments	1.54
Conscious or unconscious judicial or legislative parallelism	1.55
Contractually incorporated rules and trade terms promulgated by international organizations	1.56
Standard-term contracts	1.57
Restatements of scholars	1.58
General principles of international law	1.59
E. *Lex Mercatoria*	
The sources of the *lex mercatoria*	1.60
The normative force of usage	1.61
International conventions as evidence of usage	1.65
General principles of law	1.66
Questions	
Further reading	
2. The Conflict of Laws in Commercial Transactions	
A. The Nature of Conflict of Laws	
Definition	2.01
The structure of a conflicts rule ('meta law')	2.04
B. The Role of Conflict of Laws in International Commercial Law	
Prior to the advent of transnational commercial law	2.07
A new era: The Warsaw Convention of 1929	2.10
C. Selected Issues of General Conflict of Laws Theory	
Jurisdiction	2.14
Rules v 'approaches'	2.15
Connecting factors of particular relevance in commercial law	2.22
Contracts	2.23
Property	2.37
Other important connecting factors	2.42
Characterization	2.45

Public policy (*ordre public*)	2.48
Mandatory rules in the law of contracts	2.51
Neo-statutist theory and market regulation	2.57
Renvoi	2.58
D. The Future: Will We Continue to Need Conflict of Laws?	2.61
Questions	
Further reading	

3. International Law as It Affects Private Law Conventions Governing Cross-border Commercial Transactions

A. Nature and Sources	3.01
International law as law	3.04
Relationship between international law and soft law	3.06
Relationship between international law and domestic law	3.07
Applications of international law	3.10
Influences on international law	
Impact of sophisticated and specialized international law-making organizations	3.11
Impact of increased complexity of the international law-making process	3.12
Impact of trade and development	3.13
Impact of the enhanced role of the individual under international law	3.14
International law and the European Community	3.15
The sources of international law	3.19
Customary international law	3.21
Treaty law	3.26
B. The Typical Structure of Private Law Conventions	3.32
Preamble	3.33
Body of the Convention	3.36
Sphere of application and general provisions	3.37
Substantive rules	3.39
Final clauses	3.41
C. Interpretation of Conventions	3.47
An illustration: the Factoring Convention	3.52
Treatment of errors in a convention	3.55
A procedure for the correction of errors	3.56
Uncorrected errors and interpretation	3.57
D. Enforcement of Private Conventional Rights Against States	
The consequences of internationally wrongful acts and the concept of diplomatic protection	3.60

E. Reservations and Declarations   3.69

F. Withdrawal from a Treaty   3.70

G. Conflicts Between Conventions   3.72

Questions
Further reading

4. Comparative Law and Its Relevance to Transnational Commercial Law

A. Nature of Comparative Law and a Brief History
    Nature of comparative law   4.01
    A brief history   4.04

B. Classification of Legal Systems
    The traditional classification by family   4.07
    An issue-based classification system   4.11
    Civil law and common law   4.12
    Islamic law   4.17

C. Aims of Comparative Law   4.18
    Educational aims of comparative law   4.19
    Practical uses of comparative law   4.23
       Enhancement of understanding of one's own law   4.26
       Updating of national jurisprudence   4.28
       Aid to the drafting of new legislation   4.31
       Guide to the policy implications of a new development in national
          jurisprudence   4.32
       Development of transnational commercial law   4.33
       Refinement of the conflict of laws   4.40
       Commercial law dispute resolution   4.41
       Consistency of interpretation of uniform laws   4.42
       Consistency of determination of international trade usage 4.47
       Role of comparative law in transnational practice   4.48
    Cultural aims of comparative law   4.49

D. Methodology
    The functional approach to comparative law   4.50
    Common solutions or best solutions?   4.54
    Working methods   4.56

E. Problems
    The pitfalls of comparison
       The knowledge problem   4.59
       Language   4.62

Legal transplants and comparative law

Similarities and differences   4.63

Transplantation not attributable to comparative study   4.65

The effectiveness of legal transplants   4.70

How necessary is a knowledge of comparative law to the development
and practical application of transnational commercial law?   4.72

Questions

Further reading

5. The Harmonization of Commercial Law: Instruments and Institutions

A. Introduction

The reasons for harmonization   5.01

Substantive law harmonization and harmonization of conflicts rules   5.06

B. The Instruments of International Harmonization

International instruments intended to become legally binding   5.07

Facultative instruments   5.08

Contractually incorporated non-binding rules promulgated by
international organizations   5.11

Guides   5.15

The dialogue of sources   5.16

C. The Principal Institutions in the Harmonization of
Commercial Law

General   5.17

The Hague Conference on Private International Law   5.19

UNIDROIT   5.22

UNCITRAL   5.28

The International Chamber of Commerce (ICC)   5.32

The role of international and regional professional and industry
organizations   5.33

Co-ordination of legislative activities   5.34

Questions

Further reading

6. The Harmonization Process

A. Introduction   6.01

B. Stages in a Harmonization Project

A bright idea   6.05

Establishing the existence of a problem and support for its solution   6.06

Is the agency the most suitable for the project?   6.08

Survey of the current legal environment   6.10

Approval of the project by the relevant organ of the agency   6.13
Establishment of a study or working group and sub-groups   6.14
What type of instrument?   6.15
Distribution of drafts and consideration at meetings   6.16
Approval of the text   6.17
Committee of governmental experts   6.18
Diplomatic Conference/Session   6.19
Explanatory Report/Official Commentary   6.25
Promotion of the instrument   6.26

C. Problems of Harmonization   6.27
Over-ambition   6.30
Tensions arising in the preparation of international conventions   6.33
Technical problems   6.35
Differences in legal concepts   6.36
Drafting and language   6.37
Interpreters   6.38
Organizational problems   6.39

D. Harmonization and Regionalization   6.43

Questions
Further reading

II A VIEW THROUGH ILLUSTRATIVE CONTRACTS AND HARMONIZING INSTRUMENTS

7. International Sales and the Vienna Sales Convention

A. General Introduction   7.01

B. The Genesis of the Convention   7.02
Rabel and UNIDROIT   7.03
Assessment of the Hague Conventions   7.04
The origin of the CISG   7.07
Entry into force   7.08

C. The Sphere of Application   7.09
Types of contract covered   7.11
The internationality requirement   7.12
The connecting factor   7.14
Both parties in Contracting States   7.15
Rules of private international law leading to law of Contracting State   7.16
Exclusions from the Convention   7.30
Contracting out of the Convention   7.32

D. Interpretative Rules and the Role of Good Faith   7.36
    Autonomous interpretation   7.38
        The problem of uniformity   7.39
        Access to case law and commentaries on the CISG   7.44
    The problem of good faith   7.46
    Three views on good faith   7.47
        First view: no positive duty   7.48
        Second view: Article 7(1) imposes positive duty of good faith 7.51
        Third view: good faith as a general principle   7.55

E. Usages   7.66

F. Formation   7.70

G. The Rights and Duties of the Parties   7.72
    General provisions   7.73
    The obligations of the seller and the remedies of the buyer   7.75
    The obligations of the buyer and the remedies of the seller   7.77
    Fundamental breach   7.78
        'Breach'   7.81
        'Fundamental'   7.82

H. Interest   7.88
    Does the Convention govern determination of the rate of interest? 7.92
    What is the general principle?   7.94

I. *Force Majeure* and Exemptions for Non-Performance   7.97

J. Risk   7.101

K. Conclusion   7.104

Questions
Further reading

8. **Agency and Distribution**

A. Introduction   8.01

B. The First Company Directive (EEC)   8.06

C. The EEC Directive on Commercial Agents
    Introduction   8.09
    Scope of application   8.11
    Rights and obligations   8.12

D. The UNIDROIT Convention on Agency in the International
    Sale of Goods   8.17
    The relationship with CISG   8.20

Sphere of application 8.21
The legal effect of the acts of the agent 8.22
Termination of the agent's authority 8.24
Assessment 8.25

E. The UNIDROIT Principles of International Commercial
Contracts and the Principles of European Contract Law 334

F. Franchising
Introduction 8.29
UNIDROIT Model Franchise Disclosure Law 8.31
Scope of application 8.32
Delivery of disclosure document and information to be disclosed 8.33
Remedies 8.34
No waivers 8.35

Questions
Further reading

9. International Bank Payment Undertakings

A. Introduction
The role of banks in financing international trade 9.01
Some terminological problems 9.07
The different interests 9.08
Rules of banking practice and the International Chamber of Commerce 9.09
Why bank payment undertakings are interesting 9.10
The contract of sale as the central contract 9.13

B. Documentary Credits: The UCP and the eUCP 9.14
Classification of credits by payment method 9.17
Principles of documentary credits law 9.18
Autonomy of the credit 9.19
A documentary credit takes effect upon issue 9.20
Documentary character of the credit 9.21
Banks are concerned only with the apparent good order of the documents 9.22
Banks deal as principals, not as agents 9.23
The terms of a credit must be strictly complied with 9.24
A credit is not transferable unless expressly designated as such 9.25
The eUCP 9.26

C. Demand Guarantees: the URDG
Purpose of the URDG 9.29
Nature of a demand guarantee
Distinguished from letter of credit 9.31

Distinguished from suretyship guarantee	9.33
International character of demand guarantees	9.34
Guarantee structures	9.35
Advantages	9.36
Fundamental principles	9.37
Irrevocability and coming into effect	9.39
The demand for payment	9.40
Extend or pay demands	9.42
Termination of the guarantee	9.43
Governing law and jurisdiction	9.44
D. The International Standard Practices (ISP98)	9.46
E. The United Nations Convention on Independent Guarantees and Stand-by Letters of Credit	
Features of the UN Convention	9.51
Relationship between the Convention and the URDG	9.53
F. ICC Uniform Rules for Contract Bonds	9.54
Default	9.56
Governing law and jurisdiction	9.57
Questions	
Further reading	

10. Financial Leasing: the 1988 UNIDROIT Convention and the UNIDROIT Draft Model Law

Introduction	10.01
Background to the Leasing Convention	10.02
Sphere of application	10.07
Exclusion of Convention	10.14
Purposes of the Convention	10.15
Removal of responsibility from the lessor to the supplier	10.16
Conferment of rights against the supplier	10.19
Exculpation of lessor from liability under the leasing agreement	10.21
Liability to third parties	10.23
Protection against lessee's insolvency	10.24
Default remedies of lessor	10.26
Evaluation of the Leasing Convention	10.27
Leasing under the mobile equipment Convention and Protocol	10.28
The UNIDROIT draft Model Law	10.29
Questions	
Further reading	

11. **Receivables Financing: the UNIDROIT Convention on International Factoring and the United Nations Convention on the Assignment of Receivables in International Trade**

   A. Introduction

      The nature of receivables financing   11.01

      The need for an international regime   11.03

   B. Some Facts about Factoring

      What is factoring?   11.05

   C. The UNIDROIT Convention on International Factoring

      Genesis of the Convention   11.11

      Sphere of application   11.13

         Sphere of application ratione materiae   11.14

         Internationality   11.16

         Connecting factor   11.17

         Derogation   11.18

      Interpretation   11.19

      Removal of barriers to acquisition of receivables   11.21

      Other provisions   11.26

      Evaluation   11.28

   D. The United Nations Convention on the Assignment of Receivables in International Trade   11.29

      Nature of Convention: substantive rules and conflicts rules   11.30

      Sphere of application   11.31

      Effectiveness of assignments   11.36

      Relations between assignor and assignee   11.37

      Debtor provisions   11.38

      Priorities

         Conflict of laws rules   11.39

         Substantive law rules   11.40

   Questions

   Further reading

12. **International Interests in Mobile Equipment and the Cape Town Convention and Aircraft Protocol: Adding a New Dimension to International Law-making**

   A. Background and Key Features   12.01

      Underlying principles   12.12

      Five key features of the Convention   12.14

      Three key features of the Protocol   12.16

B. The Two-Instrument Approach   12.17

C. Sphere of Application
    When the Convention applies   12.21
    Principal matters covered by the Convention   12.22
    Definitions   12.24
    Interpretation   12.25
    Relationship between the Convention and national law   12.26

D. The Concept of the International Interest
    The international interest defined   12.27
    The nature of the international interest   12.28
    Formalities   12.31
    The connecting factor   12.32

E. Default Remedies   12.33

F. The International Registry and the Registration System
    The International Registry   12.37
    A fully automated system   12.39
    What is registrable?   12.40
    Searches and search certificates   12.42
    Duration of registration   12.43
    Liability of the Registrar   12.44
    Jurisdiction   12.45

G. Priorities
    The approach to priority rules   12.46
    Assignments   12.48

H. Insolvency   12.49

I. The Declaration System   12.50

J. Evaluation of the Convention and Protocol   12.52

Questions
Further reading

13. **Transactions in Securities**

A. Introduction
    Securities market law as amalgam of commercial and regulatory law   13.01
    Types of transaction   13.03

B. Dematerialization, Immobilization, Netting and Technology:
    Effects on Custody, Settlement and the Use of Securities
    as Collateral
    Facts and issues   13.05

C. Conflict-of-Laws Issues in the New Environment: Characterization and Connecting Factor Revisited

Framing the questions and searching for answers 13.08

Regional and global solutions 13.11

   The Hague Convention: introduction 13.12

   The PRIMA approach 13.14

   Scope of the Convention 13.15

   The Article 2(1) issues 13.16

   Characterization 13.17

   Internationality 13.19

   The applicable law: the primary rule and the fall-back rules 13.20

   The primary rule 13.22

   The fall-back rules 13.23

   Insolvency 13.24

   Public policy (ordre public*) and internationally mandatory rules* 13.25

   Relationship between transferor's law and transferee's law 13.26

   The European Community Settlement Finality Directive 13.28

   The EC Collateral Directive 13.32

National solutions 13.34

D. Substantive Issues and Solutions—National and Transnational 13.37

Questions

Further reading

III HARMONIZATION OF GENERAL CONTRACT LAW

14. Restatements of Contract Law

A. Introduction 14.01

B. Restatements of Contract Law

Introduction 14.04

The nature of the Principles 14.07

The purposes of the Principles 14.10

The scope of the Principles 14.15

The sphere of application of the Principles 14.17

   The Principles 'shall' be applied 14.18

   The Principles 'may' be applied 14.28

The substantive content of the Principles 14.41

   Freedom of contract 14.42

   Pacta sunt servanda 14.43

   Good faith 14.44

   Interpretation 14.49

   Adequate assurance of performance 14.50

Specific performance as a primary remedy	14.51
Other remedies	14.53
Hardship and change of circumstances	14.54
Assignment and novation	14.56
Agency	14.57
The Principles and mandatory rules	14.58
Questions	
Further reading	

IV TRANSNATIONAL INSOLVENCY

15. Harmonization and Co-operation in Cross-border Insolvency

A. Introduction	15.01
B. The Opposing Jurisdiction Principles	15.06
C. The UNCITRAL Model Law on Cross-Border	
Insolvency	15.13
Nature and purpose	15.14
Sphere of application	15.16
Access by foreign representative and recognition of foreign proceedings	15.18
Automatic stay	15.20
Co-operation with foreign courts and foreign representatives	15.21
D. Judicial Co-operation in Concurrent Insolvency Proceedings	15.22
E. The European Insolvency Regulation	
Background to the Regulation	15.24
Scope of the Regulation	15.25
Type of insolvency proceeding	15.26
The COMI	15.27
Applicable law	15.29
The principle of recognition	15.31
Insolvency of corporate groups	15.35
Questions	
Further reading	

V INTERNATIONAL DISPUTE RESOLUTION

16. International Civil Procedure

A. Introduction	
The nature of the problem and the challenges ahead	16.01
Sources	16.06

B. Jurisdictional Immunities   16.09

C. Jurisdiction to Adjudicate

Traditional autonomous rules in national systems   16.13

Modernization, international co-ordination and the needs of
international business

General   16.20

Party autonomy and forum selection   16.29

Discretionary limitations of jurisdiction: the doctrine of forum non
conveniens   16.38

D. Provisional and Protective Measures   16.43

E. Conduct of the Proceedings and Judicial Assistance

Service abroad of judicial documents   16.51

Taking of evidence   16.56

F. Recognition and Enforcement of Foreign Judgments

Brussels I Regulation   16.60

The Las Leñas and Buenos Aires Protocols   16.61

G. From International to Transnational Civil Procedure: the
ALI/UNIDROIT Principles of Transnational Civil Procedure

Objectives   16.62

Selected solutions   16.64

Questions

Further reading

17. **International Commercial Arbitration**

A. The Nature of International Commercial Arbitration and its
Distinguishing Features

Arbitration and litigation   17.03

Arbitration and expert determination   17.07

Arbitration and adjudication   17.10

Arbitration and alternative dispute resolution   17.12

When is arbitration 'international'?   17.14

When is arbitration 'commercial'?   17.19

B. The Harmonization of the Law of International Commercial
Arbitration   17.23

The UNCITRAL Model Law   17.27

The arbitration agreement   17.28

The composition of the arbitral tribunal   17.30

Jurisdiction of the arbitral tribunal   17.31

Conduct of arbitral proceedings   17.32

Making of award and termination of proceedings	17.33
Recourse against the award and the recognition and enforcement of awards	17.34
1958 New York Convention on the Recognition and Enforcement of Foreign Arbitral Awards	17.35
Rules of arbitration as party-determined framework for dispute settlement through arbitration	
Ad hoc arbitration and institutional arbitration	17.39
Major arbitration institutions and their rules	17.41
An outline of the UNCITRAL Rules and the ICC Rules	
Commencing the arbitration	17.43
Arbitral Tribunal	17.45
Arbitral proceedings	17.50
Arbitral awards	17.56
Costs	17.59
The principles which underpin the harmonization of international arbitration and the tensions in the modern law	17.60
C. Arbitration and the Conflict of Laws	17.67
The law governing the parties' capacity to enter into an arbitration agreement	17.70
The law governing the arbitration agreement and the performance of that agreement	17.71
The law governing the existence and proceedings of the arbitral tribunal—the *lex arbitri*	17.74
The 'delocalization' debate	17.79
The law, or the relevant legal rules, governing the substantive issues in dispute	17.110
The law governing the recognition and enforcement of the award	17.123
D. The Review of Arbitral Awards	17.124
E. Recognition and Enforcement of Arbitral Awards	17.133
Questions	
Further reading	

VI RECURRENT ISSUES OF HARMONIZATION

18. The Sphere of Application of a Convention; the Role of the Conflict of Laws; Determining the Connecting Factor; Co-existence and Conflicts of Instruments

A. Sphere of Application in General	18.01
B. The Role of the Conflict of Laws	18.06

C. The Selection of the Connecting Factor 18.08

D. Co-existence, Concurrence, and Conflicts of Conventions 18.11

Questions

Further reading

19. **Uniformity in Transnational Commercial Law**

A. The Obstacles to Achieving and Maintaining Uniformity 19.01

B. Responses (I): Public International Law and its Reception in
    Domestic Law 19.05

C. Responses (II): Devices in Private-Law Instruments 19.07

D. Uniformity Through Interpretation in a Uniform System? 19.10

E. Reservations and Declarations 19.13

F. Structural Issues and Technical Support Devices for Achieving and
    Maintaining Uniformity 19.15

G. Contract Practice 19.22

H. Do Divergences Matter? 19.23

Questions

Further reading

20. **Getting to Yes: Practical and Political Problems of Harmonization**

A. Introduction 20.01

B. Organizational Issues 20.04

C. Cultural and Economic Issues 20.18

D. Post-Adoption Stage: Imperatives and Shortcomings 20.21

Questions

Further reading

Index 741

TABLE OF CASES

Aegean Sea Continental Shelf case (Greece v Turkey) ICJ Rep 1978 p 3 . . . . 16.43
'Agent Orange' Product Liability Litigation, re 580 F Supp 690 (ED NY, 1984) 2.12
Air France v Haddad, judgment of 19 June 1997, Cour d'Appel de Paris 4.44
Air France v Saks 470 US 392, 105 S Ct 1338 (1985) 4.44
Aiton v Transfield, unreported 1 October 1999, SC New South Wales 14.45
Alfred Dunhill of London Inc v Republic of Cuba 425 US 682 (1976), 69 S Ct 1854,
      15 ILM (1976) 735 . . . . 4.29
Ali Shipping Corp v Shipyard Trogir [1999] 1 WLR 314, CA 17.06
AMB Imballaggi Plastici Srl v Pacflex Ltd [1999] 2 All ER (Comm) 249, CA 8.15
AMCO Asia Corp and others v Republic of Indonesia (1983) 1 ICSID Rep 389 . . . . 3.20
Arab Republic of Egypt v Chromalloy Air Services 939 F Supp 907
      (DCC 1996) 17.91–17.109
Asahi Metal Industry Co Ltd v Superior Court of California, Solano County 480 US 102,
      107 S Ct 1026 (1987) 16.22
Associated Electric and Gas Insurance Services Ltd v European Reinsurance Company of
      Zurich [2003] UKPC 11, [2003] 1 WLR 1041 . . . . 17.06
Atlantic Star, The [1974] AC 436 . . . . 16.38

Babanaft International Co SA v Bassatne [1990] Ch 13, CA 16.47
Baker Marine (Nig) Ltd v Chevron (Nig) Ltd 191 F 3d 194 (US Ct App
      (2nd Cir) 1999) 17.91
Banco Santander SA v Bayern Ltd [2000] 1 All ER (Comm) 776 . . . . 9.17
Bank Mellat v Helleniki Techniki SA [1984] QB 291, CA 17.94
Barcelona Traction, Light and Power Case (Belgium v Spain) (1970) ICJ
      Rep 3 . . . . 3.20, 3.63
Barrett McKenzie & Co v Escada (UK) Ltd [2001] ECC 50, QBD 8.16
Beam Technology (Mfg) Pte Ltd v Standard Chartered Bank [2003] 1 SLR 597 . . . . 9.22
Black and White Taxicab & Transfer Co v Brown and Yellow Taxicab & Transfer Co 276 US 518,
      533–4 (1928) 2.12
Bobux Marketing Ltd v Raynor Marketing Ltd [2002] 1 NZLR 506 . . . . 14.45
Bottling Companies v Pepsi Cola Panamerica, 9 October 1997, SC Venezuela 14.37
Bremen (The) v Zapata Off-Shore Co 407 US 1, 92 S Ct 1907 (1972) 2.26
Bruynzeel Deurenfabrik NV v Ministre d'Etat aux Affaires Etrangères de la République
      Malgache, Cass le civ 30 June 1976, 104 JDI 114 (1977) 17.85
Butler Machine Tool Co Ltd v Ex-Cell-O Corporation (England) Ltd [1979]
      1 WLR 401, CA 7.71

Cable and Wireless plc v IBM United Kingdom Ltd [2003] EWHC 316, QBD 17.13
Carnival Cruise Lines Inc v Shute 499 US 585, 111 S Ct 1522 (1991) 16.30
Castell v De Greef, Cape High Court Full Bench, South Africa 1994 (4) SA 408 (c) 4.61
Chorzów Factory Case (Interpretation of Judgments 7 and 8, Germany v Poland)
      (1928) PCIJ (Series A) No 17, 47 . . . . 3.20, 3.60
Colonial Bank v Cady, London Chartered Bank of Australia v Cady (1890)
      15 App Cas 267, HL; affg sub nom Williams v Colonial Bank, Williams v London
      Chartered Bank of Australia (1888) 38 Ch D 388, CA 13.08

Compania Naviera Vascongada v SS Cristina [1938] AC 485 . . . . 16.10
Corocraft v Pan American Airways [1969] 1 QB 616 . . . . 19.05
Cox v Troy (1822) 5 B & Ald 474, 480; 106 ER 1264, 1266 . . . . 4.14
Crédit Suisse Fides Trust SA v Cuoghi [1998] QB 818, CA 16.47, 16.49
Culmer, *re* 25 BLR 621 (Bankr. SDNY 1982) 15.08
Custom Made Commercial Ltd v Stawa Metallbau GmbH Case C-288/92 [1994]
    ECR I-2913 . . . . 16.27, 19.09

Delchi Carrier SpA v Rotorex Corp 71 F 3d 1024 (US Ct of Apps (2nd Cir)
    1995) 7.40, 7.85
Deutsche Schachtbau und Tiefbohrgesellschaft mbH v Shell International Petroleum Co Ltd
    [1990] 1 AC 295 (HL) 310 . . . . 17.73
Direction der Disconto-Gesellschaft v US Steel Corp 267 US 22, 45 S Ct 207 (1925) 13.08
Director General of Fair Trading v First National Bank [2001] UKHL 52,
    [2002] 1 AC 481 . . . . 14.44
Duffen v Frabo SPA (No 2) [2000] 1 Lloyd's Rep 180
    (CC (Central London)) 198 . . . . 8.16

Eastern Airlines Inc v Floyd 499 US 530 (1991), US SC 19.04
Edward Owen Engineering Ltd v Barclays Bank International Ltd [1978]
    QB 159 . . . . 9.22
Erie RR v Tompkins 304 US 64, 90 F 2d 603 (US Ct of Apps (2nd Cir)) (1938) 2.12
Esso Australia Resources Ltd v Plowman (1995) 183 CLR 10, HC. 17.06
Eurofood IFC Ltd [2004] 1 EHC 54, [2004] BCC 383 Irish HC; [2006]
    1 ESC 41 Irish SC; Case C-341/04, Opinion 27 September 2005; ECJ Grand
    Chamber, 2 May 2006 . . . . 15.28, 15.32, 15.33, 15.34
Everfresh Beverages Inc and Sundance Beverages Inc US Bankcy Ct SDNY Case Nos
    B45405 and 45406 (JHG), Ontario Ct (General Division) in Bankcy,
    Case No 32–077978 (1995) 15.22

Fairchild v Glenhaven Funeral Services Ltd [2002] 1 AC 32, HL 4.30, 4.61
Fontaine et Bertin v France Nos 38410/97 and 40373/98 [2003] ECHR 336 . . . . 4.54
Forgo, *re* 10 Clunet 64 (1883), Cour de Cassation 2.58, 2.59
Fothergill v Monarch Airlines Ltd [1981] AC 251, HL. 4.45, 19.04, 19.05
Fung Sang Trading Ltd v Kai Sun Sea Products and Food Co Ltd [1992]
    1 HKLR 40, HC. 17.17

GEC Marconi Systems Pty Ltd v BHP Information Technology Pty Ltd, unreported
    12 February 2003, Federal Ct Australia 14.45
General Reinsurance Corp v Forsakringsaktiebolgat Fennia Patria [1983]
    QB 856, CA 1.61
Gian Singh & Co Ltd v Banque de l'Indochine [1974] 1 WLR 1234 . . . . 9.22
Gillies Ramsay Diamond v PJW Enterprises Ltd [2004] BLR 131, Court of Session
    (Inner House) 17.11
Greatorex v Greatorex [2000] 1 WLR 1976, QBD 4.30

Hadley v Baxendale (1854) 9 Exch 341, 156 ER 145 . . . . 7.40
Hans-Hermann Mietz v Intership Yachting Sneek BV Case C-99/96 [1999]
    ECR I-2277 . . . . 16.48
Haya de la Torre Case (Colombia v Peru), ICJ Rep 1951, p 71 . . . . 3.23
Hazell v Hammersmith and Fulham LBC [1992] 2 AC 1, HL. 1.09
Helicopteros Nacionales de Colombia SA v Hall 466 US 408, 104 S Ct
    1868 (1984) 16.22

Hilmarton Ltd v Omnium de Traitement et de Valorisation (OTV) (1995) XX Ybk
      Commercial Arbitration 663, [1993] Revue de l'arbitrage 317 . . . . 17.87–17.90,
                                                                        17.93, 17.99, 17.105, 17.138
Hollandia, The [1983] AC 565 . . . . 19.04
Hughes Aircraft Systems International v Airservices Australia (1997) 146 ALR 1, Federal Ct,
      Australia 14.45

Ingmar GB Ltd v Eaton Leonard Technologies Inc [2002] ECC 5, QBD. 8.16
International Shoe Co v State of Washington 326 US 310, 66 S Ct 154
      (1945) 16.20, 16.21
International Trustee for the Protection of Bondholders Aktiengesellschaft v R [1936]
      3 All ER 407, CA 4.47

J I McWilliam Co Inc v Mediterranean Shipping Co SA [2005] 2 AC 423 . . . . 19.04
James Buchanan & Co Ltd v Babco Forwarding & Shipping (UK) Ltd [1978]
      AC 141, HL 4.45, 18.12, 19.05
Jones v Sherwood Computer Services plc [1992] 1 WLR 277, CA 17.08

King v T Tunnock Co Ltd 2000 SC 424, 435, 438 . . . . 8.15
Kleinwort Benson Ltd v Lincoln CC [1999] 2 AC 349, HL. 4.32
Kress v France no 39594/98 [2001] ECHR-VI 382 . . . . 4.54

Libyan Arab Foreign Bank v Bankers Trust Co [1989] QB 728 . . . . 1.62
Libyan General National Maritime Transport Co (LGN)/Götaverken Arendal AB case
      Court of Appeals, Paris, 21 Feb 1980, (1980) Rev de l'Arb 107, (1981)
      6 YB Comm Arb 221. . . . . 17.81–17.86, 17.138
Livent (US) Inc, *re* (Ontario Superior Ct of Justice, 1999) 15.23
Lotus Case (France v Turkey) (1927) PCU Rep Series A No 10, p 18 . . . . 3.23
Loucks v Standard Oil Co of New York 224 NY 99, 120 NE 198 (1918). 2.49
Lubbe v Cape plc [2000] 1 WLR 1545, HL. 16.38
Luke v Lyde (1759) 2 Burr 883, 887; 97 ER 614, 617 . . . . 2.12

M/S Bremen v Zapata Off-Shore Co 407 US 1, 92 S Ct 1907 (1972) 16.30
McFarlane v Tayside Health Board [2002] 2 AC 59, HL. 4.61
Macmillan Inc v Bishopsgate Investment Trust plc (No 3) [1995] 1 WLR 978, 987–1010;
      [1996] 1 WLR 387, CA. 2.46, 13.08, 13.10
Macob Civil Engineering Ltd v Morrison Construction Ltd [1999] BLR 93
      (QBD) 97 . . . . 17.10
MacShannon v Rockware Glass Ltd [1978] AC 795 . . . . 16.38
Mainschiffahrts-Genossenschaft eG (MSG) v Les Gravières Rhénanes SARL Case
      C-106/95 [1997] ECR I-911 . . . . 16.33, 16.34
Mareva Compania Naviera SA v International Bulkcarriers SA [1975]
      2 Lloyd's Rep 509 . . . . 16.46, 16.49
Metropolitan Life Insurance Company v Robertson-Ceco Corp 84 F 3d 560
      (2nd Cir 1996) 16.22
Mitsubishi Motors Corp v Soler Chrysler-Plymouth Inc 473 US 614, 105 S Ct 3346
      (1985) 16.30, 17.29
Montrod Ltd v Grundkötter Fleischvertriebs GmbH [2002] 1 WLR 1975 . . . . 9.22
Moore v Piretta PTA Ltd [1998] 1 All ER 174, QBD 8.15
Morris v KLM Royal Dutch Airlines [2002] QB 100, CA 19.04

North Sea Continental Shelf Case, ICJ Rep 1969, p 3; ILR, p 29 . . . . 3.06, 3.23
Nottebohm Case (Liechtenstein v Guatemala) (1955) ICJ Rep 4, ICJ 3.63

Omni Capital International Ltd v Rudolf Wolff & Co 484 US 97,
    108 S Ct 404 (1987) 16.22
Omnium de Traitement et de Valorisation (OTV) v Hilmarton Ltd [1999] 2 All
    ER 146, QBD. 17.90
Orbisphere Corp v United States 726 F Supp 1344 (US Court Intl Trade, 1989) 7.33
Owusu v NB Jackson (t/a Villa Holidays Bal-Inn Villas) and others Case C-281/02 ECJ,
    1 March 2005 . . . . 16.40

Page v Combined Shipping and Trading Ltd [1997] 3 All ER 656, CA. 8.15
Paul Smith Ltd v H & S International Holding Inc [1991] 2 Lloyd's Rep 127,
    QBD 17.74
Pennsylvania Co for Insurance on Lives and Granting Annuities v United Rlys of Havana and
    Regla Warehouses Ltd (1939) 26 F Supp 379 . . . . 13.08
Petromec Inc v Petroleo Brasileiro SA Petrobas [2005] EWCA Civ 891, [2005]
    All ER (D) 209 . . . . 14.44
Philippine Admiral, The [1977] AC 373, 402 . . . . 4.29
Playa Larga v I Congreso del Partido [1983] 1 AC 244, HL. 4.30

Rahimtoola v Nizam of Hyderabad [1958] AC 379, 422 . . . . 4.29
Republic of Haiti v Duvalier [1990] 1 QB 202, CA 16.47
Richards v Lloyd's of London 135 F 3d 1289 (9th Cir 1998). 16.30
Rodriguez de Quijas v Shearson/American Express Inc 490 US 477,
    109 S Ct 1917 (1989) 16.30
Roy v MR Pearlman Ltd 1999 SC 459 (OH) 469 . . . . 8.15

Scherk v Alberto-Culver Co 417 US 506, 94 S Ct 2449 (1974) 16.30
Shaffer v Heitner 433 US 186, 97 S Ct 2569 (1977) 16.22
Shierson v Vlieland-Boddy [2005] EWCA Civ 974, [2005] 1 WLR 3966, CA. 15.34
Société Nationale Industrielle Aérospatiale v US District Court for the Southern District of
    Iowa 482 US 522 (1987). 16.57
South West Africa Cases, ICJ Rep 1966, p 3. . . . . 3.23
Spiliada Maritime Corp v Cansulex Ltd [1987] AC 460. . . . . 16.38
SS Wimbledon Case (Britain v Germany) (192) PCIJ (Series A) No 1, 25 . . . . 3.09
Stag Line Ltd v Foscolo Mango & Co Ltd [1932] AC 328, 350. . . . . 4.45, 19.05
Star Shipping SA v China National Foreign Trade Transportation Corp (The Star Texas)
    [1993] 2 Lloyd's Rep 445. . . . . 17.94
Swift v Tyson 41 US 1, 10 L Ed 865 (1842) 2.12

Thai-Europe Tapioca Service Ltd v Government of Pakistan, Directorate of Agricultural Supplies
    [1975] 1 WLR 1485, 1491 . . . . 4.29
Tigana Ltd v Decoro Ltd [2003] EWHC 23, QBD 8.16
Timeload Ltd v British Telecommunications plc [1995] EMLR 459 . . . . 14.44

TABLE OF STATUTES AND STATUTORY INSTRUMENTS

CANADA

Business Corporations Act, RSO 1990,
    Cb-16 . . . . 15.23
Companies Creditors Arrangements
    Act, RSO 1985, c C-36 . . . . 15.23

FRANCE

Law on International Arbitration,
    1981 . . . . 1.67
Loi Badinter, 1985 . . . . 4.31
Loi Dailly, 2 January 1981, modified
    by law 24 January 1984 . . . . 11.30

GERMANY

Kartellgesetz, 1923 . . . . 4.31
Law of Obligations, 2002 . . . . 4.31, 4.33
Law on Securities Custody
    (Depotgesetz) §17a 13.35

PRUSSIA

Allgemeine Landrecht 1794 . . . . 1.10
Company Law 1843 . . . . 4.31

UNITED KINGDOM

Statutes

Arbitration Act 1979 . . . . 17.124
Arbitration Act 1996 . . . . 17.14
    s 1 . . . . 17.61
    s 69 . . . . 17.131, 17.132
    s 69(1) 17.132
    s 69(3) 17.132
    s 70(2) 17.131
    s 70(3) 17.131
Carriage of Goods by Road Act
    1965 . . . . 19.05
Carriage of Goods by Sea Act
    1924 . . . . 19.05
    Schedule (Hague Rules), Art III,
        r 1 . . . . 19.05

Companies Act 1985
    s 425 . . . . 15.22
Contracts (Applicable Law)
    Act 1990 . . . . 13.08
Contracts (Rights of Third Parties)
    Act 1999 . . . . 4.31
Housing Grants, Construction and
    Regeneration Act 1996 . . . . 17.10
Insolvency Act 1986
    s 426 . . . . 15.22
Law Commissions Act 1965
    s 3(1)(f) 4.31
Local Government Act 1997
    ss 5–7 . . . . 1.09
Sale of Goods Act 1979
    s 13 . . . . 7.86
    s 14 . . . . 7.86
    s 15 . . . . 7.86
    s 15A 7.86
    s 17 . . . . 19.02
    s 18, r 1 . . . . 2.05
State Immunity Act 1978 . . . . 16.10
Supreme Court Act 1981
    s 37(3) 16.46

Statutory Instruments

Commercial Agents (Council Directive)
    Regulations 1993,
        SI 1993/3053 . . . . 8.09
    Reg 17(6) 8.15
    Reg 17(7) 8.15
Civil Procedure Rules (CPR)
    r 25(1)(f) 16.46
Sale and Supply of Goods to
    Consumers Regulations 2002,
        SI 2002/3045 . . . . 7.13

UNITED STATES OF AMERICA

Constitution, Art VI (Supremacy
    clause) 16.52
Foreign Sovereign Immunities
    Act 1976 . . . . 4.29, 16.10

Securities Exchange Act 1934 (15 USC 78
    (m)–(n))
  ss 13(d), (e) 13.02
  ss 14(d)–(f) 13.02
Sherman Antitrust Act 1890. . . . . 4.31
Williams Act 1968. . . . . 13.02

Federal Rules of Civil Procedure
    (FRCP)
  r 28(b) 16.56

New York
  CPLR §302(a)(1) 16.23

TABLE OF CODES

CANADA

Québec
  Civil Code, 1994 . . . . 4.31
  Art 1438 . . . . 19.02

CHINA

Contract Code, 1999 . . . . 4.31

FRANCE

Civil Code 1.10, 4.07, 4.13,
                     4.31, 4.66, 4.67, 6.06
  Art 14 . . . . 16.14
  Art 1494 . . . . 17.73
Commercial Code, 1807 . . . . 1.10, 4.31, 8.03

GERMANY

Civil Code 1900 . . . . 4.31
Civil Code (Bürgerliches
    Geseztbuch—BGB) 1.24, 4.07,
               4.67, 4.68, 7.13, 16.65
  §242 . . . . 19.02
  §987 ff 4.24
Civil Procedure Code
  §23 . . . . 16.16, 16.18, 16.19
Commercial Code 1900 . . . . 1.10
Commercial Code (Handelsgesetzbuch—
    HGB) 1.13
  §§84–92c 8.03
  §89b 8.15

JAPAN

Civil Code, 1896 . . . . 4.31

NETHERLANDS

Civil Code, 1838 . . . . 20.19
Civil Code (Burgerlijk Wetboek), 1992 . . . 4.31
  Art 126(3) 16.47
  Art 289 *et seq* 16.47

  Arts 428–45 . . . . 8.03
  Art 1022(2) 16.47

SWITZERLAND

Code of Obligations 7.16
Civil Code, 1907 . . . . 4.31, 4.68, 8.03

UNITED STATES OF AMERICA

Federal Bankruptcy Code
  Ch 7 . . . . 15.23
  Ch 11 . . . . 15.22, 15.23
  s 101(41) 15.23
  s 304 . . . . 15.08
  s 363 . . . . 15.23
  s 363(m) 15.23
  s 365 . . . . 15.23
  s 508a 15.23
  s 510 . . . . 15.23
  s 544 . . . . 15.23
  s 545 . . . . 15.23
  s 546 . . . . 15.23
  s 547 . . . . 15.23
  s 548 . . . . 15.23
  s 549 . . . . 15.23
  s 550 . . . . 15.23
  s 551 . . . . 15.23
  s 1107 . . . . 15.23
  s 1108 . . . . 15.23
  s 1110 . . . . 12.49
  s 1121 . . . . 15.23
Uniform Commercial Code 1.11, 4.13,
             4.67, 5.08, 7.20, 7.23,
                  11.22, 14.11
  §1–205 . . . . 1.64
  §1–205(2) 1.64
  §1–301 . . . . 2.33
  Art 2 . . . . 7.41, 7.106
  §2–207 . . . . 7.71
  §2–609 . . . . 14.50
  Art 8 . . . . 13.06, 13.37, 13.38, 13.41

Uniform Commercial Code (*cont.*)

§8–110 . . . . 13.34

§8–503–8–508 . . . . 13.38

Art 9 . . . . 11.39, 12.04

§9–406(d) 11.24, 11.25, 14.56

New York

Uniform Commercial Code (NYUCC)

Art 8 . . . . 13.08

Art 8.105(1) 13.08

Art 8.106 . . . . 13.08

TABLE OF INTERNATIONAL CONVENTIONS
AND MODEL LAWS

Agreement between Estonia and Poland on
    Granting Legal Assistance and Legal
    Relations in Civil, Labour and
    Criminal Matters, 1998 . . . . 16.07
Berne Copyright Convention (Revised)
    1886 . . . . 6.45
Brussels Convention on Jurisdiction and
    Recognition and Enforcement, 1968
    (see also EC Regulation 44/2001
    (Brussels I Regulation)) 14.03,
        16.06, 16.24, 16.39, 19.09
    Title II, ss 2–6 . . . . 16.47
    Title III 16.48
    Art 1 . . . . 16.47
    Art 2 . . . . 16.40
    Art 2(1) 19.09
    Art 3 . . . . 16.17, 16.47
    Arts 5–18 . . . . 16.47
    Art 5 . . . . 16.47
    Art 5(1) 19.09
    Art 17 . . . . 16.29
    Art 24 . . . . 16.45, 16.47
Brussels International Convention on
    Civil Liability for Oil Pollution
    Damage, 1969 . . . . 10.23
Cape Town Convention on International
    Interests in Mobile Equipment,
    2001 . . . . 1.28, 2.40, 2.62,
        3.02, 3.31, 3.33, 3.38, 3.40, 3.41,
        3.42, 3.43, 3.44, 3.53, 3.56, 3.57,
        3.65, 5.05, 5.34, 6.20, 6.22, 6.33,
        6.39, 6.42, 6.44, 6.45, 10.27, 10.28,
        10.29, 11.04, 11.15, 11.29, Ch 12,
        18.05, 18.12, 18.15, 19.07, 19.08,
        19.14, 19.18, 19.21, 19.22, 20.01,
        20.07, 20.08, 20.10, 20.12, 20.14,
            20.19, 20.22
    Ch III 12.22, 12.31, 12.33, 12.35
    Ch VIII 12.22
    Ch IX 12.48
    Preamble 19.07
    Art 1 . . . . 2.47, 12.26, 12.27, 12.37
    Art 1(a) 11.04
    Art 1(c) 11.04

Art 1(2)(p) 12.32
Art 2 . . . . 12.19, 12.21, 12.26, 18.05
Art 2(2) 12.26, 12.27, 18.08
Art 2(2)(c) 12.30
Art 2(3) 18.05
Art 2(4) 18.06, 18.08
Art 3 . . . . 12.19, 12.21, 12.32, 18.05
Art 3(1) 18.09
Art 4 . . . . 12.21, 12.32, 18.05
Art 4(1)(a) 2.47
Art 5 . . . . 12.25, 19.07
Art 5(1) 2.47, 19.08, 19.11
Art 5(2) 2.47, 12.26
Art 5(3) 2.47, 12.25
Art 7 . . . . 2.47, 12.21, 12.26, 12.31
Art 7(b) 12.30
Art 8 . . . . 12.29
Arts 8(3)–(6) 12.33
Art 8(3) 3.65
Arts 8(5)–(6) 12.33
Art 9 . . . . 12.29
Arts 9(1)–(2) 12.33
Art 9(1) 12.50
Art 9(3) 12.33
Art 9(4) 12.33
Art 10 . . . . 12.29, 12.33, 12.50
Art 12 . . . . 12.26, 12.33, 18.06
Art 13 . . . . 3.65, 3.66, 12.34, 16.45
Art 13(2) 12.33
Art 14 . . . . 12.33
Art 15 . . . . 12.33
Art 16 . . . . 12.37, 12.40
Art 16(1)(a) 12.37
Art 17 . . . . 3.67
Art 17(2)(d) 12.37
Art 17(3) 3.28
Art 20 . . . . 12.40
Art 20(1) 12.43
Art 21 . . . . 12.43
Art 22(1) 12.42
Art 22(3) 12.42
Art 24(4) 3.43
Art 26 . . . . 12.42
Art 27 . . . . 3.67

Cape Town Convention on International
   Interests in Mobile Equipment (*cont.*)
   Art 27(1) 3.28
   Art 27(3). 3.28, 3.67
   Art 28(1) 12.44
   Art 28(2) 12.37
   Art 28(3) 12.37
   Art 29 . . . . 12.46
   Art 29(1) (*ex* Art 28(1)) 12.37, 12.46
   Art 29(3)(b). 12.47
   Art 29(4) 12.29, 12.47
   Art 29(7) 18.06
   Art 30 . . . . 12.49, 18.06
   Art 31(1) 12.48
   Art 32 . . . . 12.48
   Art 32(3) 12.48
   Art 36 . . . . 12.48
   Art 39 . . . . 12.26, 12.50, 18.06
   Art 40 . . . . 12.50, 18.06
   Art 42 . . . . 3.66, 16.31
   Art 43 . . . . 3.65, 3.66, 16.45
   Art 44 . . . . 3.66
   Art 44(1) 12.45
   Art 45*bis*. 3.44, 18.15
   Art 48 . . . . 3.14
   Art 48(2) 12.50
   Art 48(3) 6.45
   Art 52 . . . . 12.50
   Art 53 . . . . 12.50
   Art 54 . . . . 12.15, 12.33
   Art 54(2) 3.46, 12.50
   Art 55 . . . . 3.65
   Art 60 . . . . 12.50
   Art 61 . . . . 19.20
   Art 61(2)(b). 19.20
Aircraft Protocol to the Cape Town
   Convention 2001. . . . . 2.47, 3.57,
           3.65, 3.67, 5.05, 6.33, 10.27,
           10.28, Ch 12, 18.15, 19.14,
                19.22, 20.14
   Art I 12.21
   Art II. 12.19
   Art III. 12.27
   Art IV. 18.09
   Art IV(1) 12.21, 12.32
   Art VIII 12.16, 12.25
   Art IX. 12.36
   Art X. 12.34
   Art X(2) 3.66
   Art XI 3.16, 12.16, 12.34, 12.49
   Art XI (Alt A). 12.16
   Art XI (Alt A(5)(b)) 18.06
   Art XI (Alt A(11)) 18.06
   Art XI (Alt B(2)(b)). 18.06

Art XIII 12.16, 12.36
Art XVI 12.47
Art XVI(2). 18.06
Art XVII. 3.68
Art XIX 12.47
Art XXI. 3.66, 16.31
Art XXXVI. 19.20
Art XXXVI(2)(b) 19.20
Rail Protocol to the Cape Town Convention
   (draft) (*see also* Luxembourg
   Protocol) 12.09, 12.17
Space Protocol to the Cape Town Convention
   (draft) 12.09,
                12.17, 20.08
Chicago Convention on International
   Civil Aviation 1944 . . . . 12.32
   Art 47 . . . . 3.68
Contractual Joint Venture Model
   Agreements, 2004, ITC 5.13
Convention between Belgium and France on
   Jurisdiction and the Validity and
   Enforcement of Judgments, Arbitration
   Awards and Authentic Instruments,
   1899. . . . . 16.10
Convention Concerning International
   Carriage by Rail (COTIF)
   1980. . . . . 20.01
Convention for the Execution of Foreign
   Arbitral Awards, Geneva, 1927. . . . 17.23
Convention for the Unification of Certain
   Rules Relating to Maritime Liens and
   Mortgages, 1926
   Art 1 . . . . 2.39
Convention for the Unification of Certain
   Rules Relating to the Precautionary
   Attachment of Aircraft,
   Rome, 1933. . . . . 12.10
Convention on Agency in the International
   Sale of Goods, Geneva
   1983. 6.30, 8.27
Convention on International Civil
   Aviation, Chicago, 1944 . . . . 12.10
Convention on the Contract for the
   International Carriage of Goods by
   Road (CMR), Geneva,1956. . . . . . 5.07,
              18.12, 18.13, 19.05,
             19.11, 19.16, 20.01
   Art 1(2) 18.12
   Art 23(4) 19.05
Convention on the Limitation
   Period. 18.15
Council of Europe Convention on Certain
   International Aspects of Bankruptcy,
   Istanbul, 1990. . . . . 15.04

EC Contracts Convention
Art 3 . . . . 14.23, 14.24, 14.25
European Bank for Reconstruction and
    Development (EBRD) Model law on
    secured transactions, 1994 . . . . 1.14
European Convention on Human Rights
    Art 6 . . . . 4.54
European Convention on Insolvency
    Proceedings, 1995 . . . . 15.04, 15.24
European Convention on State Immunity,
    Basle 1972 . . . . 16.10
Art 4(1) 4.29
Art 20 . . . . 16.12
European Convention Providing a Uniform
    Law on Arbitration, 1962 . . . . 5.10
General Conditions of the United Nations
    Economic Commission for Europe
    (UNECE) 1.67
Geneva Convention on Maritime Liens and
    Mortgages, 1993
    Art 1 . . . . 2.39
    Art 2 . . . . 2.39
Geneva Convention on the International
    Recognition of Rights in Aircraft,
    1948 . . . . 2.39, 12.10
Grain and Feed Trade Association (GAFTA)
    Contract Form No. 100 . . . . 1.50
Hague Agency Convention, 1978 . . . . . . 2.30,
                    2.36, 2.53, 18.15
    Art 16 . . . . 2.53
Hague Choice of Forum Convention,
    2005 . . . . 6.44
Hague Conference on Private International
    Law 1.25, 3.11, 5.19–5.21, 20.11
    Statute of the Hague Conference on Private
    International Law, 1955 . . . . . 5.19, 5.20
    Amendment 2005 . . . . 5.20
Hague Convention on Choice of Court
    Agreements, 2005 . . . . 16.41, 17.35
    Art 3(c)(i) 16.37
    Art 5(1) 16.37
    Art 6 . . . . 16.37
Hague Convention on Civil Procedure,
    1954 . . . . 16.55
Hague Convention on Marriage, 1902 . . . 5.06
Hague Convention on the International
    Protection of Adults, 2000 . . . . 6.45
Hague Convention on the Law Applicable
    to Certain Rights in Respect of
    Securities held with an Intermediary
    (Hague Securities Convention)
    2002 . . . . 5.20, 6.42, 6.44, 11.15,
                13.12–13.27, 13.33, 13.36,
            18.07, 19.04, 19.14, 19.18, 20.01

Art 1(1)(f) 13.15
Art 2(1) 2.30, 6.34, 13.15,
                    13.16, 13.18, 13.20,
                        13.22, 13.25
Art 2(2) 13.18
Art 3 . . . . 13.19
Art 4 . . . . 2.41, 13.22
Art 4(1) 2.30, 6.34, 13.26
Art 5 . . . . 13.19, 13.22, 13.23
Art 6 . . . . 13.21
Art 8 . . . . 13.24
Art 11(1) 2.50, 13.25
Art 11(2) 13.25
Art 11(3) 2.56, 13.25
Hague Convention on the Service Abroad
    of Judicial and Extrajudicial Documents
    in Civil and Commercial Matters,
    1965 . . . . . . 16.06, 16.51, 16.52, 16.55
    Art 1 . . . . 16.52
    Arts 2–6 . . . . 16.51
    Art 8 . . . . 16.51
    Art 9 . . . . 16.51
    Art 10 . . . . 16.51
    Art 13 . . . . 16.55
    Art 13(1) 16.54
    Art 13(2) 16.54
Hague Convention on the Taking of Evidence
    Abroad in Civil and Commercial
    Matters, 1970 . . . . 16.06, 16.56
    Art 1 . . . . 16.56
    Art 2 . . . . 16.56
    Art 3 . . . . 16.56
    Art 9 . . . . 16.57
    Arts 15–22 . . . . 16.58
    Art 23 . . . . 16.57
    Art 27 . . . . 16.56
Hague Convention on Uniform Sales Law
    1964 . . . . 1.67, 2.12, 2.61, 7.03,
                    7.06, 14.11, 18.01,
                        18.09, 18.15
Hague Custody Convention, 1996 . . . . . 6.45
Hague Sales Convention, 1980 . . . . 18.09
    Art II 18.14
Hague Sales Convention, 1986 . . . 2.30, 2.36
Hague-Visby Rules on Bills of Lading,
    1924 . . . . 1.03, 6.45
Hamburg Rules 1978 . . . . 1.65
Havana Convention on Private
    International Law, 1928 (Bustamante
    Code) 5.06, 15.04
Inter-American Convention on
    Commercial Arbitration, 1975,
    OAS (Panama Convention) 6.45,
                    14.37, 17.24, 18.13

Inter-American Convention on the Law
    Applicable to International Contracts,
    1994. . . . . 14.01, 14.03, 14.20
Art 7 . . . . 2.29, 14.21, 14.22
Art 9 . . . . 2.32
Art 9(2) 14.22, 14.24
Art 11(1) 2.53
Art 11(2) 2.53
Art 12 . . . . 2.33
Art 13(1) 2.33
Art 17 . . . . 2.60, 14.22
Art 18 . . . . 2.50
International Convention for the Unification
    of certain rules relating to Maritime
    Liens and Mortgages, 1926 . . . . . . 12.05
International Convention for the Unification
    of certain rules relating to Maritime
    Liens and Mortgages, 1967 . . . . . . 12.05
International Convention on Aerial Navigation
    (Paris Convention), 1919 . . . . 12.10
International Convention on Civil Liability
    for Bunker Oil Pollution Damage,
    2001 . . . . 6.45
International Convention on Maritime Liens
    and Mortgages, 1993 . . . . 12.05
Lugano Convention on Jurisdiction and
    Recognition, 1988 . . . . 16.06, 16.24,
                                          16.39
Art 24 . . . . 16.45
Luxembourg Protocol to the Cape Town
    Convention 2007 . . . . 12.09
Model Contract for the International
    Commercial Sale of Perishable Goods,
    1999 (ITC) 5.13, 5.16
Mercosur Agreement on International
    Commercial Arbitration, 1998 . . . 17.24
Montevideo Convention on Extraterritorial
    Validity of Foreign Judgments and
    Arbitral Awards, 1979 . . . . . 6.45, 18.13
Montevideo Treaty of International
    Procedural Law, 1940 . . . . 15.04
Montreal Convention for the Unification of
    Certain Rules Relating to International
    Carriage by Air, 1999 . . . . 2.12, 5.17,
                                  6.45, 19.23, 20.01
Art 53(2) 6.45
New York Convention on the Recognition
    and Enforcement of Foreign Arbitral
    Awards, 1958 . . . . 1.29, 3.10, 6.45,
              14.37, 17.04, 17.07, 17.23,
              17.25, 17.26, 17.35–17.38,
              17.85, 17.106, 17.133,
              17.136, 17.137, 18.13,
              19.20, 19.23, 20.01

Art I(1) 17.36, 17.37
Art I(2) 17.37
Art I(3) 17.21, 17.37, 19.13
Art II 17.71, 17.135
Art II(3) 17.38
Art IV 17.38, 19.24
Art V 17.34, 17.38, 17.70, 17.107,
                      17.126, 17.135, 17.137,
                      17.138, 17.142
Art V(1) 17.139
Art V(1)(e) 17.138
Art VII 17.38, 17.138, 17.139,
                      17.141, 17.142
Art VII(1) 17.140
Ottawa Convention on International
    Factoring, 1988 *see* UNIDROIT
    Convention on International Factoring
Panama Convention on International
    Commercial Arbitration 1975 *see*
    Inter-American Convention on
    Commercial Arbitration
Paris Union Convention on the Protection
    of Industrial Property, 1883 . . . . . . 6.45
Rome Convention on Damage Caused by
    Foreign Aircraft to Third Parties on the
    Surface, 1952 . . . . 10.23
Rome Convention on the Law Applicable
    to Contractual Obligations,
    1980 . . . . 1.40, 11.30, 14.01,
              14.03, 14.20, 14.24, 16.24,
              18.13, 19.09
Art 1(1) 2.28
Art 3 . . . . 14.19, 14.21, 14.22
Art 3(1) 2.05, 2.28, 2.31
Art 3(3) 2.51, 2.54
Art 3(4) 2.33
Art 4(1) 2.31
Art 4(2) 2.35
Art 5 . . . . 2.51
Art 6 . . . . 2.51
Art 7 . . . . 2.51, 2.54
Art 7(1) 2.51, 2.53, 2.55
Art 7(2) 2.51, 2.53, 2.55
Art 8(1) 2.33
Art 9(1) 2.33
Art 12(1) 13.08
Art 15 . . . . 2.60
Art 16 . . . . 2.50
Art 18 . . . . 2.28
Art 21 . . . . 18.13, 18.14
Brussels Protocol 1988 . . . . 2.28
Rome Convention on the Return of Stolen
    and Illegally Exported Cultural
    Objects, 1995 . . . . 5.07

Rules of the Iran-US Claims Tribunal,
 1983. . . . . 17.23
Statute of the International Court of Justice
 Art 36 . . . . 1.67
 Art 38 . . . . 3.04, 3.19, 4.05
 Art 38(1) 1.64
 Art 38(1)(b) 3.23
 Art 38(1)(c) 16.43
 Art 59 . . . . 3.19
Treaties of Montevideo, 1889 . . . . 5.06
Treaty between the Government of the
 United States of America and the
 Hashemite Kingdom of Jordan
 Concerning the Encouragement and
 Reciprocal Protection of Investment, 1997
 Art 1 . . . . 3.13
Treaty of Asunción on the Common Market
 of the South (MERCOSUR Treaty),
 1991 . . . . 6.45
 Protocol of Las Leñas,
 1992 . . . . 6.45, 16.24, 16.61
 Art 20 . . . . 16.61
 Art 20(c) 16.61
 Protocol of Buenos Aires, 1994 . . . . 16.24,
 16.61
 Art 4 . . . . 16.36
 Art 5 . . . . 16.36
UN Charter
 Art 92 . . . . 3.09
UN Convention on Contracts for the
 International Sale of Goods (CISG),
 1980 (Vienna Convention) 1.67,
 2.12, 3.07, 3.33, 3.47, 4.61,
 5.07, 5.16, 5.34, 6.09, 6.31,
 6.36, 6.39, 6.45, Ch 7,
 8.20, 10.12, 10.20, 11.16,
 11.17, 11.20, 12.01, 14.11,
 16.27, 18.01, 18.09, 18.17,
 18.18, 19.07, 19.08, 19.09,
 19.19, 20.01, 20.12
 Part II 7.70
 Part III 7.72
 Part IV 7.101, 19.08
 Preamble 19.07
 Arts 1–6 (Ch I) 18.01
 Art 1 . . . . 7.10, 7.12, 7.14, 7.16, 7.24, 9.51
 Art 1(1)(a) 7.15, 7.16, 7.26,
 7.29, 18.02
 Art 1(1)(b) 2.61, 6.45, 7.15, 7.16,
 7.17, 7.18, 7.20, 7.22, 7.23,
 7.26, 7.27, 7.29, 8.21, 18.06
 Art 2 . . . . 7.11, 7.39, 18.03
 Art 2(a) 18.03
 Arts 2(b), (c) 18.03

 Art 2(d) 13.01, 18.03
 Art 2(f) 18.03
 Art 3 . . . . 7.11, 7.33, 7.45, 18.03
 Art 3(1) 7.11
 Art 3(2) 7.11
 Art 4 . . . . 7.30, 7.60, 7.99, 18.04
 Art 4(a) 2.47
 Art 5 . . . . 7.31, 7.60, 18.04
 Art 6 . . . . 6.45, 7.32, 7.51, 7.52, 7.53,
 7.62, 11.20
 Art 7 . . . . 3.37, 5.07, 7.36, 7.40, 7.42,
 7.47, 7.48, 7.50, 7.53, 7.55,
 7.106, 8.20, 14.44, 19.07,
 19.08, 19.09, 19.11
 Art 7(1) 7.46, 7.50, 7.51, 7.54,
 7.55, 7.56, 7.58, 7.59, 7.62,
 7.106, 19.08, 19.11
 Art 7(2) 7.40, 7.50, 7.55, 7.57, 7.58,
 7.60, 7.62, 7.64, 7.65, 7.92, 7.93,
 19.08, 19.09
 Art 9 . . . . 7.51, 7.67, 7.68, 7.69, 8.20
 Art 9(1) 7.50, 7.66, 7.67, 16.33
 Art 9(2) 1.64, 7.66, 7.67, 7.69, 14.39
 Art 10 . . . . 7.12, 8.20
 Art 11 . . . . 7.62
 Art 12 . . . . 7.32
 Arts 14–17 . . . . 7.70
 Art 16 . . . . 7.70
 Art 16(2) 7.70
 Art 16(2)(b) 7.56
 Arts 18–22 . . . . 7.70
 Art 18(2) 7.58, 7.70
 Art 19 . . . . 7.70, 7.71
 Art 19(2) 7.49, 7.55
 Art 20(2) 7.62
 Art 21(2) 7.49, 7.55, 7.56, 7.70
 Art 24 . . . . 7.52, 7.70
 Art 25 . . . . 7.73, 7.79, 7.82, 19.24
 Art 26 . . . . 7.54
 Art 27 . . . . 7.55
 Art 28 . . . . 7.73, 7.74, 7.105, 14.51
 Art 29(2) 7.56
 Arts 31–34 . . . . 7.75
 Art 33(c) 7.50
 Art 34 . . . . 7.55
 Arts 35–44 . . . . 7.75
 Art 37 . . . . 7.55, 7.56
 Art 38 . . . . 1.65, 7.55
 Art 39 . . . . 1.65, 7.55, 7.75
 Art 39(1) 7.42, 19.08
 Art 40 . . . . 1.65, 7.55, 7.56
 Art 43 . . . . 7.75
 Art 44 . . . . 7.55
 Art 45(1)(b) 7.76

UN Convention on Contracts for the
    International Sale of Goods (CISG),
    1980 (*cont.*)
  Art 46 .... 7.56
  Art 46(1) 7.76
  Art 46(2)................... 7.76, 7.79
  Art 46(3)................... 7.55, 7.76
  Art 47 .... 7.39, 7.49, 7.51, 7.76
  Art 47(2) 7.56
  Art 48 .... 7.55, 7.76
  Art 49 .... 6.45, 7.54, 7.76
  Art 49(1)(a) 7.79
  Art 49(2) 1.41
  Art 50 .... 6.45, 7.76
  Art 51 .... 7.79
  Arts 54–59 .... 7.77
  Art 57(1)(a) 19.09
  Art 60 .... 7.77
  Arts 61–65 .... 7.77
  Art 61(1)(b) 7.77
  Art 62 .... 7.77
  Art 63 .... 7.49, 7.51, 7.77
  Art 63(2) 7.77
  Art 64 .... 7.77
  Art 64(1)(a) 7.79
  Art 64(2) 7.56
  Art 65 .... 7.55
  Arts 67–69 .... 7.79
  Art 67 .... 7.102
  Art 67(1) 7.102
  Art 67(2) 7.62, 7.102
  Art 67(3) 7.102
  Art 68 .... 7.62, 7.102, 7.103
  Art 69 .... 7.101
  Art 69(2) 7.62, 7.101
  Art 69(3) 7.101
  Art 70 .... 7.79
  Art 72........................... 19.24
  Art 73 .... 7.79
  Arts 74–77 .... 7.76, 7.77
  Art 74 .... 7.40, 7.45, 7.88, 7.89, 7.92
  Art 77 .... 7.55
  Art 78........... 7.61, 7.88, 7.89, 7.92,
          7.95, 14.06, 14.37, 14.40
  Art 79........... 7.62, 7.81, 7.97, 7.98,
          7.99, 7.100, 7.105, 14.06,
          14.43, 14.55
  Art 79(3) 7.98
  Arts 81–84...................... 7.76
  Art 82.......................... 7.56
  Arts 85–88 .... 7.55, 7.56
  Arts 89–101..................... 7.32
  Art 90 .... 6.45, 7.13, 18.14, 18.15
  Arts 92–96...................... 19.13

  Art 92 .... 2.61, 3.69, 7.70, 7.72
  Art 94............... 3.69, 18.14, 18.15
  Art 94(1) 19.13
  Art 95....... 2.61, 3.69, 7.16, 7.18, 7.19,
          7.20, 7.21, 7.22, 7.23, 7.25,
          7.29, 18.06, 19.13
  Art 99...................... 7.08, 18.15
UN Convention on Independent
    Guarantees and Stand-By Letters of
    Credit, 1995 .... 6.09, 9.09, 9.51–9.53
  Art 1 .... 9.53
  Art 1(1)......................... 9.51
  Art 1(2)......................... 9.51
  Art 4(1)......................... 9.51
  Art 13(1) 9.53
  Art 13(2) 9.53
  Art 14(1) 9.53
  Art 16(1) 9.53
  Art 19 .... 9.51, 9.52, 9.53
  Art 19(1) 9.51
  Art 19(2) 9.51
  Art 20 .... 9.51
  Art 20(1) 9.52
  Art 22 .... 9.52
UN Convention on Jurisdictional
    Immunities of States and Their
    Property, 2005............ 3.03, 16.10
  Art 10 .... 3.03
UN Convention on the Assignment of
    Receivables in International Trade,
    UNCITRAL, 2001 .... 2.62,
        3.44, 5.34, 6.45, 11.29–11.40,
        14.56, 18.10, 18.15
  Ch V........................... 11.30
  Section II 11.38
  Art 1 .... 11.33
  Art 1(1)(a) 18.10
  Art 1(3) 18.10
  Art 1(4) 11.30
  Art 2 .... 11.33
  Art 2(a)......................... 11.31
  Art 3 .... 10.12, 11.33, 18.10
  Art 4 .... 11.33, 11.35
  Art 4(3) 11.35
  Art 5(a)......................... 18.10
  Art 7 .... 11.30
  Art 8 .... 11.36
  Art 8(3) 11.36
  Art 9 .... 11.36
  Art 9(1) 14.56
  Art 9(3) 11.32
  Art 10 .... 11.36
  Art 11 .... 11.25
  Art 12 .... 11.37

UN Convention on the Assignment of
    Receivables in International Trade,
    UNCITRAL, 2001 (*cont.*)
  Art 15 . . . . 11.38
  Art 17 . . . . 11.38
  Art 18 . . . . 11.38
  Art 18(1) 11.26
  Art 22 . . . . 11.39, 11.40
  Art 26 . . . . 11.30
  Art 38(1) 3.72
  Art 39 . . . . 11.30, 11.33
  Art 41 . . . . 11.32
  Art 42 . . . . 11.33
  Art 42(2) 11.40
  Annex section II 11.40
UN Convention on the Carriage of
    Goods by Sea 1978 *see* Hamburg
    Rules 1978
UN Convention on the Law of the Sea,
    1982 . . . . 1.65, 3.01
UN Convention on the Privileges and
    Immunities of the Specialised
    Agencies, 1947 . . . . 3.68
  Art II 3.68
  Annex III 3.68
UN Convention on the Recognition and
    Enforcement of Foreign Arbitral Awards,
    1958 *see* New York Convention on the
    Recognition and Enforcement of
    Foreign Arbitral Awards, 1958
UN General Assembly Resolution 2205
    (XXI), 1966 establishing
    UNCITRAL 4.03, 5.28
UNCITRAL Convention on Independent
    Guarantees and Standby Letters of
    Credit, 1995 . . . . 9.11
UNCITRAL Guide for Privately Financed
    Infrastructure Projects 5.09
UNCITRAL Model Law on Cross-Border
    Insolvency, 1997 . . . . 15.02,
            15.05, 15.09, 15.12,
            15.13–15.21, 15.31
  Ch IV 15.21
  Art 1 . . . . 15.16
  Art 2(a) 15.17
  Art 9 . . . . 15.18
  Art 11 . . . . 15.18
  Art 13 . . . . 15.18
  Art 15(1) 15.18
  Art 17(2) 15.17, 15.18
  Art 20 . . . . 15.20
  Art 21 . . . . 15.19
UNCITRAL Model Law on Electronic
    Commerce 1.28

UNCITRAL Model Law on International
    Commercial Arbitration, 1985 . . . . 1.29,
        4.61, 5.09, 17.18, 17.23, 17.26,
            17.27–17.34, 17.35, 17.60,
        17.64, 17.79, 17.108, 17.109,
        17.116, 17.118, 17.119, 17.124,
            17.130, 17.132, 17.137,
                20.01, 20.12
  Ch V 17.32
  Art 1(1) 17.19
  Art 1(3) 17.16
  Art 1(4) 17.16
  Art 5 . . . . 17.34, 17.130
  Art 6 . . . . 17.125
  Art 7 . . . . 17.28, 17.125, 17.135
  Art 7(2) 17.28
  Art 8(1) 17.28
  Art 10(2) 17.30
  Art 12(2) 17.30
  Art 16(1) 17.31
  Art 16(3) 17.31
  Art 18 . . . . 17.32, 17.66
  Art 19 . . . . 17.32
  Art 20 . . . . 17.32
  Art 22 . . . . 17.32
  Art 24(1) 17.64
  Art 28 . . . . 17.112, 17.113, 17.117
  Art 28(1) 17.33, 17.113
  Art 28(2) 17.33, 17.115
  Art 28(3) 17.33
  Art 29 . . . . 17.33
  Art 31(1) 17.33
  Art 31(2) 17.33
  Art 32(2)(a)(iv) 17.64
  Arts 34–35 . . . . 17.34
  Art 34 . . . 17.125, 17.126, 17.127, 17.136
  Arts 34(a)(ii), (iii), (iv) 17.128
  Arts 34(b)(i), (ii) 17.129
  Art 34(2)(a)(i) 17.73
  Art 36 . . . . 17.135
UNCITRAL Model Law on Procurement
    of Goods, Construction and
    Services, 1994 . . . . 5.09, 5.34
UNIDROIT Convention on Agency in
    the International Sale of
    Goods, 1983 . . . . 6.09, 8.03, 8.17–8.27
  Ch IV 8.24
  Art 2(1) 8.21
  Art 2(1)(a) 8.21
  Art 2.2.1 . . . . 8.27
  Art 2.2.3 . . . . 8.27
  Art 6 . . . . 8.20
  Art 7 . . . . 8.20
  Art 8 . . . . 8.20

UNIDROIT Convention on Agency in
   the International Sale of
   Goods, 1983 (*cont.*)
   Arts 12–16 . . . . 8.22
   Art 12 . . . . 8.22
   Art 13 . . . . 8.22
   Arts 13(2)–(6) 8.22
   Art 14(1) 8.23
   Art 14(2) 8.23
   Art 15 . . . . 8.23
   Art 17 . . . . 8.24
   Art 18 . . . . 8.24
   Art 28 . . . . 8.21
UNIDROIT Convention on Harmonised
   Rules regarding Intermediated
   Securities (draft) . . . 13.40, 18.07, 20.12
UNIDROIT Convention on International
   Factoring, Ottawa, 1988 . . . . 3.37, 5.07,
            5.34, 11.11–11.28, 14.56,
                     18.15, 20.06
   Art 1 . . . . 3.37
   Art 2 . . . . 3.37
   Art 2(2) 10.12
   Art 3 . . . . 3.37, 11.20
   Art 3(1) 11.20
   Art 3(2) 11.20
   Art 4 . . . . 3.52, 11.19
   Art 4(1) 3.53, 11.20
   Art 4(2) 3.54
   Art 5 . . . . 11.20, 11.21, 11.22
   Art 6 . . . . 11.20, 11.22
   Art 6(1) 11.20, 11.24, 11.25
   Art 6(2) 11.24
   Art 7 . . . . 11.22
   Art 9(1) 11.26
   Art 10 . . . . 11.27
   Art 10(1) 11.20
   Art 15 . . . . 3.72
   Art 20 . . . . 2.61
   Art 38(2) 3.72
UNIDROIT Convention on International
   Financial Leasing, 1988 . . . . . 1.50, 3.33,
                 6.09, 6.33, Ch 10,
                11.20, 12.50, 18.15
   Art 1 . . . . 10.03
   Art 1(2) 10.08
   Art 1(2)(a) 10.22
   Art 3(1) 10.13
   Art 3(2) 10.12
   Art 5(h) 10.12
   Art 7 . . . . 10.22, 10.24, 10.25
   Art 7(1) 10.25
   Art 7(2) 10.25

Art 7(3) 10.25
Art 8(1) 10.22
Art 8(1)(b) 10.23
Art 8(1)(c) 10.23
Art 8(2) 10.21
Art 10 . . . . 10.19, 10.21
Art 11 . . . . 10.19, 10.21
Art 12 . . . . 10.21
Art 12(3) 10.21
Art 12(4) 10.21
Art 12(5) 10.21, 10.22
Art 13 . . . . 10.26
Art 13(3) 10.26
Art 17 . . . . 3.72
UNIDROIT Convention on International
   Interests in Mobile Equipment *see* Cape
   Town Convention
UNIDROIT Guide to International Master
   Franchise Agreements 8.04, 8.30
UNIDROIT Model Franchise Disclosure
   Law 8.03, 8.30, 8.31–8.35
   Art 1 . . . . 8.32
   Arts 3–4 . . . . 8.33
   Art 5 . . . . 8.33
   Art 6 . . . . 8.33
   Art 7 . . . . 8.33
   Art 8(1) 8.34
   Art 8(2) 8.34
   Arts 8(3)–(4) 8.34
   Art 10 . . . . 8.35
UNIDROIT Model Law on Leasing
   (draft) 10.29–10.31
UNIDROIT Statute 1940 (amended
   1993) 5.07, 5.23
   Art 1 . . . . 4.03
Vienna Convention on Contracts for the
   International Sale of Goods (CISG) *see*
   UN Convention on Contracts for the
   International Sale of Goods
Vienna Convention on the Law of
   Treaties, 1969 . . . . 3.06, 3.52, 3.71,
                19.05, 19.06, 19.15
   Art 2(1)(a) 3.26
   Art 2(1)(d) 3.69
   Art 14 . . . . 3.57
   Arts 19–23 . . . . 19.14
   Art 19 . . . . 3.69, 19.05
   Art 30 . . . . 3.73
   Art 31 . . . . 3.47, 3.49, 4.42, 19.05
   Art 31(2) 3.48
   Art 31(3) 3.48, 3.49
   Art 31(3)(b) 19.05, 19.21
   Art 31(3)(c) 3.50

Vienna Convention on the Law of
    Treaties, 1969 (*cont.*)
    Art 31(4) 19.05
    Art 32 . . . . . . 3.49, 3.57, 3.59, 4.42, 19.05
    Art 33 . . . . 3.47, 3.56
    Art 33(1) 4.42
    Art 33(3) 4.42
    Art 34 . . . . 3.30
    Art 35 . . . . 3.30
    Art 36 . . . . 3.30
    Art 39(1)(B). 3.57
    Art 42(2) 3.71
    Art 53 . . . . 1.43
    Art 70 . . . . 3.71
    Art 76(2) 3.45
    Art 77 . . . . 3.45
    Art 78 . . . . 3.46
    Art 79 . . . . 3.47, 3.56
    Art 80 . . . . 3.45
Vienna Convention on Treaties concluded
    between States and International
    Organisations, 1986. . . . . 3.28
Warsaw Convention, 1929 (Convention for
    the Unification of Certain Rules

Relating to International Carriage
    by Air) 2.10, 2.12, 5.07, 6.45,
                     19.05, 19.11, 20.01
    Art 17 . . . . 4.44, 4.45
    Art 18 . . . . 4.45
    Art 18(1) 4.45
    Art 19 . . . . 4.45
    Art 20 . . . . 4.45
    Art 22(2)(b) 4.45
    Art 25 . . . . 4.45
    Art 26 . . . . 4.45
    Art 26(2) 4.45
    Art 28(1) 2.10
    Art 36 . . . . 4.44
    Hague Protocol 1955. . . . . 2.10, 6.45,
                               19.05
Washington Convention, 1965
    (Convention on the settlement
    of investment disputes between
    States and nationals of other
    States). 3.02, 3.65, 17.23
    Art 27(1) 3.65
    Art 42(1) 3.10
World Copyright Convention, 1996. . . . 6.45

TABLE OF EC TREATIES AND LEGISLATION

TREATIES

Accession Convention 1978
    Art 17 . . . . 16.33, 16.34
EC Treaty (Treaty of Rome) 6.44, 8.06,
    18.18
    Art 65 . . . . 2.28
    Art 68(1) 16.24
    Art 100A 3.34
    Art 234 . . . . 16.24
    Art 281 (*ex* Art 210) 3.17, 6.45
    Art 300 (*ex* Art 228) 3.17
    Art 307(2) (*ex* Art 234(2)) 6.45
    Art 310 . . . . 6.45
Treaty of Amsterdam 5.07, 6.44, 6.45,
    16.24, 16.62

DIRECTIVES

Collateral Directive, Dir
    2002/47/EC 13.32–13.33, 13.36
    Art 9 . . . . 13.33
First Company Directive
    (EEC) 8.06–8.08
    Art 3 . . . . 8.07
    Art 7 . . . . 8.08
    Art 8 . . . . 8.08
    Art 9(1) 8.07
    Art 9(2) 8.07
    Art 9(3) 8.07
Self Employed Commercial Agents,
    1986 . . . . 6.09, 8.03, 8.09–8.16
    Art 1(2) 8.11
    Art 1(3) 8.11
    Art 3 . . . . 8.11
    Art 3(1) 8.12
    Art 3(2) 8.12
    Art 4(1) 8.12
    Art 4(2) 8.12
    Art 4(3) 8.12
    Art 5 . . . . 8.12
    Arts 6–12 . . . . 8.13
    Art 13(1) 8.13
    Arts 15–20 . . . . 8.14
    Art 16 . . . . 8.14
    Art 17(2) 8.14

    Art 17(3) 8.14, 8.15
    Art 19 . . . . 8.14
Settlement Finality Directive, Dir 98/26/EC,
    1998 . . . . 13.28–13.31, 13.32,
    13.33, 13.35, 13.36
    Art 2(a) 13.29
    Arts 2(b)–(g) 13.29
    Art 2(k) 13.30
    Art 9(2) 13.10, 13.31
Takeover Bids, Dir 2004/25/EC 13.02
Unfair Terms in Consumer Contracts,
    Dir 93/13/EEC 5 April 1993 . . . . . 3.34
    Art 1(2) 3.34

REGULATIONS

Air Carrier Liability, Reg 2027/97 . . . . . . 6.45
Certain Aspects of the Sale of Consumer
    Goods and associated guarantees,
    Reg 44/1999 [1999] OJ L171/12 . . . 7.13
Cooperation in the taking of evidence in civil
    or commercial matters, Reg (EC)
    1206/2001 [2001] OJ L174/1 . . . 16.59
Insolvency Proceedings, Reg (EC)
    1346/2000 [2000] OJ L/160 . . . . . 3.16,
    3.35, 15.04, 15.05, 15.09,
    15.12, 15.24–15.35
    Art 1(1) 15.33
    Art 2(g) 15.30
    Art 3 . . . . 15.28, 15.33
    Art 3(1) 15.27, 15.28
    Art 3(2) 15.28
    Art 3(4) 15.26
    Art 4 . . . . 15.29, 15.30
    Art 4(1) 15.27, 15.28
    Arts 5–15 . . . . 15.29
    Art 5 . . . . 15.30
    Art 5(1) 15.30
    Art 7 . . . . 15.30
    Art 7(1) 15.30
    Art 16(1) 15.31, 15.33
    Art 17 . . . . 15.31
    Art 18 . . . . 15.26
    Art 26 . . . . 15.32
    Art 29 . . . . 15.33
    Art 29(a) 15.26

Insolvency Proceedings (*cont.*)
    Art 33 . . . . 15.26
    Art 38 . . . . 15.33
    Annex A 15.25, 15.33
    Annex C 15.33
    recital 13 . . . . 15.28
Insolvency Proceedings (Amendment)
    Regulation, Reg (EC) 603/2005
    [2005] OJ L100/1 . . . . 15.24
    Annexes A, B, C 15.24
Jurisdiction and the recognition and
    enforcement of judgments in civil
    and commercial matters (Brussels I
    Regulation *see also* Brussels
    Convention), Reg (EC) 44/2001
    [2001] OJ L12/1 . . . . 16.07, 16.24,
                          16.60, 19.09
    Arts 2–7 . . . . 16.47
    Arts 2–24 . . . . 16.45
    Art 2 . . . . 16.26
    Art 4 . . . . 16.24, 16.39
    Arts 5–24 . . . . 16.47
    Art 5(1) 16.24
    Art 5(1)(b) 16.27
    Art 5(5) 16.28
    Art 5(7) 16.24
    Arts 8–14 . . . . 16.24
    Art 23 . . . . 16.29, 16.32, 16.33
    Art 27 . . . . 16.41
    Art 31 . . . . 16.45, 16.47
    Art 32 . . . . 16.60
    Art 33 . . . . 16.60
    Art 34 . . . . 16.60
    Art 34(2) 16.60

    Art 34(3) 16.60
    Art 34(4) 16.60
    Art 35 . . . . 16.60
    Art 36 . . . . 16.60
    Art 38 . . . . 16.60
    Art 41 . . . . 16.60
    Art 43 . . . . 16.60
    Art 45 . . . . 16.60
    Art 47 . . . . 16.60
    Art 57 . . . . 16.60
    Art 58 . . . . 16.60
    Art 60 . . . . 16.28
    Art 69 . . . . 16.07
    Art 70 . . . . 16.07
    Art 71 . . . . 16.07
    Art 72 . . . . 16.07
Service of judicial and extrajudicial
    documents in civil or commercial
    matters, Reg (EC) 1348/2000
    [2000] OJ L160/37 . . . . . . 16.55, 16.59
    Ch II 16.59
    Art 1(1) 16.55
    Art 2 . . . . 16.55, 16.59
    Art 3 . . . . 16.55, 16.59
    Arts 4–11 . . . . 16.55
    Art 8 . . . . 16.55
    Art 10 . . . . 16.59
    Art 19 . . . . 16.55
Rome I Regulation (proposed) . . . 2.28, 14.03
    Art 3(2) 2.31
    Art 3(4) 2.54
    Art 8(1) 2.54
    Art 8(2) 2.55
    Art 8(3) 2.55

TABLE OF UNIFORM RULES, UNIFORM TRADE TERMS, RESTATEMENTS AND MODEL FORMS

American Law Institute

Model Penal Code 4.31
Principles of Transnational Civil
    Procedure (PTCP), 2004,
    ALI/UNIDROIT 16.62–16.65
    Preamble 16.62
    Pr 2.1–2.4 . . . . 16.64, 16.65
    Pr 2.5 . . . . 16.64
    Pr 2.6 . . . . 16.64
    Pr 6 . . . . 16.65
    Pr 8 . . . . 16.50
    Pr 11 . . . . 16.65
    Pr 14 . . . . 16.65
    Pr 16 . . . . 16.65
    Pr 22 . . . . 16.65
Restatement of the Law (first), Conflict
    of Laws, 1934 . . . . 2.18
    §332 . . . . 2.18
Restatement of the Law (second), Conflict
    of Laws, 1971 . . . . . . 2.18, 14.03, 16.18
    §6 . . . . 2.18, 2.19
    §187 . . . . 2.33
    §188(2) 2.35
    §244 . . . . 2.18
    §244(2) 2.38
    §303 (comment) 13.08
Restatement (second), Contracts 14.03
Restatement (third), Foreign Relations
    Law, 1987
    §102 . . . . 1.64, 3.20
    §402–3 . . . . 2.57
    §416 . . . . 2.57
    §421(2) 16.22

Commission on European Contract Law (CECL)

Principles of European Contract Law
    (PECL) . . . 1.58, 2.31, 3.06, 4.33, 5.14,
           6.09, 7.95, 7.100, 8.27–8.28,
           14.01, 14.05–14.62, 17.01,
        17.114, 17.115, 17.118, 19.09

Part I 14.06
Part II 14.06
Part III 14.06, 14.08
Art 1:101 . . . . 14.10, 14.15
Art 1:102 . . . . 14.42
Art 1:102(2) 14.42
Art 1:103 . . . . 14.58
Art 1:104 . . . . 14.48
Art 1:108 . . . . 14.48
Art 1:201 . . . . 14.44, 14.48, 14.59
Art 1:201(2) 7.53
Art 1:202 . . . . 14.48
Art 2:101 . . . . 14.48
Arts 2:208–9 . . . . 7.71
Art 2:301 . . . . 14.48
Art 2:302 . . . . 14.48
Ch 3 . . . . 8.05, 14.57
Art 3:101 . . . . 8.27
Art 3:102 . . . . 8.27
Art 3:201(3) 14.48
Arts 3:201–9 . . . . 8.27
Art 3:202 . . . . 8.27
Art 3:203 . . . . 8.27
Arts 3:301–4 . . . . 8.27
Art 4:107 . . . . 14.48
Art 4:109 . . . . 14.48
Art 5:101(1) 14.49
Art 5:102 . . . . 14.49
Art 6:105 . . . . 14.59
Art 6:111 . . . . 14.06, 14.43, 14.54
Art 6:111(2) 14.54
Art 6:111(3) 7.100, 14.54
Art 8:103 . . . . 14.48
Art 8:104 . . . . 14.53
Art 8:105 . . . . 14.50
Art 8:108 . . . . 14.43
Art 8:109 . . . . 14.59
Art 9:102 . . . . 7.74, 14.51
Art 9:401 . . . . 14.53
Art 9:505 . . . . 14.48
Art 9:508 . . . . 7.96, 14.06

Principles of European Contract Law
(PECL) *(cont.)*
  Art 9:509(2). 14.59
  Ch 11 . . . . 14.56
  Art 11:204 . . . . 11.37
  Art 11:301 . . . . 11.23, 11.25, 14.56
  Art 11:303 . . . . 11.38
  Art 11:307(2)(b) 11.26

Institute of International Banking Law
and Practice

International Standby Practices 1998
    (ISP98). 9.09, 9.46–9.50
  r 1 . . . . 9.49
  r 1.06 . . . . 9.47
  r 1.07 . . . . 9.47
  r 1.09 . . . . 9.47
  r 1.09(c) 9.27
  r 1.11(b) 9.49
  r 2.04 . . . . 9.48
  r 3.06(d) 9.47
  r 3.09 . . . . 9.47
  r 4.11 . . . . 9.47
  r 6 . . . . 9.48
  r 10 . . . . 9.48

Inter-American Commercial Arbitration
Commission (IACAC)

Rules of Procedure. 17.24

International Centre for the Settlement of
Investment Disputes (ICSID)

Rules 17.23

International Chamber of Commerce (ICC)

Commercial Agency Model Contract,
    2002 . . . . 5.13, 6.09, 8.04, 9.11
Incoterms, 1990 . . . . 1.56, 5.12, 7.35,
                      9.11, 20.01
International Franchising Model Contract,
    2000 . . . . 8.04, 8.30
Model Distributorship Contract-Sole
    Importer-Distributorship,
    2002 . . . . 5.13
Model Occasional Intermediary
    Contract, 2000 . . . . 5.13
Rules of Arbitration, 1975 . . . . 17.82
  Art 11 . . . . 17.82, 17.83
Rules of Arbitration, 1998 . . . . . 14.26, 17.23,
         17.26, 17.42, 17.43–17.59,
        17.64, 17.118, 17.119, 17.120
  Art 1 . . . . 17.18

Art 1(2) 17.42
Arts 4(4)–(5) 17.43
Art 4(5) 17.43
Art 5 . . . . 17.43
Art 6 . . . . 17.44
Art 6(3) 17.44
Art 6(4) 17.44
Art 7(1) 17.47
Art 7(2) 17.47
Art 7(3) 17.47
Art 7(4) 17.47
Arts 8(2)–(4) 17.45
Arts 9(1)–(2) 17.45
Arts 9(3)–(6) 17.45
Art 9(5) 17.46
Art 10(2) 17.45
Art 11 . . . . 17.48
Art 11(1) 17.48
Arts 12(2)–(3) 17.49
Art 12(4) 17.49
Art 14(1) 17.50
Arts 15(1)–(2) 17.50
Art 15(1) 17.82
Art 17 . . . . 17.117
Art 17(1) 14.26, 17.51
Art 17(3) 17.51
Art 18 . . . . 17.52
Art 18(4) 17.52
Art 19 . . . . 17.52
Art 20 . . . . 17.53
Arts 20(2)–(5) 17.53
Art 20(4) 17.53
Art 21 . . . . 17.53
Art 22 . . . . 17.54
Art 23 . . . . 17.55
Art 24 . . . . 17.57
Art 25(1) 17.56
Art 25(2) 17.56
Art 27 . . . . 17.57
Arts 28–29 . . . . 17.58
Art 28(6) 17.58
Art 30 . . . . 17.43, 17.59
Art 31(3) 17.59
Uniform Customs and Practice for
    Documentary Credits (UCP 500, 600)
    1933, 1993, 2007 revisions 1.56,
               1.64, 9.09, 9.11, 9.12,
          9.14–9.28, 9.51, 9.52,
          9.53, 12.50, 20.01
  UCP 500 . . . . 9.46, 9.47
    Art 13(c) 9.21
    Art 14 . . . . 9.22
  UCP 600 . . . . 9.46, 9.47

Uniform Customs and Practice for
    Documentary Credits (UCP 500, 600)
    1933, 1993, 2007 revisions (*cont.*)
    UCP 600 (*cont.*)
        Art 1 . . . . 9.14, 9.22, 9.46
        Art 2 . . . . 9.11, 9.17
        Art 3 . . . . 9.11, 9.15
        Art 4 . . . . 9.11
        Art 4(a) 9.17
        Art 5 . . . . 9.21
        Art 7(b) 9.20
        Art 7(c) 9.17, 9.19
        Art 9 . . . . 9.22
        Art 10(a) 9.17
        Art 12(b) 9.17
        Art 14(a) 9.22
        Art 14(d) 9.22
        Art 14(h) 9.21
        Art 16(d) 9.21
        Art 17(a) 9.24
        Art 17(b) 9.24
        Art 17(c) 9.24
        Art 48(b) 9.25
        Art 48(c) 9.25
        Art 49 . . . . 9.25
Uniform Customs and Practice for
    Documentary Credits—Electronic
    presentation for UCP 500—eUCP
    Version 1.0 . . . . 9.09, 9.14–9.28
    Art e1(b) 9.14
    Art e2(a) 9.14
Uniform Customs and Practice for
    Documentary Credits—Electronic
    Supplement for UCP 600—eUCP
    Version 1.1 . . . . 9.26
    Art e3 . . . . 9.28
    Art e3(b)(i) 9.27
    Art e4 . . . . 9.28
    Art e5(a) 9.28
    Art e5(c) 9.28
    Art e5(d) 9.28
    Art e7(a)(i) 9.28
Uniform Law on the Formation of
    Contracts for the International
    Sale of Goods 14.37
Uniform Rules for Contract Bonds (UCB),
    1993 . . . . 9.07, 9.54–9.58
    Art 7(i) 9.56
    Art 7(j) 9.56
    Art 8(a) 9.57
Uniform Rules for Contract Guarantees,
    1978 . . . . 9.29
Uniform Rules for Demand Guarantees
    (URDG), 1992 . . . . 6.09, 9.09,

          9.11, 9.29–9.45, 9.46, 9.47,
          9.52, 9.53, 9.54
    Art 2(a) 9.31, 9.40
    Art 2(c) 9.44
    Art 2(d) 9.40
    Art 5 . . . . 9.39
    Art 6 . . . . 9.39
    Art 7 . . . . 9.36
    Art 9 . . . . 9.54
    Art 13 . . . . 9.36
    Art 17 . . . . 9.36
    Art 18 . . . . 9.36, 9.43
    Art 19 . . . . 9.43
    Art 20 . . . . 9.37, 9.40, 9.41
    Art 20(a) 9.31, 9.41
    Art 20(b) 9.40
    Art 22 . . . . 9.43
    Art 23 . . . . 9.36, 9.43
    Art 24 . . . . 9.36
    Art 25 . . . . 9.36
    Art 26 . . . . 9.36, 9.42
    Art 27 . . . . 9.44
    Art 28 . . . . 9.44
Uniform Law on International Sales
    (ULIS), 1964 . . . . 1.65, 14.37, 18.09
    Art 1(1) 18.09
    Art 2 . . . . 18.09
    Art 5(1)(a) 13.01
    Art 74 . . . . 7.99

International Law Association

Principles on Provisional and Protective
    Measures in International Litigation
    (Helsinki Principles) 16.50

International Law Commission

Draft Articles on Responsibility of
    States 3.61

**ISDA (International Swaps and
Derivatives Association)**

Model Netting Act 11.31

**OHADA (Organisation for
the Harmonisation of Business Law
in Africa)**

Uniform Act on General Commercial
    Law 6.45, 18.17
    Art 1 . . . . 6.45
    Art 10 . . . . 6.45
    Arts 202–205 . . . . 6.45
    Art 249 *et seq* 6.45

Uniform Act on General Commercial
  Law (*cont.*)
  Art 254 . . . . 6.45
Uniform Act on Securities, 1997 . . . . 9.30

**UNCITRAL (United Nations Commission
on International Trade Law)**

Arbitration Rules, 1976 . . . . 17.23, 17.26,
        17.27, 17.40, 17.43–17.59,
        17.60, 17.64, 17.85, 20.01
  Art 3(1) 17.43
  Arts 3(3)–(4) 17.43
  Art 6(1)(b) 17.45
  Arts 6(2)–(4) 17.45
  Art 6(4) 17.46
  Arts 7(2)–(3) 17.45
  Art 8 . . . . 17.45
  Art 9 . . . . 17.47
  Arts 10–12 . . . . 17.48
  Art 12(2) 17.49
  Art 15(1) 17.50
  Art 15(2) 17.53
  Art 16 . . . . 17.50
  Art 17 . . . . 17.50
  Arts 18–19 . . . . 17.53
  Art 20 . . . . 17.52
  Arts 24–25 . . . . 17.52
  Art 25 . . . . 17.53
  Art 27 . . . . 17.53
  Art 27(1) 17.53
  Art 27(4) 17.53
  Art 28 . . . . 17.55
  Art 29 . . . . 17.54
  Art 31(1) 17.56
  Art 31(2) 17.56
  Art 32(2) 17.58
  Art 32(3) 17.56
  Arts 32(6)–(7) 17.58
  Art 33 . . . . 17.120
  Art 33(1) 17.51, 17.121
  Art 33(2) 17.51
  Art 35 . . . . 17.58
  Art 36 . . . . 17.58
  Art 38 . . . . 17.59
  Art 40(1) 17.59
  Art 41 . . . . 17.59

UNIDROIT

Principles of International Commercial
  Contracts (UPICC), 1994,
  2004 . . . . 1.58, 1.64, 2.13, 2.31,
        3.06, 4.33, 4.38, 5.07, 5.14,
        5.16, 5.34, 6.09, 6.15, 6.18,
        7.60, 7.63, 7.64, 7.65,
        7.95, 7.96, 7.100, 8.27–8.28,
        11.20, 14.01, 14.05–14.62,
        17.01, 17.114, 17.115,
        17.118, 19.09, 19.19,
        19.22, 20.01
  Preamble 14.10, 14.15, 14.40
  Art 1.1 . . . . 14.42
  Art 1.3 . . . . 14.43
  Art 1.4 . . . . 14.58
  Art 1.5 . . . . 14.42
  Art 1.7 . . . . 14.40, 14.44, 14.45,
        14.46, 14.59
  Art. 1.7(2) 7.53
  Ch 2, s 2 . . . . 8.05
  Arts 2.2.1–10 . . . . 8.27
  Art 2.2.1 . . . . 8.27, 14.57
  Art 2.2.2(2) 8.27
  Art 2.1.11 . . . . 7.71
  Art 4.1.1 . . . . 14.49
  Art 4.3 . . . . 14.49
  Art 4.3(c) 14.38
  Art 5.1.7(2) 14.59
  Art 6.2.2 . . . . 14.06, 14.40,
        14.43, 14.54
  Arts 6.2.2–3 . . . . 7.100
  Art 6.2.3 . . . . . . 14.06, 14.40, 14.43, 14.54
  Art 7.1.4 . . . . 14.53
  Art 7.1.6 . . . . 14.59
  Art 7.1.7 . . . . 14.43, 14.55
  Art 7.2.2 . . . . 7.74, 14.51
  Art 7.3.4 . . . . 14.50
  Art 7.4.9 . . . . 7.42, 7.92, 14.06, 14.40
  Art 7.4.9(2) 7.95
  Art 7.4.13 . . . . 14.59
  Ch 8 . . . . 14.40
  Ch 9 . . . . 14.40, 14.56
  Art 9.1.9 . . . . 11.25, 14.56
  Art 9.1.13 . . . . 11.26
  Ch 10 . . . . 14.40

TABLE OF OTHER DOCUMENTS

Amalfitan Tables 1.16
Black Book of the Admiralty 1.16
Code of Hammurabi, 1900 BC 1.15,
          4.04, 4.31
Consulate of the Sea. 1.16, 1.19
     Art 170 . . . . 1.16

Laws of Wisby 1.16, 1.19
Lübeck Law 1.21
Privilegium of 1635, Bozen (Bolzano) . . . 16.02
Rhodian Maritime Code. 1.15
Rolls of Oléron 1.16, 1.19, 4.04
Twelve Tables (of Roman Law) 4.04, 4.31

TABLE OF ABBREVIATIONS

A	Atlantic Reporter
AC	Law Reports, Appeal Cases
All ER	All England Law Reports
All ER (Comm)	All England Law Reports (Commercial Cases)
Am J Comp L	American Journal of Comparative Law
B&Ald	Barnewall & Alderson's King's Bench Reports
BCC	British Company Cases
BGB	Bürgerliches Gesetzbuch [German Civil Code]
BLR	Building Law Reports
Brook J Intl L	Brooklyn Journal of International Law
Burr	Burrow's King's Bench Reports
Bus Law	Business Lawyer
BYIL	British Year Book of International Law
CA	Court of Appeal [England]
CISG	Convention on Contracts for the International Sale of Goods
CJEL	Columbia Journal of European Law
CLR	Commonwealth Law Reports (Australian)
Clunet	Journal du droit international
CPLR	Civil Practice Law and Rules [New York]
Dick L Rev	Dickinson Law Review
ECC	European Commercial Cases
ECHR	European Convention on Human Rights
ECJ	European Court of Justice
ECR	European Court Reports
ER	English Reports
Eur Rev Priv Law	European Review of Private Law
EWCA Civ	Court of Appeal (Civil Division)
EWHC	England and Wales High Court [neutral citation]
Exch	Exchequer Reports [England]
F 2d	Federal Reporter, Second Series
F 3d	Federal Reporter, Third Series
F Supp	Federal Supplement

Harv L Rev	Harvard Law Review
HL	House of Lords [England]
I L Pr	International Litigation Procedure
ICAO	International Civil Aviation Organization
ICC	International Chamber of Commerce
ICJ Rep	Reports of Judgments, Advisory Opinions and Orders of the International Court of Justice
ICLQ	International and Comparative Law Quarterly
IEHC	Irish High Court [neutral citation]
IESC	Irish Supreme Court [neutral citation]
ILA Rep	International Law Association Report
Ind Int & Comp L Rev	Indiana International and Comparative Law Review
IPRax	Praxis des Internationalen Privat- under Verfahrensrechts
Isr L Rev	Israel Law Review
J L & Com	Journal of Law and Commerce
JBL	Journal of Business Law
La L Rev	Louisiana Law Review
Lloyd's Rep	Lloyds Law Reports
Loy LA L Rev	Loyola University of Los Angeles Law Review
Mich J Intl L	Michigan Journal of International Law
Mich L Rev	Michigan Law Review
MLR	Modern Law Review
NE	North Eastern Reporter
NY	New York Reports
NYU J Intl L & Pol	New York University Journal of International Law & Politics
NZLR	New Zealand Law Reports
Ohio St L J	Ohio State Law Journal
OJ	Official Journal of the European Communities
OUP	Oxford University Press
PC	Privy Council
PECL	Principles of European Contract Law
PICC	[UNIDROIT] Principles of International Commercial Contracts
QB	Law Reports, Queen's Bench Division
RabelsZ	Rabels Zeitschrift für ausländisches und internationales Privatrecht
RDAI	Revue de Droit des Affaires Internationales

Rev dr int pr	Revue de Droit International Privé
RIDC	Revue Internationale de Droit Comparé
Riv.dir.int.priv.proc.	Rivista di diritto internazionale privato e processuale
S Ct	Supreme Court Reporter [USA]
SC	Session Cases [Scotland]
SI	Statutory Instrument
SLR	Scottish Law Reporter
SLR	Singapore Law Reports
Tex Intl L J	Texas International Law Journal
Tul J Intl & Comp L	Tulane Journal of International and Comparative law
Tul L Rev	Tulane Law Review
U Chi L Rev	University of Chicago Law Review
U Ill L Rev	University of Illinois Law Review
U Pa L Rev	University of Pennsylvania Law Review
UCC	Uniform Commercial Code [USA]
UCC LJ	UCC Law Journal
UCLA L Rev	University of California at Los Angeles Law Review
UKPC	United Kingdom Privy Council
UNCITRAL	United Nations Commission on International Trade Law
Unif L Rev	Uniform Law Review [journal of UNIDROIT] Old series 1973–95 New series 1996 –
UPICC	UNIDROIT Principles of International Commercial Contracts
US	United States Supreme Court Reports
WLR	Weekly Law Reports
ZEuP	Zeitschrift für Europäisches Privatrecht

INTRODUCTION

With the growth of international trade has come a growing recognition of the benefits to be obtained through the harmonization of international trade law. Transnational commercial law consists of that set of rules, from whatever source, which governs international commercial transactions and is common to a number of legal systems. Such commonality is increasingly derived from international instruments of various kinds, such as conventions and model laws, and from codifications of international trade usage adopted by contract, as exemplified by the Uniform Customs and Practice for Documentary Credits published by the International Chamber of Commerce and the Model Arbitration Rules issued by the United Nations Commission on International Trade Law (UNCITRAL). Legislative guides of the kind published by UNCITRAL and UNIDROIT are also contributing to the process of harmonization at international level. So too are 'soft law' restatements, such as the UNIDROIT Principles of International Commercial Contracts, which though not binding are regularly resorted to by arbitral tribunals and influence the shaping of domestic legislation in developing as well as 'developed' countries. Underpinning these is the *lex mercatoria*, consisting of the unwritten customs and usages of merchants and general principles of commercial law.

Though the primary focus of this work is on harmonization at the international level, the growth of regional harmonization must also not be overlooked. The most powerful and wide-ranging regional organization is, of course, the European Union, which has issued a number of directives and regulations affecting commercial transactions, a selection of which are included in this work. Other regional organizations which have produced and are continuing to develop regional uniform laws include the Organization of American States (OAS), the membership of which embraces all thirty-five independent American States, and the Organisation for the Harmonisation of Business Law in Africa (OHADA), consisting of fifteen francophone African countries wishing to update their business law.

From the materials contained in this work (which are necessarily very selective in character) the student should gain a perception of what drives commercial law, the reasons for harmonization, the institutions involved, the various ways in which transnational law is created, and the major problems and policy issues which have to be confronted. Extracts from articles are reproduced without footnotes, but occasionally we have inserted footnotes ourselves for clarification.

This volume is divided into six main sections. The first, devoted to general principles, sets the scene by describing the nature and sources of transnational commercial law, the roles of comparative law and the conflict of laws in the harmonization process and the harmonizing instruments and agencies. In the second, and central, section we examine the issues referred to earlier in the context of specific international instruments (conventions, model laws, international restatements, etc.) arranged by subject: international sales, agency and distribution, international bank payment undertakings, international financial leasing, receivables financing, international interests in mobile equipment and transactions in securities. The third section is devoted to the harmonization of general contract law through international and regional restatements by groups of scholars. This is followed by a section on transnational insolvency. The fifth section focuses on international dispute resolution and instruments designed to harmonize the law and practice of international civil procedure and international commercial arbitration. In the concluding section we draw the threads together, examine recurrent issues of harmonization and consider the future direction of transnational commercial law, with particular reference to the harmonization of general principles of private law and the practical and political problems obstructing progress.

The student is not expected to be familiar with the detail of the instruments discussed, which could not possibly be covered in a single course. Rather the purpose is to focus on the influences leading to the making of the instrument, its objectives, scope and interpretation, the fundamental concepts it embodies, the key policy questions it seeks to address and the methods used to reconcile the differing viewpoints of different legal families and systems. Accordingly each seminar sheet will direct the student's attention to specific provisions to be examined in class in these contexts.

We have provided a short list of introductory reading that students will find it helpful to pursue before the start of the course. Additional reading specific to each topic is set out at the end of each chapter. Some of the literature listed consists of works of reference and these works are not intended to be read in full but should be used as a source of background information and more detailed discussion of particular issues. Students are encouraged to read the full text of extracted law reports and articles in legal periodicals. Seminar questions, for which students should prepare a week in advance, assume they have done this and cannot be answered simply by reference to the commentary.

INTRODUCTORY READING

Cheng, Chia-Jui (ed.), *Clive M. Schmitthoff's Selected Essays on International Trade Law* (Martinus Nijhoff/Graham and Trotman, Dordrecht/Boston/London, 1988) 20–37

David, René, *The International Unification of Private Law, in International Encyclopaedia of Comparative Law* (JCB Mohr, Tübingen, 1971), ch 5

Fletcher, Ian, Mistelis, Loukas, and Cremona, Marise (eds), *Foundations and Perspectives in International Trade Law* (Sweet & Maxwell, London, 2001), ch 1

Goode, Roy, 'Rule, Practice and Pragmatism in Transnational Commercial Law', (2005) 54 ICLQ 539

Gutteridge, H C, *Comparative Law* (2nd edn, Cambridge University Press, Cambridge, 1949), Chapters IX and XI–XII

Hobhouse, J S, 'International Conventions and Commercial Law: The Pursuit of Uniformity' (1990) 106 LQR 530

Horn, Norbert, and Schmitthoff, Clive M (eds) *The Transnational Law of International Commercial Transactions* (Kluwer, Deventer, 1982), chs 1 and 2

Mustill, Lord Justice, 'The New *Lex Mercatoria*: The First Twenty-Five Years' in *Liber Amicorum for Lord Wilberforce* (eds Maarten Bos and Ian Brownlie), (Oxford University Press, Oxford, 1987), ch 9

Wool, Jeffrey, 'Rethinking the Role of Uniformity in the Drafting of International Commerical Law: A Preliminary Proposal for the Development of a Policy-Based Unification Model' (1997) II Unif L Rev 46

Zweigert, Konrad, and Kötz, Hein, *An Introduction to Comparative Law* (3rd edn, transl Tony Weir) (Oxford University Press, 1998), ch 1

PART I

GENERAL PRINCIPLES

1

THE NATURE, HISTORY AND SOURCES OF COMMERCIAL LAW

A. The Nature of Commercial Law
Three definitions 1.01
  Commercial law 1.02
  Transnational commercial law 1.03
  Lex mercatoria 1.04
What drives commercial law? 1.05
  A medieval example 1.06
  A later example 1.07
  A modern example 1.08
Commercial law and civil law 1.10
The transition from planned
  economies to market economies 1.14

B. The History of Commercial Law
The early and medieval codes 1.15
Characteristics of the medieval law
  merchant 1.20
The nationalization of commercial law ... 1.24
The return to internationalism and
  the growth of transnational
  commercial law 1.25
The growth of regionalism 1.31

**C. The Sources of National
  Commercial Law** 1.32
Contract 1.33
Usage 1.34
Suppletive rules of common law 1.35
Domestic legislation 1.36

**D. The Nature and Sources of
  Transnational Commercial Law** ... 1.37
Is there an autonomous transnational
  commercial law? 1.38

The *lex mercatoria* and
  the conflict of laws 1.39
External validation by a court
  or tribunal 1.45
Determination in accordance
  with law 1.47
The sources of transnational
  commercial law 1.52
  Lex mercatoria 1.53
  International and regional
    instruments 1.54
  Conscious or unconscious judicial or
    legislative parallelism 1.55
  Contractually incorporated rules and
    trade terms promulgated by
    international organizations 1.56
  Standard-term contracts 1.57
  Restatements of scholars 1.58
  General principles of
    international law 1.59

E. *Lex Mercatoria*
The sources of the *lex mercatoria* 1.60
The normative force of usage 1.61
International conventions as
  evidence of usage 1.65
General principles of law 1.66

A. The Nature of Commercial Law

Three definitions

1.01 We shall begin by defining three terms: commercial law, transnational commercial law and *lex mercatoria*. These are not terms of art, and different writers use them in different senses. But for our purposes, they denote the following:

Commercial law

1.02 The totality of the law's response to mercantile disputes, encompassing 'all those principles, rules and statutory provisions, of whatever kind and from whatever source, which bear on the private law rights and obligations of parties to commercial transactions'.[1] In this conception, commercial law is concerned with transactions between professionals, whether they are merchants, financiers or intermediaries. This definition thus excludes: (1) institutional law, such as the law of corporations and partnerships and the law governing the establishment and capital adequacy of financial enterprises; (2) consumer law (since one party is not a professional), and (3) public law, even if affecting the enforceability of agreements, for example, competition (antitrust) law.

Transnational commercial law

1.03 We use this phrase to denote that set of private law principles and rules, from whatever source, which governs international commercial transactions and is common to legal systems generally or to a significant number of legal systems. Again, the focus is on private law and on transactions, particularly cross-border transactions. Our subject is thus to be distinguished from international economic law, which is a branch of public international law and is concerned primarily with dealings between States and resolution of inter-State disputes by organs of the World Trade Organization.

Norbert Horn, 'Uniformity and Diversity in the Law of International Commercial Contracts' in Norbert Horn, Clive M Schmitthoff and J Barrigan Marcantonio (eds), *The Transnational Law of International Commercial Transactions* (Kluwer, Boston, 1982) 4 and 12

B. Three concepts of Transnational Law

Despite the usual connection between a private contract and its applicable national contract law, the transnational (i.e. cross-border) character of a commercial transaction entails specific legal problems and consequences. The most suitable way to describe them is to adopt the modern term 'transnational law'. This term in fact points to a variety of inter-related and complex problems which are of daily concern for the international business

---

[1] Roy Goode, *Commercial Law in the Next Millennium* (Sweet & Maxwell, London, 1998) 8.

lawyer. In order to avoid confusion, however, we must strictly distinguish three separate usages of the term 'transnational law':

(1) as a general description of the legal regime of an international commercial transaction;
(2) as a label for the factual uniformity or similarity in contract laws applicable to or contractual patterns used in international commercial transactions; and, finally,
(3) as a term to denote international sources of commercial law, i.e. internationally uniform law in the proper sense.

Each of these different concepts of transnational law is relevant to understanding the legal regime of international commerce and requires some further explanation. In addition, we should bear in mind that the term 'law' is sometimes used not only to denote the objective norms created by the legislative power of a state or states but also to describe the contracts concluded by the parties which are legally binding between them; in this respect, individual contracts as well as typical and widely used contractual patterns may be termed 'contract law' (*lex contractus*).

1. All Law Pertaining to Transnational Transactions

'Transnational law' in the broadest sense has been defined by Jessup as 'all law which regulates actions or events that transcend national frontiers'. This is just a label for all legal norms governing international business contracts and might serve as a mere description of the complex legal circumstances surrounding international transactions. It is common that a variety of norms outside the *lex contractus*, from at least two and often more national legal systems, have an impact on the contract. These may be laws on exchange controls, taxation, safety rules, etc. This is in addition to the strict rules of national contract, business or company law which must be respected.

The drafters of international commercial contracts have to take into account the various legal environments and complex legal situations, which might be relevant not only when drafting clauses on choice of law and forum, but also when deciding on the time and manner of delivery and payment (including the role of banks and the use of specific sureties), and clauses on specific dispute settlement procedures. These contractual provisions dealing with the transnational situation might equally be labelled 'transnational law' in so far as they constitute legally binding *lex contractus*.

2. De facto Uniform Law and Contractual Patterns

But we can go one step further and single out those legal rules, principles and contractual patterns which are internationally used or recognised in a uniform or similar way although they may stem partly from different national laws. Here, 'transnational law' describes an actual uniformity or similarity of rules and patterns. In fact, international commerce is, to a growing extent, guided and co-ordinated by such uniform rules and patterns. This phenomenon of uniform rules serving uniform needs of international business and economic co-operation is today commonly labelled *lex mercatoria*.

3. International Sources of Law; Uniform Law

Finally, the term transnational law can also be used as a label for internationally uniform law in the proper sense, based on international sources of law, i.e., either on conventions ('international legislation') or on customary law. In addition, we should note commercial custom which, though not a legal source in a technical sense, has some important functions similar to those of a true legal source.

Examples of international conventions can be found in the law of international transportation of goods by sea, air and land. . . . Such conventions, once signed by the signatory states and embodied in their national legal systems, will be an important international source of uniform commercial law. This source has the great advantage of clarity and is a suitable vehicle for imposing mandatory rules of law on the persons to whom it is addressed. For example, the Hague-Visby Rules on Bills of Lading cannot be contracted out. On the other hand, the drafting, negotiating and ratification procedures necessary to bring such conventions to life (often followed by procedures to transform them into municipal law as prescribed by the national constitution) are time-consuming and difficult. International legislation, therefore, can be confined only to select and particularly important legal issues.

International customary law, on the other hand, is only of limited assistance in solving legal problems of international commerce. There are few legal principles, such as *pacta sunt servanda*, which are generally recognised and can be termed international customary law. It is true that the general principles of customary law provide common ground for lawyers from civil law and common law countries. But these principles are difficult to apply in specific cases, and courts in various countries have been extremely reluctant to resort to rules of international customary law when deciding issues involving private contracts.

Lex mercatoria

1.04 Some writers equate this with transnational commercial law. Thus, the Danish scholar Professor Ole Lando, in a much-cited article,[2] lists the following elements of the law merchant (which he describes as non-exhaustive): public international law, uniform laws, general principles of law, rules of international organizations, customs and usages, standard form contracts, and reporting of arbitral awards. But we prefer to confine the *lex mercatoria*, or law of merchants, to what Roman lawyers described as *ius non scriptum*, and thus to define it as that part of transnational commercial law which consists of the unwritten customs and usages of merchants, so far as these satisfy certain externally set criteria for validation. That is certainly how it was seen by the anonymous author of the thirteenth century *Lex Mercatoria*, the earliest known English treatise on the law merchant and the practice of the mercantile courts in England.[3] It is also traditional to include general principles of law as an aspect of the *lex mercatoria*, but there is a strong argument in favour of excluding such principles in that they are not specific to international transactions or even to commercial dealings, and thus can scarcely be regarded as a manifestation of the creative power of trade usage.[4]

What drives commercial law?

1.05 In order to understand commercial law in general and transnational commercial law in particular, it is important to realize that commercial law is not devised in

---

[2] Ole Lando, 'The *Lex Mercatoria* in International Commercial Arbitration' (1985) 34 ICLQ 747.
[3] See: Mary Elizabeth Basile et al, *Lex Mercatoria and Legal Pluralism: A Late Thirteenth-Century Treatise and Its Aftermath* (The Ames Foundation, Cambridge (MA), 1998).
[4] See below, paras 1.66–1.67.

the abstract but is a response to the practices and legitimate needs of merchants. It is mercantile practice that fashions commercial law;[5] and mercantile practice evolves as a response to impediments to trade, whether legal or practical, that has to be surmounted and to the driving force of competition as each enterprise strives to attract increased business by developing new products in goods and services. Three examples will help to make the point.

A medieval example

In the Middle Ages, exporters and importers of goods by sea were anxious to have a mechanism by which the goods could be sold or pledged in transit. This led to the creation of the bill of lading, a document of title issued by the carrier who undertook that on arrival of the goods at the end of the sea transit, the carrier would deliver them to whoever was the current holder of the bill of lading and presented it at the port of arrival. The bill of lading thus gave control of the goods to the holder of the document, who could transfer that control by delivery of the bill of lading with any necessary endorsement. This neat technique enabled the buyer of the goods to resell them in transit or to borrow against them by delivering the bill of lading to the buyer or lender in exchange for the price or loan, which itself might be paid by a bill of exchange.

1.06

A later example

A company wishes to obtain funds to buy equipment, but it has given covenants to a lender which restrict its right to borrow from a third party on the security of its assets. The company concludes an arrangement with a finance house by which the latter will buy the equipment and supply it to the company under a conditional sale or leasing agreement. In most jurisdictions, this is not an advance on security and does not entail the breach of any covenants in the loan agreement.

1.07

A modern example

A creditor holding a portfolio of mortgage receivables would like to have this taken off its balance sheet in order, for example, to reduce its capital adequacy requirements, which are geared to its risk-weighted assets, and to use the receivables to raise money from the securities market. Both these objectives can be achieved by a technique known as securitization. This may take different forms, but a common one is for the creditor (known as the originator) to sell the receivables to a special-purpose vehicle (SPV) which will then issue notes to investors, the proceeds of the issue being used to pay the originator the purchase price. The

1.08

---

[5] It is also, of course, true that businessmen shape their contractual arrangements around the law in order to produce or avoid a particular legal result.

receivables are then charged by the SPV to trustees for the investors to secure the issuer's obligations under the notes.

1.09 Of course, all these techniques rely on the willingness of courts, in case of a dispute, to uphold the validity of the transaction and to give it the effect intended by the parties. Experience has shown that, in most developed countries, the courts are sensitive to the need to avoid damaging commercial instruments that are fulfilling a useful and legitimate purpose, if only because of the potentially adverse effects this could have on the stability of the industry and on the attractiveness of the jurisdiction to foreigners wishing to deal with its traders. The more widespread the market practice, and the more damaging the effects of invalidating it, the more likely it is to be upheld by the courts. Even so, there are occasional upsets which either force the modification or abandonment of the practice or lead to corrective legislation. Such was the case in England in the 1990s, when the House of Lords held that swaps transactions entered into by local authorities were *ultra vires* and wholly invalid,[6] a decision that caused widespread consternation among financial institutions, particularly foreign banks, and for a while, did some damage to London's reputation as a world financial centre.[7]

Commercial law and civil law

1.10 Whether commercial law should be formally distinguished from the general civil law is a question that has exercised both legislators and scholars over the years, and approaches vary widely from jurisdiction to jurisdiction. Many legal systems have a commercial code, many others do not. In some, the applicability of the code is used as the determinant of the commercial nature of the transaction, in others, the function of the code is simply to provide rules governing some of the more important types of commercial transaction without thereby implying that other transactions are necessarily non-commercial. In those legal systems that treat commercial law separately from civil law, the character of the transaction may be determined subjectively by the status of the parties as carrying on a business (*commerçants, Kaufleute*) or objectively by reference to the type of transaction or activity (*actes de commerce, Handelsgeschäfte*) or by a combination of the two. Whatever the legal system involved, it is clear that commercial law and commercial transactions cannot be isolated as self-contained compartments of contract or of commercial law.

---

[6] *Hazell v Hammersmith and Fulham LBC* [1992] 2 AC 1 (HL).

[7] As was subsequently acknowledged by Lord Goff (who had not been a member of the panel hearing that case) in *Westdeutsche Landesbank Girozentrale v Islington LBC* [1996] AC 669 (HL) 680. For a not unsympathetic approach to the decision, see: Ewan McKendrick, 'Local Authorities and Swaps: Undermining the Market?' in Ross Cranston (ed), *Making Commercial Law: Essays in Honour of Roy Goode* (Clarendon Press, Oxford, 1997) ch 8. The hardship imposed on third parties entering into an *ultra vires* transaction with a local authority in good faith was subsequently alleviated by the Local Government Act 1997 ss 5–7.

Boris Kozolchyk, 'The Commercialization of Civil Law and the Civilization of Commercial Law' 40 Louisiana L Rev 3, 3–5 (1979–80)

This topic requires that one first clarify what is meant by civil law and by commercial law. One might be tempted to assert positivistically that civil law is the law found in civil codes and commercial law is the law found in commercial codes. Yet, legal history proves that it has been very difficult, if not impossible, to draft a code that applies exclusively to civil or commercial transactions. Even where the draftsmen of separate civil and commercial codes adopted what they thought to be neat lines of differentiation or scope criteria, it was clear, almost before the ink had dried, that they had failed in their attempts at separation.

The first to try separation was Napoleonic France with its so-called *objective* criterion, a criterion followed by the majority of other civil law countries. The scope of the French Commercial Code of 1807 was determined by inquiring whether the parties had entered into 'an act of commerce', such as, a purchase and sale of goods or merchandise for their resale, enterprises of manufacture, commission agency, transportation, public spectacles, exchange, banking and brokerage, construction, or maritime commerce, or whether the parties had signed or endorsed a promissory note or a bill of exchange. By contrast, the *subjective* criterion defined the scope of a commercial code on the basis of the merchant's professional affiliation. A subjective commercial code applied only to those who qualified as habitual and professional merchants. This approach, which was implicit in the eighteenth century Prussian *Allgemeine Landrecht*, was expressly adopted by some of Germany's nineteenth century commercial codes and prevails in the German Commercial Code of 1900. The professionals chosen under the subjective criterion included predominantly bankers and traders. Primary producers were not included because they treasured their monopolistic status, inconsistent as it was with the competition principles of the commercial codes. Agricultural business was similarly uninterested in the competitive capitalism of the commercial code. Also exempted from the commercial characterization were those who thought better of themselves, such as members of the liberal professions, including physicians (however enterprising), actors, attorneys, authors, composers and teachers.

By defining the commercial code as objective, the French codifiers attempted to avoid the stigma of conferring a privileged status to a class of citizens, anathema as privileges were to the revolutionary principle of equality before the law. Thus, in principle, the French Commercial Code applied to acts of commerce by merchants, as well as to those acts of commerce entered into by non- merchants, such as law professors, opera singers, or priests.

On the other hand, the French Civil Code dealt with matters such as a person's legal status, regulating that status from birth until death. Included in the regulation of a person's status were such aspects as: his domestic and family relations; his obligations, both contractual and extra-contractual; his non-profit associations; and his acquisition, use, and disposition, both *inter vivos* and *mortis causa*, of personal and real property. In addition, it provided principles of general application to transactions both within and beyond its confines, such as:

Laws relating to public order and morals cannot be derogated from by private agreement. Contracts lawfully entered into have the force of law for those who have made them. They can only be cancelled by mutual consent or by causes allowed by law. They must be carried out in good faith. Possession is the equivalent of title with respect to personal property. Any human act which causes damage to another obligates the person through whose fault damage occurred to make reparation for the damage. The generality of these and other principles contributed to the civil code's status as the unofficial constitution of France's private law.

The problem with the objective–subjective dichotomy is that the life of the law in general, and of commercial life in particular, is not, as Justice Holmes continually reminds us, quite that syllogistic. One who disagrees with Holmes should try to define an act of commerce, such as 'brokerage', without referring to the activity of the broker. To make sense you would have to define brokerage by describing brokers and vice versa; if you wish to define a broker, you must describe what he, as a broker, does. Moreover, consider the case of the so-called 'mixed act', the act which is commercial for one of the parties, say the seller, and civil i.e., not profit making . . . for the consuming buyer. Additionally, consider the act which starts out as a civil act on the part of the buyer, but becomes profit-making once the buyer realizes that he can profit by reselling that which he bought with the initial purpose of only consuming.

The difficulty of drawing a neat line between that which is civil and that which is commercial in everyday legal affairs does not mean that there are no significant differences between the rules, concepts, and principles of interpretation that characterize each of these major branches of private law. The differences emerge once one examines how civil and commercial law treat a simple, everyday transaction such as a sale or conveyance of valuable property.

1.11 Commercial codes in Europe tend to be rather fragmented in character and to embody only a small part of what is considered to constitute commercial law. The American Uniform Commercial Code, by contrast, adopts an integrated approach to the more important types of transaction—sale, leasing, negotiable instruments, secured transactions, for example—but does not seek either to insulate these from the general law or to characterize transactions outside the code as non-commercial. Systems such as English law that have no commercial code and no formal separation of commercial law from the general law nevertheless have a conception of commercial law as a distinct branch of law, though its scope and content are nowhere defined and are very much a matter of individual perception. As Professor Ernst von Caemmerer so elegantly put it:

> The consequence of this [historical] development is that there is no special, separate commercial law in the Anglo-American systems. If the commercial or mercantile law has its own special literature even in the Anglo-American countries, that is only a result of selection and organization of materials, which lies in the discretion of the particular author.[8]

1.12 To this, one may add that in common law jurisdictions commercial law is conceived as essentially transactional in character, and thus distinct from company (or corporation) law, while civil law jurisdictions tend to treat company law as part of commercial law.

1.13 As a generalization, one can say that commercial contracts are governed by the general law, except so far as this is qualified by rules particular to commercial

---

[8] Ernst von Caemmerer, 'The Influence of the Law of International Trade on the Development and Character of the Commercial Law in the Civil Law Countries' in Clive M Schmitthoff (ed), *The Sources of the Law of International Trade* (Stevens, London, 1964) 90.

transactions. Such rules are designed to accommodate the need of the business community for informality, flexibility and respect for commercial practice. So rules requiring writing for ordinary contracts, in particular contracts entered into by consumers, may dispense with this requirement in the case of commercial contracts. Those who deal in goods as merchants are generally expected to assume certain basic obligations—for example, that the goods are of proper quality and fit for their purpose—which are not required of a person selling as a consumer. Most jurisdictions recognize in different degrees the binding force of trade usage, whether as an implied term of a contract or as an independent legal norm. Traders frequently engage in repeat dealings among themselves, so that terms may be implied from a course of dealing that would not arise in one-shot consumer transactions. Persons engaged in commerce are generally held to a standard of commercially reasonable behaviour that is not necessarily expected of others. Consumers are in most countries protected by special legislation, which in large part does not apply to those entering into contracts in the way of business.

JH Dalhuisen, *Dalhuisen on International Commercial, Financial and Trade Law* (2nd edn, Hart Publishing, Oxford, 2004) 24–5

Tying the commercial law to acts of commerce (as enumerated) is often presented as the *objective* approach as distinguished from the *subjective* approach to commercial law, in France also referred to as the *droit réel v droit personnel* approach. This latter approach ties commercial law to the activities of merchants. France in essence opted for the objective approach (enumeration of the acts of commerce) . . . In Germany it was the reverse: all merchants are in principle in their activity governed by the commercial code, but of course only for the activities that it covers . . . So even in Germany, a definition of commercial acts (*Handelsgeschäfte*) comes in, although some activity is considered commercial *per se*. On the other hand, some commercial activity may be engaged in by non-merchants, like the writing of cheques or the drawing of bills of exchange, which is now covered by a separate statute. Where in other instances non-merchants engage in commercial activity, it may still be covered by the commercial code, but this activity is then considered commercial only in a more generic or wider sense. In fact, many provisions of the HGB [*Handelsgesetzbuch*, or Commercial Code] do not cover specific commercial matters at all and apply equally to non-merchants. The distinctions are therefore not so clean and clear in Germany either . . . The real problem in all this, in both France and Germany and in all countries that still maintain similar criteria for the application of commercial law, is that merchants are not only engaging in commercial activity but also in non-commercial acts. The consequence is that neither the concept of merchant nor the concept of commercial activity can be defined exclusively in terms of the other. Hence the confusion.

The transition from planned economies to market economies

What has been described above is based on the concept of a market economy in **1.14** which, within the constraints prescribed by law, parties are free to conclude bargains, to acquire property, to accumulate wealth and to pursue the goals of a capitalist society. That was not, of course, the case in the communist countries in

Central and Eastern Europe, where property was state owned, private rights were subordinated to the collective interest and the state had a monopoly over foreign trade, which it exercised through a foreign trade organization. But with the collapse of communism in those countries, collective rights began to be replaced by private rights, and planned economies by market economies. It is only relatively recently that the former communist countries have been able to turn their efforts to restoring and modernizing their commercial laws. This has been done partly by dusting off old commercial codes and partly by introducing new codes or other legislation. The transition process is being facilitated by the Legal Transition Programme of the European Bank for Reconstruction and Development, which has devoted particular attention to legal regimes for secured transactions and insolvency. The EBRD's model law on secured transactions, published in 1994, was a pioneer in its field and was later supplemented by its set of core principles for a secured transactions law and, more recently, its set of guiding principles for the efficient and effective development of charges registries.[9]

B. The History of Commercial Law

The early and medieval codes

1.15 Commercial law in one form or another is probably as old as trade itself. The Code of Hammurabi, believed to date back to 1900 BC, contained a number of rules of commercial law, and that code itself derived in no small measure from Sumerian laws made several centuries earlier. Much of the earlier content of commercial law remains shrouded in mystery. What we do know is that its history is a story of constant reinvention of the wheel. The Italians are generally credited with the creation of the bill of exchange in the Middle Ages, but instruments recognizable as bills of exchange are to be found in clay tablets from Karkhemish in Assyria as far back as the seventh century BC.[10] English law is credited with the development of the floating charge in the nineteenth century, yet the *hypotheca* of Roman law was not so very different. From biblical times trade was both local and international and was conducted by land, along the great caravan routes linking West to East, including the elaborate network of roads constituting the famous Silk Road, which ran from the shores of the Mediterranean through Samarkand in Central Asia to Tunhwang and Changan (Xian) in China, and by sea from Greece to India. In international trade, commercial law was closely allied to maritime law, and it is in the field of maritime law that we see one of the great codifications of our ancestors: the Rhodian Maritime Code in the second or third century BC, which was accepted equally by Greeks and Romans and was the first known law to embody the principle of general average in

---

[9] See: EBRD, 'Law in Transition 2005' <http://www.ebrd.com/pubs/legal/6215.pdf> p 17.
[10] Wyndham A Bewes, *Romance of the Law Merchant* (Sweet & Maxwell, London, 1923) 50.

maritime insurance. Remarkably, the Code lasted 1,000 years, being replaced in the seventh or eighth century AD by the Rhodian sea laws, an influential compilation of maritime customs. The connection between the law merchant and maritime law was noted long ago by Gerard Malynes in his famous seventeenth century work *Consuetudo, vel Lex Mercatoria: or, The Ancient Law-Merchant.*[11]

> Are not the Sea-Laws established to decide the controversies and differences happening between Merchants and Marriners? And is it not convenient for Merchants to know them? Considering that Merchants maintain the Fisher-men, and (by way of Trade) cause the Sea and Land Commodities to be dispersed every where? So that the prerogatives do also appertain to the Law-Merchant, as properly inherent unto commerce, and the observation of Merchants being of like condition to all People and nations.[12]

Between the eleventh and fifteenth centuries, there were several compilations of mercantile customs, mostly maritime. These included: the eleventh century Amalfitan Tables and the hugely influential Rolls of Oléron, which were largely, though not exclusively, concerned with maritime law; the British mid-thirteenth century Black Book of the Admiralty; the Laws of Wisby, a fourteenth century text heavily inspired by the Rolls of Oléron; and, the Consulate of the Sea, a massive codification from Barcelona in the fourteenth or fifteenth century consisting of some 334 articles and covering a wide diversity of subjects ranging from the procedures of consulate courts and the rights and obligations of investors in a ship construction project to the punishment of a seaman for undressing for the night when his vessel was still at sea.[13]   **1.16**

The medieval law merchant evolved because of urbanization and the consequent growth of the merchant class, the creation of merchant and consular courts, and the need for new commercial instruments in international trade. European rulers, anxious to attract international trade to their countries, enacted special laws for the protection of merchants, and recognition of their customs and the jurisdiction of their courts. Other factors were the opening up of caravan routes between East and West in the constant search for new markets, and the impact of the Crusades. But international trade could flourish only if underpinned by rules and practices which themselves enjoyed international recognition. The great fairs, such as those of Champagne and Flanders, were highly organized institutions. Granted numerous privileges, they had their own merchant courts, they were centres of banking and money exchange and they even operated their own courier service. Their   **1.17**

---

[11] Commonly referred to in the abbreviated form *Lex Mercatoria*. A much fuller treatment of the law is to be found in the eighteenth century work by Wyndham Beawes, *Lex Mercatoria Redivia: Or, The Merchant's Directory* (J Rivington, London, 1783).

[12] Gerard Malynes, *Consuetudo, vel Lex Mercatoria: or, The Ancient Law-Merchant* (3rd edn printed by Thomas Basset et al, London, 1686, reprinted Professional Books, Abingdon, Oxon, 1981) Pt I, 2–3.

[13] Which was to be tied and dunked in the ocean three times while held by a rope: Art 170.

importance was well described by the eminent French legal historian, Professor Paul Huvelin.

P Huvelin, *Essai historique sur les marchés et les foires* (Arthur Rousseau, Paris, 1897) 594–7

The influence of the fairs on our public law, on the movement towards freeing of the towns and enfranchisement of the third estate is undeniable. More striking still is the influence on links with the law of nations; the term *fair* is the equivalent of the term *peace*. The reaction against the primitive instinct of hostility comes about under the influence of commercial needs. If it is, perhaps, inexact to say that hospitable relations, in which are to be found the germ of the institutions most characteristic of international law, derive solely from the needs of commerce, it must nevertheless be recognised that in this matter these needs have contributed powerfully to affinities between religions and between races. Little by little, thanks to the spread of peace and the management of the fairs, dealings between foreigners become more secure; international relations multiply; transactions are supported by guarantees; and there increasingly develop the ideas of good faith and loyalty which must govern commerce. At the same time there is an improvement in the means of transport . . . The peace of commerce conquers the world. And the fairs disappear only after they have accomplished their work.

Their role is no less remarkable in economic matters. They are the first centres in which the notions of value can develop; the law of supply and demand, the law of the balance of trade find their first application. It is at the fairs that merchandise and money cease to be mere objects of consumption and become capital. Thanks to the fairs, trade is regularised and submitted to the great law of competition.

At the same time, the law of the fairs, born of the peace of commerce, acts strongly on the institutions of the general law, which are still steeped in their old rigidity. Little by little the law of nations penetrates the civil law; in the Middle Ages it is commercial law, derived from Roman law and based on good faith, which reacts against the rigour and the materialism of German law and which, without destroying all traces, fashions this law and transforms it so as to accommodate it to the needs of the new world. A tendency to uniformity becomes stronger. In the midst of diversity of local laws, the law of the great fairs everywhere remains the same in its essential features. This law is universal, almost of the same status as the canon law. The courts of the fairs command obedience everywhere. And thus emerges the conception of the law merchant, which remains outside and above the civil ordinances and the local commercial usages. This conception is a reaction against the spirit of fragmentation and particularism which prevails in all the laws and in all the customs, and at the same time as it affirms the notion of the unity of commercial law it shows a distinct tendency to unify other laws. It is by this route that the principles of commerce enter into civilisation . . .

So the fairs, the original form of terrestrial commerce, have been, in the history of civilisation, unrivalled instruments of rapprochement, of unification, of peace. Today they are disappearing. Little by little, periodic trade has become permanent. The tides of economic life are increasingly coming together. However, there still remains something of the old norm of periodicity; commerce remains generally subservient to the periodic return of days and of nights. Dealings which at one time were effected annually, monthly or weekly now take place every day. Meanwhile we can predict that soon, preceding as always the other functions of social life, commerce will no longer be subject to any interruption. And the circulation of capital, of credit, of work, will continue without respite, liberated at last from the bonds of periodicity, waiting for a new evolution to carry it towards destinies unknown.

To Italy, whose merchants were the dominant influence at the fairs of Champagne, **1.18** belongs pride of place in the development of the medieval law merchant. Several factors contributed to this: the unifying force of the received Roman law (particularly its maritime law), which became a European *ius commune*; the presence of Italian merchants throughout Europe; and, the recognition by Italian cities that their prosperity depended upon the provision of institutions and procedures that met the needs of the mercantile community and on their willingness to recognize and uphold mercantile custom. Thus, it is in Italy that we see the development of the bill of exchange as a means of localizing payment obligations in international trade,[14] the bill of lading as a vehicle to facilitate the sale or pledge of goods in sea transit, the adaptation of Roman law rules governing the distribution of maritime risks, the evolution of new forms of business association such as the joint venture (*commenda*) and the maritime partnership (*societas maris*), and the institution of bankruptcy. In Italy also, there came into being mercantile courts possessed of the widest powers, of which the most famous was the Mercanzia in Florence, the court formed by the five Florentine guilds.

Frederic R Sanborn, *Origins of the Early English Maritime and Commercial Law* (The Century Co, London c1930: reprinted Professional Books, Abingdon, 1989) 143 and 145

[Despite its title, half this work is devoted to European medieval maritime and commercial law].

The court of the Mercanzia had jurisdiction of all complaints directed against members, whether made by members or by non-members, the latter having complete liberty to sue in the ordinary courts, where, however, the canon law and procedure made cases complex and long drawn-out. On the contrary, justice was rapid and summary before the Mercanzia: 'Quod procedatur sine strepitu et figura judicii', reads the classical formula. Nor was this the only advantage, for the spirit of the regulations, the equity of each separate case, rather than the strict letter of the rule, was considered with scrupulous care. Because of these advantages the Florentine merchants who were not members of the guilds came to use the court of the Mercanzia more and more, although, as yet, there was nothing to compel them to do so. They were still quite free to go before the common law judges, but they did not do so, and the field of commercial jurisdiction was enlarged . . . It was left to the notary of the Mercanzia to settle all the little international difficulties which had previously caused so much trouble when settled by force, and the method was at once simple and expeditious. The *notarius mercanzie* proceeded upon a complaint against a

---

[14] For example, an Italian buyer from a French exporter, instead of shipping gold as payment of the purchase price, would arrange for his Italian bank (with which he had funds or a line of credit) to draw a bill of exchange on one of its French correspondents in favour of the seller, to whom the draft would be delivered and who would present it for payment to the French bank and collect payment in France. The two banks, between whom there might be many mutual dealings, would typically settle their accounts at one of the great international fairs.

debtor, compelling him to pay immediately, or to put up a guarantee if he claimed to be in the right, under pain of expulsion. The debtor's associates, brothers, and dependent sons were summoned, too. These remedies were copied elsewhere, and brought in a better commercial security. The results following the intervention of the Mercanzia were so successful that it was decided to give this organization an official sanction, and on March 21, 1308, a Florentine law recognized it as a State court. Soon afterwards, there was conceded to this court an advantage which none of the others enjoyed—the long and inconvenient forms of procedure in use by the judicial authorities elsewhere were abolished, but the judgment retained the same validity as if they had been followed.

1.19 Periodically, the rules established by mercantile practice were codified in compilations such as the Rolls of Oléron (an island commune of Acquitaine off the west coast of France whose rules of maritime law were hugely influential throughout Europe), the Laws of Wisby and the Consulate of the Sea, a remarkably detailed and diverse collection of merchant and maritime practices emanating from Barcelona.

Characteristics of the medieval law merchant

1.20 Professor Harold Berman has identified six qualities of the medieval law merchant:

(1) Objectivity: '. . . a movement away from mere custom in the sense of usage (patterns of behaviour) to a more carefully defined customary law (norms of behaviour).'

(2) Universality: that is, the law merchant was cosmopolitan and transnational in character.

(3) Reciprocity of rights: procedural and substantive fairness in entry into an exchange.

(4) Participatory adjudication: the judges were elected from among the merchants themselves.

(5) Integration: a coherent and integrated body of rules governing the rights of parties to transactions, particularly after reduction to writing.

(6) Growth: the organic growth of commercial instruments and institutions.[15]

1.21 In the settlement of mercantile disputes in the Middle Ages, particular importance was attached to the flexibility of rules of evidence and proof, the speed of adjudication and the observance of good faith. But one has to be careful not to romanticize the mediaeval *lex mercatoria*. Apart from maritime codifications, it was not an organized body of law at all, but rather a disparate assortment of customary rules which varied from place to place and which, administered by merchant courts and also recognized and applied by central courts, fulfilled its allotted function of responding to commercial needs and practices. As important as the substantive rules were the procedures for dispute resolution by the merchant courts and commercial consuls.

---

[15] Harold J Berman, *Law and Revolution: the Formation of the Western Legal Tradition* (Harvard U Press, Cambridge (MA), 1983) 341, 343.

**Franz Wieacker, 'On the History of Supranational Legal System of Commerce'
in Aarhus University Faculty of Social Sciences (eds),** *The Legal Organization of
Commerce and its Relation to the Social Conditions* **(Aarhus University,
Provinsbanken, 1979) 11–12**

In a second snapshot I now come to the 'international' commercial law of the high and late
Middle Ages. From the viewpoint of a legal historian, this was the golden age for a European
lex mercatoria. The simple proof of this is that—with the exception of the great anonymous
capital associations—the first pillar of the legal technical figures of the international
exchange of goods, payments and services developed within this period: banking, securities
and financial intercourse, mortgage and registration of land, maritime law, insurance, even
protection of firms and trade marks, finally the legal organization of the commercial mining
industry and the first forms of miners' associations which have survived until today . . .

1. A negative condition was the weakness of the particular, i.e. national, territorial or local
   legislative powers of the epoch. When according to a quotation of Professor Schmitthoff,
   René David from this weakness deduces the necessity of a self-made commercial and
   business law, then this may be extended to mean that this law was first made possible
   through this weakness. Not only in the flourishing business areas of the Holy Roman
   Empire, such as Northern Italy and Southern and Northern Germany, but also in
   Scandinavia, England before the Tudor-epoch and even in France and the county of
   Flanders the royal central power was not yet strong enough or, at least not willing, to ham-
   per this growth.
2. A positive condition for the filling of this vacuum was that the city community *internally* had autonomy to develop a mediaeval municipal law adapted to their social and
   economic needs, and *externally* was free to make agreements with other cities and states
   also concerning the regulation of the law to be used and its adjudication, i.e. as to the
   two most important conditions for a supraregional *lex mercatoria*. Only to mention
   Central Europe: no doubt the (relatively loose) relations between the Hanseatic towns
   has been the first condition of the spread of the Lübeck Law beyond this circle and of
   the acquisition of judgements at foreign 'Oberhöfe' and 'Schöffenstühles'.
3. Another favourable condition was the *legal conception* of the late Middle Ages. In the
   cities, law is not yet understood as a compulsory law nor as a codification made by a
   particular legislator with legislative monopoly and not any more as old custom (which
   had only little importance for the new forms of the local economic production and the
   business life and for the supralocal commercial law), but, on the contrary, as Ebel has
   demonstrated, it is understood as a contractual law, 'Verwillkürungs', i.e. as an agreement between the citizens of the community. This also implied—a long time before
   the justification according to natural law of the private autonomy and freedom of contract—the recognition of the *lex contractus* agreed upon by the parties (and consequently also of the typical content of the contract) as objective law.

In England, there were statutes making express provision for the law merchant, **1.22**
yet English law made relatively little contribution to the development of substantive law rules and concerned itself mainly with procedure, constituting 'the factual
matrix within which certain types of contract are made'.[16] Yet, the concept of the

---

[16] John Baker, 'The Law Merchant as a Source of English Law' in William Swadling and Gareth
Jones (eds), *The Search for Principle: Essays in Honour of Lord Goff* (OUP, Oxford, 1999) 79 at 96.

law merchant has long exercised a powerful hold on the imagination of those writing about it, in whose hands what were essentially practical rules devised by hard-headed businessmen to address day-to-day issues became elevated into some supra-national—indeed, one might almost say supernatural—law akin to the Roman *ius gentium*. Typical of the genre is the following passage from Malynes, *Lex Mercatoria*:

> This Law of merchants, or *Lex Mercatoria*, in the fundamentals of it, is nothing else but (as *Cicero* defineth true and just Law) *Recta Ratio, natura congruens, diffusa in omnes; Constans sempiterna*. True Law is right Reason, agreeable to Nature in all points; diffused and spread in all Nations, consisting perpetually without abrogation: howbeit some do attribute this definition unto *jus gentium*, or the Law of Nations, which consisteth of Customs, Manners and Prescriptions of all Nations, being of like conditions to all People, and observed by them as a Law. But the matter being truly examined, we shall find it more naturally and properly belongeth to the Law-Merchant.[17]

1.23 Legal historians have shown that these rather grandiose descriptions of the law merchant have little factual basis.[18]

The nationalization of commercial law

1.24 The international character of the medieval *lex mercatoria* was eventually eroded—in England, through the desire of the central courts to expand their jurisdiction and in continental Europe through the rise of the nation state and the elaboration of civil and commercial codes which, in producing integrated national laws,[19] fragmented European law and substantially reduced the influence of the *ius commune*. The consequences were fourfold: the narrowing of university legal education; the development of separate national laws for international trade; the decline of the law merchant; and the growth of private international law as a branch of national law to determine, in cases involving a foreign element, questions of jurisdiction, the applicable law and the recognition and enforcement of foreign judgments. So by the end of the eighteenth century, commercial law had lost much of its international character and coherence.

---

[17] Malynes (n 12) Pt I, 2.

[18] See Baker, above, n 16; Albrecht Cordes, 'The Search for a Medieval *Lex Mercatoria*', (2003) Oxford U Comp L Forum 5; Nicholas H D Foster, 'Foundation myth as legal formant: The medieval Law Merchant and the new *lex Mercatoria*', Forum Historiae Iuris 2005, accessible at <http://www.forhistiur.de/zitat/0503foster.htm>.

[19] Professor Zimmermann records that 'on the eve of the enactment of the BGB, the front page of the *Deutsche Juristenzeitung* was graced by a large heading 'Ein Volk, Ein Reich, Ein Recht' (One People, One Empire, One Law). See: Reinhard Zimmermann, 'Civil Code and Civil Law: The "Europeanization" of Private Law within the European Community and the Re-emergence of a European Legal Science' 1 Col J Eur L 63, 65 (1995).

Reinhard Zimmermann, 'Civil Code and Civil Law: "The Europeanization" of Private Law within the European Community and the Re-emergence of a European Legal Science' 1 CJEL 63, 65 (1995)

The history of the European codifications is inextricably linked with the rise of the modern nation state. The law of a country came to be regarded as a characteristic expression of its national spirit. This view was bound to lead to the particularization of legal science that is still with us today, and it has set legal science apart from almost all the other sciences taught at a modern university. There is no such subject as German chemistry or French medicine. But for the past hundred years or so there have been, in principle, as many legal systems (and, consequently, legal sciences) in Europe as there are nation states. This is reflected in our modern law curricula and examination requirements, which are oriented almost exclusively toward the law of the respective countries for which they have been devised.

The return to internationalism and the growth of transnational commercial law

The second half of the nineteenth century saw the beginnings of a return to inter- **1.25** nationalism and the development of transnational commercial law, though in the form of exploration rather than achievement,[20] which had to wait till well into the twentieth century. There came a growing recognition that an international commercial transaction cannot be treated in the same way as a domestic one. Typically, the parties come from different jurisdictions with different laws and commercial practices, and they may have different expectations. Laws fashioned for a purely domestic transaction are not necessarily well adapted to a cross-border transaction. Moreover, the choice of law rules vary according to the place where proceedings are brought, encouraging forum shopping. This last problem can largely be resolved by uniform conflict of laws rules, and a number of private international law conventions have been concluded under the auspices of the Hague Conference on Private International Law. But this does not address the problem of differences in national laws and, in certain fields, uncertainty as to whether a legal right or property interest created under the law of one State will be recognized and enforceable in another. Indeed, though private international law remains indispensable for the foreseeable future, it is inherently inimical to substantive uniformity and its effect is to apply a national law which may not be well suited to an international transaction. Moreover, resort to the conflict of laws frequently involves the court of one jurisdiction adjudicating on the laws of another with which the court is not familiar, making it dependent on what may be conflicting expert evidence and adding to both the cost of the proceedings and to the risk of legal error. Hence, the drive towards the harmonization of commercial law and, more generally, of private law, particularly in relation to cross-border transactions. One of the world's greatest

---

[20] HC Gutteridge, *Comparative Law* (2nd edn CUP, Cambridge, 1949) 146.

comparative lawyers, the French scholar René David, put the matter with customary elegance in his superb essay on unification.

René David, 'The International Unification of Private Law' in the *International Encyclopaedia of Comparative Law II* (JCB Mohr, Tübingen, 1971) ch 5 [33]

The international unification of law is of the greatest practical interest in the field of international legal relations. These are at present subject to a system, the application of one or more national laws being independently chosen by the various national courts, which creates a situation bordering on chaos, unfavourable to the development of international contracts, and without compensating advantages. The certainty of international commercial relations requires that the situation be clarified: there must be agreement on the national law to be applied, in any country, to a particular transaction, or a system of law governing this transaction in every country must be set up. Intrinsically, the second solution is to be preferred.

On the other hand, the complete independence of the national systems from one another can be recognized, in principle, when the legal relations in question are not of an international character. In this way, legal relations will be free from uncertainty despite the diversity of the systems.

If every country retires behind its frontiers and cuts itself off from neighbouring legal systems, the development and the progress of the law are likely to suffer. In the world today, studies in comparative law are necessary for many reasons. Many reforms in the various national systems of law profit from experiments made abroad. It can be asked whether the various legal systems would not, in many circumstances, benefit from a more systematic harmonization. Better statutes could be enacted, and better tools created for legal theory, if states confronted with similar problems or sharing a common cultural tradition were to work together.

The example of the *jus commune*, which existed in EUROPE before the days of codification without in any way derogating from national sovereignty, ought in our times to be the inspiration for a regrouping which would cure the weakness due to the excessive fragmentation of the law among too many sovereign states.

1.26   In the middle of the nineteenth century Leone Levi, a remarkable Italian from Ancona, emigrated to England, settled in Liverpool and, though a statistician by training and retaining a keen interest in that field, became an eminent English jurist who developed a passion for the modernization of English commercial law and, more broadly, the internationalization of commercial law. Founder of the Liverpool Chamber of Commerce, and later appointed to the first Chair of commercial law in England, at King's College London, he established relations with leading parliamentary figures and successfully prepared and procured the passing of several enactments for the improvement of certain aspects of commercial law and dispute resolution procedure. Meanwhile, he played a leading role in urging the improvement of statistical systems both nationally and internationally. But his most ambitious project was a remarkable comparative study of the commercial laws of the world covering fifty-nine different countries and widely welcomed as of international significance. He included in this work an address to Prince Albert, Prince Consort to Queen Victoria, proposing an international code of commerce.

Leone Levi, *Commercial Law, its Principles and Administration* (W Benning and Co, London, 1850–52) xv–xvi

TO HIS ROYAL HIGHNESS PRINCE ALBERT

. . . Jurisprudence has made rapid advancement in every country—an advancement directed everywhere in conformity with the established laws of other nations. Commercial legislation, in its onward course, has manifested in especial degree a tendency to an equalization of general principles. To foster such a development, and to lay the basis for the universal adoption of those great fundamental laws which regulate commercial intercourse, deserve the most strenuous efforts.

To your Royal Highness, who has conceived the noble idea of centralising mind and matter from all countries, that the riches of nature may be displayed, the skill of art appreciated, and the depth of intellect developed, I venture to propose the formation of what, it is generally acknowledged, would be an invaluable benefit to this and to all nations—

A NATIONAL AND INTERNATIONAL CODE OF COMMERCE AMONG ALL CIVILIZED COUNTRIES . . .

An inspection of the present work will strikingly demonstrate the similarity of principles laid down by each country, although clothed in different expressions and detailed in a different order. The references in italics from the Code of one country to that of others will show that many articles are verbatim reciprocally adopted; and if to these be added those differing merely in the mode of explaining them, we shall see a very considerable portion of the law to be identical in every country.

Leone Levi's grand design of an international commercial code was never to be real- **1.27** ized; indeed, with different countries at so many different stages of development it is hard to see that it could be. Nevertheless, his writings and energetic canvassing of support triggered a great interest in the promotion of greater convergence of national commercial laws, and a century later a number of distinguished scholars were to carry the torch for the internationalization of commercial law, among them a German émigré to Britain who was to become one of the foremost champions of a modern *lex mercatoria*.

Clive M Schmitthoff, 'Nature and Evolution of the Transnational Law of Commercial Transactions', in Horn, Norbert and Schmitthoff, Clive M (eds) *The Transnational Law of International Commercial Transactions* (Kluwer, Deventer, 1982) 19, at pp 21–22

We have so far ascertained that the area of contract law is, subject to exceptions and restrictions, governed by optional law, founded on the principle of the autonomy of the parties' will. This is the area in which a transnational law of international trade has developed and can be further evolved. This law is essentially founded on a parallelism of action in the various national legal systems, in an area in which, as we have seen, the sovereign national state is not essentially interested. The aim of this parallelism of action is to facilitate the conduct of international trade by establishing uniform rules of law for it. In some international activities the need for such rules is stronger than in others. International transportation by sea, air and road, for instance, can hardly be conducted without established uniform rules. The parallelism of action in the various national laws, which is really the essence of transnational law as the term is understood here, serves, however, another aim, which is of great importance to international trade, namely a far-reaching reduction of the national rules of conflict of laws and their substitution by a uniform, worldwide legal system of international trade regulation. The apotheosis of private international law is a side-effect of an exaggerated notion of the national state. It is an attempt at localising an international legal relationship in a national legal system. As such, it runs counter to the object and purpose of the international relationship.

1.28 More recently the benefits of harmonization of commercial law have been well set out by another scholar.

Loukas A Mistelis, 'Is Harmonisation a Necessary Evil? The Future of Harmonisation and New Sources of International Trade Law' in Ian F Fletcher, Loukas A Mistelis and Marise Cremona (eds), *Foundations and Perspectives of International Trade Law* **(Sweet & Maxwell, London, 2001) 20–21**

It is essential to restate some of the advantages of harmonisation:

- First, it facilitates commerce with the lifting of barriers resulting from the complexities of different legal regimes.
- Secondly, harmonisation of international commercial law creates a legal framework tailor-made for international transactions, disregarding differences in the regulation of domestic transactions.
- Thirdly, harmonisation normally produces neutral law, e.g. the CISG is a system of international sales law which is compatible with both civil and common law.
- Fourthly, harmonisation often fills a legal vacuum by providing rules in a field where national law was previously non-existent, e.g. UNCITRAL Model Law on Electronic Commerce, or obscure, e.g. the draft UNIDROIT Convention of Security Rights in Mobile Equipment.
- Fifthly, *effective* harmonisation substitutes a single law for a proliferation of national laws and thus within the given field dispenses with the need to resort to conflict of laws rules and the opportunity these give for forum shopping. Ineffective harmonisation, on the other hand, results in increased conflict of laws and wider possibilities for forum shopping.
- Sixthly, harmonisation of law with the collateral reduced conflict of laws results in significant reduction of transactional costs.
- Seventhly, in a field of law where conflict of laws has little or no role to play, there is increased predictability and legal certainty and consequent reduction of legal risk.
- Finally, for a number of legal systems harmonisation of law bears fruits of law reform. While in some countries law reform is a complicated and thorny issue, reforms can more easily be achieved once a provision has been adopted at international level.

1.29 A powerful impetus has been given to transnational commercial law by the huge growth in international commercial arbitration. In various respects, arbitrators have wider powers than courts—for example, in rules of evidence and procedure, in determination of the applicable law where not chosen by the parties, and in the nature of the materials of which they can take cognizance—and the effect of the 1958 New York Convention on the recognition and enforcement of foreign arbitral awards,[21] and the UNCITRAL Model Law on International Commercial Arbitration in limiting the grounds on which an arbitral award may be set aside by the courts,[22] has resulted in arbitrators having a much greater freedom from the constraints of national law than was formerly the case and an enhanced ability to look to international rather than national solutions. Scholars of international repute have also been very influential in developing the concept of transnational commercial law, among them Professors Ernst Rabel of Austria, René David and Berthold Goldman of France, Clive Schmitthoff, a German émigré who settled in England, and Alekšander Goldštajn of the former Yugoslavia.

Alekšandar Goldštajn, 'The New Law Merchant Reconsidered' [1961] JBL 12

NOTWITHSTANDING the differences in the political, economic and legal systems of the world a new law merchant is rapidly developing in the world of international trade. It is time that recognition be given to the existence of an autonomous commercial law that has grown independent of the national systems of law . . . Two legal factors have made this development possible in the laws of Western countries: the optional character of the law relating to the sale and purchase of goods, and the ever-growing use of arbitration in commercial disputes. The optional nature of commercial law is due to the fact that that branch of law is founded on the autonomy of the parties' will—freedom of contracting enables those engaged in international trade to overcome the historical peculiarities of the various national systems of law and to adopt a national legal regulation which accords with the requirements of international commerce. In this way, a new, autonomous law is being developed in practice, expressed in model contracts, standard clauses, general terms of delivery, commercial customs and trade usage. Moreover, to the extent that the settlement of disputes is referred to arbitration, a uniform legal order is being created. Arbitration tribunals often apply criteria other than those applied in courts. Arbitrators appear more ready to interpret rules freely, taking into account customs, usage and business practices. Further, the fact that the enforcement of foreign arbitral awards is generally more easy than the enforcement of foreign court decisions is conducive to a preference for arbitration.

The causes for the emergence of an autonomous international commercial law seem to lie in the diversity and inadequacy of many traditional national systems of law in the changed circumstances of modern international trade on a world market.

What has given rise to much debate is the concept of what Professor Goldštajn **1.30** referred to, in the passage quoted above, as 'an autonomous international commercial law'. We will return to this a little later.

The growth of regionalism

We cannot leave this section of the discussion without reference to the major effect **1.31** of regional laws, powered by the desire to establish a framework for the development of regional markets. By far the most important in terms of legal development

---

[21] See para 17.35.
[22] See para 17.112.

is the European Union, a group of twenty-seven States which conducts much of its business in twenty-one different official languages. But there has been a considerable volume of regional harmonization outside the EU, occasioning much debate as to whether this is beneficial as bringing together laws of countries linked by geography for the mutual advantage of all members of the region or whether its effect is to weaken the process of harmonization at international level. We will address this important subject in chapter 6.

C. The Sources of National Commercial Law

1.32   The sources of commercial law may vary from State to State but the principal sources are the following:

Contract

1.33   At the heart of commercial law in every developed legal system is contract. The law of contract underpins all commercial transactions, and in most systems, a core principle is party autonomy, the freedom of parties to 'make their own law' in the relations between themselves, though as we shall see a contract cannot speak to its own validity, and is thus not law in the full sense. Contractual terms may be express or implied. In some legal systems, the concept of the implied term covers not only terms implied from the express terms, from the surrounding circumstances or from a prior course of dealing but also terms implied by usage or by law. In other legal systems, usage is treated as an independent source of commercial law, while what common lawyers are accustomed to describe as the implication of terms by law is more accurately conceived by civil law systems as having nothing to do with the terms of the contract as such, but is simply the conferment of rights and the imposition of duties by law on parties to a particular kind of contractual relationship.

Usage

1.34   Usage is the observance of a commercial practice from a sense of obligation, as opposed to mere courtesy, expediency or convenience.[23] Our focus is on unwritten usage. A usage may become enacted in a statute or embodied in a contract or set of trade rules incorporated by contract, but in all these cases its character changes.[24] Formerly, writers distinguished usage from custom, but nowadays, at least in relation to commercial transactions, the terms tend to be used interchangeably and we shall use the term 'usage'. A usage may be that of a particular trade or a particular locality such as a town or a port, and in the former case, may

---

[23]   We return to this rather complex topic later. See below, para 1.61.
[24]   See para 1.60.

be national or international. The existence and content of usage, so far as not pre-scribed by legislation, are questions of fact to be determined by the court.

Suppletive rules of common law

Court decisions may supply default rules to deal with cases not covered by the par- **1.35**
ties' agreement or by usage.

Domestic legislation

Finally, rules of commercial law may be prescribed by legislation. **1.36**

D. The Nature and Sources of Transnational Commercial Law

In traditional legal thinking, rights and obligations are to be determined by refer- **1.37**
ence to a particular national legal system, the relevant system being identified by ref-erence to the rules of private international law of the forum. But under the influence of scholars such as those mentioned above, it became recognized that this was too narrow an approach and that courts and arbitrators should be free to draw on a wider range of sources when determining issues arising in connection with cross-border transactions to which a given national law might not by itself be sufficiently respon-sive. Even so, there has been much controversy as to the nature of transnational com-mercial law and even as to its existence. It should be borne in mind that while we regard the *lex mercatoria* as a subset of transnational commercial law and as raising distinctive issues, a number of scholars equate the *lex mercatoria* with transnational commercial law, so that what is discussed in the ensuing paragraphs is examined in much of the literature under the label *lex mercatoria*, or the new law merchant.

Is there an autonomous transnational commercial law?

In essence, transnational commercial law is the product of the convergence of **1.38**
national legal systems, but this does not mean that it can be found only by refer-ence to legislation and case law. It is now recognized that regard may be had to a variety of sources, including scholarly writings, international restatements, and contractually incorporated rules of international organizations. Yet the central ques-tion remains whether these sources can be drawn on as establishing an autonomous corpus of legal rules, or even a legal system which the parties can select as the appli-cable law, or whether they merely offer a means by which a rule of national law not previously formulated can be supplied. For example, where there is an undeter-mined question of, say, Dutch law in relation to which the tribunal finds that the question is answered by a rule common to a number of other legal systems, the tri-bunal might then apply it as a rule of Dutch law rather than as an independent, non-national legal norm. As we shall see, there are powerful proponents of the concept of a new autonomous *lex mercatoria*, but also serious objections to it.

The *lex mercatoria* and the conflict of laws

1.39   Many years ago, Professor Friedrich Juenger, in supporting the idea of the new law merchant as a body of law not deriving from sovereign states, drew attention to the threat this posed to conflict of laws theories and hence to teachers of the subject.

Friederich K Juenger, 'American Conflicts Scholarship and the New Law Merchant'
28 Vanderbilt J of Transnational L 487, 498–9 (1995)

VI. THE NEW LAW MERCHANT: THREAT AND PROMISE

There are, of course, good reasons for the conflicts teachers' reluctance to discuss the topic. The emergence of a supranational law undermines the very foundations on which their doctrines rest—the positivist notions Beale and Currie shared with Justice Holmes. Preoccupied with the idea of sovereignty, U.S. traditionalists find it difficult enough to accept the principle of party autonomy, even though it is recognized by most advanced legal systems. Those who question the parties' freedom to choose the law governing their contract are likely to feel even more uncomfortable about the emergence of rules that owe their existence to the realities of an international marketplace, rather than a sovereign's fiat. Such a law is inexplicable in their terms of reference; its 'brooding omnipresence' must be anathema to those who believe that the *raison d'état* must control international as well as purely domestic transactions. Interest analysts in particular, ought to feel uneasy, for what interests are left to analyze if those that states and nations supposedly harbor do not matter?

Worse yet, the *lex mercatoria* threatens the very existence of the conflict of laws because once supranational norms emerge choice-of-law rules and principles become superfluous. In addition, the new law merchant poses a challenge by virtue of its qualitative superiority. Merchants are, of course, interested in the quality of the rules that govern their transactions, whereas unilateralists and multilateralists alike take the position that substantive considerations should play no role in the choice of the applicable law. Even if the emerging supranational rules were confined to commercial matters, the internationalization of this vitally important field should grieve those about whom René David said:

> [T]hey have the greatest difficulty in conceiving that the theory of conflict of laws might not be the only suitable method of solving the problems posed by international legal relations. They cling to this method, seeking to perpetuate its use even in cases where it is manifestly bad: they are 'conflictualists' not true 'internationalists'.

Yet, whether conflicts scholars like it or not, cases and statutory authority support the existence of such a law merchant . . .

1.40   The ability to use rules of the *lex mercatoria* does not depend upon its being accorded the status of a legal system, since the rules in question may be sufficient to answer the question at issue and if they are not then resort can be had to an appropriately determined national law. On the other hand, the purported selection of the *lex mercatoria* as the applicable law will be ineffective as a choice of law in those jurisdictions whose conflict rules require the selection of the law of a legal *system*, a concept which embodies not only particular rules, but a comprehensive set of laws linked by an organized structure and supported by adjudication and enforcement mechanisms. Thus, within the European Union, choice of law is governed by the Rome Convention on the law applicable to contractual obligations, which plainly predicates the choice of a national law, so that a purported choice of transnational commercial law or of the *lex mercatoria* will at most amount to a contractual incorporation of such rules of transnational commercial law as can be identified, and these will enjoy contractual status only and therefore be subject to domestic mandatory rules of the applicable law. Work is now under way to convert the Convention into a European regulation, and in that connection, the question whether selection as the applicable law of rules not constituting a legal system and not in themselves having normative force should be permitted was raised but has encountered fierce criticism.

As a rule, arbitral tribunals are less constrained in their use of sources than national **1.41** courts, which usually feel obliged to apply a rule of national law determined by their own conflict of laws rules, whereas in an international commercial arbitration the wide powers enjoyed by arbitral tribunals, coupled with relatively strict limits on the review of arbitral awards, give arbitral tribunals a much greater freedom to determine the rules they will apply in the absence of party choice. So a number of legal systems now allow arbitrators to select their own conflicts rule or to apply 'rules of law' or even non-law considerations where so empowered by the parties.

Ole Lando, 'The *Lex Mercatoria* in International Commercial Arbitration' (1985) 34 ICLQ 747, 752–5

An arbitrator applying the *lex mercatoria* will act as an inventor more often than one who applies national law. Faced with the restricted legal material which the law merchant offers, he must often seek guidance elsewhere. His main source is the various legal systems. When they conflict he must make a choice or find a new solution. The *lex mercatoria* often becomes a creative process by this means.

Arbitrators of different nationalities who have applied the *lex mercatoria* in collegiate arbitral tribunals have not experienced great difficulties in reaching consensus. When the law merchant has been silent and the national laws connected with the subject-matter have not led to the same result, few arbitrators have insisted on the solution provided by their own legal systems. They have sought the most appropriate and equitable solution for the case.

Applying the *lex mercatoria*, arbitrators may take advantage of their freedom to select the better rule of law which courts sometimes miss. For instance, the Scandinavian Sale of Goods Act provides that the buyer who wished to invoke a late delivery of the goods must give notice immediately upon delivery. This rule is not fit for international sales. Non-Scandinavian buyers do not know of it, and for them it may be a trap. The rule in Article 49(2) of the Convention on the International Sale of Goods, under which notice must be given within a reasonable time, offers a better solution . . .

In many situations national law will give the parties greater certainty than the *lex mercatoria*, especially where the parties have agreed to have the contract governed by a national law system and the arbitrator is familiar with the law chosen. In many cases, however, the parties have not chosen the law applicable to the contract. Then it is often doubtful which law applies. Although the choice-of-law rules for contracts are becoming more uniform, they still create problems. One arises where the arbitrator has to apply the rules of a system which is alien to him. The cases show that his difficulties may be considerable, and that mistakes are not infrequent. The *lex mercatoria* has the advantage that it does away with the choice-of-law process which many lawyers abhor.

Even when applying a national law well known to him, the arbitrator may run into difficulties which make his decision less predictable. Several national law rules are made for domestic relationships only; they are not suitable for cases containing foreign elements. Faced with such rules, the arbitrator is sometimes in a dilemma between law and equity. In these cases the *lex mercatoria* may in fact provide more certainty.

Emmanuel Gaillard, 'Transnational Law: A Legal System or a Method of Decision-Making?' in Klaus Peter Berger (ed), *The Practice of Transnational Law* (Kluwer, The Hague, 2001) 55–6

The first area of controversy among the supporters of *lex mercatoria* has to do with the extent to which transnational rules are characterized by their purported specificity, from a substantive viewpoint, *vis-à-vis* rules found in national legal orders. From this viewpoint, international transactions require added flexibility, which the requirements found in national laws would seldom accommodate. This school of thought is related to the theory of 'specific needs of international business', which has subsequently been derided as a new form of the *laissez-faire* doctrine.

Another view, which we believe to be the better one, finds the specificity of transnational rules to lie in the fact that these rules are derived from various legal systems as opposed to a single one, and more generally from various sources, rather than in their allegedly differing content. In other words, their specificity is one of source, not of content. Indeed, there is no reason to believe that national legal orders are unable to accommodate adequately the specific needs of international situations, for example, by creating a separate set of substantive rules to govern international situations.

Admittedly, because they are chiefly derived from various national legal systems, transnational rules run a better chance not to reflect the outdated rules which may still be found in certain legal systems. In that, they may help to meet the concerns of modern business, but this is not to say that by nature, national laws cannot achieve the same result. On the contrary, it is because a sufficient number of legal systems have adopted modern rules that transnational rules will be able to follow them in embracing the most appropriate solution.

These two ideas of the specificity of content and the formation from comparative law sources were present, in the most intricate way, in the early writings on *lex mercatoria*, but they now merit to be segregated if one does not want to exacerbate an artificial distinction between national legal orders—which are not confined to domestic rules and do not necessarily contain outdated rules—and transnational rules. This is why, in our opinion, *lex mercatoria* should be defined today by its sources . . . as opposed to its content.

1.42 In short, rules of transnational commercial law are not necessarily different in content from those of national law and should not be set up in opposition to national law rules but rather should be seen as drawing upon and as complementary to those rules.[25]

---

[25] A thesis previously developed by Professor Gaillard in 'Thirty Years of *Lex Mercatoria*: Towards the Selective Application of Transnational Rules' (1995) 10 Foreign Investment LJ 208.

Klaus Peter Berger, 'The New Law Merchant and the Global Market Place' in Klaus Peter Berger (ed), *The Practice of Transnational Law* (Kluwer, The Hague, 2001) 17, 21

The states' loss of their formerly dominant position in international policy and rule-making which goes along with this process, the decreased significance of sovereignty and the freedom of parties in international contract law have caused a reconsideration of the traditional theory of legal sources which has 'moved beyond yesteryear's narrow-minded positivism.' A non-positivist notion of the law is beginning to emerge. Since this law has to take account of the complexities of society, it is not the public reason represented by the state or by inter-governmental organizations *alone* but also the power for self-regulation and coordination of the individual and of private organizations and federations which justifies normative force. The traditional theory of legal sources which was centered around the notion of sovereignty is being replaced by a legal pluralism which accepts that society's ability for self-organization and coordination is more than a mere factual pattern without independent legal significance. Today, it assumes a normative quality of its own . . .

. . . *Raiser*, even though being a proponent of the traditional positivist view of the theory of legal sources, has summarized these views in his famous studies on general contract conditions as follows:

> 'Since it turns out to be impossible to quantify general contract conditions as parts of contracts or as parts of the traditional catalogue of the sources of objective law, the option remains to put into question the distinction between a legal norm and a legal transaction. Is the thinking correct that parties, in concluding a transaction, are merely setting a factual pattern to which the law attributes or denies legal effect at its will? Aren't the parties themselves able to regulate their living conditions without the intermediation of the legal order of the state, *thus creating law among themselves?*'[26]

The principles and rules which make up the *lex mercatoria* are of a normative character, not because they are fair and reasonable from an objective viewpoint but because businessmen, arbitral tribunals and formulating agencies alike consider them to be fair and reasonable and act accordingly by way of self-regulation of international commerce and trade. The new law merchant applies due to its inherent rationality: '*veritas non auctoritas facit legem*'.

From these passages we see two distinct ideas which should not be elided. The **1.43** first, articulated by Professor Gaillard, is that in relation to international commercial transactions rights and obligations need not necessarily derive from a particular national legal system but may be drawn from a variety of sources, using the comparative method. The second, expressed in the above passage by Professor Berger, is that as between the parties contract creates law. This, however, should not be misunderstood. If the legal force of a contract derives from its 'inherent rationality', a contract must be open to challenge as not inherently rational and, indeed, as oppressive or injurious to the wider public interest. Insofar as this conclusion requires further support, it is to be found in the concept of *jus cogens* in international law under which a treaty is void if at the time of its conclusion it conflicts with a peremptory norm of international commercial law.[27] If this is true

---

[26] *Das Recht der Allgemeinen Geschäftsbedingungen* (1935), 63 (transl Berger).
[27] Vienna Convention on the Law of Treaties 1969 Art 53.

even of agreements between sovereign states, how much more so of agreements between private parties.

1.44 Thus, there has to be a control mechanism by which a contractual provision can be validated and thus treated as legally operative as from the time it is agreed. This mechanism has two limbs, both of which involve the application of legal norms.

External validation by a court or tribunal

1.45 Whether a contract term is valid is, in case of a dispute concerning the contract, a matter to be determined by a court or other tribunal of competent jurisdiction. Judges are appointed by the state in accordance with the law, and it is the law which confers jurisdiction upon them. This is not to say that a contractual term is only binding once a court has so decided, merely that a contract cannot speak to its own validity and that one of the control factors is review by a court in order to ensure that a purported contract satisfies the criteria laid down by law for a valid contract. It has, indeed, been argued that the arbitral process surmounts the difficulty of a '*contrat sans loi*'.

Gunther Teubner, '"Global Bukowina": Legal Pluralism in the World Society' in Gunther Teubner (ed), *Global Law Without a State* (Ashgate/Dartmouth, 1997) 15–17

In *lex mercatoria* it is the practice of contracting that transcends national boundaries and transforms a merely national law production into a global one—numerous international business transactions, standardized contracts of international professional associations, model contracts of international organizations and investment projects in developing countries. However, as soon as these contracts claim transnational validity, they cut off not only their national roots but their roots in any legal order. This may be fatal. It is not only lawyers who declare contracts without law unthinkable: the idea that any contract needs to be 'rooted' in a pre-existing legal order is not merely a legal axiom. Sociologists, too, will protest against *contrat sans loi*. From the work of Emile Durkheim onwards it has been the great sociological objection to any autonomous contractualism that the binding force of contract needs to be rooted in broader social contexts . . . Of a purported contractual *lex mercatoria* sociologists would ask the famous Durkheimian question: where are the non-contractual premises of global contracting?

Why not in the contracts themselves? Apparently this is a dead-end. Any self-validation of contracts leads directly into the paradox of self-reference, into the contractual version of the Cretan liar paradox . . . In the positive version ('We agree that our agreement is valid') it is a pure tautology. In the negative version ('We agree that our agreement is not valid') it is the typical self-referential paradox which leads to nothing but endless oscillation ('valid-not valid-valid . . . ') and blockage. The result is undecidability. This underlying paradox is the principal reason why lawyers, as well as sociologists, declare self-validating contracts unthinkable and talk *lex mercatoria* out of existence.

Social practice, however, is more creative than legal doctrine and social theory. *Kautelarjurisprudenz*, the practice of international draftsmen, has found a way to conceal the practice of self-validation in such a way that global contracts have become capable of doing the apparently impossible. Global contracts are creating their non-contractual foundations themselves. They have found three ways of de-paradoxification—time, hierarchy and externalization—that mutually support each other and make it possible, without the help of the state, for a global law of the economic periphery to create its own legal centre.

Empirically, we find the most perfect 'de-paradoxification' in those commercial contracts that construct a so-called 'closed circuit arbitration' . . . This is a self-regulatory contract which goes far beyond one particular commercial transaction and establishes a whole private legal order with a claim to global validity. Apart from substantive rules it contains clauses that refer conflicts to an arbitration 'court' which is identical with the private institution that was responsible for 'legislating' the model contract. This is the 'closed circuit'.

In the first place, these contracts establish an internal *hierarchy* of contractual rules. They contain not only 'primary rules' in the sense established by Hart . . . which regulate the future behaviour of the parties, but also 'secondary rules' which regulate the recognition of primary rules, their identification, their interpretation and the procedures for resolving conflicts. Thus the paradox of self-validation still exists, but it is concealed in the separation of hierarchical levels, the level of rules and meta-rules. Unlike the rules, the meta-rules are autonomous, although both have the same contractual origin. The hierarchy is 'tangled', but this does not hinder the higher echelons from regulating the lower ones . . .

Second, these contracts *temporalize* the paradox and transform the circularity of contractual self-validation into an iterative process of legal acts, into a sequence of the recursive mutual constitution of legal acts and legal structures. The present contract extends into the past and into the future. It refers to a pre-existing standardization of rules and it refers to the future of conflict regulation and, thus, renders the contract into one element in an ongoing self-production process in which the network of elements creates the very elements of the system.

Third, and most importantly, the self-referential contract uses the de-paradoxification technique of *externalization*. It externalizes the fatal self-validation of contract by referring conditions of validity and future conflicts to external 'non-contractual' institutions which are nevertheless 'contractual', since they are a sheer internal product of the contract itself. The most prominent of these self-created external institutions is arbitration which has to judge the validity of the contracts, although its own validity is based on the very contract the validity of which it is supposed to be judging! Here, the vicious circle of contractual self-validation is transformed into the virtuous circle of two legal processes—contracting and arbitration . . . An additional externalization of this reference to quasi-courts is the reference to quasi-legislative institutions—to the International Chamber of Commerce in Paris, the International Law Association in London, the International Maritime Association in Antwerp . . . Thus transnational contracting has created *ex nihilo* an institutional triangle of private 'adjudication', 'legislation' and 'contracting'.

Arbitration, by contrast with litigation, depends on agreement and arbitrators are **1.46** appointed in accordance with that agreement. This consensual character of arbitration, which is emphasized in the arbitration laws of most countries, might lead one to suppose that the process by which an arbitral tribunal is set up and the jurisdiction of the arbitrator are not subject to legal norms at all. But that would be to commit the error of a *'contrat sans loi'* in a disguised form. It is true that agreement lies at the heart of the arbitral process and that it is for the parties to appoint the arbitral tribunal. But we know that freedom of contract is not unlimited and that there are in every legal system grounds on which a purported contract may be impeached or an otherwise valid contract set aside, and arbitration agreements do not enjoy any special form of immunity from rules limiting contracts generally. Hence, the agreement to arbitrate and the jurisdiction of the arbitral tribunal, though in most cases not open to question, depend ultimately on meeting stated legal criteria. So the appointment of an arbitrator will be invalid if the arbitration agreement is invalid, and an arbitrator validly appointed may be removed for bias or other improper conduct.

Determination in accordance with law

1.47 In most systems, a court is not free to decide a contractual dispute on the basis of what it considers fair or reasonable but must apply certain legal norms, and it is widely accepted that even in international commercial arbitration, the tribunal has no power to decide *ex aequo et bono* unless so authorized by the parties.[28] From this it must follow that even an arbitral tribunal must, if the parties do not agree otherwise, apply legal norms—though not necessarily the law of a particular national legal system unless designated by the parties as the applicable law—to determine the validity and effect of contractual provisions; the tribunal cannot give a decision simply on its personal view of what would be fair and reasonable. The point is well made by Berger in his analysis of the dogmatic foundations of the *lex mercatoria* doctrine:

> A transnational understanding of modern commercial law has an important effect on the doctrine of private international law. Neither the parties' agreement to have the lex mercatoria applied to their contract nor the application of this transnational law by international arbitrators in the absence of a choice of law by the parties lead to a '*contrat sans loi*'. International arbitrators who apply the lex mercatoria do not act in a legal vacuum, nor do they render a decision in equity. Instead, they apply the rules and principles of a transnational legal system, and their award will be respected by domestic courts.[29]

1.48 What, then, are we to make of the proposition that contract makes law and that commercial practice constitutes a legal norm? First, we can say that *within the framework of external legal* norms, parties *can* make their own law; and since for commercial transactions generally and cross-border transactions in particular, the principle of party autonomy is accorded pride of place, what the parties to a contract agree will usually be binding on them and respected by courts and arbitral

---

[28] It does not, of course, follow that a tribunal empowered to decide *ex aequo et bono* is thereby precluded from reliance on legal norms; indeed, it may consider its role to be to take a legal rule as its starting point but temper its rigour by reference to considerations of equity and fairness as appropriate. See: Klaus Peter Berger, *The Creeping Codification of the Lex Mercatoria* (Kluwer, The Hague, 1999) 59; Emmanuel Gaillard and John Savage (ed), *Fouchard, Gaillard, Goldman on International Commercial Arbitration* (Kluwer, The Hague, 1999) [1506].

[29] Klaus Peter Berger, *The Creeping Codification of the Lex Mercatoria* (Kluwer Law International, The Hague/London/Boston) 113.

tribunals. In practice, the validity of a contractual provision will not normally arise unless it is challenged by one of the parties or raises a question of international public policy which the tribunal should address of its own motion, so that the contractual terms will in most cases be applied without the need to refer to any legal norms at all. That does not mean that the contract is free from such norms—for it would be repugnant to public policy to allow contracts to be self-legitimating—merely that in the particular case they do not need to be examined. Second, commercial practice consistently adopted is a guide to what right-thinking members of the commercial community regard as a proper response to a particular fact situation and may therefore be indicative of a legal norm. For example, in international banking practice, a documentary credit is considered to become binding on the issuing bank from the time of issue, so that a purported revocation would be ineffective even if dispatched before the letter of credit was received or after receipt and before any act of reliance upon it; and courts responsive to legitimate commercial practice and understanding would be minded to treat the practice as establishing a legal norm even if this ran counter to general contract theory.

Is the same true of standard contractual terms? There is a tendency on the part of **1.49** the more ardent proponents of the *lex mercatoria* to make rather extravagant claims for standard contract terms as a legal norm. Rarely do they lay down criteria to delineate the types of standard-term contract that should qualify for this elevated status. In particular, no distinction is drawn between standard terms drafted by one of the parties and standard terms or model contracts prepared by a neutral third party, or by two or more such parties representative of the competing interests, to reflect a fair balance of those interests. Moreover, the assumption is made that in any given field of trading activity there is a homogenous set of standard terms an analysis of which will reveal the golden rule, whereas in real life there are as many terms as there are term-providers and they vary widely in scope and content. Different professional bodies may produce standard-term contracts covering the same field and even a single body may have a variety of standard-term contracts.[30]

When the 1988 UNIDROIT convention on international financial leasing was in **1.50** preparation, there was some complaint by leasing specialists that the rules governing the rights and duties of lessor and lessee did not correspond to the terms found in typical leasing contracts. But this was a misconception of the purpose of an international convention, which is not to follow contract terms that very often are prepared from the perspective of one of the parties but to lay down a set of neutral provisions and leave the parties to negotiate departures from them. There are many sales contracts which are designed primarily to protect the interests of sellers, but that does not mean that these should be reflected in sales legislation, nor

---

[30] A good example is the Grain and Feed Trade Association (GAFTA), which has issued some eighty standard forms of contract. See <http://www.gafta.com/index.php?page=contracts>.

are they. By contrast, standard-term contracts drawn up by trade or professional bodies which are designed to balance the competing interests may give a guide to the legitimate expectations of the market and can form the basis of a legal norm. Examples are the standard-term contracts produced by such bodies as FIDIC,[31] for construction works and the International Chamber of Commerce for distributorship, agency and international sales. Even so, a distinguished jurist has cautioned against the use of standard forms as indicative of a legal rule.

Rt Hon Lord Justice Mustill, 'The New *Lex Mercatoria*: The First Twenty-five Years' in Maarten Bos and Ian Brownlie (eds) *Liber Amicorum for Lord Wilberforce* (OUP, Oxford, 1987) 158.

There is, however, a different form of usage to which some of the proponents have had recourse, namely the practice of contracting within various trades, on standard terms of contract. The mechanism whereby these terms become part of a standing body of law is rarely spelt out. One suggestion is that they express the sense of justice of those who draft and enter into them. I confess to some reservations about this proposition. Often, one party to a standard form contract adopts it because the other gives him no choice. More important, the form does not, it seems to me, reflect the ideas of anybody as to the justice of the transaction, if indeed this concept has any meaning in the field of commercial transactions negotiated between parties on an equal footing. Rather, the form is designed to serve as a convenient peg on which the parties can hang the specifically negotiated terms, without having to work out all the details of the transaction from scratch. Experienced traders are aware of the general financial balance of the transaction contemplated by the standard form, and know the way in which it distributes the commercial risks between the parties. With this in mind they can negotiate towards agreement on matters such as price, delivery date, insurance, demurrage, and so on. If the standard form is altered so as to throw more obligations or risks on to one of the parties, the negotiated terms will have to be adjusted to restore the balance. The second form will be neither more nor less 'just' than the first. It simply calls for a different assessment of the price in the widest sense of the term.

Furthermore, there are serious practical objections to the use of standard forms as a source of law. Quite apart from the fact that a single institution within a single trade may publish a repertoire of mutually inconsistent documents from which contracting parties may choose the most suitable to reflect the balance of their bargain, there coexist in many trades a number of institutions, each offering its own standard form; and it is, of course, a commonplace that parties alter the standard forms to suit their own purposes. There is thus no guarantee of homogeneity even within a single trade. Moreover it may legitimately be asked why a participant in one trade should be supposed to have his contract governed by rules drawn from contract forms current in a quite different trade.

Finally, it must be confessed that the mechanism whereby the use of standard forms becomes a source of law is nowhere clearly explained. The simple repetition of contracts on the same terms is as consistent with the exercise of freedom of contract as with subordination to a system of binding norms; indeed, far more so, since if the parties to a commodity transaction do not wish to bind themselves to, say, the GAFTA Contract Form No. 100, there is no legal or other institution which can compel them to do so. Moreover,

---

[31] The Fédération Internationale des Ingénieurs-Conseils.

the repetition of transactions in the same form could at most create a group of norms peculiar to the individual trade, thereby creating a network of para-legal systems. This is quite inconsistent with the theoretical premises of the *lex mercatoria*, which is that it springs spontaneously from the structure of international commerce—which is quite plainly regarded as an indivisible whole.

We may conclude that international commercial practice does not of itself consti-　**1.51**
tute an autonomous body of law, and that reliance on standard-term contracts as a source of law is fraught with difficulties, but that it is legitimate to speak of transnational commercial law as a set of legal norms not based on any one legal system but derived from a variety of sources, some of which—for example, international restatements by groups of scholars—may not be legal instruments but may nevertheless be resorted to as evidence of a consensus on an appropriate legal rule. This move from national laws determined by conflicts rules towards rules to be extracted from a variety of sources, including non-binding instruments, has been powered by international commercial arbitration, in which panels of arbitrators drawn from different jurisdictions strive to produce awards that, while conforming to legal norms, are fair and commercially acceptable. The wide degree of freedom conferred on arbitral tribunals by national legislation and international instruments, coupled with the restriction of judicial review in order to secure finality, means that arbitrators can be much more responsive than courts to non-national sources of law, and it is this that has provided the motive power for the development of what has become known as the new *lex mercatoria*, albeit ill-defined and not readily ascertainable.

The sources of transnational commercial law

Transnational law is drawn from many sources. Leaving aside individual contracts—　**1.52**
for we have shown that a contract cannot speak to its own validity, so that the parties can make their own law only in conformity with certain externally set criteria—the sources of transnational commercial law may be broadly divided into seven groups:

Lex mercatoria

We examine this in some detail later in this chapter.[32] Suffice it to note at this　**1.53**
point that there are said to be two limbs to the *lex mercatoria*, namely international trade usage and general principles of law. Once a usage has acquired such general acceptance as to become independent of any particular form of international trading activity, it ceases to be usage and becomes elevated into a general principle which, it will be argued, is best regarded as a distinct source of transnational commercial law and does not form part of the *lex mercatoria*.[33]

---

[32] Para 1.60.
[33] Roy Goode, 'Usage and Its Reception in Transnational Commercial Law' (1997) 46 ICLQ 1, 16.

35

International and regional instruments

1.54 These may in turn be divided into two sub-groups:

(a) Instruments intended to become legally binding. At the international level, these consist of multilateral conventions and uniform laws appended to such conventions. Such an instrument is not legally operative until ratified by the number of States specified in it and, within a Contracting State, until completion of whatever constitutional process (for example, legislation) is required by the law of that State to give the instrument the force of law within the State and not merely at the international level. There is also a growing number of regional instruments, the most prominent being those produced by the European Community, which is tasked with (among other things) the harmonization of law within the European Union, and achieves this through the various EC treaties and through the issue of directives and regulations. Hitherto, Community law has been confined to rules of a mandatory character and rules which outlaw or restrict various kinds of activity, such as that which breaches the Community's competition policy.

(b) Facultative instruments, namely model laws and model rules, which are not legally operative, are not, therefore, ratified and may be rejected, accepted wholly or in part or amended as a State considers fit. Such instruments, therefore, constitute a facility on which States may draw as they wish. Even where a State does not adopt the drafting it may find the model law or model rules a useful source of ideas for domestic legislation.

Conscious or unconscious judicial or legislative parallelism

1.55 A degree of harmonization may come about through conscious borrowing by the courts or legislatures of one State of ideas developed in other States. An example is the doctrine of State immunity, which in its origin gave sovereign States absolute immunity from suit but, as States began to enter the commercial arena through state trading enterprises, became limited to the acts of States in the exercise of sovereign power (*acta jure imperii*) and ceased to apply to State involvement in commercial transactions (*acta jure gestionis*). Alternatively, the courts and legislatures of different countries may arrive at broadly the same result independently of each other. Work on international and regional restatements of contract law[34] has shown a surprisingly high degree of commonality of solutions to different problems even though this may be achieved by different legal routes.

---

[34] Paras 1.58, 5.14, 14.04 ff.

Contractually incorporated rules and trade terms promulgated by international organizations

Pride of place belongs to the International Chamber of Commerce (the inter- **1.56**
national non-governmental organization representing world business) which has
produced numerous uniform rules that are given effect by incorporation into contracts. Of these, the most successful are the Uniform Customs and Practice for
Documentary Credits (UCP 600), which is in use by bankers, and incorporated
into documentary credits, all round the world. Another very popular publication
of the ICC is Incoterms, which contains a set of the price and delivery terms most
frequently used in international sales (for instance f.o.b., c.i.f., d.d.p) and sets out
in relation to each term the respective obligations of seller and buyer. These terms,
too, take effect by incorporation into contracts. The result of these contractual
incorporations into all relevant agreements is to produce through a series of bilateral transactions the effect of a multilateral contractual network and thereby facilitate not only uniformity of practice—which is the primary objective of ICC
rules—but also a harmonization of contractual rights and obligations.

Standard-term contracts

The limited significance of these has been discussed earlier. **1.57**

Restatements of scholars

A more recent phenomenon, the restatement, has taken its inspiration from the **1.58**
American Restatements, produced by leading scholars under the aegis of the
American Law Institute. Such restatements do not have the force of law, but they are
extremely influential in the development of jurisprudence in their respective fields.
They are not restatements in the strict sense (since obviously a single set of rules cannot be equally responsive to all the laws of the different States); their purpose is rather
to identify and adapt to modern conditions the best rules from the different State
systems and thereby to secure both the harmonization and the improvement of the
law. In the field of contract law, two restatements have been produced by different
groups of scholars from different countries, the Principles of International
Commercial Contracts,[35] designed for use in international commercial transactions,
and the Principles of European Contract Law,[36] which is concerned with contracts
between nationals of Member States of the European Community. These restatements[37] are in course of being supplemented by principles governing specific

---

[35] Prepared by a UNIDROIT group under the chairmanship of Professor Joachim Bonell and issued with the imprimatur of UNIDROIT. See ch 14.

[36] Produced by the Commission on European Contract Law chaired by Professor Ole Lando. A third text, a codification rather than a restatement, is the Code Européen des contrats, prepared by the Academy of European Private Lawyers (the Pavia Group) under the direction of Professor Giuseppe Gandolfi. [37] Discussed ch 14.

contracts (such as sales and the supply of services) in course of preparation as part of the European Civil Code project and the Bonell Group is engaged in a similar exercise as Phase 3 of the UNIDROIT Principles.[38] The restatements have much the same status as the American Restatements; they are not legally operative instruments but a form of 'soft' law. Nevertheless, they have already proved very influential both in international commercial arbitrations and in the preparation of legislation as indicative of an international consensus on a reasonable and neutral set of rules.[39]

General principles of international law

1.59 It may seem odd to relegate general principles of international law to the bottom of our list, but there is much uncertainty as to the meaning and content of this concept, which is rarely invoked explicitly by international tribunals.[40] It is, therefore, mentioned only for completeness and has little significance as a source of transnational commercial law.

E. *Lex Mercatoria*

The sources of the *lex mercatoria*

1.60 We have said earlier that for our purposes the *lex mercatoria* is that part of transnational commercial law which consists of the unwritten customs and practice of merchants, so far as satisfying externally set criteria for validation. This definition excludes written codifications of customs and practice.[41] Many types of documents may be resorted to as *evidence* of the unwritten rules, but they do not in our view constitute part of the *lex mercatoria*, for in stating usage they almost invariably change it. Moreover, to the extent that previously unwritten rules are given effect by contract or international convention, they change their character and thereafter derive their force from the contract or the convention (as incorporated into national law), not from the usage, so that criteria determining the legal validity of the usage—for example, consistency of adoption and reasonableness—cease to be relevant. *Lex mercatoria* is thus best seen as being, true to its origins, the product of spontaneous activity on the part of merchants. We shall, however, say something a little later about general principles of law as a possible source of the *lex mercatoria*.

The normative force of usage

1.61 A central question to be confronted is whether a usage is legally operative merely by virtue of its existence or whether it has to satisfy certain external criteria of

---

[38] Under the direction of Professor Christian von Bar.   [39] See further ch 14.

[40] Michael Byers, *Custom, Power and the Power of Rules: international relations and customary international law* (CUP, Cambridge, 1999) 189.

[41] For a detailed discussion of the various theories relating to the *lex mercatoria*, see Filip de Ly, *International Business Law and Lex Mercatoria* (TMC Asser Instituut, The Hague, 1992) ch 4.

validity. In other words, can merchants make their own law merely by adopting a particular usage, or is something more needed to give that usage legal effect? This question mirrors that previously posed in relation to the ability of parties to a particular contract to make their own law. It is obvious that a consistent course of practice cannot by itself suffice as a legal rule, for the practice may be observed purely as a matter of courtesy or convenience or from a desire to accommodate one's customer. That is why it is often said that, to become a binding usage, a practice needs to be adopted from a sense of binding obligation. There are difficulties with this formulation,[42] which finds its counterpart in international law,[43] but at least it conveys the basic idea that practice must be distinguished from law:

> There is, however, the world of difference between a course of conduct which is frequently, or even habitually, followed in a particular commercial community as a matter of grace and a course which is habitually followed, because it is considered that the parties concerned have a legally binding right to demand it.[44]

In *Libyan Arab Foreign Bank v Bankers Trust Co*,[45] the plaintiffs claimed repayment of a Eurodollar deposit with the London branch of the defendant bank. The defendants disputed liability on the ground that they were precluded from paying because of an executive order of the President of the United States freezing all Libyan property in the possession or control of United States persons, including their overseas branches. The plaintiffs contended that they were entitled to repayment in cash in London or by any other means which did not involve an act in the United States contravening the Presidential order. The defendants asserted that it was a usage of the Eurodollar deposit market that deposits could be withdrawn only by a transfer effected through the clearing system of the country in whose currency the account was denominated—in the case in question, the New York CHIPS. Staughton J held that while this was the method by which withdrawals were commonly effected, the evidence did not show a binding usage to this effect. The plaintiffs' claim to withdraw their deposit in London therefore succeeded.

1.62

Nevertheless, some authorities seem to regard international trade usage as self-validating. Once identified, it has force by reason of its very existence, without need of any external validating authority. But this cannot be right. Though it is in the nature of transnational commercial law that it need not be derived from any particular sovereign authority and may be established by reference to sources that are not in themselves legally operative instruments, yet external validation of some kind—whether by legislation, jurisprudence or doctrine—is an essential prerequisite of a

1.63

---

[42] See below.

[43] See below, para 1.64 ff, as to this parallelism and the extent to which literature on the relationship between customary international law and treaty law may be of assistance in analysing the relationship between international trade usage and conventions.

[44] *General Reinsurance Corp v Forsakringsaktiebolaget Fennia Patria* [1983] QB 856 (CA) 874 (Slade LJ).   [45] [1989] QB 728.

legal norm. As shown above, mere contracts cannot be law in the full sense, for they do not derive from authority and do not themselves possess limiting mandatory rules or *lois de police*, which are essential to a legal system in order to be able to invalidate unconscionable bargains or those which produce distortion of competition or are otherwise contrary to the public interest. So to allow merchants unfettered freedom to make their own law by usage would be to by-pass constraints which all legal systems impose on freedom of contract. And just as contracts are not law, but derive their force from external criteria for recognition, so also international trade usage cannot be self-validating but depends for its recognition on conformity with certain legal norms. Moreover, it does not suffice that such norms exist in the abstract; they must be capable of determination by a court or other tribunal of competent jurisdiction as being satisfied by the usage in question.

1.64 There is, of course, a dilemma: do judicial decisions make law, which is contrary to the orthodox view of the role of the judge and raises the question how a usage could affect rights under a contract concluded before the judicial decision, or do they merely declare law, in which case usage exists as a binding rule independently of the judicial decision? The probable answer is that the law recognizes usage where it satisfies certain criteria, but in case of dispute it is for the relevant court or other competent tribunal to decide whether those criteria have been satisfied. In this sense, usage is no different from contract. Indeed, in many legal systems, usage is considered as essentially contractual in character, though the attribution of contractual intent has been criticized as artificial in cases where a usage is binding on a party who neither consents to it nor even knows of it. An alternative approach is to say that a judicial decision validates a usage retrospectively. But commercial certainty is best promoted by a principle that a usage is to be presumed to meet the criteria for legal recognition unless, and until, a court or other competent tribunal decides otherwise.

Roy Goode, 'Usage and Its Reception in Transnational Commercial Law (1997) 46 ICLQ 1, 7–18

II. THE NATURE, ELEMENTS AND SCOPE OF INTERNATIONAL TRADE USAGE

A. The Nature of Unwritten International Trade Usage

Unwritten trade usage is a practice or pattern of behaviour among merchants established by repetition which has in some degree acquired normative force. There are two theories as to the nature of unwritten trade usage. One is that it is a particular form of international customary law. The other, adopted by *(inter alia)* English law and by Article 9(2) of the 1980 UN Convention on Contracts for the International Sale of Goods (the 'Vienna Sales Convention'), is that it takes effect as an implied term of a contract. Though the contract theory has been criticised as artificial, in that it ascribes to the parties a knowledge of the usage which they may not possess, this is entirely consistent with the objective theory of contract by which terms are interpreted not according to the subjective intention of the parties but as a reasonable person would interpret them. Usages depend for their efficacy on the settled practices of parties to contracts; they are essentially contractual in nature. Proponents of the *lex mercatoria* tend to be hostile to the contract theory, seeing it as inconsistent with the status of international trade usage as 'law'. But the practical effect of the distinction between the two theories appears to be slight.

B. The Normative Force of Unwritten International Trade Usage

Until relatively recently it has been widely accepted that for an international trade usage to have normative force it is not sufficient to establish a pattern of repetitive behaviour among merchants; it must also be shown that this pattern of behaviour is observed from a sense of legally binding obligation, not from mere courtesy, convenience or expediency . . .

. . . This principle finds an exact parallel in international customary law, which requires a conjunction of *usus* and *opinio juris sive necessitatis* to establish a principle or rule of customary law. Thus Article 38(1) of the Statute of the International Court of Justice identifies as one of the sources of international law the Court is required to apply: 'b. international custom, as evidence of a general practice accepted as law'. To much the same effect is the elegantly worded rule in the *American Restatement (revised), Foreign Relations Law of the United States* §102:

(1) A rule of international law is one that has been accepted as such by the international community of states

(a) in the form of customary law:

. . .

(2) Customary international law results from a general and consistent practice of states followed by them from a sense of legal obligation.

The problem with the requirement of observance of custom from a sense of legally binding obligation is that it is based either on circularity or on paradox, for it presupposes a belief in an existing legal duty which if correct would make the belief itself superfluous and if erroneous would convert non-law into law through error. It is interesting to note that §1–205 of the American Uniform Commercial Code and Article 9(2) of the Vienna Sales Convention have jettisoned the *opinio juris* element. Under §1–205(2): 'A usage of trade is any practice or method of dealing having such regularity of observance in a place, vocation or trade as to justify an expectation that it will be observed with respect to the transaction in question.' Article 9(2) of the Vienna Sales Convention (which as previously mentioned attributes, the binding force of usage to implied agreement) takes the same position, though in rather more prolix terms:

> The parties are considered, unless otherwise agreed, to have impliedly made applicable to their contract or its formation a usage of which the parties knew or ought to have known and which in international trade is widely known to, and regularly observed by, parties to contracts of the type involved in the particular trade concerned.

Yet these two formulations are not without their problems either, for they fail to distinguish usage observed as binding from usage followed purely as a matter of habit, courtesy or convenience or simply a desire to accommodate one's business counterparty voluntarily where this is not detrimental to one's own interests. Clearly there must be some perception of obligation, even if it is not obligation in the full legal sense of that which has been ordained by law. Perhaps the most satisfactory way of capturing the element of obligation without reference to law is to say that the usage relied on must be one which is considered by the relevant mercantile community to bear on the making, proof, interpretation, performance or enforcement of the parties' commercial engagements towards each other.

A vexed question, which has long been debated in discussions on the nature of customary law and, indeed, of the common law itself, is whether the combination of *usus* and *opinio juris* suffices or whether it is also necessary that the customary rule contended for has received judicial, arbitral or legislative recognition. What exactly is the status of an uncodified usage before it has been the subject of an adjudication in a dispute? There are at least two divergent views on this question. The first is that before the usage has been formally recognised it does not exist, for its normative force is dependent on satisfying certain criteria—consistency of practice, reasonableness, notoriety and conformity with international public policy and any applicable national mandatory law—which are imposed externally by the law and which can be shown to be satisfied only by a decision of a court. This Austinian view of custom fails to address the paradox that if the function of the court or the arbitrator is to declare the law, including any rule of customary law, the rule contended for must exist already. The decision is the authority for the existence of the rule but is not the rule itself. Moreover, if the custom has no normative force until declared, how can it affect the rights of the parties under a contract necessarily made before the decision? The alternative position, advocated by Hart, Salmond and others, is that a ruling by the court in favour of a custom as meeting certain legally defined criteria is purely declaratory and is not the source of the custom's legal force any more than it is the source of, say, subordinate legislation that is challenged but upheld by the court as *intra vires*. This position, which is paralleled in the field of transnational commercial law by advocates of the new *lex mercatoria*, seems the preferable solution. It also surmounts another problem, namely, that a finding of usage in an arbitration binds only the parties to it and cannot be constitutive of the usage as regards third parties. Only a consistent upholding of the usage in a series of awards could have this effect. To a lesser degree this is true of decisions of national judges at first instance, for these too are not binding on anyone except the parties. And if this is the case as regards local usage, how much more so of international usage, which cannot be ruled on authoritatively by any national court so as to bind the courts of other jurisdictions. The problem, then, is to determine by whom or by what standards the external criteria against which the validity of an international trade usage must be tested are to be set.

. . .

III. HOW UNCODIFIED USAGE IS ESTABLISHED

A. The Nature of the Problem

The difficulty with uncodified usage, as with any other customary law, is to establish its existence. Individual members of the commercial community may have, or believe that they have, a broad perception of what a given usage is or means, but typically the postulated usage will lack definition, its boundaries and qualifications will be hazy and even its central core may prove to be a matter of debate.

That this is so can readily be demonstrated by everyday experience and by the process of litigation, and it applies with equal force to asserted but previously unexplored rules of the common law. A young lawyer practising in England and not familiar with the workings of English bank settlement systems attends a gathering of experienced bankers who are discussing problems of daylight exposure arising from a multilateral settlement system which nets out obligations only at the end of the day. The young lawyer is curious to know whether a payment order given by a customer to his bank can be countermanded after it has gone into the bank clearing but before the conclusion of the daily settlement. He would like to ask about this but is reluctant to expose his ignorance on what must obviously be such an elementary matter. Eventually he plucks up courage and poses the question. He may then quite possibly find to his surprise that half the assembly replies yes and the other half no. He would almost certainly have had a similar experience if, before the decision in the *Banque de l'Indochine* case, he had enquired as to the meaning and effect of a payment 'under reserve' to the beneficiary of a documentary credit. One group of bankers would have said that the paying bank could recover the payment from the beneficiary if the account party could demonstrate that the documents were not in conformity with the credit, whilst the other half would have answered (correctly, as it would turn out) that the bank could recover if the account party declined to take the documents, even if the reason for his refusal to take them was not legitimate.

In fact, every case in which there is a dispute between expert witnesses as to the fact and content of an unwritten trade usage makes the point that, not being reduced to writing, the usage is exposed to challenge as to its meaning or even its very existence. Precisely the same situation obtains where there is a dispute as to whether a right or remedy is given by the common law on a point not previously the subject of a judicial decision or scholarly writing. It is worth emphasising this point because there are arbitrators who seem willing to infer international trade usage on the flimsiest of evidence or even on no evidence at all beyond their own personal experience.

B. Usage as It Exists and Usage as the Merchants Would Like It to Be

Before considering the various conditions in which an international trade usage may be received by a court or arbitral tribunal I should like to focus on a point which hitherto appears to have escaped attention, namely, whether so much emphasis should be placed on usage as it stands, and whether there is not a case for admitting evidence that the usage is no longer acceptable to the mercantile community and is observed solely because it has been given contractual force. In international law it is recognised that there may be a fine line between *lex lata* and *lex ferenda*. Indeed, *lex ferenda* may quickly become *lex lata*, as in the case of scholarly compilations such as the UNIDROIT Principles of International Commercial Contracts where what are offered are in effect best solutions adapted from existing principles, solutions which within a year or two of publication of the Principles have already been applied in a number of arbitrations and at least one court decision.

What should a tribunal do when a rule of codified usage becomes seen as obstructive or unhelpful and in need of replacement and is observed solely because it is seen as having contractual force? The problem is less acute in the case of uncodified usage, for all the business community has to do is to abandon the usage and replace it with a new one. But where a usage becomes embodied in a codification incorporated into contracts it acquires contractual force and, unless negated or modified by express contractual provision, can be changed only by altering the code. It might be said that the duty of the tribunal is to ignore dissatisfaction with the existing rule and to apply it. But in the typical case where a tribunal applies a codified rule as evidence of existing usage it is usually prompted to do so because the rule is seen to reflect what is desirable, not simply what is done.

By way of illustration, when the Uniform Customs and Practice for Documentary Credits was first published by the International Chamber of Commerce in 1933 it contained a rule that credits were to be deemed revocable unless otherwise indicated. Given the fact that a beneficiary under a revocable credit was almost wholly unprotected, it was not surprising that the vast majority of credits were issued as irrevocable credits. In other words, the rule, if it had ever reflected the needs and practices of the merchant community, long ago ceased to do so. Nevertheless the rule remained in force for 60 years; not until the 1993 revision was it changed to make credits irrevocable unless otherwise indicated. Now suppose that in

1990 a documentary credit had been issued which was in traditional form and appearance in all respects except that it did not state whether it was revocable or irrevocable and omitted any reference to the UCP, and that an arbitral tribunal was called upon to decide whether, in mercantile usage, the credit was to be considered revocable or irrevocable. What position should it take? On the one hand there was a clear rule of the UCP that a credit was to be presumed revocable unless otherwise indicated; on the other a long-settled practice of calling for irrevocable, rather than revocable, credits. Should not the tribunal rely on the practice (if duly proved or capable of judicial notice) rather than treating the rule as evidence of usage or of a general principle of documentary credits law? To generalise the question, if parties to a set of contractually incorporated rules consistently exclude one of them, should that rule continue to be presumptive of the intention of business generally so as to bind parties who have not adopted the rules and thus have no contractual commitment to apply the presumptive rule if they have not excluded it?

Unfortunately a negative answer to this question confronts an immediate difficulty, namely, that most parties do in fact adopt the UCP and therefore the presumptive rule. There is no argument about what the former rule was, merely about what it ought to be. It is not, therefore, a case where the parties decided to create a new usage by acting outside the former UCP; on the contrary, what they did was to apply the freedom given by the UCP itself to displace the presumptive rule by declaring the credit irrevocable. Thus, however much the commercial world might have thought the rule out of touch with commercial needs, there can be no doubt that they accepted its binding force, so while the *usus* of issuing irrevocable credits could readily have been established, there would have been no basis for inferring an *opinio juris* that the issue of a credit imposed an irrevocable commitment on the part of the issuer . . .

G. Is the *Lex Mercatoria* Anational?

Does this mean, then, that the *lex mercatoria* is truly anational and autonomous? Put in this way the question is ambiguous, as becomes apparent when one considers the diversity of ways in which objections to the whole concept of *lex mercatoria* have been expressed. The first objection is that the *lex mercatoria*, consisting of general principles of law and international trade usage, is not a complete legal system, so that it is futile for the parties to seek to designate it as the law applicable to their contract. It is certainly the case that the *lex mercatoria* is not a complete legal system. But that does not mean that to choose it as the applicable law is wholly ineffective, merely that so far as its principles do not cover the question in dispute it will be necessary to refer to some applicable national law. Whether they do cover the question is for the tribunal to decide, drawing on whatever materials are to hand. Second, it is objected that the *lex mercatoria* is not an autonomous body of principles, for it is controlled by rules of public policy and mandatory rules of national law. This also is true, but it does not follow that the *lex mercatoria* lacks normative force, merely that it is subordinate to higher norms, in much the same way as principles laid down by the courts may be affected by legislation. Third, it is contended that every international usage depends for its normative force on recognition by national law. To the extent that it consists of general principles of law common to States (or to relevant States, however these might be defined) this condition is met. More debatable is whether the usage has to be shown to have been received into national law. If by this is meant a particular national law then it necessarily predicates selection of a given legal system as the applicable law, for that is the national law that is relevant to the question. Since arbitrators do from time to time decide cases according to international trade usage without reference to a national law and have their awards upheld by courts it would be rather futile to deny the efficacy of awards made on this basis. Nor can we even say, conformably with arbitration practice, that international usage is necessarily to be found in a convergence of rules in different legal systems, for such usage can also be inferred from conventions which have not yet come into force or, if in force, have not yet been ratified by the relevant States.

It is everywhere admitted that the normative force of usage, whether domestic or international, depends on its satisfying certain essential criteria. But where do we look to find what these are? The usage itself cannot speak as to its own validity. There are no doubt some usages that are so broad in character and so universal of application that they would be recognised in any developed legal system, and would, indeed, be likely to have lost their distinctive status as trade usages and to have acquired the status of a general principle of law. But broad principles of this kind, such as *pacta sunt servanda*, are so hedged about with qualifications which vary from one legal system to another that they serve little purpose except as a device by which an arbitral tribunal can claim support for its conclusions without having to determine an applicable law. Outside these broad principles we cannot point to some universal law against which to measure the validity of a usage, for such a law does not exist; both the character of a trade usage and the conditions of its validity vary from jurisdiction to jurisdiction. How, then, can arbitral tribunals satisfy themselves that an international usage is valid without resorting to national law?

A short answer to this is that if the usage is truly international it cannot depend for its existence on any particular national law or decisions of any particular national court. That would be to localise and domesticate what is *ex hypothesi* international. But the admission of international usage as a determinant of rights is dependent on national law in a different sense in that (quite apart from mandatory rules and rules of public policy) the existence of international usage can be ruled upon only by a tribunal of competent jurisdiction—and in the case of an arbitral tribunal, jurisdiction is determined by the *lex loci arbitri*. It is everywhere the case that an award may be set aside where the arbitrators have exceeded their jurisdiction, and that is also a ground for refusing enforcement under the New York Convention. It is primarily the *lex loci arbitri* which controls the conditions in which arbitrators can make valid awards, within the limits set by those conditions, and in the absence of a choice of law by the parties, arbitrators can draw on whatever sources seem to them proper in order to determine the rights of the parties. Accordingly, the normative force of international trade usage depends not on what national law says about the usage but upon whether the power to decide on the existence and content of such usage has been exercised by a tribunal having competence under the *lex loci arbitri* and conforming with its procedural requirements. National laws, through their conferment of decision-making powers on arbitral tribunals, have delegated to them the power to decide whether the requisite criteria for recognising an international usage have been satisfied and for that purpose to draw on such materials as seem to them proper. As Professor Clive Schmitthoff so perceptively observed many years ago: '. . . the new law merchant, as an autonomous legal regulation, is founded on the complementary interaction of party autonomy and arbitration'.

International conventions as evidence of usage

Arbitral tribunals sometimes look to international conventions as evidence of **1.65** existing usage, a technique which enables them to give effect to a convention provision even when the convention as such is not applicable. The following extract examines the legitimacy of this approach.

Roy Goode, 'Usage and Its Reception in Transnational Commercial Law' (1997) 46 ICLQ 1, 7–18

The relationship of conventions to usages is as complex in transnational commercial law as it is in international law. A convention may be evidence of a usage, so as to allow its admission where the convention would not as such be applicable; it may operate concurrently with the usage; it may displace the usage; and it may create or evidence new usage through consistent adoption in cross-border commercial transactions or by non-contracting States. Further, if a convention is evidence of usage it may equally be the case that its non-adoption negates its significance as evidence of usage.

1. International trade conventions as evidence of existing trade usage

An international trade convention may legitimately be relied on in given conditions as evidence of pre-existing usage, in the same way as an international treaty may be relied on as evidence of international customary law. It is a characteristic of conventions that they can never exhaustively determine the scope of their own application, which may be extended by contract, usage or acquiescence.

The crucial question is whether the convention does in fact reflect pre-existing usage or whether, on the contrary, it changes the usage. It has been pointed out by a number of writers that it is impossible for *jus scriptum* accurately to capture any unwritten law, if only because the scope of the latter is inherently uncertain and changeable and may also when reduced to writing, be found in some respects to be incomplete or unsatisfactory. The notion that 'codifiers' sit down faithfully to reproduce rules of customary law is pure mythology, particularly at the international level where there are likely to be significant differences between the rules of one legal system and those of another. When legal experts gather together to frame a convention or a set of uniform rules they will normally have the advantage of a report by the secretariat of the sponsoring international organisation setting out in broad terms the existing law and practice in selected jurisdictions. Each of the participating experts will bring to bear a knowledge of his or her own legal system and, understandably enough can be expected to test each proposed rule against the rules of that system to see whether it overlooks a problem or on the contrary, represents an improvement. But the drafters of the convention or uniform rules would make no progress at all if they conceived their task as being to assemble before them all the known rules and practices and strive to create an amalgam of them all. Even if such a task were feasible its product would negate any notion of mere reproduction of existing law, for necessarily the amalgam could be created only by changing in some degree the existing rules of its various constituents. In any event, that is simply not how the process of harmonisation works. What those involved in the project seek to achieve is best solutions to typical problems, being solutions which are not so far removed from existing practice as to make them unacceptable. Accordingly, change is inherent in any redaction of rules, whether written or unwritten. The resulting text will thus be a combination of rules that existed before, modifications of existing rules and entirely new rules.

How, then, is a court or arbitral tribunal to determine whether a convention or codification reproduces existing usage or changes it? If the usage has already been embodied in an earlier convention or codification the task is relatively easy, for all the tribunal has to do is to compare the two texts. But where the convention or codification is relied on as evidence of existing unwritten usage this resource is not available. If the alleged usage is disputed then unless it is of the near-universal kind of which judicial notice can be taken a national court is likely to require it to be established by evidence. Such evidence could take a variety of forms, of which the most compelling would be the *travaux préparatoires* and the rapporteur's report. What is interesting is the readiness of some arbitral tribunals to assume, without any evidence whatsoever, that the best reflection of existing usage is the provisions of an international convention or codification.

A striking example of this is the award in an ICC arbitration, case no, 5713 of 1989.[46] The seller of goods under a contract of sale made in 1979 brought arbitration proceedings to recover the balance of the price. The buyer claimed the right to set off loss suffered from the fact that the goods did not conform to the contract of sale. An issue arose as to whether the buyer had given notice of the lack of conformity in due time. The tribunal applied generally accepted conflict of laws rules to decide that the law governing the contract was that of the seller's country. However, the applicable law as thus determined was considered by the tribunal to impose time requirements for the giving of notice of defects that were so short and specific as to run counter to generally accepted trade usages. The tribunal therefore declined to apply the law applicable under conflict of laws rules, and instead applied Articles 38 and 39 of the Vienna Sales Convention.

> The Tribunal finds that there is no better source to determine the prevailing trade usages than the terms of the United Nations Convention on the Inter-national Sale of Goods of 11 April 1980; usually called "the Vienna Convention". This is so even though neither [the country of the buyer] nor [the country of the seller] are parties to that Convention. If they were, the Convention might be applicable to this case as a matter of law and not only as reflecting the trade usages.

> The Vienna Convention, which has been given effect to in 17 countries, may be fairly taken to reflect the generally recognized usages regarding the matter of the non-conformity of goods in international sales.

The tribunal went on to hold that the buyer had given notice of non-conformity within the time laid down by Articles 38 and 39, that in any event the seller was debarred by Article 40 from invoking the time limits laid down in those articles because he had known of the non-conformity and did not disclose it, and that accordingly the buyer was entitled to compensation which could be set off against the seller's claim. It can reasonably be inferred from the rather truncated report of the award that under the applicable law the buyer would have been held to have given notice of non-conformity out of time.

What is surprising about the award is not that it extended the scope of the Convention beyond its own stated boundaries—for this can happen in a variety of ways, including treatment of the Convention as the embodiment of existing usage—but that it completely disregarded the applicable law and, in doing so, assumed without discussion that the Vienna Sales Convention did in fact embody relevant trade usage. On the latter point there are at least four matters which should have given the tribunal pause for thought.

(1) When the contract was concluded (which is accepted as the point where rights and duties are established) the Vienna Convention not merely lacked the necessary number of ratifications to bring it into force, it had not even been made! All the more curious, then, that the tribunal indicated that the Convention could have applied directly if both parties had carried on business in contracting States.

---

[46] Summarized in (1990) XX ICC *Yearbook of Commercial Arbitration* (Kluwer, Deventer 1990) 70; Sigvard Jarvin et al, *Collection of ICC Arbitral Awards: 1991–1995* (Kluwer, Boston, 1990) vol II, 223.

(2) There *was* a convention in force at the time of the contract, namely, Vienna's predecessor, the 1964 Uniform Law on International Sales. Why, then, did the tribunal not
apply (or even refer to) ULIS? One can only speculate. Perhaps the tribunal considered that the ULIS rules on the time for examination were too rigid and would have
left the buyer remediless. Another answer might be that by 1979, 15 years after it was
made, ULIS had attracted only eight ratifications and one accession, compared with
the 17 ratifications, etc, referred to in the award, and that a total of nine adopting
States was not considered strong enough evidence of prevailing international trade
usage. But if this is true of ULIS, then how much more so of a convention that was
still only in draft at the time of the contract and might conceivably have proved as
unsuccessful as ULIS.

(3) At the 1980 Diplomatic Conference there was protracted debate on what became
Article 39 and was then Article 37, and two delegates on separate occasions made the
point that the article in question was one of the most controversial in the entire
Convention—hardly the strongest basis for treating the article as evidence of an internationally established usage! It is true that the UNCITRAL Commission text which
came forward for consideration by the Diplomatic Conference and embodied what is
now Article 39 could be given some weight as representing the views of the working
group and the full UNCITRAL Commission, but why should it be accorded greater
weight than the stricter provisions of a convention which had then already been in
force for 14 years?

(4) International trade conventions are made by States, not by businessmen and accordingly are not formulated by the members of the community whose usages they are supposed to embody. Not uncommonly conventions fail to gain acceptance precisely
because they do not reflect the practices or perceptions of the dominant commercial
community. A good example is provided by the Hamburg Rules, which though technically operative have proved very much of a damp squib. Nowadays more determined
efforts are made to consult business interests on a proposed international trade convention—indeed, their representative organisations may be involved in the preparatory work as observers—but the policy decisions and the drafting are undertaken
almost entirely by lawyers, and it is primarily lawyers who will lead the representation
of their governments at a diplomatic conference to conclude a convention.

Unfortunately there is no indication from the report of the award (which, as is customary,
has been filleted to preserve the anonymity of the parties) as to whether any of the above
arguments were placed before the tribunal or, indeed, whether there was any opportunity
given, or any attempt made, to challenge the assumption that Article 39 of the Vienna
Sales Convention reflected current usage at the time of the contract or, indeed, at the time
of the making of the Convention.

There is a further problem to be considered. A purely dispositive provision of an international trade convention, even if accurately reflecting existing usage, may be displaced by
subsequent usage. How can a tribunal be sure that the convention still reflects trade usage?
No doubt there is a presumption in favour of continuing validity of a convention as evidence of usage but it should certainly be capable of being rebutted by evidence.

The drawing of inferences of uncodified usage from an international trade convention
raises a number of other conundrums. How far is the tribunal entitled to rely on hindsight? In the arbitral award referred to above the tribunal, deciding a case ten years after the
contract, relied on the fact that the Vienna Sales Convention had been carried into effect
in 17 countries. Suppose that the hearing had taken place not in 1989 but in 1981, when

there had been no ratifications at all. Would that have made a difference? Certainly there would be no clear indication at that stage of the level of support the Convention would command. The absence of ratifications would have had no significance either, because it would have been too soon to draw any inferences. Suppose that, at the time when the case was in fact heard, there had still been no ratifications. That would be a clear indication that the Convention had attracted no support from Governments and was unlikely to do so. Should the tribunal take this fact into account in giving an award in 1989, when if it had made the adjudication in 1981 no real significance could have been attached to the lack of ratifications?

If the adoption of a convention is to be relied on as evidence of usage, or its non-adoption as evidence to negate usage, do we not need to know why it gained acceptance or, on the contrary, did not? It is conceivable that the particular provision invoked in the dispute was highly controversial and considered out of touch with commercial reality but that the benefits of the convention as a whole were considered to outweigh the drawbacks of this one provision. Conversely, States may have been unanimously in favour of the provision as reflecting current usage but opposed to the convention on other grounds. Further, the fact that a convention may not have come into force does not necessarily deprive it of significance, for it may be sufficiently persuasive within the commercial community to generate new usages. Similarly, in the field of international law the ability of treaties to generate customary law prior to their coming into force is widely recognised, as in the case of recognition of the 200-mile exclusive economic zones in the course of negotiation and after adoption of the final text of the 1982 UN Convention on the Law of the Sea.

Reliance on conventions as evidence of international trade usage is at once a virtue and a danger. As previously indicated, the effect may be to extend the scope of the convention well beyond its stated sphere of application. Reference has already been made to an arbitral award which applied Article 39 of the Vienna Sales Convention to a case where the Convention was not in existence at the time of the contract, and even at the time of the award many years later the Convention would not have been applicable on its own terms, since neither of the parties carried on business in a country that had become party to the Convention. Extensions of this kind may not trouble arbitrators; they are of much graver concern to national judges, for their effect may be to impose on a national court the duty to apply the provisions of a convention which its own State has declined to ratify. The same objection applies to the theory advanced by some scholars that parties may subject their contract to the terms of a convention not as a method of incorporation of contractual terms but as the choice of an applicable law under conflict of laws rules. There is no objection to the former, for the incorporated terms of the convention become subject to the mandatory rules of the applicable law in just the same way as any other contract terms, but strong objection to the latter, which if valid would give private parties the right to invoke the convention against the wishes of a non-ratifying State in which the dispute was tried. Again, however, it has been argued that while this is a valid argument as regards national judges it should have no application to arbitrators, who typically will not occupy any position of authority in or indeed have any connection with, the State where they sit.

Of course, it has to be recognised that courts and arbitral tribunals and the parties appearing before them are unlikely to have detailed knowledge of more than a very small number of legal systems and that they cannot be expected either to engage in a major comparative study or to expend huge effort in tracking the antecedents of conventions presented to them. In meeting the exigencies of dispute resolution they cannot be said to be acting unreasonably in assuming, in the absence of evidence or argument to the contrary, that a particular convention reflects pre-existing usage. But that is a matter of evidence and of onus of proof. The difficulty in using prior arbitral awards as precedents is that we know so little about the facts and arguments. Often the reports do not show even the date of the contract in dispute, though that may be highly relevant. The countries involved and the commercial background to the dispute will usually be omitted for reasons of confidentiality, and it can be difficult even to deduce the arguments advanced or to know to what extent the arbitral tribunal was relying on its own knowledge rather than on evidence.

General principles of law

1.66 Once a usage gains such general acceptance as to be applicable independently of a particular trade or locality, it becomes elevated into a general principle of law. Such principles can be identified without too much difficulty. In the same paper as that from which an extract was quoted earlier,[47] Lord Justice Mustill identified twenty rules 'as representing a tolerably complete account of the rules said to constitute the *lex mercatoria*', including such general principles as *pacta sunt servanda*, *rebus sic stantibus*, performance of a contract in good faith, and the inability of a party to rely on failure of a condition precedent caused by its own non-performance. Since rules of this kind are to be found in most legal systems, it is usually unnecessary to invoke the *lex mercatoria*, as recourse to national law will suffice.

1.67 While general principles of law are undoubtedly a source of transnational commercial law, their relevance to the *lex mercatoria* as reflected in the usages of merchants is questionable. If there were such a thing as general principles of *commercial* law that would certainly qualify for inclusion in the *lex mercatoria*! But such principles are not to be found, which is why scholars almost invariably refer to general principles of law, not to general principles of commercial law. There is a strong argument for confining the *lex mercatoria* to international trade usage and treating general principles of law as a distinct source of law, in the same way that public international lawyers treat general principles of international law separately from customary international law. It is interesting to note that almost all the rules said to form part of the *lex mercatoria* are general principles of law common to most states and owe nothing to the spontaneous generation of rules and practices of the mercantile community, which are hardly to be found in the lists of *lex mercatoria* rules. Moreover, most such rules are not confined to international transactions but are equally applicable to domestic contracts, a number apply to contracts generally, not merely commercial contracts, and some are not dependent on a contractual relationship at all. One might add that attention has been devoted almost exclusively to trade transactions, whereas there is at least as much development in the world of international finance, through instruments such as the documentary credit, the standby credit and the demand guarantee.

---

[47] 'The New *Lex Mercatoria*', above, para 1.50 at 174–7.

Berthold Goldman, 'The applicable law: general principles of law—the *lex mercatoria*'
in Julian DM Lew (ed) *Contemporary Problems in International Arbitration* (Centre for
Commercial Law Studies, Queen Mary College, London, 1986) 113–16[47a]

There is a wide conception of the *lex mercatoria*, according to which it might be defined by the *object* of its constituent sources. *Lex mercatoria* would thus, irrespective of the origin and the nature of these sources, be the *law proper to international economic relations*. One would encompass not only transnational customary law, whether it is codified or not (and in the latter case revealed and clarified by arbitral awards), but also law of an interstate, or indeed state, which relates to international trade. Thus, for example, the successive Hague (1964) and Vienna (1980) Conventions Establishing Uniform Laws for the International Sale of Goods would be part of *lex mercatoria*. This would also be the case with respect to national legislation whose specific and exclusive object is international trade, such as that of the German Democratic Republic. The same applies to rules specific to international trade established by national case law, such as, for example, the French notions of the autonomy of the parties, the general validity of international arbitration agreements, and the capacity of the state and of public entities to bind themselves by such agreements. All this is considered as being well established by the 1981 French Law on International Arbitration, although the Law did not expressly incorporate these notions so as not to constrain the evolution of the case law.

This wide view has always been that of Clive Schmitthoff, and it may be compared to that of Philip Jessup in his classical work on 'Transnational Law'. I will state at once that I do not share it. For it is obvious that the specific problems of transnational commercial custom (ie, is it a rule of law? does it constitute a transnational legal order, distinct from national legal systems as well as from the international legal order *stricto sensu?*), do not arise with respect to rules of inter-state or state origin. No one contests that the latter are rules of law, nor that they are part of the legal order of the states having adopted them. I note in this respect that this is clearly so even when the origin of these rules is solely to be found in case law, as is the case with the French rules I cited as examples. The criterion for determining the ambit of *lex mercatoria* that I would follow thus does not solely reside in the *object* of its constituent elements, but also in its *origin* and its *customary*, and thus *spontaneous* nature.

It should be noted, however, that like many boundaries, the one thus drawn does not escape controversy, or if I may say, 'transboundary hypotheses'. Thus, the General Conditions of the United Nations Economic Commission for Europe (UNECE)—which are, in fact, Standard Contracts—have a transnational object, but were established under the auspices of an international organisation. Should they, for this latter reason, be eliminated from the domain of the *lex mercatoria?* One may oppose this, because they were prepared by the representatives of the concerned business sectors, whom the UNECE simply provided with logistical assistance and legal expertise, so that they are actually of professional and customary origin. Do they, however, have the status of customary law? It should be contended that the businessmen elevate them to this status only insofar as they refer to the standard contracts with such a degree of frequency that it might finally be concluded that such a reference is implicit. In fact, one meets this issue in more than one instance of the forming *lex mercatoria*.

[47a] This paper was delivered at the 1985 inaugural conference of the School of International Arbitration, Centre for Commercial Law Studies, Queen Mary, University of London. It was originally published in Julian DM Lew (ed), *Contemporary Problems in International Arbitration* (jointly published by Centre for Commercial Law Studies, Queen Mary, University of London and Kluwer Law International, The Hague, 1986) pp 113–116. © 1986 Kluwer Law International/CCLS. Reprinted with kind permission. All Rights Reserved.

A second 'transboundary', or at least open to discussion, hypothesis is the one where a specific rule of international trade, and in particular of international arbitration, is affirmed by a state court, without any reference to an international convention, or to a domestic statute, one may wonder whether such judicial decisions embody a rule pertaining merely to the legal system of the particular court, or rather a transnational unwritten principle or rule which the state court wishes to affirm and to apply.

At least provisionally, I would here conclude that the *lex mercatoria* comprises rules the *object* of which is mainly, if not exclusively, transnational, and the *origin* is customary and thus spontaneous, notwithstanding the possible intervention of interstate or state authorities in their elaboration and/or implementation.

Does the *lex mercatoria*, as tentatively defined according to its origin and nature, comprise both the usages of international trade which become customary rules, and *general principles of transnational law?* Furthermore, is it possible to draw a clear distinction between customary rules and general principles?

This is a difficult issue, if only because the general principles of law are themselves of double origin. There are, firstly, principles common to all, or to a large majority of national legal systems (such are the general principles mentioned as a source of international law by Article 36 of the Statute of the International Court of Justice); *pacta sunt servanda* is here the simplest, but not the only, example. Secondly, there are rules that are specific to international trade, insofar as they are not embodied in the majority of the national legal systems; an example could be here the obligation for the creditor to *minimise the prejudice* due to the non-performance by the debtor of his obligations. Indeed, while generally admitted in Common Law—as far as I know—such obligation is not clearly embodied in civil law (except, possibly, as implied in the general requirement of good faith).

Does this mean, at least, that the general principles of the first category are generated by the international *societas mercatorum*, or are specific to the international *societas mercatorum*? I do not think this first objection is decisive. Indeed (to take the example already mentioned), where a transnational contract is governed by the *lex mercatoria, pacta sunt servanda* is not referred to by the parties, nor by the arbitrators, as a principle taken from a particular national law, but as a principle dominating transnational law. The practical consequence is that the interpretation of this principle and its possible limitations (for instance, *force majeure*), which may differ from one national system to another, are themselves elaborated in the framework of the transnational law.

It might be more difficult to draw a clear distinction, in the framework of the *lex mercatoria*, between general principles and transnational customary rules. A good example is here the one of *minimisation of damages:* is the creditor's obligation to minimise his loss based on a general principle of law, or on a transnational customary rule? I would personally be inclined to choose the second solution. Indeed, a general principle is not purported to govern just one particular situation; it is the source of more than one rule of law, applicable to several sets of facts. Thus, *pacta sunt servanda* generates not only the obligation of each party to a contract to fulfill its promises, but also the obligation to perform them in good faith, to compensate for the damage caused to the other party by their non-fulfillment, and not to terminate the contract unilaterally where such termination is not contractually or legally provided for. One could say that a general principle of law is engendering rules of law and dominates their interpretation, while a transnational customary rule (like any other rule of law) governs a specific situation of fact; and one could think that according to this distinction the obligation to minimise the prejudice is a customary rule, rather than a general principle.

It remains to be seen whether the distinction, if so drawn, is of some practical interest. The same could be found in the mandatory and even the *public policy* character of the general principles, or at least of some of them, as opposed to the 'suppletory' character of the customary rules (which would mean that the parties could depart from the latter, but not from the general principles). Such a distinction implies that there is a 'public policy of the *lex mercatoria*', which one author has recently denied, but which arbitral awards have effectively applied, in respect of the state's capacity to conclude arbitral statements or in cases of bribery.

Whatever the case, the reading of court decisions or arbitral awards shows that when referring to transnational law, judges and arbitrators mention general principles as well as general usages of international trade, not taking very much care to distinguish clearly between them, as being two components of the *lex mercatoria*. Consequently, I shall here conclude that *lex mercatoria* is, at the least, *a set of general principles and customary rules spontaneously referred to or elaborated in the framework of international trade, without reference to a particular national system of law.*

Roy Goode, 'Rule, Practice and Pragmatism in Transnational Commercial Law' (2005) 54 ICLQ 539, 546–9

The idea of a new autonomous *lex mercatoria*, reviving the traditions of the mediaeval law merchant based on the practices of merchants and administered by powerful, largely independent, bodies such as the Italian *Mercanzia*, has gripped the imagination of modern scholars. It is not a new idea—the great Leone Levi published a draft international commercial law code as far back as 1863—but is much in vogue among scholars. Many years ago, at a conference on international commercial arbitration organised by the School of International Arbitration within the Centre for Commercial Law Studies at Queen Mary College, that remarkable French scholar Professor Berthold Goldman, sitting as a member of a distinguished group of panellists, commented: 'I think that here, in London, it would not be prudent for me to speak of the *lex mercatoria*!'

Since Goldman was rightly considered one of the founding fathers of the subject, this was self-restraint of truly heroic proportions. Happily it did not last, and he went on to give a paper of crystal clarity on general principles of law and the *lex mercatoria*. The concept of the *lex mercatoria*, initially propounded by Fragistas, Goldstajn, Goldman and Schmitthoff, has been powerfully developed by modern scholars, in particular Filip De Ly, Ole Lando, Klaus Peter Berger and Emmanuel Gaillard, to name only a few. But what is the *lex mercatoria*? And is it truly autonomous?

A. *The nature of the* lex mercatoria

Unfortunately there is no agreement on what the *lex mercatoria* comprises. To some, it is merely another label for transnational commercial law and thus encompasses all kinds of harmonisation, formal and informal. To others, it is the product of so-called spontaneous international law-making through international trade usage as evidenced by rules of trade associations, standard-term contracts and general principles and rules and restatements formulated by international agencies. The *lex mercatoria* is propounded as a set of rules which can not only be applied by arbitrators after the event but selected as the applicable law in contracts.

My own preference is to confine the *lex mercatoria* to international trade practice. To equate the *lex mercatoria* with the entirety of transnational commercial law deprives us of a useful label to denote that part of transnational commercial which derives from the international practice of merchants. To treat as part of the *lex mercatoria* standard-term contracts, codes of practice promulgated by international business organisations and even international conventions seems to me to confuse customary law, which is surely the essence of the *lex mercatoria*, with contract and treaty law, and to treat as a homogeneous mass things that are quite different in character. In a brilliant essay many years ago, Lord Justice Mustill (as he then was) pointed out that the *lex mercatoria* is not intentionally fashioned as an instrument of harmonisation; it simply exists as a product of spontaneous generation, whereas international conventions and standard-term international contracts have as their objective the harmonisation of rights, duties and practices. International conventions derive their force from the exercise of sovereign power through the process of ratification and thus form part of national law, not of some independent legal order. In principle, private law conventions, like private contracts, bind only those who become parties to them, in sharp contrast to customary law, which is more general in character. As to the utility of standard-term contracts as a source of law it would be helpful to be given some specifics of the rules to be extracted from such contracts so that we could form a judgment on whether they were sufficiently precise to be useful and how far they could be said to represent a generally adopted market approach.

Though a number of scholars claim that contracts create law, my view is that contracts cannot by themselves constitute a source of law; they have effect only by virtue of recognition by a national legal system. Clive Schmitthoff, who was one of the leading exponents of the modern *lex mercatoria*, is regularly invoked as a progenitor of the idea that there is an autonomous law of international trade created by spontaneous generation and owing nothing to national laws or sovereign powers, and that an important aspect of this was the international contract. What is often overlooked is that while Schmitthoff accepted that parties to international contracts were largely free to make their own law, his clearly stated view was that the parties enjoyed this power only by the will of sovereign states, alone or acting in concert, and was subject to important exceptions, for example, those based on public policy or overriding mandatory rules. It is true that Schmitthoff frequently referred to the autonomous law of international trade but it is clear that by that he meant only that, *under the authority given by States*, parties were free to subject themselves by contract to sources of law other than national laws and to organise their relations as they thought fit.

No contract can speak to its own validity and no legal system allows complete freedom to contracting parties, whose agreement is everywhere bounded by rules of public policy and mandatory rules. Accordingly, though a valid contract is undoubtedly a source of legal rights, every contract is required to satisfy certain external criteria of validity. Nor can the arbitration process elevate the status of contracts, as some have claimed, for it is everywhere accepted that unless otherwise agreed arbitrators must decide in accordance with legal rules. In Mann's words, *lex facit arbitrum*.

What of general principles of law? Though it is common to treat the *lex mercatoria* as including general principles of law, and I myself used to follow this approach, it seems to me on further reflection that these principles—for example, *pacta sunt servanda*, the *nemo dat* rule and the duty to mitigate loss suffered from a breach of contract—are not particular to international trade or even to commercial contracts, are qualified by numerous exceptions and tell us nothing about the process of spontaneous lawmaking which is said to be the hallmark of the *lex mercatoria*. If we look at the lists of rules of the *lex mercatoria* propounded by modern scholars and remove from it general principles of law and we find that almost nothing is left, while on the other hand there is a conspicuous absence of references to important modern usages in relation to documentary credits, demand guarantees, and clearing and settlement systems for the transfer of funds and investment securities. Professor Jan Dalhuisen is one of the few scholars to draw attention to the fact that usages of the financial markets are every bit as important as usages of trade. It would be different if we had general principles of *international trade* law, but these are never mentioned, for what is to me the self-evident reason that they do not exist; we simply have usages of a particular trade or locality. So I would follow the international lawyers in treating general principles of law as a separate source, thus confining the *lex mercatoria* to international trade usage, which is surely the epitome of spontaneous law-creation.

B. Is the lex mercatoria *autonomous?*

The concept of autonomy means different things to different people. There is *de facto* autonomy in that for the most part the business community is left free to develop its own practices and give effect to them through its own rules, contracts and dispute resolution procedures. Since the legality of what is done and decided is not usually questioned we can say that as a practical matter the custom of merchants and the rules they formulate for the future conduct of transactions do operate as law within the business community, whether or not they have the force of law. I believe that the failure to distinguish *lex mercatoria as law* from its observance as a matter of *practice* accounts for much of the misunderstanding that exists between those who propound the existence of a *lex mercatoria* and those who deny it. As law the *lex mercatoria* consists of binding usage and depends in the last resort on recognition by national law. As observed practice the *lex mercatoria* is not dependent on external legal recognition at all, for it is not truly *lex*. It simply exists, and it is effective because business people in the relevant community perceive its observance as necessary to the fair and efficient conduct of business, so that the sanction for failure to follow the practice is not a legal sanction but opprobrium from fellow businessmen, their unwillingness to deal with the culprit and, in the last resort, expulsion from the relevant mercantile community. *Lex mercatoria* as practice is thus almost as potent as a true law, and this is why it has been described by some leading scholars as operating at the periphery of the legal process and as soft law but not weak law.

There is also *de jure* autonomy to the extent that merchants are left free by sovereign authority to make their own laws and settle their own disputes without regard to the ordinary laws of the land. But while the parties to a contract may to a large degree subject themselves to rules which do not depend on any particular national legal system, their autonomy is not absolute, since it is universally recognised that contracts must give way to internationally mandatory rules and *lois de police*. As Montesquieu pointed out long ago, in his great work *De L'Esprit des Lois*, it is necessary to distinguish freedom of contract from freedom of commerce:

> The freedom of commerce is not power granted to the merchants to do what they please; this would be more properly its slavery. The constraint of the merchant is not the constraint of commerce . . . The English constrain the merchant, but it is in favour of commerce.

Questions

1. What were the salient characteristics of the old law merchant and the methods and tribunals by which commercial disputes were resolved?
2. Describe the typical commercial transactions and instruments developed by the old law merchant.
3. What factors were responsible for the decline of the old law merchant?

4. Why did States begin to develop rules for the conflict of laws (private international law)?
5. 'Contract is law.' Discuss.
6. How far is it true to say that rules of transnational commercial law can be identified by reference to sources that do not themselves constitute legally operative instruments?
7. What is 'the new law merchant'? In what sense can it be considered autonomous?
8. The status of the *lex mercatoria* as an autonomous legal system appears to conflict with the principle that there cannot be a contract without law. Consider the passage from Professor Teubner's paper,[48] in which this dilemma is addressed. What is the external validating factor that, in Professor Teubner's view, makes what would otherwise be a *contrat sans loi* binding? Do you consider this to be sufficient?
9. Is usage law? How is usage established?
10. What is the paradox in the concept of *opinio juris*? Can it be that the belief that something is legally binding is what makes it binding?

Further reading

Berger, Klaus Peter, Dubberstein, Holger, Lehmann, Sascha and Petzold, Victoria, 'The CENTRAL Enquiry on the Use of Transnational Law in International Contract Law and Arbitration—Background, Procedure and Selected Results' in Berger, Klaus Peter (ed), *The Practice of Transnational Law* (Kluwer, The Hague, 2001) 91–113

Berger, Klaus Peter, *The Creeping Codification of the Lex Mercatoria* (Kluwer, The Hague, 1999) ch XXVIII

Gaillard, Emmanuel, 'Transnational Law: A Legal System or a Method of Decision-Making', in Berger, K P (ed), *The Practice of Transnational Law* (Kluwer Law International, The Hague, 2001), 53

Goode, Roy, 'Rule, Practice and Pragmatism in Transnational Commercial Law' (2005) 54 ICLQ 539

Procaccia, Uriel, 'The Case Against *lex mercatoria*' in Ziegel, Jacob S (ed), *New Developments in International Commercial Law and Consumer Law: Proceedings of the 8th Biennial Conference of the International Academy of Commercial and Consumer Law* (Hart Publishing, Oxford, 1998) 87–95

Teubner, Gunther, ' "Global Bukowina": Legal Pluralism in the World Society', in *Global Law Without a State* (ed Teubner) (Ashgate, Dartmouth, 1997), ch 1

Van Houtte, Hans, *The Law of International Trade* (2nd edn, Sweet & Maxwell, London, 2002)

---

[48] Above, para 1.45.

2

THE CONFLICT OF LAWS IN COMMERCIAL TRANSACTIONS

A. **The Nature of Conflict of Laws**
Definition | 2.01
The structure of a conflicts rule
('meta law') | 2.04
B. **The Role of Conflict of Laws in International Commercial Law**
Prior to the advent of transnational
commercial law | 2.07
A new era: The Warsaw Convention
of 1929 | 2.10
C. **Selected Issues of General Conflict of Laws Theory**
Jurisdiction | 2.14
Rules v 'approaches' | 2.15

Connecting factors of particular
relevance in commercial law | 2.22
Contracts | 2.23
Property | 2.37
Other important connecting factors | 2.42
Characterization | 2.45
Public policy (*ordre public*) | 2.48
Mandatory rules in the law of contracts | 2.51
Neo-statutist theory and market
regulation | 2.57
Renvoi | 2.58
D. **The Future: Will We Continue to Need Conflict of Laws?** | 2.61

A. The Nature of Conflict of Laws

Definition

Conflict of laws is a term of art originally used primarily in the United States. Its **2.01** most common European equivalent is 'private international law' (*droit international privé, Internationales Privatrecht, diritto internazionale privato, derecho internacional privado*). But 'conflicts' illustrates exactly what is meant, and other languages are coining similar terms (*Kollisionsrecht, conflictenrecht*). In this chapter these terms are used interchangeably.

Conflict of laws is that branch of any *national* legal system that deals with cases **2.02** (fact patterns) having a foreign element and that determines which national law governs the solution of the various problems involved in the case. A 'foreign element' is any contact, be it factual or normative, with some system of law other than the national system concerned.

2.03 Rules of private international law may be entirely national (common law or statutory) in origin (the so-called 'autonomous' conflicts rules) or they may originate from an international convention (treaty) or other type of instrument.

The structure of a conflicts rule ('meta law')

2.04 A rule of substantive law provides the answer of the legislator or the courts to a question of law, for example, the seller's duties under a contract of sale or the formal requirements for the valid issue of a cheque. A rule of private international law does nothing of that kind: it just indicates where, that is in which domestic legal system, to look for the answer to any such question. In other words, conflicts rules identify the relevant substantive law. If one looks at a legal system as archaeologists look at a site of layers of soil and clay covering what is eventually found underneath, then conflicts rules may properly be described as the upper layer, and that is why some quite graphically call it 'meta law'.[1] However, rules of private international law do not 'rise above' the ordinary substantive rules of law but are subject to the same rules of legitimacy, interpretation and the like.

2.05 Given the difference in purpose, the structure of a rule of private international law differs from the structure of a rule of substantive law.

Rule 1 of section 18 of the Sale of Goods Act 1979 (UK) provides:

> Where there is an unconditional contract for the sale of specific goods in a deliverable state the property in the goods passes to the buyer when the contract is made . . .

On condition that a certain fact pattern exists (premise) the law imposes certain legal consequences (passing of ownership).

Article 3(1) of the Rome Convention on the Law Applicable to Contractual Obligations reads:

> A contract shall be governed by the law chosen by the parties . . .

2.06 However, nothing in terms of rights and duties of the parties to a contract can be derived from this rule. It merely establishes the principle that the parties' will is paramount in determining the legal system to which to look for those rights and duties.

---

[1] Albert A Ehrenzweig, *Private International Law—A Comparative Treatise on American International Conflicts Law, Including the Law of Admiralty* (Sijthoff, Leiden/Oceana, Dobbs Ferry, 1974) 64 speaks of the 'non-existing superlaw' rejecting the notion of determining the applicability of any rule of domestic law by reference to connecting factors (such as 'most significant relationship') or theoretical concepts (such as 'vested rights').

B. The Role of Conflict of Laws in International Commercial Law

Prior to the advent of transnational commercial law

Assume that on 1 February 1933 French seller/consignor S and German carrier **2.07** C entered into a contract for the carriage by air of a box containing diamonds from Paris to Warsaw. The box was handed over to A, C's local agent in Paris, and it was agreed that the consignee and buyer of the diamonds, S's customer B, would receive them on the same day that B was under an obligation to deliver a certain quantity of that type of diamonds to X. But when B received the box on 5 February, the box only contained nails. In order to comply with his obligation vis-à-vis X, B had to procure the necessary quantity of diamonds on the local market at a price 35 per cent higher than what he had paid S. B brings an action for damages against C in Warsaw.

B's counsel, and subsequently the Polish court, would have been faced with a **2.08** formidable number of problems:

(a) Does the court have jurisdiction?
(b) Is it an action in contract and/or in tort (the problem of 'characterization')?
(c) What law governs the contract between S and C?
(d) What law governs a delictual claim, if any?
(e) What happens if the law governing the contract and the different law governing C's liability in tort provide for contradictory or otherwise incompatible solutions?
(f) Under the applicable law(s), is there a basis for C's vicarious liability for A's acts or omissions?
(g) Does B, who is not a party to the contract, have any (direct) contractual rights against C under the applicable law and which law governs in this respect?

The foregoing issues are typical of conflict of laws problems. In addition, for B's **2.09** action to succeed, the issues of ascertaining what happened to the diamonds (burden of proof) and available heads of damages (*damnum emergens, lucrum cessans,* consequential damages) would have to be addressed. Moreover, the burden of proof is in some legal systems a matter of procedure, while in others it is a matter of substantive law. Its characterization may have a bearing on the outcome of the case.

A new era: The Warsaw Convention of 1929

On 12 October 1929, the delegations of thirty-two States signed the Convention **2.10** for the Unification of Certain Rules Relating to International Carriage by Air (Warsaw Convention) which, in its original version and in subsequent protocols (most important being the Hague Protocol of 1955), addresses the key issues raised above through uniform substantive rules. As such, it provides an immediate solution, without needing to identify the laws applicable according to the conflict rules of the court seised. Article 28(1) of the Convention also provides for jurisdiction of, *inter alia*, the courts at the place of destination, that is, Warsaw in the above scenario.

2.11 The *travaux préparatoires*[2] leave no doubt that the majority of the delegates deeply distrusted the 'black magic' of conflict of laws analysis: that was typical lawyers' law, whereas they were hoping to create sound and reliable rules leading to predictable (and insurable) results which permitted their 'infant industry' to grow.

> 'Nous ferons tous nos efforts pour trouver une formule qui donne satisfaction', replies the French delegate Georges Ripert to Sir Alfred Nevis (UK) who had proposed that the question of whether the carrier's liability would be triggered only by certain qualified types of intention, negligence etc. be governed by the applicable domestic law (as determined by the relevant conflicts rule), 'mais il est bien entendu . . . que nous sommes absolument opposés à une formule qui renverrait à l'application de la loi nationale . . . A notre point de vue, on arriverait ainsi à détruire la convention . . . [J]e supplie les Délégués de ne pas entrer dans cette voie dangereuse qui consisterait à réserver la solution du litige à la loi nationale.'[3]

2.12 The Warsaw Convention entered into force for France and Poland on 13 February 1933 and for Germany on 29 December 1933. It is true that the Convention provides only '*certain rules*' relating to the carriage of goods by air and that, despite the lapse of seventy years since its entry into force and the fact that it has been substantially modified by the 1999 Montreal Convention,[4] conflict-of-laws rules have so far not become entirely superfluous. Nevertheless it is fair to say that in providing a set of substantive law rules governing carriage by air the Convention introduced a new era. Over the decades that followed, intergovernmental organizations and conferences produced numerous instruments aimed at providing harmonized substantive law. The focus was on transport law, the law of negotiable instruments and, most importantly, the sale of goods, work on which culminated, first, in the 1964 Hague Uniform Sales Law and, ultimately, in the 1980 UN Convention on Contracts for the International Sale of Goods (CISG).[5] The interested commercial circles contributed massively through their (non-governmental) organizations, most prominent among those the International Chamber of Commerce, to unearthing old and creating new merchants' law. Under the intellectual leadership of towering figures such as Professors Berthold Goldman and

---

[2] See 1ère Conférence Internationale de Droit Privé Aérien, octobre–novembre 1925 (Imprimerie Nationale, Paris, 1926); Comité International Technique d'Experts Juridiques Aériens (CITEJA)—1ère Session, Paris, mai 1926, 2ème Session, Paris, avril 1927, 3ème Session, Madrid, mai 1928; IIème Conférence Internationale de Droit Privé Aérien, 4–12 Octobre 1929, Varsovie.

[3] IIème Conférence Internationale de Droit Privé Aérien, 4–12 Octobre, Varsovie, pp 44 ff.

[4] Convention for the Unification of Certain Rules Relating to International Carriage by Air, which came into force in September 2003.   [5] See below, ch 7.

Clive Schmitthoff an alternative route to labouring in the vineyards of conflict of laws seemed to open up.

Friedrich K Juenger, 'The *lex mercatoria* and private international law' (2000) V Unif L Rev, 171, 171–82

I. CONFLICTUALISM AND INTERNATIONALISM

From first blush, the title of this article appears to be paradoxical because private international law (a term used here to connote choice-of-law rules applied to international transactions) and the *lex mercatoria* represent radically different approaches to the same problem. Whereas private international law submits these transactions to the law of a particular state or nation, the *lex mercatoria*, a concept that connotes a set of transnational norms, would govern them directly, without the intervention of choice-of-law rules. To link these divergent approaches with the conjunctive 'and' may look odd given the abyss that, in the opinion of representatives of these two approaches, separates their respective schools of thought. There are, on the one side, the internationalists, such as the late Berthold Goldman and, on the other side, the 'conflictualists', such as the late Francis A Mann. The scholars found in one camp have little use for the views of those from the other and sometimes mince no words when expressing their disdain, witness the following observation of the late comparativist René David:

> [T]he lawyer's idea which aspires to submit international trade, in every case, to one or more national systems of law is nothing but bluff. The practical men have largely freed themselves from it, by means of standard contracts and arbitration, and states will be abandoning neither sovereignty nor prerogatives, if they open their eyes to reality and lend themselves to the reconstruction of international law.

No less scathingly, Mann rejected the notion of a non-national law merchant, saying that the *lex mercatoria* is 'as obscure as the equally unfortunate word "transnational"'. These remarks suggest that private international law and the *lex mercatoria* are incompatible notions, between which there cannot be any common ground. How, indeed, should it be possible to reconcile the internationalists' idea to submit transactions that transcend national frontiers to an overarching law merchant with the conflictualists' insistence that one or the other domestic law must of needs govern because such a body of transnational law simply does not exist?

Wherever one's sympathies lie, however, neither of these two approaches is indefensible and both of them have long been used in practice. The idea of a legal order specifically designed for transfrontier transactions is the older one . . .

II. THE PROBLEMS WITH PRIVATE INTERNATIONAL LAW

To answer the question which domestic law should govern a particular multistate transaction, courts and legislatures have looked to the writings of conflict of laws scholars. Ironically, the glossators and commentators were the first to discuss the choice-of-law issues. Although their primary activity had been the elaboration of a universal law, the *ius commune* that once prevailed throughout continental Europe, these medieval jurists dealt with the subject because they were of course familiar with the diversity of the legal rules and institutions found in the *statuta* of the cities of Upper Italy, where they taught and practiced . . . The intricate problems posed by the attempt to deal with multistate activities by applying domestic rules attracted some great legal scholars such as Bartolus of Sassoferrato, Friedrich Carl von Savigny and Joseph Story. As might be expected, not only the rules they advocated but also their fundamental approaches . . . differed considerably. Nor have these differences of opinion been resolved. Thus, to this day it remains doubtful whether the statutists' unilateralist approach—recently revived by American scholars such as Brainerd Currie—which attempts to determine the spatial reach of substantive rules, the multilateralist methodology Story and Savigny advocated, or perhaps an admixture of the two, is the most appropriate one to accomplish this delicate task. Obviously, methodological uncertainties of this kind hardly serve the needs of international commerce between enterprises that treasure certainty and predictability in legal relationships.

The clash of different schools of thought is not the only problem with private international law. Unilateralism as well as multilateralism are beset by a number of inherent difficulties, which the proponents of these choice-of-law methodologies have yet to resolve in a satisfactory fashion . . . There is, first of all, the multilateralists' 'General Part' of the conflict of laws, which contains an odd assortment of constructs as characterization, *renvoi*, public policy, the preliminary (or 'incidental') question and other puzzles engendered by the questionable premises on which multilateralism rests. Nor is unilateralism immune to such self-inflicted difficulties. For the past thirty years, Currie's followers have been discussing the oddities of 'true' and 'false conflicts', the 'unprovided-for case' and *dépeçage* that their approach creates. In spite of all the intellectual efforts wasted on dealing with the problems their methodologies spawn . . . [N]either of the two schools can offer satisfactory answers to the simple question which law the courts of different nations will actually apply to a particular international transaction. Both . . . reward forum shoppers by letting the decision of transnational disputes hinge on where the dispute is litigated . . . To be sure, it is the multilateralist school's objective to safeguard these values [i.e. certainty and predictability]. In fact, uniformity of decision was the rationale Savigny offered to justify the multilateralist system he advocated and multilateralists still pursue the elusive goal of 'decisional harmony' . . .

To accomplish the remarkable feat of tying down a transaction that straddles state lines to one territory or another, multilateralists use the white magic of connecting factors. These, however, have an arbitrary quality, they may even unduly favour one of the parties by invoking that party's home state law. Moreover, private international law rules differ widely from state to state, as the variations between recent European conflicts codifications demonstrate . . . Hence it cannot be predicted . . . what substantive law will be held to control a given dispute . . . Moreover, in practice, judges, after paying lip-service to the forum's conflicts rules, tend to favour the application of domestic law . . .

Even less apt to provide certainty, predictability and uniformity of result than the traditional multilateral conflicts rules is the unilateralist methodology, especially the current version that attempts to derive solutions to choice-of-law problems from the 'interests' states are said to have in the application of their laws. That approach obviously favors the *lex fori* . . . Worse yet, neither unilateralism nor multilateralism offers any guarantee of just decisions in multistate cases.

. . .

IV. IS THERE A ROLE FOR THE LEX MERCATORIA IN PRIVATE INTERNATIONAL LAW?

. . . .

Luckily, not all of us who teach private international law are entirely averse to the *lex mercatoria* . . . In fact, Justice Story—who coined the term 'private international law'— was a firm believer in the existence of a supranational law of commerce, as shown by his opinion in *Swift v Tyson*.[6] In that case, which dealt with the issue whether the endorsement of a negotiable instrument requires consideration, he said that 'the true interpretation of [contracts and other commercial instruments] are to be sought, not in the decisions of the local tribunals, but in the general principles and doctrines of commercial jurisprudence'. For this proposition he relied on an opinion in an admiralty case by Lord Mansfield (one of whose accomplishments was the incorporation of the law merchant into English common law), which quoted Cicero's observation about the *ius gentium*. In *Swift*, Story used the same quotation: '*Non erit alia lex Romae, alia Athenis, alia nunc, alia posthac, sed et apud omnes gentes, et omni tempore, una eademque lex obtinebit*'.[7]

Of course, the eminent American judge and scholar penned his opinion before the old *lex mercatoria* was nationalized; once legal positivism became rampant, *Swift v Tyson* came under attack. Justice Holmes debunked this precedent, saying that 'law in the sense in which courts speak of it today does not exist without definite authority behind it'[8] and 'the authority and only authority is the State',[9] a passage on which Justice Brandeis relied in *Erie RR v Tompkins*,[10] the decision that overruled *Swift*. The consequence of the doctrine the Supreme Court adopted in *Erie* illustrate the hazards of conflictualism. That case has helped balkanize American law and prompted innumerable choice-of-law problems, especially in mass disaster cases. The difficulties it created induced Judge Weinstein, the eminent judge and scholar, to revive—in the *Agent Orange*[11] litigation—the rule in *Swift* under the guise of a 'national consensus law'.[12] This bold move had the purpose of promoting an acceptable outcome of the staggering number of lawsuits brought for injuries armed services personnel had suffered during the Vietnam war in Indochina. As this case shows, an overarching law designed to take into account international realities is apt to produce more sensible and practical solutions than the conflictualists' insistence on the need to invoke domestic laws to dispose of disputes that, by their very nature, are not confined to the borders of a single state.

The late Professor Juenger went on to argue that, by virtue of the principle of party **2.13** autonomy, as recognized by most systems' rules regarding choice of law in contracts, parties should be free to choose transnational principles and rules of law, notably the UNIDROIT Principles of International Commercial Contracts,[13] as the law governing their contract. This point is discussed below.[14]

---

[6] 41 US 1, 10 L Ed 865 (1842), overruled by *Erie RR v Tompkins*, 304 US 64.

[7] See *Luke v Lyde* (1759) 2 Burr 883, 887; 97 ER 614, 617. The quotation is a somewhat inaccurate rendering of a passage from Cicero's *De Republica*, 3.22.33, which in fact reads: '. . . *nec erit alia lex Romae, alia Athenis, alia nunc, alia posthac, sed et omnes gentes et omni tempore una lex et sempiterna et immutabilis continebit* . . .' ('. . . there shall not be one law at Rome, another at Athens, one now, another hereafter, but one everlasting and unalterable law shall govern all nations for all time . . .'). See Roy Goode, *Commercial Law* (3rd edn, Penguin Books/Lexis Nexis, 2004), 1210, text and n 29.

[8] *Black and White Taxicab & Transfer Co v Brown and Yellow Taxicab & Transfer Co*, 276 US 518, 533–4 (1928) (Holmes, J, dissenting).   [9] Ibid 535.

[10] *Erie* (n 6) 79.

[11] *In re 'Agent Orange' Product Liability Litigation*, 580 FSupp 690 (ED NY, 1984).

[12] Ibid 696–9, 708–9, 711 and 713.   [13] Below, ch 14.   [14] See para 2.31.

C. Selected Issues of General Conflict of Laws Theory

Jurisdiction

2.14 In common law systems, jurisdiction to adjudicate is customarily treated as the first topic of treatises on the conflict of laws. In this book, it is treated as one of the key issues of international civil procedure in chapter 17 on international dispute resolution.

Rules v 'approaches'

2.15 In his article quoted above, Professor Friedrich Juenger referred to Bartolus of Sassoferrato (1314–57), by far the most important among the post-glossators or commentators who shaped conflicts theory in medieval Upper Italy. The two scholars he mentioned then, the American Supreme Court Justice and Harvard law professor Joseph Story (1779–1845) and the German Roman law scholar Friedrich Carl von Savigny (1779–1861), were towering figures of their time: the former author of the first comprehensive treatment of the subject in English, the latter visionary of multilateralism.

Joseph Story, 'Commentaries on the Conflict of Laws' (5th edn, Little, Brown & Co, Boston, 1857) 26–46.

§ 18. I. The first and most general maxim or proposition is that . . . that every nation possesses an exclusive sovereignty and jurisdiction within its own territory. The direct consequence of this rule is, that the laws of every state affect, and bind directly all property . . . within its territory; and all persons, who are resident within it . . . ; and also all contracts made and acts done within it . . .

§ 20. II. Another maxim . . . is, that no state or nation can, by its laws, directly affect, or bind property out of its own territory, or bind persons not resident therein . . .

§ 23. III. From these two maxims . . . there flows a third, and that is, that whatever force and obligation the laws of one country have in another, depend solely upon the laws . . . of the latter, that is to say, upon its own proper jurisprudence and polity, and upon its own express or tacit consent . . .

§ 25. The real difficulty is to ascertain, what principles in point of public convenience ought to regulate the conduct of nations on this subject in regard to each other, and in what manner they can be best applied to infinite variety of cases, arising from the complicated concerns of human society in modern times. No nation can be justly required to yield up its own fundamental policy and institutions in favor of those of another nation . . . The laws of one nation may be founded upon a narrow selfishness, exclusively adapted to promote its own peculiar policy . . . A particular nation may refuse all reciprocity of commerce, rights, and remedies to others. It may assume a superiority of powers and prerogatives, for the very purpose of crushing those of its neighbors, who are less fortunate, or less powerful. In these, and in many other cases . . . there would be extreme difficulty in saying, that other nations were bound to enforce laws . . . of that nation, which were subversive to their own morals, justice, interests, or polity . . .

§ 38. There is, then, not only no impropriety in the use of the phrase, 'comity of nations', but it is the most appropriate phrase to express the true foundation and extent of the obligation of the laws of one nation within the territories of another. It is derived altogether from the voluntary consent of the latter; and it is inadmissible, when it is contrary to its known policy, or prejudicial to its interests. In the silence of any positive rule, affirming, or denying, or restraining the operation of foreign laws, courts of justice presume the tacit adoption of them by their own government, unless they are repugnant to its policy, or prejudicial to its interests. It is not the comity of the courts, but the comity of the nation, which is administered, and ascertained in the same way, and guided by the same reasoning, by which all other principles of the municipal law are ascertained and guided . . .

Mr Justice Story developed his analysis and rules under the influence of the Dutch **2.16** internationalist Ulrich Huber (1636–94) and his concept of territorial sovereignty. Obviously, any legislature's acts have force of law as such only as far as that legislature's power extends (*Geltungsbereich*). But since—especially in a world of continually increasing commercial exchange—it is unthinkable that the legal position of persons, goods, contractual rights and obligations changes, as Voltaire said, each time 'when the horses of the post carriage are changed', a mechanism needed to be designed which allowed to grant those laws a sphere of application (*Anwendungsbereich*) which was larger and different from the enacting sovereigns' sphere of sovereignty. Huber and Story identified the nations' *comitas* (comity) as the device.

Although Story and von Savigny were born in the same year, had studied the same **2.17** sources, must have been observing similar developments in international commerce and taught the subject around the same time in Cambridge, Mass. and Berlin, Savigny's reasoning reveals fundamentally different views.

William Guthrie (tr), Friedrich Carl von Savigny, 'Private international law—A Treatise on the Conflict of Laws, and the Limits of Their Operation in Respect of Place and Time' (T & T Clark, Edinburgh, 1869) 26–33 and 88–9

Many have attempted to determine these questions by the principle of independent sovereignty alone, laying down the two following postulates: (1) Every state is entitled to demand that its own laws only shall be recognised within its bounds; (2) No state can require the recognition of its law beyond its bounds . . . I will not only admit the truth of these propositions, but even allow their extension to the utmost conceivable limits; yet I believe that they afford little help in the solution of our problem.

To carry out the principle of the independent sovereignty of the state to the utmost possible extent with regard to aliens, would lead to their complete exclusion from legal rights. Such a view is not strange to the international law of the Romans . . . ; and even where it was not enforced by them against foreign countries, a great distinction as to the capacity for rights was always maintained between Romans and foreigners. Modern law, on the contrary, has gradually tended towards the recognition of complete legal equality between natives and foreigners . . .

The strict right of sovereignty might certainly, among other things, go so far as to require all judges of the land to decide the cases that come before them solely according to the national law, regardless of the perhaps different rules of some foreign law with whose territory the case in question may have come in contact. Such a rule, however, is not to be found in the legislation of any known state; and its absence is to be accounted for by the following consideration:

> The more multifarious and active the intercourse between different nations, the more will men be persuaded that it is not expedient to adhere to such a stringent rule, but rather to substitute for it the opposite principle. This has resulted from the reciprocity in dealing with cases which is so desirable, and the consequent equality in judging between natives and foreigners, which, on the whole, is dictated by the common interest of nations and individuals. For it is the necessary consequence of this equality, in its full development, not only that in each particular state a foreigner is not postponed to the native (in which equality in the treatment of persons consists), but also that, in cases of *conflict of laws*, the same legal relations (cases) have to expect the same decision, whether the judgment be pronounced in this state or in that.

The standpoint to which this consideration leads us, is that of an international common law of nations having intercourse with one another; and this view has in the course of time always obtained wider recognition, under the influence of a common Christian morality, and of the real advantage which results from it to all concerned . . .

[T]he question may be stated thus:

> *To ascertain for every legal relation (case) that law to which in its proper nature, it belongs or is subject.*

Our inquiry has now brought us to this result, that in deciding cases (legal relations) which come in contact with different independent states, the judge has to apply that local law to which the case (legal relation) pertains, whether it is the law of his own country or the law of a foreign state . . .

While, therefore, the object of our inquiry has hitherto been the *person* as to whom we sought out the tie connecting him with a particular locality, the territory of a special law, our attention must now be directed to the *legal relations*, for which we have to establish a similar connection with a definite locality—a particular legal territory. But in order to bring the two parts of the investigation nearer to one another by the analogies of language, we can say that, in the sequel, a definitive *seat* is to be sought for each such class of legal relations . . .

[T]he whole problem comes to be:

> *To discover for every legal relation (case) that legal territory to which, in its proper nature, it belongs or is subject (in which it has its seat).*

This formula is, in essentials, equally applicable to the collision of local laws of the same state and of different states.

2.18   Professor AV Dicey's *Conflict of Laws*,[15] the seminal choice-of-law work for England, was based on the theory that the courts' task in conflicts cases was to enforce 'vested rights', a theory combined by Professor Joseph H Beale in1934, in his preparation

---

[15] AV Dicey, *A digest of the law of England with reference to the conflict of laws* (1st edn Stevens, London, 1896). The current edition is *Dicey, Morris and Collins on The Conflict of Laws* (14th edn, Sweet & Maxwell, London, 2006).

of the American Law Institute's (first) *Restatement of the Law, Conflict of Laws*,[16] with elements of traditional territorialism. The *Restatement of the Law Second, Conflict of Laws*,[17] prepared by Professor Willis Reese in 1971 as the ALI's Reporter took yet another route in that rules are based on the assumption that there will always be a 'most significant relationship' of a fact pattern or legal relationship. However, all these theories have something in common: they formulate rules.

Restatement, Conflict of Laws § 332 provides:

Law Governing Validity of a Contract

The law of the place of contracting determines the validity and effect of a promise with respect to [follow (a) capacity to make the contract to (h) the absolute or conditional character of the promise].

Restatement, Second, Conflict of Laws § 244 provides:

Validity and Effect of Conveyance of Interest in Chattel

(1) The validity and effect of a conveyance of an interest in a chattel as between the parties to the conveyance are determined by the local law of the state which, with respect to the particular issue, has the most significant relationship to the parties, the chattel and the conveyance under the principle stated in § 6.

(2) In the absence of an effective choice of law by the parties, greater weight will usually be given to the location of the chattel, or group of chattels, at the time of the conveyance than to any other contact in determining the state of the applicable law.

The Restatement, Second, sets forth its founding and overarching objectives and **2.19** technique almost in the manner of a 'General Part' of European provenance in its introductory § 6:

Choice-of-Law Principles

(1) A court, subject to constitutional restrictions, will follow a statutory directive of its own state on choice of law.

(2) When there is no such directive, the factors relevant to the choice of the applicable rule of law include:
    (a) the needs of the interstate and international systems;
    (b) the relevant policies of the forum;
    (c) the relevant policies of other interested states and the relative interests of those states in the determination of the particular issue;
    (d) the protection of justified expectations;
    (e) the basic policies underlying the particular field of law;
    (f) the certainty, predictability and uniformity of result; and,
    (g) the ease in the determination and application of the law to be applied.

---

[16] American Law Institute, *Restatement of the Law, Conflict of Laws* (American Law Institute Publishers, St Paul (MI), 1934).

[17] American Law Institute, *Restatement of the Law, Second, Conflict of Laws* (American Law Institute Publishers, St Paul (MI), 1971).

2.20   A significant number of the most influential conflicts scholars of the twentieth century defined choice-of-law objectives in a less 'mechanical' and more 'political' sense. Consequently, methods changed. Professor Brainerd Currie (1912–65), the leading exponent of one known as 'interest analysis', summarized his views as follows: conflict of laws rules that pointed to a particular jurisdiction were unacceptable. Unless a court was directed by statute to do otherwise, it would normally take the applicability of a rule of decision found in the law of the forum as a starting point. When a court was asked to apply the law of a foreign State different from the law of the forum, it should inquire into the policies expressed in the respective laws, and into the circumstances in which it is reasonable for the respective States to assert an interest in the application of those policies. If one State had an interest in the realization of its policies and the other(s) had none, the law of the interested State should be applied. If a court identified an obvious conflict between the interests of the States in question, it should reconsider with a view to finding out whether a restrained or otherwise mitigated interpretation of the policies involved might be capable of avoiding the conflict. If, upon reconsideration, the court found that there was an unavoidable conflict between the legitimate interests of more than one State and one of them was the forum State that State's law should apply. If the forum was disinterested, but an unavoidable conflict existed between the interests of States but no way to decline jurisdiction to adjudicate, then the court should apply the law of the forum, at least if that law corresponded with the law of one of the other States. Alternatively, the court might decide the case by a candid exercise of 'legislative discretion', resolving the conflict as it would have been resolved by a supreme legislative body having power to determine whose interest should prevail and whose should be required to yield. It must be emphasized that Currie—like other contemporary conflicts lawyers in the United States—built his theory looking primarily at inter-State rather than international conflicts. This is why the line of reasoning terminates as follows: if, with respect to a particular problem, the outcome of the resolution of the conflict were to depend entirely on where the action was brought entailing thereby a serious infringement of a strong national interest in uniformity of decision, the court should not attempt to improvise a solution sacrificing the legitimate interest of its own State, but should leave the determination of which interest should prevail to Congress.[18]

2.21   It becomes clear why the content-oriented solutions advanced by Currie and others are broadly referred to as the modern 'approaches', that is, in the parlance of literary criticism, (more or less) fine-spun webs, flexible and delicate, designed to catch meaning rather than to express it. In the United States, conflicts-of-laws theory thrived in the 1950s, 1960s and 1970s. Suffice it to mention Professor

---

[18] The statement paraphrased here was made shortly before Brainerd Currie's untimely passing away and is reproduced in HH Kay, 'A Defense of Currie's Governmental Interest Analysis' (1990) 215 Recueil des Cours 9, 76.

Albert A Ehrenzweig's 'proper law in a proper forum' and 'rule of validation', the 'better law approach' associated with Professor RA Leflar's 'choice-influencing considerations', and the 'functional analysis' of Professors Arthur von Mehren and Donald Trautman. They were all part of a formidable effort (a) to describe more what the courts were actually doing, and (b) to give them guidance in defining the general objectives of private international law. Given its intellectual intensity and the underlying ambitions, this effort was quite appropriately called the 'conflicts revolution'. With respect to some contributions, commentators referred to the 'counter revolution', and, in 1964, Professor Gerhard Kegel, observing the developments from a European perspective, gave his seminal general course at the Hague Academy of International Law under the title 'The Crisis of Conflict of Laws'.[19] Despite criticism, scepticism and outright hostility, the US revolution proved contagious in some parts of continental Europe, but less so in Britain. The European instruments dealing with conflicts issues do show that, in particularly politically sensitive areas, such as consumer contracts and transactions involving regulated industries and markets, multilateralist concepts are by no means ruling supreme. And, as has been shown elsewhere, at least courts and commentators in the US are increasingly prepared to 'think multilateral'.

Peter Hay, Russell J Weintraub and Patrick J Borchers, *Conflict of Laws: Cases and Materials* **(12th edn, Foundation Press, New York, 2004) 5**

Here there has been revolutionary change. In 1960, every United States court would have chosen Tamaulipas law to apply to the bus accident discussed previously. This was because Tamaulipas was the place of the injury. As of January 1, 2004, forty states plus the District of Columbia and Puerto Rico would choose law by a rule or method that took into account the content and purposes of the Tamaulipas and Texas laws. Similar changes in conflicts theory have also occurred in other countries.

The abandonment of territorial conflicts rules, such as place of injury, has ameliorated some problems, but has generated new difficulties. Richard Posner has listed the change in choice-of-law method among the 'legal reforms [that] have miscarried [resulting in] the destruction of certainty in the field of conflict of laws as a result of the replacement of the mechanical common law rules by "interest analysis"'. The choice-of-law materials in this book focus on the issues of whether this criticism is justified and whether there is a desirable via media between territorial rules that select law without regard to its content, and methods that result in *ad hoc* chaos.

Connecting factors of particular relevance in commercial law

A key element for any multilateralist conflicts rule is the so-called connecting factor. It indicates the nature of the fact that constitutes the necessary connection of the issue to a particular legal system in order for the rules of that system to apply. For example, in the law of tort, by far the most common connecting factor is the **2.22**

---

[19] (1964) 112 Recueil des Cours 91.

locus delicti, that is, the place of the wrong. The predominant connecting factors in matters regarding a person's own legal position or family relationships are domicile, habitual residence and nationality.

Contracts

2.23 Today, party autonomy, that is, the parties' freedom to choose the law governing their contract, is widely accepted and forms the basis of most modern bodies of conflicts rules, though certain common law jurisdictions, such as the United States and Latin American legal systems, were slower in adopting the rule than others. Party autonomy is considered as of crucial importance for the proper functioning of international business transactions. For our purposes, it is of secondary importance whether the reason for the adoption of this rule is philosophical or whether it is just convenience, in that it is the only practical device for bringing certainty and predictability into the area of transnational contracts. The courts are spared the pains of weighing theoretically relevant factors and making a decision.

2.24 Contract choice-of-law issues arise in three contexts: validity, interpretation and mode of performance. As a rule of thumb, if one of the contact States' law refused to give effect to the contract notwithstanding the parties' intentions, that was traditionally likely to be more fatal for the contract than if the issue was only one of interpretation (where there has always been a greater chance of the courts' benevolent analysis, the *favor negotii*). Modern conventions tend to take a bolder and more comprehensive approach, subjecting formation, validity, obligations of the parties, consequences of non-performance as well as the extinction of those obligations to the same law. With respect to the mode of performance, it makes obvious sense to at least take into account the law of the place where the contract is to be performed. Many conventions do indeed make provision for that.

2.25 There are three issues of significant relevance for parties to international business transactions and their counsel that continue to be the subject of theoretical debate and which are still quite regularly brought up in international disputes before courts and arbitral tribunals.

2.26 First, the question whether party autonomy regarding the determination of the applicable law is unfettered in the sense that the parties are free to choose any law or whether they are limited to selecting one which has a connection with the transaction. The reasons to do so may be many. For example, the Russian and Greek parties to a construction contract may choose English law to govern because that law is functionally compatible with the FIDIC conditions upon which the contract is largely based. Likewise, the Macedonian and French parties to a joint venture may choose Swiss substantive law to govern their agreement because the dispute resolution clause calls for arbitration in Switzerland. Again, two multinational corporations of equal bargaining power, one American and the other one Italian, may have been unable to impose their own law on the other party—obviously their first choice—and, for reasons unrelated to the substance and notwithstanding mutual unfamiliarity with it, have chosen German law, coupled with an arbitration clause calling for the nomination of three German arbitrators, just because during the negotiations the 'champagne hour' was approaching and there was no other alternative for saving the deal but to agree on a neutral law. In the US, it was the landmark case *The Bremen v Zapata Off-Shore Co,* [20] in which the Supreme Court gave effect to a contractual choice-of-forum provision in a maritime towage agreement, negotiated at arm's length, between the US owner of a drilling rig (Zapata) and a German company (Unterweser) to tow Zapata's rig from Louisiana to Italy. While being towed by the *Bremen*, the rig was damaged in a storm. Zapata, ignoring a clause providing that '[a]ny dispute arising must be treated before the London Court of Justice', commenced a suit in the US Federal Courts. The forum chosen, England, had no connection with the transaction, and the effect of limiting suit to the chosen English court was to validate contractual stipulations limiting the liability for negligent towage which were invalid under US law. Unterweser, invoking the forum-selection clause, moved to dismiss, or, alternatively, for a stay pending submission of the dispute to the High Court of Justice in London. At the same time, Unterweser brought an action for breach of contract against Zapata in England. The US District Court refused to dismiss or stay the action, and the Court of Appeals affirmed this decision. Mr Chief Justice Burger delivered the opinion of the Supreme Court:

> Here we see an American company with special expertise contracting with a foreign company to tow a complex machine thousands of miles across seas and oceans. The expansion of American business and industry will hardly be encouraged if, notwithstanding solemn contracts, we insist on a parochial concept that all disputes must be resolved under our laws and in our courts . . . We cannot have trade and commerce in world markets and international waters exclusively on our terms, governed by our laws, and resolved in our courts.
>
> There are compelling reasons why a freely negotiated agreement, unaffected by fraud, undue influence or overweening bargaining power . . . should be given full effect. In this case . . . we are concerned with a far from routine transaction between companies of two different nations . . . Manifestly much uncertainty and possibly great inconvenience to both parties could arise if a suit could be maintained in any jurisdiction in which an accident might occur . . . [in this context, the Court also mentions that it was reasonable to conclude that the forum clause, given the approach taken by English courts at the time, was also an effort to obtain certainty as to the applicable substantive law] . . .
>
> Thus, in the light of present-day commercial realities and expanding international trade we conclude that the . . . correct approach [of the court below] would have been to enforce the forum clause specifically unless Zapata could clearly show that

---

[20] 407 US 1, 92 S Ct 1907 (1972).

enforcement would be unreasonable and unjust, or that the clause was invalid for such reasons as fraud or overreaching . . .

2.27 In England, the authority most cited in this context is *Vita Food Products Inc v Unus Shipping Co Ltd*,[21] where it had been argued that a choice of English law to govern a bill of lading was not valid because the transaction contained nothing to connect it with England. Lord Wright, speaking for the Privy Council, on appeal from Nova Scotia, said that 'connection with English law is not as a matter of principle essential' as parties might reasonably desire that the 'familiar principles of English commercial law' that enjoy worldwide importance should apply.

2.28 The Rome Convention on the Law Applicable to Contractual Obligations 1980 leaves no doubt in this respect.[22] The combined effect of Article 1(1) and Article 3(1) is that there is almost unlimited freedom to choose the law of any country and irrespective of any connection with that country, subject to what is said below about mandatory rules.

2.29 The same is true for the 1994 Inter-American Convention on the Law Applicable to International Contracts. Article 7 of that instrument likewise grants freedom of choice unfettered by any requirement of an 'objective' link between the contract and the law chosen.

2.30 Whilst the 1978 Hague Agency Convention and the 1986 Hague Sales Convention are based on the same principle, the 2002 Hague Convention on the Law Applicable to Certain Rights in Respect of Securities Held With an Intermediary moves away from it. Article 4(1) of the Securities Convention leaves it to the parties to the account agreement—the investor and its intermediary—to choose the governing law and to make a statement to that effect in their account agreement. What is distinctive—indeed, counter-intuitive—is that the law so chosen, which applies to all the issues listed in Article 2(1) of the Convention, governs proprietary effects not only between the parties to the account agreement but also vis-à-vis

---

[21] [1939] AC 277 (PC).

[22] This most successful instrument in the area of conflict of laws is about to change 'pillars' and become an EC Regulation. Under the Amsterdam version of Article 65 EC, private international law and international civil procedure, which have so far been dealt with in intergovernmental conventions are now 'communitarized' and have become a branch of judicial co-operation. They therefore pass from the 'third pillar' to the 'first pillar', that is genuine Community legislation. The Commission's proposal for a 'Rome I Regulation' (for a reference see below) is now before Governments and the EU Parliament. The Brussels Protocol of 19 December 1988 on the interpretation of the Convention by the European Court of Justice was short-lived; it entered into force only on 1 August 2004. Before that date, Article 18 of the Convention and a very special document, the official report drawn up by Professors Giuliano and Lagarde and published with the Convention (OJ 1980 C 282, 1), provided the glue which maintained a remarkable uniformity in the Convention's interpretation and application by the courts of the various Member States. The ECJ's jurisdiction will shortly flow from the instrument's nature.

third parties, and extends to priority issues between competing claimants to an interest in the securities account. The underlying idea is to subject all relevant relationships derived from the securities account to a single, readily ascertainable law, and thereby remove uncertainty and enhance predictability. However, the provision goes on to limit the parties' freedom in that the law so designated applies only if the relevant intermediary has, at the time of the agreement, an office in the State whose law the parties have chosen which is in some way involved or identified as being involved in the maintenance of securities accounts, though not necessarily the account of any particular account holder. Here, the old-fashioned theory of an 'objective link' comes back into play. But we have obviously left the realm of contracts and moved into property (see below, 2.37, 13.22).

The second issue of particular interest for the evolution of transnational commer- **2.31** cial law and the role of conflict-of-laws rules in this context is the question of whether the parties may only choose the law of a country or whether they may also opt for the applicability of a non-national body of rules of law, such as the *lex mercatoria*, the UNIDROIT Principles of International Commercial Contracts, or the European Principles of Contract Law. For the time being, the predominant view in England, as well as in many continental jurisdictions, is that the Rome Convention does not sanction the choice of a non-national system of rules of law.[23] However, Dutch authorities, as well as a minority of commentators in Germany, hold a different view, pointing to the difference in the language used in Article 3(1) on the one hand ('law chosen by the parties') and that used in Article 4(1) on the other hand ('law of the country with which it [the contract] is most closely connected'). In any event, the matter is currently being reconsidered in the context of amending the Convention and transforming it into a regulation. In this connection, a number of authoritative submissions to the European Commission are advocating clarification and the explicit inclusion of texts such as the Principles of European Contract Law and the UNIDROIT Principles among the bodies of rules which the parties may select. Article 3(2) of the Commission's *Proposal for a Regulation of the European Parliament and the Council on the law applicable to contractual obligations (Rome I)*, the future Regulation, provides:

> 2. The parties may also choose as the applicable law the principles and rules of the substantive law of contract recognised internationally or in the Community.

> However, questions relating to matters governed by such general principles or rules which are not expressly settled by them shall be governed by the general principles underlying them or, failing such principles, in accordance with the law applicable in the absence of a choice under this Regulation.[24]

---

[23] See below, ch 14.
[24] 15 December 2005: COM (2005) 650 final, 2005/0261 (COD). On 12 December 2006 the Council proposed deletion of Art 3(2).

The Commission's Explanatory Memorandum states in this connection:

> To further boost the impact of the parties' will, a key principle of the Convention [*in futuro:* the Regulation], paragraph 2 authorises the parties to choose as the applicable law a non-State body of law. The form of words used would authorise the choice of the UNIDROIT principles, the *Principles of European Contract Law* or a possible future optional Community instrument, while excluding the *lex mercatoria*, which is not precise enough, or private codifications not adequately recognised by the international community. Like Article 7(2) of the Vienna Convention on the international sale of goods, the text shows what action should be taken when certain aspects of the law of contract are not expressly settled by the relevant body of non-State law.

2.32   Article 9 of the 1994 Inter-American Convention explicitly mentions 'the general principles of international commercial law recognized by international organizations', but does so with respect to the objective determination of the governing law by the court, that is in the absence of a choice by the parties.

2.33   The third issue is what law governs the existence and the validity of consent as to the choice. The solution adopted by Article 3(4) of the Rome Convention is a reference to Article 8(1): that is, one based on the law which the parties purported to choose. The same rule is adopted in Article 12 of the Inter-American Convention. In the US, both § 187 of the Restatement (Second), Conflict of Laws and § 1–301 of the Uniform Commercial Code limit the parties' freedom to choose the law governing validity. As regards the *formal validity*, modern rules are liberal. The old rule that the law of the place where the contract was concluded governs (*locus regit actum*) is usually one alternative, the other one being that the contract is also formally valid if it satisfies the formal requirements of the *lex causae*, namely the law governing the substance be it by virtue of the parties' choice or be it by virtue of one of the rules based on objective connecting factors.[25]

2.34   Absent parties' choice (a 'subjective' connecting factor) or in the event that their choice was not effective, the governing law will be determined on the basis of some 'objective' connecting factor. There is wide agreement that the law of the State which has the most significant relationship with the transaction—some rules also add most significant relationship with the parties—should govern. The follow-up question is how to ascertain which one of the many contacts a transaction may have is to be more significant than others and, therefore, decisive for our purposes. During the first half of the twentieth century, apart from some legal systems' overt or covert preference for applying the *lex fori*, the nationality or domicile of the parties, the place where the contract had been entered into, and the place where the contract was to be performed were the most widely used objective connecting factors.

---

[25]   cf. Rome Convention, Art 9(1); Inter-American Convention, Art 13(1).

§ 188(2) of the Restatement Second, Conflict of Laws (1971) lists the contacts to   **2.35**
be taken into account for identifying the most significant relationship and then
states, among the four just mentioned: 'These contacts are to be evaluated according to their relative importance with respect to the particular issue'. Two Swiss
scholars, Professors Adolf Schnitzer and Frank Vischer, are to be considered the
fathers of an immensely influential inquiry into the 'anchoring' of contracts in
their 'social function'. They concluded—and courts and writers in other countries
followed quickly—that, apart from contracts where money was the subject of the
transaction, such as exchange contracts, the role of any contract in 'man's existence' was never characterized by the money paid by one of the parties, but by the
other party's performance: a sale, by the seller's performance; a contract for the
carriage of goods, by the carrier's performance; a contract between a home owner
and an architect, by the services rendered by the latter. Legislators too were soon
seduced by the concept of the 'characteristic performance' and Article 4(2) of the
1980 Rome Convention on the Law Applicable to Contractual Obligations adopted
it as the principal connecting factor for ascertaining the most significant relationship:

> . . . it shall be presumed that the contract is most closely connected with the country
> where the party who is to effect the performance which is characteristic of the contract
> has . . . his habitual residence, or, in the case of a body corporate or unincorporated,
> its central administration . . .

The same approach had been taken by the 1978 Hague Agency Convention,   **2.36**
where the agent's performance had been identified as characteristic, and the 1986
Hague Sales Convention followed as a matter of course.[26]

Property

We have seen that the conflicts rule for the law of contracts identifies the governing   **2.37**
law by referring, primarily, to the parties' choice and, secondarily, to other elements
thought to be obvious or essential for establishing the most significant link to a
country and its laws. Which are the relevant interests—both private and public—
that legislators and courts should take into consideration in selecting the appropriate connecting factor for determining the law governing rights *in rem*?

It would appear that never in the history of private international law in any legal   **2.38**
system has there been any doubt that the law governing rights in an immovable
(land) must be the law of the country where the immovable is situated (*lex situs* or
lex rei sitae). Already at the time of the statutists[27] the rule was extended to movables
where those movables belonged to the inhabitants of the territory in question or, in
other words, the subjects of the local sovereign (*res subditae*). An exception was

---

[26] For the role of mandatory rules and their impact on the law determined on the basis of the
aforementioned connecting factors, see below, para 2.51.
[27] See above, para 2.12 (quoting FK Juenger).

made where the movables were just passing through the rule giver's territory (as, for example, goods during transport from the seller's to the buyer's home town—*res in transitu*). The choice of the connecting factor reflected in § 244(2) of the Restatement Second, Conflict of Laws (1971) was deeply rooted in legal history and, like no other conflicts rule, almost universally recognized. Moreover, it is usually not only the validity of a transfer of a movable and its effect on the proprietary rights of the parties that is governed by the *lex situs*, but all rights *in rem*: their creation, their giving in security and their extinction. The *lex rei sitae* has been adopted as the basic rule by most courts and most modern private international law statutes. There are, however, both in statutes and case law of advanced legal systems, important qualifications and examples of functional fine-tuning, in particular with respect to means of transportation (such as lorries, vessels, aircraft) and security interests (including the functional equivalents of retention of title in a sale and the lessor's title in financial leasing). For example, the steps for the creation of a non-possessory security interest that are required and were taken in jurisdiction A (the exporter's country) may be recognized in country B, or 'translated' into their functional equivalent or combined with elements required by the laws of B (the importer's country) with a view to ensuring that the parties' intention to create a valid and enforceable interest is not thwarted by re-locating the object in which security was taken. The drive for modernization of the conflict-of-laws rules in those advanced jurisdictions was fuelled by a series of conventions which addressed the specificity of movables that were at least capable of—or even destined to—moving regularly across national frontiers. The outer—and yet uncharted—limits of these more recent developments is the recognition of party autonomy, that is the parties' right to choose the law governing security interests in—maybe only certain categories of—movables.

2.39 Transnational commercial law treaties have addressed the issue of how security interests are to be protected—against the background of, on the one hand, the *situs* being the main connecting factor and, on the other hand, the encumbered movables being frequently re-located from one jurisdiction to another—for a number of decades. Article 1 of the 1926 Convention for the Unification of Certain Rules Relating to Maritime Liens and Mortgages is based on the principle of recognition of any such rights created in accordance with the laws of the Contracting State to which the vessel belongs in all other Contracting States if those rights have been properly recorded. Similarly, Article 1 of the 1993 Geneva Convention on Maritime Liens and Mortgages looks to the law of the State in which the vessel is registered for determining whether a charge has been created, while Article 2 which relates to the ranking and effects of mortgages, *hypothèques* and charges, applies both the law of the State of registration and the State where enforcement takes place. In other words, the Convention distributes competences among Contracting States, and provides for the recognition of acts done and effects arising in a competent Contracting State. The system of attribution of competences is based on universally accepted connecting factors that are typical to maritime law as well as international civil procedure. As its title shows, the 1948 Geneva Convention on the International Recognition of Rights in Aircraft equally provides for the recognition of rights that have been created in one Contracting State in all other Contracting States. The Convention thus modifies two elements of the conflict-of-property-laws situation: the registration of the aircraft as to nationality becomes the connecting factor, and the legal position that exists under the national law so identified is recognized by all other Contracting State. It is clear that these Conventions are one of the sources of the ongoing quest for the modernization of conflicts rules regarding property.

The 2001 Cape Town Convention on International Interests in Mobile Equipment **2.40** is not only another step forward in that direction but a qualitative leap: it is not based on the concept that interests created in accordance with the *lex situs* in one jurisdiction should be recognised in other jurisdictions. Instead it provides for a genuinely international property interest which will be recognized in all Contracting States, regardless of the location of the object to which the interest relates.[28]

Similarly, the 2002 Hague Convention on the Law Applicable to Certain Rights **2.41** in Respect of Securities held with an Intermediary boldly presses ahead where it recognizes, in Article 4, for the first time, the principle of party autonomy as the principal connecting factor in a conflicts rule on property rights. Admittedly, the securities contemplated are not every-day chattels.[29]

Other important connecting factors

As regards *companies* and other incorporated or unincorporated bodies, the world **2.42** was traditionally divided into roughly two equally strong camps. One of them, mainly common law jurisdictions, but also important civil law countries, favoured the place where the company had been incorporated or founded as the connecting factor. The other camp strongly advocated the principal place of the company's administration (*siège social*). The arguments put forward in the century-old battle between the proponents of both 'religions' (no less seemed to be at stake if one reads the leading cases and texts on the matter) are highly instructive for the understanding of the moving forces of commercial law in general. Party autonomy versus general interests; unfettered freedom of shaping business transactions versus transparency and publicity; unregulated versus regulated constitution of markets and market participants. The battle has been decided in a series of judgments by the European Court of Justice on grounds of Community law in favour of the *lex incorporationis* (or *lex societatis*), at least as regards companies incorporated in a Member State of the European Union and their position in all other

---

[28] For detailed discussion, see below, ch 12.   [29] For detailed discussion, see below, ch 13.

Member States. It is an open question whether the 'seat' in the sense of the 'real' place of administration will survive in Europe. It continues to enjoy strong support, however, in Japan and South America.

2.43 Other important connecting factors in business law contexts include the debtor's centre of main interests in insolvency,[30] the territory of the country for which protection is claimed regarding intellectual property rights and the *locus laboris* for labour law.

2.44 It is worthwhile to note that interest in domicile and nationality, connecting factors of significant weight in many areas until the early 1970s, waned and is unlikely to regain force in jurisdictions where conflicts rules are developing against the background of economic realities and ambitions.

Characterization

2.45 Every conflicts rule classifies the facts and the legal issues to be assigned to the law of a country. As we have seen, 'contracts' are governed by the law chosen by the parties or in the absence of choice by the place of business of the party whose performance is characteristic of the contract, 'torts' are governed by the law of the place of the wrongdoing, 'proprietary rights' are governed by the *lex situs*, 'issues of company law' are governed by the *lex societatis*. However, it may be far from certain whether a given question a court is faced with is, for example, one of contract law or of property law. The process of determining the nature of the issue (the cause of action) for the purposes of putting it into its proper conflict-of-laws pigeon hole, or opening the right conflicts drawer is called characterization or classification (*Qualifikation, qualification*). This process, which consciously or unconsciously must always be performed, is usually accomplished automatically and without difficulties. It may, however, become highly contentious where the outcome of the case depends on whether the court seised has, in light of the correct qualification, jurisdiction or not, whether the law of country A is to be applied because the parties wish to have it applied, or whether it is the law of country B because the asset in dispute is situated there.

2.46 There are a number of theories as to what law should govern the process. For our purposes, it is sufficient to note that a court might either adopt a narrow and inward-looking perspective in making the characterization or rise to the occasion and analyse the facts and the issues at hand in an open-minded and cosmopolitan manner with a view to identifying the appropriate conflicts rule from a comparative and internationalist point of view. This approach was forcefully advocated by Professor Ernst Rabel (1874–1955). Rabel himself emphasized that his was a

---

[30] See below, ch 15.

method rather than a theory,[31] and it may not come as a surprise that, given that few judges dispose of his vast and profound comparative knowledge, judgments based on this approach are and will remain a rarity. The most common method used to allocate an issue to a conflicts rule is to characterize it according to the court's own substantive law, the *lex fori*.[32] The most recent prominent English case in which the issue of characterization was subjected to thorough judicial analysis was *Macmillan Inc v Bishopsgate Investment Trust plc (No 3)*.[33] In that case, it was stated that 'the proper approach is to look beyond the formulation of the claim and to identify according to the *lex fori* the true issue or issues thrown up by the claim and the defence'.[34]

Generally speaking, transnational commercial law instruments try to avoid ambiguities and the danger of de-unification through judicial interpretation by extensive lists of defined terms, an approach they share with statutes enacted by legislatures in common law jurisdictions. For example, Article 1 of the 2001 Cape Town Convention on International Interests in Mobile Equipment defines each and every essential term used in the instrument from '(a) agreement' to '(nn) writing', and further definitions are provided by the Aircraft Protocol. Combined with these are the provisions of Article 5(1) and (2) calling for interpretation that promotes international uniformity, predictability and safeguarding the Convention's underlying principles and policies. However, issues of characterization and so-called 'incidental questions'—a related topic of general conflicts theory which cannot be discussed here—continue to arise because, in particular, recent uniform law instruments increasingly accept that they cannot aspire to create self-sufficient systems. They leave a great number of questions to be resolved by the domestic law applicable by virtue of the conflicts rules of the forum State.[35] For example, whether an entity was validly 'incorporated or formed',[36] or whether there actually was an 'agreement'[37] are issues the treaty does not address. **2.47**

Public policy (*ordre public*)

Public policy is usually invoked to justify the application of the *lex fori* where the normal play of conflicts rules would lead to the application of foreign law. It is an emergency brake. **2.48**

---

[31] Ernst Rabel and Ulrich Drobnig, *Conflict of Laws* (2nd edn, University of Michigan Law School Press, Ann Arbor, 1958) 54.

[32] Some distinguished writers think that the process of characterization should be performed in accordance with the *lex causae*, that is, the law appropriately governing the issue. It is a hotly debated question whether this is a circular argument.   [33] [1996] 1 WLR 387 (CA).

[34] Ibid 407 (Auld LJ).   [35] See Article 5(3) of the Cape Town Convention.

[36] See Article 4(1)(a) of the Cape Town Convention.

[37] See Article 7 of the Cape Town Convention and, more explicitly, Article 4(a) of the UN Convention on Contracts for the International Sale of Goods 1980.

2.49   Professor Albert A Ehrenzweig, as we have seen, the father of the *lex-fori-in-foro-proprio* approach, observes:

> Reliance on . . . public policy for application of the law of the forum has always been a last resort of any court faced with an over-generalized rule of choice of law . . . Where non-discriminating invocation of foreign 'personal' or 'real' statutes and customs seemed unworkable in the growing commerce among the Italian city states . . . , foreign 'statuta odiosa' were rejected in a partly regained discretion of the forum. When in nineteenth century Europe the nationality principle and vested rights . . . began to arrogate a universal regime based on non-existing superlaws, the forum's ordre public was called in as a corrective.

This analysis is confirmed by Mr Justice Cardozo's opinion which, however, on the whole is much more in line with modern legislation, case law and doctrine—more internationalist, provided one applies the essence of the case involving Massachusetts and New York to an international situation. In *Loucks v Standard Oil Co of New York*,[38] an action was brought to recover damages for injuries resulting in death. The plaintiffs were administrators of the estate of Mr Loucks who, while travelling in Massachusetts, was killed in a car accident through negligence of the defendant's servants. A Massachusetts statute provided for punitive damages to be assessed with reference to the degree of culpability of the employer or its employees. The question was whether a right of action under that statute was enforceable in New York courts.

> 'The courts of no country execute the penal laws of another' . . . The defendant invokes that principle as applicable here. Penal in one sense the statute indisputably is . . . But the question is not whether the statute is penal in some sense. The question is whether it is penal within the rules of private international law. A statute penal in that sense is one that awards a penalty to that state, or to a public officer in its behalf, or to a member of the public, suing in the interest of the whole community to redress a public wrong . . . The Massachusetts statute has been classified in some jurisdictions as penal, and in others as remedial . . . The courts of Massachusetts have said that the question is still an open one . . . No matter how they may have characterized the act as penal, they have not meant to hold that it is penal for every purpose . . . We think the better reason is with those cases which hold that the statute is not penal in the international sense . . .

> Another question remains. Even though the statute is not penal, it differs from our own. We must determine whether the difference is a sufficient reason for declining jurisdiction. A tort committed in one state creates a right of action that may be sued upon in another unless public policy forbids . . .

> Our own scheme of legislation may be different. We may even have no legislation on the subject. That is not enough to show that public policy forbids us to enforce the foreign right. A right of action is property. If a foreign statute gives the right, the mere fact that we do not give a like right is no reason for refusing to help the plaintiff in

---

[38]   224 NY 99, 120 NE 198 (1918).

getting what belongs to him. We are not so provincial as to say that every solution of a problem is wrong because we deal with it otherwise at home . . .

The misleading word 'comity' has been responsible for much of the trouble. It has been fertile in suggesting a discretion unregulated by general principles: Beale, *Conflict of Laws*, § 71. The sovereign in its discretion may refuse its aid to the foreign right . . . From this it has been an easy step to the conclusion that a like freedom of choice has been confided to the courts. But that, of course, is a false view . . . The courts are not free to enforce a foreign right at the pleasure of the judges, to suit the individual notion of expediency or fairness. They do not close their doors, unless help would violate some fundamental principle of justice, some prevalent conception of good morals, some deep-rooted tradition of the common weal . . .

This opinion, as well as countless more recent ones expressed by the courts in many **2.50** countries, may be seen as a template for the language chosen in Article 16 of the 1980 Rome Convention on the Law Applicable to Contractual Obligations, Article 18 of the 1994 Inter-American Convention on the Law Applicable to International Contracts, and Article 11(1) of the 2002 Hague Convention on the Law Applicable to Certain Rights in Respect of Securities held with an Intermediary, as well as more recent national reform statutes in Europe and other parts of the world.

Mandatory rules in the law of contracts

Even in legal systems that have carried the concept of party autonomy to the point **2.51** where neither the parties nor the contract need to have any contact with the law chosen, there are limits beyond which the courts are given the discretion to enforce mandatory rules. For example, Article 3(3) of the 1980 Rome Convention provides that, where 'all the other elements relevant to the situation . . . are connected with one country only', the parties' choice of a foreign law 'shall not prejudice the application of rules of the law of that country [that is, the all-contacts country] which cannot be derogated from by contract, hereinafter called "mandatory rules"'. As regards the Rome Convention, the utmost care is to be taken in reading and applying provisions referring to 'mandatory rules'. In Article 3(3) the meaning is clear: it encompasses *all* rules that, according to the law of the all-contacts State, are mandatory, that is, of a nature that excludes any derogation by the parties to that contract. No further specification is to be read into it. Conversely, Article 7(1) implicitly distinguishes 'simple mandatory rules' (those of the kind referred to above which a given law would not allow to be excluded by contract if that law were the applicable law but which could be avoided by choice of a different law) and 'internationally mandatory rules', which apply regardless of the otherwise applicable law. Only the latter are elevated to a special status. Article 7(2) acknowledges that the forum is unlikely to renounce its discretion to impose rules considered mandatory in the circumstances on the parties. The meaning of 'mandatory' for the special purposes of consumer and labour contracts in Articles 5 and 6, and the latter's relationship with Article 7 are subject to continued debate.

2.52 The issue of how mandatory rules ought to be treated in the private international law of contracts is historically connected with, yet to be kept separate from, the role of public policy. In some legal systems, the connection is described in terms of defence (negative operation of public policy) and attack (positive function of public policy as expressed in certain rules of law). Mandatory rules in other languages are accordingly called: *lois de police, lois d'application immédiate, leyes de policía, norme di applicazione necessaria, bepalingen van bijzonder dwingend recht, Eingriffsnormen.* Provisions of this kind and their recognition in international treaties obviously reflect a statutist or unilateralist approach. The rules themselves indicate their desired sphere of application, not the multilateral conflicts rule of the forum. What must be kept in mind, however, is that not all rules that a system considers mandatory for domestic purposes are to be characterized as such in an international context.

2.53 Article 16 of the 1987 Hague Convention on the Law Applicable to Agency is an early harbinger of the universal acceptance of the underlying theories. Even before the entry into force of that Convention and, shortly thereafter, the 1980 Rome Convention, the generally accepted principle was that a court is free to apply its own internationally mandatory rules irrespective of the law otherwise applicable to the contract.[39] The innovation introduced by Article 7(1) Rome Convention,[40] previously known only from the case law in a few jurisdictions and rejected by way of a reservation by some Contracting States, is that effect may also be given to the mandatory rules of a 'third country'—that is, a country which is neither the forum, nor the country whose law is otherwise applicable—provided that the situation has a close connection with that country and under the law of that country (and regardless of the position under the *lex fori*) those rules must be applied whatever the law applicable to the contract. The areas where non-forum mandatory rules are potentially significant are land law, labour law and the law regulating the relationship between principal and agent,[41] securities regulation and investor protection, antitrust law and the law relating to unfair competition, export controls, protection of cultural objects and exchange contracts.

2.54 The future Community instrument (the Rome I Regulation) leaves the language unchanged as regards the current Article 3(3), which is going to be Article 3(4). As regards current Article 7, however, the Commission is taking a common law style approach and introduces a definition in future Article 8(1):

> Mandatory rules are rules the respect for which is regarded as crucial by a country for safeguarding its political, social or economic organisation to such an extent that they are applicable to any situation falling within their scope, irrespective of the law otherwise applicable to the contract under this Regulation.

---

[39] Article 7(2) Rome Convention and Article 11(1) Inter-American Convention.

[40] And, fourteen years later, Article 11(2) Inter-American Convention, but in a less guided way.

[41] See ch 8 below.

This provision reflects five decades of case law and doctrinal writing across Europe **2.55** devoted to this issue. Future Article 8(2) and 8(3) correspond to current Article 7(2) and 7(1) respectively.

An interesting feature of the most recent conflicts convention, the 2002 Hague **2.56** Convention on the Law Applicable to Indirectly Held Securities, is a provision which limits the mandatory force even of rules of the *lex fori*. According to Article 11(3), the application of mandatory provisions of the law of the forum imposing requirements with respect to perfection or relating to priorities between competing interests in the securities is not permitted unless the law of the forum is the applicable law under the Convention. The purpose of this is to prevent a Contracting State from invoking its rules of public policy to undermine the efficacy of perfection or priority of an interest under the Convention law. For example, a provision in domestic legislation invalidating an unregistered security interest granted by a company which later goes into liquidation cannot be invoked in a Contracting State in which the Convention has become law where the effect would be to negate a valid pre-liquidation perfection of the security interest under the Convention law. A Contracting State, by its act of ratification, renounces the mandatory applicability of those provisions for the purposes of cases that come under the Convention. It will be interesting to see whether Article 11(3) will be used as a model by Governments in the negotiation of future uniform law instruments.

Neo-statutist theory and market regulation

Whereas mandatory or interventionist rules used to be both few and isolated **2.57** exceptions in nineteenth and early twentieth centuries' bourgeois society, the advent of mixed economies as well as growing conscience that markets as well as other institutions of society need permanent protection made them a common and widespread phenomenon. When legislators do define their sphere of application, the conflicts rules are usually unilateral. The connecting factors are typically physical location, conduct or effects on the legislator's own territory or markets. When legislators do not define the sphere of application of public-policy rules or mandatory rules, and courts and regulators have to take care of finding the appropriate connecting factors, they tend to tailor them similarly. This means, in particular, that they will always apply the *lex fori* when there is such connection with the forum and the forum's policies require that the rule in question be applied. They will do so because the underlying policies are, in many instances and at least for the time being, not interchangeable. For example, the securities regulation in the US continues to be distinct in many respects and more comprehensive than in most other jurisdictions. Regulatory law is, in principle, obviously relevant for transactions on the regulated markets and the commercial law governing them. However, a note of caution is appropriate. The fact that a market is highly regulated by rules that reflect strong economic and social persuasions does not, in the absence of clear legislative guidance, justify simply applying, as frequently suggested, 'the law of the market'. The conflict-of-laws analysis must, at the outset, keep the two bodies of law separate. A sale of securities or the taking of security in securities is, as such, governed by the law identified by the relevant conflicts rule regarding contracts, dispositions, etc. That some regulatory requirement might then intervene unilaterally is a different matter. Finally, it deserves mentioning that this type of unilateralism is not carved in stone, as case law in both Europe and the US[42] shows.

Renvoi

2.58 Owing to the differences in the private international law of countries, there are a number of different solutions to when a, say, English judge is referred by his conflict-of-laws rules to, say, French law. For instance, (1) he may take 'French law' to mean the domestic substantive law only; (2) or he may take 'French law' to mean French law including French conflicts rules. If he does, French law may (3) also declare French substantive law applicable, or (4) refer back to English law, or (5) refer to the law of a third State. The English judge will then have to decide what to do if French law refers back to English law or onward to some other law. Both depend on whether English private international law accepts in principle the doctrine of *renvoi* and how it operates in the various fact patterns. The doctrine is best exemplified by the well-known decision of the French *Cour de Cassation* in *Forgo's case*.[43]

2.59 Forgo, a Bavarian national, died intestate in Pau, where he had lived since early childhood. The question before the French courts was whether his movables in France should be distributed according to the internal law of France or of Bavaria. Collateral relatives were entitled to succeed by Bavarian law, but under French law the property passed to the French Government to the exclusion of collaterals. French private international law referred the matter of succession to Bavarian law, but Bavarian private international law referred it to French law. The *Cour de Cassation* accepted the remission and applied French law.

2.60 Legal systems differ widely as to how one should deal with this issue. In the law of contracts, and in particular where the parties have chosen the governing law, there is a strong tendency to exclude *renvoi* by stating that the 'law' specified as applicable means the rules of law in force in the designated country other than its conflict-of-laws rules. This is the solution of Article 15 of the Rome Convention 1980, of Article 17 of the Inter-American Convention 1994, as well as the one chosen in most commercial-law conventions where there are issues referred to the (otherwise) 'applicable law'.

---

[42] For the United States, see: American Law Institute, *Restatement (Third) of Foreign Relations Law* (American Law Institute Publishers, St Paul (MI), 1987) §§ 402–3 and § 416 (with respect to its 'jurisdiction to prescribe' regarding transactions in securities).

[43] *Re Forgo* 10 Clunet 64 (1883).

D. The Future: Will We Continue to Need Conflict of Laws?

In his article quoted above, Professor Juenger asked whether there is a role for the **2.61**
lex mercatoria in private international law. The inverse question is equally legitimate: is there a role for conflict of laws in modern transnational commercial law?
It is submitted that the answer will be in the affirmative for a number of reasons,
the most obvious one being the delay, the limited resources and the selectivity with
which governments and international organizations are following commercial and
financial practice and its creativity. Second, even where a particular field or issue of
commercial law is covered by an international instrument that enjoys wide or even
universal support, factors such as lack of parliamentary time in major trade or
financial centres may prevent the negotiated substantive rules from getting on the
statute book. Third, a Contracting State may have substantially limited the substantive scope of application of a convention. Article 92 of the 1980 UN Sales Convention (CISG) and Article 20 of the 1988 Ottawa Convention on International
Financial Leasing may be cited as examples. Fourth, many conventions allow for
the parties to contractually exclude their application. On the other hand, it may
actually be the conflicts rule of the court seised of a dispute that leads the judge to
the international uniform law instrument because, through ratification by the
State whose law governs the matter by virtue of the rules of private international
law, the instrument has become that country's law for international cases. That was
the basis for the application of the 1964 Hague Uniform Sales Laws in a considerable number of cases. Consequently, the draftsmen of the successor instrument
CISG[44] deliberately provided for this avenue to become one of the entry points
into the Convention, Article 1(1)(b). However, Article 95 provides that a Contracting State may declare that it will not be bound by Article 1(1)(b).

Most important from a conceptual point of view, however, is the fact that neither **2.62**
practising lawyers nor, consequently, drafters of more recent substantive uniform
law instruments are as beset by that hostility vis-à-vis conflict of laws as their counterparts in the 1920s. Whilst at the diplomatic Conference for the adoption of the
Warsaw Convention, the mere threat of becoming hostage to the choice-of-law
process was sufficient at least to paper over disagreement regarding the substance
of an envisaged solution, this threat is gradually subsiding. Both the 2001 Cape
Town Convention on International Interests in Mobile Equipment and the 2001
UN Convention on the Assignment of Receivables testify to the perceived ability
to predict with reasonable precision the economic consequences likely to flow
from the choice of particular rules.

For all these reasons, it is neither tenable nor helpful to portray uniform substantive
law, the *lex mercatoria* on the one hand, and conflict of laws on the other as strategic

---

[44] See below, ch 7.

and conceptual alternatives available to legislators and adjudicators. They are complementary tools,[45] for the development of a modern legal framework for transnational commerce.

Questions

1. To what extent do you consider it feasible or desirable to dispense with the rules of private international law and to harmonize all substantive rules governing cross-border transactions?
2. What criteria would you apply in deciding whether in a particular field one should harmonize substantive rules of law or merely the conflict of laws rules?
3. How should one decide what is the appropriate connecting factor in determining the scope of a commercial law convention?
4. Should contracting parties have complete freedom when choosing the law or principles of law that is applicable to their contract? If they should not, to what extent should the law limit the autonomy of the parties and on what basis?
5. What is:
   (a) a 'simple mandatory rule',
   (b) an internationally mandatory rule?
   What role do such rules play in transnational commercial law?
6. What is meant by the *renvoi* doctrine? Does *renvoi* have any role to play in transnational commercial law?
7. Article 4(1) of the 2002 Hague Convention on the Law Applicable to Indirectly Held Securities would appear to be a departure from contemporary conflict of laws standards regarding the parties' freedom to choose the applicable law. Comment on the nature of this departure and the presumed underlying rationale for it.

Further reading

Audit, Bernard, 'A Continental Lawyer Looks at Contemporary American Choice-of-Law Principles' 27 Am J Comp L 589 (1979)

---

[45] For a thorough analysis, in particular their relationship as developed over 'three legislative generations', see: C Kessedjian, 'Codification du droit commercial international et droit international privé' (2004) 300 Recueil des Cours 79, 224–59.

Basedow, Jürgen, 'Souveraineté territoriale et globalisation des marchés; le domaine d'application des lois contre les restrictions de la concurrence' (1998) 264 Recueil des Cours 9

Cheatham, Elliott E, Book review of Ernst Rabel, *The Conflict of Laws: A Comparative Study*, 48 Col L Rev 1267 (1948)

Fawcett, James, Harris, Jonathan, and Bridge, Michael, *International Sale of Goods in the Conflict of Laws* (OUP, Oxford, 2005)

Ferrari, Franco, 'CISG and Private International Law' in Franco Ferrari (ed), *The 1980 Sales Law: Old Issues Revisited in the Light of Recent Experiences* (Giuffrè, Milan, 2003), 19

Goode, Roy, 'Rule, Practice, and Pragmatism in Transnational Commercial Law' (2005) 54 ICLQ 539

Hay, Peter, 'Flexibility versus Predictability and Uniformity in Choice of Law' (1992) 226 Recueil des Cours 281

Juenger, Friedrich K, *Choice of Law and Multistate Justice* (Nijhoff, Dordrecht, 1992)

Kay, Herma Hill, 'A Defense of Currie's Governmental Interest Analysis' (1990) 215 Recueil des Cours 9

Kronke, Herbert, 'Capital Markets and Conflict of Laws' (2000) 286 Recueil des Cours 245

Kronke, Herbert, 'Most Significant Relationship, Governmental Interests, Cultural Identity, Integration: "Rules" at Will and the Case for Principles of Conflict of Laws' (2004) 9 Unif L Rev 467

Lando, Ole, 'The Conflict of Laws of Contracts. General Principles' (1985) 189 Recueil des Cours 226

von Mehren, Arthur T, 'Theory and Practice of Adjudicatory Authority in Private International Law: A Comparative Study of the Doctrine, Policies and Practices of Common- and Civil-Law-Systems' (2002) 295 Recueil des Cours 9

Muir Watt, Horatia, 'Aspects économiques du droit international privé (Réflexions sur l'impact de la globalisation économique sur les fondements des conflits de lois et de juridictions)' (2005) 307 Recueil de Cours 25

North, Peter, 'Private International Law in Twentieth-Century England' in Jack Beatson and Reinhard Zimmermann (ed), *Jurists Uprooted—German-speaking Emigré Lawyers in Twentieth-century Britain* (OUP, Oxford, 2004) 483

Picone, Paolo, 'Les méthodes de coordination juridiques en droit international privé' (1999) 276 Recueil des Cours 9

Reese, Willis LM, 'Power of Parties to Choose Law Governing Their Contract' 54 Am Soc Intl L Proceedings 49 (1960)

Torsello, Marco, *Common Features of Uniform Commercial Conventions: a comparative study beyond the 1980 uniform sales law* (Sellier European Law Publishers, Munich, 2004) 249–59

Winship, Peter, 'Private International Law and the UN Sales Convention' 21 Cornell J Intl L 487 (1988)

3

INTERNATIONAL LAW AS IT AFFECTS PRIVATE LAW CONVENTIONS GOVERNING CROSS-BORDER COMMERCIAL TRANSACTIONS

A. **Nature and Sources**	3.01	Body of the Convention	3.36
International law as law	3.04	Sphere of application and general	
Relationship between international law		provisions	3.37
and soft law	3.06	Substantive rules	3.39
Relationship between international law		Final clauses	3.41
and domestic law	3.07	C. **Interpretation of Conventions**	3.47
Applications of international law	3.10	An illustration: the Factoring	
Influences on international law		Convention	3.52
Impact of sophisticated and specialized		Treatment of errors in a convention	3.55
international law-making		A procedure for the correction	
organizations	3.11	of errors	3.56
Impact of increased complexity of the		Uncorrected errors and interpretation	3.57
international law-making process	3.12	D. **Enforcement of Private**	
Impact of trade and development	3.13	**Conventional Rights**	
Impact of the enhanced role of the		**Against States**	
individual under international law	3.14	The consequences of internationally	
International law and the European		wrongful acts and the concept of	
Community	3.15	diplomatic protection	3.60
The sources of international law	3.19	E. **Reservations and Declarations**	3.69
Customary international law	3.21	F. **Withdrawal from a Treaty**	3.70
Treaty law	3.26	G. **Conflicts Between Conventions**	3.72
B. **The Typical Structure of Private**			
Law Conventions	3.32		
Preamble	3.33		

A. Nature and Sources

International law is primarily concerned with States and international organi- **3.01**
zations, not with individuals or bodies lacking international legal personality or
with relations between private parties to a commercial transaction. Traditionally,
such persons had no standing to bring proceedings for treaty violations by a foreign

State, and had to pursue remedies through the State of which they were nationals under the doctrine of diplomatic protection. That has changed in that, in more recent times, direct rights of suit have been conferred on individuals and corporations under treaties made for their protection, particularly in the fields of human rights, foreign investment, European Community law, and even under the United Nations Convention on the Law of the Sea. But it remains the general rule that individuals and corporations who are injured by violation of a treaty by a foreign State must seek redress through the intermediation of their own State.

3.02 The focus of this book is on legal harmonization as it affects cross-border commercial transactions between private parties. International economic law is outside the scope of this book. So too is the legal regime established by contracts between a private party and a State or State entity pursuant to a treaty, such as a bilateral investment treaty. Indeed, the greater part of international law concerns issues which we shall not be addressing. Nevertheless, international law does possess some significant points of contact with transnational commercial law in the sense in which that term is used in this book. In particular:

(1) the literature and case law on the nature of customary international law and its relationship to treaty law are relevant to the nature of trade usage and its relationship to the commercial law conventions examined in this book;

(2) the general law of treaties—for example on interpretation, taking effect, amendment, withdrawal, reservations and declarations—governs private law conventions;

(3) it is necessary to be aware of the conditions set by constitutional law in which parties to a private law convention may treat its provisions as part of domestic law and may be able to invoke it directly;

(4) a few conventions that are predominantly private law conventions impose duties on States, or involve or create organizations that may have legal personality in international law—for example the Cape Town Convention on International interests in Mobile Equipment 2001;

(5) private law conventions may contain distinctive provisions governing the functions of the depositary or may involve or create organizations that are already or may become subjects of international law;

(6) transnational law governing the resolution of commercial disputes, discussed later in this work, has had to address the special considerations arising where the dispute springs from a commercial contract in which one of the parties is a State or State entity and the other a commercial enterprise, as in the case of the 1965 Washington Convention.[1]

---

[1] Convention on the settlement of investment disputes between States and nationals of other States. This established the International Centre for the Settlement of Investment Disputes (ICSID)

The present chapter is confined to some general observations and to issues of the **3.03** above kind arising from international instruments covered by the book. For the history, theory and other aspects of international law reference should be made to standard textbooks on the subject. The complex topic of State immunity, now governed by the 2005 UN Convention on Jurisdictional Immunities of States and Their Property,[2] is briefly discussed in chapter 16. Suffice it to say, at this point, that whereas until relatively recently a State enjoyed absolute immunity from suit, even when engaging in a commercial transaction, modern law adopts a principle of restrictive State immunity by which immunity from suit is confined to acts of a State done in exercise of its sovereign powers (*acta jure imperii*) and does not extend to acts relating to commercial activity (*acta jure gestionis*), for which a State cannot plead immunity from jurisdiction.[3] However, enforcement against a State by a process of execution is governed by different rules (so that, for example, waiver of immunity from jurisdiction does not constitute waiver of immunity from execution), though there is a trend towards the removal of immunity for property used or to be used in commercial activities of the State in question.

International law as law

An infallible means of enraging an international lawyer is to ask whether inter- **3.04** national law is law at all! We need not spend time on such abstractions. It is clear that norms have developed governing international relations, and that in appropriate cases these are accepted as law by States. The International Court of Justice, replacing earlier bodies, was established as the principal judicial organ of the United Nations with the function of determining in accordance with international law disputes between subjects of international law (Article 38 of the Statute of the Court identifies the sources of international law). It is, therefore, indisputable that, even if international law does not constitute a legal system in the full sense, because of the lack of a formal legislature or of courts with universal compulsory jurisdiction, nevertheless it exists as law in the sense of conferring rights and imposing binding obligations on those who are subject to it. International legal norms typically arise from consent, so that in principle a State cannot be bound by a new rule of customary law to which it objects or by a treaty to which it has not consented. However, in contemporary international law, there is a tendency for some newly negotiated rules to become quickly transformed into

---

to which a national of a State involved in a dispute with another State under an investment agreement can resort for conciliation or arbitration where the other State has given its consent. Such consent is commonly given in a bilateral investment treaty between two States pursuant to which a national of one of them may invoke the dispute resolution procedure laid down by the treaty. The investor is not a party to the treaty, but this is considered to embody an offer of conciliation/arbitration by the host State which the investor is deemed to accept by making a request for conciliation/arbitration to ICSID.

  [2] See (2006) 55 ICLQ, where all the shorter articles are devoted to the Convention.
  [3] This rule is now embodied in Art 10 of the 2005 State Immunity Convention.

customary law binding on individual States once there is a general consensus on the part of all States regarding their adoption and implementation.

3.05 For our purposes, the interesting questions include the relationship between international law and soft law and between international law and municipal law, the extent to which customary international law and its relationship to treaty law find their parallels in international trade usage and its relationship to international conventions, the duties of States parties to a private law convention designed primarily to regulate private rights, and the conditions in which a person enjoying such rights can pursue a remedy against a State party to the convention for a breach of its treaty obligations.

Relationship between international law and soft law

3.06 It is only in relatively recent times that the influence of so-called soft law has come to be recognized. Soft law consists of non-binding rules or statements of practice which are intended to influence behaviour or to be a resource for those seeking the best rule for a particular situation. They take a variety of forms: codes of practice, restatements such as the Principles of European Contract Law and the UNIDROIT Principles of International Commercial Contracts, communications and non-binding declarations, legislative guides, and even treaties where they impose no real obligations on the parties. Soft law may also contribute to the development of a rule of customary international law or even a treaty.

Alan Boyle, 'Some Reflections on the Relationship of Treaties and Soft Law'
(1999) 48 ICLQ 901, 902–4 and 906–7

(1) Soft law as an alternative to law-making by treaty

There are several reasons why soft law instruments may represent an attractive alternative to law-making by treaty. First, it may be easier to reach agreement when the form is non-binding. Use of soft law instruments enables states to agree to more detailed and precise provisions because their legal commitment, and the consequences of any non-compliance, are more limited. Secondly, it may be easier for some states to adhere to non-binding instruments because they can avoid the domestic treaty ratification process, and perhaps escape democratic accountability for the policy to which they have agreed. Of course this may also make it comparably harder to implement such policies if funding, legislation, or public support are necessary. Thirdly, soft law instruments will normally be easier to amend or replace than treaties, particularly when all that is required is the adoption of a new resolution by an international institution. Treaties take time to replace or amend, and the attempt to do so can result in an awkward and overlapping network of old and new obligations between different sets of parties . . . Lastly, soft law instruments may provide more immediate evidence of international support and consensus than a treaty whose impact is heavily qualified by reservations and the need to wait for ratification and entry into force.

Given the relative advantage of soft law over treaties, it is perhaps surprising that the multilateral treaty has until now been the International Law Commission's preferred instrument for the codification of international law. Although a treaty basis may be required when creating new international organisations or institutions, or for dispute settlement provisions, soft law instruments appear to be just as useful a means of codifying international law as treaties. Provided they contain no binding dispute settlement clauses, the Commission's draft articles on the law of state responsibility could equally well be codified using either a General Assembly resolution or an intergovernmental declaration. Indeed this may be more effective than using a treaty, which, like the Vienna Convention on the Law of Treaties, runs the risk of securing only a small number of parties. The Commission's work on treaties is among its most successful and authoritative codifications, but it is difficult to suggest that this owes much to its treaty status, or to the number of states parties.

The argument for using a treaty rather than a soft law instrument is stronger in the case of new law-making, such as the re-negotiation of the law of the sea or the elaboration of human rights law, although in many of these cases institutions with extensive powers were already being established at the same time and a treaty was thus desirable in any event. But even for new law, non-binding instruments may still be useful if they can help generate widespread and consistent state practice and/or provide evidence of *opinio juris* in support of a customary rule ...

What all of this suggests is that the non-binding form of an instrument is of relatively limited relevance in the context of customary international law-making. Treaties do not generate or codify customary law because of their binding form but because they either influence state practice and provide evidence of *opinio juris* for new or emerging rules, or because they are good evidence of what the existing law is. In many cases this is no different from the potential effect of non-binding soft law instruments. Both treaties and soft law instruments can be vehicles for focusing consensus on rules and principles, and for mobilising a consistent, general response on the part of states ...

(4) Soft law as General Norms or Principles

The point was made many years ago by Judge Baxter that some treaties are soft in the sense that they impose no real obligations on the parties. Though formally binding, the vagueness, indeterminacy, or generality of their provisions may deprive them of the character of 'hard law' in any meaningful sense ... This is probably true of many, if not most, treaties, a point recognised by the International Court in the *North Sea Continental Shelf Case* when it specified that one of the conditions to be met before a treaty could be regarded as law-making is that it should be so drafted as to be 'potentially normative' in character.

There is, however, a second and more significant sense in which a treaty may be potentially normative, but still 'soft' in character, because it articulates 'principles' rather than 'rules'. Such principles do have legal significance in much the same way that Dworkin uses the idea of constitutional principles. They may lay down parameters which affect the way courts decide cases or the way an international institution exercises its discretionary powers. They can set limits, or provide guidance, or determine how conflicts between other rules or principles will be resolved. They may lack the supposedly harder edge of a 'rule' or an 'obligation', but they are certainly not legally irrelevant. As such they constitute a very important form of law, which may be 'soft', but which should not be confused with 'non-binding' law.

Relationship between international law and domestic law

An important question is the extent to which international law forms part of **3.07** domestic law without the need for incorporation into it. For example, if a State ratifies the 1980 Vienna Convention on Contracts for the International Sale of Goods, does that fact alone suffice to enable a party to a contract falling within the Convention to invoke its provisions in proceedings before the courts of the ratifying State? The answer to this kind of question was formerly thought to depend on whether one subscribed to the theory of monism, on the one hand, or dualism, on the other. The monist theory postulated that international law and domestic law constituted a single legal system in which international law was paramount and applied within a given legal system without the need for it to be transformed into domestic law by legislation or judicial decision. The dualist theory, by contrast, held that international law and domestic law operated at different planes, international law governing relations between States and domestic law relations within a State, so that, for example, ratification of a treaty by a State would impose obligations upon it at international level, but would have no effect on the State's domestic law unless adopted by the legislature or the courts.

3.08 Modern practice suggests that this theoretical division is rather sterile, in that in relation to each State, the relevant question is the constitutional process by which a rule of international law takes effect as part of domestic law, and that there is a whole range of national responses to this question. In the United Kingdom, it is established that a treaty or convention does not form part of domestic law unless transformed into domestic law by legislation, so that in the absence of such transformation, failure to observe the treaty constitutes a breach of international law, but not a breach of domestic law. The position is otherwise as regards customary international law, which is considered to apply as part of domestic law unless incompatible with statute or binding judicial decision. In the United States, a similar position is taken as regards customary law, but in relation to treaties the position is more complex. Many international agreements are concluded by the President without Congressional approval: these 'executive agreements' will be binding only in international law. 'Treaties' so-called must have the assent of the Senate for the United States to become a party. Some of these treaties are self-executing in the sense that the constitutional process by which they are given effect does not require legislation, others are not self-executing and require Congressional legislation before they can take effect as law within the United States. It is often difficult for constitutional experts to determine on which side of the line a treaty falls. Even a self-executing treaty will not be given effect if it is inconsistent with the constitution of the United States, whereas in some countries, for example the Netherlands, a treaty can override a provision of the constitution if approved by a two-thirds majority of the legislature. Where the constitution of a State requires legislation to give effect to a treaty as part of the State's municipal law, the safest course is to enact the legislation before ratifying the treaty, which is the practice of the United Kingdom. If ratification takes place first there is the risk that the legislation will not be approved, thereby placing the State in question in breach of its international obligations.

With all these divergent approaches to the relationship between international law **3.09** and municipal law, one principle at least has gained general acceptance, namely that a State cannot invoke its domestic law as a defence to a claim based on a breach of its international obligations. Nor can a State walk away from its treaty obligations by invoking the doctrine of State sovereignty. This was settled by a decision of the Permanent Court of Justice (PCIJ) over eighty years ago.[4]

SS Wimbledon Case (Britain v Germany) (1923) PCIJ (Series A) No 1, 25

The court declines to see in the conclusion of any treaty by which a State undertakes to perform or refrain from performing a particular act an abandonment of sovereignty. No doubt any convention creating an obligation of this kind places a restriction upon the exercise of the sovereign rights of the State, in the sense that it requires them to be exercised in a certain way. But the right of entering into international engagements is an attribute of State sovereignty.

Applications of international law

Examples of the application of international law in cross-border commercial **3.10** transactions are numerous, and include the following. First, commercial law treaty provisions may set out rules specifying which municipal courts are to have jurisdiction. Such treaty provisions, once operative in a contracting State, must be respected by the courts of that State, who must then interpret the treaty and apply any relevant rules of international law. Second, in a large and increasing number of cases, rules of international law are applied under choice of law clauses, particularly in investment treaties, which commonly provide for the application of the law of the host State and principles of international law. In case of a conflict between them, tribunals consistently give priority to international law over municipal law, typically in situations where the host State is alleged to have expropriated the investor's investment without due compensation.[5] Under Article 42(1) of the Washington Convention,[6] Tribunals appointed by ICSID are required to apply the rules of law agreed by the parties, and in the absence of such agreement, 'such rules of international law as may be applicable'. The investor will thus have two sets of rights, which not infrequently overlap: rights under international law conferred by the treaty, and rights under domestic law conferred by the investment agreement.[7] Third, the involvement of States and State entities in commercial

---

[4] The PCIJ, established through procedures of the League of Nations (1921), was replaced by the International Court of Justice (ICJ), established by Article 92 of the United Nations Charter as its 'principle judicial organ'. The ICJ is essentially a continuation of the PCIJ.

[5] For a detailed analysis, see : Christoph H Schreuer, *The ICSID Convention: A Commentary* (CUP, Cambridge, 2001), commentary to Art 42 [55] ff.   [6] See above, para 3.02.

[7] These have to be treated distinctly. Disputes under the investment agreement are usually referred to the exclusive jurisdiction of the host State, while disputes under some or all of the treaty provisions are commonly referred to an international panel of arbitrators under the ICSID procedure.

activities may raise questions of State immunity from jurisdiction, succession and acts of government interfering with contractual relationships, to be resolved, wholly or partly, by reference to international law. Fourth, arbitral tribunals in other commercial disputes often apply elements of international law, and their awards are usually enforceable under the 1958 New York Convention on the Recognition and Enforcement of Foreign Arbitral Awards.[8]

Influences on international law

Impact of sophisticated and specialized international law-making organizations

3.11 The impact of sophisticated and specialized law-making bodies cannot be over-stated. These organizations have developed a body of knowledge, technical expertise and materials that enables them to play a major role in the preparation and conclusion of international instruments and other texts. Their secretariats have an international orientation, often shared by member State participants, particularly those that remain involved over a significant period of time. The work of UNIDROIT, the Hague Conference, UNCITRAL and other specialized agencies of the United Nations, and of regional bodies such as the European Union fall within this category. These bodies, and other specialist multilateral and regional organizations, have produced a large number of important commercial law instruments, many of which are reproduced in Volume 2 of this work.

Impact of increased complexity of the international law-making process

3.12 This salutary shift to specialist law-making agencies is all the more important given the parallel multiplication of sovereign States, and, correspondingly, the complexity of the process. The numbers of States operatively engaged in law making has expanded at an intense rate. The United Nations had fifty-one member States in 1951, and has 192 at present. In addition, expert, assertive, and politically powerful non-governmental organizations are now a fixed part of the law-making landscape.

Impact of trade and development

3.13 There are now a large number of multilateral and other governmental bodies that in one way or other finance trade. They often do so by financing commercial activity. Not only do these bodies require international standards supporting their transactions, they are increasingly active participants in the law-making process. The World Bank, the International Monetary Fund, the European Bank for Reconstruction and Development, a number of United States aid agencies, and

---

This confluence of private law and public international law can give rise to intricate questions as to the relationship between them.

[8] See below, para 17.135.

various government entities providing export finance fall within this category. The distinction between commerce and trade is becoming increasingly tenuous. In particular, the explosion of bilateral investment treaties, which address commercial law items, is accelerating the unity of commercial, trade, and economic categories.[9]

Impact of the enhanced role of the individual under international law

The individual is increasingly being recognized as a subject of international law. **3.14** This is seen in a variety of contexts, including, as mentioned below, the field of trade and investment. A related development involves human right jurisprudence, which increasingly permits the direct assertion of private rights, not only by natural persons but also by corporations, for even these have 'human rights', for example, privacy, the right to a fair hearing and the protection of property.

International law and the European Community

The position as regards the penetration of international law into municipal law, **3.15** which has been the subject of much controversy, is still more complex in relation to international conventions entered into by the European Community on matters in which it has legal competence. In some cases, its competence is exclusive, displacing what would otherwise be the competence of Member States. In other cases, it is shared, as in the case of mixed conventions, parts of which fall within the competence of the Community, while others lie within the exclusive competence of Member States. The Cape Town Convention 2001 provides a good example. Article 48 of that Convention empowers the Community as a regional economic integration organization to sign up to the Convention.

Article 48—Regional Economic Integration Organisations

1. A Regional Economic Integration Organisation which is constituted by sovereign States and has competence over certain matters governed by this Convention may similarly sign, accept, approve or accede to this Convention. The Regional Economic Integration Organisation shall in that case have the rights and obligations of a Contracting State, to the extent that that Organisation has competence over matters governed by this Convention. Where the number of Contracting States is relevant in this Convention, the Regional Economic Integration Organisation shall not count as a Contracting State in addition to its Member States which are Contracting States.

2. The Regional Economic Integration Organisation shall, at the time of signature, acceptance, approval or accession, make a declaration to the Depositary specifying the matters governed by this Convention in respect of which competence has been

---

[9] The definition of protected 'investments' in a typical BIT includes 'contractual rights', 'tangible property', and 'intangible property, including rights such as leases, mortgages, liens, and pledges'. See, for example, Treaty Between the Government of the United States of America and the Government of the Hashemite Kingdom of Jordan Concerning the Encouragement and Reciprocal Protection of Investment 1997 Art 1.

transferred to that Organisation by its Member States. The Regional Economic Integration Organisation shall promptly notify the Depositary of any changes to the distribution of competence, including new transfers of competence, specified in the declaration under this paragraph.

3. Any reference to a 'Contracting State' or 'Contracting States' or 'State Party' or 'States Parties' in this Convention applies equally to a Regional Economic Integration Organisation where the context so requires.

3.16 The great bulk of the convention falls outside the Community's competence. It does, however, have competence on matters relating to jurisdiction and through the Commission it asserted a competence which it almost certainly did not have over the insolvency provisions embodied in Article XI of the aircraft equipment protocol, claiming that these might in some unexplained way affect the European Union Insolvency Regulation,[10] whereas Article XI deals with substantive law and the Regulation is essentially a conflict-of-laws Regulation. It is in fact impossible to see how the former could in any way affect the latter, but the Commission's position was somewhat reluctantly accepted by Member States as part of a compromise, the Commission in turn agreeing that each Member State would be free to decide for itself which option, if any, of Article XI to adopt instead of all Member States being required to make the same decision.

3.17 An important issue is whether an international convention entered into by the Community can have a direct effect on Community law, and thus expose Community measures to challenge.

Paul Craig and Gráinne de Búrca, *EU Law: Text, Cases and Materials* **(3rd edn, OUP, Oxford, 2003) 193**

By virtue of Articles 281 (ex Article 210) and 300 (ex Article 228) of the EC Treaty, the Community has legal personality and is empowered to enter into contractual relations with other persons and organizations. The question arising within the current discussion concerns the legal effect of international agreements entered into by the EC. We shall see that in this context the 'direct effect' of international agreements concerns the capacity for such agreements to be directly invoked and enforced not only within the legal orders and courts of the Member States, but also within the legal order of the EU before the Court of Justice.

One the one hand, as treaties concluded with other States or international organizations, these could be seen as traditional international agreements binding only on the States or organizations which signed them and having no specific effect upon individuals. On the other hand, as agreements entered into by the Community, they could share some of the key characteristics of EC law, and in particular could be capable of direct effect and enforcement by individuals whenever sufficiently precise and unconditional. Opting broadly for the approach which would integrate agreements made by the Community into the law of the Member States, the Court held that international agreements can, *under certain circumstances*, be directly effective.

---

[10] Council Regulation (EC) 1346/2000 on insolvency proceedings [2000] OJ L/160. See below, paras 15.24 ff.

This question has arisen primarily in the context of the impact of GATT and the **3.18**
WTO on Community law, a subject outside the scope of the present work.

The sources of international law

Article 38 of the Statute of the International Court of Justice is generally consid- **3.19**
ered to be the authoritative statement of the sources of international law.

Statute of the International Court of Justice, Article 38

1. The Court, whose function is to decide in accordance with international law such
   disputes as are submitted to it, shall apply:
   a. international conventions, whether general or particular, establishing rules
      expressly recognized by the contesting states;
   b. international custom, as evidence of a general practice accepted as law;
   c. the general principles of law recognized by civilized nations;
   d. subject to the provision of Article 59,[11] judicial decisions and teachings of the
      most highly qualified publicists of the various nations, as subsidiary means for
      determination of rules of law.
2. This provision shall not prejudice the power of the Court to decide a case *ex aequo
   et bono* if the parties agree thereto.

This enumeration does not indicate any hierarchical ranking of sources.[12] However, **3.20**
the sources in paragraph 1(d) are subsidiary only, while the reference to general
principles was inserted primarily to avoid the possibility of a gap in international
law and a consequent ruling of *non liquet*, that is, that the court cannot decide the
case because of uncertainty as to the applicable rule. General principles of law
derived from national legal systems are regularly invoked in human rights cases
and by arbitrators involved in disputes between States and corporations, and have
been invoked by the International Court of Justice and international arbitral
tribunals to support a variety of rights, including the right to performance of contractual undertakings (*pacta sunt servanda*), reparations,[13] compensation on the
basis of *damnum emergens* and *lucrum cessans*,[14] and 'lifting of the veil' to enable
claims arising from breaches of obligations by a company to be pursued in certain

---

[11] To the effect that the ICJ's decisions do not bind non-litigants.
[12] Compare: American Law Institute, *Restatement (Third) of Foreign Relations Law* (American
Law Institute Publishers, St Paul (MI) 1987) § 102: (1) A rule of international law is one that has
been accepted as such by the international community of states (a) in the form of customary law; (b)
by international agreement; (c) by derivation from general principles common to the major legal
systems of the world. (2) Customary international law results from a general and consistent practice
of states followed by them from a sense of legal obligation. (3) International agreements create law
for the states parties thereto and may lead to the creation of customary international law when such
agreements are intended for adherence by states generally and are in fact widely adopted. (4) General
principles common to the major legal systems of the world, even if not incorporated or reflected in
customary international law or international agreement, may be invoked as supplementary rules of
international law where appropriate.   [13] See the *Chorzów Factory* case, below, para 3.60.
[14] *AMCO Asia Corp and others v Republic of Indonesia* (1983) 1 ICSID Rep 389.

cases against the persons behind the company.[15] But the two primary sources are treaty and custom. We shall deal with the latter first.

Customary international law

3.21 We have seen earlier[16] that the sources of international law include international custom, by which is meant the practice of States accepted as law, and that just as, according to the traditional view, international commercial practice does not constitute a normative usage unless observed from a sense of obligation, so also State practice does not constitute a source of international law unless observed in the belief that it is legally binding. In other words, *usus* must be conjoined with *opinio juris*.

3.22 This parallelism between trade usage and international customary law suggests that literature and case law on each may be of assistance in unravelling the other. Yet to date, the two streams, though involving similar issues, have developed in isolation from each other, international lawyers working out theories of customary international law while commercial lawyers are separately engaged in a comparable exercise in relation to international trade usage. No doubt this lack of mutual engagement reflects the fact that, in the words of a leading transnational commercial law scholar, Professor Norbert Horn:

> International customary law, on the other hand, is only of limited assistance in solving legal problems of international commerce. There are few legal principles, such as *pacta sunt servanda*, which are generally recognised and can be termed international customary law. It is true that the general principles of customary law provide common ground for lawyers from civil law and common law countries. But these principles are difficult to apply in specific cases, and courts in various countries have been extremely reluctant to resort to rules of international customary law when deciding issues involving private contracts.[17]

3.23 The requirement of *opinio juris* remains controversial. Some see it as creating a paradox. If the belief that the practice is legally binding is correct, it is unnecessary, whilst if the belief is incorrect, it seems a strange basis for a legal rule. Moreover, how could a new customary rule develop? These difficulties have led several commentators to suggest that *opinio juris* is not an essential element at all. Others point out that it is necessary to introduce some subjective element in order to exclude practice observed for convenience or out of courtesy or for some other reason unconnected with legal obligation. Proponents of this latter view argue

---

[15] *Barcelona Traction, Light and Power Case (Belgium v Spain)* (1970) ICJ Rep 3, [55] and following. See generally: Malcolm N Shaw, *International Law* (5th edn, CUP, Cambridge, 2003) 92 and following. [16] Para 3.19.

[17] Horn, Norbert, 'Uniformity and Diversity in the Law of International Commercial Contracts' in Horn, Norbert and Schmitthoff, Clive M, *The Transnational Law of International Commercial Transactions* (Kluwer, Deventer, 1982) 14–15.

that it is the acceptance of the binding nature of the practice that is the element that makes it binding, so that the question of correctness of the belief simply does not arise. Perhaps the basis for a new customary rule could be an *intention* that it should be binding, rather than a *belief* in a current status quo which *ex hypothesi* does not exist. Thus, the subjective element would look forward, not backward.

Michael Akehurst, 'Custom as a Source of International Law'
(1974–5) 47 BYIL 1, 31–7

IV. *OPINIO JURIS*

The traditional approach

Practice on its own is not enough to create a rule of customary law; it must be accompanied by evidence of *opinio juris*. The traditional approach to *opinio juris* was well summarized by the International Court in the *North Sea Continental Shelf* cases, where it said that the acts constituting the practice in question

> ... must also be such, or be carried out in such a way, as to be evidence of a belief that this practice is rendered obligatory by the existence of a rule of law requiring it ... The states concerned must therefore feel that they are conforming to what amounts to a legal obligation. The frequency, or even habitual character of the acts, is not in itself enough. There are many international acts, e.g. in the field of ceremonial and protocol, which are performed almost invariably, but which are motivated only by considerations of courtesy, convenience or tradition, and not by any sense of legal duty.

Statements of the same approach are found in other judgments of the Court and of its predecessor, the Permanent Court of International Justice. Moreover, Article 38 (1)(b) of the Court's Statute, by providing that practice must be 'accepted as law', seems to require *opinio juris*, although it leaves the meaning of *opinio juris* uncertain.

However, the traditional approach gives rise to difficulties. It seems to require that states must believe that something is *already* law before it can *become* law. Such a belief is by definition mistaken, and, although such mistakes are possible, they are likely to be rare. It is stretching credulity to suggest that all the many rules of customary law existing today originated on the basis of such mistakes. Moreover, such an approach leaves no room for the *deliberate* creation of new rules to meet new needs, in the future.

It is not surprising, therefore, that various attempts have been made to reformulate the requirement of *opinio juris*, in order to escape from the difficulties caused by the traditional approach.

Writers denying or minimizing the need for opinio juris

The most radical approach is a denial of any requirement of *opinio juris*. In many cases courts have concluded from an examination of practice that a rule of customary law exists, without requiring or finding any evidence of *opinio juris*. However, such cases may simply represent an elision in judicial reasoning; although there are many cases which do not mention *opinio juris*, there are none which say expressly that it is unnecessary.

Besides, there are many judgments of the Permanent Court of International Justice and of the International Court of Justice affirming the need for *opinio juris*. (These cases are not merely *obiter dicta:* the absence of *opinio juris* was fatal to the French claim in the *Lotus* case, and to the Netherlands and Danish claim in the *North Sea Continental Shelf* cases.)

Some writers conclude that the cases conflict, and that the judge has an unfettered discretion to insist on, or dispense with, the requirement of *opinio juris*. But such an approach is useless as a means of *predicting* how the judge will decide a case, nor does it provide any solution for cases which never come to court (such cases are even more frequent in international law than in municipal legal systems, because states are often reluctant to accept the jurisdiction of international courts).

International law, like all legal systems, contains permissive rules as well as rules imposing obligations. If states habitually act in a particular way (e.g. by writing to one another on white paper), is this because international law requires them so to act, or because international law merely permits them so to act? The frequency or consistency of the practice provides no answer to this question; *opinio juris* alone can provide the answer. Moreover, *opinio juris* is also needed in order to distinguish legal obligations from non-legal obligations, such as obligations derived from considerations of morality, courtesy or comity.

If *opinio juris* is abandoned, some other criterion for making such distinctions will be needed to take its place. Most authors who seek to eliminate *opinio juris*, in whole or in part, do not face this problem, although Quadri is an exception. He suggests that the difference between customary law and comity is based on the relative importance of the issue involved—*de minimis non curat lex*. This would explain why there is no rule of law requiring states to use white paper; but it does not explain why the enforcement of foreign judgments, which is important enough to merit the conclusion of treaties, is not important enough to be regulated by customary law. Nor does Quadri's criterion provide any means of distinguishing between permissive rules of law and rules of law imposing duties.

Some authors argue that consistent practice should be regarded as giving rise to a rule of law imposing a duty, in the absence of indications that the practice was not intended to be legally obligatory; instead of looking for *opinio juris*, a court should look for *opinio non-juris*. States do sometimes do things while denying that they are under any legal obligation to do so, as when they pay compensation *ex gratia*. But such disclaimers are often not made. For instance, so far as the present author is aware, no state has ever said that it is *not* under a duty to use white paper for its diplomatic correspondence. A theory which is liable to force us to treat as legally obligatory a practice like that, which we all know instinctively not to be legally obligatory, is obviously unsound.

Opinio juris *as the consciousness of moral or social needs*

The weakness of the traditional theory of *opinio juris* is that it appears to require that states should regard conduct as obligatory before it can become obligatory. One way round this difficulty has been suggested by a number of writers who define *opinio juris* as a belief that conduct is required by some extralegal norm; such a belief, coupled with practice, creates a rule of customary law ...

Of course many customary rules reflect prevailing ideas of justice and social needs, but the overlap is not nearly as complete as the theories mentioned in the previous paragraph would seem to require. Practice accompanied by a sense of moral or social obligation does not always create a rule of customary law. The immorality of aggressive war was recognized centuries before its illegality. Most, if not all, developed countries give aid to poorer countries and would probably admit that they have a moral obligation to do so, but how many of them recognize a legal obligation to give aid? Conversely, there are many illogical distinctions and exceptions in customary law which have grown up for historical reasons, but which cannot be regarded as a response to moral or social needs ...

The International Court has emphasized that moral considerations do not necessarily produce rules of law. In the *South West Africa* case the Court said:

> Throughout this case it has been suggested ... that humanitarian considerations are sufficient in themselves to generate legal rights and obligations ... The Court does not think so. It is a court of law, and can take account of moral principles only in so far as these are given a sufficient expression in legal forms.

Similarly, in the *Haya de la Torre* case the Court drew a distinction between legal obligations and considerations of courtesy and good neighbourliness.

D'Amato's theory of articulation

Professor D'Amato substitutes for *opinio juris* the requirement that the practice in question must be preceded or accompanied by the 'articulation' of a rule of customary law. 'The articulation of a rule of international law ... in advance of or concurrently with a positive act (or omission) of a state gives a state notice that its action or decision will have legal implications. In other words, given such notice, statesmen will be able freely to decide whether or not to pursue various policies, knowing that their acts may create or modify international law. The absence of prior notification that acts or abstentions have legal consequences is an effective barrier to the extrapolation of legal norms from patterns of conduct that are noticed ex post facto.' A rule can be articulated by a state, a court, an international organization or a writer, provided it receives sufficient publicity for states to have actual or constructive notice of it.

D' Amato says that 'a single writer or a single state may effectively articulate a new rule of international law', provided that there is no articulation of a conflicting rule; where a conflicting rule has been articulated, the rule which has been articulated more often will prevail. At first sight this echoes his views about the quantity of practice needed to establish a customary rule, but it is open to suspicion. For instance, when Japan adopted the western calendar in 1872, she said she was doing so in response to a duty imposed by international law. So far as the present author is aware, no state has ever articulated the view that the western calendar is permitted but not required by international law: that view has been taken for granted, but never stated expressly. On D'Amato's reasoning, all states which have used the western calendar since 1872 have been confirming a rule of international law making such use obligatory—which is manifestly absurd. In order to establish a rule of customary law requiring particular conduct, it is not necessary to prove that all or even most of the instances of such conduct have been accompanied by acknowledgments of its obligatory character; but the view that such conduct is required (and not merely permitted) does become questionable when the instances of such conduct infinitely outnumber statements that it is obligatory.

Statements, not beliefs

Yet, although D'Amato's theory can be criticized on matters of detail, it does recognize the essential truth that what matters is statements, not beliefs. Practice creates a rule of customary law that particular conduct is obligatory, if it is accompanied by statements on the part of states that such conduct is obligatory.

This is not really very different from the traditional view of *opinio juris*. The traditional view seeks evidence of what states believe; the present author prefers to look for statements of belief by states. The similarity between the two views is worth stressing; the traditional view is open to objections, but the judicial support for the traditional view is so strong that the traditional view ought not to be modified except to the minimum degree necessary to meet these objections.

**Michael Byers, *Custom, Power and the Power of Rules* (CUP, Cambridge 1999)
130–31 and 148**

Most international lawyers agree that customary international law results from the co-existence of two elements: first, the presence of a consistent and general practice among states; and, secondly, a consideration on the part of those states that their practice is in accordance with law. The second, subjective element is usually referred to as *opinio juris sive necessitates*, or simply *opinio juris*. It is clear that something in addition to state practice should be necessary for customary international law, for it is essential that one should be able to distinguish between legally binding rules and patterns of behaviour which are not legally required. Yet there are many problems associated with *opinio juris* and the traditional bipartite concept of customary international law ...

The chronological paradox

One problem with the traditional bipartite conception of customary international law is that it involves the apparent chronological paradox that states creating new customary rules must believe that those rules already exist, and that their practice, therefore, *is* in accordance with law ... This requirement would seem to make it impossible for new customary rules to develop, since *opinio juris* would only exist in respect of those rules which were *already* in force ... Although traditional theories reply on *opinio juris* to distinguish state practice which is relevant to the customary process from state practice which is not, writers advocating those theories have had difficulty explaining the character of *opinio juris* and in identifying this second element of customary international law. However, if the customary process is understood as involving a 'collective knowledge' or set of shared understandings, *opinio juris* may then be understood as being those shared understandings which enable states to distinguish between legally relevant and legally irrelevant state practice.

**International Law Association, Committee on Formation of Customary (General)
International Law: Final Report, *Statement of Principles Applicable to the
Formation of General Customary International Law* (International Law
Association, London, 2000) section 1(iii)**

Where a rule of general customary international law exists, for any particular state to be bound by that rule it is not necessary to prove either that state's consent to it or its belief in the rule's obligatory or (as the case may be) permissive character.

3.24   The practice which gives rise to a rule of international customary law may itself be generated by 'statements' in normative form in a treaty or declaration, negotiated by consensus, which in influencing State practice create new rules of customary international law.

3.25   Others issues of customary international law are capable of arising in the same way in the context of international trade usage. What kinds of act are relevant? How settled and consistent must the practice be in order to constitute a binding usage? Must the practice be adopted universally and, if not, who are to be considered the relevant players and how many must there be? Must they act with a common intention, or are uncoordinated acts which embody the same practice sufficient? Can a party refuse to be bound by the practice? It is beyond the scope of this work to explore these questions in relation to international law.[18] We simply draw attention to the fact that similar questions have to be addressed in determining whether the practice of merchants has given rise to a binding international trade usage.

Treaty law

The principal source of treaty law is the Vienna Convention on Treaties 1969, **3.26** Article 2(1)(a) of which defines a treaty (though for the purposes of the Convention only) as:

> an international agreement between states in written form and governed by international law, whether embodied in a single instrument or in two or more related instruments and whatever its particular designation.

The word 'treaty' is a generic term covering all forms of agreement within the above **3.27** definition, including international conventions. Treaties or conventions may be bilateral or multilateral. We are concerned only with multilateral private commercial law conventions open to all States.

Despite the above definition, the treaty-making power is not confined to States: it **3.28** extends to international organizations so far as conferred, expressly or impliedly, by the relevant rules of the organization in question.[19] Examples of such international organizations are the specialized agencies of the United Nations, the European Community and, more recently, the European Union, and the World Trade Organization. New international organizations with treaty-making powers may always be created by or under the authority of a State or an association of States or by a treaty between States. But international organizations, though possessing legal personality, do not on that account alone enjoy the power to conclude treaties: that power must either be found, expressly or by implication from functional necessity, in their constitutive documents or must evolve from subsequent practice. Thus, the Cape Town Convention, in establishing a Supervisory Authority to set up and supervise the International Registry, provides that it is to have international legal personality so far as not already possessing it.[20] However, its functions are very limited, and while it may enter into any agreement requisite

---

[18] For a valuable and wide-ranging, if in some respects controversial, review, see the Final Report of the International Law Association's Committee on Formation of Customary (General) International Law, *Statement of Principles Applicable to the Formation of General Customary International Law* (International Law Association, London 2000) endorsing the analysis of its chairman Professor Maurice Mendelson in his Hague Academy lectures, reproduced in 'The Formation of Customary International Law' (1998) 272 Recueil des cours 155.

[19] Vienna Convention on treaties concluded between states and international organisations in 1986.

[20] Art 27(1). At the time of conclusion of the convention it was envisaged that the Supervisory Authority would be the International Civil Aviation Organisation, which already possesses international legal personality, but at that time ICAO had not accepted the position of Supervisory Authority. It has done so since.

for the performance of its functions, including any agreement with its host State governing exemption from taxes and other privileges,[21] it has no general power to conclude international agreements.

3.29 International organizations of different kinds have assumed great importance in recent years, and some of them have acquired by transfer or delegation from States extensive, even sovereign, powers and immunities, raising concerns as to their accountability.[22]

3.30 The fundamental principle of treaty law is that a treaty binds only those who become parties to it,[23] usually by ratification or accession,[24] followed by fulfillment of the conditions necessary for entry of the treaty into force if it is not already in force prior to or as the result of the ratification. A State party becomes bound to perform in good faith the obligations imposed on it once the treaty has come into force: *pacta sunt servanda*. Though in general States not party to a treaty ('third States') are not bound by it, there are certain exceptions. For example, a third State may become bound by a treaty the provisions of which it accepts in accordance with Articles 35 and 36 of the Vienna Convention, and on this basis there are certain types of treaty which potentially confer rights and impose obligations *erga omnes*, though this is not true of any of the conventions discussed in the present work. Moreover, non-parties not bound by the treaty itself will nevertheless have to comply with any rules of customary law codified by the treaty.

3.31 Treaty law is a complex subject to which major texts have been devoted. We shall confine ourselves to examining it in the context of the structure, general provisions and selected final clauses of some of the conventions discussed in this book. There will be a particular focus on the 2001 Cape Town Convention on International Interests in Mobile Equipment, which raises most of the public international law issues likely to arise from a private commercial law convention, including the means by which a private party to a transaction governed by an international convention can seek redress for a State's breach of its obligations under that convention where the breach impairs that party's ability to enforce its rights under the convention against another party to the transaction.

---

[21] Cape Town Convention 2001 arts 17(3) and 27(3).

[22] See Dan Sarooshi, *International Organizations and their Exercise of Sovereign Powers* (OUP, Oxford, 2005); Final Report of the Committee on Accountability of International Organisations of the International Law Association, *Report of the 71st Conference* (International Law Association, London 2004) 164, which includes a detailed discussion of remedies against IOs and recommends, for example, that disputes arising out of contracts between private persons and IOs should be settled by an independent body such as an arbitral tribunal set up in accordance with the rules of a permanent institution. [23] Vienna Treaty Art 34.

[24] Ratification is confined to States who have signed the Convention; others accede. For brevity future references are to ratification and ratifying states. A ratifying state is termed a 'Contracting State'; once the treaty has come into force (if not already in force at the time of or consequent on the ratification) the ratifying state becomes a 'State Party'.

B. The Typical Structure of Private Law Conventions

Most private law conventions in the field of transnational commercial law are **3.32** structured in the following way.

Preamble

First, there is a preamble which sets out the purpose of the convention, the advan- **3.33** tages it is expected to bring and the fact that the States involved have agreed on the ensuing text. Drafting of the preamble is best left till after the substantive provisions have been agreed. There is a tendency to treat the preamble as unimportant and even to omit it altogether in compilations of international conventions. This is unfortunate, because much care may be devoted to the exact wording of the preamble at the Diplomatic Conference, and it may be a helpful guide to interpretation of the convention. In addition, it gives the States involved an opportunity to convey a political message. In international conventions, the preamble is usually quite short. Here are some examples. For further examples, see below, paras 19.07–08.

Vienna Convention on Contracts for the International Sale of Goods 1980

The States Parties to this Convention,

Bearing in mind the broad objectives in the resolutions adopted by the sixth special session of the General Assembly of the United Nations on the establishment of a New International Economic Order,

Considering that the development of international trade on the basis of equality and mutual benefit is an important element in promoting friendly relations among States,

Being of the opinion that the adoption of uniform rules which govern contracts for the international sale of goods and take into account the different social, economic and legal systems would contribute to the removal of legal barriers in international trade and promote the development of international trade,

Have agreed as follows:

UNIDROIT Convention on International Financial Leasing 1988

THE STATES PARTIES TO THIS CONVENTION,

RECOGNISING the importance of removing certain legal impediments to the international financial leasing of equipment, while maintaining a fair balance of interests between the different parties to the transaction,

AWARE of the need to make international financial leasing more available,

CONSCIOUS of the fact that the rules of law governing the traditional contract of hire need to be adapted to the distinctive triangular relationship created by the financial leasing transaction,

RECOGNISING therefore the desirability of formulating certain uniform rules relating primarily to the civil and commercial law aspects of international financial leasing,

HAVE AGREED as follows:

Convention on International Interests in Mobile Equipment 2001

THE STATES PARTIES TO THIS CONVENTION,

AWARE of the need to acquire and use mobile equipment of high value or particular economic significance and to facilitate the financing of the acquisition and use of such equipment in an efficient manner,

RECOGNISING the advantages of asset-based financing and leasing for this purpose and desiring to facilitate these types of transaction by establishing clear rules to govern them,

MINDFUL of the need to ensure that interests in such equipment are recognised and protected universally,

DESIRING to provide broad and mutual economic benefits for all interested parties,

BELIEVING that such rules must reflect the principles underlying asset-based financing and leasing and promote the autonomy of the parties necessary in these transactions,

CONSCIOUS of the need to establish a legal framework for international interests in such equipment and for that purpose to create an international registration system for their protection,

TAKING INTO CONSIDERATION the objectives and principles enunciated in existing Conventions relating to such equipment,

HAVE AGREED upon the following provisions:

3.34   To be contrasted with these is the style of European Community legislation, where the preamble usually runs to several pages. Here is one of the shorter examples.

COUNCIL DIRECTIVE 93/13/EEC of 5 April 1993 on unfair terms in consumer contracts

THE COUNCIL OF THE EUROPEAN COMMUNITIES,

Having regard to the Treaty establishing the European Economic Community, and in particular Article 100 A thereof,

Having regard to the proposal from the Commission,

In cooperation with the European Parliament,

Having regard to the opinion of the Economic and Social Committee,

Whereas it is necessary to adopt measures with the aim of progressively establishing the internal market before 31 December 1992; whereas the internal market comprises an area without internal frontiers in which goods, persons, services and capital move freely;

Whereas the laws of Member States relating to the terms of contract between the seller of goods or supplier of services, on the one hand, and the consumer of them, on the other hand, show many disparities, with the result that the national markets for the sale of goods and services to consumers differ from each other and that distortions of competition may arise amongst the sellers and suppliers, notably when they sell and supply in other Member States;

Whereas, in particular, the laws of Member States relating to unfair terms in consumer contracts show marked divergences;

Whereas it is the responsibility of the Member States to ensure that contracts concluded with consumers do not contain unfair terms;

Whereas, generally speaking, consumers do not know the rules of law which, in Member States other than their own, govern contracts for the sale of goods or services; whereas this lack of awareness may deter them from direct transactions for the purchase of goods or services in another Member State;

Whereas, in order to facilitate the establishment of the internal market and to safeguard the citizen in his role as consumer when acquiring goods and services under contracts which are governed by the laws of Member States other than his own, it is essential to remove unfair terms from those contracts;

Whereas sellers of goods and suppliers of services will thereby be helped in their task of selling goods and supplying services, both at home and throughout the internal market; whereas competition will thus be stimulated, so contributing to increased choice for Community citizens as consumers;

Whereas the two Community programmes for a consumer protection and information policy underlined the importance of safeguarding consumers in the matter of unfair terms of contract; whereas this protection ought to be provided by laws and regulations which are either harmonized at Community level or adopted directly at that level;

Whereas in accordance with the principle laid down under the heading 'Protection of the economic interests of the consumers', as stated in those programmes: 'acquirers of goods and services should be protected against the abuse of power by the seller or supplier, in particular against one-sided standard contracts and the unfair exclusion of essential rights in contracts';

Whereas more effective protection of the consumer can be achieved by adopting uniform rules of law in the matter of unfair terms; whereas those rules should apply to all contracts concluded between sellers or suppliers and consumers; whereas as a result inter alia contracts relating to employment, contracts relating to succession rights, contracts relating to rights under family law and contracts relating to the incorporation and organization of companies or partnership agreements must be excluded from this Directive;

Whereas the consumer must receive equal protection under contracts concluded by word of mouth and written contracts regardless, in the latter case, of whether the terms of the contract are contained in one or more documents;

Whereas, however, as they now stand, national laws allow only partial harmonization to be envisaged; whereas, in particular, only contractual terms which have not been individually negotiated are covered by this Directive; whereas Member States should have the option, with due regard for the Treaty, to afford consumers a higher level of protection through national provisions that are more stringent than those of this Directive;

Whereas the statutory or regulatory provisions of the Member States which directly or indirectly determine the terms of consumer contracts are presumed not to contain unfair terms; whereas, therefore, it does not appear to be necessary to subject the terms which reflect mandatory statutory or regulatory provisions and the principles or provisions of international conventions to which the Member States or the Community are party; whereas in that respect the wording 'mandatory statutory or regulatory provisions' in Article 1(2) also covers rules which, according to the law, shall apply between the contracting parties provided that no other arrangements have been established;

Whereas Member States must however ensure that unfair terms are not included, particularly because this Directive also applies to trades, business or professions of a public nature;

Whereas it is necessary to fix in a general way the criteria for assessing the unfair character of contract terms;

Whereas the assessment, according to the general criteria chosen, of the unfair character of terms, in particular in sale or supply activities of a public nature providing collective services which take account of solidarity among users, must be supplemented by a means of making an overall evaluation of the different interests involved; whereas this constitutes the requirement of good faith; whereas, in making an assessment of good faith, particular regard shall be had to the strength of the bargaining positions of the parties, whether the consumer had an inducement to agree to the term and whether the goods or services were sold or supplied to the special order of the consumer; whereas the requirement of good faith may be satisfied by the seller or supplier where he deals fairly and equitably with the other party whose legitimate interests he has to take into account;

Whereas, for the purposes of this Directive, the annexed list of terms can be of indicative value only and, because of the cause of the minimal character of the Directive, the scope of these terms may be the subject of amplification or more restrictive editing by the Member States in their national laws;

Whereas the nature of goods or services should have an influence on assessing the unfairness of contractual terms;

Whereas, for the purposes of this Directive, assessment of unfair character shall not be made of terms which describe the main subject matter of the contract nor the quality/price ratio of the goods or services supplied; whereas the main subject matter of the contract and the price/quality ratio may nevertheless be taken into account in assessing the fairness of other terms; whereas it follows, inter alia, that in insurance contracts, the terms which clearly define or circumscribe the insured risk and the insurer's liability shall not be subject to such assessment since these restrictions are taken into account in calculating the premium paid by the consumer;

Whereas contracts should be drafted in plain, intelligible language, the consumer should actually be given an opportunity to examine all the terms and, if in doubt, the interpretation most favourable to the consumer should prevail;

Whereas Member States should ensure that unfair terms are not used in contracts concluded with consumers by a seller or supplier and that if, nevertheless, such terms are so used, they will not bind the consumer, and the contract will continue to bind the parties upon those terms if it is capable of continuing in existence without the unfair provisions;

Whereas there is a risk that, in certain cases, the consumer may be deprived of protection under this Directive by designating the law of a non-Member country as the law applicable to the contract; whereas provisions should therefore be included in this Directive designed to avert this risk;

Whereas persons or organizations, if regarded under the law of a Member State as having a legitimate interest in the matter, must have facilities for initiating proceedings concerning terms of contract drawn up for general use in contracts concluded with consumers, and in particular unfair terms, either before a court or before an administrative authority competent to decide upon complaints or to initiate appropriate legal proceedings; whereas this possibility does not, however, entail prior verification of the general conditions obtaining in individual economic sectors;

Whereas the courts or administrative authorities of the Member States must have at their disposal adequate and effective means of preventing the continued application of unfair terms in consumer contracts,

HAS ADOPTED THIS DIRECTIVE:

This is pretty long compared with the preamble in international conventions. **3.35** Even so, it is one of the shorter European Community instruments. For instance, the EC Insolvency Regulation has thirty-three recitals and is nearly twice as long.[25] The preamble is used in EC instruments to lay the foundation for each of the operative articles in the body of the instrument, and its length reflects the much greater importance attached to it. Indeed, the preamble often goes beyond the substantive articles, so that the answers to various questions are to be found only in the recitals. An example is the meaning of 'centre of main interests' in the Insolvency Regulation, which features only in the preamble and is nowhere defined in the body of the text.

Body of the Convention

After the preamble comes the body of the convention. This is usually divided into **3.36** chapters, which in turn are divided into articles each consisting of one or more paragraphs. Nowadays, it is customary to have headings not only for chapters, but also for individual articles so as to indicate their subject matter, though the latter is not invariable.

Sphere of application and general provisions

The first part of any commercial law convention is devoted to such matters as the **3.37** sphere of application, definitions, and other general provisions. A common approach is to begin by defining the types of transaction covered and excluded, and then follow with the test of internationality where (as is usual) the convention is to be confined to cross-border transactions, the connecting factor (that is, the required link to a Contracting State) and an interpretation provision, which usually takes its inspiration from Article 7 of the Vienna Convention on Contracts for the International Sale of Goods.

UNIDROIT Convention on International Factoring 1988

CHAPTER I—SPHERE OF APPLICATION AND GENERAL PROVISIONS

> *Article 1*
> 1. This Convention governs factoring contracts and assignments of receivables as described in this Chapter.

---

[25] See below, paras 15.24 ff.

2. For the purposes of this Convention, 'factoring contract' means a contract concluded between one party (the supplier) and another party (the factor) pursuant to which:

   (a) the supplier may or will assign to the factor receivables arising from contracts of sale of goods made between the supplier and its customers (debtors) other than those for the sale of goods bought primarily for their personal, family or household use;

   (b) the factor is to perform at least two of the following functions:
       – finance for the supplier, including loans and advance payments;
       – maintenance of accounts (ledgering) relating to the receivables;
       – collection of receivables;
       – protection against default in payment by debtors;

   (c) notice of the assignment of the receivables is to be given to debtors.

3. In this Convention references to 'goods' and 'sale of goods' shall include services and the supply of services.

4. For the purposes of this Convention:

   (a) a notice in writing need not be signed but must identify the person by whom or in whose name it is given;

   (b) 'notice in writing' includes, but is not limited to, telegrams, telex and any other telecommunication capable of being reproduced in tangible form;

   (c) a notice in writing is given when it is received by the addressee.

Article 2

1. This Convention applies whenever the receivables assigned pursuant to a factoring contract arise from a contract of sale of goods between a supplier and a debtor whose places of business are in different States and:

   (a) those States and the State in which the factor has its place of business are Contracting States; or

   (b) both the contract of sale of goods and the factoring contract are governed by the law of a Contracting State.

2. A reference in this Convention to a party's place of business shall, if it has more than one place of business, mean the place of business which has the closest relationship to the relevant contract and its performance, having regard to the circumstances known to or contemplated by the parties at any time before or at the conclusion of that contract.

Article 3

1. The application of this Convention may be excluded:

   (a) by the parties to the factoring contract; or

   (b) by the parties to the contract of sale of goods, as regards receivables arising at or after the time when the factor has been given notice in writing of such exclusion.

2. Where the application of this Convention is excluded in accordance with the previous paragraph, such exclusion may be made only as regards the Convention as a whole.

3.38 Most commercial law conventions are confined to cross-border transactions—typically defined by reference to the fact that the parties concerned have their places of business in different States—and exclude agreements for goods or services acquired primarily for personal, family or household use. This negative formulation, rather than a positive limitation to business-to-business transactions, is designed to avoid doubt as to the status of agreements entered into by embassies, charities and other bodies not primarily engaged in business. Interestingly, the Cape Town Convention has no provision directly excluding consumer agreements, but in practice the classes of objects covered in the convention and the further limitations imposed by the protocol will almost invariably have the effect of excluding consumer transactions. In his work on comparative law, Gutteridge, writing in 1949, records that the English practice of inserting definitions in Acts of Parliament is viewed with disfavour on the Continent.[26] But times change. The Cape Town Convention and Aircraft Protocol provide striking examples, the Convention containing no fewer than forty definitions, while the Protocol adds a further sixteen definitions. Moreover, these are not relegated to obscurity at the end of the instruments but in both cases are boldly listed in the very first article.

Substantive rules

The second and central part of the convention is devoted to substantive rules lay- **3.39** ing down the rights, duties, liabilities and immunities of the relevant parties. In commercial law conventions, great importance is attached to party autonomy, so that there is almost always a provision allowing the parties, in the relations between themselves, to exclude, add to or vary the convention except as regards certain mandatory rules which cannot be excluded by agreement, though even these may effectively be disapplied by the parties' choice of the law of a non-Contracting State to govern their agreement.

The Cape Town Convention on international interests in mobile equipment is **3.40** unusual in combining public law with private law provisions. So in addition to dealing with various kinds of interest, rights of parties to agreements, priority rules governing competing interests and assignments of rights, it contains provisions for access to speedy interim judicial relief, the establishment of an International Registry and the functions of a Supervisory Authority and a Registrar, as well as providing Contracting States with a range of options exercisable by deposit of a declaration with UNIDROIT as the depositary. These provisions raise some interesting questions of public international law which we will come to later.

Final clauses

The last part of the convention consists of the final clauses, usually drafted by **3.41** a final clauses committee, whose draft is then referred back to the drafting

---

[26] HC Gutteridge, *Comparative Law* (2nd edn CUP, Cambridge, 1949) 182.

committee or alternatively directly to the Committee of the Whole.[27] Final clauses are often treated as rather boring boiler-plate, but they are very important because they embrace a range of matters covering entry into force, amendments, withdrawals, revision of the convention, denunciation by a State, reservations, and the like, and may also include matters which are far from boiler-plate, such as transitional provisions, the treatment of pre-existing rights, and the like. They therefore deserve careful attention. The final clauses of the Cape Town Convention merit particular mention because they include some unusual provisions, particularly on regional economic integration organizations, internal transactions, declarations and transitional provisions.[28]

3.42 In general, a Convention enters into force on some designated date after deposit of the last instrument of ratification required to bring the number of ratifications up to that specified in the Convention. In the case of the Cape Town Convention, three ratifications were required for the Convention other than those provisions (the great majority) relating to objects covered by the Aircraft Protocol, for which eight ratifications were required.

3.43 Certain technical provisions in a treaty 'regulating matters arising necessarily before the entry into force of the treaty' apply from the time of adoption of the treaty.[29] These include provisions regarding the authentication of the text, ratification and declaration procedures, and the functions of the depositary. In the case of the Cape Town Convention, it was also necessary to be able to take steps to set up the International Registry, since this had to be in place before the Convention and Protocol came into force. This was dealt with by a Provision in Resolution No 2 to set up a Preparatory Commission to act with full authority as Provisional Supervisory Authority pending entry into force of the Convention and Protocol.

3.44 The Diplomatic Conference for the Cape Town Convention is distinctive for the range of devices employed to achieve different objectives: the two instruments themselves; the Final Act, to record the agreement on linguistic alignment; and the Resolutions, to prepare the way for entry into force. One further device may be mentioned. The Diplomatic Conference was anxious to ensure that in case of conflict between the assignment provisions of the Convention and the then forthcoming United Nations Convention on the assignment of receivables in international trade the Cape Town Convention should have priority. This could readily have been assured if, as had been expected, the United Nations Convention had been concluded first. In fact, it was not concluded until the following month, and although by inference it subordinated itself to the Cape Town Convention it was felt desirable to make the position crystal clear. This was achieved by another

---

[27] See further ch 6.
[28] See above, para 3.15 as to regional economic integration organisations and below, paras 12.50 ff as to the declaration system in the Cape Town Convention.   [29] Art 24(4).

device, an Annex approved by the Conference, which provided that after deposit of the UN Convention with the Secretary-General of the UN a new Article 45 *bis* should be inserted into the Cape Town Convention to the effect that the latter is to prevail as it relates to the assignment of receivables which are associated rights related to international interests in aircraft objects, rolling stock and space assets.[30]

Finally, mention must be made of the role of the depositary, that is, the State or **3.45** international organization having custody of the original convention. The functions of the depositary are set out in Article 77 of the Vienna Convention 1969 and are often supplemented by provisions of the particular convention itself. They are 'international in nature', and, above all, the depositary has an obligation to 'act impartially' (that issue being more acute if it is a State).[31] Its particular duties generally relate to:

(a) custody of documents relating to the treaty and the participation therein of States parties;
(b) checking each instrument of ratification or accession to ensure that it is in conformity with the convention;
(c) notifications of these to other States which are entitled to become parties to the convention; and,
(d) registration and publication of the treaty.[32]

A depositary also has certain responsibilities regarding the correction of errors **3.46** after authentication of the text.[33] The duties imposed on the depositary of the Cape Town Convention by UNIDROIT, are particularly onerous because of the Convention's complex system of declarations, on which UNIDROIT has issued an explanatory memorandum with thirty-six specimen forms of declaration, one of which, under Article 54(2), is mandatory, whereas the others are permissive.

C. Interpretation of Conventions

In interpreting a Convention, it is necessary to apply any rules of interpretation laid **3.47** down in the Convention itself. Even without such rules, a Convention must be interpreted autonomously in the light of its international character: it is not permissible to resort to rules of interpretation laid down in domestic law, nor should it be assumed that a term in a Convention has the same meaning as it would in domestic law. For example, several provisions of the 1980 UN Convention on Contracts for the International Sale of Goods (CISG) refer to 'breach of contract', which in common law systems means an *unexcused* non-performance and, thus, does not cover a non-performance induced by frustration or by the other party's own breach of duty,

---

[30] As to 'associated rights' see para 12.48.   [31] Art 76(2).   [32] Arts 77 and 80.
[33] Art 78.

whereas it is clear from Article 79 of the Convention that for the purposes of the Convention *any* non-performance is characterized as a breach of contract, though if it falls within Article 79 there is no liability to pay damages.[34] We examine the principle of autonomous interpretation in more detail in chapter 19.

Interpretation under the Vienna Convention on Treaties, 1969

SECTION 3. INTERPRETATION OF TREATIES

Article 31

General rule of interpretation

1. A treaty shall be interpreted in good faith in accordance with the ordinary meaning to be given to the terms of the treaty in their context and in the light of its object and purpose.
2. The context for the purpose of the interpretation of a treaty shall comprise, in addition to the text, including its preamble and annexes:
    (a) any agreement relating to the treaty which was made between all the parties in connection with the conclusion of the treaty;
    (b) any instrument which was made by one or more parties in connection with the conclusion of the treaty and accepted by the other parties as an instrument related to the treaty.
3. There shall be taken into account, together with the context:
    (a) any subsequent agreement between the parties regarding the interpretation of the treaty or the application of its provisions;
    (b) any subsequent practice in the application of the treaty which establishes the agreement of the parties regarding its interpretation;
    (c) any relevant rules of international law applicable in the relations between the parties.
4. A special meaning shall be given to a term if it is established that the parties so intended.

Supplementary means of interpretation

Recourse may be had to supplementary means of interpretation, including the preparatory work of the treaty and the circumstances of its conclusion, in order to confirm the meaning resulting from the application of Article 31, or to determine the meaning when the interpretation according to Article 31:

(a) leaves the meaning ambiguous or obscure; or
(b) leads to a result which is manifestly absurd or unreasonable.

Article 33

Interpretation of treaties authenticated in two or more languages

1. When a treaty has been authenticated in two or more languages, the text is equally authoritative in each language, unless the treaty provides or the parties agree that, in case of divergence, a particular text shall prevail.

---

[34] See further para 7.81.

2. A version of the treaty in a language other than one of those in which the text was authenticated shall be considered an authentic text only if the treaty so provides or the parties so agree.

3. The terms of the treaty are presumed to have the same meaning in each authentic text.

4. Except where a particular text prevails in accordance with paragraph 1, when a comparison of the authentic texts discloses a difference of meaning which the application of Articles 31 and 32 does not remove, the meaning which best reconciles the texts, having regard to the object and purpose of the treaty, shall be adopted.

Thus, the general rule of treaty interpretation set out in the Vienna Convention is **3.48** that a treaty shall be interpreted in good faith 'in accordance with the ordinary meaning to be given to the terms of the treaty in their context and in the light of its object and purpose'. This is a single rule with three elements: the text (provisions), context (including preamble and annexes and other materials surrounding the conclusion of the treaty, such as agreements in a final act),[35] and objects and purpose (often seen in the preamble as well). In addition to context, subsequent agreements on the interpretation of the treaty or the application of its provisions and any subsequent practice in the application of the treaty which establishes the agreement of the parties regarding its interpretation) must also be taken into account.[36]

The *travaux préparatoires* constitute an essential tool of the interpretive process. **3.49** Of course, there are many provisions that can be readily understood without them, but there will usually be at least some provisions so carefully nuanced that without the *travaux préparatoires* even the most skilled lawyer is liable to misunderstand them if he or she took no part in the preparatory work or the Conference proceedings. So Article 32 of the Vienna Convention permits recourse to the *travaux préparatoires* in order to confirm the meaning resulting from the application of Article 31 or to determine the meaning when the interpretation according to Article 31 leaves the meaning ambiguous or obscure or leads to a result which is manifestly absurd or unreasonable.

Just as resort may be made to the preparatory work to interpret a convention, so **3.50** also under Article 31(3) the meaning of a Convention provision may be gleaned from subsequent agreement or practice or, under Article 31(3)(c), by reference to 'any relevant rules of international law applicable in the relations between the parties'. This provision, which until very recently 'languished in obscurity',[37] has become invigorated by decisions of the International Court of Justice and other international tribunals in demonstrating that treaties are, in appropriate cases, to

---

[35] Art 31(2). Also included are instruments made by one State-party at the conclusion of the treaty and accepted by the others.   [36] Art 31(3).
[37] Campbell McLachlan, 'The Principle of System Integration and Article 31(3)(C) of the Vienna Convention' (2005) 54 ICLQ 279.

be interpreted within the broader framework of general international law. There is also a well-established practice in modern commercial law treaty-making to provide detailed materials in aid of uniform interpretation. These include official commentaries and explanatory reports. This trend reflects the need for commercial predictability, and has been assisted by greater reliance on rule-based drafting techniques. Municipal legislation implementing international conventions not infrequently provides that regard may be had to such commentaries and explanatory reports in interpreting the legislation giving effect to the convention provisions.

3.51 It is not always easy to determine whether an issue is to be regarded as covered by the principles underlying a convention or as outside its scope altogether. For example, the better view is that set-off falls outside the scope of CISG altogether, while a right to withhold performance for the other party's breach could be deduced as a general principle, but not all scholars are in agreement with these propositions.[38]

An illustration: the Factoring Convention

3.52 In commercial law conventions, the general rules of interpretation laid down by the Vienna Convention on Treaties are usually supplemented or modified by express provision. Article 4 of the Convention on International Factoring contains a common form of interpretive clause.

Article 4

1. In the interpretation of this Convention, regard is to be had to its object and purpose as set forth in the preamble, to its international character and to the need to promote uniformity in its application and the observance of good faith in international trade.

2. Questions concerning matters governed by this Convention which are not expressly settled in it are to be settled in conformity with the general principles on which it is based or, in the absence of such principles, in conformity with the law applicable by virtue of the rules of private international law.

3.53 Article 4(1) is now standard, though in the Cape Town Convention the usual reference to good faith is replaced by a reference to predictability, the concern being that in transactions involving very high value a requirement of good faith would inject uncertainty into a set of rules based to a high degree on party autonomy and on the predictability of the outcome of disputes. Reference to the international character shows that domestic rules of interpretation are to be avoided, whilst the mention of uniformity is designed to encourage a national court to ensure that as far as possible its decisions are in line with any consensus emerging from decisions of other jurisdictions. The reference to the object and purpose of the convention

---

[38] See the discussion in Peter Schlechtriem and Ingeborg Schwenzer (eds), *Commentary on the UN Convention on the International Sale of Goods* (2nd edn (English) OUP, Oxford, 2005) 72–3.

suggests a teleological approach to interpretation, as opposed to a textual approach, that is, one that seeks to focus purely on the 'plain meaning' of a provision, or an 'intention' approach which seeks to identify the common will of the parties. Yet this is not a licence to ignore the language of the text.

Article 4(2) of the Factoring Convention, which lays down a hierarchy of inter- **3.54** pretive rules, is also typical. First, comes the language of the convention itself. Only if this is silent may recourse be had to the general principles on which the convention is based. These may be ascertained from the preamble, or from the fact that a particular principle is common to a number of provisions. Inevitably, writers looking for general principles tend to do so from the standpoint of their own legal system. Thus, a German scholar may find in CISG a general principle of good faith by reference to requirements of reasonable conduct in a number of articles, since in German law this is an aspect of good faith, whereas in English law good faith generally denotes honesty rather than reasonableness. So an English scholar may consider that CISG provisions requiring reasonable behaviour do not in themselves support the inference of a general principle of good faith. If no solution is to be extracted from the principles on which the Convention is based then, and then only, must resort be had to the law applicable under the rules of private international law of the forum.

Treatment of errors in a convention

How should errors in a convention be dealt with? This may seem a strange ques- **3.55** tion. Surely an international convention ought not to contain errors! But errors are common and arise either through oversight or because of pressure of time at a Diplomatic Conference. Errors may take a variety of forms: spelling or punctuation mistakes, erroneous cross-references (usually arising because of the insertion or deletion of an article and the failure to make consequential amendments to cross-references), inconsistencies between one provision and another, lack of concordance between different language texts, or just plain mistakes in expression which produce a result different from that intended.

A procedure for the correction of errors

Article 79 of the Vienna Convention lays down a procedure for the correction of **3.56** agreed errors, but this is rather cumbersome. A better approach is for the Diplomatic Conference to authorize the correction of errors by the depositary, perhaps in conjunction with the President of the Conference, within a stated period. Again, the Cape Town Convention provides an instructive example. Let us take first the question of linguistic alignment. Prior to the Diplomatic Conference, the text of the draft convention had been produced by a drafting committee in the two working languages of UNIDROIT, English and French. But the International Civil Aviation Organization, which co-hosted the Conference, has five working languages and Chinese was added as a Conference language. The six languages of the Conference were therefore Arabic, Chinese, English, French, Russian and Spanish. Now it is impossible, at least with complex instruments such as the Cape Town Convention and Protocol, for a drafting committee to work in more than two languages at a Diplomatic Conference. Accordingly, the drafting committee worked in English and the text was then sent down the wire from Cape Town to ICAO's team of translators in Montreal. These were highly skilled professional translators, but the product of work by a drafting committee consisting of experts in the relevant field is of a different order of quality from what emerges from translation under time pressure by translators not familiar with the subject-matter and working on their own rather than in a group of subject specialists. Unsurprisingly, therefore, as the other language texts were distributed to the Conference, the delegates rose one after another to protest against the perceived inaccuracy, or even incomprehensibility, of the translations. Some improvements were made by delegations themselves, but in the end, in order to ensure that texts in all six languages could be annexed to the Final Act and signed, it was agreed that the texts of the two instruments would be subject to verification by the Joint Secretariat of the Conference under the authority of the President within a period of ninety days as to the linguistic changes required to bring the texts in the different languages into conformity with each other. This agreement was incorporated into the Final Act and various linguistic changes were subsequently made. This does not preclude the possibility—even the likelihood—that there remain divergences between the different texts, in which case resort must be had to Article 33 of the Vienna Convention, set out above. During the ninety-day period, opportunity was also taken to correct cross-referencing and other errors. So the published text departs in some respects from that which was adopted at the Conference, though not, of course, so as to change any of the intended substance of the provisions.

Uncorrected errors and interpretation

3.57 Where errors still remain, the convention should where possible be interpreted in such a way as to overcome them. As we have seen, Article 32 of the Convention authorizes reference to the *travaux préparatoires* in order to avoid a result which is manifestly absurd or unreasonable. Despite all the care that went into the final perusal of the Cape Town Convention and Protocol, certain errors passed undetected. How should these be dealt with? For example, Article 39(1)(b) of the Convention speaks of the right of arrest or detention of an object to secure payments due to a State entity, intergovernmental organization or other private provider of public services, but through a drafting slip omits reference to payments due to the State itself. Clearly such payments are intended to be covered. Again, in Article 14 there is an inconsistency between paragraph 1 and paragraph 2. Paragraph 1 provides a priority rule based on the first to register, whilst paragraph 2 gives priority to one who *acquires* an aircraft object prior to registration of another party's interest. It is therefore necessary to interpret paragraph 2 as referring to a buyer under a *registered* interest. In both cases, the necessary corrective interpretation is given by the Official Commentary on the Convention and Protocol.

The correction of errors in interpreting an instrument necessarily involves the **3.58** application of non-interpretive techniques. Where the ordinary language of the instrument is self-contradictory or otherwise produces absurd results, the task of the reader is not to interpret the meaning of the words, but to disregard them or to treat them as if they had said something different. In his magisterial work *Purposive Interpretation in Law*, Chief Justice Aharon Barak, President of the Supreme Court of Israel, discusses the limits of interpretation. Though these are described in the context of constitutions, statutes and contracts rather than international conventions, there seems no reason why they cannot equally be applied to the latter.

Aharon Barak, *Purposive Interpretation in Law* (Princeton U Press, Princeton, 2005) 18 and 65[38a]

Language and the Limits of Interpretation

What, then, are the boundaries of interpretation? Tribe says[39] that, because of the multiplicity of systems of interpretation, all that can be said is that the boundary of interpretation is set by the good faith of the interpretive process. In his opinion, there are no additional standards, because we have no standards with which to select among the various systems of interpretation. I accept that there are numerous systems of interpretation, most of which I cannot disqualify as illegitimate. When I claim that most, if not all—except for purposive interpretation—are improper, I do not claim that they exceed the bounds of interpretation. From my point of view, in order for a system to be interpretive—to belong to the interpretive family of law—it must adhere to one critical principle: interpretation is a rational activity that gives a legal text a meaning that it can bear in its language (public or private). This condition is both necessary and sufficient for the existence of a system of interpretation ... my position is that the limits of the text set the limits of interpretation in law, and the limits of language set the limits of the text. An activity is interpretive if it confers meaning on a text that is consistent with one of its (explicit or implicit) meanings, in the (public or private) language of the text. Giving a text a meaning beyond its semantic meaning is not an act of interpretation, and it must rely on non-interpretive doctrines. Interpretation ends at the point at which language ends ...

Non-interpretive doctrines are important both practically and theoretically. On the practical level they allow a judge to reach the proper solution without the need for interpretive rules. This is important for cases in which interpretive rules, used in the ordinary way, fail to reach the proper solution. On the theoretical level, the doctrines impart legitimacy to judicial activity without the need to try to force the proper solution into the framework of interpretive rules—an attempt that will ultimately break the rules ... The

---

[38a] © 2005 Princeton University Press. Reprinted by permission of Princeton University Press.
[39] Laurence H Tribe, *American Constitutional Law* (3rd edn, Foundation Press, New York, 2000) 92.

list of non-interpretive doctrine is ever-expanding. Their source is mostly in case law, as opposed to statutory law. [They include] five such doctrines: (1) filling in a gap in a text; (2) resolving a contradiction between two separate texts; (3) correcting a mistake in a text; (4) changing the language of the text in order to prevent an absurdity; and (5) fulfilling the purpose of the text by making a change ('doctrine of approximation' [*cy-pres*]).

3.59 In international law, non-interpretive doctrine is sanctified by Article 32 of the Vienna Convention, which reflects customary international law, and by decisions of the International Court of Justice. But it has to be applied with great caution, and only when the solution proposed can reasonably be seen as reflecting the intention of the parties to the convention in question. The primary task of the tribunal is to determine the meaning of a treaty provision, not to change it.

D. Enforcement of Private Conventional Rights Against States

The consequences of internationally wrongful acts and the concept of diplomatic protection

3.60 The remedy for breach of an international obligation for which a State is responsible is reparation, which may take the form of restitution (restoration to the status quo existing prior to the breach), compensation, non-monetary satisfaction, such as a formal acknowledgement of wrongdoing or an apology, or any combination of these.

Chorzów Factory Case (Interpretation of Judgments Nos 7 and 8, Germany v Poland) (1928) PCIJ (Series A) No 17, 47

The essential principle contained in the actual notion of an illegal act—a principle which seems to be established by international practice and in particular by the decisions of arbitral tribunals—is that reparations must, as far as possible, wipe out all the consequences of the illegal act and re-establish the situation which would, in all probability, have existed if that act had not been committed. Restitution in kind, or, if this is not possible, payment of a sum corresponding to the value which a restitution in kind would bear; the award, if need be, of damages for loss sustained which would not be covered by restitution in kind or payment in place of it—such are the principles which should serve to determine the amount of compensation due for an act contrary to international law.

3.61 More recently, the International Law Commission has produced a set of Draft Articles on Responsibility of States for internationally wrongful acts. The draft articles were adopted by the Commission at its fifty-third session in 2001. The first three of the 59 articles read as follows:

Article 1

Responsibility of a State for its internationally wrongful acts

Every internationally wrongful act of a State entails the international responsibility of that State.

Article 2

Elements of an internationally wrongful act of a State

There is an internationally wrongful act of a State when conduct consisting of an action or omission:

(a) is attributable to the State under international law; and

(b) constitutes a breach of an international obligation of the State.

Article 3

Characterization of an act of a State as internationally wrongful

The characterization of an act of a State as internationally wrongful is governed by international law. Such characterization is not affected by the characterization of the same act as lawful by internal law.

The United Nations has periodically considered what should be done with the draft articles—in particular, whether a Diplomatic Conference should be convened to embody them in an international convention—but has again deferred further consideration, until its sixty-second session in 2007.[40] **3.62**

As mentioned earlier, although in principle a treaty may be invoked directly only by a State or international organization, many treaties, particularly investment treaties, confer direct rights of action on the private enterprise against an infringing host State.[41] In the absence of a treaty provision conferring such a right, the traditional mechanism for a private party seeking compensation is 'diplomatic protection': a State asserts a claim on behalf of its 'nationals'.[42] The assertion may be made to another State,[43] or, where applicable, before an international tribunal. A range of issues may arise in establishing nationality in this context. Such issues are not necessarily susceptible to resolution by reference to the domestic law of the asserting State. In the *Nottebohm* case,[44] the International Court of Justice required an 'effective link' (subsequently referred to at times as a 'genuine connection'—in either case, a close, factual connection) between the State and the national. Commentators disagree on whether the effective link test has extended or restricted diplomatic protection. **3.63**

---

[40] For an up-to-date description of progress, see: James Crawford and Simon Olleson, 'The Continuing Debate on a UN Convention on State Responsibility' (2005) 54 ICLQ 959.

[41] See further below, para 3.65.

[42] Interestingly, not many States have express rules entitling transaction-parties to compensation received from another State, yet this has not posed a problem in practice.

[43] Typically, requiring the exhaustion of local remedies, which can take many years, unless expedited by use of agreed arbitration procedures, which are common.

[44] *Nottebohm Case* (*Liechtenstein v Guatemala*) (1955) ICJ Rep 4 (ICJ).

Ian Brownlie, *Principles of Public International Law* (6th edn, OUP, Oxford, 2003) 466–7

THE *BARCELONA TRACTION CASE* AND THE PROTECTION OF CORPORATIONS

The decision in the Barcelona Traction case (Second Phase)[45] ... must be considered in relation to the diplomatic protection of corporations. The Barcelona Traction Company was incorporated under Canadian law and had its registered office in Canada. The International Court, in reaching the conclusion that Belgium had no capacity to espouse the claims of the, as alleged, Belgian shareholders in the Company, considered the argument that such a claim was the only possibility of redress for the loss suffered since the company's national state lacked capacity to act on its behalf. This argument raised the question whether Canada was the national state of Barcelona Traction. The Court explained its view that Canada was the national state in these terms:

> In allocating corporate entities to States for purpose of diplomatic protection, international law is based, but only to a limited extent, on an analogy with the rules governing the nationality of individuals. The traditional rule attributes the right of diplomatic protection of a corporate entity to the State under the laws of which it is incorporated and in whose territory it has its registered office. These two criteria have been confirmed by long practice and by numerous international instruments. This notwithstanding, further or different links are at times said to be required in order that a right of diplomatic protection should exist. Indeed, it has been the practice of some States to give a company incorporated under their law diplomatic protection solely when it has its seat (*siège social*) or management or centre of control in their territory, or when a majority or a substantial proportion of the shares has been owned by nationals of the State concerned. Only then, it has been held, does there exist between the corporation and the State in question a genuine connection of the kind familiar from other branches of international law. However, in the particular field of the diplomatic protection of corporate entities, no absolute test of the 'genuine connection' has found general acceptance. Such tests as have been applied are of a relative nature, and sometimes links with one State have had to be weighed against those with another. In this connection reference has been made to the *Nottebohm* case. In fact the Parties made frequent reference to it in the course of the proceedings. However, given both legal and factual aspects of protection in the present case, the Court is of the opinion that there can be no analogy with the issues raised or the decision given in that case.

> In the present case, it is not disputed that the company was incorporated in Canada and has its registered office in that country. The incorporation of the company under the law of Canada was an act of free choice. Not only did the founders of the company seek its incorporation under Canadian law but it has remained under that law for a period of over 50 years. It has maintained in Canada its registered office, its accounts and its share registers. Board meetings were held there for many years; it has been listed in the records of the Canadian tax authorities. Thus a close and permanent connection has been established, fortified by the passage of over half a century. This connection is in no way weakened by the fact that the company engaged from the very outset in commercial activities outside Canada, for that was its declared object. Barcelona Traction's links with Canada are thus manifold.

---

[45] *Barcelona Traction Case* (n 15) 42.

This passage is of considerable importance. The Court rejects the analogy of the *Nottebohm* case and the 'genuine connection' principle applied in the case in the context of the naturalization of individuals. Nevertheless, the authority of this expression of opinion is reduced by three circumstances. First, since neither Belgium nor Spain contested the Canadian character of the Barcelona Traction Company the reference to the issue of 'genuine connection' was quite without point. Secondly, the Court in fact takes the trouble to set out the 'manifold' links of the company with Canada. Thirdly, there is a considerable body of opinion both on the Court and elsewhere in favour of the application of the *Nottebohm* principle to the diplomatic protection of limited companies. It would seem that the process whereby an individual embarks on a voluntary naturalization and the incorporation of a company in the country of choice are significantly similar. Fears that the 'genuine' or 'effective' link principle will lead to instability and absence of diplomatic protection are by no means groundless. However, municipal law, international law has a reserve power to guard against giving effect to ephemeral, abusive, and simulated creations. Moreover, there is probably a presumption of validity in favour of the nationality created by incorporation and, in the case of multi-national corporate bodies, no very exacting test of substantial connection should be applied.

The existence of appropriate links between the person invoking the diplomatic   **3.64** protection and the State whose intervention is invoked is not the only prerequisite. Unless that State is also itself a claimant in its own right, it is necessary to show that the injured party has exhausted all local judicial and administrative remedies against the respondent State. The injured party has no right to demand that its own State takes up its case: this is entirely within that State's discretion, the theory being that the exercise of diplomatic protection is the right of the State, not the person on whose behalf it is acting,[46] though more recently this view has sustained criticism.[47]

In multilateral private law conventions, it is relatively uncommon to find duties   **3.65** imposed on States or international organizations for the benefit of private transacting parties. A notable exception is the Washington Convention on the Settlement of Investment Disputes between States and Nationals of other States 1965, which entitles an investor in the host State to resort to conciliation or arbitration through the World Bank's International Centre for the Settlement of Investment Disputes (ICSID), very often under a bilateral investment treaty between the host State and the investor's home State. Where such direct right of recourse exists diplomatic protection is excluded.[48] The Cape Town Convention provides a further exception to the rule that a private party cannot assert treaty rights except through the State of which it is a national. Let us start with State responsibility.

---

[46] Ibid [78]–[79].
[47] Phoebe Okowa, 'Issues of Admissibility and the Law on International Responsibility' in Malcolm D Evans, *International Law* (1st edn, OUP, Oxford, 2003) ch 15.
[48] Washington Convention Art 27(1).

CONVENTION ON INTERNATIONAL INTERESTS IN MOBILE
EQUIPMENT 2001

Article 13—Relief pending final determination

1. Subject to any declaration that it may make under Article 55, a Contracting State shall ensure that a creditor who adduces evidence of default by the debtor may, pending final determination of its claim and to the extent that the debtor has at any time so agreed, obtain from a court speedy relief in the form of such one or more of the following orders as the creditor requests:
   (a) preservation of the object and its value;
   (b) possession, control or custody of the object;
   (c) immobilisation of the object; and
   (d) lease or, except where covered by sub-paragraphs (a) to (c), management of the object and the income therefrom.

2. In making any order under the preceding paragraph, the court may impose such terms as it considers necessary to protect the interested persons in the event that the creditor:
   (a) in implementing any order granting such relief, fails to perform any of its obligations to the debtor under this Convention or the Protocol; or
   (b) fails to establish its claim, wholly or in part, on the final determination of that claim.

3. Before making any order under paragraph 1, the court may require notice of the request to be given to any of the interested persons.

4. Nothing in this Article affects the application of Article 8(3) or limits the availability of forms of interim relief other than those set out in paragraph 1.

. . .

Article 55—Declarations regarding relief pending final determination

A Contracting State may, at the time of ratification, acceptance, approval of, or accession to the Protocol, declare that it will not apply the provisions of Article 13 or Article 43, or both, wholly or in part. The declaration shall specify under which conditions the relevant Article will be applied, in case it will be applied partly, or otherwise which other forms of interim relief will be applied.

3.66 The purpose of Article 13 is to guarantee a creditor who adduces evidence of default speedy interim judicial relief pending final determination of its claim on the merits. 'Speedy relief' is not defined in the Convention, but Article X(2) of the Aircraft Protocol defines it as 'such number of working days from the date of filing of the application for relief as is specified in a declaration made by the Contracting State in which the application is made'. But what is the remedy of a creditor who suffers loss because a Contracting State fails to ensure such relief is in fact provided, so that, for example, an aircraft which a lessor desires to preserve and immobilize is flown to a destination out of reach of the lessor? The Convention confers no direct right of action on the lessor, who must invoke the aid of the State of which it is a national. It is arguable that as that State would have a claim in its own right for breach by the respondent State of its obligations under the Convention it would be unnecessary for the lessor to exhaust local remedies.

The practical difficulty lies in finding a forum that has jurisdiction. The jurisdiction provisions of the Cape Town Convention itself offer no assistance here. The parties to a transaction can agree on a choice of forum under Article 42, but such an agreement cannot confer jurisdiction against a State. The other articles on jurisdiction are confined to claims for interim relief under Article 13 (see Article 43 and Protocol, Article XXI) and claims against the Registrar under Article 44. The International Court of Justice could have jurisdiction, but only if the respondent State consents. So the threat of proceedings for breach of a Contracting State's duties under Article 13 may be a mere *brutum fulmen*, leaving that Article simply as a lever to exert moral suasion.

The Cape Town Convention also imposes duties on the Supervisory Authority, **3.67** while conferring such immunities as are provided by the Protocol.

Article 17—The Supervisory Authority and the Registrar

1. There shall be a Supervisory Authority as provided by the Protocol.
2. The Supervisory Authority shall:
   (a) establish or provide for the establishment of the International Registry;
   (b) except as otherwise provided by the Protocol, appoint and dismiss the Registrar;
   (c) ensure that any rights required for the continued effective operation of the International Registry in the event of a change of Registrar will vest in or be assignable to the new Registrar;
   (d) after consultation with the Contracting States, make or approve and ensure the publication of regulations pursuant to the Protocol dealing with the operation of the International Registry;
   (e) establish administrative procedures through which complaints concerning the operation of the International Registry can be made to the Supervisory Authority;
   (f) supervise the Registrar and the operation of the International Registry;
   (g) at the request of the Registrar, provide such guidance to the Registrar as the Supervisory Authority thinks fit;
   (h) set and periodically review the structure of fees to be charged for the services and facilities of the International Registry;
   (i) do all things necessary to ensure that an efficient notice-based electronic registration system exists to implement the objectives of this Convention and the Protocol; and
   (j) report periodically to Contracting States concerning the discharge of its obligations under this Convention and the Protocol.

3. The Supervisory Authority may enter into any agreement requisite for the performance of its functions, including any agreement referred to in Article 27(3).
4. The Supervisory Authority shall own all proprietary rights in the data bases and archives of the International Registry.
5. The Registrar shall ensure the efficient operation of the International Registry and perform the functions assigned to it by this Convention, the Protocol and the regulations.

. . .

Privileges and immunities of the Supervisory Authority and the Registrar

Article 27—Legal personality; immunity

1. The Supervisory Authority shall have international legal personality where not already possessing such personality.
2. The Supervisory Authority and its officers and employees shall enjoy such immunity from legal or administrative process as is specified in the Protocol.
3. (a) The Supervisory Authority shall enjoy exemption from taxes and such other privileges as may be provided by agreement with the host State.
   (b) For the purposes of this paragraph, 'host State' means the State in which the Supervisory Authority is situated.
4. The assets, documents, data bases and archives of the International Registry shall be inviolable and immune from seizure or other legal or administrative process.
5. For the purposes of any claim against the Registrar under Article 28(1) or Article 44, the claimant shall be entitled to access to such information and documents as are necessary to enable the claimant to pursue its claim.
6. The Supervisory Authority may waive the inviolability and immunity conferred by paragraph 4.

3.68 Article XVII of the Protocol provides that the Supervisory Authority is to be the international entity designated by a Resolution of the Diplomatic Conference or, if it is unwilling to act, a Supervisory Authority designated by a Conference of Signatory and Contracting States. The Supervisory Authority and its officers are to enjoy such immunity from legal and administrative process as is provided under the rules applicable to them as an international entity or otherwise. Resolution No 2 invited ICAO to accept the functions of Supervisory Authority, which it subsequently agreed to do. ICAO is an international, intergovernmental organisation with international legal personality and contracting powers under Article 47 of the Chicago Convention on International Civil Aviation 1944 and, as a specialized agency of the United Nations, under Article II of the 1947 UN Convention on the Privileges and Immunities of the Specialised Agencies. Its 'personal law' is international law and it enjoys the privileges and immunities set out in the standard clauses in the UN Immunities Convention and in Annex III to that Convention.

E. Reservations and Declarations

Article 2(1)(d) of the Vienna Convention defines a reservation as:

> a unilateral statement, however, phrased or named, made by a state, when signing, ratifying, accepting, approving or acceding to a treaty, whereby it purports to exclude or modify the legal effect of certain provisions of the treaty in their application to that state.

3.69 In general, a state is entitled to make a reservation if it is not prohibited, or outside the categories of reservation permitted, by the convention and is not incompatible with its object and purpose.[49] Reservations are to be distinguished from interpretative declarations by which a state declares its understanding of the meaning of a particular provision. But frequently, the term 'declaration' denotes a reservation, as in Articles 92, 94 and 95 of the CISG. It is nowadays common to include in the final clauses a provision that no reservations are permitted except as provided by the convention.

F. Withdrawal from a Treaty

All modern commercial law treaties are of indefinite duration with broad rights in favour of States parties to withdraw from the treaty. Typically, all that is required is notice to the Depositary followed by the passage of a specified period of time. That act, technically a 'denunciation' (unilateral act by which a State terminates its participation in a treaty), may affect transaction-parties that have relied upon the treaty provisions in entering into and structuring their contracts.   **3.70**

The Vienna Convention, following the treaty-as-contract paradigm, endorses treaty provisions permitting denunciation.[50] As to the consequences of withdrawal, it states that, unless a treaty otherwise provides, denunciation (a) releases that withdrawing State from any further obligation to perform the treaty, and (b) 'does not affect any right, obligation or legal situation *of the parties* created through the execution of the treaty prior to its termination [emphasis added].'[51] As 'parties' means States parties, the italicized words, viewed by experts as underscoring that the provision does not protect vested interests of transaction-parties, have given rise to commercial law treaty provisions that expressly provide such protection. The same issues, and the same express treaty provisions, apply to the related concept of the effect of future declarations or modifications of existing declarations.   **3.71**

G. Conflicts Between Conventions

The growth of international conventions has greatly increased the risk of inconsistency between overlapping conventions. In some conventions, use of what had become a standard form of deference to other conventions positively invited conflict. For example, several conventions provide that they are not to prevail over any international agreement that has been entered into *or may be entered into* concerning matters covered by the convention. It only needs two such conventions adopting this formula to produce a stand-off, each deferring to the other. Article 17 of the UNIDROIT Leasing Convention and Article 15 of the UNIDROIT   **3.72**

---

[49] Vienna Convention on Treaties Art 19.   [50] Art 42(2).   [51] Art 70.

Factoring Convention both use this formula, though they do not occupy the same field. Article 38(1) of the UN Convention on receivables financing likewise provides for deferment to prior and subsequent international agreements but, alive to the danger of inconsistency with the Factoring Convention, provides in Article 38(2) that the UN Convention is to prevail.

3.73 Article 30 of the Vienna Convention provides a set of residuary rules to govern successive treaties dealing with the same subject matter. Of course, the possibility of conflict arises only as regards States parties to both conventions. Subject to this, there are certain additional rules that can be called into play: for example, there is a presumption that as between parties to both conventions the later overrides the earlier in case of inconsistency. General provisions in one convention will give way to *lex specialis* in another, so that, for example, if there were a convention governing contracts generally and another earlier convention governing the sale of goods, provisions of the latter would generally prevail over those of the former.

Questions

1. An international convention has been concluded governing the rights of the parties to an agency agreement where the principal and the agent carry on business in different States. These rights include compensation for the agent on termination of the agreement.
   (1) What conditions have to be satisfied before the agent can invoke the provisions of the convention in the courts of Ruritania?
   (2) What additional factors may have to be considered in the case of a State which is a member of the European Union?
2. 'The notion that *opinio juris* is an essential element in the formation of a rule of customary international law is untenable.'
   (1) What is *opinio juris*?
   (2) What is the basis for the above criticism?
3. To what extent does the controversy in public international law surrounding the requirement of *opinio juris* have its parallel in debates on international trade usage?
4. What principles govern the interpretation of an international convention, and what sources may be relied on to show the meaning of a text? Is the process of determining the effect of a convention provision governed exclusively by interpretive techniques?
5. A State party to a convention which creates private rights breaches one of its obligations under the convention, to the detriment of a private party upon

whom such rights are conferred. What forms of redress does that party have, and subject to what conditions? Give an example of a convention of this kind.

6. What principles are applied to determine conflicts between conventions covering the same subject matter?

Further reading

Aust, Anthony, *Modern Treaty Law and Practice* (CUP, Cambridge, 2000)

Brownlie, Ian, *Principles of Public International Law* (6th edn OUP, Oxford, 2003), particularly chs 1–2, 21–22 and 24

Crawford, James, *The International Law Commission's articles on state responsibility: introduction, text, and commentaries* (CUP, Cambridge, 2002)

Damrosch, Lori F, Henkin, Louis, Pugh, Richard Crawford, Schachter, Oscar, and Smit, Hans, *International Law: Cases and Materials* (4th edn, West Group, St Paul (MI), 2001), particularly chs 1–3, 9–11 and 20

Fox, Hazel, *The Law of State Immunity* (OUP, Oxford, 2002)

Hart, HLA, *The Concept of Law* (2nd edn, OUP, Oxford, 1994) ch X

International Law Association, Committee on Formation of Customary (General) International Law: Final Report, *statement of Principles Applicable to the Formation of General Customary International Law* (International Law Association, London, 2000)

Jacobs, Francis G, and Roberts, Shelley (eds), *The Effect of Treaties in Domestic Law* (Sweet & Maxwell, London, 1987)

Lowenfeld, Andreas F, *International Economic Law* (OUP, Oxford, 2002) chs 13–15

Mendelson, Maurice H, 'The Formation of Customary International Law' (1998) 272 Recueil des cours 155

Mann, FA, 'British Treaties for the Promotion and Protection of Investments' (1981) 52 BYIL 241

Mann, FA, 'Foreign Investment in the International Court of Justice: The *ELSI* Case' 86 American J of Intl L 92 (1992)

Shaw, Malcolm N, *International Law* (5th edn, CUP, Cambridge, 2003)

von Mehren, Robert B, and Kourides, P Nicholas, 'International Arbitrations between States and Foreign Private Parties: The Libyan Nationalization Cases' 75 American J of Intl L 476 (1981)

Wolfke, Karol, *Custom in Present International Law* (2nd rev edn, Nijhoff, Dordrecht, 1993)

4

COMPARATIVE LAW AND ITS RELEVANCE TO TRANSNATIONAL COMMERCIAL LAW

A. Nature of Comparative Law and a Brief History

Nature of comparative law	4.01
A brief history	4.04

B. Classification of Legal Systems

The traditional classification by family	4.07
An issue-based classification system	4.11
Civil law and common law	4.12
Islamic law	4.17

C. Aims of Comparative Law 4.18

Educational aims of comparative law	4.19
Practical uses of comparative law	4.23
Enhancement of understanding of one's own law	4.26
Updating of national legal jurisprudence	4.28
Aid to the drafting of new legislation	4.31
Guide to the policy implications of a new development in national jurisprudence	4.32
Development of transnational commercial law	4.33
Refinement of the conflict of laws	4.40
Commercial law dispute resolution	4.41
Consistency of interpretation of uniform laws	4.42
Consistency of determination of international trade usage	4.47
Role of comparative law in transnational practice	4.48
Cultural aims of comparative law	4.49

D. Methodology

The functional approach to comparative law	4.50
Common solutions or best solutions?	4.54
Working methods	4.56

E. Problems

The pitfalls of comparison	4.59
The knowledge problem	4.59
Language	4.62
Legal transplants and comparative law	
Similarities and differences	4.63
Transplantation not attributable to comparative study	4.65
The effectiveness of legal transplants	4.70
How necessary is a knowledge of comparative law to the development and practical application of transnational commercial law?	4.72

A. Nature of Comparative Law and a Brief History

Nature of comparative law

4.01 We may begin with a rather simplistic definition of comparative law as the systematic study of the institutions and rules of at least two different legal systems on a comparative basis. *Comparison* is the key feature. Merely to examine a foreign legal system without comparing it with another is not engaging in comparative law. So whilst the examination of foreign laws in order to assist a court in deciding which direction its own law should take is a true exercise in comparative law, the study and presentation of evidence of a rule of a particular foreign legal system because it is the applicable law under the forum's conflict of laws rules does not in itself involve comparative law at all. Indeed, for the court it is an altogether different exercise, because it may involve a close examination of the detail of the rule of foreign law under consideration, whereas, as we shall see, reference to foreign law to assist the court in deciding on the future direction of one of its own legal rules looks more to the underlying policy of the foreign law and its approach to the solution of a common problem.

4.02 As a subject, comparative law encompasses both the comparative activity itself and the purposes and methodology of comparison. The phrase 'comparative law' is unfortunate, as it misleadingly suggests a body of extant, substantive law, whereas comparative law is a process of comparison which does not in itself have any normative content. That is one of the reasons why it is so difficult to define it in a meaningful way.

> Legal definitions are notoriously unsatisfactory and apt to lead to controversies which are often barren of result. This, in particular, is the case when any attempt is made to define 'Comparative Law' as law, since the subject-matter, being non-existent, is one which defies definition.[1]

4.03 Yet the result of the comparative law process in the context of transnational commercial law ('comparative commercial law') is rich. It lies at the very foundation of the transnational commercial law enterprise. One need look no further than the constitutional documents of the principal organizations involved in the development of substantive transnational commercial law, UNIDROIT and UNCITRAL.

Statute of UNIDROIT (International Institute for the Unification of Private Law) 1940, as amended in 1993

Article 1

The purposes of the International Institute for the Unification of Private Law are to examine ways of harmonising and coordinating the private law of States and of groups of

---

[1] HC Gutteridge, *Comparative Law* (2nd edn, CUP, Cambridge, 1949) 2.

States, and to prepare gradually for the adoption by the various States of uniform rules of private law.

To this end the Institute shall:

. . .

(c) undertake studies in comparative private law . . .

General Assembly of the United Nations, Resolution 2205 (XXI), 17 December 1966

The General Assembly . . .

Decides to establish a United Nations Commission on International Trade Law (hereinafter referred to as the Commission), which shall have for its object the promotion of the progressive harmonization and unification of the law of international trade, in accordance with the provisions set forth in section II below . . .

8. The Commission shall further the progressive harmonization and unification of the law by . . .

(e) Collecting and disseminating information on national legislation and modern legal developments, including case law, in the field of the law of international trade . . .

A brief history

Comparative law has been a feature in the development of law from time imme-   **4.04**
morial. The history of law includes a history of legal borrowing. That process has been described as the reception, export, import, imposition, migration, diffusion, circulation, transfer, assimilation, transplantation, or transposition of ideas, rules and institutions, depending on the objectives of the author.[2] Thus, the Code of Hammurabi, dating back to approximately 1914 BC,[3] drew on the laws of various Sumerian cities and other Near East sources. In Ancient Greece, Plato's *Laws* compared the laws of the Greek City States. The Twelve Tables of Roman Law are said to have been compiled between 450 and 451 BC by a group of commissioners after a visit to Athens and a study of its laws, particularly those of Solon. In the Middle Ages, the Rolls of Oléron, embodying rules of maritime law adopted by the Commune of Oléron, were applied widely throughout continental Europe and in England.[4] Turning to more modern times, many consider that the great eighteenth century French political thinker Montesquieu has a claim to be the founder of comparative law,[5] while the law reform movement of early nineteenth century England, powerfully led by Jeremy Bentham, and later by John Austin, clearly perceived the advantages that can flow from a comparative approach,

---

[2] Bernard S Jackson, 'Evolution and Foreign Influence in Ancient Law' 16 Am J Comp L 372 (1968). See also: Alan Watson, *Legal Transplants: an approach to comparative law* (2nd edn, U of Georgia Press, London 1993).

[3] A S Diamond, *Primitive Law* (2nd edn, Watts, London, 1950) 22.   [4] See para 1.16.

[5] See, for example, Gutteridge, *Comparative Law* (2nd edn, CUP 1946) 12; Otto Kahn-Freund, 'On Uses and Misuses of Comparative Law' (1974) 37 MLR 1, 6.

though except in matters of criminal reform the movement's work proved more influential on the Continent of Europe than in England. This approach gained pace in the nineteenth century in all major systems[6] even though the emergence of the nation states, each with its own Codes (or codal ambitions) also acted as a brake. But it is from the turn of the twentieth century onwards that we begin to see the first fruits of the scientific cultivation of the subject.

Konrad Zweigert and Hein Kötz, *An Introduction to Comparative Law* (Tony Weir tr) (3rd edn, Clarendon Press, Oxford, 1998) 2–3

Comparative law as we know it started in Paris in 1900, the year of the World Exhibition. At this brilliant panorama of human achievement there were naturally innumerable congresses, and the great French scholars EDOUARD LAMBERT and RAYMOND SALEILLES took the opportunity to found an International Congress for Comparative Law. The science of comparative law, or at any rate its method, was greatly advanced by the occurrence of this Congress, and the views expressed at it have led to a wealth of productive research in this branch of legal study, young though it is.

The temper of the Congress was in tune with the times, whose increasing wealth and splendour had given everyone, scholars included, an imperturbable faith in progress. Sure of his existence, certain of its point and convinced of its success, man was trying to break out of his local confines and peaceably to master the world and all that was in it. Naturally enough, lawyers were affected by this spirit; merely to interpret and elaborate their own system no longer satisfied them. This outgoing spirit permeates all the Congress papers; the whole Congress was dominated by a disarming belief in progress. What LAMBERT and SALEILLES had in mind was the development of nothing less than a common law of mankind (*droit commun de l'humanité*). A world law must be created—not today, perhaps not even tomorrow—but created it must be, and comparative law must create it. As LAMBERT put it ... comparative law must resolve the accidental and divisive differences in the laws of peoples at similar stages of cultural and economic development, and reduce the number of divergencies in law, attributable not to the political, moral or social qualities of the different nations but to historical accident or to temporary or contingent circumstances.

4.05 Nothing ever came of the majestic grand design to recreate a *jus gentium*, a task noble in its ambition but wholly impracticable, given the diversity of legal cultures. Even so, it provided the motive power for the development of comparative law which has persisted to this day.

HC Gutteridge, *Comparative Law* (2nd edn, CUP, Cambridge, 1949) 6–7

So far as the views held by these two famous jurists [Lambert and Saleilles] were based on the existence of certain principles common to all systems of law, they rest on a somewhat flimsy foundation and appear to have been abandoned to a very large extent at present day.

---

[6] See generally Helmut Coing, 'European Common Law: Historical Foundations' in *New Perspectives for a Common Law of Europe* (ed. Mauro Cappelletti 1978), 31 ff. For the impact on the English law of contract see, inter alia, Brian Simpson, 'Innovation in Nineteenth Century Contract

Nevertheless, the 'universalist' view of law has exercised a marked influence on the development of modern comparative law. It formed the starting point for the wave of unificationary enthusiasm which swept Europe in the years following the war of 1914–1918, and it still provides a motive for much of the comparative study and research which is carried out at the present time. It also finds expression in Article 38 of the Statute of the International Court of Justice, which directs the court to apply, among other rules, 'the general principles of law recognized by civilized nations'. It has been suggested, moreover, that a search for 'common principles' conducted on analytical lines may result in a solution of a problem which is created in the domain of private international law by the varying interpretation given in different jurisdictions to the same legal concept, a problem which is known as that of 'Qualification', 'Classification' or 'Characterisation'. It is, however, doubtful whether the universalist theory can be regarded as more than a pious aspiration founded, partly, on the need for collaboration between the nations in the legal as well as in other spheres, but, in the main, on a belief in the essential unity of mankind. If this view of the matter is put to a test in the conditions of everyday life, it is apt to break against the obstacles created by the differences in national mentality, by habits deeply rooted in tradition, and by variations in the structure of legal institutions and legal technique from country to country.

Although the 'universalist' theory may still be invoked in aid of projects for the unification of private law, it is no longer regarded as explaining the necessity for the employment of the comparative method. At the present day the tendency is to stress the value of the method by indicating the different purposes which may be served by its employment, and this has led to various attempts to classify comparative law in accordance with the objects which can be attained by its utilisation.

The International Academy of Comparative Law was founded in The Hague **4.06** in 1924, and its international Congresses, which began in 1932, are now held in different countries every four years. Many countries now have Institutes of comparative law, and numerous journals of comparative law are published by the Institutes and by university law schools. Comparative law has come of age, though it has to be said that interest in it as a subject of undergraduate study remains limited. Yet, the work of harmonization of law, and in particular of commercial law, could not be undertaken without comparative law studies.

B. Classification of Legal Systems

The traditional classification by family

Scholars have long sought for a rational taxonomy of legal systems. The accepted **4.07** method at the general level is to divide systems into groups known as families. The

---

Law' (1975) 91 LQR 247 ff. For the scene in America and the Germanic impact on academe and intellectual thinking see, among others, Mathias Reimann (ed. and contr.) *The Reception of Continental Ideas in the Common Law World 1820–1920* (1993). Finally, for France, and the growing influence of German thought in that country, especially after the disastrous Franco-Prussian War, see, inter alia, Philippe Jestaz and Christoph Jamin, *La Doctrine* (2004).

problem is to know what criteria to apply in making the division. The underlying concept, as described by Zweigert and Kötz, is that of legal *style*.[7] By this is meant that congeries of characteristics which mark off one legal system from another. Systems possessing similar characteristics are then allocated to a particular family. Among the characteristics considered as principal elements of a legal style are: historical development, mode of legal thinking, distinctive legal institutions (such as the trust in the common law, and the doctrine of *cause* in the civil law), the sources of law recognized by a legal system, and the ideology of a system, for example, whether it is a socialist system, in which law is subordinate to political considerations and the rights of the individual to those of the community, or a capitalist system, characterized by adherence to the rule of law, a free market economy and the protection of individual rights, including rights of property. Roman law exercised an influence on all European legal systems, though much less so in England than elsewhere, because of the practice orientation and vigour of the common law. Hence, the legal systems of continental Europe together constitute the *Romanist* family, though a number of scholars consider that Germany and the countries adopting the German civil code (*Bürgerliches Geseztbuch* or BGB) belong to a distinct *Germanic* family because of the marked differences in approach between the French *code civil* and the German BGB. Both are treated as civil law systems. The *common law* family consists of present and most former members of the British Commonwealth, including Canada and the United States,[8] though in some of these countries, notably the countries of southern Africa, the legal system is a mixture of common law and Roman-Dutch law. The *Scandinavian* countries are generally considered to constitute a distinct legal family, so too are *socialist* countries, such as China and formerly Russia and its satellite countries. Other groupings are the *Islamic* family and *Hindu* law, the latter applying mainly in India. Finally, there are unclassified legal systems, some of which, such as the South African and Israeli systems, are sometimes described as hybrid systems.

4.08 Classifications of this kind are not without their advantages, at least as a starting point for dealing with the ever-growing number of state and supra-state legal cultures. But their limitations must also be noted, however briefly. First, they are predominantly based on private law, becoming fashionable at the time of creation or modernization of Civil Codes, and largely ignore public law, a subject which has acquired a much greater influence from the beginning of the second half of the twentieth century. Secondly, they ignore the often significant shift of some legal

---

[7] Konrad Zweigert and Hein Kötz, *An Introduction to Comparative Law* (Tony Weir (tr)) (3rd edn, Clarendon Press, Oxford, 1998) 67 ff. A more recent and seemingly broader concept is that of legal culture. See below, para 4.49.

[8] Apart from Quebec in Canada and Louisiana in the United States, both of which are civil law systems. The United States, though initially deriving its jurisprudence from England, has moved in a substantially different direction and is therefore a distinct subset of common law jurisdictions. The same is true to a lesser extent of Canada and Australia.

systems from their original sources towards different systems. To give but two instances, systems such as the Dutch and the Portuguese, traditionally under the umbrella of French law, have in more recent times made significant switches towards German law, while other systems, such as the Italian, which are traditionally included in the Romanistic family, have in some branches (e.g. civil procedure) demonstrated a strong leaning towards Germanic thought, whereas in others (e.g. commercial law) they are showing themselves increasingly willing to seek guidance from the common law.

Thirdly, yet another group of systems, originally highly dependent on Roman and French law, have re-oriented themselves in some subjects towards German law whereas in others they have come under the influence of American law. Brazil provides a good example. In this third group of systems one might include a subcategory of systems which have remained faithful to their progenitors in some areas of the law but look for inspiration towards a new source of ideas. The nuanced differences of the practice of the South African Supreme Court and the South African Constitutional Court may provide illustrations worth further examination. **4.09**

In the light of the above, it is not surprising that some authors have felt obliged to develop their own classifications, more tailor-made to the exigencies of their own subjects. Professor Philip Wood, a former practising lawyer and one of the world's leading experts in international financial law, is one who has done just that. His own classifications of the financial laws of the world are based on his long experience of international banking and business transactions. Wood's primary focus is on the general style of a jurisdiction, and in particular, on the following characteristics: **4.10**

- the emphasis on predictability;
- the degree of liberalism in commercial law;
- the degree of criminalization of commercial law;
- the attitude to 'big pocket' liability;
- attitudes to dispute resolution; and,
- policies on hard law, including insolvency law, property and secured transaction rights, and soft law, such as regulatory guidelines and administrative indications lacking legal force but nevertheless compelling in their impact.[9]

Philip Wood, *Comparative Financial Law* (Sweet & Maxwell, London, 1995), para 3–2 (footnotes to the table have been added but are taken from the author's text)

One may attempt a broad classification of financial law of jurisdictions into families of the law on the basis of the tests discussed in the previous chapter and on the basis of other

---

[9] Philip Wood, *Comparative Financial Law* (Sweet & Maxwell, London, 1995) paras 2–10 ff. Note that this work was published in 1995, and some changes may have taken place since publication.

criteria which are noted in more detail in subsequent chapters. This grouping is not a grading between good and bad. There are no moral implications whatsoever: the classification is neutral on ethics. The differences do not arise out of moral differences between peoples. Further, the current legal culture of a jurisdiction can be, and often is, quite different from the bare legal rules, Nor is the classification a guide as to which states have a stable legal and judicial system with high standards and those which do not. Efficient commercial law systems are very expensive to run and many countries are more preoccupied with survival than legal refinement. Some legal systems in a grouping are stagnant, while others in that group are on the move . . .

The classification is tentative. It has not been possible to check the position on all issues in all states and the research required to do so would be stupendous. Hence, some jurisdictions may be wrongly categorised.

Subject to these qualifications, the suggested classification is as follows:

GROUP	CLASS	JURISDICTIONS	GLOBAL POPULATION
1A	Traditional English[10]	146/79[12]	1797m (33.4%)
1B	American common law[11]		
2	Mixed Roman/common law[13]	15	243m (4.5%)
3	Germanic and Scandinavian[14]	13	360m (6.7%)
4	Mixed Franco-Latin/Germanic[15]	13	279m (5.2%)
5	Traditional Franco-Latin[16]	76	982m (18.3%)
6	Emerging jurisdictions[17]	18	1488m (27.7%)
7	Islamic jurisdictions[18]	14	108m (2%)
8	Unallocated jurisdictions[19]	13	116m (2.2%)

An issue-based classification system

4.11 The value of Wood's approach is that his classification by legal family in a general sense is followed by second-order groupings according to the particular issue

---

[10] England; Australia; Canada (except Quebec); India; New Zealand; Hong Kong; Malaysia; Singapore. Many other small territories.

[11] All US states save Louisiana, together with Liberia and a few affiliated island territories.

[12] The latter if federal systems, for instance, if Australia, Canada, and the United States, each count as one.

[13] Japan; Korea; the Southern Africa group (for example, South Africa, Botswana, and Zimbabwe); Scotland; Quebec; Sri Lanka; Liechtenstein; the Channel Island group, e.g. Jersey.

[14] Germany; Netherlands and its related states (for example, Indonesia, Aruba); Poland; Finland; Norway; Sweden; Switzerland; Taiwan.

[15] Austria; Czech Republic; Slovak Republic; Denmark; Hungary; Italy; Thailand; Turkey.

[16] Belgium; Egypt; France; Greece; Luxembourg; Portugal; Spain; most Latin American countries; most former French, Belgium, and Portuguese possessions in Africa, the Caribbean, and Indochina.

[17] These are rapidly modernizing their laws, thus grouping is premature: China; Russia; Vietnam; the former Yugoslav States; the three Baltic States; some of the Eastern European members of the former USSR.

[18] Most western Arabian States; Afghanistan; Asian members of the former USSR, for instance Kazakhstan, Tajikistan, Uzbekistan.

[19] Antarctica jurisdictions; Bhutan; Cambodia; Eritrea; Ethiopia; North Korea, Laos, Maldives, Nepal, San Marino, Somalia, Vatican City, Western Sahara.

under discussion. For example, jurisdictions are identified whose laws embody the 'false wealth' principle by which assets in the apparent or reputed ownership of the debtor are treated as his assets so as to be available to creditors upon his insolvency, the real owner being expropriated because he was the secret owner. The impact of the principle varies, but is typically reflected in rules which deny efficacy to non-possessory security interests, trusts, assignments of debts not registered or notified to the debtors, or other invisible interests.[20] Similarly, jurisdictions are classified according to the degree of liberality shown towards the recognition of different types of security interest, property rights, insolvency set-off, and the like. Such an approach moves below the surface of a general classification to an issue-based classification, which does not necessarily correlate with the general taxonomy, and is of particular value to those advising on international financial transactions.

Civil law and common law

The two legal families most often contrasted are the civil law[21] and the common law. These two families are far from homogeneous: there are significant differences between common law systems, and even more between civil law systems. Nevertheless, there are certain contrasts that can be made between the two families as a whole. Certain supposed distinctions can be largely consigned to history. For example, it is said that the civil law system is deductive, reasoning from general principle to specific case, whereas the common law is inductive, extracting the general principle from specific cases, and that the common law is fashioned by practice, the civil law by principle. But these distinctions are of much less significance in modern law. The common law has concepts and principles as highly developed as the civil law, and while it may be true that common law judges, in striving to arrive at a just result, are strongly influenced by the facts of a case, they nevertheless render their decisions in accordance with settled principles and rules.   **4.12**

On the other hand, it is also the case that the common law, being uncodified, is much less accessible to the citizen than, say, the French *code civil*.[22] Moreover, whereas the *code civil* has proved a highly exportable product, spreading the influence of France and French law around the world, the English have nothing in exportable form, not even an equivalent of the American Uniform Commercial Code.   **4.13**

---

[20] Wood (n 9) paras 2–27 ff.

[21] The civil law is Roman law, and particularly Justinian's *Corpus Juris Civilis*, as received and developed in Europe in the Middle Ages.

[22] Though this advantage of the civil law systems, especially the French, must not be exaggerated since the law actually in force must be sought in an ever-growing case law—which at times, bears little resemblance to the wording of the Code—as well as detailed legislation. The law of contracts in favour of third parties and what common lawyers would call the law relating to liability for negligence provide good illustrations.

4.14   There is also a difference in the approach to judicial decisions. As Merryman put it, common law judges are problem solvers rather than theoreticians, whereas the scientific, formal approach of the civil law tends to impede effective problem solving.[23] This is not to say that the common law is superior to the civil law—on the contrary, many of its principles have been influenced by the civil law[24]—merely that it is different.

4.15   There are other points of distinction between the two legal families. The common law gives a wide measure of freedom to the parties to a transaction, whether in relation to contractual rights and obligations, or in relation to the organization of property rights. The civil law adopts a more paternalistic, formal attitude which imposes constraints on what can be done. For example, an assignment may take effect in equity at common law without any formalities, whilst in the civil law, formal requirements are imposed to prevent collusive arrangements, for instance in antedating an assignment. Civil law systems tend to require specificity in the creation of property rights, and would, thus, view with disfavour an all-assets security interest or a transfer of unparticularized future property. Common law systems tend to be creditor oriented, civil law systems debtor oriented. The trust is a concept peculiar to the common law, though it has analogues in the civil law designed to protect the beneficiary from the consequences of a fiduciary's insolvency, without, however, necessarily treating the beneficiary as having a full-blooded property right.

4.16   It is fair to say that the common law laissez-faire approach is more receptive to modern commercial transactions than that of the civil law, whilst the latter is more rigorously systematic and usually more protective of the rights of the weaker party. But there are other important factors, extraneous to law, which have contributed to the dominant position acquired by the commercial law of the common law world: the importance of the English language in the international world of trade; the dominance of the Anglo-American world of finance; and the emergence of the new multi-national law firms which, though internationally staffed, are structured in an Anglo-American way and dominate a substantial part of the legal business related to trade and finance.

---

[23] John H Merryman, *The Civil law Tradition: An Introduction to the Legal Systems of Western Europe and Latin America* (Stanford U Press, Stanford (Cal), 1969) 71.

[24] Thus, in the English case, *Cox v Troy* (1822) 5 B & Ald 474, 480; 106 ER 1264, 1266, Best J said of the great French jurist Pothier that:

> the authority of Pothier is expressly in point. That is as high as can be had, next to the decision of a Court of Justice in this country. It is extremely well known that he is a writer of acknowledged character; his writings have been constantly referred to by the Courts, and he is spoken of with great praise by Sir William Jones in his Law of Bailments, and his writings are considered by that author equal in point of luminous method, apposite examples, and a clear manly style, to the works of Littleton on the laws of this country. We cannot, therefore, have a better guide than Pothier on this subject.

Islamic law

Most of the legal systems that feature in classifications are the systems of a State **4.17** and are thus territory-based. By contrast, Islamic Law, the *Shari'a*, which governs the lives of hundreds of millions of Muslims, is distinct in that it is not a territorial law, but a personal law, and, moreover, one which, deriving from God, is immutable in its precepts, though nonetheless susceptible to diverse interpretations. Islamic law had little impact in modern times until the overthrow of the Shah of Iran, which led to its resurgence throughout the Muslim world. This brought in its wake a distinctive form of internal comparative law which involved testing the validity of legislation against the tenets of the *Shari'a*. Again, however, an important caveat must be made. For even in systems where *Shari'a* law applies, it tends to affect principally what one might describe as family law matters, leaving other parts of the law of these countries—typically contract and tort—to retain a strong European, French or English origin.

**Chibli Mallat, 'Comparative Law and the Islamic (Middle Eastern) Legal Culture'
in Reinhard Zimmermann and Mathias Reimann (eds),** *The Oxford Handbook
of Comparative Law* **(OUP, Oxford, 2006)**

In fact, Islamic law is only a small, discrete component of a larger frame of reference within Islamic culture . . . That said, Islamic law is increasingly all-encompassing and, in fact, is equivalent to the rule of law in the modern state. Every aspect of life is regulated by (Islamic) law . . .

Besides constituting a special type of nomocracy and operating at a multi-level order in society, Islamic law is also unique in that it represents a personal, rather than a territorial system of law. It thus stands in sharp contrast to the post-Westphalian order that dominates the rest of the world. This characteristic, which is typical of any religious-based social order, is also typically Middle Eastern. The application of law to a person on the basis of religious affiliation is an increasingly important source of tension in the world order, one that is based on personal, or communitarian, law, as opposed to the territorial law that dominates the rest of the world. This contrast is possibly the most pervasive and divisive issue that arises when regarding the different legal systems and cultures at play from a comparative perspective.

From a historical perspective, Islamic law consistently elicits an array of autonomous references. Looking at its uninterrupted flow since the Muslim revelation in the 7th century, the *shari'a* appears as the common law in the region and beyond, reaching Mauritania and West Africa on its western fringes and Indonesia to the east. Beyond its textual differences with other major legal systems, the *shari'a* is increasingly studied for its immense diversity across history. In the early period, the Qu'ranic text, the *hadiths* (aphorisms attributed to the Prophet) and the *sira-maghazi* literature (the *sira* consists of biographical accounts of the Prophet, the *maghazi* of the early conquests), were all elaborated upon in many legal genres after the death of the Prophet Muhammed (d 632 CE). Added to this legacy were the classical books of doctrine (*fiqh*), the customary rules, the case law available from extant archival courts, the literature on the art of judgments, the *fatwas* (individual legal opinions), formularies, deeds and contracts, the statute law (*qanun*) since the 15th century, as well as the relevant histories and literature at large, such as chronicles or *belles lettres*. Recent scholarship brings all these genres within the purview of Islamic law. This has led to profound changes in the appreciation of the concept of sources, the development of law and its interpretation, the phenomenon of the Islamic legal 'schools' or *madhhabs* ... all the way to the emergence of codified national laws in the 19th and 20th centuries.

Werner Menski, *Comparative Law in a Global Context* (2nd edn, CUP, Cambridge, 2006) 281–3

The difficulties in understanding Islamic law are exacerbated because it is, similar to Hindu and African laws, a complex family of laws rather than one single legal system. The terminology 'Islamic' or 'Muslim' law itself gives rise to debate. Protracted politics over terms like 'Muhammadan law', which is specific to Indo-Muslim law and the historically grown 'Anglo-Muhammadan law' continue to excite some authors. Muslims themselves tend to emphasise the unity of the worldwide community of believers (*ummah*) and resent being divided, more so after 9/11. As Islam is a way of life manifested in widely disparate local traditions which might cause some raised eyebrows, the immense plurality of locally coloured customary and religious practices leads some scholars to speak of 'Islams' rather than 'Islam'.

While nobody seriously doubts that Islamic law is law, in contrast to perceptions of African laws, many questions arise about the nature, structure and development of Muslim law. The central problematic in Islamic law is the tension between its doctrinal and religious claims to global validity and its practical application in diverse and complex socio-cultural contexts ...

Islamic law asserts itself ... as first and foremost a religious law based on divine revelation. But it is also a scholars' or jurists' law, which raises at once the clash of revelation and reason as a core problem in Muslim jurisprudence. If God made all law, what is the scope for human law-making? ...

But there has always been an overlapping consensus, often hidden by strategic silences and external politics: accepting that Islamic law is more than God's law and has man-made elements as well, requires pluralist perspectives.

C. Aims of Comparative Law

4.18 Comparative law serves various objectives,[25] which can be divided broadly into three categories: educational, practical and cultural.

Educational aims of comparative law

4.19 One of the purposes of the study of comparative law, as of all subjects, is knowledge for its own sake, fuelled by intellectual curiosity. The subject can be studied from a number of different perspectives: *historical*, depicting the progress of social

---

[25] One scholar, in a non-exhaustive list, has identified nine objectives. See: Roger Cotterrell, 'Comparatists and sociology' in Pierre Legrand and Roderick Munday (eds), *Comparative Legal Studies: traditions and transitions* (CUP, Cambridge, 2003) 134–5.

and legal development;[26] *taxonomic*, examining the classification of legal families and systems;[27] *sociological*, in which laws are interpreted and their impact and that of their transplantation into other legal systems assessed in their social context;[28] or *technical*, in terms of legislative, judicial or administrative technique. Again, the subject of the comparison may be as broad or as narrow as the comparatist chooses. It may, for example, be a comparison of legal families,[29] grouped by juristic ideology and style[30] (for instance, the civil law and the common law); legal systems within the same family (such as English law and Australian law) or within different families (for example, French law and Danish law); or the examination of particular fields (for example, contract law, tort law); or of particular subjects within a field (for example, the treatment of consequential loss in the law of contract); and it may be a comparison of substantive laws, of the rules of private international law or of procedural law and the administration of justice. In the case of multi-jurisdictional States, such as the United States, Canada and Mexico, comparative studies may be conducted at an internal level between different law districts within the same State.

4.20 For the scholar, a study of one or more foreign legal systems enhances his understanding of his own system, highlighting characteristics which he may previously have assumed to be common to systems generally rather than particular to his own, and thereby facilitating a critical re-examination of his own system's rules.

4.21 A focus exclusively on one's own legal system leads to a parochial, inward-looking perception of the law: a belief that the solutions offered are the only ones that are fair and sensible, and even an innate sense of the superiority of one's own legal system over others untrammeled by any knowledge that might suggest otherwise. The limiting effect of such a nationalistic approach was long ago pointed out by the brilliant jurist Rudolf von Jhering, who exerted a lasting influence on the development of comparative law.

Rudolf von Jhering, *Geist des römischen Rechts auf den verschiedenen Stufen seiner Entwicklung* (2nd edn, Breitkopf und Härtel, Leipzig, 1866) vol 1, 14

The formal unity of legal science as it formerly existed through the commonalty of one and the same Code in use throughout the greater part of Europe, and that working together by legal science in the most diverse countries on the same subject matter and the

---

[26] Which may provide a guide to the present. See: James Gordley, 'Comparative Law and Legal History' in in Reinhard Zimmermann and Mathias Reimann (eds), *The Oxford Handbook of Comparative Law* (OUP, Oxford, 2006)

[27] See: Patrick Glenn, 'Comparative Legal Families and Comparative Legal Traditions' in Reinhard Zimmermann and Mathias Reimann (eds), *The Oxford Handbook of Comparative Law* (OUP, Oxford, 2006)　　　　　　　　　　　　　　[28] See: Cotterrell (n 25).

[29] See above, para 4.07.

[30] See, for example, René David's classic work, *Les grands systèmes de droit contemporains* (11th edn, René David /Camille Jauffret-Spinosi, Dalloz, Paris, 2002).

same tasks is gone forever, along with the formal community of law. Legal science has been degraded to provincial jurisprudence, and the boundaries of legal science coincide with political boundaries. How humiliating and unworthy such form for a science! But it is for science alone to transcend these boundaries and to preserve for the future its old character of transnationality in the new form given by comparative jurisprudence. This will carry different methods, a broader outlook, a judgment more mature, and a greater freedom in the treatment of materials, and therefore the apparent loss will be turned effectively to its true advantage by raising science to higher levels of scholarly pursuit.[31]

Konrad Zweigert and Hein Kötz, *An Introduction to Comparative Law* (3rd edn, transl. Tony Weir, Clarendon Press, Oxford, 1998) 15

The primary aim of comparative law, as of all sciences, is knowledge. If one accepts that legal science includes not only the techniques of interpreting the texts, principles, rules and standards of a national system, but also the discovery of models for preventing or resolving social conflicts, then it is clear that the method of comparative law can provide a much richer range of model solutions than a legal science devoted to a single nation, simply because the different systems of the world can offer a greater variety of solutions than could be thought up in a lifetime by even the most imaginative jurist who was corralled in his own system. Comparative law is an 'école de vérité' which extends and enriches the 'supply of solutions' (ZITELMANN) and offers the scholar of critical capacity the opportunity of finding the 'better solution' for his time and place.

4.22　　These obvious advantages of comparison have not appealed to everyone, especially to those who see in the study and possible use of foreign law an opportunity for a judge, jurist, or legislator to 'cherry pick' ideas which simply reinforce his own value preferences. This mistrust of foreign law has been particularly strong in the United States during the last two decades, when much ink has been spilt over the appropriateness of using foreign law to frustrate the internal democratic process. Space does not permit us to discuss, even briefly, these American debates and the literature to which they have given rise,[32] but two observations are not out of place. The first is that in the USA this voluminous literature has shifted much of the debate about the study of foreign law from private law to public law. Secondly, this has made it even more necessary to examine and discuss the legal rules shaped by the courts against the existing political realities. This tendency to study law in conjunction with politics, economics, sociology etc, referred to generically in the USA under the heading 'Law and . . .', can both provide a deeper understanding of the link between legal rules and the societies in which they exist and help show some of the potential difficulties—real or exaggerated—in any attempt at legal borrowing or transplants.

---

[31] Extracted from Konrad Zweigert and Kurt Siehr, 'Jhering's Influence on the Development of the Comparative Legal Method' 19 Am J Comp L 215, 218 (1971). See below.

[32] For a recent comparative survey see Sir Basil Markesinis and Jörge Fedtke, *Foreign Law in National Courts: A New Source of Inspiration?* (2006, UCL Press London/Routledge-Cavendish Press Abingdon).

Practical uses of comparative law

4.23 While the acquisition of knowledge for its own sake is the essence of academic activity, comparative law is of great practical importance.[33] Indeed, for Zweigert and his followers, comparisons are made not for their intrinsic interest but as tools to be put to work.

Konrad Zweigert and Kurt Siehr, 'Jhering's Influence on the Development of Comparative Legal Method' 19 Am J Comp L 215, 220–2 (1971)

1. Modern legal comparison is *critical* in its attitude. The comparatist is not interested in the differences or similarities of various legal orders merely as facts, but in the fitness, the practicability, the justice, and the *why* of legal solutions to given problems. The mere description of a certain legal order might be interesting and illuminating; however, such 'foreign legal data' are not comparative law. True, comparative method can put the treasure chest of foreign experience to good use, but this does not get to the essence of legal comparison, which is the critical exploration of the usefulness of foreign solutions for the needs of domestic or international rule-making. Moreover, comparative law is not a museum of foreign legal systems. Its determinant feature with respect to policy choices and critiques is related to Jhering's abhorrence for antiquarianism . . .

2. Legal comparison is *undogmatic*. In this respect we mean the following: It is the fate of every legal order to see its principles and guiding rules turn eventually into the rigidity of dogmas. This applies equally to the codified systems and to the unwritten common law. These dogmas may acquire such a weight of their own that they will obfuscate and even distort the views of scholars and practitioners in finding better solutions . . . Thus, the legal comparatist turns a skeptical eye towards dogmas. As a consequence, functional legal comparison discards in its investigations any provincial, dogmatically tainted national legal language, and endeavors to use notions which are free of any kind of value-judgment and are gained through the investigation of sociological classification. As a legal sociologist, Jhering was again a pioneer in this field.

3. Finally—to borrow a word from Jhering—comparative legal method is *realistic*. It is realistic in covering in its investigations not merely the domains of legislation, adjudication, and doctrine but 'all the real motives which rule the world: the ethical, the psychological, the economic [and] those of legislative policy.'

4.24 There is, of course, an obvious link between legal education and practical application.

Reinhard Zimmermann, 'Comparative Law and the Europeanization of Private Law' in Reinhard Zimmermann and Mathias Reimann (eds), *The Oxford Handbook of Comparative Law* (OUP, Oxford, 2006)

It is widely accepted today that the Europeanization of private law decisively depends on a Europeanization of the legal training provided in the various universities throughout

---

[33] It may be noted at this point that the use of foreign law by the lawyers and judges of a particular national legal system is not easy and, as one author has put it, it requires careful 'packaging' to make the foreign ideas useable. This point is discussed at great length by Sir Basil Markesinis in many of his works, most recently in *Comparative Law in the Courtroom and the Classroom* (Hart Publishing, Oxford, 2003), ch 1–3.

Europe. For if students continue to be taught the niceties of their national legal systems without being made to appreciate the extent to which the relevant doctrines, or case law, constitute idiosyncrasies explicable only as a matter of historical accident, or misunderstanding, rather than rational design, and without being made to consider how else a legal problem may be solved, a national particularization of legal scholarship that takes the mysteries of the owner-possessor relationship (§§ 987 ff BGB) or the abracadabra of conditions, warranties, and intermediate terms for granted, threatens to imprint itself on the next generation of lawyers. Europeanization of the legal training, therefore, requires the strengthening of subjects which are not only of a foundational character but also inherently international in nature: Roman law, the history of private law and constitutional law in Europe, comparative law and jurisprudence. Sadly, however, in the law curricula of virtually all European countries these common elements tend to be reduced rather than enhanced in importance. A much more positive development has been the introduction of the Erasmus/Socrates programme by the Commission of the European Communities as a result of which the mobility of students across Europe has been very significantly increased. Every year, thousands of law students spend at least one semester at a university in another EU member state; and even if that period is not normally a fully integrated part of their degree programme, it encourages the kind of distance from the respective student's own legal system that is required for an interest in comparative law.

4.25 So a legal education in comparative law is an important element in ensuring that the practitioner of the future is able to put comparative law to practical use. What, then, do comparatists seek to achieve in practical terms?

Enhancement of understanding of one's own law

4.26 The use of comparative law to obtain a better understanding of one's own legal system and its distinctive characteristics has been elegantly described by Chief Justice Aharon Barak, then President of the Israel Supreme Court.

Aharon Barak, *Purposive Interpretation in Law* **(transl. Sari Bashi, Princeton U Press, Princeton, 2005,) 169–70**

Comparative law helps a judge understand the objective purpose of a text. You get to know yourself better by comparing yourself to others. Comparative law helps a judge 'expand his horizons and interpretive field of vision. Comparative law enriches our options.' The same legal institution (like 'good faith', for example) may play similar roles in different legal systems. To the extent that is so, comparative literature serves as a source of the objective purpose of a piece of legislation ('micro-comparison'). Furthermore, basic democratic principles are common to democratic countries. One democracy may inform or inspire the other ('macro-comparison').

Still, the technique has its limits. Comparative law is not just about comparing laws. Comparative interpretation can take place only among legal systems that share a common ideological basis. An interpretation must be sensitive to the uniqueness of each system. Sometimes, comparison is impossible ...

Above all, comparative law is important for its ability to expand the interpreter's horizons. It offers the judge guidance about the text's latent interpretive potential. It shows the interpreter what may or may not be accomplished through the text. It gives the judge information about the successes or failures of the different possibilities latent in the text. It makes the interpreter aware of links between a solution to an interpretative problem he or she faces and other legal problems. Comparative law serves as an experienced friend. Of course, judges have no obligation to resort to comparative law, and even when they do, the final adjudication must always be 'local' . . . Comparative law does not provide an answer to a specific problem troubling the judge; the judge consults comparative law at a higher level of abstraction, in order to expand his or her interpretive horizons. Judges should be careful, however, not to let intellectual curiosity lead them to imitate at the cost of self-denial. The purpose of consulting comparative law is to understand the local text better. The comparison must not interfere with the normative harmony of local law.

This distinguished judge returned to the theme in his most recent publication, in **4.27** which he referred to the widespread use of comparative law by Israeli courts and those of many other jurisdictions, whilst at the same expressing regret that the same approach was not adopted by the United States Supreme Court.

Aharon Barak, *The Judge in a Democracy*, **Princeton University Press, Princeton, 2006), 202–4** [33a]

The use of comparative law for the development of the common law and the interpretation of legal texts is determined by the tradition of the legal system. Israeli law, for example, makes extensive use of comparative law. When Israeli courts encounter an important legal problem, they frequently examine foreign law. Reference to United States law, United Kingdom law, Canadian law, and Australian law is commonplace. Those with linguistic ability also refer to Continental law, and sometimes we use English translations of Continental (mainly German, French and Italian) legal literature.

In countries of the British Commonwealth, there is much cross-fertilisation. Each such nation refers to the United Kingdom case law, the United Kingdom judges refer to Commonwealth case law, and Commonwealth judges in turn refer to each other's case law. The Supreme Court of Canada is particularly noteworthy for its frequent and fruitful use of comparative law. As such, Canadian law serves as a source of inspiration for many countries around the world. The generous use of comparative law can be found in the opinions of the South African Constitutional Court. In South Africa's Constitution, it is explicitly determined that:

When interpreting the Bill of Rights, a court, tribunal, or forum—

(a) must promote the values that underline an open and democratic society based on human dignity, equality and freedom;
(b) must consider international law;
(c) may consider foreign law.

Regrettably, until very recently the United States Supreme Court has made little use of comparative law. Many democratic countries draw inspiration from the United States Supreme Court, particularly in its interpretation of the United States Constitution. By contrast, some Justices of the United States Supreme Court do not cite foreign case law in their judgments. They fail to make use of an important soure of inspiration, one that enriches legal thinking, makes law more creative, and strengthens the democratic ties and foundations of different legal systems.

[33a] © 2006 Princeton University Press. Reprinted by permission of Princeton University Press.

Updating of national legal jurisprudence

4.28 A second objective is to bring specific rules evolved in national jurisprudence into line with modern thinking. If other jurisdictions have found better solutions to a common problem than those formulated by courts in one's own country, then why not adopt them? Lord Mansfield, the founder of English commercial law, was equally at home in the civil law and the common law, and frequently imported civil law concepts into his judgments.

4.29 A good modern example is furnished by the characteristically vivid judgment of one of England's greatest judges, Lord Denning, in a case concerning the scope of sovereign immunity. English law had traditionally adopted a principle of absolute immunity, while in other jurisdictions a distinction had been drawn between acts of a state done in exercise of its sovereign power and commercial activity, only the former attracting sovereign immunity. The question the English Court of Appeal had to decide was whether to throw over the traditional English law approach and adopt the distinction that had developed elsewhere.

Trendtex Trading Corp v Central Bank of Nigeria [1977] **QB 529, CA Lord Denning MR, 555–7**

In the last 50 years there has been a complete transformation in the functions of a sovereign state. Nearly every country now engages in commercial activities. It has its departments of state—creates its own legal entities—which go into the market places of the world. They charter ships. They buy commodities. They issue letters of credit. This transformation has changed the rules of international law relating to sovereign immunity. Many countries have now departed from the rule of absolute immunity. So many have departed from it that it can no longer be considered a rule of international law. It has been replaced by a doctrine of restrictive immunity. This doctrine gives immunity to acts of a governmental nature, described in Latin as jure imperii, but no immunity to acts of a commercial nature, jure gestionis. In 1951 Sir Hersch Lauterpacht showed that, even at that date, many European countries had abandoned the doctrine of absolute immunity and adopted that of restrictive immunity—see his important article, 'The Problem of Jurisdictional Immunities of Foreign States' in *The British Year Book of International Law*, 1951, vol 28, pp 220–272. Since that date there have been important conversions to the same view. Great impetus was given to it in 1952 in the famous 'Tate letter' in the United States. Many countries have now adopted it. We have been given a valuable collection of recent decisions in which the courts of Belgium, Holland, the German Federal Republic, the United States of America and others have abandoned absolute immunity and granted only restrictive immunity. Most authoritative of all is the opinion of the Supreme Court of the United States in *Alfred Dunhill of London Inc v Republic of Cuba*. It was delivered on May 24, 1976, by White J with the concurrence of the Chief Justice, Powell J and Rehnquist J:

> Although it had other views in years gone by, in 1952, as evidenced by . . . (the Tate letter) . . . the United States abandoned the absolute theory of sovereign immunity and embraced the restrictive view under which immunity in our courts should be granted only with respect to causes of action arising out of a foreign state's public or governmental actions and not with respect to those arising out of its commercial or

proprietary actions. This has been the official policy of our government since that time, as the attached letter of November 25, 1975, confirms ... 'Such adjudications are consistent with international law on sovereign immunity'.

To this I would add the European Convention on State Immunity (Basle 1972), Article 4, paragraph 1, which has been signed by most of the European countries.

Are we to follow likewise?

Seeing this great cloud of witnesses, I would ask: is there not here sufficient evidence to show that the rule of international law has changed? What more is needed? Are we to wait until every other country save England recognises the change? Ought we not to act now? Whenever a change is made, someone some time has to make the first move. One country alone may start the process. Others may follow. At first a trickle, then a stream, last a flood. England should not be left behind on the bank. ' ... We must take the current when it serves, or lose our ventures.': *Julius Caesar*, Act IV, sc III.

In one respect already the Privy Council have abandoned the absolute theory and accepted the restrictive theory. It is in respect of actions in rem: see *The Philippine Admiral* [1977] AC 373, 402. But unfortunately the Privy Council seem to have thought that the absolute theory still applied to actions in personam. They said, at p 402:

> ... it is no doubt open to the House of Lords to decide otherwise but it may fairly be said to be at the least unlikely that it would do so.

That is a dismal forecast. It is out of line with the good sense shown in the rest of the judgment of the Privy Council. This is how they put it, at pp 402–403:

> ... the trend of opinion in the world outside the Commonwealth since the last war has been increasingly against the application of the doctrine of sovereign immunity to ordinary trading transactions ... Their Lordships themselves think that it is wrong that it should be so applied ... Thinking as they do that the restrictive theory is more consonant with justice they do not think that they should be deterred from applying it.

Such reasoning is of general application. It covers actions in personam. In those actions, too, the restrictive theory is more consonant with justice. So it should be applied to them. It should not be retained as an indefensible anomaly.

I see no reason why we should wait for the House of Lords to make the change. After all, we are not considering here the rules of English law on which the House has the final say. We are considering the rules of international law. We can and should state our view as to those rules and apply them as we think best, leaving it to the House to reverse us if we are wrong.

The modern rule

What then is the modern rule of international law? I tried to state it nearly 20 years ago in *Rahimtoola v Nizam of Hyderabad* [1958] AC 379, 422:

> If the dispute brings into question, for instance, the legislative or international transactions of a foreign government, or the policy of its executive, the court should grant immunity if asked to do so, because it does offend the dignity of a foreign sovereign to have the merits of such a dispute canvassed in the domestic courts of another country: but, if the dispute concerns, for instance, the commercial transactions of a foreign government (whether carried on by its own departments or agencies or by

setting up separate legal entities), and it arises properly within the territorial jurisdiction of our courts, there is no ground for granting immunity.

I recently re-stated it in *Thai-Europe Tapioca Service Ltd v Government of Pakistan, Directorate of Agricultural Supplies* [1975] 1 WLR 1485, 1491:

> . . . a foreign sovereign has no immunity when it enters into a commercial transaction with a trader here and a dispute arises which is properly within the territorial jurisdiction of our courts. If a foreign government incorporates a legal entity which buys commodities on the London market; or if it has a state department which charters ships on the Baltic Exchange: it thereby enters into the market places of the world: and international comity requires that it should abide by the rules of the market.

Since those cases, there have been two very recent cases on the subject: *The Philippine Admiral* [1977] AC 373 in November 1975, in the Privy Council; and *Alfred Dunhill of London Inc v Republic of Cuba* on May 24, 1976, in the Supreme Court of the United States. There is a Bill also before the House of Representatives of the United States reported on September 9, 1976 (now passed into law, Foreign Sovereign Immunities Act of 1976) which is very much on the lines I suggested. All this confirms me in the view which I have expressed.

4.30 Lord Denning's approach was subsequently approved by the House of Lords in *Playa Larga v I Congreso del Partido*.[34] Since then, English courts, and the House of Lords in particular, have shown an increasing interest in legal doctrines and developments in continental Europe.[35]

Aid to the drafting of new legislation

4.31 Just as courts sometimes look to the jurisprudence of other jurisdictions to help resolve a problem, so also legislatures borrow from enactments elsewhere.

Jan Smits, 'Comparative Law and its Influence on National Legal Systems' in Reinhard Zimmermann and Mathias Reimann (eds), *The Oxford Handbook of Comparative Law* (OUP, Oxford, 2006)

The use of comparative law while drafting new legislation is as old as the phenomenon of statutory law itself. It is well known that the law of the Twelve Tables (450 BC) was influenced by Roman visits to foreign (in particular Greek) cities and even the Code of Hammurabi (1,700 BC) is presumably based upon the laws then prevailing in the Near East. In fact, the modern science of comparative law was primarily provoked by the wish to look at foreign law to improve national legislation. This discipline of 'législation comparée', as propagated by the *Société de Législation Comparé* (founded in 1869), led to the study of foreign codes not only in France but also in other countries. Famous examples of drawing inspiration from foreign law are to be found in Germany, where the Prussian company law of 1843 was partly based upon the French Commercial Code of 1807 and

---

[34] [1983] 1 AC 244 (HL).
[35] See, for example, *Fairchild v Glenhaven Funeral Services Ltd* [2002] 1 AC 32 (see below, para 4.61); *White v Jones* [1995] 2 AC 207, HL; *Greatorex v Greatorex* [2000] 1 WLR 1976 QBD; and Basil Markesinis, *Comparative Law in the Courtroom and Classroom* (Hart Publishing, Oxford, 2003) ch 4.

where the large nineteenth century unification projects in the areas of private law, procedural law and criminal law were inspired by extensive comparative research as well. There is also abundant evidence of such influence of foreign law on national legislation in other countries. When Alan Watson held that the migration of ideas between legal systems is 'the most fertile source of (legal) development', he referred mainly to legislation being adopted by countries other than those for which it was originally passed. More examples include income tax, which was imported from England to the European Continent around 1800, Austrian competition law, which formed the basis for the German *Kartellgesetz* of 1923, the Swedish institution of the ombudsman, which was taken over in many countries, and the French *Loi Badinter* (1985), which regulates the compensation of victims of traffic accidents and which was itself based upon comparative research and subsequently influenced other European countries' legislation. The wholesale importation of civil codes into other countries is also a well known phenomenon. Thus, not only did the French *Code civil* serve as a model for many countries in Europe and South America, the Swiss Civil Code of 1907 was taken over in Turkey (1926), and the drafts of the 1900 German Civil Code, together with French law, played a large role in the drafting of the Civil Code of Japan (1896). The new civil codes of the Netherlands (1992) and Québec (1994), and the new German law of obligations of 2002, were also based upon extensive comparative reasoning. Likewise, it is no coincidence that most European countries have enacted rather similar laws in the fields of environmental liability, company law, social security and family law. Sometimes it seems as if one can meticulously trace the migration of an institution from one country to another: thus, same-sex-marriage was first recognised by statute in the Netherlands in 2002, subsequently accepted in Belgium and most of the Canadian provinces in 2003 (followed by the whole of Canada in 2005), accepted in the state of Massachusetts (2004) and Spain (2005), and its introduction is now being discussed in many other countries. Of special importance is the influence of Western law on the former communist countries of Central and Eastern Europe: the new codes in the areas of civil, commercial and criminal law were usually based upon extensive comparative considerations. The same is true for China, which also based its new contract code of 1999 on comparative research.

In most of the above examples, the respective governments had resources available to integrate comparative law findings into the drafting of new legislation. In civil law countries such as Germany and France this has even become routine: in the drafting of any major new statute, the ministry of justice usually looks for inspiration to the laws of other countries. In this respect, it sometimes solicits opinions on foreign law from comparative law research centres, but not infrequently it relies on research by its own civil servants. This is different in many common law jurisdictions, where a ministry of justice in the Continental style does not exist. However, one cannot say that there is less influence of foreign law on these countries' legal systems, only that such influence takes a different form. In the United Kingdom, it is through the English and Scottish Law Commissions that comparative law finds its way into legislation. Section 3(1)(f) of the Law Commissions Act 1965 states that one of the functions of the Law Commissions is 'to obtain such information as to the legal systems of other countries as appears to the Commissioners likely to facilitate the performance of any of their functions' (that is: systematically developing and reforming the law of England and Scotland). An example is the (English) Law Commission's report on 'Privity of Contracts: Contracts for the Benefit of Third Parties'. It not only discussed the laws of other common law jurisdictions, but also stated that a factor in support of reform of the third party rule in English law was that 'the legal systems of most of the member states of the European Union recognise and enforce the rights of third party beneficiaries under contracts.' The report led in the end to the Contracts (Rights of Third Parties) Act 1999.

In the United States, the American Law Institute (founded in 1932) makes use of comparative law in drafting the Restatements of Law. Model codes (like the Model Penal Code) are also inspired by other legal systems, and even in the field of competition law the federal legislature benefited from European experience in reviewing the Sherman Antitrust Act of 1890. Generally speaking, however, the American debate is less enlightened by foreign law than is the case in Europe: reference to foreign law is made, but it seems to play a less important role than in European countries. This may be linked to the fact that inter-state comparison (ie among the fifty three American jurisdictions) is much more important than comparison with legal systems outside the United States. 'The American common law', as Zaphiriou states, 'contains contrasts that are almost as instructive and often more constructive than any comparison with the law of a foreign country.'

When confronted with these examples, one can only agree with Schlesinger: little new legislation is enacted, in Europe and elsewhere, without at least some comparative research, and *every* legal system contains imported elements.

Guide to the policy implications of a new development in national jurisprudence

4.32 Comparative law may also assist judges in deciding whether a proposed step-change in a legal rule to extend the boundaries of liability would produce adverse consequences. Thus, in *Kleinwort Benson Ltd v Lincoln CC*, [36] the House of Lords in England was called on to consider whether money paid under a mistake of law should be recoverable. A long line of authority had held that recovery was limited to mistake of fact. But materials presented to the House on the policy adopted in a number of civil law systems on the continent of Europe showed that there was no blanket rule excluding recovery of money paid under a mistake of law, that such a rule was considered unnecessary and that the experience of the systems in question assisted in dispelling the fears expressed in the early English cases that a right of recovery for mistake of law might lead to a flood of litigation.[37] Guy Canivet, First President of the French *Cour de Cassation*, has described the utility of comparative law for the judge.

Guy Canivet, 'The Use of Comparative Law Before the French Private Law Courts' in Guy Canivet, Mads Andenas and Duncan Fairgrieve (eds), *Comparative Law Before the Courts* (British Institute of International and Comparative Law, London, 2004) 188

What are the uses a national judge can make of comparative law? We can start by stating the obvious, that is that comparison with other legal cultures unquestionably enlarges the judge's horizon. Comparative law multiplies the available viewpoints and interpretative options. With globalization, different national institutions are increasingly called to treat the same kinds of legal problem. Therefore, to the extent that similarities exist between legal values, the judge can better fulfil his role because of the enhancement of his stock of possibilities. But at a deeper level we can see that many fundamental principles

---

[36] [1999] 2 AC 349 (HL).   [37] Ibid 374–5 (Lord Goff).

underpinning a legal system are common between democratic societies. It is only natural that legal comparison can reveal those options by bringing them out into the open.

The structure of comparison is always more complicated than a simple lining up of rules or institutions coming from different countries. We should not simply compare individual legal solutions on this or that problem; we should also examine the failures and successes of these solutions vis-à-vis the fundamental principles of the legal system in question. In other words, comparative law is always useful for the local judge because it makes him understand the coherence between a judicial precedent and a body of fundamental principles that underlie a legal system. Thus, the judge will be better equipped to perform this work of harmonization in his own legal system.

If two legal systems share basic cultural features, it should be possible to use comparative law as a source of inspiration for the judge's task of interpreting written law. The judge can learn a lot from foreign constitutions or statutes about the aims pursued by another legal system and about the arrangement of legal means with a view to obtaining these aims. Once more, the utility of the comparison does not consist so much in the alignment of concrete legal solutions as in the interpretative methodology, that is, in the way a legal culture approaches a problem and arranges the means it has at its disposal in order to resolve it. The judge will not be so much influenced by concrete legal solutions found in another legal system; he will be mostly influenced by this hermeneutic back-and-forth between the specific or general goals of a legal rule or institution and the practical solutions that foreign judges have conceived in order to pursue those goals. The judge will, in the end, be inspired more by the mechanisms of interpretative decoding he will find in a legal culture that is not his own than by ready-made solutions he can easily discern by simply consulting legal textbooks.

Development of transnational commercial law

If comparative law can be of assistance to judges and to legislators who are con- **4.33** sidering whether to adopt or to change a particular regime, it is also an essential tool for those engaged in the international or regional harmonization of law, whether by multilateral conventions or by restatements such as the UNIDROIT Principles of International Commercial Contracts or the Principles of European Contract Law prepared by the Commission on European Contract Law (CECL), both of which were taken into consideration in the later stages of work on an Act to reform the German law of obligations which came into force in 2002.[38]

A comparative study may reveal a convergence of national solutions to a common **4.34** problem, and even where this is not the case, the contrasts it throws up between one approach and another may facilitate a search for best solutions.

The needs of commerce have always made special demands on applied compar- **4.35** ative law, in helping to assess, allocate and mitigate cross-border transaction risk, particularly through the harmonization of commercial law. The first major

---

[38] See: Reinhard Zimmermann, *The New German Law of Obligations: historical and comparative perspectives* (OUP, Oxford, 2005) 41 and 77; Basil S Markesinis, Hannes Unberath and Angus Johnston, *The German Law of Contract* (2nd edn, Hart Publishing, Oxford, 2006), ch 9.

comparative law analysis in England was driven by the requirements of trade. This was Leone Levi's great four-volume treatise published between 1850 and 1852 comparing the mercantile laws of the United Kingdom with those of no fewer than sixty other countries, together with the Institutes of Justinian.[39] In this remarkable work, Levi addresses the law applicable to merchants generally, commerce generally, partnership, agency, carriage of goods, contracts, sales, bills of exchange, mortgages (less extensively), shipping, bankruptcy, commercial jurisdiction, and tribunals, not to mention statistical charts, a history of commerce, chronological tables and a table of usances.[40] He summarizes the laws of Great Britain, then of each of the other fifty-nine jurisdictions, following which he sets out an analysis, highlighting core similarities and differences.

4.36   Foreshadowing efforts to follow, Levi was the first to propose the unification of international commercial law, a 'Universal Code', on the basis of extensive comparative law analysis.[41] Levi believed that his work identified 'comprehensive universal principles, such as any country professing to have regard to justice may readily consent to.' Like the quest for the holy grail of a new *jus commune*, this pursuit of universal principles of commercial law has so far proved fruitless, though vigorous attempts have been made to revive it through the concept of the new *lex mercatoria*.[42]

4.37   In the 150 years since Levi's great work, there have been a considerable number of international instruments in the field of commercial law, as well as regional commercial law-making, most notably in the European Union, for both of which purposes existing national laws have provided the inspiration, though without precluding entirely new solutions. Moreover, in interpreting a European Community instrument, the European Court of Justice frequently refers to those national laws of Member States from which the instrument derived its inspiration.[43] Comparative law may also help to identify a general principle from which to fashion a new rule of international law.

---

[39]   Leoni Levi, *Mercantile Law of Great Britain compared with the Codes and Laws of Commerce of Anhalt, Austria, Baden, Bavaria, Belgium, Brazil, Bremen, British Colonies, British Guiana, Brunswick, Canada, China, Denmark, East Indies, France, Frankfort, Greece, Guernsey, Hamburgh, Hanover, Hayti, Hesse Electorate, Hindustan, Holland, Hungary, Ionian Islands, Lombardy, Louisiana, Lubeck, Llucca, Luxemburg, Malta, Mecklenburg, Mexico, Modena, Nassau, Norway, Normandy, Papel States, Parma, Portugal, Prussia, Russia, Sardinia, Saxe-Coburg-Gotha, Saxe-Weimar Saxony, South America, St. Lucia, Sweden, Switzerland (Cantons), Spain, Tunis, Turkey, Tuscany, Two Sicilies, United States, Wallachia, Wurtemburg, and the Institutes of Justinian* (William Benning & Co, London, 1850–52).

[40]   Usages between countries with respect to the time of payment of bills of exchange. These disappeared, and it is nowadays left to the bill itself to specify the time of payment.

[41]   For an extract from Levi's letter to Prince Albert making that unification proposal, see above, para 1.25.   [42]   See ch 1.

[43]   See generally: Patrick Glenn, 'Aims of Comparative Law' in Jan M Smits (ed), *Elgar Encyclopaedia of Comparative Law* (Edward Elgar Publishing, Cheltenham (UK), 2006) ch 4.

Konrad Zweigert and Hein Kötz, *An Introduction to Comparative Law* (3rd edn, transl. Tony Weir, Clarendon Press, Oxford, 1998) 24–5

The final function of comparative law ... is its significant role in the preparation of projects for the international unification of law. The political aim behind such unification is to reduce or eliminate, so far as desirable and possible, the discrepancies between national legal systems by inducing them to adopt common principles of law. The method used in the past and still often practiced today is to draw up a uniform law on the basis of work by experts in comparative law and to incorporate it into a multipartite treaty ...

Unification cannot be achieved by simply conjuring up an ideal on any topic and hoping to have it adopted. One must first find what is common to the jurisdictions concerned and incorporate that in the uniform law. Where there are areas of difference, one must reconcile them either by adopting the best existing variant or by finding, through comparative methods, a new solution which is better and more easily applied than any of the existing ones. Preparatory studies in comparative law are absolutely essential here; without them one cannot discover the points of agreement or disagreement in the different legal systems of the world, let alone decide which solution is the best. A model of such a preparatory study is ERNST RABEL, *Das Recht des Warenkaufs* ... , which was of vital importance for the unification of international sales law.

Of particular significance is the interest of both developing and developed countries and regions in international and regional restatements. Thus, UNIDROIT is advising the Organization for the Harmonization of Business Law in Africa (OHADA) on a draft Uniform Act on Contracts, and Professor Marcel Fontaine has completed a preliminary draft based on the UNIDROIT Principles of International Commercial Contracts.[44] Similarly, the European Commission has commissioned a study of European contract law with a view to the preparation of a European Contract Code based on the Principles of European Contract Law produced by the Commission on European Contract Law.[45] In both cases, the basic text is the work of international scholars, not of governments, yet if adopted, it has the potential to make a profound impact on business transactions. **4.38**

There are three overriding contemporary reasons for reference to such foreign and comparative input. First, there has been a significant increase, in aggregate and percentage terms, in cross-border commercial transactions. Second, the pace of change in commercial legal systems in developing jurisdictions has accelerated. Many of these countries are wrestling with the dual, and not always consistent, tasks of (a) rediscovering historical legal principles affected by recently removed political influences (for example, the Central and Eastern European countries formerly under Soviet sway), and (b) bringing their legal framework for commercial transactions into line with emerging international norms. Third, there has been a rapid expansion of regional commercial law-making, most notably in the European Union. The role of international development and lending bodies, such as the World Bank, the International Monetary Fund, the European Bank for **4.39**

---

[44] As to which see below, paras 14.04 ff.   [45] See below, paras 14.04 ff.

Reconstruction and Development, as well as national experts providing technical support, in encouraging reference to foreign and best practice law and supporting materials in the law reform process, can hardly be overstated. The law and economics justification for commercial law reform also seeks use of foreign and best practice sources, although the factual basis for that justification often seems anecdotal.

Refinement of the conflict of laws

4.40 There are at least three situations in which comparative law has a role to play in the field of the conflict of laws. In the first place, resort to comparative law may be necessary in order to enable the court to characterize an issue in a case involving a foreign element.[46] Second, a comparative analysis of conflict of laws rules may lead a court to discard its own rule governing a particular case, and to adopt that fashioned by another jurisdiction. Third, such a comparative analysis, in showing the relative advantages and disadvantages of different legal systems, may influence a choice of law in a contract, while the merits and demerits of a system in terms of efficiency and predictability of decision-making may influence a choice of forum.

Horatia Muir Watt, 'Private International Law' in Jan M Smits (ed), *Elgar Encyclopaedia of Comparative Law* (Edward Elgar Publishing, Cheltenham (UK), 2006) 571–2

Firstly, the competitive paradigm invests comparative law with a new importance, since in highlighting differences between legal systems, it can point to the factors which make them more or less attractive to investors. The recent, controversial report of the World Bank, 'Doing Business' ... has pointed out some of the normative and institutional factors which may be more or less conducive to international investment. Comparative law can help show that the competitiveness of a given legal system in this respect, for instance in offering greater legal certainty, may depend not only on the content of its legal rules, but also on the efficiency of its courts, or the availability of effective remedies ... Thus it may be that interjurisdictional competition is realistic only in the case of heterogeneous products, where regulatory policies create winners and losers. Rules which may appear to be 'neutral', or even 'natural' from an internal perspective, such as the rules on formation and validity of contracts, can, when confronted with other legal systems, prove not only to be one legal construct among many other possibilities, but also to comprise an implicit regulatory regime ...

A second role of comparative law within the interjurisdictional paradigm consists in confronting the systems of private international law themselves, to determine the extent to which they are liberalizing or regulating competition. In this respect, mobility is essentially metaphorical, as it signifies less the possibility of moving physically from one jurisdiction to another (voting with one's feet) than the possibility to exit a legal system in favour of another. This is precisely where it becomes apparent that, to a certain extent, law is a product on a market.

---

[46] Zweigert and Kötz (n 7) 6–7.

Commercial law dispute resolution

Because of the huge growth in cross-border trade and finance, with many financial **4.41** and securities transactions having points of contact with a number of jurisdictions, comparative law is increasingly relevant to dispute resolution, both by courts and by arbitrators, as parties search for the law (or alternatively a conflict rule leading to the law) most helpful to their case.

Consistency of interpretation of uniform laws

Comparative law is not infrequently utilized when the interpreter is called upon **4.42** to apply uniform texts. All modern commercial law conventions—which are pluri-lingual with each text being 'equally authentic'[47]—expressly state that, in their interpretation, regard is to be had to their 'international character' and the 'need to promote uniformity' in their application. One of the variants further emphasizes the need to promote 'predictability' and the other 'the observance of good faith in international trade'.

While these will be taken up in subsequent chapters, we here observe that this **4.43** is a clear directive to take into account, at least in the case of ambiguity, foreign language texts and related legislative materials, and, to some degree, foreign decisions. Questions and problems are ever present, more so relating to foreign decisions. First, differing weight is given to the case law across the spectrum of legal systems. Much has been written, for example, on the differing form, logic, function, degrees of authoritativeness, and role of *stare decisis* of case law as between common and civil law systems. Second, a court may be reluctant to have regard to decisions in legal systems with fundamentally different characteristics and interpretative principles. Third, many rules of interpretation limit the use of supplemental material when a text is thought by the court interpreting it to be clear. Fourth, national courts often, as a matter of practice, interpret international uniform law in a manner that avoids inconsistency with national law. Yet international legal data bases have been and are being set up to facilitate the use of foreign decisions on international texts.

Much experience in comparative judicial interpretation derives from the treat- **4.44** ment of uniform texts in the field of transportation law, namely, the treaty systems addressing international carriage by air, rail, sea and road, most notably under the Hague Rules (shipping—unification relating to bills of lading) and the Warsaw System (air—unification relating to carriage by air). Language problems are

---

[47] See: Article 33(1) and (3) of the Vienna Treaty on the Law of Treaties 1969. Where a treaty is authenticated in more than one language, each is 'equally authoritative' unless otherwise agreed. Where a 'comparison of the authentic texts discloses a difference of meaning' (not removed by application of the Vienna Treaty's general rule of interpretation, Article 31, or through supplemental means of interpretation, Article 32), then the meaning which 'best reconciles the texts, having regard to the objects and purpose of the treaty' is to be adopted.

sometimes acute, and courts may find that a foreign language text is clearer and more precise than the text in its own language, even where the latter is equally authentic.

Air France v Saks 470 US 392, 105 S Ct 1338 (1985)

[This case, before the United States Supreme Court, addresses the interpretation of the word 'accident' under Article 17 of the Convention for the Unification of Certain Rules Relating to International Carriage by Air 1929 ('Warsaw Convention'). Under Article 36 of the Warsaw Convention, the authentic text is French.]

Justice O'Connor delivered the opinion of the Court at 396–404:

Air France is liable to a passenger under the terms of the Warsaw Convention only if the passenger proves that an 'accident' was the cause of her injury … The narrow issue presented is whether respondent can meet this burden by showing that her injury was caused by the normal operation of the aircraft's pressurization system. The proper answer turns on interpretation of a clause in an international treaty to which the United States is a party. '[Treaties] are construed more liberally than private agreements, and to ascertain their meaning we may look beyond the written words to the history of the treaty, the negotiations, and the practical construction adopted by the parties.'

[The court then highlights the pertinent wording from the French text ('*lorsque l'accident qui a causé le dommage*') and the official American translation ('if the accident which caused the damage') which was before the Senate at the time of advice and consent to ratification.]

The word 'accident' is not a technical legal term with a clear legal meaning … To determine the meaning of the term 'accident' in Article 17 we *must consider its French meaning* [emphasis added] … This is true not because 'we are forever chained to French law' by the Convention … but because it is our responsibility to give the specific words of a treaty a meaning consistent with the shared expectations of the contracting parties … We look to the French legal meaning for guidance as to these expectations because the Warsaw Convention was drafted in French by continental jurists … A survey of French cases and dictionaries indicate that the French legal meaning of the term 'accident' differs little from the meaning of the term in Great Britain, Germany, and the United States … In determining precisely what causes can be considered accidents, we 'find the opinions of our sister signatories to be entitled to considerable weight' … While few decisions are precisely on point, we note that, in *Air France v Haddad, Judgment of June 19, 1997, Cour d'appel de Paris* … , a French court observed that the term 'accident' in Article 17 of the Warsaw Convention embraces causes of injuries that are fortuitous or unpredictable. European legal scholars have generally construed the word 'accident' in Article 17 to require that the passenger's injury be caused by a sudden or unexpected event other than the normal operation of the plane.

4.45 English courts have taken a similar approach and, indeed, have on occasion quoted extensively from foreign language texts.

Fothergill v Monarch Airlines Ltd [1981] AC 251 (HL)

[In this case the House of Lords had to consider the meaning of the word 'damage' in Article 26(2) of the 1929 Warsaw Convention on carriage by air.]

Lord Diplock at 281–82:

The language of an international convention has not been chosen by an English parliamentary draftsman. It is neither couched in the conventional English legislative idiom nor designed to be construed exclusively by English judges. It is addressed to a much wider and more varied judicial audience than is an Act of Parliament that deals with purely domestic law. It should be interpreted, as Lord Wilberforce put it in *James Buchanan & Co Ltd v Babco Forwarding & Shipping (UK) Ltd* [1978] AC 141, 152, 'unconstrained by technical rules of English law, or by English legal precedent, but on broad principles of general acceptance.'

Lord Wilberforce at 272–74:

My Lords, some of the problems which arise when the courts of this country are faced with texts of treaties or conventions in different languages were discussed in *James Buchanan & Co Ltd v Babco Forwarding & Shipping (UK) Ltd* [1978] AC 141. It is obvious that the present represents a special and indeed unique case.

Here it is not only permissible to look at a foreign language text, but obligatory. What is made part of English law is the text set out *in Schedule 1*, ie in both Part I and Part II, so both English and French texts must be looked at. Furthermore, it cannot be judged whether there is an inconsistency between two texts unless one looks at both. So, in the present case the process of interpretation seems to involve:

1. Interpretation of the English text, according to the principles upon which international conventions are to be interpreted (see *Buchanan's* case and *Stag Line Ltd v Foscolo, Mango & Co Ltd* [1932] AC 328, 350).
2. Interpretation of the French text according to the same principles but with additional linguistic problems.
3. Comparison of these meanings.

Moreover, if the process of interpretation leaves the matter in doubt, the question may have to be faced whether 'travaux préparatoires' may be looked at in order to resolve the difficulty.

I start by considering the purpose of Article 26, and I do not think that in doing so I am infringing any 'golden rule.' Consideration of the purpose of an enactment is always a legitimate part of the process of interpretation, and if it is usual—and indeed correct— to look first for a clear meaning of the words used, it is certain, in the present case, both on a first look at the relevant text, and from the judgments in the courts below, that no 'golden rule' meaning can be ascribed. The purpose of Article 26, on the other hand, appears to me to be reasonably clear. It is: (1) to enable the airline to check the nature of the 'damage', (2) to enable it to make inquiries how and when it occurred; (3) to enable it to assess its possible liability, to make provision in its accounts and if necessary to claim on its insurers; (4) to enable it to ensure that relevant documents (for example, the baggage checks or passenger ticket, or the air waybill) are retained until the issue of liability is disposed of.

If one then inquires whether these considerations are relevant to a case of partial loss of objects contained in baggage, the answer cannot be doubtful: they clearly are. Moreover, prompt notification may give the airline an opportunity of recovering the objects lost.

In particular, as regards (4), preservation of the baggage check is important in order to establish the relevant weight upon which the limit of liability is fixed—see Article 22 (2) (*b*) which explicitly mentions 'any object contained therein' (for example, in registered baggage).

There seems, on the contrary, to be no sense in making a distinction between damage to baggage—which presumably must include damage to contents—and loss of contents.

What then of the language? No doubt in an English legal context loss is one thing, damage another. But the nature of the text in question does not suggest that it was drafted with strict English meanings in mind. First, in the *English text*, the word 'damage' in the Convention is used in more than one sense. Sometimes it means 'monetary loss'—for example in Article 17, or Article 19. Sometimes it means 'physical damage'—for example, Article 22 (2)(*b*). In some articles it is used with both meanings, for example, Article 18. Whether it can include 'partial loss' is, textually, open to argument. There can be no doubt that the carrier is liable for loss, total or partial, of the contents of baggage—the appellant does not contend the contrary. Article 22 (2)(*b*) indeed makes provision for this. But when one looks for the word which covers this, the search yields no clear result. Article 18 refers to 'loss of' registered baggage, and 'damage to' registered baggage. Nothing there is really apt to cover loss of something contained in the baggage. I am inclined to agree with Lord Denning MR when he says [1980] QB 23, 36: 'In Article 18(1) I think "loss of" means loss of the *whole* suitcase . . .' In this state of the text we must see whether the French text can assist.

The *French text*. This, at least, avoids part of the English difficulty, in that it confines the use of the word 'dommage' to monetary loss (Articles 17, 18, 19, 20, 25). When it refers to physical 'damage' it uses the word 'avarie.' So what does 'avarie' mean? This raises, once more, the question how the court ought to ascertain the meaning of a word or an expression in a foreign language.

My Lords, as in *James Buchanan & Co Ltd v Babco Forwarding & Shipping (UK) Ltd* [1978] AC 141, I am not willing to lay down any precise rule on this subject. The process of ascertaining the meaning must vary according to the subject matter. If a judge has some knowledge of the relevant language, there is no reason why he should not use it: this is particularly true of the French or Latin languages, so long languages of our courts. There is no reason why he should not consult a dictionary if the word is such that a dictionary can reveal its significance: often of course it may substitute one doubt for another. (In *Buchanan's* case I was perhaps too optimistic in thinking that a simple reference to a dictionary could supply the key to the meaning of 'avarie.') In all cases he will have in mind that ours is an adversary system: it is for the parties to make good their contentions. So he will inform them of the process he is using, and, if they think fit, they can supplement his resources with other material—other dictionaries, other books of reference, text-books and decided cases. They may call evidence of an interpreter, if the language is one unknown to the court, or of an expert if the word or expression is such as to require expert interpretation. Between a technical expression in Japanese and a plain word in French there must be a whole spectrum which calls for suitable and individual treatment.

In the present case the word 'avarie' would not I think convey a clear meaning to an English mind without assistance. The courts (both Kerr J and the Court of Appeal) therefore looked at dictionaries and at certain text-books and articles and in my opinion this process cannot be criticised. Neither could they have been criticised if they had allowed expert evidence to be called—for 'avarie' is, or may be, a term of art. There were five dictionaries involved, of evidently different standards: some of English publication, others of French. I regard the latter, which provide an analysis, as of greater value than the former, which provide a translation—since then we have to interpret the translation. Two are of high quality—that of M Raymond Barraine, docteur en droit [*Nouveau Dictionnaire de Droit et de Sciences Economiques*, 4th ed (1974)], and the *Trésor de la Langue Française* (1974) published by the Centre National de la Recherche Scientifique. They seem to me to show that 'avarie' has both an ordinary meaning and a special meaning as a term of maritime law. In the ordinary meaning, the word signifies physical damage to a movable; in its special meaning, it is capable of meaning physical damage, or loss, including partial loss. In my opinion this does not carry the matter much beyond the English text: both use words of some ambiguity; perhaps the French text points somewhat more in the direction of partial loss than does the English. The text-book writers (to be considered) do not favour the view that 'avarie' naturally means partial loss and I do not think that we can so hold. An attempt was made to carry the argument from the French text further by suggesting that 'avarie' means 'average' and 'average' means partial loss. But I cannot accept that it is sound, in effect, to retranslate 'avarie' by 'average' when in fact it is translated by 'damage.' Clearly 'average' could not be sensibly inserted in the English text in replacement for 'damage.' Nor am I persuaded that 'average,' though it may have to do with partial loss, means partial loss.

The linguistic argument, alone, remains to my mind inconclusive.

The text-books and articles, however, do take the matter further. Professor du Pontavice in 'Maritime Law and Air Law' [Revue Trimestrielle de Droit Commercial, vol XXI (1968), p 472] expresses a clear opinion that 'avarie' in Article 26 includes partial loss following a theft, approving a decision to this effect by an Argentine court. M Max Litvine, of the Free University of Brussels, writes, referring to Article 26:

> Where the loss or destruction is only partial, it is necessary to decide that Article 26 must be effective since the partial loss or destruction a fortiori constitutes damage. (*Droit Aérien* (Brussels, 1970), p 250.)

Professor Rodière of the University of Paris in his book on transport law (*Droit des Transports* (Paris, 1977) writes (s 607): 'The text' (of Article 26) ' . . . relates only to average' (ie, 'avarie'). 'In my view, it must be *extended to the partial loss, . . .*' agreeing with M Litvine whose work 'is the safest there is.' He appears to express a contrary view in the *Précis Dalloz* (*Droit des Transports Terrestres et Aériens*, 2nd ed (Paris, 1977) s 271), but the fuller treatment in his own work is, in my view, to be preferred. Dr Werner Guldimann, attorney at Zurich, often acting as expert for the Swiss Government, writes in *Internationales Lufttransportrecht* (Zurich, 1965) p 155:

> [Article 26, paragraph 2] stipulates time limits for complaints made in respect of damage . . . and delays . . . to goods and baggage . . . No time limit is set for destruction and loss, since in such cases it may be assumed that the carrier is already aware of the occurrence and is able to make the necessary arrangements required to secure proof—since this is the aim of such time limits. Thus the term damage is given a broad interpretation: simply partial loss and partial destruction are both basically considered to be damage . . .

I quote also from an extract from the Argentine *Compendio de Derecho Aeronáutico* (1975) written by Juan A Lena Paz because this well states the reasoning (section 461, p 286):

> As paragraph 2 of Article 26 only mentions 'damage,' it is necessary to determine whether the protest (ie complaint) is relevant in the case of 'loss' of the merchandise or luggage. A distinction should be made here between total loss and partial loss. Since the first is a fact which can be verified at any time without the need for proof, a protest is not necessary to bring an action against the transporter and paragraph 3 of Article 13 … is applicable:… On the other hand, in the case of partial loss, it is vital to establish what is missing as quickly as possible since, as time goes by, the probability of the loss being the result of an event occurring after delivery increases.

My Lords, this consensus is impressive. It supports an interpretation of Article 26(2) to which a purposive construction, as I hope to have shown, clearly points. The language of both texts is unsatisfactory: some strain, if not distortion, seems inevitable but of the governing French text it can at least be said that it does not exclude partial loss from the scope of the paragraph. I am of opinion therefore, on the whole, that following the sense of the matter and the continental writers we should hold that partial loss of contents is included in 'damage' and that consequent action may be barred in the absence of a timeous complaint.

4.46 What is true of international conventions embodying substantive law rules is also true of private international law conventions.

Mathias Reimann, 'Comparative Law and Private International Law' in Reinhard Zimmermann and Mathias Reimann (eds), *The Oxford Handbook of Comparative Law* (OUP, Oxford, 2006)

In our time, an increasing number of private international law norms originate not in a particular domestic order but rather stem from international conventions adopted by a growing number of states. This is especially true among the member countries of the Hague Conference on Private International Law. The construction of norms in, or those based on, such conventions poses particular challenges and is especially dependent on a comparative approach.

This is mainly because the very purpose of such conventions is the (worldwide or regional) unification of private international law rules. Obviously, courts would defeat that purpose if they were to interpret convention rules in different ways, eg, by looking only to their respective forum laws for purposes of qualification. It is therefore widely recognized that conventions must be interpreted on their own terms ('autonomously') and that guidance must be sought by looking to the other signatory states' substantive laws and practices.

The most impressive manifestation of this approach is the rich case law of the European Court of Justice pertaining to the so-called Brussels Convention. Here, one can see private international law and comparative law go hand-in-glove in the routine practice of an international tribunal. Today, such a comparative approach is also embraced by many national courts, especially in Europe. The track record of American courts is decidedly mixed in that regard. In two major decisions interpreting private international law conventions, the United States Supreme Court duly looked at the negotiation history of the respective conventions and at the foreign law background but made no visible effort to consider whether foreign courts had faced the same, or similar, issues and how they had decided them. Lower courts, however, have occasionally considered foreign decisions and strived to construe international conventions from an international, rather than a domestic, point of view.

Consistency of determination of international trade usage

International trade usages[48] are vehicles for the harmonization of commercial law. **4.47** Courts should, but often do not, take into account decisions and related analysis from other jurisdictions when faced with questions relating to such international usages. There are countless examples of fact patterns in which doing so would be justified, prudent, and serve the objective of unifying the law applicable to commercial transactions. Lord Wright's observations in 1937 in *International Trustee for the Protection of Bondholders Aktiengesellschaft v R*[49] show the pedigree and capture the objective of references to foreign interpretations of international commercial usages:

> The gold clauses[50] in bond and obligations are very common in international contracts and in every part of the world. It would be a very serious matter if contracts of that character were treated by particular courts as having a different meaning, in the absence of language and surrounding circumstances of decisive character compelling that conclusion. The construction of such clauses ought to be as far as possible uniform unless there are the strongest considerations involving a different construction.[51]

Role of comparative law in transnational practice

In view of the fine line between law and practice in this field, a final function of **4.48** comparative commercial law requires special note. Comparative legal analysis is practised in the ordinary course by lawyers around the world when advising on international transactions or involved in dispute resolution. They rely heavily on the outcome of that analysis in deciding how to structure transactions, the choice of law to govern contracts, the arrangement of key factors such as the location of entities and the occurrence of legal acts to influence the determination of the law applicable to proprietary aspects, and the manner in which risks will be allocated and minimized. Similar practical considerations arise in connection with decisions on the mode of dispute resolution and choice of the litigation forum, or the seat of an arbitration. In short, international lawyers today use comparative law offensively. The study of comparative method, therefore, should be an increasingly important part of legal education and training.

---

[48] See above, paras 1.60 ff.   [49] [1936] 3 All ER 407, CA.

[50] Such clauses, which require the payment of principle and interest by reference to the value of gold, were widely used internationally. The case arose as a result of the British government's refusal to pay amounts it owed with reference to that gold standard, on an obligation expressed to be governed by New York law, on account of changes in United States law rendering payments so calculated illegal. See: M Schmitthoff, 'The Gold Clause in International Loans' (1936) 18 J Comp Legis & Intl L (3rd series) 266.   [51] *International Trustee for the Protection of Bondholders* (n 49) 426.

Cultural aims of comparative law

4.49 We have earlier referred to legal styles as the basis for classifying legal systems. A parallel concept is that of legal cultures, which go beyond style, in the sense of professional approaches to law, and encompass popular expectations and understandings of law—'a more general consciousness or experience of law that is widely shared by those who inhabit a particular legal environment, for example, a particular region, nation, or group of nations'.[52] A good example is furnished by Islamic law, to which reference has previously been made.[53]

Roger Cotterrell, 'Comparative Law and Legal Culture' in Reinhard Zimmermann and Mathias Reimann (eds), *The Oxford Handbook of Comparative Law* (OUP, Oxford, 2006)

The primary difficulties, which affect all uses of the concept of legal culture, are twofold. First, how are components of legal culture to be identified in an acceptable way? (Whose acceptance matters? Those who see themselves as inhabiting the culture? Those who observe it as outsiders?) Secondly, how are the boundaries of legal culture to be recognized? Friedman is prepared to recognize innumerable legal cultures, overlapping and interacting. For comparatists who start from an idea of national legal cultures, the presumption will be of common legal experience within nation states and different experiences between them. But a recognition of European, Western, modern or post-modern legal cultures (and many other possible varieties) will indicate other boundaries, other parameters, determining when and where similarity, on the one hand, or difference, on the other, will be the governing presumption about legal experience.

It can, at least, be said that to invoke legal culture is *always* to imply both similarity (within) and difference (between) cultures. Culture is invariably invoked *against* something, however much it is used to emphasize the common interests, beliefs, values, traditions or allegiances of those who share the culture . . .

One does not need to accept the various positions that have been taken, in the politics of difference in comparative law, to recognize that the call to appreciate difference has the capacity to reinvigorate aspects of comparative legal scholarship, merely by emphasizing aspects of culture that raise issues about non-instrumental objectives of legal comparison. The dominant trend in modern comparative law scholarship has been to assume that unification or harmonization of law is a primary objective of comparative legal studies. While many reasons for valuing the search for similarity in law have been given, the main one has surely been to foster trade and transnational commerce, and more generally to facilitate international legal communication and co-operation—a more effective use of law in regulating relations between individuals and corporations in different jurisdictions. Thus, a primary focus has been on law's role in regulating instrumental relations, the relations of people engaged in convergent or common projects.

The emphasis on legal culture in recent comparative law can be understood as, in part, an effort to bring into sharp focus law's contributions to many other kinds of relations apart from instrumental ones. Law is not merely valuable as a facilitator of contractual, commercial and corporate relations. It is also a protector and shaper of traditions, an expression of shared beliefs and ultimate values, and—in much less definable ways—an

---

[52] Cotterrell, 'Comparative Law and Legal Culture', below.   [53] Above, para 4.17.

expression of national expectations, allegiances and emotions. Savigny tried to grasp this elusive aspect of law in the *Volksgeist* idea, which threatens always to slide into a dangerous mysticism. Nevertheless, the suggestion that law has an important role in expressing or recognizing aspects of emotional experience in personal or collective life is not absurd. While at one level this focus on affective relations is extremely abstract—for example, on the nation, or even on 'Europe' or the 'West'—at another it is found in everyday aspects of the regulation of domestic, fiduciary or caring relations at interpersonal level.

D. Methodology

The functional approach to comparative law

The method of comparative study of different legal systems may be either formal **4.50** or functional. The formal method examines the concepts and doctrinal base of each of the systems under comparison, the functional method addresses their purpose and utility. Zweigert followed Rabel in emphasizing that if the practical aims of legal comparison are to be achieved, the functional approach to comparative law is the only one worth adopting. This is explained in the following illuminating passage.

K Zweigert, 'Methodological Problems in Comparative Law' (1972) 7 Isr L Rev 465, 466–7 and 471–2

The basic principle of comparative law methods is that of functional equivalence; and all other methodical rules–for the selection of legal systems for analyzing a given problem, the scope of investigation, the setting up of a system, etc—derive from this principle. You cannot compare the incomparable, and in law, the comparable is only that which fulfils the same task. That might appear to be self-evident except that it comprehends a wealth of experience in the field of comparative law, the full implications of which the beginner will not at once grasp. The one fundamental experience which goes to the very roots of comparative law is that every society poses the same problems to be solved by its law but the different valid legal orders solve these problems by very different means, although in the end and for practical reasons the solutions are about equal. The starting question of every analysis should therefore be put in purely functional terms, the subject of analysis should be formulated without reference to the concepts of one's own legal order. For example, it would not be feasible to ask what forms does foreign law prescribe for a sales contract? One should better ask by what means a legal system protects a party from entering into a transaction without due deliberation or from being bound by a contract which was not seriously intended to be a contract?

A focal point at which everyone of us (and not just the beginner) is confronted with the principle of functionality, is the premature conclusion when researching a problem that nothing is to be found in that system with regard to the problem. Such a conclusion should normally send you back to review your starting point, your 'problem', and see whether in formulating it you have really freed yourself from the concepts, thinking attitudes and reasoning of your own system.

. . .

About the working techniques of comparative law I need only add a few general words. I am referring to the problems of selecting the systems of law which are to be included in the process of comparison and to the order of comparative studies, reports by country and then a comparative and critical analysis of significant solutions which have been found. This comparative analysis is fairly difficult, for it means viewing the different solutions in a new and—above all—common perspective. In the reports by country, which are really nothing but reports, every solution which a legal problem has found in a certain system of law is presented comprehensively but on its own terms, in its own rules of statute or case law, its own concepts and systematic reference. In the comparative analysis every one of these solutions is set against the background of, and judged by, all other solutions rather than in the context of its own legal order. This is one new perspective, that of comparison in its proper meaning. The second which is the premise of the first and inseparably linked to it is the functional perspective. For it is the same function, the fulfillment of the same task, which provides the only possible basis for a meaningful comparison of the institutions of different legal systems. Function is the starting point and the basis of all comparative law. It is the *tertium comparationis* (common point of reference) which earlier comparatists have long searched for in vain. This means for the process of comparison that the solutions which the different legal systems have arrived at must be stripped of all systematic concepts of these systems and be viewed solely and exclusively with regard to their function, to the fulfilment of the problem which has originated them.

4.51 As a good illustration of the point Zweigert was making, consider the case of a seller who sells goods knowing that they are subject to a hidden defect making them unfit for their purpose. Under French law, the seller has a duty to disclose such a defect and his failure to do so may enable the buyer to avoid the contract. A comparative lawyer examining English law would look in vain for a duty of disclosure in this situation, and might well be mistakenly led to conclude that if the contract were governed by English law the buyer would have no remedy. Nothing could be further from the truth. English law imposes a liability on the seller to supply goods that are fit for their known purpose. Breach of this duty entitles the buyer to reject goods and/or recover damages. There is, therefore, no need for a duty of disclosure; the buyer is given protection comparable to that furnished by French law but by a different route. Moreover, the seller's liability is strict and does not depend on his prior knowledge of the defect.

4.52 Thus, what in one system is characterized as a pre-contractual duty of disclosure is treated in another as a contractual duty to furnish goods fit for their purpose. Both approaches lead to a broadly comparable solution to the problem posed. The experienced comparatist will come to this result by ignoring the conceptual boxes in which the respective duties are placed, and focusing on the function of the duty in either case, which is to protect the buyer against the supply of non-conforming goods.

Max Rheinstein, 'Comparative Law and Conflict of Laws in Germany' 2 U Chi L Rev 232, 247–8 (1934–5)

. . . we must start with the small concrete detail, but we must never look at it as an isolated fact; we must always see it as part of an entirety. The isolated rule is meaningless, its significance does not appear except in connection with other rules ... [what is relevant is] the *function* of a legal institution not its conceptual shape; the *purposes* it serves not its formal place in the legal system. How are the problems set by life, how are the actual conflicts of social interests solved by the legal order? Such a comparison very often shows that different legal systems may use different technical means for the same purpose. The Anglo-American institution of trust does not exist as such in continental laws. But its purposes may be achieved to a considerable extent by using other institutions: *fiducia* and authorization, institution of a reversionary heir and usufruct, foundation, purpose-gift, gift under a charge and others ... It is only when we observe a legal institution with regard to its functions and as a part of its entire legal system, and when we have found which institutions of another legal system can be used for the same or for kindred purposes, that we may see whether, and in what respects, the two systems really differ. It is striking to observe how comparatively seldom such real differences exist. The unity of our occidental civilization becomes apparent under all the dissimilarities on the surface.

Such a functional approach opens our eyes to an understanding of the role of legal concepts and of techniques in law. Each legal system uses fundamental concepts in order to express its rules. In different legal systems, these concepts often differ, but comparative observation reveals how little such concepts constitute ends in themselves, that they are nothing but blocks with which to build structures.

4.53 The functional method continues to be the subject of controversy among comparatists, some of whom complain that it lacks a theoretical underpinning, and is only one of several legitimate approaches to the use of comparative law.[54] But Rabel was both an outstanding scholar and a leading arbitrator and judge and was very sensitive to the need to combine theory with practice. The functional approach has been applied with success by experts from all over the world involved in the practical, as well as the theoretical, application of commercial law.

Common solutions or best solutions?

4.54 Is the base-line objective of international harmonization to identify and build on common approaches or to devise the best practical solution to the problem under consideration? This is fundamental, as its answer affects all aspects of the comparative law and law reform processes, in particular, which questions are posed and against what criteria they are assessed. The modern trend is decidedly from the former to the latter approach. To the extent that a traditional 'common solution' approach is followed, generalities inevitably result. That may well serve political considerations—in the sense that national law is not being superseded and there remains a wide scope for judicial discretion—but it does not serve the requirements of commerce, which needs laws that address practical problems and facilitate rather than impede business. Maintenance of the lowest common denominator

---

[54] For a recent overview, see: Ralf Michaels, 'The Functional Method of Comparative Law' in Reinhard Zimmermann and Mathias Reimann (eds), *The Oxford Handbook of Comparative Law* (OUP, Oxford, 2006).

neither advances the law nor responds to changing commercial needs, nor does it usually provide the higher degree of specificity—rules, as opposed to standards— required for modern cross-border transactions. The formulation of rules on the basis of the lowest common denominator is a serious temptation to those involved in the ever-growing number of projects which try to discover the common foundations of European law in order to propose possible uniform laws or, if sitting in supranational courts, to shape the law on the basis of 'general principles of law'. Legal rules so manufactured run the risk not only of displeasing everyone but also of creating a new, synthetic law, cut off entirely from the legal and cultural roots of any particular country. The First President of the French Court of Cassation M Guy Canivet described vividly this new and very contemporary danger, and his views deserve to be quoted more fully.

Guy Canivet, 'La convergence des systèmes juridiques par l'action du juge', in *De tous horizons* (Mélanges Xavier Blanc-Jouvan (2005),11, 20–1

This [entire] dispute illustrates the contrast between the abstract formalism of human rights and the reality of historical traditions. This is an old debate, at least as old as that over human rights. Can we endanger what is dear to our history in the names of disembodied principles running roughshod over traditions, habits and existing realities in the name of an ideal? The rights of man, from their first appearance at the end of the 18th century, were accused of ignoring concrete realties in the name of abstract principles [citation of Burke]. And one could already discern emerging a disagreement between the English attachment to pragmatism and the French preference for the tabula rasa. To be honest, it is no longer a mater of conflict between [these] cultures but, rather, a clash, on the one hand, between a long-established and prestigious culture and, on the other, a non-culture, an aggregate of many national legal cultures. Even though many European lawyers feel that they share something in common with one another, they do not have the same feelings towards the Strasbourg case law that they nourish towards their home grown culture. Indeed, in some extreme cases, jostled by such attitudes, national lawyers are thus forced to react by adopting nationalistic positions denying the legitimacy of the European judge. In this way Europe succeeds in bringing closer to us the agony of globalisation. For can we ever be satisfied by a synthetic culture? National culture is alive with stories, symbols, traditions, which is another way of saying a shared consciousness. For by being omnipresent it needs not to be proclaimed. To articulate it risks proving fatal to it for it would be tantamount to admitting that it is threatened. Article 6 of the Convention of Human Rights is not, therefore, the antidote, a way of ridding the law of its impurities, but a solvent of national legal cultures. If people that do not have myths are left in the cold, the globalisation that follows the clash of these two ways of thinking will lead us to a world which may attain some peace through trade but which will have become glacial. This example of convergence enforced from the top thus presents us with a paradox of globalisation. For as legal cultures slowly integrate into their systems the principles of superior values, the more the local pockets of resistance tend to develop.[55]

---

[55] The English translation is taken from Sir Basil Markesinis and Jörg Fedtke, *Foreign Law in National Courts: A New Source of Inspiration?* (Routledge-Cavendish, New York, 2006), 53 ff. The comment refers to the decisions of the European Court of Human Rights in *Fontaine et Bertin v*

In the field of transnational commercial law, at any rate, the search is for best **4.55** solutions, not for lowest common denominators. In this context, the 'best solution' is the one that is pragmatic, serving the predictability and efficiency objectives of commercial law (albeit with due deference to principles of reasonableness and fairness) by taking the transaction structure as a starting point. Examples include new rules concerning negotiable instruments, demand and standby guarantees, dealings in securities held with an intermediary, and secured financing.

Working methods

The comparative law method will depend on the purpose of the exercise, the **4.56** problem to be resolved, the time and resources available and, in the case of an international harmonization project, the practice of the organization undertaking it. The scholar will follow established research methods: identifying the problem and a working hypothesis for its solution; a survey of the relevant legislative and secondary materials of the countries to be surveyed; a questionnaire to academic and practising experts; interviews with selected respondents; and a report, paper or monograph setting out the nature and results of the survey. International organizations engaged in a harmonization project may have to work within the limitations of a tighter time frame and fewer resources, and will rely more heavily on questionnaires and on the accumulated expertise of members of the Study Group. International law firms will rely on the expertise available in their own offices or in those of other firms with whom they have a relationship and, where relevant, on academic experts. The web is, of course, a particularly fruitful source of information, offering links to a number of databases on transnational law.

The preparation of a questionnaire requires careful thought. It is important to **4.57** ensure that the questions are neutral, and do not embody value judgments or give a steer towards a particular solution. The questions should be short, clear and unambiguous and should be kept down to a reasonable number in order to increase the prospects of a good response rate. It is useful to send a draft of the questionnaire to selected respondents as a pilot to ensure that the questions are properly directed and understood. It is useful to include open-ended questions which allow the respondent to identify issues that the researcher or Study Group may have missed. But responses to questionnaires and published materials should not be the sole source of information. It is important to have discussions with a range of foreign academics, practising lawyers and (where available) government experts to tease out the issues and get an up-to-date picture of the real problems and possible solutions. This process is also useful in generating interest in the

---

France, nos 38410/97 and 40373/98, [2003] ECHR 336, and *Kress v France*, no 39594/98, ECHR-VI 382 declaring that the posts of Avocat Général in the Cour de Cassation and the Commissaire du Gouvernement de la Republique in the Conseil d' Etat run counter to Art 6 of European Convention on Human Rights.

project and, later, support for it if the evidence justifies its being carried forward. The results of the survey should then be embodied in a paper prepared by a member of the Study Group appointed as reporter for the project, and this should then be circulated to all interested parties and the paper should form the basis of future work by the Study Group.

4.58 Professor Ole Lando, the President of the Commission on European Contract Law and the driving force behind the Principles of European Contract Law, has described the process adopted by the Commission on European Contract Law for work on the Principles.

Ole Lando, 'Comparative Law and Lawmaking' 75 Tul L Rev 1015, 1020 (2000–2001)

The way in which the CECL has worked has changed over the years, but the main features have remained the same. For each subject, a Reporter is selected from among the members of the Commission. On the basis of the comparative research he has made, he submits a position paper in which he presents the leading ideas of his coming draft.

The position paper is then discussed in a drafting group of four or five members, each belonging to one of the European legal families. If the Reporter has overlooked or omitted an important rule in a legal system, this will be considered and included in the report by the drafting group.

Several international organizations utilize a reporter—for instance the UNIDROIT group and the Hague Conference on Private International Law. Some organizations have no reporter and the group makes the proposal. It is, however, my experience that it is useful that one person does the research, conceives and formulates the ideas, and ensures consistency. Without a reporter, the necessary research work has not always been done when the group meets. In addition, if the proposals are to be made by a group, the several cooks have no initial and common recipe to work with, and, without that, it is difficult to make a good broth.

E. Problems

The pitfalls of comparison

The knowledge problem

4.59 The comparative lawyer adopting a functional approach faces formidable challenges in his endeavours to draw sensible conclusions from comparisons between one system and another. It is very difficult to evaluate a particular legal rule without a knowledge of the system of rules of which it forms part. We have already given an illustration of this in showing that the absence of a seller's duty of disclosure in a contract of sale of goods governed by English law does not, as one might have supposed, mean that the buyer is without a remedy, but merely that the remedy lies elsewhere. Again, while it is generally true that under English law specific performance is exceptional except in relation to contracts for the sale of land, and under German law its equivalent, enforced performance, is a primary remedy, the concept of enforced performance in German law is wider, embracing the creditor's right to have performance carried out by a third party at the debtor's expense,[56] whereas in English law this is treated not as specific performance but as grounding a claim for damages. This exemplifies a wider problem, namely that lawyers trained in a particular legal system tend to look at other law from the cultural and legal perspective of their own system and to assume the superiority of the latter. Moreover, if one is not a comparative lawyer in the fullest sense it is difficult, if not impossible, to familiarize oneself with another jurisdiction's legal system, ways of thinking and reasoning, instinctive responses to particular types of issue. Indeed, leading scholars have raised the question how far it is possible for a person not trained in a given legal system to understand it.

> ... rules and concepts alone actually tell one very little about a given legal system and reveal even less about whether two legal systems are converging or not. They may provide one with much information about what is apparently happening, but they indicate nothing about the deep structures of legal systems. Specifically, rules and concepts do little to disclose that legal systems are but the surface manifestation of legal cultures and, indeed, of culture *tout court*. In other words, they limit the observer to a 'thin description' and foreclose the possibility of the 'thick description' that the analyst ought to regard as desirable.[57]

BS Markesinis, *Foreign Law and Comparative Methodology: A Subject and a Thesis* (Hart Publishing, Oxford, 1997) 195–6

But if a *ius commune* existed in the past and is likely to appear again within the European context, this will in the future (as it was in the past) be in no small measure due to the kind of jurists who will develop it: devoid of nationalistic arrogance, extrovert in disposition, able to withstand the special kind of isolation that their approach often brings in its initial phases. That, in my opinion, is the definition of the modern comparatist who, whether he is an academic or an open-minded judge, is thus forced to realise that he *has* to study more than he can ever fully digest. This leads to an intense, omnivorous erudition; but it also comes with a sense of desperation as he realises early on in his career what Socrates proclaimed towards the end of his: that the more one reads the less one really knows. Yet the quest for understanding others as much as learning about them must and will continue, especially in our shrinking world. And often, by accident rather than by design, it leads to some unique insights into the law and its rules, as well as underscoring the commonness of human suffering and the universality of the basic notions of justice which one's nationalistic schooling has done so much to blur ...

So how does one go about encouraging such an internationalist approach? In my view by promoting, among other things, a greater partnership between academic and judge, and thus ensuring that they meet their colleagues from other jurisdictions as often as

---

[56] See: Basil Markesinis, Hannes Unberath and Angus Johnston, *The German Law of Contract* (2nd edn, Hart Publishing, Oxford, 2006) 404.

[57] Pierre Legrand, 'European legal systems are not converging' (1996) 45 ICLQ 52, 56. See also: David Nelken, 'Legal Cultures' in Jan M Smits (ed), *Elgar Encyclopaedia of Comparative Law* (Edward Elgar Publishing, Cheltenham (UK), 2006) 372.

possible ... Through such meetings judges can also ask themselves to what extent the similarity of the problems they face may be forcing them to consider implicitly, but not explicitly, the same underlying policy factors, thereby in most cases being pushed towards similar solutions.

4.60   A leading comparatist has openly acknowledged the limitations of comparative law, devoting a whole chapter of his book to what he describes as 'the perils of comparative law'.

Alan Watson, *Legal Transplants: an Approach to Comparative Law* (2nd edn, U of Georgia Press, London, 1993) 10–12

In a book on Comparative Law it may seem perverse to write a prominent chapter on 'The Perils,' but it is important to stress the dangers inherent in the study and its limitations. Much has been claimed for Comparative Law yet so far it has contributed relatively little to the understanding of law or legal development. At times sadly it has obscured the truth. An awareness of the perils, whether they are inevitable or only normal, should lead to a more just appreciation of the contribution which Comparative Law can make. Some of the dangers stem from the comparative method in general; others are particular to Comparative Law.

To begin with, Comparative Law is superficial. As astounding as this may seem as a bald statement, the fact is admitted by some leading comparatists. FH Lawson has indeed gone further and claimed: 'Now, in a sense, a comparative lawyer is bound to be superficial; he would soon lose himself in the sands of scholarship.' The explanation is patent: it is hard enough to know in detail one branch of the law of one system, but to know the history of that branch and its relationship with that of some other system (and thus to possess a knowledge of that as well) is well-nigh impossible...

This peril of Comparative Law is then compounded with another, even more serious, getting the foreign law wrong. Error of law is probably more common in Comparative Law than in any other branch of legal study. Again the reason is only too plain. Too much has to be taken on trust from other writers, including other comparatists; too often knowledge is derived from too few original sources, and too frequently linguistic deficiencies interpose a formidable barrier between the scholar and his subject. What in other contexts would be regarded as a good knowledge of a foreign language may not be adequate for the comparatist ...

The fragility of conclusions dependent on a superficial knowledge combined with frequent error of law should be underlined.

A third peril is that Comparative Law can scarcely be systematic. Again we are indebted to law for the insight: 'I do not know how a comparison between two laws can be systematic.' Hence even where there is a relationship between the two systems ... there will always be a considerable element of selection in the objects of study. In the very nature of things the choice can scarcely ever be made in full knowledge of all the relevant facts ...

Another weakness is that the systems chosen for study may have no proper relationship, and the conclusions will be lacking in significance. Even worse, the faults of this approach may be compounded and the systems be examined at different points in their evolution. Though this last danger has long been recognized by comparatists it remains distressingly tempting.

This leads to one of the greatest (and strangest) perils of Comparative Law, the desire to see a particular legal pattern common at least in outline to all, or to many divergent, systems.

Nevertheless, though we should be alert to the dangers described above, it is **4.61** important not to be overawed by the challenges of comparative law. The best is often the enemy of the good. If we spend too much time reflecting on the dangers of comparative law we shall make no progress at all. The task, then, is to make proper use of comparative law by showing the policy issues underpinning the approach of courts of other jurisdictions to the solution of a common problem and by utilizing these to avoid a violation of the forum's conception of justice.

McFarlane v Tayside Health Board [2002] 2 AC 59, HL

[The case involved a claim for damages for negligent advice as the result of which the claimant and her husband ceased to take contraceptive precautions and the claimant became pregnant and gave birth to a healthy child. The House of Lords, on appeal from the Inner House of the Scottish Court of Session, reviewed case law not only in Scotland but in England, Australia, France, Germany, the Netherlands, New Zealand and the United States. The various courts adopted widely differing views on the legal and ethical issues involved.]

Lord Steyn at 81:

From this comparative survey I deduce that claims by parents for full compensation for the financial consequences of the birth of a healthy child have sometimes been allowed. It may be that the major theme in such cases is that one is simply dealing with an ordinary tort case in which there are no factors negativing liability in delict. Considerations of corrective justice as between the negligent surgeon and the parents were dominant in such decisions. In an overview one would have to say that more often such claims are not allowed. The grounds for decision are diverse. Sometimes it is said that there was no personal injury, a lack of foreseeability of the costs of bringing up the child, no causative link between the breach of duty and the birth of a healthy child, or no loss since the joys of having a healthy child always outweigh the financial losses. Sometimes the idea that the couple could have avoided the financial cost of bringing up the unwanted child by abortion or adoption has influenced decisions. Policy considerations undoubtedly played a role in decisions denying a remedy for the cost of bringing up an unwanted child. My Lords, the discipline of comparative law does not aim at a poll of the solutions adopted in different countries. It has the different and inestimable value of sharpening our focus on the weight of competing considerations. And it reminds us that the law is part of the world of competing ideas markedly influenced by cultural differences.

Fairchild v Glenhaven Funeral Services Ltd [2003] 1 AC 32, HL

[Claims were brought by former employees for exposure to asbestos dust during different periods of employment with different employers. The onset of the disease could not be attributed to any particular or cumulative wrongful exposure.

The question was whether the necessary requirement of causation had been satisfied. In holding that it had, the House of Lords had regard to decisions on the issue from a number of foreign jurisdictions, both common law and civil law]

Lord Bingham of Cornhill at para 32:

This survey shows, as would be expected, that though the problem underlying cases such as the present is universal the response to it is not. Hence the plethora of decisions given in different factual contexts. Hence also the intensity of academic discussion, exemplified by the articles of the late Professor Fleming ('Probabilistic Causation in Tort Law' 68 Canadian Bar Review, No 4, December 1989, 661) and Professor Robertson ('The Common Sense of Cause in Fact' (1997) 75 Tex L Rev 1765). In some jurisdictions, it appears, the plaintiff would fail altogether on causation grounds, as the Court of Appeal held that the present appellants did. Italy, South Africa and Switzerland may be examples (see *Unification of Tort Law: Causation*, ed Jaap Spier (2000), at pp 90, 102 and 120). But it appears that in most of the jurisdictions considered the problem of attribution would not, on facts such as those of the present cases, be a fatal objection to a plaintiff's claim. Whether by treating an increase in risk as equivalent to a material contribution, or by putting a burden on the defendant, or by enlarging the ordinary approach to acting in concert, or on more general grounds influenced by policy considerations, most jurisdictions would, it seems, afford a remedy to the plaintiff. Development of the law in this country cannot of course depend on a head-count of decisions and codes adopted in other countries around the world, often against a background of different rules and traditions. The law must be developed coherently, in accordance with principle, so as to serve, even-handedly, the ends of justice. If, however, a decision is given in this country which offends one's basic sense of justice, and if consideration of international sources suggests that a different and more acceptable decision would be given in most other jurisdictions, whatever their legal tradition, this must prompt anxious review of the decision in question. In a shrinking world (in which the employees of asbestos companies may work for those companies in any one or more of several countries) there must be some virtue in uniformity of outcome whatever the diversity of approach in reaching that outcome.

B S Markesinis and Jörg Fedtke, *Judicial Recourse to Foreign Law; A New Source of Inspiration?* (Routledge-Cavendish, New York, 2006), 167–72

For us the role of the trained comparatist is to avoid, and also help the judge avoid, the haphazard (or wrongly motivated) use of foreign law. Recourse to foreign law is primarily a mind-broadening experience. It is meant to give the observer, here the judge, a new optic and show him how a common problem is solved by an equally qualified fellow judge. This it will do, not only if the rule is carefully selected but also clearly and 'properly' presented to the judge for him to see its relevance. This is where the tasks of the academic and the advocate end and that of the judge begins. Depending on his observational powers, knowledge, experience, and intuition, *he* will then have to decide if the foreign idea is of use to him. This use may vary in content. It may lead him to understand the problem facing him better; it may encourage him to re-adjust his own law; or it may alert him to the kind of consequences that may follow if he adopts (or not) a particular solution. In other words, as Guy Canivet, the First President of the French Cour de Cassation, observed, he may be able to discern both the good but also the potentially harmful results of a particular rule. For us, none of these endeavours leaves room for the haphazard, amateur, or random; on the contrary—it is (and should be seen to be) strictly scientific if it is to serve its purpose and allay the fears we are addressing in this sub-section.

These reactions … do not mean … that there is no merit in the basic demand for some kind of rational process of deciding what is chosen, how it is chosen, and then how it is used. The objections raised by colleagues … must thus be addressed; and if what follows is far from perfect, it is because it represents, so far as we know, a first attempt to answer a question which has surfaced only recently thanks to American scholarship. Here then are some criteria we would like to advance for consideration and further elaboration. They are not meant to be read cumulatively; nor should one of them be seen as being more important than others. Often all may have to be weighed carefully, even if at the end of the day only one may prove to be decisive.

First, we must remember that the range of possible references/systems may be determined by the subject-matter, itself. If, for instance, the question before the court involves the understanding of a particular term found in an international convention or EU directive, the search would normally be limited to the countries that are signatories to that convention or bound by the directive. For it is from this usage and understanding that guidance should be sought and only rarely (and, for instance, for the purpose of comparison) will there be any need to go outside this 'closed' circle of systems. The contaminated blood case we discussed in chapter two, above, offers a good illustration; the Vienna Convention on the International Sale of Goods or the UNCITRAL model on international commercial arbitration (enacted by a number of States in the US such as California and Texas) would be another. No one could possibly object that such a limitation of the comparative exercise would be anything other than sensible.

Second, one must realise (and accept) that the search for inspiration must be justified by rational criteria—but this does not mean that it must be exhaustive …

A similarity of the socio-economic environment will, for example, usually make the comparison more meaningful as well as facilitate (if so desired) the use or (even) transplantability of the foreign idea should it prove its worth in the eyes of the potential borrower.

But by placing the emphasis on the broad similarity in the socio-economic environment we are thus deliberately excluding the idea that comparison should be limited to systems that belong to the same legal family. This is partly because we do not find the divisions thus made of the various legal systems entirely convincing but mainly because this (old) concept was only based on their private laws (which dominated the legal scene when this division was devised) and ignores their public law rules (which can fall into entirely different categories) …

Third, and it follows from the underlying premise of the previous observations, recourse to one (major) legal system may often, in itself, be both useful and legitimate. For instance, a legal system may in its rules reflect a traumatic period in its past and a concerted effort to address these experiences in its current phase. The German approach to informed consent in medical malpractice cases offers such an example; and it has proved its worth in countries which have been open-minded to the need of greater sensitivity towards all aspects of human dignity including the right to decide freely what is done with one's body. Thus, in the South African case of *Castell* v. *De Greef* Judge Ackermann (prior to his appointment to the Constitutional Court) wrote the judgment for the Cape High Court Full Bench in which the English solution (favouring doctors) was roundly rejected in favour of the

German, the judgment making good use of the leading German (and comparative) treatise of that time written by the late Professor Dieter Giesen of the Free University of Berlin.
Despite the vast differences between South Africa and Germany—in terms of geography,
size of the population, culture, economy, and (in general) the way of living—the fact that
Germany had emerged from its dark years in 1949 with a new vision of human rights
protection thus proved a powerful factor in the choice of German legal approaches not
only in the area of constitutional law but private law, as well.

Fourthly, the richness or maturity of a legal system and its related literature is also a factor
militating in favour of a careful determination (and delimitation) of the range of the necessary research. There may be some overlap between this factor and the previous one; yet
they are not coterminous.

For a country and the system looked at for the purposes of inspiration may be more
varied, ethnically mixed, and living under a 'variant' of the free economy model which
pertains in the system of the potential borrower, but nonetheless have managed to
develop a sophisticated jurisprudence worth a closer look. South Africa can, again, serve as
an example that illustrates this point since in many ways—historically, ethnically, legally
and economically—it may present many differences with, say, England, France, or
Germany. Yet its case law (especially, one is inclined to suggest, its constitutional case
law) has more than earned its spurs during the last decade or so and, in our view at least,
deserves to be considered . . .

Fifth, the time and location of the potential borrower may, for pragmatic reasons, delimit
the range of the comparative survey which his legislator or his courts may be realistically
expected to undertake. Under this heading we are not envisaging the omni-present difficulty of access to foreign material but a more political kind of difficulty. American constitutional law was thus an obvious 'choice'—and we deliberately put the words in inverted
commas—for the Japanese when they were called upon to draw up a new constitution
after the end of World War II. The dynamics of the current situation in Iraq are, by contrast, very different, as the second of us (acting as an advisor for the 'Democratisation
Assistance Programme' of the German Foreign Office) has found out at many recent
meetings with members of the Iraqi Parliament and political or religious groups involved
in the search for a new constitutional settlement for the country. For, in this last instance,
purely political reasons did *not* make the American model (despite its undisputable qualities) 'an ideal' choice in the search for inspiration. The German and South African variations did, on the other hand, offer intriguing and (more importantly) *politically acceptable*
possibilities to an emerging nation desperately trying to come to grips with a model of
federalism and human rights protection which best suits its troubled realities.

Thoughts such as the above can lead to three basic (albeit tentative) conclusions.

First, the choice of systems studied or used for the purposes of inspiration must not be
undertaken randomly and solely because they help bolster an individual choice. The purpose of comparison is to help widen horizons and not to back already formed narrow and
personal views.

Second, the choice of systems to be looked at must be made on the basis of pragmatic
considerations which should include such matters as relevance, affinity, accessibility, and
the like. In the preceding paragraphs we have advanced some suggestions which can, no
doubt, be refined and adapted.

Third, the presentation should be primarily left to the attorneys (with or without the
co-operation of academics) rather than UN Agencies or various interested groups acting

through the medium of amicus briefs which, in our view, do not necessarily offer the best tool for undertaking this demanding task in a scholarly manner. Yet we accept that the practice is too well entrenched in the United States to be easily modified. The disputes about the reliability of the foreign material thus assembled will therefore continue to affect adversely the wider debate in America.

Finally, a wider observation—indisputably showing our preferences (or biases)—needs to be made. American academy is right in identifying these difficulties in the use of comparative law by the courts the world over. Yet, paradoxically, their discussions are 'academic' in the extreme. They are thus often keen to invent (or import) words, broaden the horizon of the search to include 'less developed' systems, and quick to confuse (we think) the bounds of comparative law and comparative anthropology—often lacing all of the above with a good dose of political ideology. All of these habits are to be expected in work done in academic cloisters; but they are also unlikely to give any real guidance to judges who are asked to conduct (or not to conduct) research into foreign law. These writings are thus likely to make other academics think but *not* likely to make judges follow. And, surely, this must be one of the aims these authors have in mind given that their academic work was, itself, born out of the activities of practitioners.[58]

Language

The true comparatist needs to be multilingual, for otherwise he will be unable to **4.62** study foreign legal materials not in his own language and will be dependent on translations, which in many cases will not be available. Moreover, it is not possible to understand the nuances of rules of a foreign legal system without familiarity with the language in which those rules are expressed. The dominance of English as a *lingua franca* does, of course, assist discourse in comparative law, but it also impoverishes language and creates a barrier to full understanding, if, indeed, full understanding is possible.

Vivian Grosswald Curran, 'Comparative Law and Language' in Reinhard Zimmermann and Mathias Reimann (eds), *The Oxford Handbook of Comparative Law* (OUP, Oxford, 2006)

For present purposes, it is sufficient to posit that there are irreducible untranslatables between languages. A vast and varied literature links the phenomenon of untranslatability to the conclusion that language uniqueness arises from, and in turn also fortifies, a unique world perspective, an irreproducible manner of seeing and understanding. This attribute of language has significance for comparative law beyond the similarity of the field to translation. It means that knowing a second language allows entry into another world, a way of seeing through another lens, into 'incommensurable systems of concepts'. Consequently, for comparatists, knowing the languages of legal systems they study signifies access to all that the texts of law imply and connote, but do not state, to their infinity of links to the contexts that spawned them and that they also affect. It has been suggested that communication always lies beyond language. The kind of openings to perspective, to ways of thinking and feeling, that an additional language offers, also allows one to intuit the

---

[58] Ch 5 of the same work also contains an extended and fruitful analysis of the mental disposition of the national judge as a factor impeding recourse to foreign law.

nature of the closures and barriers to intercontextual understanding that are comparative law's greatest challenges, even before one locates, identifies, and learns to overcome the particular impediments in the particular study at hand.

The polyglot knows that much alterity is not apparent. The polyglot legal comparatist knows that legal orders reside as much beneath and aside from words as they do in the words that purport to embody them. Ernst Rabel's insistence on multilinguism for legal comparatists, like George Steiner's for literary comparatists, stems from the premise that, since knowing another language is a powerful and crucial entry into another world vision and universe of thought, it more importantly indirectly transmits the fact that other world visions and universes of thought exist and are to be apprehended. Beyond the particulars of two differing underlying networks of meaning, knowing another language expands one's imaginative capacities to encompass an understanding of the nature of differences, the imperfections of translation, the pitfalls to constructing equivalences, and the likelihood that newness and difference will have unexpected locations and provenances in another system of thought.

Immersion in more than one language, and the struggle to translate between languages, highlights tapestries of interlinking threads that are woven into infinity, connections between past and present, and among spiralling associations inspired by words and phrases in a unique syntax, endless links of threads to connecting ties. It is a messiness that one can approach but not reduce without distortion. Just as comparison is an act of translation, so too translation is an act of comparison, and the word 'comparison', after all, admits of being less than exact correspondence. Comparison is of the order of simile, not metaphor.

The process of translating from one language to another is the basic pattern not just of comparative law, but of all analysis, of cognition.

Legal transplants and comparative law

Similarities and differences

4.63 These problems have led scholars to question the validity of the comparatist's assumptions of similarity among legal systems and, more broadly, the contribution of comparative law to the process of legal transplants. Professor Pierre Legrand, to whom we intend no disrespect in describing him as one of the world's leading legal iconoclasts, is particularly sceptical about the tendency to begin with an assumption of similarities between systems.

Pierre Legrand, 'The same and the different' in Pierre Legrand and Roderick Munday (eds), *Comparative Legal Studies: traditions and transitions* (CUP, Cambridge, 2003) 245–8 and 299–300 [58a]

In a very important sense, the recent history of comparative legal studies must be read as a persistent, albeit not always adroit, attempt to identify sameness across laws and to demote difference to a *modus deficiens* of sameness. As John Merryman observes, '[d]ifferences between legal systems have been regarded ... as evils or inconveniences to be overcome.' Not surprisingly, '[w]hen differences are discovered, gentility seems to require that [they] be dissolved' ... The desire for sameness breeds the expectation of sameness which, in turn, begets the finding of sameness ... Konrad Zweigert and Hein Kötz, indeed, postulate

---

[58a] © Cambridge University Press, reproduced with permission.

'*presumptio similitudini*' to the effect that 'legal systems give the same or very similar solutions, even as to detail, to the same problems of life', so that a finding of difference should lead comparatists to start their investigations afresh. In these authors' words, 'the comparatist can rest content if his researches through all the relevant material lead to the conclusion that the systems he has compared reach the same or similar practical results, but if he finds that there are great differences or indeed diametrically opposite results, he should be warned and go back to check again whether the terms in which he posed his original question were ... purely functional, and whether he has spread the net of his researches quite wide enough ... , Do comparatists, as they disclose a comprehensive attitude *preceding* the facts which are supposed to call it forth, act out of *wishful thinking* or in *bad faith*? Perhaps more accurately, do they indulge in *double belief* through two contrary reactions, simultaneously and rejecting 'reality', that is, acknowledging the 'reality' of the difference through the persistence of perception and yet disavowing or repressing it in order to make themselves believe something else? Does the main goal of ideology not become the consistency of ideology itself? ...

Today's comparatists in law faculties everywhere, perhaps especially in Europe, are expected to subscribe to a script of underlying unity and transcendental universalism where particularism is assumed to be secondary and fated to play but a peripheral role in the future of human affairs. It is easy to sympathize with the desire for a more orderly, circumscribed world. The obsession to find and impose order possibly answers a most basic human drive. But it is quite another thing to underwrite the search for a monistic unifying pattern not unlike the Platonic or Hegelian belief in a final rational harmony ...

Comparison must not have a unifying, but a multiplying effect. It must stand athwart the self-deluding investment in the excision of the incommensurable. It must avoid complicity in the disregard for different ways of doing things and the ensuing exclusion of alterity, in the refusal to recognize other worlds as other worlds. It must aim at organizing the diversity of discourses around different (cultural) forms and counter the intellectual tendency towards assimilation ... The comparatists must emphatically rebut any attempt at the extravagant axiomatization of sameness. I argue that comparatists need to recall how the diversity of legal traditions and the diversity of forms of life-in-the-law these traditions embody remain the expression of the human capacity for choice and self-creation, that is, how the differences at issue are not just superficial or technical distinctions but play a constituting role in shaping cultural identity.[59]

4.64 Though many scholars would argue that common problems are more often than not met by common solutions, even if the routes to them are different, Professor Legrand's warning not to under-estimate the importance of diversity should be heeded. Diversity not only enriches in a general sense but at the practical level provides choice.[60]

---

[59] For a response, see: David Nelken, 'Comparatists and Transferability' in Pierre Legrand and Roderick Munday (eds), *Comparative Legal Studies: Traditions and Transitions* (CUP, Cambridge, 2003) 440 ff. See also: Cotterrell (n 25) 147 ff, and Gerhard Dannemann, 'Comparative Law: Study of Similarities or Differences?' in Reinhard Zimmermann and Mathias Reimann (eds), *The Oxford Handbook of Comparative Law* (OUP, Oxford, 2006).

[60] See: Roger Cotterrell, 'Is it so bad to be different? Comparative law and the appreciation of diversity' in Esin Örücü and David Nelken (eds), *Comparative Legal Studies: a Handbook* (Hart Publishing, forthcoming).

Arthur T von Mehren, 'The Rise of Transnational Legal Practice and the Task of Comparative Law' 75 Tul L Rev 1215, 1215–17 (2000–2001) [60a]

Comparatists fall into one of three camps. First, there are those who see legal systems as differing so greatly in fundamental respects that each is essentially unique. They sometimes see the task of comparative law as consisting only of highlighting these differences; sometimes they use the insights provided by comparative law to improve their own law. A second camp is comprised of those comparatists who believe that our rapidly shrinking world is moving inexorably towards convergence in many areas of law, driven by transnational activities in all spheres of economic and social life; they see their task as helping this convergence come about. Finally, there are those who take the position that neither uniqueness nor convergence does now, or ultimately will, characterize non local law. According to them, until such time as convergence has come about, comparative law bears the responsibility for making clear the degree to which, and the way in which, convergence has occurred and for providing analytical tools that enable jurists from different legal cultures to achieve a shared understanding of their respective intentions, positions, and views. Comparatists map the forests into which practitioners venture and provide concepts and tools of analysis that enable them to find their way. One possessed of comparative law training can better judge whether there is sufficient reciprocity and coherence of interest to justify assuming legal obligations and, if so, how the transaction can best be structured for legal purposes.

In the second half of the twentieth century the once predominant belief in uniqueness as a characteristic of legal systems has lost ground to the belief in convergence. International conventions have made progress in harmonizing certain areas of law—for example, the substantive law applicable to the international sale of goods. Also, the ancient concept of the *lex mercatoria*, based on the customs of merchants, rather than on state sovereignty, has grown in influence and importance. Today the convergenist camp challenges even the third camp's view that, in our 'globalizing' contemporary world, important elements of diversity will persist. Thus, whole areas, for example contract law, in which convergence—real or assumed—has occurred have been systematically restated. Further, such projects for other areas are on their way.

Experience suggests, and reflection supports, the proposition that to achieve a high measure of convergence in private-law matters, two conditions must be satisfied: there must be a supra-national starting point for legal reasoning, and it must be administered by a supra-national judicial system whose judges are trained in a shared legal tradition with a common conceptual structure and common values. Except in regional federations, the likelihood of these conditions being satisfied is small.

Transplantation not attributable to comparative study

4.65 Several scholars have cautioned against the tendency to make exaggerated claims for comparative law.

> The effort to justify comparative law by its practical uses sometimes verges on the ridiculous. According to some sentimentalists, comparison is supposed to increase understanding among peoples and foster the peaceful coexistence of nations. According to that idea, the statesmen who triggered the two world wars would have stopped at the brink of catastrophe had they only attended courses in comparative

---

[60a] Reprinted with the permission of Tulane Law Review Association, which holds the copyright.

law. Napoleon himself would have given up his imperialistic dreams had he spent less time over the code that bears his name and more on the *gemeines Recht*, the common law and the *kormchaia Pravda*.[61]

We do not need to go quite as far as this sardonic *reductio ad absurdum* to conclude **4.66** that whilst a comparative study is nowadays an essential prelude to a project of uniform law, the incorporation of foreign legal concepts into a particular jurisdiction is not necessarily attributable to comparative work in the true sense, but may result from other factors. Thus, transplantation may occur through imperialism, as in the case of Roman law, the common law, and in some degree French law; through the spread of liberal values and revolutionary ideas, which led to the reception of the French *code civil* throughout a large part of continental Europe and in sub-Saharan Africa, Québec and Louisiana; and in recent times through the urgent need, in the new market economies, for an off-the-shelf set of laws governing investment and commercial transactions. In all these cases, comparative law studies were not the motive power for the adoption of foreign laws; rather, this was either the imposition of a foreign law by a conqueror or settler or the lack of a developed system of law for a prospective market economy and the consequent need to borrow from elsewhere.

The exportability of a significant branch of private law, as opposed to one or more **4.67** specific rules, depends very much on its form. The French *code civil*, for example, has been shown to be readily exportable, being systematic and at the same time elegant and responsive to the aspirations of the populace. By contrast, English law, even if producing better solutions for problems arising from commercial transactions, has nothing to export, for the common law is not a codified system but a mass of case law which has to be reduced to structure and organization by the works of scholars. Hence, in the preparation of the American Uniform Commercial Code, its chief architect, Karl Llewellyn, who studied and taught at Leipzig University, drew heavily on his knowledge of codes in general and the German BGB in particular.

William D Hawkland, 'The Uniform Commercial Code and the Civil Codes' 56 La L Rev 231, 232–9 (1995–6)

Llewellyn . . . now faced the formidable job of creating on the state level commercial law that would operate uniformly throughout a country in which many regions held divergent views on what the law of private commercial transactions should be. How was this goal to be accomplished? Llewellyn's answer, though never directly articled by him in so many words, was codification . . . If Llewellyn had publicized his intention to codify commercial law, his Uniform Commercial Code probably would have died aborning. But he almost certainly had elected to use the code structure in building his new UCC because he knew that the common law methodology had broken down in the commercial arena . . . [Prior] uniform commercial statutes lacked preemption, system, and comprehension—the key

---

[61] Rodolfo Sacco, 'Legal Formants: A Dynamic Approach to Comparative Law' 39 Am J Comp L 1, 2 (1991).

elements of a true code. Codification of the commercial laws, therefore, became the answer ... And it was Llewellyn's answer, though, as I have indicated, he was very reluctant for political reasons ever to admit this fact.

I have also indicated that while most American lawyers seem hostile to the concept of codification, they could not, if put to the test, distinguish a code from a statute. As all of us in Louisiana know, there is a wide difference between a statute and a true code. A 'code,' in my view, is a preemptive, systematic, and comprehensive enactment of a whole field of law. It is preemptive in that it displaces all other law in its subject. It is systematic in that all of its parts, arranged in an orderly fashion and stated with a consistent terminology, form an interlocking, integrated body, revealing its own plan and containing its own methodology. It is comprehensive in that it is sufficiently inclusive and independent to enable it to be administered in accordance with its own policies. A mere statute ... is neither preemptive, systematic, nor comprehensive, and, therefore, its methodology is different from a code ... A 'code,' on the other hand, remains at all times its own best evidence of what it means: cases decided under it may be interesting, persuasive, cogent, but each new case must be referred for decision to the undefiled code text ... Since a true code preempts a large body of law and comprehensively deals with all of its parts, it obviously must be construed systematically. That requires: (1) that its provisions be logically presented and coordinated and stated in language employing a chosen and consistent terminology; (2) that means be made available to handle competing and conflicting rules; (3) that means be provided to fill the gaps; and (4) that supereminent ('safety-valve') provisions be present to mitigate harshness which might otherwise flow from rigid rules. The Uniform Commercial Code meets these requirements. Its provisions, following the organizational plan of most European codes, are logically divided into interlocking 'articles,' each handling one major subdivision of the entire subject ... the UCC is not drafted as elegantly as the French Civil Code. Nor does it employ its highly abstract principles. Yet ... it meets the formal requisites of a true code and ought to be treated as such, at least for purposes of legal method.[62]

4.68   Other legal systems have likewise drawn on European civil codes. So Eugen Huber's elegant Swiss Civil Code was adopted in Turkey and the German BGB in Japan.

4.69   The problem we now face is that the time horizon for law reform has changed dramatically over the years, as have the financial realities associated with it. Governments and industry expect faster, less expensive processes, without compromises in quality. That is unrealistic, and that should be acknowledged. What is important for our purposes is to assess the implications of time and cost issues on the comparative law and law reform processes. How much literature may be consulted? How wide is the net of those consulted? How much time is given for study, reaction, and revision? How interactive is the comparative law process? In short, in today's world, can comparative law do more than provide an insight into the need for, and feasibility of, law reform, and, perhaps, the form of a proposed instrument?

---

[62]   See also: William L Twining, *Karl Llewellyn and the Realist Movement* (Weidenfeld and Nicolson, London, 1973) ch 12.

The effectiveness of legal transplants

Montesquieu long ago pointed out that laws should be so adapted to the people **4.70** for whom they were made that it would be a great coincidence if those of one country were to suit another.[63] More recently, while drawing on Montesquieu, Professor Otto Kahn-Freund added a comment which is highly relevant in the context of international lawmaking:

O Kahn-Freund, 'On Uses and Misuses of Comparative Law' (1974) 37 MLR 1, 12

But there is a third political element, and in many ways it is from a practical point of view the most important. It is the enormously increased role which is played by organised interests in the making and in the maintenance of legal institutions. Anyone contemplating the use of foreign legislation for law making in his country must ask himself: how far does this rule or institution owe its existence or its continued existence to the distribution of power in the foreign country which we do not share? How far would it be accepted and how far rejected by the organised groups which, in the political sense, are part of our constitution? And if I say 'organised groups' I am not only thinking of groups representing economic interests: big business, agriculture, trade unions, consumer organisations, but equally of organised cultural interests, religious, charitable, etc. All these share in the political power, and the extent of their influence and the way it is exercised varies from country to country. Here perhaps is the strongest 'organic' element in the law today: its close link with the infinite variations of the organisation of power in culturally, socially, economically very similar countries.

There are a number of additional factors affecting the ability of a country to **4.71** borrow the laws of another effectively.[64] These include problems of language, which are incapable of adequate resolution.[65] But perhaps the most important factor is the lack of a developed infrastructure, in particular a banking system with multilateral clearing and settlement facilities, a stock exchange, a system for the registration of security interests, and, most importantly of all, an independent and efficient judiciary.

How necessary is a knowledge of comparative law to the development and practical application of transnational commercial law?

It might be thought that in the ideal world all those involved in work of harmo- **4.72** nization would be fully equipped as comparative lawyers. However, this is neither feasible nor necessary, nor, indeed, is it desirable. Relatively few members of a study group engaged in a harmonization project would consider themselves true comparative lawyers. While a comparative study is an essential preliminary to any work on international uniform law, and it is useful if the study group

---

[63] C Montesquieu, *De L'Esprit des Lois* (Barrillot, Geneva, 1749) Book I, s 3.

[64] Many scholars have discussed the problem of legal transplants. See in particular: Alan Watson, *Legal Transplants: an Approach to Comparative Law* (2nd edn, U of Georgia Press, London, 1993).

[65] See above, para 4.62, and Sacco (n 61) 10 ff.

contains one or two comparative lawyers to provide an overall perspective of existing systems, the functional approach reduces the need for any detailed knowledge of foreign legal systems by most of those engaged in the work, for the task is to identify the practical problems to be addressed and best solutions to those problems. Where a proposed rule might create difficulties for a particular jurisdiction we can rely on an expert from that jurisdiction to identify them and to suggest a modification that might resolve them. Those engaged in work on international harmonization do not have either the time or the resources needed to conduct the kind of comparative study that would be undertaken by a comparatist scholar.

4.73 In the case of transnational commercial law, it is increasingly found that most national legal systems have failed to keep pace with evolving international practice, so that these may have little to bring to the table. The usual method of proceeding in such cases is for one or more experts in the field to draft a set of rules designed to resolve the problems that have been identified by the study group and then expose these to critical comment by the study group, every member of the group testing each proposed rule against his or her own legal system, knowledge and experience to identify the rule's strengths and weaknesses. The combined expertise of the participants will thus inform the work and enable the rules to be adjusted where these would create significant difficulties for particular legal systems. So the need is less for comparative lawyers in the full sense than for lawyers equipped with a knowledge and understanding of the type of international transaction under review and its treatment by their own legal systems, aided by specialists from the particular industry sector involved equipped to explain why a uniform law is necessary and what issues it has to address.

4.74 The same is true of international legal practice. International law firms with offices in many parts of the world consider themselves well placed to obtain sufficient information about other legal systems to structure cross-border transactions, and to provide opinions on their legal efficacy, without having been trained as comparative lawyers. Since their concern is with transactions and problem solving, they are not concerned with foreign legal systems as a whole or even with a field of law within such a system but focus on the particular issues that the particular transaction under consideration is seen to raise.[66]

Alan Watson, *Legal Transplants: an Approach to Comparative Law* (2nd edn, U of Georgia Press, London, 1993) 17

... I should here like to stress the value which a knowledge of foreign law can have even where the knowledge is by no means detailed or systematic.

---

[66] See in this connection H Patrick Glenn, 'Comparative Law and Legal Practice' 75 Tul L Rev 977 (2000–2001).

Even unsystematic knowledge can be very useful in a practical way for, say, law reform. A person whose function it is to consider possible improvements in the law of bankruptcy in Scotland may well set out to discover the legal approach in England, France, Sweden, South Africa, New Zealand and so on. He may have no knowledge of these systems to begin with, and at the end he may know little about them except for an outline of their bankruptcy laws. He may, indeed, have little idea of how well or badly these laws operate. But his concern is with the improvement of bankruptcy law in Scotland. What he is looking for in his investigation of foreign systems is an idea which can be transformed into part of the law of Scotland and will work there well. A rule of Swedish law which is successful at home might be a disaster in the different circumstances existing in Scotland; a rule of French law which there works badly might provide an ideal rule for Scotland.

When the available evidence for the system which a scholar, especially a legal historian, is studying points towards a particular development then his conclusions may receive some support if he can refer to a similar development elsewhere. Here, too, the scholar need not have a systematic knowledge of that other system nor need there even be a relationship between the two systems. The essential point to notice, however, is that the foreign system is thus used only to confirm the results already obtained in the primary system. A gap in the knowledge of the primary system cannot be filled in this way from unsystematic knowledge of a related system or even from systematic knowledge of an unrelated system.

Questions

1. What is comparative law? What purposes does it serve?
2. What do you understand by the functional approach to comparative law?
3. To what extent has the development of commercial law in your own legal system been influenced by foreign law? And what were the factors motivating your courts in referring to foreign law?
4. 'It is a basic assumption underlying comparative law methodology that legal systems face similar problems, address them differently, yet reach similar results.'

   Discuss this statement. To what extent do you consider it to be borne out by the UNIDROIT Principles of International Commercial Contracts and the Principles of European Contract Law?
5. In what ways may comparative law assist a national judge in considering a question arising under his or her own law?
6. What are the dangers that have to be confronted in comparative law studies?
7. 'Recourse to foreign law for the purpose of shaping a rule of domestic law is incompatible with the democratic principle by which the governed are entitled to a voice in the formulation of laws by those who govern them.' Discuss.

Further reading

Canivet, Guy, Andenas, Mads, and Fairgrieve, Duncan (eds), *Comparative Law Before the Courts* (British Institute of International and Comparative Law, London, 2004)

de Cruz, Peter, *Comparative Law in a changing world* (2nd edn, Cavendish Publishing, London, 1999), especially ch 1 and 7

David, René, 'The International Unification of Private Law' in the *International Encyclopaedia of Comparative Law II* (JCB Mohr, Tübingen, 1971) ch 5

Drobnig, Ulrich, and van Erp, Sjef (eds), *The Use of Comparative Law by Courts* (Kluwer, The Hague, 1999)

Gordley, James, and von Mehren, Arthur Taylor, *An Introduction to the Comparative Study of Private Law: Readings, Cases, Materials* (Cambridge University Press, 2006)

Hesselink, Martijn W., The New European Legal Culture (Kluwer, Deventer, 2001)

Jacobs, Francis, 'Judicial Dialogue abd the Cross-fertilisation of Legal Systms: The European Court of Justice', 38 Texas International Law Journal 553 ff (2003)

Kahn-Freund, Otto, 'On Uses and Misuses of Comparative Law' (1974) 37 MLR 1

Kronke, H, 'The "Functional Approach" in Corporative Law, Private International Law and Transnational Commercial Law: Promises and Challenges', Annales Universitatis Scientiarum Budapestiensis de Rolando Eötvös nominatae, Sectio Juridica, Tomas XLVII (forthcoming)

Koopmans, T, 'Comparative Law and the Courts' (1996) 45 ICLQ 545

Legeais, Raymond, 'L'utilisation du droit comparé par les tribunaux' (1994) 46 RIDC 7

Markesinis, B S, *Foreign Law and Comparative Methodology: A Subject and a Thesis* (Hart Publishing, Oxford, 1997)

Markesinis, Basil (ed), *The British Contribution to the Europe of the Twenty-First Century: The British Academy Centenary Lectures* (Hart Publishing, 2002)

Markesinis, Basil, 'Understanding American Law by Looking at it Through Foreign Eyes: Towards a Wider Theory for the Study and Use of Foreign Law', 81 Tulane L. Rev (November 2006)

Pescatore, Pierre, 'Le recours, dans la jurisprudence de la Cour de justice des Communautés européennes, à des normes déduites de la comparaison des droits des États membres' (1980) 32 RIDC 337

Pound, Roscoe, 'The Revival of Comparative Law' 5 Tul L Rev 1 (1930–31)

Rabel, Ernst, *Aufgabe und Notwendigkeit der Rechtsvergleichung* (Max Hueber, München 1925) as reprinted in Leser, Hans G (ed), *Rabel, Gesammelte Aufsätze III* (JCB Mohr, Tübingen, 1965) 1

Reimann, Mathias, 'The Progress and Failure of Comparative Law in the Second Half of the Twentieth Century,' 50 Am J Comp L 671 ff (2002)

Schlesinger, Rudolf B, 'The Uniform Commercial Code in the Light of Comparative Law' 1 Inter-Am L Rev 11 (1959)

Tushnet, M, 'The Possibilities of Comparative Law' 108 Yale Law Journal 1225 (1999)

Winship, Peter, 'As the World Turns: Revisiting Rudolf Schlesinger's Study of the Uniform Commercial Code "In the Light of Comparative Law"' 29 Loy LA L Rev 1143 (1995–6)

5

THE HARMONIZATION OF COMMERCIAL LAW: INSTRUMENTS AND INSTITUTIONS

A. Introduction		C. The Principal Institutions in the	
The reasons for harmonization	5.01	Harmonization of Commercial Law	
Substantive law harmonization and		General	5.17
harmonization of conflicts rules	5.06	The Hague Conference on Private	
B. The Instruments of International		International Law	5.19
Harmonization		UNIDROIT	5.22
International instruments intended to		UNCITRAL	5.28
become legally binding	5.07	The International Chamber of	
Facultative instruments	5.08	Commerce (ICC)	5.32
Contractually incorporated non-binding		The role of international and	
rules promulgated by international		regional professional and industry	
organizations	5.11	organizations	5.33
Guides	5.15	Co-ordination of legislative activities	5.34
The dialogue of sources	5.16		

A. Introduction

The reasons for harmonization

As we have seen in previous chapters, throughout history, merchants as well as the **5.01** polities concerned—for example the 'maritime republics' and merchant cities—in some way organized, or at least recognized and documented, 'spontaneous production' of rules governing national and international commerce. There are many reasons for scholars, businessmen, governments, practising lawyers and trade associations to look into the feasibility, start substantial research and, at a later stage, to recommend or demand systematic and organized harmonization of commercial law at the international level. Not all the groups and institutions just mentioned took an interest in this at the same time, and not all shared the views of all others. The various stakeholders had varying priorities and strategic objectives, and some at times had strong reservations or even opposed initiatives and activities undertaken by others. However, four reasons can be identified.

5.02 First, as seen in chapter 2, the utter distrust and hostility most practitioners harboured (and continue to harbour) vis-à-vis the rules of conflict of laws. To many, they seem esoteric and, in any event, typical 'lawyers' law' or even 'scholars' law'. Whilst the greater degree of certainty provided by modern conflicts legislation and greater familiarity with the subject, thanks to its being regularly taught in the law schools of most countries, have eased these tensions and the practitioners' insecurity, they continue to be an incentive for the development of harmonized or uniform substantive law. Suffice it to recall the late Professor Friedrich Juenger's strong-worded position which is extensively quoted above.[1]

5.03 Second, the desire to reduce the difficulties and, therefore, expenses connected with entering into international business transactions without being familiar with the laws and regulations applicable to the 'foreign tier' of any such transaction. In today's parlance, inspired by economic theory, the transaction costs, that is, the expenses one incurs to obtain information about the rights and obligations as well as the risks inherent in such matters as concluding a contract, are presumably lower if the law applicable to all parts of the transaction is the same, irrespective of whether these are domestic or foreign. The records of the preparatory work for an instrument to unify sales law carried out at UNIDROIT since the 1920s and culminating in the acts and proceedings of the 1964 Diplomatic Conference for the adoption of the Uniform Law on International Sales and of the 1980 Diplomatic Conference for the adoption of the CISG[2] reflect that desire, as well as the belief that internationally harmonized sales law is in fact capable of producing those economic benefits. The same is true for the vast majority of uniform law instruments.

5.04 Third, there is a political or ideological reason which is to be seen in the historical context of the institutionalized harmonization movement. It is, obviously, not a mere coincidence that UNIDROIT was launched as a specialized agency of the League of Nations in the wake of World War I. The League's *raison d'être* and its mandate was to avoid future catastrophes of that nature through a framework of rules of international law and procedures capable of resolving potential and real conflicts by peaceful means.[3] In the same vein, it was thought that armed conflicts could best be avoided if there was trust and understanding among nations; that such trust and understanding were effectively fostered by more trade; and, that more trade and, consequently, economic opportunities, for all would be facilitated by a framework of harmonized and, therefore, reliable rules of commercial law. In sum, peace through internationally generated and adopted commercial law. Similarly, the creation of the United Nations Commission on International Trade

---

[1] See para 2.12.   [2] Below, ch 7.   [3] See the inaugural speech quoted below, para 5.22.

Law (UNCITRAL) in 1966 was rooted in ethical considerations, when it was argued that the new independent nations who had just shaken off the yoke of colonialism now needed to be involved in universal harmonization of trade law. This time, development through harmonized commercial law could have been the motto.

Today, we are much more cautious in formulating the reasons for harmonizing **5.05** commercial law than the pioneers in the late nineteenth and the first half of the twentieth centuries, or the idealists among academics and politicians supporting the good cause. Universal unity based on universal private law, a noble scholarly dream of some of our forefathers, is not the objective. Nowadays, the intergovernmental organizations tend to define their objective as the development of new (commercial law) solutions for new problems. And, to the extent that these new problems are by their very nature transnational, the solutions should from the outset be internationally compatible and harmonized solutions. To take but two examples: first, there are probably no—or very few—securities held by intermediaries within the boundaries of one State's territory. Consequently, the rules governing the multi-tiered and multi-national holding patterns should be harmonized.[4] Second, the taking of security in aircraft, space assets and other categories of mobile equipment that are not tied to any country's territory should be governed by one set of rules which are applicable irrespective of where the encumbered asset, the security giver and the security taker are located. It is against this background that governments negotiated and adopted the 2001 Cape Town Convention on International Interests in Mobile Equipment and various equipment-specific protocols.[5]

Substantive law harmonization and harmonization of conflicts rules

Historically, the efforts to harmonize conflict of laws rules—and first results—are **5.06** older than the beginnings of substantive law harmonization. On 12 February 1889, Argentina, Bolivia, Paraguay, Peru, and Uruguay adopted three treaties and a protocol on international private law, international commercial law and international procedural law (Treaties of Montevideo). These were later adopted by Colombia as well, though not until 1993. Apart from a conference held in Caracas in 1911, and a second conference in Montevideo held in 1940, the 'Código Bustamante' of 20 February 1928, an impressive codification of conflicts rules which reached as far as criminal law and were named after its principal drafter (a Cuban professor), was adopted by a number of Latin American States and is still in force in some of them.[6] Conferences for the elaboration and adoption of uniform

---

[4] See below, ch 13.   [5] See below, ch 12.

[6] See: G Parra-Aranguren, 'La primera etapa de los tratados sobre Derecho Internacional Privado in América (1826–1940)' (1996) 98 Caracas 59. For an exhaustive analysis, see: Jürgen Samtleben,

conflicts rules in form of conventions were held in The Hague from 1893, and the first of those treaties (on marriage) was adopted in 1902. However, during a rather long period, these efforts were confined to Latin America, Continental Europe and Japan. The common law countries joined only after World War II. Given the 'meta-law' character of conflict-of-laws rules,[7] that is, the fact that often deeply rooted policies of domestic private law norms are not at stake, it is easy to understand why governments are prepared to harmonize conflicts rules much earlier than the substantive law at issue. As discussed in chapters 2 and 13, the harmonization of substantive law and the harmonization of conflicts rules are completely different issues. Given the frequently narrow fields of substantive private and commercial law which are subject of harmonization efforts, and in view of those areas that remain non-uniform (because of options and reservations provided for in the treaties and designed to render the harmonization process and its results responsive to individual national preferences) both will continue to be needed in the future.

B. The Instruments of International Harmonization

International instruments intended to become legally binding

5.07 Today, we are looking at a wide range of international instruments which are capable of bringing about different degrees of harmonization of commercial law. However, the evolution leading to this variety of options, one may even say the menu to choose from, is fairly recent. In the beginning, there was but one tool, namely bilateral and multilateral treaties or conventions which either required that a ratifying State implemented them by adapting its domestic laws accordingly, or which created themselves uniform laws applicable *tel quel* in all contracting States.

Herbert Kronke, 'International uniform commercial law Conventions: advantages, disadvantages, criteria for choice' (2000) V Unif L Rev 13, 13–20

[. . .] I was only asked to address the advantages and disadvantages of the classic vehicle for achieving harmonisation . . . However, as pinpointing 'advantages' and 'disadvantages' only makes sense against the backdrop of the alternatives available . . . this paper unavoidably also deals with the criteria for choosing the appropriate type of instrument.

II.—The institutional framework

[. . .] Notwithstanding the success that not only the UNIDROIT Principles,[8] but also even 'softer' instruments are enjoying, the choice of type and form does pose institutional

---

Internationales Privatrecht in Lateinamerika: der Código Bustamante in Theorie und Praxis (Mohr Siebeck, Tübingen 1979); Jürgen Samtleben, *Derecho internacional privado in América Latina: teoría y práctica del Código Bustamante* , (tr Bueno-Guzmán) (Depalma, Buenos Aires 1983); Diego Fernández Arroyo, *La codificación del derecho internacional privado in América Latina: ambitos de producción juridica y orientaciones metodológicas* (Editorial Beramar, Madrid, 1994).

[7] See above, ch 2.   [8] For a detailed analysis, see ch 14, below.

questions. On the one hand, the Organisation is accountable to Governments. On the other hand, Governments, just as any other body, corporate or indeed individual, tend to entertain more interest in matters in which they are actively involved and which are or will shortly be of immediate concern to them. . . .

How important *inter-governmental* exchange on the objectives and content of uniform or harmonised law is—and such exchange occurs primarily in the preparation of Conventions—is reflected by the fact that the United States of America acceded to the UNIDROIT Statute barely a month before the diplomatic Conference leading to the Hague Sales Laws, and that since the Conference and in the run-up to Vienna, Ottawa and Rome[9] no fewer than 20 States from all continents have acceded or re-acceded to [UNIDROIT].

After the Treaty of Amsterdam, an institutional *dis*advantage of working on Conventions is the rather far-reaching and not always predictable and convincing views as to competence and substance put forward by some Member States and by the EU Commission. As soon as it becomes clear that the Organisation working on the basis of a *global* mandate does not envisage a binding form, their interest in being actively involved and in determining the limits of individual States' competence appears to wane.

III.—Measures for determining appropriateness and success

How do we know whether the classical form of harmonising . . . private law, *ie* the Convention, is suitable for tackling a given issue, problem area or type of transaction? A large number of ratifications, a rapidly growing body of case law from many countries which succeeds in maintaining uniformity, no calls for revision enable us, with hindsight, to dub "advantageous" those Conventions that succeed in eliciting such a response. . . .

No matter how many ratifications and accessions it collected, the sponsors of an instrument would still be dissatisfied if, despite its intrinsic technical qualities, traders regularly excluded its application to their transactions.

By the same token, there is no evidence whatsoever that those Conventions which, though praised sky-high, have been blessed with few or no ratifications would have known a different fate had a different form been preferred.

And again, does the ascertainable success of a Convention—*eg* the CMR[10]—in one region of the world necessarily mean that it might be a good idea to 'export' it to other regions? While some might regard this as advantageous compared to the *status quo*, others will disagree and cite advantages, *in terms of uniformity*, of the Convention-less situation. . . .

However, there is some experience on which we may draw and which would seem to support certain hypotheses.

IV.—Disadvantages

In the abstract, the disadvantages of the treaty form are numerous and they have been discussed many times. In particular, drumming up support for the UNIDROIT Principles

---

[9] These are references to the diplomatic Conferences that adopted the CISG, the 1988 Conventions on Leasing and Factoring and the 1995 Convention on the Return of Stolen and Illegally Exported Cultural Objects.

[10] Convention on the Contract for the International Carriage of Goods by Road, signed at Geneva on 16 May 1956.

of International Commercial Contracts required some stark language. As Professor Goode, member of the UNIDROIT Governing Council, put it,

> the treaty collections are littered with Conventions that have never come into force, for want of the number of required ratifications, or have been eschewed by the major trading States. There are several reasons for this: failure to establish from potential interest groups at the outset that there is a serious problem which the proposed Convention will help to resolve; hostility from powerful pressure groups; lack of sufficient interest of, or pressure on, Governments to induce them to burden still further an already over-crowded legislative timetable; mutual hold-backs, each State waiting to see what the others will do, so that in the end none of them does anything.

However, most of this, except for the packed legislative agendas and the hold-back games between States regarding ratifications, could apply to other instruments as well. So, much depends on the structure of the elaboration process . . .

A. *The elaboration process*

[The article goes on discussing a number of key problems regarding the elaboration process; for details, see chapter 6 below[11]].

B. *The Convention in place*

Once a Convention has received the blessing of a diplomatic Conference, the following aspects may make themselves felt as disadvantages.

First, Conventions are normally rather specific and fragmentary in character. Let us call it the isolated-position syndrome. For example, a Convention on agency may find itself implanted in a body of law—codified or judge-made—whose domestic rules on contracts, restitution, property or tort are hard to reconcile with the Convention's solutions but against whose background the uniform law must be interpreted.

The state of the art in mitigating the effects of this unpleasant situation is to draft a provision like Article 7 CISG. I shall not here embark on a discussion of the issues raised in this respect. Suffice it to recall that the general principles on which a *Convention* as such ('it') is based are usually few or vague or hard to ascertain and that, therefore, further progress derived from different kinds of instruments (*eg* the UNIDROIT Principles) or, indeed, any 'outside' principles depends chiefly on drafting those references to outside sources in a broader and more liberal fashion. Some of the road ahead may be covered by 'creeping unification', but Conventions themselves could . . . lend a helping hand.

The second disadvantage . . . is the international community's still underdeveloped ability to respond to changing circumstances. The Warsaw Convention, but other Conventions in the area of transport law as well, are prominent examples . . .

Third, the impact of most Conventions on domestic law reform around the world seems to be smaller than the impact which various model laws, the Principles of International Commercial Contracts, etc have enjoyed. The influential role to which the CISG may lay claim . . . , or the impact that the draft UNIDROIT Convention on International Interests in Mobile Equipment will undoubtedly have on many countries' law on secured transactions are a-typical in this respect . . .

---

[11] For an instructive 'guide' by a very experienced negotiator, see: Jean-Paul Béraudo, 'La négociation internationale institutionelle de droit privé (1ère partie)' (1997) 2 Unif L Rev 9.

Fourth, a Convention often poses problems for latecomers who find a body of existing case law interpreting and developing rules to the elaboration of which they have made practically no contribution.

[. . .]

V.—Advantages

[. . .] In the abstract . . . , there is one considerable advantage which, however, is not a distinctive characteristic of uniform law *Conventions* and, again as in other sources of law, is offset by a disadvantage. I refer to . . . *certainty of law v flexibility.* . . . Hard-and-fast Convention rules (even more so mandatory ones), to the same extent as codified law, provide the former and . . . lack the latter. Unfettered freedom of contract, Principles and other sources of 'soft law', to the same extent as judge-made law, allow for the latter . . .

B. Which Conventions? Proposals for improvement

Strong evidence suggests that uniform law Conventions may have quite a bright future. Provided, that is, that changes are made in both the general approach and the structure of such Conventions, as and where appropriate.

[. . .] Conventions should be innovative and create the devices needed . . . in international trade. The 1929 Warsaw Convention is a striking example, as there was hardly any national legislation on the matter in those days and the international character of the subject was obvious from the outset . . .

[. . .]

Facultative instruments

Historically, the first alternative means to bring about *harmonization*—and this **5.08** was a conscious step back from the initial ambition to *unify* private law—was the model law (in French, *loi-type*). The example was clearly the Uniform Commercial Code which, in the United States, had been the only constitutionally conceivable— as well as hugely successful—vehicle for the harmonization of commercial law across the many States of the Union. A model law proposes, in more or less detailed provisions, a way of regulating a certain type of transaction (for example leasing) or a certain area of law (such as international commercial arbitration). National legislatures are then free to either not make use of the proposal at all, to take the model law as it is and transplant it into their domestic law, or, finally, to adopt it in part and provide for amendments and variations required by or considered to be desirable in light of a specific domestic situation. More generally, the differences between legislative styles may entail that the model is very detailed (common law style), whereas its domestic echo resounds in fewer and rather abstract provisions (as traditionally preferred in civil law systems). In that case, the details may then be reflected in the *travaux préparatoires*, such as the government's explanatory report as it accompanies the bill submitted to parliament. Model laws adopted and proposed by intergovernmental organizations, like conventions, are negotiated by governments. However, since the objectives and the ambition are different, and since the discussions are not exposed to considerations of national sovereignty, the style of negotiation is different and the gestation periods are typically (but not always) shorter.

5.09 The model-law technique has been breathtakingly successful in some instances. Undoubtedly, the most successful model law so far is the 1985 UNCITRAL Model Law on International Commercial Arbitration.[12] Unlike other model laws, its degree of success is measurable, and the number of jurisdictions that have adopted it is by all means impressive. Strikingly, although it is not a binding treaty, but (only) an offer submitted to national legislatures, and although its drafters deliberately and expressly limited its scope to *international* and *commercial* arbitration, a number of States took it as a blueprint for modernizing their laws which govern both national and domestic, as well as commercial and non-commercial, arbitration. Why did they do that?

Gerold Herrmann, 'The Role of UNCITRAL' in Ian F Fletcher, Loukas A Mistelis, Marise Cremona (eds), *Foundations and Perspectives of International Trade Law* (Sweet & Maxwell, London, 2001) 33

[. . .] Being the most widely and best known arbitration law in the world, it provides (with this 'hi-fi factor') confidence and certainty to potential users, which is of particular interest to investors or traders.

Two other good examples are our Model Law on Procurement of Goods, Construction and Services [of 1994] as well as, though below the level of unification, our recently adopted Guide for Privately Financed Infrastructure Projects. In both fields, the effect of 'certainisation' instills confidence into would-be investors and either encourages them to participate in that economically important activity or, at least, to reduce their prices.

5.10 Many other model laws have been drafted over the years, and other intergovernmental organizations (for example, the Organization of American States (OAS), the *Organisation pour l'Harmonisation en Afrique du Droit des Affaires* (OHADA) and UNIDROIT) have used this method since. Not all model laws have, however, been successful: some were outright failures. The great French comparatist René David once wrote that 'model laws end up in the waste-paper basket'. This was true for one he himself drafted, namely the 1962 European Convention Providing a Uniform Law on Arbitration. Dressed up as a Convention, this instrument consisted of thirty-one articles and an annex providing for fifteen possible reservations. The latter makes it essentially a model law—a reminder that one cannot always trust the terminology chosen by the drafters of an instrument but that a functional analysis is required.

---

[12] See ch 17, below.

Contractually incorporated non-binding rules promulgated by international organizations

Under this heading, a great number and variety of instruments come to mind. **5.11**
Again, notwithstanding their non-binding character, some of them are remarkably successful and some literally govern their area of the law worldwide.

The first category are *international trade terms*, most prominently the INCOTERMS **5.12**
(see also para 1.56) as well as (other) *rules codifying custom and usage* such as the ICC's Uniform Customs and Practice for Documentary Credits (UCP) discussed in chapter 9.

The second category consists of *model contracts and (model) general conditions of* **5.13**
contract. Of particular interest are those issued by the International Trade Centre UNCTAD/WTO (ITC), such as the Model Contract for the International Commercial Sale of Perishable Goods (1999) and the Contractual Joint Venture Model Agreements (2004),[13] and by the ICC, such as the Model Occasional Intermediary Contract (2000), the Model Commercial Agency Contract (2002) and the Model Distributorship Contract–Sole Importer–Distributorship (2002).

The third category is the most interesting one in that its addressees and potential **5.14**
users (and, as we now know, actual users) are not only contract drafters, but national and international legislators, arbitral tribunals and courts as well. This is, obviously, a reference to 'codifications' and *restatements* (as a commentator rightly noted, and *pre*-statements) by international groups of scholars and distinguished practitioners, such as the UNIDROIT Principles of International Commercial Contracts (UPICC) and the Principles of European Contract Law (PECL). Both instruments are discussed in chapter 14 below.

Guides

Yet another category of instruments, which international organizations have in **5.15**
recent years developed and put at the disposal of governments and businesses, are guides of various kinds. 'Best practice guides' are typically addressed at professional and trade associations. The (potential) users of 'legislative guides' are governments and legislators. The UNIDROIT Guide to International Master Franchise Arrangements (2002) briefly described in chapter 8 below has traits of both types. The UNCITRAL Legislative Guide on Secured Transactions, which is expected to be adopted in 2007, clearly addresses legislators. The term 'soft law'

---

[13] *ITC Contractual Joint Venture Model Agreements* (International Trade Centre, UNCTAD/WTO, Geneva, 2004). For in-depth comment, see: Jean-Paul Vulliéty, 'Le contrat type pour les *Joint Ventures* contractuelles du Centre du Commerce International au regard des Principes d'UNIDROIT et d'autres normes d'unification du droit des contrats' (2004) 9 Unif L Rev 295.

would be a misnomer in this context. Guides are truly educational exercises, the authors being the teachers and the government officials and parliamentarians being the pupils: a guide discusses in depth the structure of legal problems (for example, the taking of security in movables, the issues to be dealt with in the contract between franchisor and franchisee), including their economic, technical and other factual background, outlines possible solutions and explains the underlying legal concepts, and ideally concludes by making recommendations.

The dialogue of sources

5.16 It is most interesting to note that 'hard law' Conventions and the whole range of non-binding instruments are by no means autistic. They communicate among each other. For example, as is well known, the UPICC and the PECL, rather than re-inventing solutions where those proposed by the CISG are state of the art, sound and considered appropriate for contracts generally, simply adopt those solutions.[14] Only where there are none, or where a rule barely disguises the fact that the delegations present at the Diplomatic Conference in Vienna papered over their disagreements, do the UPICC and the PECL affirm their autonomy. In other words, the Convention, on the one hand, and the restatements on the other hand, are complementary. In the same vein, the above mentioned ITC Model Contract for the International Commercial Sale of Perishable Goods contains a choice-of-law clause providing that it is to be governed by the CISG and the UPICC as applicable. Similarly, the Model Contracts issued by the International Chamber of Commerce make reference to the general framework regarding contractual obligations offered by the UNIDROIT Contract Principles.[15] Whether this dialogue of sources, possibly emphasized by one law-formulating organization endorsing the adoption and the use of other organizations' consonant instruments, in the long run prepares the ground for systematically pulling the strings together—some even use the term codification[16]—makes for interesting speculation.

---

[14] For details, see: Michael J Bonell, *An International Restatement of Contract Law* (3rd edn, Transnational Publisher, Ardsley(NY), 2005) 305–13.

[15] For an exhaustive overview and detailed analysis of the reception of the UPICC in ICC model contracts, see Alexis Mourre and Emmanuel Jolivet, 'La réception des Principes d'UNIDROIT dans les contrat modèles de la Chambre de Commerce Internationale' (2004) 9 Unif L Rev 275.

[16] Professor Clive Schmitthoff is often cited as the father of the idea. See also: Note by the Secretariat of the International Institute for the Unification of Private Law (UNIDROIT), 'Progressive codification of the law of international trade' (1968–70) 1 UNCITRAL Ybk 285; G Herrmann, 'The Role of UNCITRAL' in Ian F Fletcher, Loukas A Mistelis, Marise Cremona (eds), *Foundations and Perspectives of International Trade Law* (Sweet & Maxwell, London, 2001) 36; Michael J Bonell, 'Do We Need a Global Commercial Code?' (2000) 5 Unif L Rev 469; O Lando, 'A Global Commercial Code' (2004) 50 Recht der Internationalen Wirtschaft 161. On this intriguing notion, albeit in a different perspective, see also Klaus Peter Berger, *The Creeping Codification of the Lex Mercatoria* (Kluwer, The Hague, 1999).

C. The Principal Institutions in the Harmonization of Commercial Law

General

The drafting of legal instruments is part of the activities of a great number of inter- **5.17**
national and supranational organizations, both at the global and the regional level.
For example, the International Civil Aviation Organization (ICAO) and the
International Maritime Organization (IMO), notwithstanding their being primarily tasked with matters such as navigation, technical standards and security, from
time to time convene their Member States for the purpose of drafting private and
commercial law texts under their auspices. The Montreal Convention for the
Unification of Certain Rules for International Carriage by Air of 28 May 1999[17] is
a very prominent example. The World Intellectual Property Organization (WIPO)
is obviously an agency with a brief for a special and increasingly autonomous
branch of commercial law. The United Nations Economic Commission for Europe
has in the past contributed to the harmonization of commercial law aimed at facilitating trade between the former Eastern bloc and the West. Important regional
organizations dealing with private, commercial and, more generally, economic law
are the European Community/European Union, a supranational entity *sui
generis*, the Organization of American States (OAS), the South American common market MERCOSUR/MERCOSUL, the *Organisation pour l'Harmonisation
en Afrique du droit des Affaires* (OHADA). Organizations in the Asia-Pacific region
such as the Asia-Pacific Economic Cooperation (APEC) and the Association of
South East Asian Nations (ASEAN) are beginning to show interest and to develop
policies in these areas.[18] Moreover, the World Bank and its affiliates, the International Monetary Fund (IMF) and the regional development banks (EBRD,
ADB, Inter-American Development Bank), are key facilitators of commercial law
reform in developing countries and transition economies. Finally, the United
Nations Conference on Trade and Development (UNCTAD) and the Organization for Economic Cooperation and Development (OECD), the industrialised
countries' economic policy think tank, have occasionally produced commercial
law instruments.

However, only the three intergovernmental organizations described below are spe- **5.18**
cialized in the field of private and, in particular, commercial law, and are exclusively

---

[17] Text reproduced in (1999) 4 Unif L Rev 948, with introductory comment by Michael Milde,
'Liability in international carriage by Air—The new Montreal Convention' (1999) 4 Unif L Rev 835.

[18] See: the Resolution of the Ministers of Commerce and the APEC Business Advisory Council,
Los Cabos 2002, and Manon Dostie, 'APEC Symposium on International Financing Instruments—
Singapore, 14–16 Dec 2004' (2004) 9 Unif L Rev 906; Lawan Thanadsillapakul, 'The Harmonisation
of Asian Competition Laws and Policy and Economic Integration' (2004) 9 Unif L Rev 479.

mandated to develop legislative instruments and to contribute in other ways to private and commercial law reform at the global level.

The Hague Conference on Private International Law

5.19   The Hague Conference's mandate is to work on the progressive unification of the rules of private international law.[19] First meetings (conferences) with a view to elaborating international conventions in this field were held in 1893 in The Hague. In 1955, the Hague Conference was given international legal personality under public international law by a Statute elaborated by sixteen States which were all European except for Japan. The Organization currently has sixty-five Member States from all continents.[20] Noteworthy is an amendment to the Statute adopted in 2005 that opens membership to Regional Economic Integration Organizations such as the European Community. Its direct and full membership is desirable as under the European Community Treaty in its Amsterdam version, part of the power to negotiate and conclude treaties on conflict of laws and international civil procedure vests in the European Community as a whole and not in its individual Member States. The European Community is expected to become a member of the Hague Conference in April 2007.

5.20   The Statute provides for the Hague Conference to hold an 'ordinary session' every four years. That session is prepared by 'Special Commissions' and the work of the 'Permanent Bureau', the Organization's Secretariat. The Permanent Bureau is headed by a Secretary-General who is assisted by qualified lawyers drawn from Member States. The objective is the elaboration of draft Conventions on all areas of conflict of laws. The Special Commissions and Diplomatic Sessions are open to Member States and observers such as non-Member States, intergovernmental organizations and non-governmental organizations. The Diplomatic Session, held every four years, adopts draft Conventions as well as the work programme for the following years. The 2005 amendment to the Statute also provides for the former 'Special Commission' on General Affairs and Policy to be called 'Council' which reflects its more permanent character and its increased importance. Since 1954, thirty-six Hague Conventions have been adopted. Many are on matters of family law, others are on international civil procedure and various areas of private and commercial law. A number of them are discussed in various chapters of this book, in particular the 2002 Convention on the Law Applicable to Certain Rights in Respect of Securities held with an Intermediary in chapters 2 and 13. The Hague Conference places great importance on its post-adoption work: the implementation, interpretation and application of its conventions are closely monitored, and

---

[19] In the sense of conflict of laws. See ch 2 above.
[20] Details on this and the following can be found on the Hague Conference on Private International Law website <http://www.hcch.net>.

guides, databases and training programmes are offered to such organizations as Member States' governments and members of the judiciary.

As regards the Organization's working methods,[21] dramatic changes have taken **5.21** place over recent years. In particular, texts are not adopted any more by voting but by consensus; the interested private sector is more deeply and regularly involved in informal inter-sessional work; and electronic developments, such as communication by email have significantly sped up the procedure.

UNIDROIT

The International Institute for the Unification of Private Law (UNIDROIT)[22] **5.22** was set up in 1926 as an auxiliary organ of the League of Nations.[23] On 30 May 1928, in the presence of His Majesty the King of Italy, the members of the Diplomatic Corps, other dignitaries and the members of the Governing Council of UNIDROIT (Scialoja, President; Adachi, Japan; Colin, France; Destrée, Belgium; Fernandes, Brazil; Sir Cecil Barrington Hurst, United Kingdom; Loder, Netherlands; Rabel, Germany; Rocco, Italy; Rundstein, Poland; Titulescu, Romania; Unden, Sweden; Villegas, Chile; Sanchez Roman y Gallifa, Spain), the Prime Minister of Italy, Benito Mussolini, opened the session. The representative of the President of the Council of the League of Nations replied:

> *Sire,*
>
> *[. . .] Votre Majesté, dont le nom symbolise tout ce qu'il y a de grand, de noble, de majeustueux dans le people italien, a bien voulu par son Auguste presence rendre plus solennelle la présente cérémonie. C'est avec le plus grand plaisir que je renouvelle en même temps, au nom du Conseil de la Société des Nations, les voeux de reconnaissance de l'offre généreuse du Gouvernement Italien.*
>
> *Dès la fin de la grande guerre mondiale, tous les efforts des peoples ont été dirigés vers la creation de rapports réciproques de collaboration, en resserrant les liens mutuels de solidarité; ils visaient au but d'assurer une paix durable à l'humanité, en l'acheminant sur la voie du progrès . . . Pourtant, pendant que cet heureux travail s'accomplissait, de nouveaux champs d'action s'offraient à l'activité du Conseil de la Société des Nations; parmi ces derniers, nous voyons, au premier plan, le droit, dont les nombreuses et variées dispositions actuellement en viguer présentaient une possibilité d'unification du plus grand intérêt pour l'humanité.*
>
> *[. . .]*

---

[21] For details of the harmonization process, see ch 6 below.

[22] The short form is not an acronym but taken from its French name *Institut International pour l'Unification du Droit Privé.*

[23] The most complete and readily accessible account of the historical details in English is Lena Peters, 'International Institute for the Unification of Private Law (UNIDROIT)' in Roger Blanpain (ed), *International Encyclopaedia of Laws—Intergovernmental Organizations (Suppl 23)* (Kluwer, The Hague, 2005) 11–13.

Unifier les règlements du droit privé, cela signifie travailler à la création d'une loi universelle, cela signifie . . . abattre une des barrières les plus formidables qui séparent les individus d'origine diverse; cela signifie, en un mot, assurer le développement tranquille et productif de la vie des peuples . . .

[. . .]

Vous n'avez pas manqué d'indiquer . . . les graves difficultés afférent à notre tâche. Le Conseil de la Société des Nations, aussi, s'en est bien rendu compte et il a tâché de les surmonter par le seul moyen dont il disposait, en choisissant les membres du nouvel Institut parmi les juristes les plus illustres des différentes nations et en désignant surtout comme Président de l'Institut une personnalité dont la renommé est mondiale: M. Vittorio Scialoja. Il ne m'en voudra pas si je me permets de rappeler en cette circonstance quelques passages d'un ouvrage essentiel dans le champ du droit, à la parfaite traduction duquel M. Scialoja a dédié les premières années de sa jeunesse: Je parle du système du droit romain de Charles Frédéric Savigny.[24] Je crois trouver, en effet, dans les premières phrases de cet ouvrage les grandes lignes descriptives du nouvel institut. Lorsque sur un champ scientifique comme le nôtre s'est accumulé le travail ininterrompu de plusieurs siècles, nous qui appartenons au siècle présent, pouvons nous offrir un riche héritage. Ce ne sont pas seulement la quantité de vérités acquises dont nous pouvons bénéficier, mais aussi toute nouvelle tentative intellectuelle, tout effort du passé, fut-il fécond ou vain, nous sert d'exemple et de règle de conduite.

Nous travaillons, en quelque sorte, avec le concours des siècles passés. Si nous voulions négliger par inertie ou par orgueil, avantage naturel de notre positions en laissant au hasard le choix entre les diverses parties de ce riche héritage, nous renoncerions aux dons précieux communs à l'essence de toute vraie science: la communauté des idées scientifiques et le progrès continuel de l'humanité. Sans cela, cette communauté même pourrait dégénérer en conventionalisme stérile. Nous devons donc souhaiter que de temps en temps les diverses tentatives et les résultats remportés soient réunis dans un ensemble unique de connaissances . . . Il ne s'agit point ici de choisir une chose plutôt que l'autre; il faut réunir en une unité supérieure les divergences qui se présentent . . .

Il s'agissait, au temps de Savigny, d'accomplir un travail purement scientifique. Il s'agit aujourd'hui d'une œuvre essentiellement pratique, et, pourtant, plus difficile et plue utile à l'humanité. Réunir dans une unité supérieure les divergences qui se présentent: voilà la méthode de travail et le but suprême de la Société des Nations dans ses différents champs d'action, voilà la méthode de travail et le but du nouvel Institut. Il s'ouvre aujourd'hui sous les meilleurs auspices, dont le plus important c'est d'avoir son siège a Rome; lorsqu'on parle de droit, on ne peut penser qu'à Rome, où toute chose acquiert les lignes de l'éternité et où même les pierres éparpillés parmi les ruines de ses anciens monuments portent l'empreinte ineffaçable de l'esprit juridique du peuple qui, de cette enceinte sacrée, dicta ses lois au monde.[. . .][25]

5.23 Following the demise of the League, the Organization was re-established in 1940 on the basis of a multilateral treaty known as the UNIDROIT Statute. Membership

---

[24] The reference is to the eight volumes of Friedrich Carl von Savigny, *System des heutigen römischen Rechts* (Veit und Comp, Berlin, 1840–49). See also above, ch 2, para 2.17.

[25] Séance d'ouverture, Rome, le 30 mai 1928, in Société des Nations Institut International de Rome pour l'Unification du Droit Privé, Actes et Documents, Année 1928 (Rome 1934—XIII) 5–8.

was restricted to States. The Organization's current sixty-one Member States are drawn from all five continents,[26] and represent a variety of different legal, economic and political systems as well as different cultural backgrounds.

UNIDROIT has an essentially three-tiered structure, made up of the General **5.24** Assembly, the Governing Council and the Secretariat. The General Assembly is the ultimate decision-making organ of the Institute: it votes the Organization's budget each year; it adopts the work programme every three years; it elects the Governing Council every five years. The General Assembly is made up of one diplomatic representative from each member government (and/or officials from that Member State's Ministry in charge of UNIDROIT matters) and chaired by the ambassador of one member government appointed on a rotating basis from amongst the Member States of one of the five continents. The Governing Council, made up of the President of the Institute and twenty-five members, is a unique institution that, together with the great flexibility of its rules and practices, distinguishes UNIDROIT from other intergovernmental organizations and reflects the spirit of the 1920s (as well as the decades following World War II, when the Organization was often described as a 'republic of scholars'). What make it so unique are, first, the members of the Council and their professional background and, second, their independent status. Once a candidate is proposed by his government[27] and has been elected, he or she does not represent the government but sits in his personal capacity as an expert. The Secretariat is the executive organ of the Organization, and is responsible for the day-to-day running of its work programme and the general administration. It is run by a Secretary-General, who is appointed by the Governing Council upon nomination of the President. The Secretary-General is assisted by a staff of international civil servants. They are qualified lawyers and drawn from different Member States.

As regards the working methods,[28] the feature which most visibly distinguishes **5.25** UNIDROIT from other intergovernmental organizations engaged in elaborating legislative instruments and other texts aimed at the modernization and harmonization of private and commercial law is the use of study groups. Study groups are traditionally very small groups of first-rate experts, both academics and practitioners, in the field under consideration. They are drawn from Member States and selected so as to represent the various legal systems and economic backgrounds relevant for reliable analysis of the subject matter. In addition, private sector advisors may be invited to provide their specific expertise, and their industry's views and

---

[26] For the updated list as well as the identification of the ministries or other government agencies in charge of the respective government's involvement in the organization's activities, see its website <http://www.unidroit.org>.
[27] Certain governments traditionally present senior officials dealing with private and commercial law in the relevant ministries; others, distinguished scholars; others still, senior members of the judiciary or Bar. [28] For details regarding the harmonization process, see ch 6 below.

concerns. Study groups are chaired by a member of the Governing Council. Governments are not represented at this stage. The task of the study groups and the Secretariat at the pre-governmental stage is to draw up a feasibility study and/or a comparative law study designed to ascertain the desirability and feasibility of law reform. Recent experience shows that, where deemed useful or necessary and provided funding is available, an economic impact assessment study may be of equal importance if meaningful law reform is the objective. A preliminary draft instrument established by a study group will be laid before the Governing Council for approval and advice as to the most appropriate further steps to be taken. Typically, in the case of a preliminary draft convention, the Secretariat will convene a Committee of governmental experts for the discussion and finalization of a draft capable of being submitted for its adoption to a Diplomatic Conference. Again, the Governing Council will need to approve the draft and authorize its transmission to a Diplomatic Conference. Such a Conference will be convened by one of UNIDROIT's Member States. In the case of one of the alternative types of instrument discussed above (such as model laws, general principles or guides) either the Council or a Committee of governmental experts may finalize, approve or adopt the text. The Council may even seise the General Assembly of a proposed non-convention text with a view to giving it governmental *imprimatur*.

5.26 Full participation in UNIDROIT Committees of governmental experts is open to representatives of all Member States. Non-Member States may be invited depending on the subject matter concerned and the Organization's desire to have those States involved in the discussions. Non-Member States, intergovernmental and international non-governmental organizations as well as professional and trade associations are observers, but participate fully in the discussions. All States, not just Member States, are invited to participate in Diplomatic Conferences.

5.27 Essential support for UNIDROIT's legislative activities is provided by its maintaining a world-renowned specialized library, its publications—notably the Uniform Law Review/*Revue de droit uniforme*—and databases as well as outreach activities such as a scholarship programme for lawyers from developing countries and transition economies, assistance in the implementation of international instruments and the elaboration of regional or national legislation connected with transnational private law texts.

UNCITRAL

5.28 The United Nations Commission on International Trade Law (UNCITRAL) was set up in 1966 as a commission of the United Nations General Assembly,[29] with the general mandate to further the progressive harmonization and unification of

---

[29] GA Resolution 2205 (XXI) (UN GAOR 6th Comm, 21st Sess, 1497th plen mtg) reprinted in (1966) 1 UNICITRAL Ybk 65.

international trade law. Special emphasis was placed on the Commission's role to co-ordinate work carried out by other organizations. That co-ordination was needed had been felt for some time. Professors Gutteridge in 1949,[30] and Schmitthoff in 1966,[31] had urged the setting up of a kind of international clearing house tasked with co-ordination and supervision of activities in the many regional and universal, general and specialized organizations, both governmental and non-governmental.

Initially, UNCITRAL had twenty-nine Member States, but from 2002 its membership consists of sixty Member States. The General Assembly elects members for terms of six years. The membership is structured so as to ensure that the various geographic regions, the principal legal and economic systems of the world and in particular developing countries are represented. **5.29**

UNCITRAL's legislative activities are conducted at three levels.[32] Firstly, the Commission itself where, at annual sessions, draft texts referred to the Commission by working groups are finalized and adopted. Its chairperson, vice-chairpersons and reporters are drawn from amongst Member States representing the five geographic regions. The proceedings are set forth in a report prepared by the Secretariat to be formally adopted by UNCITRAL for submission to the UN General Assembly. Second, the working groups, which to a large extent carry out the substantive work on topics included in the Commission's work programme. Proposals for topics to be included in the work programme may be made by governments or be the result of consultations with other entities such as non-governmental organizations and trade associations. Working groups generally hold one or two sessions per year. In 2006–7, six working groups (procurement, international arbitration and conciliation, transport law, electronic commerce, insolvency law, security interests) were in session. In addition to its own Member States, UNCITRAL invites as observers other United Nations Member States as well as intergovernmental and non-governmental organizations who have an interest in the topics under discussion. Observers participate fully in the discussions. Under its practice, decisions taken both by the Commission and its working groups reconcile the different positions put forward by its members by consensus rather than by vote. Finalized instruments are either adopted by a Diplomatic Conference or, more frequently, the United Nations General Assembly, and it would be interesting to analyse more closely whether there is evidence that the mode of adoption and the ultimate success of an instrument are related to each other. The Secretariat is in charge of the third level. It assists the Commission and the working groups in their deliberations. The International Trade Law Division of the United Nations Office of Legal **5.30**

---

[30] HC Gutteridge, *Comparative Law* (2nd edn, CUP, Cambridge, 1949) 183.
[31] The 'Schmitthoff Report' (UN Doc A/6396) reprinted in (1966) 1 UNCITRAL Ybk 2.
[32] For details regarding the harmonisation process, see ch 6 below.

Affairs, with its headquarters in Vienna, provides the Secretariat for UNCITRAL. The Director of the Division serves as the Secretary of UNCITRAL. He or she is assisted by a small number of international civil servants of different nationalities who are all qualified lawyers.

5.31   Apart from its legislative activities, UNCITRAL is engaged in documenting and making accessible sources relevant for the harmonization of trade law and in providing database infrastructure assisting governments, judges and advocates in the implementation, interpretation and application of its text (Case Law on UNCITRAL Texts—CLOUT).

The International Chamber of Commerce (ICC)

5.32   The International Chamber of Commerce was founded in 1919. Today, it has member companies and associations, such as associations of national chambers of commerce and national committees, in some 130 countries. The ICC is the 'voice of international business'.[33] Commissions of experts from the private sector are working in specialized fields of concern to international business. A number of the ICC's products aimed at standards and rules setting—a substantial part of what is frequently referred to as the 'creeping codification of the *lex mercatoria*'—in particular, in the areas of sales and banking transactions, is extensively discussed in other chapters of this book. The ICC and its commissions of experts closely co-operate with the intergovernmental organizations engaged in the development of transnational commercial law. In the field of international dispute resolution, the ICC Court of International Arbitration is a leading institution.

The role of international and regional professional and industry organizations

5.33   Governments and their intergovernmental organizations are keenly aware that the drafting of commercial law instruments that aspire to address real problems posed by cross-border conduct of business in a meaningful way and to become successful requires in-depth analysis of the factual situation in any given area of commerce and finance as well as the advice from the professionals and the industry concerned. Therefore, international and regional professional organizations and industry associations are regularly consulted and invited to participate in the work of the Hague Conference, UNIDROIT and UNCITRAL. Some of them customarily even take the lead in the development of instruments which are at a later stage transmitted to one of the intergovernmental organizations. Examples are the *Comité Maritime International* (CMI), the International Road Transport Union (IRU), the International Air Transport Association (IATA), the International Bar Association (IBA),

---

[33]   For details, see its website <http://www.iccwbo.org>.

the International Securities and Derivatives Association (ISDA) and the insolvency specialists of INSOL International.

Co-ordination of legislative activities

Looking at the extended panorama of intergovernmental and non-governmental organizations involved in the drafting of legislative instrument rules and standards, it is clear that co-ordination of these activities must be a matter to which the greatest priority is given. As we have seen, UNCITRAL's original and principal brief was indeed co-ordination. **5.34**

José Angelo Estrella Faria, 'The Relationship Between Formulating Agencies in International Legal Harmonization: Competition, Cooperation, or Peaceful Coexistence?—A Few Remarks on the Experience of UNCITRAL' 51 Loy L Rev 253, 269–80 (2005)

[. . .]

II. Main Obstacles to Effective Coordination

[. . .] this paper will focus on three circumstances that, in the view of UNCITRAL, are the main obstacles to an ideal level of cooperation in commercial law harmonization: the insufficient institutional relationship between formulating agencies, the sometimes difficult interface between international negotiations and internal consultations, and the growing role of regional organizations.

A. Institutional Relationship between Formulating Agencies

The most famous and ambitious product of UNCITRAL, the . . . ['CISG'], is a prime example of cooperation. The CISG would not have been successfully completed had the ground not been leveled by the extensive work done by UNIDROIT in the preparation of the Hague Uniform Laws.

[. . .] Similarly, UNIDROIT, after having carried out a substantial part of the preliminary work on a convention concerning the liability of operators of transport terminals in international trade, handed over the project in 1984 to UNCITRAL, which carried it until its adoption . . . in 1991 . . .

Cooperation has also taken the form of exchange of input and expertise in the preparation of uniform law instruments. A recent example is the cooperation between the Hague Conference and UNCITRAL in the formulation of the choice-of-law rules contained in chapter 5 of the United Nations Convention on Assignment of Receivables in International Trade (2001) . . . Another way in which cooperation can be achieved is through allocation of work among the various organizations, as is currently the case in the field of secured transactions between UNIDROIT (currently working on transactions on transnational and connected capital markets), the Hague Conference (law applicable to certain rights on securities held by an intermediary), and UNCITRAL (on-going draft legislative guide on secured transactions).

Needless to say, drawing the lines between respective projects is not always an easy task, as is evidenced by the time that was needed to arrive at a satisfactory interplay between the UN Receivables Convention, the UNIDROIT Convention on International Interests in

Mobile Equipment (the 'Cape Town Convention'), and the UNIDROIT Convention on International Factoring (the 'Ottawa Convention').

Despite these efforts, duplications or even contradictions—real or potential—persist, and sometimes the compromise to avoid them is translated in a complex (some might even say 'artificial') delimitation of the respective field of application of the various instruments being prepared by each organization in question. Unfortunately, the resulting fragmentation of uniform commercial law adds another ground for criticism to the lists drawn up by those who regard the harmonization of private law basically as a futile, harmful, or simply inefficient process.

[. . .]

In the context of increased demand for legal harmonization, it is clear that inter-agency coordination cannot create a web of monopolies where each organization would claim to handle entire areas of law alone. Indeed, certain topics may require harmonizing efforts at different levels or even at different forums simultaneously. All organizations specially devoted to legal harmonization (the Hague Conference, UNIDROIT, and UNCITRAL) commonly and chronically lack secretariat resources, which severely limits the number of initiatives each organization is capable of handling at any given time. Where further harmonization cannot await the completion of work in one organization, States may agree to ask another one to take up work in a related area.

[. . .]

Could better coordination have been achieved through a more proactive role of UNCITRAL? Maybe yes, but the effectiveness of the tools available to UNCITRAL should not be overestimated.

As a subsidiary body of the UN General Assembly, UNCITRAL is undoubtedly well placed to make recommendations to other organizations without the same degree of universality, exhorting them to take certain measures necessary to ensure the coordination of their efforts. But one should not expect too much from these recommendations: they will be followed or not according to opinion of the organizations concerned. As independent subjects of public international law, intergovernmental organizations are not obliged to follow recommendations addressed to them by UNCITRAL or even the UN General Assembly . . .

This is a problem even for the coordination between organizations sharing a close relationship, such as UNIDROIT, the Hague Conference, and UNCITRAL, or between UNCITRAL and other bodies of the United Nations, such as the Economic Commission on Europe or UNCTAD. To some extent, the direct, almost collegial relationship between the staff of the multilateral organizations . . . and the national experts who take part in their activities, has substituted for the lack of institutional ties and has had some success in preventing conflicts between formulating agencies. After all, as an experienced observer has noted, '[the] task of formulating new law rests on a small number of people, a few tens, certainly less than one hundred, that at any given time are in charge of international negotiations of private law in the various States.'

Ensuring adequate coordination, however, becomes more difficult when we leave this circle. Though the magnitude of the problem varies depending on the scale of the organizations involved–cooperation being in general easier with small secretariats than with large bureaucracies–the root of the problem is the same: how to ensure cooperation between independent organizations, without hierarchical relationships, having their own governing bodies and sometimes even different membership.

[. . .]

B. Shortcomings of Domestic Coordination

[. . .]

While a ministry—Foreign Affairs in most countries—is often in charge of the internal role of coordination for a great part—if not all—of the multilateral organizations (like UNIDROIT, UNCITRAL, or the Hague Conference), this function may often involve various units within the Ministry . . .

[. . .]

One . . . explanation is that States may consider that some level of competition between formulating agencies is beneficial, as it allows them to make use of the agencies' comparative advantages and to decide in each case which is the one best suited to handle a given project. Arguably, an organization with an extensive academic network, smaller membership, and lighter machinery than the United Nations, like UNIDROIT, is much better placed to carry out a project such as the Principles of International Commercial Contracts than UNCITRAL. Conversely, an organization with a broad constituency, such as UNCITRAL, may be better suited to carry out projects aimed at promoting law reform in developing countries, such as the UNCITRAL Model Law on Procurement of Goods, Construction and Services. Furthermore, the particular mechanics and likelihood of building consensus within the various agencies, which are largely—although not exclusively—predicated by their respective membership and methods of work, may render one of them more attractive than the others in the eyes of States having an interest in a particular project.

[. . .]

C. Supranationality as an Additional Challenge

[On this issue, see below, chapter 6]

Conclusion

[. . .] The current situation is certainly not ideal, but some coordination exists nonetheless. The challenge, therefore, is to look for ways to build further on the positive achievements.

One such way to build is to establish institutional mechanisms and institutional ties between the various organizations specialized in the unification of the private or international law. For instance, a joint coordinating committee comprised of representatives of the respective secretariats and a number of Member States appointed by each organization is one possible improvement. Closer cooperation might provide an opportunity to further explore the comparative advantages of various agencies (such as the specificity of mandate and the expertise on the Conference of the Hague, the academic network and the flexibility of the methods of UNIDROIT, the universality and the political authority of UNCITRAL), while avoiding duplication.

Also in need of review is the role of the private sector in the harmonization of laws. The usefulness of standard clauses and contract terms in the creation of a 'common language of international trade' is well known. ICC and other similar institutions have made a remarkable contribution in this field . . .

[. . .]

The book of Genesis teaches us that chaos itself was a step in creation. The world is what we got out of that. For whatever it is worth, we have not seen a better one.

Questions

1. What criteria would you apply in evaluating the success of a uniform law project? What might these indicate as to the questions that should be asked and the kind of research that should be carried out *before* one embarks on a project for the harmonization of the rules governing an area of law?

2. Did the drafters of the 1980 UN Convention on Contracts for the International Sale of Goods (CISG) choose the most advantageous type of instrument in opting for a binding treaty?

3. A disadvantage inherent in substantive commercial law conventions, frequently cited by critics of harmonization in general and the use of the (binding) treaty mechanism in particular, is that such conventions reduce the space for competition among legal systems. Discuss.

4. Are there areas of the law where, in your view, the binding international treaty will continue to be the only type of instrument for meaningful harmonization? Are there other areas where one would not even attempt to bring about harmonization by means of a convention?

5. In an article cited above,[34] Professor Ole Lando, sometimes referred to as the 'father' of the Principles of European Contract Law, recommends that, drawing on the experience of the United States, a Global Commercial Code be developed and that in that context the UNIDROIT Principles of International Commercial Contract be elevated to the status of rules having the force of law. This has also been advocated by the European Commission in its proposal for a regulation (Brussels I) to replace the Rome Convention on the law applicable to contractual obligations.

   Do you support this recommendation?

6. Consider the following questions in the light of the formulating agencies' different institutional structures and their working methods (see also chapter 6 below):

   (a) Was UNCITRAL the organization best equipped to negotiate and promote the CISG and, if so, why?

   (b) Was UNIDROIT the organization best equipped to negotiate and promote the Cape Town Convention on International Interests in Mobile Equipment?

   (c) Assume your government wishes to encourage the development of a *Guide to Principles of Corporate Governance* within the institutional framework of an intergovernmental organization. Which one(s) would you consider and recommend, and why?

---

[34] See para 5.16 (n 16).

Further reading

Béraudo, Jean-Paul, 'La négociation internationale institutionelle de droit privé (1ère partie)' (1997) 2 Unif L Rev 9

David, René, 'The International Unification of Private Law' in the *International Encyclopaedia of Comparative Law II* (JCB Mohr, Tübingen, 1971) ch 5

Drobnig, Ulrich, 'Vereinheitlichung von Zivilrecht durch soft law: neuere Erfahrungen' in Basedow, Jürgen, Drobnig, Ulrich and others (eds), *Aufbruch nach Europa—75 Jahre Max-Planck-Institut für Privatrecht* (Mohr Siebeck, Tübingen, 2001) 745

Droz, Georges AL, 'La Conférence de la Haye de droit international privé et les méthodes d'unification du droit: traités internationaux ou lois modèles?' (1961) 13 Revue internationale de droit comparé 507

Hardjowahono, Bajuseto, *The Unification of Private International Law on International Commercial Contracts within the Regional Legal System of ASEAN* (Ulrik Huber Institute for Private International Law, Groningen, 2005)

Goldring, John, 'Globalisation, National Sovereignty and the Harmonisation of Laws' (1998) 3 Unif Law Rev 435

Kronke, Herbert, 'Ziele–Methoden, Kosten–Nutzen: Perspektiven der Privatrechtsvereinheitlichung nach 75 Jahren UNIDROIT' (2001) Juristenzeitung 1149

Kronke, Herbert, 'Methodical Freedom and Organizational Constraints in the Development of Transnational Commercial Law' 51 Loy L Rev 287 (2005)

Kronke, Herbert, 'From International Uniform Conventions to Model Laws—From Guides to Principles: The Choice of Approach', in Perret, Louis, Bisson Alain-François, and Mariani, Nicola (eds), *Evolution des systèmes juridiques, bijuridisme et commerce international (The Evolution of Legal Systems, Bijuralism and International Trade)* (Wilson & Lafleur, Montréal, 2002) 283

Kropholler, Jan, *Internationales Einheitsrecht—Allgemeine Lehren* (Mohr Siebeck, Tübingen, 1975)

Kropholler, Jan and Neuhaus, Paul Heinrich, 'Rechtsvereinheitlichung—Rechtsverbesserung?' ('Unification of Law–Improvement of Law?' with English summary) (1981) 45 Rabels Zeitschrift 73

Peters, Lena, 'International Institute for the Unification of Private Law (UNIDROIT)' in Blanpain, Roger (ed), *International Encyclopaedia of Laws—Intergovernmental Organizations (Suppl 23)* (Kluwer, The Hague, 2005)

Rabel, Ernst, 'Zwei Rechtsinstitute für die internationalen privatrechtlichen Beziehungen' (1932) Juristische Wochenschrift 2225

Rodinò, Walter 'UNIDROIT', in *Digesto, IV Edizione, Discipline Privatistiche—Sezione Civile* (UTET, Turin, 2000) 742

Sauveplanne, Jean Georges, 'Eenvormig Privaatrecht' (1961) Rechtsgeleerd Magazijn Themis 225

Trompenaars, BWM, 'Pluriforme unificatie en uniforme interpretatie' (Kluwer, Deventer, 1989)

Van Houtte, *The Law of International Trade* (2nd edn, Sweet & Maxwell, London, 2002)

Wallace Jr, Don, 'International Agencies for the Formulation of Transnational Economic Law: A Comment about Methods and Techniques' in Horn, Norbert, Schmitthoff, Clive M and Marcantonio, J Barrigan (eds), *The Transnational Law of International Commercial Transactions* (Kluwer, Boston, 1982) 81

Wieacker, Franz, 'Historische Bedingungen und Paradigmen supranationaler Privatrechtsordnungen' in Bernstein, Herbert, Drobnig, Ulrich, and Kötz, Hein (eds), *Festschrift für Konrad Zweigert zum 70. Geburtstag* (Mohr Siebeck, Tübingen, 1981) 575

Winship, Peter, 'Introduction to Harmonization of Private Law' in Raisch Marylin J and Shaffer, Roberta I, *Introduction to Transnational Legal Transactions* (Oceana Publications, New York, 1995) 159

Winship, Peter, 'Karl Llewellyn in Rome' (1998) 3 Unif L Rev 725

6

THE HARMONIZATION PROCESS

A. Introduction	6.01	Committee of governmental experts	6.18
B. Stages in a Harmonization Project		Diplomatic Conference/Session	6.19
A bright idea	6.05	Explanatory Report/Official	
Establishing the existence of a problem		Commentary	6.25
and support for its solution	6.06	Promotion of the instrument	6.26
Is the agency the most suitable for		C. Problems of Harmonization	6.27
the project?	6.08	Over-ambition	6.30
Survey of the current legal environment	6.10	Tensions arising in the preparation of	
Approval of the project by the		international conventions	6.33
relevant organ of the agency	6.13	Technical problems	6.35
Establishment of a study or		Differences in legal concepts	6.36
working group and sub-groups	6.14	Drafting and language	6.37
What type of instrument?	6.15	Interpreters	6.38
Distribution of drafts and consideration		Organizational problems	6.39
at meetings	6.16	D. Harmonization and	
Approval of the text	6.17	Regionalization	6.43

A. Introduction

While there is a vast amount of literature on the products of harmonization of contract **6.01** and commercial law, relatively little attention has been paid to the working methods used by the different international organizations in the harmonization process itself. Yet much of the success of a uniform law project depends on its planning and organization and on the skill with which the project and its boundaries are delineated. In the second edition of his small but outstanding work on comparative law Professor H C Gutteridge devoted an entire chapter to the mechanics of unification.

H C Gutteridge, *Comparative Law* (2nd edn, CUP, Cambridge, 1949) 173–5*

Unification is at best a protracted and laborious enterprise; it must of necessity pass through several stages, and the difficulties encountered cannot be appreciated unless each

---

* © Cambridge University Press, reproduced with permission.

of these stages is considered apart from the others. The first, which may be described as the 'preliminary' or 'exploratory' stage, consists in the employment of the comparative method in order to ascertain whether unification is possible and, if so, along what lines. The second or 'formulatory' stage involves the formulation of proposals for unified law, which will furnish the necessary groundwork for discussion and negotiation between the countries, or between the private interests which are concerned in the matter. The nature of such proposals is indicated by the term which is sometimes applied to them, i.e. *bases de discussion*. The third stage, which may be referred to as the 'operative' stage consists in the drafting of uniform laws or rules which can be submitted to the governments or private interests for formal ratification. The mere fact that the proposals are adopted by an international assembly does not mean that unification has been achieved. A final stage is necessary in which the resolutions of the assembly are ratified by the governments or other interests concerned, and are, if necessary, put into effect, either by legislation, or, in the case of private interests, by the incorporation of the draft rules in printed forms of contract, or in some other way . . .

The Formulatory Stage

It is at this stage that the difficulties connected with unification begin to appear. Concrete proposals must be framed for the consideration of an international assembly, and this gives rise to a series of problems. It must be ascertained how far the interests which may be affected would welcome unification, and how far and in what way the obstacles created by certain difficulties, which are inherent in all proposals to unify law, can be overcome. In particular, care must be exercised to interfere as little as possible with the procedural rules of the systems of law concerned, and vigilance is necessary to avoid any invasion of the extremely debatable territory occupied by the bogey of all unificationists and private international lawyers, namely the national rules of public policy. In general, it is essential to ascertain in advance how far the interests concerned are prepared to abandon their national rules and to accept uniformity of law. A method which is often employed for this purpose is to issue a questionnaire addressed either to government departments or associations of lawyers, chambers of commerce and similar bodies. The value of this expedient is doubtful, because experience suggests that a questionnaire seldom produces the information which is desired. It is extremely difficult, without undue prolixity, to frame a questionnaire in such a way that it will produce the replies which are needed. Moreover, government departments and private organizations are reluctant to commit themselves in advance and however carefully the questionnaire may be framed, the replies will often be incomplete or evasive.

6.02 The methods adopted by harmonizing agencies for selecting, initiating and carrying through to completion a particular harmonization project vary from agency to agency but there are key steps common to them all. After outlining these we will discuss a number of the more significant problems that may impede progress towards completion and adoption of an international instrument, taking the international convention as the paradigm. At various points in this chapter we will take one major international instrument that is clearly going to be successful and use this as the vehicle to examine in more detail the different stages of a harmonization project, from its conception to the coming into force of the instrument, and the ways in which various obstacles were overcome.

This chapter is concerned only with the four international harmonizing agencies **6.03** that are not subject specific, namely UNIDROIT, UNCITRAL, the Hague Conference on Private International Law and the International Chamber of Commerce. But it should be borne in mind that there are many specialist international organizations, both intergovernmental and non-governmental, which promote uniform laws and with which the general agencies collaborate. Intergovernmental organizations include the United Nations Conference on Trade and Development (UNCTAD), which is concerned with trade, development and related issues; the United Nations Educational, Scientific and Cultural Organization (UNESCO), which promotes education and culture; the International Civil Aviation Organization (ICAO)—another intergovernmental organization within the UN family— which is devoted primarily to issues of safety, security and efficiency in air transport but which also co-sponsored the mobile equipment convention with UNIDROIT; and the International Maritime Organization (IMO), a UN agency which fulfils a similar function for ships. Each of the last two bodies has an NGO counterpart, the International Air Transport Association (IATA) for aviation and the Comité Maritime International (CMI) for ships, which in addition to their other activities are also closely involved in measures for international harmonization of the law within their respective fields.

In all four of the agencies considered in this chapter the Secretariat plays an impor- **6.04** tant role, organizing meetings, preparing minutes and reports, circulating papers, and sometimes initiating projects itself, as well as negotiating with prospective host States for a Diplomatic Conference.

B. Stages in a Harmonization Project

A bright idea

Someone comes up with a bright idea for a project. The idea may come from the **6.05** Secretariat of the relevant agency or from an individual, business organization or government which communicates it to the Secretariat.

Establishing the existence of a problem and support for its solution

Nowadays all agencies seek to ascertain, by a survey or otherwise, whether the **6.06** problem which the harmonizing instrument is designed to address really exists and, if so, whether it is susceptible of solution by harmonization and is supported by the relevant interests as sufficiently serious to justify the time, effort and money that goes into the preparation, conclusion and promotion of an international instrument. This was not always done with sufficient care in the past, and it was only after the instrument had been made that it was discovered that there was no great demand for it, or even hostility, from the sectors affected. This partly accounts for the substantial number of international instruments that adorn libraries and government offices around the world but have either never come into force or have lacked ratification by states with a particular interest and influence in the field covered by the instrument. To quote Gutteridge again in the same work at 157–8:

It would seem that much of the blame for the failure to achieve more definite and permanent results must be attributed to an excess of zeal fostered by an exaggerated belief in the need for unification and over-confidence in its feasibility. It is, perhaps, difficult for an enthusiast—and most 'unificationists' fall within that category—to realize that he is engaged in promoting a cause which is unpopular among lawyers and makes little appeal to the general public. One cannot, for instance, conceive of a situation in which there would be popular demonstrations in favour of the uniformity of the law of Negotiable Instruments, or even for the assimilation of the Laws of Marriage and Divorce. Unification can only be achieved by lengthy and patient efforts which will ultimately convince those in all countries, who are in a position to sponsor and carry through changes in the law, that it is a matter of urgent necessity to take steps in order to remove sources of inconvenience and friction in the international sphere. Unification cannot be achieved by a stroke of the pen, nor can it be carried out within the four walls of law libraries, practitioner's offices or professorial studies. The ground must be very carefully surveyed, and the interests concerned must be won over before any action is undertaken. It is necessary, for our present purposes, to underline the fact that many of the woes from which the movement for unification suffers are undoubtedly due to premature and ill-advised attempts to draft schemes for unified law which have little or no prospect of acceptance. Apart from these errors of judgment which are largely responsible for the setbacks hitherto experienced, it is beyond doubt that unification is, in any circumstances, confronted by other obstacles of a psychological character. National pride makes itself felt in the realm of the law as well as in other spheres. The abandonment of national rules of law seems to imply that there is something amiss with the rules which are to be displaced, and national *amour propre* suffers accordingly. The citizens of many countries are deeply attached to their national law: at one extreme we have, for instance, the Frenchman, who carries in his pocket the *Code Civil*, the dog-eared leaves of which bear witness to the frequency with which it is consulted, and, at the other end of the line, we find the Englishman who never looks at a law book but is nevertheless convinced that his common law is the quintessence of human wisdom and justice. It must not be forgotten that to invite the citizen to give up a rule of law to which he has become accustomed may be to demand almost as great a sacrifice as the abandonment of his national speech or religion. Moreover, lawyers of all nationalities are apt to be hostile to unification, very largely because they may not have the leisure or the inclination to investigate the reasons by which it is prompted. Judges and practitioners have a distinct and not altogether unreasonable suspicion of proposals for the reform of law which have an international flavour.

6.07 Where there is found to be a problem it is typically not confined to the existence of differences in national laws but results from their unsuitability for modern conditions. So the task is not simply to select existing aspects of different laws but to develop an international legal regime which improves and modernizes the rules, particularly those governing cross-border transactions and activities. Thus fact-finding is an indispensable precondition of work on a harmonization project. Questionnaires continue to be used for this purpose, though Gutteridge's wise warning about their limited utility needs to be kept in mind. Indeed, further caveats may be made. One of the difficulties of constructing a questionnaire is that one cannot be sure that the right questions are being asked. There are various techniques available to address this problem. One is to ensure that the questionnaire contains not merely specific questions but also open-ended questions which allow the respondent to offer the benefit of its own experiences. Another is to test the questionnaire on a few specialists and see if it works for them. In any event, it is desirable not to place exclusive reliance on questionnaires but to engage in a series of discussions with different interest groups to get a feel for the subject and to identify pressure points and difficulties arising from the lack of an international regime and the inadequacies of existing national laws.

Is the agency the most suitable for the project?

This depends partly on the nature of the instrument envisaged, partly on agreements reached in inter-agency co-operation and partly on the eagerness of the agency to be seen to provide a lead in the field in question.[1] In general an agency is not likely to be deterred by the existence of competitors from engaging in a project which it wishes to pursue; indeed, there is a degree of healthy competition between agencies whose spheres of interest overlap. But there are certain factors which either lead to or exclude a particular agency. The Hague Conference on Private International Law is the specialist agency for private international law conventions, so that while it would be open to UNIDROIT or UNCITRAL to prepare such a convention their practice is to leave these to the Hague Conference and to focus on substantive law conventions and model laws. The International Chamber of Commerce is not a law-making body and therefore is not engaged in the preparation of international conventions or model laws. In its work on rules governing transactions[2] the ICC produces uniform rules, uniform trade terms and model forms which take effect by incorporation into contracts or, in the case of model forms, by adoption by contracting parties. Necessarily such instruments are confined to matters which can be governed by contract. The ICC would therefore not be a suitable institution for the preparation of uniform rules on secured transactions, priority of competing property rights or the jurisdiction of courts. On the other hand within the sphere of contract its influence, through such instruments as Incoterms, the Uniform Customs and Practice for Documentary Credits, the Uniform Rules for Demand Guarantees, and its standard forms of agency and sale agreement, is enormous. There is some overlap between the work

6.08

---

[1] See further ch 5.

[2] The ICC is also the international non-governmental body representing world business and a number of its Commissions are devoted not to the preparation of rules but to the development of positions and the presentation of views on policy issues arising from the work of the United Nations and other international organizations.

of UNIDROIT and that of UNCITRAL in that UNIDROIT was set up to promote the progressive harmonization of private law, including commercial law, whereas UNCITRAL is a specialist organ of the United Nations devoted to the harmonization of international trade law and is very influential in that field. In practice the Secretariats of the two organizations work together to avoid duplication and turf wars.

6.09   Not infrequently two or more agencies occupy the same field but through different kinds of instrument. For example, demand guarantees are the subject of the ICC's Uniform Rules for Demand Guarantees and the UN Convention on independent guarantees and stand-by letters of credit.[3] The Convention contains provisions on judicial remedies that would be outside the competence of ICC rules to provide but both the convention and the rules deal with the rights and duties of the parties, duplication being avoided by the convention's deferment to party autonomy and thus to the rules where incorporated by contract. Then again, different agencies may address different facets of a particular activity. For example, contractual relations arising from international sales of goods are the subject of the UN Convention on contracts for the international sale of goods and, at regional level, the EC Directive on Commercial agents, the UNIDROIT Convention on agency in the international sale of goods is devoted to relations between the principal or agent on the one hand and the third party buyer on the other; and the ICC has produced a model form of commercial agency contract for use in the appointment of commercial agents to promote and effect sales. Agency itself also features in the UNIDROIT Principles of International Commercial Contracts and in the Principles of European Contract Law. UNIDROIT was responsible for the Convention on international financial leasing but is also currently engaged in the preparation of a model law on leasing as a means of harmonizing domestic leasing law.

Survey of the current legal environment

6.10   An essential part of the process of identifying problems and possible solutions is to ascertain the existing laws of different states governing the field in question, and particularly (though not exclusively) the laws of those states that are members of the harmonizing agency. It is important for such a survey to include legal systems from all significant legal families. Comparative law thus plays an important role in the development of transnational commercial law.[4]

K. Zweigert and Hein Kötz, *An Introduction to Comparative Law* (3rd edn, transl. Tony Weir, Clarendon Press, Oxford, 1998), 24

The final function of comparative law to be dealt with here is its significant role in the preparation of projects for the international unification of law. The political aim behind

---

³ See ch 9.   ⁴ See ch 4.

such unification is to reduce or eliminate, so far as desirable and possible, the discrepancies between the national legal systems by inducing them to adopt common principles of law. The method used in the past and still often practised today is to draw up a uniform law on the basis of work by experts in comparative law and to incorporate it in a multipartite treaty which obliges the signatories, as a matter of international law, to adopt and apply the uniform law as their municipal law . . .

Unification cannot be achieved by simply conjuring up an ideal law on any topic and hoping to have it adopted. One must first find what is common to the jurisdictions concerned and incorporate that in the uniform law. Where there are areas of difference, one must reconcile them either by adopting the best existing variant or by finding, through comparative methods, a new solution which is better and more easily applied than any of the existing ones. Preparatory studies in comparative law are absolutely essential here; without them one cannot discover the points of agreement or disagreement in the different legal systems of the world, let alone decide which solution is the best.

To this one must add the cautionary note that the different legal systems governing the subject under consideration must be comparable and in particular that they must be at a similar stage of evolutionary development. This is a matter determined more by the degree of sophistication of the systems under comparison than by chronology. **6.11**

Sir Frederick Pollock, 'The History of Comparative Jurisprudence' (1903) 5 J Soc Comp Legis, (N.S.) 74, 76

If we compare the Roman law of property which Papinian administered at York seventeen centuries ago with the English law of real property which the Court of Appeal now administers in London, it will be for the purpose of throwing light not on anything in the past history of English law, but on what English law may tend to become in the days of our children or grandchildren; for the classical law of Rome is, in all essentials, far more modern in everything relating to the ownership and disposition of landed property than the mediaeval system, eked out with cumbrous and piecemeal alterations, which still serves our turn. On the other hand, the commercial law of the Roman Empire under the Antonines and even under Justinian was rudimentary as compared with the modern development of the law merchant.

As we note a little later,[5] the degree of development of a system of commercial law in a given area is a function of the volume, diversity and sophistication of its commercial institutions, instruments and practices, for it is these that throw up the problems to which the law must find an answer, and the greater the level of economic activity the more developed the infrastructure needed to accommodate it and the richer the laws governing it. This might suggest that US law, which offers the most developed commercial law in the world, and to a lesser extent English law have little to learn from civil law systems even in highly developed countries. Nothing could be further from the truth. What the civilians have to offer are system and values, and these are a necessary corrective to laws which, to the outsider **6.12**

---

[5] See the extract in para 6.33.

at least, might sometimes seem to consist mainly of a series of solutions to practical problems rather than a coherent legal structure and to be focused too exclusively on meeting the demands of the commercial community, subordinating other interests. Moreover, it has to be borne in mind that over 60 per cent of the world's countries, representing a similar percentage of the world's population, utilize the civil law, while only 27 per cent of the world's countries, accounting for a little over 34 per cent of the world's population, utilize the common law.[6] So the level of development, while important, is not everything, though obviously some legal systems are so relatively undeveloped that their inclusion in a comparative survey serves little purpose but to underscore their need for improvement of their commercial laws.

Approval of the project by the relevant organ of the agency

6.13 The next step is for the relevant organ of the agency considered to examine the material collated by its Secretariat and to consider whether the project should be included in its future work programme. This decision is taken, in the case of UNIDROIT by its Governing Council; in the case of the Hague Conference by a Diplomatic Session or by the Commission on General Affairs and Policy of the Conference (now to be called the Council); in the case of UNCITRAL by the Commission; and in the case of the ICC by the particular Commission responsible for the project—for example, the Commission on Commercial Law and Practice for business-to-business transactions or the Commission on Banking Technique and Practice for uniform rules on banking practice. It has been a common practice of UNIDROIT to have a new harmonization project examined in the first instance by a restricted exploratory working group to make a preliminary determination of the need for and feasibility of the project and to suggest a framework within which any study group established by the Governing Council might work. Only when this exploratory working group has reported favourably will the Governing Council consider giving its approval to the setting up of a study group.

Establishment of a study or working group and sub-groups

6.14 The organ that approves the project in each of the four organizations usually establishes a study group or working group, or in the case of the Hague Conference a Special Commission, under the leadership of a designated chairman and in collaboration with the Secretariat,[7] to carry the project forward and draft the requisite instrument for consideration by the organ in question, though in the

---

[6] University of Ottawa, '*World Legal Systems*', <http://www.droitcivil.uottawa.ca/world-legal-systems/eng-monde.html>, cited by Wayne R Barnes, 'Contemplating a Civil Law Paradigm for a Future International Commercial Code' 65 L A L Rev 677, 681 (2005).

[7] The Hague Conference Secretariat is called the Permanent Bureau.

case of UNCITRAL drafts are not infrequently prepared by the Secretariat. In a UNIDROIT project the members of the Study Group are individual experts—principally academics and practising lawyers—who act in that capacity and not as government representatives. UNCITRAL Working Group members and members of a Hague Conference Special Commission act as government representatives, though a number of these may be academics. ICC working groups consist of a mixture of business people, bankers and academic and practising lawyers. Each body welcomes the participation of representatives of other international governmental and non-governmental organisations as observers. Observers have no voting rights and in theory cannot speak unless invited to do so, but in practice it has been found convenient to allow them to take part in the same way as other participants, particularly because they often have expertise to contribute on a particular issue that might not otherwise be available to the group. The group or Commission may decide to set up sub-groups. UNIDROIT, for example, invariably establishes a drafting committee to prepare texts in accordance with decisions of the group and submit them for discussion and approval, and may set up specialist sub-groups to examine issues requiring special expertise. The ICC Commission on Commercial Law and Practice has established a number of task forces to examine particular areas decided upon by the Commission, including a task force on Incoterms. The study or working group or Special Commission may present reports of work in progress, which is standard procedure in UNCITRAL, and a final report with accompanying text on completion of the work.

What type of instrument?

To some extent this depends on the institution undertaking the project. The **6.15** International Chamber of Commerce, not being a law-producing body, seeks to harmonize *practice* by formulating contractually adopted uniform rules, trade terms, model forms and guides. Though the objective is to promote consistency of practice the effect, of course, is that when rules are contractually incorporated they help to determine the rights and obligations of the parties. Where the sponsoring organization is the Hague Conference on Private International Law, the instrument takes the form of an international conflict-of-laws convention. UNIDROIT and UNCITRAL use a wide range of instruments and publications, including multilateral conventions, model laws, legal or legislative guides and (in the case of UNIDROIT) an international restatement of contract law. In determining the choice of instrument (see paras 5.07–5.16) a preliminary question is whether governments will be involved. In the case of the UNIDROIT Principles of International Commercial Contracts the view was taken that since the Principles were to be non-binding rules, that is, a form of soft law, the work should be undertaken exclusively by scholars and governments should not be involved. Where what is envisaged is an instrument that will be adopted by States the choice is between a multilateral convention and a model law. Where there is a reasonable expectation of acceptance by relevant States the convention route is preferable in that it ensures uniformity, whereas a model law may be adopted with modifications which vary from State to State. On the other hand a model law is very useful where it is anticipated that it will be difficult to secure agreement to a convention or there are States in different stages of development who wish to be able to adapt the law to their particular needs.

Distribution of drafts and consideration at meetings

6.16 Each successive draft of a text is circulated for comment—in the case of the ICC interim and final drafts of a proposed instrument are circulated to all National Committees for approval prior to final indorsement by the relevant Commission— and may attract extensive comments and proposed redrafts of particular provisions, all of which will be considered by the group at a formal meeting. It is usually necessary to have a series of meetings before agreement is reached. It is not the usual practice to have votes; instead, decisions are taken by consensus. An exception was the Hague Conference, which used to take decisions by vote both at the last meeting of the Special Commission meetings and at the ensuing Diplomatic Session, but the Conference also has now moved to decision by consensus.

Approval of the text

6.17 Once the group has completed its work its report and annexed text are presented for approval, in the case of UNCITRAL by the Commission, in the case of UNIDROIT by the Governing Council for submission to a committee of governmental experts (see below), in the case of the Hague Conference by the Special Commission and in the case of the ICC by the Commission which initiated the project and then the Executive Committee of the ICC.

Committee of governmental experts

6.18 Since members of a UNIDROIT Study Group act as individuals, not as government representatives, the Governing Council has to approve the text of any draft convention or model law for submission to a committee of governmental experts. This stage is unnecessary for the other three bodies, since for two of them the participants are government representatives while the third, the ICC, is a non-governmental body. Exceptionally, the UNIDROIT Principles of International Commercial Contracts (UPICC) did not go before a committee of governmental experts; indeed, governments were not involved in its preparation, which was purely the work of scholars, because the UPICC is not a legislative text, rather a source of reference and inspiration for legislators, courts and arbitral tribunals.

Diplomatic Conference/Session

6.19 An international convention, having been approved by the sponsoring body, has then to be adopted by the Member States of the body concerned. This is done either at a regular Diplomatic Session of the body in question, in the case of an UNCITRAL or Hague Conference text, or at a specially convened Diplomatic Conference, for which a State has to be found willing to host it. UNCITRAL texts are presented to the General Assembly of the United Nations for approval. This is usually a formality and no textual amendments are made. Where the instrument is an international convention, what began as an UNCITRAL draft convention becomes a UN Convention, UNCITRAL being a subsidiary body of the General Assembly. In the case of UNIDROIT the text is submitted to a Diplomatic Conference, together with a detailed Explanatory Report and other documents. The Explanatory Report is usually prepared by or on behalf of the Secretariat or by a rapporteur appointed for the purpose and typically consists of an overview of the convention followed by an article-by-article analysis of its provisions.

The Diplomatic Conference is far from a formality and involves a fairly elaborate **6.20** apparatus. Organisation of the Conference is a major undertaking. For some projects States may be reluctant to act as host, for others, such as the Cape Town Convention, there was keen competition, and eventually South Africa was selected. It is important for the Conference to be located in a country equipped to provide the necessary administration and facilities. Though the Diplomatic Conference leading to the Cape Town Convention was the very first to be held in the continent of Africa it was superbly organized and this did much to contribute to its successful conclusion.

The Conference, attended by representatives of governments and observers from **6.21** international organizations and specialist groups, initially meets in plenum to elect the president, vice-presidents and other officers of the Conference, and to establish and elect chairpersons of the Conference, the Committee (or Commission) of the Whole, and drafting, credentials, final clauses and other committees.[8] The Conference is conducted in accordance with rules previously laid down and circulated by the responsible Secretariat or Secretariats. The role of the President of the Conference is largely formal, being to preside over the plenary sessions which meet at the beginning and end of the Conference and to ensure observance of rules of the Conference. The main responsibility for the efficient conduct of the Conference falls on the chairman of the Committee of the Whole. The Conference

---

[8] The drafting committee is responsible for preparing drafts to give effect to decisions of the Committee of the Whole as the Conference proceeds (see below). The credentials committee is responsible for examining the credentials of representatives of participating states to ensure that they are properly authorized (usually by the head of State or foreign minister of the state concerned) to represent their respective states. The final clauses committee is responsible for preparation of clauses dealing with such matters as signature, ratification, accession, amendment, denunciation, and the like. Final clauses are often erroneously regarded as standard provisions requiring no special attention, which is very far from the truth. After being drafted by the final clauses committee they then go either to the drafting committee to ensure consistency with the rest of the text and to deal with any anomalies or direct to the Committee of the Whole.

may also appoint a rapporteur, whose function is to give an overview of the draft instrument, introduce each article by explaining its purpose and meaning, and answer questions from delegates, some of which may be highly technical. The text is then examined article-by-article and paragraph-by-paragraph by the Committee of the Whole, which may decide on substantial additions, deletions and amendments. Chairmanship of the Committee of the Whole is a crucial post requiring the highest legal competence and a combination of firmness, fairness and tact, coupled with an ability to crystallize issues, suggest compromises and bring the Committee to decisions. At different stages the text is sent to a drafting committee, and working parties may be established in the course of the Conference to address difficult substantive issues and report back. It is good practice for the Chair to summarize decisions made on each article before it is referred to the drafting committee. This helps to avoid misunderstandings and also ensures that the Committee of the Whole has reached clear conclusions on the relevant policy issues. The drafting committee is the workhorse of the Conference and its members have to be prepared to burn the midnight oil, as it is essential to keep pace with the Committee of the Whole. Where there are no more than two working languages of the Conference—typically English and French—it is the responsibility of the drafting committee to produce parallel texts, an arduous and time-consuming task but one which is essential to the success of the work.[9]

6.22 For some reason everyone participating in a Diplomatic Conference wants to be able to serve on the drafting committee! Perhaps this reflects a misunderstanding of the function of a drafting committee, which is not to decide policy issues but to produce texts which implement the decisions of the Committee of the Whole.[10] Some may be influenced by a Machiavellian desire to regain in the drafting points on which they lost on the substance! Drafting committees should not be too large. On the other hand, it is important to ensure that there is representation of all the legal families represented at the Conference and a fair balance between developed and less developed countries. For the leasing and factoring conventions there were delegates from nine countries and about fifteen people attended; for the Cape Town Convention fifteen *countries* were designated and no fewer than fifty delegates attended the first meeting of the drafting committee! It is, of course, impossible to draft in a group of this size, and it was quickly agreed that a small 'friends

---

[9] For the qualitative difference between the product of work by a drafting committee and that of translators, however capable these may be, see above, para 3.56.

[10] In practice, the line cannot always be so clearly drawn, because there is a tendency to try to save time by referring to the drafting committee matters which are really unresolved policy issues; and it can happen that there is a lack of clarity as to what the Committee of the Whole decided on particular issues. In either case the drafting committee then has to do the best it can, if necessary producing alternative texts for the issue in question.

of the Chairman' group of some seven or eight experts would be responsible for preparing drafts to be considered by the full drafting committee.

There is likely to be a series of papers from governments and international organ- **6.23** izations taking part in the conference as observers. Much important work is also done outside the Committee of the Whole, through formal working groups set up by the Committee or its Chair or through informal meetings designed to improve a text or to hammer out a compromise that may avoid the necessity for further debate. The beneficial effect of breaks for morning coffee and afternoon tea should not be underestimated! If all goes well the Committee of the Whole reaches agreement on the text, which is then presented to the Conference for formal adoption. On the last day of the Conference the convention is opened for signature of the Final Act—a formal summary record of the proceedings, including the text of the convention and any resolutions passed—and of the convention itself. Government representatives usually sign the Final Act, which is merely an authentication of the proceedings involving no commitment, and may also sign the convention, which under the final clauses of most modern private law conventions does not commit the signatory state unless and until it ratifies the convention.

From time to time during the Diplomatic Conference delegates may raise ques- **6.24** tions as to the need to introduce an additional provision here or there or may seek clarification of an issue which the chairman of the drafting committee considers adequately covered by the existing text. In such cases the drafting committee may be asked to consider the question, but a common and convenient alternative solution is to say that the question will be dealt with in the Explanatory Report; and as the Conference proceeds the list of matters to be covered in the Explanatory Report tends to become longer and longer. But the device is useful in that it saves time—always a precious commodity at diplomatic conferences—and enables the text to be kept light rather than being cluttered up with unnecessary detail.

Explanatory Report/Official Commentary

At some stage after conclusion of the Convention it is necessary to produce a **6.25** new Explanatory Report or Official Commentary which gives the history and background of the project and provides an article-by-article and paragraph-by-paragraph analysis of the provisions of the Convention. This may be left to the Secretariat or prepared by the rapporteur or joint rapporteurs, the chairman of the drafting committee or some other designated person or persons. Even if there are rapporteurs the Secretariat usually plays a significant role in work on the Report. It is good practice to circulate drafts to a select group of participating experts from different jurisdictions in the first instance and, when the text has been finally settled, to distribute this for comment to all governments and organizations that participated in the Diplomatic Conference. Comments received should be carefully considered but in the end the Report is that of the person or persons responsible for it, including the Secretariat.

Promotion of the instrument

6.26 Adoption at a diplomatic Conference, thought by some to be the culmination of the work, in reality represents only a halfway house. At least as much work has to be done to promote the instrument and to secure ratifications and accessions (see further paras 20.21–22).

C. Problems of Harmonization

6.27 Earlier attempts to promote uniform law instruments were often frustrated because of insufficient care in selecting the subject matter and constraining it within reasonable bounds and because of inadequate planning and preparation. But there are other factors which have little to do with the intrinsic merit of a harmonization project.

René David, 'The International Unification of Private Law', in *International Encyclopaedia of Comparative Law II* **(J C B Mohr, Tübingen, 1971), Ch 5, paras 56–9**

The unification of law can come up against three types of obstacles which jeopardize its realization. The first category, which comes to mind immediately, concerns the divergence of views as to what is *just*, moral, and in the interest of society. A second category, less obvious to the uninitiated but all-important to the lawyer, concerns the varying techniques employed for expounding rules of law. However, the principal obstacle, which we shall deal with first, consists simply of the weight of inertia, routine, and prejudice . . .

The principal difficulty hindering projects for international unification of the law consists of routine, and of the prejudice of those who would have to be convinced before a new order can be constructed . . .

It is traditional to point out lawyers' conservative attitudes, obvious in their dress, their language and their manner, their way of life and their system of recruiting. There is much truth in the usually critical remarks made in many countries on this subject; the problem of the unification of law cannot begin to be considered in practical terms without taking into account, and allowing for, the psychological state of the lawyers.

However, the inertia of the law is not due only to the lawyers. The whole population is involved and it is not always the lawyers who are the most conservative. It is natural for a man to consider as just, reasonable and necessary rules of conduct to which he has been accustomed since childhood and has always seen observed . . .

International unification of law inevitably implies some reforms in the law of each country. Lawyers and businessmen are attached to the *status quo*, to the order of things which they know, and to which their behaviour and their ways of doing things have been adapted. They view all reform with suspicion, seeing primarily the trouble it will cause, rather than its beneficial effects and the progress which it is intended to produce. When the reform has been carried out, they will be reconciled and recognize that it may have improved matters. Until then, many circles will be against it on principle, even if no acquired right or vested interest is threatened or questioned.

This attitude can be clearly seen when the international unification of law is considered. Everyone accepts unification, provided this means all the others falling into line with national law. Leaving aside any feeling of national pride, it is everywhere required of the uniform law that it should not change the existing law, meaning, in each country, its national law.

The various harmonizing agencies have learnt from these experiences and much   **6.28** more thought now goes into the whole process. Even so, there is a tendency to focus on substantive content and to neglect consideration of promotional activity and working methods and assume that the self-evident merits of the project will suffice to carry it through, when the reality is that every project has to be sold to governments and the relevant private interest sectors and every stage in the process carefully planned. We have already noted the importance of adequate preparation to establish that there is a significant problem that can and should be resolved by an international convention and that there is a reasonable indication of support for the project. Let us assume that this has been done and that work is now ready to commence. What difficulties lie ahead? Several of these have been neatly summarized by the Secretary General of UNIDROIT in the following terms:

Herbert Kronke, 'International uniform commercial law Conventions: advantages, disadvantages, criteria for choice' (2000) V Unif L Rev 13, 17–18

A. The elaboration process

The choice of subject is the first step, and it is this step where in the past most mistakes have been made and where we are likely to make mistakes in the future. Traditionally, the subject was chosen by academics and/or intellectual leaders in decision-making centres such as Governments and international Organisations. In some instances—we need but think of the Sales and Carriage-of-Goods Conventions—the initial choice was good, but subsequently the parameters changed. Some projects were either too broadly or too narrowly tailored. Some tackled problems which commercial circles did not see at all or which were not felt to be really serious. Uncertain support from such quarters should in any event be an orange, if not a red traffic light for law-makers. More specifically, if the result envisaged by the sponsoring States or Organisation, on average, is not clearly a win-win situation for both parties to the transaction envisaged (carrier/shipper, creditor/debtor, bank/client, seller/buyer), the chances of wide-spread acceptance recede.

Another pitfall is when participating Governments are not sufficiently committed to the Convention and/or when the latter is not connected with adjacent work. For example, in one important UNIDROIT member State the official in charge not only of relations with the Organisation as such but dealing also with the substance of its most important current work, in the light of the other international and purely domestic tasks assigned to his unit is able to allot barely one tenth of his time to the Institute's work. Again, only four out of roughly forty States participating contemporaneously in an UNIDROIT and an UNCITRAL project with one rather tricky interface manage to provide for some form of tangible co-ordination between the two delegations.

Third, a project may be aimed at an insufficient number of Governments and their domestic constituencies.

Fourth, Governmental delegations to expert committees or diplomatic Conferences still often seem to have trouble viewing issues raised in negotiating private law Conventions from a strictly economic, technical or legal perspective; instead, they perceive their own private law solutions as forming part of their national sovereignty.

Fifth, progress in negotiations is often too slow because the substance is poorly understood or because of psychological incompatibilities between the key players, both on the part of Governments and on that of the Conference sponsors. This can be avoided to some extent by more careful manning of delegations and selection of Conference officers.

Lastly, an increasingly perceptible disadvantage is that negotiations too often aim for a compromise between legal systems as their main or, for that matter, only objective. But as one head of delegation from a common law country (not the UK or the US) recently told my UNCITRAL colleagues and myself, to make an established and well-functioning common law rule look a little more like civil law (and vice versa) is not an incentive but a serious impediment to negotiation and the will to succeed.

6.29 We have referred earlier to the importance of preparation and to the problems that arise if insufficient care is taken to ensure that there is a need for the project in question and the likelihood of support for it from relevant interest groups. We take up some of the other ideas mentioned in the above extract, together with some additional issues

Over-ambition

6.30 Several projects have failed because they sought to achieve too much, particularly at the outset. A case in point is the ill-fated UNIDROIT project on agency in the international sale of goods.[11] As originally conceived this was to take the form of a convention providing a uniform law on agency of an international character in the sale and purchase of goods covering both the internal relations of principal and agent—itself a large and complex topic—and the external relations between principal or agent and the purchaser. The Diplomatic Conference was held in Bucharest from 28 May to 13 June 1979 but unhappily failed to finish its work and was reduced to recording the progress made and annexing the set of articles on which agreement had been reached, with a request to UNIDROIT to take steps to ensure that the work was completed as soon as possible.[12] Subsequently a restricted group of experts was appointed by UNIDROIT to examine the existing texts. This group recommended deletion of the chapter of the draft convention dealing with relations between principal and agent and to focus on third-party relationships. This recommendation was endorsed and a revised text prepared, and the Convention on agency in the international sale of goods adopted at a second Diplomatic Conference, in Geneva, in February 1983. However, it has so far attracted only five of the ten ratifications required to bring it into force.

---

[11] See ch 8.
[12] The text of the Resolution will be found at the end of the Explanatory Report by the UNIDROIT Secretariat reproduced in 1981 II Uniform Law Review 59.

By contrast, the initial draft prepared by the restricted exploratory working group **6.31** on international interests in mobile equipment began from a smaller canvas, with a mere five articles, whilst as work progressed industry experts demonstrated the need for an ever-wider range of provisions, so that the resulting product consists of a convention of sixty-two articles and an aircraft protocol of thirty-seven articles—ninety-nine articles in total, just two short of the CISG. Concluded in November 2001 the convention and protocol came into force on 1 March 2005, a remarkably speedy adoption which demonstrates the value of organic growth of an instrument during the course of its development rather than an initial grand design. This allows time for the development of a consensus in support of the project and the introduction of new ideas and provisions as it unfolds.

A distinguished French judge has commented that harmonization is easier in a **6.32** field where the economic activity is relatively recent and has not attracted much attention from the legislature or judiciary.

Jean-Paul Béraudo, 'La négociation internationale institutionnelle de droit privé' (Ière partie) (1997) II Unif L Rev, 9, 11

Mais l'élaboration de règles uniformes communes à une large partie de la société inter-nationale n'est pas toujours realizable. Lorsque l'institution à organizer est complexe, du fait de la multiplication des situations concretes ou à cause du poids de l'histoire, il est chimérique de les envisager. Nous pensons au droit des successions et des régimes matri-moniaux ou, meme, au droit du marriage et du divorce. En revanche, lorsque une activité économique est relativement récente et n'a donné lieu de la part des législateurs nationaux ou de la jurisprudence qu'à des règles générales sommaires, l'unification matérielle peut-être sérieusement envisagée. Dans cet ligne, l'idée d'unifier les règles relatives au crédit-bail international ou à l'affacturage international était rationnellement fondée. La France qui ne connassait qu'une legislation embryonnaire sur le crédit-bail et seulement des pratiques contractuelles pour l'affacturage s'est enrichie juridiquement en ratificant les deux Con-ventions d'Unidroit ouvertes à la signature à Ottawa le 28 Mai 1988 . . .

Tensions arising in the preparation of international conventions

In every harmonization project there are bound to be points of stress. These may **6.33** arise from a variety of causes: differences in political perspectives, a perception by one group of participants that another is assuming too dominant a role, language difficulties, and personality clashes. The growing dependence on specialists in par-ticular forms of commercial transaction, though inevitable, also raises concerns as to the maintenance of a fair balance of interests. These problems cannot be entirely avoided but they can be managed.

Roy Goode, 'Rule, Practice and Pragmatism in Transnational Commercial Law' (2005) 54 ICLQ 539, 558–60

The preparation of international conventions is arduous and time-consuming and calls for immense patience, mutual respect and a very great deal of hard work. Even where these qualities are present—as they usually are. particularly in drafting committees, which are the work horse of study groups and Diplomatic Conferences—tensions can arise which are not related to the quality of the work . . .

The first arises from the fact that the sophistication of commercial law is directly related to the volume and diversity of business transactions. The greater the volume of business, the more diverse the instruments and the wider the range of problems that will be encountered by the business community and the courts. This in turn is a factor of the degree of freedom given to business people to make their own law and to devise their own instruments, structures and governing rules. This laissez-faire approach is much less acceptable to civil law jurisdictions, particularly in the field of property law, where there are many rules that constitute a serious impediment to modern methods of dealing and finance. I refer in particular to strict formalities, a restricted view of admissible property rights, a requirement of specificity of subject-matter, a hostile attitude towards non-possessory security interests, difficulties with the concept of real rights in after-acquired property, the absence of effective perfection requirements and facilities, the lack of the trust except in attenuated form and restrictions on resort to contractual self-help remedies.

In a highly developed financial centre whose laws embody a laissez-faire philosophy, there will be more solutions to a greater number of problems than in a jurisdiction which has a lower degree of commercial activity. It is an undisputed fact that although substantial volumes of business are transacted in many commercial capitals of the world, the leaders by a long margin are New York and London, the laws of whose countries are in consequence regularly chosen as the governing law by parties to contracts that have no necessary connection with the United States or England. And this creates a problem, because those from other jurisdictions, particularly the major civil law jurisdictions, rightly take pride in their own legal systems and do not wish to find the preparatory proceedings dominated by Anglo-American laws and lawyers. This is a point to which the English and Americans have to be particularly sensitive. My own experience of working with colleagues from a variety of countries, including France, Germany, Italy, the Netherlands, the Scandinavian countries, Japan, and China, is that they are very open-minded but find a number of concepts of the common law unfamiliar and requiring explanation, so that one has to proceed step by step in a process of familiarization. Some of the difficulties of civil law to which I have alluded in regard to property rights have begun to be resolved as a response to the needs of international commerce and finance and the desire of countries to ensure that their legal systems remain competitive, though the changes have been gradual and fragmented.

But the learning process is by no means one-way. The civilians have just as much to contribute as to receive. They bring with them a concept of system, a high degree of intellectual rigour and a keen perception of the need to balance other interests against commercial interests. So they may feel that some proposed rules are too creditor-friendly and give insufficient weight to the interests of debtors, while other rules fail to take account of long-established legal traditions, such as rules restricting self-help. These sensitivities need to be respected and accommodated. The civilians also appreciate drafting that is not only accurate but elegant and light.

The second tension relates to new players on the international scene. There has long been a feeling that transnational law is dominated by developed countries and is then imposed on developing countries and new market economies, who may feel that their views are not being adequately considered. In most cases these concerns can be overcome by mutual respect and attentiveness to differing viewpoints and by ensuring that representatives of developing countries are included in study groups, working parties and drafting committees.

Sometimes it helps if a State with well-developed laws is given a leadership role within its region. For example, at the Diplomatic Conference in Cape Town on the mobile equipment convention—a conference superbly hosted by the Government of South Africa—the African States, though represented and participating individually, were happy to entrust leadership of their interventions to South Africa, with very good results.

The third tension relates to the maintenance of a balance between pressure from commercial interests and respect for the rights of others. We have to face the reality that the business community, by virtue of its intimate knowledge of the workings of commerce and finance, is best equipped to identify the problems and to come up with solutions and international business organizations must be major players from the very outset of a harmonization project. At the same time we must ensure that other interests are respected, and where the balance is drawn is likely to vary from State to State. It is not the function of an international convention simply to reproduce provisions found in standard-term contracts. This is not always understood. There were some practitioners in the leasing industry who complained that the dispositive provisions of the UNIDROIT Convention on International Financial Leasing did not reflect the typical terms of a finance lease, with its hell-or-high-water clauses for payment of rent, its provisions for damages on termination for default, and the like. I pointed out that the function of any transactional law is to maintain a balance of interests. We do not frame our sales legislation to reflect sellers' standard terms of business. Similarly with leasing. If lessors want additional rights, they must do what they have always done, namely negotiate to have their own standard terms accepted.

There are various ways in which a balance may be achieved in the preparation of convention rules: a compromise approach to a proposed rule; the provision of variants, leaving it to each Contracting State to decide which it prefers; the insertion of provisions allowing a State to opt out of rules too much at variance with its legal traditions or limiting the application of rules to those States that opt into them. All these techniques are to be found in the Mobile Equipment Convention, and there is no doubt that they were in no small measure responsible for the fact that on the last day of the Diplomatic Conference no fewer than 20 States signed a Convention of 62 Articles and an Aircraft Equipment Protocol of 37 Articles—a total of 99 Articles in all and in my view a major achievement.

6.34 The exigencies of business practice may dictate solutions which are highly fact-specific and out of accord with general theory. This is as true of issues of private international law as it is of questions of substantive law. A striking illustration is to be found in the 2002 Hague Convention on the law applicable to certain rights in respect of securities held by an intermediary, where under Article 4(1) the law chosen by the parties to an account agreement between an investor and a securities intermediary to govern the issues laid down in Article 2(1) of the Convention applies not only to the relationship between those parties but to rights vis-à-vis third parties and even priorities between competing claims to an interest in the account.[13]

---

[13] See Roy Goode, 'Rule, Practice and Pragmatism in Transnational Commercial Law' (2005) 54 ICLQ 539, 541–4.

Technical problems

6.35 The above passage identifies various stress points in the harmonization process that can lead to tension between individuals or groups of participants. There are also a number of technical issues which are often hard to resolve.

Differences in legal concepts

6.36 It is inevitable that those taking part in work on the unification of law take as their starting point their own national legal systems, with which they are familiar. There is nothing wrong with this. On the contrary, the best way of testing a proposed new rule is to compare it with a rule on the same issue in one's own law, identify the differences and see which rule is to be preferred. There is, however, a great danger of misunderstanding rules of a foreign legal system, particularly where the legal expressions used appear to be identical but in fact reflect very different ideas—the *faux amis*. For example, the French word *compensation* appears to be readily translatable into English as compensation but in legal terminology is more likely to refer to something quite different, namely set-off. It may still be necessary to use similar expressions in parallel texts for want of any better ones—for example, what is encompassed in the English term 'possession' is significantly different from that in the French word *possession*, yet it is usually necessary to treat them as equivalent for want of a word or phrase capturing the essence of both—but this should at least be done in the awareness that the parallelism of the concepts is at best approximate. The most reliable way of avoiding misunderstandings when discussing a proposed new rule is to present a series of typical fact situations and invite each participant to state how the legal issues arising from them would be resolved by the new rule. Indeed, the wider the range of problems thrown at the rule, the greater the likelihood that ambiguities will be teased out and unforeseen difficulties resolved. Professor John Honnold, a former Secretary of UNCITRAL, noted the use of this technique in the preparation of CISG:

> One device used by the Secretariat in presenting issues to UNCITRAL seemed to facilitate agreement and, perhaps, a more direct mode of expression. At points where the proposed legal texts might be read differently by delegates from different legal backgrounds the crucial issues were posed initially in terms of concrete factual examples. It proved to be easier to reach agreement on the results of concrete cases than to agree on legal drafts; and starting with agreement on the substance of the rule made it easier to draft a text that was direct and clear.[14]

Drafting and language

6.37 It is impossible to over-emphasize the importance of clear and accurate drafting in order to avoid ambiguities in a text and consequent misunderstandings. The

---

[14] John Honnold, *Uniform Law for International Sales under the United Nations Convention* (3rd edn, Kluwer Deventer, 1999) para 33.

drafting style for a Convention should be light and uncluttered by the mass of detail that so often befogs domestic legislation, particularly in common law jurisdictions. The problem, of course, is that inevitably the preparation of a preliminary text reflects the legal background of the person who drafts it. At one time French was the preferred language for the basic text, from which parallel texts in English and, where appropriate, other languages would be produced. Today the basic text is more often than not prepared in English. However, where English and French are the working languages it is customary to proceed paragraph by paragraph. The golden rule here is that if the formulation of a rule in the one language cannot be rendered accurately and elegantly in the other it is not a good formulation and should be modified. So, not infrequently, difficulties with the French text result in clarification of the English text to align it with the French or to allow a more elegant rendering. It should be borne in mind that the work is not one of translation, which implies the primacy of a particular language text, but of the production of parallel texts, each equally authentic. Drafting committees face the same problem as translators in deciding how far a parallel text can depart from a literal rendering of the basic language version in order to convey more accurately the spirit of the text. Certainly some leeway must be allowed to accommodate differences in the structure of different languages. On the other hand, legal accuracy and parity of meaning must be given priority over elegance and brevity. To take a simple example, the phrase 'to the extent that' in one language is not accurately rendered by 'if' in another. Drafting is difficult and time-consuming and requires not only a thorough conversance with the substantive subject-matter but also drafting skills that enable sometimes complex ideas to be expressed in simple language.

Interpreters

Where a Diplomatic Conference uses more than one working language inter- **6.38** preters must be employed. Almost invariably interpretation is simultaneous, for otherwise too much time is lost. Though many interpreters are also translators, the skills required, while overlapping, are not the same. For one thing, interpreters have very little time at their disposal, they have to start interpreting as soon as they have the sense of what is being expressed. Inevitably, therefore, mistakes can occur which can cause misunderstandings. These are less likely to occur when the interpreters can have recourse to prepared texts; the pressure comes from extempore interventions of delegates, some of whom make little allowances for the interpretation process and speak very fast. Skilled interpreters cope remarkably well with these problems, but any assistance that can be given is usually appreciated, for example, by arranging for an expert to meet the interpreters before the start of the Conference, run through the principal technical terms that will be used and explain their meaning.

Organizational problems

6.39 It has been a characteristic of international law-making that it has a lengthy gestation period. The Convention on Contracts for the International Sale of Goods was over a decade in preparation, while the Cape Town Convention took thirteen years from conception to completion, though the process was greatly accelerated once the Aviation Working Group came into being. The problem is partly one of finance. Meetings entail substantial expense, with participants from many parts of the world having to fund themselves, or be funded by governments or private organizations, for their travel, accommodation and subsistence costs. Where, as is common, there are two or more working languages, the costs of interpretation have to be provided and these are substantial. All these factors limit the frequency of meetings, so that often the relevant group meets no more than once a year and sometimes less frequently than that. Time is another factor. Most participants are heavily engaged in government work, legal practice or business and the time they can devote is limited, particularly as this is given *pro bono*. It would be impossible to finance a harmonization project if professional fees were to be paid. Then there are delays because of a change in the composition of the relevant group, so that new members have to be given time to play themselves in and are likely to ask questions over issues thought to have been settled long ago, though sometimes the questions turn out to be highly pertinent and to expose weaknesses in what had previously been agreed. Allied to this is the effect of the involvement of larger groups at later stages of the project, a point succinctly made by Professor John Honnold, a former Secretary of UNCITRAL.

John Honnold, 'Process and value of the unification of commercial law: lessons for the future drawn from the past 25 years', in UNCITRAL, *Uniform Commercial Law in the Twenty-First Century* (United Nations New York, 1995) 11, 15

The principal drawback, in my view, is the consideration of draft texts by larger groupings at successive stages of the process. It is a problem that does not arise solely from UNCITRAL. Most, if not all, representatives to the Commission and observers participating in UNCITRAL meetings are lawyers. Any lawyer worth his salt will be of the view that a legal text is capable of improvement. Since there are many ways in which a legal text may be drafted, one sees, in the final stages of the process, a fair number of proposals for amendments. Amendments tend to lead to compromises. Compromises may be in the interest of acceptability of legal rules, but they do not always make good law.

There is a fundamental difference between the measured, thoughtful work of a working group, from meeting to meeting over a period of years, and the abruptness of almost instant decisions that often must be taken on a great many matters in the larger groupings of committees of the whole, the full Commission or in a diplomatic conference. The process of drafting legal rules in the smaller working groups whose membership tends to remain stable over the years with ample time for studying proposals, for redrafting and consideration, cannot be duplicated in the larger forums where quite a number of participants come to the subject for the first time, and where legal texts must often be redrafted on the spot.

The problem to which Professor Honnold alludes becomes particularly acute at **6.40** the Diplomatic Conference, where there are delegations from many countries and most of the delegates will previously have had little or no involvement in or knowledge of the text to be examined. The entire text produced for the conference is examined afresh, article-by-article, paragraph-by-paragraph. Paragraphs or whole articles may be deleted, added or amended as the result of interventions from the floor which may seem reasonable at the time and be given approval without much discussion, only for difficulties to be encountered in the drafting committee. Though the Conference may begin in what seems a leisurely fashion, taking two or three days to get down to the substance of the Conference, the time pressures build up as the Conference proceeds, and towards the end there is likely to be a scramble to finish on time. In this process it is all too easy for errors of one kind or another to occur and for some of the coherence of the original draft to be lost. There is little that can be done about this. The greater the preparation in advance, the less likely it will be for serious errors to occur. The key objective is to produce an agreed text before the end of the conference, for which purpose it is invariably necessary to produce compromises which may weaken the text, but this is not the fault of those responsible for the drafting, a fact all too frequently overlooked by critical commentators.

But the most fundamental weakness in the harmonization process is that insuffi- **6.41** cient thought is given to the planning and management of a project. Meetings are sometimes not long enough to make significant progress. Work on a convention is usually allowed to proceed stage by stage in accordance with a well-established pattern but not always with a proper plan for the enterprise as a whole. It is frequently the case that there is little activity between formal meetings, and much time is thereby lost. A major construction contract would have a project manager, but harmonizing agencies do not have funds for such a post, though it could considerably accelerate their work.

There are things that can be done to speed up completion of a harmonization proj- **6.42** ect. One is to plan the timetable for the project. It may not be feasible to do this until the shape and complexity of the project become clearer, but fairly soon the point should be reached where a provisional timetable can be set for all the stages prior to the Diplomatic Conference, this last being dependent on the willingness of a State to host the Conference. A second way of expediting the process is to identify a person knowledgeable in the field who is able and willing to act as the driver of the project and to carry it forward by the organization of regular meetings to enlist interest and support, conference calls, preparation of drafts, invitations to submit papers, and the like. Work on both the Cape Town Convention on mobile equipment and the Hague convention on indirectly held securities benefited immensely from drivers of this kind. Thirdly, it is helpful to identify in good time prior to the Diplomatic Conference aspects of the work calling for specialist input. In the case of the Cape Town Convention there were at various stages working groups on the international registry, public international law aspects and insolvency law aspects, as well as an international registry task force, and their input substantially facilitated progress at the Diplomatic Conference itself. Finally, those involved in work on the Hague convention devised an innovative technique by which the drafting committee, when working during the preparatory stages to produce a text to give effect decisions of the plenum, was mandated to test the water for different solutions and, if changes were supported by a consensus, to draft for these without waiting for the next meeting of the plenum. This enabled the substance of the text to be improved between meetings and much time saved at the meetings themselves. The combination of these two last features resulted in the conclusion of the Hague Convention a mere two and a half years after the project began—an astonishing achievement and one which offers a pointer to future working methods.

D. Harmonization and Regionalization

6.43 As a response to the de-localization of economic and political processes and the real or perceived loss of local and national control over them, societies around the world have in recent decades been placing ever greater emphasis on the regions as a geographical space or political entity capable of defining and protecting cultural identity and, in some cases, a vehicle designed to regain some authority to establish the 'rules of the game'. The harmonization of private and, in particular, commercial law has always had to take the relevance of regions into account. Historically, the main reason was that the geographical regions of the world tended to coincide with areas where one of the legal families dominated. In large parts of continental Europe and in Latin America this was, and still is, quite obvious. Indeed, some commentators have described the universal harmonization of private law in the late nineteenth and the first half of the twentieth centuries as 'regional harmonization in disguise'. While it must not be forgotten that the historical beginnings of the harmonization movement were by no means disguised but consciously regional, to wit Latin American,[15] and that Brazil, Chile and Japan were represented on the first UNIDROIT Governing Council, there can be no doubt that the agenda of institutional harmonization at a worldwide level was largely driven by a regional, to wit European, political and scientific discourse.

---

[15] See ch 5 above.

René David, 'The International Unification of Private Law', in *International Encyclopaedia of Comparative Law II* (J C B Mohr, Tübingen, 1971), ch 5, **paras 131, 133**

It must be frankly recognized that the modern world contains many different situations. If international law is to progress it mst, in most fields, pass through a 'regional' stage before becoming a world system, if a world system ever comes to pass . . . .

Dangers of regional harmonisation.—One of the principal questions on the agenda of the third meeting of organizations concerned with the unification of law, organized by Unidroit in 1963, was that of the relations between unification of law on a world scale and unification of law on a regional scale . . . The fear is that the attainment of certain regional unifications will constitute an obstacle to the unification which, it is thought, might have been realized on a larger scale.

This is certainly a danger. In some countries, the unification of law on a national scale resulted in a weakening of the international idea and the universal ideals in the law. It may be feared that, if a degree of unification is attained in the BENELUX countries, it will be more difficult to attain unification, in the same fields, on the level of the Council of Europe—that the unification of the law in the ROMANO-GERMANIC group will be an obstacle to the harmonization of the legal systems of this group and the SOCIALIST systems or the COMMON LAW . . .

On the other hand, as David went on to point out, not all manifestations of **6.44** regionalization and not even all efforts to harmonize private law within a regional institutional framework are posing new problems for worldwide harmonization and the organizations charged with it. The fact that the United Nations Economic Commission for Europe (UNECE), the Organization of American States (OAS) or the *Organisation pour l'Harmonisation en Afrique du Droit des Affaires* (OHADA) have been engaged in drafting and promoting private law texts for some time and that intergovernmental organizations in other regions of the world are currently joining them or are about to do so required 'only' effective co-ordination.[16] The fundamental novelties and the change of paradigms are, firstly, that harmonization of private law in an increasing number of regional organizations is seen as a function of those organizations' agenda regarding the respective region's economic integration and, secondly, that the Member States of one Regional Economic Integration Organization, the European Union, under the Treaty of Amsterdam have transferred parts of their sovereign legislative (and judicial) powers to the supranational entity. Organizations such as the Hague Conference, UNIDROIT and UNCITRAL, while remaining the only or primary theatres of private law harmonization in and for many regions of the world, are assuming a dramatically changed function for their European members: first, to provide a bridge to the 'outer world', second, to provide minimum levels of harmonization needed for universal and inter-regional compatibility and, third, to constitute a forum for

---

[16] See ch 5, para 5.10, above.

sectorial efforts in areas where there is neither an unambiguous competence of the Community nor the political will to move forward even in its absence. It is obvious that the additional presence of the European Commission at the negotiation table has a significant impact on the negotiation of transnational commercial law instruments between EU Member States and the rest of the world. This became apparent—at times in a rather traumatic way—at certain stages of negotiations of what are now the 2001 Cape Town Convention, the 2002 Hague Securities Convention and the 2005 Hague Choice of Forum Convention. The holder of constitutional powers to legislate in yet to be clearly defined areas of private law and, in particular, conflict of laws and international civil procedure is unlikely to pursue its brief in the way a simple observer—the EC's formal status in those fora—would have done. As is obvious, the harmonization process becomes multi-layered if States and their common supranational legislative and executive powers first have to consult internally in order precisely to define each other's sphere of competence, substantive objectives, and negotiation strategy. Moreover, the consent of non-Member States to whatever result may be reached in these complex and time-consuming consultations cannot be taken for granted. With respect to competences, both the internal and external consequences of the constitutional changes we are witnessing in Europe will need to be further explored and clarified. While the supremacy of Community law over national law and uniform private law Conventions, even if the latter were concluded prior to the EC Treaty, has been confirmed by the European Court of Justice and by Member States' courts, both the premises—in particular the true dimensions of the Community's so-called 'mixed competences'—and many incidental and preliminary questions are not yet settled. Traumatic experiences do, as we know, not infrequently assist individuals and, indeed, organizations in reaching a better understanding of who they are and how they wish to relate to their peers and to their environment. Not surprisingly there are now encouraging signs of a positive learning curve: at the first sessions of an UNIDROIT Committee of governmental experts for the preparation of a Convention on harmonized substantive rules regarding intermediated securities in 2005 and 2006,[17] i.e. a field where the Community's competence is undisputed but where the subject matter of legislative intervention is by definition not confined to the EU's territory, it was acknowledged that it may be wise to start harmonizing at the worldwide level and to follow up with measures deemed necessary to deepen regional harmonization and to go into more detail if and where required in an internal market. The EC's impending admission to membership of the Hague Conference[18] is a logical institutional step, and the accession to UNIDROIT may and should follow.

---

[17] See ch 13 below.
[18] The process is expected to be completed by mid-2007.

In 2002, the Congress to celebrate the seventy-fifth anniversary of the founding of UNIDROIT was entirely devoted to launching an in-depth inquiry into the facts and analysis of the objectives as well as the legal implications of regional economic integration for worldwide harmonization of private law. The papers and panel discussions focused on areas ranging from the law of contracts, in particular sales and carriage of goods, to secured transactions, and from civil procedure to the protection of mankind's cultural heritage. The following extensive quotation is from the General Report by Professor Jürgen Basedow, where a vast panorama of challenges for the harmonization process unfolds.

6.45

Jürgen Basedow, 'Worldwide Harmonisation of Private Law and Regional Economic Integration—General Report', (2003) VIII Unif L Rev 31, 31–49

I.—Introduction

In 1997, the Treaty of Amsterdam conferred upon the European Community the power to harmonise private international law. It did not take long before Professor *Struycken*, the chairman of the Dutch State Committee on private international law which operates as a steering body in the framework of the Hague Conference on Private International Law, identified this new competence on the part of the Community as a threat to the Hague Conference, warning of 'the shadows of Brussels over the Hague'. A more recent statement by the Secretary-General of UNIDROIT, Herbert *Kronke*, appears less concerned and more detached. He pointed out that we know little about the relationship between the universally harmonised modernisation of private law and the regional approximation of laws. . . .

II. The Evolution of Universalism and Regionalism

[. . .]

1. The first phase: regionalism in disguise

[. . .] Their [intergovernmental organizations,'] . . . bid for universality could not be satisfied until the USA and other States of the Western Hemisphere acceded to them in the wake of World War II. . . .

[. . .] These observations . . . are essentially confirmed by a closer look at the pre-war ratifications of, and accessions to, some early substantive law conventions. In 1940, the Paris Union Convention on the protection of industrial property of 1883 was in force in 32 States, 21 of which European. The 1886 Revised Berne Copyright Convention had been ratified and acceded to by 26 States, and only seven of them were extra-European countries. The 1929 Warsaw Convention on international air transport had been implemented by 27 countries, 21 of which European and only six non-European States. The only exception are the 1924 Hague Rules on bills of lading; in 1940, no fewer than 30 out of the 48 Contracting Parties were extra-European countries. However, this exception does not prove the existence of a world-wide unification of private law since the vast majority of the 30 extra-European States were colonies and other dependent territories to which Britain and France had extended the operation of the Convention. These observations relate to areas of the law which have an inherent global dimension and not to matters such as road transport which, by the nature of things, do not require unification beyond continental confines. The reported data also support the view that throughout the first phase, the unification of private law was essentially regional in character.

2. The second phase: the rise of universalism

Things changed . . . in particular from the 1970s onwards. The reasons . . . were manifold: the loss of influence of the European powers at the universal level, the corresponding increase of power of other regions, the quest of dozens of newly independent States intent on building their own legal systems for equal participation in diplomatic exchange, the growing gap between East and West and the consequential rise in lobbying activities of both sides in international organisations, the improvement of international transport and communication networks which allowed for unprecedented growth in international exchange and trade from which a need for universal legal co-ordination and harmonisation ensued, and the like.

[. . .]

As to the international instruments, two observations can be made with regard to this second phase of uniform private law: first, the number of ratifications of and accessions to several of the pre-existing international conventions has greatly increased, thereby imparting to these instruments a truly universal character. Thus, the number of participating States as regards the above-mentioned Conventions on intellectual property, maritime and airborne transport is well over a hundred. Second, some new conventions have been concluded which can boast world-wide approval. In particular, the Convention on the International Sale of Goods (CISG), which is the first example of successful unification of a core component of substantive private law.

At the same time, the rise of universalism has drawn attention to the potential for conflict that may occur between universal, regional and bilateral conventions. These issues have naturally not only formed the subject of thorough scholarly analysis, but they have moreover produced a number of clauses which have become familiar in more recent treaties. These clauses seek to reconcile conflicting conventions by giving priority to the *lex posterior*, the *lex prior*, the *lex specialis* or the *lex favorabilior*. In the absence of such clauses and sometimes even despite their incorporation, the solution is far from clear. . . .

3. The third phase: the dawn of inter-regionalism

A third phase of international uniform law has been sparked by another change in the relevant players in the diplomatic arena. In the recent past, regional organisations have made their appearance that have availed themselves of legislative procedures to accelerate the unification process in their respective parts of the world. Thus, the institutional framework of MERCOSUR in South America certainly favours the adoption of uniform law instruments, and this is even more true of the Organisation for the Harmonisation of Business Law in Africa (OHADA), whose Council of Ministers is empowered unanimously to adopt uniform law instruments which take effect in all Member States, apparently without any further ratification procedure at the national level.[19] While these institutional innovations foster the production of regional law, they do not generally impair national sovereignty as

---

[19] The author refers to Joseph Issa-Sayegh, 'Quelques aspects techniques de l'intégration juridique: l'exemple des actes uniformes de l'OHADA' (1999) IV Unif L Rev 5. See also, in the same

the ultimate source of legislation and they do not affect the right of Member States to nego-tiate and conclude international conventions. Conflicts between regional instruments and the existing universal treaties are therefore not all that different compared to traditional conflicts of conventions.

The case of the European Community is quite different. . . . Indeed, there is ample evi-dence for the proposition that the Community has succeeded in implementing harmon-isation in areas where all previous attempts to put into effect international treaties had failed. What is more important for the universal unification of laws, however, is that the European Community . . . is endowed with legal personality (Article 281 EC), and that certain provisions of the Treaty, such as Article 310, empower it to conclude international agreements with one or more States or international organisations. The European Court of Justice has even enlarged the treaty-making powers. It is now firmly established that the Community is competent to conclude international agreements even in the absence of an express affirmation by the Treaty if it is vested with internal legislative competence in a given area. . . . [I]t is common ground that there is an external authority of the Community insofar as it has made use of its internal legislative powers and insofar as a treaty concluded with third States may affect the operation of existing Community legislation. Depending on the particulars, such external competence may even be exclusive of that of individual Member States.

It follows that the European Community is in fact a new player in the diplomatic arena where treaties . . . are negotiated. The growing body of internal European Community legislation in the field of private law is reflected by the simultaneous growth of its external competence. In the light of the great numerical significance of European countries for the unification of private law in the past, their obligations under Community law—which may go as far as to refrain from participating in international negotiations—indicate a fur-ther and decisive step into a new era of unification of private law. Organisations from other regions of the world may perhaps follow in the future, and this would change the entire institutional framework of international negotiations into inter-regional negotiations. For the time being, however, the European Community is the only organisation that has the power to intervene in international negotiations and which must therefore be taken into account by States and international organisations interested in the unification of private law.

The preceding observations can be summarised as follows: the need for harmonisation of private law has always been felt most clearly within the regions where transboundary social and commercial exchange is particularly intense. World-wide unification has been a kind of free-rider of that need for many years. After World War II, demand for univer-sal harmonisation has grown considerably, however, and now requires more and more initiatives which have an inherently global dimension. . . . However, universal harmoni-sation is slow and has to cope with many divergent interests. Therefore, the unaltered and even increased demand for regional harmonisation will more and more frequently be sat-isfied by efficient legislative procedures, a kind of fast-track harmonisation at the regional level. As a consequence, this will generate inter-regional conflicts sooner or later which can be accommodated by inter-regional harmonisation. The mandate of the European Community to negotiate treaties at the universal level is a first step in that direction.

---

special issue of the Unif L Rev where this article is taken from, KL Johnson, 'L'OHADA et la mod-ernisation du droit des Affaires en Afrique', (2003) VIII Unif L Rev 71.

III.—Illustrations

[. . .]

1. Traditional conflicts of Conventions

A traditional conflict of Conventions is highlighted by the co-existence, in the field of arbitration, of the universal *United Nations Convention on Recognition and Enforcement of Foreign Arbitral Awards* of 1958[20] and two inter-American Conventions, one on *International Commercial Arbitration* of 1975 (Panama Convention), the other on the *Extraterritorial Validity of Foreign Judgments and Arbitral Awards* of 1979 (Montevideo Convention). While conflicts between the Panama and the U.N. Conventions do not appear to be very numerous, they are generally decided on the basis that the regional Convention is given priority as the *lex specialis*. . . . Matters grow more complicated when it comes to conflicts between the 1979 Montevideo Convention and the U.N. Convention. . . .

2. Regional fast-track instruments and international Conventions

(a) *MERCOSUR*—In 1991, Argentina, Brazil, Paraguay and Uruguay concluded the Treaty of Asunción on the *Common Market of the South* (MERCOSUR). Inspired by the model of the European Union, the four States created an institutional framework aimed at accelerating integration and economic growth. This treaty has triggered a great many initiatives for the unification of laws in various areas, among them arbitration. One of the various measures adopted by the 1992 Protocol of Las Leñas was MERCOSUR Council Decision No. 5/92 containing a Protocol on co-operation and judicial assistance on civil, commercial, labour and administrative matters[21] which also deals with the recognition of arbitral awards. The relationship between this instrument and the pre-existing international Conventions, both at regional and universal level, naturally gives rise to further questions which may appear novel, since the MERCOSUR instrument is designated as a 'decision', not as another Convention. However, the MERCOSUR terminology, which contains echoes of the supra-national legislation of the European Community, is misleading. First, acts of secondary MERCOSUR legislation such as decisions will usually have to be implemented in national law before they take effect. Second and as a matter of fact, Decision 5/92 is a Protocol which even needs to be ratified by Member States and therefore does not differ from a traditional Convention. It follows that the conflicts between such acts and traditional international Conventions do not pose any new problems either.

(b) *OHADA Uniform Acts*—This appears to be different in the case of the uniform acts adopted by the *Organisation for the Harmonisation of Business Law in Africa* (OHADA). One of the achievements of that organisation is a *Uniform Act on General Commercial Law* which contains a Book V on commercial sales. Its rules sometimes differ from the corresponding provisions of CISG. Thus, in contrast to Article 50 CISG, the buyer of defective goods is not entitled to reduce the price under Article 249 *seq* of the Uniform Act, while under Article 254 a claim for avoidance of the contract may only be filed in court, not implemented by a private declaration by the buyer as is possible under Article 49 CISG. Finally, the Uniform Act replaces the national sales laws and cannot be avoided by appropriated contract clauses, while Article 6 CISG explicitly allows such contractual exclusion of CISG.

---

[20] See ch 17 below.   [21] Reproduced in vol 2, p 685.

Such conflicts in substance raise the question of the scope of application of the conflicting instruments. Articles 202 to 205 only deal with the subject matter of the Book on sales, which is by and large the same as that of CISG. The geographical scope of application of the entire Uniform Act is conditional upon whether the merchant—be it a natural or legal person—is established in the territory of a Contracting State of OHADA (see Article 1). The significance of this rule for the application of the provisions on commercial contracts is not quite clear, but it appears to follow that a seller established in the Republic of Guinea, which is a Contracting State to both CISG and OHADA, is subject to both, at least in its transactions with other Francophone African countries. CISG will be applicable by virtue of its Article 1(1)(b) as the law of the seller, and the OHADA Uniform Act on general commercial law will govern those transactions under its Article 1 and in view of its purpose to unify the law of sales throughout the OHADA member States. This conflict could be accommodated by Article 90 CISG in favour of the Uniform Act which can be viewed as an 'agreement' for the purposes of that provision.

But what about a transaction between a seller from Guinea and a buyer established outside the OHADA region? Here too, both instruments might be applicable. The issue of such conflicts has not been tackled expressly. A solution might be inferred from Article 10 of the basic OHADA Treaty which confers a direct and overriding effect upon the uniform acts in respect of previous or subsequent enactments of *internal laws*. But it is not clear whether this provision also purports to deal with conflicts between uniform acts and other international commitments of single Contracting States. If it does not, the conflict outlined above cannot be said to differ very much from a traditional conflict of Conventions.

Just as in the traditional cases, the acting entities are Nation States, and the main difference with the conflicts discussed previously consists in the fact that the OHADA uniform acts are adopted using a kind of fast-track procedure, *i.e.* by unanimous decision of a Council of Ministers, and take effect without any ratification procedures being required at the national level. It appears doubtful whether this really comes down to a transfer of sovereignty; it might also be viewed as an authorisation by national Governments to legislate without any control by national institutions, and in particular, national parliaments. In the latter case the uniform acts could hardly be said to differ very much from international agreements. Therefore, the solution of a conflict between the OHADA Uniform Act and CISG will probably have to make use of the same general principles which have been outlined above in respect of the traditional conflicts of Conventions, until the Common Court of Justice and Arbitration of OHADA hands down a decision on the actual significance of Article 10 of the OHADA Treaty. A finding of that court that the uniform acts, under Article 10 of the basic OHADA Treaty, take priority over international Conventions to which the single OHADA Member States are Party would, however, change the situation. It would then come close to what is already the state of the law in Europe.

3. Supranational regional instruments and international Conventions

(a) *European Community Law and uniform law Conventions*—A new quality of relations between regional and universal instruments is indicated by some recent legislation of the European Community. Such legislation may adopt different forms, and it may be either in line with or opposed to international Conventions. In some cases, as for example during the preparation of the consumers sales directive, the European Commission took an international Convention like CISG as a blueprint for its own act. The interest in international harmony reaching beyond Community borders may be strong enough to cause express reference being made in the Community Act to the international Convention and to produce almost complete identity of texts. Such is the case of the Community Directive relating to the transport of dangerous goods by road which practically extends the scope of application of the previous European Convention on the matter to intra-State transport. Alternatively, the Community may also, by adopting appropriate legislation, work towards the ratification of international Conventions by the single Member States; this has happened with regard to some instruments related to shipping. While, in the previous cases, the Community rather supports and affirms the policies expressed in international Conventions, problems may arise when those international instruments come into conflict with Community law or policy. Take the example of rules on jurisdiction and the recognition and enforcement of judgements which are contained in so many private law Conventions. While those rules appear to be necessary supplements of international liability regimes, there will always be an overlap with the detailed Community regulation on the matter.

In view of the precedence of Community law over national law, including the international commitments of Member States, conflicts arising from such overlap have to be cleared lest the international instrument lose its practical effect. So far, two solutions have been explored: the Community may either leave the whole negotiation process to the Member States and confine itself to the adoption of legislation that sets forth the conditions for an eventual ratification of the international Convention by the Member States 'in the interest of the European Community'; this option was chosen with regard to the 1996 *Hague Custody Convention* and the *International Convention on Civil Liability for Bunker Oil Pollution Damage* of 2001. Alternatively, the Community may also join the negotiation process and try to bring the content of the international instrument in line with its own law and policy before eventually becoming a Contracting Party to the new Convention; this way has been paved by appropriate ratification and accession clauses in the 1996 *World Copyright Convention*, in the 1999 *Montreal Convention on International Air Transport* and in the recent *UNIDROIT Convention on International Interests in Mobile Equipment* signed at Cape Town in 2001. It is easy to see that the first of these options is a risky endeavour for the international community. It will be negotiating a treaty with single Member States of the European Community, possibly acting *ultra vires* although this will be unclear at the time of negotiation. Thus, the treaty might contain commitments which the EC Member States will not be allowed to honour due to some subsequent EC legislation. It follows that the international community should have a strong interest in the implementation of the second option, *i.e.* participation by the Community as such in international negotiations lest commitments accepted at diplomatic Conferences be qualified by internal legislation at a later stage.

(b) *The example of the air transport liability regime*—The most conspicuous example of such qualification is the adoption of *EC Regulation No. 2027/97 on air carrier liability in the event of accidents*. It is well-known that the liability limits established by the 1929 Warsaw Convention have been long outdated. Except for the 1955 Hague Protocol, attempts to raise those limits to amounts which would appear acceptable by today's economic and social standards have failed again and again. Under these circumstances, the Community adopted Regulation 2027/97 to implement a provisional liability regime which was to remain in force until a modernised universal regime took effect. The Regulation basically deprives Community air carriers of the privilege of limiting their liability, but allows them to do so to an amount of 100 000 SDR if they can successfully prove to have taken all necessary measures to avoid the damage or that it was impossible for them to take such measures, *i.e.* in the case of no-fault liability.

The International Air Transport Association (IATA) challenged, in the English High Court, the validity of an Order which the British Government had issued to ensure implementation of Regulation 2027/97. Plaintiff alleged Regulation 2027/97 to be invalid as it required Member States to act in breach of their obligations under the Warsaw Convention. The Court held that the Warsaw Convention did not permit Contracting States to impose upon their own air carriers a liability exceeding that established by the Convention and that Regulation 2027/97 was therefore in conflict with the Warsaw Convention. In an elaborate opinion with ample references to the case law of the European Court of Justice the judge however upheld the Regulation. His principal argument was derived from Article 307(2) EC (formerly Article 234(2)) which provides that, to the extent that pre-existing international agreements are not compatible with the EC Treaty, 'the Member State or States concerned shall take all appropriate steps to eliminate the incompatibilities established.' As pointed out by the learned judge, this provision in fact presupposes the validity of EC legislation despite its being in conflict with international commitments of the Member States.

This opinion has been questioned by commentators, but it appears to be in line with the constant practice of the European Court of Justice. Its effect is the affirmation of the supremacy of Community law over Conventions on uniform private law even if the latter were concluded prior to the EC Treaty. This may be deplored, but lacking an authoritative universal dispute settlement concerning the interpretation of uniform law Conventions, it has to be accepted as a fact by the international community. Instead of lamenting the decline of uniform law, we should rather think about appropriate measures which might help to preserve or re-establish the international legal order.

IV.—Some Consequences for the International Law-Making Process

The appearance, in the diplomatic arena, of new actors which, while not States, may have a strong impact on, and even the final say in certain matters raises several problems. These are connected to the need for integration of the new actors into the negotiation process and call for a response on the part of the international community.

The use of Agreements as an instrument of co-ordination depends on the powers of the parties to implement what they promise. As applied to international relations this means that an international treaty, *i.e.* an agreement concluded *inter nationes*, relies on the assumption that the sovereign legislative power is vested in the Nation State. It follows that Nations which transfer part of their legislative powers to supranational organisations will become less attractive to the international community as potential treaty-making partners. Conversely, the international organisations to which these powers are transferred will gain importance for third States. Sooner or later, the international community will insist on those organisations being integrated into the international law-making process. This implies two changes in the present structure of the international system: first, supranational organisations such as the European Community would have to be integrated into the existing international law-making bodies, and second, they would have to be admitted as Parties to international Conventions.

1. The European Community as a member of uniform law organisations

[Here, the author discusses the *potential* advantages and difficulties of the EC's accession to the universal private-law formulating agencies. The European Community is expected to become a member of the Hague Conference in April 2007.]

2. The European Community as a Contracting Party to uniform law Conventions

Whatever the answer to the issue of membership, the European Community even now has the power to influence and even block the adoption of certain international instruments by its Member States. As pointed out *supra*, the best way to accommodate that new situation would be to open these instruments to ratification by the Community. For that purpose, appropriate provisions must be inserted into the uniform law Conventions. Such provisions have emerged from a development which began more than thirty years ago in areas such as fishing, commodities, world trade, and the law of the sea, where the European Community's external competence has been recognised for a long time. The latest version of such clauses does not explicitly refer to the European Community but to organisations of regional economic integration which are endowed with legislative competence for the subject matter of the respective Convention. In case of ratification or accession, that regional organisation is required to make a declaration concerning its competence which if not contradicted by Member States of that organisation, will be deemed to be accepted.

While this type of clause has already been added to some uniform law Conventions, it is by no means generally approved and cannot be regarded as a general principle or a custom implied in international Conventions. Thus, neither the UNCITRAL *Convention on the Assignment of Receivables* of 2001 nor the Hague *Convention on the International Protection of Adults* of 2000 admit participation of entities other than States. While such shortcomings may be avoided in future international instruments, it is difficult to cure them in the Conventions of the past. A feasible although risky solution would probably be the tacit approval, by the Contracting Parties, of a declaration of accession by the European Community; as a subsequent practice, such tacit approval could have the effect of modifying the original Convention.

The accession clauses outlined above do not solve all the problems. They do not upgrade the role of the regional organisations in the course of negotiating a universal treaty; they confer rights upon regional organisations which become effective *after* the adoption of a treaty, but do not necessarily entitle such organisations to vote or bring motions while it is being prepared. Moreover, the new accession clauses carry the risk of split ratification by the regional organisation and its Member States. So far, the European Community has avoided that risk by issuing internal rules providing for the deposit of the ratification instrument by the Community only after the Member States have taken the appropriate measures for the implementation of the treaty and have ratified the treaty themselves. . . .

V.—Some Consequences at the Stage of Adjudication

1. Internal and international fact situations

If States and regional organisations are put on an equal footing as Contracting Parties to an international Convention, the traditional borderline between internal and international fact situations is blurred. It is sometimes both the objective and the consequence of regional economic integration that transborder fact situations within the integration area are subject to the same legal regime as purely internal cases of the single Member States. An example is provided by the internal market in the European Community, which has given rise to numerous enactments, such as the Regulation on air carrier liability in case of accidents, which no longer distinguish between international and internal cases. However, the application of many traditional uniform law Conventions presupposes the presence of some kind of international element. It follows from the equation of States and regional economic integration organisations that transborder fact situations which are entirely located within the territory of a regional economic integration organisation are internal affairs of a Contracting Party and do not come within the scope of application of the international Convention.

As a practical consequence, the new Montreal Convention on international carriage by air would not be applicable to intra-Community flights such as a link between Rome and Paris. In order to avoid such an outcome, the equation of States and regional economic integration organisations has been explicitly excluded in Article 53(2) of the Montreal Convention in respect of the geographical scope of application of that instrument. The authors of the Montreal Convention have in fact analysed each provision of their treaty in view of the aforementioned equation and have restricted its purview by no less than seven exceptions. This is different in the case of the UNIDROIT Convention on International Interests in Mobile Equipment; its Article 48(3) also provides for an equation of States and regional economic integration organisations, but only 'where the context so requires.' It is questionable whether this flexible provision can cope with the need for precision which is inherent in the law of secured transactions and which otherwise has had such a visible impact on the Cape Town Convention. International legislators would be well advised to follow the example of the Montreal Convention and to analyse carefully the extent of the equation of States and regional organisations.

2. Regional courts and international Conventions

Regional economic integration organisations have their own institutional framework which may have to deal with international Conventions ratified by that regional organisation. Thus, the European Court of Justice has repeatedly held that treaties concluded by the European Community with third States or international organisations form an integral part of Community law. Such Conventions are regarded as 'acts of the institutions of the Community' which are subject, as to their interpretation, to the jurisdiction of the Court of Justice (see Article 234 EC). The Court has also pointed out that provisions contained in international Conventions of the Community which are liable to be directly applied must not produce different effects depending on whether institutions of the Community or of single Member States are called upon to enforce them. It is up to the Court to guarantee the uniform application of such Conventions within the whole Community.

While the resulting decisions cannot be binding outside the European Community, they will certainly have considerable authority in third States. The reasons for this are threefold: first, the absence of an authoritative supranational interpretation of uniform law Conventions is perceived as a serious deficit by many judges. Second, litigation dealings with uniform private law Conventions usually does not involve strong national interests; therefore, judges outside the European Community would basically be prepared to follow a European precedent if based on persuasive arguments. Third, the multi-linguistic practise of the European Court of Justice would allow judges all over the world to read the opinions of the European Court in a language that they can understand.

It would therefore appear not unlikely that the European Court system could acquire a key role in the application of uniform law Conventions and that it would attract litigation from all over the world. This perspective might disconcert the legal industry in some extra-European countries which have traditionally refrained from committing themselves to international dispute settlement mechanisms and induce those States to change their minds and accept, in future Conventions, some kind of institutional framework which would allow for a neutral and supranational interpretation of the respective instruments. . . .

Questions

1. What is the relevance of comparative law in a given field to work on a harmonization project in that field?
2. Describe the typical stages in a project to produce an international convention.
3. 'A number of projects for harmonization through an international convention either never come to fruition or result in conventions which fail to enter into force or to secure ratification by a sufficient number of relevant States.'
   Discuss, identifying what you regard as among the principal causes of failure and steps that can be taken to enhance the prospects of success.
4. What do you see as the respective roles of the academic and the practitioner in the fashioning of international commercial law conventions?
5. Compare and contrast the style of drafting of an international convention such as CISG or the Cape Town Convention with that of the legislation of your own country. What would you regard as the key elements of good drafting for an international convention or model law?
6. 'The final stage of a harmonization project leading to an international convention is the conclusion of the convention at a Diplomatic Conference, thus bringing the project to a successful conclusion.'
   Comment on this statement.
7. (a) Identify the provisions aimed at accommodating participation of so-called *Regional Economic Integration Organisations* in post-1997 transnational commercial law Conventions and discuss the premises on which they are founded.
   (b) Would the 1980 Vienna Sales Convention (CISG), if negotiated in 2006, contain a final clause regarding Regional Economic Integration Organisations? If so, how should it be drafted?

Further reading

David, René, 'The International Unification of Private Law', in *International Encyclopaedia of Comparative Law II* (J C B Mohr, Tübingen, 1971), ch 5

Gutteridge, H C, *Comparative Law* (2nd edn, 1949, Cambridge University Press), ch XIII

Hartjowahono, Bajuseto, 'The Unification of Private International Law on International Commercial Contracts within the Regional Legal System of ASEAN' (Ulrik Huber Institute for Private International Law, Groningen, 2005)

Kronke, Herbert, 'International uniform commercial law Conventions: advantages, disadvantages, criteria for choice' (2000) Unif L Rev 13

Of particular relevance is the special issue of the Uniform Law Review, (2003) 8 Unif L Rev, *Worldwide Harmonisation of Private Law and Regional Economic Integration—Acts of the Congress to celebrate the 75th Anniversary of the Founding of the International Institute for the Unification of Private Law (UNIDROIT)*, which contains contributions by leading experts from many jurisdictions and international organizations.

Marquis, Louis, *International Uniform Commercial Law—Towards a Progressive Consciousness* (Ashgate, Aldershot, 2005)

Van Houtte, *Law of International Trade* (2nd edn, Sweet & Maxwell, London, 2002)

PART II

A VIEW THROUGH ILLUSTRATIVE CONTRACTS AND HARMONIZING INSTRUMENTS

7

INTERNATIONAL SALES AND THE
VIENNA SALES CONVENTION

A. General Introduction	7.01	Second view: Article 7(1) imposes positive duty of good faith	7.51
B. The Genesis of the Convention	7.02	Third view: good faith as a general principle	7.55
Rabel and UNIDROIT	7.03		
Assessment of the Hague Conventions	7.04	E. Usages	7.66
The origin of the CISG	7.07	F. Formation	7.70
Entry into force	7.08	G. The Rights and Duties of the Parties	7.72
C. The Sphere of Application	7.09		
Types of contract covered	7.11	General provisions	7.73
The internationality requirement	7.12	The obligations of the seller and the remedies of the buyer	7.75
The connecting factor	7.14		
Both parties in Contracting States	7.15	The obligations of the buyer and the remedies of the seller	7.77
Rules of private international law leading to law of Contracting State	7.16	Fundamental breach	7.78
		'Breach'	7.81
Exclusions from the Convention	7.30	'Fundamental'	7.82
Contracting out of the Convention	7.32	H. Interest	7.88
D. Interpretative Rules and the Role of Good Faith	7.36	Does the Convention govern determination of the rate of interest?	7.92
Autonomous interpretation	7.38	What is the general principle?	7.94
The problem of uniformity	7.39	I. *Force Majeure* and Exemptions for Non-Performance	7.97
Access to case law and commentaries on the CISG	7.44		
The problem of good faith	7.46	J. Risk	7.101
Three views on good faith	7.47	K. Conclusion	7.104
First view: no positive duty	7.48		

A. General Introduction

Having examined the nature and scope of transnational commercial law and some **7.01** of the general principles which underpin the subject, we now turn in this Part to an examination of various illustrative contracts and harmonizing instruments. In doing so, our aim is not to provide a comprehensive analysis of the substantive legal content of these instruments. Rather, it is to use these instruments as a vehicle for an examination of some of the difficulties and issues which can and do arise in the harmonization process. Our examination extends to six topics, namely (i) contracts of sale, (ii) agency and distribution contracts, (iii) international bank payment undertakings, (iv) finance leasing, (v) receivables financing and (vi) international interests in mobile equipment. Each topic has been given its own chapter. The subject matter of this chapter is the contract of sale, in particular the regulation of the contract of sale through the Vienna Convention on Contracts for the International Sale of Goods.

B. The Genesis of the Convention

7.02 The most significant legal instrument operative in the field of international sales is the Vienna Convention on Contracts for the International Sale of Goods (hereafter 'CISG'). It has been ratified by most of the major trading nations of the world and it exerts considerable influence over sales law across the world. It is, however, necessary to place the CISG in its context. Most international conventions build on work done by their predecessors and the CISG is, in this respect, no exception.

Rabel and UNIDROIT

7.03 The inspiration for the work that culminated in the CISG can be found in the work of the great Austrian jurist, Professor Ernst Rabel. He began work on the creation of an international uniform sales law in the late 1920s and published his influential comparative work in sales law, *Recht des Warenkaufs*. His work was taken on and developed by UNIDROIT who began the task of preparing an international law on the sale of goods. A draft document was approved in 1939 by the Governing Council of UNIDROIT, but the work was suspended on the outbreak of World War II. Work was resumed on the project after the end of the war and it did ultimately bear fruit in the form of two Hague Conventions, namely the Uniform Law on the International Sale of Goods and the Uniform Law on the Formation of Contracts for the International Sale of Goods. The text of both instruments was agreed in 1964, but they did not come into force until 1972, when they obtained the necessary ratifications.

Assessment of the Hague Conventions

7.04 Neither Convention can be termed a resounding success. Only nine States ratified them.[1] But it would be a mistake to conclude that they were therefore devoid of practical significance. Professor Peter Schlechtriem, one of the leading authorities on sales law, has offered the following conclusion on the Hague Conventions:

> the Hague Sales Law in the end proved to be very successful. In 1987, when my Institute [in Freiburg] published a collection of cases decided under this Uniform

---

[1] United Kingdom, Belgium, West Germany, Italy, Luxembourg, Netherlands, San Marino, Israel and Gambia.

Sales Laws and asked all district courts and courts of appeal to send us cases decided by them in which these Uniform Sales Laws were applied, we received almost 300 decisions, although only 5% of the courts responded to our request.[2]

This conclusion is rather more favourable to the Hague Conventions than the generally accepted view which is that they failed to have the impact which those responsible for their creation had hoped. While they did have an impact on the continent of Europe (albeit the precise extent of that impact is difficult to assess), their impact elsewhere was extremely muted, if not non-existent. **7.05**

Why was it that the Hague Conventions failed to secure acceptance in the international market place? A number of reasons can be given. First, it was perceived as a European project and the role of States beyond the shores of Europe in the preparation of the Conventions was very limited. This can be seen in the fact that almost all of the ratifying States were European States. In particular, the Conventions failed to secure the participation of the developing nations of the world. They also failed to secure ratification by a large number of the major trading nations of the world. Second, and relatedly, the lack of participation resulted in a lack of ownership of the project; in other words, States which had not participated in the drafting of the Conventions felt no obligation to ratify them. Third, the Conventions could be ratified on an opt-in basis. This had the consequence that, even in the case where they were ratified, they did not necessarily have any practical effect. That this is so can be seen by the example of the United Kingdom, which availed itself of the opportunity to ratify the Conventions on an opt-in basis. Thus the Uniform Laws on International Sales Act 1967 provided that it was open to the parties, should they wish to do so, to agree to incorporate the Conventions into their contracts. But the fact that it was possible for the parties to do so did not have the consequence that they took advantage of the opportunity so given to them. On the contrary, it would appear that the parties declined to do so and continued their practice of contracting by reference to the law of a nation State (usually English law). Finally, the Conventions themselves were thought to suffer from a number of technical weaknesses; that is to say, the substantive legal content of the Conventions was thought by many to be less than satisfactory. The Conventions represented a good first attempt at the creation of a uniform law of international sales but they were not sufficiently good to persuade States to ratify them. Thus the primary significance of the Hague Conventions is to be found in the fact that they provided a significant starting point for the drafting of the CISG. While it is true that the CISG departs from the Hague Conventions at a number of points, it did so only after careful consideration of the competing issues. **7.06**

---

[2] Peter Schlechtriem, 'Uniform Sales Law—The Experience with Uniform Sales Law in the Federal Republic of Germany' (1991–2) 3 *Juridisk Tidskrift* 1, 2.

The origin of the CISG

7.07 The immediate origin of the CISG is to be found in the work of the United Nations Commission on International Trade (UNCITRAL). UNCITRAL was launched in 1966. Its first step was to send the Hague Conventions, together with a commentary by Professor André Tunc, to all governments and to invite them to comment on the Conventions and to indicate their attitude towards ratification. This consultation process established that a number of major trading nations, including the United States, the Soviet Union and China, did not intend to ratify the Hague Conventions. Once this point had been established, work began on the preparation of a new Convention and the consultation process was much more extensive than was the case in relation to the Hague Conventions. As Herrmann observes, the 'crucial value added by UNCITRAL was the universal representation'.[3] A working group was formed in 1968 and it produced its first draft in 1976. Matters then moved relatively swiftly. The work culminated in a diplomatic conference which was held in Vienna between 10 March and 11 April 1980. The conference was attended by sixty-two States and eight international organizations. The Convention itself was adopted on 11 April 1980.

Entry into force

7.08 The Convention did not come into force immediately. Article 99 provided that it would not come into force until the first day of the month following the expiration of twelve months after the date of deposit of the tenth instrument of ratification, acceptance, approval or accession. The necessary ratifications were secured by December 1986 and the Convention came into force on 1 January 1988. The number of ratifications or accessions has increased steadily over the years and it has now been ratified by seventy States, including most of the major trading nations of the world.[4] Thus it has been ratified by countries such as the United States, China, Singapore and Australia. Most European nations have ratified the Convention, with the exception of the United Kingdom, Ireland and Portugal. The United Kingdom Government has indicated its willingness in principle to ratify the Convention. The pragmatic obstacle which remains to be overcome is apparently the need to find Parliamentary time for ratification.[5] The Convention

---

[3] Gerold Herrmann, 'The Role of UNCITRAL' in Ian F Fletcher, Loukas A Mistelis and Marise Cremona (eds), *Foundations and Perspectives of International Trade Law* (Sweet & Maxwell, London, 2001) 30.

[4] A list of the States who have ratified the CISG can be found at <http://www.uncitral.org/en-index.htm>.

[5] The extent of the difficulty is, perhaps, open to question given that with a few exceptions the Convention must be taken as it stands or rejected, so that no article-by-article examination is involved. In the light of this, the demands on Parliament, whether of time or otherwise, would not appear to be great.

has also been ratified by a number of South American States, but African involvement is more limited.[6]

C. The Sphere of Application

A fundamental part of any international convention regulating transnational com-   **7.09**
mercial law is the part that deals with the sphere of application of a Convention. To which contracts is the Convention to apply? If it is only to apply to 'international' contracts, how is internationality to be defined for this purpose? What connection, if any, must there be between the contract and the State which has ratified the Convention?

One of the principal provisions of the CISG which assists in the definition of the   **7.10**
sphere of application of the Convention is Article 1 which is in the following terms:

(1) This Convention applies to contracts of sale of goods between parties whose places of business are in different States:
   (a) when the States are Contracting States; or
   (b) when the rules of private international law lead to the application of the law of a Contracting State.

(2) The fact that the parties have their places of business in different States is to be disregarded whenever this fact does not appear either from the contract or from any dealings between, or from information disclosed by, the parties at any time before or at the conclusion of the contract.

(3) Neither the nationality of the parties nor the civil or commercial character of the parties or of the contract is to be taken into consideration in determining the application of this Convention.

A number of issues arise out of this Article.

Types of contract covered

The first relates to the reference to 'contracts of sale'. The Convention does not pur-   **7.11**
port to define a contract of sale. Instead, it excludes certain contracts from its scope. Thus, Articles 2 and 3 exclude consumer sales from the scope of the CISG, attempt to distinguish a contract for the sale of goods from a contract for services (or a contract for work and materials) and they provide a partial definition of goods. The general rule is that contracts for the sale of goods to be manufactured or produced are to be considered as contracts of sale.[7] The rule is subject to an exception in the case where the buyer 'undertakes to supply a substantial part of the materials necessary for such manufacture or production'.[8] The word 'substantial' would appear to

---

[6] To date the Convention has been ratified by Lesotho, Zambia, Ghana, Uganda and Liberia.
[7] Art 3(1).   [8] Ibid.

indicate a quantitative rather than a qualitative assessment.[9] Article 3(2) of the Convention provides that the Convention shall not apply 'to contracts in which the preponderant part of the obligations of the party who furnishes the goods consists in the supply of labour or other services'. This raises the vexed issue of the distinction between a contract of sale on the one hand and a contract for services on the other hand. The distinction has never been an easy one to draw and it can be argued that it has become even harder to draw in the modern world given the service obligations which are often assumed by sellers of, for example, electrical goods and computers. Indeed, it is possible to go further and question the wisdom of attempting to distinguish sharply between contracts of sale and contracts for the provision of services given the increasing inter-connection between these obligations in the modern market place. Is this a case in which the legal categories which we have inherited from our ancestors have been allowed to exert an influence which is no longer appropriate? Whatever doubts we may harbour about the continued significance of the distinction, it must still be drawn for the purposes of the CISG. The word 'preponderant' in Article 3(2) is required to do a lot of work here and it is not entirely clear whether it is to be understood in a quantitative or a qualitative sense. The cases on balance support the adoption of a quantitative approach, so that the vital question becomes whether the monetary value of the services exceeds the monetary value of the goods supplied.[10]

The internationality requirement

7.12   The second issue relates to the meaning to be given to the word 'international'. The word 'international' can, of course, be defined in different ways. It can be defined by reference to the place of business of the parties or by reference to the movement of goods between different States. As far as Article 1 of the CISG is concerned, the definition turns on the place of business of the parties to the contract.[11] In other words, what matters is the place of business of the parties to the contract of sale and not whether the goods themselves have crossed international borders (although, as a matter of fact, where the parties have their places of business in different States the goods themselves will often also cross borders). This differentiation between 'international' sales and other (domestic) sales may require justification. Why not create a uniform law which applies to all contracts of sale,

---

⁹ Contrast the French text which uses the phrase '*une part essentielle*' which does appear to be apt to encompass a qualitative as well as a quantitative assessment.

¹⁰ See generally: CISG Advisory Opinion No 4, 'Contracts for the Sale of Goods to be Manufactured or Produced and Mixed Contracts (Article 3 CISG)' <http://cisgw3.law.pace.edu/cisg/CISG-AC-op4.html>.

¹¹ The definition of 'place of business' is to be found in Art 10. Where a party has more than one place of business, the relevant place of business will be the place which has the closest relationship to the contract and its performance. In the case where a party does not have a place of business, the reference shall be made to that party's habitual residence.

whether international or domestic? One answer is that international sales give rise to problems which simply do not arise in domestic sales. The principal difference is that the conflict of laws poses problems for international sales, whereas such considerations do not generally arise in the case of domestic sales. The case for uniformity is also greater in the case of international sales because of the perceived need to provide a common floor of rights and obligations for parties who come from a wide variety of legal and commercial backgrounds. Finally, a convention which is confined to international sales is less of an intrusion into national sovereignty. But there are arguments the other way and examples can be found, particularly in the context of regional harmonization, where a distinction is not drawn between international and domestic sales contracts. Thus OHADA[12] has created a new law for commercial sales contracts which came into force on 1 January 1998. This instrument unifies international and national commercial sales between and within member States of OHADA.

Developments are also taking place within Europe. Thus, the European Community Directive on Certain Aspects of the Sale of Consumer Goods and Associated Guarantees[13] makes significant inroads into the law of consumer sales in the domestic law of Member States. The Directive and the implementing regulations have altered the terms which are to be implied into contracts of sale concluded between a professional seller and a consumer buyer and have also made important changes in terms of the remedies to which buyers are entitled.[14] The significance of the Directive lies in the fact that it may herald the beginnings of a future European law of sale and, were such a law to develop, it would presumably encompass domestic sales, whether of a consumer or a commercial variety. The creation of a European law of sales would also raise difficult questions about the relationship between regional harmonization instruments and the CISG. In the case of a contract of sale concluded between a German party and a French party, would the contract be governed by a future European law of sales or by the CISG? This raises a technical legal difficulty[15] but it also raises a difficult issue of policy, namely the level at

7.13

---

[12] Organization for the Harmonisation of Commercial Law in Africa (OHADA). The membership of OHADA consists of Benin, Burkina Faso, Cameroon, Central African Republic, Islamic Federal Republic of the Comoros, Congo, Gabon, Equatorial Guinea, Mali, Niger, Senegal, Chad and Togo.

[13] Council Regulation (EC) 44/1999 of the European Parliament and of the Council of 25 May 1999 on certain aspects of the sale of consumer goods and associated guarantees [1999] OJ L171/12. The Regulations have been enacted into English law in the form of the Sale and Supply of Goods to Consumers Regulations 2002 SI 2002/3045. See generally: Robert Bradgate and Christian Twigg-Flesner, *Blackstone's Guide to Consumer Sales and Associated Guarantees* (OUP, Oxford, 2003).

[14] The Directive has had a significant impact on the law in Germany and the United Kingdom. In the case of the former, it provided the occasion for significant changes to the BGB. In the case of the latter, the Directive has introduced remedies which were previously unknown to sales law in the United Kingdom.

[15] The CISG itself contains two provisions which might provide an answer to this question. The first is Art 90 which states that the CSIG does not prevail over any international agreement which

which sales law should be regulated. Is it a subject which is more suitable for regulation at national level, regional level or at international level? Or is it the case that it is not possible to prescribe one solution for this problem which will hold good for all cases? Thus it may be the case that some sales are more appropriately regulated at international level than others (so, for example, it could be argued that commercial sales are more appropriate for regulation at international level, whereas consumer sales are more appropriately regulated at national level, although the growing significance of consumer contracts concluded over the internet may ultimately throw into doubt the validity of the proposition that consumer sales should be regulated nationally).

The connecting factor

7.14 The third issue relates to the connecting factor that must exist between the contract and a Contracting State. In terms of the sphere of application of the Convention, Article 1 has proved to be a provision of some controversy. It has two limbs which provide alternative connecting factors.

Both parties in Contracting States

7.15 Article 1(1)(a) is relatively straightforward in so far as it provides that the Convention applies to contracts for the sale of goods between parties whose places of business are in different States when the States are Contracting States. Where both parties have their places of business in Contracting States, they are unlikely to be taken by surprise by the Convention and, to the extent that they are surprised, they, or their lawyers, must be taken to shoulder the responsibility for their failure to appreciate the law that is applicable to their contract. Article 1(1)(a) is now the most important provision in terms of the sphere of application of the Convention. This was not so in the early days of the life of the Convention when the number of Contracting States was low. At that point in time the principal connecting factor was Article 1(1)(b). But, as the number of States ratifying the Convention increases, more and more cases will fall within the scope of Article 1(1)(a) and the practical significance of Article 1(1)(b) can be expected to diminish.

---

has already been or may be entered into and which contains provisions concerning matters governed by the CISG provided that the parties have their places of business in States which are parties to such agreement. It is, however, uncertain, whether Directives can claim priority under Art 90 (see, for example: Peter Schlechtriem and Ingeborg Schwenzer (eds), *Commentary on the UN Convention on The International Sale of Goods (CISG)* (2nd (English) edn, OUP, Oxford, 2005) 921–3). The second provision of the CISG which may be relevant is Art 94 which entitles States to declare that the CISG will not apply to contracts of sale or to their formation where the parties have their places of business in those States where the States have 'the same or closely related legal rules on matters governed by this Convention'.

Rules of private international law leading to law of Contracting State

Article 1(1)(b) has proved to be much more troublesome than Article 1(1)(a).   **7.16**
Article 1(1)(b) extends the sphere of application of the Convention so that it
applies when the rules of private international law lead to the application of the
law of a Contracting State. The controversy that lurks behind this provision is
reflected in Article 95 which entitles a State, at the time of ratification, acceptance,
approval or accession, to declare that it will not be bound by Article 1(1)(b). A
number of States have entered an Article 95 reservation.[16] In the following extract,
Professor Christophe Bernasconi explains the rationale behind Article 1(1)(b) and
the motivation of certain States to enter an Article 95 reservation to prevent its
application.

**Christophe Bernasconi, 'The Personal and Territorial Scope of the Vienna
Convention on Contracts for the International Sale of Goods (Article 1)' (1999) 46
Netherlands Intl L Rev 137, 160–5 [16a]**

3.3.3 *The expediency of Article 1(1)(b)*

3.3.3.1 An enlargement of the Convention's scope

The conflictual method of determining the CISG's applicability is based on the notion
that it is not only justified and appropriate to apply the Convention when both parties
have their places of business in different contracting states, but also when an analysis of the
transaction on the grounds of private international law principles reveals that its center of
gravity is located in a state that has ratified the Vienna Convention. Article 1(1)(b) considerably enlarges the Convention's sphere of application. In order for the Convention to
be applied, it will be sufficient if the transaction is international in character (ie, places of
business in different states), and the conflicts rules of the forum lead to the law of a State
Party to the Convention. Since the Convention is well-suited to international transactions, the more it applies, the more legal certainty that may be achieved. Usually, decisions
based on the modern (and 'neutral') law of the Convention are more acceptable to both
parties than one party's domestic law, often unfamiliar to the other party.

Furthermore, it may be argued that it is often easier for the courts of a non-contracting
state to apply the Convention than to try to determine, understand and apply the rules
of a foreign domestic law; as there is a wealth of largely accessible information on the
CISG, the judge sitting in a non-contracting state has an easier access to useful information on the CISG than on almost any foreign substantive law. On the whole, Article
1(1)(b) may fairly be regarded as a logical development and ultimate achievement of the
idea of a *loi uniforme*. Indeed, as far as international sales transactions are concerned, it
may be legitimately presumed that a state that has ratified the CISG has substituted its
domestic rules on (internal) sales for the more suitable rules of the Convention. It seems,
therefore, appropriate that the judge of a foreign forum honors the contracting state's
decision.

---

[16] States that have entered an Article 95 reservation include the United States. The list is kept up
to date at UNCITRAL <http://www.uncitral.org/en-index.htm>.

[16a] Permission granted by the Netherlands International Law Review, The Hague.

3.3.3.2 Internationally harmonized judgments?

However, the expansion of the Convention's scope by reference to the mechanisms of private international law is still not unanimously accepted. Opponents of Article 1(1)(b) assert that this provision does not assist in achieving internationally harmonized judgments and that the originated diversity may lead to forum shopping. If only one party to the contract has its place of business in a contracting state, the action is brought before a judge of that contracting state and private international law leads to the application of the law of the forum (or any other contracting state), the Convention applies. If, however, the same action is brought before the courts of the non-contracting state and private international law leads to the application of the law of this (or any other) non-contracting state, the Convention does not apply. As a result, the same contract could be governed by different laws depending on where the action is launched. This critique cannot be questioned in its result. It points, however, to the wrong source of the problem. Indeed, in cases like the previous example, the stumbling block is not Article 1(1)(b), but rather the fact that the two fora apply different conflict of laws principles. Essentially, even if the contracting state excluded Article 1(1)(b), the countries would still apply divergent substantive laws. The purpose of Article 1(1)(b) is not to ensure harmonized decisions, but to enlarge the Convention's sphere of application.

3.3.3.3 The CISG as an unwelcome surprise?

According to another argument that is quite often presented to condemn Article 1(1)(b), the enlargement of the Convention's scope through the means of private international law may cause an unwelcome surprise to parties who have their places of business in different non-contracting states but who decide to bring their actions before a court sitting in a contracting state. The next example illustrates the problem:

> X has his place of business in London. He sells goods to a buyer Z, whose place of business is in Tokyo. According to an express choice embodied in their contract, the transaction is governed by 'the law of Switzerland' [Switzerland being a Contracting State] and any action has to be brought before the commercial court in Zurich.

According to the strict wording of Article 1(1)(b), the Swiss judge should apply the Vienna Convention to this transaction, although neither X nor Z have their places of business in member states of the CISG. According to the opponents of Article 1(1)(b), it is inadequate to apply the CISG in such cases: to allow the parties' contract to be governed by the CISG would violate their prime intention.

This apprehension is comprehensible; its practical impact, however, should not be overemphasized. If the parties made an express choice in favour of the law of a contracting state . . . without having any links or previous attachments to that country, it is likely that the judge of the forum will also examine the conditions of Article 6 of the Vienna Convention which allows the parties to opt out of the CISG's application. The judge will first look at the precise wording of the parties' choice of law rule: does it refer, for example, to Swiss law in general or to the Swiss Code of Obligations? In the latter case, the judge will (likely) not apply the CISG but rather the Swiss domestic law on sales . . .

Despite all sympathy one may have for the uniform law . . . in cases where two parties, who have their places of business in non-contracting states, choose the law of a contracting state to govern their contractual relationship, the question of the applicability of the CISG should be considered very carefully. In such cases, the parties' presumable intention seems to point to the domestic law rather than to the CISG, even if the latter may be better tailored to international sales transactions. As a matter of fact, parties wanting their contract to be governed by the Swiss Code of Obligations—or by any other domestic law—would be well advised to make the point clear and unequivocal in their contractual choice of law provision.

3.3.3.4 The position of the United States

In addition to the arguments pleading in favour of certainty and international harmony, the US possessed a further reason for excluding Article 1(1)(b) . . . The US made an Article 95 reservation because it desired to preserve as much as possible the applicability of its UCC, apparently preferring its own law to that embodied in the CISG. This conviction . . . is legitimate; however, contrary to the express allegation of the US, such a position considerably reduces the frequency of the Convention's applicability to international sales transactions. The CISG's international rules do not supplant US domestic law in a transaction involving, for example, an American seller and a Japanese buyer—two of the principal trading blocks in the world. This clearly rebuts the CISG's goal of establishing an international sales code. The US attitude also illustrates the inherent tension between sovereignty and multilateral treaties embodying substantive rules.

7.17 The balancing act conducted by Article 1(1)(b) is a difficult one. On the one hand, it enables the sphere of application of the Convention to be extended so that it does not only apply as between contracting parties both of whom have their place of business in Contracting States. As a result of Article 1(1)(b), the Convention can apply to a contract concluded between a party that has its place of business in a Contracting State and a party that has its place of business in a non-Contracting State. Yet it is this extension which is the source of the problem because its effect is that, where the rules of private international law of the forum State lead to the application of the law of a non-Contracting State, then that State's domestic law will govern the contract, but where those rules lead to the application of the law of a Contracting State, the law applicable will be the CISG and not the domestic law of that Contracting State. The consequence of Article 1(1)(b) is therefore to diminish the significance of the domestic law of a Contracting State in favour of the CISG. For some States, as can be seen from the example of the United States of America quoted above, this was a step too far. While they were prepared to accept the displacement of their own domestic law in contracts concluded with businesses in Contracting States, they were not willing to accept the same displacement of their domestic law in contracts concluded with businesses in non-Contracting States.

7.18 The controversy over the legitimacy of Article 1(1)(b) was only resolved by allowing States to enter an Article 95 reservation. Article 95 has been criticized by commentators on two grounds. The first relates to the policy which underpins it. Thus Bernasconi states:

> A reservation under Article 95 considerably reduces the reach of CISG and constitutes a break-block to the effective spreading of a modern, well-suited tool. There is

no persuasive justification to the restriction of the Convention's sphere of application generated by Article 95. If private international law principles establish that an international sales transaction has its closest ties with a contracting state, the application of the well-suited, largely accepted CISG seems generally more appropriate than the domestic rules on internal sales . . . Additionally, the belief that the Convention should only be applicable to sales transactions concluded between parties who have their places of business in different contracting states cannot be justified by referring to the principle of reciprocity rooted in public international law. Indeed, the CISG is not aimed at ensuring the exchange of two equivalent performances between contracting states; the CISG has rather been designed to make sure that international sales transactions be governed by suitable rules.[17]

7.19 The second criticism relates to the technical legal difficulties which have been generated by Article 95. As Bernasconi explains:

Given the great number of variables one must consider (where the forum sits; where each party has his place of business; which state's laws are applicable under the conflicts rules of the forum; which state has made a reservation under Article 95), there are many possible cases in which the question of the Convention's sphere of application might arise. Fortunately, in most cases, the answer is clear. There are, however, some particular situations that continue to cause considerable—and harmful—uncertainty.[18]

7.20 There are a number of situations which give rise to technical legal difficulties, of which it will suffice to note three. The first is where a judge sitting in a Contracting State, through his rules of private international law, is directed to apply the law of a State which has made an Article 95 reservation. Suppose that a manufacturer in France sells goods to a buyer in England. France is a Contracting State; the United Kingdom is not. The seller brings a claim in France against the buyer and the judge concludes that, according to the French conflict-of-law rules, the law applicable to the dispute is that of a state within the United States of America, a Contracting State which has entered an Article 95 reservation excluding the application of Article 1(1)(b). Which law is applicable to this dispute? Is it the CISG or is it the domestic law of sales in the United States (that is, the Uniform Commercial Code)? According to Winship,[19] the question which needs to be considered is 'whether a State which makes a declaration under Article 95 remains a "Contracting State" under para. (1)(b) in jurisdictions where this paragraph is in effect'.[20] He continues:

A forum in a Contracting State which has not made an Article 95 declaration is bound by para. (1)(b) to apply the convention if its conflict-of-laws rules lead to the law of a 'Contracting State'. It would appear that a declaring State is not a Contracting State.

---

[17] Christophe Bernasconi, 'The Personal and Territorial Scope of the Vienna Convention on Contracts for the International Sale of Goods (Article 1)' (1999) 46 Netherlands Intl L Rev 137, 165.
[18] Ibid.
[19] Peter Winship, 'The Scope of the Vienna Convention on International Sales Contracts' in Nina M Galston and Hans Smit (eds), *International Sales: The United Nations Convention for the International Sale of Goods* (Matthew Bender, New York, 1984) 25.   [20] Ibid 27.

The Vienna conference rejected an alternative version of Article 95 . . . which would have answered the question in the negative. The reports of the conference debates suggest, however, that this rejection was based more on the complexity of the last minute proposal rather than on its content. Moreover, a negative answer is consistent with the result when the forum sits in a declaring State or a non-Contracting State to consider similar cases and a uniform answer will discourage forum shopping.[21]

This solution is also adopted by Bernasconi. He likens the effect of an Article 95 reservation to that of a

switch-signal, indicating which set of substantive rules within the designated *lex causae* is applicable. The *lex causae* has not enacted the CISG for cases similar to this one, thus the Convention's rules are inapplicable. By refusing to consider the reservation filed under Article 95, the forum judge would fail to recognize the *lex causae* altogether.[22]

This would appear to be the soundest solution. Enabling the forum State to apply the CISG in such cases would be to ignore another State's decision to file a reservation under Article 95. Arguments to the contrary, based on the intent and underlying aim of the Convention to ensure its largest possible sphere of application, do not justify such a total disregard for a Contracting State's wishes. Nevertheless, this seems to have been the approach taken by the Oberlandsgericht in Düsseldorf in 1993.[23] At that time Germany was not a Contracting State and the court was called upon to resolve a dispute between a United States seller and a German buyer. Applying the German conflict-of-law rules, the court held that the CISG was applicable as the conflict rules pointed to United States law, thus largely ignoring the fact that the United States had made an Article 95 reservation. However, the decision has been heavily criticized, and it is suggested that it should be regarded as having been wrongly decided on the ground of the detrimental impact which it has on the reservation entered by a State. **7.21**

The second situation which has given rise to difficulty is the case where a judge sitting in a State which has made an Article 95 reservation is led by his conflict-of-law rules to apply the law of a Contracting State which has not made an Article 95 reservation. Let us modify the example given above. Suppose that the French seller decides to file suit in a Court in the United States, which has made an Article 95 reservation. The American court concludes that its conflict-of-law rules point to the law of France as the applicable law. France is a Contracting State that has not made an Article 95 reservation. Must the United States court apply the CISG, or is it prevented from doing so by its Article 95 reservation? According to Thieffrey, the **7.22**

---

[21] Ibid.   [22] Bernasconi (n 17) 168.
[23] Oberlandesgericht Düsseldorf 17 U 73/93 (2 July 1993); discussed by Michael J Bonell and Fabio Liguori, 'The UN Convention on the International Sale of Goods: a critical analysis of current international case law (Part 1)' (1996) 1 Unif L Rev 147, 154.

United States has made an Article 95 declaration according to which it will not be bound by Article 1(1)(b) and that:

> [t]herefore, courts in the United States will not apply the Convention to sales between parties whose concerned places of business are not both in Contracting States [as required by Article 1(1)(a) of CISG]. This would be true even in instances where their rules of conflict of law lead to the application of the law of a Contracting State.[24]

7.23　This view is not, however, shared by the majority of commentators. Thus Bernasconi argues:

> . . . Article 95 eliminates the applicability of the Vienna Convention only in favour of the domestic law of the reservation state. If, for example, a New York court has to sit on a sales contract concluded between an American buyer and a Japanese seller [Japan not being a Contracting State], and the American conflicts rules point to the law of New York, the CISG will not apply. However, if the conflicts rules of the reservation state point to the law of a contracting state that has not made the reservation, the Vienna Convention does apply . . . regardless of the US reservation under Article 95.

> This conception of the interplay of Article 1(1)(b) and Article 95 is supported by the legislative history of the latter. The goal of the promoters of Article 95 was to make sure that a judge sitting in a reservation state would not have to apply the Convention if private international law would lead to the application of the law of the forum.

> Unfortunately, this unequivocal purpose of Article 95 is sometimes misunderstood. According to Thieffry, for example, courts in the United States should not apply the Convention even in instances where their conflict rules lead to the application of the law of a contracting state that has not filed a reservation under Article 95. This opinion clearly contradicts both the legislative history and the basic purpose of Article 95. It is not supported by the official US statement justifying the reservation: US conflicts rules point to a foreign legal order, thus the problem of displacing US law (ie, the UCC) is not an issue at all in this case. Furthermore, Thieffry's opinion violates the foreign contracting state's will to apply the Convention in such an event. Finally, it might also provoke forum shopping since courts of different countries would adopt different positions. For these reasons, Thieffrey's opinion must be rebutted. Hence, the effects of Article 95 on a court sitting in a reservation state . . . may be summarized as follows: a sales contract to which at least one of the parties is from a non-contracting state and which, according to the forum's conflicts rules, is subject to the law of the forum (or the law of another reservation state) is not governed by the CISG but rather by the forum's domestic rules on sales.[25]

7.24　This view is also supported by the UNCITRAL Commentary on Article 1, paragraph 7 of which states:

> Even if one or both parties to the contract have their places of business in a State which is not a Contracting State, the Convention is applicable if the rules of private

---

[24] Patrick Thieffry, 'Sale of Goods Between French and US Merchants: Choice of Law Considerations Under the UN Convention on Contracts for the International Sale of Goods' (1988) 22 Intl Lawyer 1017, 1018 (fn 3).　　[25] Bernasconi (n 17) 168–69.

international law of the forum lead to the application of the law of a Contracting State. In such a situation the question is then which law of sales of that State shall apply. If the parties to the contract are from different States, the appropriate law of sales is this Convention.[26]

A third situation of difficulty arises in the case where the court hearing the dispute **7.25** is located in a non-Contracting State. If we use the example above, assume that the dispute between the French seller and the English buyer is brought before a court in England. Assume that the court's conflict-of-law rules point to the law of France, a Contracting State. Is the English court entitled or obliged to apply the CISG in such a case? Bernasconi deals with this question as follows:

> We have already seen that in a non-contracting state, the CISG cannot be applied autonomously. However, what about an application of the CISG through the means of the conflicts rules of the forum? Firstly, it seems to be unequivocal that when the conflicts rules of the forum point to the (domestic rules) of either a non-contracting state or a state that has filed a reservation under Article 95, the CISG does not apply. However, if the private international law of the forum points to the law of a contracting state, it is suitable to apply the CISG, since for international sales transactions, the directed state has substituted its domestic rules for the uniform law of the Vienna Convention. It must be emphasized, though, that in such instances, public international law does not impose any obligation on the judge of the forum to apply the Convention.[27]

This approach has also been adopted in a number of jurisdictions, most notably in **7.26** Germany before the Convention came into force there.[28] One example is the decision of the Landgericht Baden-Baden in 1991.[29] An Italian manufacturer brought an action against a German buyer because of the latter's failure to make payment in respect of two deliveries of wall tiles. The buyers brought a counter-claim in which they sought to recover damages as a result of an alleged non-conformity in the tiles supplied. The sellers disputed the entitlement of the buyers to bring such a counter-claim on the ground of the buyers' delay in giving notice of the alleged non-conformity. The court held that the parties' relationship was governed by the CISG so that it governed the rights and obligations of the parties. The Convention was not applicable as a result of the operation of Article 1(1)(a) because Germany was not, at the date of entry into the contract, a party to the Convention. Rather it was applicable in accordance with Article 1(1)(b). The application of its conflict-of-law rules led the court to the conclusion that the contract was governed by Italian law. The CISG entered into force in Italy on 1 January 1988 and on that basis it was applicable to the contract concluded between the parties.

---

[26] UNCITRAL, <http:www.cisg.law.pace.edu/cisg/text/secomm/secomm-01.html>.
[27] Bernasconi (n 17) 168–9.
[28] These cases are summed up in: Bonell and Liguori (n 23) 153 (fn 36).
[29] Landgericht Baden-Baden 4 OJ113/90 (14 August 1991); translated 12 J L & Com 277 (1993).

7.27   One final complication which may arise in the application of Article 1(1)(b) is whether a forum should 'take into account the rules of private international law recognized by a Contracting State to whose laws the forum's conflict rules would lead'.[30] An example of this would be the following: a French manufacturer brings a suit against an English buyer in England and the English rules of private international law point to the law of France, a Contracting State, as the applicable law. In applying that law should the English judge decide whether the private international law rules of France also point to the law of a Contracting State before declaring the CISG applicable? According to Winship:

> This question takes on importance because different jurisdictions recognize different rules of private international law . . . There is a general reluctance to inquire into the conflict-of-laws rules recognized by another jurisdiction, as suggested, for example, by general disapproval of the doctrine of *renvoi*. This reluctance is supported by the difficulty of the inquiry and the possibility of circularity of the inquiry because of the difference in conflicts rules. The drafting history [of the CISG] also suggests that the forum should apply the convention if its own rules lead to a Contracting State.[31]

7.28   The problem is essentially a question of private international law and will not be dealt with at any length here. However, the question is of some importance to the application of the CISG in international sales, as an Austrian case shows. The Bundesgericht für Handelssachen was called upon to decide a dispute between an Italian seller and two Austrian buyers.[32] The court held that, although the Austrian conflicts rules pointed to Italian law as the applicable law, and Italy was a Contracting State, the Convention was not applicable because Italian conflicts rules made a *renvoi* to Austrian law (the Convention had not entered into force in Austria at that time). The question, thus, comes down to whether a forum's conflict rules recognize the doctrine of *renvoi*, an issue which is beyond the scope of this chapter.[33]

7.29   The significance of this debate about the proper scope of Article 1(1)(b) is, however, likely to diminish in the future. As the number of States ratifying the Convention increases, the consequence will be that more and more cases will fall within the scope of Article 1(1)(a) and the controversy associated with the application of Article 1(1)(b), and its relationship with Article 95, should gradually fade away.

Exclusions from the Convention

7.30   Excluded from the scope of the Convention are matters relating to the validity of the contract and the effect which the contract may have on the property in the

---

30   Winship (n 19) 28.   31   Ibid 28–9.
32   Bezirksgericht für Handelssachen Wien, n 9 C 3486/90w (20 February 1992).
33   *Renvoi* is discussed in more detail at paras 2.58–2.60.

goods sold.[34] At first sight, it seems strange to exclude from the Convention matters relating to the validity of the contract and the passing of property, given the centrality of both issues to the defining characteristics of a contract of sale, namely that it is a contract under which property in the goods passes from seller to buyer. The reason for their exclusion is essentially a pragmatic one. The law relating to the validity of contracts and the passing of property differs sharply as between different nation States and the task of producing a uniform set of rules on these intractable topics would have been a formidable one. The sphere of application of the Convention was therefore narrowed so that it applies, in essence, to the formation of a contract of sale, the contractual rights and obligations of buyers and sellers and the remedial consequences that flow from non-performance of one or more of these obligations. The effect of the exclusion of issues relating to the passage of property is particularly important given that it removes from the scope of the Convention issues such as the validity of retention of title clauses, the problems that have arisen in relation to the passage of property in the case of bulk sales and the question whether a non-owner of goods can transfer property in the goods to a third party.

Article 5 is also an exclusionary provision in that it excludes from the scope of the Convention the liability of the seller for death or personal injury caused by the goods of any person. **7.31**

Contracting out of the Convention

Article 6 is also significant, in so far as it provides that, subject to Article 12, the parties to a contract of sale are entitled to exclude the application of the Convention. This is an important point. The Convention is not mandatory in the sense of precluding the parties from contracting out of it.[35] Parties can contract out of it, or parts of it, but the onus is put on them to do so; unless they do so they will be bound by the terms of the Convention where it is otherwise applicable. **7.32**

Exclusion is a relatively straightforward matter where the parties expressly exclude the application of the CISG or parts of it. More difficult is the case where it is submitted that the parties have impliedly excluded the CISG. Some controversy has arisen here as a result of the difference in wording between the CISG and Article 3 of the Uniform Law on the International Sale of Goods which provides that the 'exclusion may be express or implied'. The lack of an express reference in the CISG to the possibility of an implied exclusion has not, however, led courts and arbitrators **7.33**

---

[34] Art 4. See generally: Helen E Hartnell, 'Rousing the Sleeping Dog: the validity exception to the convention on contracts for the international sale of goods' 18 Yale J Intl L 1 (1993).

[35] The exception is Art 12 which expressly states that the parties may not derogate from or vary its effect. It must also be the case that Arts 89–101 of the CISG cannot be excluded by the parties, given that these Articles are not directed towards the parties.

to conclude that the CISG cannot be impliedly excluded. Although the case law has not been entirely consistent,[36] the generally accepted view is that the CISG can be impliedly excluded, although this implication will not lightly be made.[37] The difficulty which has arisen is one of identifying the circumstances in which the exclusion of the CISG will be implied. We have already noted this controversy in the context of choice of law clauses.[38] The choice of the domestic law of a State which has not ratified the CISG will amount to an exclusion of the CISG, whereas the choice of the domestic law of a State which has ratified the CISG is unlikely to be held to amount to an exclusion of the CISG.

7.34 Suppose, for example, that the parties choose French law to govern their contract. In such a case, is the choice of French law a choice of the domestic law of sale in France (the word 'domestic' being used here to denote French law excluding the CISG) or is to be regarded as a choice of the CISG given that the CISG has been incorporated into French domestic law? The answer is ultimately a question of interpretation of the relevant contract clause. While the case law does not speak unanimously on the subject,[39] it is suggested that the most likely interpretation of such a clause is that the choice of French law will be held to be a reference to French law including the CISG. Slightly more difficult is the case where the parties phrase their choice of law clause in the following terms: 'this contract shall be governed by the domestic law of France'. In such a case, it could be argued that the word 'domestic' is intended as a reference to French law excluding the CISG. This is not, however, a conclusive argument because, as has been noted, the CISG has been incorporated into the domestic law of France and so may fall within the scope of the word 'domestic'. Contracting parties who wish to ensure that the CISG has been effectively excluded would be well advised to say so in express terms or to choose the law of a State which has not ratified the CISG. Choice of the law of a State which has ratified the CISG is an ill-advised approach to take if the desired goal is the exclusion of the CISG.

7.35 Another case which has given rise to some difficulty is the incorporation of Incoterms into the contract of sale. It is very unlikely that Incoterms will operate to displace the CISG in its entirety because they do not purport to be comprehensive.[40] They therefore leave room for the CISG to operate but, where a particular

---

[36] There are some cases which have concluded that CISG can only be excluded expressly. See, for example: *Orbisphere Corp v United States* 726 F Supp 1344 (US Court Intl Trade, 1989). These cases are, however, in the minority.

[37] See, for example: Franco Ferrari, Harry M Flechtner and Ronald A Brand (eds), *The Draft UNCITRAL Digest and Beyond: cases, analysis and unresolved issues in the UN sales convention* (Sellier European Law Publishers, München, 2004) 531–2.   [38] See above paras 2.25–2.33.

[39] For a summary of the relevant case law, see: Ferrari, Flechtner and Brand (n 37) 532–3.

[40] See, for example: Oberster Gerichtshof, Austria, [1 Ob 77/01] (22 October 2001), available at <http://cisgw3.law.pace.edu/cases/011122a3.html>.

Incoterm is inconsistent with a provision in the CISG which would otherwise have governed the issue, the provision in the CISG will generally give way to the term of the contract (unless the term of the contract and the relevant provision in the CISG can be read together in an harmonious fashion).

D. Interpretative Rules and the Role of Good Faith

Article 7 of the Convention deals with a number of difficult issues. It states: **7.36**

(1) In the interpretation of this Convention, regard is to be had to its international character and to the need to promote uniformity in its application and the observance of good faith in international trade.

(2) Questions concerning matters governed by this Convention which are not expressly settled in it are to be settled in conformity with the general principles on which it is based or, in the absence of such principles, in conformity with the law applicable by virtue of the rules of private international law.

The opening words of this provision indicate that it is concerned with issues which **7.37** arise in the interpretation of the Convention. But, as we shall see, it has been argued that the Article cannot be so confined. The Article raises a number of issues.

Autonomous interpretation

The first arises out of the direction that, in the interpretation of the Convention, **7.38** regard is to be had to its 'international character and to the need to promote uniformity in its application'. The aim of these words is clear; it is to ensure that, as far as possible, the Convention is interpreted in the same way in different jurisdictions. In this respect the Convention is to have an autonomous interpretation.[41] The meaning of 'autonomous' in this context has proved to be somewhat elusive. The following definition has been provided:

Martin Gebauer, 'Uniform Law, General Principles and Autonomous Interpretation' (2000) 5 Unif L Rev 683, 686–7

. . . an interpretation may be qualified as 'autonomous' if it does not proceed by reference to the meanings and particular concepts of a specific domestic law. However, this is a

---

[41] See, more generally: Martin Gebauer, 'Uniform Law, General Principles and Autonomous Interpretation' (2000) 5 Unif L Rev 683; Harry M Flechtner, 'The Several Texts of the CISG in A Decentralized System: observations on translations, reservations and other challenges to the uniformity principle in Article 7(1)' (1997–8) 17 J L & Comm 187; Franco Ferrari, 'CISG Case Law: a new challenge for interpreters' (1997–8) 17 J L & Comm 245; Phanesh Koneru, 'The International Interpretation of the UN Convention on Contracts for the International Sale of Goods: an approach based on general principles' 6 Minn J Global Trade 105 (1997); Robert A Hillman, 'Applying the United Nations Convention on Contracts for the International Sale of Goods: the elusive goal of uniformity' (1995) Cornell Review of the Convention on Contracts for the International Sale of Goods 21.

negative definition, stating that regard is not to be had to a particular external concept. This autonomous interpretation of uniform law can also be defined in a positive sense. The Convention's terms and concepts are to be interpreted in the context of the Convention itself. If they are to be regarded as independent terms and concepts, they must be interpreted by reference to the Convention's own system and objectives. Autonomous interpretation, in this sense, may be said to rest on systematic and teleological arguments. This does not mean that in interpreting a uniform law other elements, such as literal or historical considerations, are less important, only that they do not constitute the autonomy of the interpretation. If a certain term or concept is well-known in domestic law, and the same term or concept is used in a Convention but with a different meaning, the difference in interpretation is not a literal argument, not a matter of different meaning of the words. If a Convention is drafted in more than one language, autonomous interpretation requires that the literal meaning in all authentic versions is taken into account. But the imperative not to focus on one single language, with its specific literal meaning, does not follow from any literal argument, but is dictated by the need to give an independent interpretation to the Convention. Likewise, if the legislative history of the uniform law favours a certain interpretative choice that differs from the solutions offered by domestic law, it is not that history that promotes autonomy of interpretation. It is merely an argument in favour of a certain choice of interpretation, not of an independent solution. Thus, autonomous interpretation is not a method of interpretation *in addition* to other methods, such as literal, historical, teleological or systematic interpretation. Rather, it would seem to be a *principle* of interpretation that gives preference to a particular kind of teleological and systematic argument in interpreting a legal text.

The problem of uniformity

7.39   In the following section, Camilla Baasch Andersen examines the problems which can arise when national courts strive for uniformity in the interpretation of the CISG:

Camilla Baasch Andersen, 'Uniformity in the CISG in the first decade of its application' in Ian F Fletcher, Loukas A Mistelis and Marise Cremona (eds), *Foundations and Perspectives of International Trade Law* **(Sweet & Maxwell, London, 2001) 293–5**

[H]ow uniform is 'uniform'? If it is . . . elusive to define positively, then perhaps we should look at what constitutes a problem of uniformity and define it negatively. It appears that one of the best definitions, to date, of what constitutes a problem of uniformity was offered by Professor Sundberg on the subject of a different uniform convention (Warsaw Air Charter) a decade before the CISG was even drawn up. He stated that a margin of imperfection is not a defect with regards to uniformity as long as it does not encourage forum shopping . . . Although the definition is perhaps a tad vague . . . it is still a valid guideline for determining that which is a problem of uniformity . . .

Most of the problems of uniformity fall into some 'categories' of different problems, and although I realise the danger of rigidly pigeonholing case law into categories, it is nonetheless an efficient way of lending an overview, so I will briefly try to illustrate some of them and give you examples of provisions which present problems:

   (i)   First of all, the *sphere of application of the Convention*, a problem which spills over into the other categories, but nonetheless deserves its own, for how can we begin to speak of uniformity if the CISG does not even apply to the same cases in the different member states? One of the examples of this is one of interpretation of terms, found in Article 2: is software 'goods'? If it is, then the convention will apply to software trans-actions, lending itself to the security of both buyer and seller in the absence of any other contract, and giving predictability to such transaction *providing*, of course, that it is predictable whether or not it applies, *ie* whether or not software is 'goods'. Now, any legal counsel representing a party who has breached an agreement in some way would be well advised to encourage his client to hurriedly forum-shop to a venue where software is not considered goods, to avoid the provisions of the pro-contractual CISG for breach.

(ii) Another example is that of *Faux Amis*, ie the 'false friend' in a term which seems famil-iar to a practitioner but which in fact is defined differently in the uniform law than it is in the system where the practitioner is used to it. This is found in Article 47, which was—rather unfortunately—referred to as a '*Nachfrist*' rule by the Secretariat's com-mentary, prompting some German courts to equate it to their own Nachfrist rule in the BGB, and causing them to apply it to cases of delay in delivery and not just in cases of non-conformity of goods as was intended. The forum shopping advantages here are clear; a buyer who has not given a seller Nachfrist in a case of late delivery, should flee from all German courts as it is only here that such a Nachfrist would be required under Article 47.

A possible case of *faux amis* is the US case of *Delchi Carrier SpA v Rotorex Corp.*[42] **7.40** The defendants, a New York corporation, sold compressors for use in portable room air conditioners to the claimants, an Italian manufacturer of air condition-ers. The compressors were found to be non-conforming and the claimant buyers terminated the contract. The claimants sought replacement compressors from other suppliers, but to no avail. They brought a claim for damages against the defendants in the United States in which they sought to recover, *inter alia*, lost profits resulting from the fall in sales of their units caused by the non-conformity of the compressors supplied by the defendants. The entitlement of the claimants to recover damages turned on the proper interpretation of Article 74 of the CISG, which states that 'damages may not exceed the loss which the party in breach fore-saw or ought to have foreseen at the time of the conclusion of the contract'. The court understood this as a reference to the 'familiar principle of foreseeability established in *Hadley v Baxendale*'.[43] The latter case is one of the leading English cases on remoteness of damage,[44] and it is a case which has crossed the Atlantic remarkably well.[45] Here, we can see an example of a court instinctively reaching for an analogy from its own jurisdiction in order to give a meaning to a phrase found within the CISG. There was no attempt to investigate the meaning of Article 74 by reference to the *travaux preparatoires* nor, apparently, to refer to case law decided under the Convention. Instead, the court equated the interpretation of 'foresaw or ought to have foreseen at the time of the conclusion of the contract'

---

[42] 71 F 3d 1024 (US Ct of Apps (2nd Cir) 1995).   [43] Ibid 1029.
[44] *Hadley v Baxendale* (1854) 9 Exch 341, 156 ER 145.
[45] See, for example: Melvin A Eisenberg, 'The Principle of *Hadley v Baxendale*' (1992) 80 Cal L Rev 563.

with the meaning given to that phrase in *Hadley v Baxendale*. On the facts of *Delchi*, the homeward-bound tendency in the interpretative process probably did little by way of harm. This is so for two reasons. The first is that the rule in Article 74 is, in all probability, a reflection of a rule which, if not identical with the rule in *Hadley v Baxendale*, is at least crafted in very similar terms. Second, the court in *Delchi* was not in fact unaware of Article 7. After referring to Article 7, Winter CJ continued as follows:

> Because there is virtually no caselaw under the Convention, we look to its language and to 'the general principles' upon which it is based. See CISG Art 7(2). The Convention directs that its interpretation be informed by its 'international character and . . . the need to promote uniformity in its application and the observance of good faith in international trade.'[46]

7.41 But it did not take Winter CJ long to drop from the international realm back down to the more familiar terrain of domestic law. The next sentence in his judgment states that 'caselaw interpreting analogous provisions of Article 2 of the Uniform Commercial Code ('UCC'), may also inform a court where the language of the relevant CISG provisions tracks that of the UCC'.[47] The readiness of courts to interpret the Convention through the lens of domestic law concepts makes the process of achieving a uniform or harmonious outcome to the interpretation of the Convention more difficult.

7.42 Baasch Andersen continues her categorization of the case law on Article 7 as follows:

> (iii) *domestic influence on uniform law* is felt throughout many of the problems of uniformity, including the instances of vague terms and the interpretation of the more flexible provisions. One of the best examples of this is found in Article 39(1) concerning the timeliness of a notice of non-conformity from a buyer to a seller in cases where the buyer wishes to exercise any rights under the convention. Such a notice must be given within '*reasonable time*', and what is that? In available case law this time-period has varied from several days to over a month, and there is evidence that there is a tendency for the buyer-friendly French courts to allow longer time-frames, whereas German courts, which I think I can safely call seller-friendly, lean towards much briefer timeframes. There is a rising trend for standardising the way the timeframe is measured by using a 'grosszügige Monat' as a vantage point to which accepted criteria for setting a time frame are applied, but to date this has only been applied in three member States.
>
> (iv) The last example of a problem category regarding uniformity that I share with you today is that of *Gap-filling* and *Article 7*. According to Article 7, gaps in CISG provisions which are within the sphere of the convention are to be resolved either via otherwise applicable law or general principles. On top of these options, some courts have referred to standard gap-fillers (such as the UNIDROIT principles) in lieu of CISG solutions. An example of a provision with such a gap is the question of rate of interest in Article 78. Some courts apply the principle of full compensation found throughout the convention as a principle to award compensatory interest at the cost of not having the money, others

---

[46] *Delchi Carrier SpA v Rotorex Corp* (n 42) 1027–8.   [47] Ibid.

apply the otherwise applicable law (using private international law) in determining the rate, and then there is a worrying trend to apply UNIDROIT principle 7.4.9 as a standard gap-filler to the question, regardless of whether the parties have agreed to apply them in part or in whole or otherwise have referred to general principles of international law. This question of interest rate, which is relevant for almost every CISG case lodged, is a central issue which must in my mind find some standardised solution in the interest of predictability; it is difficult to point to any nationalised trends which may promote forum shopping, but there are fundamental differences, and the issue is certainly a problem of uniformity.

We shall return to the question of the rate at which interest is to be paid at a later **7.43** point in this chapter.[48] The extracts from the article by Baasch Andersen serve to demonstrate the difficulties inherent in the adoption of a uniform approach to the interpretation of the CISG. But the courts and arbitrators are not left without resources in the pursuit of a uniform interpretation.

Access to case law and commentaries on the CISG

Two important steps have been taken. The first is the provision of information. **7.44** Databases now exist which contain the text of many court decisions and arbitral awards relating to the Convention. The most important databases are CLOUT[49] and Unilex.[50] Other good websites exist.[51] A court or an arbitration tribunal that wishes to discover the interpretation that has previously been placed upon a provision of the Convention can now take steps in order to do so. The weight to be given to these precedents is not an entirely straightforward matter.[52] In the first place, the decision may be in a language which is either unknown or (worse) partially known to the court or arbitral tribunal which is called upon to consider the decision.[53] The second point concerns the weight to be given to a decision of a foreign court. A court or arbitrator is not bound to follow previous decisions. It should have 'regard' to them, but it is not bound by them. A lawyer who works within one legal system quickly learns which court decisions and which judgments carry the most weight. But this information is unlikely to be known in the case of a foreign judgment. What weight can a court in one jurisdiction be expected to give to a judgment in another jurisdiction when it is unsure of the quality of the decision making in that particular jurisdiction? Perhaps the best solution is to conclude that 'foreign case law should be used as a source from which to draw either arguments or counter-arguments'.[54] It follows from this that

---

[48] See below paras 7.88–7.96.   [49] See: <http://www.uncitral.org/english/clout/>.

[50] See: <http://www.unilex.info/dynasite>.

[51] See, for example: PACE <http//:www.cisg.law.pace.edu> and University of Freiburg <http://www.cisg-online.ch>.

[52] See, for example: Ferrari 'CISG Case Law: a new challenge for interpreters' (n 41).

[53] Although from the point of view of an English speaker, the availability of translations in English has considerably reduced this problem.

[54] Ferrari 'CISG Case Law: a new challenge for interpreters' (n 41) 259.

'an arbitral award could have more influence on a specific solution than a decision of a supreme court of a country whose judges are not accustomed to dealing with international issues in general, and the CISG in particular'.[55] This view seems clearly preferable to an attempt to create some kind of 'supranational *stare decisis*'.[56]

7.45 The second step relates to the existence of academic commentaries on the Convention.[57] These commentaries may help to achieve a more harmonious interpretation of the Convention. A further step has been taken with the formation of a private body, the International Sales Convention Advisory Council ('CISG-AC'). It consists of a panel of experts whose declared function is to support the understanding of the CISG and to assist in the promotion of its uniform interpretation. It will do so through, *inter alia*, the preparation of opinions on issues which have been the subject of divergent interpretations in national courts and arbitral tribunals. As at the end of 2006, the CISG-AC had issued six opinions dealing with electronic commerce, notice of lack of conformity, parol evidence, a number of issues relating to the proper interpretation of Article 3, the buyer's right to avoid the contract in case of non-conforming goods or documents and the calculation of damages under Article 74.[58] One difficulty is that these opinions and commentaries lack official status. However, in the long run, they may help to iron out inconsistencies in the interpretation of the Convention.

The problem of good faith

7.46 The second problem with Article 7 relates to the role of good faith. This is a vexed issue which has divided civil law and common law jurisdictions. Article 7(1) provides that in the interpretation of the Convention regard is to be had to '. . . the observance of good faith in international trade'. The text is the result of a compromise between those who wished to see good faith as a positive obligation directed to the parties' behaviour in the formation and performance of the contract (as is found in many civil law countries) and those who thought that there should be no such general duty on the ground that it would lead to great uncertainty in determining the rights and obligations of the contracting parties (an approach associated with common lawyers in general and English lawyers in particular). The outcome of the negotiations between the different parties in Vienna is a provision

---

[55] Ibid.

[56] A view which has some support, see: Larry A DiMatteo, 'An International Contract Law Formula: the informality of international business transactions plus the internationalization of contract law equals unexpected contractual liability' 23 Syracuse J Intl L & Com 67 (1997).

[57] See, for example: Schlechtriem and Schwenzer (n 15); John Honnold, *Uniform Law for International Sales under the 1980 United Nations Convention* (3rd edn, Kluwer, Deventer, 1999); Cesare M Bianca and Michael J Bonell (eds), *Commentary on the International Sales Law* (Giuffrè, Milan, 1987).

[58] These opinions are available on the PACE web-site, on which see n 51 above.

which has since given rise to even greater debate than the extensive debate which took place during the drafting of the Article.

Three views on good faith

Traditionally, three different views on the role of 'good faith' in Article 7 can be located in the literature and the case law.[59] **7.47**

First view: no positive duty

The first view is that the Convention does not impose a positive duty of good faith on the parties to an international sales contract. Rather, good faith is a criterion that is to be applied by judges and arbitrators only in the interpretation of the Convention so as to reduce, if not avoid, the possibility of interpreting the Convention in such a way as to produce results which are perceived to be inequitable or unfair. This view is based upon a literal reading of the provision. Thus Professor Allan Farnsworth speaks of 'seemingly harmless words'[60] with respect to the use of 'good faith' in Article 7. His view, as one of the delegates who opposed any reference to good faith, is that the provision does not settle the question of whether a duty of good faith exists in an international sales transaction. This means that, unless a duty of good faith can be extracted from the general principles on which the Convention is based (which he contends it cannot), the Convention itself does not impose a duty of good faith directly on to the parties. To let a general principle of good faith in by the back door, Farnsworth contends, would be 'a perversion of the compromise'[61] achieved by the delegates in Vienna. **7.48**

Professor John Honnold agrees, yet his view is less restrictive, as can be seen from the following passage: **7.49**

> [T]he Convention rejects 'good faith' as a general requirement and uses 'good faith' solely as a principle for interpreting the provisions of the Convention. What content

---

[59] Disa Sim ('The Scope and Application of Good Faith in the Vienna Convention on Contracts for the International Sale of Goods' <http://www.cisg.law.pace.edu/cisg/biblio/sim1.html>) has put forward a more sophisticated analysis in which she recognizes six different views on the role of good faith in the Convention; these are (i) 'an obligation of good faith established by the practice of parties or by international trade usage'; (ii) 'the doctrine of good faith as an interpretative guide'; (iii) 'the doctrine of good faith as a prerequisite to the exercise of rights and remedies provided in the Convention'; (iv) 'the doctrine of good faith as a substantive principle in the resolution of matters not expressly governed by the Convention'; (v) 'the doctrine of good faith as a source of rights and obligations which may contradict or extend those in the Convention'; and (vi) 'the doctrine of good faith merely serves as an interpretative guide. In cases not expressly governed by the Convention, general principles may be derived which are, at best, particular manifestations of good faith; a general doctrine of good faith, however, does not exist to serve as a fount of additional rights and obligations.'

[60] E Allan Farnsworth, 'The Convention of the International Sale of Goods from the Perspective of the Common Law Countries' in Franco Ferrari (ed), *La vendita internazionale: applicabilità ed applicazioni della Convenzione di Vienna del 1980* (Guiffrè, Milan, 1981) 18.

[61] E Allan Farnsworth, 'Duties of Good Faith and Fair Dealing under the UNIDROIT Principles, Relevant International Conventions and National Laws' 3 Tul J Intl & Comp L 47, 56 (1995).

should be given to 'good faith' as an aid to interpretation? The Convention's goal 'to promote uniformity' should bar the use of purely local definitions and concepts in construing the international text. But this objection does not apply to 'good faith' principles that reflect a consensus—a 'common core' of meaning—in domestic law . . . '[G]ood faith' probably would be promoted by a liberal application of Articles like 19(2) and 21(2), which require a party to inform another who is known to be subject to a misapprehension. One who demands performance within an additional period (Arts. 47 & 63) may not, in good faith, refuse to accept the performance that he requested. Delay in compelling specific performance or avoiding a contract after a market change or construing ambiguous acts as acceptance—situations that could permit a party to speculate at another's expense—may well be inconsistent with the Convention's provisions governing these remedies when they are construed in the light of the principle of good faith.[62]

7.50 The claim that good faith is simply a criterion to be applied by judges and arbitrators in the interpretation of the Convention gains support from the fact that the good faith obligation is located in an article the subject matter of which is the interpretation of the Convention. It was applied in the case of *W v R*[63] in an ICC Arbitration. There, a German manufacturer of industrial equipment had concluded an exclusive distribution agreement with a Spanish distributor. The parties made several individual sales contracts subsequent to that agreement. Four years after the conclusion of the initial distribution agreement, the German seller informed the Spanish buyer that, as a result of insufficient sales, it wished to sell its products through another distributor with whose parent it had recently merged. The Spanish buyer subsequently refused to pay for certain deliveries and so the sellers brought an action in respect of the unpaid invoices. The buyer counterclaimed for damages on the basis of an alleged breach by the sellers of the exclusive distributorship agreement, the delivery of allegedly non-conforming goods and an alleged failure to deliver spare parts. The sole arbitrator held that the CISG was applicable to the individual sales contracts concluded on the basis of the distribution agreement. The arbitrator noted that in German law the source of the seller's collateral obligation to have replacement parts ready for delivery, even in the absence of a special agreement between the parties, could be found in the principle of good faith in Article 242 of the BGB but concluded that no such collateral obligation could be derived from Article 7. Thus he stated that 'since the provisions of Art 7(1) CISG concern only the interpretation of the Convention, no collateral obligation may be derived from the "promotion of good faith"'. However, it did not follow from this that there was no obligation on the seller to provide replacement parts. The arbitrator found the existence of such an obligation by a more circuitous route. He found that prompt delivery of spare parts had become 'normal practice' between the parties under Article 9(1) of the CISG and, further,

---

[62] Honnold (n 57) 94–5.
[63] ICC Arbitration Case No 8611/1997. A case abstract can be found at UNILEX, D.1997–3.

that Article 33(c) read in conjunction with Article 7(2) of the CISG obliged the German manufacturer to deliver subsequent replacement parts 'within a reasonable time after receiving the buyer's order'. In this way, the arbitrator was able to reach a conclusion similar to, but not identical with, the conclusion which would have been reached by a direct application of the good faith principle to the parties.

Second view: Article 7(1) imposes positive duty of good faith

A second view is that Article 7(1) does impose a duty of good faith on the parties **7.51** to the contract. In favour of this view is the proposition that it is not possible to draw a clear line of distinction between a good faith duty that is directed to the interpretation of the Convention and a duty that is directed to the interpretation and enforcement of the contract of sale itself. Interpretation does not exist in the abstract; it inevitably impacts on the rights and duties of the parties that are the subject of the interpretative exercise. Professor Joachim Bonell explains the position in the following passage:

Michael J Bonell, 'Interpretation of Convention' in Cesare M Bianca and Michael J Bonell (eds), *Commentary on the International Sales Law* **(Giuffrè, Milano, 1987) 84–5**

[T]here are those who insist on the literal meaning of the provision and conclude that the principle of good faith is nothing more than an additional criterion to be used by judges and arbitrators in the interpretation of the Convention . . . Others, moving from a broader interpretation of the reference to good faith as contained in Article 7(1), point out that 'the need to promote . . . the observance of good faith in international trade' is also necessarily directed to the parties to each individual contract of sale . . .

Of the two opinions the latter is preferable. Indeed, even as a simple aid to the interpretation of the Convention's specific provisions the principle of good faith may have some impact on the behaviour of the parties. It has been rightly observed [see Honnold above] that, for instance, a party who demands performance within an additional period according to Articles 47 or 63 may not, in good faith, refuse to accept the performance that he requested. Similarly, compelling specific performance or avoiding a contract after a market change that permits a party to speculate at the other's expense, may well be inconsistent with the Convention's provisions governing these remedies, when they are construed in the light of good faith. Other examples of cases where in particular circumstances a party is prevented from invoking rights and remedies normally granted to him under the Convention could be added. Even contractual agreements or usages may be disregarded if their application in accordance with Articles 6 and 9 of the Convention would in the specific case appear to be contrary to good faith . . .

A similar example is provided by Eörsi in the following passage: **7.52**

Gyula Eörsi, 'General Provisions' in Nina M Galston and Hans Smit (eds), *International Sales: the UN Convention on Contracts for the International Sale of Goods* **(Matthew Bender, New York, 1984) [2.03]**

Under Article 24, a declaration of acceptance 'reaches' the addressee when 'it is . . . delivered . . . to his place of business or mailing address . . .' If a party knows that the other party who has a place of business is away from his home for a considerable period of time, and he nevertheless sends the declaration to the mailing address, he may violate the requirement of good faith. Again, a party sends declarations regularly to place of business 'A' but on one occasion he directs the declaration to place of business 'B' intending that it should reach the other party late; the principle of good faith is again violated and the court may hold that the proper place of business was 'A'. Thus, interpretation of the Convention may indeed lead to application of the good faith clause. It might be argued that in such cases it was not the Convention which was interpreted but the contract. In my humble opinion, however, interpretation of the two cannot be separated since the Convention is necessarily interpreted by the parties also; after all, the Convention constitutes the law of the parties insofar as they do not make use of Article 6 on freedom of contract.

7.53 The difficulty with this argument is the obvious one, namely that it appears to undermine the compromise supposedly created by Article 7. The suggestion that the parties are interpreters of the Convention also gives rise to potential difficulties. If Article 7 is indeed directed to the parties, it would appear that they are permitted to exclude its application by means of Article 6, as Eörsi suggests. Such a conclusion appears distinctly odd given that one would ordinarily expect a good faith duty not to be capable of exclusion by the parties.[64]

7.54 Examples can be found of cases in which courts have apparently been willing to impose a good faith duty directly on the parties. A possible example is a decision of the *Oberlandesgericht München* (Munich Court of Appeal) in 1995.[65] A buyer claimed to be entitled to terminate a contract for the sale of eleven BMW cars on the ground of non-delivery of the cars. However, the buyer waited two and a half years before seeking to exercise the right to declare the contract avoided and the court held that, in these circumstances, it was not entitled to do so. The court stated that 'in the light of such situation, it would be against the principles of good faith if the [buyer] were entitled to claim any rights with regard to the non-performance of the sales contract'. It is dangerous to build a theory on the foundation of this case given the brevity of the reasoning of the court. It has, however, been argued that the decision can be explained on the ground that the court interpreted Articles 26 (declaration of avoidance) and 49 (avoidance within a reasonable time) in the light of Article 7(1) to promote good faith in international trade.[66] Sim[67] explains the case on the basis that 'it must have been predicated on an unspoken assumption that all parties had to observe good faith before they could invoke the rights and remedies of the Convention' and that this 'amounts to the imposition of substantive obligations of good faith on the party and contradicts the express wording of Article 7(1)'.

---

[64] UNIDROIT Principles Art 1.7(2); PECL Art 1.201(2).
[65] Oberlandesgericht München, No 7 U 1720/94 (8 February 1995), case law on UNCITRAL texts (CLOUT) abstract no 133.
[66] Troy Keily, 'Good Faith and the Vienna Convention on Contracts for the International Sale of Goods (CISG)' (1999) 3 Vindobona J Intl L & Arb 15, 18.   [67] Sim (n 59).

Third view: good faith as a general principle

A third view is that Article 7(1) does not impose a duty of good faith on the parties, **7.55** but that this duty is one of the 'general principles' on which the Convention is based. Article 7(2) provides that, where the Convention does not expressly settle a matter which it governs, such matters are to be decided in conformity with 'the general principles on which [the Convention] is based or, in the absence of such principles, in conformity with the law applicable by virtue of the rules of private international law'. Thus, if it can be established that 'good faith' is a general principle upon which the Convention is based, such a duty will be imposed on the parties by Article 7(2), rather than 7(1). This is the approach followed by Professors Schlechtriem and Kastely in the following two extracts:

Peter Schlechtriem, *Uniform Sales Law*. The UN Convention on Contracts for the International Sale of Goods (Manz, Vienna, 1986) 39

The reference to the observance 'of good faith in international trade' in Article 7(1) indicates one of the general principles that must be regarded in interpreting and extending the uniform law. Whether or not effective international standards of good faith can actually be determined must be left to studies in comparative law. The principle has affected the formulation of a number of provisions in CISG and the leading commentary on CISG cites Articles 21(2) and 19(2) as likely 'candidates' for an interpretation based on the principles of good faith.

There is naturally some cause for uncertainty when the principle of good faith, as embodied in the Convention, concerns only the interpretation of the Convention and not the conduct of the parties in the formation and performance of the contract or the interpretation of their intentions . . . [C]oncerns . . . that such broadly formulated principles could be interpreted and applied in different ways, that domestic views about their content varied, and that sanctions were lacking, finally led to the withdrawal of [the proposal that the principle should be generalised to include the conduct of the parties]. The [civilian] jurist may regret this rejection of a 'good faith rule' . . . However, the function of such a general clause can probably be fulfilled by the rule that the parties must conduct themselves according to the standard of the 'reasonable person' which is expressly described in a number of provisions and, therefore, according to Article 7(2), must be regarded as a general principle of the Convention.

Amy H Kastely, 'Unification and Community: a rhetorical analysis of the united nations sales convention' 8 Northwestern J Intl L & Bus 574, 596–7 (1987–8) [67a]

The notion of good faith in international trade is explicitly stated as a principle of the Convention in Article 7. In addition, this value is implied throughout the Convention's detailed provisions. It is reflected in the commitment to honest communication between the parties and in provisions requiring the parties to act with some concern for each other's interests. The best examples of this are the provisions on preservation of goods and the mitigation of damages [Articles 85–88 of the Convention]. If the buyer has wrongfully failed to take delivery or the seller has made a defective delivery, the party in possession of the goods is obligated to preserve them for the benefit of the other. This duty may include arranging

---

[67a] Reprinted by special permission of Northwestern University School of Law, Northwestern Journal of International Law and Business.

for storage or resale of the goods. If the person in possession does resell the goods, he or she must account to the other party for the proceeds. Similarly, Article 77 provides that a party injured by the other's breach must take reasonable steps to mitigate his or her damages.

The value of good faith concern for the other party is also seen in provisions regarding errors in transmission, performance of the contract, and the exercise of rights in the event of breach. The recipient of an erroneously transmitted acceptance, notice of defect, or other such communication is obligated either to notify the other side of the error or to treat it as effective [Articles 21(2), 27]. The recipients in these cases must consider the interests and expectations of the other party; in most cases the sender will not know of the error in transmission, and the recipient must take account of this. Similarly, the seller must consider the interests of the buyer when arranging for carriage and insurance [Article 32] or when specifying the goods to be sold [Article 65].

When there has been some defect in the goods delivered or in documents relating to the goods, the seller normally has a right to cure the defect; yet in exercising this right, the seller must consider any inconvenience or extra expense to the buyer [Articles 34, 37, 48]. In like fashion, a buyer must consider the interests of the seller by promptly inspecting the goods and giving notice of any defect [Articles 38, 39, 40, 44]. The buyer normally has a right to require the repair of any defect, yet in exercising this right, the buyer must consider whether this would entail excessive difficulty or expense for the seller [Article 46(3)].

7.56   Whether such a general principle can be extracted from the various other provisions of the Convention depends very much on how broadly the concept of good faith is to be understood. For example, it has been alleged that manifestations of the principle of good faith are to be found in Articles 16(2)(b), 21(2), 29(2), 37, 40, 46, 47(2), 64(2), 82 and 85–88.[68] The proposition that good faith is a general principle which underpins the Convention encounters a number of difficulties, of which Sim points out three.[69] The first is that 'there is no coherent content to the concept of good faith in the Convention'. In particular, the fact that there is an express reference to good faith in Article 7(1) cannot, of itself, turn good faith into a principle which underpins the CISG. Further, the conception of good faith alleged to underpin the various cited articles is so broad as to be practically useless. As Sim points out, 'commentators tend to latch onto whatever promotes justice or fairness in the Convention' in order to substantiate their claim that the foundation of the article is the promotion of good faith. It should not occasion surprise that many articles of the CISG are consistent with ideas of fairness, justice and reasonableness. Most if not all rules of law should be consistent with those ideas. The fact that individual articles are consistent with good faith does not of itself justify the creation of a general duty of good faith which transcends the scope of the individual articles.

7.57   Second, Sim points out that the 'imposition of substantive obligations of good faith on contracting parties would undermine the objective of the CISG to promote certainty and predictability in international trade.' The recognition of a broad

---

[68] See, for example: Ferrari, Flechtner and Brand (n 37) 537.   [69] Sim (n 59).

notion of good faith is not conducive to the certainty and predictability which the CISG was intended to introduce. Third, Sim argues that reliance on Article 7(2) in order to impose a substantive obligation of good faith and fair dealing on the parties would undermine the compromise that was achieved at Vienna because it would, in effect, impose a duty of good faith on the parties by the back door.

The view that is most consistent with the drafting history of the CISG is that good **7.58** faith is a doctrine which is to be taken into account in the interpretation of the CISG. This conclusion leaves us with two problems. First, what conception of good faith is to be found in Article 7(1)? Second, what is meant by 'interpretation'? Sim argues that the word 'interpretation' should be given its natural and ordinary meaning, namely 'to explain or tell the meaning of'. Thus 'regard should be had to the need to promote the observance of good faith in international trade in order to resolve cases of textual ambiguity'. On this view there is a difference between interpretation and gap-filling or 'implying qualifications into the CISG which the instrument has not expressly provided for'. Good faith, on this view, should be confined to the former and should not become a gap-filler. More difficult is the meaning of 'good faith'. We have already noted, in relation to Article 7(2), the claim that there is no coherent content to the concept of good faith in the CISG. Sim returns to this claim in her discussion of the role of good faith as an interpretative tool. She states:

> Ironically, perhaps, we are thus forced to fall back on the very same conception of good faith that we used for the purposes of Article 7(2). . . . [T]he conclusion there was that the CISG does not embody a general principle of good faith, at least not in a form that it is capable of independently generating concrete rights and obligations. It was argued, however, that the Convention does contain several principles that can be said to be particular manifestations of a broad idea of good faith. Examples of such principles were the principles of reasonableness, estoppel and favor contractus.

> It is submitted that this conception of good faith can also be utilised for the purposes of Article 7(1). The term 'good faith' in Article 7(1) should not be read to refer to some general doctrine of good faith, for no coherent one can be formulated. Instead, it should be read as a compendious term referring to the collection of more specific good faith principles in the Convention. Thus, when a question of interpretation arises, the tribunal should first decide which of these principles are implicated and resolve the problem in a way that upholds that principle. Thus, the definition of 'good faith' for the purposes of Article 7(1) is one that is derived from the CISG itself. It is true that there are a number of other good faith definitions that can be externally derived, either from national jurisprudence or academic literature on the subject. It is submitted, however, that these definitions are not as strong as one that is internally derived from the CISG. This is because there is no guarantee that any of these 'external' definitions will meet with the approval of those countries that have adopted (or will adopt) the Convention. At a minimum, however, they must accept those principles embodying the idea of good faith because they are contained in the Convention itself.

> The upshot of all this is that the one reference that the CISG does make to the concept of good faith should not be understood as sanctioning the adoption of a legal doctrine of good faith, even if it is only for interpretative purposes.

The following example will illustrate how the above points would apply. A provision that has taken on an especially ambiguous meaning in this technological age is Article 18(2) which provides: 'An acceptance of an offer becomes effective at the moment the indication of assent *reaches* the offeror [emphasis added].'

In so far as an acceptance by electronic mail is concerned, an acceptance may be deemed to have 'reached' the offeror at any one of three points—when it is stored in the computer, when it is read or when it is reproduced in a tangible form. The matter is further complicated if the offeror fails to check his electronic mail diligently and only discovers the message after the date for acceptance has passed or intentionally waits until the time has passed for acceptance before reading his e-mail.

The concept of good faith as explained above can be used here to identify the appropriate definition of 'reaches'. The specific good faith principle that is implicated here is the one that requires the observance of reasonable behaviour in the absence of any other specific regulation. The message should thus not be deemed to have 'reached' the offeror when the message first arrives and is stored on the computer's hard disk. It would be unreasonable for the offeree to expect that that the offeror has knowledge of the acceptance even before he has had a chance to read it. It is only fair that the offeror should be given a reasonable opportunity to read the message. Thus, the acceptance should be considered to have 'reached' the offeror only after he has had a reasonable opportunity to read the message. What qualifies as a 'reasonable opportunity' would depend on factors such as the offeror's known access to an e-mail server and whether the offeree sent the message outside office hours. It would constitute bad faith, however, for the offeror to insist that an acceptance 'reaches' him only after he has printed it because he is, by then, already cognisant of the acceptance. If it were otherwise, the offeror would be free to act in bad faith and print the message only after the time for acceptance has passed, thus thwarting the reasonable expectations of the offeree.

7.59 Later on, Sim substantiates her view and her rejection of the broad concept of good faith on the following grounds:

> As long as the reference to good faith in the Convention remains, the problem of uncertainty and vagueness can never be completely eliminated. The only thing we can do is to minimise the problem. Restricting the definition of 'good faith' in Article 7(1) to encompass only those principles in the CISG that constrain the behaviour of contracting parties in order to promote justice, fairness and ethical behaviour achieves this in three ways.

> Firstly, it severely circumscribes the scope of decision-makers' discretion by limiting the menu of options they can choose from. Instead of giving them the option to resort to a free-ranging principle of good faith, decision-makers now are limited to those general principles of the CISG that manifest this idea of good faith. This is far better than leaving a loose cannon in their hands. In order to ensure that this version of good faith actually does operate as a significant constraint, decision-makers should be expected to demonstrate that the principle that they seek to use is indeed one on which the CISG is based and to articulate precisely how that principle promotes justice and fairness, or moderates unethical behaviour.

> Secondly, even if decision-makers were to use a general principle that does not promote the cause of good faith to resolve an issue of interpretation, the damage done is not

acute. This is because the role of good faith is restricted to issues of textual interpretation only. Thus its impact cannot be as severe as a substantive, wide-ranging principle.

Thirdly, even if the principle used does not embody some specific idea of good faith, we can at least seek solace from the fact that the errant decision-maker must be promoting some other value of the Convention since he is employing one of the principles on which the CISG is based.

As we have noted, Article 7(2) also directs courts and arbitrators to have regard to **7.60** 'the general principles' on which the Convention is based. It does so only where the matter is 'governed by' the Convention but the Convention does not expressly answer the problem that has arisen on the facts of the case. In such a case the court or arbitrator is to resolve the problem by reference to the general principles on which the Convention is based and only to revert to national law as a last resort. A court or tribunal must therefore first determine whether the matter for evaluation is governed by the Convention. If so, it then needs to examine whether there is a gap in the Convention on the relevant point. If there is a gap, it first needs to look at the general principles upon which the Convention is based in order to fill that gap. In the following extract, Dr Gebauer explains this process:

Martin Gebauer, 'Uniform Law, General Principles and Autonomous Interpretation' (2000) V Unif L Rev 683, 696–7

. . . a distinction must be drawn between matters governed by the Convention and matters not so governed, eg the validity of the sales contract or the transfer of property. Matters not governed by CISG because they do not fall within the scope of Article 4 [dealing with matters of the validity of the sales contract and the transfer of property] or because they fall under the exception in Article 5 [which provides that the Convention does not apply to the liability of the seller for death or personal injury caused by the goods to any person], cannot constitute a gap in the Convention. They are governed by domestic law to be determined by the private international law rules of the forum.

For there to be a gap in CISG requires the matter to be in general governed by the Convention. How can such a gap be filled? . . . the Convention's approach is a mixed one, a two-step combination of application of the Convention's general principles and, if such principles cannot be found or developed, application of domestic law, to be determined by the private international law rules of the forum. The old *Uniform Law on the International Sale of Goods (ULIS)*, predecessor of CISG, did not provide for subsidiary recourse to private international law, relying on the general principles in all cases. The mixed approach however presents a realistic view and is anyway better than applying the *lex fori* dressed up as 'general principles'. As far as the first step is concerned, ie recourse to the general principles on which the Convention is based, these are primarily . . . *internal* principles . . . and, according to some authors, *externally* codified principles such as the UNIDROIT Principles as well. Autonomous gap-filling through recourse to the Convention's general principles can be based on the same arguments as those connected with autonomous interpretation in general, ie mainly on systematic and teleological arguments.

Two comments may be made at this point. First, the distinction between matters **7.61** governed by the Convention and those not so governed is not as straightforward as it might at first sight appear. An example, to which we shall return, relates to the rate at which interest is payable in the event that a party fails to pay 'the price or any other sum that is in arrears'. Article 78 of the CISG provides that the other contracting party is entitled to recover interest in such circumstances but it is silent on matters such as the rate at which interest is payable. Is the rate at which interest is payable a matter that is 'governed' by the Convention or does the silence of Article 78 indicate that it is a matter which falls outside its scope? As we shall see,[70] this is a question to which courts and arbitral tribunals have given divergent answers. Other examples can be given of the same problem. Are matters such as pre-contractual liability, set-off and the location of the burden of proof 'governed' by the Convention?

7.62   The second point relates to the distinction between principles which are 'internal' to the Convention and principles which are 'external' to it. An internal general principle is a principle which underpins the Convention itself, whereas an external general principle is one which is derived from outside of the Convention. In the case of 'internal' principles, the difficulty lies in locating the existence of these principles, whereas in the case of 'external' principles, the difficulty is a different one, namely the justification for resorting to principles which are not to be found in the Convention itself. The first of these issues has been considered in the following extract:

Ulrich Magnus, 'General Principles under the UN Sales Law' 3 Intl Trade & Bus L Ann (1997) 33, 40

General principles can regularly be derived from the CISG—and other Uniform Law Conventions—in four ways: First, some provisions explicitly claim their applicability to the entire Convention, for example in the CISG Art 6 (principle of party autonomy), Art 7(1) (principle of good faith) or Art 11 (principle of lack of form requirements). Their character as a general provision results both from their wording and their position in the Convention's system. In the CISG, they are incorporated in the part 'General Provisions'. Strictly speaking, they might not be included in the general principles contemplated by Art 7(2) CISG, since they expressly indicate their general applicability and thus do not constitute principles 'hidden in the law [. . .] without having been directly expressed'. However, due to their fundamental importance, which occasionally goes beyond their wording, it appears justified to regard them as part of the Convention's general principles.

Further, a separate comprehensive thought can be derived from several provisions. For example, Art 67(2) and 69(2) CISG provide that passing of risk requires identification of the goods to the respective contract. This rule can be extended to those cases in which the question—as in Art 68—is not expressly regulated.

In addition, single provisions might include legal thoughts which are subject to generalization and are to be applied in similar situations. Art 20(2) CISG can serve as an example.

---

[70] See further paras 7.92–7.96.

According to this provision, holidays generally do not extend the period for making a declaration, except if the respective notice could not be delivered due to the holiday. This thought can be generalized to the effect that holidays are included in all time limits (eg, also for delivery), except if the respective action (eg, delivery) could not have been taken due to the holiday. In this case the time limit is extended accordingly.

Finally, the overall context can show that a certain basic rule is implicitly assumed. An example in the CISG is the rule 'pacta sunt servanda'. The sentence is not expressed anywhere, but apparently constitutes the basis for the exemption provision of Art 79 which determines the cases in which an obligor is discharged from his obligation.

The justification for resort to principles 'external' to the Convention is perhaps more difficult to find and has been discussed in the following terms: **7.63**

Martin Gebauer, 'Uniform Law, General Principles and Autonomous Interpretation'
(2000) V Unif L Rev 683, 695

External principles can also be taken from other uniform law instruments in order to interpret or supplement a Convention's rule. For example, some authors hold the UNIDROIT Principles to be a means of interpreting and supplementing CISG. Such recourse to the external codified rules of another uniform law instrument is a convincing choice where two Conventions can form a coherent body of rules, using the same concepts for similar purposes. In interpreting the Rome Convention, for example, regard should be had to parallel concepts of the Brussels Convention and their interpretation by the European Court of Justice. However, caution is indicated when attempting to embody external concepts, since they should generally be understood in their own context. Also, at times identical words used in a neighbouring Convention turn out to be *faux amis*, conflicting with the aims and fundamental principles of a Convention if transferred to a different context. Many Conventions can be regarded as small legal systems, and to rely on external uniform solutions may help avoid recourse to a national law. However, in case of a conflict between external and internal principles, the latter are to be preferred because they can be based on the system and aims of the uniform law in question.

As Gebauer notes, this debate has assumed primary significance in relation to the role of the UNIDROIT Principles of International Commercial Contracts[71] in the interpretation and supplementation of the CISG. Arbitral awards can be found in which arbitrators have resorted to the UNIDROIT Principles in this way (for example, to ascertain the rate at which interest is payable when the buyer fails to pay the price at the contractual date for payment[72]). The legitimacy of this approach is open to question. The difficulty lies in providing a coherent rationale for the application of the UNIDROIT Principles in such a context. The UNIDROIT Principles were, after all, drawn up subsequent to the coming into effect of the CISG and it is not altogether easy to see the basis on which it can be said that the interpretation of one Convention can be influenced by a document drawn up at a later point in time   **7.64**

---

[71] See further ch 14.   [72] See further paras 7.95–7.96.

which does not itself have the force of law. However, the justification for resort to the UNIDROIT Principles probably lies in more pragmatic considerations:

Michael Bridge, *The International Sale of Goods Law and Practice* (OUP, Oxford, 1999) [2.39]

Shortage of time and the need for compromise meant that the CISG suffers from vagueness of expression and a number of omissions. It is here that the Unidroit Principles, assuming the legitimacy of their use, might assist tribunals to fill gaps in the CISG despite the lack of any particular or general mention of them in the text of Article 7(2). Except where they would contradict the CISG, the Unidroit Principles may stimulate the search for unstated general principles in the CISG. There is a clear need for them: the CISG can be changed only by means of a diplomatic conference. Nothing in the CISG corresponds to the continuing editorial work provided for in the American Uniform Commercial Code. The Unidroit Principles are not the product of a diplomatic conference and may be modified with relative ease in the future. Moreover, they are drafted in much the same way as the Uniform Commercial Code with hypothetical illustrations and comment attached to each Article . . . Although, if they are invoked, the Unidroit Principles cannot be allowed to contradict the CISG, the position they adopt may be influential in settling the uncertain position taken [on certain issues] in the CISG.

7.65 A court or tribunal which does not resort to the UNIDROIT Principles in this way may find itself confronted by the difficulty of finding an alternative source of legal principle which will resolve the question which confronts it. If it is not possible to resort to the UNIDROIT Principles or some similar instrument in order to locate the applicable general principle, what other option is open to the judge or arbitrator? The answer given by Article 7(2) is that the court or arbitrator must resort to the national law applicable by virtue of the rules of private international law. Thus cases can be found in which national courts and arbitrators have resorted to national law in order to determine the rate at which interest is payable in a case where the buyer fails to pay the price for the goods at the contractually agreed time. The problem with this approach is that national law tends to yield different answers and, to that extent, the quest for uniformity is undermined. Courts and arbitrators are here involved in a difficult balancing act. On the one hand, they tend to want to pursue the goal of uniformity but, on the other hand, they do not wish illegitimately to expand the sphere of application of the Convention. It would appear that courts tend to be rather more willing to resort to national law than is the case with arbitrators who seem to be more willing to find the existence of an applicable general principle on which the Convention is based. In many cases, it should be possible to find such a general principle. As Professor Michael Bridge has observed, with a 'modicum of creative energy' a court or tribunal ought not to have to resort to national law but 'should find the answer to a problem within the CISG itself.'[73] Too

---

[73] Michael Bridge, *The International Sale of Goods Law and Practice* (OUP, Oxford, 1999) [2.40].

great a willingness to resort to national law will destroy the uniformity which the Convention was intended to create.

E. Usages

The parties are bound by any usage to which they have agreed and by any practices **7.66** which they have established between themselves (Article 9(1)). This agreement need not be express; it can be implied. Article 9(2) further provides that the:

> parties are considered, unless otherwise agreed, to have impliedly made applicable to their contract or its formation a usage of which the parties knew or ought to have known and which in international trade is widely known to, and regularly observed by, parties to contracts of the type involved in the particular trade concerned.

There are important differences between Articles 9(1) and (2). In the case of **7.67** Article 9(1) the usage need not be international, nor need it be widely known and observed; it suffices that it has been agreed to or established between the parties to the particular contract of sale. Article 9(2), by contrast, is broader in its scope because it can incorporate well-known and regularly observed usages, even if they have not been agreed to or established between the particular parties to the contract. Incoterms can be incorporated into a contract of sale via Article 9. As has been noted, the Incoterms do not themselves have the force of law; they must be incorporated into the contract.[74] The most obvious method of incorporation is as usage and a number of cases support the implication of Incoterms in this way.[75]

Usages that are binding on the parties by virtue of Article 9 take priority over any **7.68** conflicting articles in the CISG and, in this sense, can be said to be hierarchically superior to the provisions of the CISG. The fact that it is possible to contract out of CISG in this way demonstrates that the CISG is not a mandatory convention; it gives way in the face of a contrary agreement between the parties, whether that agreement is express or implied. Article 9 has been invoked for a wide range of purposes, including the implication of a term into a contract of sale setting the rate at which interest was to be paid and even to imply a duty which performs a function which is similar to that achieved by a duty of good faith and fair dealing.[76]

One of the difficulties with Article 9 relates to the meaning to be given to the **7.69** word 'usage'. The range of views surrounding the meaning of this word has already been canvassed in some detail.[77] There are two principal views. The first

---

[74] The test applied by the courts when deciding whether or not to incorporate the Incoterms into the contract may vary as between States. In some countries, the courts may be very willing to find that the Incoterms have been incorporated into the contract, while in other cases, the courts may require more by way of evidence to establish that incorporation has taken place.

[75] See further: Ferrari, Flechtner and Brand (n 37) 563.   [76] See paras 7.47–7.59 above.

[77] See paras 1.34 and 1.60–1.65 above.

is that unwritten trade usage is a particular form of international customary law. The second is that it takes effect as an implied term of the contract. The latter is the view which, in essence, is taken in Article 9(2). The provision itself is open to criticism in so far as it fails explicitly to distinguish between usage which is observed as a matter of habit, courtesy or convenience and usage which is observed because it is believed to be legally binding. It is unlikely that Article 9(2) intended to jettison the *opinio juris* element entirely: there must be some perception of an obligation to comply with the relevant usage before the operation of Article 9 can be triggered.[78]

F. Formation

7.70 Part II of the Convention deals with the formation of a contract of sale. This part was a source of some controversy, in particular for Scandinavian countries. As a consequence, Article 92 makes it possible for a State to make a declaration that it will not be bound by Part II.[79] The framework adopted by the Convention is the offer and acceptance framework,[80] with appropriate modifications.[81] The Convention provides answers to old problems, in particular the time at which a contract is concluded when the parties make use of the post,[82] the battle of the forms[83] and the revocability of offers.[84] Some of these issues have proved to be matters of considerable debate within national legal systems. For example, in relation to acceptances sent through the post, some legal systems have adopted the rule that the acceptance is generally effective at the moment at which the acceptance is put in the post, whereas others take the view that the acceptance does not take effect until it is received. The rule adopted in the CISG is that acceptance takes place upon receipt, not posting.[85] The fact that the rule adopted in the CISG differs from that adopted by English law is unlikely to act as a barrier to ratification of the Convention (although, in the case of Scandinavian countries it was a more important obstacle). Professor Francis Reynolds has summarized Part II of the CISG in the following terms:

> I propose to spend little time on Part II, which deals with formation of contract. I suggest that it is of little importance. The problems which it attacks, those of the offer and acceptance model, are well known to common lawyers, and probably to all lawyers, from their student days. The main differences from what is understood to be the current position in English law are that an offer can by its terms be irrevocable, ie without consideration to support the promise to keep it open, or may become

---

[78] See further para 1.64 above.
[79] A list of the States that have made such a reservation can be found at UNCITRAL <http://www.uncitral.org/en-index.htm>.
[80] Arts 14–17 define and regulate offers, whilst Arts 18–22 regulate the acceptance.
[81] For example, in the case of the battle of the forms, see: Art 19.
[82] Arts 16(2), 18(2), 21(2) and 24.   [83] Art 19.   [84] Art 16.
[85] Arts 18(2) and 24.

irrevocable because the offeree has acted in reliance on it; and that acceptance of an offer becomes effective at the moment the indication of assent reaches the offeror rather than on dispatch. So long as one has rules, it need not matter much what they are: even if one disagrees with them, I doubt whether accommodation to these solutions would be difficult.[86]

This robust view may not be to everyone's taste. But there is a lot to be said for it. **7.71** In many cases lawyers simply want to know what the rules are on the formation of a contract. Once they know the rules, they can plan their affairs accordingly. However, the certainty for which lawyers yearn may not be achievable in all cases. This is apparent in areas such as the battle of the forms. If commercial parties insist on using their own standard terms and conditions which differ in various respects from the standard terms and conditions of their counter-parties, the law will inevitably find it difficult to find consensus (and the terms of that consensus) when the terms used by the parties vary in different degrees. The solution to the battle of the forms to be found in Article 19 is not without its difficulties,[87] but it is probably as good as, if not better than, solutions devised in other international instruments or in national legal systems.[88]

G. The Rights and Duties of the Parties

Part III of the Convention is, in many ways, the heart of the Convention. It con- **7.72** sists of sixty-four articles. It is divided into five chapters and these chapters are often split into sections. A State can enter a declaration that it will not be bound by Part III.[89]

General provisions

Chapter I deals with general provisions. Two issues stand out. The first is the def- **7.73** inition of fundamental breach in Article 25, an issue to which we shall shortly return. The second relates to the remedy of specific performance. Here we encounter the divide between common law and civil law jurisdictions because specific performance is traditionally a primary remedy in the latter jurisdictions, but has only a secondary

---

[86] FMB Reynolds, 'A Note of Caution' in Peter Birks (ed), *The Frontiers of Liability* (OUP, Oxford, 1994) 20.

[87] See, for example: Francis Vergne, 'The "Battle of the Forms" Under the 1980 United Convention on Contracts for the International Sale of Goods' 33 Am J Comp L 233 (1985).

[88] For attempts to resolve the problem of the battle of the forms in other international instruments, see: UNIDROIT Principles of International Commercial Contracts Art 2.1.11 and PECL Arts 2:208–9. For examples drawn from national law, see § 2–207 of the UCC and, in England, *Butler Machine Tool Co Ltd v Ex-Cell-O Corporation (England) Ltd* [1979] 1 WLR 401 (CA).

[89] Art 92. A list of the States that have made such a reservation can be found at UNCITRAL <http://www.uncitral.org/en-index.htm>.

role in the former.[90] Article 28 does not attempt to resolve this problem; rather it relegates the issue to national law by providing as follows:

> If, in accordance with the provisions of this Convention, one party is entitled to require performance of any obligation by the other party, a court is not bound to enter a judgement for specific performance unless the court would do so under its own law in respect of similar contracts of sale not governed by this Convention.[91]

7.74   The failure to prescribe a uniform solution has been criticized on the ground that it may lead to the application of the CISG in a 'highly parochial'[92] way. These fears can be over-stated in that Article 28 has in fact given rise to very little case law. The remedy of specific performance may not be particularly important in practice in sale of goods cases and in this sense it can be said that the role of the remedy is of greater academic than practical significance. Article 28 can be contrasted with the solutions devised in Article 7.2.2 of the UNIDROIT Principles of International Commercial Contracts and Article 9:102 of the Principles of European Contract Law ('PECL').[93] Both instruments provide for a general right to specific performance but then set out exceptions to the rule (for example, where performance would cause the obligor unreasonable effort or expense). In this way both sets of Principles seek to strike a balance, or effect a compromise, between common law and civil law systems. The advantage which they have over Article 28 is that the compromise which they effect is apparent on the face of the text and consistency will hopefully emerge as the provisions are, over time, subject to interpretation in courts and arbitral tribunals. Article 28, by contrast, effects what may be described as a 'hidden' compromise in so far as it requires lawyers in practice to be familiar with the domestic rules of law in the jurisdiction in which enforcement of performance is likely to be sought. However, one should not, perhaps, be unduly critical of Article 28. The advantage which the UNIDROIT Principles and the PECL enjoyed was that they were able to build on the work of the CISG and to learn from any mistakes made. It may also have been the case that it was easier to reach agreement in the Principles because of their non-binding nature. Had the Principles assumed the form of binding rules of law, common lawyers may not have been willing to assent to the primacy that these texts give (at least initially) to specific performance.

---

[90] There may also be a difference in the meaning given to the phrase 'specific performance.' Common lawyers tend to use it to describe the order given by the court that the defendant performs its primary obligations under the contract. Civilian lawyers, by contrast, use the phrase in a more expansive manner in order to encompass remedies such as repair or replacement of the goods.

[91] See further: Amy H Kastely, 'The Right to Require Performance in International Sales: Towards an International Interpretation of the Vienna Convention' 63 Wash L Rev 607 (1988) and Steven Walt, 'For Specific Performance under the United Nations Sales Convention' 26 Tex Intl LJ 211 (1991).

[92] John Fitzgerald, 'CISG, Specific Performance and the Civil Law of Louisiana and Quebec' (1997) 16 J L & Com 291, 292.   [93] See further para 14.51.

The obligations of the seller and the remedies of the buyer

Chapter II sets out the obligations of the sellers and is, in turn, divided into three **7.75** sections. The first section[94] regulates the delivery obligations of the seller (and delivery here extends to the delivery of documents). The second section[95] deals with the obligations of the seller in relation to the conformity of the goods and claims by third parties. This section has generated numerous interpretative difficulties, particularly in relation to the notification obligations of the buyer.[96]

The third section deals with the remedies for breach of contract by the seller. The **7.76** section contains within it a multiplicity of remedies, including delivery by the seller of substitute goods,[97] repair of the goods,[98] avoidance of the contract,[99] the fixture of an additional period of time of reasonable length for performance by the seller of its obligations (followed by avoidance in the case of non-compliance by the seller),[100] cure by the seller (either before or, in certain cases after, the time for performance),[101] price reduction[102] and damages.[103] Viewed from the perspective of a common lawyer, a striking feature of the remedial regime is its complexity. It provides for a broader range of remedies than that found in many common law jurisdictions. A second feature is that termination (or, in the language of the CISG, avoidance) appears to play a subsidiary role. The philosophy underpinning the Convention appears to be that the law should encourage the parties to a contract of sale to stick together and to work out their difficulties. The response should not be to encourage parties to walk away from the transaction at the first sign of difficulty, via a wide right of termination.

The obligations of the buyer and the remedies of the seller

Chapter III regulates the obligations of the buyer. The obligations of the buyer are **7.77** to pay the price[104] and to take delivery of the goods.[105] The remedies for breach of contract by the buyer[106] in many ways mirror the remedies available to the buyer in the event of a failure by the seller to perform its obligations under the contract. Thus we find that the seller may be entitled to require the buyer to pay the price, take delivery or perform its other obligations under the contract.[107] Alternatively, the seller may fix an additional period of time of reasonable length for performance

---

[94] Arts 31–34.   [95] Arts 35–44.

[96] Art 39 and, albeit to a lesser extent, Art 43. On Art 43, see generally: Schlechtriem and Schwenzer (n 15) 460–76 and 507–10.   [97] Art 46(1) and (2).

[98] Art 46(3).

[99] Art 49. The effects of avoidance are set out in Arts 81–84. Avoidance releases both parties from their obligations to perform under the contract (subject to any damages claim which may arise) but, crucially, a party who has performed his obligations under the contract is entitled to restitution from the other party.   [100] Art 47.

[101] Art 48.   [102] Art 50.   [103] Arts 45(1)(b) and 74–7.   [104] Arts 54–9.

[105] Art 60.   [106] Arts 61–5.   [107] Art 62.

by the buyer of its obligations,[108] and in default of such performance may avoid the contract[109] and/or claim damages.[110]

Fundamental breach

7.78 One issue which has produced a sharp difference of view among commentators, courts and arbitrators relates to the circumstances in which a party to a contract of sale should be entitled to avoid the contract as a result of defective performance or non-performance by the other party to the contract.[111] There is an observable difference between common law systems (in particular, English law) and civilian legal systems in relation to the importance of termination in the scheme of rights and remedies which arise in the event of defective performance or non-performance. English lawyers, particularly lawyers dealing with commodity sales, tend to perceive termination as an important remedy and contend that its availability ought not to be unduly circumscribed by the law. Civilian lawyers, by contrast, tend to view termination as a subsidiary remedy and therefore are more willing to place limits on the ability of contracting parties to avoid the contract between the parties.

7.79 This difference of view can be seen in the drafting, and the interpretation, of Article 25 of the CISG which defines the concept of 'fundamental breach'. The existence of a fundamental breach is important for a number of reasons within the CISG. The following remedies are dependent upon the occurrence of a fundamental breach: (i) the right of the buyer to demand substitute goods if the goods delivered do not conform with the contract (Article 46(2)), (ii) the right of one party to avoid the contract on the ground of non-performance by the other party (Articles 49(1)(a), 64(1)(a) and 73) and (iii) the right of the buyer to avoid the contract for partial delivery (Article 51). Fundamental breach is also relevant in relation to the transfer of risk (Article 70).[112] Fundamental breach is defined in Article 25 in the following terms:

> A breach of contract committed by one of the parties is fundamental if it results in such detriment to the other party as substantially to deprive him of what he is entitled to expect under the contract, unless the party in breach did not foresee and a reasonable person of the same kind in the same circumstances would not have foreseen such a result.

7.80 A number of points should be noted about this definition of fundamental breach.

---

[108] Art 63.   [109] Art 64.   [110] Arts 61(1)(b), 63(2) and 74–7.

[111] See, generally: CISG Advisory Opinion No 5, 'The buyer's right to avoid the contract in case of non-conforming goods or documents' <http://cisgw3.law.pace.edu/cisg/CISG-AC-op5.html>.

[112] Art 70 provides that if the seller has committed a fundamental breach of contract, Arts 67–9 (which deal with the passage of risk and are discussed at paras 7.101–7.103) do not impair the remedies available to the buyer on account of the breach.

'Breach'

The first point is that the word 'breach' is not defined in the Convention. However, **7.81**
it is clear that it encompasses not only an unexcused failure in performance (the
sense in which English law uses the word breach) but any failure to perform,
whether that failure to perform is excused or not.[113] The Convention adopts a unitary conception of breach; that is to say, 'all violations of any obligation by any
party to the contract are dealt with, in principle, on the same footing and attract
the selfsame remedies'.[114] In particular, the definition of breach encompasses failures to perform which are attributable to non-delivery as well as those that are
attributable to the delivery of non-conforming goods.

'Fundamental'

The word 'fundamental' is also important. From the perspective of a common **7.82**
lawyer, particularly the perspective of an English commercial lawyer, the definition
is a narrow one in that it appears to be an objective test which leaves it principally
to the court or arbitrator (rather than the parties[115]) to decide whether or not the
breach which has occurred is fundamental or not. When deciding whether or not
a breach is fundamental, the court or arbitral tribunal is directed to consider the
'detriment' caused to the other party. This 'detriment' will normally take the form
of economic loss but it would appear that it may in an appropriate case extend
beyond economic loss on the basis that 'detriment' is a broader concept than damage. The breach must also substantially deprive the other party to the contract of
what it was entitled to expect under the contract. The reference to the expectations
of the other party suggests that it is open to the parties to define for themselves what
is and what is not 'fundamental'. The word 'substantial' is not defined and it is left
to the courts or arbitrators to carry out the evaluative exercise of deciding whether
or not the effects of any breach are 'substantial'. The result of the breach of contract
must have been foreseeable to the party in breach or to a reasonable person in that
party's position. The burden of proving that the result is unforeseeable rests on the
party who is in breach. The time at which the foreseeability test is to be applied is
not stated in Article 25 and it has given rise to a difference of view between commentators and in the courts. Account must clearly be taken of matters that were
foreseeable at the time of entry into the contract. The controversial issue is whether
or not the court can take account of circumstances arising after the conclusion of

---

[113] The fact that the word breach is used in this wider sense becomes apparent from an examination of Art 79, on which see paras 7.97–7.100 below.

[114] See: Gerhard Lubbe, 'Fundamental Breach under the CISG: a source of fundamentally divergent results' (2004) 68 *Rabels Zeitschrift für ausländisches und internationales Privatrecht* 444.

[115] Cf CISG Advisory Opinion No 5 (n 111) [4.2] where it is stated that 'first and foremost, it is
up to the parties to stipulate what they consider to be of the essence of the contract'. The question
whether the parties have agreed that a particular obligation is to be of the essence of the contract is a
question of the interpretation of the contract, which must be decided in accordance with the principles laid down in Art 8.

the contract. There is much to be said for the view that the test is to be applied at the time of entry into the contract on the basis that that is the time at which the parties carry out the task of allocating the risks between themselves.

7.83 Given the vagueness inherent in the definition it is, perhaps, no surprise to find that the meaning of 'fundamental' breach has given rise to a considerable volume of case law,[116] much of which turns on its own facts. Cases can be found in which the courts have been reluctant to conclude that a breach is fundamental, particularly where the buyer can still use or resell the goods. Equally, cases can be found in which the focus of attention has not been on the question whether the buyer can still use or resell the goods but on the nature and extent of the default by the seller. Certain broad propositions do, however, emerge with reasonable clarity from the case law. The first is that a delay in delivery or a delay in payment does not in itself amount to a fundamental breach. It is generally necessary to examine the consequences which have resulted from the delay in performance: if these consequences are sufficiently serious, then the other party to the contract may be entitled to avoid the contract. Matters may be otherwise in the case where the parties have attached particular importance to the contractual date for performance. This may be readily inferred where the goods are seasonal in nature or are liable to perish. Alternatively, the parties may agree expressly that the time for performance is to be regarded as 'fundamental' or 'essential'. The second is that a 'final' refusal to perform one's contractual obligations will generally amount to a fundamental breach, unless the refusal relates to a minor part of these obligations. The third is that the delivery of defective or non-conforming goods can constitute a fundamental breach, although here the case law does exhibit a degree of instability. In this connection it may be helpful to contrast some of the cases which have been the subject of discussion in the literature.

7.84 The first is a German case where the sellers sold four different quantities of cobalt sulphate to the buyer, a German company.[117] The parties agreed that the goods must be of British origin and it was also agreed that the sellers would supply a certificate of origin and a certificate of quality. After the sellers had tendered the documents, the buyer purported to avoid the contract on various grounds, including that the cobalt sulphate had been manufactured by a South African firm, that the certificate of origin was consequently inaccurate and that the goods delivered were of an inferior quality when compared with the contractual specification. The

---

[116] See generally: Leonardo Graffi, 'Case Law on the Concept of "Fundamental Breach" in the Vienna Sales Convention' (2003) 3 Revue de droit des affaires internationales 338; Alastair Mullis, 'Avoidance for Breach under the Vienna Convention: a critical analysis of some of the early cases' in Mads Andenæs and Nils Jareborg (eds), *Anglo-Swedish Studies in Law* (Iustug Förlag, Uppsala, 1999) 326; Lubbe (n 114).

[117] Bundesgerichtshof, VIII ZR 51/95 (3 April 1996) <http://cisgw3.law.pace.edu/cases/960403g1.html>.

sellers brought an action for payment of the price. The buyer resisted the claim and one of the grounds on which it sought to do so was that the sellers had committed a fundamental breach of contract in delivering goods of the wrong origin and of inferior quality. The Bundesgerichtshof held that the sellers had not committed a fundamental breach of contract. In so concluding, the court attached importance to a number of factors. First, the contract did not state that the obligations which the sellers had broken were essential or fundamental to the contract. Second, the court attached considerable significance to the ability or otherwise of the buyer to put the goods to 'another reasonable use.' The significance of this factor was particularly apparent in relation to the buyer's complaint concerning the origin of the goods. The buyer alleged that the difference between goods of British origin and goods of South African origin was important to it because it could not export goods of South African origin to its principal customers in India and South East Asia as a result of an embargo which then existed in these countries over goods of South African origin. The court rejected this submission on the facts (in that it held that the buyer had not proved its case by reference to individual, named customers) and, more significantly, it stated that the buyer did not submit that a 'disposal in Germany or an export to another country was not possible or only possible with unreasonable difficulties'. The court thus envisaged that a buyer may be required to look for alternative uses for the goods in a domestic market, notwithstanding the fact that the goods were bought for export. Third, the court rejected the submission that a defect which cannot be repaired is, by definition, a fundamental breach. Thus, the fact that the defect in the present case could not be repaired did not suffice to establish the fundamental nature of the breach. On the facts the buyer could not show that its interest in performance essentially ceased as a result of the sellers' breaches and so it could not prove that the breaches were fundamental. Perhaps the most significant aspect of the decision of the court is the statement that 'avoidance of contract is only supposed to be the [buyer's] last resort to react to a breach of contract by the other party which is so grave that the [buyer's] interest in the performance of the contract essentially ceases to exist'. This is a very difficult test to satisfy and the circumstances in which it is likely to be satisfied are few.

However, other cases can be found in which courts have applied a less restrictive test. **7.85** A case which is commonly contrasted with the decision of the *Bundesgerichtshof* is a decision of the *Cour de Cassation* in which it was held that French wine buyers were entitled to avoid a contract for the purchase of Italian wine on the ground that the sellers had imported adulterated wine into France in the same year.[118] However, the decision does not contribute greatly to our understanding of the nature of a 'fundamental' breach because of the very brief nature of the report.

---

[118] 173 P/B 93-16.542 (23 January 1996) available at <http://cisgw3.law.pace.edu/cases/960123f1.html>.

A decision which is more helpful in this respect is *Delchi Carrier SpA v Rotorex Corp*[119] to which reference has already been made.[120] On the facts it was held that the buyers were entitled to avoid the contract on the ground of the seller's breach of contract in delivering non-conforming compressors. The compressors were rejected because they had lower cooling capacity and consumed more power than the sample which had been provided to the buyers. The court concluded that 'because the cooling power and energy consumption of an air-conditioner compressor are important determinants of the product's value, the district court's conclusion that Rotorex was liable for a fundamental breach of contract under the Convention was proper'.[121] The reasoning of the court on the point is brief and stated largely in the form of a conclusion. However, in many ways the significance of *Delchi* and the decision of the *Cour de Cassation* are to be found in the matters which the courts did not see fit to explore. Thus neither court considered whether or not the buyers could have made some alternative use of the goods (the wine or the compressors), nor did they consider whether damages would have been an adequate remedy for the buyers. Instead, they appeared to infer that the breach was fundamental from the importance of the term to the buyer.

7.86 The case law has been helpfully reviewed by Professor Alastair Mullis who concludes as follows:

Alastair Mullis, 'Avoidance for Breach under the Vienna Convention: A Critical Analysis of Some of the Early Cases' in Mads Andenæs and Nils Jareborg (eds), *Anglo-Swedish Studies in Law* (Iustug Förlag, Uppsala, 1999) 344–5

It is undoubtedly the case that judges applying the Convention have had in the forefront of their minds the undesirability of allowing avoidance of the contract unless the breach achieves at least a minimum degree of seriousness. In assessing the seriousness of the breach at least three factors appear to be relevant, namely: whether the buyer can make some use of the goods without undue difficulty for the purpose for which he purchased the goods; how important in the circumstances of the individual case to the buyer was the term broken; and, thirdly, the relevance of any offer to cure. The exact inter-relationship between these factors and the likely weight to be attached by courts to each remains a question of some difficulty and something which may not be particularly productive of certainty. Inevitably each case will depend upon its own facts but in the absence of express provisions in the contract making it absolutely clear what the parties value as fundamental for their respective expectations, the tendency of courts has been to refuse to allow avoidance unless the goods are so defective that the buyer cannot use them for his original purpose. While there is much to be said for the approach of the courts in relation to contracts for the sale of machinery and consumer goods (which is what most of the cases so far decided have been about), the application of such an approach to contracts for the sale of commodities on documentary terms will undoubtedly engender uncertainty in an area of commercial activity where certainty is of paramount importance.

---

[119] *Delchi Carrier SpA v Rotorex Corp* (n 42).   [120] See para 7.40 above.
[121] *Delchi Carrier SpA v Rotorex Corp* (n 42).

Even if it is clear that the Convention test of fundamental breach is likely to engender uncertainty, it might be argued that this is a price worth paying as a way of promoting justice, in the sense that it restricts the right to avoid the contract to cases of serious breaches. Certainly there is much to be said for this policy, at least in respect of contracts for the sale of goods other than commodities. Indeed it should be noted that even English law, which has traditionally allowed the innocent party to avoid contracts on somewhat insubstantial grounds, has recently recognised the injustice of allowing the 'innocent party' to terminate the contract for trivial breaches: a new section, s 15A, has been inserted into the Sale of Goods Act 1979, to prevent the buyer from rejecting where breach of the terms implied by ss 13, 14 and 15 of the Sale of Goods Act is 'so slight that it would be unreasonable for him to reject.' Contracts are after all made to be performed and, particularly in the case of some international sales contracts, to allow avoidance after expensive shipment would be wasteful of resources. However, while there is much to be said for this policy in relation to most types of international sales, the same cannot be said, for the reasons mentioned above, for sales of commodities on documentary terms. Interestingly most of the cases decided under the Convention do not involve sales of commodities on documentary terms but instead involve sales of machinery or consumer goods. Provided courts applying the Convention have regard to the commercial background when considering whether to allow avoidance for breach, the fundamental breach test could work adequately enough. Unfortunately, cases such as the recent decision of the Bundesgerichtshof raise doubts as to whether the commercial background is given sufficient weight in all cases.

As Mullis points out, the limited role given to avoidance may not suit all tastes. In **7.87** particular, it may not suit the commodity markets where the greater emphasis on certainty may require a clearer remedial regime. But in such a case the remedy lies in the hands of the parties. It is open to them to agree to exclude the operation of the Convention. Commodities markets are generally well organized and many contracts are made on standard terms. These standard terms typically exclude the CISG in express terms and so the problem of the alleged unsuitability of the CISG for commodity sales should not arise in practice.

H. Interest

Another Article which has given rise to difficulty is Article 78 which makes provi- **7.88** sion for the payment of interest. The Article is in the following terms:

> If a party fails to pay the price or any other sum that is in arrears, the other party is entitled to interest on it, without prejudice to any claim for damages recoverable under Article 74.

The entitlement of the creditor to claim interest is not dependent on proof by the **7.89** creditor that it has suffered loss as a result of the non-payment or late payment by the debtor. In this way the claim to recover damages under Article 74 in respect of loss suffered must be distinguished from the entitlement to recover interest on sums that are in arrears. While Article 78 establishes the principle that there is an entitlement to recover interest, it does not define the scope of that entitlement.

Thus, it is silent on important matters such as the rate at which interest is payable and the date from which it is payable. The failure of Article 78 to address these issues has given rise to considerable difficulty in practice, given that a claim for interest plays a not insignificant role in the majority of cases.

7.90 Why did those responsible for drafting the CISG not provide answers to these questions? The reason is not that they were not anticipated. On the contrary, they were clearly foreseeable and foreseen by those responsible for the drafting of the CISG. The reason for the silence is to be found in the fact that it was only possible to obtain agreement on the issue of principle that interest was to be payable; it was not possible to secure agreement on other issues. There were at least two principal causes of the failure to reach agreement on these matters. The first was that interest was a difficult issue for Islamic States, given that the Shari'a expressly forbids the charging of interest. In the light of the disagreement on the issue of principle, it was thought to be sufficient to establish the existence of the right to recover interest and to leave secondary issues, such as the rate at which interest was to be payable, to be resolved at a later point in time. In other words, what mattered was the recognition of the principle rather than its scope. The second difficulty was caused by the fact that, at the time of the negotiation of the CISG, interest rates diverged sharply between western industrialized nations and the then socialist economies of Eastern Europe. Interest rates were much higher in the former than the latter. This made it much more difficult to reach agreement on the rate at which interest was to be payable. Take the case where an Eastern European buyer defaulted on a contract to purchase goods from a seller in Western Europe. What is the seller entitled to by way of interest on the failure by the buyer to pay the sum stated to be due in the contract? If the seller is entitled to recover interest at the rate prevailing in its own country, then the buyer will be required to pay interest at a much higher rate than that applicable in its own country. Assume now that, in a contract between the same two parties, we have a case of seller default. If the buyer can only recover the interest which it would have recovered in its own country, the result is that the seller pays less by way of interest than it would have been required to pay in its own country. Eastern European countries were not prepared to give Western European nations the right to recover interest at the rate prevailing in their own country while only being obliged to pay interest at the much lower rate applicable in Eastern European countries.

7.91 Given that the Convention is silent on the rate at which interest is to be paid, how is a court or arbitral tribunal to resolve this particular issue? Perhaps not surprisingly, it has given rise to a not insignificant amount of case law and considerable academic commentary.[122]

---

[122] See, for example: Karin L Kizer, 'Minding the Gap: determining interest rates under the UN Convention for the International Sale of Goods' 65 U Chi L Rev 1279 (1998); Christian Thiele,

Does the Convention govern determination of the rate of interest?

The first issue to be decided is whether or not this is an issue that is governed by **7.92** the Convention. If it is not governed by the Convention, then the answer must be found outside the Convention and this will require the court or arbitral tribunal to ascertain the applicable law for the purpose of identifying the rate at which interest is payable. A number of cases can be found in which this course of action has been taken.[123] In some of these cases the courts appear to have assumed that the applicable law is the domestic law of the creditor, whereas in others the courts have endeavoured to ascertain the relevant law by resort to the rules of private international law of the forum State. The case for concluding that the matter falls outside the scope of the Convention rests on the proposition that the rate at which interest is payable is a matter which is not 'governed' by the Convention. But this may be to frame the question too narrowly. The entitlement of the creditor to recover interest is a matter which is governed by the Convention and it can be argued that issues relating to the scope of that entitlement should similarly fall within the Convention. Thus cases can be found in which courts have concluded that the rate at which interest is payable is a matter which is governed by the Convention and then, via Article 7(2), have sought to identify the principle which enables them to identify the rate at which it is payable.[124] An example of the latter approach is to be found in the following arbitral award:

> Article 78 of the CISG, while granting the right to interest, says nothing about the level of the interest rate payable. In international legal writings and case law to date it is disputed whether the question is outside the scope of the Convention—with the result that the interest rate is to be determined according to the domestic law applicable on the basis of the relevant conflict-of-laws rules (see inter alia HERBER/ CZERWENKA, *Internationales Kaufrecht*, 1991, 347; Oberlandesgericht Frankfurt, 13 June 1991 in *Recht für internationale Wirtschaft* 1991, 591)—or whether there is a true gap in the Convention within the meaning of Article 7(2) so that the applicable interest rate should possibly be determined autonomously in conformity with the general principles underlying the Convention (see in this sense, for example, JO HONNOLD, *Uniform Sales Law*, 2nd edition, Denver- Boston 1991, 525–526; ICC arbitral award No. 6653 (1993), Clunet 1993, 1040). This second view is to be preferred, not least because the immediate recourse to a particular domestic law may lead to results which are incompatible with the principle embodied in Art 78 of the CISG, at least in the cases where the law in question expressly prohibits the payment

---

'Interest on Damages and Rate of Interest Under Article 78 of the UN Convention on Contracts for the International Sale of Goods' (1998) 2 Vindobona J Intl Com L & Arb 3; Alan F Zoccolillo Jnr, 'Determination of the Interest Rate under the 1980 United Nations Convention on Contracts for the International Sale of Goods: general principles vs national law' (1997) 1 Vindobona J Intl Com L & Arb 3.

[123] See, for example: Oberlandesgericht Frankfurt, 13 U 51/93 (20 April 1994) available at <http://cisgw3.law.pace.edu/cases/940420g1.html>.

[124] See, for example, arbitral award dated 15 June 1994 (Austrian Arbitral Tribunal, Vienna, SCH-4318), available at http://cisgw3.law.pace.edu/cases/940615a3.html.

of interest. One of the general legal principles underlying the CISG is the requirements of 'full compensation' of the loss caused (cf Art 74 of the CISG). It follows that, in the event of failure to pay a monetary debt, the creditor, who as a business person must be expected to resort to bank credit as a result of the delay in payment, should therefore be entitled to interest at the rate commonly practiced in its country with respect to the currency of payment, ie the currency of the creditor's country or any other foreign currency agreed upon by the parties (cf Art 7.4.9 of the Principles of International Commercial Contracts prepared by the International Institute for the Unification of Private Law (UNIDROIT), on which see MJ BONELL, An International Restatement of Contract Law. The UNIDROIT Principles of International Commercial Contracts, Transnational Juris Publications, Irvinton—NY, 1994, 114–115). The information received from the leading Austrian banks is that the average 'prime borrowing rates' for US dollars and DM in Austria in the period in question were 4.5% and 8%, respectively. The interest due from the respondent should be calculated at those rates.[125]

7.93 The difficulty with the latter approach is twofold. First, it is contrary to the majority view in the case law and in the academic literature which is that the rate at which interest is payable is not a matter governed by the Convention so that the solution should be found outside the Convention. The second is that, in so far as reliance is placed upon Article 7(2) of the Convention, it is no easy task to identify the 'general principle' on which the Convention is based which tells us the rate at which interest is to be paid.

What is the general principle?

7.94 There are some possible candidates. The first is the principle of 'full compensation' for losses that have been inflicted on a contracting party (and this is the principle invoked in the arbitration award above) and the second is the principle that unjust enrichments must be reversed. These principles can lead to different results in practice. The full compensation principle suggests that the interest rate should be based on the credit costs which the creditor has incurred. Thus, if the creditor has had to borrow money in order to replace the money which the debtor has failed to pay, the interest rate should be based on the average commercial borrowing rate in the country of the creditor's place of business. The focus of the unjust enrichment principle is different in that it looks at the position of the debtor on the basis that the law should not permit the debtor to make a profit from the use of money to which the creditor is entitled. On this basis the interest rate should reflect the rate of return which the debtor would earn if it invested the money. These possibilities do not exhaust the field. There are decisions in which courts or arbitrators have attempted to find a 'usage' which enables them to set the rate at which interest is payable. Thus LIBOR (the London Inter-Bank Offered Rate) has been used by

---

[125] Arbitral award dated 15 June 1994 (Austrian Arbitral Tribunal, Vienna, SCH-4318), available at http://cisgw3.law.pace.edu/cases/940615a4.html.

some courts but the claim of LIBOR to constitute a usage may be limited on the basis that it is confined to the London market (important though that market is).

Thus, cases can be found which support recourse to (i) the domestic law of the **7.95** creditor's state, (ii) the average bank lending rate of interest, (iii) the rate determined by the domestic law of the debtor's State, (iv) the rate determined by the domestic law governing the contract in the absence of the CISG and (v) the rate determined by the domestic law of the place of payment. The weight of authority supports option (iv).[126] An alternative option, which has some support in the case law and academic literature, is resort to the UNIDROIT Principles or to the PECL for the purpose of supplementing Article 78. Thus Article 7.4.9(2) of the UNIDROIT Principles provides:

> The rate of interest shall be the average bank short-term lending rate to prime borrowers prevailing for the currency of payment at the place for payment, or where no such rate exists at that place, then the same rate in the State of the currency of payment. In the absence of such a rate at either place the rate of interest shall be the appropriate rate fixed by the law of the State of the currency of payment.

To similar effect, is Article 9:508 of the PECL which provides that interest shall **7.96** be recoverable 'at the average commercial bank short-term lending rate to prime borrowers prevailing for the contractual currency of payment at the place where payment is due'. Once again we can see the advantage which the UNIDROIT Principles and the PECL enjoy in terms of being able to learn from the experience of the CISG and to construct more elaborate solutions where the CISG has been found to be inadequate. They also benefit from the fact that their non-binding nature makes it easier to secure agreement on issues of controversy. We have already noted the difficulties which arise in terms of justifying resort to the Principles in this type of case but, assuming that the pragmatic justifications set out above command general acceptance,[127] then it may be that the Principles will play a greater role in future cases in terms of setting the rate at which interest is payable and that resort to domestic law will diminish.

I. *Force Majeure* and Exemptions for Non-Performance

Article 79 proved to be one of the most difficult and controversial provisions in **7.97** the Convention. As Professor Barry Nicholas observed, this Article 'is one of the longest in the Convention and its drafting took up a great deal of time, but the outcome is in several ways unsatisfactory'.[128] While it has generated a considerable amount of academic discussion, it has not proved to be such a controversial issue in

---

[126] Ferrari, Flechtner and Brand (n 37) 817.   [127] See above para 7.64.

[128] Barry Nicholas, 'The Vienna Convention on International Sales Law' (1989) 105 LQR 201, 234.

practice, at least in terms of the number of cases in which the issue has arisen. The reason for this may be that excuse for non-performance is frequently regulated by the contract itself (either through a *force majeure* clause or a hardship clause) so that the Article is in practice frequently displaced by the terms of the contract.

The text of the Article provides as follows:

(1) A party is not liable for a failure to perform any of his obligations if he proves that the failure was due to an impediment beyond his control and that he could not reasonably be expected to have taken the impediment into account at the time of the conclusion of the contract or to have avoided or overcome it or its consequences.

(2) If the party's failure is due to the failure by a third person whom he has engaged to perform the whole or a part of the contract, that party is exempt from liability only if:
 (a) he is exempt under the preceding paragraph; and
 (b) the person whom he has so engaged would be so exempt if the provisions of that paragraph were applied to him.

(3) The exemption provided by this Article has effect for the period during which the impediment exists.

(4) The party who fails to perform must give notice to the other party of the impediment and its effect on his ability to perform. If the notice is not received by the other party within a reasonable time after the party who fails to perform knew or ought to have known of the impediment, he is liable for damages resulting from such non-receipt.

(5) Nothing in this Article prevents either party from exercising any right other than to claim damages under this Convention.

7.98 The Article is headed 'exemption' but deals with what, in civilian terms, may be called '*force majeure*'. There is no direct equivalent in common law systems. The doctrine of frustration operates in a very different manner in the common law, largely because the effect of the operation of the doctrine is to bring the contract between the parties to an end. However, the content of Article 79 does not reflect the doctrine of *force majeure* in any one legal system. In this respect, the provision is a compromise. From the perspective of a common lawyer, a striking feature of the Article is that it shields a party from liability in damages but purports to leave all other remedies intact.[129]

7.99 Article 79 gives rise to a number of interpretative difficulties.[130] The principal difficulty is probably the meaning of the word 'impediment'. It clearly encompasses

---

[129] Including specific performance. This qualification is not as strange as it might appear because an impediment may be temporary in nature (see Art 79(3)). The existence of an entitlement to terminate is not regulated by Art 79 but by the general provisions of Part III dealing with avoidance for non-performance.

[130] One issue concerns the relationship between Art 79 and Art 4, which provides that issues of validity do not fall within the scope of the Convention. The problem is that some cases of impossibility may be thought to raise issues of validity of the contract so that the issue thereby falls outside the scope of the Convention.

events which make it physically impossible to perform in accordance with the terms of the contract but the position is less clear in relation to events which do not physically prevent performance from taking place but, instead, make it economically more difficult to perform. The predominant view is that economic difficulties do not, except possibly in extreme cases, amount to an 'impediment'. Support for this conclusion can be found in the drafting history of Article 79. It is a revised version of Article 74 of Uniform Law on International Sales ('ULIS') where the word used was 'circumstance'. The choice of the latter word in ULIS was criticized on the ground that it was too liberal, in the sense that it made it too easy for a promisor to find an excuse for the non-performance of its contractual obligations. The word 'impediment' was chosen principally because it was thought to convey a narrower meaning; in particular, it was intended to ensure that the exemption from liability did not include defective performance such as the supply of non-conforming goods. The 'impediment' must be something which is beyond the party's control and be such that it could not reasonably be expected to have taken it into account or have avoided it or overcome it. Thus it is unlikely that changed economic circumstances will amount to an 'impediment' unless the change could not reasonably have been taken into account by the parties at the time of entry into the contract and it is a change of a particularly extreme nature.[131]

Article 79 is less innovative than the corresponding provisions to be found in both **7.100** the UNIDROIT Principles and the Principles of European Contract Law. The latter instruments also contain provisions the effect of which is to impose upon the parties a duty to enter into negotiations with a view to adapting or ending the contract in cases of 'hardship'[132] or 'change of circumstances'.[133] This is an area in which it may be possible for a court or an arbitral tribunal to resort to the UNIDROIT Principles or to the PECL for the purpose of supplementing Article 79.

J. Risk

Chapter IV deals with the passage of risk. To say that a party to a contract for the **7.101** sale of goods bears the risk means that it will bear the loss if the goods are damaged or destroyed without the fault of either party to the contract.[134] The notion of 'risk' is thus used by the law to allocate as between the seller and the buyer the responsibility for accidental loss or damage to the goods. In many cases, the allocation of

---

[131] See, for example: Schlechtriem and Schwenzer (n 15) 822–4.
[132] UNIDROIT Principles Arts 6.2.2–3, on which see paras 14.54–14.55.
[133] PECL Art 6:111(3), on which see paras 14.54–14.55.
[134] Matters are otherwise where the loss or damage is occasioned by a breach of contract by the other party. In the latter case, the innocent party will have a claim against the breaching party for the losses suffered as a result of the breach. The essence of the 'risk' cases is that the loss or damage has been caused by an event for which neither party to the contract was responsible.

risk is governed by the express terms of the contract. The law therefore does no more than lay down default rules. The presumptive rule under the CISG for the passage of risk is that risk passes with control or custody of the goods. The default rule is contained in Article 69 which, in paragraph (1) provides that the risk passes to the buyer 'when he takes over the goods or if he does not do so in due time, from the time when the goods are placed at his disposal and he commits a breach of contract by failing to take delivery'. However, if the buyer is bound to take over the goods at a place other than a place of business of the seller, then risk passes to the buyer when delivery is due and the buyer is aware of the fact that the goods are placed at his disposal at that place.[135]

7.102 Articles 67 and 68 deal with the passage of risk in the case of contracts which involve the carriage of goods (in the case of Article 68 goods which are sold in transit). If the contract of sale is one which involves carriage of the goods and the seller is not bound to hand the goods over at a particular place, the risk passes to the buyer when the goods are 'handed over to the first carrier for transmission to the buyer in accordance with the contract of sale'.[136] The policy which lies behind this provision is that risk should pass to the buyer at the beginning of the agreed transit on the basis that the buyer is normally in a better position than the seller to assess any damage which has occurred in transit and to pursue claims in respect of any such loss. In the case where the seller is bound to hand the goods over to a carrier at a particular place, the risk does not pass to the buyer until the goods are handed over to the carrier at that place.[137] The fact that the seller is authorized to retain a document controlling the disposition of the goods, such as a bill of lading, does not affect the passage of risk.[138]

7.103 Article 68 deals with the situation where goods are sold which, at the time of sale, are already in transit. It provides that the risk in such cases passes to the buyer 'from the time of the conclusion of the contract'. This rule has been criticized by some commentators on the ground that it fails to provide for the retroactive passage of risk. Yet in many documentary sales, particularly contracts concluded on cif terms, the generally accepted rule is that risk passes on shipment or as from shipment. Where risk passes 'as from shipment', the risk in back-dated to the time at which the shipment took place. This rule should not cause hardship for the buyer because one of the documents which the buyer will obtain from the seller is an insurance policy and that policy will cover the goods against the usual risks from the time of shipment. So, in the event that the goods are lost or damaged as a result of an insured event, the buyer will have a claim under the policy. This commercial allocation of risk is not reflected in the opening sentence of Article 68 and this fact

---

[135] Art 69(2). However, if the contract relates to goods not then identified, the goods are considered not to be placed at the disposal of the buyer until they are clearly identified to the contract: Art 69(3).
[136] Art 67(1).   [137] Art 67(2).   [138] Art 67(3).

has been used by some commentators in order to demonstrate that the CISG does not deal satisfactorily with documentary sales. It is, however, important to read Article 68 as a whole because it is the second sentence which makes provision for the retroactive passage of risk. The second sentence provides that, 'if the circumstances so indicate, the risk is assumed by the buyer from the time the goods were handed over to the carrier who issued the documents embodying the contract of carriage'.[139] This sentence does appear to be apt to deal with the retroactive passage of risk in the case of cif contracts and, to this extent, the criticisms levelled against Article 68 seem to be misplaced. The problem is not that the Article does not deal with the issues that have arisen in the context of documentary sales. Rather, the criticism is that the emphasis has been placed in the wrong place. The general rule should be found in the second sentence, not the first and so it can be argued that the order of the Article should be reversed in order to reflect the commercial realities in modern day documentary sales.

K. Conclusion

The CISG must be considered to be a considerable success. It has been ratified by **7.104** most of the major trading nations of the world; it has been tested in thousands of cases and arbitral hearings in many of the world's jurisdictions and it has been the subject of exhaustive academic commentary. This exposure to practice and to critical commentary has, it is true, exposed gaps and weaknesses in the Convention. But the same can be said of almost any legal instrument. In general it can be said that the CISG has proved to be a workable instrument in practice which produces sensible results in the vast majority of cases. To the extent that the CISG may not produce satisfactory results, the remedy lies in the hands of the parties who are free to exclude the application of the CISG where they wish to do so. This point carries particular force in the case of documentary sales. It has been argued by some that the CISG is not appropriately drafted to deal with documentary sales. However many commodities markets are well-organized, make use of standard form contracts and thus are in a position to exclude the CISG where it is appropriate to do so.

The CISG has been successful in bringing together common law and civil law prin- **7.105** ciples within the one instrument. This 'marriage' of common law and civil law traditions has not always been an easy one. At times, the failure to agree is explicit on the face of the text, as in the case of Article 28 and the compromise over the role of

---

[139] However, if at the time of the conclusion of the contract of sale the seller knew or ought to have known that the goods had been lost or damaged and did not disclose this to the buyer, the loss or damage is at the risk of the seller.

specific performance. At other times, the failure to agree is not so obvious (as in the case of the disagreement over the role of 'good faith') but has nevertheless proved to be troublesome. It cannot be said that the text of the CISG favours the common law over the civil law or vice versa; in truth, it partakes of elements of both systems. The reduced significance given to termination as a remedy in the event of non-performance, the (limited) role given to good faith, the notification obligations that are imposed on both buyers and sellers and the '*force majeure*' provisions to be found in Article 79 of the Convention are more familiar to a civil lawyer than a common lawyer. Conversely, the unitary notion of 'breach', the fact that fault does not generally play a part in deciding whether or not there has been a breach of contract and the provisions relating to the assessment of damages are probably more familiar to common lawyers than they are to civil lawyers.

7.106   The biggest challenge in terms of the future of the Convention lies in ensuring that the Convention is interpreted in a harmonious fashion in the many different jurisdictions of the world. It is probably both unreasonable and undesirable to expect absolute uniformity in the interpretation and the application of the CISG. But it should be possible to achieve a more modest outcome, namely the development of a 'truly international CISG jurisprudence'. The means by which this ideal may be realized is outlined by Professor Harry Flechtner in the following extract:

Harry M Flechtner, 'The Several Texts of the CISG in A Decentralized System: observations on translations, reservations and other challenges to the uniformity principle in Article 7(1)' (1997–8) 17 J L & Com 187, 214–17

It is worthwhile to recall the text of Article 7(1), which provides that, '[i]n the interpretation of this Convention, regard is to be had . . . to the need to promote uniformity in its application.' . . . this treats uniform application of the CISG as a consideration, or a factor to be weighed. In other words, the uniformity principle in Article 7(1) is a matter of *process*—specifically, the decision-making process of those interpreting the Convention, which is supposed to be informed with an awareness of the value of uniform application, as well as an awareness of other values articulated in Article 7(1). Complying with the Article 7(1) mandate to consider the need to promote uniform application when interpreting the Convention is unlikely to result in the strict and absolute uniformity of international sales rules that some seek. It should, however, permit those applying the CISG an opportunity to identify and avoid unintended and undesirable non-uniformity, and will thus facilitate progress toward the ideal of a uniform system of general rules with sufficient flexibility to accommodate the extraordinarily diverse types and conditions of international sales transactions. What Article 7(1) envisions is relative, not absolute, uniformity.

Some reasons to be hopeful about the possibility of maintaining a relatively high level of uniformity by following the process-oriented mandate of Article 7 can be found in the experience of US courts applying Article 2 of our Uniform Commercial Code (UCC). The analogies between the CISG and UCC Article 2 are striking. . . . Both sales regimes were promulgated for the purpose of increasing the uniformity of sales law, they were adopted by separate sovereign governments in textual versions that varied to some degree, and they are interpreted and applied by multiple independent judicial systems. Despite the obstacles created by the fact that the UCC is embodied in multiple state laws rather than a single federal law. . . . I think most would agree that the UCC has, on the whole, succeeded in creating an acceptable level of uniformity in internal US sales law.

Of course the uniformity achieved under the UCC is by no means perfect. The imperfections have arisen, furthermore, despite the shared language and legal culture of those interpreting the UCC, advantages not available under the CISG. Nevertheless, as an experiment in nurturing a uniform regime of sales law through the promulgation of a relatively uniform text to be adopted by independent sovereigns and applied by independent judiciaries, the UCC experience is a hopeful one. The attitude of the judges who construe the UCC has, I believe, been the key to this success. Although courts in one state are not bound by decisions of courts in other states, judges show a healthy respect for the decisions of sister states construing the UCC. This respect is informed by appreciation for the importance of maintaining a relatively uniform national system of sales laws. Respect for the demands of uniformity, however, is balanced against a regard for proper results, and the balance sometimes favors a departure from the approach in other jurisdictions. Despite such deviations, a workably uniform system of sales law—one that may in fact be enriched over the long term by the opportunity for experimenting with alternative solutions in different jurisdictions—has resulted. This 'federalist' vision of uniform law may produce a weaker version of uniformity but, over time, a stronger substantive law. It is a vision that could easily be applied to the CISG, and that seems particularly well suited to the conditions of Convention and to the uniformity principle articulated in Article 7(1).

The key to honoring the mandate of the uniformity principle in Article 7(1) is ensuring that the deliberations of decision-makers are informed by knowledge of how pertinent issues have been handled by others, particularly courts and commentators representing different legal traditions. This requires developing both a research methodology that unearths such materials, and a decision-making process that takes them into account. The evidence to date is that we in the United States have not done a good job in this regard, although that certainly does not doom future efforts. In this country, realizing the process-oriented mandate of the uniformity principle articulated in Article 7(1) will probably depend much more on the practicing bar rather than judges and scholars. In this time of crowded dockets, it is the litigators who must, in their briefs and arguments, bring to a court's attention relevant foreign commentary and case law, and incorporate those sources into arguments that the court may find persuasive. And it is legal counsel who must have an awareness of foreign authority in order to give sound advice to clients. To serve their clients properly with respect to Convention issues, practicing lawyers must make the effort to master unfamiliar research sources and to grapple with language problems. They should be encouraged by the knowledge that implementing the vision of a truly international CISG jurisprudence—one that will foster a shared vision of sales law and thus uniform application of the Convention—is increasingly practicable. Furthermore, their pioneering efforts in creating an international law methodology appropriate for the CISG may well facilitate the success of future initiatives directed to international unification of law . . .

Compared to the 'Babel of diverse domestic legal systems' that it replaced, the Convention represents vast progress towards a uniform international sales law. However, it does not and could not achieve perfect uniformity. The uniformity principle of Article 7(1) recognizes this significant but incomplete achievement. It does not mandate an absolutist approach to uniformity, but rather requires a process and a mind set—a 'regard' for 'the need to promote uniformity.' This mandate is quite in keeping with the fact that the

Convention will be applied by autonomous judicial systems and arbitral tribunals not answerable to a single final authority. Attempts to promote a more authoritarian vision of uniformity in the Convention not only misconstrue Article 7, but also could be harmful in a broader sense. They can undermine the flexibility required to allow the CISG to deal with the vast diversity of trading conditions around the world, and they can sacrifice the sometimes slow development of well-conceived and just principles to the false god of absolute conformity.

Implementation of the Article 7 uniformity principle along the lines described here could be an important step in spreading acceptance of an international law methodology—a methodology that, by mandating knowledge of and respect for (but not necessarily submission to) the perspectives of legal systems beyond one's national boundaries, clears the way for more ambitious ventures in international law. As Professor Honnold has written, 'international acceptance of the same rules gives us a common medium for communication—a *lingua franca*—for the international exchange of experience and ideas. It is not too much to expect that this dialogue will contribute to a more cosmopolitan and enlightened approach to law.'

Of course, Professor Honnold has long beaten me to all my punches. Ten years ago in his concluding remarks at the first University of Pittsburgh Symposium on the CISG, he said:

> Throughout the work on uniform laws realists have told us: Even if you get uniform laws you won't get uniform results
>
> . . .
>
> . . . As our sad-faced realists predicted, international unification *is* impossible. But before we despair, perhaps we should consider the alternatives: conflicts rules that are unclear and vary from *forum to forum*; national systems of substantive law expressed in doctrines and languages that, for many of us, are impenetrable. The relevant question is surely this: Is it possible to make law for international trade a bit more accessible and predictable?

Improvements to the accessibility and predictability of the law governing international trade not only are possible, but through the efforts of those involved with the CISG—Professor Honnold in particular—they have been achieved to a far greater extent than any of us could reasonably have expected when work on the Convention began.

Questions

1. You are a judge of the High Court of State X, a state which has ratified the CISG. You are hearing an action relating to a contract of sale of goods made between Seller having its place of business in State Y and Buyer having its place of business in State Z. The contract is of a kind covered by the CISG. To what extent do you consider yourself bound to apply the CISG in each of the following situations:

   (a) States Y and Z are Contracting States but (applying the conflict of laws rules of State X) the contract is governed by the law of State A, which is not a Contracting State.

(b) State Y is a Contracting State but State Z is not. The contract contains the following provision: 'This contract shall be governed by the law of State Y'.

(c) States Y and Z are Contracting States. The contract contains the following provision: 'This Contract shall be governed by the law of State A (a non-Contracting State)'.

(d) States Y and Z are Contracting States. The contract contains the following provision: 'This Contract shall be governed by the domestic law of State Y'.

(e) States Y and Z are not Contracting States. The contract contains the following provision: 'This Contract shall be governed by the Vienna Sales Convention'.

(f) State Y is a Contracting State, State Z is not. Under the rules of private international law of State X, the contract is governed by the law of State Y. State X has made a declaration under Article 95 disapplying Article 1(1)(b), State Y has not.

(g) State Y is a Contracting State, State Z is not. Under the rules of private international law of State X, the contract is governed by the law of State Y which has made a declaration under Article 95.

Would your answer be different if State X was not a Contracting State?

2. S enters into a contract to sell goods to B. S and B have their places of business in different States, both of which have ratified the Vienna Convention on Contracts for the International Sale of Goods. A dispute has broken out between S and B and the case will shortly come before a judge in a court of State C, a State that has also ratified the Vienna Convention. In the litigation B has advanced a number of arguments on which S now seeks your advice. B's submissions are as follows:

(i) Article 7 of the Vienna Convention imposes on the parties an obligation to act in good faith both in relation to pre-contractual negotiations and in the performance of the contract;

(ii) economic hardship can never amount to an 'impediment' for the purposes of Article 79 of the Convention so that S cannot rely on a sudden increase in the price of raw materials in order to justify its failure to deliver the goods to B. Further, B submits that the judge in State C is bound to adopt this construction of 'impediment' on the basis that it was adopted last year by an appeal court in State D and that the judge in State C is obliged to follow that decision;

(iii) it is entitled to an order of the court requiring S to deliver the goods to it at the contractually agreed price.

Advise S.

3. (a) S enters into a contract to sell goods to B. The contract states that 'this contract shall be governed by the Vienna Sales Convention'. Neither S nor B

has its place of business in a State that has ratified the Vienna Convention. A dispute occurs between the parties and it comes before a judge in a court of State Z, a State that has ratified the Vienna Convention. Is the judge obliged to apply the Vienna Convention?

Would your answer differ if S had its place of business in a Contracting State but B did not and the rules of private international law of State Z provide that the contract is governed by the law of S's jurisdiction which has made a declaration under Article 95 of the Convention?

(b) S has its place of business in State C and B has its place of business in State D. States C and D have both ratified the Vienna Convention. The contract between S and B provides that 'this contract shall be governed by the law of State C'. S is required by the contract to deliver goods to B 'before 17.00 hours on 31 March 2002'. S delivers the goods to B at 17.15 on 31 March but B refuses to take delivery of them and informs S that he has terminated the contract between them. B claims that S knew that B required the goods before 17.00 so that it could supply the goods to its sub-buyer, for whom the time of delivery was extremely important. S, on the other hand, claims that trade practice is not to insist on precise compliance with time stipulations and that the real reason for B's refusal to take delivery of the goods is that their market price has fallen.

Advise S.

4. 'Despite its narrow wording, Article 7(1) [of the Vienna Convention on Contracts for the International Sale of Goods (CISG)] cannot be confined to the interpretation of the CISG's express rules' (SCHLECHTRIEM). Discuss.

Further reading

The Convention generally

Benicke, Christoph, 'Warenhandel' in Kronke, Herbert, Melis, Werner and Schnyder, Anton K (eds), *Handbuch Internationales Wirtschaftsrecht* (Dr Otto Schmidt, Köln, 2005) 13

Bridge, Michael, *The International Sale of Goods: Law and Practice* (OUP, Oxford, 1999) chs 2–3

Bridge, Michael, 'The Bifocal World of International Sales: Vienna and Non-Vienna' in Cranston, Ross (ed), *Making Commercial Law: Essays in Honour of Roy Goode* (Clarendon Press, Oxford, 1997) 277

De Ly, Filip, 'The relevance of the Vienna Convention for International Sales Contracts: Should we stop contracting out?' (2003) 4 Bus L Intl 241

Heuzé, Vincent, 'La vente internationale de marchandises—droit uniforme' (GLN Joly éditions, Paris, 1992)

Lee, Robert G, 'The UN Convention on Contracts for the International Sale of Goods—OK for the UK?' [1993] JBL 131

Lookofsky, Joseph, 'Understanding the CISG in Scandinavia' (2nd edn, DJØF, Copenhagen, 2002)

Nicholas, Barry, 'The Vienna Convention on Contracts for the International Sale of Goods' (1989) 105 LQR 201

Reynolds, FMB, 'A Note of Caution' in Birks, Peter (ed), *The Frontiers of Liability* (OUP, Oxford, 1994) 18–28

Rosett, Arthur, 'Critical Reflections on the United Nations Convention on Contracts for the International Sale of Goods' (1984) 45 Ohio St LJ 265

Schlechtriem, Peter, and Schwenzer, Ingeborg (eds), *Commentary on the UN Convention on The International Sale of Goods (CISG)* (2nd (English) edn, OUP, Oxford, 2005)

Article 1

Petrochilos, Georgios, 'Arbitration Conflict of Laws Rules and the 1980 International Sales Convention' (1999) 52 *Revue Hellenique de Droit Intl* 191

Article 7

Baasch Andersen, Camilla, 'Uniformity in the CISG in the first decade of its application' in Fletcher, Ian F, Mistelis, Loukas A, and Cremona, Marise (eds), *Foundations and Perspectives of International Trade Law* (Sweet & Maxwell, London 2001) ch 20

Ferrari, Franco, 'CISG Case Law: a new challenge for interpreters' (1999) 17 J L & Com 245

Flechtner, Harry M, 'The Several Texts of the CISG in A Decentralized System: observations on translations, reservations and other challenges to the uniformity principle in Article 7(1)' (1997–8) 17 J L & Com 187

Gebauer, Martin, 'Uniform Law, General Principles and Autonomous Interpretation' (2000) 5 Unif L Rev 683

Hillman, Robert A, 'Applying the United Nations Convention on Contracts for the International Sale of Goods: the elusive goal of uniformity' (1995) Cornell Review of the Convention on Contracts for the International Sale of Goods 21

Koneru, Phanesh, 'The International Interpretation of the UN Convention on Contracts for the International Sale of Goods: an approach based on general principles' 6 Minn J Global Trade 105 (1997)

Powers, Paul J, 'Defining the Undefinable: good faith and the United Nations Convention on Contracts for the International Sale of Goods' (1998–9) 18 J L & Com 333

van Alstine, Michael P, 'Dynamic Treaty Interpretation' 146 U Pa L Rev 687 (1997–8)

Zeller, Bruno, 'The UN Convention on Contracts for the International Sale of Goods—a leap forward towards unified international sales law' 12 Pace Intl L Rev 79 (2000)

Article 25

Graffi, Leonardo, 'Case Law on the Concept of "Fundamental Breach" in the Vienna Sales Convention' (2003) Revue de droit des affaires internationales 338

Mullis, Alastair, 'Termination for Breach of Contract in C.I.F. Contracts Under the Vienna Convention and English Law: Is there a substantial difference?' in Lomnicka, Eva Z, and Morse, CGJ (eds), *Contemporary Issues in Commercial Law: Essays in Honour of AG Guest* (Sweet and Maxwell, London, 1997) 137

Mullis, Alastair, 'Avoidance for Breach under the Vienna Convention: a critical analysis of some of the early cases' in Andenæs, Mads, and Jareborg, Nils (eds), *Anglo-Swedish Studies in Law* (Iustug Förlag, Uppsala 1999) 326

Articles 65–69

Bollée, Sylvain, 'The Theory of Risks in the 1980 Vienna Sales Convention' in the *Review of the Convention on Contracts for the International Sale of Goods (CISG) 1999–2000* (Kluwer, The Hague, 2000) 245

Article 78

Thiele, Christian, 'Interest on Damages and Rate of Interest under Article 78 of the UN Convention on Contracts for the International Sale of Goods' (1998) 2 Vindobona J Intl Com L & Arb 3

Zoccolillo Jnr, Alan F, 'Determination of the Interest Rate under the 1980 United Nations Convention on Contracts for the International Sale of Goods: general principles vs national law' (1997) 1 Vindobona J Intl Com L & Arb 3

Article 79

Howard Jenkins, Sarah, 'Exemption for non-performance: UCC, CISG, UNIDROIT Principles—a comparative assessment' 72 Tul L Rev 2015 (1998)

Rimke, Joern, 'Force majeure and hardship: application in international trade practice with specific regard to the CISG and the UNIDROIT Principles of International Commercial Contracts' in the *Review of the Convention on Contracts for the International Sale of Goods (CISG) 1999–2000* (Kluwer, The Hague, 2000) 197

Weitzmann, Todd, 'Validity and Excuse in the UN Sales Convention' (1996–7) 16 J L & Com 265

8

AGENCY AND DISTRIBUTION

A. **Introduction**	8.01		E. **The UNIDROIT Principles of**	
B. **The First Company Directive**			**International Commercial Contracts**	
(EEC)	8.06		**and the Principles of European**	
C. **The EEC Directive on Commercial**			**Contract Law**	334
Agents			F. **Franchising**	
Introduction	8.09		Introduction	8.29
Scope of application	8.11		UNIDROIT Model Franchise	
Rights and obligations	8.12		Disclosure Law	8.31
D. **The UNIDROIT Convention on**			Scope of application	8.32
Agency in the International Sale			Delivery of disclosure document and	
of Goods	8.17		information to be disclosed	8.33
The relationship with CISG	8.20		Remedies	8.34
Sphere of application	8.21		No waivers	8.35
The legal effect of the acts of the agent	8.22			
Termination of the agent's authority	8.24			
Assessment	8.25			

A. Introduction

'Agency' is both a term of art known to all legal systems and a less technically per- **8.01** ceived business model for reaching customers through middlemen to which the commercial law in many systems has devoted a number of special rules. Agency and distribution have proved to be extremely difficult subjects to regulate at transnational level. The reason for this lies largely in the complexity of the topics. This complexity arises in part from the number of parties involved. Agency involves three parties; namely the principal, the agent, and the third party. The three relationships thus generated (between principal and third party,[1] agent and third party, and principal and agent[2]) give rise to a diverse range of issues. Agency relationships can arise in a wide variety of contexts: for example, the sale of goods

---

[1] Here referred to as the 'external' aspect of agency.
[2] Here referred to as the 'internal' aspect of agency.

317

and the sale of land, financial services, insurance, partnerships and the organization of companies. As a matter of fact, modern economic theory concerning the structure of the corporation and functional and efficient corporate governance is based on the paradigm of 'agency costs', that is, the risk that the owners of the enterprise (shareholders) take in having their corporation run by management which, under certain conditions, tends to behave in an opportunistic way rather than being guided by the interests of the owners and the fiduciary duties which it owes towards them. Agency relationships are often contractual in nature, but need not be: they can arise gratuitously, or as a matter of law. Certain agents may benefit from employment protection legislation enacted in many States, and so trigger questions of labour law. All of these factors have conspired to make agency law a subject of considerable complexity and difficulty. One of the greatest American jurists of all time set out to explore the universe of agency as follows:

Oliver Wendell Holmes Jr, 'Agency' 4 Harv L Rev 345, 345–50 (1890–91); 5 Harv L Rev 1, 1–2, 6, 14 and 19 (1891–92)

I propose in these lectures to study the theory of agency at common law, to the end that it may be understood upon evidence, and not merely by conjecture, and that the value of its principles may be weighed intelligently. I shall first endeavor to show why agency is a proper title in the law. I then shall give some general reasons for believing that the series of anomalies or departures from general rule which are seen wherever agency makes its appearance must be explained by some cause not manifest to common sense alone; that this cause is, in fact, the survival from ancient times of doctrines which in their earlier form embodied certain rights and liabilities of heads of families based on substantive grounds which have disappeared long since, and that in modern days these doctrines have been generalized into a fiction, which, although nothing in the world but a form of words, has reacted upon the law and has tended to carry its anomalies still farther. The fiction is, of course, that, within the scope of agency, principal and agent are one. I next shall examine the early law of England upon every branch of the subject—tort, contract, possession, ratification—and show the working of survival of fiction in each. If I do not succeed in reducing the law of all these branches to a common term, I shall try to show at least they all equally depend upon fiction for their present existence. I shall prove incidentally that agency in its narrower sense presents only a special application of the law of master and servant, and that the peculiar doctrines of both are traceable to a common source. Finally I shall give my reasons for thinking that the whole outline of the law is the resultant of a conflict at every point between logic and good sense—the one striving to work fiction out to consistent results, the other restraining and at last overcoming that effort when the results become too manifestly unjust. . . .

The first question proposed is why agency is a proper title in the law. That is to say, Does agency bring into operation any new and distinct rules of law? Do the facts which constitute agency have attached to them legal effects which are peculiar to it, or is agency only a dramatic situation to which principles of larger scope are applied? And if agency has rules of its own incapable of being further generalized, what are they?

If the law went no farther than to declare a man liable for the consequences of acts specifically commanded by him with knowledge of circumstances under which those circumstances were the natural results of those acts, it would need no explanation and introduce no new principle. . . .

But however this [ie the reason for establishing liability for the acts of third persons in Roman law] may be, it is plain good sense to hold people answerable for wrongs which they have intentionally brought to pass, and to recognize that it is just as possible to bring wrongs to pass through free human agents as through slaves, animals or natural forces. This is the true scope and meaning of '*Qui facit per alium facit per se*', and the English law has recognized that maxim as far back as it is worth while to follow it. . . .

No additional explanation is needed for the case of a contract specifically commanded. A difficulty has been raised concerning cases where the agent has a discretion as to the terms of the contract and it has been called 'absurd to maintain that a contract which in its exact shape emanates exclusively from a particular person is not the contract of such person [ie the agent], but is the contract of another'. But I venture to think that the absurdity is the other way, and that there is no need of any more complex machinery in such a case than where the agent is a mere messenger to express terms settled by his principal in every detail. Suppose that the principal agrees to buy a horse at a price to be fixed by another. The principal makes the contract, not the referee who settles the price. If the agreement is communicated by messenger, it makes no difference. If the messenger is himself the referee, the case is still the same. But that is the case of an agent with discretionary powers, no matter how large they may be. So far as he expresses his principal's assent to be bound to terms to be fixed by the agent, he is a mere messenger; in fixing the terms he is a stranger to the contract, which stands on the same footing as if it had been before his personal function began. The agent is simply a voice affording the marks provided by the principal's own expression of what he undertakes. Suppose a wager determined in amount as well as event by the spinning of a teetotum, and to be off if numbers are turned up outside certain limits; is it the contract of the teetotum?

If agency is a proper title of our *corpus juris*, its peculiarities must be sought in doctrines that go farther than any yet mentioned. Such doctrines are to be found in each of the great departments of the law. In tort, masters are held answerable for conduct on the part of their servants, which they not only have not authorized but forbidden. In contract, an undisclosed principal may bind or may be bound to another, who did not know of his very existence at the time he made the contract. By a few words of ratification a man may make a trespass or a contract his own in which he had no part in fact. The possession of a tangible object may be attributed to him although he never saw it, and may be denied to another who has it under his actual custody or control. The existence of these rules is what makes agency a proper title in the law.

Then [after discussing the reasons for the general principles being applied to torts] with regard to undisclosed principals in contract, it might be said that it was no hardship to hold a man bound who had commanded his servant to bind him. And as to the other and more difficult half of the doctrine, the right of an undisclosed principal to sue, it might be observed that it was first asserted in cases of debt, where the principal's goods were the consideration of the liability, and that the notion thus started was afterwards extended to other cases of simple contract. . . .

Looking at the whole matter analytically it is easy to see that if the law did identify agents with principals, so far as that identification was carried the principal would have the burden and the benefit of his agent's torts, contracts or possession. So, framing a historical hypothesis, if the starting-point of the modern law is *patria potestas*, a little study will show that the fiction of identity is the natural growth from such a germ.

There is an antecedent probability that the *patria potestas* has exerted an influence at least upon existing rules. I have endeavored to prove elsewhere that the unlimited liability of an owner for the torts of his slave grew out of what had been merely a privilege of buying him off from a surrender to the vengeance of the offended party, in both the early Roman and the early German law. . . . Of course it is unlikely that the doctrines of our two parent systems should have been without effect upon their offspring, the common law. . . .

In this branch of the law [ie contract] there is less of anomaly and a smaller field in which to look for traces of fiction than the last [ie tort]. A man is not bound by his servant's contracts unless they are made on his behalf and by his authority . . . It seems always to have been recognized that an agent's ostensible powers were his real powers; and on the other hand it always has been the law that an agent could not bind his principal beyond the powers actually given in the sense above explained.

There is, however, one anomaly introduced by agency even into the sphere of contract—the rule that an undisclosed principal may sue or be sued on a contract made by an agent on his behalf; . . . The rule would seem to follow very easily from the identification of agent and principal . . . It is therefore well to observe at the outset that the power of contracting through others, natural as it seems, started from the family relations, and that it has been expressed in the familiar language of identification. Generally speaking, by the Roman law contractual rights could not be acquired through free persons who were strangers to the family. But a slave derived a standing to accept a promise to his master *ex persona domini*. . . .

I gave some evidence, at the beginning of this discussion, that notions drawn from the *familia* were applied to free servants, and that they were extended beyond the domestic relations. All that I have quoted since tends in the same direction. For when such notions are applied to freemen in a merely contractual state of service it is not to be expected that their influence should be confined to limits which became meaningless when servants ceased to be slaves. The passage quoted from Bracton proved that already in his day the analogies of domestic service were applied to relations of more limited subjection. I have now only to complete the proof that agency in the narrower sense, the law more familiar to the higher and more important representatives employed in modern business, is simply a branch of the law of master and servant. . . .

I said that finally I should endeavor to show that the whole outline of the law, as it stands to-day, is the resultant of a conflict between logic and good sense—the one striving to carry fictions out to consistent results, the other restraining and at last overcoming that effort when the results become too manifestly unjust. To that task I now address myself.

I assume that common-sense is opposed to making one man pay for another man's wrong unless he actually has brought the wrong to pass according to the ordinary canons of legal responsibility—unless, that is to say, he has induced the immediate wrongdoer to do acts of which the wrong, or at least a wrong, was the natural consequence under the circumstances known to the defendant. I assume that common-sense is opposed to allowing a stranger to my overt acts and to my intentions, a man of whom I have never heard, to set up a contract against me which I had supposed I was making with my personal friend. I assume that common-sense is opposed to the denial of possession to a servant and the assertion of it for a depositary, when the only difference between the two lies in the name by which the custodian is called. And I assume that the opposition of common-sense is intensified when the foregoing doctrines are complicated by the additional absurdities introduced by ratification. I therefore assume that common-sense is opposed to the fundamental theory of agency, although I have no doubt that the possible explanations of its various rules which I suggested at the beginning of this chapter, together with the fact that the most flagrant of them now-a-days often presents itself as a seemingly wholesome check on the indifference and negligence of great corporations, have done much to reconcile men's minds to that theory . . .

The restrictions which common-sense has imposed on the doctrine of undisclosed principal are well known. An undisclosed principal may sue on his agent's contract, but his recovery is subject to the state of accounts between the agent and third person. He may be sued, but it is held that the recovery will be subject to the state of accounts between principal and agent, if the principal has paid fairly before the agency was discovered; but it is, perhaps, doubtful whether this rule or the qualification of it is as wise as the former one . . .

The 'battle between logic and commonsense' was for centuries waged not only in **8.02** the common law jurisdictions but in all legal systems. This was especially the case in German law, as it developed in the nineteenth century and codified in 1900, as well as other legal systems influenced by it. Purism and admirable summits of abstraction sometimes prevailed over commonsense. The endeavours by Holmes[3] to pierce the doctrinal veil—scrupulously analysing ancient sources, precedent and scholarly writings in a number of languages and legal systems, in what we would today call a 'functional approach'—are as precious as they are rare.

Two consequences have followed from the complexity mentioned (one is tempted **8.03** to say that these consequences have flowed, at least in part, from the lack of lucid insight based on historical and comparative research such as Justice Holmes' monograph). The first is that the success rate of instruments, the aim of which has been to bring about a greater degree of harmonization, has been limited. An example of this is provided by the 1983 UNIDROIT Convention on Agency in the International Sale of Goods, which, notwithstanding the passage of more than two decades since its conclusion, has failed to secure the necessary ten ratifications required in order to bring it into force. Second, attempts at harmonization have generally been partial in nature; that is to say, they have not attempted to deal with all aspects—and not even all contractual aspects—of agency law or of distribution agreements, but have chosen to concentrate on particular aspects. Thus, the UNIDROIT Convention deals with the external aspects of agency,[4] but does not address the internal ones. Conversely, the 1986 European Community Directive on Self-Employed Commercial Agents regulates the internal aspects but no external aspects. Similarly, the UNIDROIT Model Franchise Disclosure Law deals with only one aspect of the legal relationship between franchisor and franchisee, namely, the information owed to the latter during the negotiation and formation of the contract, but does not regulate any other aspect of that contract. In particular,

---

[3] Oliver Wendell Holmes Jr (1841–1935) served briefly as professor at Harvard Law School. He had practised law in Boston, became Chief Justice of the Supreme Judicial Court of Massachusetts and, later on, one of the Associate Justices of the United States Supreme Court. His work 'The Common Law' is generally considered the most important 19th century book on law in the United States. He states right at the beginning: 'The life of the law has not been logic; it has been experience.' For further information, see: Oliver Wendell Holmes Jr, 'The Common Law' (Little Brown, Boston, 1881).   [4] Art 1(3).

continental Europeans are accustomed to detailed and analytical bodies of agency law, either as part of their civil code,[5] or as part of their commercial code.[6]

8.04   While it has not been possible to draft a Convention or Model Law which has enjoyed widespread acceptance and been implemented in practice, it has been possible to secure a measure of agreement through the formulation of contract standard terms which regulate particular aspects of agency or distribution agreements. Two documents are worthy of note here, although neither is reproduced in the volume of primary materials which accompanies this book. The first is the International Chamber of Commerce Agency Model Contract,[7] which consists of a set of contract terms designed to regulate the relationship between a principal and an agent. Therefore, it deals with the internal, but not the external, aspects of agency. The model form has been prepared on the assumption that it will apply to international agency agreements involving self-employed commercial agents acting in connection with transactions for the sale of goods. The aim of the model form is to strike a fair balance between the respective interests of the agent and the principal. While the contract as a whole seeks to balance the rights and duties of the parties in a fair and equitable manner, the balance is not, of course, binding on the parties who remain free to depart from its terms as they see fit (or as bargaining power dictates). Second, in the context of distribution agreements, UNIDROIT has published a 'Guide to International Master Franchise Agreements' and the International Chamber of Commerce has published an International Franchising Model Contract, both of which are mentioned later in this chapter.[8]

8.05   Chapter 2 Section 2 of the UNIDROIT Principles of International Commercial Contracts 2004 (UPICC),[9] and Chapter 3 of the Principles of European Contract Law (PECL),[10] have provisions which deal with the external aspects of agency law, but not the purely internal aspects. The nature of those sets of Principles is one of the main issues discussed in chapter 14 below. The substantive content of the agency provisions to be found in both sets of Principles is discussed in more detail in section E of this chapter.

B. The First Company Directive (EEC)

8.06   The First Council Directive of 9 March 1968 on the harmonization of company safeguards for Member States was a milestone in the history of the European Economic Community (as it then was) in that it was the first instrument dealing

---

[5]   See: the Netherlands, *Burgerlijk Wetboek* Arts 428–45; Switzerland, *Obligationenrecht* Arts 418a–v.
[6]   See: France, *Code de Commerce* Arts L 134-1–17; Germany, *Handelsgesetzbuch* §§ 84–92c.
[7]   ICC, *The ICC Model Commercial Agency Contract* (2nd edn ICC Publishing, Paris, 2002).
[8]   See paras 8.29–8.35 below.   [9]   See paras 8.26–8.28 and ch 14.
[10]   See paras 8.26–8.28 and ch 14.

with commercial law designed to achieve the policy objectives of the Treaty of Rome. Of the three problem areas addressed by the Directive, only one, namely the validity of obligations entered into by a company, is relevant in this context. Put the other way round: the capacity of agents of a company, in particular its directors, to bind the company.

Alfred F Conard, *Corporations in Perspective* **(The Foundation Press, Mineola (NY), 1976) 32 ff**

Early corporation codes (and the officials who administered them) required articles of incorporation to be very specific about the business that the corporation proposed to follow. If the corporation was a railroad, the termini must be named without equivocation. But circumstances often made some change in the business plan imperative or desirable, and the practical businessmen who ran the corporation usually trimmed their sales [sic] to the wind. As long as all went well, no one was likely to complain. But when things went badly, someone was sure to remember that the corporation had strayed from its sworn objective.

Legislatures had usually been quite positive about the essentiality of the incorporators' declaring their purpose, but almost never said anything about what would happen if the enterprise strayed from it. When judges were presented with this tangled skein, many found an easy way out by pretending that whatever was done wrong was not done at all; it was 'ultra vires'. Often the ridiculous consequence was to reward the transgressor by relieving it of paying for value received. This bit of judicial futility was endured in England until 1972 when abandonment was required by European community rules. In the United States, it was first mitigated by conflicting opinions of a more practical if less logical bent; but today, virtually all legislatures have provided more sensible solutions, and relieved the judges from groping in the dark.

Under the relevant provision of the First Directive, Article 9(1), acts done by the organs of the company (mainly the directors) are binding upon it, even if those acts are not within the objects of the company unless such acts exceed the powers conferred upon them by *law*. Domestic law may provide, however, that the company is not bound by such acts if it proves that the third party knew or ought to have known that they were outside the company's objects. Internally fixed limits on the organs' authority—whether in the articles of incorporation, the statute, or limits set by decisions of its organs—are never sufficient to prevent the company from from being bound, even if those limits had been disclosed.[11] There is one exception to this general rule. Where domestic law provides that authority to represent a company may, in derogation from the legal rules governing the subject, be conferred by the particular articles or the statutes on a single person or on several persons acting jointly, such a limit may be relied on as against third parties if it relates to the general power of representation and if it has been publicized.[12] **8.07**

In respect of acts on the company's behalf before its having acquired legal personality, the persons so acting are liable without any limit unless the company assumes **8.08**

---

[11] Art 9(2).   [12] Art 9(3) and 3.

the obligations arising from such action.[13] Irregularities in the appointment of a person as an organ of the company, after completion of the disclosure formalities, may not be relied upon as against third parties. They may be relied upon, however, if the company proves that the third party had knowledge of those irregularities.[14]

C. The EEC Directive on Commercial Agents

Introduction

8.09   This EC Directive[15] addresses key issues regarding the internal relationship between the *agent and the principal*. The Directive is 'based on the civil law assumption that commercial agents deserve protection'.[16] This is in contrast to the assumption which has tended to underpin the common law rules, namely that it is the principal who is the party in need of protection. The fact that the common law did not recognize, at least explicitly, a special category of commercial agents who stood in need of protection,[17] created a certain amount of difficulty for legislators in the United Kingdom and for the English and Scottish courts when called upon to interpret the Regulations which implemented the Directive.[18]

The commercial background to the Directive has been explained in the following terms:

Séverine Saintier, *Commercial Agency Law: a comparative perspective* (Ashgate, Aldershot (UK), 2002) 87

Commercial agents are representatives whose main role is to create, develop or maintain a customer base (goodwill), within a given territory, for manufacturers who want to expand their businesses. Commercial agents are therefore appointed in order to sell or purchase goods and/or services on behalf of their principals. During the life of the commercial agency contract, both parties benefit from the commercial agent's efforts since the principal acquires more customers through the sale or purchase of the goods and/or services and the commercial agent receives more commissions. Because commercial agents do not act for themselves, civil law recognises the risk that once commercial agents have created or developed the customer base, manufacturers might terminate the contract, by-pass commercial agents and deal directly with the clients which would deny commercial agents their legitimate share of the profits. This would cause them to suffer a loss and would create an imbalance, since the principal is the only one who can continue to benefit from the goodwill. Commercial agents must be protected from the risk of such a loss, hence they deserve protection. The protection of the Directive comes in the form of termination payments

---

¹³ Art 7.   ¹⁴ Art 8.   ¹⁵ Or EEC, as it still was in 1986.

¹⁶ Séverine Saintier, *Commercial Agency Law: a comparative perspective* (Ashgate, Aldershot (UK), 2002) 263.

¹⁷ See, for example: *Bowstead and Reynolds on Agency* (18th edn, FMB Reynolds, Sweet & Maxwell, London, 2006), para 1-040 ('the term "commercial agent" stems from continental legal systems and is not known to the common law').

¹⁸ See: The Commercial Agents (Council Directive) Regulations 1993 (UK) SI 1991/3053.

that principals must pay on termination, unless termination is justified by a just cause. The aim of the termination payments is to remedy, as far as money can, this imbalance.

The position of commercial agents is very different from that of other types of intermediaries such as distributors, franchisees and licencees. Commercial agents could be described as a half way house between employees and distributors. In fact, although commercial agents are independent businessmen, they do not act for their own account but for that of the manufacturer they represent. The latter has a high level of control over the terms of the contracts and the goods the commercial agent is in charge of selling. Distributors, franchisees and licencees however do not represent the manufacturers since they act for their own account.

The difference is of crucial importance because on termination, distributors, franchisees and licencees are therefore not faced with the same risk of loss as commercial agents, i.e. being deprived of a part of the goodwill generated.

For many countries in Europe, the Directive did not require fundamental changes **8.10** to be made to domestic law: the changes required were ones of detail. However, this was not the case in the United Kingdom where more significant changes had to be made to the common law rules. As has been noted, the 'common law rules as to the relationship between principal and any agent are based on the assumption that freedom of contract prevails' and, in so far as one party is in need of protection, that person is the principal who is in need of 'protection against misuse of his powers by the agent'.[19] The need to enact a set of rules, the aim of which was to protect the agent against the misuse of his powers by the principal, required the legislators in the United Kingdom to view the principal/agent relationship through a very different lens.

Scope of application

The Directive applies to self-employed intermediaries who have continuing **8.11** authority to negotiate—or to negotiate and conclude—the sale or the purchase of goods on behalf and in the name of a principal.[20] The Directive is applicable to any commercial agent, whether that agent is an individual, a partnership or a company.

Rights and obligations

Both parties owe each other a duty to act in good faith,[21] and these duties are **8.12** mandatory so that it is not open to the parties to derogate from them.[22] The Directive does not attempt to define the scope of the duty of good faith. This is, perhaps, an unfortunate omission, given the divergent approaches to the existence and content of the duty of good faith in the common law and the civil law.[23]

---

[19] *Bowstead and Reynolds on Agency* (n 17), para 11–001.
[20] Art 1(2). There are specific exclusions in Arts 1(3) and 3.
[21] Arts 3(1) and 4(1). As far as English law is concerned, this is a departure from the common law rule in its application to the duty owed by the principal to the agent. At common law, a principal was not generally regarded as owing a fiduciary duty to its agent.   [22] Art 5.
[23] On which see further paras 7.47–7.59.

However, the Directive does give some content to the duty in so far as its sets out some specific instances of the application of the duty. Thus, while the agent is obliged to make the necessary efforts in the interest of the principal (to keep the latter fully informed and to follow his instructions),[24] the principal must provide the agent with the necessary documentation and other relevant information.[25]

8.13   The protective stance of the Directive can be seen in the various provisions which have been enacted for the benefit of the commercial agent. Thus, there are very detailed provisions on the remuneration to which the agent is entitled.[26] The parties are entitled to receive from each other a document setting out the terms of the agency contract including any subsequent amendments and this right cannot be waived.[27]

8.14   The Directive regulates in some detail the termination of an agency contract.[28] Most strikingly for many domestic legal systems, the Directive provides for an indemnity or compensation to be paid to the agent on the termination of the contract.[29] The agent is entitled to an indemnity if the agent's activities have brought the principal new customers or have otherwise significantly increased the volume of business with existing customers, and the principal continues to derive benefit or if it is equitable to do so having regard to all the circumstances, in particular the commission lost by the commercial agent on business transacted with such customers.[30] A commercial agent is also entitled to 'compensation for the damage which he suffers as a result of the termination of his relations with the principal'.[31] The parties may not derogate from the entitlement of the agent to obtain an indemnity or compensation.[32]

8.15   The UK case law on the entitlement of a commercial agent to recover an indemnity or compensation is of interest in so far as it demonstrates the willingness of the courts to depart from the meaning which the common law would ordinarily attribute to the words 'indemnity' and 'compensation'. The word 'indemnity' is generally used in the common law to denote an obligation to compensate for defined loss or damage.[33] However, it is clear that this is not the meaning of 'indemnity' as used in the Directive. In *Moore v Piretta PTA Ltd*,[34] the judge recognized that the source

---

[24] Art 3(2).   [25] Art 4(2) and (3).   [26] Arts 6–12.   [27] Art 13(1).

[28] Arts 15–20.

[29] The right to an indemnity or to recover compensation does not arise in every case. Article 16 of the Directive provides that the Directive shall not affect the application of the law of a Member State where the latter provides for the immediate termination of the agency contract 'because of the failure of one party to carry out all or part of his obligations' and 'where exceptional circumstances arise'. The intent behind these exceptions would appear to be to preserve the rights of the parties in the event that the contract is discharged by a breach of contract, by a frustrating event or by a *force majeure*.

[30] Art 17 (2).   [31] Art 17(3).   [32] Art 19.

[33] Thus, it is often used in relation to an obligation to make good a liability incurred by one party to a third party.   [34] [1998] 1 All ER 174 (QBD).

of the concept of an 'indemnity' was to be found in German law,[35] and consequently that it was 'permissible to look into the law and practice' of Germany 'for the purpose of construing the English regulations and to use them as a guide to their application'.[36] Thus, the judge concluded that 'the purpose of the indemnity seems to me to be to award a share in the goodwill built up by the efforts of the agent to him on the termination of his agency'.[37] A similar approach can be seen at work in the context of the entitlement of the agent to recover 'compensation'. Here again, the courts have acknowledged that the word 'compensation' is not to be understood as it would generally be understood in English or Scots law. The phrase which is used in the Directive is 'compensation for the damage which he suffers', and this is not the same thing as compensation for loss. Initially, the courts in England did equate compensation with contractual damages for loss,[38] but later cases have shown a greater awareness of the need to pay attention to the origins of the word in the Directive itself. The most likely source of the concept of 'compensation for the damage which he suffers' is to be found in French law, although the extent to which this concept is in fact derived from French law is disputed.[39] Thus, cases can be found in which the courts have had regard to French law for the purpose of ascertaining the level of compensation to which the agent is entitled.[40] The leading example is probably the decision of the Scottish Inner House of the Court of Session in *King v T Tunnock Co Ltd*.[41] Lord Caplan, who gave the judgment of the court, stated:

> [44] We were given material on the view taken by French law of the compensation provisions in the Directive . . . It seems clear from the material produced that the French courts will regard compensation as being reparation for the loss of the value of the terminated agency agreement. The agent gets a reward for the value of the agency he has built up and which he suddenly loses. We were referred to *Dalloz Repertoire Droit Commercial* (2nd edition 1996) section 3 where, at paragraph 87, referring to the calculation of compensation for a commercial agent whose agency has been terminated, the author (as translated) says:
>
> > The compensation or indemnity due on termination of the contract is customarily calculated either on the last two years of the proper or normal performance of the contract or on the last three years (taking the annual average of the commissions in these years and multiplying them by two). In order to reach the total commission courts and tribunals take into account: the commissions due to the agent (and not simply the commission paid) so that the principal may not

---

[35] The source is to be found in Article 89b of the *Handelsgesetzbuch* (the German Commercial Code).   [36] *Moore* (n 34) 176.

[37] Ibid 181 (John Mitting QC).

[38] See: *Page v Combined Shipping and Trading Ltd* [1997] 3 All ER 656 (CA).

[39] See, for example, Bowstead and Reynolds (n 17) 11-049.

[40] See, for example: *AMB Imballaggi Plastici Srl v Pacflex Ltd* [1999] 2 All ER (Comm) 249 (CA); *Roy v MR Pearlman Ltd* 1999 SC 459 (OH) 469; and *King v T Tunnock Co Ltd* 2000 SC 424, 435, 438.

[41] n 40.

minimise the compensation by retaining commission properly due without distinguishing among the origin of the customer base.

The author then cites certain other matters that are not taken into account and continues in relation to the calculation of compensation:

> Without taking into account events subsequent to the termination of the contract; what is lost is part of the market on the day the contract ended—the damage to the agent as suffered at that moment (accordingly the cessation of business by the principal is of little relevance). The mode of fixing the compensatory indemnity as reparation for damage and prejudice suffered (by the agent) is therefore based on the commissions earned during the last years of the proper performance of the contract. This is, effectively, the only certain element without any element of supposition for measuring the incorporeal value lost by the agent. Similarly it is the same element which is taken into account in the case of transfers of the agencies between agents.

[45] In respect of the report of the European Commission dated 23 July 1996 we find acknowledgement that the compensation system was based on French law, and that judgments of the French court have justified payment of compensation on the ground that it represents the cost of purchasing the agency to the agent's successor or the time it takes to reconstitute the client base which the agent has forcibly been deprived of. The report also confirms what the other authorities set forth, namely that compensation in France is customarily paid on the basis of two years' purchase of gross commission, although the court always has an ultimate discretion to deviate from that standard.

[46] The report of the Select Committee of the House of Commons on European Legislation dated 30 October 1996 equally has no apparent difficulty in declaring that the relevant French system on which Article 17(3) is based compensates the agent for that part of the market lost to him at the time of the termination. Thus future circumstances are not taken into account and the agent is not required to mitigate his loss.

[47] Within the limited area of law we have been referring to we have no difficulty in being persuaded as to the approach of the French law . . .

[48] It is obvious, in our view, that on the basis of their own terms Regulation 17(6) and Regulation 17(7) [of the UK Regulations which implement the Directive] provide for a different basis of making compensation than our traditional common law approach. However, as stated, the Regulation does fit in well with the French approach to such compensation. The legislation provides for valuation at the date of termination rather than requiring an explanation of the future prospects for the agency. During the currency of the agency the agent has owned a valuable asset and what he chooses or omits to do after he has lost that asset has no bearing on the value of what he has lost. If he had assigned the agency he would normally have received some compensation for that assignation observing that he could do so only with the principal's agreement and been free thereafter to do as he chose. Thus the French conclusion that mitigation of loss by the agent is not a factor when compensation is approached as we have described, is in our view persuasive. The implication would be (and in our view we consider this to be inevitable) that in the present case the post-termination activities of the pursuer and any sums of sickness benefit he received have no application to the measure of his loss. The Directive and Regulations, as presented, seem to

harmonise with the French approach and given their terms, and the general objective of achieving harmonisation, we see no justification for construing the Regulations as being radically different from the French approach.

[49] The matter of fixing an appropriate level of compensation remains. It seems that even in France the two-year rule is only a benchmark and can be varied at the discretion of the judge. However, this does not mean that we are precluded from considering what will happen in France for the rulings of a judicial system applying the same legislation (intended indeed to operate in the same way between the relevant systems) must be entitled to some respect. There are also practical considerations. The French law obviously considers that there is some merit in finding a clear and practical basis for determining a fair level of loss. We equally consider that given the particular type of loss we are dealing with a broad approach is both inevitable and a practical requirement of the law. This approach is emphasised when we consider that they are seeking an overview of the commercial situation where one of the dominant aims is to protect the agent.

Applying this principle to the facts of the case, the court awarded the agent compensation based on two years' gross past commission. However, it would be misleading to state that the courts in the United Kingdom have uncritically followed the lead of French law. They have not: indeed, in some cases, there has been marked hostility to the notion that the courts should seek to 'mimic what a French court would have done'.[42] In particular, the judges want to avoid the situation where it is necessary to call expert evidence on French law before any decision can be made as to the level of compensation to which an agent is entitled.[43] There has also been a reluctance to develop a default rule to the effect that an agent is entitled to two years' worth of commission because such a rule would confer a windfall on the agent.[44] However, as was noted in the extract above, French law does not positively require the award of two years' worth of commission, albeit there is evidence of judicial practice to this effect.[45] While the courts in the United Kingdom are not under a legal obligation to follow the approach which would be taken by a French court when assessing the level of compensation for agents, the courts seem to have regard to French law for the purpose of ascertaining the essential nature of the concept of 'compensation' as used in the Directive. However, having identified that nature, they are likely to develop what has been referred to as 'UK-based criteria' for assessing the level of compensation that is appropriate on the facts of the individual case.[46] The experience of the courts in the United Kingdom in respect to the task of interpreting the word 'compensation' underlines the difficulties involved in transplanting a legal concept from one jurisdiction to another.

8.16

---

[42] *Duffen v Frabo SPA (No 2)* [2000] 1 Lloyd's Rep 180 (CC (Central London)) 198. To similar effect, see: *Tigana Ltd v Decoro Ltd* [2003] EWHC 23 (QBD).

[43] See, for example: *Barrett McKenzie & Co v Escada (UK) Ltd* [2001] ECC 50 (QBD) [21].

[44] See, in particular: *Ingmar GB Ltd v Eaton Leonard Technologies Inc* [2002] ECC 5 (QBD) [22].

[45] See: Jeremy Scholes and Séverine Sainter, *Commercial Agents and the Law* (LLP, London, 2005) 177–90.   [46] Ibid 195–202.

D. The UNIDROIT Convention on Agency in the International Sale of Goods

8.17   The UNIDROIT Convention on Agency in the International Sale of Goods was concluded in Geneva in 1983. However, it has not as yet come into force: ten ratifications are required before it can do so but, as at 31 December 2006, it had been ratified by only five nation states.[47] Accordingly, the impact of the Convention has been, at best, muted.

8.18   The origins of the Convention can be traced back to work commenced by UNIDROIT in the 1930s. But that work made slow and difficult progress. The divide between common law and civil law jurisdictions proved to be particularly troublesome. Broadly speaking, civil law countries distinguish between direct and indirect representation. Agency is 'direct' where the principal and the agent agree that the agent shall act in the principal's name and on his behalf when dealing with a third party. Correspondingly, agency is 'indirect' where the principal authorizes the agent to carry out transactions on his behalf in his (the agent's) own name so that the agent, and not the principal, assumes contractual responsibility towards the third party (but the agent nevertheless remains accountable as an agent to his principal). The paradigm example of indirect agency is the commission agent, an institution which is not explicitly recognized in common law countries, though it finds some support in older cases on commission agents.[48] The most significant distinction in common law countries is between disclosed and undisclosed agency. In many respects, 'disclosed agency' parallels 'direct agency', but undisclosed agency differs from indirect agency in one very important respect: the undisclosed principal can, within limits, both sue and be sued by the third party. As such, the legal effects of the doctrine of undisclosed agency more closely resemble direct agency than indirect agency. These differences between indirect agency and undisclosed agency have been at the root of many of the problems faced by those seeking to introduce greater uniformity into this area of law.

8.19   Notwithstanding these difficulties, two draft uniform rules were produced in the 1960s,[49] but they failed to secure agreement because they were thought to be a reflection of civil law rather than common law principles. The work stumbled through the 1970s, but once the decision was made by the Governing Council of UNIDROIT to adopt a less ambitious approach and to confine the scope of the Convention to the external aspects of agency law, it became possible to secure a

---

[47]   A list of the States that have ratified the Convention is given in Vol 2, ch 4, XII.

[48]   See *Bowstead and Reynolds on Agency* (n 17), para 1.020.

[49]   UNIDROIT Draft Convention providing a Uniform Law on Agency in Private Law Relations of an International Character and the UNIDROIT Draft Convention Providing a Uniform Law on the Contract of the Commission Agent on the International Sale or Purchase of Goods.

sufficient consensus to enable agreement to be reached on the content of the Convention. This led to a diplomatic conference in Geneva in 1983, attended by delegates from fifty-eight countries, at which the final text of the Convention was approved. Notwithstanding the unanimous approval of delegates, the Convention has not been a success. The Convention nevertheless remains a document which is worthy of further study. A number of points can be noted.

The relationship with CISG

The first point relates to the link between this Convention and the Vienna Convention on Contracts for the International Sale of Goods (CISG).[50] The Geneva Convention deals with agency in the context of international sale contracts and expressly refers to the CISG in its Preamble. The two Conventions share a number of common techniques and rules. Thus, there are similar provisions relating to the approach to be adopted in the interpretation of the Convention,[51] the role of usages,[52] and the definition of 'place of business'.[53] The test of internationality and the rules relating to the sphere of application of the Convention are similar, albeit that the rules are slightly more complex in the case of the Agency Convention as a result of the fact that there are three actors, not two.

8.20

Sphere of application

This leads us into the second point which relates to the sphere of application of the Convention. The test of internationality is based on the place of business of the principal and the third party (not the place of business of the agent).[54] Given that the aim of the Convention is to regulate the external aspects of agency law, the decision to focus attention on the position of the principal and the third party seems a sensible one given that this is the more important of the two external relations. It will also result in the greatest degree of overlap with the CISG because, where the principal (seller) and the third party (buyer) have their places of business in different States, the CISG may also regulate the contract of sale. However, in terms of the connecting factor with a Contracting State, it is the place of business of the agent that is crucial.[55] The proposal that it sufficed for the principal, the agent *or* the third party to have his place of business in a Contracting State was rejected on the ground that it was too liberal. The place of business of the agent was chosen as the connecting factor because it provided an objective standard, in the sense that the principal and the third party are most likely to be aware of the place of business of the agent. As in the case of CISG,[56] the Convention contains

8.21

---

[50] See ch 7 above. [51] See: Art 6, and compare it with Art 7 of CISG.
[52] See: Art 7, and compare it with Art 9 of CISG.
[53] See: Art 8, and compare it with Art 10 of CISG. [54] Art 2(1). [55] Art 2(1)(a).
[56] See: Art 1(1)(b) on which see para 7.16 above.

an alternative connecting factor, namely that the rules of private international law lead to the application of the law of a Contracting State. This provision was as controversial as the equivalent provision in CISG and, consequently, States may declare at the time of signature, ratification, acceptance, approval or accession that they will not be bound by this provision.[57]

The legal effect of the acts of the agent

8.22 The most important provisions in the Convention are Articles 12–16, and they have been described as a 'serious attempt to bridge the gap between the Common law and the Civil Law systems'.[58] Article 12 is relatively straightforward in so far as it provides that, where an agent acts within the scope of his authority and the third party knew, or ought to have known, that the agent was acting as an agent, a direct contractual relationship is generally created between the principal and the third party. In essence, this is an extended form of direct representation in so far as it removes the need for the agent to represent that he is acting in the name of a principal, and replaces it by a test that focuses on the knowledge of the third party as to the capacity in which the agent is acting. More difficult is the case where the third party neither knew nor ought to have known that the agent was acting as an agent or where the third party knows that the undertaking of the agent is to bind himself only. This situation is governed by Article 13 which attempts to strike a delicate balance between common law and civil law jurisdictions. Article 13 draws from civil law jurisdictions in so far as its starting point is that the acts of the agent in such a case shall 'bind only the agent and the third party'.[59] However, it then gives something to the common law systems by providing that, where the agent fails to fulfil his obligations to the principal or the third party, these two may, within limits, sue each other directly.[60] While this compromise (or, if one prefers, balancing act) was sufficient to secure agreement in Geneva in 1983, it has not proved to be sufficient to turn that initial consensus into subsequent ratifications.

8.23 In the case where the agent acts without authority or outside the scope of his authority, the general rule is that his acts do not bind the principal and the third party to each other.[61] This rule is subject to an exception where the principal conducts himself in such a way as to lead the third party reasonably and in good faith to believe that the party acting as an agent did in fact have authority and was acting within the scope of that authority.[62] Further, a principal can, within limits, ratify an unauthorized act of his agent, and the effect of the ratification may be to give the principal rights enforceable against the third party.[63]

---

[57] Art 28.
[58] Malcolm Evans, 'Explanatory Report on the Convention on Agency in the International Sale of Goods' [1984] II Unif Law Rev 119.   [59] Art 13.
[60] Art 13(2)–(6).   [61] Art 14(1).   [62] Art 14(2).   [63] Art 15.

Termination of the agent's authority

Chapter IV deals with the termination of the agent's authority. This chapter occu-
pies an uneasy position within the structure of the Convention as a whole because
it begins to stray into internal aspects of agency, that is to say, the relationship
between the principal and the agent. At this point, we see that the internal aspects
of agency cannot be cleanly separated from its external aspects in that the authority of the agent to bind the principal in his relations with a third party is largely
derived from the relationship between the principal and the agent. This being the
case, it was agreed that some minimum provision should be made for the termination of the agent's authority. Article 17 contains grounds of termination which
are recognized by almost all legal systems, and therefore, excites little controversy
(with the possible exception of sub-paragraph (c)). Article 18 further provides a
supplement to these generally accepted rules by reference to the grounds of termination recognized by the applicable law.

8.24

Assessment

The fact that the Convention has so far only secured five ratifications is a major
disappointment in the light of the optimism that was apparent immediately after
agreement was reached in Geneva in 1983. Writing shortly after the text of the Convention had been agreed, Professor Bonell wrote that 'the new Convention . . .
deserves serious attention in that it represents an impressive effort to find, in an
area characterized by marked differences between the various legal systems, new
solutions capable of being universally accepted'.[64] However, while the bridge
between the common law and the civil law was spanned for the purpose of securing agreement in Geneva, the consensus, compromise or balancing act (depending on one's point of view) has failed to translate itself into ratifications. There
may be many reasons for this. First, the need for such a Convention may be
debated. The differences between agency law in national legal systems may be
considerable in theory, but do they present considerable problems in practice?
And, to the extent that problems do arise in practice, are they not solved by the
applicable national law? Second, the Convention is incomplete. As Professor
Bonell points out, the Convention only applies to agency in the purchase or sale
of goods, and so has no application to 'other equally important transactions, such
as leasing, factoring, warehousing, insurance, transportation contracts, and . . .
various banking operations'.[65] It is also limited in that, as we have noted, it is confined to the 'external relations between the principal and the agent on one hand,
and the third party on the other',[66] and does not apply to the internal relations

8.25

---

[64] Michael J Bonell, 'The 1983 Convention on Agency in the International Sale of Goods' 32
Am J Comp L 717, 718 (1984).   [65] Ibid 747.
[66] Ibid.

between the principal and the agent. In this respect, Professor Bonell concludes as follows:

> What causes greater concern is the fact that within the scope of the Convention there are other omissions which are far from negligible. In some cases, eg, the lack of regulation of certain causes of termination of authority or of the effects of acts performed on behalf of a corporation or other legal entity prior to its incorporation—such omissions can be justified by the objective difficulty of agreeing on a uniform, substantive regulation. This explains why there is an express reference to the applicable national law for the regulation of these questions, sometimes accompanied by a uniform choice of law provision. At other times, on the contrary, the draftsman preferred to exclude from the very outset certain questions from consideration, fearing that even simply attempting to find a universally acceptable solution could have compromised the fate of the Convention in its entirety. This was the case, for instance, with regard to the issues of the capacity of the principal and the agent, defects in consent, the relevance of the subjective mood, the abuse of agency power in general, contracting with oneself, substitution and sub-agency, the so-called confirming agent (the agent who, upon the request of the third party exporter, assumes the responsibility of personally guaranteeing the solvency of the principal importer) and agency *in rem propriam* . . . The fact that in reference to these questions one must continue in the future to refer to national laws does undoubtedly diminish the practical importance of the Convention.[67]

8.26 It may be that States have preferred a domestic law that is complete to an international Convention which is incomplete.

8.27 It would, however, be a mistake to write off the Convention as an instrument devoid of consequences. Whilst it has not yet attained the force of law, it has, nevertheless, been influential on subsequent developments, in particular the content of the relevant provisions in the PECL and the UPICC. While the latter instruments depart from the Geneva Convention at various points, it is nevertheless clear that the Convention constituted an influential starting point for their work. After setting both sets of Principles against the backdrop of the differences between common law and civilian systems, we turn to consider the principal differences that exist between the Principles.

E. The UNIDROIT Principles of International Commercial Contracts and the Principles of European Contract Law

Michael J Bonell, 'Agency' in Arthur S Hartkamp and others (eds), *Towards a European Civil Code* (3rd edn, Kluwer, New York, 2004) 517–31

The law of agency, emphatically described as 'a subject of never-ending fascination' if not even 'a legal miracle', broadly speaking deals with the situation where a party enters into legal relationships with another party by acting not personally but through an intermediary. As

---

[67] Ibid 748–49.

such it represents an essential supplement to general contract law and may be seen as the legal response to division of work indispensable in modern societies.

Yet despite the fact that the practical needs it is meant to meet are basically the same everywhere, the law of agency differs, at least at first sight, significantly among the various jurisdictions, leading to considerable linguistic difficulties and conceptual confusion.

Notions such as 'agency', *'Stellvertretung'*, *'représentation'*, *'rappresentanza'*, *'vertegenwoordiging'* or the like, only apparently express the same concept, while in fact they have quite different meanings within the respective legal systems.

Thus, the common law notion of 'agency' has a very broad meaning, covering all cases where a person, the principal, consents that another person, the agent, acts on its behalf so as to affect its relation with a third party, irrespective of whether or not the agent reveals to the third party the identity or even the very existence of the principal.

By contrast, civil law systems traditionally distinguish between 'direct' and 'indirect' agency— *rectius: Stellvertretung, représentation, rappresentanza* or *vertegenwoordiging*—depending on whether the agent, when dealing with the third party, acts in the name of the principal or in its own name, and only in the first case provide that the agent's acts directly bind the principal, while in the second case it is the agent who becomes party to the contract with the third party even if the third party knows that it is dealing with an agent.

Doubts may arise as to whether such conceptual contrasts are really justified or whether the time has not come to try to find a common ground between the common law and civil law approaches to the law of agency. . . .

Both the European Principles and the UNIDROIT draft,[68] rather than providing a comprehensive set of rules on agency, focus on the authority of an agent to bind its principal in relation to a contract with a third party. In other words, they are concerned only with the external relations between the principal or the agent on the one hand and the third party on the other, and not with the internal relations between the principal and the agent which continue to be governed by the otherwise applicable law.

This approach, which is the same as that taken by the Geneva Convention but not by the Draft Restatement,[69] is based on the so-called principle of separation (*'Trennungsprinzip'*), i.e. the distinction between the unilateral act of the principal's granting the authority to an agent to affect its relations with a third party, and the underlying contract that may or may not exist between the agent and the principal.

This principle, while adopted in most, though not all, civil law systems, is as such unknown in common law systems. However, as has been pointed out, the contrast between the two systems lies 'rather in the nature and extent of the conclusions drawn from the initial reasoning than in the reasoning itself'. Indeed, also at common law the authority of an agent stems not from any contract between principal and agent (for indeed there need not to be one) but from the unilateral grant of authority.

Where civil law and common law really diverge is with respect to the so-called abstract nature of the authority (*'Abstraktion der Vollmacht'*), ie the impossibility of the principal to

---

[68] At the time when Professor Bonell wrote the article, the UNIDROIT Governing Council had not yet adopted the 2004 version of the UPICC.

[69] The reference is to *the draft Restatement (Third) of Agency*, Reporter Professor Deborah DeMott. The Working Group for the preparation of the UPICC 2004 had at its disposal drafts, including the American Law Institute Council Draft No 4 (26 November 2002).

invoke against third parties the limitations of the agent's authority as established in the internal relationship. However, it should be noted that this principle, which is the most important corollary of the *Trennungsprinzip*, is fully recognised as such only in some civil law systems and even then only with respect to the holder of a statutory commercial authority. At any rate it is not accepted by either the European Principles or the UNIDROIT draft. . . .

More substantial are the differences between the European Principles and the UNIDROIT draft with respect to the effects of the acts of the agent. . . .

Commission on European Contract Law, *Principles of European Contract Law: Parts I and II* **(ed Ole Lando and Hugh Beale, Kluwer, The Hague/London/Boston, 2000) 199–201**

Article 3:101: Scope of the Chapter

(1) *This Chapter governs the authority of an agent or other intermediary to bind its principal in relation to a contract with a third party.*

(2) *This Chapter does not govern an agent's authority bestowed by law or the authority of an agent appointed by a public or judicial authority.*

(3) *This Chapter does not govern the internal relationship between the agent or intermediary and its principal.*

COMMENT

[. . .]

Article 3:102: Categories of Representation

(1) *Where an agent acts in the name of a principal, the rules on direct representation apply (Section 2). It is irrelevant whether the principal's identity is revealed at the time the agent acts or is to be revealed later.*

(2) *Where an intermediary acts on instructions and on behalf of, but not in the name of, a principal, or where the third party neither knows nor has reason to know that the intermediary acts as an agent, the rules on indirect representation apply (Section 3).*

COMMENTS

A. *Direct Representation*

Following a more or less explicit division recognized by all European countries, these Principles distinguish between two categories of representation, direct and indirect. The decisive criterion is whether or not an agent acts in the name of a principal and the third party knows or ought to know this. In this case, the rules on direct representation apply (cf. Section 2).[70] This is the normal situation. Direct representation also covers the case where an agent acts in the name of 'a' principal but does not, at first, disclose that principal's name. The agent may not even have a principal at the time of the conclusion of the contract. The agent is, however, bound to reveal the name if the third party so requests; cf. for details Article 3:203.

By virtue of direct representation an agent establishes a direct relationship between his principal and the third person, cf. Article 3:202.

---

[70] The Comments refer to Articles 3:201–9 of the PECL.

B. *Indirect Representation*

By contrast, where an intermediary acts in his own name but on behalf of a principal, there is indirect representation. That is so even if the intermediary discloses that he acts on behalf (but not in the name) of a principal. The most typical commercial example is a so-called commission agent in the Continental countries.

There is indirect representation also if the intermediary acts in his own name and does not even disclose that he acts on behalf of a principal. This description covers the undisclosed agency of the English common law and the so-called strawman (*prête-nom*) in the Continental countries. The rules on indirect representation are to be found in Section 3.[71] Subject to exceptions, and in contrast to direct representation, no direct relationship between the principal and the third person comes into being. Rather, two separate relationships exist side by side: one between the principal and the intermediary and another between the intermediary and the third party.

UNIDROIT Principles of International Commercial Contracts 2004

Article 2.2.1

(Scope of the Section)

  (1) *This Section governs the authority of a person ('the agent') to affect the legal relations of another person ('the principal') by or with respect to a contract with a third party, whether the agent acts in its own name or in that of the principal.*
  (2) *It governs only the relations between the principal or the agent on the one hand, and the third party on the other hand.*
  (3) *It does not govern an agent's authority conferred by law or the authority of an agent appointed by a public or judicial authority.*

COMMENT

[. . .]

Contrary to a number of legal systems that distinguish between 'direct representation' and 'indirect representation' depending on whether the agent acts in the principal's name or in its own name, no such distinction is made in this Section.[72]

[. . .]

Article 2.2.3

(Agency disclosed)

  (1) *Where an agent acts within the scope of its authority and the third party knew or ought to have known that the agent was acting as an agent, the acts of the agent shall directly affect the legal relations between the principal and the third party and no legal relation is created between the agent and the third party.*
  (2) *However, the acts of the agent shall affect only the relations between the agent and the third party, where the agent with the consent of the principal undertakes to become the party to the contract.*

---

[71] The Comments refer to Articles 3:301–4 of the PECL.
[72] The Comment refers to Section 2: Authority of Agents, Articles 2.2.1–10.

COMMENT

[. . .]

For the establishment of a direct relationship between the principal and the third party it is sufficient that the agent acts within the scope of its authority and that the third party knows or ought to know that the latter acts on behalf of another person. By contrast, it is as a rule not necessary for the agent to act in the principal's name (see also Art 2.2.1(1)).

In practice, however, there might be cases where it is in the agent's own interest to indicate expressly the identity of the person on whose behalf it is acting. Thus, whenever the contract requires the signature of the parties, the agent is well advised not simply to sign in its own name, but to add language such as 'for and on behalf of' followed by the principal's name, so as to avoid any risk of being held personally liable under the contract. . . .

[. . .]

An agent, though openly acting on behalf of a principal, may exceptionally itself become a party to the contract with the third party (para (2)). This is the case, in particular, where a principal, who wants to remain anonymous, instructs the agent to act as so-called 'commission agent', i.e. to deal with the third party in its own name without establishing any direct relation between the principal and the third party. This is also the case where the third party makes it clear that it does not intend to contract with anyone other than the agent and the agent, with the consent of the principal, agrees that it alone and not the principal will be bound by the contract. In both cases it will follow from the terms of the agreement between the principal and the agent that, once the agent has acquired its rights under the contract with the third party, it will transfer them to the principal.

[. . .]

Francis Reynolds, 'Authority of Agents' in *UNIDROIT Principles: New Developments and Applications* 2005 Special Supplement ICC International Court of Arbitration Bulletin (ICC Publishing, Paris, 2005) 9–16

It is probably fairly well-known to those working in the area that the distinction between direct and indirect representation, as a matter of the exposition of agency law, is not known to the common law. There are some well-known descriptions of the commissionaire in nineteenth century decisions, but after that the matter dropped out of prominence. There can be no theoretical objection to an intermediary operating commercially on the basis that externally it deals as a principal, but internally owes obligations to its principal that are the same, or more or less the same, as those owed by an agent who has power to affect the legal relations of his principal, ie is a direct representative. But there are few cases about such a situation, and virtually none attributing a special status to persons who act in this way professionally. Common law decisions tend to assume in the sale context, for example, that either the agent is a true agent (with an undisclosed, unidentified or identified principal) and makes contracts for its principal; or it buys from third parties and resells to its principal; or it buys from its principal and resells to third parties.

The Principles of European Contract Law (hereinafter 'PECL') base themselves on the distinction between direct and indirect representation. I think that if international comprehensibility is sought, the position adopted by the UNIDROIT Principles is better as making them easier to understand for common lawyers, for instance common law trained arbitrators, not all of whom have heard of indirect representation at all (though they have no difficulty in understanding it when it is explained to them). As I understand it, in the UNIDROIT Principles the indirect representation situation is covered almost incidentally in Article 2.2.3(2), on the simple basis that this is a situation where 'the agent with the consent of the principal undertakes to become the party to the contract'. (I wonder however whether it is appropriate, as the comment does, to describe such situations as 'exceptional'.)

It seems that it is not infrequently believed by comparative lawyers whose first training is in civil law that the common law doctrine of the undisclosed principal corresponds to the civil law notion of indirect representation, and thus provides a more direct way to liability of the principal on the indirect representative's contracts, and the right of the principal to intervene on them. As I understand the common law, and the notion of indirect representation, this is not a true parallel. The undisclosed principal doctrine requires that the principal authorise the agent to contract on his or her behalf, and expect a right and accept liability on the contract which is not (at any rate initially) known to the third party. An example would be that of a purchaser of land who wishes to accumulate a lot of different but contiguous sites, but wishes it not to be known that one person is seeking to buy them, because this could affect the price at which vendors might sell, so buys through an agent or agents whom he directs not to disclose that he is interested. The converse occurs where the principal assumes the agent will disclose that he is acting for another, but the agent for his own reasons does not do so. The first is rather a doubtful function for justifying a juridical institution, and neither is, as I understand it, the central example of indirect representation.

I therefore approve of the policy of the UNIDROIT Principles in not making use of the distinction between direct and indirect representation, and in disallowing the doctrine of the undisclosed agent as a separate exercise. But when the opening provision on agency, states almost immediately that it applies 'whether the agent acts in its own name or in that of the principal', I do have to express regret that the phrase *'acts in the name of'* survives even for the limited purpose of saying that it is not relevant. It has always puzzled me that this phrase in the English language emerges from other, non-English speaking countries, when it is little used by common lawyers (most of whom are English-speaking) and would have no agreed meaning for them. I have always thought that it would be better to use the language of one of the countries where the phrase is used, and to treat 'in the name of' as a technical term which needs definition when employed in the English language. If the UNIDROIT Principles are to be readily understood by common lawyers, I would have thought it might have been sensible to say something like 'whether under any particular legal system (or 'legal system in which this distinction is taken') the agent would be regarded as acting in its own name or as acting in the name of the principal'.

That apart, I regard the formulation of Article 2.2.3(2) as most ingenious in accommodating indirect representation in a different garb. I have one—highly technical—reservation about it. It seems to postulate a person with authority to bind the principal (which is the nearest one gets to a definition of an agent in Article 2.2.1) who acts exceptionally (by becoming the party to the contract) in certain circumstances. This is appropriate to the second situation given in the comment as triggering off paragraph (2)—that where the third party says it will only deal with (the person who was willing to act as) the agent. . . .

Professor Reynolds approves of the considerable degree of simplification achieved **8.28** by the authors of the UNIDROIT Principles and their primary objective of not indulging in specialities developed in many domestic systems. In this case, comparative research reduced conceptual complexity in the interest of international trade. But comparative analysis may also assist in identifying distinctions—and, therefore, increase complexity—that were hitherto unknown or, in any event, not brought to fruition in domestic legal systems. Professor Ernst J Cohn, one of the many great jurists who had to flee Germany in 1933 and who became a highly regarded advocate in England, 'discovered' the full potential of 'contracts for whom it may concern', a category akin to, yet to be distinguished from, undisclosed agency (*verdeckte Stellvertretung*) as understood in German law, by employing detailed comparative research in Swiss, Austrian, Italian and English law.[73] Students who read German may wish to have a look at his work.

F. Franchising

Introduction

8.29 International franchising is playing an ever greater role in refining the 'distribution' of goods and services in the widest sense in that it introduces commercial know-how into countries and markets where those goods or services had not been originally developed. The countries which stand to gain the most in terms of accelerated build-up of such know-how are arguably developing countries and countries with economies in transition. Some countries may be pushed into admitting franchising under bilateral investment treaties or the WTO framework, although they neither have experience nor even basic traditional legislation, or case law, on commercial agents who, in some countries, served as a useful starting point for tackling certain issues raised by this new business device. Legislative activity at the domestic level can be observed around the globe. However, rumour has it that fully fledged legislation specifically devoted to these types of distribution arrangements has in certain jurisdictions literally suppressed franchising as a business model.

8.30 At the international level, three documents deserve mention. First, there is the UNIDROIT *Guide to International Master Franchise Arrangements*,[74] which was prepared by a UNIDROIT Study Group and the publication of which was authorized by the Governing Council of UNIDROIT in 1998. While devoted particularly to the top-tier franchise agreement, that is the agreement between a franchisor and its partner (the sub-franchisor in a different country), the Guide may be referred to as a compendium of high-level information regarding all problem areas, starting with the analysis of fundamental concepts of franchise agreements (including a description of rights and duties of the parties, financial issues, issues of intellectual

---

[73] Ernst J Cohn, 'Das rechtsgeschäftliche Handeln für denjenigen, den es angeht, in dogmatischer und rechtsvergleichender Darstellung (Elwert, Marburg, 1931). On Cohn and his contributions to many areas of German, English, comparative, international and uniform commercial law, see: Werner Lorenz, 'Ernst J Cohn (1904–1976)' in Jack Beatson and Reinhard Zimmermann (eds), *Jurists Uprooted: German-speaking émigré lawyers in twentieth-century Britain* (OUP, Oxford, 2004) 325–44.

[74] Rome, 1998.

property, trade secrets, liability and insurance) through to regulatory problems and issues of conflict of laws. Second, the International Chamber of Commerce has published an International Franchising Model Contract in 2000. Third, there is the UNIDROIT Model Franchise Disclosure Law, to which we shall shortly turn.

Philip F Zeidman, 'The UNIDROIT Guide to International Master Franchise Arrangements: An Introduction and a Perspective' (1998) 3 Unif L Rev 746–69

I.—Background

[. . .]

Now that the Guide has been published, it may be useful to place it in the context of what has been occurring in this rapidly evolving field of commercial law and business . . .

In 1985, franchising was largely the province of American companies, with developments elsewhere most evident in more limited activities in Canada, Western Europe, Japan and Australia. The intervening years have seen:

- slow but continuing growth in those areas, especially in Western Europe and Japan;
- the emergence of indigenous franchising in almost every area of the world;
- rapid growth of international cross-border franchising, with its attendant and inevitable complexities;
- the beginnings of franchise activity in countries and regions where it would have been unthinkable only a few years earlier—in China and Russia and India; in the Middle East; in South Africa and Morocco and elsewhere in Africa; in many parts of the former Soviet Union; . . .
- changes in the nature of what is franchised. While food service operations, hotels and other businesses associated with catering and tourism continue to be in the vanguard of franchising, rapid development is now occurring in service industries generally, including business services and other activities responding to economic, demographic and social changes;[75] . . . .
- that, while the largest franchisors continue to dominate the economic scene, franchisors are appearing everywhere, reflecting the capacity of franchising to leverage the resources of retail operators to augment the contributions by the originators of the concepts;
- that, although franchising remains an attractive option for the small business person, or an employee seeking to become a business owner, cross-border franchising has prompted the emergence of considerably larger franchisees—in some cases larger than their franchisors; . . .
- the continued proliferation of variations on the theme of franchising—perhaps most significantly, 'conversion franchising', the placing of an existing business under the 'umbrella' of a franchising organization; . . .

[. . .]

---

[75] A service industry not mentioned is health care, including general medical and dental services. Also, there are countries where the postal services are organized as franchises.

VI.—MATERIAL NOT AVAILABLE ELSEWHERE

The *Guide* contains a number of features which may prove invaluable because there are few, if any, other sources for the information they provide in the context of international franchising. These discuss, for example:

- some important clauses that can be found in a master franchise agreement, alerting the reader to the need to consider the effectiveness of each clause when assessed against the relevant applicable laws. In addition to a discussion of the importance of the preamble, the clauses discussed include those dealing with severability; 'entire agreement'; waivers; *force majeure* and hardship; cumulative rights; notice provision; and damages;

- the use of ancillary documents to record obligations imposed on the parties but which have not been incorporated into the master franchise agreement. The ancillary documents may precede the master franchise agreement (eg, joint venture agreements or letters of intent) or follow its execution (eg, a transfer agreement). Some may only be necessary in certain circumstances (eg, letters of credit and financing agreements). An ancillary document may also be used to separate out negotiated, one-time terms from the terms central to the master franchise agreement, or to bind a party which may not be bound by the terms of the master franchise agreement (eg, employees who execute a non-competition agreement). Changes to the parties' relationship may also be documented through ancillary agreements; and an ancillary document can be used to comply with the laws of a particular jurisdiction;

- ancillary documents commonly used with a master franchise agreement (dealing with, eg, confidentiality, non-competition, guarantee and indemnity, transfer, termination, and release); those required for the franchised business (dealing with, eg, supply, equipment purchase or lease, and software license); those required by the structure of certain transactions (dealing with, eg, letters of intent, joint venture, methods of payment, evidencing financing arrangements); and those required by local law (dealing with, eg, trademark license and registered users);

- certain legislative requirements which a franchisor may encounter when executing an international agreement, and which may not be applicable in the execution of a domestic agreement. This could prove to be an invaluable checklist. The chapter concludes with a discussion of the allocation of responsibilities for meeting these requirements.

[. . .]

UNIDROIT Model Franchise Disclosure Law

8.31 The document reproduced in the primary materials volume is devoted to the franchisor's duties to disclose material information to the franchisee. The Model Law focuses on this aspect because there is evidence that a significant part of litigation between franchisees and franchisors in a number of jurisdictions is about whether the franchisee was able to make an informed decision when he entered into the contractual relationship with the franchisor. At the contractual level, everything from sophisticated US-style—that is, exceedingly detailed—documentation to the consistent and strategic avoidance of any written agreement between franchisor (in one case even a franchisor whose brand and goods enjoy a worldwide reputation) and franchisee could be found. The Model Law deliberately refrains from covering issues of general contract law. In this respect, parties may wish to refer to one of the two 'restatements' of contract law, namely the UNIDROIT Principles of International Commercial Contracts or the Principles of European Contract Law.[76] As a model law, the document places its rules at the disposal of national legislators who may adopt it as it is or modify it so as to accommodate their specific needs. In any event, the Model Law needs implementation. The implementation, interpretation, and application of the Model Law is facilitated by an official Explanatory Report.[77]

Lena Peters 'The Draft UNIDROIT Model Franchise Disclosure Law and the Move Towards National Legislation' (2000) 5 Unif L Rev 717, 717–19

I. WHY A MODEL LAW?

[. . .]

This growth of interest was largely due to the increasing attention devoted to franchising by national legislators and the consequent proliferation of franchise laws . . . The members of the Study Group felt that the legislation adopted in a number of countries demonstrated a certain lack of understanding of franchising and risked severely hampering its development. Considering the moves towards the adoption of franchising legislation that were underway in other countries, they feared that similarly controversial legislation might be adopted there and felt that this should, if possible, be avoided. If instead UNIDROIT prepared a Model Law, which by definition would be a balanced instrument given the nature of the Organisation and the guarantees offered by its past history, this would, they felt, make available to legislators an instrument that was clearly aimed at promoting the development of franchising. . . .

The decision to go ahead with a Model Law was . . . not uncontroversial . . . Although the majority of the Study Group were . . . in favour . . . some members questioned the decision, fearing that to make an instrument available would incite Governments to adopt legislation. Instead, they suggested that UNIDROIT should rather act as a consultant to Governments. . . .

Of the different types of instrument that are possible, international Conventions are the most rigid. The intention with an international Convention is that it should become part of the national law of the Contracting States more or less as it stands. Opportunities to vary the contents of Conventions are very limited, as States will only be able to make reservations to specific provisions [. . .]

Model Laws are more flexible than international Conventions. Here, the intention is from the beginning to permit States to make the changes they consider necessary to cater for the country's specific needs. A further advantage is that it is possible to include in a

---

[76] On which see further ch 14.

[77] Available, together with the text of the Model Law, as a publication: UNIDROIT, 'Model Franchise Disclosure Law' (2002) 7 Unif L Rev 107, or at UNIDROIT's website: <http://www.unidroit.org/english/franchising/modellaw/modellaw-e.pdf>.

model law provisions that the experts preparing the law deem to constitute the most appropriate solution to a specific problem, even if some States may wish to modify the suggested provision when they take inspiration from it for their national legislation. . . .

Scope of application

8.32   The law applies,[78] as mentioned, only to a limited aspect of a franchise granted or renewed. Except as otherwise expressly provided it is not concerned with the validity of the franchise agreement or any of its provisions.[79]

Delivery of disclosure document and information to be disclosed

8.33   A franchisor must give every prospective franchisee a disclosure document, to which the proposed franchise agreement must be attached. The document must be regularly updated.[80] Only in certain prescribed circumstances is no disclosure document required.[81] The Model Law's core provision is Article 6. It lists in great detail the items of information which the franchisor is required to provide. These range from the identification of the franchisor, its affiliates, and officers, to their business, financial and criminal record, other franchisees of interest for the party negotiating for a new franchise, intellectual property rights, the description of the goods or services that the franchisee is required to purchase or lease and financial matters, including estimates of the prospective franchisee's investment, description of the relevant market, training, and limitations imposed on the franchisee. At the franchisor's request, the prospective franchisee must acknowledge in writing the receipt of the disclosure document.[82]

Remedies

8.34   If the disclosure document or notice of material change has not been duly delivered or contains a misrepresentation of a material fact, the franchisee may terminate the franchise agreement and/or claim damages.[83] The remedies must be exercised within a determined timeframe.[84] The remedies provided for in the Model Law do not derogate from any other right the franchisee may have under the applicable law.[85] This is a reference to the conflict-of-laws rules of the forum which will identify the law governing these matters.

No waivers

8.35   Any waiver by a franchisee of a right given by the Model Law is void.[86]

---

[78] The instrument refers to itself as 'the law'. However, in light of its nature, this has to be read as a reference to 'the national law implementing the Model Law'.   [79] Art 1.
[80] Arts 3–4.   [81] Art 5.   [82] Art 7.   [83] Art 8(1).   [84] Art 8(2).
[85] Art 8(3)–(4).   [86] Art 10.

Questions

1. A company is an artificial legal person and it can act only through natural legal persons. Thus, the central issue becomes the determination of which people in which circumstances can be regarded as having acted as the company. On what basis should a legal system resolve this issue?
2. To what extent is it true to say that the experience of the UK courts in the interpretation of the Commercial Agents Directive underlines the difficulties involved in transplanting a legal concept (such as 'compensation') from one jurisdiction to another?
3. What significance, if any, should be attached to the distinction between 'direct' and 'indirect' agency? Is 'indirect agency' the same thing as the doctrine of the undisclosed principal? If it is not, what is the difference between the two?
4. Why has the 1983 Geneva Convention on Agency in the International Sale of Goods failed to achieve the necessary ratifications required to bring it into force?
5. If a person *never* (or very rarely) acts (at any rate professionally) except in the capacity of 'indirect representative' and is known to do so, does—and should— that person qualify as an 'agent' within the meaning of, and so far as defined by, the UNIDROIT Contract Principles at all?
6. Why does the Model Franchise Disclosure Law take the form of a Model Law? What other form could it have taken? Assess the relative advantages and disadvantages of the different forms.
7. Read the Preamble to the Model Franchise Disclosure Law. What purpose does it serve? Why do you think it sets out a list of 'elements' which State legislators may wish to consider when enacting legislation based on the Model Law? How might State legislators respond to these 'elements'?
8. Read Article 6(1)(G) of the Model Franchise Disclosure Law. What is its underlying rationale? Why has it proved to be such a controversial provision?

Further reading

Berle, Adolf A, and Means, Gardiner C, *The Modern Corporation and Private Property* (MacMillan Co, New York, 1932)

American Law Institute, *Restatement (Third) of the Law, Agency: tentative draft no 7* (September 2005)

Binder, Olivier, 'Les initiatives d'UNIDROIT en matière de franchisage: vers un système moderne et plus transparent de distribution des merchandises et des services' (2000) 5 Unif L Rev 707

Bonell, Michael J, 'The 1983 Convention on Agency in the International Sale of Goods' 32 Am J Comp Law 717 (1984)

Davies, Paul L, *Gower & Davies' Principles of Company Law* (7th edn, Sweet & Maxwell, London, 2003) 129–75

Demott, Deborah A, 'A Revised Prospectus for a Third Restatement of Agency' 31 UC Davis L Rev 1035 (1997–8)

Easterbrook, Frank H, and Fischel, Daniel R, *The Economic Structure of Corporate Law* (Harv U Press, Cambridge (MA), 1991)

Evans, Malcolm, 'Explanatory Report to the Convention on Agency in the International Sale of Goods' (1984) II Unif L Rev 119

Fernlund, Anders, 'Harmonised Legislation on Franchise Disclosure and National Law: the Case of Sweden' (2000) 5 Unif L Rev 737

Giesler, Jan Patrick, 'Franchisevertrag' in Kronke, Herbert, Melis, Werner and Schnyder, Anton K (eds), *Handbuch Internationales Wirtschaftsrecht* (Dr Otto Schmidt, Köln, 2005)

Hartkamp, Arthur S, 'Indirect Representation According to the Principles of European Contract Law, the Unidroit Agency Convention and the Dutch Civil Code' in Basedow, Jürgen, Hopt, Klaus J, and Kötz, Hein (eds), *Festschrift für Ulrich Drobnig zum siebzigsten Geburtstag* (Mohr Siebeck, Tübingen, 1998) 45–56

Killias, Laurent, 'Vertragshändlervertrag' in Kronke, Herbert, Melis, Werner and Schnyder, Anton K (eds), *Handbuch Internationales Wirtschaftsrecht* (Dr Otto Schmidt, Köln, 2005)

Presti, Gaetano, Rescigno, Matteo, Mazza, Francesca and Garrido, José M Garrido, 'Capacità della società e rappresentanza degli amministratori' in Campobasso, Gian F (ed), *'Armonie e disarmonie nel diritto comunitario delle società commerciali'* (Giuffrè, Milano, 2003) 573

Sainter, Séverine, and Scholes, Jeremy, *Commercial Agents and the Law* (LLP, London, 2005)

Schmitthoff, Clive M (ed), *The Harmonisation of European Company Law* (UKNCCL, London, 1973)

Thume, Karl-Heinz, 'Handelsvertretervertrag' in Kronke, Herbert, Melis, Werner and Schnyder, Anton K (eds), *Handbuch Internationales Wirtschaftsrecht* (Dr Otto Schmidt, Köln, 2005) 603

9

INTERNATIONAL BANK PAYMENT UNDERTAKINGS

A. Introduction
The role of banks in financing
    international trade   9.01
Some terminological problems   9.07
The different interests   9.08
Rules of banking practice and the
    International Chamber of Commerce   9.09
Why bank payment undertakings are
    interesting   9.10
The contract of sale as the central
    contract   9.13

B. Documentary Credits: the UCP and
    the eUCP   9.14
Classification of credits by
    payment method   9.17
Principles of documentary credits law   9.18
Autonomy of the credit   9.19
A documentary credit takes effect
    upon issue   9.20
Documentary character of the credit   9.21
Banks are concerned only with the
    apparent good order of the
    documents   9.22
Banks deal as principals, not as agents   9.23
The terms of a credit must be strictly
    complied with   9.24
A credit is not transferable unless
    expressly designated as such   9.25
The eUCP   9.26

C. Demand Guarantees: the URDG
Purpose of the URDG   9.29
Nature of a demand guarantee
    Distinguished from letter of credit   9.31
    Distinguished from suretyship
        guarantee   9.33
    International character of demand
        guarantees   9.34
Guarantee structures   9.35
Advantages   9.36
Fundamental principles   9.37
Irrevocability and coming into effect   9.39
The demand for payment   9.40
Extend or pay demands   9.42
Termination of the guarantee   9.43
Governing law and jurisdiction   9.44

D. The International Standard
    Practices (ISP98)   9.46

E. The United Nations Convention
    on Independent Guarantees and
    Stand-by Letters of Credit
Features of the UN Convention   9.51
Relationship between the Convention
    and the URDG   9.53

F. ICC Uniform Rules for Contract
    Bonds   9.54
Default   9.56
Governing law and jurisdiction   9.57

A. Introduction

The role of banks in financing international trade

9.01 Where goods are ordered by a buyer in one country from a seller in another and the parties do not enjoy an existing business relationship, each party may wish to ensure that the other's commitment is buttressed by an undertaking from a third party. This role is traditionally fulfilled by banks. In transactions involving the international sale of goods by sea transit it would, of course, be possible in theory for the parties to agree that the buyer shall collect the goods from the seller's factory or warehouse and pay on the spot, but such an arrangement is rarely practicable. Generally the buyer finds it convenient to leave it to the seller to organize the shipment of the goods. But the seller may be unwilling to ship without an assurance of payment and the buyer to pay without an assurance of delivery.

9.02 One way of overcoming this dilemma is to arrange for exchange of a payment instrument against shipping documents through the banking system. For example, if the seller is in London and the buyer in New York, the seller's bank in London could arrange with its correspondent in New York to hand over the bill of lading and other shipping documents to the seller's New York bank in exchange for payment by a sight draft (delivery against payment, or 'D/P') or acceptance of a term bill (delivery against acceptance, or 'D/A'). This gives the parties some protection but for the seller this is not complete, because he will already have incurred the expense of manufacturing or acquiring the goods and shipping them to New York, so that if the bill is not given or is dishonoured he will have the trouble and expense of finding another buyer and in what is for him a foreign jurisdiction.

9.03 So what the seller of the goods needs is an assurance in advance of the commencement of performance that he will be paid. This is the function of the documentary credit, an undertaking by a bank to the buyer that on or at some time after presentation of specified shipping documents it will make payment, accept a draft (bill of exchange) or purchase a draft or documents. With the letter of credit in his hand the seller can proceed to fulfil the order, secure in the knowledge that the buyer's payment undertaking is now reinforced by that of the issuing bank. But if the bank is not known to the seller and he is nervous about its financial status he may be able to stipulate for a confirmed credit, in which the issuing bank's undertaking is reinforced by an independent undertaking from another bank (the confirming bank), usually located in the seller's country.

9.04 Under a documentary credit the issuing or confirming bank, as the case may be, is the first port of call for payment. The seller as beneficiary of the credit is not entitled to by-pass the agreed payment mechanism by seeking payment direct from the buyer unless the bank fails to issue or honour the credit.

To be contrasted with the documentary credit is the demand guarantee. This is a **9.05** bank assurance given in favour of the intended *recipient* of goods or services. Take the case of a government in, say, Saudi Arabia that is proposing to place a contract for major construction works to be carried out by a French construction company. The government may want some safeguard against the failure of the construction company to carry out the work in accordance with the contract. This can be provided in the form of a demand guarantee, an undertaking by a bank that it will, on first written demand and on presentation of any other specified documents, pay a sum or maximum sum to the beneficiary. In contrast to the issuer of a documentary credit, a bank issuing a demand guarantee is not intended as the first port of call for payment. The purpose of the demand guarantee is to provide a safeguard against the contractor's default; the employer as beneficiary would thus be acting in breach of duty if it made a demand under the guarantee without an honest belief that a default had taken place. However, the bank is not concerned with that; it is both entitled and obliged to make payment against the requisite documents whether or not there has in fact been default. As with a documentary credit, the demand guarantee may be issued direct by a bank in the contractor's country or it may be issued by a bank in the beneficiary's country against a counter-indemnity, or counter-guarantee, from the contractor's bank. Thus a mechanism is in place to protect both parties, the supplier by a documentary credit and the employer by a demand guarantee.

The standby credit, which evolved in America, is conceptually a form of demand **9.06** guarantee but has a much greater diversity of use and in many aspects tends to follow banking practice governing documentary credits. Nevertheless it is conceived as secondary in intent in that it should be called only if the beneficiary honestly believes there has been default. A hybrid is the rather strangely named direct pay standby, which contains payment undertakings some of which are standby in character while for others the issuing bank is the first port of call for payment.

Some terminological problems

This area of commercial practice is unfortunately bedevilled by terminological **9.07** confusion. Reference has already been made to the 'direct pay' standby, which is a contradiction in terms. The word 'guarantee' is frequently used to describe both demand guarantees, which are purely documentary in character, and suretyship guarantees, under which the guarantor is liable only upon actual default. To add to the confusion, instruments developed in Germany, France and the Netherlands have been labelled 'suretyship' guarantees payable on first demand, leaving it unclear whether the obligation was accessory because of the word 'suretyship' or independent because of the phrase 'first demand'.[1] Then there is the word 'bond',

---

[1] See Roeland F. Bertrams, *Bank Guarantees in International Trade: The Law and Practice of Independent (First Demand) Guarantees and Standby Letters of Credit in Civil Law and Common Law Jurisdictions* (3rd edn, Kluwer Law International, The Hague, 2004), paras 4-17–19.

used indiscriminately to cover both suretyship and independent guarantees. However, where qualified by the word 'performance', 'bid', 'tender', and the like, it is an independent guarantee, while on the other hand the unhappily named 'contract bond' referred to in the ICC's Uniform Rules for Contract Bonds is a suretyship bond.[2] In all these cases it is necessary to look beyond the label to the terms of the instrument to see whether it is an accessory or an independent guarantee.

The different interests

9.08   The rules governing bank payment undertakings have to balance at least three sets of interests. First, of course, is that of the beneficiary, who as we have seen needs an advance assurance of payment before commencing performance and the benefit of a payment undertaking which is conditioned solely on presentation of documents and is independent of the underlying transaction. Then there is the principal, who wishes to ensure that payment is made only against specified documents which conform to the credit or guarantee—in default of which he may refuse to take up and pay for the documents—and, in the case of a demand guarantee, that he receives at least some safeguards against an abusive call on the guarantee. But the issuing bank also has its own interests to protect, so that while it is primarily for the beneficiary to stipulate what form of payment it will accept, the banking community exercises a powerful influence, through its codified customs and practice, to ensure that banks are not exposed to excessive risk. There are three basic conditions necessary to protect the bank. First, there needs to be certainty as to the commencement, duration and amount or maximum amount of the bank's liability. All these things are provided by the terms of the credit. Next, the issuing bank does not wish to concern itself with external facts or transactions. Hence the principle that banks deal only in documents, not in goods or services, and the related principle that the engagement established by the issue of the credit is independent of the underlying transaction. This principle is embodied in the relevant rules of banking practice.[3] Finally, since the bank is not in a position to ensure that documents and signatures are genuine it must be given the right to pay against documents which appear on their face, after reasonable examination, to be genuine and in conformity with the credit. That, too, is provided by the rules.

Rules of banking practice and the International Chamber of Commerce

9.09   One of the most striking aspects of the law governing international bank payment obligations is that, to a very large degree, it is governed by uniform rules of banking practice published by bodies such as the International Chamber of Commerce and given effect by contractual incorporation into all relevant contracts entered

---

[2] See below, para 9.54. The first-named author attempted unsuccessfully to have the label changed to 'suretyship' or 'conditional' bond when the UCB were in preparation.   [3] See below.

into by banks with their customers and with beneficiaries of payment undertakings. The four sets of rules relating to abstract payment undertakings that we shall examine in outline in the present chapter are the Uniform Customs and Practice for Documentary Credits (2007 revision), known in the industry as UCP 600; the supplement to their predecessor, UCP 500, covering electronic presentation (eUCP); the Uniform Rules for Demand Guarantees (URDG), published in 1992; and the International Standby Practices (ISP98) published in 1998 by the Institute of International Banking Law & Practice. To these must be added the 1995 UN Convention on Stand-By Letters of Credit and Independent Guarantees. We will also refer briefly to the ICC's 1993 Uniform Rules for Contract Bonds (UCB), dealing with suretyship bonds. It should be borne in mind that, as previously stated, the two Institutes are not law-making bodies, and their rules are designed to produce consistency of banking practice. They therefore embody not only firm directions, which when incorporated into contracts give rise to legal rights and obligations in the same way as any other contractual provisions, but also certain exhortations as to good practice which banks are urged but not legally bound to follow. Of these various rules the oldest and most successful are the UCP, which were first published in 1933 and are used by banks all over the world. The 2007 revision replaces UCP 500 as from 1 July 2007.

Why bank payment undertakings are interesting

In this book we are not concerned with the minutiae of the rules governing the different forms of bank payment undertaking. Rather we explore them for the insights they give into the development of transnational commercial law. All these forms of bank undertaking constitute a class that may be compendiously referred to as abstract payment undertakings, the characteristics of which are that they take effect independently of the underlying transaction pursuant to which they are given (the principle of the autonomy of the credit) and become binding immediately upon issue, regardless of the time of receipt and without the need for acceptance or reliance by the beneficiary. These characteristics evolved solely through the international usages of bankers, not through any formal legal underpinning by courts or legislatures, and in terms of traditional contract theories they raise acute doctrinal difficulties, with which scholars and courts in a number of different countries have grappled over the years. Few people doubt the binding force of a documentary credit or demand guarantee; the problem is to know what precisely makes the promise binding. Then there is the question of how far the principle of autonomy of the credit admits of exceptions. Fraud is almost everywhere regarded as an exception, though there is still much debate over questions such as whose fraud is relevant, whether fraud in the underlying transaction rather than in the credit facility suffices and whether the tender of forged documents can be rejected independently of fraud on the basis of failure to conform to the terms of the credit. Finally, in what circumstances can, say, rules embodied in the UCP be

9.10

invoked where the UCP have not been expressly incorporated into the contract? This is a question addressed a little later.[4]

9.11 Apart from these conceptual questions we should take note of the surprising power of rules formulated by the ICC as a body which, though international and enjoying special United Nations status, is not itself a law-making body. The ICC has rightly claimed that the UCP are the most successful private rules for trade ever developed. Their success is due in no small measure to the extensive consultations and rigorous analysis undertaken each time the UCP are revised. Thus UCP 600 were three years in preparation and the UCP Drafting Group and the Banking Commission distributed numerous drafts through its national committees and elsewhere throughout the world and sifted through no fewer than 5,000 comments before reaching agreement on the final version in October 2006.

Roy Goode, 'Abstract Payment Undertakings in International Transactions', XXII Brook J Int Law 1. 3–4, 12–17, 19–20 (1996)

I. GENERAL CONSIDERATION

Payment undertakings of the kind I shall be examining do not fall within ordinary contract principles. They do not involve offer and acceptance (being considered binding as from the time of issue unless and until rejected by the beneficiary); they do not depend on consideration or reliance by the promisee; they are not governed by any special formal requirements (such as a deed); and they fit neither the definition of a bilateral contract nor that of a unilateral contract. They are best regarded as mercantile specialties, undertakings which, by the usage of merchants, have effect by virtue of their issue without any additional requirements. Leading American scholars treat such undertakings as engagements rather than as contractual promises in the strict sense. English writers tend to regard them as contractual in character since the grounds for avoiding them and the remedies for their breach are determined by ordinary contract principles. We need not be overly concerned about the difference in approach, which (once one accepts the binding force of such undertakings) will in most cases be of little practical consequence.

Documentary credits and demand guarantees have several characteristics in common. Both are abstract payment undertakings, so that they are not required to conform to the ordinary conditions for a valid and binding contract. Both are autonomous in character, so that in principle the bank's duty is to pay against conforming documents without regard to whether, in the case of documentary credits, there has been proper performance of the underlying contract by the beneficiary or, in the case of demand guarantees, there has been a breach of the underlying contract. Both are documentary in character, so that the obligation is triggered solely by presentation of documents within the time and on the terms specified in the undertaking without regard to external facts or events. In both cases the bank fulfills its duty by paying against documents which appear, on reasonable examination, to conform to the credit. This occurs even if it transpires that without the bank's knowledge one or more of the documents has been forged or fraudulently altered or contains false data. But in other respects there are crucially important differences between documentary credits and demand guarantees to which I shall advert a little later . . .

---

[4] See below, para 9.14.

II. DOCUMENTARY CREDITS

. . .

A fundamental principle of documentary credits law is the autonomy of the credit, that is, its independence both from the underlying trade transaction between the applicant for the credit and the beneficiary, and from the relationship between the former and the issuing bank. This concept, enshrined in Articles 3 and 4 of the UCP, is widely recognised and applied by courts around the world. So, in general, it is not a defence to a claim on the credit that the beneficiary appears to have committed a breach of the underlying contract, that the contract is unenforceable (e.g., for illegality), or that the applicant for the credit has failed to put funds in the issuing bank. This is scarcely surprising, for the typical letter of credit transaction sets up a series of engagements involving different parties, and it would be strange if a breach of contract between, for example, the beneficiary and the applicant for the credit, were to constitute a defence to a claim under an entirely separate engagement between issuing bank and beneficiary, an engagement to which the applicant for the credit is not a party.

The extension of the UCP to cover credits issued by a bank for its own account—namely, to discharge an obligation incurred to the beneficiary by the bank itself—raises the question whether in this two-party situation the letter of credit still remains independent of the underlying transaction. Here, the parties to the two engagements are identical, so that the doctrinal arguments for treating one engagement as independent of the other are less compelling. Nevertheless, the general principle must still apply. There is nothing particularly novel in an arrangement by which the payment obligation under a commercial contract is tapped off into a separate contract insulated from the main agreement. The typical case is the bill of exchange given in payment for goods or services and considered to generate a distinct contract between holder, drawer, and acceptor.

What is distinctive about the letter of credit is the degree of insulation which is afforded as a result of its abstract character. Except as against a holder in due course, a party who would otherwise be liable on a bill of exchange can plead a total or partial failure of the consideration for which the bill was given. So a buyer of goods sued on a bill, who has exercised a right to reject the goods for non-conformity with the sale contract, can plead that the consideration for the bill has wholly failed. But, as we have seen, a documentary credit is a form of abstract payment undertaking which is not required to be supported by consideration in the first place. It follows that the question of failure of consideration cannot arise. This must apply just as much to a credit issued for the issuer's own account as to one issued for the account of a third party, for the payment undertaking is just as abstract in the former case as in the latter.

All jurisdictions admit of certain exceptions to the autonomy principle. In particular, fraud on the part of the beneficiary or his agent in relation to documents tendered under the credit disentitles the beneficiary to payment. In England, other defences have been admitted, such as illegality affecting the letter of credit transaction, set-off between beneficiary and issuing bank, and rescission of the letter of credit transaction on the ground that it was induced by misrepresentation. In the United States it is not necessary that the fraud should relate to the documents; fraud in the underlying transaction suffices. In many jurisdictions the ambit of the exceptions to the autonomy principle has been a matter of considerable debate and controversy. Is there conduct short of fraud which nevertheless makes a claim on the credit abusive? Is fraud on the part of a third party for whose acts the beneficiary is not legally responsible a defence? Suppose that such fraud consists in the forgery of a document presented under the credit. Can the beneficiary say that he is innocent of the fraud and entitled to payment, or can the bank plead that while it is entitled to pay against a forged document which appears on its face to be genuine it is not obliged to do so, since a forged document is not a document that conforms to the credit? What is meant by fraud in the underlying transaction (for example, does it cover fraud not reflected in the documents at all, such as a fraudulent misrepresentation by the seller inducing the buyer to enter into the contract of sale) and how far is this a defence? There is a divergence of views not only between different law systems, but even within the same law system both on what constitutes a defence to a claim on a credit and on the approach to be taken by the court on an application for interim injunctive relief. It is therefore helpful that the UNCITRAL Convention on Independent Guarantees and Standby Letters of Credit has addressed these issues. Indeed, it is this part of the Convention which is one of the most likely to be of practical utility . . .

III. DEMAND GUARANTEES AND STANDBY CREDITS

A. *Demand Guarantees and Documentary Credits: Comparisons and Contrasts*

I now turn to demand guarantees. As noted earlier, the documentary credit is designed to ensure the discharge of a payment obligation. By contrast, the demand guarantee is used almost exclusively to secure the performance of a non-monetary obligation—typically the execution of construction works or the delivery of conforming goods under a contract of sale—and is conceived as a default mechanism. It is the principal (the equivalent of the applicant for the credit in a documentary credit transaction) who is primarily responsible for the performance to which the demand guarantee relates, and the agreement between principal and beneficiary requires, expressly or by implication, that the beneficiary resort to the bank only if the principal defaults. So whereas a bank pays a documentary credit only if things go right, in the case of a demand guarantee it is intended that the bank will be called upon to pay only if things go wrong. But the agreement as to the default nature of the demand guarantee is internal to the principal-beneficiary relationship and does not concern the bank, whose duty is to pay against a written demand and such other documents, if any, as the guarantee may specify. Thus the demand guarantee shares with the documentary credit the characteristic that it is an abstract payment undertaking, insulated from the underlying trade transaction, but differs from the documentary credit in that it is improper for the beneficiary to call the guarantee if he does not honestly believe that the principal has committed a breach of the underlying contract. Accordingly, the problem of unfair or abusive calls is peculiar to demand guarantees and cannot arise in relation to documentary credits, where it is agreed from the outset that the bank, not the principal, is to be the first port of call for payment.

Three further differences between documentary credits and demand guarantees may be noted. First, the former usually involve the presentation of a substantial volume of documents, and more often than not these fail to conform to the credit on first presentation, whereas the documentation required for a claim on a demand guarantee is skeletal in the extreme, entailing in most cases presentation of no more than the written demand itself. Second, the making of 'extend or pay' demands is a particular feature of demand guarantee practice for which the URDG (though not the UNCITRAL Convention) made special provision. Third, in a four-party demand guarantee transaction the position of the parties to the counter-guarantee has to be covered.

B. *Standby Letters of Credit*

Standby letters of credit were brought within the UCP for the first time in the 1983 revision, primarily to alleviate the concerns of American banks, most of whom were prohibited from issuing suretyship guarantees and were anxious to send a signal to American courts that standby credits were to be equated with autonomous documentary credits, not with suretyship guarantees. Are standby credits also within URDG?

The treatment of standby credits in relation to URDG has an interesting history. A late draft of the URDG actually contained a provision declaring that the URDG were inapplicable to standby credits. I pointed out that such a provision would set the courts an impossible task, for from a legal viewpoint demand guarantees and standby credits are indistinguishable, and the latter clearly falls within the definition of a demand guarantee in Article 2. Accordingly, the first draft, prepared by the Drafting Group established to finalise a text and resolve the impasse reached in the original Working Party, made explicit reference to standby credits in Article 2. However, bankers were understandably keen to keep the UCP as the applicable set of rules, since it was more detailed and the courts were familiar with the concept. In the end a compromise was reached. The draft was revised to omit specific reference to standby credits in the text of the rules, whilst the introduction made it clear that standby credits were technically within the rules but that banks were advised to continue using the UCP. This solution was approved by the two Commissions involved in the preparation of the rules, the Banking Commission and the Commission on International Commercial Practice.

It has to be said that the treatment of standby credits is not entirely satisfactory. On the one hand, the UCP are much more detailed and therefore deal with matters that are not at present covered by the URDG, including the issue of a credit for the insurer's own account and the confirmation of a credit. On the other hand, the UCP are conceptually inappropriate for standby credits, since almost all of the provisions are designed for situations in which the obligation under the underlying trade transaction is a payment obligation and the issuing bank is the first port of call for payment. The UNCITRAL Convention produces the converse situation in which, as a last minute addition to the text, parties to a commercial credit can opt into the Convention, despite the fact that all its other provisions are geared to instruments that cannot properly be called except in the event of the principal's default.

. . .

E. *The UNCITRAL Convention*

In the light of the URDG, it is at first sight somewhat surprising that UNCITRAL has invested such time and effort in producing its 1995 Convention on Independent Guarantees and Standby Letters of Credit covering much of the same ground. The reason for this is historical. Soon after UNCITRAL first began to look at demand guarantees, the ICC began its project to formulate a set of demand rules designed to be more accommodating of prevailing practice than the 1978 rules. Thereupon, UNCITRAL agreed to halt further work and defer to the ICC project. Unfortunately, this proceeded much more slowly than had been expected, and when after the lapse of several years it showed no signs of reaching finality, UNCITRAL understandably decided to proceed with its own proposals for a convention or uniform law. By the time the URDG had got back on track, the UNCITRAL project was considered too far advanced to be abandoned. Moreover, being a work designed to lead either to a Convention or to a uniform law capable of adoption in national legislation it was able to deal with matters that could not properly be the subject of contractually incorporated rules, notably the effect of fraud and the grant of interim injunctive relief. In its treatment of contractual relations between the parties, the Convention follows the URDG fairly closely in scope and effect, though the drafting is somewhat different and the draft Convention does not contain any equivalent of Article 20, nor does it deal with extend or pay demands.

Given that the contractual aspects of the Convention can be excluded by agreement of the parties, it is unlikely that in relation to these aspects the Convention will ever play a significant role, for in the great majority of cases the parties will incorporate either the URDG or the UCP, and in either case the effect will be to displace those provisions of the Convention dealing with contractual rights and duties. It is in the field of defences to a payment claim and the ground for interim injunctive relief that the influence of the Convention is most likely to be felt. It will be interesting to see how effective it will be in reducing the divergences of approach between national courts.

Guillermo Jiménez, 'The International Chamber of Commerce: Supplier of Standards and Instruments for International Trade', (1996) I Unif Law Rev 284, 284, 286, 292

The International Chamber of Commerce (ICC), a world business organisation based in Paris, is of such central importance in international trade that it deserves an extended introduction. Although the ICC's activities are diverse, of primary interest to the international legal practitioner (as well as to exporters, importers, carriers and insurers) is the ICC's role as a developer of international commercial, legal and banking *standards*.

Thus, the ICC has developed the rules that govern global letter of credit (documentary credit) practice—the *UCP 500*, as well as rules intended to govern guarantee and surety bond practice—the *URDG 458* and *URCB 524*. On the legal side, the ICC's *International Court of Arbitration* is probably the world's foremost international commercial dispute-resolution forum. The *ICC Incoterms 1990*,[5] comprising standard trade terms such as FOB and CIF, define the legal content of price quotes in international transactions. *ICC Model Contracts*, such as those for Agency and Distributorship, provide a reliable alternative to unbalanced or incomplete contracts.

Objectives

The ICC serves world business by promoting trade and investment and open markets for goods and services, as well as the free flow of capital. It defends the private enterprise system and encourages self-regulation by business. Founded in 1919 (and launched at its first World Congress in 1920), the ICC is a non-governmental organisation of thousands of companies and business associations in more than 140 countries. 60 ICC National Committees throughout the world present ICC views to their governments and alert Paris headquarters to national business concerns.

Membership and revenues

As a private, non-profit trade association, the ICC is financed partially through revenues received from dues paid by its 7000 member companies and associations to ICC National Committees. A further important share of the ICC's revenues is derived from administrative fees earned by the ICC Court of International Arbitration; additional income is generated by the marketing of ICC rules and codes, as well as other books (ICC Publishing) and seminars.

Special status

The ICC has class I (top-level) consultative status with the United Nations, where it puts forward the views of business in industrialised and developing countries. It also maintains

---

[5] Later replaced by Incoterms 2000.

close working relations with the newly-stablished *World Trade Organisation* (*WTO*), the *Organisation for Economic Cooperation and Development* (*OECD*), the *European Commission* (*EU*) and other intergovernmental and non-govemmental bodies. ICC permanent representatives at the UN in New York and Geneva monitor developments affecting business within the UN and its specialised agencies . . .

Specialist ICC *Commissions* meet regularly to review issues affecting world business. They cover a wide range of sectors, among them banking, competition, the environment and energy, financial services, insurance, intellectual property, marketing, air, maritime and surface transport, taxation, and trade and investment policy. These Policy Commissions are, in effect, large international committees of top-level lawyers, bankers and trade professionals (commonly, approximately 5–100 members from 25–35 countries). When a particular Commission decides to undertake a specific project, it creates a sub-committee, known as a *Working Party*, to accomplish the given task.

Many of the ICC's key instruments are products of these high-level Working Parties. For example, the revision of the Incoterms or UCP is initially entrusted to a small Working Party operating as a drafting team. Revised drafts are then circulated broadly and internationally through ICC National Committees, with the resulting comments and criticism channelled back to the Working Party. Final drafts, once approved by the Working Party and Commission, are submitted for adoption by the ICC Executive Board. Although the broad international consultation entailed by this procedure is quite time-consuming, it ensures that official ICC products carry a certain authority as representing the true consensus view-point of the world business community.

. . .

Documentary credits (also called letters of credit or 'U/Cs') substantially reduce payment-related risks for both exporter and importer. Not surprisingly, therefore, the letter of credit is the classic form of international export payment, especially in trade between distant partners. Payment, acceptance or negotiation of the credit is made by the bank upon presentation by the seller of stipulated documents. These documents (e.g., bill of lading, invoice, inspection certificate) provide a basic level of proof that the right merchandise has been properly sent to the importer—although, of course, there is always the chance that the documents may prove inaccurate or even fraudulent. It may seem paradoxical, but the very exporters who insist on payment by documentary credits often encounter difficulties with them later. This is because the documentary procedures are so strict that it is easy for the inexperienced exporter to submit documents containing discrepancies, which can impede or seriously delay payment . . .

International letter of credit practice has been standardised by ICC rules known as the Uniform Customs and Practice for Documentary Credits ('UCP 500'). The UCP is frequently cited as the foremost example of how international business self-regulation can be more efficient than treaties, government regulation or case law. Indeed, legal commentators have called the UCP the most successful act of commercial harmonisation in the history of world trade, with the UCP 500 currently observed by banks in approximately 180 countries.

Letter of credit law developed primarily in the United Kingdom in the 19th century, and since the First World War, also extensively in United States courts, as well as in other national courts and legal systems around the world. The first adopted version of the UCP dates from 1929; the 1933 revision of this text gained broad acceptance in Europe. The next revision was adopted in 1951 and brought the UCP to truly global scope, being used by banks in Asia, Africa, Latin America, the United States and Europe. The 1962 revision provided a major breakthrough, gaining the acceptance of the influential UK and Commonwealth banking community. Further revisions, adding technical refinements and improvements, were approved in 1974 and 1983. The currently valid version, UCP 500, entered into effect on 1 January 1994. Periodic revisions have allowed the UCP to keep in step with advances in banking practice. As a result, the UCP is arguably more useful and practical than an international law or treaty could ever be.

With regard to the legal effect around the world of the ICC's rules for letters of credit, the basic rule is that the UCP rules are creatures of contract, and thus apply principally when they have been voluntarily incorporated by the parties. After more than 60 years of existence, the UCP has achieved such universal effect that in some countries the UCP is recognised as having the force of law, or at least that of a strong trade custom. However, in other countries, such as the UK, the UCP does not have formal legislative status.

9.12   Near-universal adoption of the UCP in international trade and their incorporation into all relevant contracts—between the applicant for the credit and its bank, the issuing bank and a correspondent and confirming bank, the issuing/confirming bank and the beneficiary—has had the result of producing, through a series of bilateral contracts, a multilateral network of contractual engagements all based on a set of uniform rules by which the parties make their own law, which is largely independent of national legal systems.

Boris Kozolchyk, 'Letters of Credit', in Boris Kozolchyk and John F. Molloy (eds.), *United States Law of Trade and Investment* (F B Rothman Publications, Littleton (CO), 2001) 24.6–24.7

. . . UCP 500 is the most influential source of LOC law both in the United States and abroad. Its standardization of practice including terms as well as procedures, provides the soundest basis for uniformity and predictability of LOC law. Thanks to the practice standardized by the UCP, a bank in Europe or in Latin America can expect that LOC terms such [as] 'advice', 'confirmation', 'expiration' or 'transfer' will have the same meaning in Asia, Africa or North America. Similarly, a bank in the United States can expect that banks elsewhere will follow the same procedures it follows when examining, accepting or returning LOC documents, making payments or accepting drafts. And when these procedures are not followed, the bank in the United States can rely on the UCP's non-judicial, but nonetheless, effective remedies in the same manner a foreign bank would if the bank in the United States was negligent in its duties to other banks and their clients.

The contract of sale as the central contract

9.13   The seller cannot demand nor the buyer proffer payment by way of a documentary credit unless the contract of sale or some other agreement so provides. Typically it is the contract of sale which will determine the payment method, the type of credit to be issued (payment, acceptance or negotiation and confirmed or unconfirmed) and the documents to be presented under it. A credit issued otherwise than in accordance with the contract may be rejected by the seller/beneficiary. The buyer's instructions to its bank for the issue of the credit must follow the requirements of the contract of sale and the resulting credit must correspond to the buyer's instructions as applicant for the credit. In practice the same form is used.

B. Documentary Credits: the UCP and the eUCP

Most documentary credits issued in connection with international transactions are **9.14** expressed to be governed by UCP 500, now replaced by UCP 600, operative from 1 July 2007. Unless otherwise indicated, references that follow are to UCP 600. The primary method by which these instruments are given effect is express contractual incorporation; indeed, in the case of the UCP this is the only method specified,[6] though where the eUCP are adopted (which under Article e1(b) requires an indication to that effect) the UCP apply automatically without express incorporation.[7] Nevertheless there are other means by which these two instruments may become applicable. One is by a consistent course of dealing, another by international trade usage. In addition, some of the rules embody fundamental principles, such as the autonomy of the credit, which have become accepted as part of documentary credit law in the sense of judicial recognition of international usage. This demonstrates that no set of contractual rules is capable of exhaustively defining the scope of its own application.

The key documents required to be presented are a transport document (e.g. a bill **9.15** of lading), an insurance document (for example, a policy or certificate of insurance) and a commercial invoice, with others being furnished as required by the underlying contract, such as a certificate of origin, a certificate of quality, and a weight certificate. A credit is irrevocable even if there is no indication to that effect,[8]

The opening of a credit is frequently advised by a bank other than the issuing **9.16** bank—for example, the latter's correspondent in the beneficiary's country, the credit calling for presentation of documents to the advising bank. The latter does not itself incur any obligation to the beneficiary to honour the credit unless it adds its own separate undertaking (confirmation), in which case the credit becomes a confirmed credit.

Classification of credits by payment method

Article 10(a) of the UCP requires that all credits clearly indicate whether they are **9.17** available by sight payment, deferred payment, acceptance or negotiation. A sight payment credit entitles the beneficiary to payment at sight, that is, on presentation of the documents. A deferred payment credit, now very common, is one under which payment is to be made on the maturity date or dates determinable in accordance with the stipulations of the credit, typically on expiry of a specified period after shipment date, bill of lading date or presentation of documents, so

---

[6] Art 1.   [7] Art e2(a).

[8] Art 3. Prior to UCP 500 the rules provided that a credit was presumed to be revocable unless otherwise stated. This was so contrary to the basic purpose of a credit and to banking usage that in UCP 500 the presumption was reversed. UCP 600 makes no reference to revocable credits at all.

that in the ordinary way payment will not be made until some time after the documents have been presented. A bank which is authorized by the issuing bank to incur a deferred payment undertaking may now prepay, as by negotiating a draft or purchasing documents, and collect reimbursement from the issuing bank at maturity of the credit even if there is no provision in the credit to that effect.[9] An acceptance credit is one which entitles the beneficiary to call for acceptance of a draft by the issuing bank or other bank named in the credit and payment of the draft at maturity. When the draft has been accepted, the purpose of the credit is completed and thereafter the beneficiary's rights stem from the draft, which must be presented at maturity. A credit which is available only to the named beneficiary is known as a straight credit. It is to be contrasted with a negotiation credit, which extends the payment promise to cover a bank which purchases the draft and/or other documents. The negotiation credit authorizes a named bank, or in the case of a freely negotiable credit any bank, to purchase drafts and/or documents under a complying presentation by advancing or agreeing to advance funds to the beneficiary on or before the banking day on which reimbursement is due to the nominated bank,[10] that is, on or before maturity of the credit. The issuing bank then has to reimburse the nominated bank provided that the documents comply with the credit and have been forwarded to the issuing bank.[11]

Principles of documentary credits law

9.18   The UCP incorporate certain fundamental principles of documentary credit transactions:

Autonomy of the credit

9.19   A credit by its nature is a separate transaction from the sale or other contract on which it may be based.[12] It follows that in the absence of fraud the beneficiary's breach of the underlying transaction does not entitle the bank to withhold payment of a credit, for the letter of credit engagement is between different parties and the payment obligation is conditioned only on tender of the relevant documents within the period of the credit and in conformity with its terms.[13] Accordingly a bank's undertaking is not subject to claims or defences by the applicant resulting

---

[9] Art 12(b). UCP 500 contained no such provision, and in *Banco Santander SA v Bayern Ltd* [2000] 1 All ER (Comm 776) the English Court of Appeal held that a confirming bank which without authorization from the issuing bank discounted its own deferred payment obligation assumed the risk that the issuing bank would refuse to pay if fraud on the part of the beneficiary were discovered prior to the maturity of the credit. Art 12(b) is designed to reverse the effect of that decision.

[10] Art 2, definition of 'negotiation'.   [11] Art 7(c).   [12] Art 4(a).

[13] Ibid. Similarly confirmation of a credit sets up a direct relationship between the confirming bank and the beneficiary which is separate from the relationship between the latter and the issuing bank.

from its relationship with the issuing bank or the beneficiary, and a beneficiary cannot avail itself of the contractual relationships existing between banks or between the applicant and the issuing bank.[14] The guiding rule is 'pay first, argue later'. Fraud by the beneficiary or its agent is everywhere accepted as a ground for non-payment, though this is a rule of law and is not to be found in the UCP. Legal systems differ as to whether the fraud must be in the documents or whether fraud in the underlying transaction suffices, and, in the case of forgery of documents, whether the beneficiary's good faith is irrelevant.[15]

A documentary credit takes effect upon issue

A credit becomes irrevocable upon issue[16]—that is, upon its release from the con- **9.20** trol of the issuer or confirmer—irrespective of the time it is delivered to or received by the beneficiary. The question of how, if at all, this is to be reconciled with traditional contract theory has perplexed scholars from many different countries. Most of the theories advanced founder on being inconsistent with the nature of the transaction and the intention of the parties. The most satisfactory answer is that the binding force of mercantile usage suffices to displace the ordinary contract rules.[17]

Documentary character of the credit

A corollary of the first principle is that all parties concerned deal with documents, **9.21** and not with goods, services or performances to which the documents may relate.[18] Banks have to decide within a very short time—a maximum of five banking days following the day of presentation[19]—and an examination of goods or investigation of facts is incompatible with the need for a speedy payment mechanism. Accordingly banks have to concern themselves only with whether the documents appear on their face to conform to the credit.[20] The loose practice of specifying non-documentary conditions was thought to undermine the letter of credit mechanism, and Article 14(h), restating Article 13(c) of UCP 500, therefore provides that if a credit contains non-documentary conditions these are to be treated as not stated and disregarded.

Banks are concerned only with the apparent good order of the documents

The duty of a bank is to examine the documents presented to it with reasonable **9.22** care to determine, on the basis of the documents alone, whether or not they

---

[14] Art 7(c).

[15] For a detailed comparative analysis of fraud in relation to demand guarantees see Bertrams (n 1), ch 14–16.   [16] Art 7(b).

[17] See Roy Goode, *Commercial Law* (3rd edn, Penguin Books/Lexis Nexis, 2004) 970–71 and literature there cited.   [18] Art 5.

[19] Art 16(d). Under UCP 500 presentation had to be made within a reasonable time and in any event within not more than seven banking days. The period has been shortened and the reference to reasonable time removed.   [20] See below, para 9.22.

appear on their face to constitute a complying presentation.[21] A document is non-complying if it contains data which conflict with data in the same document or any other stipulated document or in the credit.[22] Compliance is to be determined by international standard banking practice[23] as reflected in the UCP and elaborated in the ISBP.[24] It should be borne in mind that the rule allowing reliance on the apparent good order of documents is a rule for the protection of the banks; there is no warrant for the proposition that the good-faith beneficiary is entitled to be paid against documents that appear to be genuine but are in fact forgeries or are issued on behalf of a person who has given neither actual nor ostensible authority for their issue. It is unfortunate that courts in England, in their laudable desire to protect the certainty of payment of bank undertakings, have converted what was designed as a condition of actual compliance with the terms of a credit into a condition of apparent compliance and have thereby extended to good-faith beneficiaries a protection designed exclusively for the banks, while at the same time imposing on banks the duty to pay for documents which they know to be forged and therefore worthless. In this connection it is interesting to compare decisions of the House of Lords and Court of Appeal with a decision of the Singapore Court of Appeal.

United City Merchants (Investments) Ltd v Royal Bank of Canada (The American Accord) [1983] 1 AC 168

Lord Diplock at 184–7

It has, so far as I know, never been disputed that as between confirming bank and issuing bank and as between issuing bank and the buyer the contractual duty of each bank under a confirmed irrevocable credit is to examine with reasonable care all documents presented in order to ascertain that they appear *on their face* to be in accordance with the terms and conditions of the credit, and, if they do so appear, to pay to the seller/ beneficiary by whom the documents have been presented the sum stipulated by the credit, or to accept or negotiate without recourse to drawer drafts drawn by the seller/beneficiary if the credit so provides. It is so stated in the latest edition of the Uniform Customs. It is equally clear law, and is so provided by Article 9 of the Uniform Customs, that confirming banks and issuing banks assume no liability or responsibility to one another or to the buyer 'for the form, sufficiency, accuracy, genuineness, falsification or legal effect of any documents.' This is well illustrated by the Privy Council case of *Gian Singh & Co. Ltd. v. Banque de l'Indochine* [1974] 1 W.L.R. 1234, where the customer was held liable to reimburse the issuing bank for honouring a documentary credit upon presentation of an apparently conforming document which was

---

[21] Art 14(a). 'Complying presentation' means a presentation that is in accordance with the terms and conditions of the credit, the applicable provisions of the UCP and international standard banking practice (Art 1).

[22] Art 14(d). This does not require that the data be identical (for example, the bill of lading may not contain all the data in the commercial invoice), merely that they are consistent (ibid ISPB para 24).

[23] Ibid.

[24] International Standard Banking Practice (ISBP) for the examination of documents under documentary credits (ICC publication No 645). The ISBP is to be revised so as to conform to UCP 600.

an ingenious forgery, a fact that the bank had not been negligent in failing to detect upon examination of the document.

It would be strange from the commercial point of view, although not theoretically impossible in law, if the contractual duty owed by confirming and issuing banks to the buyer to honour the credit on presentation of apparently conforming documents despite the fact that they contain inaccuracies or even are forged, were not matched by a corresponding contractual liability of the confirming bank to the seller/beneficiary (in the absence, of course, of any fraud on his part) to pay the sum stipulated in the credit upon presentation of apparently confirming documents. Yet, as is conceded by counsel for the confirming bank in the instant case, if the broad proposition for which he argues is correct, the contractual duties do not match. As respects the confirming bank's contractual duty to the seller to honour the credit, the bank, it is submitted, is only bound to pay upon presentation of documents which not only appear on their face to be in accordance with the terms and conditions of the credit but also do not in fact contain any material statement that is inaccurate. If this submission be correct, the bank's contractual right to refuse to honour the documentary credit cannot, as a matter of legal analysis, depend upon whether *at the time of the refusal* the bank was virtually certain from information obtained by means other than reasonably careful examination of the documents themselves that they contained some material statement that was inaccurate or whether the bank merely suspected this or even had no suspicion that apparently conforming documents contained any inaccuracies at all. If there be any such right of refusal it must depend upon whether the bank, when sued by the seller/beneficiary for breach of its contract to honour the credit, is able to prove that one of the documents did in fact contain what was a material misstatement.

It is conceded that to justify refusal the misstatement must be 'material' but this invites the query: 'material to what?' The suggested answer to this query was: a misstatement of a fact which if the true fact had been disclosed would have entitled the buyer to reject the goods; date of shipment (as in the instant case) or misdescription of the goods are examples. But this is to destroy the autonomy of the documentary credit which is its raison d'etre; it is to make the seller's right to payment by the confirming bank dependent upon the buyer's rights against the seller under the terms of the contract for the sale of goods, of which the confirming bank will have no knowledge.

Counsel sought to evade the difficulties disclosed by an analysis of the legal consequences of his broad proposition by praying in aid the practical consideration that a bank, desirous as it would be of protecting its reputation in the competitive business of providing documentary credits, would never exercise its right against a seller/beneficiary to refuse to honour the credit except in cases where at the time of the refusal it already was in possession of irrefutable evidence of the inaccuracy in the documents presented. I must confess that the argument that a seller should be content to rely upon the exercise by banks of business expediency, unbacked by any legal liability, to ensure prompt payment by a foreign buyer does not impress me; but the assumption that underlies reliance upon expediency does not, in my view, itself stand up to legal analysis. Business expediency would not induce the bank to pay the seller/beneficiary against presentation of documents which it was not legally liable to accept as complying with the documentary credit unless, in doing so, it acquired a right legally enforceable against the buyer, to require him to take up the documents himself and reimburse the bank for the amount paid. So any reliance upon business expediency to make the system work if the broad proposition contended for by counsel is correct, must involve that as against the buyer, the bank, when presented with apparently conforming documents by the seller, is legally entitled to the option, *exercisable at its own discretion and regardless of any instructions to the contrary from the buyer,* either (1) to take up the documents and pay the credit and claim reimbursement from the buyer, notwithstanding that the bank has been provided with information that makes it virtually certain that the existence of such inaccuracies can be proved, or (2) to reject the documents and to refuse to pay the credit.

The legal justification for the existence of such an independently exercisable option, it is suggested, lies in the bank's own interest in the goods to which the documents relate, as security for the advance made by the bank to the buyer, when it pays the seller under the documentary credit. But if this were so, the answer to the question: 'to what must the misstatement in the documents be material?' should be: 'material to the price which the goods to which the documents relate would fetch on sale if, failing reimbursement by the buyer, the bank should be driven to realise its security.' But this would not justify the confirming bank's refusal to honour the credit in the instant case; the realisable value on arrival at Callao of a glass fibre manufacturing plant made to the specification of the buyers could not be in any way affected by its having been loaded on board a ship at Felixstowe on December 16, instead of December 15, 1976.

My Lords, in rejecting this broad proposition I have dealt with it at greater length than otherwise I would have done, because it formed the main plank of the confirming bank's argument on the documentary credit point before Mocatta J.—who, however, had no hesitation in rejecting it, but found for the confirming bank on the Bretton Woods point. It formed the main ground also in the confirming bank's notice of cross-appeal to the Court of Appeal upon which the confirming bank would seek to uphold the judgment in its favour if the sellers' appeal should succeed upon the Bretton Woods point. It was not until half-way through the actual hearing in the Court of Appeal that the notice of cross-appeal was amended to include a narrower proposition referred to as a 'half-way house' which the Court of Appeal accepted as being decisive in the confirming bank's favour. This rendered it unnecessary for that court to rule upon the broad proposition that I have so far been discussing, although Stephenson L.J. indicated obiter that for his part he would have rejected it. In the confirming bank's argument before this House a marked lack of enthusiasm has been shown for reliance on the 'half-way house' and the broad proposition has again formed the main ground on which the confirming bank has sought to uphold the actual decision of the Court of Appeal in its favour on the documentary credit point.

The proposition accepted by the Court of Appeal as constituting a complete defence available to the confirming bank on the documentary credit point has been referred to as a 'half-way house' because it lies not only half way between the unqualified liability of the confirming bank to honour a documentary credit on presentation of documents which upon reasonably careful examination appear to conform to the terms and conditions of the credit, and what I have referred to as the fraud exception to this unqualified liability which is available to the confirming bank where the seller/beneficiary presents to the confirming bank documents that contain, expressly or by implication, material representations of fact that to his own knowledge are untrue; but it also lies half way between the fraud exception and the broad proposition favoured by the confirming bank with which I have hitherto been dealing. The half-way house is erected upon the narrower proposition that if any of the documents presented under the credit by the seller/beneficiary contain a material misrepresentation of fact that was *false to the knowledge of the person who issued the document* and intended by him to deceive persons into whose hands the document might come, the confirming bank is under no liability to honour the credit, even though, as in the instant case, the persons whom the issuer of the document intended to, and did, deceive included the seller/beneficiary himself.

My Lords, if the broad proposition for which the confirming bank has argued is unacceptable for the reasons that I have already discussed, what rational ground can there be for drawing any distinction between apparently conforming documents that, unknown to the seller, in fact contain a statement of fact that is inaccurate where the inaccuracy was due to inadvertence by the maker of the document, and the like documents where the same inaccuracy had been inserted by the maker of the document with intent to deceive, among others, the seller/beneficiary himself? Ex hypothesi we are dealing only with a case in which the seller/beneficiary claiming under the credit has been deceived, for if he presented documents to the confirming bank with knowledge that this apparent conformity with the terms and conditions of the credit was due to the fact that the documents told a lie, the seller/beneficiary would himself be a party to the misrepresentation made to the confirming bank by the lie in the documents and the case would come within the fraud exception, as did all the American cases referred to as persuasive authority in the judgments of the Court of Appeal in the instant case.

The American cases refer indifferently to documents that are 'forged or fraudulent,' as does the Uniform Commercial Code that has been adopted in nearly all states of the United States of America. The Court of Appeal reached their half-way house in the instant case by starting from the premiss that a confirming bank could refuse to pay against a document that it knew to be forged, even though the seller/beneficiary had no knowledge of that fact. From this premiss they reasoned that if forgery by a third party relieves the confirming bank of liability to pay the seller/beneficiary, fraud by a third party ought to have the same consequence.

I would not wish to be taken as accepting that the premiss as to forged documents is correct, even where the fact that the document is forged deprives it of all legal effect and makes it a nullity, and so worthless to the confirming bank as security for its advances to the buyer. This is certainly not so under the Uniform Commercial Code as against a person who has taken a draft drawn under the credit in circumstances that would make him a holder in due course, and I see no reason why, and there is nothing in the Uniform Commercial Code to suggest that, a seller/beneficiary who is ignorant of the forgery should be in any worse position because he has not negotiated the draft before presentation. I would prefer to leave open the question of the rights of an innocent seller/beneficiary against the confirming bank when a document presented by him is a nullity because unknown to him it was forged by some third party; for that question does not arise in the instant case. The bill of lading with the wrong date of loading placed on it by the carrier's agent was far from being a nullity. It was a valid transferable receipt for the goods giving the holder a right to claim them at their destination, Callao, and was evidence of the terms of the contract under which they were being carried.

But even assuming the correctness of the Court of Appeal's premiss as respects forgery by a third party of a kind that makes a document a nullity for which at least a rational case can be made out, to say that this leads to the conclusion that fraud by a third party which does not render the document a nullity has the same consequence appears to me, with respect, to be a non sequitur, and I am not persuaded by the reasoning in any of the judgments of the Court of Appeal that it is not.

Montrod Ltd v Grundkötter Fleischvertriebs GmbH [2002] 1 WLR 1975

Potter LJ at 1991–2

The fraud exception to the autonomy principle recognised in English law has hitherto been restricted to, and it is in my view desirable that it should remain based upon, the fraud or knowledge of fraud on the part of the beneficiary or other party seeking payment under and in accordance with the terms of the letter of credit. It should not be avoided or extended by the argument that a document presented, which conforms on its face with the terms of the letter of the credit, is none the less of a character which disentitles the person making the demand to payment because it is fraudulent *in itself*, independently of the knowledge and bona fides of the demanding party. In my view, that is the clear import of Lord Diplock's observations in the *Gian Singh* case [1974] 1 WLR 1234, 1238, and in the *United City Merchants* case [1983] 1 AC 168, 183–188, in which all their Lordships concurred. As I understand it, Lord Diplock was of the view that a seller/beneficiary who was ignorant of forgery by a third party of one of the documents presented, or of the fact that the document contained a representation false to the knowledge of the person who created it, should not be in a worse position than someone who has taken a draft drawn under a letter of credit in circumstances which rendered him a holder in due course. While he left open the position in relation to a forged document where the effect of the forgery was to render the document a 'nullity', there is nothing to suggest that he would have recognised any nullity exception as extending to a document which was not forged (ie fraudulently produced) but was signed by the creator in honest error as to his authority; nor do I consider that such an exception should be recognised.

That being so, I do not consider that the fact that in this case it was the seller/beneficiary himself who created the document said to be a nullity should *of itself* disentitle him to payment, assuming (as the judge found) that such creation was devoid of any fraudulent intent and was effected in the belief that GK enjoyed the authority of Montrod, as applicant for the credit, to sign and issue the certificate. Although the circumstances were highly unusual, they may none the less be regarded as no more than an illustration of the wide variety of circumstances in which documents come into existence in a commercial context which do not necessarily reflect the factual situation but which parties may none the less employ as a convenient means of progressing a particular transaction. If, in the circumstances of a multipartite transaction, a seller/beneficiary is indeed led to believe that he has authority to create and present a certificate of inspection for the purpose of triggering payment by letter of credit, I do not see why he should be regarded as any less entitled to payment in accordance with UCP 500 than in a case where he receives from a third party a document regular on its face which has, unknown to him, been created without authority.

In my view there are sound policy reasons for not extending the law by creation of a general nullity exception. Most documentary credits issued in the United Kingdom incorporate the UCP by reference. Various revisions of the UCP have been widely adopted in the USA and by United Kingdom and Commonwealth banks. They are intended to embody international banking practice and to create certainty in an area of law where the need for precision and certainty are paramount. The creation of a general nullity exception, the formulation of which does not seem to me susceptible of precision, involves making undesirable inroads into the principles of autonomy and negotiability universally recognised in relation to letter of credit transactions. In the context of the fraud exception, the courts have made clear how difficult it is to invoke the exception and have been at pains to point out that banks deal in documents and questions of apparent conformity. In that context they have made clear that it is not for a bank to make its own inquiries about allegations of fraud brought to its notice; if a party wishes to establish that a demand is fraudulent it must place before the bank evidence of clear and obvious fraud: see *Edward Owen Engineering Ltd v Barclays Bank International Ltd* [1978] QB 159; cf *Turkiye Is Bankasi AS v Bank of China* [1996] 2 Lloyd's Rep 611, 617 per Waller J. If a general nullity exception were to be introduced as part of English law it would place banks in a further dilemma as to the necessity to investigate facts which they are not competent to do and from which UCP 500 is plainly concerned to exempt them. Further such an exception would be likely to act unfairly upon beneficiaries participating in a chain of contracts in cases where their good faith is not in question. Such a development would thus undermine the system of financing international trade by means of documentary credits.

Beam Technology (Mfg) Pte Ltd v Standard Chartered Bank [2003] 1 SLR 597 [24a]

31 In summary, the current position of the law would appear to be this. The House of Lords in United City Merchants had left open the question whether there is a nullity exception although at the Court of Appeal all the three members of the quorum thought there was. In Montrod, the Court of Appeal (of a different quorum) was inclined to the view that, apart from the traditional fraud exception (ie fraud or knowledge of fraud on the part of the beneficiary or other party seeking payment), there was no separate nullity exception. In any case, even if there was such a nullity exception, it held that the certificate issued by the seller in Montrod in honest belief that he had the authority of the applicant of the letter of credit could not be a nullity. Perhaps another way of differentiating Montrod from the present case is that there the certificate required was not an essential document but one touching on the question as to the quality of the goods sold. In short, there is no definite authority on point, although the views of the Court of Appeal in United City Merchants are no doubt highly persuasive.

32 It seems to us that the issue must be approached on first principles. It is clear that the obligation of the issuing/confirming bank towards the beneficiary is independent and separate from the contractual obligations between the seller and the buyer, and the obligation to pay is absolute irrespective of any dispute that may arise between the seller and the buyer. As far as the confirming or negotiating bank is concerned, their duty is only to verify whether what appears on the documents conforms with what is required by the credit. If there is prima facie compliance, the bank is authorised to pay and may claim reimbursement from the issuing bank notwithstanding that a document tendered may subsequently turn out to be a forgery: Gian Singh. This is to protect the bank and to ensure the smooth flow of international trade and the avoidance of delay. But we are unable to see why such a rule should also lead to the result that if the confirming or negotiating bank, from whatever source, is able to establish within the prescribed seven-day limit that a material document tendered is a forgery, being null and void, the bank is, nevertheless, obliged to pay.

33 While the underlying principle is that the negotiating/confirming bank need not investigate the documents tendered, it is altogether a different proposition to say that the bank should ignore what is clearly a null and void document and proceed nevertheless to pay. Implicit in the requirement of a conforming document is the assumption that the document is true and genuine although under the UCP 500 and common law, and in the interest of international trade, the bank is not required to look beyond what appears on the surface of the documents. But to say that a bank, in the face of a forged null and void document (even though the beneficiary is not privy to that forgery), must still pay on the credit, defies reason and good sense. It amounts to saying that the scheme of things under the UCP 500 is only concerned with commas and full stops or some misdescriptions, and that the question as to the genuineness or otherwise of a material document, which was the cause for the issue of the LC, is of no consequence.

34 As the judge below observed, UCP 500 does not provide that a bank is obliged to accept a document which is a nullity notwithstanding that the time prescribed under Art 14 for the bank to reject the document has not expired. Thus the nullity exception which

---

we postulate is a limited one and would not have given rise to the sort of problems which Potter LJ had expressed concern (at 274):

> If a general nullity exception were to be introduced as part of English law it would place banks in a further dilemma as to the necessity to investigate facts which they are not competent to do and from which UCP 500 is plainly concerned to exempt them.

We are not in any way suggesting that the bank is obliged to investigate into any document tendered. The nullity exception would only permit a bank to refuse payment if it is satisfied that a material document is a nullity.

35 Here, we would like to refer to the following comments of Professor R M Goode in an article in Centre Point entitled 'Reflections on Letters of Credit -1', where he, in discussing the position of the bona fide plaintiff, said:

> Is a plaintiff who seeks to enforce a letter of credit affected by forgery of the documents or other fraud in the transaction if he himself acted in good faith? There is a remarkable dearth of authority on this question. Let us start with the beneficiary. He himself has a duty to tender documents which are in order, and the fact that he acted in good faith in tendering forged documents is thus irrelevant. This fundamental point appears to have been overlooked by Mr Justice Mocatta in The American Accord when he held that the beneficiary was entitled to collect payment despite the insertion of a fraudulent shipping date on the bill of lading, since the fraud had been committed by the loading broker who was the agent of the carrier, not of the seller/beneficiary. But this, with respect, is not to the point. The beneficiary under a credit is not like a holder in due course of a bill of exchange; he is only entitled to be paid if the documents are in order. A fraudulently completed bill of lading does not become a conforming document merely because the fraud is that of a third party.

36 It is our opinion that the negotiating/confirming bank is not obliged to pay if it has established within the seven-day period that a material document required under the credit is forged and null and void and notice of it is given within that period. While we recognise that there could be difficulties in determining under what circumstances a document would be considered material or a nullity, such a question can only be answered on the facts of each case. One cannot generalise. It is not possible to define when is a document a nullity. But it is really not that much more difficult to answer such questions than to determine what is reasonable, an exercise which the courts are all too familiar with.

Banks deal as principals, not as agents

9.23 A bank issuing a letter of credit assumes a payment liability as principal, not as agent for the account party, who cannot be sued on the credit, though if it is dishonoured he may be sued under the original contract. It follows from the fact that banks act as principals and from the autonomy of the credit that a bank's duty to pay against conforming documents is not dependent on its customer's consent and that, absent compelling evidence of fraud, the bank must refuse to accept its customer's instruction to withhold payment if the documents are in order.

The terms of a credit must be strictly complied with

9.24 The general rule is that the documents must conform strictly to the terms of the credit and be presented within the credit period. The fact that the non-conformity is minor or that the credit is presented only a day late does not entitle the beneficiary to claim payment. However, the principle of strict compliance is to be applied in a commercially sensible fashion. So misspellings or typing errors that do not affect the meaning of the word or sentence in which it occurred do not make a document discrepant.[25] At least one original of each document specified in the credit must be presented.[26] What constitutes an original document under UCP 500 gave rise to much debate and a number of court decisions. The position was helpfully clarified by an ICC Banking Commission Policy Statement[27] the key elements of which are now embodied in UCP 600.[28]

A credit is not transferable unless expressly designated as such

9.25 The general rule is that only the named beneficiary or its agent has the right to present documents under the credit and collect payment. A credit is not transferable unless it is designated as such[29] and even then it is transferable only to the extent and in the manner expressly consented to by the transferring bank.[30] In banking practice the form of transfer is not an assignment but a novation, the transferee replacing the transferor as beneficiary to the extent of the transfer. The fact that a credit is not stated to be transferable does not affect the beneficiary's right to assign the proceeds.[31]

The eUCP

9.26 The eUCP Version 1.1 are the electronic supplement to UCP 600 and replace Version 1.0 used with eUCP 500. They do not deal with the electronic issue of letters of credit, a well-established practice calling for no particular rules, but are directed to the presentation of electronic records, either alone or with paper-based documents. When fully developed, a system of electronic presentation embodying a standardized electronic format will have many advantages. In particular, it will enable presentation by the beneficiary direct to the issuer rather than to an advising or confirming bank and, more importantly, will provide an automated mechanism for checking the conformity of presented data with the terms of the credit, thus substantially reducing the currently high percentage of non-conforming presentations and enabling such presentations to be rapidly identified and rectified.

9.27 The definition of an electronic record embodies three distinct elements. The first describes the concept of an electronic record, namely the creation, generation, dispatch, communication, receipt or storage of data by electronic means. The second is that the electronic record is capable of being authenticated as to the apparent

---

[25] ISBP, para 28.   [26] UCP Art 17(a).
[27] 'The Determination of an 'Original' document in the context of UCP sub-Article 20(b)', (document 470/871 (Rev.)), discussed by James E Byrne, *The Original Documents Controversy: from Glencore to the ICC Decision* (Institute of International Banking Law & Practice Inc, Montgomery Village (MD), 1999). See para 9.26 below as to electronic credits.   [28] Art 17(b), (c).
[29] Art 48(b).   [30] Art 48(c).   [31] Art 49.

identity of the sender and the apparent source of the data and as to whether it has remained complete and unaltered. The third is that it is capable of being examined for compliance with the terms of the eUCP credit.[32]

9.28 Article e3 of the eUCP modifies for electronic presentations terms used in UCP 600 and supplies definitions. Under Article e4 a eUCP credit must specify the formats in which electronic records are to be presented, and if it does not then presentation may be made in any format. The credit must state a place for presentation of the electronic record and, if the presentation is to be partly by paper documents, a place for their presentation.[33] However, a presentation under an eUCP credit is considered not received unless and until the beneficiary has provided a notice to the bank to which the presentation is made signifying when the presentation is complete and the presentation identifies the eUCP credits under which it is presented.[34] The time of receipt of the notice of completeness marks the commencement of the period allowed for the examination of documents.[35]

C. Demand Guarantees: the URDG

Purpose of the URDG

9.29 The URDG are designed to provide a set of rules for demand guarantees that are more in keeping with international practice than the 1978 Uniform Rules for Contract Guarantees. The latter made payment conditional on the production of a judgment or arbitral award or the principal's written approval of the claim. Though technically documentary in character, these requirements made demand guarantees almost indistinguishable from suretyship guarantees. The URCG thus failed to provide beneficiaries with the near-equivalent of cash which the needs of the market dictated, so that instead of a beneficiary being able, upon a breach, to make an immediate call for payment by the issuing bank it had to engage in a protracted process leading to a judgment or arbitral award. The URDG, by contrast, recognize the practice of issuing guarantees payable on first written demand without need for further documents, though they impose an additional requirement in the form of a statement of breach.[36] Technically the URDG are applicable to standby letters of credit, which do not differ in legal concept, only in the breadth and diversity of their business application and the adoption of a number of practices used in relation to documentary credits. However, the ISP are specifically designed for standbys and it is these rather than the URDG that are incorporated into standbys. The International Chamber of Commerce has also published Model Forms for Issuing Demand Guarantees.[37]

---

[32] Art E3(b)(i). Compare rule 1.09(c) of the ISP.   [33] Art E5(a).   [34] Art E5(c), (d).
[35] Art E7(a)(i).   [36] See below.   [37] ICC 503, 1993.

After a slow start the URDG are now gaining widespread acceptance, due in no **9.30** small measure to promotion by the ICC's Task Force on Guarantees. They have been incorporated into the forms of guarantee issued by FIDIC[38] and the World Bank; they have been approved by UNCITRAL and strongly recommended by SITPRO;[39] the ICC's Documentary Instruments Dispute Resolution Expertise (DOCDEX) has been amended to cover the servicing of disputes concerning the URDG; the OHADA Uniform Act on Securities 1997 has chapters on demand guarantees closely modelled on the URDG; and they are now used by banks around the world.

Nature of a demand guarantee

Distinguished from letter of credit

A demand guarantee differs from a letter of credit in that the guarantor is not **9.31** intended as the primary source of payment. It is, indeed, improper for the beneficiary to make a demand unless he genuinely believes that the principal has defaulted in his obligations. However, this concerns only the relationship between beneficiary and principal. So far as the guarantor is concerned its payment undertaking is in no way dependent on proof of default; it is purely documentary in character. This makes it difficult to formulate a definition which distinguishes a demand guarantee from a documentary credit. Indeed, Article 2(a) of the URDG does not attempt to do so; it offers a definition which could equally be applied to a documentary credit. The relevance of default features indirectly in Article 20(a), which provides as follows:

> Any demand for payment under the Guarantee shall be in writing and shall (in addition to such other documents as may be specified in the Guarantee) be supported by a written statement (whether in the demand itself or in a written document or documents accompanying the demand and referred to in it) stating:
>
> (i) that the Principal is in breach of his obligation(s) under the underlying contract(s) or, in the case of a tender guarantee, the tender conditions; and
> (ii) the respect in which the Principal is in breach.

This Article, which attracted much controversy, is discussed below. **9.32**

Distinguished from suretyship guarantee

A demand guarantee differs from a suretyship guarantee in that under the latter the **9.33** guarantor's liability is dependent on default by the principal and, unless otherwise agreed, is limited to the loss resulting from that default. The suretyship guarantee

---

[38] *Fédération Internationale des Ingéieurs-Conseils* (International Federation of Consulting Engineers).
[39] Formerly the Simpler Trade Procedures Board, SITPRO Ltd is a body established in the United Kingdom to promote the simplification of international trade.

is therefore not documentary in character but depends on proof of facts establishing default.

International character of demand guarantees

9.34 The demand guarantee shares with the documentary credit the character of being independent of the underlying transaction, so that liability is triggered by presentation of a demand and other specified documents and does not depend on default. This, of course, was an entirely novel conception in national legal systems, for all of whom it was axiomatic that a guarantee was accessory in nature and the guarantor's liability secondary. The concept of a free-standing guarantee was thus a novel one derived exclusively from international trade usage.

Roeland F Bertrams, *Bank Guarantees in International Trade: The Law and Practice of Independent (First Demand) Guarantees and Standby Letters of Credit in Civil Law and Common Law Jurisdictions* (3rd revised edn, Kluwer Law International, The Hague, 2004), para 1–7

The phenomenon of the independent guarantee as it is encountered in practice has been the point of departure [from a comparative study of national legal systems]. Several factors account for this approach. The modern guarantee and notably the guarantee payable on first demand is a product of international trade in response to the changing needs for a more suitable and convenient security instrument in the light of changing trade patterns, the increasing significance of risk and risk avoidance as a factor, a shift in bargaining power, the demand for new and versatile financing instruments and the need for intermediation by banks. These modern guarantees developed autonomously and independently of national law with its traditional concepts, categories, principles and its domestic peculiarities. As independent guarantees are born and bred in a transnational setting, the law on such guarantees is and should also be developed on a transnational level, taking the phenomenon of the guarantee as it functions in international trade as the point of reference. It is true that, in the absence of generally adopted international conventions, the law on independent guarantees is necessarily national law and has developed in national courts. But it is equally true that, from the beginning, there has been a general awareness that guarantees are an international phenomenon and that national law should be finely tuned to developments elsewhere. Indeed, case law and legal writing in the various countries have drawn on developments from elsewhere. In fact, a significant degree of uniform law across jurisdictional boundaries has spontaneously emerged. This is also borne out by the fact that the role of private international law is relatively unimportant. On the other hand, there are many areas which continue to give rise to controversies and where the law is unsettled and inconsistent. However, these uncertainties in the law do not run along national boundaries, but tend to occur in all jurisdictions equally. Accordingly, in respect of these areas too, the law in the various countries cannot be said to differ.

Guarantee structures

9.35 Demand guarantees are typically issued in favour of employers under construction contracts and buyers under contracts of sale, the purpose being to secure proper performance of obligations that are usually non-monetary in character. The URDG apply both to direct (three-party) guarantees and to indirect (four-party) guarantees.

In a three-party guarantee the principal (the contractor, seller, etc.) instructs its bank (the guarantor), which is usually in the same country as the principal, to issue a guarantee directly in favour of the beneficiary, who is usually a foreign party. A four-party guarantee is issued where the beneficiary requires the assurance of payment from a bank in its own country and the principal does not have an account with such a bank. The principal then instructs its own bank (which in this situation is designated 'the instructing party') to request a local bank in the beneficiary's country to issue a guarantee against a counter-guarantee (or counter-indemnity) by the instructing party, which thus has no relationship with the beneficiary.

Advantages

The URDG provide advantages for all parties: the principal, the instructing party, **9.36** the guarantor and the beneficiary. They are designed to strike a fair balance of competing interests, giving the beneficiary the assurance of prompt payment in case of default while building-in certain protections for the principal.

Georges Affaki, *ICC Uniform Rules on Demand Guarantees: A User's Handbook to the URDG* (ICC Publishing, Paris, 2001), paras 39, 42, 49

THE BENEFICIARY'S ADVANTAGES IN USING THE URDG

The beneficiary of a URDG guarantee (and the guarantor beneficiary of a URDG counter-guarantee) derive a number of advantages from the incorporation of the rules.

The most important is the indisputably independent nature of the URDG guarantee and counter-guarantee. Today's guarantee litigation overwhelmingly revolves around the determination of the guarantee's true nature: *independent undertaking or accessory suretyship?* Hundreds of court decisions, the result of lengthy, costly and highly adversarial proceedings, have been rendered to answer that simple problem.

At stake is the possibility for the guarantor to raise defences against the beneficiary's demand. In a nutshell, if the disputed guarantee is found to be a demand guarantee, the beneficiary is entitled to obtain payment if he presents a demand conforming with the guarantee's terms, regardless of whether or not any breach has occurred in the underlying transaction. In a suretyship, the beneficiary first has to prove the principal's breach and, second, to expect his claim to be set off against any counterclaim or defence arising from the underlying transaction . . .

ADVANTAGES TO THE INSTRUCTING PARTY AND GUARANTOR IN USING THE URDG

Independence. It is beyond the guarantor and the instructing party's scope of normal operations, especially when they are banks, to assess the fairness of the beneficiary's assertion of breach, the amount of the exact loss resulting from that breach and the validity of the defences available to the principal under the contract. Neither are they in a position to determine before payment any disputed issues of fact or law arising from the underlying transaction. Accordingly, unless he knowingly chooses to issue a suretyship, the guarantor will wish to see his undertaking insulated from the underlying transaction, and subject only to its own terms.

. . .

THE PRINCIPAL'S ADVANTAGES IN USING THE URDG

It has occasionally been claimed that the URDG have sacrificed the principal's interests on the altar of a beneficiary's interest-driven compromise. That is not the case. If a URCG hybrid guarantee is taken as a benchmark, a principal is likely to find a URD guarantee more severe because he will not be asked to give his consent before the guarantee is paid. However, such a benchmark would be unrealistic in today's buyer-driven market. Principals who do not offer equivalent-to-cash guarantees are automatically excluded from many major projects.

A more positive and more realistic approach for a principal would be to identify the advantages offered by a URDG guarantee compared to the cash deposit he would have been obliged to place in the hands of the beneficiary. These advantages can be divided into two categories:

1. **New rights for the principal.** The URDG directly benefit the principal by entitling him to rights he might not have enjoyed under the governing law without the URDG or a specific contractual agreement, including:
    (i) Force majeure. It is the beneficiary—and not the principal—who bears the risks linked to uncontrollable events (Article 13). Under the URDG, uncontrollable events do not result in suspending and extending the validity of the guarantee or the counter-guarantee until the event ceases. Indeed, if as a result of any uncontrollable event, the beneficiary is unable to present a demand before the expiry of the guarantee, he will not be entitled to claim payment later if the guarantee expires in the meantime. Accordingly the principal will be released from his obligations upon the agreed expiry date or event, regardless of the *force majeure* . . .

    (ii) **Duties to provide information.** Under the URDG the guarantor owes the principal a duty of providing comprehensive information. Instructing parties are also entitled to the same information in indirect (four-party) guarantees. Absent the URDG, the principal (or the instructing party) may not be entitled to claim the same information, since such a right may not be available to him under the applicable law . . . [reference is then made to Articles 7, 17, 26 and 25]

    (iii) **Safe regulatory harbour.** Principals are often concerned about the risk of contracting under unknown foreign laws. To a reasonable extent, the URDG can offer them a safe regulatory harbour. This is possible because the majority of national commercial code provisions are optional. As such, they can be superseded by the URDG . . .

    (iv) **Termination.** [Reference is made to the termination provisions in Articles 24, 18 and 23]

2. **A streamlined negotiation environment.** The URDG also benefits the principal by streamlining the negotiation process, thereby saving him time and cost. Above all, the rules allow the negotiations to take place in a more serene environment, for example:
    (i) **Bases for negotiation.** Offering the URDG as a framework for the guarantee, whether at the outset or as a means to break a negotiating stalemate, is more likely to obtain the beneficiary's consent than, for instance, the principal suggesting clauses drafted by his legal counsel . . .

    (ii) **A shortened text.** Agreeing to issue a URDG guarantee spares the parties the effort of drafting extensive clauses to describe the independence of the guarantee, its irrevocability, its non-assignability, the guarantor's duties, the treatment of extend or pay demands, the conditions to accept a demand for payment, applicable law and jurisdiction, etc. . . . .

Fundamental principles

Many of the principles governing documentary credits apply with equal force to   **9.37**
demand guarantees. These are documentary in character, they are separate from
the underlying transaction and from internal mandates between the same parties,
the beneficiary is entitled to payment only on presentation of the relevant documents, and the guarantor's duty is limited to exercising reasonable care to ensure
that the documents appear to be in conformity with the guarantee. But the documents are usually much simpler (typically, a written demand and, if Article 20 is
not excluded, a statement of breach) and, whereas in the case of a documentary
credit the bank is the first port of call for payment, a demand guarantee is intended
as a fall-back position in the event of the principal's default, though such default is
not a condition of payment as between guarantor and beneficiary. Both the liability to pay and the amount to be paid are governed solely by the terms of the guarantee and are not conditioned on actual default or actual loss.

Roy Goode, *Guide to the Uniform Rules for Demand Guarantees* (ICC Paris, 1992) 8

The essential point to bear in mind is that demand guarantees, being a substitute for cash,
are designed to provide the beneficiary with a speedy monetary remedy against the counterparty to the underlying contract and to that end are primary in form and documentary
in character. That is to say, in contrast to the suretyship guarantee, which is an undertaking
to be answerable for another's debt or default, and is thus triggered only by proof of actual
default and to the amount of loss suffered from the default within the maximum amount
stated in the guarantee, the demand guarantee is expressed to be payable solely on presentation of a written demand. Accordingly any demand within the maximum amount must
in principle be paid by the guarantor, regardless whether the underlying contract has in fact
been broken and regardless of the loss actually suffered by the beneficiary.

The demand guarantee is independent not only of the underlying transaction but   **9.38**
also of (a) the mandate given by the principal to the guarantor, (b) any counter-
guarantee, and (c) any mandate given to the counter-guarantor (or, in the words
of the URDG, instructing party).

Irrevocability and coming into effect

Like a documentary credit, a demand guarantee becomes irrevocable on issue[40] and   **9.39**
takes effect from the same time unless otherwise provided.[41]

---

  [40] Art 5.   [41] Art 6.

The demand for payment

9.40 The requirements for the demand under the guarantee contain a feature unique to the URDG. The demand must be in writing (which includes electronic data interchange)[42] and must be presented on or before the expiry date and before the expiry event[43] and in conformity with the requirements of the guarantee, together with such other documents (if any) as the guarantee may specify. But Article 20, reproduced earlier, also requires an additional document to be presented, whether or not specified in the guarantee, namely a statement (whether in the demand itself or in a separate document accompanying the demand and referred to in it) stating that the principal is in breach of his obligations under the underlying contract or in the case of a tender guarantee the tender conditions and the respect in which the principal is in breach.[44] The requirements for a demand under a counter-guarantee are simpler still. The demand must be accompanied by a written statement that the guarantor has received a demand for payment under the guarantee in accordance with its terms and with Article 20.[45]

9.41 Though Article 20(a) can be expressly excluded by the terms of the guarantee, it nevertheless demonstrates that in the relationship between beneficiary and principal the guarantee should not be called if the beneficiary does not believe that the principal has committed a breach of the underlying contract. The purpose of Article 20 is to provide some check on abusive calling without interfering with the immediacy of performance of the payment undertaking. The check is a limited one only, since it is the beneficiary itself which provides the statement of breach. But the thinking was that a beneficiary who might otherwise be tempted to make an abusive call might be reluctant to put its name to a false statement. Article 20 proved to be the most controversial of the provisions of the URDG; indeed, they almost foundered because of it. The principal objection was that it created a trap because the requirement to present a statement of breach applied even if not so stated in the terms of the guarantee. That objection never had much substance, given that parties to a guarantee incorporating the URDG are expected to be familiar with the Rules in the same way that parties to a documentary credit are expected to be familiar with the UCP. In any event, the objection is readily overcome by setting out the requirements of Article 20 in the guarantee itself, as in the ICC *Forms for Issuing Demand Guarantees* (ICC Publications, Paris, 1994).

---

[42] Art 2(a), (d).

[43] An expiry event means the presentation of a document specified for the purpose of expiry (Art 22), for example, an architect's certificate of completion, the presentation of which results in expiry of the guarantee.

[44] The statement of breach can be quite general, for example that the contract was not completed by the due date.   [45] Art 20(b).

Extend or pay demands

Article 26 deals with the extend or pay (alternatively pay or extend) demand, that **9.42** is, a demand to extend the period of the guarantee or if not then to pay it. Such a demand is not necessarily improper, for there may in fact have been a breach or the beneficiary may believe a breach to have occurred. When such a demand is made the guarantor must inform the principal and suspend payment for such period as is reasonable to enable the beneficiary and the principal to reach agreement. If an extension is agreed, it takes effect on issue of the requisite amendment to the guarantee by the guarantor. If the extension is refused, the guarantor must pay, and the same is the case if negotiations are still current when the reasonable time elapses. But expiry of the guarantee before then does not affect the beneficiary's right to payment, since all that is required is that the demand be made before expiry of the guarantee.

Termination of the guarantee

The guarantee ends on payment,[46] on expiry,[47] on cancellation[48] or by force of law. **9.43** Termination is not dependent on return of the guarantee except where this act is itself relied on as an act of cancellation. [49]

Governing law and jurisdiction

Unless otherwise provided, the law governing the guarantee is that of the place of **9.44** the business of the guarantor, while the law governing a counter-guarantee is that of the place of business of the instructing party.[50] Similarly, unless otherwise provided it is the competent court of the same place that has jurisdiction.[51] The significance of the autonomy of the counter-guarantee is not always understood, even by courts. In *Wahda Bank v Arab Bank plc*[52] one of the issues was the law governing the counter-guarantee. Staughton LJ clearly thought little of Articles 2(c) and 27 of the URDG.

> We were referred to a set of rules propagated by the International Chamber of Commerce. They are called the ICC Uniform Rules For Demand Guarantees, ICC Publication No. 458, Copyright 1992. They provide in Art. 2b:
>
> > Guarantees by their nature are separate transactions from the contract(s) or tender conditions on which they may be based, and Guarantors are in no way concerned with or bound by such contract(s), or tender conditions, despite the inclusion of a reference to them in the Guarantee.
>
> They then go on in Art. 2c to deal with 'counter-guarantees' and says that they:
>
> > . . . are by their nature separate transactions the Guarantees . . . and Instructing Parties are in no way concerned with or bound by such guarantees. . . .

---

[46] Art 18. [47] Arts 19, 22. [48] Art 23. [49] Art 22. [50] Art 27.
[51] Art 28. [52] [1996] 1 Lloyd's Rep 470.

> I would not agree with that at all, I must say. The party who gives the performance bond is vitally concerned, I would say, in the counter guarantee.

Article 27 of those so-called Uniform Rules provides:

> Unless otherwise provided in the Guarantee or Counter-Guarantee, its governing law shall be that of the place of business of the Guarantor or Instructing Party (as the case may be), or, if the Guarantor or Instructing Party has more than one place of business, that of the branch that issued the Guarantee or Counter-Guarantee.

> This case shows, to my mind, for the reasons that I have given, that that solution will not be very attractive to bankers. I should not be surprised if they decide to adopt something which is more suitable for their needs. However, that is for another day.[53]

9.45   It is fair to say that the learned Lord Justice was far from being alone in these views. Nevertheless it is evident that he did not have brought to his attention a number of salient facts. In the first place, the URDG were not prepared as a theoretical study by academics; they were the product of intensive work by a joint working party of two commissions of the ICC, the Banking Commission and the Commission on International Commercial Practice, the former consisting of highly experienced bankers from all over the world, including the United Kingdom, and the latter from business interests in many countries, including those well versed in exports and imports. The work occupied several years, took account of hundreds of comments from ICC national committees all over the world as well as from international organizations and, having been largely accomplished by the working party, was eventually completed by a small drafting group and approved without dissent at separate meetings of both commissions. Secondly, since banks are not equipped to examine external facts and do not wish to do so, the payment obligation of the instructing party (i.e. the counter-guarantor) is geared entirely to documents and is not dependent on the validity of the claim under the guarantee or even on production of the beneficiary's demand, a fact which emphasizes the deliberate intention to insulate the counter-guarantee from the guarantee itself as regards the instructing party's payment obligation. Thirdly, it is widely accepted that the appropriate law to govern a guarantee is the guarantor's place of business and to govern a counter-guarantee is the instructing party's place of business, this being in both cases the place where the payment obligation has normally to be performed. Fourthly, the analogy drawn in an earlier part of the judgment between counter-guarantees and confirmed credits is false, for as an experienced commentator who is also a senior lawyer in a major French bank has pointed out the undertaking given in a confirmed credit is parallel and additional to that of the issuing bank, whereas a counter-guarantee is given only to the guarantor, not to the beneficiary.[54]

---

[53]   Above, at 473–4.
[54]   Georges Affaki, *ICC Uniform Rules on Demand Guarantees: A User's Handbook to the URDG* (ICC Publishing, Paris, 2001), paras 158 and 159.

D. The International Standard Practices (ISP98)

UCP 600 are expressed to apply (to the extent to which they may be applicable) **9.46** to standby credits as well as documentary credits.[55] This follows UCP 500, but while the goal of broadening the scope of the UCP is understandable it would have been better to say nothing of standby credits, since most of the provisions of the UCP are geared to presentation to the bank as the first port of call for payment and are thus wholly unsuited to standbys. The URDG were thus more appropriate, since from a legal perspective demand guarantees and standbys are indistinguishable. However, as stated earlier, standbys are used for a much wider variety of purposes and involve a number of techniques also used in documentary credit operations, so that what was required was a set of rules which utilized those aspects of the UCP that could be applied to standbys but were otherwise specifically geared to the nature of a standby as a fall-back recourse for the beneficiary.[56] This is what the International Standard Practices (ISP98) are designed to provide.

Like the UCP and the URDG, ISP98 embodies the concepts of irrevocability, **9.47** independence of the credit from the underlying transaction, and documentary character.[57] It also provides for electronic presentation where so permitted by the credit.[58] As with the URDG there is a specific rule for extend or pay demands[59] but it is differently structured. There is no suspension of the duty to pay; the issuer is allowed the maximum period of seven days to complete its examination of the documents and has a discretion whether to consult the applicant as to the extension or to pay if the demand is compliant. This is logical because an extension involves increased risk for the issuer, and since an amendment to the credit can only be effected with the issuer's consent there is no point in requiring the issuer to go through the consultation process if it has anyway decided not to grant the extension. If an amendment granting the extension is issued (which needs to be done within the seven days allowed for examination of the documents) the beneficiary is considered to have retracted its demand.

ISP98 contains a number of other rules reflecting standby practice, including pro- **9.48** visions for nomination of a person to advise, receive a presentation, effect a transfer, confirm, etc.,[60] transfer of drawing rights,[61] and syndication of and participation in the issuer's rights.[62]

---

[55] Art 1.

[56] Standby letters of credit have featured prominently in disputes before the Iran-US Claims Tribunal

[57] R 1.06 and 1.07. As under the UCP, non-documentary terms or conditions are to be disregarded (r 4.11).   [58] R 3.06(d), 1.09.

[59] R 3.09.   [60] R 2.04.   [61] R 6.   [62] R 10.

9.49 Interestingly, while ISP98 describes the characteristics of a standby credit—irrevocability, independence, documentary character, binding force on issue—it nowhere offers a definition. Professor James Byrne's official commentary explains why.

James E Byrne, *The Official Commentary on the International Standby Practices* (ed James G Barnes, Institute of International Banking Law & Practice, Montgomery Village (MD), 1998) 2

This Rule [Rule 1] uses the term 'standby' in two distinct senses. Subrules (a) and (b) refer to a 'standby letter of credit.' No definition of a standby letter of credit is provided in these Rules. A precise definition has not been given because the distinction between commercial letters of credit and standby letters of credit is not precise. A standby letter of credit is any letter of credit and undertaking which is not a commercial letter of credit. This approach, however, only shifts the difficulty. The question becomes what constitutes a commercial letter of credit, hardly a matter which is appropriate for standby rules. That there may be some overlap is not a source of significant difficulty. Rather than being overly concerned with a technical definition, ISP98 leaves it to the market to decide with which undertakings it is best used . . . As recognized in ISP98 Rule 1.11(b) (Interpretation of these Rules), 'standby letter of credit' and 'standby' have different meanings in the Rules. A 'standby letter of credit' is the type of letter of credit which is understood to be a letter of credit. A 'standby' is any undertaking subject to these Rules. Thus, an independent guarantee subject to ISP98 would be a 'standby' for purposes of these Rules.

9.50 In other words, ISP98 is intended to be applied to standby letters of credit as these are understood in the market but any undertaking which is expressed to be subject to ISP98 is a standby even if it is not of a kind that would ordinarily be described in the market as a standby letter of credit. ISP98, like the URDG, does not itself identify any characteristics which distinguish a standby credit from a documentary credit. Moreover, the difficulty of so doing is compounded by the curiously named 'direct pay' standby, to which ISP98 is expressed to apply but which, being payable independently of default, is surely a contradiction in terms and is indistinguishable from an ordinary documentary credit. Direct pay standbys are frequently coupled with an undertaking also making them payable on default. It is hard to see what additional benefit this further undertaking confers on the beneficiary.

James E. Byrne, 'Standby Rulemaking: A Glimpse at the Elements of Standardization and Harmonization of Banking Practice', in Jacob S. Ziegel (ed), *New Developments in International Commercial and Consumer Law* (Hart Publishing, Oxford, 1998), 138–40

The standby letter of credit has suffered through identification of its legal nature with its function. To some extent this can be explained by its historical antecedents, as the standby emerged from the commercial letter of credit to back up (or 'stand-by') another payment mechanism. In this sense, it became readily confused with an accessory or suretyship guarantee. Similarly, its character was associated with the occurrence of a default. Strictly speaking, neither characterization is satisfactory or complete.

Standbys are, of course, used in default situations. Classified by the Bank of International Settlements as 'performance standbys', default standbys assure performance of various undertakings which run the gamut of human and commercial conduct. In this sense, they are similar in many respects to the uses with which independent guarantees are almost exclusively associated. Another use of standbys has emerged, however, which illustrates the remarkable flexibility of this device and which demonstrates the limitations of a system of classification predicated upon function. Since the mid-1980s, the capital markets have relied heavily on standby letters of credit to assure payment of principal and interest to trustees on behalf of purchasers of bonds and commercial paper. The volume of these issuances exceeds all other uses of standbys. Although these financial standbys provide for payment in the event of default, they also provide for regular payment of interest and principal as the ordinary avenue of payment. As a result, it is incorrect to describe them as 'default' instruments.

This so-called 'direct pay' feature of a financial standby makes the definition of a standby almost impossible. The only satisfactory definition is that it is an independent undertaking to pay against the presentation of documents which is not predicated upon payment against documents related to the sale of goods. Even this attempt at a definition is rendered difficult by the existence of so-called 'commercial standbys' which are used as a back-up for payment of commercial transactions and which require the presentation of many of the same documents which would have been expected to be presented under a commercial letter of credit.

E. The United Nations Convention on Independent Guarantees and Stand-by Letters of Credit

Features of the UN Convention

The UN Convention results from a project by UNCITRAL to harmonize the law **9.51** governing cross-border independent guarantees and standby letters of credit. For the Convention to apply the internationality requirement must be satisfied[63] and there must be the requisite connection to a Contracting State.[64] The Convention is limited to independent undertakings (standbys, demand guarantees, counter-guarantees) and does not apply to suretyship guarantees. It can also be applied to international letters of credit.[65] At first sight this seems as inappropriate as the inclusion of standby letters of credit in the UCP; but whereas the UCP takes effect by contractual incorporation the Convention, on coming into force and being brought into effect in Contracting States, becomes a legally operative instrument and contains useful provisions on defences to payment and on provisional court

---

[63] That is, the places of business, as specified in the undertaking, of any two of the following persons are in different States, guarantor/issuer, beneficiary, principal/applicant, instructing party, confirmer (Art 4(1)).

[64] That is, either the place of business of the guarantor/issuer at which the undertaking is issued must be in a Contracting State or the rules of private international law lead to the application of the law of a Contracting State (Art 1(1)). cf CISG, Art 1.   [65] Art 1(2).

measures[66] which could not have been inserted into the UCP and which give useful support to the latter.

9.52 In general, the provisions track those of a kind contained in the UCP and URDG. Distinctive are the rules governing exceptions to the payment obligation and the ordering of provisional measures. Article 19(1) entitles the guarantor/issuer, acting in good faith,[67] to withhold payment from the beneficiary if 'it is manifest and clear that (a) any document is not genuine or has been falsified, (b) no payment is due on the basis asserted in the demand and the supporting documents, or (c) judging by the type and purpose of the undertaking, the demand has no conceivable basis'. Article 19(2) provides a list of situation types in which a demand has no conceivable basis. These include the beneficiary's wilful misconduct in preventing fulfilment of the underlying obligation. In any case in which the guarantor/issuer is entitled to withhold payment the principal/applicant or the instructing party may apply to the court, on the basis of immediately available strong evidence, for an order preventing the beneficiary from receiving payment or blocking the process paid to the beneficiary.[68] The choice of law rule is the same as under the URDG.[69]

Relationship between the Convention and the URDG

9.53 Because for the most part the Convention defers to the agreement of the parties to a demand guarantee and expressly recognizes international rules and usages, the Convention rules do not present any serious obstacle to the operation of the URDG; rather they serve as gap-fillers where the URDG do not apply and, through Article 19, reinforce the rights of the parties.

Rafael Illescas-Ortiz, 'International Demand Guarantees: The Interaction of the Uncitral Convention and the URDG Rules of the ICC', in Jacob S. Ziegel (ed), *New Developments in International Commercial and Consumer Law* **(Hart Publishing, Oxford, 1998), 162–4**

Because of the separate nature of the Convention and the Rules, any conflict between them is not likely to be very serious. Furthermore, the opting-out and opting-in mechanism provided by Article 1 of the Convention gives considerable freedom to the parties to the undertaking to choose whether to submit their undertaking to one or other set of rules in specific cases. In addition, the URDG and UCP clearly and explicitly establish the manner in which the guarantee and standby fall under the jurisdiction of the specific ICC Rules . . .

---

[66] Arts 19 and 20.

[67] It is not clear in what circumstances a guarantor/issuer invoking Art 19 could ever be said not to be acting in good faith.

[68] Art 20(1). The court may require the applicant for the order to furnish such security as the court deems appropriate, eg to cover the cost of compensating the beneficiary establishing its claim for loss suffered as the result of the order.   [69] Convention, Art 22.

In five different contexts the UN Convention makes reference to external sources of the dynamics of the undertaking embodied in a demand guarantee or a standby letter of credit. These situations are:

(1) The accurate determination of all the rights and obligations of the guarantor/issuer and the beneficiary of the undertaking. That determination, as stated by Article 13(1) of the Convention, must be made by the 'terms and conditions set forth in the undertaking, *including any rules, general conditions or usages specifically referred to therein, and by the provisions of this Convention*' (emphasis added).

(2) The correct interpretation of the terms and conditions of the undertaking and the settlement of questions not addressed by those terms and conditions must be done with regard to '*generally accepted international rules and usages of independent guarantee or standby letter of credit practice*': Article 13(2) of the Convention (emphasis added).

(3) The standard of conduct of the guarantor/issuer in discharging its obligations under the undertaking of good faith and reasonable care. In order to fix the meaning of both standards—the good faith and the reasonable care—'*due regard shall be had to generally accepted standards of international practice of independent guarantees or standby letters of credit*': Article 14(1) of the Convention (emphasis added).

(4) When demand for payment is made by the beneficiary to the guarantor/issuer, Article 16(1) of the Convention states that 'the guarantor/issuer shall examine the demand and any accompanying documents in accordance *with the standard of conduct referred to in paragraph (1) of Article 14*' (emphasis added).

(5) Examination of the document mentioned above obligates the guarantor/issuer to honour the promise of payment contained in the undertaking if the guarantor/issuer concludes that the beneficiary's demand is a proper demand. As Article 16(1) of the Convention requires, in determining whether documents are in facial conformity with the terms and conditions of the undertaking and are consistent with one another,—upon which is based the conformity of the demand of payment—the guarantor/issuer shall have due regard to *the applicable international standard of independent guarantee or standby letter of credit practice*' (emphasis added).

F. ICC Uniform Rules for Contract Bonds

The UCB differ from the URDG in that the beneficiary must establish that there **9.54** has been a default by the contractor (or 'principal' to use the language of the rules) before it is entitled to payment from the guarantor: it does not suffice for the beneficiary to issue a demand for payment accompanied only by a statement that the principal is in breach and the respect in which he is in breach. In this respect the UCB partakes of the nature of a traditional suretyship bond; that is to say, the liability of the guarantor is an accessory liability, dependent upon a prior breach of one of his obligations by the contractor. The bond remains documentary in nature but the documentary obligations accepted by the beneficiary are more onerous than in the case of the URDG.9.

9.55 The UCB are a set of contract terms and depend for their effect on incorporation by the parties into their contracts. In this respect, the rules depend for their use upon the operation of the market. The rules are most likely to be used in the construction industry, where an insurance company issues to the employer a contract bond under which the insurance company agrees to guarantee the obligations of the contractor under the building contract. But the rules are not confined in their scope to the construction industry. They can be incorporated into any contract where the parties so choose.

Default

9.56 The obligation of the guarantor to honour the guarantee given is dependent upon the occurrence of a 'default'.[70] A default is deemed to have been established for the purposes of the rules (i) upon issue of a certificate of default by a third party if the bond so provides, (ii) if the bond does not provide for the issue of a certificate by a third party, upon the issue of a certificate of default by the guarantor or (iii) by the final judgment, order or award of a court or tribunal of competent jurisdiction.[71] These rules provide substantial protection for the guarantor and, accordingly, it was not necessary to incorporate into the rules provisions protecting the guarantor against unfair or abusive calls.

Governing law and jurisdiction

9.57 In the absence of a choice of law by the parties, the law applicable to the bond shall be the law applicable to the contract between the principal (contractor) and the beneficiary.[72] This presumptive link to the underlying contract between the principal and the beneficiary, illustrates the closeness of the link between the obligation to pay under the bond and the liability of the principal to the beneficiary.

9.58 Further, the rules provide that all disputes arising between the beneficiary, the principal and the guarantor in relation to a bond governed by the rules shall, unless otherwise agreed, be 'finally settled under the Rules of Conciliation and Arbitration' of the ICC. The parties remain free to exclude the application of the ICC rules of conciliation and arbitration and to make their own provision for the determination of any dispute. Where they exclude the application of the ICC rules but do not make their own provision for the determination of disputes, any dispute shall be determined by a competent court of the guarantor's principal place of business or, at the option of the beneficiary, the competent court of the country in which the branch of the guarantor which issued the bond is situated.

---

[70] Art 7(i).
[71] Art 7(j). In the case of (i) and (ii) the parties retain the right to require the determination of any dispute or difference arising under the contract or the bond or the review of any certificate of default or payment made pursuant thereto by a court or tribunal of competent jurisdiction.
[72] Art 8(a).

Questions

Bank payment undertakings generally

1. (1) What do you understand by the phrase 'abstract payment undertaking'?
    (2) What are the principal types of abstract payment undertaking? By whom are these usually issued?
    (3) What is the commercial reason for the emergence of the abstract payment undertaking?

Documentary credits

2. What is a documentary credit? How is it to be distinguished from:
    (1) a suretyship guarantee;
    (2) a standby letter of credit?
3. (1) What theoretical difficulties do you see, under the law of your own country, in reconciling the binding nature of an abstract payment undertaking, and the UCP rules governing it, with traditional contract theory?
    (2) What is the legal status of the UCP? In what circumstances may they be applied?
    (3) Discuss the significance of the UCP as an instrument of harmonization of the law governing bank payment undertakings.
4. Analyse the passages set out above in the speech of Lord Diplock in *United City Merchants (Investments) Ltd v Royal Bank of Canada* Read and the judgment of Potter LJ in *Montrod Ltd v Grundkötter Fleischvertriebs Gmbh* [2002] 1 WLR 1975.
    (1) Do you agree with the reasoning in those passages?
    (2) What would be the result under Article 19 of the UN Convention on Independent Guarantees and Stand-By Letters of Credit?
    (3) What is your view of the approach to the nullity question taken by the Singapore Court of Appeal?

Demand guarantees

5. What is a demand guarantee? How, if at all, is it distinguishable from:
    (a) a standby letter of credit;
    (b) a documentary credit;
    (c) a suretyship guarantee?
6. Prior to issuing the URDG, the ICC had published a set of rules in 1978 governing demand guarantees.
    (1) What were they?
    (2) Why were they unsuccessful? And what lessons can we learn from this experience in making rules to harmonize commercial practice?

7. (1) What problems have national courts confronted in characterizing a demand guarantee? How have courts in your country overcome these difficulties? And why have they been willing to do so?

   (2) What must the beneficiary of a demand guarantee do in order to be entitled to obtain payment under a demand guarantee? What unique rule is contained in the URDG relating to this—and why is it there?

The UNCITRAL Convention on Independent Guarantees and Stand-By Letters of Credit

8. (1) What is the purpose of the UNCITRAL Convention on Independent Guarantees and Stand-By Letters of Credit?

   (2) To what extent will the rules of the convention override or be overridden by the URDG or UCP?

   (3) What does the answer to (2) tell you about the relationship between conventions and codified usages in the hierarchy of legal norms governing commercial transactions?

9. To what extent are such conventions and codifications reliable evidence of existing usage?

Further reading

Brindle, Michael, and Cox, Raymond (eds), *Law of Bank Payments* (3rd edn, Sweet & Maxwell, London, 2004), ch 8

De Ly, Filip, 'The U.N. Convention on Independent Guarantees and Stand-by Letters of Credit', (1999) 33 The International Lawyer 831–46

Dolan, John F, *The Law of Letters of Credit* (3rd revised edn, A S Pratt & Sons, Washington DC, 1996, with semi-annual supplements)

Ehrlich, Dietmar, 'Dokumentäre Zahlungsverkehrsinstrumente' in Kronke, Herbert, Melis, Werner and Schnyder, Anton K (eds), *Handbuch Internationales Wirtschaftsrecht* (Dr Otto Schmidt, Köln, 2005) 1017

Gao, Xiang, *The fraud rule in the law of letters of credit: a comparative study* (Kluwer Law International, The Hague, 2002)

Goode, Roy, *Commercial Law* (3rd edn, Penguin Books/Lexis Nexis, London, 2004), ch 35

Goode, Roy, 'Abstract Payment Undertakings in International Transactions', XXII Brook J Int Law 1 (1996)

Jack, Raymond, Malek, Ali, and Quest, David, *Documentary Credits* (3rd edn, Butterworths, 2001)

Mugasha, Agasha, 'Enjoining the Beneficiary's Claim on a Letter of Credit or Bank Guarantee' [2004] JBL 515

Seppala, Christopher R, 'The ICC Uniform Rules for Demand Guarantees ('URDG') in Practice: A Decade of Experience', presentation at an ICC Conference Paris, 15 May 2001, accessible on the FIDIC web site

Weller, Matthias, 'Sicherheiten' in Kronke, Herbert, Melis, Werner and Schnyder, Anton K (eds), *Handbuch Internationales Wirtschatsrecht* (Dr Otto Schmidt, Köln, 2005) 908

10

FINANCIAL LEASING: THE 1988 UNIDROIT CONVENTION AND THE UNIDROIT DRAFT MODEL LAW

Introduction	10.01	Exclusion of Convention	10.14
Background to the Leasing Convention	10.02	Purposes of the Convention	10.15
Sphere of application	10.07	Removal of responsibility from the	
The transaction is a financial		lessor to the supplier	10.16
leasing transaction	10.08	Conferment of rights against	
The equipment is not to be used		the supplier	10.19
primarily for the lessee's personal,		Exculpation of lessor from liability	
family or household purposes	10.11	under the leasing agreement	10.21
The lessor and the lessee have their		Liability to third parties	10.23
places of business in different States	10.12	Protection against lessee's insolvency	10.24
Those States and the State in which		Default remedies of lessor	10.26
the supplier has its place of		Evaluation of the Leasing Convention	10.27
business are Contracting States		Leasing under the Mobile Equipment	
or both the supply agreement		Convention and Protocol	10.28
and the leasing agreement are		The UNIDROIT Draft Model Law	10.29
governed by the law of a			
Contracting State	10.13		

Introduction

There are three principal methods of financing the acquisition of business equip-   **10.01**
ment: sale, lease and secured loan. The first two are forms of title finance, the creditor's security for performance deriving from its ownership of the asset or its other
rights as lessor, in contrast to a secured loan, in which the creditor advances funds
on the security of an asset owned by the debtor. Of course, many sales and leases are
not financing instruments at all, since they are not designed to provide financial
accommodation. The typical financing sale is one in which the creditor reserves
title until payment. The finance lease, as explained in more detail below, is one
which is structured to provide the creditor with reimbursement for its outlay on the
equipment and the desired return on capital, and is to be contrasted with the operating lease. Straddling these two forms of title finance is the sale and lease back.

Background to the Leasing Convention

10.02   UNIDROIT first began preliminary work on a proposed convention on international financial leasing in 1974, and the Convention was finally concluded in Ottawa on 28 May 1988. Fourteen years may seem a long time for a convention which, apart from the final clauses, is only fourteen articles long. But the issues proved more complex than had been appreciated, and constraints of time and resources meant that meetings of the Study Group responsible for the preparation of the text were infrequent.

10.03   A key reason for undertaking this project was the fact that in most, if not all, legal systems the law did not respond adequately to the distinctive characteristics of financial leasing transactions or to the tripartite relationships they set up.[1] What are these characteristics? First, though from a legal viewpoint financial leasing is a form of rental, with or without an option to purchase,[2] in substance it is a financing transaction in which equipment is acquired by a lessor from a manufacturer or supplier for the purpose of being leased for the greater part of its expected working life to a single lessee at a rent based not on the use-value of the equipment but on what is required to amortize the capital cost of the equipment over the primary period of the lease[3] and provide the lessor with its desired return on capital. Second, both the supplier and the equipment are selected by the intending lessee, not the intending lessor, and it is the former who conducts negotiations with the supplier concerning the specification of the equipment, the price, the delivery terms, and the like. The intending lessee thus relies on its own skill and judgment in its dealings with the supplier, not on the lessor, who may have limited or no experience of the type of equipment in question. These features are captured in Article 1 of the Convention. The finance lease is thus to be distinguished from the operating lease, in which the lessor manufactures or buys equipment for the purpose of leasing it to several lessees in succession at a rental equivalent to the use-value of the goods. Reflecting this distinction, accounting rules in a number of jurisdictions require future rentals under finance leases to be capitalized in the accounts of the lessor and the lessee in much the same way as on an instalment sale, whereas in the case of a true operating lease rentals are treated in the balance sheet of the parties as accruing year by year.[4]

10.04   Finance leasing has always been driven by tax considerations, and this was particularly true of cross-border leasing, where parties to transactions were able to

---

[1] Frequently, of course, there are more than three parties involved, but this does not affect the analysis which follows.

[2] In many common law countries the inclusion of an option to purchase creates a distinct category of agreement known as hire purchase, possessing its own legal characteristics.

[3] Typically the equipment is leased for a specified primary period at the end of which the lessee is given the right to renew it for one or more secondary periods at a substantially reduced rental. If and when the equipment is given up the lessee is usually appointed agent of the lessor to sell it and is paid or credited most of the proceeds of sale.

[4] This is a very simplified description. In practice the distinction between a finance lease and an operating lease is often not clear-cut.

utilize differences in national laws concerning the characterization of a transaction in such a way that the lessor would be treated as owner of the equipment so as to be entitled to depreciation allowances under the law of its jurisdiction while under the law of the lessee's jurisdiction it would be considered the owner and would thus be able to claim depreciation allowances as well. This 'double dip' came under increasing scrutiny from tax authorities and in a number of jurisdictions legislation has been introduced to disallow it. Financial and tax considerations led to the development of the leveraged lease by which a third party was brought in to fund the purchase from the supplier, either by way of non-recourse loan to the lessor on the security of the equipment and lease rentals or by purchasing the equipment itself and letting it on lease to the leasing company with permission to sub-lease to the end-user.

Leasing structures can be quite complex, particularly in cross-border transactions, **10.05** which may involve a multiplicity of parties and may include arrangements for securitization of the lease rentals, that is, their packaging and transfer into a special-purpose vehicle as security against which bank loans may be made or notes or bonds issued on the market.

The characterization of a finance lease varies from jurisdiction to jurisdiction. In **10.06** the United States, Canada and New Zealand many finance leases are treated as security agreements, though the criteria vary from jurisdiction to jurisdiction and within Canada the Ontario legislation differs from that of the Western provinces. In England a lease is a mere bailment in which the lessee enjoys possession but the lessor retains full ownership; inclusion of an option to purchase converts the agreement from a lease into a hire-purchase agreement, which is legally distinct. In France an option to purchase is an essential element of a *credit-bail.*

Ronald C C Cuming, 'Model Rules for Lease Financing: A Possible Complement to the UNIDROIT Convention on International Financial Leasing' (1998) III Unif L Rev 371, 377–80

Finance leasing is not a complete substitute for an effective, modern secured financing regime. It has an important, but limited role. As such, it can be viewed as a first step in a transition to a complete regime of secured financing law.

Finance leasing is a device that works well when financing is required for the acquisition of equipment or other high-priced durable movable property ... it can be used in cases where the financing is being provided by a supplier of the equipment or where it is being provided by an independent financier. In addition, it is possible to use a highly formalistic version of financing lease, the sale and lease-back, as a method of securing a loan made by the lessor to the lessee essentially on the security of the lessee's equipment. In technical terms, the borrower sells the property to the lender and then leases it from the lender under a financing lease arrangement. In effect, the lessee is buying back the property.

However, finance leasing cannot be used as a vehicle for financing the acquisition of inventory. It is fundamental to a finance leasing contract that the lessee-buyer retains the equipment, since this is the lessor's security. By definition, inventory collateral will be sold by the debtor in the ordinary course of its business. Further, lease financing law provides no conceptual basis on which to recognize a security interest in proceeds received by the lessee-buyer from use of the leased equipment. The only security available to a lessor under a finance lease is its 'ownership' of the leased property.

A modern secured financing regime does not have these deficiencies. A central feature of such a regime is the recognition that an obligation can be secured, not only by property of any kind owned by the debtor at the date of execution of the security agreement, but also property acquired by the debtor at a future time during the currency of the agreement. Consequently, the purchase price of property and any other obligation of the debtor to the secured party can be secured through a security interest not only in the property itself, but also by other property then owned or later acquired by the purchaser . . . a financing lease is in substance not a lease, but a secured financing device in the guise of a lease. While this form of legal fiction can be useful, it can also be a source of confusion and injustice. If the rights of the parties to a financing lease are regulated on the basis that the contract between them is a true lease, the law becomes distorted and important economic interests can be overlooked.

The paradigm for a secured financing regime is a debt or other obligation that is collaterally secured by an interest in property of the debtor. In substance, a security agreement is one under which the owner of property recognizes through an agreement that another person has or will automatically acquire an interest in that property in order to secure an obligation. The function of a security agreement is to provide to an obligee an in rem interest in property of the debtor that secures the obligation.

A lease is a fundamentally different transaction. The lessor 'owns' the leased property; the lessee has temporary possession of it under the terms of the lease contract. Unlike a secured financing transaction, the purpose of a true lease is not to finance the acquisition of the property by the lessee. The lessor expects to get its property back at the end of the lease term. Consequently, when a transaction cast in the form of a lease is used as a financing device, what is hidden in the relationship between the lessor and the lessee is the fact that the lessee is acquiring under the transaction an economic interest in the leased property that goes well beyond temporary use of it. By making the lease payments, the lessee is 'buying' an interest in the leased property.

The commercial realities of financing leases present an important conceptual and functional question: what type of legal regime is needed to recognize fully and accurately the relative rights of the parties to a financing lease and the rights of third parties who acquire interests in leased property from lessees in possession? It is clear that traditional leasing law is inadequate; it does not reflect the fact that the purpose of the transaction is to finance purchase price property[5] being acquired by the lessee. Further, it is not possible in most jurisdictions to describe the rights of lessors and lessees under financing leases by analogy to the seller-buyer relationship arising under a title retention sale of goods contract. Under most legal systems, a buyer is not recognized as acquiring any proprietary interest in the goods until the full purchase price is paid. This approach is not confined to systems based on traditional civil law, which does not accept the concept of 'equitable' or limited interests in property. It is applied as well in most common law jurisdictions, including England. The problem for many legal systems in accepting that the lessee has an in rem interest in the leased property commensurate with the payments made to the lessor is that this conclusion cannot be supported by analogy to any existing legal construct.

---

[5] *Sic.* Probably 'the purchase price of property' is intended.

Legal systems that give explicit recognition to the interest of the lessee-buyer and provide a conceptual basis for this recognition treat the lessee as an owner of the property who has charged that property. This is possible because these systems adopt function, not form, as the primary factor on which characterization of transactions is based. Transactions in the form of leases that function as secured financing devices are treated as secured financing devices and, consequently, are fully integrated into secured financing regimes. This is not an option for many countries that are looking to lease financing as a device that can address at least in part the lack of other modern forms of secured financing. While strict adherence to formalism may be weakening in many parts of the world, it is too much to expect many legal systems to recognize that a lessee under a financing lease is to be treated in law as the owner of the leased property subject to a charge held by the lessor.

It is the view of the author that the most realistic approach is to provide special measures in the context of the law applicable generally to leasing which recognize the peculiar relationships that arise in the context of lease financing. In practice, if not in theory, this would entail accepting that the lessee has a legally recognized interest in the leased property beyond temporary possession which requires legal protection. As the secured financing law of a jurisdiction develops to the point where it can absorb lease financing as a secured financing device, these special measures can be repealed and the legal fiction that the transaction is a lease can be dropped.

Sphere of application

In order for the Convention to apply four conditions must be satisfied. These **10.07** relate to (1) the structure and financial nature of the transaction, (2) the purpose for which the equipment is to be used, (3) the internationality of the transaction and (4) the connection to a Contracting State.

The transaction is a financial leasing transaction   The characteristics that a **10.08** transaction must possess in order to qualify as a financial leasing transaction within the Convention are set out in Article 1(2):

(a) the lessee specifies the equipment and selects the supplier without relying primarily on the skill and judgment of the lessor;
(b) the equipment is acquired by the lesssor in connection with a leasing agreement which, to the knowledge of the supplier either has been made or is to be made between the lessor and the lessee; and
(c) the rentals payable under the leasing agreement are calculated so as to take account in particular of the amortization of the whole or a substantial part of the cost of the equipment.

Thus the key features are the lessee's reliance on its own skill and judgment rather **10.09** than that of the lessor in selecting the equipment and the supplier, the acquisition of the equipment from a third-party supplier (thus excluding, for example, leases by the manufacturer itself) and computation of the rentals to recover the capital cost (and, of course, the desired return on capital) rather than to reflect the use-value of the equipment. It is because the finance lease is in essence a capital transaction in which the economic risks and benefits flow to the lessee that the

Convention confers on the lessor substantial immunities that would not be appropriate for a lessor under an operating lease. That is why the Convention is confined to finance leases. The Convention does not apply to bipartite transactions in which the lessor is the supplier itself. This is because it is in the three-party situation that most of the problems arise.

10.10 The Convention applies whether or not the leasing agreement confers on the lessee an option to purchase or to renew the lease and whether or not the option price or rental is nominal.

10.11 **The equipment is not to be used primarily for the lessee's personal, family or household purposes** In other words, the convention is confined to business equipment. This is a standard feature of modern commercial law conventions, reflecting the fact that in most jurisdictions consumer transactions are heavily regulated by laws which have a strong policy orientation. Such transactions are much less susceptible to uniform treatment at the international level.

10.12 **The lessor and the lessee have their places of business in different States** This has been the principal test of internationality since the conclusion of CISG, though the formulation is not uniform. For example, Article 3 of the 2001 United Nations Convention on the assignment of receivables in international trade refers to the place where the parties are 'located'. What if a party has more than one place of business? Article 3(2) of the leasing convention, like Article 2(2) of the factoring convention, points to the place of business which has the closest relationship to the relevant contract and its performance, having regard to the circumstances known to or contemplated by the parties at any time before or at the conclusion of that contract. Article 5(h) of the UN Convention is to similar effect, though it omits the phrase 'having regard to . . .'

10.13 **Those States and the State in which the supplier has its place of business are Contracting States or both the supply agreement and the leasing agreement are governed by the law of a Contracting State** Article 3(1) provides alternative connecting factors. The first requires that all three parties have their places of business in Contracting States. The alternative is that both contracts are governed by the law of a Contracting State. The reason for this is that the inter-relationship between the sale contract and the leasing contract makes it essential to provide a connecting factor which links all three parties to a Contracting State (though not necessarily the same Contracting State), either through their places of business or through the governing law.

Exclusion of Convention

10.14 Just as the inter-relationship of the supply agreement and the leasing agreement influences designation of the alternative connecting factors, so also it affects the ability of the parties to exclude the Convention. This can be done only by agreement of each of the parties to the supply agreement and each of the parties to the leasing agreement. It is not, however, necessary for all the parties to do this in the same agreement; it suffices that the Convention is excluded both in the supply agreement and in the leasing agreement.

Purposes of the Convention

The Convention has four key objectives: to transfer responsibility for non-conforming equipment from the lessor to the supplier; to restrict the lessor's liability to third parties; to safeguard the lessor's property interest in the event of the lessee's insolvency; and to ensure the effectiveness of provisions for liquidated damages.   **10.15**

Removal of responsibility from the lessor to the supplier

It will be apparent that if the substance of the transaction were the basis of distribution of legal rights and obligations any claims of the lessee for failure of the equipment to meet specifications or the requisite quality standard would lie against the supplier, not the lessor. However, since the sale contract is between supplier and lessor and the leasing agreement is between lessor and lessee there is usually no contractual relationship between lessee and supplier, and the person entitled to pursue the supplier for any non-conformity of the equipment with the supply contract is not the lessee but the lessor. It is true that the lessee may have rights against the lessor, but the standard terms of the lease usually make it clear that the equipment is selected by the lessee, who exercises its own skill and judgment, and that the lessor has no responsibility for non-conformity of the equipment and is entitled, under so-called 'hell or high water' clauses, to be paid the agreed rental come what may.   **10.16**

Two techniques have evolved to deal with this problem. In the first, the lessor agrees to make claims against the supplier on the lessee's behalf as well as, or as an alternative to, its own claims. The problem here is that the lessor can recover only for its own loss, and its exclusion of liability and right to payment of rentals in any event usually mean that it suffers no loss. In the second, the lessor agrees to assign to the lessee any claim it may have against the supplier. Again, however, the lessee, claiming in right of the lessor, can recover only for the lessor's loss, which is usually zero.   **10.17**

One of the most interesting features of the Convention for our purposes lies in the ingenious techniques used to overcome the difficulties created by the tripartite relationship. To achieve this objective it was necessary, first, to give the lessee direct rights against the supplier and, second, to remove liability from the lessor, though not completely.   **10.18**

Conferment of rights against the supplier

10.19   Article 10 of the Convention provides as follows:

> 1. The duties of the supplier under the supply agreement shall also be owed to the lessee as if it were a party to the agreement and as if the equipment were to be supplied directly to the lessee. However, the supplier shall not be liable to both the lessor and the lessee in respect of the same damage.
>
> 2. Nothing in this Article shall entitle the lessee to terminate or rescind the supply agreement without the consent of the lessor.

The lessee's position is reinforced by Article 11, under which:

> The lessee's rights derived from the supply agreement under this convention shall not be affected by a variation of any term of the supply agreement previously approved by the lessee unless it consented to that variation.

10.20   So the lessee can invoke the terms of the supply agreement as if it were a buyer. As deemed buyer he has whatever rights are conferred on him by the law governing the supply agreement, and in any proceedings in a state that is party to the Vienna Convention on Contracts for the International Sale of Goods (CISG) the lessee's rights as deemed buyer will be governed by that convention if the agreement falls within its scope.[6]

Exculpation of lessor from liability under the leasing agreement

10.21   The corollary of the principle that the lessee can proceed directly against the supplier for non-delivery of the equipment or the tender of equipment not in conformity with the supply contract is that what would ordinarily be the corresponding liability of lessor to lessee under the leasing agreement is removed. At the same time, it was felt that it would not be reasonable to give the lessor full immunity. The effect of Article 12 is that if the equipment is not delivered at all or is not in conformity with the contract then the lessee has the same right as against the lessor to reject the equipment or to terminate the leasing agreement, and the lessor has the same right to cure the breach, as if the lessee had agreed to buy the equipment from the lessor under the same terms as those of the supply agreement. Thus the combined effect of Articles 10 and 11 is that for the purpose of claims against the supplier the lessee is treated as if it were a buyer from the supplier, while for the purpose of its rights against the lessor the lessee is treated as if it were a buyer from the lessor. In addition to its right (subject to the lessor's right of cure) to reject non-conforming equipment or to terminate the agreement for non-delivery the lessee is entitled to withhold payment of rentals until the breach has been remedied or until it has lost the right to reject, and if it exercises a right to terminate the lease it can recover rentals and other sums paid in advance.[7] But apart from a warranty of quiet possession[8] the lessee has no other

---

[6] See above, ch 7.   [7] Art 12(3), (4).   [8] Art 8(2).

claim against the lessor except to the extent to which the breach results from the act or omission of the lessor.[9]

The basic idea underlying these provisions is that the lessor should not incur any **10.22** positive liability to damages for non-delivery or for delivery of non-conforming goods, these being events over which it normally has no control, but at the same time should not be able to recover or retain lease rentals for undelivered or non-conforming equipment unless the lessee chooses to retain the equipment and thereby lose its right to reject, in which case it must pay the agreed sum for possession and use of the equipment. There is some overlap between Article 12(5), referring to the act or omission of the lessor, and the rather differently worded Article 8(1), which was intended primarily to exclude liability in tort but also covers contractual liability and which, except as otherwise provided by the convention or the leasing agreement, excludes the lessor's liability to the lessee in respect of the equipment 'save to the extent that the lessee has suffered loss as the result of its reliance on the lessor's skill and judgment and of the lessor's intervention in the selection of the supplier or the equipment'. The rationale for limiting the lessor's liability to the lessee in a financial leasing transaction was cogently stated in the Explanatory Report on the draft Convention prepared by Mr Martin Stanford, then UNIDROIT's Principal Research Officer and now a Deputy Secretary General.

Martin Stanford, 'Explanatory Report on the Draft Convention on International Financial Leasing' (1987) I Unif L Rev 169, 271[10]

At first sight the provisions of Article 7 [which later became Article 8] might appear to involve a fairly radical departure from the law of most countries. In fact, they do little more than reflect the situation existing in practice, in that financial leases invariably contain detailed provisions absolving the lessor from responsibility for defective or non-conforming equipment and requiring the lessee to indemnify the lessor against claims brought by third parties. It reflects the general philosophy underlying the draft Convention, that is the special nature of financial leasing, seen both in the lessor's role and in that of the lessee, in excluding the lessor's liability in contract and tort in most situations in which it would otherwise normally have been held liable in its capacity of lessor of the equipment. The finance lessor will in most cases have no technical expertise with respect to the equipment's specifications, will never take delivery of the equipment and normally will not even have reason to see it. Its role is limited to supplying the capital needed for the acquisition of the equipment. It is the lessee, we have seen in Article 1(2)(a) above, who relies primarily on its own skill and judgment in selecting both equipment and

---

[9] Art 12(5). There is some overlap with Art 8, which is primarily intended to limit liability in tort but also defines the lessor's contractual liability to the lessee in terms somewhat different from Art 12(5). See below.

[10] Study LIX—Doc. 48, also reproduced in *Diplomatic Conference for the Adoption of the Draft Unidroit Conventions on International Factoring and International Financial Leasing: Acts and Proceedings* UNIDROIT, Rome 1999–2000), Vol. I, 27 ff. This also contains a paragraph-by-paragraph analysis of the draft Convention presented to the Diplomatic Conference.

supplier, and who typically conducts negotiations with the supplier on its own as a reasonably informed user. If there is any reliance on the knowledge and representations of another party in this context, indeed it is the lessee's reliance on the supplier's knowledge of the equipment and its representations in this regard, so much so indeed that it is the supplier rather than the lessor who places the equipment into the stream of commerce.

Liability to third parties

10.23 As a logical concomitant of the special features of financial leasing Article 8(1)(b) provides that 'the lessor shall not, in its capacity of lessor, be liable to third parties for death, personal injury or damage to property caused by the equipment'. But Article 8(1)c) makes it clear that this provision 'does not govern any liability of the lessor in any other capacity, for example as owner'. There are relatively few cases in which ownership as such attracts liability in national legal systems, and these typically derive from international conventions, such as liability of the owner of a vessel for oil pollution under the 1969 Brussels International Convention on Civil Liability for Oil Pollution Damage and of an aircraft for ground damage under the 1952 (Rome) Convention on Damage Caused by Foreign Aircraft to Third Parties on the Surface.

Protection against lessee's insolvency

10.24 Article 7 provides that the lessor's real rights are valid against the lessee's trustee in bankruptcy and creditors, including creditors who have obtained an attachment or execution. By 'real rights' is meant rights *in rem*, or proprietary rights, as opposed to purely personal rights. The words 'ownership' and 'proprietary' (which might be thought to imply ownership) were avoided because the lessor may not be the owner but may itself hold the goods under a head lease or a conditional sale agreement. Nevertheless, such a lessor will in many systems be considered to have real rights in the equipment in the sense of rights available against persons generally, not merely contractual rights against its own lessor or conditional seller. Article 7 is confined to bankruptcy. The Convention does not lay down any rules governing priority outside bankruptcy.

10.25 Article 7 is designed to prevent the leased assets from being treated as part of the insolvent lessee's estate so as to be available to its general creditors. However, under Article 7(2) any public notice requirements prescribed by the applicable law as a condition of validity against the above parties must be satisfied. For example, if the applicable law is the law of New York State and under that law the leasing transaction is characterized as a security agreement which is effective against a trustee only if previously perfected by filing, then failing such perfection the lessor will be unable to invoke the protection conferred by Article 7(1). Rules for determining the applicable law are set out in Article 7(3). Article 7 does not affect the priority of lien creditors or, in the case of ships or aircraft, creditors having rights of arrest or detention, which are almost invariably given primacy in national laws.

Default remedies of lessor

Article 13 confers on the lessor a set of basic default remedies of the kind given by national laws. The lessor is entitled to recover unpaid rentals with interest and, in the case of substantial default, may require accelerated payment of the value of the future rentals[11] or alternatively terminate the leasing agreement and recover such damages as will place it in the position in which it would have been if the lessee had performed the agreement in accordance with its terms. Article 13(3) validates a provision in the agreement for liquidated damages, which is expressed to be enforceable unless it would result in damages substantially in excess of what is necessary to put the lessor in the position in which it would have been if the contract had been properly performed. This sends a signal to national courts not to apply a principle such as the common law rule against penalties unless the disconformity between the liquidated damages and the lessor's loss is substantial.

10.26

Evaluation of the Leasing Convention

Viewed purely in terms of the number of ratifications the Convention on International Financial Leasing, despite its merits in overcoming the problems created by the tripartite relationship of supplier, lessor and lessee, has not been as successful as its progenitors had hoped. Although coming into force on 1 May 1995 it has so far attracted only nine ratifications and in the case of leases of aircraft objects it has been superseded by the 2001 Convention on International Interests in Mobile Equipment.[12] The relatively low level of adoption may reflect the point made in the UNIDROIT Explanatory Report on the draft Convention that one of the major facts to emerge from the questionnaire sent out by the UNIDROIT Secretariat to leasing operators and experts all over the world was that the successful mounting of truly cross-border leasing transactions was still a rare occurrence, even if the sums involved in the relatively small number of transactions actually mounted successfully were enormous.[13] But the number of ratifications is not the sole measure of the Convention's success. It has influenced the domestic legislation of a number of jurisdictions—indeed, it is the model adopted

10.27

---

[11] That is, the present value, the rentals being discounted to take account of the acceleration of liability for payment.

[12] Protocol to the Convention on international interests in mobile equipment on matters specific to aircraft equipment 2001, Art XXV. See ch 12.

[13] Martin J. Stanford, '*Explanatory Report on the Draft Convention on International Financial Leasing*' (1987) I Unif L Rev 169, para 3. The Explanatory Report was first reproduced in 1987 I Uniform Law Review 169 and later republished in the *Diplomatic Conference for the Adoption of the Draft UNIDROIT Conventions on International Factoring and International Financial Leasing: Acts and Proceedings, Volume I*, Study LIIX—Doc. 48 (UNIDROIT, Rome, 1999–2000), 27 ff.

by those engaged in running projects for the International Finance Corporation for the building up of leasing industries in developing countries—and it forms the basis of work now being undertaken by UNDROIT in the preparation of a model law on leasing.[14]

Leasing under the Mobile Equipment Convention and Protocol

10.28 The UNIDROIT Convention on international financial leasing is not the only convention dealing with leases. The 2001 Convention on international interests in mobile equipment with its associated aircraft Protocol is a convention of major importance in the field of leasing and, in contrast to the 1988 Convention, it is not confined to cross-border leasing or to financial leasing agreements.

The UNIDROIT Draft Model Law

10.29 The special need of developing countries and countries in transition to a market economy to have modern legal rules governing equipment financing led the UNIDROIT Governing Council to draw up a model law on leasing targeted at such countries and based on the Convention but broader in scope. In accordance with its established practice the Governing Council first sought to satisfy itself that the project was indeed both economically necessary and legally viable. A detailed note prepared by the Secretariat in mid-2006 explains the approach.

UNIDROIT Secretariat, Preparation of a Model Law on Leasing—Study LIX A

Recent developments, whether it be in relation to the UNIDROIT Convention on International Financial Leasing (hereinafter referred to as the *UNIDROIT Convention*), or the Cape Town Convention on International Interests in Mobile Equipment (hereinafter referred to as the *Cape Town Convention*), have highlighted the special need that developing countries and countries engaged in the transition to a market economy have for the introduction of modern legal rules governing the financing of equipment, of every level of value, in order to develop their economic infrastructure. In particular, those engaged in running the projects of the International Finance Corporation (I.F.C.) for the development of leasing industries in such countries have invariably taken the rules contained in the UNIDROIT Convention as the model for the leasing laws to underpin such new leasing markets. On occasions, the UNIDROIT Secretariat was approached by Governments seeking UNIDROIT's assistance in the development of leasing legislation. The States Parties to the UNIDROIT Convention are, moreover, almost all either developing countries or countries in transition.

A similar pattern has emerged with the Cape Town Convention. In particular, not only was the diplomatic Conference that saw the adoption of this Convention attended by an unusually high proportion of developing economies but the majority of the States that have to date become Parties to that Convention and the Protocol thereto on Matters specific to Aircraft Equipment are also developing countries.

---

[14] See below, para 10.29.

These considerations led the UNIDROIT Governing Council to decide that it would be appropriate for UNIDROIT to draw up a model law on leasing, in particular targeted at just such developing countries and countries in transition. It was considered that this would be a more efficient way of developing basic leasing laws in developing countries and countries in transition than to reinvent the wheel each time a new leasing industry was being established, in particular since it would be primarily on the basis of the aforementioned UNIDROIT Convention, as, in effect, the latest expression of the international legislators' will in this area, and through making use of UNIDROIT's unique expertise in this area.

Before, however, embarking on the preparation of such a model law, the UNIDROIT Secretariat considered it expedient to consult some of the potential key economic stakeholders in such a project, in particular the World Bank, the I.F.C. and the Equipment Leasing Association of the United States of America (E.L.A.). The idea behind this consultation was to ascertain both the economic and legal expediency of the project, as exemplified by such Organisations' willingness to contribute thereto. The favourable outcome of this consultation, significantly, reflected the undoubted enthusiasm of such potential stakeholders to be able to avail themselves, at the earliest possible opportunity, of the use of such a model law. In particular, it was pointed out that the countries of Africa stood to benefit enormously from the sort of contribution that leasing might be expected to give to the overcoming of their serious infrastructure financing shortcomings. In addition, the model law was considered to a particularly helpful tool for those countries currently engaged in the drafting of leasing legislation.

From the beginning, therefore, the parameters of the project were clearly delimited by reference to the needs of developing countries and countries in transition, the end-product of the Institute's work in this area being perceived as a particularly apposite and efficient method of ameliorating the inadequate investment capacities of such countries. In the first place, the UNIDROIT Secretariat, in establishing the composition of the Advisory Board to which the preparation of a preliminary draft model law was entrusted, had especial regard to the need to reflect adequately those legal and economic systems that were intended to be the essential beneficiaries of the project amongst its membership: in addition to a minimum number of experts from Europe and North America, the Advisory Board thus included experts from North Africa and the Arab-speaking world, sub-Saharan Africa, the People's Republic of China, Latin America and countries of the Former Soviet Union ...

Whilst it is not the purpose of this brief Note to provide an exhaustive introduction to the substantive provisions of the preliminary draft, it might, nevertheless be useful to introduce its basic structure. First, it is intended to cover both what are commonly referred to as financial leases and operating leases, the idea being that it should be as broad as possible in its substantive sphere of application so as not only to encompass the present-day needs of developing countries and transition economies but also to envisage likely trends in the development of such markets. Secondly, it provides uniform rules governing the effects of the leasing agreement (enforceability, the running of the supplier's duties to the lessee, priority in relation to liens and liability for death, personal injury or property damage to third parties), the performance of the leasing agreement (the irrevocability of the lessee's duties as from the time when the leasing agreement is entered into, the risk of loss under a lease, the lessee's rights in the event of damage to the leased asset, the conditions for, and consequences of the lessee's acceptance and rejection of the leased asset, the extent of the right of the parties to the leasing agreement to transfer their rights and duties thereunder, the extent of the warranties of the parties to a leasing agreement, the extent of the lessee's duty to maintain and return the leased asset), thirdly, default remedies (the definition of default, the need for the giving of notice, the measure of damages, liquidated damages, termination of the leasing agreement and the lessor's right to recover possession and dispose of the leased asset where the leasing agreement comes to an end or is terminated). Thirdly, it has been structured as a model law expressly with a view to enabling national legislators to adapt it to their specific needs . . .

10.30 The draft model law is wider than the Convention in that it covers operating leases as well as financial leases and domestic as well as cross-border transactions, and also contains more detailed provisions generally. In relation to financial leases the draft tracks the Convention, as one would expect. For operating leases additional rules are provided covering risk of loss, damage to the asset, lessee's right of rejection, warranty of acceptability and fitness and duties of the lessee to maintain the asset and to return it when the leasing agreement comes to an end.

10.31 The selection of a model law rather than a convention is particularly appropriate for developing countries and new market economies in that it enables them to adapt the instrument to their particular needs and thus provides a greater degree of flexibility than is usually possible in the case of a multilateral convention. But it is desirable for adopting States to adhere as closely as possible to the model law in order to bring about through domestic legislation the harmonization which will be achieved at the international level only if greater support for the Convention is forthcoming.

Questions

1. Why is the Convention made applicable only to:
   (1) financial leasing agreements
   (2) leasing transactions between parties carrying on business in different States?
2. We have seen that different legal systems characterize leases in different ways.
   (1) Why does characterization matter?
   (2) What characteristics must a lease possess to fall within the Convention on International Financial Leasing?
   (3) To what extent, if at all, is the application of the Convention influenced by the way in which a lease is characterized under the applicable national law?
3. Does the Convention seek to cover the whole field of financial leasing law? If not, should it have done so?
4. In what respects does the Convention break new ground in structuring the rights, duties and liabilities of the parties involved in a financial leasing

transaction? In what ways does it differ in this respect from the law of your own country?

5. You are asked to act as reporter for a project on the harmonization of the law governing cross-border financial leasing and to prepare a report for the Study Group set up to produce a draft Convention. List what you see as the key issues to be considered by the Study Group on which a comparative law analysis should be prepared (you may wish to refer back to the issues discussed in chapter 4 to help you answer this question).

6. (1) What law governs the lessee's rights against the supplier under Article 10(1)?
   (2) In what circumstances, if at all, could the Vienna Convention on Contracts for the International Sale of Goods be relevant in answering the question in (1) above?

7. The lessee under a leasing transaction governed by the Convention wishes to terminate the supply agreement because of failure by the supplier to deliver goods conforming to the contract of sale, but the lessor refuses to agree. Can the lessee nevertheless terminate the supply agreement? And what law governs this question?

8. (1) Article 10(1) provides that the supplier is not to be liable to both the lessor and the lessee in respect of the same damage. How could a procedural rule ensure that the interests of both lessor and lessee were protected? Does the Convention contain any such rule—and if not, why not?
   (2) Does Article 10(1) entitle the lessee to recover for its own loss or for that of the lessor?

9. Why does the Convention not contain rules governing priorities of competing rights outside bankruptcy of the lessee?

10. Article 6(2) of the Convention contains what has now become a standard provision in private law conventions:

    Questions concerning matters governed by this Convention which are not expressly settled in it are to be settled in conformity with the general principles on which it is based or, in the absence of such principles, in conformity with the law applicable by virtue of the rules of private international law.

    Can you identify any such general principles?

11. 'The leasing industry does not favour the UNIDROIT Convention on International Financial Leasing because it fails to reflect the standard terms of a finance lease.'
    Discuss the validity of this criticism.

12. What do you see as the advantages of a model law on leasing of the kind in course of preparation by UNIDROIT? To what extent does the adoption in domestic legislation of provisions comparable to those of the leasing Convention provide an effective substitute for ratification?

Further reading

Ferrari, Franco, 'General Principles and International Uniform Commercial Law Conventions: A Study of the 1980 Vienna Sales Convention and the 1988 Unidroit Conventions' (1997) II Uniform Law Review 451

Girsberger, Daniel, 'Leasing' in Kronke, Herbert, Melis, Werner and Schnyder, Anton K (eds), *Handbuch Internationales Wirtschaftsrecht* (Dr Otto Schmidt, Köln, 2005) 757

Levy, David A, 'Financial Leasing under the UNIDROIT Convention and the Uniform Commercial Code: A Comparative Analysis' 5 Ind Intl & Comp L Rev 267 (1994–5)

Stanford, Martin, 'Explanatory Report on the Draft Convention on International Financial Leasing' (1987) I Unif L Rev 169

11

RECEIVABLES FINANCING: THE UNIDROIT CONVENTION ON INTERNATIONAL FACTORING AND THE UNITED NATIONS CONVENTION ON THE ASSIGNMENT OF RECEIVABLES IN INTERNATIONAL TRADE

A. Introduction		Other provisions	11.26
The nature of receivables financing	11.01	Evaluation	11.28
The need for an international regime	11.03	**D. The United Nations Convention**	
B. Some Facts about Factoring		**on the Assignment of Receivables**	
What is factoring?	11.05	**in International Trade**	11.29
C. The UNIDROIT Convention on		Nature of Convention: substantive	
International Factoring		rules and conflicts rules	11.30
Genesis of the Convention	11.11	Sphere of application	11.31
Sphere of application	11.13	Effectiveness of assignments	11.36
Sphere of application *ratione materiae*	11.14	Relations between assignor and assignee	11.37
Internationality	11.16	Debtor provisions	11.38
Connecting factor	11.17	Priorities	
Derogation	11.18	Conflict of laws rules	11.39
Interpretation	11.19	Substantive law rules	11.40
Removal of barriers to acquisition of			
receivables	11.21		

A. Introduction

The nature of receivables financing

The supplier of goods or services does not necessarily wish to tie up his capital while **11.01** awaiting payment. Receivables financing, by which the supplier can sell its receivables to a factoring company or charge them to a bank, thus provides a useful source of liquidity, as well as other facilities referred to below. The term 'receivables', which is short for 'accounts receivable', is not a term of art, and its meaning depends on the context in which it is used. Primarily it denotes monetary obligations, whether earned or to be earned, derived from the supply of goods, services or facilities and recorded in an account rendered, or invoice. Receivables are intangible assets and can be transferred in the same way as other forms of property. This was not always the case. Both Roman law and the common law initially took the position that personal rights were non-transferable, but over time the needs of commerce led to the modification and eventually the abolition of this restriction. Receivables financing is typically effected by assignment,[1] though other forms of transfer are also found, such as subrogation.

11.02 Receivables financing is typically not a one-shot affair but constitutes financing against a continuing stream of receivables, so that there is an ongoing relationship between assignor and assignee. Receivables financing can be regarded as a particular form of asset-based finance. Indeed, in the case of non-recourse loans the cash flow may represent the sole source of repayment of the loan, the borrower having no personal obligation to repay. Similarly receivables may be sold on a non-recourse basis, meaning that the buyer bears the risk of default by the debtor. Examples of non-recourse transactions are project finance, full service factoring (described below) and forfaiting, which is the non-recourse discounting of international credit instruments such as drafts drawn under a letter of credit or backed by a bank.[2] Receivables may be securitized, that is, converted from non-marketable into marketable form by being packaged and transferred to a special-purpose vehicle (SPV) which issues bonds or notes on the market or procures bank loans on the security of the receivables and other assets of the SPV. But the transfer of the receivables remains governed by the normal rules of private law applicable to the assignment of debts, so that securitization does not raise issues relevant to our present discussion.

The need for an international regime

11.03 Despite the advantages of receivables financing in allowing a trader to obtain liquidity and off-load risk, most legal systems have historically displayed hostility towards security over or transfers of streams of contract debts. This has long ceased to be the case in major common law jurisdictions but in varying degrees remains true to this day of civil law jurisdictions, where typical constraints are:

(a) restrictions on the assignment of future receivables;
(b) the concept of specificity—the impractical requirement of specifying each assigned contract; and

---

[1] For specimen assignment clauses and commentary, see Roy Goode, 'Assignment Clauses in International Contracts', (2002) Intl Bus Law J 389.

[2] Forfaiting is not further discussed, the focus of the present chapter being on the purchase of accounts rather than instruments.

(c) the imposition of externalization requirements, such as notification to the
debtor, as a condition of the validity of the transfer even as between the parties.

A substantial volume of receivables financing is international in nature, the sup- **11.04**
plier/assignor and the debtor having their places of business in different countries,
and this trend will continue in the future. That has given rise to the need to
address the legal impediments to receivables financing at the international level.
Two international instruments are of particular interest and form the subject of
the present chapter. They are the 1988 UNIDROIT Convention on international
factoring and the 2001 UN Convention on the assignment of receivables in international trade. Mention should also be made at this point of the provisions of the
2001 Cape Town Convention on international interests in mobile equipment, a
chapter of which is devoted to the assignment of 'associated rights', that is, rights
to payment or other performance by a debtor under a security agreement, a title
reservation agreement or a leasing agreement, which are secured by or associated
with the aircraft or other object comprised in the agreement.[3] We shall begin with
the factoring convention before proceeding to an analysis of the much broader
convention on receivables financing, deferring treatment of the assignment of
associated rights to a later chapter.[4]

R M Goode, 'A Uniform Law on International Factoring', in *Unification in*
Comparative Law Theory and Practice: Contributions in Honour of Jean Georges
Sauveplanne **(Kluwer, Deventer, 1984), 91**

1. INTRODUCTION

For those who believe only in what they can see and touch the wealth of an enterprise consists essentially of its land and buildings, its equipment and its stock in trade. For the self-
made man these are the physical manifestations of his success, the demonstration of his
achievements to the world at large. Yet the possession of such tangible assets involves both
labour and expense. They must be stored, and take up space which may be costly to rent.
They must be kept in repair, safeguarded and insured. They are not always readily saleable
and in the case of fixed assets are a very illiquid species of property. They attract taxes and
licensing requirements, and their value may fluctuate wildly with market variations.

By contrast, an enterprise's receivables—the debts and other money obligations due and
becoming due from its obligors—represent a relatively uncomplicated form of wealth.
They are not susceptible to physical damage or destruction, their maintenance requires no
outlay beyond that involved in supervising and collecting the accounts and they may be
readily converted into cash by way of sale or mortgage.

The huge growth in the extension of credit over the last fifty years has meant that the
trader finds more and more of his capital locked up in the form of receivables; and to help
him convert these into cash he has turned increasingly to receivables financiers who will
either buy the receivables at a discount or advance money on the security of them. Yet
despite the enormous volume of receivables financing that is now undertaken, the

---

[3] See the Convention, Art 1(c),(a).   [4] See below, para 12.48.

lawmakers of most countries continue to devote most of their legislative efforts to the regulation of rights relating to tangible assets. For these, the most elaborate rules have been devised for the attachment and perfection of security rights and the resolution of priority disputes, whilst the treatment of interests in receivables has remained largely untouched by legislation. In the result there are many issues in receivables financing on which the law remains unclear; and the analysis of receivables financing in the conflict of laws is still largely undeveloped . . .

II WHY UNIFORM RULES ON INTERNATIONAL FACTORING?

. . .

Where a given type of commercial activity is legally more difficult to undertake in one State than in another, distortion of an intended common market is likely to occur. It may be difficult for the parties to predict what law will be applied by the forum, and whilst this problem can in large measure be resolved by an express choice of law clause in the contract the party whose law is not chosen may feel unhappy about being subjected to a law and legal system with which he is not familiar.

But experience has shown that harmonization is a lengthy and laborious process and that it is wise not to be too ambitious. If the task of harmonization is heavy in the field of public law—eg. the regulation of companies and financial institutions—it is still more formidable where fundamental concepts of property and obligation are concerned . . .

It was with these thoughts in mind that the Governing Council of Unidroit, instead of embarking on a project to formulate uniform rules governing the whole field of intangible movables, or even the narrower field of receivables financing, decided to concentrate its efforts on a very specific form of international receivables financing, namely international factoring. There were several advantages in such a choice. First, the efficacy of the international assignment of debts depends in the last resort on the willingness of the courts in a particular jurisdiction to recognise and enforce rights created in a different jurisdiction, and in several countries the law relating to the transfer of future receivables is not well suited to the needs of international business. Secondly, factoring is carried on within a defined institutional structure, through membership of national and international factoring associations, so that there is a corpus of accepted practice, indeed even a code of international factoring customs, and representative bodies whose expertise can be tapped. Thirdly, the fact that this area of receivables financing is occupied by professionals using standard contracts and procedures makes it unnecessary to formulate a general code of contract rules and allows work to be concentrated on the practical problems of removing legal obstacles to the international factoring of receivables.

Thus work in this restricted field has a practical utility . . . and the acceptance and use of uniform rules on international factoring may lay the foundation for a broader harmonization of laws governing the transfer of tangible movables.

B. Some Facts about Factoring

What is factoring?

11.05   Modern factoring as a form of receivables financing is derived from the practice of mercantile agents who bought or sold goods for others. Factors were mercantile agents who also bought and sold on their own account, and among the services they offered were the grant of loans to those for whom they were selling, repayable from the proceeds of sale they collected. Eventually delivery of goods direct to the customer instead of consignment to the factor for resale led to the disappearance of the factor's sale function and its replacement by the purchase of the customer's trade receivables. Factoring takes a variety of forms and only the barest outline can be given here.

Noel Ruddy, Simon Mills and Nigel Davidson (eds), *Salinger on Factoring* **(4th edn, Sweet & Maxwell, London, 2006) 2**

... factoring is:

[t]he purchase of debts (other than debts incurred for goods or services purchased by a debtor for his personal, family or domestic use and debts payable on long terms or by instalments) for the purpose of providing finance, or relieving the seller from administrative tasks or from bad debts or for all or any of such purposes.

Factoring is confined to the purchase of trade debts and to receivables payable **11.06** in a single sum. Factors do not buy debts due from consumers—that is a function performed by finance houses—nor do they usually purchase debts payable by instalments or over a period longer than six months. There is a common misconception that factoring is a service provided for suppliers whose customers are considered a poor risk. This is not the case. Quality control is essential to successful factoring.

Factoring arrangements involve at least three parties: the supplier (also called the **11.07** client), who assigns the debts by way of sale; the debtor (also called the customer), to whom the supplier has supplied goods or services for the purposes of the debtor's business which remain to be paid for; and the factor, who buys the debts due to the supplier. In the case of international factoring, involving foreign customers of the client, the factor may assign the debts for collection to a factor based in the debtor's country, as described below. Factoring is characterized by the offer of four essential facilities, though any particular supplier may have need of only one or some of them. They are: the transfer of risk of default to the factor, who buys approved receivables on a non-recourse basis up to an approved limit for any particular debtor; the provision of finance through payments on account of the price in advance of collection; the maintenance of accounts; and the collection of the debts. The last two functions are not strictly services for the client but activities which the factor performs for its own benefit as the new owner of the debts. It is for the supplier to decide which of the various functions it wishes the factor to perform. Full-service, or old-line, factoring involves the performance of all four functions. Obviously the performance of each function involves a cost. A client not needing finance will select maturity factoring, that is, factoring under arrangements by which payment for the debts is made at maturity as defined by the agreement. A supplier happy to keep the risk of default will sell its debts on a recourse basis, the factor having the right to require the client to repurchase debts due from defaulting debtors. A supplier wishing to maintain its own account-keeping and not wishing its direct relationship with its customers to be disturbed will ask for non-notification factoring, usually known as invoice discounting, by which debtors are not notified of the sale of the debts to the factor, the supplier continues to collect, ostensibly on its own behalf but in reality as agent of the factor, and the debts are purchased by the factor with recourse. Invoice discounting has now become the dominant form of service offered by factoring companies.

11.08   There are two alternative forms of sale agreement. One is the facultative agreement in the sense that while the supplier has to offer for sale to the factor all the debts falling within the scope of the agreement the factor has a discretion as to which to purchase. The other, which has become the preferred form, is the whole turnover agreement under which all the debts are turned over to the factor, though in certain cases on a recourse basis. In both cases there is a continuing arrangement under which debts are offered or sold in batches at a time.

11.09   Factoring is designated international when supplier and debtor are in different countries. The factor may be in the country of the supplier or in the country of the debtor. In the former case the factor may either (1) collect direct or, in the event of default, through a correspondent member of a chain of international factors ('direct export factoring'), or (2) as 'export factor' transfer ownership of the debt to a factor ('import factor') in the debtor's country for collection, but with the import factoring guaranteeing payment in respect of approved debts. In direct import factoring the factor is in the debtor's country and concludes arrangements with a foreign supplier.

11.10   Factoring thus offers a varied and flexible service which has led to a steady growth year by year.[5] It is also seen as a cheaper and more efficient mode of financing international sales than letters of credit.

C. The UNIDROIT Convention on International Factoring

Genesis of the Convention

11.11   The UNIDROIT Convention on international factoring was concluded in Ottawa in 1988 at the same time as the Convention on international financial leasing and came into force on 1 May 1995. Its genesis lay in the perception of the considerable obstacles to international factoring caused by differences in national legal systems governing the assignment of receivables.

---

[5] For some figures, see *Salinger on Factoring*, above, app 1.

Frédérique Mestre, Explanatory Report on the Draft Convention on International Factoring (1987) I Unif L Rev, 85, 93[6]

It is apparent from this brief description of factoring that it presents many economic advantages ... it provides financial liquidity, the certainty of payment and the handling and recovery of receivables, the choice of the combination of services being left to the parties. In each system, legal means have been sought to ensure the development of this relatively recent technique of financing in the most satisfactory manner possible, in terms not only of facilitation and flexibility, but also of certainty and cost, and this explains the fact that while in most countries it is the assignment of receivables which provides the underlying legal basis for factoring transactions, the procedures whereby such assignments are effected and the rules which govern the different aspects of them differ considerably. In consequence, when the supplier has commercial dealings with foreign buyers, the problem of distance and the difficulties facing the former in obtaining information as to the financial position of the latter, language barriers and frequently ignorance of the applicable foreign law make the services offered by factors all the more attractive. It is nevertheless true that the divergencies in national law and the frequent uncertainty as to the law applicable to a given transaction or to one or another aspect of it create problems which the factoring industry must constantly face and which it seeks to overcome by passing on to suppliers the increased cost of its services ...

It is in these circumstances that the Unidroit committee of governmental experts, endorsing the conclusions of the study group, recognized that trade would be encouraged by facilitating factoring and that it would therefore be desirable to draw up uniform rules in this connection.

11.12 Uncertainties as to the applicable law governing the different relationships could, of course, have been overcome by uniform conflict-of-laws rules, but this is very much a second-best option, since the applicable law is then dependent on the conflict rules of the forum, so that the governing law and thus the outcome of a dispute may vary according to the place where proceedings are brought. Thus uniform rules within a tightly defined area were seen as the only sensible solution.

Sphere of application

11.13 Like several other commercial law conventions, the first part of the Convention lays down rules for the sphere of application *ratione materiae*, the test of internationality and the connection to a Contracting State.

Sphere of application ratione materiae

11.14 Article 1 sets out the sphere of application of the Convention in terms of the types of transaction covered. Various points should be noted. In line with factoring practice the Convention is concerned only with assignments of receivables due

---

[6] Study LVIII—Doc. 33, also reproduced in the *Diplomatic Conference for the Adoption of the Draft Unidroit Conventions on International Factoring and International Financial Leasing, Acts and Proceedings* (UNIDROIT, Rome 1991), Vol. I, 85 et seq. This also contains a paragraph-by-paragraph analysis of the draft Convention presented to the Diplomatic Conference.

from business debtors. The Convention is also confined to transactions where notice of assignment is given to the debtor. Invoice discounting thus falls outside the scope of the Convention. It was felt that non-notification financing raises different issues and its inclusion might unduly broaden the scope of the Convention.

11.15 In framing the issues to be covered the progenitors of the Convention proceeded cautiously. The focus is on the efficacy of the assignment, the relations between factor and debtor and subsequent assignments, that is, by the factor or a later assignee. The formulation of priority rules governing successive assignments was at that time considered too delicate a subject for harmonization, though later experience with the Cape Town Convention on international interests in mobile equipment was to show the feasibility of laying down a relatively simple set of priority rules and the importance of so doing. The UN Convention on the assignment of receivables in international trade, concluded a month after the Cape Town Convention, adopted a halfway house, opting for a conflict rule to govern priorities rather than a set of substantive rules. So the Factoring Convention has been criticized as insufficiently ambitious. Nevertheless in many ways it was in advance of its time and it has to be viewed in the context of severe problems in civil law jurisdictions in providing a workable method for the simple assignment of a continuing stream of future receivables. If these problems were to be overcome and receivables financing liberated from the shackles of obsolete doctrine it was necessary to provide a simple mechanism by which an agreement for the transfer of future receivables could operate according to its terms without requiring some new act of transfer upon a receivable coming into existence and without the need either to specify the debts to be assigned or to identify the debtors, for neither would be known at the time of entry into the factoring agreement. This was the focal point of the Convention and as we shall see it achieved its objective neatly and without fuss. The Convention can thus be seen as a prototype for the movement away from doctrinal and towards commercially oriented solutions, a trend later reinforced by the more detailed provisions of the Cape Town Convention on international interests in mobile equipment and the Hague Convention on indirectly held securities.

Internationality

11.16 Prescription of the internationality test is a little less straightforward than under the Vienna Convention on contracts for the international sale of goods (CISG) because factoring involves three parties. The factoring Convention applies only to international factoring, that is, the factoring of receivables arising from a contact of sale between a supplier and a debtor whose places of business are in different States. It is the relationship between these two parties that typically generates conflict-of-laws problems. So what attracts the Convention is the internationality of the receivables, not the internationality of the assignment. By contrast, as we shall see, the UN Convention on the assignment of receivables in international trade covers both the assignment of international receivables and the international assignment of domestic receivables.

Connecting factor

Here, too, the presence of three players and two separate contracts makes the **11.17** designation of the connecting factor more complex. There are alternative tests. The first requires all three parties to have their places of business in a Contracting State, though not necessarily in the same Contracting State. The second and alternative test is that both the sale contract and the factoring contract are governed by the law of a Contracting State—again, not necessarily the same State. This alternative basis of application stems from the CISG and reflects a desire to ensure a wide scope of application. It does, of course, mean that the applicability of the Convention depends on the conflict-of-laws rules of the forum, so that the Convention may be held to be applicable in proceedings in State A, whereas the conflict rules of State B may lead to the law of a non-Contracting State in relation to either or both of the contracts.[7]

Derogation

The entire Convention may be excluded by the parties to the factoring contract; **11.18** the assent of the debtor is not required. The Convention may also be excluded by the parties to the sale contract , but they should give notice in writing of such exclusion to the factor since it is only as regards receivables arising after such notice that the exclusion can be effective. This is to prevent the factor from being misled. But the Convention must be excluded in its entirety; for obvious reasons it is not possible for parties to exclude some provisions and retain others.

Interpretation

Article 4 embodies the standard canons of interpretation of a commercial law **11.19** convention.

> 1.–In the interpretation of this Convention, regard is to be had to its object and purpose as set forth in the preamble, to its international character and to the need to promote uniformity in its application and the observance of good faith in international trade.
>
> 2.–Questions concerning matters governed by this Convention which are not expressly settled in it are to be settled in conformity with the general principles on which it is based or, in the absence of such principles, in conformity with the law applicable by virtue of the rules of private international law.

Can we identify general principles on which the Convention is based? **11.20**

---

[7] A point made by Marco Torsello, *Common Features of Uniform Commercial Law Conventions: A Comparative Study Beyond the 1980 Uniform Sales Law* (Sellier European Law Publishers, Munich 2004) 109.

Franco Ferrari, 'General Principles and International Uniform Commercial Law Conventions: A Study of the 1980 Vienna Sales Convention and the 1988 UNIDROIT Conventions on International Factoring and Leasing and the UNIDROIT Principles' (1999) Eur J of Law Reform 217, 234–6

One of the general principles upon which the Factoring Convention is based appears to be, at least at first sight, that of party autonomy; this view is based upon the text of Article 3(1) which establishes that the parties may exclude the application of the Convention at hand, thus confirming its dispositive nature. However, in the light of Article 3, and its comparison with Article 6 of the CISG, it is doubtful whether party autonomy should really be considered a general principle of the Factoring Convention. This is due to its somewhat limited scope compared to that of party autonomy under the CISG: according to the CISG, the parties may not only exclude the Convention's application *in toto* or even partially, but they may also derogate from its provisions (with one exception) or modify its effects, whereas according to Article 3(2) of the Factoring Convention, the parties may only exclude its application *in toto*.

A 'true' general principle of the Factoring Convention seems to be the principle whereby assignments of receivables are encouraged as much as possible, a principle which can be derived not only from Article 6(1), according to which the assignment of receivables is allowed even in the presence of a *pactum de non cedendo*, but also from Article 5, which considers valid not only the assignment of single existing receivables but also the assignment of single future receivables as well as bulk assignments, and from Article 10(1), which—as a general rule—bars the debtor from being allowed to recover a sum which he paid to the assignee if he is entitled to recover that sum from the supplier, thus protecting the assignee's reliance and, consequently, his willingness to purchase receivables.

Not unlike the CISG, the Factoring Convention seems to be based upon the principle of good faith. Indeed, good faith is not only mentioned as an interpretative criterion—provided for by Article 4(1) of the Factoring Convention—but it is also mentioned in the provision (Article 6) which validates the assignment of receivables despite the existence of a non-assignment clause; in effect, this provision places upon the supplier 'an indispensable general duty of good faith [. . .] towards the debtor for breach of the non-assignability clause contained in the sales contract.'

Another general principle underpinning the Factoring Convention is the principle whereby the assignment shall not place the debtor in a disadvantageous position compared to that in which he would find himself had the assignment not taken place. This principle may be readily deduced from the Convention's provision which—in a claim by the assignee against the debtor—allows the latter to set up against the former all defences which he could have set up against the supplier if such claim had been made by the latter, and it may also be inferred from the provision which, even though it validates the assignment of receivables in the presence of a *pactum de non cedendo*, upholds the supplier's liability towards the debtor.

Removal of barriers to acquisition of receivables

11.21   Article 5 is a key provision:

As between the parties to the factoring contract:

(a) a provision in the factoring contract for the assignment of existing or future receivables shall not be rendered invalid by the fact that the contract does not specify them individually, if at the time of conclusion of the contract or when they come into existence they can be identified to the contract;

(b) a provision in the factoring contract by which future receivables are assigned operates to transfer the receivables to the factor when they come into existence without the need for any new act of transfer.

This Article removes at a stroke the barriers to modern receivables financing **11.22** created by a number of legal systems. It renders unnecessary any listing of the receivables to be assigned or of the debtors from whom they are to become due, requiring only that the receivables be identifiable by the time they come into existence as falling within the factoring agreement. So it would suffice for the factoring agreement to specify 'all debts due or to become due to the supplier', though in practice the factoring agreement would introduce qualifications, for example to exclude consumer debtors. Further, Article 5 gives proprietary effect to an assignment of future receivables automatically upon their coming into existence without need of a new act of transfer. Thus the contract also functions as a transfer, abandoning the sharp distinction in many legal systems between contract and conveyance. Article 5 reflects the laissez-faire approach of common law systems, which through the development of equity and, in America, the advent of the Uniform Commercial Code, have pared to a minimum the formalities needed to effect the assignment of present and future receivables. Article 5 is reinforced by Article 7, which empowers the parties to provide in the factoring contract for the transfer of all the supplier's rights under the sale agreement, including any reservation of title in the supplier's favour.

Article 6 removes another barrier to the free movement of receivables in the stream **11.23** of trade, namely the no-assignment clause in contracts by which the creditor is prohibited from assigning its rights without the debtor's prior consent. Such clauses are not capricious but have sound commercial reasons. First, the debtor may be happy to deal with the original creditor, with whom it may have a relaxed relationship, but uncomfortable about the prospect of a relationship with a new creditor whose attitude may be more severe. Second, a debtor involved in a large number of contracts can easily overlook a notice of assignment and pay the assignor instead of the assignee, which in the ordinary way creates no problem but exposes the debtor to liability to make a second payment if the assignor becomes insolvent without having paid over the proceeds of the debt to the assignee. Third, if the debtor is going to have a continuing relationship with the original creditor involving mutual dealings and claims on both sides the debtor may not want to lose its right to set off against its liability on a particular claim its own cross-claim arising from the subsequent supply of goods or services to its creditor. Nevertheless, no-assignment clauses are inherently inimical to modern receivables financing, and it is this fact that justifies what might otherwise be thought an unwarranted interference with freedom of contract.

Ole Lando, Eric Clive, André Prüm and Reinhard Zimmermann (eds), *Principles of European Contract Law, Part III* (Kluwer Law International, The Hague, 2003) Article 11:301 and Comment B (Reporter for Article 11: Roy Goode)

ARTICLE 11:301: CONTRACTUAL PROHIBITION OF ASSIGNMENT

(1) An assignment which is prohibited by or is otherwise not in conformity with the contract under which the assigned claim arises is not effective against the debtor unless:
  (a) the debtor has consented to it; or
  (b) the assignee neither knew nor ought to have known of the non-conformity; or
  (c) the assignment is made under a contract for the assignment of future rights to payment of money.
(2) Nothing in the preceding paragraph affects the assignor's liability for the non-conformity.

COMMENT

B. *Exceptions*

The general rule stated in the first part of paragraph (1) [that an assignment prohibited by the contract is ineffective] works well enough in circumstances where it is commercially practicable for an intending assignee to obtain sight of the contract under which the assigned claims arise and to discover the existence of the no-assignment clause. But there may be cases in which the assignee would not know of the prohibition, for example where this is contained in a separate contract the existence of which was unknown to the assignee. Accordingly, apart from the obvious case stated in paragraph (1)(a) where the debtor consents to the assignment, paragraph (1)(b) allows the assignment to have effect against the debtor where the assignee neither knew nor ought to have known of the prohibition.

A further exception relates to future money claims (that is, money claims arising under future contracts, as opposed to claims which arise under existing contracts but are payable in the future). In this case too the assignment is effective. This exception is particularly necessary where the assignment relates to a continuing stream of future debts, for example, by a supplier to a factor under a factoring agreement. In this type of arrangement it is manifestly impossible to expect the factor to scrutinise the individual contracts, which may run into hundreds, in order to see whether these contain a provision against assignment. Even where, as will usually be the case, the contract is a standard-term contract which does not embody such a provision, the assignee who examines one such contract cannot be sure that the assignor will not at some stage change the terms without notifying him. So paragraph (1)(c) allows the assignment to take effect where it is made under a contract for the assignment of future money claims. While it may seem hard on the debtor to override a no-assignment clause in this way, it needs to be borne in mind that a debtor who is able to insist on such a clause will almost invariably hold the stronger bargaining position and is therefore not the party primarily in need of protection. In such a situation the debtor may be able to resist the creditor's request for security for payment, such as a letter of credit or bank guarantee. If the creditor were also to be prevented from laying off risk by assigning the receivables to a factor under a non-recourse factoring agreement the creditor could be severely prejudiced. This second exception is confined to the assignment of debts, for it is in the field of receivables financing that the no-assignment clause typically creates problems. Claims to non-monetary performances are outside the scope of paragraph (1)(c).

Hence Article 6(1) of the Factoring Convention, following what is now § 9-406(d) **11.24** of the American Uniform Commercial Code, provides that an assignment is effective notwithstanding any prohibition against assignment. However, respecting the sensitivity of States who might feel unable to accept such an interference with party autonomy, Article 6(2) allows a Contracting State to make a declaration disapplying Article 6(1) in relation to a debtor having its place of business in that State at the time of the supply agreement.

The lead set by UCC § 9-406(d) and Article 6(1) of the Factoring Convention was **11.25** followed in Article 11:301 of the Principles of European Contract Law, as indicated above, and in Article 9.1.9 of the UNIDROIT Principles of International Commercial Contracts and Article 11 of the UN assignments Convention. In all of these the provisions giving effect to an assignment even where made in breach of a no-assignment clause are limited to the assignment of rights to the payment of money; assignments of rights to non-monetary performance which are prohibited by the agreement remain ineffective.

Other provisions

Article 9(1) enables the debtor to assert against the factor all defences arising **11.26** under the sale contract which would have been available against the supplier and all rights of set-off in respect of claims against the supplier available at the time of notice of assignment to the debtor. This broadly reflects the position under existing national laws, though it is defective in failing to allow set-off for post-notification cross-claims closely connected with the assigned claim, a set-off rightly allowed by Article 11:307(2)(b) of the PECL[8] though not followed in this respect by Article 9.1.13 of the UNIDROIT Principles.

There remains to note an Article dealing with the vexed question whether a debtor **11.27** who has paid the factor but receives no performance from the supplier is entitled to recover his payment from the factor. The basis of such a claim would be unjust enrichment. To this it might well be answered, first, that there is nothing unjust in allowing the factor to retain the proceeds of a debt for which it has given value to the supplier, and, second, that just as assignment should not prejudice the debtor, so also it ought not to enhance his position by giving him a right against an additional party which he would not have had but for the assignment. The question is only of practical importance if the supplier has become insolvent. Reflecting the above arguments Article 10 denies liability in general but makes exceptions where the factor has not paid the supplier (and would normally be entitled to withhold payment either under the general law or under the terms of the factoring agreement)

---

[8] See also a similar provision in Art 18(1) of the UN Convention on the assignment of receivables in international trade.

or has paid the supplier in the knowledge of the latter's non-performance, in which case the factor has only itself to blame for its predicament. Article 10 is interesting in providing a solution to a knotty problem which probably differs in some respects from the laws of most national legal systems but provides solutions which make commercial sense.

Evaluation

11.28 Some eighteen years have elapsed since the Factoring Convention was concluded, and it has now been in force for over ten years. Despite this it has secured only six ratifications, which even by the long time-scales for implementation of international conventions is disappointing. The factoring industry was certainly supportive; indeed, it made a valuable contribution to the shaping of the convention. But it seems that the political will was lacking, and industry pressure to implement it was insufficient to persuade governments to make legislative time available. The experience with this and the only slightly more successful Leasing Convention shows the importance of building support at every level as the project proceeds and to follow it up after completion with intensive promotion. The difficulty is that this involves time and resources and the availability of people to undertake the very considerable work involved. Time will tell whether, belatedly, either of these instruments will become more widely adopted.

D. The United Nations Convention on the Assignment of Receivables in International Trade

11.29 The 2001 UN Convention on the assignment of receivables in international trade is an altogether more ambitious instrument. The Convention was prepared by the UNCITRAL Working Group on International Contract Practices and was concluded in December 2001, a month after the Cape Town Convention on international interests in mobile equipment. It requires five ratifications in order to enter into force. So far, Liberia is the only State that has ratified the Convention.

Nature of Convention: substantive rules and conflicts rules

11.30 The Assignment Convention is a somewhat complex mixture of substantive rules and conflict-of-laws provisions. Article 7, dealing with interpretation, follows what has become the traditional pattern, so that matters not *expressly* settled in the Convention are to be settled in conformity with the principles on which it is based or, in the absence of such principles, in conformity with the law applicable by virtue of the rules of private international law. Chapter V of the Convention lays down a set of priority rules which in Article 26 are stated as applying to matters within the scope of the Convention as provided by Article 1(4) *'and otherwise* *within the scope of this Convention but not settled elsewhere in it*.[9] The term 'settled' as opposed to the phrase 'expressly settled' in Article 7 indicates that the hierarchy laid down in Article 7 is to be preserved, so that it is only in the absence of an applicable general principle of the Convention that resort is to be had to the rules of private international law, at which point Chapter V comes into play to provide the appropriate conflict rule unless excluded by a declaration by the forum State under Article 39. Interestingly, Part V is not confined to cases in which the Convention is applicable but is applicable in a Contracting State to cases outside the Convention altogether, and thus operates as a free-standing mini private international law Convention.[10] The conflict rules of the Convention are interesting and complex.

Catherine Walsh, 'Receivables Financing and the Conflict of Laws: The UNCITRAL Draft Convention on the Assignment of Receivables in International Trade' 106 Dick L Rev 159 (2001)

Private international law solutions to legal problems created by differences among legal systems are often distrusted. Instead of a substantive solution, a choice of law rule merely provides a signpost—and not always a clear one—to the source where the solution may be found. Moreover, a solution incubated in a domestic factual and legal context may not prove appropriate or workable beyond local borders.

Distrust of private international law is matched by distrust of the private international lawyer. Although considered a speciality in itself, private international law covers the entire spectrum of private law. As such, it requires the skills of the generalist. Yet a generalist may not be sufficiently attuned to the practical contexts in which a conflicts rule must operate to recognize when a theoretically defensible solution may turn out to be unworkable. On the other hand, to leave the matter exclusively to the substantial law specialist risks undermining carefully cultivated conflicts norms.

In the area of assignment of receivables, the challenges are particularly fearsome. The assignment matrix is a complex one, involving not one but two sets of contractual relations; the original contract between the assignor and debtor which generates the assigned receivable and the contract between the assignor and assignee by which the assignment of that receivable is accomplished.

From a choice of law perspective, the original contract and the contract of assignment are sufficiently independent to justifying subjecting each to its own proper law. But what of the impact of the assignment on the debtor? Should this be governed by the proper law of the contract of assignment or the original contract? Is a contract-based choice of law approach even appropriate? Consensus, after all, is the essence of contract, and the assignee/debtor relationship is typically an involuntary one from the debtor's perspective.

The dual juridical nature of the assigned debt adds a further layer of complexity. From the perspective of the debtor/assignor relationship, the debt is a purely personal obligation—the debtor's creditor does not own the debt, the creditor is owed it. But it becomes a species of property when the original creditor assigns the right to payment to another. As with any

---

[9] Art 26.

[10] Spiros V Bazinas, 'UNCITRAL's Contribution to the Unification of Receivables Financing Law: The United Nations Convention on the Assignment of Receivables in International Trade' (2002) VII Unif L Rev 49, 63.

contract involving the divestment of property rights in favour of another, competing third party claimants may enter the picture: the recipient of a competing assignment, attaching creditors of the assignor, or the assignor's insolvency administrator. This makes a contractual approach inappropriate because freedom of contract ends where third party rights begin both in substantive law and in the conflict of laws. Yet solutions drawn from choice of law for property, where the *lex situs* dominates, are not readily transplanted to a right which lacks a corporeal object, and therefore a physical situs . . .

As the experience under the Rome Convention attests, the most controversial choice of law issue in the area of assignment concerns the appropriate law to govern the priority of the assignee's interest against competing assignees and the assignor's creditors or insolvency administrator. Not surprisingly, priority is also the issue on which there is the greatest range of difference among legal systems at the substantive level. All systems adopt a first-in-time rule, at least as a starting point, but differ on the relevant event.

In some systems, priority turns simply on when the first assignee reached agreement with the assignor. This is based on pure property doctrine: after the assignor's rights are vested in the assignee under the first assignment, there is nothing left that the assignor can transfer or that the assignor's creditors or insolvency administrator can attach. However, uniformity even among states adopting this technique is undercut by non-uniform exceptions. Some regimes, for instance, impose special additional requirements in the case of assignments for security purposes. In others, the prominent example being German law, a first-in-time bank assignee of a general bulk assignment may be subordinated to a subsequent inventory supplier who takes an assignment of the receivables arising on the assignor's authorized resale of the inventory.

In other systems, an assignment is not effective against third parties until the debtor is either notified of or accepts the assignment, and the first assignee to give notice prevails. The notification theory of priority is justified on two complementary rationales: notice to the debtor is the closest functional equivalent for intangibles to the general rule that title to tangible goods passes on physical delivery; and the rule enables a prospective assignee or interested creditor to assess their priority risk by inquiry of debtor as to whether there have been any previous notices. Again, however, systems that agree on this general rule do not necessarily agree on the appropriate exceptions, or some have legislated partial alternatives, as in the case of the *Loi Dailly* in France, and the fragmented statutory registration regimes available in England.

In still other systems, notice of assignment must be registered in a public registry to take effect against third parties, and ranking among successive assignees depends on the order of registration. The rationale for this approach is obvious: a public registry for giving notice of assignment protects assignees by enabling them to preserve their priority status through timely registration, and it protects third parties by providing an objective accessible means for them to find out about prior assignments. Once again, however, matters are not so simple, and there is disagreement among systems adopting the first-to-register rule on the appropriate exceptions.

The Working Group charged with preparing the Draft Convention initially favoured a uniform substantive rule for priority. However, there was no consensus on what that rule should be . . .

Faute de mieux, the Convention instead attempts international uniformity only at the choice of law level.

Sphere of application

The most striking feature of an earlier draft of the UN Convention was the width **11.31** of its coverage, as is shown by the following comment of the UNCITRAL Secretariat on the convention while still in draft.

United Nations Commission on International Trade Law, Analytical Commentary on the draft Convention on Assignment [in Receivables Financing] [of Receivables in International Trade] (2000) 3rd Session, A/CN.9/470

Transactions covered

6. In view of the broad definition of a 'receivable' in Article 2 (a) ('contractual right to payment of a monetary sum'), the draft Convention applies to a wide array of transactions. In particular, the draft Convention covers the assignment of trade receivables (arising from the sale of goods or services between businesses), consumer receivables (arising from consumer transactions), financial receivables (arising from financial transactions, such as loans, deposit accounts, swaps and derivatives) and sovereign receivables (arising from transactions with a governmental authority). With a view to clarifying the context of application of the draft Convention, those practices are described briefly in the following paragraphs. The list of practices cannot be exhaustive, in particular in view of the fact that new practices are rapidly developing which the draft Convention cannot ignore.

7. First of all, included are traditional financing techniques relating to trade receivables, such as factoring (the outright sale of a large number of receivables with or without recourse) and forfaiting (the outright sale of single, large-value receivables, whether they are documentary or not, without recourse). In these types of transactions, assignors assign to financiers their rights in receivables arising from the sale of the assignors' goods or services. The assignment in such transactions is normally an outright transfer but may also, for various reasons (e.g. stamp duty), be for security purposes. The purchase price is adjusted depending on the risk and the time involved in the collection of the underlying receivable. Beyond their traditional forms, those transactions have developed a number of variants tailored to meet the various needs of parties to international trade transactions. For example, in invoice discounting, there is an outright sale of a large number of receivables without debtor-notification but with full recourse against the assignor in the case of debtor default; in maturity factoring, there is full administration of the sales ledger, collection from debtors and protection against bad debts, but without any financial facility; in international factoring, receivables are assigned to a factor in the country of the assignor ('export factor') and then from the export factor to another factor in the country of the debtor ('import factor') for collection purposes, while the factors do not have recourse against the assignor in the case of debtor default (non-recourse factoring). All those transactions are covered in the draft Convention regardless of their form.

8. The draft Convention also covers innovative financing techniques, such as securitization and project finance, which may relate to a wide range of receivables, including consumer receivables. In a securitization transaction, an assignor, creating receivables through its own efforts ('originator'), assigns, usually by way of an outright transfer, these receivables to an entity ('special purpose vehicle' or 'SPV'), fully owned by the assignor and specially created for the purpose of buying the receivables and paying their price with the money received from investors to whom the SPV sells the receivables or securities backed by the

receivables. The segregation of the receivables from the originator's other assets allows the price paid by investors (or the money lent) to be linked to the financial strength of the receivables assigned and not to the creditworthiness of the assignor. It also insulates the receivables from the risk of the insolvency of the originator. Accordingly, the originator may be able to obtain more credit than would be warranted on the basis of its own credit rating. In addition, by gaining access to international securities markets, the originator may be able to obtain credit at a cost that would be lower than the average cost of commercial bank-based credit. In large-scale, revenue-generating infrastructure projects, sponsors raise the initial capital costs by borrowing against the future revenue stream of the project. Thus, hydroelectric dams are financed on the security of the future income flow from electricity fees, telephone systems are paid for by the future revenues from telecommunications charges and highways are constructed with funds raised through the assignment of future toll-road receipts. Given the draft Convention's applicability to future receivables, these types of project finance may be reduced to transfers, usually for purposes of security, of the future receivables to be generated by the project being financed. In this context, it should be emphasized that the draft Convention's exclusion of assignments made for personal, family or household purposes will not act to exclude consumer receivables.

9. Many other forms of traditional transactions relating to the assignment of a receivable generated in the context of a financial transaction will also be covered. These include the opening of a credit line on the security of the balance in a deposit account; the refinancing of loans for improving capital to obligations ratio or for portfolio diversification purposes; the assignment of the insurance company's contingent obligation to pay upon loss; and the assignment of rights arising under a letter of credit. Also covered are less traditional transactions, such as loan syndications and participations, swaps and other derivatives, repurchase agreements ('repos') and interbank payments.

10. A 'swap' is a transaction in which two parties agree to exchange one stream of obligations for another. The first swaps related to interest payments involved currencies, commodities, energy and credit obligations, and the range continues to expand. The underlying rationale for entering into a swap is to transfer the risks involved with a particular obligation to another party better able or willing to manage them. In a traditional interest swap, a creditworthy entity borrowing money at a fixed interest rate exchanges that interest with a variable interest rate at which a less secure entity borrows a similar sum. As a result, a less creditworthy entity, for a fee, in effect borrows money at a fixed rate. No payment of capital occurs between the parties to the swap (that comes from the underlying loan transactions). Between such parties, only interest payments take place. In practice, the interest payments are offset against each other and only a net payment is made by the party with the larger payment due. This residual payment is a contractual right to a monetary sum and is, therefore, within the broad definition of Article 2. There are several variations of a simple interest rate swap. For example, an investor may buy a fixed rate bond and swap the fixed rate for a floating rate from a bank; the bank may take security over the bond to secure the investor's obligations to pay amounts equal to the fixed rate.

11. Derivatives are a more general class of transaction of which swaps are a specific instance. They share the common characteristic of creating payment obligations that are determined by the price of an underlying transaction (this is why they are described as being

'derived' from those transactions). With the exception of interest swaps, most derivative contracts relate to the difference between the agreed future price of an asset on a future date and the actual market price on that date. For example, in a futures contract, one party agrees to deliver to the other party on a specified future date ('the maturity date') a specified asset (e.g. a commodity, currency, a debt, equity security or basket of securities, a bank deposit or any other category of property) at a price agreed at the time of the contract and payable on the maturity date. Futures are usually performed by the payment of the difference between the price agreed upon at the time of the contract and the market price on the maturity date, and not by physical delivery and payment in full on that date (they are called derivatives because settlement is not by actual performance of the sale or deposit contract but by a difference payment derived from an actual asset and an actual price; the contract is derived from an ordinary commercial contract). In options, the buyer has the right (but not the obligation) to acquire ('call option') or to sell ('put option') an asset in the future at a price fixed when the option is entered into. Repurchase agreements (or repos) are contracts under which one party sells a (usually fixed interest) security to another and simultaneously agrees to repurchase the security at a future date at an agreed price that includes allowance for the interest on the cash consideration and the accrued interest on the security. The payments are contingent upon the delivery or return of security. Within inter-bank payment systems and securities settlement systems, participants have obligations to make a large number of individual payments and also rights to receive similar numbers of payments from other participants. These obligations and rights are resolved into payments due to or from the system as a whole (typically using a central counter-party) or due between each pair of participants.

12. Derivatives, including swaps and repos, are usually transacted within a master netting agreement (e.g. the Master Netting Agreement prepared by the International Swaps and Derivatives Association ('ISDA')), which provides for the net settlement of payments due in the same currency on the same date. The agreement may also make provision, upon the default by a party, for the termination of all outstanding transactions at their replacement or fair market cost, conversion of such sums into a single currency and netting into a single payment by one party to the other (issues relating to netting are addressed in the ISDA Model Netting Act, adopted by 21 States). Set off (the discharge of reciprocal claims to the extent of the smaller claim) and netting (at its simplest, the ability to set off reciprocal claims on the insolvency of a counter-party) may come within the ambit of the draft Convention to the extent that the net obligation arising under a derivatives contract may be assigned.

It will be apparent from the above that the draft Convention then under consideration covered not only factoring and invoice discounting but a huge range of other assignment arrangements—including assignments of consumer receivables, securitizations, swaps, options and repos—some of which involved highly specialized operations that were subject to detailed master agreements prepared by international trade organizations, such as the International Swaps and Derivatives Association (ISDA). But in the final text, assignments of receivables arising from a variety of market-oriented transactions were sensibly excluded, notably transactions on a regulated exchange, financial contracts governed by netting agreements (except on termination of all outstanding transactions), foreign exchange **11.32** transactions, inter-bank payment systems, securities clearing and settlement systems and dealings in financial assets held with an intermediary. The reason given for these exclusions is that such transactions are already subject to market regulation. To this one might add that rules governing non-market assignments could seriously interfere with transactions on an organized market, which are best left to the systems and regulation of the market itself. The exclusion of assignments arising in relation to securities held with an intermediary 'reflects verbatim the text suggested by the securities industry',[11] an indication of the importance of involving industry specialists and of the influence they wield. A Contracting State may also make a declaration excluding other categories of assignment so far as not falling within Article 9(3).[12]

11.33 Like other commercial law conventions, the Assignment Convention is confined to international transactions and to those having the necessary connection to a Contracting State. The coverage both of assignments of international receivables and of international assignments of receivables, whether these are themselves domestic or international, made it necessary to provide two different tests of internationality.[13] In order for the Convention to apply it is necessary for the assignor to be located in a Contracting State at the time of conclusion of the contract of assignment, and in addition the Convention does not affect the rights and obligations of the debtor unless at the time of conclusion of the supply contract from which the assigned receivables arises either the debtor is located in a Contracting State or the law governing that contract is governed by the law of a Contracting State. However, the debtor's location is irrelevant to provisions of the Convention relating solely to the relations between assignor and assignee or to priorities between competing assignees or other issues not affecting the debtor.

Article 1

Scope of application

1. This Convention applies to:
   (a) Assignments of international receivables and to international assignments of receivables as defined in this chapter, if, at the time of conclusion of the contract of assignment, the assignor is located in a Contracting State; and
   (b) Subsequent assignments, provided that any prior assignment is governed by this Convention.
2. This Convention applies to subsequent assignments that satisfy the criteria set forth in paragraph 1 (a) of this Article, even if it did not apply to any prior assignment of the same receivable.

---

[11] Spiros V Bazinas, 'Multi-Jurisdictional Receivables Financing: UNCITRAL's Impact on Securitization and Cross-Border Perfection' 12 Duke J of Comp and Intl L 365 (2002).
[12] Art 41.   [13] Art 3.

3. This Convention does not affect the rights and obligations of the debtor unless, at the time of conclusion of the original contract, the debtor is located in a Contracting State or the law governing the original contract is the law of a Contracting State.
4. The provisions of chapter V apply to assignments of international receivables and to international assignments of receivables as defined in this chapter independently of paragraphs 1 to 3 of this Article. However, those provisions do not apply if a State makes a declaration under Article 39.
5. The provisions of the annex to this Convention apply as provided in Article 42.

Article 2

Assignment of receivables

For the purposes of this Convention:

(a) 'Assignment' means the transfer by agreement from one person ('assignor') to another person ('assignee') of all or part of or an undivided interest in the assignor's contractual right to payment of a monetary sum ('receivable') from a third person ('the debtor'). The creation of rights in receivables as security for indebtedness or other obligation is deemed to be a transfer;

(b) In the case of an assignment by the initial or any other assignee ('subsequent assignment'), the person who makes that assignment is the assignor and the person to whom that assignment is made is the assignee.

Article 3

Internationality

A receivable is international if, at the time of conclusion of the original contract, the assignor and the debtor are located in different States. An assignment is international if, at the time of conclusion of the contract of assignment, the assignor and the assignee are located in different States.

Article 4

Exclusions and other limitations

1. This Convention does not apply to assignments made:
    (a) To an individual for his or her personal, family or household purposes;
    (b) As part of the sale or change in the ownership or legal status of the business out of which the assigned receivables arose.
2. This Convention does not apply to assignments of receivables arising under or from:
    (a) Transactions on a regulated exchange;
    (b) Financial contracts governed by netting agreements, except a receivable owed on the termination of all outstanding transactions;
    (c) Foreign exchange transactions;
    (d) Inter-bank payment systems, inter-bank payment agreements or clearance and settlement systems relating to securities or other financial assets or instruments;
    (e) The transfer of security rights in, sale, loan or holding of or agreement to repurchase securities or other financial assets or instruments held with an intermediary;
    (f) Bank deposits;

(g) A letter of credit or independent guarantee.

3. Nothing in this Convention affects the rights and obligations of any person under the law governing negotiable instruments.

4. Nothing in this Convention affects the rights and obligations of the assignor and the debtor under special laws governing the protection of parties to transactions made for personal, family or household purposes.

5. Nothing in this Convention:

    (a) Affects the application of the law of a State in which real property is situated to either:

      (i) An interest in that real property to the extent that under that law the assignment of a receivable confers such an interest; or

      (ii) The priority of a right in a receivable to the extent that under that law an interest in the real property confers such a right; or

    (b) Makes lawful the acquisition of an interest in real property not permitted under the law of the State in which the real property is situated.

11.34 It is not only assignments by way of sale that are covered by the Convention. The term 'assignment' is widely defined so as to pick up both assignments by way of security—a useful provision, since a number of civil law systems do not recognize the fiduciary transfer of ownership (*fiducia cum creditore*)—and the creation of security rights in receivables without a transfer.

11.35 The definition of 'assignment' is wide enough to cover novation, that is, the transfer of a receivable by contractual substitution of the transferee for the transferor as the obligee. However, transfers of bank accounts and investment securities, which are the principal cases in which novation is used, are excluded by Article 4, reflecting a concern not to disturb established market regulation and practice. The assignment of rights under negotiable instruments is not excluded as such but under Article 4(3) nothing in the Convention affects the rights and obligations of any person under negotiable instruments law. The effect of this is that where rights to payment embodied in a negotiable instrument are transferred by negotiation of the instrument (by delivery with any necessary indorsement) it is negotiable instruments law that will control the rights and obligations of the parties. If, however, such rights are transferred by assignment under the general law instead of by negotiation of the instrument the Convention will govern the assignment, assuming other conditions of application of the Convention are satisfied. Assignment is an inferior method of transfer because the rights of the assignee will usually be overridden by or subordinate to an indorsee of the instrument. So the only situation in which assignment will normally occur is where rights embodied in a negotiable instrument form an undifferentiated part of a bulk assignment.

Effectiveness of assignments

11.36 This is dealt with in Article 8 and shows the influence of the Factoring Convention in its provisions negating any requirement of specificity. It is complemented by

Article 9, which, within defined limits, gives effect to an assignment even if made in breach of a no-assignment provision of the supply contract (the policy reasons for this have already been discussed) and by Article 10, which allows future receivables to vest automatically without need of a new act of transfer. However, while the lack of specificity cannot be raised as an objection to the validity of an assignment, other limitations imposed by national law—for example, the prohibition in some legal systems of a bulk assignment of future debts—are preserved.[14]

Relations between assignor and assignee

These are left to be dealt with by agreement of the parties. There are only two provisions of the Convention relevant to the relations between assignor and assignee. The first is the set of representations the assignor is deemed to make unless otherwise agreed, namely that the assignor has the right to assign the receivable and has not previously assigned it to another assignee and that the debtor does not have and will not have any defences or rights of set-off.[15] This is mirrored in Article 11:204 of the Principles of European Contract Law. The second provision establishes the right of the assignee to receive payment from the debtor and, if the latter pays the assignor, from the assignor. **11.37**

Debtor provisions

Section II of the Convention has a set of provisions concerning the debtor. The general principle is that assignment does not, without the debtor's consent, affect the debtor's rights or obligations except that a payment instruction may change the person to whom payment is to be made and the address or account to which payment is to be made (for otherwise the assignee would not be able to collect payment) but not the State or the currency of payment.[16] Article 17 provides that until receipt of notice of assignment the debtor can pay the assignor but after notice must pay the assignee. Though this formulation follows national laws it is not quite as good as Article 11:303 of the PECL, which improves on national laws by providing that the notice of assignment is effective only if it requires the debtor to give performance to the assignee. Article 17 assumes that somehow the debtor is expected to infer from the notice of assignment that payment is to be made to the assignee. The provisions of Article 18 as to defences and rights of set-off follow the principles adopted in national laws. **11.38**

Priorities

Conflict of laws rules

Of particular interest are the provisions of the Convention relating to priorities. The body of the Convention does not lay down substantive priority rules, which **11.39**

---

[14] Art 8(3).   [15] Art 12.   [16] Art 15.

obviously depend on whether a State does or does not have a system of registration of assignments, but leaves these to be determined by reference to the law of the assignor's location.[17] This is a welcome departure from the traditional rule of the conflict of laws under which the law governing the debt also governs priorities, a rule quite unsuited to modern receivables financing because the competing claims may be governed by different laws, and while the debtor has an interest in ensuring that its rights and obligations remain governed by the law applicable to them there is no good policy reason for making the same law apply to a competition between creditors. Designation of the law of the assignor's location has the advantage of subjecting all priorities to the same law.

Harry C Sigman and Edwin E Smith, 'Towards Facilitating Cross-Border Secured Financing and Securitization: An Analysis of the United Nations Convention on the Assignment of Receivables in International Trade', 57 Bus Law 727, 747–8 (2002)[17a]

The choice of law pointer to the law of the assignor's State to determine priority is subject to 'the exception of matters settled elsewhere in this Convention' and to the exceptions discussed below. The decision to limit the Convention's priority rules largely to choice of law rules deserves further comment. Although ideally the Convention might have provided substantive priority rules, UNCITRAL was not able to reach consensus on what those rules should be. Providing choice of law rules for issues of priority was the next preferred alternative.

At first glance, the limitation of the priority rules of the Convention to choice of law rules may appear problematic when considered together with the Convention's party location rules. Those planning transactions that might be within the scope of the Convention will need to assess whether the Convention applies to a particular transaction and, if so, whether the priority rules of the assignor's State, as determined under the party location rules of the Convention, have been satisfied. The party location rules of the Convention will have an impact on both determinations: whether the requisite internationality and other scope requirements have been met so as to make the Convention applicable, and which State's law will provide the operative priority rules. That assessment may well also have an impact on opinion practice.

In fact, in a few instances, the application of the Convention's choice of law rules for priority, when considered with the Convention's party location rules, may produce a result different from that under the national law of a particular State. To take one example, let us assume that the United States and the United Kingdom are Contracting States. Consider an assignor Delaware corporation, centrally administered from the United Kingdom, that borrows funds secured by its receivables owed by debtors located in the United States. Assume that the receivables are 'accounts' as defined in U.C.C. Article 9. The assignor is, under the Convention's party location rules, located in the United Kingdom, and the test of internationality would be met (i.e., the receivables would be international under the Convention) by the fact that the assignor is located in one State (United Kingdom) and the account debtors are located in another State (United States). Whether or not the assignee is located in the United States, the assignee would, under the Convention, achieve priority for its security interest in the receivables by satisfying

---

[17] Art 22.
[17a] © 2002 by the American Bar Association. Reprinted with permission.

whatever priority requirements exist under the laws of the United Kingdom. This would be the case notwithstanding that, in the absence of the Convention, U.C.C. Article 9 would view the assignor to be located in Delaware, with the perfection and priority steps to be taken by the assignee being those required under internal Delaware law. If a challenge to the assignment were made in the United States, the Convention would require that the assignee have complied with the priority requirements of United Kingdom law even though the assignee had taken all steps required under U.C.C. Article 9 to perfect its security interest and to obtain the desired priority

M. Michel Deschamps, a member of the Canadian delegation to UNCITRAL in work on the Assignment Convention, has provided a valuable set of examples of the way in which the conflicts rules would work in practice.

Michel Deschamps, 'The Priority Rules of the United Nations Receivables Convention: A Comment on Bazinas', 12 Duke J Comp & Intl L 389, 396–9 (2002)

This section examines the way the Convention would work in certain scenarios likely to occur in commercial transactions. For simplicity's sake, each scenario assumes that all states in which the assignee might need to assert its priority are parties to the Convention. The term 'perfection' is used in the examples below to describe all requirements that have to be satisfied to render an assignment effective against third parties, and to establish the priority of the right of the assignee. The definition of priority in the Convention is broad and includes the determination of whether these requirements have been satisfied. Accordingly, the reference in the Convention to the law of the assignor as the governing law for priorities must be construed as including perfection issues.

Example 1

On day one, A, a manufacturer with places of business in Canada and the United States, assigns all of its present and future receivables to Bank B. The assignment secures a line of credit made available to the manufacturer by a branch of Bank B located in the province of Quebec, in Canada. The manufacturer has its place of central administration in the province of Quebec, but is incorporated and has its registered office in the state of Delaware. Bank B has its place of central administration in the province of Quebec. Bank B perfects its assignment under the laws of the state of Delaware and, accordingly, makes the filing required by the Uniform Commercial Code of Delaware. A search in Delaware reveals no other entry against A's name.

On day two, the manufacturer assigns to C, a bank whose place of central administration is in New York City, a pool of receivables arising under a supply agreement with D, a corporation whose sole place of business is in the state of New York. The assignment secures a loan made by Bank C to finance the manufacturing by A of the goods sold to D under the supply agreement. Bank C perfects its assignment under the laws of the province of Quebec and a filing against A's name is made in the Quebec registry for security rights. No other entry appears in the registry in relation to A.

In the event of a priority contest between B and C with respect to the receivables owed by D, C will prevail. The receivables are international because the assignor and the debtor are located in different states within the meaning of the Convention: the assignor's place of central administration is in Canada and the debtor's sole place of business is in the United States. The Convention, therefore, applies to the priority contest between the two assignees with the result that the law of the location of the assignor, namely, the law of the province of Quebec, determines who is entitled to priority. Since Bank C has perfected its assignment under the laws of the province of Quebec but Bank B has not, Bank C will prevail over Bank B.

It is noteworthy that Bank C will prevail despite the fact that under the internal conflict-of-laws rules of both the province of Quebec and the state of New York, the law applicable to priority would have been the laws of Delaware. The conflict rules of the Convention displace the internal conflict-of-laws rules of the countries that are parties to the Convention.

Example 2

In this example, the fact pattern is the same as in example 1, except that D, the debtor, has its sole place of business in the province of Quebec.

Under this new scenario, the assignment between A and B is not per se governed by the Convention insofar as its relates to the receivables owed by D: the location of each of A, B, and D is in the province of Quebec within the meaning of the Convention, with the result that neither the assignment nor the receivables owed by D are international. As previously mentioned, for the Convention to apply to an assignment, either the assignment or the assigned receivables (or both) must be international; that is, the parties to the assignment or to the contract under which the receivable arises must be in different states.

Nonetheless, a dispute between Bank B and Bank C will be settled in the same manner as in example 1: C will have priority over B. This is so because the assignment between A and C is an international assignment (A being located in Canada and C being located in the United States) with the consequence that C is entitled to rely on the Convention to establish its priority right. B is a competing claimant in relation to assignee C and the Convention defines a competing claimant as including another assignee whose assignment would not otherwise be subject to the Convention. In other words, in the case of priority contest between two assignees, the priority provisions of the Convention govern if at least one of the two assignments is an assignment to which the Convention applies.

Therefore, in example 2, the priority provisions of the Convention will point to the law of the province of Quebec (that is, the law of the location of the assignor). In the example, Bank C has taken all steps required to perfect its assignment, including filing a notice of its assignment in the Quebec filing system for security rights. Therefore, Bank C will prevail over Bank B, given that Quebec law grants priority in a scenario like this to the claimant who is first to file in Quebec

Example 3

On day one, a bank, whose place of central administration is in Germany, lends money to a manufacturer also with its place of central administration in Germany. As security for the repayment of the loan, the manufacturer executes in favor of the bank an assignment of a receivable owing to the manufacturer by a customer located in Pennsylvania. Nothing else is done by the German bank to establish its priority right, assuming, for the purposes of the example, that the law in Germany states that a first in time assignee prevails over a subsequent assignee without any need to register the assignment or to notify the debtor.

On day two, the manufacturer, through its Philadelphia office, sells the same receivable to a factor located in Pennsylvania; on the same day, the factor perfects its assignment in Pennsylvania and in the District of Columbia and makes the appropriate filings under the laws of these jurisdictions. Searches show no other filing against the name of the manufacturer.

On day three, a priority contest arises between the two assignees. Who wins? According to the Convention, the German bank has priority over the American factor because, under German law, a first in time assignment ranks ahead of a subsequent assignment. The fact that the German bank's assignment has not been perfected under the law applicable to such issue in Pennsylvania or the District of Columbia is not relevant: the Convention specifies that the governing law for priorities is the law of the state in which the assignor is located, Germany in the above scenario.

This example may serve as a reminder that the application of the law of the jurisdiction of the assignor is not conditioned on such jurisdiction having a public filing or recording system for security rights. In the example, the Convention would direct the court to apply German law, even if German law does not provide for public registration or recording of assignments of receivables. **11.40**

Substantive law rules

What is also interesting is that an Annex to the Convention allows a Contracting State to make a declaration that it will be bound by a given set of priority rules, the State being offered a choice between three substantive law provisions according to whether under that State's law priority is or is to be determined by (a) registration under an international registration system established under section II of the Annex or under the State's own registration system or (b) the order of the competing assignments or (c) the order in which notification of the respective assignments is given to the debtor. This approach is designed to accommodate different stages of development among States as to registration of assignments whilst providing a common set of priority rules for all States selecting the same priority system. Where a State makes such a declaration then for the purposes of Article 22, which as stated above applies the law of the assignor's location, that law is the particular set of rules in the Annex selected by the declaration.[18] The effect is to produce an ingenious combination of a choice of law rule leading, where the assignor's State is a State that has made the requisite declaration, to the application of a set of substantive law rules in the Convention itself.

Questions

1. Why is receivables financing important in international trade?
2. What are the 'obvious reasons' why the factoring Convention can only be excluded in its entirety?
3. 'To allow an assignment to be effective despite a prohibition against assignment in the assigned agreement is a wholly unwarranted interference with the principle of freedom of contract, which is a central principle of transnational commercial law.' Discuss.

---

[18] Art 42(2).

4. In what respects, if any, does the Assignment Convention distinguish between the international assignment of receivables and the assignment of international receivables:

   (1) in defining internationality;

   (2) in specifying the connection to a Contracting State?

   In both cases explain the policy underlying the Convention's approach.

5. What types of transfer are excluded from the scope of the Assignment Convention—and why?

6. Read Article 1(3) of the Assignment Convention. What general principle can be deduced from this?

7. Is Article 26 of the Convention compatible with the hierarchy of interpretation rules laid down in Article 7?

8. Why do you think it was found possible to reach agreement on a set of substantive priority rules in Article 29 of the Cape Town Convention on international interests in mobile equipment but not in the Factoring Convention or the Assignment Convention? Do you think the conflicts rule adopted by the latter is a sound one?

Further reading

Bazinas, Spiros V, 'UNCITRAL's Contribution to the Unification of Receivables Financing Law: the United Nations Convention on the Assignment of Receivables in International Trade' (2002) 7 Unif L Rev 49

Ferrari, Franco, 'The International Sphere of Application of the 1988 Ottawa Convention on International Factoring' (1997) 31 Intl Law 41

Kötz, Hein, 'Rights of Third Parties: Third Party Beneficiaries and Assignment' (1992) 27 Intl Encyc Comp L, chs 13 and 52

Papeians de Morchoven, J-C, 'UNIDROIT Convention on International Factoring and its Implementation in French Law and Belgian Law' [1996] Revue de droit des affaires internationales 835

Sigman, Harry C, and Smith, Edwin E, 'Towards Facilitating Cross-Border Secured Financing and Securitization: an analysis of the United Nations Convention on the Assignment of Receivables in International Trade' 57 Bus Law 727 (2002)

Trager, Mara E, 'Towards a Predictable Law on International Receivables Financing: the UNCITRAL Convention' 31 NYU J Intl L & Pol 611 (1998–9)

Walsh, Catherine, 'Receivables Financing and the Conflict of Laws: The UNCITRAL Draft Convention on the Assignment of Receivables in International Trade' 106 Dick L Rev 159 (2001)

Wagenknecht, Claus-Rainer and Iffland, Hans-Gerhard, 'Factoring' in Kronke, Herbert, Melis, Werner and Schnyder, Anton K (eds), *Handbuch Internationales Wirtschaftsrecht* (Dr Otto Schmidt, Köln, 2005) 743

12

INTERNATIONAL INTERESTS IN MOBILE
EQUIPMENT AND THE CAPE TOWN
CONVENTION AND AIRCRAFT
PROTOCOL: ADDING A NEW
DIMENSION TO INTERNATIONAL
LAW-MAKING

A. Background and Key Features	12.01	E. Default Remedies	12.33
Underlying principles	12.12	F. The International Registry and	
Five key features of the Convention	12.14	the Registration System	
Three key features of the Protocol	12.16	The International Registry	12.37
B. The Two-Instrument Approach	12.17	A fully automated system	12.39
C. Sphere of Application		What is registrable?	12.40
When the Convention applies	12.21	Searches and search certificates	12.42
Principal matters covered by the		Duration of registration	12.43
Convention	12.22	Liability of the Registrar	12.44
Definitions	12.24	Jurisdiction	12.45
Interpretation	12.25	G. Priorities	
Relationship between the Convention		The approach to priority rules	12.46
and national law	12.26	Assignments	12.48
D. The Concept of the International		H. Insolvency	12.49
Interest		I. The Declaration System	12.50
The international interest defined	12.27	J. Evaluation of the Convention	
The nature of the international interest	12.28	and Protocol	12.52
Formalities	12.31		
The connecting factor	12.32		

A. Background and Key Features

We have referred earlier to the long-standing reluctance of those engaged in the **12.01** international harmonization of private law to move into the field of property law, which has traditionally been seen as too complex and too jurisdiction-specific to lend itself to the formulation of uniform substantive law rules. That is why one of the most successful of the modern law conventions, the 1980 Vienna Convention on Contracts for the International Sale of Goods, is confined to contract formation and contractual relations between seller and buyer and says nothing about property rights. But given the ever-increasing importance of property in international transactions, resistance to the treatment of property rights began to crumble, particularly with the advent of the conventions on international financial leasing and international factoring.

12.02 The idea of building on the leasing convention to provide an international regime for security interests in equipment of high unit-value of a kind regularly moving across national frontiers was first mooted in 1988 by a leading Canadian lawyer, Mr TB Smith QC, the Canadian member of the Governing Council of UNIDROIT, who had presided over the 1988 Diplomatic Conference in Ottawa. The rationale for such a regime was that a security or quasi-security (title retention) interest valid and enforceable in one jurisdiction might be unprotected or less efficacious when the equipment moved to another jurisdiction, so that creditors, conditional sellers and lessors could not be confident of the validity and ready enforceability of their interests outside their own jurisdiction, and this uncertainty could inhibit financing or make it significantly more expensive. Even the ordinary conflict-of-laws rule, the *lex situs* (or *lex rei sitae*), was unsuited to dealings in equipment having no fixed *situs*, and while this problem was in some degree overcome in the case of ships and aircraft by international conventions providing for the application of the law of the state of nationality registration,[1] this still left the problem of wide differences in the substantive laws of different States, some of which were considerably less favourable to security interest and retention of title rights than others.

12.03 A questionnaire was prepared by Professor Ron Cuming of the University of Saskatchewan to ascertain the extent of the interest in and need for such a regime and, the responses being positive and the key issues identified, the Governing Council of UNIDROIT set up a restricted exploratory working group to examine the project and to ascertain the feasibility of preparing uniform rules. This group consisted of a mixture of academic and practising lawyers, assisted by representatives of relevant business organizations. The group concluded that the project was not only useful but feasible so long as its scope was restricted. In particular, it should be confined to security interests in mobile equipment which were international in character and should either create a new form of international interest or provide for the recognition of foreign security interests, and should lay down certain default remedies, priorities and protection of the security interest in the event of the debtor's insolvency. Following the group's report to the Governing

---

[1] See commentary at n 2.

Council a study group was established to carry the project forward, and meanwhile comments were invited from governments of the Member States of UNIDROIT and a number of international gatherings organized to explain the project.

From the start the study group favoured the idea of a new international interest **12.04** rather than merely a recognition of national interests. Its initial inclination was to advocate the creation of an international security interest conceived in functional terms not dissimilar to those embodied in Article 9 of the American Uniform Commercial Code and thus encompassing conditional sale agreements, leases with an option to purchase, and perhaps finance leases as well. But it soon became clear that this approach would not find favour in Europe, where title retention under sale agreements was not characterized as security and there was a strong feeling that parties should continue to be free to choose different forms of instrument with different legal consequences. In principle, the Convention should encompass international interests in all mobile equipment of a kind normally moving from one State to another in the ordinary course of business and there should be an international public notice system recording the international interests. The Secretariat was asked to conduct an enquiry into public notice systems.

As the work proceeded, it became evident that the original conception had to be **12.05** modified in a number of respects. First, it should be confined to aircraft, railway rolling stock, satellites and perhaps ships, though as it turned out the shipping industry did not wish ships to be included, preferring to rely on three existing international conventions, though these were very different in character (being essentially conflict-of-laws conventions) and had been singularly unsuccessful.[2] Second, the registration system should be asset-based, not debtor-based, that is to say, the international interest should be registered against such items as particular aircraft or railway rolling stock, not against the name of the debtor. This meant that the assets to be covered by the convention had to be uniquely identifiable. It also meant that in principle the convention had to be confined to existing assets and those in course of construction which had reached the point of identifiability, and that the convention could not cover future property, nor in general could it extend to proceeds, for such an extension would then move the project away from asset-based financing and into general receivables financing, which was not the intention. Third, the convention should treat separately security interests in the

---

[2] The three conventions are the 1926 International Convention for the unification of certain rules relating to maritime liens and mortgages, in force but not ratified by a single common law jurisdiction; the 1967 convention of the same name, requiring five ratifications but so far securing only three; and the 1993 international Convention on maritime liens and mortgages, which came into force on 5 September 2004 but, like the 1926 Convention, has not been ratified by any common law jurisdiction. See: Roy Goode, 'Battening Down Your Security Interests: how the shipping industry can benefit from the UNIDROIT Convention on international interests in mobile equipment' [2000] LMCLQ 161, which was published before entry into force of the 1993 Convention.

narrow sense, conditional sale agreements and leasing agreements and should not conflate these into a unified security interest.

12.06   The involvement of lawyers specializing in aviation, and in due course the creation at UNIDROIT's request of an Aviation Working Group (AWG) which included representatives of aircraft manufacturers, leasing companies and financial institutions, proved crucial to progress. The technical nature of the subject made the involvement of industry experts essential. For example, how should airframes and aircraft engines be defined? What limiting factors should be incorporated to exclude light aircraft? What factors were peculiar to aviation? Clearly the study group could not resolve these issues on its own, nor could its drafting committee. Indeed, it took the industry specialists many months to come up with suitable definitions, and even then, a delegate at one of the joint UNIDROIT-ICAO[3] sessions was able to point to a missing element. These problems led in turn to consideration of the structure of the convention, a complex question which led to much discussion and division of opinion but was ultimately resolved in favour of the so-called two-instrument approach discussed below.

12.07   Several other specialist groups were established to address specific problems. Much preparatory work on the registration system was carried out initially by a Registration Working Group, later transmuted into an International Registry Task Force; issues of insolvency law were addressed by an Insolvency Working Group; and a Public International Law Working Group was set up to examine questions of public international law. Finally, a Steering and Revisions Committee, consisting of representatives of the Governing Council of UNIDROIT and of the ICAO Secretariat, IATA and the AWG, was established by the UNIDROIT Governing Council to finalize the texts of the two instruments from a technical perspective.

12.08   The aviation industry devoted a huge effort and substantial resources to the project as it affected aircraft, and this paid dividends, not only in helping to ensure that the convention and protocol would meet the needs of the different players in the aviation industry but also in gaining their support. The participation and support of the International Air Transport Association gave valuable additional impetus to the project. The final stage was to invite the participation of the intergovernmental aviation body, ICAO, which joined UNIDROIT in hosting three joint sessions of UNIDROIT's committee of governmental experts and ICAO's Legal Sub-Committee and also had the text examined in detail by its Legal Committee. UNIDROIT and ICAO co-sponsored the Diplomatic Conference in Cape Town in October and November 2001 at which the Convention and Aircraft Protocol were concluded. It is a measure of the interest and support that had been garnered by the end of the Diplomatic Conference that no fewer than

---

[3] International Civil Aviation Organization, which joined forces with UNIDROIT in the latter stages of the work in relation to aircraft objects and co-sponsored the Diplomatic Conference.

twenty States signed the Convention and Protocol at the closing ceremony. Eight ratifications were required to bring the Convention fully into force, together with its associated Aircraft Protocol, and this was reached with the ratification by Malaysia in November 2005. The Convention and Protocol thus came into force on 1 March 2006, by which time Senegal had brought the number of ratifications to nine.[4]

Similar working groups were subsequently established for railway rolling stock **12.09** and space assets, and draft protocols have been produced for each. The Rail Protocol was concluded in Luxembourg on 23rd February 2007 (too late to include in volume 2) under the title 'Luxembourg Protocol to the Convention on International Interests in Mobile Equipment on Matters Specific to Railway Rolling Stock'. Wherever possible it follows the wording of the Aircraft Protocol, avoiding the temptation to improve on the text for fear of implying a different meaning. However, the Luxembourg Protocol contains some interesting departures. One resulted from the insight that the criteria for unique identification of railway rolling stock did not have to be as tight for the purposes of an agreement constituting an international interest as it did for the purposes of registration. Hence Article V does not require specificity in an agreement; it allows a description by class or even 'all present and future railway rolling stock', on the basis that as between the parties it suffices that an item of railway rolling stock can be identified as falling within the scope of the agreement. This useful provision, which permits an agreement over after-acquired railway rolling stock, avoids the need to have a fresh agreement each time the debtor acquires a new item of rolling stock. Another major departure from the Aircraft Protocol is an Alternative C to the remedies on insolvency in Article IX of the Luxembourg Protocol. Alternative C enables the creditor to repossess railway rolling stock from a defaulting debtor without need of a court order unless the insolvency administrator, within the cure period, cures all defaults and agrees to perform all future obligations or applies for and obtains a court order suspending its obligation to give the creditor an opportunity to take possession. Article XXV, which requires an opt-in declaration by a Contracting State, allows for a freeze on the exercise of creditors' remedies in the case of public service railway rolling stock. Finally, Article XXIII, dealing with entry into force, addresses a problem overlooked when the Cape Town Convention was concluded, namely the danger that the Convention and Aircraft Protocol might come into force before the International Registry had become operational. That, indeed, would have happened in the case of aircraft objects but for a block on progress towards adoption of the Convention within the European Community for political reasons, which turned out to be a blessing in disguise. The Diplomatic Conference recognized the danger as regards the International

---

[4] For details of signatures and ratifications, see vol 2, pp 402, 421.

Registry for railway rolling stock, and Article XXIII precludes the Luxembourg Protocol from entering into force before the Secretariat of the Supervisory Authority has deposited with UNIDROIT as Depositary a certificate confirming that the International Registry is fully operational.

It is hoped that a Space Protocol will be concluded in 2008, completing the initial trilogy envisaged when the project began, and there is some interest in developing a fourth Protocol, devoted to agricultural and other equipment of high unit value.

12.10 The joint involvement of two international, intergovernmental organizations, UNIDROIT and ICAO, meant that the various drafts of the Convention and Protocol were subjected to particularly stringent scrutiny, a process which undoubtedly strengthened the final product.

Ludwig Weber and Silvério Espinola, 'The development of a new Convention relating to international interests in mobile equipment, in particular aircraft equipment: a joint ICAO-UNIDROIT project' (1999) IV Unif L Rev 463, 463–5

Early in 1997, the International Civil Aviation Organization (ICAO), a Specialized Agency of the United Nations system with 185 member States, and the International Institute for the Unification of Private Law (UNIDROIT), an intergovernmental organization independent of the United Nations system, with 57 member States (56 of which are also members of ICAO) decided to join efforts to develop a legal project aiming at the creation of an 'international interest in mobile equipment', an innovative legal concept of security rights independent of the various kinds of analogous rights created under national laws. The project also provides for the creation of an international registry, operating as a central registry, where all records of titles and conveyances relating to international interests are to be registered and kept up to date. It is considered that the envisaged legal system would not be effective without such a registry.

This project had been initiated within UNIDROIT nearly a decade earlier and, as it stands now, provides for the elaboration of an international Convention which would set forth general rules applicable to the different categories of high-value mobile equipment covered by its scope of application, to be supplemented by specific protocols relating to each category of such equipment, including aircraft equipment. A basic draft Convention and a draft Protocol relating to aircraft equipment have been developed and are currently undergoing intergovernmental consultation process within the joint framework of ICAO and UNIDROIT. The project provides for both instruments to be adopted simultaneously and read together as a single instrument.

The institutional co-operation between ICAO and UNIDROIT regarding this project, which resulted from the already existing co-operation between UNIDROIT and representatives of aviation industry as it will be referred to below, can be particularly fruitful in dealing with security rights in aircraft which is considered by academics and practitioners to be one of the most complex areas of private international air law. The joint expertise of both organizations is essential to make this project successful, as far as aircraft equipment is concerned. For example, the question will need to be addressed whether to pursue the idea of a basic Convention with general provisions and a protocol with specific provisions, or whether it would be better to adopt a single instrument. A proposal has been tabled to consolidate the two draft texts under consideration into a single Convention to serve the specific needs of the aviation sector. Other, similarly difficult questions remain to be resolved in the framework of co-operation between ICAO and UNIDROIT in the project. According to the arrangement under which the two organizations co-operate in moving forward the draft texts through the intergovernmental consultation process, this co-operation is to be carried out as far as the project is consistent with the specificity and interests of the civil aviation sector in general.

By providing for the creation of an international security interest, the proposed Convention, as far as it would apply to aircraft by virtue of the Protocol, addresses issues which are not or not adequately covered by the *Convention on the International Recognition of Rights in Aircraft*, adopted at Geneva on 19 June 1948, already within the framework of ICAO, which had come into existence in 1947 with the entry into force of the *Convention on International Civil Aviation*, signed at Chicago on 7 December 1944 (the Chicago Convention). The Geneva Convention has so far been ratified by 81 States, which represents a considerable degree of acceptance. It is however recognized that the ability of the Geneva Convention to protect a creditor's security interest in an asset is limited and may not serve the industry fully satisfactorily in a market where new trends and commercial practices have developed.

The proposed new Convention/Protocol would also have implications for the *Convention for the Unification of Certain Rules Relating to the Precautionary Attachment of Aircraft*, signed at Rome on 29 May 1933, which has been so far ratified by 29 States. Implications for both the Geneva and Rome Conventions are addressed in the draft Protocol.

It should be noted that it has always been considered by the international civil aviation community that questions of private international law, insofar as they affect civil aviation, should be handled by the appropriate international civil aviation bodies. This view dates back to a time long before the establishment of ICAO, during the existence of its predecessor, the International Commission on Aerial Navigation (ICAN) created under the International Convention on Aerial Navigation (the Paris Convention, 1919). This responsibility was then carried out by the *Comité International Technique d'Experts Juridiques Aériens (CITEJA)* created in 1926 as an independent committee. Among other international private air law instruments, the above-mentioned Geneva and Rome Conventions resulted from texts which had been prepared by CITEJA.

High value is not the only characteristic of mobile equipment qualifying to be covered by the proposed draft Convention. Regular mobility across international frontiers and the possibility of being easily identified, typically by manufacturer's serial number, are other essential characteristics. Aircraft equipment, namely airframes, aircraft engines and helicopters as considered for the purpose of the draft instruments, fulfilling all these intrinsic characteristics, was a natural candidate to be included in the scope of application of the prospective Convention, the question being then to know whether there was sufficient economic and political interest in having aircraft equipment included.

As regards the economic interest, the answer came soon from the aviation industry, first from manufacturers, leasing companies and lending institutions, which in 1994 aggregated in the *ad hoc* Aviation Working Group (AWG), later joined by the International Air Transport Association (IATA) in 1996, representing its member airlines' interests. The AWG and IATA took the view that the UNIDROIT initiative should be promoted with a view to establishing an international legal regime which would increase aviation credit and reduce its cost by enhancing legal certainty for parties contemplating the extension of secured transactions and creating rights in aircraft equipment that are easily and expeditiously enforceable. This would facilitate asset-based financing for purchase and leasing of aircraft, thus bringing economic benefits to civil aviation. Consequently, these two private organizations advised that the envisaged legal system would be more effective if it was composed of a basic Convention and supplementary specific protocols relating to each relevant category of mobile equipment, the idea being that each specific protocol be oriented to serve the specific needs of the concerned sector, and proposed the establishment of a group to draft the protocol to be applicable to aircraft equipment. This proposal being accepted by UNIDROIT, it was natural that ICAO be asked to also enter in project. During this first phase of ICAO's involvement, the Organization, together with UNIDROIT, AWG and IATA, set up the Aircraft Protocol Group (APG) in order to produce the first draft of the aircraft equipment protocol.

The somewhat strange symbiosis between aircraft suppliers and aircraft operators in a provider-consumer commercial relationship would be enough to show the overall real economic interest involved in the project, as far as the industry is concerned. Nevertheless, the AWG and IATA commissioned an independent study, namely the Economic Impact Assessment, to identify, assess and quantify economic benefits, with a view to promoting the project and motivating governments to adhere to it. This study tends to demonstrate that the approval of the proposed draft instruments, with a commercially oriented aircraft equipment protocol as it stands, would generate considerable economic advantages from which not only the industry but also the consumers could benefit: manufacturers would be able to expand their markets; leasing companies and lending institutions would be able to enhance security of their transactions and reduce their rates; airlines would gain increased access to aircraft financing and leasing at lower costs, which would allow them to purchase or lease aircraft at lower rates, thus benefiting consumers as well.

Even governments would directly benefit from the new system to the extent that asset-based financing and leasing would replace sovereign guarantees they are normally required to provide for their airlines transactions. In sum, the current project is likely to contribute to further develop civil aviation activity in general and international air transport in particular. Furthermore, it is possible that the economic benefits from the proposed legal system for airlines would help them to comply with high safety and environmental standards of international civil aviation by facilitating renewal of their fleets and aircraft engines.

12.11 In this chapter we shall focus on certain key features of these two instruments which it is necessary for the student to understand, in particular, the concept and nature of the international interest, the sphere of application of the Convention and Protocol, an overview of the default remedies, priority rules and protection against insolvency, and the unique character of the international registration system. We shall refer only fleetingly to the complex provisions relating to the assignment of associated rights and to the protection of non-consensual rights and interests, and students will not be expected to grapple with the details of these or with the rules relating to pre-existing rights and interests.

Underlying principles

12.12 The Convention and Aircraft Protocol are governed by five underlying principles,[5] namely practicality in reflecting the salient features of asset-based financing,

---

[5] See: Roy Goode, *Convention on International Interests in Mobile Equipment and Protocol thereto on Matters Specific to Aircraft Equipment: Official Commentary* (UNIDROIT, Rome, 2002) 13.

party autonomy in contractual relationships, predictability in the application of the Convention, transparency in providing information about the existence of an international interest through the international registration system, and sensitivity to national legal cultures in allowing a Contracting State to avoid the application of Convention rules incompatible with the fundamental principles of its legal system by utilizing the system of declarations referred to below. Key to the success of the project was the willingness of members of the Study Group from different legal families to recognize the need to accept new concepts and modifications of rules long settled in their own domestic laws.

The central purpose is to provide an international legal regime for international **12.13** interests which, by enhancing the security and enforceability of such interests and the predictability of outcome of disputes, will facilitate the acquisition and financing of mobile equipment, particularly in developing countries, and will enhance the credit rating of equipment receivables and reduce borrowing costs, to the advantage of all interested parties. The Aircraft Protocol Group, which was established by invitation of the President of UNIDROIT for the purpose of preparing a Protocol relating to aircraft equipment and which included representatives of ICAO, IATA and the AWG, commissioned an economic impact study by Professor Anthony Saunders and Ingo Walter under the auspices of the *Institut Européen d'Administration des Affaires* (INSEAD) and the New York University Salomon Centre. This study concluded that the international regime established by the Convention could reduce borrowing costs by several US$ billion a year, an analysis later reinforced by the fact that a little over a year after the conclusion of the Convention the Export-Import Bank of the United States, the official United States export credit agency, announced that buyers of large US commercial aircraft in foreign countries that ratified the Cape Town Convention in suitable form would qualify for a significant reduction in Ex-Im Bank's exposure fee.

Five key features of the Convention

The Convention embodies three features that are unique in international law- **12.14** making. First, it is a base Convention that, while covering three distinct categories of equipment, is not itself designed to be equipment-specific, matters particular to a given category being left to a Protocol that relates exclusively to that category and can modify or override the provisions of the Convention. This two-instrument approach was agreed only after a long struggle between its proponents and those who advocated a series of stand-alone conventions, each devoted to a single category. The second unique feature is the creation of an international interest in mobile equipment which derives its force from the provisions of the Convention, not from national law, and which, on registration, is accorded priority over purely national interests and over subsequently registered and unregistered interests, as well as legal validity in the debtor's insolvency. We shall examine the distinctive characteristics of the international interest a little later. Suffice to say at this point that in order for the interest to come into existence under the Convention it is necessary not only that the creditor has ownership of or other rights in the equipment but that it has entered into a security, title reservation or leasing agreement with the debtor. Outright transfers, for example, by way of sale, are outside the scope of the Convention but the registration and priority provisions of the Convention are extended by the Aircraft Protocol to the sale of aircraft objects. (The recently concluded Luxembourg Protocol for railway rolling stock permits registration of sales for information purposes only, so that while registration may constitute notice of a sale for the purposes of national law it has no effect under the Convention or Protocol.) The third unique feature is the provision of an international registry, a body established under the aegis of a Supervisory Authority to provide a wholly electronic system for recording international interests and dealings in such interests, as well as certain other rights and interests, and for making searches for registered interests. The great advantage of such a centralized international system is that it avoids the need to resort to a variety of national registration systems of varying degrees of efficiency and sophistication and provides a single modern, highly developed and fully electronic means of effecting registrations and searches, underpinned by a single set of standard rules and procedures. Fourth, the registration system covers not only the interest of a chargee under a security agreement but also that of a conditional seller or lessor, whereas in most jurisdictions outside the United States, Canada and New Zealand conditional sales and leases are not characterized as security agreements and are not registrable.

12.15 To these four features may be added a fifth which, though not unique to the Cape Town Convention, has been taken to a new level of sophistication, namely the elaborate system of declarations of various kinds by which those provisions that in some States would be considered an unacceptable interference with a long-established principle or policy would either not come into force in a Contracting State unless it made a declaration to that effect ('opt-in declaration') or could be disapplied by a Contracting State by a declaration ('opt-out declaration'). For example, a State whose municipal law does not permit the exercise of self-help remedies may make a declaration under Article 54 declaring that any remedy given by the Convention may be exercised only with leave of the court. Though such system is, of course, open to the objection that it weakens the uniform application of the Convention its great merit is that on certain key issues it provides a measure of flexibility which will enable States to ratify the Convention when they might otherwise feel unable to do so.

Three key features of the Protocol

12.16 The Aircraft Protocol also contains three distinctive features which enhance the security of financiers and lessors of aircraft objects. First, to the basic default remedies provided by the Convention Article XIII of the Protocol adds two more, namely de-registration (enabling the creditor to change the nationality registration of the aircraft) and export. Second, where a Contracting State has made a declaration applying Article VIII the parties to an agreement may choose the applicable law, and their choice will be effective even if the State whose law is selected has no connection with the parties or the transaction. Finally, and again subject to a declaration, Alternative A of Article XI gives the creditor strong rights on the debtor's insolvency, requiring the insolvency administrator, within a given waiting period, to cure all defaults and agree to perform all future obligations, failing which the creditor must be given possession of the aircraft. The waiting period cannot be extended and the court cannot intervene to grant relief. These provisions are reinforced by a duty on the courts of a Contracting State where the aircraft object is situated to co-operate to the maximum extent possible with foreign courts and foreign insolvency administrators in carrying out the provisions of Article XI.

B. The Two-Instrument Approach

At the start of the project the intention was to have a single convention covering all **12.17** three categories of equipment. But very soon technical problems began to emerge which necessitated a review of the structure of the instrument. In the first place, there were the definitional issues already mentioned, the resolution of which in the case of aircraft objects was to necessitate a major input from the aviation industry. Second, it soon became clear that not all three sectors were in a position to proceed at the same pace. The aviation experts were well ahead of both rail and space. If completion of the project in regard to aircraft objects was not to be delayed, it was necessary to find some mechanism by which work on the Convention could be advanced as regards these in isolation from matters concerning railway rolling stock and space assets. The ingenious and novel solution devised by the Aviation Working Group and IATA was to have a base Convention consisting of provisions not specific to any particular category of equipment and then supplement and modify these provisions, so far as necessary to meet the needs of a particular industry sector, by a series of Protocols, one for each category of equipment. The novelty lay in the fact that, as regards aircraft objects at least, the Aircraft Protocol would not be a separate instrument concluded later as a supplement to the Convention but would come into force at the same time and would both control the coming into force of the Convention and amend or add to its provisions as necessary, so that the Convention would be subordinate to the Protocol.

Roy Goode, 'The Preliminary Draft UNIDROIT Convention on International Interests in Mobile Equipment' (1999) IV Unif L Rev 265, 269–71

III.—THE TWO-INSTRUMENT APPROACH

As the project proceeded, it became clear that while most of the provisions of the Convention were likely to be appropriate for all types of equipment, it was inevitable that differences in the nature of equipment would necessitate at least some provision that would be equipment-specific. For example, each type of equipment needs to be defined. To the layman the meaning of 'aircraft' or 'space property' might seem obvious, but defining each of these terms has proved more complex than even the experts had expected. The Aviation Working Group and the Aircraft Protocol Group devoted considerable attention over a significant period of time to the definition of 'aircraft engines'; even so, a number of suggestions for amendment were made by delegates. Moreover, what is involved in the definition is not merely a description of the character of the equipment but also a component which limits the definition to equipment of high unit value. In the case of aircraft engines this was done by reference to thrust or horsepower. Again, objects located in outer space may have to be treated different from those situated within the jurisdiction of a State. Moreover, it would not be practicable to devise a single registration system covering all categories of equipment.

At one point it was envisaged that the Convention should be divided into separate parts, one part consisting of provisions that were not equipment-specific while each of the other parts would be devoted to particular types of equipment calling for provisions peculiar to that type. It was quickly seen, however, that this would make the Convention excessively long and cumbersome. Moreover, the technique would work only for those categories of equipment in respect of which the industry sector concerned had been able to complete work on the equipment-specific provisions in time for the Diplomatic Conference. The Aviation Working Group and the International Air Transport Association (IATA) then came up with the imaginative idea of a general convention supplemented by equipment-specific protocols. Each protocol would deal with a particular type of equipment and would control the Convention in the sense that the Convention would come into force as regards that type of equipment only when the protocol relating to it had been concluded, and the particular provisions of the Protocol would override the general provisions of the Convention as regards such equipment. Of course, it is important that the protocol procedure is not used to interfere with the basic structure and provisions of the Convention and is confined to those amendments which are considered necessary for the particular type of equipment involved. This test has largely been met by the draft Aircraft Protocol, which, though making a number of additions and amendments, leaves the great bulk of the Convention provisions untouched.

There is a third option, namely to have a series of stand-alone Conventions, each devoted to a particular type of equipment. The German delegation made a proposal that the Joint Session should work on a single, integrated text for aircraft, merging the Convention and the Aircraft Protocol. One reason given for this is the perceived uncertainty as to whether draft protocols would emerge for other types of equipment. However, it may not have been appreciated that a great deal of work had already been undertaken by the Rail Working Group and the Space Working Group, each of which had produced a draft Protocol, and that the two Protocols were in an advanced state of preparation, though not yet quite ready for consideration by governments. Moreover, the Intergovernmental Organisation for International Carriage by Rail (OTIF) had agreed to co-ordinate the intergovernmental consultation procedure in respect of the preliminary draft Protocol on railway rolling stock ...

In fact, UNIDROIT had given some thought to the idea of separate conventions for each class of equipment, but further consideration revealed serious disadvantages in this procedure. First, it would multiply the work, since there would need to be a separate study group to consider each convention and a separate Diplomatic Conference to agree upon it. Secondly, there would be a constant reinvention of the wheel, with each group drafting its own proposals while looking back to the work of its predecessors. Thirdly, there would inevitably be divergences between one convention and another even in relation to provisions that were not equipment-specific. This would undermine the unison and integrity of a single convention and would require courts and arbitral tribunals to interpret each convention separately, thus undermining the harmonising effect of a single convention. Fourthly, the single-instrument approach would lose the advantages of the fast-track procedure now being devised which would allow for additional protocols without the need for further Diplomatic Conferences, since it could be assumed that the single Convention would remain largely untouched and it would be necessary to examine only those matters related to the specific needs of the relevant industry for the types of equipment concerned. As a corollary, States would be deprived of the ability to choose from a menu of protocols and select only those they considered suitable to their situation. So the two-instrument approach possesses many advantages which one would not want to lose. It is significant that both the Rail Working Group and the Space Working Group strongly support the two-instrument approach.

However, the German proposal embodies an idea which, suitably extended, deserves serious consideration, namely the production of an integrated text which would not itself be an international legal instrument but would be prepared after the adoption of each protocol and would, for the convenience of those involved in the industry concerned, reproduce in a single text the combined effect of the Convention and the protocol. The relevant legal instruments would, as now, be the Convention and the Aircraft Protocol and the advantages of the two-instrument approach would be preserved, while on the other hand each industry would be able to make use of an integrated text for its own purposes as a convenient working tool.

12.18 Despite these compelling arguments, the choice between stand-alone conventions and the two-instrument approach remained contested right up to the final stage and was only resolved in favour of the latter at the beginning of the Diplomatic Conference itself. However, it was recognized that for those involved in the financing of aircraft objects it would be a great practical advantage to have a consolidated text in which the provisions of the Aircraft Protocol would be integrated into the Convention. Accordingly, pursuant to Resolution No 1 of the Diplomatic Conference, the Secretariats of UNIDROIT and ICAO together produced a Consolidated Text which, though not itself a legally operative document, provides a safe and convenient tool for those in the industry.[6]

12.19 The two-instrument approach represented a new departure in terms of treaty-making, for the normal function of a protocol is to supplement a treaty, not to control its commencement and qualify its provisions from the outset. Two distinguished international lawyers were invited by UNIDROIT to explore some of the implications of this approach.

---

[6] The Resolution and Consolidated Text are reproduced in Goode, *Official Commentary* (n 5) Annex IV. Annex IX provides a Table of Concordance between the Convention/Protocol and the Consolidated Text.

Christine Chinkin and Catherine Kessedjian, 'The legal relationship between the proposed UNIDROIT Convention and its equipment-specific Protocols' UNIDROIT document Study LXXII—Doc 47 and ICAO ref LSC/MEE-WP/12, reproduced (1999) IV Unif L Rev 323, 323–5

The legal framework for the proposed regulation of international interests in mobile equipment is innovative in terms of treaty law and rests upon the partnership between public and private sectors in establishing industry-specific international regimes. The important and unusual role of the private sector in developing international legal norms pushes at the boundaries of public international law and necessitates so rethinking in some important areas of treaty law.

The proposed instruments comprise a base Convention that provides for the 'constitution and effects of an international interest in mobile equipment' (Article 2) and equipment-specific Protocols prepared in conjunction with, and benefiting from, sector experts. The base Convention is envisaged as applying to a range of categories of 'uniquely identifiable objects': airframes; aircraft engines; helicopters; [registered ships;] oil rigs; containers; railway rolling stock; space property (Article 3). It is not foreseen that the base Convention will stand by itself so as to apply in general to all such equipment apart from that specifically regulated by a Protocol. The base Convention 'shall be read and interpreted as a single instrument' with each relevant protocol (Article U and reiterated within each Protocol, see preliminary draft Protocol to the preliminary draft UNIDROIT Convention on International Interests in Mobile Equipment on Matters specific to Aircraft Equipment *(the preliminary draft Aircraft Protocol)*, Article II).

At the time of the first meeting of governmental experts in February 1999, only one equipment-specific preliminary draft Protocol will be ready for the consideration of Governments, namely, the preliminary draft Aircraft Protocol. While this can be seen as a model for other Protocols it does of course have regard to unique aspects of the aircraft industry and current international aviation law and practice. The experience of drafting the preliminary draft Aircraft Protocol alongside the base Convention (and with participation of experts from the aircraft sector in the drafting of the base Convention) has shown that there are a number of legal consequences of the relationship that require careful and explicit consideration. These result from the understandings that:

1 In each case the base Convention and relevant Protocol are to be read as a single instrument. Provisions in the base Convention apply to all relevant equipment unless there are sector-specific provisions contained within a Protocol. In this sense it is the Protocol, not the base Convention, that is controlling with respect to each category of equipment.

2 The base Convention can only become applicable with respect to any category of equipment with the coming into force of the relevant Protocol, and only for the Parties to the relevant Protocol.

3 Each equipment-specific Protocol is controlling. It can amend or modify the base Convention where the special characteristics of the relevant sector make this necessary.

4 Consequently States' obligations under the base Convention will vary according to which Protocols they have adhered to, and there may be different obligations for the same Party if it has entered into more than one Protocol.

The challenge presented by this structure is therefore to ensure that there is sufficient flexibility within the base Convention to accommodate the needs of different sectors within the relevant Protocols, while ensuring that the essential structural coherence of the UNIDROIT registration system and the legal effects of international registration are maintained, that is that equipment-specific modifications do not undermine the basic objectives of the base Convention (which do however include the facilitation of asset-based financing). It will be necessary to ensure both that any amendment to the base Convention is compatible with each Protocol and, conversely, that no Protocol amendment entails an amendment to the base Convention that will undermine another Protocol. These requirements are especially important in the contexts of adopting future equipment-specific Protocols and for processes for amendment and review of all Protocols and the base Convention. In all these contexts, States may wish to consider the impact of the innovative framework upon the traditional processes of treaty law and whether they wish to depart from them.

In theory, a Protocol could virtually rewrite the Convention, but this would frustrate the whole purpose of the two-instrument approach, which is to enable additions and amendments to be made to reflect the needs of the particular industry sector affected by the Protocol while leaving intact provisions having no special implications for a particular category of mobile equipment. **12.20**

C. Sphere of Application

When the Convention applies

The Convention applies if the following conditions are satisfied:[7] **12.21**

(1) The equipment belongs to one of following categories:
    (a) airframes, aircraft engines and helicopters; [8]
    (b) railway rolling stock;
    (c) space assets.
(2) The equipment is of kind in respect of which a Protocol has been made
(3) The equipment is uniquely identifiable as provided by the Protocol
(4) The interest in the equipment is a security interest or an interest vested in a person who is a seller under reservation of title or a lessor under a leasing agreement
(5) The agreement is constituted in accordance with Article 7 of the Convention
(6) At the time of the agreement the debtor is situated in a Contracting State[9] or, the agreement relates to a helicopter, or to an airframe pertaining to an aircraft, registered in an aircraft register of a Contracting State which is the State of registry.[10]

We shall examine some of these conditions in a little more detail below.

Principal matters covered by the Convention

The main purpose of the Convention is to provide for the creation, enforcement, perfection, priority and protection against insolvency of an international interest **12.22**

---

[7] Arts 2, 3 and 7.   [8] For definitions, see: Protocol Art I.   [9] Arts 3 and 4.
[10] Protocol Art IV(1).

as defined by the Convention. The first set of substantive provisions is contained in Chapter III, which provides a set of basic default remedies available to the creditor, which may be modified or, within limits, expanded by agreement of the parties and which include an important provision for speedy interim relief from a court upon evidence of default being adduced. The next four chapters are devoted to the International Registry, the system for registration and searches, the respective roles of the Supervisory Authority and Registrar, their privileges and immunities and the liability of the Registrar for system failure and errors and omissions of the Registry.

12.23   Chapter VIII deals with the effects of an international interest as against third parties, laying down a set of rules governing the priority of an international interest and dealing with the effects of the debtor's insolvency.

Definitions

12.24   The Convention and Protocol together contain an unusually large number of definitions—forty in the Convention, sixteen in the Protocol—which should always be consulted when seeking to interpret any of the Convention's substantive provisions, for often ordinary words are used in a special sense. Examples are 'agreement', 'creditor', 'debtor', and 'proceeds', in the Convention, and 'aircraft engines', 'airframes', 'guarantee contract', and 'guarantor', in the Protocol. The heavy dependence on special terms is a further distinctive feature of these two instruments and results partly from the complexity of the matters covered by their provisions and partly from a desire to avoid tedious repetition.

Interpretation

12.25   Article 5 contains what has become the standard interpretation provision in international private law conventions,[11] except that the need to promote predictability in its application replaces the usual reference to good faith, which was considered to inject too much uncertainty into a convention dealing with equipment of high unit-value. The Convention does not provide for an express choice of law by the parties; that is left to the rules of private international law of the forum State.[12] However, Article VIII of the Protocol contains an interesting provision to the effect that where a Contracting State has made a declaration applying that Article the parties may agree on the law which is to govern their relations, wholly or in part. The effect of this is that the courts of a Contracting State which has made the declaration are bound to give effect to a choice of law clause even where the State whose law is selected has no connection with the parties, the aircraft object or the transaction.

---

[11] See above, para 3.52.   [12] Art 5(3).

Relationship between the Convention and national law

12.26 We have seen that the Convention establishes an autonomous regime for international interests in that any interest provided under an agreement conforming to Articles 2 and 7 of the Convention is effective to create an international interest even if it would otherwise be without effect under the applicable law. Nevertheless, national law is by no means wholly displaced. In the first place, interests created by national law continue to subsist despite registration of an international interest, though they are subordinate to a registered international interest. Second, it is for the applicable law to determine into which of the three categories of agreement referred to in Article 2(2) a particular agreement falls, though the meaning of 'security agreement', 'title reservation agreement' and 'leasing agreement' is determined by Article 1, not by national law. Third, the question whether an agreement was validly created in the first place or was void, for example, for want of consensus or legal incapacity, is left to the applicable law. Fourth, the requirement that the charger, conditional seller or lessor must have power to dispose of the object may be satisfied either by a rule of the applicable law or implicitly by the registration requirements and priority rules of the Convention. Fifth, non-consensual rights or interests which under Article 39 are to have priority without registration must be rights or interests which would have priority under the law of the declaring State over interests equivalent to registered international interests. Finally, any matter not settled by the Convention expressly or in conformity with the general principles on which it is based is to be determined by the applicable law,[13] in addition to which default remedies available under the applicable law over and above those conferred by the Convention are available to the extent that they are not inconsistent with the Convention's mandatory rules.[14]

D. The Concept of the International Interest

The international interest defined

12.27 Article 2(2) defines an international interest in mobile equipment. In order for an interest to constitute an international interest, it must relate to an object within one of the three categories of object referred to above, the object must be uniquely identifiable as provided by the Protocol, and the interest must be granted by the chargor under a security agreement or be vested in a person who is the conditional seller under a title reservation agreement or a lessor under a leasing agreement, each of these terms being defined in Article 1. As previously stated, an outright sale does not confer an international interest under the Convention; however, by Article III of the Protocol an outright sale of an aircraft object, while not creating

---

[13] Art 5(2). [14] Art 12.

an international interest, is brought within the scope of the Convention's registration and priority provisions, though it should be noted that this applies only to transfers by way of sale, not to original ownership. Interestingly, the Convention nowhere defines either the concept of internationality or the phrase 'mobile equipment'.

The nature of the international interest

12.28　It is important to appreciate that the holder of an international interest in an object need not be the owner of the object. Indeed, ownership as such is not sufficient to establish an international interest, which by definition is an interest:

(a) granted by the chargor under a security agreement;
(b) vested in a person who is the conditional seller under a title reservation agreement; or
(c) vested in a person who is the lessor under a leasing agreement.

12.29　The distinction between category (a) and categories (b) and (c) is relevant in at least two respects. First, the default rules for security agreements are more detailed, on the theory that the conditional seller or lessor still owns the object and, once entitled to recover possession for default, is free to deal with the object as it chooses. Secondly, there are special rules in Article 29(4) governing the priority of a conditional buyer or lessee vis-à-vis a competing third party. However, the Convention does not itself characterize agreements; it is left to the applicable law (which will usually be the *lex situs* of the object at the time of the agreement) to determine into which category the agreement falls. In the United States, most of the Canadian Provinces and New Zealand conditional sale agreements and many leases are treated as security agreements. It was therefore necessary to provide that an interest falling within category (a) does not also fall within category (b) or (c). So the default rules applicable to a conditional sale agreement characterized by, say, New York law will be those set out in Articles 8 and 9, not the rules governing conditional sale agreements in Article 10.

12.30　The interest of a seller or lessor does not derive from the contract of sale or lease; typically it precedes these agreements and results from manufacture by the seller or lessor or purchase from a third-party manufacturer or other supplier. That is why Article 2(2)(c) carefully avoids the phrase 'vested in a person *as* seller' or 'vested in a person *as* lessor'. The interest arises only at the point where the agreement between seller/lessor and buyer/lessee is concluded; until then the seller/lessor has at best a registrable prospective international interest and even this only if there are negotiations for an agreement which relate to an already identifiable object. The term 'creditor' is used to denote a chargee, seller or lessor and the term 'debtor' to denote a chargor, buyer or lessee. Not every debtor is competent to grant a charge nor every creditor to reserve title. A chargor under a security agreement and a seller/lessor under a title reservation or leasing agreement must be someone who has power to dispose of the object,[15] a requirement which may be satisfied either by national law or by operation of the provisions of the Convention itself.

Formalities

Article 7 lays down the formalities for the constitution of an international inter- **12.31**
est. These are fairly simple, and most agreements within one of the above three categories which satisfy the requirements of national law are likely to meet the conditions laid down in Article 7. It will be seen that registration is not included, for the function of this is purely to give notice of the existence of the international interest to third parties and preserve its priority. However, until registration the only benefits conferred on the creditor by the Convention are the default remedies set out in Chapter III, and failure to register risks loss of priority and also avoidance in the debtor's insolvency unless the interest is independently validated by the applicable law.

The connecting factor

The Convention applies only where there is the requisite connection with a **12.32**
Contracting State. Under Article 3 of the Convention this is the State in which the debtor is situated at the time of conclusion of the agreement. Article 4 sets out a number of alternative ways in which the test of situation in a Contracting State may be satisfied, the object being to give the widest scope to the application of the Convention. Article IV(1) of the Aircraft Protocol provides an alternative connecting factor for helicopters and airframes, extending the Convention to cover a helicopter, or an airframe pertaining to an aircraft, registered in an aircraft register of a Contracting State which is the State of registry as defined by Article I(2)(p).[16] Though the time at which the registration has to be in place is not stated, it is implicit that, as under Article 3 of the Convention, the condition must be satisfied at the time of conclusion of the agreement. However, where the registration is made pursuant to an agreement for registration of the aircraft it is deemed to have been effected at the time of the agreement. This means that a delay in implementing the agreement for registration does not preclude the application of the Convention, if that agreement is subsequently implemented and was in place at the time of the security or other agreement. This alternative connecting factor is not available in relation to aircraft engines, for which there is no system of nationality registration.

---

[15] Art 7(b).
[16] This means a nationality registration effected under the 1944 Convention on International Civil Aviation (the Chicago Convention).

E. Default Remedies

12.33 Chapter III of the Convention sets out a set of remedies available to the creditor in the event of the debtor's default. As mentioned above, these remedies and
the conditions in which they are given vary according to whether the agreement is characterized as a security agreement on the one hand (in which case
they are available only to the extent that the chargor has at any time so agreed)
or a conditional sale or leasing agreement on the other (where no such agreement is required). The creditor may also invoke any additional remedies permitted by the applicable law, including any remedies agreed upon by the
parties, to the extent that they are not inconsistent with the mandatory provisions of Chapter III,[17] that is, the provisions of Articles 8(3) to (6), 9(3) and
(4), 13(2) and 14.[18] The provisions relating to the remedies of the chargee
under a security agreement are designed to ensure that it cannot recover more
by enforcement than the amount of the secured obligations, any surplus being
handed over to the holders of subsequently ranking interests which have been
registered or of which the chargee has been given notice, in order of priority,
any balance being paid to the chargor.[19] But Article 9 provides for vesting of the
object in satisfaction of the debtor where agreed by all interested parties or so
ordered by the court on the chargee's application.[20] The default remedies of a
conditional seller or lessor are much simpler, namely termination of the agreement and repossession or application to the court for an order authorizing
either of these acts.[21]

12.34 Of particular importance to the rating of credit risk is the availability under
Article 13 of speedy interim relief[22] to a creditor who adduces evidence of
default. In the case of aircraft objects Article X of the Protocol reinforces these
provisions in various ways, among them by a requirement that the relief be given
within such number of working days from the filing of the application for relief
as is specified in a declaration made by the Contracting State in which the application is made. The difficult question of whether a creditor suffering loss because
of a Contracting State's failure to observe its obligations under Article 13 of the
Convention or Article XI of the Protocol has any right of recourse, directly or

---

[17] Art 12.   [18] Art 15.   [19] Art 8(5)–(6).

[20] Art 9(1)–(2). But the court may grant an application only if the amount of the secured obligation to be satisfied by the vesting is commensurate with the value of the object after taking account
of any payment to be made by the chargee to any of the interested persons (Art 9(3)).

[21] Art 10. Self-help will not, however, be available in a Contracting State which has made a declaration to that effect under Art 54.

[22] More accurately, relief pending final determination of the creditor's claim.

through the concept of diplomatic protection, has been discussed already in chapter 3.[23]

The provisions of Chapter III give considerable leeway to the principle of autonomy but qualify this in various respects in order to protect the debtor and other parties having an interest in the object. Moreover, to respect the sensitivities of States for whom some of the remedies, such as self-help, are contrary to their legal tradition, they can opt out by means of a declaration. **12.35**

The Aircraft Protocol provides two additional remedies, namely de-registration of an aircraft and its export and physical transfer from the territory in which it is situated.[24] This enables the creditor to have the aircraft re-registered in a nationality registration of its choice and to have the aircraft moved to a jurisdiction where the creditor has greater control. **12.36**

F. The International Registry and the Registration System

The International Registry

We have previously referred to the establishment of an International Registry for registration of international interests as a unique feature of the Cape Town Convention. To carry forward the registry project an *ad hoc* International Registry Task Force was formed in March 2000 which prepared a series of reports on registration issues that were submitted jointly to UNIDROIT and ICAO and helped lay the foundations for the registration system. The establishment and supervision of the International Registry are the responsibility of the ICAO, under whose auspices a competitive tender was organized and a Preparatory Commission set up which, acting as the provisional Supervisory Authority, awarded the contract for the Registry to Aviareto, a joint venture company of the Irish government and SITA SC, a leading provider of communication services to the air transport community. The International Registry is now up and running and registrations are already being effected at a more rapid rate than envisaged. The registration system is governed partly by the Convention, partly by the Protocol, partly by regulations made by the Supervisory Authority pursuant to Article 17(2)(d) of the Convention and dealing with operational matters, and partly by International Registry procedures established by the Supervisory Authority pursuant to regulation 15 of the regulations. **12.37**

---

[23] See above, para 3.60ff.   [24] Art IX. See also: Art XIII.

Ronald CC Cuming, 'Considerations in the design of an International Registry for interests in mobile equipment' (1999) IV Unif L Rev 275, 276–9

II.—WHAT IS MEANT BY 'REGISTRATION'?

The word 'registration'[5] is not a term of art in English; it has a number of different meanings. What it means in any particular situation can only be determined through examination of the context within which it is used.

The term 'registration' is often used to refer to the act of recording data relating to a person or an object in a government database. The purposes for requiring the data may vary widely and include revenue collection, public security or the collection of statistics. For example, in Canada all motor vehicles must be 'registered' under provincial legislation. The principal purposes for requiring this are to collect road taxes and determine who is legally responsible for loss caused by negligent operation of a vehicle. Registration does not create or record property rights in motor vehicles.

Another use of the term 'registration' is to describe the final step in the creation of property rights in assets. In other words, property rights in the assets vest in a named person when that person becomes the registered owner of the assets as a result of an entry in a public record or registry. In this context, rights are created through the registration process.

The term is also used to refer to a legal requirement that must be met if rights in property created by contract or otherwise arising under law are to be enforceable against other persons claiming interests in the property. Registration does not create the right, but it is a prerequisite to legal recognition of the priority of the right in the context of a conflict resulting from a competing claim to the property.

The third meaning described above is the one that is relevant in the context of the Convention and the Protocol. Article 28(1) of the Convention[25] provides that a 'registered interest has priority over any other interest subsequently registered and over an unregistered interest.' It is clear that the section is referring to an interest that is not created through registration, but to one that already exists or has potential existence. The effect of this provision is to apply the principle *qui prior est tempore potior in jure* to registration of competing interests rather than to their creation. This is supplemented by the rule that a registrable but unregistered interest is subordinate to the interests of subsequent buyers and representatives of creditors.

However, registration in an international registry created under the Convention and a Protocol is more than that encompassed in the third meaning of the term set described above. To the extent that the Convention gives priority to an international interest that is represented by a prospective registration (*ie*, a registration effected before the international interest was created), the system introduces another dimension to the concept. Registration is not a public record of the existence of an interest; it is a record of the potential existence of such an interest or of a potential contract that affects an existing property right. While ordinarily the creation of the interest predates the registration, in this context the registration predates the creation of the interest or rights affecting the interest. For priority purposes, effectively, the interest is deemed to have been created or affected at the date of registration.

It is often assumed that a registry system of the kind contemplated by the Convention is one that is designed to 'give notice' of the existence of a prior interest to the public. In a

---

[25] Now Art 29(1).

functional sense this is correct; in a technical sense it is not. While registration provides the facility through which a third party can acquire information as to the existence or potential existence of the registered interest, the priority of the registered interest is not dependent upon the state of knowledge of the third party. The function of registration is to preserve the priority that the registered interest would normally have under the *prior tempore* rule. In other words, the focus is on the fact of registration and not on the state of knowledge of the holder of a competing interest. This feature is made explicit by Article 28(2) and (3) of the Convention which provides that the state of knowledge of the holder of a competing interest is irrelevant to the application of the priority rules.

III.—WHAT TYPE OF REGISTRY?

As noted above, it is clear that an international registry created under the Convention and Protocol will not affect the creation of international interests. Its role is to provide a functionally efficient and commercially acceptable method for setting the priority rights of competing claimants to property in which international interests are held. However, this role does not dictate all of the features of the registry; it can be fulfilled in a number of different ways ... While the observations in this paper are presented, for the most part, in the context of a registry for international interests in aircraft equipment, most of them apply to any registry created under a protocol to the Convention.

IV.—NOTICE REGISTRATION OR DOCUMENT FILING

Most states of the United States and provinces of Canada have long had registry systems for security interests that were designed to fulfil functions very similar to those required of a registry system established under the Convention and Protocol. For many years, these systems required that a registrant file in a government office a copy of the contract that created the security interest. Searching parties were entitled to examine these documents at the public registry or obtain abstracts from the registrar setting out the central terms of the agreements creating the interests. Because these systems were inefficient and very costly and difficult to maintain, they were eventually discarded and replaced by notice registration systems. In many jurisdictions, the switch to notice registration was accompanied by a change from manual databases to computerized databases. Under a notice registration system, what is entered into the registry database is basic information concerning the transaction that gave rise to or that will give rise to the interest involved. This is much less information than would be included in the written record of the contract under which the interest was created or affected.

It is the view of the author that it would be inconceivable to create a document filing system under the Convention or Protocol. A document filing system would effectively preclude the use of a computerized registry database. Given the need for efficiency and accessibility, an international registry will have to employ a computerized database. It is, of course, possible to use optical scanning to digitalize contracts providing for international interests. However, the costs of this approach would be prohibitive, particularly in view of the need to have software that would address many languages.

V.—NOTICE REGISTRATION—WHAT DATA MUST BE SUBMITTED?

The decision to implement a notice registration system does not obviate the need to make additional choices with respect to the basic characteristics of the system. One of the choices that must be made concerns the amount of data that must be included in a registration. At one end of the spectrum is a system requiring that many of the details of the relationship set out in the agreement between an obligor and the obligee be included as registration information. At the other end of the spectrum is a system that requires minimum information to effect a registration: the names and addresses of the obligor and the obligee and a specific description of the equipment involved.

There is no demonstrable need to include extensive details of the agreement between the parties. In the few circumstances in which these details are relevant, they can be obtained from the obligee directly or through the obligor. In the bulk of cases, the functions of the international registry are fully served simply by providing public notice of the existence or potential existence of an international interest. A person who discovers this fact through a search of the registry will be able to take the steps necessary to remove the legal risk associated with being subordinate to a prior interest in the equipment. That person may refuse to deal further with the obligor, require a discharge of the registration (in cases where the registration does not support an extant international interest) or go directly to the obligee to attempt to buy out or obtain a contractual subordination of its interest.

Important benefits are associated with a notice registration system that requires disclosure of little more than the identity of the obligor, the obligee and the equipment. There is an inverse relationship between the amount of information that must be included in a registration and the extent to which the confidentiality of business relations between the obligor and obligee can be protected. A system that requires only minimal information about these relations is one that best provides the necessary balance between adequate disclosure through registration and the preservation of confidentiality of business information. There is a direct relationship between the amount of information that must be included in the registration and the incidence of error on the part of registrants in recording that information or on the part of registry clerks who enter data into the registry database from hardcopy records of registration information. In addition, the amount of information that must be included in registrations is an important consideration when designing a system that must function in more than one language. One feature of the Convention in particular demands a minimalist approach to registration data. Article 16(1)(a) contemplates the registration of a 'prospective international interest'. This term is defined in Article 1 as 'an interest that is intended to be created or provided for as an international interest in the future upon the occurrence of a stated event (which may include the obligor's acquisition of an interest in the object) whether or not the occurrence of the event is certain.' Article 16 provides for registration at a time before an agreement exists between the persons who later become obligor and obligee. If no agreement exists at the date of registration, it is not possible to require that detailed information concerning such an agreement be included in the registration.

12.38 With this helpful introduction to registration systems we can focus on a few key points embodied in the system finally established under the Convention, which follows quite closely that advocated by Professor Cuming.[26]

A fully automated system

12.39 The registration system is designed as a fully automated system requiring no human input at the Registry end, all registration applications and searches being

---

[26] For an up-to-date and informative account of the registry system, see: Ronald CC Cuming, 'The International Registry for Interests in Aircraft: an overview of its structure' (2006) XI Unif L Rev 18.

checked, registrations effected and search certificates issued, by computer. The system is therefore fast, reliable and relatively inexpensive, and does not involve the filing of agreements or copies or the checking of filed particulars against the agreements to which they relate.

What is registrable?

Article 16 sets out the matters capable of registration. Pride of place belongs, of **12.40** course, to the international interest, but there are several other kinds of registration. Particularly useful is the ability to register a prospective international interest, that is, one that is intended to be created or provided for in an object as an international interest in the future. It is, of course, necessary that the parties and the object be identified. Registration of a prospective international interest enables the intending creditor to secure a priority position for the interest itself when created, since priority goes back to the time of registration of the prospective international interest. In the case of aircraft objects the registration and priority provisions of the Convention are extended to sales, and the Protocol permits registration of a prospective sale, including an option to purchase given to the lessee under a leasing agreement. Other registrable items include assignments and prospective assignments of international interests and subordinations. Most of the interests can be registered only by or with the consent of the person against whom they are registered.[27]

The registration system is, of course, confined to objects falling within the scope **12.41** of the Convention, that is, airframes, aircraft engines and helicopters, railway rolling stock and space assets. Airframes and aircraft engines are treated separately, reflecting the fact that it is now quite common to have separate financing for engines, for which there is no system of nationality registration as there is for aircraft.

Searches and search certificates

Any person may make a search in the manner prescribed by the Protocol and regu- **12.42** lations.[28] To avoid the need for a fresh registration when the interest comes into existence the Convention provides that a search certificate is to indicate that the creditor named has acquired or intends to acquire an international interest but is not to indicate whether what is registered is an international interest or a prospective international interest.[29] This also has the effect of preventing the issue of a certificate misleadingly referring to a prospective interest when this has already become an actual interest.

---

[27] See: Art 20.

[28] Art 22(1). Under Art 26, no person may be denied access to the registration and search facilities on any ground other than failure to comply with the prescribed procedures.

[29] Art 22(3).

Duration of registration

12.43 Registration remains effective until discharged or until expiry of the period specified in the registration[30] and may be extended prior to expiry by either party with the other's consent.[31]

Liability of the Registrar

12.44 In order to provide assurance to registrants, the Registrar is made strictly liable not only for its own acts and omissions but also for system malfunction except where caused by 'an event of an inevitable and irresistible nature, which could not be prevented by using the best practices in current use in the field of electronic registry design and operation, including those related to back-up and systems security and networking'.[32]

Jurisdiction

12.45 Only the courts of the country in which the Registrar has its centre of administration have jurisdiction over claims against the Registrar.[33] This reflects the international function of the Registry, the fact that national courts in other jurisdictions would have no control over it, and the need to avoid conflicting decisions of national courts in different jurisdictions.

G. Priorities

The approach to priority rules

12.46 The rules of national legal systems governing the priority of competing interests tend to be refined and complex. By contrast the drafters of the Convention opted for simplicity, avoiding the myriad of classifications and exceptions that characterize national laws. This has enabled all the rules governing the priority of registered international interests to be gathered together in a single article, Article 29.[34] It should be noted at the outset that Article 29 is confined to priorities involving a registered international interest. The priority of competing unregistered interests is not covered by the Convention and remains governed by the applicable law.

12.47 The basic rule is contained in Article 29(1). A registered international interest has priority over a subsequently registered interest and over an unregistered interest even if the latter is not capable of registration under the Convention. The fact that the holder of the registered interest acquired it with knowledge of an earlier unregistered interest or gave value with such knowledge is irrelevant. Under Article 29(3)(b), there is an exception in favour of an outright buyer, whose interest is not

---

[30] Art 21.   [31] Art 20(1).   [32] Art 28(1).   [33] Art 44(1).
[34] But there are separate rules in Art 36 governing the priority of assignments of associated rights.

capable of registration under the Convention and who therefore is protected if acquiring its interest prior to registration of the international interest. That exception is disapplied by the Protocol as regards international interests in aircraft objects because the Protocol gives the outright buyer the right to register its interest. The priority of a conditional buyer or lessee vis-à-vis a registered interest of a third party depends on that of its own conditional seller or lessor.[35] In the case of aircraft objects, further priority provisions are to be found in Article XIX, as well as provisions for debtor protection in Article XVI.

Assignments

Chapter IX of the Convention deals with the assignment of associated rights and international interests and rights of subrogation. Associated rights are defined by Article 1 as all rights to payment or other performance by a debtor under an agreement which are secured by or associated with the object. Article 31(1) provides that except as otherwise agreed by the parties, an assignment of associated rights made in conformity with Article 32 also transfers to the assignee the related international interest and all the interests and priorities of the assignee under the Convention. This paragraph was originally drafted in a quite different way to provide that an assignment of the international interest transferred the associated rights. However, several delegations, particularly those from civil law jurisdictions, objected to this as being contrary to the principle that security interests are accessory to the secured claim and not vice versa. From a conceptual point of view this was, of course, correct, but it overlooked the fact that the Convention is not concerned with the assignment of receivables and its effects but rather with the assignment of international interests and its effects. It would therefore have been preferable to adhere to the original formulation. But a desire to maintain the purity of the legal concept carried the day, causing some complications in the drafting, because it was then necessary to provide that the Convention should not apply to an assignment of associated rights which is not effective to transfer the international interest.[36] The moral is, of course, that we should seek to make legal concepts our servants, not our masters. Chapter IX deals with the formalities of assignment, the debtor's duty to the assignee, default remedies in respect of an assignment by way of security, the priority of competing assignments and the assignee's priority with respect to associated rights. Article 36, which deals with this last question, is interesting in that for sound policy reasons it qualifies the priority of an assignee of associated rights over a subsequent assignee. We do not need to go into the rather complicated provisions here.[37]

12.48

---

[35] Art 29(4).   [36] Art 32(3).
[37] For a detailed analysis with illustrations, see: Goode, *Official Commentary* (n 5) 128–34.

H. Insolvency

12.49 The acid test of a security interest is its efficacy in the debtor's insolvency. The Convention contains rules designed to protect the creditor against invalidation of its interest when the debtor becomes insolvent, while the Protocol has additional rules governing the creditor's right to the return of aircraft objects on the debtor's insolvency if certain conditions are not met by the insolvency administrator. Under Article 30 of the Convention, an international interest registered prior to the commencement of insolvency proceedings is effective—that is, enforceable against the insolvency administrator and creditors—except so far as it is subject to avoidance under rules of insolvency law relating to preferences and transfers in fraud of creditors. Even an unregistered interest is effective if given effect under the applicable law. Article XI of the Protocol, which applies only in a Contracting State which has made a declaration to that effect, goes much further. It is expressed in two alternatives, and a Contracting State making a declaration must specify which alternative it selects. Alternative A, the so-called 'hard' option, provides in effect that on the occurrence of an insolvency-related event the insolvency administrator must either cure all defaults and agree to perform all future obligations within a specified waiting period, or give up possession of the aircraft object. This Article is based on section 1110 of the American federal Bankruptcy Code and leaves the court no discretion to impose a stay. Alternative B, the so-called 'soft' option, requires the insolvency administrator, on the request of the creditor, to give notice within the time specified in the Contracting State's declaration whether it will cure all defaults and agree to perform all future obligations or give the creditor an opportunity to take possession of the aircraft object. On failure of the insolvency administrator to give such notice or to fulfil its undertaking to give possession the court may permit the creditor to take possession. It is not incumbent on a Contracting State to make any declaration under Article XI. In that event its own insolvency law will continue to apply.

I. The Declaration System

12.50 The Convention does not permit unilateral reservations but to accommodate the different legal philosophies of Contracting States it allows for a range of declarations by a Contracting State. These fall into four categories. First, there are opt-in declarations which a Contracting State is required to make if a particular provision of the Convention is to have effect. Into this category fall Articles 39, 40 and 60. Then there are opt-out declarations which enable a Contracting State that feels a particular provision to be incompatible with its legal system to exclude the application of a Convention provision. For example, a Contracting State whose legal system does not permit self-help may wish to make a declaration excluding resort to extra-judicial remedies under Articles 9(1) and 10. There are two mandatory declarations, under Articles 48(2) and 54(2), the failure to provide which would preclude UNIDROIT as depositary from accepting the deposit of an instrument of accession. There is also a residual category of declaration under Articles 52 and 53. The Protocol adds provision for a battery of additional declarations, most of which are opt-in declarations, for example, those relating to choice of law or to the creditor's rights on insolvency. A declaration matrix has been prepared by IATA and the AWG,[38] and UNIDROIT has produced a guide to declarations containing more than thirty recommended forms. The declaration system is thus undeniably complex and it is open to the criticism that it weakens the uniformity which the Convention and Protocol are designed to provide. But the best is often the enemy of the good, and it was considered more important to maximize the prospects of adoption of the Convention than to maintain strict uniformity.

Jeffrey Wool, 'Rethinking the Notion of Uniformity in the Drafting of International Commercial Law: a preliminary proposal for the development of a policy-based unification model' (1997) II Unif L Rev 46, 46–53

The belief that commercial law ought to be gradually unified is a salient feature of orthodox thought on international commercial law reform. This Article will, as a starting point, take issue with an often-unstated assumption in this orthodoxy. The assumption is that no principled distinction need be made between the types of rules that ought to be unified. It will be argued that this assumption is misguided, and that a distinction ought to be made between the unification of rules reflecting public policy and rules embodying legal constructs. It will also be suggested that the failure to make this distinction has adverse implications which an alternative model of international commercial law reform would avoid . . .

I. INTRODUCTION: THE INTERNATIONALISATION OF COMMERCE AND FINANCE AND THE NEED FOR AN APPROPRIATE INTERNATIONAL LEGAL FRAMEWORK

Little need be said on the internationalisation of commerce and finance as a factual matter, nor on its theoretical and practical incompatibility with a network of incongruous and uncoordinated national legal systems. Such matters have been discussed at length in the literature. More illuminating, perhaps, would be to identify and distinguish between the two lines of reasoning supporting the proposition that international commercial law reform is desirable, and the type of law reform each inspires.

The first line of thought focuses on the costs and risks of a non-unified and uncoordinated international legal system. These would include unnecessarily high transaction, compliance and enforcement costs. They would also include the greater risks attributable to transacting with a relatively high degree of legal uncertainty. Concerns of this kind often lead to law reform efforts that seek to minimise such costs and risks by harmonising justiciability

---

[38] See: ibid Annex X. For an overview of the declaration system, see [51] and [71].

issues, including choice of law, jurisdictional, and enforceability of judgments issues, and typically do so by laying down law-selecting rules of decision rather than substantive rules.

The second rationale has at its base the objective of encouraging or promoting international commercial standards and practices and, more recently, even legal principles and concepts perceived by some to be general in nature and thus supra-national. Included under this general heading are, for example, the incorporation of best practice provisions in the 1993 revisions to the ICC Uniform Customs and Practice for Documentary Credits and the framing of a *sui generis* form of financial leasing as the conceptual foundation of Unidroit's Convention on International Financial Leasing 1988. Efforts driven by this objective tend to result in the preparation of substantive rules, either private in nature (and thus applicable by express or implied incorporation into a contract) or the subject of international conventions (and thus applicable, subject to their provisions permitting exclusion, on a mandatory basis).

The second rationale is justifiably gaining currency since it is consonant with the nature of contemporary international commerce and finance and, at its best, represents the embodiment of the revered, if at times overstated, principles associated with historical mercantile law. It encourages law reform that is transnational in nature, and commercial in orientation. It is consistent with a future in which sophisticated international business practices will play an even greater role, and in which legal rules, on policy and efficiency grounds, will increasingly accommodate and often encourage such practices.

For the reasons stated above and others, few would take issue with the need for, and inevitability of, an increasing number of international commercial law reform initiatives. The purpose of this Article, starting from the proposition that such law reform, particularly in the form of international substantive law conventions—our particular focus—is desirable, seeks to provide a model for the drafting of such conventions that promotes *commercially beneficial unification of law* to the maximum extent consistent with the principle that important *policy-based decisions* relevant to the subject convention should reside with contracting States. Before doing so, however, let us consider the intellectual centrepiece of international commercial law orthodoxy, the undifferentiated unification model.

II. UNDIFFERENTIATED UNIFICATION MODEL: FEATURES AND CONSEQUENCES

The unification of commercial law has a venerable past. Efforts in the field have been undertaken by powerful minds for lofty purposes, as well as practical ones. It is only a slight distortion to view the genesis of, or at least the ideals underlying, such efforts in high-minded scientific terms, and it is perfectly fair to trace its contemporary incarnation to the optimism surrounding, and commendable objectives of, the early inter-war period.

This distinguished pedigree, unfortunately, produced a somewhat flawed model of international commercial law reform. Worse still, it would appear that this flaw has been undetected or, at any rate, underanalysed. What is the model, what is its flaw, and what are the consequences of this flaw?

Let us start with an innocuous description of the principal objectives of contemporary international commercial law reform. With great deference to the interests and sensitivities of the ultimate actors in the drama—nation States—law reform orthodoxy seeks, through the tool of comparative methodology, to propose widely acceptable rules in furtherance of international trade. Put more pithily, international commercial law reform is a diplomatic effort, with a commercial objective, reliant upon comparative methodology.

The basic conceptual problem stems from the nature of, and interaction among, these three components: comparative methodology, diplomacy, and commerce. The comparative method—identifying and articulating common foundational principles underlying different national concepts, terms and constructs—is *policy-neutral in its application*. It seeks to identify a common language by which vastly different nations, with different legal concepts and different terminological conventions, may reach agreement in service of overarching transnational objectives. While the comparative method may serve other functions, it is this analytical function that is central to the law reform process. For our purpose, the essential point is that the comparative method and its application *neither differentiates between types of rules nor provides any guidance as to the normative value of the rules so produced.*

Those expressing views on the product of this comparative methodology—suggested undifferentiated uniform rules—*ie* commercial diplomats, as representatives of their respective States, often view matters from a different perspective. They are, or should be, keenly interested in the policy implications of the suggested rules. In the context of commercial law, such policy implications are bound to include the impact of an international convention's provisions on important areas of its national law, such as insolvency law, procedural law, and so-called mandatory law. In a diplomatic effort, great efforts must be made to accommodate these policy-type concerns.

The manner in which such accommodations are made is the source of the problem. Orthodox practice seeks *text-based solutions to confrontations with policy*. Which techniques are employed? First, compromise wording, often open-textured and general in nature, will be drafted in an attempt to, if possible, avoid or, if not, obscure the policy issue. Secondly, the rules of a convention may simply defer to categories of (generally, rather than precisely, described) national law. Thirdly, the convention may include a range of rules contemplating its own partial or complete inapplicability. Fourthly, the convention may include provisions, frequently prepared in the very final stages of the process, permitting reservations on points of policy. These provisions are often prepared in some haste, typically in an effort to accommodate the objection of one or more outspoken participants, rather than, as proposed below, as part of a deliberate and systematic approach to certain questions of policy. Fifthly, the text of the convention may simply avoid important commercial subjects for fear of policy confrontations.

The harm of such text-based solutions to policy confrontations is only fully appreciated in light of the principal objective underlying the commercial law reform enterprise, the furtherance of international trade. *The proximate cause of the furtherance of international trade, all else constant, is greater levels of certainty and predictability*. Greater levels of legal certainty and predictability facilitate clear risk allocations and rational pricing determinations. These are the most basic of elements in investment and financing decisions. International commercial law reform efforts should be, but in general are not, guided by this as the first, rather than as a subsidiary, principle of reform. One need only consider the adverse effects of the above-mentioned text-based solutions on the matter of commercial certainty and predictability to reach this empirical conclusion. Supporting evidence is available from another source: the position of potential contracting States and action of transacting parties. Notwithstanding the diplomatic, rather than commercial, orientation of the law reform process, international conventions, as a general proposition, have neither had as significant an impact, nor been as widely adopted, as the very great time, cost and effort required to produce them would merit.

How, then, should we summarise the orthodox undifferentiated unification model of international law reform, its fundamental flaw, and the consequences of this flaw? The undifferentiated unification model is designed to produce, as a starting point in an essentially diplomatic process, a set of uniform rules. Derived from application of comparative methodology, such rules do not differentiate matters of policy from more technical common points of law. The fundamental flaw in the undifferentiated unification model is the unacceptable tension between such undifferentiated uniform rules, on the one hand, and the diplomatic nature of the law reform process, on the other, as well as the manner in which this tension is relieved. As part of an essentially diplomatic effort, the undifferentiated unification model is forced to accommodate the policy concerns of governments by seeking text-based solutions and compromises, typically in a reactive and unsystematic manner. These text-based solutions and compromises, in turn, are inconsistent with the overriding commercial objective of achieving materially greater levels of certainty and predictability. As a consequence, the resulting international conventions are not as well received and relevant to international trade as they ought to be.

III. POLICY-BASED UNIFICATION MODEL: A PRELIMINARY PROPOSAL

In this section, we will outline the principal objectives and characteristics of an alternative model of international commercial law reform by means of substantive conventions: the policy-based unification model. We will also consider the main benefits of, and likely objections to, this alternative model.

The threshold objective of the policy-based unification model is to produce substantive conventions that, to the extent consistent with achieving the underlying legal objectives and maintaining the theoretical integrity of the convention, leaves important related policy-type decisions with contracting states. This approach, ever mindful of the increasing internationalisation of commerce and finance, encourages the clear and mandatory *unification of legal concepts and constructs*, yet defers to State decision-making on *points of policy*.

In one sense, this approach simply makes explicit that which is implicit in the traditional approach, to wit, that the prerogatives of contracting States on questions of policy must be accommodated. This, however, is where the similarity between the models ends. The *deliberateness and purposefulness* of this alternative approach avoid the need to seek textual solutions to policy problems that, experience has shown, produce unacceptable results from a commercial vantage point. As importantly, it permits individual contracting States to make conventions considerably more important commercially, within their respective territories, by taking certain trade-facilitating policy decisions when signing and ratifying conventions. The resulting commercial attractiveness is further augmented by the fact that contracting States are bound, through the mechanism of an international convention, to other contracting States on these policy determinations.

In broad terms, this is how the model might work in practice. First, the basic objectives of the project, and associated underlying legal concepts, would be identified. Once identified, traditional use of the comparative method would be made to devise the basic legal rules necessary to achieve these objectives, including the unification of the relevant legal concepts. These resulting rules, which we shall refer to as '*mandatory convention provisions*', would be drafted in a close-textured, that is, self-contained and self-explanatory, style. This drafting style would be designed to ensure that, as regards the subject matter addressed, such rules are clear, certain and predictable. The mandatory convention provisions would be binding upon all contracting States.

Secondly, points of policy satisfying a '*relational criterion*' would be identified *ex ante*, and would be developed in parallel with the mandatory convention provisions. The relational criterion would be formulated so as to identify the points of policy which, *inter alia*, are reasonably ancillary to, or are in the penumbra of, the objectives of the law reform project. This relational criterion, which should also include consequential considerations, might be something like this three-part test: (i) would a rule on the relevant matter significantly enhance or promote the basic objectives of the project?; (ii) if so, is its relationship to such objectives sufficiently close to justify its inclusion in the convention?; and (iii) if this is the case, is a rule on the related policy point, formulated so as to enhance or promote such objectives, reasonably likely to be acceptable to a number of States, or groups or categories of States? There are, of course, numerous other candidates for an appropriate relational criteria.

Rules satisfying the relational criteria, which we shall refer to as '*precatory convention provisions*', would be binding on a particular contracting State *if, and only if, such contracting State has not entered a reservation* in respect of any such precatory convention provision. Such reservations would be expressly authorised by the convention. All precatory convention provisions, whose terms must in all events be *compatible* with the mandatory convention provisions, would be drafted such that, if applicable, they would significantly enhance the objectives of the convention. The decision of a contracting State to enter or not to enter a reservation on the precatory convention provisions would be, in effect, a second-order policy decision: do the policy benefits of significantly furthering the objectives of the convention within its territory outweigh the policy values embedded in the provisions of its national law which such precatory convention provisions would displace? It is also a decision to which it would be bound internationally.

What are the foreseeable objections to the policy-based unification model, how forceful are they, and what are their implications?

We would anticipate the first objection to be that the policy-based unification model is undesirable in that its application reduces the overall unifying effect of substantive conventions. A terse initial response to this objection is that it is merely question-begging: for the reasons outlined above, the objective of unification, in certain circumstances, is subordinate to policy determinations in the policy-based unification model. A more satisfactory response from an orthodox law reform perspective would require consistency with traditional justifications for limiting the unifying effect of a convention. Such a response is also available. For those favouring the maximum degree of unification of international commercial law, limitations on unifying effect are viewed in largely political terms: which limitations are necessary to produce the greatest level of support for a particular convention? The policy-based unification model would provide a framework for the systematic assessment of this question.

The second objection may be that the policy-based unification model relies too heavily on the concept of reservations to international conventions or that, as a matter of precedent, reservations have not played the central, constructive role contemplated by the policy-based unification model. The first disjunct, to the extent that it is severable from the second disjunct, would be a reference either to an abstract preference or to the lack of an appropriate basis for reservations under international law. The former, by its nature, is neither rebuttable nor troubling. The rejoinder to the latter is that Articles 19 and 20(a) of the leading international instrument on the matter, the 1969 Vienna Convention on the Law of Treaties, provide clear authority for expressly permitted reservations of the kind contemplated by our model.

The second disjunct to this objection, that our assigned role for reservations ventures beyond core precedent in the field, would merit consideration. This is so since the charge is factually accurate. While expressly contemplated reservations have been an integral, even essential, element of numerous commercial and economic law conventions, they have not been used as a vehicle for the purposeful identification of policy matters. Nor have they served as a means of deliberate decision-making related to such matters. Before moving beyond established practice, therefore, this question should be considered: why, and on what basis, did this precedent develop, and are the traditional reasons for following precedent compelling in this instance?

Precedent on this point requires explanation in that it is not philosophically consistent with the model on which, in many respects, the law of treaties is based. That model is the law of contracts. Parallel concepts between the law of contracts and international treaties include requirements for valid consent to be bound, and the circumstances under which agreements may be amended or terminated. These concepts, and certain other analogies between the law of contracts and that of international treaties, are based on the *notion of autonomy*, State autonomy in the case of international treaties, and party autonomy in the case of contracts. It is somewhat surprising, therefore, that in the international commercial law reform paradigm the functional equivalent of a freedom-of-contract type notion—a qualification on one's consent to be bound—should have a negative connotation. Perhaps the best explanation as to why it does so brings us back, again, to the notion of unification as an end in itself. Such thinking has, as its basis, historical ideals of articulating a common commercial law of nations, or otherwise so legislating. It is submitted that such ideals, however enchanting, should not be an important strain in the reasoning of current international commercial law reform.

We can readily observe that, although understandable from an historical and, perhaps, ideological perspective, precedent disfavouring an important role for reservations is at odds with the central contract-model analogy applicable to international conventions. Nonetheless, should precedent be followed simply because it is precedent? It is submitted that the traditional reasons for doing so, respecting reliance interests and assisting in unifying the interpretation of phrases commonly employed in conventions, are not compelling. More broadly, policy matters surrounding a particular convention are sufficiently unique to merit separate and independent treatment in relation to the subject matter of the relevant convention.

The third, and more forceful, objection to the policy-based unification model is technical yet important. The model may require the inclusion of certain potentially difficult choice of law rules within substantive law conventions: the agreement of which contracting State is to be dispositive when different versions of a convention are potentially applicable. While it is tempting to dismiss this objection on grounds that the same problem currently exists whenever reservations are permitted—that is, in numerous important commercial law conventions—the fact remains that the policy-based unification model renders this issue more acute. Perhaps unavoidable by-products of the model are that determining the rules of decision under a particular convention will require specific attention, and that such conventions will be somewhat more complicated. This may well lead to the conclusion that use of the policy-based unification model is more justified in contexts, and in projects, in which the perceived benefits of a convention significantly increase by inclusion of a related set of provisions requiring policy determinations.

A fourth objection would consider the institutional implications of the potentially greater complexity of the policy-based unification model. The government consultations, diplomatic conference, ratification process and depository arrangements surrounding the relevant convention would necessarily be somewhat more intricate under the policy-based unification model. One may argue, therefore, that these matters are already sufficiently difficult and an approach that would make them more so should be discouraged. A response to this type of objection—which, admittedly, contains grains of truth—would be in two parts. The first would inquire how, on a comparative basis, the policy-based unification model fares against the traditional approach, the undifferentiated unification model. Much time is currently spent during government consultations and at diplomatic conferences reacting to and addressing policy-type points. The organisation and deliberateness of the policy-based unification model on such policy points may be viewed as an improvement. Similarly, even if one concludes that the relevant processes relating to the traditional approach are comparatively more simple, the result of its processes, as mentioned, is often non-ratification on policy grounds.

The second part of the response draws attention to the increased importance of the roles played by the institutions and governments sponsoring international commercial law conventions under the policy-based unification model. The success or failure of such conventions will depend to a relatively greater extent on the organisational work of such institutions and governments. Their increased responsibilities would include the organisation of government consultation and ratification processes designed to analyse policy, as well as purely legal, subject matter. The implementation of enhanced depository arrangements that contemplate (and facilitate access to and comprehension of) the more detailed and differentiated ratification instruments, as well as, most helpfully, the organisation of ongoing law review and dissemination arrangements, would also be required to support conventions produced on the policy-based unification model.

A fifth category of objections would focus on elements of the policy-based unification model itself, and may well start by questioning or drawing attention to the following: the difficulties of drawing a bright line between points of policy on the one hand, and legal concepts and constructs (which often embody policy determinations themselves) on the other; the practicalities of articulating an appropriate relational criterion designed to identify the relevant policy questions; the application of such relational criterion; and the issues associated with articulating and reaching agreement on rules relating to trade-facilitating policy matters. These are important matters that, both in theory and practice, require development and elaboration. The first such issue mentioned above may well require that a gradation or hierarchy of policy-type issues be contemplated by the model.

12.51 Having set out the argument, the writer of the above article then goes on to consider its application to what was then the draft convention on international interests in mobile equipment.

J. Evaluation of the Convention and Protocol

12.52 Only time will tell how successful these two ambitious instruments will prove to be. But the speed with which they were brought into force—only a little over four years—and the fact that the volume of initial registrations is significantly above what had been expected provide a good augury for the future. The system of declarations, though not free from complexity, provides a flexible mechanism for accommodating the concerns of States with different legal philosophies while leaving most of the key features of the Convention and Protocol undisturbed.[39] Completion of the political process leading to adoption by the European Union will lead to a substantial number of ratifications and give a strong additional impetus to the ratification process.

Questions

1. What law is usually applied under conflict-of-laws rules to determine the creation, perfection and priority of proprietary rights in tangible movables?
2. What is the difficulty in applying such rules to dealings in equipment which regularly moves from one country to another? How have the various conventions referred to earlier in relation to shipping and aircraft mortgages and liens sought to resolve that difficulty?
3. In what way do the Convention and Protocol provide a better solution to the problem of cross-border movement of equipment than that provided under the conventions referred to in question 2? And what do you see as the economic advantages of the Cape Town Convention and Aircraft Protocol?
4. What were the reasons for the adoption of the two-instrument (Convention/Protocol) approach? And what arguments were advanced against such approach?
5. (1) To what extent, if at all, does the creation of an international interest depend on national law?
   (2) Discuss the relationship between a national interest and an international interest giving security over an object within the Convention.
6. (1) What do you understand by the phrase 'mobile equipment' in the Convention?
   (2) Does the Convention set out a test of internationality? If not,
      (a) should it; and,
      (b) if so, how would you formulate the test?
7. Article 5 deals with the interpretation of the Convention. To what extent does this correspond with Article 7 of the Vienna Convention on Contracts for the International Sale of Goods? How are any differences to be explained?
8. (1) What is meant by 'power to dispose' in Article 7 of the Convention? Is it the same as a right to dispose?

---

[39] See: Iwan Davies, 'The New *Lex Mercatoria*: International Interests in Mobile Equipment' (2003) 52 ICLQ 151, 175.

    (2) Do any of the following have a power to dispose, and if so, does the power arise under the Convention or under the applicable law:

        (a) A sub-lessor;

        (b) A lessee in possession who purports to create a charge over the object;

        (c) A lessee who has not yet taken delivery and purports to create a charge over the object; and,

        (d) A person who grants a lease as agent of the true owner but acts in excess of his authority?

9. Why does the Cape Town Convention not apply to general proceeds?

10. The Convention permits a creditor, on the debtor's default, to have recourse to self-help remedies such as repossession. This is contrary to the legal policy of a number of civil law jurisdictions. In what way does the Convention respond to their concern to preserve that policy?

11. (1) Look at the priority rules in Article 29. To what extent do these correspond to the priority rules for registrable interests under the law of your country?

    (2) Article 29(2) provides that the priority of the first to register applies even if the registrant had actual knowledge of a prior unregistered interest. What is the policy reason for this rule?

12. 'The elaborate system of declarations under the Cape Town Convention and Aircraft Protocol undermines the very uniformity these instruments are designed to promote and should never have been introduced.' Discuss.

Further reading

(1999) IV Unif L Rev, A new international regimen governing the taking of security in high-value mobile assets: the legal and economic implications. (A special issue of the Uniform Law Review devoted to the Cape Town Convention and Aircraft Protocol and containing articles by numerous contributors.)

Davies, Iwan, 'The New *Lex Mercatoria*: international interests in mobile equipment' (2003) 52 ICLQ 151

Clark, Lorne, and Wool, Jeffrey, 'Entry into Force of Transactional Private Law Treaties Affecting Aviation: Case Study—Proposed UNIDROIT/ICAO Convention as Applied to Aircraft Equipment' (2000–2001) 66 J Air L & Com 1403

Cuming, Ronald CC, 'Overview of the Convention on International Interests in Mobile Equipment' 35 UCC LJ 73 (2002)

Cuming, Ronald CC, 'The International Registry for Interests in Aircraft: an overview of its structure' (2006) XI Unif L Rev 18

Goode, Roy, *Convention on International Interests in Mobile Equipment and Protocol thereto on Matters Specific to Aircraft Equipment: Official Commentary* (UNIDROIT, Rome, 2002)

Goode, Roy, 'The Cape Town Convention on International Interests in Mobile Equipment: a driving force for international asset-based financing' (2002) VII Unif L Rev 3

Graham-Siegenthaler, Barbara, *Kreditsicherungsrechte im internationalen Rechtsverkehr—Eine rechtsvergleichende und international-privatrechtliche Untersuchung* (Stämpfli, Bern, 2005)

Honnebier, B Patrick, 'The Convention on Cape Town on International Interests in Mobile Equipment: the solution of specific European property law problems' (2002) 10 Eur Rev Priv L 377

Standell, Joseph R, 'The Role of the International Registry Task Force (IRTF) in the Development of the International Registry for Interests in Aircraft' (2006) XI Unif L Rev 9

13

TRANSACTIONS IN SECURITIES

A. **Introduction**
  Securities market law as amalgam of
    commercial and regulatory law   13.01
  Types of transaction   13.03
B. **Dematerialization, Immobilization,**
  Netting and Technology: Effects
  on Custody, Settlement and the
  Use of Securities as Collateral
  Facts and issues   13.05
C. **Conflict-of-Laws Issues in the New**
  Environment: Characterization and
  Connecting Factor Revisited
  Framing the questions and searching
    for answers   13.08
  Regional and global solutions   13.11
    The Hague Convention: introduction   13.12
    The PRIMA approach   13.14
    Scope of the Convention   13.15

    The Article 2(1) issues   13.16
    Characterization   13.17
    Internationality   13.19
    The applicable law: the primary
      rule and the fall-back rules   13.20
    The primary rule   13.22
    The fall-back rules   13.23
    Insolvency   13.24
    Public policy (*ordre public*) and
      internationally mandatory rules   13.25
    Relationship between transferor's
      law and transferee's law   13.26
    The European Community
      Settlement Finality Directive   13.28
    The EC Collateral Directive   13.32
  National solutions   13.34
D. **Substantive Issues and Solutions—**
  National and Transnational   13.37

A. Introduction

Securities market law as amalgam of commercial and regulatory law

Analysis of transactions in securities is a newcomer in transnational commercial **13.01** law, although transactions on the markets for securities (shares, bonds and other financial instruments) are arguably of greater economic importance than any other branch of cross-border commerce and finance. There are two frequently cited reasons for this state of affairs. First, the relevant transactions were and sometimes still are viewed as ordinary sales, loans, the taking of security in moveables, at times touching and overlapping with certain rules of company law. Second, the law governing transactions in financial instruments is intertwined with regulatory law which, traditionally, is characterized as 'public' law designed to impose on the parties to such transactions the policies of the legislature and other arms of government relating to such matters as investor protection, liquidity, market structure and industrial development. If the former were true no special analysis might, indeed, be required. The latter, on the other hand, for decades seemed to place the subject matter well beyond the boundaries to which the harmonization process had been confined. It is telling—and this would contradict the first reason cited while confirming the second one—that instruments aiming at the unification of the law of international sales do, quite contrary to the notion that we are faced with ordinary sales transactions, not treat them as such but exclude them explicitly from their scope of application.[1] Likewise, the draft Legislative Guide on Secured Transactions which is currently being developed by UNCITRAL[2] explicitly refrains from touching upon the taking of security in securities.

13.02 The changing realities of financial markets, partly driven by technological and operational innovation but mainly caused by the needs and expectations of investors, issuers and financial intermediaries, make it increasingly difficult to keep transactional and regulatory law separate. An illustrative example is takeover bids. Not long ago they were considered to be pure and simple transactions for the sale and purchase of a majority or all shares of a company: the offeror—be it a shareholder of that company or an outsider (in particular another company)—approached the offeree (the target company or, less frequently, its shareholders individually) with a view to acquiring a controlling majority or the entirety of the target company's shares. Only in the 1960s did insights of the institutional role of business organizations and markets[3] provided by economic theory lead to the development of a regulatory framework designed to guarantee, for example, equal treatment of owners of the same class of shares, sufficient time for the offeree to make an informed decision, duties for the directors of the target company to act in the company's and/or its shareholders' interest instead of defending their own. In 1968, the United States Congress responded to these challenges by passing the Williams Act and adding sections 13 (d) and (e), 14 (d)–(f) to the provisions of the Securities Exchange Act of 1934.[4] In Europe, widely differing national solutions dominated the market for corporate control over decades. In 1974, a report for the European Community Commission drawn up by Professor Robert Pennington[5] set in motion the discussion of the issues involved. After a number of failed attempts the Directive 2004/25/EC on takeover bids entered into force on 20 May 2004. Its objective is the harmonization of transactional and regulatory

---

[1] Compare: Art 2(d) of the CISG as well as its predecessor, Art 5(1)(a) of the 1964 Uniform Law on the International Sale of Goods.

[2] Document A/CN 9/WG. VI/WP. 21 Add 1–5, Recommendation 4 (a) and Commentary, WP. 21 Add 1 para 10.

[3] Starting with Henry G Manne, 'Mergers and the Market for Corporate Control' (1965) 73 J Pol Econ 110.   [4] Section 15 USC 78(m)–(n).

[5] Doc XI/C/1.

rules from contract to company law and from labour law to administrative law and conflict of laws. The types of domestic sources affected range from hard-law market regulation to classic examples of soft law (the [English] City Code on Takeovers and Mergers and Rules Governing Substantial Acquisitions of Shares).

Types of transaction

The types of transaction in securities and the problem areas national legal sys- **13.03** tems—certainly regulatory but also private law rules—deal with in what are at times significantly diverging ways and that may benefit from the development of transnational principles and rules include:

(i) the issue of bonds and their placement with investors, including issues regarding the (often mandatory) involvement of intermediaries who stand between issuers and investors and whose involvement entails specific contractual and proprietary relationships;

(ii) the issue of shares and, alongside problems similar to the ones just mentioned, certain peculiarities of the transactional law regarding price determination; initial public offerings (IPOs) over the Internet including conflict-of-laws problems;

(iii) the role and the legal position of intermediaries and central counter parties (CCPs);

(iv) the impact of trade usages on the one hand and standard contract terms legislation and general consumer protection legislation on the other hand;

(v) securities lending;

(vi) the private law framework for disclosure, prevention of insider trading and other forms of market abuse.

The problem areas where transnational law is most visibly and forcefully coming **13.04** to the fore are securities custody and securities settlement, that is the transfer of title, and in particular the use of securities as collateral. Both the private-law formulating agencies acting at a worldwide level and the European Community have been seised of the matter and produced uniform law instruments that address a number of key issues. But much still remains to be done.

B. Dematerialization, Immobilization, Netting and Technology: Effects on Custody, Settlement and the Use of Securities as Collateral

Facts and issues

Only a few decades ago investment securities, in particular shares and bonds but **13.05** also a variety of hybrids such as debt convertible into equity etc., in all legal systems around the world were certificated. At least in everyday bilateral transactions a sale and purchase transaction could be carried out as the sale and purchase of any other movable: the seller delivered the certificate representing the underlying security against payment of the purchase price. The delivery transferred, subject to qualifications flowing from the type of security and varying according to the relevant national law, title in the securities (=settlement); the payment occurred either contemporaneously unless the parties to the transaction agreed, at the seller's risk, to defer payment of the price. The fact that owners of securities either kept the certificates under their direct control or, at the most, under a simple custody agreement with their bank contributed equally to the straightforwardness of the situation and the absence of risks—other than the risk of bad judgment—and serious legal problems. So long as all investors had physical possession of their securities in the form of certificates and notes, and trade occurred within the territorial boundaries of one country the law paid hardly any attention. However, the reality of today's capital markets is different. Together with the term 'settlement' the term 'clearing' or 'clearance' will be encountered frequently in this chapter; it refers broadly to the process of matching, registering, guaranteeing trades and calculating the participants' obligations.

Roy Goode, 'The Nature and Transfer of Rights in Dematerialised and Immobilised Securities' in Fidelis Oditah (ed), *The Future for the Global Securities Market: Legal and Regulatory Aspects* **(Clarendon Press, Oxford, 1996) 107 ff**

Developments in securities markets

The last thirty years have witnessed dramatic changes in the structure and organization of securities markets. Among the factors which have driven these developments are:

- A huge expansion in the amount of capital sought to be raised on the market
- A desire to promote cross-border investment and trading in securities
- The requirement for an efficient system of distribution among major investors
- The pressure to reduce delay, administrative burdens, risk and expense by curbing the volume and movement of paper ... and the number of transfers crossing the books of issuers
- The need to eliminate principal risk by developing systems to ensure simultaneous delivery versus payment (DVP).

Among the steps which have been taken to meet these objectives are: the move from direct holdings of investments (that is, holdings direct from the issuer by entry on its registers or possession of bearer securities) to indirect holdings through one or more tiers of custodian; the development of dematerialised (uncertificated) securities in which transfers are effected purely by book-entry (a particular feature of government securities); the immobilisation of internationally traded securities by deposit with the international securities depositories (ICSDs) ... and by the issue of permanent global notes instead of individual definitive certificates; and the linkage of securities transfer systems and funds transfer systems so as to ensure or facilitate DVP.

Risks

[...] Specific types of risk include country risk, pipeline liquidity risk[6], settlement risks of different kinds, such as principal risk[7] and replacement cost risk,[8] custody risk and legal risk. Overarching all of these is systemic risk, the risk that failure of a major player will have a domino effect on the market as a whole.

Though something will also be said about custody risk, which is of considerable importance to investors, this paper is primarily devoted to legal risk. Specifically it is concerned with the different types of risk that arise where securities, instead of being recorded in the issuer's books as held in the name of the investor or a pledgee of the investor, are held in the name of the custodian ('first-tier intermediary') with whom they have been deposited by the issuer and credited in the custodian's books to the securities account of the investor or pledgee or of some depositor ('second-tier intermediary') which itself is acting as a custodian for the investor or pledgee.[9] ...

Classification of securities by mode of transfer

[...] important for our purposes is the distinction between tangible securities, which are embodied in a negotiable certificate or note and transferable by its manual delivery, and intangible securities, which are not so embodied and transferable only in the books of the issuer. In English law this classification corresponds exactly to the unregistered/registered classification. This is because a certificate issued in connection with registered securities is not the embodiment of title, but merely evidence of title, so that the securities are not themselves transferable or negotiable by delivery of the certificate; such delivery is not effective to transfer legal title or to create a pledge and amounts at most to evidence of an intention to create a non-possessory mortgage or charge. So all registered securities, whether certificated or uncertificated, are considered intangibles in English law, and only unregistered securities represented by a negotiable certificate are tangible. By contrast under American law[10] certificates to registered, as well as unregistered, securities are considered to represent the securities and to provide the holder with an alternative mode of transfer by indorsement and delivery which is effective between the parties. Accordingly certificated securities are considered in the United States to be tangible, not intangible.

The diminishing importance of tangibility

The distinction between tangible and intangible securities has historically been of fundamental importance, affecting the mode of acquisition and transfer of the security, its pledgeability and its legal location. But tangible securities, though readily transferable, enjoy three major disadvantages. First, they entail the issue and physical movement of large quantities of paper, which in recent times grew to such dimensions that it threatened

---

[6] The risk arising from delays through gaps between processing cycles of different ICSDs, CSDs (Central Securities Depositories) and central bank payment systems.

[7] The risk that one party to a securities transaction may perform without reciprocal performance by the other.

[8] The risk of total non-performance of a transaction by one party, leading to a potential failure to realize an anticipated gain and a potential liability to others in a chain.

[9] Both the paper quoted and this ch 13 use for brevity the term 'account-holder' hereafter to denote the party to the credit of whose account the security entitlement (see para 13.37, below) is held, whether that party holds for itself or for its own customers or by way of pledge. The customer of a second-tier intermediary may itself be an intermediary ('third-tier intermediary') holding for its own customer, and so on.   [10] As well as many other legal systems.

to swamp clearing and settlement systems. Secondly, the certificates ... are expensive to produce ... Thirdly, they are risky, since title passes by manual delivery, so that if the certificates ... are stolen the thief can pass an overriding title to a bona fide purchaser for value ... Fourthly, their *situs*, and therefore the law governing their transfer, is susceptible to constant change ...

13.06 Two principal measures have been taken to deal with the problem of paper, dematerialization and immobilization. The most complete method of eliminating paper is to dematerialize the security completely by having no instruments or certificates at all, even in relation to registered securities. The investor merely receives confirmation from the issuer or its agent that securities of a stated type and amount have been issued to him. Denmark and France have been the pioneers on this path. In some countries only (or primarily) government bonds were dematerialized, in others all types of security—a paperless world where all securities exist as mere entries in electronically administered accounts with intermediaries (ICSDs or CSDs, banks and broker-dealers). Some, and over time an increasing number, of legal systems made it compulsory, others not. In a number of legal systems dematerialization entailed the need to resort to complex conceptual operations and fictions—in particular as regards possession—and, in general, encountered significant legal problems. Dematerialization does not by itself affect the direct relationship between investor and issuer.

James Steven Rogers, 'Policy Perspectives on Revised UCC Article 8' 43 UCLA L Rev 1431, 1442–5 (1996)

A generation or more ago, the principal mechanism of settlement in the securities markets was physical delivery of certificates representing securities. .... In most markets, that stage was passed long ago, at least with respect to the clearing function. Any two major players in the markets, such as large broker-dealers or banks acting as dealers and custodians, may have entered into numerous trades with each other in any given security on a given day. Rather than settling each of those trades one-by-one by passing certificates back and forth, a more efficient system can be devised by netting all of the transactions between the two parties into a single net deliver or receive obligation to the other. Even further efficiency can be achieved by moving from a bilateral to a multilateral netting system through a centralized clearing facility, so that all trading activity of each participant on a given day is netted to a single deliver or receive position in each security with all other participants. ....

Net clearing arrangements, however, simply reduce the number of transactions that need to be effected to settle a given day's trading. Some other step is needed to effect settlement itself. Even as late as the 1960s, that step was still delivery of physical certificates. Once each firm's net deliver or receive position had been determined, physical certificates were delivered from firm to firm to settle those obligations. By the late 1960s, the mechanical problems of processing the paperwork for securities settlement had reached crisis proportions. ....

One response to the inefficiency of paper settlement might have been the elimination altogether. During the 1970s, considerable attention was given to the possibility of establishing legal rules on securities transfer that would permit securities ownership to be evidenced simply by electronic records maintained by the issuers ... Those efforts resulted in the 1978 amendments to Article 8, designed to establish the commercial law rules that were thought to be necessary to permit the evolution of a system in which issuers would no longer issue certificates. The system contemplated by the 1978 amendments differed from the traditional system only in that ownership of securities would not be evidenced by physical certificates. It was contemplated that changes in ownership would continue to be reflected by changes in the records of the issuer. The main difference would be that instead of surrendering an indorsed certificate for registration of transfer, an instruction would be sent to the issuer directing it to register the transfer.

In some segments of the securities markets, physical certificates have been eliminated. Perhaps the most important example is United States Government securities, which have been issued only in book-entry form since the late 1970s ...

A direct uncertificated system ... was not, however, the mechanism by which the problems of the securities settlement system were solved. To use clearance and settlement jargon, the key development in the modern ... system in the United States has been 'immobilization' rather than 'dematerialization'. A useful starting place in understanding how the system operates is to consider where one would find the records of ownership of shares of any publicly held United States corporation.

If one examined the shareholder records of large corporations whose shares are publicly traded on the exchanges or in the over-the-counter market, one would find that one entity—Cede & Co—is listed as the shareholder of record of ... sixty to eighty per cent of the outstanding shares of all publicly traded companies. Cede & Co is the nominee used by The Depository Trust Company ('DTC'), a limited purpose trust company organized under New York law for the purpose of acting as depository to hold securities for the benefit of its participants, some six hundred or so broker-dealers and banks. Essentially all of the trading in publicly held companies is executed through the broker-dealers who are participants in DTC, and the great bulk of public securities ... is held by these broker-dealers and banks on behalf of their customers. ... By handing all their securities over to a common depository, all of these deliveries can be eliminated. Transfers can be accomplished by adjustments to the participants' DTC accounts. ...

The development of the book-entry system of settlement seems to have accomplished the objective of ensuring that the settlement system has adequate operational capacity to process current trading volumes. At the time of the 'paperwork crunch' in the late 1960s, the trading volume on the New York Stock Exchange that so seriously strained the capacities ... was in the range of ten million shares per day. Today, the system can easily handle trading volume on routine days of hundreds of millions of shares. Even during the October 1987 market break, when daily trading volume reached the current record level of six hundred eight million shares, the clearance and settlement system functioned relatively smoothly. Yet, as the ... system comes to rely increasingly on the book-entry system, the need for an adequate modern legal structure of commercial law rules concerning the system of securities holding through intermediaries becomes more and more pressing ...

13.07 Immobilization means the breaking of the link between issuer and investor. It may either be compulsory and permanent, as where a new issue is by its terms represented by a single permanent global note lodged with a CSD as a custodian and not exchangeable for definitive securities, or optional and revocable, as where certificated securities are deposited by the holder with a custodian on terms that they or their equivalent can be withdrawn at any time.

The article quoted above, para 13.05, concludes (at p 112):

The immobilisation of securities, whether it is permanent or temporary, has both legal and practical effects.

(1) Subject to the terms of the agreement and the applicable law, the investor typically gives up his ownership of the deposited security and becomes an account holder, acquiring co-ownership of a pool of fungible securities of the same class, with a personal right[11] to have securities of that class and to the value of his entitlement transferred or (if they are not permanently immobilised) to withdraw them in physical form.

(2) So long as the securities are immobilised within the system it is the book-entry recording the investor's entitlement, not the certificates representing them, that constitute the source of his rights.

(3) As a corollary of the second point, transfers are effected through book-entries in the records of the custodian, not by physical delivery of the certificates or entries on the issuer's register.

(4) In determining the applicable law under conflict of laws rules the physical location of the certificates is irrelevant.

C. Conflict-of-Laws Issues in the New Environment: Characterization and Connecting Factor Revisited

Framing the questions and searching for answers

13.08 In the early 1980s, when some legal systems moved quicker than others to embrace the new commercial realities and needs, one unusually far-sighted commentator outlined the challenges for conventional conflict-of-laws ways of dealing with transactions in securities.[12] But that the last one of the aforementioned conclusions regarding the legal consequences of immobilization (and dematerialization) of securities was far from reflecting common understanding even fifteen years on became clear when the English courts had to deal with one of the many disputes arising out of the collapse of Robert Maxwell's empire.

Macmillan Inc v Bishopsgate Investment Trust plc and others (No 3) [1995] 1 WLR 978, 987–1010

In November 1990 a number of shares in B. Inc. were transferred from the name of the plaintiff, a wholly-owned subsidiary of MCC incorporated in Delaware, into the name of the first defendant to be held as nominee. Subequently 7.6m. of the shares were transferred to the central depository system of DTC in New York without the plaintiff's knowledge or

---

[11] There are, however, legal systems where a considerable amount of constructive ingenuity has been invested to arrive at the conclusion that it is not a mere personal right but (because one wanted it to be!) ownership proper.

[12] Ulrich Drobnig, 'Vergleichende und kollisionsrechtliche Probleme der Girosammelverwahrung von Wertpapieren im Verhältnis Deutschland–Frankreich' in Herbert Bernstein, Ulrich Drobnig and Hein Kötz (eds), *Festschrift für Konrad Zweigert zum 70. Geburtstag* (Mohr Siebeck, Tübingen, 1981) 73.

consent and later used as security for loans to finance the Maxwell group of companies. The second defendants became the holders of 1.9m. shares under securities created by the deposit of share certificates in London afterwards perfected in New York through the DTC system. The third defendants acquired a security interest in 2.4m. shares by means of book entries in New York in the DTC system. The fifth defendant acquired an interest in 1m. shares through the DTC system, and in 500,000 shares by delivery of share certificates and an executed transfer form in England. At the date of the writ the transfer was not registered in the DTC system, but it was subsequently perfected.

The plaintiff, a Delaware corporation, owned the controlling interest of Berlitz Inc (B Inc), a company incorporated in New York. The plaintiff was itself a wholly-owned subsidiary of an English publicly quoted company, MCC, which was part of the group of companies controlled by Robert Maxwell (RM). In the months prior to his death RM's companies were in serious financial difficulties. He was obliged to provide ever increasing collateral in order to avoid breaches of the group's banking covenants. As part of that support operation RM called a meeting of the plaintiff's board in New York at which the board, in ignorance of RM's fraudulent purpose, resolved to transfer the B Inc shares to the first defendant, an investment trust controlled by RM and authorised him to sign the share transfers. The shares were transferred to the first defendant as nominee for the plaintiff and taken to London. The first defendant was a bare trustee of the shares and had no authority to dispose of them or to use them as security. Notwithstanding the breach of trust involved, the B Inc shares were thereafter used as security for borrowings by various of RM's companies both before and after RM's death. In order to facilitate dealings in the shares, 7.6m registered in the name of the first defendant and held by it as nominee for the plaintiff, were without the plaintiff's knowledge or consent deposited in the New York central depository system (the DTC) where they ceased to be in the registered ownership of the first defendant and were instead registered in the name of a nominee company, which held them for the account of the DTC agent of RM's companies. Three tranches of the shares were subsequently used as security for loans made by the second, third and fifth defendants, a New York financial institution (*Shearson Lehman*) and two Swiss banks (*Swiss Volksbank and Crédit Suisse*), to RM's companies. The first tranche of 1.9m shares was deposited with the second defendant in London and the security was perfected by deposit in the DTC system after RM's death; the second tranche of 2.4m shares was transferred to the third defendant by a book entry made in New York through the DTC system after RM's death; and the third tranche of 1.5m shares was transferred to the fifth defendant in two parcels. 1m shares by a book entry in New York through the DTC system and 500,000 shares delivered in London with an executed share transfer. Following RM's death on 5 November 1991 and the collapse of his group in December 1991 the plaintiff issued a writ against, inter alia, the second, third and fifth defendants claiming recovery of the shares or their proceeds of sale (more than $137m) on the grounds that they had been pledged to the defendants in breach of trust, that the plaintiff's interest in the shares was superior to that of the defendants and that they were held on constructive trust by the defendants, who in turn claimed to be entitled to the shares as bona fide purchaser for value without notice of the plaintiff's interest. At the date of the commencement of proceedings the fifth defendant had taken no steps to perfect its security in relation to the 500,000 shares received in London and it did not do so until 4 June 1992, when it became registered as the owner of the shares with full knowledge of the plaintiff's claim. The question arose whether the priority of interests was to be determined according to New York or English law.

Held—The actions against all three defendants were dismissed.

[...]

MILLETT J

[...]

CHOICE OF LAW

Characterisation of the issue

Each of the defendants maintains that the claims against it must be determined in accordance with the law of New York, though they are not agreed why this is the case. New York law has been invoked as the law governing the creation of the thing the ownership of which is in dispute (the law of incorporation) (by Shearson Lehman, Crédit Suisse); as the law of the place where the relevant transfer took place (the lex loci actus) (by Swiss Volksbank); and as the law of the place where the subject matter of the relevant transaction was situate when the transaction took place (the lex situs) (by all three defendants but only as a second choice). Macmillan insists that its claims must be determined in accordance with English law as the law with which its claim has 'the closest and most real connection' (the proper law of the restitutionary obligation).

The defendants rely variously upon the facts that Berlitz is a New York corporation, that its shares are transferable—and transferable only—in New York and consequently must be treated as located there, and that they were in fact transferred to the defendants by entries made in New York, either on the Berlitz transfer sheets or on the books of DTC. Macmillan relies cumulatively upon the facts that each of the defendants is an English company resident and carrying on business in England, that all the parties with whom the relevant transactions were entered into were resident and carrying on business in England, that all the negotiations which led to the defendants taking security over the shares took place in England, that the secured debts and all the security documentation were governed by English law, that everything which took place except the making of the relevant book entries in New York took place in England, that any inquiries which ought to have been made as to the transferor's title to the shares would have been made in England, and that where the security was taken or preceded by the physical delivery of share certificates they were delivered in England.

There is at the outset a fundamental disagreement between the parties as to the proper characterisation of the dispute for the purposes of English conflict of laws. The defendants insist that the question at issue is concerned with the priority of competing interests in a chose in action. Macmillan insists that its claim lies in restitution and, being brought by an equitable owner, must be decided in accordance with equitable principles. ...

It is manifestly correct to characterise Macmillan's claim as lying in restitution, but that is only the first step in the analysis. In order to ascertain the applicable law under English conflict of laws, it is not sufficient to characterise the nature of the *claim*: it is necessary to identify the *question at issue*. ...

In my judgment, Macmillan's claim is properly be characterised as a restitutionary claim which depends upon establishing a continuing proprietary interest in the subject matter of the claim; each of the defendants claims to have acquired a security interest in that subject matter which is superior to Macmillan's interest; and the question at issue is whether any of the defendants can identify a particular act or event which had the result of extinguishing Macmillan's interest or postponing it to that of the defendant. In my judgment the defendants have correctly characterised the issue as one of priority.

The situs of the shares

Article 8.105(1) of the New York Uniform Commercial Code (the NYUCC) provides that 'certified securities' governed by Art 8 are negotiable instruments. 'Certified securities' in Art 8 may mean the shares themselves or the share certificates or both as the context requires. ... [T]he expert witnesses agreed that the shares were ... negotiable securities under New York Law. Such shares are indistinguishable from the certificates, pass by endorsement and delivery, and are treated as situate wherever the certificates are located.

Under English law the position is different. No instrument can be transferred in England as a negotiable instrument unless it has been made negotiable by English law ... Where an instrument, whether issued by an English or a foreign person, is delivered in England, English law determines both whether that which was delivered is a negotiable instrument and the effect of its delivery upon the rights of third parties. The Berlitz share certificates, which were not bearer securities, were not negotiable instruments under English law. It follows that the shares must be distinguished from the certificates. The shares pass by registration and are treated as located where the register is located. The certificates are merely evidence of the entry on the register, though where indorsed with or accompanied by a duly executed power of transfer form in favour of a transferee and delivered into his possession they enable him to become the owner of the shares by registration.

Where the Berlitz share certificates were in England, therefore, and were dealt with in this country, the shares themselves would be regarded by New York law as being situate in England and by English law as being situate in New York. For the purposes of English conflict of laws, however, the domestic rule must prevail, for the situs of a thing, like any other connecting factor, must be ascertained by reference to the lex fori.

The applicable law

It is convenient to take each of the rival candidates in turn.

(1) *The proper law of the restitutionary obligation*

It is impossible to quarrel with the contention that the governing law should be the law which has 'the closest connection with the transaction'. In the present case, however, the incantation of the formula is not particularly helpful. It is merely to state the question, not to solve it. It is in order to identify the relevant transaction and to ascertain the law which has the closest and most real connection with it that it is necessary to undertake the process of identifying and characterising the issue in question between the parties.

That process is sufficient to dispose of Macmillan's submissions. Most of the factors on which it relies are aspects of the relationship between the parties to the relevant transactions, which consisted of assignments by way of security. Those factors would be determinative if the question at issue were concerned with the intrinsic validity of any of the assignments, its contractual effect as between the immediate parties thereto, or the mutual obligations of assignor and assignee. All such questions are governed by the proper law of the assignment: see *Dicey and Morris*, 12th ed, vol 2, p 979, r 120(1), reproducing Art 12.1 of the Rome Convention on the Law Applicable to Contractual Obligations, which is in force in England by virtue of the Contracts (Applicable Law) Act 1990 ... Such questions must be distinguished from questions of priority, which are concerned with the proprietary effect of the assignment on the assignor and third parties such as Macmillan claiming under him. An assignment is only a species of contract, and the parties to it can choose the system of law by which they intend their contract to be governed; but they cannot by their contract choose the law which will govern its effect on third parties. There is no obvious reason why most of the factors invoked by Macmillan should have any greater significance for the ascertainment of that law than would the parties' own choice of law to govern their contractual relationship inter se.

(2) *The law of incorporation*

Shearson Lehman and Crédit Suisse submit that the effect on Macmillan's pre-existing interest of every assignment by way of security, whether taking place in England or in New York, is governed by the law of New York as the law of incorporation of Berlitz. ...

In my judgment the application of the law of incorporation is contrary to principle and authority. This is not to say that the law of incorporation is irrelevant. Any question whether the manner in which a transfer of shares has been effected is such as to entitle the transferee to be registered as a shareholder must be referred to that law. The corporate rights of the transferee depend entirely on the law of incorporation. But the effect of a transfer on the company and its effect on the transferor and persons claiming under him are two different questions, and there is no rational basis for applying the law of incorporation to a question of the second kind. In my judgment this would be wrong in principle and impossible to reconcile with the law relating to negotiable instruments or with *Cady's* case.[13] It is pertinent to observe that the witnesses who gave expert evidence for the defendants on New York conflict of laws all argued for the application of the law of incorporation, but their reasoning would, if accepted, lead in fact to the application of the lex loci actus.

(3) *The* lex loci *actus*

In my judgment the issues of priority in a case such as the present fall to be determined by the lex loci actus, ie the law of the place where the transaction took place on which the later assignee relies for priority over the claim of the original owner. This does *not* lead to the adoption of English law in respect of every transaction in the present case, as Macmillan contends. The relevant transaction is not the contract to grant security, which affects only the parties to the contract, but the actual delivery of possession or transfer of title which created the security interest on which the particular defendant relies.

In my judgment the lex loci actus is in accordance with both principle and authority. The resolution of a priority dispute is a matter of legal policy. The question in every case is: in what circumstances should the security of the purchaser be preferred to that of the dispossessed owner? In English domestic law the answer frequently turns on the nature of the property in dispute ... The right to make such policy decisions which we claim for ourselves we concede to others. We accept the risk of an English owner losing his title as the result of a transaction which takes place abroad ... If, under a particular system of law, the security of the purchaser is preferred where the sale or other transaction takes place under specified conditions or where the asset sold or transferred is of a specific kind, that is because it has adopted a policy—or at least a rule having that effect—of quietening the title where those conditions are observed or of promoting the marketability of assets of that kind. It is to my mind appropriate in principle that the policy rules adopted by a particular system of law should be applied to all transactions taking place within its territory, but not elsewhere.

---

[13] According to the judge's previous analysis the leading English authority on the choice of law in regard to the transfer of shares: *Colonial Bank v Cady, London Chartered Bank of Australia v Cady* (1890) 15 App Cas 267 (HL); *affg* sub nom *Williams v Colonial Bank, Williams v London Chartered Bank of Australia* (1888) 38 Ch D 388 (CA).

The main argument which has been advanced against the lex loci actus is that the place where the certificates are delivered may be fortuitous or contrived. What, Shearson Lehman and Crédit Suisse ask rhetorically, if the certificates were handed over on an aircraft in mid-Atlantic? In my view there should be no difficulty in dealing with such cases, which can be safely left to be dealt with when they arise. They will be rare. Far more common are cases like the present in which portfolios of securities are delivered which consist of shares of companies in many different countries. On receipt of the certificates and the transfer forms, no doubt, each of them must be checked separately to see that it conforms to the formal requirements of the issuer; but, when it comes to considering whether any, and if so what, inquiries the recipient ought to make in order to verify the right of the transferor to deliver the portfolio, it would in my judgment be absurd to distinguish between the different components of the portfolio unless and until the recipient himself differentiates between them by attempting to perfect his security.

Even if the matter were free of authority, therefore, my own inclination would be to apply the lex loci actus, with the result that the effect of Macmillan's pre-existing interest in the shares of the delivery of the certificates would be governed by the law of England, because that is where the delivery was made, and effect of the entries on the books of DTC or the Berlitz transfer sheets would be governed by the law of New York, because that is where the entries were made. . . .

There may be good reason for this [ie application of the lex situs] in the case of tangible movables; but less in the case of intangibles, where the situs is somewhat artificial. In the case of shares *Cady's* case supports the lex loci actus. It is, however, unnecessary to explore this particular question further. In the present case the lex loci actus and the lex situs of the subject matter of each of the transaction in question were one and the same, and that is probably inevitable in the case of shares. Accordingly, there is no need to distinguish between the two, and I do not propose to do so.

Such textbook authority as there is treats questions of priority as governed by the lex loci actus/lex situs . . . In my judgment, unless this is fortuitous or contrived, the proper law of the transaction and the lex loci actus/lex situs can be treated as synonymous, and I use the terms interchangeably. . . .

In my judgment that [ie *Cady's*] case is authority for the following propositions: (i) the formal validity of a transfer of shares in a foreign corporation must be determined by the law of incorporation; (ii) the rights, if any, in the shares of a foreign corporation, conferred by the lawful possession of the share certificates, must be determined by the same law; but (iii) where the certificates are delivered into the possession of the holder in England, the prior question whether he is entitled to retain possession of them against the claim of the true owner must be determined by English law.

In my judgment the case is clear authority in favour of the lex loci actus and against the application of the law of incorporation for the purpose of deciding questions of priority while the transfer remains unregistered. There is also strong persuasive authority to the same effect in the United States . . .[14]

---

[14] The judge goes on to discuss *Direction der Disconto-Gesellschaft v US Steel Corp* 267 US 22, 45 S Ct 207 (1925); *United Cigarette Machine Co Inc v Canadian Pacific Rlys Co* (1926) A 12 F 2d 634; *Pennsylvania Co for Insurance on Lives and Granting Annuities v United Rlys of Havana and Regla Warehouses Ltd.* (1939) 26 F Supp 379; *Restatement of the Law, Second, Conflict of Laws* (1971), p 319, comment to § 303.

(4) *The* lex situs

It remains only for me to make good the proposition that in the present case the lex loci actus and the lex situs were one and the same.

Shearson Lehman and Crédit Suisse maintain the contrary. They submit that the lex situs was the law of New York whether the security interest in question was created by the delivery of share certificates in England or by making of book entries in New York. They point out that share certificates are merely evidence of the entries on the share register, and that the intention was to create security interests in the shares themselves and not merely in the certificates. In English law, the deposit of share certificates is evidence from which the agreement to charge the shares may be inferred, which agreement being specifically enforceable creates an equitable charge on the shares themselves and not merely a lien upon the certificates.

All that is true, but in my judgment these submissions fly in the face of *Cady's* case and confuse the intended subject matter of the security interest with the subject matter of the transaction which is relied on for the creation of that interest. The two are not necessarily the same. The effect, if any, of the possession of the share certificates on the title to the shares themselves may depend on the law of incorporation; but the prior question of the right to retain possession of the certificates does not depend upon that law. If it depends upon the lex situs of the subject matter of the transaction by which possession was obtained, the relevant transaction must be the delivery of possession and its subject matter must be the certificates.

In my judgment, if the lex situs applies, the effect on Macmillan's pre-existing interest in the shares of the delivery of the certificates is governed by the law of England because that is where the certificates were delivered into the possession of the relevant defendants, and the effect of the book entries in New York is governed by the law of New York because that is where the shares were situate when the entries were made.

(5) *Conclusion*

In my judgment, where the defendants rely for the creation of their security interests on book entries made in New York (Swiss Volksbank and Crédit Suisse in relation to the 1m shares), the effect of those entries on Macmillan's prior interest must be determined by the law of New York. There is no escape from this conclusion; the law of incorporation, the lex loci actus, the lex situs and the proper law of the transaction all coincide.

Had the parties which acquired their security interest by taking delivery of the share certificates in England (Lehman Bros and Crédit Suisse in relation to the 500,000 shares) taken no steps to perfect their security, they would have been compelled to rely upon their continued possession of the certificates in order to defeat Macmillan's claim, and their right to retain such possession against Macmillan would be determined by English law in accordance with the decision of the House of Lords in *Cady's* case. Both Lehman Bros and Crédit Suisse (in relation to the 500,000 shares), however, perfected their security by book entries made in New York, in the case of Crédit Suisse after the commencement of the present action, and neither needs to or can rely on the continued possession of the original share certificates ...

[there follows a detailed discussion of the relevant substantive English and New York priority rules and their interaction, and, finally, the position under New York conflict-of-laws rules including the question of whether the doctrine of renvoi cf above, chapter 2, might be relevant]

I reject the evidence of the defendants' witnesses that a New York court would apply the law of incorporation. I accept as an accurate statement of New York law the statement in the official comment to Art 8–106 of the NYUCC that–

'Any transfer of securities that is not effected through registration on the issuer's records is subject to the law provided by general choice of law rules. Transfers (including pledges) of certificated securities are not effected by registration on the issuer's records, and thus are subject to general choice of law rules.'

While the statement does not indicate what law should be applicable, it does indicate that it is not necessarily the same law as that which would govern a transfer effected on the books of the issuer, ie the law of incorporation. I have heard nothing which persuades me that the decisions in *Direction der Disconto-Gesellschaft v US Steel Corp* ... and *Pennsylvania Co for Insurance on Lives and Granting Annuities v United Rlys of Havana and Regla Warehouses Ltd* ... do not still represent the law in the United States. ...

Accordingly, I find that the questions whether, and if so when, a purchaser has acquired possession are pure questions of fact. Once the security has been perfected and the purchaser is no longer relying on the continued possession of the certificates which were delivered to it, I find that a New York court would determine the effect of the book entries in New York exclusively in accordance with the provisions of the NYUCC, that it would if necessary determine whether and if so when the purchaser had acquired possession *in fact* of the relevant certificates, that it would determine what the effect of the purchaser's state of knowledge at that time was by reference to the NYUCC, and that it would not find it necessary to inquire whether under the law applicable in the place where he obtained possession of the certificates the purchaser might have been required to deliver them up if he had remained in possession of them. ...

On appeal, the Court of Appeal (Staughton, Auld and Aldous LJJ)[15] held the *lex situs* to be applicable, identifying this as the law of the issuer's incorporation. In the speeches particular attention was paid to questions of conflict-of-laws analysis and methodical clarity. This theory-conscious judgment drew surprised applause from continental-European commentators.[16] However, the conflicts rule applied is the most conservative one the judges could have chosen.   **13.09**

Lord Millett, 'Foreword', in Richard Potok (ed), *Cross Border Collateral: Legal Risk and the Conflict of Laws* (Butterworths, London, 2002) V

It is a truism ... that the realities of commercial life change faster than the legal response to them. ... Securitisation, dematerialisation, indirect holdings through intermediaries, and cross-border collateralisation are all relatively recent innovations. They require a reappraisal of many of the assumptions of domestic laws and undermine the assumptions which underlie the solutions hitherto adopted in the conflict of laws.

This became uncomfortably apparent to me when trying the *Macmillan* case. The supposed rule that the applicable law governing a charge on shares depended on the *lex situs*

---

[15] [1996] 1 WLR 387.

[16] Compare: Eva-Maria Kieninger, 'Übertragung von Gesellschaftsanteilen im englischen Internationalen Privatrecht' (1997) IPRax 449.

was not obviously appropriate to dematerialised securities held through an intermediary. Struggling to maintain some kind of rational link with precedent, I applied the law of the place where the relevant electronic entries would be made, that is, the law of the immediate intermediary (though I was not sophisticated enough to describe it as such). The Court of Appeal substituted the law of the share register, which was singularly old-fashioned. Fortunately there was only one share register (many multinationals maintain share registers in different countries) and only one intermediary (there is often a chain) and both the share register and the intermediary's electronic records were maintained in New York.

So no harm was done in the particular case. But the decision will cause problems if its reasoning is applied to dematerialised securities held through a chain of intermediaries where real choice of law problems may arise. The starting point must be to undertake a rigorous analysis of the legal nature of the interest in question. In terms of English law these will inevitably be equitable; but that only creates further problems when cross-border complications involve categorisation for the purposes of the conflict of laws. . . .

One day these questions will have to be resolved. . . .

13.10 In a similar vein, one of the present writers, in his 1999 Hague Academy course on key issues of private international law regarding capital-market transactions, addresses these questions as follows:

Herbert Kronke, 'Capital Markets and Conflict of Laws' (2000) 286 Recueil des Cours 245, 320

In transnational securities trade, where specialized clearing houses and custodians . . . are operating, the main questions to be answered are the following: Are securities tangible, even if not embodied in a negotiable certificate but only in a global note or in form of a book entry? And if so, where are they located and does their *situs* matter for the purposes of determining the law applicable (*lex cartae sitae*), including the question of whether this may be accomplished by mere delivery? Moreover, as always in the area of secured transactions, can the pledgee etc. rely on his position in the case of the owner's insolvency? While it is generally accepted that the nature of a security is governed by the issuer's personal law . . . , the *lex societatis*, the proper choice-of-law rule for selecting the law governing the transfer is less certain.

The question whether the *lex cartae sitae* has a useful role to play under the changed circumstances was originally answered in the affirmative and if the transfer had to be effected from a Central Securities Depository in one country to the one in another country the *leges cartae sitae* of the transferor's and the transferee's countries were applied successively. In this situation, the result of applying the *leges loci actuum*[17] would appear to be identical and it would have the conceptual advantage of looking at the technique of the transfer rather than the nature of the security to be transferred. As Professor Goode has pointed out, both solutions are equally impracticable and in cases of dematerialization and immobilization of securities deposited with an ICSD application of the intermediary's law of incorporation or place of business is preferable. This, indeed, is also the position of Belgian and Luxembourg law with regard to Euroclear and Clearstream Banking. According to both, the *place of the administration of the account* (ie Belgium or Luxembourg, respectively)

---

[17] As advocated by Millett, J (as he then was) in *Macmillan Inc v Bishopsgate Investment Trust plc and others (No 3)* [1995] 1 WLR 978.

is the relevant connecting factor and both subject the 'pool' of securities and entitlements of the co-owners to that law even if the securities or parts thereof are physically located (eg with another custodian) in a third country. Article 9 (2) of the EU Directive on settlement finality in payment and securities settlement systems of 19 May 1998 provides, albeit with a limited scope of application, ... for the application of the law of the Member State where the account or deposit system is kept, cf below para 13.28].

There may still be doubts and imperfections as regards details, such as the Directive's limitation to the *taking of collateral*, the likelihood that any forum outside Belgium and Luxembourg will not apply the self-righteous'[18] rules if the forum's own rules require certain guarantees which the ICSD's law does not provide for, or the desire that a modern rule should place the account holder in a position to have rights against the issuer in the issuer's insolvency *and* give customers of lower-tier intermediaries direct rights against higher-tier intermediaries. However, the thrust against mechanical use of traditional private-international-law rules on securities and for their adaptation with a view to coping with modern transaction techniques on global securities markets are clear. Where conflict-of-laws rules are unable to build the bridge to overcoming the imperfections mentioned, deeper harmonization of substantive law might be needed. For complexity of the law in this area is certainly one of the factors increasing transaction costs—a main concern for both investors and financial intermediaries. And nothing makes the law and hence the parties' contractual arrangements more complex and expensive than uncertain conflicts rules against the backdrop of substantially diverging substantive rules.

Regional and global solutions

Instinctive and tentative answers to the questions raised, as proposed by courts, a **13.11** few domestic legislatures and commentators, were in a more systematic way analysed and developed in the run-up to the Hague Conference's first session of a working group of experts devoted to these matters, convened in The Hague in January 2001.[19] European Directives addressing certain isolated aspects of dealings in securities influenced the negotiations in The Hague but will in turn be influenced by the instrument adopted at the Diplomatic Session.

The Hague Convention: introduction

The 2002 Hague Convention on the Law Applicable to Certain Rights in Respect **13.12** of Securities held with an Intermediary is designed to accommodate what emerged both in the aforementioned case law and scholarly writings and in particular the normal fact patterns where there are several tiers of intermediary. Usually, where

---

[18] Compare: Gerhard Kegel, 'Die selbstgerechte Sachnorm' in Erik Jayme and Gerhard Kegel, *Gedächtnisschrift für Albert A. Ehrenzweig* (Müller, Heidelberg, 1976) 51. The context here, however, is different in that the substantive law is paired with a conflicts rule.

[19] This document came to be known as the 'Bernasconi Report', prepared by Christophe Bernasconi with the assistance of Richard Potok and Guy Morton. See also: Christophe Bernasconi, Richard Potok and Guy Morton, 'General introduction: legal nature of interests in indirectly held securities and resulting conflict of laws analysis' in Richard Potok (ed), *Cross Border Collateral: legal risk and the conflict of law* (Butterworths, London, 2002) 7.

an intermediary holds a particular issue of securities for several of its customers these are held in a common (fungible) pool, or omnibus account, which is maintained by the intermediary and does not identify any particular customer. Among the many advantages of this arrangement are that they enable huge volumes of transactions in securities to be processed without going through the books of the issuer, each investor having—at least in those models found in certain jurisdictions and generally considered to be most advanced—its relationship only with its own intermediary, and that pooled accounts give the intermediary much greater flexibility in dealings for customers.

13.13 Conflict-of-laws rules in many countries have yet to adapt to the change from direct to intermediated holdings.[20] The traditional conflicts rule in the area of property law and, in particular, proprietary interests in investment securities lead to the *lex rei (cartae) sitae.* In relation to bearer securities no questions arise. In relation to registered securities the *situs* is in many legal systems considered to be the place of incorporation or, alternatively and more in general the place where the register is kept. But this is ill-suited to holdings reflected only in the accounts kept by an intermediary, who may be based in a different country (or more than one), and it subjects all holdings and dealings, at whatever level, to a single law which may have little or no connection with the account or the dealing in question.

The PRIMA approach

13.14 Given that—in the model which served as the conceptual basis—each investor's relationship is solely with his own intermediary, a logical starting point, which was the initial focus of the draft Convention, was to adopt the law of the place of the relevant intermediary approach (PRIMA), so that the proprietary effects of a credit to a securities account and of dealings with that account are governed by the law of the place of the intermediary with whom the account is maintained. But that approach proved inadequate because in modern trading the function of maintaining accounts may be distributed among different offices of the intermediary situated in different countries or, indeed, may be centrally organized through an electronic system with no office at all. So though the concept of the relevant intermediary is retained, the primary rule is the law selected by the parties to govern the account agreement.

Scope of the Convention

13.15 The Convention is a pure conflict-of-laws instrument, having no rules of substantive law and no effect on the substantive domestic law of a State that ratifies it. It is confined to issues listed in Article 2(1) in respect of securities held with an intermediary, that is, the rights of an account holder resulting from a credit of securities

---

[20] For three strikingly differing examples, see above, para 13.10 and below, para 13.34.

to a securities account.[21] The Convention applies when the following five conditions have been satisfied: securities have been issued; they have been credited to a securities account; the account is one maintained by a 'securities intermediary', to which the Convention gives an extended definition; the issue to be decided is one falling within Article 2(1); and the case involves a choice between the laws of different States.

The Article 2(1) issues

Within its scope of application the Convention determines the law applicable to **13.16** all the issues listed in Article 2(1) in relation to the securities themselves, whether the entitlement to the securities is proprietary, co-proprietary, derived from a trust or other fiduciary relationship, contractual or mixed, or indeed of any other character. Excluded are purely contractual or other purely personal rights which do not relate to the securities themselves as credited to a securities account but derive from the account agreement, such as the intermediary's standard of care in maintaining the account, the content and frequency of account statements, the time by which instructions must be given by the account holder in order to be carried out on a certain date, fees and other obligations of the account holder.

Characterization

Different legal systems classify the investor's rights in different ways. In some sys- **13.17** tems the rights against the intermediary are only contractual; in others, there may be a fiduciary relationship which ensures that if the intermediary becomes insolvent the securities it holds for its account holders are treated as forming a separate estate which is not available to its external creditors; in yet other systems the investor may be owner of a separately designated part of what the intermediary has or a co-owner of an undifferentiated pool of securities of the same issue held by the intermediary through an account with its own intermediary. In a desire to equate dematerialized securities with physical securities as far as possible, a number of systems categorize dematerialized securities which are not held in a nominal account for the investor as bearer securities and equate the intermediary with a depositee. In several systems the nature and characterization of the account holder's rights remains unclear.

The Convention is not concerned with the substantive law governing these mat- **13.18** ters, but the question of characterization also surfaces in relation to the sphere of application of the Convention. As we have seen, it does not apply to purely contractual or other purely personal rights. But what law determines whether rights are purely contractual or otherwise purely personal? This question is answered in the following terms in the Explanatory Report on the Convention.

---

[21] See the definition in Art 1(1)(f).

Roy Goode, Hideki Kanda and Karl Kreuzer, assisted by Christophe Bernasconi,
Explanatory Report on the Hague Convention on the Law Applicable to Certain Rights
in Respect of Securities Held with an Intermediary: Hague Securities Convention
(Koninklijke Brill, The Hague, 2005), para 2–5

2–5 There may occasionally be cases where the question arises whether or not an issue falls within the Article 2(1) list. This question is to be answered by reference to the language of Article 2(1) and (2) and not by using the Convention itself. It is only when the applicable substantive law has been determined by the Convention that the Convention law comes into play to determine and give effect to any characterisation required by that substantive law. Thus, it is not necessary to classify an account holder's rights relating to the securities themselves and resulting from a credit of securities to a securities account as proprietary or personal or otherwise in order to determine whether the Convention applies. The Convention applies to the rights relating to securities credited to a securities account, however the legal nature of these rights is classified in any legal system and whether or not the account holder has rights directly against the issuer . . .

Internationality

13.19 As stated above, the Convention applies to all cases involving a choice between the laws of different States,[22] and whether or not the applicable law is that of a Contracting State.[23] Thus the concept of internationality is given the widest scope, applying where one of the players (including for this purpose the issuer or any intermediary or account holder or a transferee) and any other player are located in different States. Moreover, the fact that the forum might not consider the foreign element relevant to the issue before it is immaterial to the applicability of the Convention. But where all the factors relevant to the situation are located in the same State the fact that the forum is in another State does not attract the Convention.

The applicable law: the primary rule and the fall-back rules

13.20 It is important to note that the Convention has to be applied separately to each account and at each level. Each account holder's rights are determined by the law applicable to his holding with his own intermediary and with no one else. The Convention thus rejects the notion of some super-PRIMA governing all relationships at all levels. Once the securities in question have entered the intermediated system by being credited to a securities account with an intermediary and the other conditions for the Convention to apply are satisfied the law applicable in relation to that account governs the Article 2(1) issues, and that law continues to apply after a transfer of securities (and notwithstanding any choice of law in the transfer agreement) unless and until the securities are transferred to a new account in the name of the transferee, in which event the transferee's rights become governed by the law applicable in relation to that new account. So each new credit creates a potentially new applicable law.

---

[22] Art 3.   [23] Art 5.

The Convention lays down a primary rule for determining the applicable law and, where this does not apply, three fall-back rules are arranged in a cascade so that the first applicable fall-back rule is the one to be applied. In determining the applicable law Article 6 excludes from consideration the location of the issuer or of certificates to securities or of any intermediary other than the relevant intermediary, that is, the intermediary with whom the account holder in question has his account. **13.21**

The primary rule

Article 4 lays down the primary rule, namely that the law applicable to all the issues specified in Article 2(1), is the law of the country expressly agreed by the parties to the account agreement to govern that agreement or such other law as the parties expressly choose to govern those issues. However, the parties do not have unlimited freedom of choice. In the first place they can only select 'other law' to govern *all* the Article 2(1) issues. Choice of a law to govern some of the issues only is not a valid choice, and the applicable law will then be that expressly chosen to govern the account agreement or, failing that, the law determined by the relevant fall-back rule in Article 5. Secondly, it is necessary that the designated law satisfy the so-called 'Qualifying Office' test in being the law of a State in which the intermediary has an office that is engaged in a business or other regular activity of maintaining securities accounts or is identified by an account number, bank code, or other specific means of identification as maintaining securities accounts in that State. **13.22**

The fall-back rules

These are laid down in Article 5. They apply if the parties to the account agreement have not made an express choice or their choice is invalid or does not satisfy the 'Qualifying Office' test. Then the law to be applied is the law of the State in which is located the office of the intermediary expressly and unambiguously stated in a written account agreement as the office through which the account agreement was entered, provided that such office satisfies the Qualifying Office test. Failing such a statement, the intermediate fall-back rule looks to the place where the intermediary is incorporated or otherwise organized. If the intermediary is not incorporated or otherwise organized, the ultimate fall-back rule points to the law of its (principal) place of business. **13.23**

Insolvency

Under Article 8 an insolvency court must respect the application of the Convention-determined law to the Article 2(1) issues but this does not affect the application of the forum State's substantive or procedural insolvency rules, including those relating to the ranking of claims and the avoidance of a disposition as a preference or a transfer in fraud of creditors. The effect of this is that the insolvency court cannot **13.24** apply a different law to disturb the status, perfection, and priority of an interest in securities under the Convention law but, having respected the application of the Convention law to the Article 2(1) issues, the insolvency court may then apply any special rules of its own (or a third country's) insolvency law providing for the avoidance or insolvency ranking of such an interest.

Public policy (ordre public) and internationally mandatory rules

13.25   Article 11(1) and (2) reflect the current mainstream approach to questions of the forum's public policy and the so-called internationally mandatory rules.[24] Article 11(3), however, precludes recourse to provisions of the *lex fori* imposing requirements with respect to perfection or relating to priorities between competing interests, unless the law of the forum is the applicable law under the Convention. The purpose of this provision is to ensure that the provisions of the Convention which lie at the heart of the instrument cannot be undermined by recourse to rules of public policy or mandatory rules that would have the effect of supplanting or modifying the applicable law determined by the Convention.

Relationship between transferor's law and transferee's law

13.26   An account holder, A, pledges to P securities held by A in an account with Intermediary 1 in Ruritania. In conformity with Article 4(1) the account agreement specifies Ruritanian law as the governing law. A then fraudulently mortgages the same securities to T, the securities being transferred to a securities account held by T with Intermediary 2 in Urbania under an agreement validly expressed to be governed by Urbanian law. Under Urbanian law T acquires an overriding title. Under Ruritanian law the mortgage is ineffective to deprive P of his rights. Who wins?

13.27   The first point to note is that the fact situation here described is atypical. In the normal case the original account holder (in this example, A) merely instructs its intermediary to sell some securities and does not specify any transferee. Given that there may be several tiers of intermediary involved and that transactions will usually be netted out in one or more multilateral clearings, it will usually not be practicable to establish a link between the securities acquired by the transferee and those disposed of by the transferor. But even if it were, the drafters' analysis concluded that it was unnecessary for the Convention to provide for such case if one accepts that where there are competing dispositions governed by different laws, the law to be applied is that governing the last disposition—in this case, Urbanian law. If under that law T acquires an overriding title it is unnecessary to consider whether under Ruritanian law the pledge to P precluded A from transferring an unencumbered title to T. If on the other hand the rule under Urbanian law is that T cannot acquire a better right than A, then (assuming that T's interest was acquired

---

[24] See also above ch 2.

under a system which treated A as the direct transferor) a court applying Urbanian law will hold that the validity of the pledge to P is governed by Ruritanian law and that, if valid, that pledge will have priority over T's mortgage. It should therefore not be possible for the situation to arise where T acquires an overriding title without P losing its own interest. Even where T acquires an overriding title, Ruritanian law may still be relevant to P's rights, as where P, though losing his interest in the securities transferred, is considered by Ruritanian law to continue to hold a proportionate interest in the reduced pool of securities held by Intermediary 1 for its various account holders.

The European Community Settlement Finality Directive

The Directive 98/26/EC is part both of the European Community's prudential regulation regime and its internal-market insolvency regime. Settlement occurs mainly through settlement systems and by book entry transfer. Not all deliveries are, however, made against payment, for instance, because they are a transfer of securities against a loan. Again, the very nature of those settlement arrangements involves significant systemic risks. These are heightened in the context of transnational transactions in that the participation of foreign institutions in settlement systems entails that issues of property law, insolvency law, etc., are potentially governed by a multitude of domestic rules. The Directive is designed to limit systemic risk and to ensure both the efficiency and the stability of dealings among participants in recognized clearing and settlement systems. **13.28**

The scope of the Directive is limited. It applies to any 'system',[25] governed by the law of a Member State, to all 'participants' in such a system,[26] and to collateral security provided in connection with participation in a system or operations of Member States' central banks. **13.29**

The Directive's objectives are, first, to secure the finality of settlements in relation to transfer orders and netting,[27] second, to remove from attack under general insolvency law of Member States the position of participants under the rules of a designated settlement system and, third, to ensure the enforceability of security collateral. **13.30**

The Directive addresses the issue of which law governs the question of whether security, given in connection with participation in a system or to central banks, is valid and enforceable. Article 9(2) basically provides that, where securities are so provided and the right with respect to the securities is recorded in a register, account, or centralized deposit system located in a Member State, the rights of the **13.31**

---

[25] As defined in Art 2(a).

[26] As defined in Art 2(b)–(g).

[27] That is, the conversion into one net claim or one net obligation of claims and obligations resulting from transfer orders that a participant or participants either issue to, or receive from, one or more other participants with the result that only a net claim can be demanded or a net obligation is owed (Art 2(k)).

holders of the collateral are to be determined by the law of that Member State. This rule is likely to be amended in light of the Hague Convention's since under the Convention the location of the intermediary, account or deposit system is only of secondary relevance.

The EC Collateral Directive

13.32   The Directive 2002/47/EC complements the Settlement Finality Directive as well as insolvency related EC law. It is, however, broader and more ambitious in scope. The Directive addresses issues of legal risk associated with the taking of security in financial instruments. It covers both directly held and indirectly held securities. The Directive requires Member States to disapply certain provisions of insolvency law with a view to achieving the necessary protection of the collateral taker. The recitals are even more important for the understanding of this Directive than recitals usually are. They state the objective of establishing a 'Community regime ... for the provision of securities and cash as collateral under both security and title transfer structures including repurchase agreements (repos). This will contribute to the integration and cost-efficiency of the financial market as well as to the stability of the financial system in the Community ...'.[28]

13.33   Article 9 of the Directive provides that the legal nature and proprietary effects of book entry securities collateral, including perfection requirements, priority rules, and steps required for realization of book entry securities collateral, are to be governed by the law of the State in which the relevant account is maintained. As in the case of the Settlement Finality Directive, the conflicts provision will need to be modified in light of the Hague Convention's primary rule, that is the parties' freedom to choose the applicable law, subject to certain conditions.

National solutions

13.34   As mentioned earlier, Belgium and Luxembourg, homes to the ICSDs Euroclear and Clearstream, were leaders in embracing the new commercial and technological facts in their relevant legal framework; the applicability of the law of the account keeper was their solution. In the United States, the 1994 revision of the Uniform Commercial Code (UCC)[28a] brought the following section on the conflict of laws.

> § 8–110. **Applicability; Choice of Law.**
> (a) The local law of the issuer's jurisdiction, as specified in subsection (d), governs:
>   (1) the validity of a security;
>   (2) the rights and duties of the issuer with respect to registration of transfer;
>   (3) the effectiveness of registration of transfer by the issuer;

---

[28] Recital (3).
[28a] Uniform Commercial Code, copyright by the American Law Institute and the National Conference of Commissioners on Uniform State Laws. Reproduced with the permission of the Permanent Editorial Board for the Uniform Commercial Code. All rights reserved.

    (4) whether the issuer owes any duties to an adverse claimant to a security; and

    (5) whether an adverse claim can be asserted against a person to whom transfer of a certificated or uncertificated security is registered or a person who obtains control of an uncertificated security.

(b) The local law of the securities intermediary's jurisdiction, as specified in subsection (e), governs:

    (1) acquisition of a security entitlement from the securities intermediary;

    (2) the rights and duties of the securities intermediary and entitlement holder arising out of the security entitlement;

    (3) whether the securities intermediary owes any duties to an adverse claimant to a securities entitlement; and

    (4) whether an adverse claim can be asserted against a person who acquires a securities entitlement from the securities intermediary or a person who purchases a security entitlement or interest therein from an entitlement holder.

(c) The local law of the jurisdiction in which a security certificate is located at the time of delivery governs whether an adverse claim can be asserted against a person to whom the security certificate is delivered.

(d) 'Issuer's jurisdiction' means the jurisdiction under which the issuer of the security is organized or, if permitted by the law of that jurisdiction, the law of another jurisdiction specified by the issuer. An issuer organized under the law of this State may specify the law of another jurisdiction as the law governing the matters specified in subsection (a) (2) through (5).

(e) The following rules determine a 'securities intermediary's jurisdiction' for purposes of this section:

    (1) If an agreement between the securities intermediary and its entitlement holder governing the securities account expressly provides that a particular jurisdiction is the securities intermediary's jurisdiction for purposes of this part, this Article or this [Act], that jurisdiction is the securities intermediary's jurisdiction.

    (2) If paragraph (1) does not apply and an agreement between the securities intermediary and its entitlement holder governing the securities account expressly provides that the agreement is governed by the law of a particular jurisdiction, that jurisdiction is the securities intermediary's jurisdiction.

    (3) If neither paragraph (1) nor paragraph (2) applies and an agreement between the securities intermediary and its entitlement holder governing the securities account expressly provides that the securities account is maintained at an office in a particular jurisdiction, that jurisdiction is the securities intermediary's jurisdiction.

    (4) If none of the preceding paragraphs applies, the securities intermediary's jurisdiction is the jurisdiction in which the office identified in an account statement as the office serving the entitlement holder's account is located.

    (5) If none of the preceding paragraphs applies, the securities intermediary's jurisdiction is the jurisdiction in which the chief executive office of the securities intermediary is located.

(f) A securities intermediary's jurisdiction is not determined by the physical location of certificates representing financial assets, or by the jurisdiction in which is organized the issuer of the financial asset with respect to which an entitlement holder has a security entitlement, or by the location of facilities for data processing or other record keeping concerning the account.

13.35 In 1999, the legislature of the Federal Republic of Germany did more than was required for the implementation of the Directive 98/26/EC and crafted for the first time a general rule of private international law regarding proprietary aspects of securities. The matter had previously been dealt with according to the customary and judge-made rule providing for the applicability of the *lex rei (cartae) sitae*. At the time, the new § 17a of the Law on Securities Custody (*Depotgesetz*) was rightly hailed as an appropriate measure to complete the modernization of the country's private international law on property.[29] The provision reads (in the authors' translation):

> **§ 17a Dispositions regarding Securities**
>
> Dispositions regarding securities or interests in pools of securities that are registered in a register or credited to an account with constitutive effect are governed by the law of the State under whose regulatory supervision the register is maintained in which the constitutive entry to the credit of the transferee is made or where the principal or branch office of the custodian is located with whom the account is maintained and that makes the entry with constitutive effect in favour of the transferee.

13.36 Advanced as it was when it was enacted in 1999, this provision will need to be fundamentally redrafted if and when Germany ratifies the Hague Convention or implements the two European Community Directives as amended in light of the approach taken by the Hague Securities Convention.

D. Substantive Issues and Solutions—National and Transnational

13.37 Modernization of the conflict-of-laws rules is necessary. But it is only a first step. The substantive law identified as the one governing has to be up to the task. In the article quoted above, Professor James Steven Rogers, who served as Reporter to the Drafting Committee for the revised UCC Article 8, describes his reflections at the outset as follows:

> The commercial law rules of the securities holding and transfer system are a bit like the utility systems of a building. When they are working right, no one notices them; as they age, it takes more and more effort to keep them working, and the people who know how they work come to realize that they may break down altogether if conditions put them under heavy load. At some point prudence demands that they be replaced with systems that are designed for modern conditions and have the capacity to handle heavy loads, even though at the time they are replaced they are still 'working'. Indeed, the Article 8 revision project reminded me quite a bit of my own thought process in deciding to replace the electrical system of my nearly century-old house. When we moved in, we found an electrical system that had been 'designed' in

---

[29] Dietrich Schefold, 'Grenzüberschreitende Wertpapierübertragungen und Internationales Privatrecht' (2000) IPRax 468.

very much the same manner as old Article 8. Starting with a small main box of but four fuses, installed sometime in the early part of the twentieth century, additional boxes and panels had been patched on with the installation of each new electrical device added to the house over the decades, yielding a product that in the whole resembled something out of an MC Escher print. No doubt, any electrician could have figured how that system worked fairly quickly, and having spent many hours poring over the elaborate arrangement of boxes and cables and pulling out fuses to see what went out, I too pretty much knew how it worked. One day at work, I received a panicked phone call from my spouse, telling me that the repairmen working on our furnace had blown a fuse, putting the whole house into darkness, and none of them could figure out which of the dozens of fuses of all different sorts was the one that needed to be replaced. That experience got me thinking. Suppose the problem had not been that a fuse had blown, but that someone needed to shut off the electricity to some part of the house? Would anyone who had not spent all that time figuring out how that system worked be able to react promptly in an emergency? Not long thereafter we bit the bullet and made the investment to replace the old 'working' system with a new, modern working system. One of the things that it means when we say that a system 'works' is that people can figure out how it works and can do so quickly in times of emergency.

The present commercial law rules were designed for the system in which delivery of physical certificates was the key to the securities transfer process. Trying to use those rules for the modern system of securities holding through intermediaries is like trying to use an old electric system for a modern building; it can be done, but it takes a lot of effort and provides little protection against emergencies. Today, an inordinate amount of legal time—which, of course, means cost—is required to fit modern securities transactions into the conceptual scheme of a prior era.[30]

This statement applies, today more than when it was made, to a not insignificant   **13.38** number of legal systems and their rules on the transfer of securities. The clear and easy determination of the law applicable to proprietary aspects of the holding of and dealing in securities through intermediaries is everywhere essential but only in very few jurisdictions possible. Again Professor Rogers:

The essence of the Revised Article 8 drafting technique can be stated in a few words: First describe it, then name it. The starting point of the Revised Article 8 approach is to identify, in functional rather than categorical terms, what it means to say that a person holds a security through an intermediary. The answer to that inquiry comes in the form of a statement, in Sections 8-503 through 8-508, of the core of the package of rights and duties that define the relationship between a securities intermediary and a person ('entitlement holder') who holds a securities position through that intermediary. The elements of this package are as follows:

- the entitlement holder does not take credit risk of the intermediary's other business activities; that is, property held by the intermediary is not subject to the claims of the intermediary's general creditors;

---

[30] James Steven Rogers, 'Policy Perspectives on Revised UCC Article 8' 43 UCLA L Rev 1431, 1448 (1996).

- the intermediary will maintain a one-to-one match between the assets that it itself holds and all of the claims of its entitlement holders;
- the intermediary will pass through to the entitlement holder payments or distribution made with respect to the securities;
- the intermediary will exercise voting rights and other rights and privileges of ownership of the securities in the fashion directed by the entitlement holder;
- the intermediary will transfer or otherwise dispose of the positions at the direction of the entitlement holder; and
- the intermediary will act at the direction of the entitlement holder to convert the position into any other available form of securities holding, eg, obtain and deliver a certificate.[31]

13.39 Moreover, the national rules governing the rights and duties of investors who hold their securities not directly but through intermediaries are only in a minority of jurisdictions functionally up-to-date, efficient, easy to understand and to explain to others and workable in cross-border situations. National bodies of law governing the matter may work perfectly in a purely domestic environment but be incompatible—or be made compatible only at high (transaction) costs—with the relevant rules in other important legal systems—thus regularly requiring a number of legal opinions from lawyers in different jurisdictions where a major cross-border transaction is contemplated. Finally, there are a huge number of legal systems which have no rules capable of giving any guidance regarding intermediated securities holding at all.

13.40 Consequently, the strategic objectives aimed at by the *draft Convention on Harmonised Rules Regarding Intermediated Securities*, currently under preparation at UNIDROIT,[32] were described by the Study Group as 'internal soundness' and 'international compatibility'. While it may be tempting to take tested and readily available models 'from the shelf', the functional approach followed by the drafters—that is, that the attempt to identify what one wants to achieve in essence rather than tailoring a cloak out of pre-existing legal concepts—may make it possible to cast the net wider, not least by reaping the fruits of the ever-advancing technological infrastructure. Moreover, rules designed for achieving the necessary degree of inclusiveness at the worldwide level may be complemented by rules aiming at deeper harmonization needed in the context of a—regional—single financial market such as the European market. In light of the foregoing a clear focus and some modesty as to the envisaged scope was required for the project to stand the chance of being acceptable.

---

[31] Ibid 1450–1.
[32] UNIDROIT Study LXXVIII. Most recent version draft as adopted by the Committee of Governmental Experts at its third session, held in Rome (6–15 November 2006) Doc. 57, available at <http://www.unidroit.org/english/publications/proceedings/2006/study/78/s-78-57-e.pdf>. For the Study Group's approach, see: Position Paper of the UNIDROIT Study Group on Harmonised Substantive Rules regarding Indirectly Held Securities (August 2003) Doc 8, 5 and following, available at <http://www.unidroit.org/english/publications/proceedings/2003/study/78/s-78-08-e.pdf>.

On this basis, the preliminary conclusion regarding the scope of the project, ie the desirability of a uniform rule, encompasses the following issues:

- Preclusion of 'upper tier attachment';
- Role of book entries into a securities account;
- Role of non book-entry dispositions over securities;
- Possibility of a provisional credit, which does not correspond to the total number of securities credited to accounts maintained by an intermediary;
- Good faith acquisition;
- Net settlement;
- Finality of book entry transfers and irrevocability of instructions;
- Loss allocation, ie who bears the risk of a shortfall in securities.

There are other issues where a uniform rule may be considered, especially that of the protection of the client's assets against the claims of general creditors of the (insolvent) intermediary ...

The UNIDROIT Study Group and the Committee of Governmental Experts at **13.41** its first meeting followed the approach of the draftsmen of the revised Article 8 of the UCC in insisting on the need to address the issues in a functional way. However, unlike in a purely domestic context such as the United States, an instrument capable of reaching the desired substantive results and creating a sufficient degree of trans-border compatibility also needs to carefully avoid the use of legal concepts clearly identifiable with or only available in certain national systems or legal families. Therefore, the draft Convention in particular and deliberately does not take a stance on whether the rights of the account holder vis-à-vis the intermediary are rooted in or similar to ownership, trust or any other existing concept. Rather, it describes the content of the position leaving it to national legislatures to 'translate' that into their respective conceptual moulds.

Questions

1. In outlining the commercial and operational background of the changes from the direct holding to indirect holding patterns, the paper quoted at the beginning of this chapter refers, *inter alia*, to 'country risk' and 'custody risk'. Give examples for what these mean.
2. What do dematerialization and immobilization of securities, for the purposes of the conflict of laws, have in common and where may the consequences of a legislature's choice of one or the other differ?
3. With respect to the analytical process conflict-of-laws theory calls 'characterization', both the High Court and the Court of Appeal in the *Macmillan* case address the question what exactly is it that the courts characterize (the claim?,

the cause of action?, the issue?) and according to which law is the connecting factor of the relevant conflicts rule determined.

    (a) What are the answers to both questions?

    (b) Is there a logical sequence as to which one must be addressed first and which one follows?

    (c) What do the conflicts rule laid down by Millett J (as he then was) in the *Macmillan* case and the Hague Convention's primary and fall-back rules have in common?

4. Describe the factual and legal assumptions regarding the relationship of an investor/accountholder with the intermediaries of various tiers on which the Hague Securities Convention is based.

5. What may have been the reasons for the German legislature (§ 17a Law on Securities Custody) to focus on the transferee's account in determining the law governing a disposition?

6. Compare the provisions regarding the scope of application ('internationality') in Article 1 of the CISG, Article 1 of the United Nations Convention on the Assignment of Receivables and Articles 3 and 5 of the Hague Securities Convention.

7. It has been said that to allow parties freely to choose the law applicable to proprietary effects is 'counter-intuitive and contrary to the traditional conflict-of-laws approach'.

    (a) Why in your view, did the drafters of the Hague Securities Convention opt for it as the primary rule?

    (b) Are there other areas where conflicts rules in your own legal system or rules in transnational commercial law instruments allow for that freedom or where commentators urge that the legislator or the courts consider to grant such freedom?

8. What distinguishes in form and content the 'strategic plan' for the revision of Article 8 of the Uniform Commercial Code as formulated by Professor Rogers and the 'work programme' for an international uniform law instrument as drawn up in the UNIDROIT Study Group's position paper?

Further reading

Benjamin, Joanna, Yates, Madeleine, and Montagu, Gerald, *The Law of Global Custody* (2nd edn, Butterworths, London, 2002)

Einsele, Dorothee, *Wertpapierrecht als Schuldrecht: Funktionsverlust von Effektenurkunden im internationalen Rechtsverkehr* (Mohr Siebeck, Tübingen, 1995)

'Enhancing Legal Certainty over Investment Securities Held with an Intermediary—The preliminary draft UNIDROIT Convention, related international initiatives and national perspectives', Texts of international instruments and national draft legislation and contributions by B Sen, C Bernasconi and H Sigman, S V Bazinas, K M Löber, M Deschamps, Dong Ansheng and Han Liyu, A Maffei, D Einsele, J Than, H Kanda, L Affrell and K Wallin-Norman, M Romanowski L Thévenoz, C Reitz (2005) X Unif L Rev, 4–442

The Giovannini Group, 'Second Report on EU Clearing and Settlement Arrangements' (2003) <http://europa.eu.int/comm/economy_finance/giovannini/reports_en.htm>

Goode, Roy, *Legal Problems of Credit and Security* (3rd edn, Sweet & Maxwell, London, 2003), Chapter VI

Goode, Roy, Kandi, Hideki and Kreuzer, Karl, assisted by Bernasconi, Christophe, *Explanatory Report on the Hague Convention on the Law Applicable to Certain Rights in Respect of Securities Held with an Intermediary: Hague Securities Convention* (Koninklijke Brill, The Hague, 2005)

Gruson, Michael, 'Global Shares of German Corporations and Their Dual Listings on the Frankfurt and New York Stock Exchanges' 22 U Pa J Intl Econ L 185 (2001)

Houtte, Hans van (ed), *The Law of Cross-Border Securities Transactions* (Sweet & Maxwell, London, 1999)

Kronke, Herbert, and Haubold, Jens, 'Börsen-und Kapitalmarktrecht' in Kronke, Herbert, Melis, Werner, and Schnyder, Anton K (eds) *Handbuch Internationales Wirtschaftsrecht*, (Otto Schmidt, Köln, 2005) 1405

Mooney Jnr, Charles W, 'Beyond Negotiability: a new model for transfer and pledge of interests in securities controlled by intermediaries' 12 Cardozo L Rev 305 (1990–91)

Nizard, Frédéric, *Les titres négociables* (Economica, Paris, 2003)

Rogers, James Steven, 'Policy Perspectives on Revised UCC Article 8' 43 UCLA L Rev 1431

Schefold, Dietrich, 'Kollisionsrechtliche Lösungsansätze im Recht des grenzüberschreitenden Effektengiroverkehrs—die Anknüpfungsregelungen der Sicherheitenrichtlinie (EG) und der Haager Konvention über das auf zwischenverwahrte Wertpapiere anwendbare Recht' in Mansel, Heinz-Peter (ed), *Festschrift für Erik Jayme* (Sellier European Law Publishers, München, 2004) 805

Schwarcz, Steven L, 'Intermediary Risk in a Global Economy' 50 Duke LJ 1541 (2000–2001)

Wood, Philip R, *Comparative Law of Securities and Guarantees* (Sweet & Maxwell, London, 1995)

PART III

HARMONIZATION OF GENERAL CONTRACT LAW

14

RESTATEMENTS OF CONTRACT LAW

A. Introduction	14.01	*Pacta sunt servanda*	14.43
B. Restatements of Contract Law		Good faith	14.44
Introduction	14.04	Interpretation	14.49
The nature of the Principles	14.07	Adequate assurance of performance	14.50
The purposes of the Principles	14.10	Specific performance as a primary	
The scope of the Principles	14.15	remedy	14.51
The sphere of application of the		Other remedies	14.53
Principles	14.17	Hardship and change of	
The Principles 'shall' be applied	14.18	circumstances	14.54
The Principles 'may' be applied	14.28	Assignment and novation	14.56
The substantive content of the Principles	14.41	Agency	14.57
Freedom of contract	14.42	The Principles and mandatory rules	14.58

A. Introduction

In this chapter we shall examine the harmonization of the law of contract by **14.01** means of non-binding 'restatements' of the law, in particular the *Principles of International Commercial Contracts* and the *Principles of European Contract Law*. Before doing so, however, it is necessary briefly to return to some of the issues discussed in chapter 2, where we examined the role of the conflict of laws in commercial transactions. In that chapter we discussed various attempts at harmonizing the conflict of laws rules, in particular the 1980 Rome Convention on the Law Applicable to Contractual Obligations and the 1994 Inter-American Convention on the Law Applicable to International Contracts. In this chapter we turn to consider a distinct issue, namely the attempt to harmonize (through 'soft law' instruments) the substantive rules of the law of contract. The harmonization of conflict-of-law rules aims to ensure, as far as possible, that the same law is applied no matter where the case is, in fact, heard. The harmonization of substantive law is, in comparison, a much more ambitious project in that it aims to harmonize the substantive law of contract in the various jurisdictions which are party to the particular project.

14.02   While the two projects are separate and distinct, it remains important to consider why it was thought to be necessary to go beyond the harmonization of the con-flict-of-law rules and to embark upon the more difficult task of harmonizing the substantive rules of the law of contract.

14.03   It is clear from the Rome Convention, the Inter-American Convention and the proposed Rome I instrument that considerable progress has been made in terms of harmonizing the relevant conflict of law rules. However, for some commenta-tors, harmonization or unification of the conflict-of-law rules does not go far enough. In their view, it is necessary to take a further step and attempt to harmon-ize the substantive content of domestic law. The case for doing this in the area of the law of contract is made in the following extract:

Ole Lando 'European Contract Law' in Petar Šarcevic (ed) *International Contracts and Conflicts of Laws: A Collection of Essays* (Graham & Trotman London, 1990) 1, 3–4

Attempts at unification within the European Communities have been fruitful in one area, namely the conflict of laws. . . . Compared to the unification of substantive law, the unifi-cation of choice-of-law rules has certain advantages.

First, reforming conflict rules disturbs the national legal environment to a relatively small extent. The penetration of choice-of-law rules into society is slight, since such rules are addressed only to citizens and enterprises taking part in international trade or having some other relationship with a foreign country. In matters such as contract, tort and property, changes in conflict laws do not imply a revolution, whereas the unification of substantive law will often bring about a perceptible upheaval resulting in considerable confusion in the countries involved, especially when these rules apply to internal as well as to inter-national relationships.

Second, the unification of choice-of-law rules is also a much simpler process than the uni-fication of substantive rules. Choice-of-law rules are mostly spacious 'portfolios' with the general scope of each provision covering large areas of substantive law such as the compos-ition of corporations, torts, and rights to immovables. A whole branch of jurisprudence may be covered by a few conflicts provisions. Whereas it has been possible to unify the choice-of-law rules on contracts in a European Convention of about 20 operative articles, the unification of substantive law throughout the Community is a much more ambitious and difficult undertaking. In the United States, the part of the Restatement, Second, Conflict of Laws which deals with contracts, including several specific contracts, com-prises only 36 sections, whereas the Restatement Second, Contracts, which only treats the general principles of contract law, has 386 sections.

Uniform conflict-of-law rules promote predictability. The uniformization of jurisdiction rules reduces the number of available fora, while uniform choice-of-law rules make it eas-ier for the parties to determine which country's law will apply in an action brought in the courts of the states which have adopted the uniform rules. In addition, such rules are often codified and thus have the advantages of a codification over judge-made law. In Europe there is still some uncertainty as to which choice-of-law rules the courts will apply to an issue involving a contract. Uniform choice-of-law rules could reduce this uncertainty to some extent although one must be careful not to overestimate the level of predictability provided by uniform choice-of-law rules.

On the other hand, the unification of conflict rules also has shortcomings.

First, choice-of-law rules pose the problem of ascertaining foreign law which ... is a serious problem for parties travelling abroad. In general, a party and a court will be able to ascertain the law of a foreign country which belongs to their own 'family of laws' and which speaks their language or a familiar tongue. An Irish party or an Irish court has no trouble in ascertaining English law, nor does a French party or court have great difficulty in ascertaining Belgian or Luxembourg law.

A party or a court faced with the problem of acquiring information about the law of a country which belongs to an alien 'family' and which speaks a foreign language is often in a difficult position. It will not help a Scottish party suing in a Scottish court to know that the court will apply Greek law to the issue if neither he nor the court has a knowledge of the law of Greece. Obtaining reliable information about the contents of foreign law is often troublesome, time-consuming and costly. This difficulty increases when the foreign law itself is uncertain, for instance, when the relevant case law is obscure or contradictory. Obscurity and contradiction may also exist in the law of the forum country or in the law of a system within the 'family.' The difficulties, however, increase considerably when one is facing a legal system which, because it is alien, is doubly obscure. Courts therefore often apply the law of the forum because the parties agree in court upon its application or fail to plead the foreign law, or because reliable information on the foreign law is not provided. The EEC Conventions cannot do much to prevent this. The Brussels Convention will often give a plaintiff the choice of suing the defendant in more than one country. If he can sue in his home country or another country whose laws favour his case, he will often stand a good chance of having the law of the forum apply.

Another disadvantage of the unification of choice-of-law rules is that courts tend to be reluctant to apply a foreign law. The traditional multilateral choice-of-law rules require a leap into the unknown. In a (usually) wide variety of cases, merely showing a certain foreign contract suffices to make the court bound to apply the law of any of a large number of legal systems. This blindfolded selection of a legal system will sometimes prove offensive to the court. If a foreign rule of law 'outrages its sense of justice or decency,' a court can clearly invoke public policy considerations and refuse to apply the rule. In many cases, however, the foreign rule of law may not violate public policy but appear so alien to the forum as to provoke instinctive rejection. Decisions both in Europe and the United States reveal that courts have revolted against the remorseless mandate of the choice-of-law rule. Courts want a say in the decision on the merits and are not ready to accept a foreign substantive rule uncritically. When the court does disapprove of a foreign substantive rule for one reason or another, it frequently resorts to 'covert techniques' to avoid its application. This behaviour impairs the effectiveness of the choice-of-law rule. Few rules of law are so frequently sabotaged by the courts as choice-of-law rules.

This viewpoint has gained considerable support in recent years and a considerable amount of energy has been expended on the production of Restatements of the law of contract, the aim of which is to create a uniform set of rules for the law of contract. It is to these 'Restatements' that we now turn our attention.

B. Restatements of Contract Law

Introduction

14.04   The scholarly restatement of principles of a given field of law as a means of promoting harmonization of the laws of different jurisdictions originated in the United States with the series of Restatements published by the American Law Institute. Of course, the term 'restatement' is used in a rather loose sense, since the process necessarily involves departures from at least some of the rules from which the restatement is drawn, not only because these differ from each other but also because of a concern to produce best solutions to typical problems in the light of experience.

14.05   In the field of contract law the restatement concept has crossed national boundaries. Two separate projects have now been completed, the *Principles of International Commercial Contracts* ('the UNIDROIT Principles'), produced by a group of international scholars under the direction of Professor Joachim Bonell and published with the imprimatur of the Governing Council of UNIDROIT, and the *Principles of European Contract Law*, prepared by scholars drawn from every Member State of the European Community under the chairmanship of Professor Ole Lando ('the PECL', also sometimes referred to as the work of the 'Lando Commission').[1]

14.06   In the remaining parts of this chapter, our focus will be upon the UNIDROIT Principles and upon PECL. The first edition of the UNIDROIT Principles was published in 1994 and a second edition, the coverage of which is much more extensive, was published in 2004. A third phase is now in progress. The PECL were published in three phases: Part I was published in 1995, Parts I and II in 2000[2] and Part III in 2003. The work of those responsible for drafting both the UNIDROIT Principles and the PECL was very much influenced by the work of those who had gone before them. Thus the significance of the CISG can be seen at numerous points in both Principles, albeit that they frequently go beyond the solutions prescribed in CISG.[3] In this way, both groups made the best use of the opportunity

---

[1] In addition, the preliminary draft of a European Contract Code has been produced by the Academy of European Private Lawyers (the Pavia Group) under the direction of Professor Giuseppe Gandolfi. The European Commission had contemplated the preparation of a binding European Contract Code but for the time being seems to have moved away from this idea, though it has not been abandoned. See 'Communication from the Commission to the European Parliament and the Council: A More Coherent European Contract Law—An Action Plan' COM(2003) 68 final, 12.2.2003.

[2] The production of Part II resulted in various changes being made to the version of Part I which was published in 1995 and, consequently, an amended version of Part I was also published in 2000.

[3] See, for example, PECL, Art 6:111 and UNIDROIT Principles, Arts 6.2.2 and 6.2.3 which deal with change of circumstances. These provisions are much more elaborate than that to be found in Article 79 of CISG (on which see paras 7.97–7.100 above).

to learn from the problems and gaps that had become apparent in the final text of CISG. Further, the fact that neither set of Principles aims to produce a legally binding text gave to those responsible for drafting the Principles greater latitude in developing novel or 'best' solutions to some old and some new problems in the law of contract.[4] The two groups responsible for drawing up the Principles had a degree of commonality of membership and, to some extent, they had an influence on each other's work. The first edition of the UNIDROIT Principles was published in 1994 and was thus available to members of the Lando Commission when preparing the early drafts of their text. However, the Lando Commission quickly began to catch up on the work of UNIDROIT and, indeed, Part III of PECL was produced before the second edition of the UNIDROIT Principles made its appearance in 2004. It would perhaps be fairer to say that, latterly, the two Principles operated in tandem (or even in competition with one another) so that it would not be correct to conclude that the learning experience was a one-way process (namely that PECL always drew on the experience of UNIDROIT).

The nature of the Principles

Neither set of Principles is a legally operative instrument; that is to say, the **14.07** Principles were not drafted on the basis that they were to become legally binding rules of law. The essential nature of the Principles is explained in the following extract:

Roy Goode, 'International Restatements of Contract and English Contract Law' **(1997) II Unif L Rev 231, 234**

The characteristic common to ... these instruments is that they are not issued, endorsed or implemented by lawmaking bodies. They are essentially non-binding tools made available to the international community for adoption in contracts and use by judges and legislatures. Their influence depends on their quality, on the standing of the individuals preparing them and the institutions sponsoring them and the vigour with which they are promoted. Thus in contrast to its practice in relation to its conventions, Unidroit deliberately refrained from

---

[4] This follows from the fact that it was not necessary to secure the agreement of all members of the Commission in order to obtain approval for the text. In this way, the possibility of one member of the Commission holding the others to ransom was substantially reduced, if not eliminated. The process of reaching agreement in CISG was much more fraught, largely as a result of the need to produce a text which States would be willing to ratify. A good example of this process is provided by Article 78 of CISG dealing with the payment of interest (which is discussed in more detail at paras 7.88–7.96 above). The controversy surrounding the entitlement of a party to recover interest was such that it was only possible to secure agreement in Article 78 to the principle that interest should be paid. The Article is silent on matters such as the rate at which interest is to be paid. Article 7.4.9 of the UNIDROIT Principles and Article 9:508 of PECL, which deal with the payment of interest, are, by contrast, more elaborate. The fact that there was no need to achieve unanimity on the text of the Articles doubtless made it easier to reach agreement on the content and the scope of the respective Articles in the Principles.

seeking endorsement of the UNIDROIT Principles by the governments of its member States. In the case of the PECL the question did not, of course, arise, since the Commission on European Contract Law is a private body of scholars, not an international organization.

Yet paradoxically the impact of the two sets of principles may prove to be greater than that of an international convention, for a convention has no force at the time it is concluded and represents at most a provisional indication of support by participating States which may or may not crystallise, whereas the Principles represent the unconditional commitment and consensus of scholars of international repute from all over the world. . . .

It is a characteristic of all harmonising measures, whether normative or non-normative, that they do not merely reproduce the existing rules or usages but also change them. This is inevitable. For one thing, since national laws (and in federal systems, state or provincial laws) differ from each other, any harmonisation necessarily changes them in some respects. For another, the task of those engaged in the work of harmonisation, whether it takes the form of a convention, a set of uniform rules to be incorporated by contract, a model law or a scholarly restatement, is to find the best solutions to typical problems, and thus to improve the law, not merely to reproduce it. This is as true of the Principles as it is of the American Restatements. It is, of course, necessary to proceed judiciously. If the new rules are to have a reasonable prospect of acceptance they must advance thinking to some extent but not move too far ahead of prevailing rules or usage. The draftsmen of the Principles were very alive to the dangers of being too revolutionary. Accordingly, while observance of the Principles involves some departure from the existing rules of every legal system, and in certain cases the introduction of novel concepts, the Principles for the most part reproduce rules that will be familiar to legal systems generally.

14.08   Reference is made in this extract to the fact that the Commission on European Contract Law was a 'private body of scholars'. It consisted of a group of scholars drawn from all of the then Member States of the European Union which met under the chairmanship of Professor Ole Lando. The Commission itself is no longer in existence; its work was completed on the publication of Part III of the Principles. While the Principles themselves will continue to exert considerable influence over the development of European private law, the Commission as such will not have any further role to play in the development of a possible European Civil Code.[5] We have described the work of UNIDROIT elsewhere in this volume.[6] While UNIDROIT is an international, intergovernmental organisation, it is important to note the point made in the extract above, namely that governments were not involved in drawing up the UNIDROIT Principles.

14.09   Important consequences flow from the fact that the Principles are not legally binding rules and thus do not constitute laws of a national legal system. For example, it has the consequence that the Principles cannot, under traditional conflict-of-laws rules, be selected as to the law to govern the contract, although

---

[5] Individual members of the Commission may of course continue to play an important role in the development of European private law.   [6] See further paras 5.22–5.27 above.

they can be incorporated into the contract as contract terms, in which case they take effect subject to any applicable mandatory rules. This is, however, a question of some controversy and it is one to which we shall shortly return.

The purposes of the Principles

The Principles have several stated purposes in common. The Preamble to the **14.10** UNIDROIT Principles provides as follows:

> These Principles set forth general rules for international commercial contracts.
>
> They shall be applied when the parties have agreed that their contract be governed by them.[*]
> They may be applied when the parties have agreed that their contract be governed by general principles of law, the *lex mercatoria* or the like.
> They may be applied when the parties have not chosen any law to govern their contract.
> They may be used to interpret or supplement international uniform law instruments.
> They may be used to interpret or supplement domestic law.
> They may serve as a model for national and international legislators.
>
> [*] Parties wishing to provide that their agreement be governed by the Principles might use the following words, adding any desired exceptions or modifications:
> 'This contract shall be governed by the UNIDROIT Principles (2004) [except as to Articles …]'.
> Parties wishing to provide in addition for the application of the law of a particular jurisdiction might use the following words:
> 'This contract shall be governed by the UNIDROIT Principles (2004) [except as to Articles …], supplemented when necessary by the law of [jurisdiction X]'.

Article 1:101 of the PECL is in similar terms:

> (1) These Principles are intended to be applied as general rules of contract law in the European Union.
> (2) These Principles will apply when the parties have agreed to incorporate them into their contract or that their contract is to be governed by them.
> (3) These Principles may be applied when the parties:
>   (a) have agreed that their contract is to be governed by 'general principles of law', the 'lex mercatoria' or the like; or
>   (b) have not chosen any system or rules of law to govern their contract.
> (4) These Principles may provide a solution to the issue raised where the system or rules of law applicable do not do so.

There are obvious similarities between these two statements. Indeed, their simi- **14.11** larities are so obvious that they prompt the question why it was necessary to draft two sets of Principles. Given that the UNIDROIT Principles are intended to have a global reach and thus to include Europe within their scope, the question is most obviously directed at the Lando Commission. Why did they embark upon the task of creating a set of principles of European contract law? Professor Lando attempts to answer this question in the following extract:

Ole Lando, 'European Contract Law' in Petar Šarcevic (ed) *International Contracts and Conflicts of Laws: A Collection of Essays* (Graham & Trotman, London, 1990) 1, 5

One may ask why the UNIDROIT rules cannot be accepted by the European Communities. ... Why is a separate European effort necessary? The UNIDROIT principles are to be offered to all nations and are to be applied equally by market economy and state economy countries, by industrialized and developing countries, by nations whose trade laws have their roots in Roman law and Christianity as well as by societies with other religions and traditions. Although this enterprise will undoubtedly be of great value to the Commission on European Contract Law, we believe that the European countries should have the opportunity to choose principles of contract law which meet their requirements as industrialized, predominantly market economy countries. Principles will be needed for inter-European trade which do not have to take account of the traditions and views of countries with a political, social and economic background differing considerably from that of the EC countries. ...

The Commission has made an effort to deal with problems of contract encountered in international business life today and to propose rules which will promote trade. Unlike the UNIDROIT principles, the European principles are not intended merely to govern commercial relationships in the technical sense. There are several reasons for this.

First, in some of the Member States, commercial law has never existed as a distinct legal concept and in others it has been abandoned. In those States that have retained it, its scope and limitations are conceived differently. Second, the principles will also apply to contracts that are not 'commercial' in the sense of being strictly between merchants, for example, employment contracts, contracts between merchants and consumers, and between persons who are not merchants. Third, the principles of party autonomy governing some of the existing commercial codes should not apply to all the present rules, for instance, those reflecting a public policy such as the need to protect the weak party to a contract or the consumer. The principles will apply to consumer contracts; however, the commission will not draft special rules for such contracts. Nor are the principles intended to supersede the special legislation of the Member States relating to labour contracts.

Although intended primarily for international and intra-community trade, the principles are not confined to international relationships. In the long run, it seems inadvisable to operate two systems of contract law, one for purely domestic and another for international and intra-community relationships. ...

The principles are intended for the countries of the European Economic Communities and thus take account of the economic and social conditions prevailing in the Member States. Although the commission has paid attention to all of the legal systems of the European Communities, this does not imply that all systems have had equal influence on every issue considered, rather that the principles and terminology have not been based on any single legal system. Nor have the draftsmen of the principles taken it upon themselves to make interpolations or compromises between the existing laws. Rules of legal systems outside the Communities have also been considered as well as suggestions and ideas which have not yet materialized in the law of any State. The Commission on European Contract Law has found guidance in the American Uniform Commercial

Code, the American Restatements of the Law, and in existing uniform laws and conventions such as the Hague Uniform Laws on the International Sale of Goods and the UN Convention on Contracts for the International Sale of Goods.

It can be seen from this extract that, while the range of materials taken into account by the Lando Commission was international in nature, the intention was to create a set of Principles which were suitable for regional use, that is to say, within Europe. It is this regional limitation which distinguishes the PECL from the UNIDROIT Principles. That this is so becomes apparent when the same issue is considered from the UNIDROIT side of the fence. Thus Professor Bonell has pointed out that 'it is unlikely that there will be any real competition between the UNIDROIT Principles and the European Principles outside Europe'.[7] Thus he points out that legislators from 'Africa, the Americas, Asia or Oceania can hardly be expected to take as a model the European Principles which by their own admission "are designed primarily for use in the Member States of the European Community" and "have regard to the economic and social conditions prevailing in the Member States"'.[8] On the other hand, 'the European Principles, and not the UNIDROIT Principles, will be the obligatory point of reference for the legislative and judicial organs of the European Union when drafting or interpreting Community law'.[9] Thus Professors Lando and Beale, in their editorial introduction to *Principles of European Contract Law*,[10] state that the Principles may form a foundation for European legislation, including a possible first step in the work of preparing a future European Code of Contracts.

14.12

It is also unlikely that there will be any real competition in the context of the drafting of contracts and the resolution of contractual disputes. One would expect the UNIDROIT Principles to be used by parties who are not European and by arbitrators when the parties to the dispute are not European (or only one is European). Professor Bonell sets out his conclusions on the relationship between the two sets of Principles in the following extract:

14.13

Michael J Bonell, 'The UNIDROIT Principles of International Commercial Contracts and the Principles of European Contract Law: Similar Rules for the Same Purposes?' (1996) I Unif L Rev 229, 245

For the purpose of unification or harmonisation of law there is nothing worse than duplication of work leading to the adoption of different instruments competing with one another in the same area. At first sight it might appear that the more or less contemporaneous

---

[7] Michael J Bonell, 'The UNIDROIT Principles of International Commercial Contracts and the Principles of European Contract Law: Similar Rules for the Same Purposes?' (1996) I Unif L Rev 229, 242. [8] Ibid p 243.

[9] Ibid p 244.

[10] O Lando and H Beale (eds), *Principles of European Contract Law: Parts I and II* (Kluwer, The Hague, 2000).

preparation of two sets of rules such as the UNIDROIT Principles and the European Principles is an example of such a duplication. A closer examination demonstrates that this is not the case.

It is true that both instruments address basically the same issues of general contract law and are very similar in terms of formal presentation. However, they definitely differ as to their scope. The UNIDROIT Principles relate specifically to international commercial contracts, while the European Principles are intended to apply to all kinds of contracts, including transactions of a purely domestic nature and those between merchants and consumers. Moreover, while the territorial scope of the UNIDROIT Principles is universal, that of the European Principles is formally limited to the member States of the European Union.

It follows that the two instruments in actual practice not only do not overlap but may well coexist and play equally important, but not interchangeable, roles. Indeed, outside Europe or in commercial transactions involving non-Europeans, it will be the UNIDROIT Principles that apply, while within the European Union or in purely intra-European contracts, especially between merchants and consumers, it will be the European Principles that prevail.

14.14 Thus it is likely that the two sets of Principles will continue to co-exist, at least in the short to medium term. The lists of the purposes of the Principles set out above contain two important components: the first is the definition of their respective spheres of application and the second concerns the circumstances in which they may be applied. We shall now turn to consider these two issues.

The scope of the Principles

14.15 The Preamble to the UNIDROIT Principles states that the Principles 'set forth general rules for international commercial contracts' while Article 1:101 of PECL provides that they are 'intended to be applied as general rules of contract law in the European Union.' These statements reflect important differences in the scope of the two sets of Principles:

Roy Goode, 'International Restatements of Contract and English Contract Law' (1997) II Unif L Rev 231, 235–6

The UNIDROIT Principles are at once wider and narrower than the PECL in the range of transactions to which they are addressed. They are wider in that they are intended to be universal, whereas the PECL are designed for contracts within Europe; they are narrower in being confined to international commercial contracts (a phrase deliberately left undefined), while the PECL apply to contracts generally, whether domestic or international and whether commercial or non-commercial. However, it is a feature of international instruments, whether they are conventions, model laws or contractually incorporated trade usages, that they can never exhaustively define the scope of their own application. For one thing, parties are always free to incorporate their provisions as contract terms, whether or not the contract is one which falls within the sphere of application of the incorporated instrument. For another, courts and arbitrators may choose to apply them by analogy. So a rule in the UNIDROIT Principles could be invoked in relation to a purely domestic transaction as evidence of what is now perceived to be the best rule for the situation under consideration. Similarly, the parties or a court or arbitrator could resort to the PECL even in relation to a transaction one of the parties to which carries on business in a State which is not within the European Union.

While it is of course true that neither set of Principles can exhaustively define its **14.16** own scope of application, one would nevertheless expect the expression of their scope to be respected in the vast majority of cases in practice. The important point to note is that the PECL are of a general nature, while the UNIDROIT Principles are stated to apply only to 'international commercial contracts'. As is noted in the above extract, the drafters of the UNIDROIT Principles decided to leave the words 'international commercial contracts' undefined. However some guidance on the meaning of these words has been provided in the following extract:

UNIDROIT Principles of International Contracts 2004 (UNIDROIT, Rome, 2004) 2

The international character of a contract may be defined in a great variety of ways. The solutions adopted in both national and international legislation range from a reference to the place of business or habitual residence of the parties in different countries to the adoption of more general criteria such as the contract having 'significant connections with more than one State', 'involving a choice between the laws of different States', or 'affecting the interests of international trade'.

The Principles do not expressly lay down any of these criteria. The assumption, however, is that the concept of 'international' contracts should be given the broadest possible interpretation, so as ultimately to exclude only those situations where no international element at all is involved, i.e. where all the relevant elements of the contract in question are connected with one country only. . . .

The restriction to 'commercial' contracts is in no way intended to take over the distinction traditionally made in some legal systems between 'civil' and 'commercial' parties and/or transactions, i.e., to make the application of the Principles dependent on whether the parties have the formal status of 'merchants' (commerçants, Kaufleute) and/or the transaction is commercial in nature. The idea is rather that of excluding from the scope of the Principles the so-called 'consumer transactions' which are within the various legal systems being increasingly subjected to special rules, mostly of a mandatory character, aimed at protecting the consumer, i.e. a party who enters into the contract otherwise than in the course of its trade or profession.

The criteria adopted at both national and international level also vary with respect to the distinction between consumer and non-consumer contracts. The Principles do not provide any express definition, but the assumption is that the concept of 'commercial' contracts should be understood in the broadest possible sense, so as to include not only trade transactions for the supply or exchange of goods or services, but also other types of economic transactions, such as investment and/or concession agreements, contracts for professional services etc.

The sphere of application of the Principles

Both sets of Principles seek to define, in so far as they can, their respective spheres **14.17** of application. It should be noted that they both distinguish the case where they 'shall' or 'will' apply from the case where they 'may be applied' or 'may be used'. This distinction suggests that courts or arbitrators have a greater degree of discretion as to the applicability of the Principles in the cases where they 'may be applied'. It should therefore follow that their application will be much more straightforward in the case where they 'shall' or 'will' be applied. We shall first consider the case where the Principles 'shall' or 'will' apply before turning to the case in which they 'may' be applicable.

The Principles 'shall' be applied

14.18   The UNIDROIT Principles 'shall' be applied 'when the parties have agreed that their contract be governed by them' while the PECL 'will' apply 'when the parties have agreed to incorporate them into their contract or that their contract is to be governed by them'. The need for incorporation by the parties reflects the non-binding nature of the Principles. They do not themselves have the force of law and thus, to be applicable, they must be incorporated, either expressly or impliedly, into the contract between the parties. The proposition that the Principles can be incorporated into a contract as contract terms (and thus subject to any mandatory laws of the applicable law) does not give rise to difficulty. It is not doubted that the Principles can be incorporated into contracts in the same way as any other set of standard terms and conditions, such as the Incoterms.

14.19   Much more difficult is the proposition that the parties' contract can be 'governed' by either set of Principles. While it is true that this is what the Principles themselves state, their statements cannot be regarded as conclusive, at least in the context of litigation. The ability of contracting parties to incorporate either set of Principles into their contract as the applicable law is governed in a European context by Article 3 of the Rome Convention on the Law Applicable to Contractual Obligations.[11]

14.20   As we have seen,[12] both the Rome Convention and the Inter-American Convention give substantial freedom to the contracting parties to choose the law that is to be applicable to their contract. They can, in principle, choose a law which has no connection with the contract other than the fact that the parties have chosen to make it the law applicable to the contract. The issue which concerns us here, however, has given rise to greater difficulty and that is the question whether they can choose rules of law, such as the UNIDROIT Principles or the PECL as the law applicable to their contract.

14.21   Article 3 of the Rome Convention provides:

> A contract shall be governed by the law chosen by the parties. The choice must be expressed or demonstrated with reasonable certainty by the terms of the contract or

---

[11] On which see further paras 2.23–2.36.   [12] See paras 2.28–2.29 above.

the circumstances of the case. By their choice the parties can select the law applicable to the whole or a part only of the contract.

Article 7 of the Inter-American Convention is in similar terms:

> The contract shall be governed by the law chosen by the parties. The parties' agreement on this selection must be express or, in the event that there is no express agreement, must be evident from the parties' behavior and from the clauses of the contract, considered as a whole. Said selection may relate to the entire contract or to a part of same.

Article 7, like Article 3 of the Rome Convention, refers to 'the law' and this would **14.22** appear to be a reference to the law of a Nation State, an interpretation which derives support from Article 17 of the Inter-American Convention which states that law 'shall be understood to mean the law current in a State, excluding rules concerning conflict of laws'. However Article 9, paragraph (2) of the Inter-American Convention (which applies where the parties have not selected the applicable law or their selection proves to be ineffective) states that the court 'shall also take into account the general principles of international commercial law recognised by international organisations'. It is this latter provision which is thought by some to enable the parties to agree that their contract shall be governed by the UNIDROIT Principles.[13] In relation to Article 3 of the Rome Convention, however, the generally accepted view is that the reference to 'the law' requires the parties to choose as the law applicable to their contract the law of a Nation State.[14] An orthodox explanation of Article 3 is set out in the following extract:

Adrian Briggs, *The Conflict of Laws* (OUP Oxford, 2002) 159

The Convention . . . broadly adopts the principle of party autonomy, allowing a choice to be decisive except only in related to limited and clearly specified matters; but it requires two things: the choice to be made, and that choice to be expressed or demonstrable, and this will preclude the argument that the parties (as reasonable people) must have chosen a particular law but did not express that choice or suggest that they had made it.

A choice expressed in the form 'this contract shall be governed by the law of France' will therefore be effective to make French law the governing law; and a less artful choice, such as 'this contract shall be construed in accordance with French law', will probably be taken as a choice of governing law. In advising clients, one hopes that a legal adviser will recognize the freedom to choose, but also the responsibility to express that choice clearly, which is afforded by Article 3. But one could be forgiven for thinking that some draftsmen regard a clear expression of choice as being too easy, rejecting it for something more challenging. An expression of choice of the law of the United Kingdom, or of British law, for example, cannot be given literal effect, because there is no such law to be chosen; and

---

[13] See Friedrich K Juenger, 'The Inter-American Convention on the Law Applicable to International Contracts: Some Highlights and Comparisons' 42 Am J Comp L 381 (1994).

[14] For a helpful, balanced discussion of the issue see Ulrich Drobnig, 'The UNIDROIT Principles in the Conflict of Laws' (1998) III Unif L Rev 385.

to interpret this as an express choice of English law is to make an assumption which is probably factually correct but politically incorrect. Again, a choice of the *lex mercatoria*, or of the law of Mars, not being the law of a country, cannot be upheld, because the Convention sanctions only the choice of the law of a country and in such a case Article 3 cannot apply.

14.23 This view is not, however, one that is universally shared. Some commentators have advocated a more expansive interpretation of Article 3, as the following extract demonstrates:

Katharina Boele-Woelki, 'Terms of Co-existence: The CISG and the UNIDROIT Principles' in F W Grosheide, E Hondius and Katharina Boele-Woelki (eds), *International Contract Law 2003: Articles on Various Aspects of Transnational Contract Law* (Molengrafica Series, Intersentia, Oxford, 2004) 275, 293–4

It is stated that judges have no option but to select a national system as the applicable law. Therefore, it is to be expected that the national courts of many countries will tend to consider the parties' reference to the Principles as a mere agreement to incorporate them into the contract and proceed to determine the law governing the particular contract on the basis of their own conflicts rules. As a result, the parties' choice for the Principles will be restricted to a *materiellrechtliche Verweisung*.

One argument against this conventional or restrictive interpretation is the parallel that can be drawn with the phenomenon of opting-in, i.e., the question of the limits of a choice of law in favor of rules of an international convention not otherwise applicable. Even before the EC Contracts Convention came into force (1991), the Dutch Supreme Court ruled in a decision of 26 May 1989 that, where parties choose an international convention dealing with uniform law (in this case the CMR Convention), that choice must be regarded as a choice of law applicable to the contract, even though the formal conditions for the applicability of the Convention have not been met. On the strength of this decision, Dutch jurists take the view that, even under the EC Contracts Convention, the choice of law is not confined to national law but may also refer to uniform law as laid down in an international convention.

A broad interpretation of Article 3 of the EC Contracts Convention is preferable, particularly as there has been a profound change in circumstances since the EC Contracts Convention was drafted. These changes are the result of the growing number of autonomous uniform regulations in international commercial law. The Principles are fated to play a prominent role in this process. The following hypothetical question could be raised: What would the conflicts rule of the EC Contracts Convention have looked like if the drafters had known of the Principles?

14.24 It is no easy task to provide an answer to the hypothetical question posed by Professor Boele-Woelki. In 2003 the Commission issued a Green Paper[15] in which it posed the following question: 'should [contracting] parties be allowed to

---

[15] Green Paper on the Conversion of the Rome Convention of 1980 on the Law Applicable to Contractual Obligations into a Community Instrument and its Modernisation, COM (2002) 654 final, 14 January 2003.

directly choose an international convention, or even the general principles of law'
as the law applicable to their contract? The Commission has responded to its own
question in the affirmative and has put forward a proposal which contains a
revised version of Article 3.[16] For our purposes the critical addition is the sentence
which states that 'the parties may also choose as the applicable law the principles
and rules of the substantive law of contract recognised internationally or in the
Community'. It can be seen that this sentence bears a close resemblance to paragraph 2 of Article 9 of the Inter-American Convention. The commentary on the
revised Article 3 produced by the Commission provides as follows:

> To further boost the impact of the parties' will, a key principle of the Convention,
> paragraph 2 authorises the parties to choose as the applicable law a non-State body
> of law. The form of words used would authorise the choice of the UNIDROIT
> Principles, the Principles of European Contract Law or a possible future optional
> Community instrument, while excluding the lex mercatoria, which is not precise
> enough, or private codifications not adequately recognised by the international
> community.

The distinction drawn here between the UNIDROIT Principles and the PECL, **14.25**
on the one hand, and the *lex mercatoria*, on the other hand may give rise to some
controversy, particularly given the practice of some contracting parties of referring
to the Principles as an expression of the *lex mercatoria*. Will such a reference suffice to satisfy the requirements of the revised Article 3? It may well not do so
because the underlying choice in this case appears to be the choice of the *lex mercatoria* and that, as far as the commentary is concerned, is a choice which lacks the
necessary precision. Had the proposal been accepted, the consequence might have
been to encourage contracting parties to make greater use of the UNIDROIT
Principles and the PECL. But the Council has rejected the proposal.

As matters currently stand, the doubt concerning the ability of contracting parties **14.26**
to incorporate the Principles into their contract as the applicable law must inhibit
the use of the Principles. Parties who wish to incorporate the Principles into their
contract as the applicable law would be well advised to avoid litigation and to provide instead for arbitration as the method of dispute resolution. The reason for
this is that some arbitration rules, such as the ICC Rules of Arbitration 1998, state
that parties 'shall be free to agree upon the rules of law to be applied by the Arbitral
Tribunal to the merits of the dispute'.[17] The phrase 'rules of law' is wider than 'the

---

[16] 'Proposal for a Regulation of the European Parliament and the Council on the Law Applicable to
Contractual Obligations (Rome I)' COM (2005) 650 Final, 2005/0261 (COD), 15 December 2005.
[17] Art 17(1) of the ICC Rules of Arbitration, 1998, discussed in more detail at paras
17.117–17.119 below. On the use of the UNIDROIT Principles in international arbitration see
Fabrizio Marrella and Fabien Gélinas, 'The Unidroit Principles of International Commercial
Contracts in ICC Arbitration' *ICC International Court of Arbitration Bulletin* Vol 10, No 2 (Fall,
1999) 26 and F Marrella 'The Unidroit Principles of International Commercial Contracts in ICC
Arbitration, 1999–2001' *ICC International Court of Arbitration Bulletin* Vol 12, No 2 (Fall, 2001) 49.

law' and thus is apt to encompass non-binding rules such as the Principles. The need presently to combine a choice of the Principles as the applicable law with an arbitration agreement is emphasized in the following extract:

UNIDROIT Principles of International Contracts 2004 (UNIDROIT, Rome, 2004) p. 3

Parties who wish to choose the Principles as the rules of law governing their contract are well advised to combine such a choice of law clause with an arbitration agreement.

The reason for this is that the freedom of choice of the parties in designating the law governing their contract is traditionally limited to national laws. Therefore, a reference by the parties to the Principles will normally be considered to be a mere agreement to incorporate them in the contract, while the law governing the contract will still have to be determined on the basis of the private international law rules of the forum. As a result, the Principles will bind the parties only to the extent that they do not affect the rules of the applicable law from which the parties may not derogate. . . .

The situation is different if the parties agree to submit disputes arising from their contract to arbitration. Arbitrators are not necessarily bound by a particular domestic law. This is self-evident if they are authorised by the parties to act as *amiable compositeurs* or *ex aequo et bono*. But even in the absence of such an authorisation parties are generally permitted to choose 'rules of law' other than national laws on which the arbitrators are to base their decisions. . . .

In line with this approach, the parties would be free to choose the Principles as the 'rules of law' according to which the arbitrators would decide the dispute, with the result that the Principles would apply to the exclusion of any particular national law, subject only to the application of those rules of domestic law which are mandatory irrespective of which law governs the contract.

14.27   Thus, subject to any applicable mandatory rules[18] and provided that the applicable arbitral rules permit them to do so, an arbitrator who is confronted by a contract which states that it is governed by the UNIDROIT Principles or the PECL should give effect to the choice of the parties. However, it would appear that it is still a rare event for contracting parties to provide in express terms that their contract shall be governed by the UNIDROIT Principles or the PECL. Cases in which the UNIDROIT Principles are found to be applicable as a result of the consent of the parties tend to be cases in which the contract does not contain a choice of law clause but the parties subsequently consent to the application by the arbitrators of the Principles to the contract.[19] However, past experience is no necessary guide to future practice. In future, it may be that contracting parties will be more willing to agree that their contract should be governed by the UNIDROIT Principles or the

---

[18]   These mandatory rules are not purely domestic mandatory rules (rules applicable despite any agreement to the contrary on the assumption that the relevant domestic law applied), but overriding super-mandatory rules (rules applicable whatever the governing law).

[19]   The best source of case law on the UNIDROIT Principles is the Unilex data base, which is available at <http://www.unilex.info>.

PECL and, in such cases, the arbitrator should, in principle, give effect to the choice of the parties.

The Principles 'may' be applied

Turning now to the cases in which the Principles 'may' be applied, both sets of **14.28** Principles enumerate certain circumstances in which they may be applicable and there is a substantial degree of similarity between the two lists.

First, both the UNIDROIT Principles and the PECL state that they may be appli- **14.29** cable where the parties agree that their contract shall be 'governed by general principles of law, the *lex mercatoria* or the like'. Examples can be found of cases in which arbitrators have applied the UNIDROIT Principles in such circumstances.[20] Thus Unilex cites twelve cases in which the UNIDROIT Principles have been applied as 'general principles of law' and two cases in which they have been treated as an expression of the *lex mercatoria*.

The twelve cases in which the UNIDROIT Principles were accepted as an expres- **14.30** sion of 'general principles of law' are either cases in which the contract did not contain a choice-of-law clause but the parties consented to the application by the arbitrators of 'generally accepted principles of international commercial law' or are cases in which the parties agreed that their contract would be governed by 'the laws or rules of natural justice' or some similar phrase.

The claim of the Principles to be part of the *lex mercatoria* is less straightforward. **14.31** One cannot by means of a self-serving statement turn one's statements into the *lex mercatoria*; there must be an objective element to the question whether or not an instrument or rule can be said to be part of the *lex mercatoria*. Nevertheless, examples can be found of arbitral awards in which arbitrators have invoked the UNIDROIT Principles as an expression of the general principles of the *lex mercatoria*. Of the two cases cited in the Unilex database, the first is an arbitral award issued by the International Arbitration Court at the Chamber of Commerce and Industry of the Russian Federation[21] in which the arbitration court decided to apply the UNIDROIT Principles as an expression of the general principles of the *lex mercatoria*. The second award cited is more ambiguous. The contract provided that: 'this contract is governed by international law; any dispute arising in

---

[20] This and related issues are discussed in more detail by Pierre Lalive, 'The UNIDROIT Principles as *Lex Contractus*, With or Without an Explicit or Tacit Choice of Law: An Arbitrator's Perspective' *ICC International Court of Arbitration Bulletin—Special Supplement 2002* 77 and Julian D.M. Lew, 'The UNIDROIT Principles as *Lex Contractus* Chosen by the Parties and Without an Explicit Choice-of-Law Clause: The Perspective of Counsel' *ICC International Court of Arbitration Bulletin—Special Supplement 2002* 85.

[21] Arbitral award dated 5 November 2002, Number 11/2002. An abstract of the award can be found at <http://www.unilex.info>.

connection with this contract shall be settled amicably, and failing that, by arbitration under the ICC International Court of Arbitration'.

14.32 The parties, having failed to resolve their dispute amicably, resorted to arbitration in accordance with the terms of their contract. The arbitral tribunal concluded that the reference to 'international law' was to be understood as a statement by the parties that they did not wish their contract to be governed by any domestic law. The abstract of the case continues as follows:

> the term 'international law' was to be understood as reference to the lex mercatoria and general principles of law applicable to commercial contracts, and since such general principles are reflected in the UNIDROIT Principles it concluded that the dispute should be governed by the UNIDROIT Principles. As to the Principles of European Contract Law, the arbitral tribunal stated that 'they constitute an academic research, at this stage not largely well-known to the international business community and are a preliminary step to the drafting of a future European Code of Contracts, not enacted yet' and therefore excluded their application in the case at hand.

14.33 It is important not to attach too much significance to this abstract, especially in the absence of a text of the award itself. But it is noteworthy for the distinction drawn between the UNIDROIT Principles, on the one hand, and the PECL on the other and it suggests that it may be easier to establish that the UNIDROIT Principles are part of the *lex mercatoria*. However it should not be assumed from this award that the PECL can never constitute part of the *lex mercatoria*. Arbitral awards can be found in which references have been made to the PECL in the context of a discussion of the content of the *lex mercatoria* and so, while it may be more difficult to establish that the PECL is part of the *lex mercatoria*, it is not impossible.

14.34 Why might there be a reluctance in certain quarters to accept that the Principles are part of the *lex mercatoria*? The first difficulty is created by the definition of the *lex mercatoria*. As we have noted,[22] the content of the *lex mercatoria* is the subject of some controversy. If it is defined as the unwritten customs and practices of merchants, then it is difficult to see on what basis it can be said that either set of Principles can be part of the *lex mercatoria*. However, a broader interpretation of the scope of the lex mercatoria may be able to encompass the Principles without much difficulty.[23] The second difficulty arises from the claim made by the authors of the Principles that their aim has not simply been to reflect existing practices but to adopt, where appropriate, 'best solutions' to old and new problems within the law of contract. To the extent that the Principles prescribe such innovative solutions, it is difficult to see the basis on which it can be said that these solutions are

---

[22] See paras 1.60–1.67 above.
[23] See, for example, Ole Lando, 'The *Lex Mercatoria* in International Commercial Arbitration' (1985) 34 ICLQ 747, 750.

part of the *lex mercatoria* when they are not based, and do not claim to be based, on any established practice. The latter point suggests that the question whether the Principles are part of the *lex mercatoria* may not be susceptible of a single answer; that is to say, the answer will depend upon the particular article which is in issue between the parties and 'no provision of the ... Principles can be considered as a rule of the *lex mercatoria* before checking whether it is really in line with the standards of international trade'.[24] In the case where the article reflects existing market or legal practice it may be part of the *lex mercatoria*, but where it is innovative in nature it is unlikely to be part of the *lex mercatoria*. There are some signs of this approach in the case law itself. The provisions on hardship[25] in both Principles are among the most innovative of the solutions to be found in the Principles and it is perhaps no surprise to find that, in this context, one arbitral tribunal concluded that 'the provisions of the UNIDROIT Principles on hardship do not correspond, at least presently, to current practices in international trade.'[26]

14.35 Nevertheless, there are good pragmatic reasons which may impel an arbitrator to resort to the Principles when the parties have agreed that their contract is to be governed by the *lex mercatoria*. These reasons are set out in the following extract:

Alejandro M Garro, 'Contribution of the UNIDROIT Principles to the Advancement of International Commercial Arbitration' 3 Tulane Jnl Int & Comp L 93, 104–5 (1995)

There are at least three reasons to apply the Principles in such an instance. First, because the parties have expressed a willingness to subject the contract to some kind of international commercial law that is not connected with the national law of a particular jurisdiction, the Principles will effectuate the will of parties. Second, the Principles provide a well-defined set of rules, thereby reducing the inherent indefiniteness and uncertainty of the general principles of law and the usages and customs of international trade that make up lex mercatoria. Whereas most national courts may want to avoid use of lex mercatoria because of its vagueness, even if the parties have agreed upon its application, the parties can be confident that if a dispute arises under a contract to which the Principles are applied as governing law, their contractual rights and duties will be enforced pursuant to the Principles to the extent permitted by the domestic law. Finally, unlike the contract rules codified in civil or commercial codes or statutes, the rules embodied in the Principles are specifically tailored to international commercial disputes.

14.36 Second, both the UNIDROIT Principles and the PECL state that they 'may' be applied in the case where the parties have not chosen any law to govern their contract. Examples can be found of cases in which arbitrators have applied the

---

[24] Fabio Bortolotti, 'The UNIDROIT Principles and the arbitral tribunals' (2000) V Unif Law Rev 141, 145.   [25] Discussed in more detail at paras 14.54–14.55 below.
[26] ICC International Court of Arbitration, Paris, Arbitral Award No 8873, dated July 1997 and ICC International Court of Arbitration, Rome, Arbitral Award No 9029, dated March 1998, both available at <http://www.unilex.info>.

UNIDROIT Principles in the absence of a choice-of-law clause in the contract.[27] In one case the arbitrators construed the absence of a choice of law clause as a decision by the parties to exclude the domestic law of both parties.[28] The majority arbitrators, having dismissed the national law of both contracting parties, continued as follows:

Thus, the Tribunal will decide legal issues by having regard to the terms of the Contract and, where necessary or appropriate, by applying truly international standards as reflected in, and forming part of, the so-called 'general principles of law'. . . .

The Majority Arbitrators are aware that various terms are used, such as general principles of law, generally accepted principles of private law, a-national rules of law, transnational law rules, lex mercatoria, principles of international law etc. [. . .]

The Tribunal will apply those general principles and rules of law applicable to international contractual obligations which qualify as rules of law and which have earned a wide acceptance and international consensus in the international business community, including notions which are said to form part of a lex mercatoria, also taking into account any relevant trade usages as well as the UNIDROIT Principles, as far as they can be considered to reflect generally accepted principles and rules.

The Majority Arbitrators are of the opinion that these 'General Principles of Law' (in the wide understanding as described above) are established in sufficiently concrete fashion so as to enable the Tribunal to adjudicate any and all issues as may arise in the framework of this arbitration.

[. . .]

As regards the reference to the UNIDROIT Principles [. . .] the Majority Arbitrators believe that these Principles, prepared by a working group established in 1981 and composed of leading experts and academics of all major legal systems, contain in essence a restatement of those 'principes directeurs' that have enjoyed universal acceptance and, moreover, are at the heart of those most fundamental notions which have consistently been applied in arbitral practice.

On the other hand, the UNIDROIT Principles, as now laid down, have not as yet, in all their details, stood the test of detailed scrutiny in all their aspects, and thus it is at least conceivable that a particular rule would not seem to reflect the international consensus; because of this concern, the Tribunal has added the qualification 'as far as they can be considered to reflect generally accepted principles and rules.' In this direction see the critical comments made by HILMAR RAESCHKE-KESSEER, The UNIDROIT Principles for International Commercial Contracts: A New lex mercatoria? in: ICC/ Dossier of the Institute of International Business Law and Practice, 1995, 167 ss. who raises formal concerns that there are certain rules that differ from the principles and rules

---

[27] The Unilex database cites only one case in which the UNIDROIT Principles have been applied in the absence of a choice-of-law clause in the contract. This may, however, create a misleading impression because other cases can be found in the database in which the Principles have been applied in the absence of a choice-of-law clause in the contract. Thus the database contains eleven examples of cases in which the Principles have been applied as the rules of law which the arbitrators determine to be appropriate to the case and, in some of these cases, the contract between the parties did not contain a choice-of-law clause.

[28] ICC International Court of Arbitration, Paris, Arbitral Award No 7375, dated 5 June 1996, available at <http://www.unilex.info>.

as reflected in the United Nations Sales Convention of 1980 and, possibly, also with the 'Principles of European Contract Law' prepared by the 'Commission on European Contract Law' chaired by Professor Ole Lando (Denmark). He expressed the opinion that the United Nations Sales Convention 'already provides a rather complete set of rules on a lex mercatoria' (at p. 174, with reference to the view expressed by Drobnig in The American Journal of Comparative Law 1992, 635 ss.

Third, the UNIDROIT Principles may be used to interpret or supplement inter- **14.37**
national uniform law instruments. The equivalent provision in the PECL is cast in more general terms and provides that the PECL may be applied in order to 'provide a solution to the issue raised where the system or rules of law applicable do not do so'. The UNIDROIT Principles have played an important role in supplementing the CISG; the Unilex database cites thirteen cases in which the UNIDROIT Principles have been used in this way. Almost half of the cases cited are cases in which UNIDROIT has been used to supplement Article 78 of CISG which, as we have noted,[29] makes provision for the entitlement to recover interest but is silent on matters such as the rate at which interest is payable and the time from which it is payable. The role of the UNIDROIT Principles (and, to a lesser extent, the PECL) in supplementing the CISG is not without its controversy,[30] but it seems to be well-established in the case law. This supplementary role can also be played in relation to other international instruments; thus one case can be found in which the UNIDROIT Principles were used to supplement the Uniform Law on the International Sale of Goods (ULIS) and the Uniform Law on the Formation of Contracts for the International Sale of Goods.[31]

Fourth, the UNIDROIT Principles may be used to interpret or supplement **14.38**
domestic law. The Unilex database suggests that this is where the UNIDROIT Principles have had their greatest impact. It cites fifty cases in which the Principles have been used as a 'means for interpreting and supplementing [the] domestic law otherwise applicable'. The cases cited in this category are an interesting mix. In some of them the Principles have been used in a confirmatory role; that is to say, their function has been to confirm that the solution found by the arbitrators under domestic law corresponds with the solution to be found under modern international commercial law. In other cases, the role of the Principles has been to assist in the development of the chosen domestic law. This is particularly noticeable in common law jurisdictions where, as we shall see,[32] the UNIDROIT Principles

---

[29] See paras 7.88–7.96 above.   [30] See paras 7.64–7.65 above.
[31] ICC International Court of Arbitration, Paris, Arbitral Award No 8547, dated January 1999, available at <http://www.unilex.info>. The UNIDROIT Principles have also been used by the Supreme Court of Venezuela to support a broad interpretation of 'international contract' in the 1958 New York Convention on the Recognition and Enforcement of Foreign Arbitral Awards and the 1975 Inter-American Convention on Commercial Arbitration: *Bottling Companies v. Pepsi Cola Panamericana*, 9 October 1997, available at <http://www.unilex.info>.
[32] See para 14.44 below.

have been used by judges who wish to see the development of a doctrine of good faith and fair dealing in the common law. A few of the cases are cases in which the law chosen by the parties was found by the arbitral tribunal not to be 'fully developed' and so the Principles were used in order to interpret and supplement the chosen domestic law. But by no means all of the cases concern legal systems which are commonly regarded as 'under-developed'. Some of the cases involve well-established, widely used legal systems which simply did not provide a clear answer to the question which had arisen on the facts of the case. Thus in one arbitration held in Auckland, where the law governing the contract was the law of New Zealand, one of the issues which the arbitrators had to decide was whether they could have regard to the conduct of the parties subsequent to the making of the contract for the purpose of interpreting the contract. The arbitrators found that the law of New Zealand on this issue was in a somewhat uncertain state and so they had regard to Article 4.3(c) of the UNIDROIT Principles in order to establish that they could take such conduct into account in the interpretative process. A final interesting aspect of the use of the UNIDROIT Principles in the interpretation and supplementation of domestic law is that the case law illustrates the way in which the Principles can be used in order to influence the development of the law of contract throughout the world. In this respect it is interesting to note that some of the cases cited in this category involve the hardship provisions in UNIDROIT. As we shall see, the hardship provisions in both the UNIDROIT Principles and the PECL can be described as innovative and their innovations may yet extend into the domestic law of nation States.

14.39 Fifth, the Principles may be applied as examples of a 'trade usage'. Neither the UNIDROIT Principles nor the PECL expressly mention this possibility but Unilex cites nine arbitral awards in which the UNIDROIT Principles have been invoked as 'relevant trade usages' to be taken into account by the arbitrators. In one case recourse to the UNIDROIT Principles was justified on the ground that 'they reflect usages of which the parties knew or ought to have known and which are widely known in international trade and are therefore applicable according to' Article 9(2) of the CISG.[33] The Unilex database also includes three cases in which the UNIDROIT Principles were applied by arbitrators who were authorized by the parties to act as *amiable compositeurs*.

14.40 One of the interesting features of the Unilex database is the dominance of the Preamble in the list of citations. At the end of 2005, Unilex lists 113 cases in which the UNIDROIT Principles have been cited. Ninety of these cases are arbitral awards while twenty-three are decisions of courts in various parts of the world. These 113 cases include 107 references to the Preamble. This tends to suggest that

---

[33] International Arbitration Court of the Chamber of Commerce and Industry of the Russian Federation, Award No 229/1996 (5 June 1997) available at <http://www.unilex.info>.

the scope of the Principles and their essential nature are of greater practical significance at present than the substantive content of the Principles themselves. The
list of citations in the Unilex database is in fact very uneven. For example, there are
no case references to chapters 8, 9 or 10 of the UNIDROIT Principles and none
which relate to the provisions dealing with the authority of agents. On the other
hand, there are twenty citations which refer to Article 7.4.9 (which deals with the
award of interest for failure to pay money), eighteen which refer to Article 1.7
(which deals with good faith and fair dealing), nine which refer to Article 6.2.2
(which defines hardship) and nine which refer to 6.2.3 (which deals with the effect
of hardship). The large number of references to Article 7.4.9 can be explained on
the ground that this is the provision which has been invoked in order to supplement Article 78 of CISG and the relatively frequent references to the hardship
provisions can be attributed to their innovative nature. The references to good
faith are, perhaps, more difficult to explain. The explanation for the invocation of
the article may vary as between common law and civil law systems (or between
arbitrators from common law systems and those from civil law systems). In the
case of common law jurisdictions the references to good faith are generally part of
an attempt to introduce a doctrine of good faith and fair dealing into the common
law,[34] whereas the references in cases from civil law systems have no such reforming goal but simply reflect the important role which the doctrine of good faith and
fair dealing plays in many modern civil law jurisdictions.

The substantive content of the Principles

The Principles cover the whole spectrum of contract law, from formation, repre- **14.41**
sentation, validity and interpretation through performance and remedies for non-
performance to assignment, novation, set-off and prescription. A number of the
rules are common to many national legal systems; some are closer to one legal family or system than to others; and a few are *de lege ferenda* and are designed to advance
legal thinking beyond what any legal system currently provides, for example, the
duty of the parties to renegotiate in the event of a fundamental change of circumstances. Key features common to the Principles are set out in the following
paragraphs.

Freedom of contract

The Principles adopt the near-universal approach of general contract law in their **14.42**
insistence on party autonomy[35] (including the freedom to derogate from or vary
the Principles themselves[36]), subject only to some interesting provisions on mandatory rules discussed below[37] and to the overriding requirement of good faith.

---

34 See further paras 14.44–14.45 below.
35 UNIDROIT Principles, Art 1.1; PECL, Art 1:102.
36 UNIDROIT Principles, Art 1.5; PECL, Art 1:102(2).   37 See paras 14.58–14.62.

Pacta sunt servanda

14.43 Likewise the Principles adhere strongly to the concept *pacta sunt servanda*[38] and provide that in the absence of one party's own failure of performance only exceptional circumstances excuse performance by the other party, namely impediments outside a party's control[39] or a fundamental change in the burden of performance or the economic equilibrium of the contract.[40]

Good faith

14.44 Both the PECL and the UNIDROIT Principles impose a duty of good faith on the contracting parties. The doubts which we noted in relation to the scope of the duty of good faith in the context of Article 7 of the CISG[41] do not arise in this context. Article 1.7 of the UNIDROIT Principles and Article 1:201 of the PECL unambiguously impose a duty of good faith directly on to the contracting parties. Why did the representatives of common law systems agree to the inclusion of good faith in the Principles when they objected in such strong terms to the imposition of a duty of good faith on contracting parties in the context of CISG? Three possible answers suggest themselves. The first is the passage of time. English law in particular is less hostile to the duty of good faith than it was twenty-five years ago[42] and so it may be that the traditional hostility of common law systems to the recognition of a duty of good faith has simply abated. The second relates to the legal nature of the Principles. The fact that they do not have the force of law may have reduced the opposition to the creation of a duty of good faith. There is a significant distinction between the creation of a legal rule which is intended to be part of a national legal system and a rule which has been drafted on the basis that it is not to be binding: in other words, what is acceptable in a non-binding set of rules may not be acceptable if imposed on a national legal system. Third, much attention was given to the wishes of dissentients in the context of the CISG, given the desire to ensure that as many States as possible ratified the Convention. This factor was not present in the context of the Principles because there was no intention to turn the Principles into legally binding rules and so there was not the same need to ensure that everyone was happy with the content of each and every article. In short, the common lawyers may simply have been outvoted and have been unable to do anything about it.

---

[38] Expressly stated in the UNIDROIT Principles, Art 1.3.

[39] UNIDROIT Principles, Art 7.1.7; PECL Art 8:108. Both formulations closely follow Art 79 of the CISG.   [40] UNIDROIT Principles, Arts 6.2.2, 6.2.3; PECL, Art 6.111.

[41] See paras 7.46–7.65 above.

[42] See, for example, *Timeload Ltd v British Telecommunications plc* [1995] EMLR 459; *Director General of Fair Trading v First National Bank* [2001] UKHL 52, [2002] 1 AC 481 (although it should be noted that this case was concerned with the interpretation of a statutory instrument which implemented an EC Directive which made use of the language of good faith and so it may not be indicative of the general attitude of English law towards a doctrine of good faith); *Petromec Inc v Petroleo Brasileiro SA Petrobas* [2005] EWCA Civ 891, [2005] All ER (D) 209 at [115]–[121].

Article 1.7 of the UNIDROIT Principles provides that 'each party must act in **14.45** accordance with good faith and fair dealing in international trade'. The addition of the words 'in international trade' is important because it signifies that the definition of good faith and fair dealing is not to be found in the laws of any one Nation State but is to be located in an international context. In other words, the standards to be applied are those adopted internationally and not nationally.[43] The concept of good faith is given a very broad interpretation in the discussions in the academic literature. The provision has also been cited on a number of occasions in courts and in arbitral tribunals.[44] Interestingly, there have been some citations of Article 1.7 in the courts in common law jurisdictions where the Article has exerted some influence in nudging the courts in the direction of recognising the existence of a duty of good faith and fair dealing.[45] However, it would be going too far to conclude that, as a result of Article 1.7, all differences between common law and civil law systems have been eliminated. Common law systems generally remain more reluctant to recognize the enforceability of a duty of good faith and fair dealing. The point can be illustrated by reference to one ICC arbitral award.[46] The arbitrators concluded that the parties intended 'to obligate themselves to co-operate in good faith' but they also found that the parties had not chosen the law that was to govern the contract. The claimant submitted that the obligation to negotiate in good faith was unenforceable under any of the laws that might govern the contract.[47] However the arbitrators declined to apply a law the effect of which would have been to render the obligation to co-operate in good faith unenforceable or void. It was held that such could not have been the intention of the parties. The arbitrators found that the law applicable to the contract was the law of the State of New York and, after consideration of the rival submissions, concluded that New York law would enforce an express obligation to negotiate in good faith. While the UNIDROIT Principles were not directly applicable to this contract, the arbitrators nevertheless had regard to the Principles for the purpose of comparing 'the conclusion which results from the application of the proper law

---

[43] Michael J Bonell, *The UNIDROIT Principles in Practice: Caselaw and Bibliography on the UNIDROIT Principles of Commercial Contracts* (Transnational, Ardsley (NY), 2005) Comment 2 to Art 1.7.

[44] At the end of 2005, the Unilex database cites eighteen examples of cases in which Article 1.7 has been discussed.

[45] Thus Art 1:7 has been cited in three Australian cases in which the courts have recognized the existence of a duty of good faith and fair dealing (see *Hughes Aircraft Systems International v Airservices Australia* (1997) 146 ALR 1 (Federal Court of Australia); *Aiton v Transfield*, unreported 1 October 1999, Supreme Court of New South Wales, available at <http://unilex.info> and *GEC Marconi Systems Pty Ltd v BHP Information Technology Pty Ltd*, unreported, 12 February 2003, Federal Court of Australia, available at http://unilex.info. In New Zealand Article 1.7 was cited by Thomas J in his dissenting judgment in *Bobux Marketing Ltd v Raynor Marketing Ltd* [2002] 1 NZLR 506 but his analysis failed to convince the majority. [46] See <http://unilex.info>.

[47] These included English law where the obligation to negotiate in good faith would be unenforceable and Saudi Arabian law where the obligation would be void.

with the conclusion that would be obtained were the Tribunal to apply those general principles'. In this way the UNIDROIT Principles provided support for the conclusion which the arbitrators had reached in their application of the law of New York. In many ways the case neatly illustrates the persuasive influence which the Principles can have when arbitrators are deciding not only the law that is to govern the contract but also the substantive content of that law.

14.46   Thus far there has been no detailed analysis of the substantive content of the good faith duty in the cases that have cited Article 1.7. In most cases the reference to Article 1.7 was made for the purpose of establishing the existence of a duty of good faith and fair dealing or in order to establish that good faith and fair dealing is a basic idea underlying the Principles. However, there has been some discussion of the substantive content of the good faith duty in the literature:

UNIDROIT Principles of International Commercial Contracts 2004 (UNIDROIT, Rome, 2004) 19

A typical example of behaviour contrary to the principle of good faith and fair dealing is what in some legal systems is known as 'abuse of rights.' It is characterised by a party's malicious behaviour which occurs for instance when a party exercises a right merely to damage the other party or for a purpose other than the one for which it had been granted, or when the exercise of a right is disproportionate to the originally intended result.

14.47   But it is clear that the good faith duty extends beyond cases of obvious 'bad faith' exemplified by the abuse of rights cases. That this is so is demonstrated by the following two illustrations:

UNIDROIT Principles of International Commercial Contracts 2004 (UNIDROIT, Rome, 2004) 18 and 20

A grants B forty-eight hours as the time within which B may accept its offer. When B, shortly before the expiry of the deadline, decides to accept, it is unable to do so: it is the weekend, the fax at A's office is disconnected and there is no telephone answering machine which can take the message. When on the following Monday A refuses B's acceptance A acts contrary to good faith since when it fixed the time-limit for acceptance it was for A to ensure that messages could be received at its office throughout the forty-eight hour period. . . .

Under a contract for the sale of high-technology equipment the purchaser loses the right to rely on any defect in the goods if it does not give notice to the seller specifying the nature of the defect without undue delay after it has discovered or ought to have discovered the defect. A, a buyer operating in a country where such equipment is commonly used, discovers a defect in the equipment after having put it into operation, but in its notice to B, the seller of the equipment, A gives misleading indications as to the nature of the defect. A loses its right to rely on the defect since a more careful examination of the defect would have permitted it to give B the necessary specifications.

14.48   Article 2:101 of the PECL also requires the parties to act in accordance with good faith and fair dealing. This is buttressed by specific rules imposing a duty to co-operate in order to give full effect to the contract,[48] requiring negotiations to be conducted in good faith,[49] confidential information not to be disclosed,[50] and specifying fraud[51] and the taking of unfair advantage[52] as grounds for avoiding a contract. But these specific rules, so far as requiring the exercise of good faith, must always be read in conjunction with Article 1:201, for this is a mandatory rule, whereas the specific rules are not so designated and derive their mandatory force solely from Article 2:101. Quite apart from these specific cases, Article 2:101 exercises a pervasive influence on the Principles as a whole. The PECL do not define good faith but some guidance as to its likely scope and meaning can be gleaned from the following extract:

Ole Lando and Hugh Beale (eds), *Principles of European Contract Law: Parts I and II* **(Kluwer Law International, The Hague, 2000) 113–16**

Good faith and fair dealing are required in the formation, performance and enforcement of the parties' duties under a contract, and equally in the exercise of a party's rights under the contract. Particular applications of this rule appear in specific provisions of the present Principles. . . . The concept is, however, broader than any of these specific applications. It applies generally as a companion to Article 1:104 on Usages. Its purpose is to enforce community standards of decency, fairness and reasonableness in commercial transactions, see Article 1:108 on Reasonableness. It supplements the provisions of the Principles, and it may take precedence over other provisions in these Principles when a strict adherence to them would lead to a manifestly unjust result. Thus, even if the non-performance of an obligation is fundamental because strict compliance with the obligation is of the essence of the contract under Article 8:103, a party would not be permitted to terminate because of a trivial breach of the obligation.

The principle of good faith and fair dealing also covers situations where a party without any good reason stands on ceremony. . . . The principle covers a party's dishonest behaviour. . . . In relationships which last over a period of time (Dauerschuldverhältnisse) such as tenancies, insurance contracts, agency and distributorship agreements, partnerships and employment relationships, the concept of good faith has particular significance as a guideline for the parties' behaviour. . . . A particular application of the principle of good faith and fair dealing is to prevent a party, on whose statement or conduct the other party has reasonably acted in reliance, from adopting an inconsistent position. . . .

Article 1:201 imposes upon each party a duty to observe reasonable standards of fair dealing and to show due regard for the interests of the other party. This applies, *inter alia*, to their handling of contingencies which were not contemplated in their agreement or in the rules of law governing the contract . . . Good faith and fair dealing is required of the party which is to perform its obligations under a contract and of a party which wishes to have the contract enforced when the other party has failed to perform. Good faith and fair dealing require, for instance, the aggrieved party to limit as far as possible the loss which it will suffer as a result of a breach by the other party, thereby reducing the amount of damages, see Article 9:505 . . .

---

[48] Art 1:202.   [49] Art 2:301.   [50] Art 2:302.   [51] Art 4:107.
[52] Art 4:109.

'Good faith' means honesty and fairness in mind, which are subjective concepts. A person should, for instance, not be entitled to exercise a remedy if doing so is of no benefit to him and his only purpose is to harm the other party. 'Fair dealing' means observance of fairness in fact which is an objective test. ... The notion of good faith (*bonne foi*) as set out in Article 1:201 is different from the 'good faith' of a purchaser who acquires goods or documents of title without notice of third-party claims in the goods or documents. Article 1:201 does not deal with *bona fide* acquisitions. The notion of good faith in this Article is also different from that used in Article 3:201(3) under which a principal is treated as having granted authority to an agent when its conduct induces the third party in good faith to believe that the agent has authority ...

Good faith is to be presumed. The party which alleges that the other party has failed to observe good faith and fair dealing has to prove it. ...

What is good faith will, however, to some extent depend upon what was agreed upon by the parties in their contract. Thus, parties may agree that even a technical breach may entitle the aggrieved party to refuse performance. ...

However, a party should not have a right to take advantage of a term in the contract or of one of these Principles in a way that, given the circumstances, would be unacceptable according to the standard of good faith and fair dealing. Contract language which gives a party such a right should not be enforced.

Interpretation

14.49 The principles applied by courts and arbitral tribunals when interpreting contract terms are of enormous significance in practice, given that so many cases raise issues of interpretation. Both Principles emphasize the importance of the 'common intention' of the parties in the interpretative process and, at least in the case of the PECL, attach less weight to the literal meaning of the words used by the parties.[53] When interpreting the contract, courts and arbitral tribunals can draw on a wide range of materials,[54] including preliminary negotiations between the parties, conduct subsequent to the making of the contract, usages and, in the case of PECL, good faith and fair dealing. This list is broader than the range of materials traditionally admissible in evidence in common law jurisdictions but there have been signs recently that common law courts may be prepared to adopt a more liberal approach to the admissibility of such evidence and the Principles may, possibly, encourage them to take further steps down this road.[55]

Adequate assurance of performance

14.50 There may be cases where, though a party has not expressed his inability or unwillingness to perform, his conduct or other circumstances have generated a reasonable

---

[53] PECL, Art 5:101(1); UNIDROIT Principles, Art 4.1.1.

[54] PECL, Art 5:102; UNIDROIT Principles, Art 4.3.

[55] See further Ewan McKendrick, 'The Interpretation of Contracts: Lord Hoffmann's Restatement' in S Worthington (ed), *Commercial Law and Commercial Practice* (Hart Publishing, Oxford, 2003).

belief by the other party that there will be a fundamental non-performance by the first party. Under Article 7.3.4 of the UNIDROIT Principles the other party may demand adequate assurance of performance and if this is not forthcoming within a reasonable time he may terminate the contract. There is a similar provision in Article 8:105 of the PECL. Though inspired by §2–609 of the American Uniform Commercial Code, the UNIDROIT and PECL solutions are more restricted, requiring a reasonable belief that there *will be* a fundamental non-performance, whereas §2–609 imposes on a party the duty to ensure that the other party's expectation of receiving due performance will not be impaired and confers the right to demand adequate assurance of due performance when reasonable grounds for insecurity of performance arise. The utility of this provision, and the benefits which English law could derive from the creation of such a rule, are illustrated by the following hypothetical:

Roy Goode, 'International Restatements of Contract and English Contract Law' (1997) II Unif L Rev 231, 240–41

The parents of a young woman who is about to be married make arrangements with a catering firm to provide a reception and dinner after the ceremony. A month before the wedding is due to take place, the mother of the bride-to-be contacts the caterers to check that all the arrangements are in order, and is told: 'Well, we are in the middle of a strike at the moment, but though I can't give an absolute guarantee I'm almost sure we shall be all right on the night.' Are the parents still bound by the contract and obliged to run the risk of a ruined celebration and a huge social embarrassment? Is there any other step they can take for their protection? Astonishingly, English law does not yet provide any satisfactory answers to these questions. The case is not one of anticipatory breach, or of disablement from future performance, for the caterers have affirmed both their intention to perform and the strong likelihood of their ability to do so. Nor does English law appear to provide a right to demand an adequate assurance of performance. Such a right, with an ability to terminate the contract if the assurance is not forthcoming within a reasonable time, is given by the Principles, so that in the example given the devoted parents would have a remedy.

Specific performance as a primary remedy

Departing from the common law tradition, in which the primary remedy for non-performance is debt or damages, the Principles adopt the civil law rule by which specific performance is a primary remedy.[56] However, this is cut down by exceptions which exclude the remedy where (*inter alia*) it would cause the debtor unreasonable effort or expense or where the aggrieved party may reasonably obtain performance from another source,[57] for example, by buying equivalent goods on the market. A useful contrast can here be drawn with Article 28 of the CISG where, as has been noted,[58] those responsible for drafting the Convention failed to

14.51

---

[56] PECL, Art 9:102; UNIDROIT Principles, Art 7.2.2.   [57] Ibid.
[58] See paras 7.73–7.74 above.

reach agreement on the extent to which specific performance should be available as a remedy and, instead, relegated the matter to national law. However, the drafters of the Principles were able to achieve more, perhaps as a result of the non-binding nature of the Principles as the following extract suggests:

> What is acceptable in a non-binding set of rules may be quite different if imposed on a national legal system. In the case of the [Principles of European Contract Law] I was quite happy, for example, to accept a rule making specific performance the primary remedy and prepared, though rather less willingly, to live with a rule that did not allow the court a general discretion. It would be quite another thing to have this as a rule of English law, which in my opinion proceeds on the correct assumption that, in commercial transactions at least, what businessmen are primarily interested in is money, not specific performance.[59]

14.52 The Unilex database reveals that there has, as yet, been no reported example of a case in which the articles relating to specific performance have been invoked. This tends to suggest that the remedy is more important in theory than it is in practice.

Other remedies

14.53 Apart from the normal remedies of damages, termination, and the like, the Principles give a party whose non-conforming tender is rejected an opportunity to cure the default by a fresh and conforming tender;[60] and where the non-conforming tender is accepted then in lieu of damages the innocent party is given by PECL a claim to a reduction in price proportionate to the reduction in the value of the promised performance,[61] so that if, for example, the performance should have been worth £150,000 but by reason of the breach is only worth £100,000, and the price was £180,000, then instead of claiming damages of £50,000 the innocent party can claim a price reduction of one-third, i.e. £60,000. This *actio quanti minoris* is not available under the UNIDROIT Principles.

Hardship and change of circumstances

14.54 The most innovative provisions of the Principles are those relating to the effect of an adverse change of circumstances on a party's duty to perform. In the UNIDROIT Principles this is labelled 'hardship' and involves a fundamental change in the equilibrium of the contract because of an increase in the cost of performance or diminution in the value of the performance received.[62] The PECL equivalent is labelled 'change of circumstances'[63] and refers to performance becoming 'excessively onerous', but the concept is the same. It is clear from the comments to both provisions that only in exceptional circumstances will a party be able to invoke

---

[59] Professor Goode in his response to the Communication on European Contract Law issued by the European Commission to the European Parliament and the Council, para 11.

[60] PECL, Art 8:104; UNIDROIT Principles, Art 7.1.4.   [61] PECL, Art 9:401.

[62] Art 6.2.2.   [63] Art 6:111.

these provisions.[64] The mere fact that a contract has become unprofitable for one party does not suffice. Where the provisions do apply, then under the PECL the parties come under a duty to enter into negotiations with a view to adapting the contract or ending it,[65] while under the UNIDROIT Principles the disadvantaged party may request negotiations.[66] On the parties' failure to reach agreement within a reasonable time the court is empowered to terminate the contract or to adapt it in order to reflect the change of circumstances.[67] Though most systems have rules for dealing with the effect of a radical change of circumstances, the duty to negotiate goes further than is required by most legal systems and it has been invoked in a number of cases to date.

This is an area in which the Principles go much further than the CISG. Article 79[68] **14.55** of the CISG deals with what may, broadly, be termed *force majeure* and its true equivalent is to be found in Article 7.1.7 of the UNIDROIT Principles. The hardship provisions provide the courts and arbitrators with much greater remedial flexibility. This flexibility is likely to be important in the case of long-term contracts where the parties are more likely to wish to avoid the termination of their contract and, instead, prefer to have their contract adapted in order to meet the changed circumstances.

Assignment and novation

Both Principles contain rules on assignment and novation.[69] These do not require **14.56** comment except to note that, in line with the rule adopted in certain international conventions,[70] assignments of accounts are in general effective despite a no-assignment clause in the assigned contract.[71] The purpose of this rule is to avoid the impediments to receivables financing that would otherwise arise.

Agency

Both principles contain rules relating to the external aspects of agency,[72] that is to **14.57** say, the extent of an agent's authority to bind his principal in relation to a contract with a third party. Agency is discussed in more detail in chapter 8 of this work.

---

[64] It is, of course, open to the parties to make provision in their contract for its adjustment through change of circumstances. See in that connection the ICC Hardship Clause 2003 (No. 650).

[65] Art 6:111(2).   [66] Art 6.2.3.

[67] UNIDROIT Principles, Art 6.2.3; PECL, Art 6:111(3).

[68] On which see further paras 7.97–7.100 above.

[69] UNIDROIT Principles, ch 9; PECL, ch 11.

[70] The 1988 UNIDROIT Convention on International Factoring; the 2000 UN Convention on the Assignment of Receivables in International Trade, Art 9(1). Both of these provisions drew their inspiration from what is now §9-406(d) of the Uniform Commercial Code.

[71] UNIDROIT Principles, Art 9.1.9; PECL, Art 11:301, which, however, is limited to the three cases there mentioned.   [72] UNIDROIT Principles, Art 2.2.1ff; PECL, ch 3.

The Principles and mandatory rules

14.58   In those cases where the choice of the Principles as the applicable law is valid[73] they will override domestic mandatory rules, which cannot be excluded by contract but operate only where that law is the governing law and may thus be excluded by a choice of foreign law. By contrast, the Principles always take effect subject to mandatory rules which apply regardless of the governing law.[74] In the case where the Principles take effect as contractually incorporated terms they will take effect subject to applicable domestic mandatory rules.

14.59   As well as providing for deferment to external mandatory rules, the Principles contain mandatory rules of their own. These include the duty of good faith,[75] the reduction of a grossly excessive stipulated payment for non-performance,[76] and curbs on contractual provisions excluding or limiting liability.[77] In addition, the UNIDROIT Principles provide that where the price is to be determined by one party and that determination is manifestly unreasonable, a reasonable price shall be substituted notwithstanding any contract term to the contrary,[78] while the PECL extend this to cover to all contractual terms to be determined by one party.[79]

14.60   At first sight it seems odd that Principles which do not themselves have the force of law should incorporate mandatory rules of any kind. But this may not be as strange as it seems:

**Roy Goode, 'International Restatements of Contract and English Contract Law'
(1997) II Unif L Rev 231, 246**

It may be asked how it is possible for Principles which do not themselves have the force of law to incorporate mandatory rules of any kind. But this is not as strange as it seems. In the first place, where the parties select the Principles as rules of law governing their contract, they thereby subject themselves to the binding force of the mandatory rules. Secondly, in stating what rules are to be considered mandatory, the Principles provide evidence of a general acceptation of what is to be considered, or ought to be considered, mandatory. Thirdly, even where the Principles are merely incorporated as terms of the contract, rather than being selected as the applicable law, their adoption will indicate an intention to give overriding effect to those rules expressed as mandatory to the extent that this is not incompatible with the construction of the contract as a whole.

14.61   However, in the event that contracting parties sought expressly to exclude the application of an article which is expressed by the Principles to be mandatory, it is

---

[73] See above.

[74] UNIDROIT Principles, Art 1.4; PECL, Art 1:103. The UNIDROIT Principles are intentionally silent on the applicability of domestic mandatory rules.

[75] UNIDROIT Principles, Art 1.7; PECL, Art 1:201.

[76] UNIDROIT Principles, Art 7.4.13; PECL, Art 9:509(2).

[77] UNIDROIT Principles, Art 7.1.6; PECL, Art 8:109.   [78] Art 5.1.7(2).

[79] Art 6:105.

unlikely that a court or an arbitrator would be able to conclude that this exclusion was devoid of effect:

***UNIDROIT Principles of International Commercial Contracts 2004* (UNIDROIT, Rome, 2004) 14**

A few provisions of the Principles are of mandatory character, i.e. their importance in the system of the Principles is such that parties should not be permitted to exclude or to derogate from them as they wish. It is true that given the particular nature of the Principles the non-observance of this precept may have no consequences. On the other hand, it should be noted that the provisions in question reflect principles and standards of behaviour which are of a mandatory character under most domestic laws also.

The latter quotation expressly accepts that the Principles themselves cannot prevent exclusion of the relevant articles by the parties, at least where the exclusion is cast in express terms. However, it does not follow from this that the characterization of certain rules as 'mandatory' is devoid of effect. In the first place, it emphasizes the importance of the articles which are declared to be mandatory and renders it less likely that a court or an arbitrator will conclude that the article has been impliedly excluded by a contract term which is difficult to reconcile with the relevant article. Second, it may encourage courts and arbitrators to conclude that the article is mandatory not only in relation to the Principles themselves but also as a matter of the otherwise applicable domestic law and in this way assist in the development of internationally accepted mandatory rules. **14.62**

Questions

1. 'Much time and effort went into the preparation of the UNIDROIT Principles of International Commercial Contracts and its European counterpart, the Principles of European Contract Law, prepared by the Commission on European Contract Law. But since neither set of instruments is legally binding, they serve no useful purpose.' Discuss.
2. Why, in Europe, was it considered desirable to prepare uniform rules of substantive contract law instead of just relying on the conflict rules contained in the Rome Convention on the law applicable to contractual obligations?
3. In what circumstances may the UPICC or the PECL be applied?
4. (1) May the parties select either set of Principles as the law to govern their contract?
   (2) What has the European Commission proposed in that regard? Do you agree with its proposal?
5. Both sets of Principles contain mandatory rules. What effect can these have when the Principles themselves have no binding force?

Further reading

Basedow, Jurgen, 'Uniform Law Conventions and the UNIDROIT Principles of International Commercial Contracts' (2000) V Unif L Rev 129

Béraudo, Jean-Paul (ed), *Principles for International Commercial Contracts: a New Lex Mercatoria?* (ICC, Paris, 1995)

Berger, Klaus Peter, 'Harmonisation of European Contract Law: The Influence of Comparative Law' (2001) 50 ICLQ 877

Boele-Woelki, Katharina, 'The Unidroit Principles of International Commercial Contracts and the Principles of European Contract Law: How to Apply them to International Contracts' (1996) 1 Unif L Rev 652

Bonell, Michael J (ed), *The UNIDROIT Principles in Practice* (Transnational Publishers, New York, 2002)

Bonell, Michael J, 'The UNIDROIT Principles of International Commercial Contracts and the Principles of European Contract Law: similar rules for the same purposes?' (1996) I Unif L Rev 229

Bonell, Michael J, 'UNIDROIT Principles: a significant recognition by a United States District Court' (1999) IV Unif L Rev 651

Bonell, Michael J, 'Unification of Law by Non-Legislative Means: the UNIDROIT draft principles for international commercial contracts' (1992) 40 Am J Comp L 617

Bortolotti, Fabio, 'The UNIDROIT Principles and the arbitral tribunals' (2000) V Unif L Rev 141

Farnsworth, E Allan, 'Duties of Good Faith and Fair Dealing Under the Unidroit Principles, Relevant International Conventions and National Laws' (1995) 3 Tul J Intl & Comp L 47

Kronke, Herbert, 'The UN Sales Convention, the UNIDROIT Contract Principles and the Way Beyond' 25 J of Law and Comm 451 (2005–06)

Lando, Ole, 'Is Codification Needed in Europe? Principles of European Contract Law and the Relationship to Dutch Law' (1993) 1 Eur Rev Priv L 157

Lando, Ole, and Beale, Hugh, (eds), *Principles of European Contract Law, Parts I and II* (Kluwer Law International, The Hague, 2000)

Lando, Ole, Clive, Eric and Prüm, André (eds), *Principles of European Contract Law, Part III* (Kluwer Law International, The Hague, 2003)

Lando, Ole, Clive, Eric, Prüm, Andre, and Zimmerman, Reinhard (eds), *Principles of European Contract Law* (Kluwer, The Hague, 2003)

Ramberg, Jan, 'The Creativity of Arbitrators in the Context of the UNIDROIT Principles of International Commercial Contracts' (1998) III Unif L Rev 651

Staudenmeyer, Dirk, 'The Commission Communication on European Contract Law and the Future Prospects' (2002) 51 ICLQ 673

UNIDROIT Principles of International Commercial Contracts 2004 (UNIDROIT, Rome, 2004)

PART IV

TRANSNATIONAL INSOLVENCY

15

HARMONIZATION AND CO-OPERATION IN CROSS-BORDER INSOLVENCY

A. Introduction	15.01	D. Judicial Co-operation in Concurrent Insolvency Proceedings	15.22
B. The Opposing Jurisdiction Principles	15.06		
C. The UNCITRAL Model Law on Cross-Border Insolvency	15.13	E. The European Insolvency Regulation	
Nature and purpose	15.14	Background to the Regulation	15.24
Sphere of application	15.16	Scope of the Regulation	15.25
Access by foreign representative and recognition of foreign proceedings	15.18	Types of insolvency proceeding	15.26
		The COMI	15.27
Automatic stay	15.20	Applicable law	15.29
Co-operation with foreign courts and foreign representatives	15.21	The principle of recognition	15.31
		Insolvency of corporate groups	15.35

A. Introduction

Courts around the world have long had to wrestle with conflict-of-laws problems **15.01** arising from insolvencies having points of contact with two or more jurisdictions. A company in liquidation or insolvent reorganization which was incorporated and carrying on business in one State may also have assets to be recovered and debts to be enforced in another, and the recovery and enforcement process will usual involve proceedings in the other State in which the foreign court will be asked to recognize the title of the office-holder (liquidator, trustee, administrator, etc.)—which it may or may not do—and to lend its assistance to the recovery process. A company may operate in a number of jurisdictions through branches or offices or through subsidiaries which constitute distinct legal entities and there-fore in principle have to be the subject of separate insolvency proceedings. The institution of insolvency proceedings in one State may raise a question as to whether other States should recognize its exclusive, worldwide jurisdiction or whether each State should regard itself as free to entertain insolvency proceedings in conform-ity with its own jurisdiction rules. In the latter case, there will be parallel insolvency proceedings in the different jurisdictions, raising questions as to whether one should be treated as auxiliary to the other or should operate independently and whether there should be co-operation between the different courts and office-holders involved.

15.02 The evolution of global trading, coupled with the rise of the so-called rescue culture in which the objective has shifted from winding-up and realization of the debtor's assets to reorganization with a view to restoring the debtor to profitable trading or restructuring the company so as to maximize the prospect of returns to creditors, has made these issues much more acute and pervasive. It has come to be seen that the individual pursuit of insolvency proceedings in one jurisdiction without regard to existing or impending parallel proceedings elsewhere may impede, if not prevent altogether, a sensible restructuring of the debtor company and may thus be very detrimental to the interests of creditors.

UNCITRAL Model Law on Cross-Border Insolvency with Guide to Enactment (United Nations, New York, 1999), para 17

To the extent that there is a lack of communication and coordination among courts and administrators from concerned jurisdictions, it is more likely that assets would be dissipated, fraudulently concealed, or possibly liquidated without reference to other more advantageous solutions. As the result, not only is the ability of creditors to receive payment diminished, but so is the possibility of rescuing financially viable businesses and saving jobs. By contrast, mechanisms in national legislation for coordinated administration of cross-border insolvency makes it possible to adopt solutions that are sensible and in the best interests of the creditors and the debtor; the presence of such mechanisms in the law of a State is therefore perceived as advantageous for foreign investment and trade in that State.

15.03 Particularly complex issues arise in cases where investigation into corporate groups reveals massive fraud involving the misappropriation of a company's money or other assets to the value of millions, or even billions, of dollars. The Bank of Credit and Commerce International SA provides a case in point. The bank was incorporated in Luxembourg, but had forty-seven offices or branches in different countries. A winding-up order was made in Luxembourg and was followed soon after by a similar order in England, the English winding-up proceedings being ancillary to those in Luxembourg. Proceedings were also instituted in the United States. BCCI's parent company, the Bank of Credit and Commerce International (Overseas) Ltd, incorporated in the Cayman Islands, had sixty-three offices or branches in different jurisdictions. The group was found to be involved not only in fraudulent transactions but in a wide range of seriously unlawful activities, including establishing links with drug cartels and terrorist organizations. Depositors were said to have been defrauded of US$10 billion. The liquidators had to pursue recovery measures in a number of jurisdictions, seeking assistance from local courts, and in most cases were extremely successful, paying dividends to creditors totalling over 80 per cent.[1] Even this enormous case was later dwarfed by the insolvency of the giant Italian food company Parmalat, where €4 billion of funds supposedly held by the company did not exist, €8 million of funds supporting bond issues had disappeared and total debt exceeded €14 billion. The liquidator has brought proceedings against numerous banks in different countries seeking to recover losses which it attributes to their culpability in different ways.

Prior to the 1880s jurisdictional issues arising from cross-border insolvency were addressed by bilateral treaties. In 1889, a regional treaty on international commercial law was concluded at Montevideo by the Latin American States, Title X of which was devoted to bankruptcies. This was essentially a conflict-of-laws convention, which was supplemented in 1940 by provisions included in the Montevideo Treaty of International Procedural Law. In between, came the 1928 Havana Convention on Private International Law (generally known as the Bustamente Code), which was ratified by a number of South American and Latin America States and combined the key principles of unity and universality described below. In Europe an early attempt at harmonization was made by the distinguished judge Jabez Henry, who in 1925 wrote his *Outline of Plan of an International Bankruptcy Code for the Different Commercial States of Europe*, a very progressive document which unhappily failed to secure action. Not until 1990, after thirty years of hard work, was the Council of Europe Convention on certain international aspects of bankruptcy concluded at Istanbul, but enthusiasm for this waned with the conclusion of the European Union Convention on Insolvency Proceedings, which was signed by fourteen Member States of the European Union, leaving only one more necessary signature, that of the United Kingdom, which declined to sign,[2] whereupon the Convention fell by the wayside, though in the year 2000 it was resuscitated with largely the same text in the form of a European Community Regulation. **15.04**

In this chapter we examine two major instruments designed to address key issues arising from cross-border insolvency. The first, at international level, is the 1997 UNCITRAL Model Law on cross-border insolvency; the second, a regional instrument, is the European Community Regulation on insolvency proceedings referred to above. But as a prelude to our examination of these two instruments we shall briefly describe the rival approaches to questions of jurisdiction. **15.05**

---

[1] The major exception was proceedings against the Bank of England for $1.8 billion for misfeasance in a public office. The case dragged on for twelve years and the hearing lasted 256 days before the trial was unexpectedly abandoned, and the liquidators were ordered to pay indemnity costs estimated at in excess of £80 million as well as having to bear their own costs.

[2] Two reasons have been ascribed to this: the hostility of the then Prime Minister, John Major, because of the European Commission's refusal to remove the ban on the export of British beef because of 'mad cow' disease and the concern that signature would jeopardize the United Kingdom's sovereignty over Gibraltar, to which Spain was also laying claim.

B. The Opposing Jurisdiction Principles

15.06   Two central questions arise in relation to insolvencies with a foreign element. The first is whether jurisdiction over all the debtor's assets and affairs should be vested exclusively in the courts of a single State, for example, that of the debtor's incorporation, or whether, when proceedings have been opened in one State, it should be possible to have parallel proceedings in another State. In other words, should the principle be one of *unity* of proceedings or of *plurality*? The second is whether the jurisdiction of the insolvency court should cover all the debtor's assets worldwide or should be confined to local assets. Here the contest is between *universality* and *territoriality*. The two pairs of opposing principles, though conceptually distinct, are often treated in combination under the label 'universalism', which encompasses the concept both of a single law and of a single court whose jurisdiction covers all assets on a worldwide basis.

15.07   While in some countries jurisdiction is limited to local assets the general approach of an insolvency court is to assert jurisdiction over all the debtor's assets, wherever situated, while being rather reluctant to accept a similar assertion of jurisdiction by foreign insolvency courts. More accurately, while the universalism of a foreign court's jurisdiction may be recognized in principle, the local insolvency court may be reluctant to cede control altogether over local assets and may wish to be satisfied that the surrender of these to a foreign administrator is not incompatible with any rule of public policy. Most commentators agree that a pure concept of universalism, though good in theory, is unrealistic. Similarly, it is recognized that when insolvency proceedings have been opened in one jurisdiction, insolvency courts of other jurisdictions, though often willing to accept their role as being of an ancillary character, may be reluctant to cede ultimate control over the administration of assets within their jurisdiction. The controversy, particularly keen among American insolvency specialists, who have been at the forefront of debates on the question, has centred on whether the starting position should be that of the territorialist model, as propounded by Professors Tung, LoPucki and others, or of the universalist model, as advocated by a number of scholars, and in particular by Professor Jay Westbrook. We begin with some of the critics of the universalist approach.

Frederick Tung, 'Is International Bankruptcy Possible?' 23 Mich J Intl L 31, 32–3 and 39–47 (2001–2002).

Scholars of international bankruptcy are caught in the grip of a failed idea: universalism. Generations of scholars have advanced the universalist mantra: ie, that the assets and liabilities of a multinational firm in bankruptcy should be administered by one court applying one nation's bankruptcy laws on a worldwide basis. Until recently, this advancement of universalism occurred largely without challenge. Even with recent challenges, however, universalism dominates the debate, as scholars attempt to debunk its claimed efficiency advantages.

This debate over universalism is misguided because, simply put, universalism will not work. In this article, I argue that universalism is politically implausible and likely impossible. No nation has adopted it, and it is unlikely that any will. States will be reluctant to commit to enforcing the decisions of foreign courts applying foreign bankruptcy laws against local parties. In addition, even assuming states exist that would be interested in universalism, structural problems will preclude the achievement of workable universalist cooperation. I rely on elementary game theory and international relations theory to show that even states that prefer universalism will find themselves in a prisoners' dilemma with no ready solution. Impediments to cooperation will afflict even bilateral universalist ambitions, with multilateral universalism all the more unlikely. Because the claimed superior efficiency of universalism implicitly depends on its widespread adoption—if not ubiquity—this implausibility of multilateral universalism is particularly damning to the universalist cause. Universalism should be shelved, and the terms of the scholarly debate should shift to more plausible goals ...

I. Debating Universalism

Territoriality simply honors the age-old behavior of nations in exercising jurisdiction over assets and parties within their borders. Analysts agree that territoriality is and has always been the dominant practice. Each nation in which a multinational debtor owns assets decides under its own laws how the assets within its territory should be treated in the face of creditor claims. For example, assume that Firm A has assets, employees, and creditors in both State A and State B. When it suffers financial distress, it files for bankruptcy in State A, where its headquarters are located. This will protect the firm's assets in State A, but under the territorial system that currently dominates, the filing will have no effect on the firm's assets in State B. Creditors may still pursue the firm's State B assets, relying on State B law. The firm might additionally file for bankruptcy in State B, but that proceeding would occur under State B law administered by State B courts.

Historically, analysts have also agreed that a universalist approach is preferable to one segmented by territorial boundaries. The financial distress of a multinational firm should come under one bankruptcy regime, even though several states may claim jurisdiction over various pieces of the firm or over claimants located in or having some other connection with those states.

This Part first explains the case for universalism, and then discusses rival proposals that have recently emerged.

A. The Universalist Account

The basic universalist principle is 'one law, one court'. As most commonly envisioned by universalists, the courts of the debtor's home country, applying home country bankruptcy law, would have worldwide jurisdiction over the debtor's bankruptcy. In Firm A's bankruptcy, State A would probably be the home country, and State A bankruptcy law would govern Firm A's bankruptcy worldwide. State A courts would enjoy global jurisdiction to administer State A bankruptcy law with respect to the debtor's assets and creditors everywhere, with other states deferring to State A courts. The home country courts would depend on local courts in other states to carry out home country decisions.

Conceptually, universalism is attractive. A unified proceeding enables one court to administer the entirety of the debtor's assets. This maximizes the value that can be preserved for creditors by facilitating a coordinated disposition of the debtor's assets. It assures creditors' equal treatment, and it avoids the duplicative administrative costs that multiple proceedings would entail. Standardizing home country law as the governing law promotes predictability, thereby lowering the costs of credit and facilitating economic activity. Universalists generally agree that the home country should ordinarily be determined by the location of the debtor's principal place of business. They claim that this approach should be straightforward in most cases, and that judges should be able to handle the rare controversy that might arise.

Professor Jay Westbrook has been the leading advocate for universalism. Recent scholarship by Professors Lucian Bebchuk and Andrew Guzman has also identified other plausible efficiencies from universalism. Bebchuk and Guzman argue that to the extent territoriality is synonymous with discrimination against foreign creditors, it creates inefficient investment incentives for debtors that would not plague a universalist system. In a later piece, Guzman asserts that greater predictability and lower information costs under universalism would lower the costs of credit. Territoriality forces creditors continually to monitor the location of the debtor's assets and to ascertain the laws of the various jurisdictions to which assets might possibly be moved. Universalism, by contrast, makes asset location irrelevant, relieving creditors of such burdens.

While universalist advocates have not focused much attention on the question of how universalism might emerge, their brief comments suggest that universalism could evolve spontaneously through unilateral reciprocity policies of individual states. By those lights, any state interested in universalism could unilaterally proclaim its willingness to behave as a universalist toward any other state willing to adopt the same reciprocity policy. In this way, universalist states would reveal themselves, presumably allowing emergence of a universalist system over time.

B. Rival Proposals

Professors Lynn LoPucki and Robert Rasmussen have each questioned the claimed efficiency advantages of universalism, and each has proposed a reform alternative.

In two recent articles, LoPucki has called for cooperation on a territorial basis. Rather than overthrowing the existing territory-based order, LoPucki would build on it. Under his system of cooperative territoriality, each state would continue to exercise jurisdiction over, and apply its own laws to, the debtor's assets within its territory. Parallel bankruptcy proceedings could occur in each state with debtor assets, and cooperation would occur through the interaction of agents appointed by each state to represent the bankruptcy estate located there. States would negotiate cooperative asset disposition on a case-by-case basis. Particular inefficiencies from territoriality could be remedied through specific international arrangements, without attempting to impose an entirely new regime on recalcitrant sovereigns.

Comparing the benefits of this system to universalism, LoPucki argues that universalism cannot deliver on its promise of ex ante predictability or lower borrowing costs because the 'home country' concept is indeterminate and may be manipulated by debtors. Furthermore, the interface between local nonbankruptcy law and universalist foreign bankruptcy law would cause difficulties. The scope of bankruptcy jurisdiction ceded to a universalist court would always be open to question, and the dramatic shift from local nonbankruptcy entitlements to universalist bankruptcy entitlements would invite wasteful gamesmanship by debtors and creditors. These interface issues are much more manageable under a territorial system.

For his part, Robert Rasmussen has advocated a 'debtor's choice' approach, under which each debtor's corporate charter would specify a choice of national bankruptcy law that would apply in case of financial distress. The impetus to this approach is that the universalist choice of home country law may not necessarily be the most efficient choice. Instead, the argument goes, private parties allowed to choose their own governing law would be better able to pick the optimal set of rules.

C. Is Universalism Possible?

LoPucki seems to agree with universalists that they offer a conceptually acceptable approach, and that as states' various bankruptcy regimes converge as a result of the globalization of business, universalism might emerge. However, LoPucki and Westbrook disagree about how realistic is the hope for universalism. Westbrook seems to believe that even piecemeal and sporadic deference to foreign insolvency proceedings is appropriate—despite the unpredictability and injustices generated—as it moves us in the right direction toward universalism. By contrast, LoPucki notes that harmonization sufficient to make universalism widely acceptable might take decades or even centuries. The crucial question is 'what to do while we are waiting for the "new world society"—essentially, a world government—to arrive?'

I argue that the wait will be a long one. I agree with LoPucki's conclusion that a new and improved territoriality is the right approach to reform. However, I am even less optimistic than LoPucki that universalism is possible. At best, universalism is premature. At worst, it is futile. Without directly addressing the efficiency debate among the competing models, I am content to take universalists at their word, ignore universalist critics, and assume the strongest case for universalism. I focus instead on a prior question. Is universalism even possible as a political matter? Only regularized universalist cooperation can deliver the predictability and promised efficiencies of universalism. I argue that such a system is highly improbable.

II. The Intuitive Implausibility of Universalism

States are generally reluctant to commit to universalism . . . Bankruptcy is a particularly difficult area for international harmonization or cooperation. As I have discussed elsewhere in detail, bankruptcy has drastic wholesale effects, and the deference to foreign law and courts demanded by universalism is far greater than any commitment states have been willing to make to date. The observed limits of nations' willingness to commit to relatively narrow cooperation suggests even greater reluctance to accede to the broader cooperative arrangement demanded under universalism.

A conflict of laws arises when a legal dispute involves parties, property, or events that implicate more than one legal system. When a multinational enterprise fails, various states may assert jurisdiction over all or part of the failing firm or certain of its legal relationships. States will seek to apply their own laws to those issues over which they claim jurisdiction. Universalism simply provides a rule to resolve the conflicts of laws that arise in this context.

In the typical bankruptcy context, the debtor will enter formal bankruptcy proceedings in its home country, whose courts will apply home country bankruptcy laws. The home country court will attempt to include the debtor's foreign assets in the proceeding, claiming extraterritorial jurisdiction over those assets and extending the effect of its bankruptcy law to those assets. However, local courts in these other states will also claim jurisdiction over assets within their respective territories. They will seek to apply their own bankruptcy or other debt collection laws to those assets, typically to the benefit of local creditors or other domestic interest groups. Conflicts arise because states generally favor their own bankruptcy regimes—especially as to firms and assets within their territorial jurisdictions—and may attempt to extend extraterritorial effects to include foreign assets of their domestic debtors. At the same time, states will scrutinize and limit the local effects of foreign proceedings. They will be leery of granting recognition and giving local effect to determinations of foreign bankruptcy courts.

Universalism resolves this conflict by requiring the local court to defer to the home country court and its bankruptcy law. Universalism demands that other states recognize and enforce home country court orders applying home country bankruptcy law. However, states have shown great reluctance to concede their sovereignty in favor of home country law and courts.

Although international recognition of civil judgments is common and becoming more so, universalist bankruptcy recognition is basically nonexistent. Bankruptcy law is among the areas of law least amenable to international harmonization or cooperation, and to date, the history of multilateral insolvency cooperation has been marked by frustration.

Professor Lynn LoPucki argues that the universalist approach rests on the mistaken assumption that it is possible to identify the relevant 'home country'.

Lynn M LoPucki, 'The Case for Cooperative Territoriality in International Bankruptcy' 98 Mich L Rev 2216, 2223–28 and 2229–30 (1999–2000)

Nearly all of the putative advantages of universalism depend on the assumption that each multinational company has a single home country that will not change over time. The arguments for universalism fail because no universalist scholar has yet proposed a workable test or method for identifying that country. Without such a method, universalism cannot be implemented.

Universalism cannot operate without the ability to identify a home country for each multinational company for three reasons. First, the home country's law will determine the priorities of creditors in the debtor's estate. Contrary to the arguments presented by Professors Guzman and Rasmussen, large differences exist among the bankruptcy laws of different countries. Several examples illustrate these differences: (1) The laws of some countries treat a creditor with a right of set off as secured; the laws of others treat them as unsecured. (2) In some countries tort creditors share pro rata with commercial creditors; in other countries, tort creditors are subordinated to commercial creditors; and in yet others, tort creditors who have not yet reduced their claims to judgments before bankruptcy do not share at all. (3) In some countries employees are willing to extend substantial credit to their employers, because they know they will have first priority—ahead of even secured creditors—in the factories in which they work; in other countries such extensions would be foolish because employees' priorities are limited sharply or even nonexistent. These differences in legal doctrine occur against even sharper differences in system operation. In some countries, bribery is common. In others—particularly small nations—the local courts might be under the corrupt influence of a multinational company based there. Some countries do not yet have an operating bankruptcy system. If the identity of the home country is arguable or manipulable at the time of bankruptcy, debtors or their creditors could change both substantive rights and likely outcomes, simply by their choices of venue.

Second, under universalism, the validity of transfers the debtor made in the period before bankruptcy would be tested by the laws of the home country. Most national bankruptcy systems have laws providing for the avoidance of various kinds of transfers made by the debtor in the period before bankruptcy. The transfers typically made avoidable include those that had the effect of preferring one creditor over another, those made to insiders, and those that had the effect of reducing an already insolvent estate. But here too, the laws of the various countries differ widely. Without a clear identification of the debtor's home country in advance, prefiling transfers would be voidable or not, depending on the choice of venue.

Third, under universalism, the courts of debtors' 'home countries' will adjudicate the claims of creditors from all over the world. While the home country might, under its own conflicts rules, choose to apply the substantive law of the place where the claim accrued, that is a matter that necessarily would be left to the home country. The home countries presumably would apply their own procedures to the adjudication of the claims—and with them their own notions of due process of law. Thus, the filing of a bankruptcy in some distant part of a universalist world could deprive an injured person of his or her right to a trial by jury, to pretrial discovery, or to the effective assistance of counsel—even though the tort was perpetrated by the debtor in the United States and the injury occurred in the United States. The difference these changes in 'procedure' would make were starkly illustrated in two recent mass tort cases. What was thought to be $3 billion in claims against Union Carbide for the deaths of 4,000 people in Bhopal, India was settled for $470 million when it became apparent the cases would be tried in India rather than in the United States. The recent settlement of breast implant claims in the Dow Corning bankruptcy expressly gave foreign women lower payments than US women for the same injuries, on the theory that those injuries were worth less under foreign procedures. If the identity of the home country were unclear as bankruptcy approached, so would be the values of these claims.

1. Which Country is the 'Home Country'?

Despite the importance of the identity of the home country for any particular debtor, universalists have been unable to specify meaningful criteria for its identification. Each of four different bases is plausible. First, most courts and commentators seem to regard the country of incorporation as having the strongest claim to home country status. For example, more than half of all large public companies filing for bankruptcy within the United States today file in Delaware rather than in states where their headquarters, assets, and operations are located. They file there on the basis that Delaware is their jurisdiction of incorporation. Second, companies often are identified with a particular country, because the companies are headquartered in that country. Third, if substantially all of the employees, operations, and customers of a large company were in a single country, it is difficult to imagine that country would not be considered the 'home country,' even if the company's tiny headquarters and place of incorporation were elsewhere. Fourth, the assets of a company can be almost entirely separate from its operations, as might occur when a company rents the factories where its employees work, but has substantial land holdings in another country.

Universalists attempt to dismiss this issue with the assertion that the identity of the home country will be obvious in most cases. But that rationale contradicts their basic premise of increasing globalization. No one can deny the existence of a substantial number of multinational companies whose home countries are either not obvious or in flux. That number will grow naturally with the increasing globalization of business. In a prematurely universalist system, that growth might turn malignant, as financially ailing companies jockey to give themselves bankruptcy options.

Perhaps responding to the rampant forum shopping within the United States based on place of incorporation, Guzman and Westbrook both reject place of incorporation as the standard for home country. Declining to choose from my list of concrete options, both state a preference for 'principal place of business' as the test. Westbrook defends that choice on the ground that it is a commonplace standard in American law. But he ignores two key facts about his choice. First, the American courts have been forced to give specific meaning to the phrase 'principal place of business' and have interpreted it to mean essentially the same thing as 'headquarters'—one of the concrete choices he rejected. Second, the 'principal place of business' standard was the basis for rampant forum shopping in US bankruptcies in the 1980s.

Westbrook also suggests the possibility of a 'multidimensional test' based on some combination of factors. He gives the example of a presumption based on place of incorporation 'rebuttable only by a clear showing that the center [of the debtor's main interests] was elsewhere.' This is the test employed in a model international insolvency law that Westbrook was instrumental in negotiating . . .

2. Is the 'Home Country' That of the Entity or the Group?

Multinational companies are almost invariably corporate groups. Some corporate groups operate a single, indivisible business, such as an airline. Individual corporations within the group may perform specific functions, such as holding title to aircraft, conducting operations, or obtaining financing, but none may have a business that could operate apart from the other corporations in the group. Such a group is referred to as having an 'integrated' business. At the opposite extreme, a conglomerate, particularly one that frequently buys and sells businesses, carefully may avoid any interdependence among the businesses it owns, so that the group could sell any of them without affecting the others. Each such business might be owned by a 'stand-alone' subsidiary. Most corporate groups probably are somewhere between these extremes. They operate businesses that are integrated, to some degree, but that they can, with varying degrees of effort and expense, separate.

Regardless of how one defines 'home country,' the home country of a corporate group often will be different from the home countries of corporations within the group. For example, assume that Parent Corporation is a holding company whose only significant assets are its stock holdings in its three subsidiaries. Parent Corporation is incorporated in country P where it maintains its 'world headquarters.' Each of the three subsidiaries has its place of incorporation, headquarters, and operations in each of three countries other than P. P probably would be considered the home country of the group, but P could not be considered the home country of any subsidiary.

In which 'home country' would the bankruptcy of one or more members of this corporate group take place? That is, would all file in the home country of the group? Would each entity file in its own home country? Or might the home country determination depend on which corporations were in financial difficulty, which ones filed, or the degree of integration among them?

No answer to these questions describes a system that could capture the supposed benefits of universalism. A rule that put the bankruptcy of each entity in the home country of the entity would split the bankruptcy of the group among up to four countries. If the group operated an integrated business, that would, by the universalists' reasoning, prevent the reorganization of the business or the liquidation of its assets for their best price.

A rule that put the bankruptcy of the entire group in the home country of the group would lead to anomalous results and the resulting system would be manipulated easily. The anomalous results would occur when only a single, entirely foreign subsidiary was in financial difficulty. Even if that entity did business only in country A and had no ties to country P other than ownership by a holding company located in P, its bankruptcy would take place in P, the home country of the debtor's group. To illustrate, if the stock of the corporation that owned Rockefeller Center in New York had been owned by a Japanese company, the bankruptcy of Rockefeller Center would have been in Japan, even if the Japanese parent had not been in financial difficulty.

Professor Westbrook argues that in the long term there is no alternative but univer-   **15.08**
salism, and that the most difficult problem is to fashion an interim solution pending movement to true universalism. That solution lies in his view in the 'modified universalism' proposed in the American Law Institute Transnational Insolvency Project.

Jay L Westbrook, 'A Global Solution to Multinational Default' 98 Mich L Rev 2276, 2300–1, 2302 and 2309 (2000–2001)

Modified universalism is the approach that I have suggested as an interim or transitional solution. I believe that the 'cooperative territorialism' proposed by Professor LoPucki ... is one form of modified territorialism. The operation of modified universalism is illustrated by In re Culmer, one of the leading cases decided under section 304 of the Bankruptcy Code. There, a Bahamian corporation had assets in the United States and creditors had attached those assets, giving them certain priority rights under United States law. The Bahamian liquidators brought a petition under section 304 seeking a stay of the United States collection actions and turnover of the assets for distribution in the Bahamian proceeding. That they succeeded in both requests reflected the court's universalist view: because the Bahamian action satisfied the statute's choice-of-forum rule, ancillary relief was indicated. The universalist perspective was emphasized by the fact that the relief included turnover of assets, in effect dispatching the creditors to the Bahamas to assert their claims. On the other hand, the court did not grant the relief until it had satisfied itself that Bahamian law could be trusted to be fair and was in general terms similar to United States law. That inquiry justifies the adjective 'modified,' because the deference to the preferred universalist forum was not automatic, but required a practical finding of fairness and rough similarity. Presumably, a court committed to cooperative territorialism would have denied the petition, leaving the liquidators or other creditors to bring a full parallel United States bankruptcy, in which the court might cooperate on some level with the foreign court, but only within limits ensuring that creditors in the United States proceeding were given first access to the United States assets.

The key difference between the two approaches is that modified universalism takes a worldwide perspective, seeking solutions that come as close as possible to the ideal of a single-court, single-law resolution, while territorialism of any sort seems to me to be defined by a conviction that local creditors have vested rights in whatever assets can be seized by their courts when insolvency looms ...

The difficulties created by differing priority systems constitute one of the major complications of parallel proceedings. A creditor or group of creditors that is the beneficiary of a domestic priority may assert that this right to priority in distribution must trump an effort at cooperation, whether it be cooperation in a plan of reorganization, by transfer of assets, or otherwise. Such assertions could block any important attempt at cooperation. Priority rules may be unwaivable except by unanimous agreement, a standard that encourages certain parties to 'hold out' for their personal advantage despite agreement among the great majority of creditors, both privileged and general.

The inevitable consequence is that real cooperation in a territorial system is necessarily very limited. Instead, recoveries will turn on the fortuitous or manipulated location of assets and the results will be highly unpredictable ex ante. Modified universalism attempts to achieve some of the benefits of universalism in a multi-forum, multi-law world. It requires each court to become part of an international system for maximizing value and fairness in the management of the default. In either an ancillary or parallel approach under national law, modified universalism permits the court to view the default and its resolution (liquidation or reorganization) from a worldwide perspective and to cooperate with other courts to produce results as close to those that would arise from a single proceeding as local law will permit. Because it will develop experience, methods, and precedents through such cooperation, modified universalism will provide essential background for the development of a convention establishing a universalist system ...

A territorial system, being asymmetrical to a global market, has two serious weaknesses: the consequences of a general default depend upon the location of assets, and the laws of each jurisdiction differ greatly. International bankruptcy is reduced to a game of musical chairs in which creditors cannot know in advance where the assets of the debtor will be located when the music stops. These flaws produce three bad results: a) distribution results are unpredictable; b) the debtor, perhaps in collusion with a favored creditor, can engage in strategic behavior up to and including fraud, by manipulation of asset location; and c) claims must be made, and administration and litigation must be conducted, in multiple jurisdictions at far greater cost. By contrast, in a world with a universalist convention establishing one bankruptcy law and one court system to administer it, the law would be highly predictable, movement of assets would be irrelevant, and the entire process could be administered efficiently. The consequence would be a great reduction in risk premiums and transaction costs and a great increase in fairness and efficiency.

15.09 The principle emerging in recent years is that of qualified universality, which divides proceedings into main proceedings and territorial proceedings. Main proceedings can be instituted only in the jurisdiction where the debtor has its centre of main interests (COMI) but encompass all assets worldwide. Territorial proceedings may be instituted in other jurisdictions where the debtor has an establishment but are limited to local assets, any surplus resulting from a winding-up in the territorial proceedings being handed over to the administrator of the main proceedings. That principle is encapsulated both in the UNCITRAL Model Law on cross-border insolvency and in the EC Insolvency Regulation. In addition, national courts have increasingly accepted that there are cases in which their role is ancillary to that of foreign courts in which main proceedings are opened and is essentially that of providing assistance to such foreign courts and foreign administrators.

15.10 The theories discussed above do not exhaust the possibilities. Professor Robert Rasmussen has advanced an imaginative contractualist theory under which a company would be able to designate in advance, in its instrument of incorporation, the applicable law, forum and insolvency regime applicable in the event of a cross-border insolvency.[3] However, this has encountered strong criticism both on theoretical and on practical grounds.

A further important principle is that of non-discrimination against foreign cred-   **15.11**
itors. The concept of territorial proceedings is not incompatible with this principle. All creditors, whether local or otherwise, may participate and prove for a dividend in such proceedings as well as in the main proceedings, though to preserve the principle of equality among creditors a creditor who has already received a dividend in one proceeding will usually be precluded from receiving a dividend in the other proceeding until the creditors in the latter have received a dividend at the same rate. This is the so-called hotch-pot rule.

We turn now to consider the UNCITRAL Model Law on Cross-Border Insolvency   **15.12**
and the European Insolvency Regulation. Neither of these instruments seeks to harmonize substantive rules of insolvency law. The nearest the European Community Regulation gets to this is through its rules on the applicable law in insolvency proceedings, while the Model Law does not even have choice-of-law rules of any kind, only rules relating to jurisdiction and recognition.

C. The UNCITRAL Model Law on Cross-Border Insolvency

The UNCITRAL Model Law on cross-border insolvency, adopted in 1997, was the   **15.13**
product of collaboration between UNCITRAL and the International Association of Insolvency Practitioners (INSOL International). UNCITRAL has also included in its booklet on the Model Law a *Guide to Enactment* for the assistance of legislators and others seeking an understanding of the Model Law.

Nature and purpose

To see the factors that gave impetus to the preparation of the Model Law one has   **15.14**
only to refer to the Resolution of 30 January 1998 passed by the General Assembly of the United Nations when promulgating the Model Law.

> **RESOLUTION ADOPTED BY THE GENERAL ASSEMBLY**
> [*on the report of the Sixth Committee (A/52/649)*]
> 52/158. Model Law on Cross-Border Insolvency of the United Nations Commission on International Trade Law

---

[3] Robert K Rasmussen, 'A New Approach to Transnational Insolvencies' 19 Mich J Intl L 1 (1997).

The General Assembly,

Recalling its resolution 2205 (XXI) of 17 December 1966, by which it created the United Nations Commission on International Trade Law with a mandate to further the progressive harmonization and unification of the law of international trade and in that respect to bear in mind the interests of all peoples, in particular those of developing countries, in the extensive development of international trade,

Noting that increased cross-border trade and investment leads to greater incidence of cases where enterprises and individuals have assets in more than one State,

Noting also that when a debtor with assets in more than one State becomes subject to an insolvency proceeding, there often exists an urgent need for cross-border cooperation and coordination in the supervision and administration of the insolvent debtor's assets and affairs,

Considering that inadequate coordination and cooperation in cases of cross-border insolvency reduce the possibility of rescuing financially troubled but viable businesses, impede a fair and efficient administration of cross-border insolvencies, make it more likely that the debtor's assets would be concealed or dissipated and hinder reorganizations or liquidations of debtors' assets and affairs that would be the most advantageous for the creditors and other interested persons, including the debtors and the debtors' employees,

Noting that many States lack a legislative framework that would make possible or facilitate effective cross-border coordination and cooperation,

Convinced that fair and internationally harmonized legislation on cross-border insolvency that respects the national procedural and judicial systems and is acceptable to States with different legal, social and economic systems would contribute to the development of international trade and investment,

Considering that a set of internationally harmonized model legislative provisions on cross-border insolvency is needed to assist States in modernizing their legislation governing cross-border insolvency,

1 *Expresses its appreciation* to the United Nations Commission on International Trade Law for completing and adopting the Model Law on Cross-Border Insolvency contained in the annex to the present resolution;

2 *Requests* the Secretary-General to transmit the text of the Model Law, together with the Guide to Enactment of the Model Law prepared by the Secretariat, to Governments and interested bodies;

3 *Recommends* that all States review their legislation on cross-border aspects of insolvency to determine whether the legislation meets the objectives of a modern and efficient insolvency system and, in that review, give favourable consideration to the Model Law, bearing in mind the need for an internationally harmonized legislation governing instances of cross-border insolvency;

4 *Recommends also* that all efforts be made to ensure that the Model Law, together with the Guide, become generally known and available.

15.15 The model law has no binding force in itself: it is simply a model which Contracting States are free to adopt, adapt or ignore as they think fit. Nevertheless the Model Law has steadily grown in influence and has now been adopted in a number of countries, including Japan, Poland, South Africa, the United States and the United

Kingdom. Its primary purpose is to provide primacy to foreign main proceedings, with local jurisdiction elsewhere over local assets, to promote co-operation between courts and office-holders and to prescribe recognition of foreign proceedings and foreign office-holders ('foreign representatives') in local courts. It is thus essentially jurisdictional and procedural and contains no rules of substantive law or choice-of-law rules.

Sphere of application

The provisions of the Model Law have to be read from the standpoint of the State **15.16** that has adopted it ('the enacting State'). Courts of another State are 'foreign' courts even if they too have adopted the Model Law. Article 1 defines the sphere of application of the Model Law to cover four situations:

(1) A foreign court or a foreign representative seeks assistance in the enacting State in connection with a foreign proceeding.
(2) Assistance is sought in a foreign court in a connection with a proceeding under the insolvency law of the enacting State.
(3) A foreign proceeding and a proceeding under the insolvency law of the enacting State in respect of the same debtor are taking place concurrently.
(4) Creditors or other interested persons in a foreign State have an interest in requesting the commencement of or participating in a proceeding under the insolvency law of the enacting State.

'Foreign proceeding' means a collective judicial or administrative proceeding in a **15.17** foreign State, including an interim proceeding, pursuant to a law relating to insolvency in which proceeding the assets and affairs of the debtor are subject to control or supervision by a foreign court, for the purpose of reorganization or liquidation.[4] So only collective proceedings for the purpose of reorganization or winding-up are covered. The Model Law focuses on two types of foreign proceeding, namely foreign main proceedings, that is, proceedings which take place where the debtor has its COMI, and foreign non-main proceedings, that is, foreign proceedings, other than foreign main proceedings, taking place in a State where the debtor has an establishment. Given this dichotomy, which runs through the Model Law, one might have supposed that the definition of 'foreign proceedings' would refer to proceedings that are either main or non-main foreign proceedings, but curiously it does not. Accordingly on a literal construction there can be foreign proceedings which are neither main nor non-main, and there appear to be various provisions which apply to such proceedings. It may be, however, that the scope of the definition of 'foreign proceedings' is limited by Article 17(2), which in speaking of recognition confines itself to main and non-main proceedings.

---

[4] Art 2(a).

Access by foreign representative and recognition of foreign proceedings

15.18 A foreign representative is given a right of direct access to a court in the enacting State,[5] a *locus standi* to commence an insolvency proceeding in that State,[6] and the same right to commence and participate in a proceeding in that State as is given to local creditors.[7] In addition, a foreign representative may apply to the court of the enacting State for recognition of the foreign proceeding in which he has been appointed.[8] The effect of these provisions on proceedings in an enacting State is that problems of recognition of the status of a foreign representative or foreign proceedings are avoided. However, in contrast to the position under the European Community Insolvency Regulation recognition of foreign proceedings before a court of competent jurisdiction under the Model Law is not automatic but has to be the subject of an application by the foreign representative. The effect of Article 17(2) would appear to be that the court in the enacting State is not bound to recognize a foreign proceeding that is neither a main nor a non-main proceeding, because it is opened in a State in which the debtor has neither its COMI nor an establishment.

15.19 The foreign representative may also apply for a variety of forms of relief designed to safeguard the debtor's assets or to provide information as to the debtor's assets, affairs, rights, obligations or liabilities.[9]

Automatic stay

15.20 Recognition of a foreign main proceeding has the effect of imposing an automatic stay on the commencement or continuance of proceedings against the debtor or his assets and the levy of execution on such assets,[10] though this is subject to exceptions provided by the insolvency law of the enacting State, which might, for example, permit secured creditors and title-retention sellers to enforce their security and title-retention rights against local assets despite a foreign liquidation.

Co-operation with foreign courts and foreign representatives

15.21 A central plank of the Model Law is the set of provisions in Chapter IV directed to co-operation between courts and direct communication between courts and foreign representatives. These include specific provision for concurrent proceedings in a foreign State and the enacting State and formalize and reinforce co-operative arrangements devised by courts and office-holders themselves, based on protocols agreed between the office-holders and approved by their respective courts.[11]

---

[5] Art 9.   [6] Art 11.   [7] Art 13.   [8] Art 15(1).   [9] Art 21.
[10] Art 20.   [11] See below, paras 15.22 ff.

D. Judicial Co-operation in Concurrent Insolvency Proceedings

Independently of statute or international convention, the potential problems aris- **15.22** ing from concurrent insolvency proceedings in different jurisdictions have been greatly alleviated by the evolution of mechanisms for co-operation between the two courts concerned and between the two insolvency administrators.

Roy Goode, *Principles of Corporate Insolvency Law* (3rd edn, Sweet & Maxwell, London, 2005) [14–27]

It has long been recognised that the institution of concurrent insolvency proceedings in courts of different countries may raise complex questions, particularly where the insolvency law of both countries adopts the principle of universality, with the potential for conflicts between the laws of the two jurisdictions and the orders of their respective courts. That these problems have not proved insurmountable is largely due to the spirit of co-operation and mutual assistance prevailing among the judges and to legislation such as that embodied in s426 of the Insolvency Act which has just been examined.

One of the most remarkable examples of judicial co-operation was triggered by the collapse of the Maxwell group of companies following the death of the business tycoon Robert Maxwell, a collapse resulting in major litigation in many different jurisdictions. Maxwell Communications Corp plc ('MCC') was an English holding company with a large number of subsidiaries scattered around the world. MCC filed under Chapter 11 of the US Bankruptcy Code and soon afterwards obtained an administration order in England. The peculiar feature of the case was that both sets of proceedings were primary proceedings, so that each court had jurisdiction over the assets of the company on a worldwide basis. The English proceedings were controlled by Hoffmann J, the US proceedings by Judge Tina L Brozman, a judge of the Bankruptcy Court for the Southern District of New York. The English administrators were anxious to be heard in the US proceedings, and Judge Brozman fully recognised them as parties in interest but was anxious to create a mechanism that would facilitate co-operation and avoid conflict. To that end she appointed an examiner. The examiner and the joint administrators then collaborated with a view to harmonising the two sets of proceedings for the benefit of all creditors and eventually agreed on a Protocol to govern their respective roles and powers. Both courts then responded positively to the invitation to approve the Protocol, each court agreeing that it would to the necessary degree defer its jurisdiction to that of the other. The examiner and the administrators then settled upon a reorganisation plan under Chapter 11 and a scheme of arrangement under s425 of the Companies Act 1985. Simultaneously Judge Brozman approved the plan under Chapter 11 and Hoffmann J the scheme of arrangement under s425. The combination of the plan and the scheme produced the single distribution mechanism upon which the success of the whole operation so crucially depended, differences in the two sets of governing laws being resolved by accommodations on all sides. The result was to save substantial sums for the creditors in both jurisdictions. Thus began the practice by which protocols are agreed between the office-holders in the different jurisdictions and approved by their respective courts. Common provisions in such protocols include: a statement confirming the sovereignty and independence of the two courts involved and recording that each of the two office holders is subject only to the jurisdiction of its own court; a recognition by each court of the proceedings opened by the other and of any stays granted; the status of the two office-holders and the right of each to be heard as a foreign representative in the other proceedings; a direction to the office-holder in each court, while respecting this sovereignty and independence of the two courts, to co-operate with each other in connection with the management of the parallel insolvencies and to harmonise and co-ordinate their activities; a provision for similar co-operation between the two courts with a view to establishing methods of communication, with or without counsel, co-ordinating rulings and conducting joint hearings via a telephone link; an identification of the various cross-border issues to be addressed (*eg* reorganisation, treatment of claims, realisation of assets); a provision for mutual disclosure of relevant documents and for notice to all interested parties of any court motions; provision for the venue of applications for relief, which will depend on the nature of the relief sought and whether it relates to property within the jurisdiction of one of the courts; and a direction to the two office-holders to submit to their respective courts reorganisation plans in substantially the same form.

Evan D Flaschen and Ronald J Silverman, 'Cross-Border Insolvency Cooperation Protocols' 33 Tex Intl LJ 587, 592–3 (1998)

The Protocols created subsequent to Maxwell have built on the Maxwell example and further developed the manner in which Protocols may be utilized. One such example is the Everfresh Beverages proceedings conducted in the United States and Canada.

Everfresh Beverages Inc was a Delaware corporation headquartered in Chicago. Everfresh operated an integrated manufacturing and distribution business with plants in Illinois, Michigan, and Ontario. As a result, it had creditors and suppliers in both the United States and Canada. Needing to reorganize, Everfresh commenced a Chapter 11 petition in the US Bankruptcy Court for the Southern District of New York and filed for protection under the Canadian Bankruptcy and Insolvency Act in the Commercial Division of the Ontario Court of Justice in Toronto, each on the same day. From the outset, both the Honorable Mr Justice Farley, Chief Judge of the Commercial Division of the Ontario Court of Justice, and US Bankruptcy Judge Jeffrey Gallet encouraged the implementation of a cross-border Protocol to coordinate the US and Canadian proceedings.

Perhaps the most significant aspect of the Everfresh proceedings, and the Protocol formulated for their coordination, was the use made of the Cross-Border Insolvency Concordat (the Concordat) drafted by Committee J of the Section on Business Law of the International Bar Association. The Concordat is a nonstatutory set of guidelines, based in part on the Protocols implemented in the Maxwell and Olympia & York cases, that provides suggested avenues for coordinating multinational insolvency proceedings. In modeling the Everfresh Protocol on the Concordat, the parties were able to specify up front how a wide range of both procedural and substantive matters would be addressed by the US and Canadian courts.

The Everfresh Protocol explicitly addressed a broad range of issues likely to arise in cross-border, dual insolvency proceedings, including choice of law, choice of forum, claims resolution, and avoidance actions. For example, creditors were given the express right to file claims in either the US or the Canadian proceeding. The US court was allotted the responsibility of dealing with assets located in the United States and addressing claims governed primarily by US law. Conversely, the Canadian court was allotted the responsibility of dealing with assets located in Canada and addressing claims governed primarily by Canadian law. Likewise, proceeds of assets sold were to be dealt with by the court in the jurisdiction in which the assets were located. Ultimately, the Everfresh Protocol provided that the plans of reorganization to be implemented in the United States and Canada be coordinated to provide comparable classification and treatment of creditors. Thus, with reference to the Concordat, the Everfresh Protocol was able to express in detail the guiding principles of cooperation and coordination that were to govern many facets of the Everfresh cross-border proceedings.

In the Livent insolvency, where there were parallel proceedings in New York and **15.23** Toronto, the degree of co-operation was even more striking in that the Protocol was approved by the two courts in a joint order under the signature of the two judges and subsequently differences that had arisen between the two insolvency administrators as to the interpretation of the Protocol were resolved by a similarly signed joint order. It is, of course, important to have transparency in cross-border collaboration between courts, which should take place only with the full knowledge and consent of the parties.

UNITED STATES BANKRUPTCY COURT SOUTHERN
DISTRICT OF NEW YORK

In re	}	Chapter 11
	)	Case No 98 B 48312 (AJG)
LIVENT (US) INC, et al	)	
	)	(Jointly Administered)
Debtors	)	

ONTARIO

SUPERIOR COURT OF JUSTICE
(COMMERCIAL LIST)

THE HONOURABLE MR.	)
	)
JUSTICE GROUND	)

IN THE MATTER OF THE APPLICATION OF LIVENT INC.
under section 4,5,6,7,11,17 and 18.6(2) of the *Companies Creditors Arrangement Act*, RSO 1985, c C-36 and as amended under the *Business Corporations Act*, RSO 1990, C b-16;

CROSS-BORDER INSOLVENCY PROTOCOL **WHEREAS**, on November 18, 1998 (the 'Petition Date'), each of Livent Inc, Livent (US) Inc, Livent Realty (NEW YORK) Inc and Livent Realty (Chicago) Inc. (collectively, the 'Debtors') filed, in the United States Bankruptcy Court for the Southern District of New York (together with any other Court having jurisdiction over these bankruptcy cases, the 'Bankruptcy Court'), a voluntary petition for relief under Chapter 11 of title 11 of the United States Code (the 'Bankruptcy Code'); and

WHEREAS, the Debtors continue in the possession of their respective properties and the management of their respective businesses as debtors in possession pursuant to sections 1107 and 1108 of the Bankruptcy Code. These Chapter 11 cases (the 'Chapter 11 Cases') have been consolidated for procedural purposes only and are being jointly administered pursuant to an order of the Bankruptcy Court; and

WHEREAS, the estate of Livent Inc ('Livent'), one of the Debtors, is being substantially administered in the United States under the jurisdiction of the Bankruptcy Court; and

WHEREAS, on November 19, 1998, to protect the estate of Livent against the actions of creditors beyond the personal jurisdiction of the Bankruptcy Court, Livent sought and received protection from its creditors in the Superior Court of Justice (the 'Canadian Court'), pursuant to the Companies Creditors Arrangement Act (the 'CCAA'). In connection with that proceeding (the 'Canadian Proceeding'), the accounting firm of Ernst & Young Inc ('E&Y') has been appointed Monitor by the Canadian Court to review and oversee Livent's financial performance and to assist it in the development of its Protocol; and

WHEREAS, on December 1, 1998, the United States Trustee appointed an official committee of unsecured creditors (the 'Creditors' Committee'). On December 4, 1998, the Canadian Court, and on December 3, 1998, the Bankruptcy Court, approved on a final basis a $25 million debtor in possession financing facility (the 'DIP Facility') with Angelo Gordon & Co. (the 'DIP Lender'). On February 22, 1999, the Debtors consummated the debtor in possession financing facility with the DIP Lender. No trustee or examiner has been appointed in the Chapter 11 Cases; and

WHEREAS, Canadian Imperial Bank of Commerce ('CIBC') believes it holds security over all of the assets of the Debtors; and

WHEREAS, the Debtors are a leading, vertically integrated producer of live theatrical entertainment, as well as an operator of theatres in important North American markets. Among other things, the Debtors are engaged in the business of acquiring American, Canadian and international theatrical stage rights and ancillary rights (including foreign licensing rights, merchandising rights, sponsorships rights and cast album rights) and developing, producing, managing, marketing and licensing theatrical and other forms of live entertainment throughout the United States, Canada and elsewhere throughout the world, as well as owning and managing theatres; and

WHEREAS, a framework of general principles should be agreed upon to address, among other things, issues that are likely to arise in connection with the cross-border insolvency proceedings of Livent, including, without limitation, (a) the sale of assets; (b) the distribution and disposition or the proceeds of sale of the assets; (c) the determination of claims asserted against Livent, and the allowability and priority status of such claims; (d) the filing and implementation of a plan of reorganization under the Bankruptcy Code and a scheme or proposal under the CCAA (the 'Proposal'); and (e) general administrative matters, and that an agreement upon such matters is essential to the orderly and efficient administrative of these cross-border cases; and

WHEREAS, the purpose of this protocol (the 'Protocol') is to protect the interests of all parties in interest wherever located and to protect the integrity of the process by which the Chapter 11 Cases and the Canadian Proceeding is administered.

NOW THEREFORE, is adjudged, ordered and decreed as follows:

1. The Debtors, the Creditors' Committee and the Monitor will (i) have regard for the proceedings initiated by Livent under Chapter 11 of the Bankruptcy Code in

the Bankruptcy Court and under the CCAA in the Canadian Court; (ii) co-operate with actions taken in either the Bankruptcy Court or the Canadian Court or both; and (iii) take steps to coordinate their respective administrations under the Bankruptcy Code and the CCAA in the Bankruptcy Court and the Canadian Court. Either Court shall honor and enforce any orders of the other Court, directed to persons within the jurisdiction of the other Court or who appeared on the motion for such order, related to investigations of any of the Debtors' assets and liabilities.

2. The Debtors, the Creditors' Committee and the Monitor, and any other official representative that may be appointed by the Bankruptcy Court or the Canadian Court, and CIBC and the DIP Lender shall receive notice of all proceedings in accordance with the practices of the respective Courts, and have the right to appear in all proceedings in any forum, whether in the Bankruptcy Court or the Canadian Court. Livent and the Monitor shall be subject to jurisdiction in both for any matter related to the insolvency proceedings, but appearing in a forum shall not subject it to jurisdiction for any other purpose in the forum state, except to the extent otherwise set forth herein to the contrary.

3. All creditors, equity interest holders and other parties in interest of Livent shall have the right to appear in any forum to the same extent as creditors of the forum state, regardless of whether they have filed claims in that particular forum. All creditors or Livent shall have the opportunity to file a notice of appearance with the Clerk of the Bankruptcy Court, the Alexander Hamilton US Custom House, One Bowling Green, 5th Floor, New York, New York 10004 or to participate in the proceedings in the Canadian Court; *provided, however*, that such filing or participation shall subject such creditor, equity interest holder or party in interest to the personal jurisdiction in the Court in which the notice or appearance is filed or made only for the purposes of such proceeding; *provided, further*, that appearance by the Creditors' Committee in the Canadian proceeding shall not form a basis for personal jurisdiction in Canada over the members of the Creditors' Committee.

4. Information publicly available in any forum state shall be publicly available in both forum. To the extent permitted, non-public information shall be made available to official representatives of the Debtors, including the Creditors' Committee and any other official committee appointed in Livent's Chapter 11 Case and shall be shard with other official representative, CIBC and the DIP Lender, subject to the appropriate confidentially arrangements.

5. Any transactions outside the ordinary course of business concerning the sale or lease or use of Livent's assets located solely in Canada shall be subject to the sole approval of the Canadian Court. Any transactions outside the ordinary course of business concerning the sale or lease or use of Livent's assets located solely in the United States shall be subject to the sole approval of the Bankruptcy Court. Any transactions outside the ordinary course of business concerning the sale of lease or use of Livent's assets located both Canada and the United States, including but not limited to a sale of all or substantially all of the assets of the collective Debtors, shall be subject to the joint jurisdiction and approval of the Bankruptcy Court and the Canadian Court, unless otherwise ordered by both the Bankruptcy Court and the Canadian Court upon request of the Debtors or any other parties in interest.

6. The Bankruptcy and Canadian Courts may conduct joint hearings with respect to any matter related to the conduct, administration, determination or disposition of any aspect of the Chapter 11 Cases and the Canadian Proceedings where considered

by both Courts to be necessary or advisable and in particular, without limiting the generality of the foregoing, to facilitate or coordinate the proper and efficient conduct of the Chapter 11 Cases and Canadian Proceedings. With respect to any such hearings, unless otherwise ordered, the following directions are made:

(a) A telephone and/or video link shall be established such that both Courts shall be able to simultaneously hear the proceedings in the other Court. The Judge of the Bankruptcy Court and the Justice of the Canadian Court may appear and sit jointly in either Court as agreed between the Judge and Justice, subject to subsection (f) of this paragraph, provided, that, in such instance, creditors, equity interest holders and parties in interest may appear and be heard in person or at the courtroom of the Judge or Justice who as travelled to appear in the other courtroom.

(b) Any party, intending to rely upon any written evidentiary material in support of a submission to the Canadian Court or the Bankruptcy Court in connection with any joint application shall file in each Court materials, which shall be identical insofar as possible and shall be consistent with the procedural and evidentiary rules and requirements of each Court, in advance of such application. If a party has not previously appeared in or attorned or does not wish to attorn to the jurisdiction of either court it shall be entitled to file such material without, by the act of filing, being deemed to have attorned to the jurisdiction of the Court in which such material is filed, so long as it does not request in its materials or submissions any affirmative relief from the Court to which it does not wish to attorn.

(c) Submissions or applications by any party shall be made only to the Court in which it is appearing unless specifically given leave by the other Court to make submissions or applications to it.

(d) The Judge of the Bankruptcy Court and the Justice of the Canadian Court who will hear any such application shall be entitled to communicate with one another in advance of the said applications, with or without counsel being present, to establish guidelines for the orderly making of submissions and rendering of decisions by the Bankruptcy and the Canadian Courts, and to deal with any other procedural, administrative or preliminary matters.

(e) The Judge of the Bankruptcy Court and the Justice of the Canadian Court, having heard any such application, shall be entitled to communicate with one another after any such application, with or without counsel present, for the purpose of determining whether substantively consistent rulings can be made by both Courts having regard to the applicable jurisprudence in each jurisdiction and to coordinate and resolve procedural or non-substantive matters relating to such applications.

(f) In the event of a sale of all or substantially all of the assets of the collective Debtors in accordance with section 363 of the Bankruptcy Code and any related authority under the CCAA before the Courts, all parties wishing to launch a competing bid for the assets shall appear before the Bankruptcy Court pursuant to bidding procedures (including bidding protections) established by the Bankruptcy Court consented to by the Monitor for conducting such sale. The Justice of the Canadian Court will join with the Bankruptcy Court and appear and sit for the purpose of jointly conducting the sale.

7. All creditors of Livent (US) Inc, Livent Realty (New York) Inc and Livent Realty (Chicago) Inc (collectively, the 'US Debtors') must file their proofs of claim against the US Debtors with the Clerk of the Bankruptcy Court, the Alexander Hamilton US Custom House, One Bowling Green, 5th Floor, New York, New York 10004.

8. Any creditor or equity security holder of Livent may file a proof of claim or interest in either the Bankruptcy Court or with the Monitor in the Canadian Proceeding; provided, however, that the resolution of such claim or interest shall be governed by the provisions of paragraph 10. If a creditor files a claim both in the Bankruptcy Court and with the Monitor in the Canadian Proceeding, the last timely filed claim shall govern. A timely failed proof of claim in either the Bankruptcy Court or Canadian Proceeding will be deemed timely filed both in the Bankruptcy Court with the Monitor under the Canadian Proceeding. The Debtors and the Monitor will endeavor to co-ordinate notice procedures and established the same deadline for the filing of the claims against the Debtors in both the Bankruptcy Court and the Canadian Proceeding, and all other matters regarding the filing, reviewing and objecting to claims.

9. The Bankruptcy Court shall have exclusive jurisdiction over all claims against the US Debtors.

10. The Bankruptcy Court shall have jurisdiction over all claims asserted against Livent governed principally by the laws of the United States or any of its states unless, with respect to any particular claim, the Canadian Court is a more appropriate forum in view of all of the circumstances. The Canadian Court shall have jurisdiction over all claims asserted against Livent governed principally by the laws of Canada or any of its provinces and territories unless, with respect to any particular claim, the Bankruptcy Court is a more appropriate forum in view of all circumstances. Subject to the last sentence of paragraph 13, the adjudicating forum shall decide the amount, value, allowability, priority, classification and treatment of claims filed in any plan of reorganization or Proposal and a creditor's rights to collateral and set off using a choice of law analysis based upon the choice of law principles applicable in that forum. Nothing herein shall limit the right of any party-in-interest to object to claims to the extent permitted under Section 502 (a) of the Bankruptcy code and the Bankruptcy Rules and any related authority under the CCAA. Nothing herein shall limit or modify the Order of the Bankruptcy Court, dated April 15, 1999, authorizing and approving the Management Retention Incentive and Severance Plan.

11. All executory contracts, other than employment contracts to which Livent is a party, and unexpired leases between or among Livent and any party (including any of the U.S. Debtors) which is a Person subject to the personal jurisdiction of the Bankruptcy Court shall be subject to and governed by the provisions of section 365 of the Bankruptcy Code. All executory contracts and unexpired leases between or among Livent and parties which are Persons not subject to the personal jurisdiction of the Bankruptcy Court and all employment contracts to which Livent is a party shall be subject to and governed by the provisions of the CCAA.

12. Neither this Proposal nor any actions taken pursuant hereto is intended nor shall it have any affect on the rights of creditors, the Monitor, or the estates of the Debtors with regard to the applicability of Section 508 (a) of the Bankruptcy

Code and any similar provisions under the CCAA, it being intended that such Section 508 (a) be, to the extent applicable, enforced in both fora.

13. The proceeds of any transaction other than a transaction involving the sale of all or substantially all of the assets of the collective Debtors shall be used by the Debtors to fund working capital needs subject to further or existing order of the adjudicating Court, including but not limited to orders governing the use of cash collateral. The proceeds of any transaction involving the sale of all or substantially all of the assets of the collective Debtors shall be held in escrow, by an agent acceptable to the Debtors and the Monitor and approved by the adjudicating Court, pending distribution through a plan of reorganization and/or a Proposal or otherwise pursuant to an order approved by both Courts; provided, that nothing contained herein shall be construed to prohibit the Debtors from paying amounts owing to the DIP Lender from the proceeds of such sale pursuant to the terms of the DIP Facility and in accordance with the existing orders of the Courts approving the DIP Facility. The allocation among each of the Debtor's estates of the proceeds generated from a sale of all or substantially all of the assets of the collective Debtors shall be determined by: (i) the Bankruptcy Court and the Canadian Court at a joint hearing, in respect of the proportion of proceeds to be allocated to the estate of Livent Inc; and (ii) the Bankruptcy Court, using a choice of law analysis is applicable, based upon the choice of law principles applicable in that forum, in respect of all other allocation matters.

14. The provisions of section 363 (m) of the Bankruptcy Code shall apply in both proceedings to any transaction involving all or substantially all of the assets of the collective Debtors.

15. A 'Person' (as defined in section 101 (41) of the Bankruptcy Code) shall not be subject to a forum's substantive laws, including, without limitation, avoidance rules and sections 510, 544, 545, 546, 547, 548, 549, 550, and 551 of the Bankruptcy Code, unless, using a choice of law analysis based upon the principals of international law applicable in the forum, such Person would be subject to the forum's substantive laws in a lawsuit on the same transaction in a non-insolvency proceedings. No avoiding actions will be taken by the Monitor in Canada without the express written consent of the Debtors or as may be directed by the Canadian Court.

16. For greater particularity, all lien claims, trust claims or actions in debt by the City of Toronto or for goods and services lien claimants (the "Construction Lien Claimants") against Livent in respect of the Pantages Theather property and surrounding developments in Toronto, Ontario be subject to the jurisdiction of the Canadian Court, notwithstanding that any one or more of the Contraction Lien Claimants may have or maintain a US office or affiliate.

17. To the extent permitted by the laws of the respective jurisdiction and to the extent practicable and procedurally applicable, the Montior and Livent shall endeavor to submit a Proposal in Canada and a plan of reorganization in the United States substantially similar to each other and the Monitor and Livent shall endeavor to coordinate all procedures in connection therewith. In order to coordinate the contemporaneous filing of the Proposal, and the plan of reorganization, Livent shall take the actions necessary to seek extensions from time-to-time of the date

for the filing to the Proposal, and the Debtors shall take the actions necessary from time-to-time to seek extensions of the exclusive time period during which only the Debtors may file a plan of reorganization pursuant to Section 1121 of the Bankruptcy Code (the 'Exclusive Period'). Notwithstanding the foregoing, this paragraph is without prejudice to the rights of the Creditors' Committee or any other party in interest to oppose any extension of the Exclusive Period, seek a shortening of the Exclusive Period or file a plan of reorganization after expiration of the Exclusive Period.

18. Except with respect to matters where the Monitor and the other Canadian professionals appear before Bankruptcy Court pursuant to paragraph 2 hereof, the Canadian Court shall have sole jurisdiction and power over the Monitor, including, without limitation, its tenure in office, the conduct of the liquidation proceedings under Canadian law, the retention and compensation of the Monitor and other Canadian professionals, except as otherwise provided in paragraph (s) 19 and 20, and the hearing and determination of matters arising in the proceedings under Canadian law. The Monitor and other Canadian professionals shall be compensated for their services in accordance with Canadian principles under Canadian law, such that the Monitor and other the Canadian professionals are not required to file fee applications with the Bankruptcy Court, except as otherwise provided in paragraph 20.

19. The Bankruptcy Court shall have sole jurisdiction and power over the conduct of the Chapter 11 cases, the compensation of the professionals rendering service to the Debtors in the United States, and the hearing and determination of matters arising in the Chapter 11 cases.

20. Notwithstanding anything to the contrary, the Bankruptcy Court shall have sole jurisdiction and power over any professionals hired by the Creditors' Committee, including but not limited to Canadian professionals, and such professionals shall be retained and compensated according to the rules governing retention and compensation generally in chapter 11 cases.

21. The Protocol shall be without prejudice to the rights of the Debtors to seek the substantive consolidation of their estates before the Bankruptcy Court and the Canadian Court.

22. This Protocol shall be binding on and inure to the benefit of the parties hereto and their respective successors, assigns, representatives, heirs, executors, administrators, trustees (including any trustees of the Debtors, under Chapter 7 or 11 of the Bankruptcy Code), and receivers, receiver managers, trustees or custodians appointed under Canadian law, as the case may be.

23. Compliance with the Protocol may not be waived and the Protocol may not be amended or modified orally or in any other way or manner (including, without limitation, pursuant to a plan of reorganization of the Debtors) except with approval and authorization of the Bankruptcy Court and the Canadian Court.

24. Nothing contained herein shall alter the Debtors' obligations to pay fees due under 23 USC s 1930 (a) (6) based upon all disbursements made in any jurisdiction.

25. Nothing contained herein shall be construed to limit or modify the DIP Facility, the existing orders of the Court approving the DIP Facility, or the rights and obligations of the Debtors and the DIP Lender thereunder.

26. The Protocol shall be deemed effective upon its approval by the Bankruptcy Court and the Canadian Court.

Dated: New York, New York

June •, 1999

_____

UNITED STATES BANKRUPTCY JUDGE

Dated: Toronto, Canada

June •, 1999

_____

JUSTICE OF SUPERIOR COURT OF JUSTICE

UNITED STATES BANKRUPTCY
COURT SOUTHERN DISTRICT OF
NEW YORK

In re

LIVENT (US) INC, et al

Chapter 11
Case No 98 B 48312 (AJG)

Debtors

ONTARIO

SUPERIOR COURT
OF JUSTICE (COMMERCIAL
LIST)

THE HONOURABLE MR
JUSTICE GROUND

IN THE MATTER OF THE APPLICATION OF LIVENT INC.
under section 4,5,6,7,11,17 and 18.6(2) of the *Companies Creditors Arrangement Act*, RSO 1985, c C-36 and as amended under the *Business Corporations Act*, RSO 1990, C b-16;

CROSS-BORDER INSOLVENCY PROTOCOL

On the return of the motion for approval of the Cross-Border Insolvency Protocol in the within proceedings on June 4, 1999, objections to the draft protocol were raised by counsel for certain Canadian creditors. Having considered the submissions of counsel for the creditors, including the official committee of unsecured creditors (the 'Creditors Committee') appointed by the United States Trustee, the Debtors, the Monitor and other parties in interest, we have concluded as follows with respect to the various objections raised by counsel.

We are satisfied that the reference in the last sentence of paragraph 1 of the draft Protocol that 'Either Court shall honor and enforce orders of the other Court relating to the investigations of any of the Debtors' assets and liabilities' must, in the context of the paragraph and of the Protocol, be restricted to orders made pursuant to the Chapter 11 proceedings in the United States Bankruptcy Court and the CCAA proceedings in the Ontario Superior Court of Justice. We are aware of the concerns raised by certain parties in interest that the sentence would preclude a challenge to any such order based on lack of jurisdiction and our order will provide that such sentence be amended to add after the reference to 'orders of the other Court', the words 'directed to persons within the jurisdiction of the other court or who appeared on the motion for such order,'.

The submission that the definition of the 'Canadian Court' in the fourth recital to the Protocol should be amended to include reference to appellate courts and, presumably that the reference to the 'Bankruptcy Court' should be amended to refer to appellate courts in the United States, is in our view unnecessary. All appellate rights subsist regardless of the wording of the Protocol and to expand the definition of 'Canadian Court' and 'Bankruptcy Court' to include appellate courts would in our view be confusing and would not be an appropriate definition for many of the provisions of the Protocol.

The submissions with respect to paragraph 13 of the draft Protocol appear to us to be based on the premise that there is a clear division of dichotomy between Canadian assets, Canadian lenders, Canadian security and Canadian proceeds as opposed to United States assets, lenders, security and proceeds. This is clearly not the case. In the proceedings before the courts, there are lenders in both jurisdictions, cross-border security and cross-border guarantees and one of the stated purposes of the Protocol is to establish a process whereby the proceedings in the United States and Canada can proceed in any orderly and efficient manner to protect the interests of all creditors, the Debtors, the Monitor and other parties in interest wherever located and to avoid duplication of proceedings and conflict in the management of the Chapter 11 Cases and the Canadian Proceeding. We are conscious of the fact that the draft Protocol submitted to this Court has been approved by the most significant and representative creditors in both Canada and the United States and by the Monitor appointed by the Canadian Court. With respect to the concern expressed as to the escrow agent and the situs of proceeds of any sale of assets, it should be noted that the appointment of the escrow agent must be approved by the Monitor and by both courts and it would appear to us that this should satisfy any concerns that Canadian or US Creditors may have as to the escrow agent being located in, or holding the proceeds in, one jurisdiction or the other. As to the concern regarding the proceedings of any transaction, other than a sale of all or substantially all of the assets, being used for working capital needs, any such sale under the Protocol requires the approval of the appropriate court or courts and such court would take into account the application of the proceeds and any preferred or secured claims against the assets to be sold.

With respect to the allocation provisions of paragraph 13, it is our view that the allocation of the portion of the proceeds of a sale of all or substantially all of the assets to the estate of Livent Inc should be approved by the Canadian Court and the Bankruptcy Court in a joint hearing structured so that counsel may appear in either court to make submissions but that all other matters of allocation should be determined by the Bankruptcy Court which has jurisdiction over all five estates and our order will so provide.

With respect to the Submissions on paragraph 14 of the Protocol and the reference to section 363(m) of the Bankruptcy Code, which is cross-referenced in paragraph 10 of the draft Protocol, it is in our view essential that there be some certainty as to the risk being assumed by any prospective purchaser of assets as to the transaction being set aside in a subsequent court proceeding. The effect of these references in the Protocol is, in our view, simply that any person appealing from an order approving a sale must move for a stay of such sale, pending disposition of the appeal, within 10 days from the date of the original order of approval. It does not appear to us that it is particularly onerous on any prospective purchaser to be required to move for a stay during the time period and this does not affect the time periods during which the appellant must commence its appeal which will be governed by the applicable law, whether the Bankruptcy Code or the CCAA.

Dated: New York, New York

    June 11, 1999

UNITED STATES BANKRUPTCY JUDGE

Dated: New York, New York

    June 11, 1999

JUSTICE OF SUPERIOR COURT OF JUSTICE

E. The European Insolvency Regulation

Background to the Regulation

15.24 The failure of the 1995 EC Convention because of the United Kingdom's refusal to sign it proved a temporary setback. Within a relatively short time came a proposal for a European Community Regulation, which avoided the need for ratification by all Member States and also conferred power on the European Court of Justice to interpret the instrument without need of an express provision to that effect. The Regulation was made in 2000 and came into effect on 31 May 2002. Under European Community law a Regulation is binding on all Member States and is directly applicable without having to be implemented by domestic legislation; indeed, it is not permissible for Member States to domesticate a Regulation by transposing it into legislation. The Regulation took over most of the provisions of the 1995 Convention verbatim, thereby allowing recourse to the authoritative[12] Virgós-Schmit Report on the interpretation of the Convention to be used as a guide to interpretation of the Regulation. An amending Regulation made in 2005[13] substituted new Annexes A, B and C for those in the original Regulation.

---

[12] But not authorized, because the failure of the Convention meant that the Report was never formally endorsed. Nevertheless, it is very influential and widely cited for the purpose of interpreting the Regulation.

[13] Council Regulation (EC) 603/2005 of 12 April 2005 amending the lists of insolvency proceedings, winding-up proceedings and liquidators in Annexes A, B and C to Regulation (EC) 1346/2000 on insolvency proceedings (2005) OJ L100/1.

Scope of the Regulation

The Regulation applies only where the debtor company has its COMI within the **15.25** European Union and insolvency proceedings are opened in a Member State. Insolvency proceedings, that is, proceedings of a kind listed in Annex A to the Regulation, divide primarily into winding-up proceedings, in which the debtor's assets are collected in and realized and the proceeds distributed in accordance with the applicable insolvency law, and proceedings designed to lead to restructuring or reorganization of the debtor company.

Types of insolvency proceeding

Insolvency proceedings are of two kinds: main proceedings, that is, proceedings **15.26** opened within the territory of the debtor's COMI, and territorial proceedings, that is, proceedings opened in another Member State in which the debtor has an establishment. Main proceedings extend to all the debtor's assets worldwide, but control of assets located within a Member State in which territorial proceedings have been opened is subject to those proceedings, and only if creditors in those proceedings (which are not confined to local creditors but may include creditors in the main proceedings) are paid in full is the surplus handed over to the liquidator in the main proceedings. Territorial proceedings are limited to local assets and are themselves of two kinds: secondary proceedings, opened after the opening of main proceedings and confined to winding-up, and independent proceedings, opened prior to the opening of main proceedings and not so confined.[14] The liquidator in the main proceedings has extensive powers to intervene in any other proceedings,[15] which he may well want to do where, for example, the main proceedings are for reorganization and steps to realize assets in territorial proceedings might jeopardize a planned restructuring.

The COMI

Given that the law applicable to insolvency proceedings and their effects is that of **15.27** the Member State in the territory of which the proceedings are opened[16] and that it is only main proceedings that embrace the totality of the debtor's assets, it will be evident that the concept of the COMI is of central importance. It is thus curious that the COMI is nowhere defined in the body of the Regulation but is dealt with only in recital (13), which states that it 'should correspond to the place where the debtor conducts the administration of his interests on a regular basis and is therefore ascertainable by third parties'. In the case of a company or legal person this is presumed to be the place of its registered office,[17] but the presumption is readily rebutted, because frequently the registered office is not the place from which the company's administration is conducted.

---

[14] But they can be opened only in the circumstances described in Art 3(4).
[15] Arts 18, 29(a) and 33.   [16] Art 4(1).   [17] Art 3(1).

Ian F Fletcher, *Insolvency in Private International Law: national and international approaches* (2nd edn, Clarendon Press, OUP, 2005) para 7.75

The cases discussed above . . . can be said to have laid the foundations of a 'functional' test for locating the COMI that is within the spirit and purpose of the Regulation, and of its predecessor the 1995 Convention. What has been referred to here as the 'command and control' test—sometimes termed the 'head office function' test has emerged as the pragmatic response of the English courts to the challenge of devising a set of workable criteria for assessing whether the presumption in Article 3(1) which places the COMI of a company at its registered office can be rebutted by the party who is seeking to open insolvency proceedings in a different Member State. No doubt there is a likelihood that courts in different Member States may reveal some divergence of approach to such questions as the relative strength, or weakness, of the presumption in Article 3(1), and the corresponding degree of cogency of the evidence required to rebut it. This is a matter of fundamental importance to the sound and satisfactory working of the Regulation, and it can be anticipated that the interpretative rulings of the ECJ will be sought in relation to the meaning and effect of Article 3, perhaps more than any other provision of the Regulation. A further question concerns the attitude towards the concept of the mobility of the COMI after the point at which it is regarded as having migrated from the place of its registered office—for example where it is alleged that the company subsequently became dormant, or ceased to trade actively in the State where its COMI had become located. Prominent in the reasoning of the English courts has been their concern to give due weight to the principle of protection of creditors' expectations, by seeking to answer the question 'In what jurisdiction should the creditors expect to pursue the assets of the company?' In this way the reference in Recital (13) of the Regulation to the COMI being 'ascertainable by third parties' is construed as having special relevance to the company's creditors, who are logically the 'third parties' in contemplation in this context.

15.28 The European Court of Justice has now given an authoritative ruling in the *Eurofood* case on the approach to the determination of the COMI and has emphasized that the mere fact that a subsidiary's activities can be controlled by its parent in another jurisdiction does not suffice to displace the presumption that the COMI is the location of the registers office.

Case C-341/04, Eurofood IFC Ltd, ECJ Grand Chamber, 2 May 2006

26 By its fourth question, which should be considered first since it concerns, in general, the system which the Regulation establishes for determining the competence of the courts of the Member States, the national court asks what the determining factor is for identifying the centre of main interests of a subsidiary company, where it and its parent have their respective registered offices in two different Member States.

27 The referring court asks how much relative weight should be given as between, on the one hand, the fact that the subsidiary regularly administers its interests, in a manner ascertainable by third parties and in respect for its own corporate identity, in the Member State where its registered office is situated and, on the other hand, the fact that the parent company is in a position, by virtue of its shareholding and power to appoint directors, to control the policy of the subsidiary.

28 Article 3 of the Regulation makes provision for two types of proceedings. The insolvency proceedings opened, in accordance with Article 3(1), by the competent court of the

Member State within whose territory the centre of a debtor's main interests is situated, described as the 'main proceedings', produce universal effects in that they apply to the assets of the debtor situated in all the Member States in which the regulation applies. Although, subsequently, proceedings under Article 3(2) may be opened by the competent court of the Member State where the debtor has an establishment, those proceedings, described as 'secondary proceedings', are restricted to the assets of the debtor situated in the territory of the latter State.

29 Article 3(1) of the Regulation provides that, in the case of a company, the place of the registered office shall be presumed to be the centre of its main interests in the absence of proof to the contrary.

30 It follows that, in the system established by the Regulation for determining the competence of the courts of the Member States, each debtor constituting a distinct legal entity is subject to its own court jurisdiction.

31 The concept of the centre of main interests is peculiar to the Regulation. Therefore, it has an autonomous meaning and must therefore be interpreted in a uniform way, independently of national legislation.

32 The scope of that concept is highlighted by the 13th recital of the Regulation, which states that 'the 'centre of main interests' should correspond to the place where the debtor conducts the administration of his interests on a regular basis and is therefore ascertainable by third parties'.

33 That definition shows that the centre of main interests must be identified by reference to criteria that are both objective and ascertainable by third parties. That objectivity and that possibility of ascertainment by third parties are necessary in order to ensure legal certainty and foreseeability concerning the determination of the court with jurisdiction to open main insolvency proceedings. That legal certainty and that foreseeability are all the more important in that, in accordance with Article 4(1) of the Regulation, determination of the court with jurisdiction entails determination of the law which is to apply.

34 It follows that, in determining the centre of the main interests of a debtor company, the simple presumption laid down by the Community legislature in favour of the registered office of that company can be rebutted only if factors which are both objective and ascertainable by third parties enable it to be established that an actual situation exists which is different from that which locating it at that registered office is deemed to reflect.

35 That could be so in particular in the case of a 'letterbox' company not carrying out any business in the territory of the Member State in which its registered office is situated.

36 By contrast, where a company carries on its business in the territory of the Member State where its registered office is situated, the mere fact that its economic choices are or can be controlled by a parent company in another Member State is not enough to rebut the presumption laid down by the Regulation.

37 In those circumstances, the answer to the fourth question must be that, where a debtor is a subsidiary company whose registered office and that of its parent company are situated in two different Member States, the presumption laid down in the second sentence of Article 3(1) of the Regulation, whereby the centre of main interests of that subsidiary is situated in the Member State where its registered office is situated, can be rebutted only if factors which are both objective and ascertainable by third parties enable it to be established that an actual situation exists which is different from that which locating it at that registered office is deemed to reflect. That could be so in particular in

the case of a company not carrying out any business in the territory of the Member State in which its registered office is situated. By contrast, where a company carries on its business in the territory of the Member State where its registered office is situated, the mere fact that its economic choices are or can be controlled by a parent company in another Member State is not enough to rebut the presumption laid down by the Regulation.

Applicable law

15.29 Particularly interesting are the provisions of the Regulation on the law applicable to insolvency proceedings. These are designed to strike a balance between insolvency rules and pre-insolvency *in rem* (property) rights under the applicable law and to preclude invalidity under the insolvency law of acts governed by the law of another Member State which does not permit such acts to be challenged in the relevant case. Article 4 is the general provision on the law applicable to insolvency proceedings and brings within the *lex concursus* all those matters which traditionally fall within the *lex concursus* under national legal systems, including a determination of the assets forming part of the estate, the conditions under which set-off may be exercised, the effects of insolvency proceedings on current contracts, and the rules governing proof and ranking of claims. Articles 5–15 then set out special rules for particular cases.

15.30 Articles 4, 5 and 7 together reflect the traditional relationship between insolvency and pre-insolvency rules of law. The starting position of insolvency law is to respect pre-insolvency entitlements as determined by the *lex causae*. It is then for the insolvency law (*lex concursus*) to determine the extent to which those entitlements are modified or nullified by the insolvency rules. Thus Article 4 is confined to *insolvency* effects, Article 5(1) provides that the opening of insolvency proceedings is not to affect the *in rem* rights of creditors over assets belonging to the debtor which are situated within the territory of another Member State at the time of the opening of proceedings,[18] and in similar vein Article 7(1) preserves the efficacy of a seller's reservation of title to assets so situated.[19] Neither of these provisions lays down a conflict rule; in an issue arising in the insolvency proceedings themselves the law determining the *in rem* or title reservation rights is the applicable law under the conflict rules of the insolvency jurisdiction (*lex concursus*) as the *lex fori*, which will typically apply the law of the *situs* of the assets at the time of the opening of the insolvency proceedings. But the ranking of an *in rem* right established by the *lex causae* may be changed by the *lex concursus* for the purpose of the

---

[18] Art 2(g) deals with the question where assets are deemed to be situated, the answer depending on the category of asset.

[19] Where the assets were not then situated within any Member State, it is still the *lex causae* that has to be applied to determine the existence and content of the *in rem* or title reservation rights.

insolvency proceedings, for example, by subordinating a secured claim to the claims of preferential creditors, such as claims for unpaid wages or government taxes.

The principle of recognition

A key feature of the Regulation, as with the UNCITRAL Model Law, is the prin-   **15.31**
ciple of recognition. A judgment opening proceedings handed down by a court of
a Member State is to be recognized in all other Member States[20] and is to have the
same effects as under the law of the Member State in which the judgment was
given unless the Regulation otherwise provides, and such effects may not be challenged in other Member States.[21] One effect of these provisions is to make it
improper, save in exceptional circumstances, for a court in one Member State to
enquire into the basis on which the court of another Member State assumed jurisdiction to open proceedings. So a finding by a court of a Member State that the
debtor's COMI was situated in the territory of that State cannot be challenged in
later proceedings before a court of another Member State. Second, the rule of
recognition applies not only where the court of one Member State has assumed
jurisdiction but also where it has declined it.[22] This may in certain cases require
the court of another State to treat the debtor's COMI as situated within that State
when it might not otherwise have done so.

However, the principle of recognition is not inviolate. Article 26 provides that a   **15.32**
Member State may refuse to recognize insolvency proceedings opened in another
Member State or to enforce a judgment handed down in the context of such proceedings where the effects of such recognition or enforcement would be manifestly contrary to the first State's public policy, in particular its fundamental principles
or the constitutional rights and liberties of the individual. An example is where an
interested party was not given sufficient opportunity to be heard.[23]

In the *Eurofood* case the European Court of Justice, endorsing the Opinion of the   **15.33**
Advocate General, considered that the appointment of a provisional liquidator
constituted the opening of insolvency proceedings, and this despite the fact that

---

[20] Art 16(1).   [21] Art 17.
[22] Miguel Virgós and Francisco Garcímartin, *The European Insolvency Regulation: law and prac-tice* (Kluwer, The Hague, 2004).
[23] In *Re Eurofood IFSC Ltd* [2004] 1 EHC 54, [2004] BCC 383, a decision of the Irish High Court, affirmed by the Irish Supreme Court [2006] 1 ESC 41 after a reference to the ECJ [2004] 1 ESC 45, it was held that where a provisional liquidator appointed in Ireland was not given notice of the hearing before the foreign court or supplied with copies of relevant documents it would be mani-festly contrary to the public policy of Irish law to give effect to the foreign court's decision. This was one of the questions referred to the European Court of Justice and in Case C341-04 of 27 September 2005 Advocate General Jacobs delivered an Opinion supporting the judgment, an Opinion which has since been endorsed by the ECJ (see below). The case was one of several arising from the collapse of the Parmalat group of companies, generating proceedings in a number of jurisdictions, including England, France, Germany and Italy.

proceedings for such an appointment do not feature in the list of insolvency proceedings in Appendix A to the Regulation. The Court reasoned as follows:

45 By its first question, the referring court essentially asks whether the decision whereby a court of a Member State, presented with a petition for the liquidation of an insolvent company, appoints, before ordering that liquidation, a provisional liquidator with powers whose legal effect is to deprive the company's directors of the power to act, constitutes a decision opening insolvency proceedings for the purposes of the first subparagraph of Article 16(1) of the Regulation.

46 The wording of Article 1(1) of the Regulation shows that the insolvency proceedings to which it applies must have four characteristics. They must be collective proceedings, based on the debtor's insolvency, which entail at least partial divestment of that debtor and prompt the appointment of a liquidator.

47 Those forms of proceedings are listed in Annex A to the Regulation, and the list of liquidators appears in Annex C.

48 The Regulation is designed not to establish uniform proceedings on insolvency, but, as its second recital states, to ensure that 'cross-border insolvency proceedings ... operate efficiently and effectively'. To that end, it lays down rules which, as its third recital indicates, are aimed at securing 'coordination of the measures to be taken regarding an insolvent debtor's assets'.

49 By requiring that any judgment opening insolvency proceedings handed down by a court of a Member State which has jurisdiction pursuant to Article 3 be recognised in all the other Member States from the time that it becomes effective in the State of the opening of proceedings, the first subparagraph of Article 16(1) of the Regulation lays down a rule of priority, based on a chronological criterion, in favour of the opening decision which was handed down first. As the 22nd recital of the Regulation explains, '[t]he decision of the first court to open proceedings should be recognised in the other Member States without those Member States having the power to scrutinise the court's decision'.

50 However, the Regulation does not define sufficiently precisely what is meant by a 'decision to open insolvency proceedings'.

51 The conditions and formalities required for opening insolvency proceedings are a matter for national law, and vary considerably from one Member State to another. In some Member States, the proceedings are opened very shortly after the submission of the application, the necessary verifications being carried out later. In other Member States, certain essential findings, which may be quite time-consuming, must be made before proceedings are opened. Under the national law of certain Member States, the proceedings may be opened 'provisionally' for several months.

52 As the Commission of the European Communities has argued, it is necessary, in order to ensure the effectiveness of the system established by the Regulation, that the recognition principle laid down in the first subparagraph of Article 16(1) of the Regulation, be capable of being applied as soon as possible in the course of the proceedings. The mechanism providing that only one main set of proceedings may be opened, producing its effects in all the Member States in which the Regulation applies, could be seriously disrupted if the courts of those States, hearing applications based on a debtor's insolvency at the same time, could claim concurrent jurisdiction over an extended period.

53 It is in relation to that objective seeking to ensure the effectiveness of the system established by the Regulation that the concept of 'decision to open insolvency proceedings' must be interpreted.

54 In those circumstances, a 'decision to open insolvency proceedings' for the purposes of the Regulation must be regarded as including not only a decision which is formally described as an opening decision by the legislation of the Member State of the court that handed it down, but also a decision handed down following an application, based on the debtor's insolvency, seeking the opening of proceedings referred to in Annex A to the Regulation, where that decision involves divestment of the debtor and the appointment of a liquidator referred to in Annex C to the Regulation. Such divestment involves the debtor losing the powers of management which he has over his assets. In such a case, the two characteristic consequences of insolvency proceedings, namely the appointment of a liquidator referred to in Annex C and the divestment of the debtor, have taken effect, and thus all the elements constituting the definition of such proceedings, given in Article 1(1) of the Regulation, are present.

55 Contrary to the arguments of Mr Bondi and the Italian Government, that interpretation cannot be invalidated by the fact that the liquidator referred to in Annex C to the Regulation may be a provisionally-appointed liquidator.

56 Both Mr Bondi and the Italian Government acknowledge that, in the main proceedings, the 'provisional liquidator' appointed by the High Court, by decision of 27 January 2004, appears amongst the liquidators mentioned in Annex C to the Regulation in relation to Ireland. They argue, however, that this is a case of a provisional liquidator, in respect of whom the Regulation contains a specific provision. They note that Article 38 of the Regulation empowers the provisional liquidator, defined in the 16th recital as the liquidator 'appointed prior to the opening of the main insolvency proceedings', to apply for preservation measures on the assets of the debtor situated in another Member State for the period between the request for the opening of insolvency proceedings and the judgment opening the proceedings. Mr Bondi and the Italian Government infer from that that the appointment of a provisional liquidator cannot open the main insolvency proceedings.

57 In that respect, it should be noted that Article 38 of the Regulation must be read in combination with Article 29, according to which the liquidator in the main proceedings is entitled to request the opening of secondary proceedings in another Member State. That Article 38 thus concerns the situation in which the competent court of a Member State has had main insolvency proceedings brought before it and has appointed a person or body to watch over the debtor's assets on a provisional basis, but has not yet ordered that that debtor be divested or appointed a liquidator referred to in Annex C to the Regulation. In that case, the person or body in question, though not empowered to initiate secondary insolvency proceedings in another Member State, may request that preservation measures be taken over the assets of the debtor situated in that Member State. That is, however, not the case in the main proceedings here, where the High Court has appointed a provisional liquidator referred to in Annex C to the Regulation and ordered that the debtor be divested.

58 In view of the above considerations, the answer to the first question must be that, on a proper interpretation of the first subparagraph of Article 16(1) of the Regulation, a decision to open insolvency proceedings for the purposes of that provision is a decision handed down by a court of a Member State to which application for such a decision has been made, based on the debtor's insolvency and seeking the

opening of proceedings referred to in Annex A to the Regulation, where that decision involves the divestment of the debtor and the appointment of a liquidator referred to in Annex C to the Regulation. Such divestment implies that the debtor loses the powers of management that he has over his assets.

15.34 What remains unclear is the effect of a request to open proceedings where no such appointment is sought or there has been no hearing. In such a case the condition of divestment of the debtor's property is not satisfied. Is it therefore open to the debtor to change its COMI to that of another Member State,[24] and for insolvency proceedings to be opened in that State? This question is not answered by the Regulation, but the principle of Community respect, the importance of which was emphasized by the ECJ in the *Eurofood* case, would seem to require that the court of the other Member State defer its own judgment in order to await the outcome of the proceedings in the first Member State. It would also seem that the plea of *lis alibi pendens* could be made to support that result.[25]

Insolvency of corporate groups

15.35 The Regulation has no provision dealing with the insolvency of corporate groups; each corporate member is a separate legal entity and must be treated as such. This may create difficulties where it is desired to have an orderly administration with a view to a restructuring. Where the administrator in the main proceedings of one member of the group is also the administrator in the main proceedings of other members he is well placed to ensure co-ordination of the different insolvency proceedings. In other cases, it is necessary to depend on mutual co-operation among the administrators concerned and among the courts of their respective jurisdictions.

Questions

1. What do you understand by the terms unity, plurality, universality, territoriality and universalism?
2. How would you describe the principles underlying the modern approach to jurisdiction in cross-border insolvencies as exemplified by the UNCITRAL Model Law and the European Community Regulation? To what extent has this approach been influenced by the rescue culture?

---

[24] In *Shierson v Vlieland-Boddy* [2005] EWCA Civ 974, [2005] 1 WLR 3966 the English Court of Appeal held that there was nothing to prevent the debtor from doing this prior to the opening of insolvency proceedings in the previous COMI, even if the effect was to preclude the court of that COMI from exercising jurisdiction. [25] Virgós and Garcímartin (n 22) [70].

3. 'Assets within a given jurisdiction should be available exclusively to local creditors, and no foreign creditors or office-holders should have a right to intervene in relation to such assets or their administration.' Discuss.

4. What are the issues that divide Professors LoPucki and Tung on the one hand and Professor Westbrook on the other on the subject of universalism in cross-border insolvency? What view do you take?

5. To what extent is it possible to organize cross-border collaboration in the insolvency of a multinational company without the availability of an international or regional convention or other similar legal instrument?

6. What is the presumption in the European Insolvency Regulation as to the place of the debtor's COMI? And what must be shown in order to rebut that presumption?

7. A debtor company having its COMI in Germany, establishments in France and Belgium and assets in these countries and in Italy and Spain becomes insolvent. All five countries are members of the European Union. You are consulted by one of the largest creditors, A, seeking your advice as to whether it can institute winding-up proceedings against the debtor in each of these countries.

    (1) Advise A.
    (2) How, if at all, would your advice differ if the debtor had its COMI in Canada?

8. The facts are as in question 7. Another creditor, B, wishes to begin proceedings for insolvent reorganization in France. Advise B.

9. 'Upon the opening of insolvency proceedings in a given jurisdiction all priority rules embodied in the law of another jurisdiction which is the applicable law in relation to pre-insolvency dealings are displaced by the *lex concursus* and must be disregarded.'

    Comment on this statement.

10. How can the insolvency of a multinational corporate group best be managed?

Further reading

American Law Institute, *Transnational Insolvency Project, Principles of Cooperation in Transnational Insolvency Cases Among the Members of the North American Free Trade Agreement* (American Law Institute, Philadelphia PA 2000), especially app 2 'Guidelines Applicable to Court-to-Court Communications in Cross-Border Cases'

Bridge, Michael, and Stevens, Robert (eds), *Cross-Border Security and Insolvency* (OUP, Oxford, 2001)

Clift, Jenny, 'The UNCITRAL Model Law on Cross-Border Insolvency—A Legislative Framework to Facilitate Coordination and Cooperation in Cross-Border Insolvency' 12 Tul J Intl & Comp L 307 (2004)

Fletcher, Ian, *Insolvency in Private International Law: National and International Approaches* (2nd edn Clarendon Press, OUP, 2005)

Goode, Roy, *Principles of Corporate Insolvency Law* (3rd edn, Sweet & Maxwell, London, 2005), ch 14

LoPucki, Lynn, 'The Case for Cooperative Territoriality in International Bankruptcy' 98 Mich L Rev 2216 (1999–2000)

Moss, Gabriel, Fletcher, Ian F, and Isaacs, Stuart, *The EC Regulation on Insolvency Proceedings: a commentary and annotated guide* (OUP, Oxford, 2002)

Omar, Paul J, *European Insolvency Law* (Ashgate, Aldershot, 2004)

Rasmussen, Robert K, 'A New Approach to Transnational Insolvencies' 19 Mich J Intl L 1 (1997)

Tung, Frederick, 'Is International Bankruptcy Possible?' 23 Mich J Intl L 31 (2001–2002)

Veder, Paul Michael, *Cross-border insolvency proceedings and security rights: a comparison of Dutch and German law, the EC Insolvency Regulation and the UNCITRAL Model Law on Cross-Border Insolvency* (Kluwer, Deventer, 2004) ch II

Virgós, Miguel, and Schmit, Etienne, *Report on the Convention on Insolvency Proceedings* (European Union doc 6500/96, 1996)

Virgós, Miguel, and Garcimartín, Francisco, *The European Insolvency Regulation: Law and Practice* (Kluwer Law International, The Hague, 2004)

Westbrook, Jay Lawrence, 'A Global Solution to Multinational Default' 98 Mich L Rev 2276 (2000–2001)

Ziegel, Jacob S, and Cantlie, Susan I (eds), *Current Developments in International and Comparative Corporate Insolvency Law* (Clarendon Press, Oxford, 1994)

PART V

INTERNATIONAL DISPUTE RESOLUTION

16

INTERNATIONAL CIVIL PROCEDURE

A. **Introduction**
  The nature of the problem and the
    challenges ahead   16.01
  Sources   16.06
B. **Jurisdictional Immunities**   16.09
C. **Jurisdiction to Adjudicate**
  Traditional autonomous rules in
    national systems   16.13
  Modernization, international
    co-ordination and the needs
    of international business
  General   16.20
  Party autonomy and forum
    selection   16.29
  Discretionary limitations of
    jurisdiction: the doctrine of
    forum non conveniens   16.38

D. **Provisional and Protective**
  Measures   16.43
E. **Conduct of the Proceedings and**
  Judicial Assistance
  Service abroad of judicial documents   16.51
  Taking of evidence   16.56
F. **Recognition and Enforcement of**
  Foreign Judgments
  Brussels I Regulation   16.60
  The Las Leñas and Buenos Aires
    Protocols   16.61
G. **From International to**
  Transnational Civil Procedure:
  the ALI/UNIDROIT Principles
  of Transnational Civil Procedure
  Objectives   16.62
  Selected solutions   16.64

A. Introduction

The nature of the problem and the challenges ahead

Assume merchants from different countries enter into a contract and that only **16.01** one of them or neither is present in the country where the court seised of a dispute arising subsequently out of the contract is sitting. Or that the subject matter of a contract is located outside the country where the parties to the contract are. Or that the assets of a judgment debtor are located abroad.

Originally, courts and other tribunals tended to entertain actions only if the com- **16.02** mercial activity underlying the dispute or the assets in question or the litigants were relatively closely connected with the tribunal's territorial area of jurisdiction. For example, Article 1 of the *PRIVILEGIUM Capitul, Regul und Ordnung* of 15 September 1635 for the market court of the Tyrolian city of Bozen (Italian: Bolzano) in defining the grounds for jurisdiction, firstly, refers to the personal capacity of the parties as *Kauffleüthen* (merchants):

> *Sie seyen Auß: oder Inländische / Reich oder Arm / Lädler /Kramer / oder andere die offne Läden oder Ständt haben / was Nation / Standts oder Condition sie seyen / dieselbigen alle unnd deren Marckts Handlungen / sollen gemeltem Magistrat unterworfen seyn.*

16.03 Origin, domicile, nationality and other personal or professional qualifications as well as the typology of the merchants in question were irrelevant. The tribunal had:

> *[G]ewalt ... / privative und absonderlichen / ... / in zeit deß Marckts / und so lang derselbe wehret / ... / zuvollenden und zu urthailen alle die fürkommenden strittigen Sachen / ... / welche anvor noch nicht angefangen / noch vor anderen Richtern seyen eingefüehrt oder anhengig gemacht ...*

that is, jurisdiction to decide all civil disputes that arose during the ongoing market and which had not been brought before any other court prior to the commencement of the market.[1] The tribunal also had jurisdiction to punish carriers due to whose fault goods were delayed:

> *Doch solle diser Punct auff jenige Personen / welche die Güter per transitum durchfüehren / nicht: sondern die jhenigen / weliche dem Marckt zu guetem dienen / verstanden werden*

unless those carriers were only passing through and not considered to serve the market and provided the goods were likewise *res in transitu*.

16.04 The exercise of judicial authority was thus closely linked with concepts and ideas such as 'physical subjection', commercial transactions being entered into on the market as a regulated 'local institution', 'sovereignty', 'territoriality' of the Sovereign's power, etc. The latter continued to be relevant even in more recent times when traders had begun to organize their own adjudicatory institutions (arbitration) separate from the States' judicial systems, because those private dispute resolution mechanisms were not always available, nor were they necessarily functionally suited for all types of civil disputes. Apart from political aspects and concerns of unfair treatment it was these rather underdeveloped notions of jurisdiction that entailed a considerable degree of uncertainty and unpredictability regarding the actual worth of claims arising out of commercial transactions. This situation was likely to be a disincentive for traders to extend their activities beyond the borders of their own country, or in Europe even those of the city. Advancement of the concepts of international civil procedure is therefore clearly of considerable importance for trans-border commerce. It must, however, be emphasized that advancement

---

[1] Not relevant for our purposes here, but highly interesting is the composition of both the tribunal of first instance and the appeal panel set up by these regulations. They are made up of three adjudicators from three different regions (jurisdictions) which today would be Germany, Austria, Italy and Switzerland (Augsburg and Memmingen, Innsbruck, Rovereto, and Venice, Berne and St Gallen).

cannot mean only, or even primarily, putting an ever greater number of venues and procedural devices at the disposal of potential litigants. Commendable imaginative measures taken by counsel of international businesses to transform the legal systems of the world into a chessboard on which individual gain is sought must be countered by efforts on the part of legislatures and courts to develop a harmonious system of international civil procedure which should eventually guarantee the same degree of efficiency and consistency in the trans-border context that sophisticated systems have achieved domestically. That system has to be based on seven pillars:

(1) grounds for the courts' competence that take into account both the plaintiff's and the defendant's legitimate expectations;
(2) independence and impartiality of the court, in particular vis-à-vis foreign parties;
(3) fairness and the guarantee to fully present one's case;
(4) predictability of the structure of the proceedings and their administration by the court
(5) open-mindedness for trade usages and other special features of dealings among businessmen;
(6) expeditiousness;
(7) adequate enforceability of court decisions rendered abroad.

16.05 The phrase 'international civil procedure' is now widely used in a number of countries where it is seen as a special branch of the law of civil procedure. In others the issues coming under this umbrella are still treated as part of the conflict of laws.[2]

Sources

16.06 Firstly, there are multilateral and bilateral treaties governing jurisdiction, the conduct of proceedings, judicial assistance and recognition and enforcement of foreign judgments. The most prominent examples for the former are, at the regional level, the 1968 Brussels and the 1988 Lugano Convention on Jurisdiction and Recognition and, as regards judicial assistance and at the global level, the 1965 Hague Convention on Service and the 1970 Hague Convention on Taking Evidence.

16.07 Secondly, a Member State of a Regional Economic Integration Organization such as the European Union applies the instruments of the REIO as its own internal law, and this (subject to qualifications and exceptions) is directly applicable and takes precedence over that State's other domestic law. It is the provisions of the regional instrument which determine the State's position in relation to other treaties into which it has entered. Arguably the most important regional instrument of this kind is the EC jurisdiction and recognition of judgments regulation,[3]

---

[2] See above, ch 2.
[3] Council Regulation (EC) No 44/2001 of 22 December 2000 on jurisdiction and the recognition and enforcement of judgments in civil and commercial matters (2001) OJ L12/1.

which replaced the Brussels Convention and is therefore known as the Brussels I Regulation. Article 69 of the Regulation[4] states that the Regulation shall supersede, as between Member States, no fewer than sixty-two specified bilateral and trilateral treaties.[5] Articles 71 and 72 address the relationship between the Regulation and other multilateral[6] and bilateral treaties to which EU Member States are parties.

16.08 Thirdly, there are the so-called 'autonomous' domestic rules on jurisdiction, the conduct of proceedings and the recognition and enforcement of foreign court decisions, which may be either statutory or common law (judge-made). While details depend on the constitutional framework of the forum concerned, in particular the relationship between international law and domestic law, bilateral and multilateral treaties prevail over autonomous rules, whether these are statutory or common law in origin.

B. Jurisdictional Immunities

16.09 Both customary international law and treaties as well as municipal law provide for the immunity from jurisdiction of States, Heads of State and certain representatives of Governments, diplomats and foreign consuls. Transnational commercial contracts and transnational commercial litigation not infrequently involve issues of State immunity. Foreign Governments and foreign state-owned agencies or enterprises are often engaged in activities such as the exploitation of natural resources, maritime and air transportation, construction and operation of infrastructure projects, defence procurement, broadcasting, and others. They are typically parties to concession and joint-venture agreements, and in many developing countries and economies in transition they are quite generally the entry points for foreign investment.

16.10 Outside the scope of the 1972 European Convention on State Immunity and the 2005 UN Convention on the Jurisdictional Immunity of States and Their Property (the latter has not yet entered into force), general principles of public international law and their reception by both case law and statutes[7] as well as a multitude of treaties covering specific areas govern the subject. All are an expression of the

---

[4] But see also Art 70.

[5] The oldest one is the 1899 Convention between Belgium and France on Jurisdiction and the Validity and Enforcement of Judgments, Arbitration Awards and Authentic Instruments, the most recent one is the 1998 Agreement between Estonia and Poland on Granting Legal Assistance and Legal Relations in Civil, Labour and Criminal Matters.

[6] Of significant practical importance in this respect are provisions on jurisdiction and recognition in conventions on the carriage of goods.

[7] Eg the UK State Immunity Act 1978, the US Foreign Sovereign Immunities Act 1976, the acts on the organization of the judiciary, or the codes of civil procedure of many countries.

maxim *par in parem non habet imperium*, meaning that the courts of one country will not by their process make a foreign sovereign 'against his will a party to legal proceedings whether the proceedings involve process against his person or seek to recover from him specific property or damages'.[8] Against the background of increased state trading after the Second World War the theory of 'absolute' immunity had been gradually eroded and replaced by the 'restrictive' theory according to which States are immune in respect of acts of government (*acta jure imperii*) but not in respect of commercial acts (*acta jure gestionis*). The often difficult characterization is generally left to the forum. Contractual claims, claims arising out of the State's participation in a company or other commercial entity (at least if the latter has its seat in the forum State), and disputes concerning intellectual property, are, for example, characterized as *jure gestionis*. A sovereign may waive its immunity, and in this respect frequently the question arises as to who has the authority to waive the State's immunity and what the scope of any such undertaking is.

When a question of immunity is raised, then the issue must be decided as a preliminary one before the court can proceed. This is why many legal systems treat the issue of immunity as distinct from jurisdiction in the sense of territorial or personal competence. While the court seised has to decline to entertain such proceedings where there is immunity even if the State does not appear, the assumption of jurisdiction in the absence of an appropriate territorial or personal connecting factor would be a mere technical mistake or, more precisely, a misjudgment regarding the opportuneness of entertaining the action. **16.11**

The law distinguishes clearly between immunity from jurisdiction and immunity from execution. There is a general rule that, even if judgment against a State based on an act *jure gestionis* has been entered, measures of execution against that State's property may not be taken without the foreign State's consent if the assets in question serve governmental purposes. Article 20 of the European Convention establishes a State's duty to comply with the provisions of any judgment given in accordance with the Convention if it is final. **16.12**

C. Jurisdiction to Adjudicate

Traditional autonomous rules in national systems

Before efforts to co-ordinate and harmonize rules on jurisdiction began, both the fundamental approaches and the individual rules that addressed the issue differed widely. Firstly, some countries had code or judge-made rules specifically designed for cross-border litigation while others used primarily their rules on *venue* (that is, **16.13**

---

[8] *Compania Naviera Vascongada v SS Cristina* [1938] AC 485, *per* Lord Atkin at 490.

'*territorial*' or '*local*' *competence*)—e.g. by analogy—also to determine *jurisdiction* (i.e., as many actually call it, '*international*' *competence*). Secondly, some took a balanced line and treated their own nationals and foreigners equally while others discriminated against foreigners in that the country's own citizens were given special protection. Thirdly, roots in legal history as well as different political, economic and social conditions had generated quite different connecting factors on which courts based jurisdiction. For example, while some countries traditionally required for claims *in personam* that the defendant be physically present so as to be served with process, others required the plaintiff to follow the defendant to wherever he resided: *actor sequitur forum rei*.

16.14 The French *Code Civil*, the source of that country's traditional autonomous rules on jurisdiction, provides:

> *Art. 14—L'étranger, même non resident en France, pourra être cité devant les tribunaux français, pour l'exécution des obligations par lui contractées en France avec un Français; il pourra être traduit devant les tribunaux de France, pour les obligations par lui contractées en pays étranger avec un Français.*

16.15 A French plaintiff could therefore always rely on the jurisdiction of the French courts.

16.16 § 23 of the German Code of Civil Procedure until quite recently used to be construed as providing a ground for jurisdiction whenever the defendant had assets in Germany—whatever their value and whether in any way related to the dispute or not.

16.17 Both connecting factors, as well as the *forum actoris* under Belgian and Dutch law and others such as the common law rule that service on the defendant during very temporary physical presence (such as a stop over), were stigmatized by Article 3 of the Brussels Convention as 'exorbitant' and were excluded for disputes within the Convention's scope.[9] For the internal relations among countries forming part of a homogeneous area of justice they were as a matter of fact untenable, and they should also be gradually eliminated from autonomous sources for the courts' power to adjudicate.

16.18 § 23 of the German Code of Civil Procedure may be but is not necessarily the basis for an action *in rem*. As the US Restatement, Second, Conflict of Laws (1971) explains in its Introductory Note to Topic 2, Chapter 2:

> [E]very valid exercise of judicial jurisdiction affects the interests of persons in different ways, and it is convenient to divide the subject of judicial jurisdiction [another term for jurisdiction to adjudicate] into three main categories: jurisdictions over persons [ie jurisdiction for actions *in personam* as discussed so far], jurisdiction over things and jurisdiction over status [ie personal and family law matters] . . .

---

[9] For an earlier rejection by the American Supreme Court of the defendant's casual presence as a basis for jurisdiction in claims against a corporation, see para 16.20.

Even though personal jurisdiction over the defendant is lacking, the state may affect any interests he may have in things subject to its jurisdiction. A judgment rendered in such a proceeding binds only the defendant's interests in the specific thing at which it is directed and thus has a more limited effect than a judgement against the defendant personally ...

In English law the only claim *in rem* is an Admiralty claim. The *res* is normally a   **16.19**
ship or its cargo. If the judgment is only *in rem* it may be enforced only against the *res*—here the difference between this ground for jurisdiction and § 23 German Code of Civil Procedure where the location of the defendant's assets serves as connecting factor for an action *in personam* becomes clear. It does not affect anyone who does not have an interest in the thing and, if he does have such an interest, affects him only to the extent of that interest. Secondly, the judgment is binding, to the extent of his interest in the thing, on anyone who has such an interest.

Modernization, international co-ordination and the needs of international business

General

In many legal systems, traditional rules regarding jurisdiction to adjudicate were   **16.20**
rather parochial and sometimes utterly selfish both in granting and in denying access to the legislature's own courts. At the same time, they tended to be highly conceptualized and typical 'lawyers' law'. Ironically, the drive to modernize those rules, to make them reflect the reality of growing trans-border streams of commerce at first strengthened the latter characteristic. In the United States, the search of new jurisdictional standards began with the Supreme Court's rejection of 'mechanical or quantitative' criteria to 'justify the subjection of a corporation to suit'.[10]

> Since the corporate personality is a fiction, ... it is clear that unlike an individual its 'presence' without, as well as within, the state of its origin can be manifested only by activities carried out on its behalf by those who are authorized to act for it. To say that the corporation is so far 'present' there as to satisfy due process requirements, for purposes of ... the maintenance of suits against it in the courts of the state, is to beg the question to be decided. For the terms 'present' or 'presence' are used merely to symbolize those activities of the corporation's agent within the state which courts will deem sufficient to satisfy the demands of due process ...
>
> 'Presence' in the state in this sense has never been doubted when the activities of the corporation have not only been continuous and systematic, but also give rise to the liabilities sued on, even though no consent to be sued or authorization to an agent to accept service of process has been given ... Conversely it has been generally recognized that the casual presence of the corporate agent or even his conduct ... in a state in the corporation's behalf are not enough to subject it to suit on causes of action

---

[10] *International Shoe Co v State of Washington*, 326 US 310, 66 S Ct154 (1945) per Chief Justice Stone.

unconnected with the activities there ... To require the corporation in such circumstances to defend the suit away from its home or other jurisdiction where it carries on more substantial activities has been thought to lay too great and unreasonable a burden on the corporation to comport with due process ...

It is evident that the criteria by which we mark the boundary line between those activities which justify the subjection of a corporation to suit, and those which do not, cannot be simply mechanical or quantitative ... Whether due process is satisfied must depend rather upon the quality and nature of the activity in relation to the fair and orderly administration of the laws which it was the purpose of the due process clause to ensure ...

The obligation which is here sued upon arose out of those [previously examined more in detail] activities. It is evident that these operations establish sufficient contacts or ties with the state of the forum to make it reasonable and just according to our traditional conception of fair play and substantial justice to permit the state to enforce the obligations which appellant has incurred there ...

16.21 *International Shoe* is a landmark in the quest to craft modern rules on judicial jurisdiction. It is noteworthy that the tests of 'minimum contacts', 'fairness' and 'substantial justice'—discussed with utter scepticism in a dissenting opinion given by Justice Black—are used as devices to protect the defendant. The same is true of many modern rules regarding jurisdiction in other parts of the world. It is imperative, however, that any system of rules be balanced in this respect so as to equally protect the interests of potential plaintiffs.

16.22 The 'minimum contacts' and 'fairness' tests were no more than a sketch that required further outlining and shading. The courts contributed to that in many decisions which, over the decades, refined the test and applied it also to actions (*quasi*) *in rem*.[11] The legislatures, both Federal and State, purported to shoulder their share of the burden by enacting 'long-arm statutes' of which there is a great variety. Generally speaking, 'continuous and systematic [business] contacts' are deemed to be sufficient for assuming jurisdiction throughout the United States. The question, problematic from a non-US point of view, is how far one can go in this direction, in other words, of what nature and how substantial 'doing business' needs to be so as to justify a person's subjection to the relevant State's jurisdiction. § 421(2) of the Restatement (Third) of Foreign Relations Law (1987) states:

In general, a state's exercise of jurisdiction to adjudicate ... is reasonable, if, at the time jurisdiction is asserted, the person ... (h) regularly carries on business in the state; (i) ... had carried on activity in the state, but only with respect to such activity.

---

[11] See, in particular, *Helicopteros Nacionales de Colombia, SA v Hall* 466 US 408, 104 S Ct 1868 (1984); *Asahi Metal Industry Co, Ltd v Superior Court of California, Solano County* 480 US 102, 107 S Ct 1026 (1987); *Omni Capital International, Ltd v Rudolf Wolff & Co* 484 US 97, 108 S Ct 404 (1987); *Metropolitan Life Insurance Company v Robertson-Ceco Corp* 84 F 3d 560 (2nd Cir 1996). For the *quasi in rem* constellation, see *Shaffer v Heitner* 433 US 186, 97 S Ct 2569 (1977) where a derivative suit against the directors of a company was brought by another shareholder and based on the statutory presence of the directors' shares in the company's home State Delaware.

New York CPLR § 302(a)(1) seem to go very far when they subject to that State's **16.23**
jurisdiction anyone:

> who in person or through an agent ... transacts any business within the state or con-
> tracts anywhere to supply goods or services in the state.

In Europe,[12] modernization and co-ordination are synonyms of 'communitariza- **16.24**
tion'. On 1 March 2002, the Brussels Convention on Jurisdiction and Recognition
and Enforcement of 1968 changed 'pillars' because under the Treaty of Amsterdam
private international law and international civil procedure, which had so far been
dealt with in intergovernmental conventions (e.g. the 1980 Rome Convention, see
above chapter 2), became a branch of judicial co-operation and passed from the
'third pillar' to the 'first pillar', i.e. genuine Community legislation. The Brussels
Convention became EC Regulation 44/2001. By definition the Regulation is in
force in all Member States except Denmark. The Brussels Convention will remain
in force with respect to that country. One of the reasons that had made the
Convention the most successful transnational law instrument of all time was the
European Court of Justice's competence to authoritatively rule on its interpretation—and Member States' courts' specular duty to refer queries as to its interpretation which they consider relevant for their own decision to the ECJ.[13] The Lugano
Convention of 16 September 1988 (the 'parallel convention' to Brussels) will
continue to govern the relationship between EU Member States and the other
Member States of the European Economic Area. The Regulation's system is exclusive. Autonomous domestic rules on jurisdiction come into play only outside the
Regulation's substantive scope of application or where the Regulation refers to
them (e.g. Article 4). Apart from Article 2, which establishes the general principle
that, subject to specific provisions, persons domiciled in a Member State shall,
whatever their nationality, be sued in the courts of that Member State, there are
three rules (plus one addressing typical maritime-law issues, Article 5(7), and an
entire section on matters relating to insurance, Articles 8–14) which are of particular interest in the context of disputes arising out of transnational commercial
transactions.

Article 5(1) confers jurisdiction 'in matters relating to a contract' on 'the courts **16.25**
for the place of performance of the obligation in question'. For the purposes of this
provision the place of performance is, unless otherwise agreed, in the case of the

---

[12] For South America, the 1992 Las Leñas and the 1994 Buenos Aires Protocols to the MER-
COSUR Treaty are the most important regional instruments. For details, see below, at paras 16.36,
16.61.

[13] Between its entering into force on 1 February 1973 and 2002 the ECJ had rendered more than
100 decisions regarding the interpretation of the Convention. While the ECJ's competence and the
details regarding the reference for a preliminary ruling by national courts' used to be a matter governed by a special Protocol to the Convention, the relevant provisions are now Article 68(1) and
Article 234 of the EC Treaty.

sale of goods or in the case of provision of services, the place in a Member State where, under the contract, the goods were delivered or should have been delivered or where the services were provided or should have been provided.

16.26 Among the numerous issues that fuelled the judicial and scholarly discussion over the years two are worth mentioning here. The first one takes us back to the problem of 'characterization', a conflict-of-laws classic discussed in chapter 2. When is a claim to be characterized as 'contractual'? Different legal systems give different answers. The law of one Member State may characterize as contractual in nature claims arising out of the repudiation of a commercial agency agreement, membership of an association, a company's relationship with its directors or breach of pre-contractual duties or claims for restitution as part of the unwinding of a failed contract, whereas the laws of other Member States may characterize them as delictual, 'corporate' or in other ways which, within their system, are clearly not 'contractual claims' or even 'matters relating to a contract'. From early on, the European Court of Justice has firmly rejected all suggestions to construe the term 'contract' in accordance with the *lex fori* or the substantive law indicated by the forum's conflict of laws rules as governing (*lex causae*). Instead, the Court insists on an 'autonomous' interpretation with a view to maintaining and strengthening uniformity in the application of the Convention/Regulation. Commentators of transnational commercial law frequently refer to this example when the various sources of many other instruments' failure to achieve uniformity are analysed.

16.27 With respect to the second issue, that is, how to determine where the 'place of performance' is, the Court, from its first two decisions rendered in 1976 on, took the view that the law governing the obligation in question, whether national law identified by the forum's conflicts rules or international uniform law conventions, determines the place of its performance. The ECJ was much criticized on this point, chiefly because, quite contrary to the Convention's system and policies, this rule frequently led to giving the plaintiff (for example, a seller suing for the purchase price under the CISG[14]) a forum in his own country. Against the view expressed by a number of national courts, the Advocate General's advisory opinion and the prevailing view amongst commentators, the Court defended the line taken citing reasons of legal certainty and predictability. The emerging tensions between the basic system and approach of the Convention/Regulation on the one hand and predictability as one of the prime objectives of transnational commercial law on the other hand have now been settled by the Community legislature for sales contracts and contracts for services.[15]

16.28 Article 5(5) provides that, as regards a dispute arising out of the operation of a branch, agency or other establishment, a person (including a company, cf. Article 60)

---

[14] Case C-288/92 *Custom Made Commercial Ltd v Stawa Metallbau GmbH* [1994] ECR I–2913; [1994] I L Pr 516. [15] See Art 5(1)(b) of the Regulation.

domiciled in a Member State may be sued in another Member State if the branch, agency or other establishment is situated there. The ECJ has carefully developed the various elements of this provision, not always without hesitations and ambiguities. And the state of the law is still a far cry from the United States' refined— but likewise not crystal clear—system of procedural handling of parent-subsidiaries situations. There, in certain circumstances, the corporate veil is pierced and a subsidiary is treated as the parent company's 'alter ego' or 'mere department' for purposes of ascertaining jurisdiction. However, Article 5(5) does have considerable potential to properly address cases where groups of companies deliberately use the group structure to distribute the roles of transacting parties and parties benefiting from the transaction entered into with a view to shielding one member of the group from—substantive or procedural—risk.

Party autonomy and forum selection

The third rule on jurisdiction, and one which is of utmost importance for inter- **16.29** national commerce and finance, is Article 23 of Regulation 44/2001 (largely identical with Article 17 of the Brussels Convention). If the parties—provided at least one of them is domiciled in a Member State—have agreed that the courts of a Member State are to have jurisdiction to settle any disputes which have arisen or which may arise in connection with a particular legal relationship, those courts have, in principle, exclusive jurisdiction. The conferment of jurisdiction by means of contractual agreement, also known as prorogation, is the procedural twin of the parties' freedom to choose the substantive law that is to govern their contract.[16] The parties' freedom to prorogate encompasses their right to derogate, that is, to stipulate that courts other than those they have selected refrain from exercising jurisdiction the law would normally confer on them. Other courts must honour the stipulation and decline to entertain an action brought in violation of the forum selection clause. As the European Court of Justice has repeatedly stated, it is in keeping with the spirit of certainty, which constitutes one of the aims of the Regulation, that the national court seised should be able readily to decide whether it has jurisdiction on the basis of its provisions, without having to consider the substance of the case. It is for those reasons that the Court continues reminding national courts that Article 23 of the Regulation (Article 17 of the Convention) dispenses with any objective connection between the relationship in dispute and the court designated.

In the United States—as in other countries outside continental Europe—courts **16.30** had historically often disregarded the parties' choice on the ground that parties to a private agreement cannot dispose of a court's jurisdiction conferred upon it by law. As we have seen in the context of the development of the concept of party

---

[16] See ch 2.

autonomy (see chapter 2), the US Supreme Court's landmark decision *M/S Bremen v Zapata Off-Shore Co*[17] had opened new horizons citing the changing needs of businesses in global markets. Against resistance, mainly from lower courts but also from dissenting Justices within the Supreme Court, this line was confirmed in a series of decisions even where the chosen tribunal was not another US court but an arbitral tribunal, even where parties had combined forum-selection clauses and choice-of-law clauses so as to make sure that the chosen court would apply the law specifically chosen by the parties for the underlying transaction rather than select one following its own conflict-of-laws rules, and even where the effect of the combined clauses was that Federal regulatory law (antitrust, securities law, maritime law) was disapplied.[18]

16.31 Modern transnational commercial law instruments explicitly reflect and approve widespread contract practices in this respect. Article 42 of the 2001 Cape Town Convention on International Interests in Mobile Equipment and Article XXI of the Aircraft Protocol (see chapter 12), for example, are based on the established contract practice to prorogate certain courts experienced in the handling of disputes arising out of secured transactions in high-value mobile equipment.

16.32 For the forum-selection clause to be valid Article 23 EC Regulation 44/2001 requires that it be either (a) in writing or evidenced in writing; or (b) in a form which accords with practices which the parties have established between themselves or,

> (c) in international trade or commerce, in a form which accords with a usage of which the parties are or ought to have been aware and which in such trade or commerce is widely known to, or regularly observed by, parties to contracts of the type involved in the particular trade or commerce concerned.

16.33 While alternative (b) is a simple and welcome recognition that the parties ought to be the masters of their agreements, and that the law should not intervene imposing formalism where they themselves considered formal requirements unnecessary (cf. Article 9(1) CISG), alternative (c) is calling for some more reflection. As a starting point it must be noted that the prerequisites for assuming jurisdiction established by Article 23 are to be examined autonomously under Community law and not by reference to any domestic law. In 1995, the Bundesgerichtshof

---

[17] 407 US 1, 92 S Ct 1907 (1972).

[18] *Scherk v Alberto-Culver Co* 417 US 506, 94 S Ct 2449 (1974); *Mitsubishi Motors Corp v Soler Chrysler-Plymouth, Inc* 473 US 614, 105 S Ct 3346 (1985); *Rodriguez de Quijas v Shearson/American Express, Inc* 490 US 477, 109 S Ct 1917 (1989); *Vimar Seguros y Reaseguros, SA v M/V Sky Reefer* 515 US 528, 115 S Ct 2322 (1995); *Richards v Lloyd's of London* 135 F 3d 1289 (9th Cir 1998) (*en banc*). A case deserves special mention which, at first sight, seems to be an example of consumer-protection law but which contains valuable analysis of the problem of choice-of-forum clauses in standard form contracts, *Carnival Cruise Lines, Inc v Shute* 499 US 585, 111 S Ct 1522 (1991). For the implications regarding international securities regulations, see H Kronke, 'Capital Markets and Conflict of Laws', Recueil des Cours 286 (2000), 245, at p 359 et seq.

(German Federal Supreme Court) referred to the European Court of Justice for a preliminary ruling two questions on the interpretation of the Convention, one of which regarded alternative (c).

ECJ, 20 February 1997, Case C—106/95 *Mainschiffahrts-Genossenschaft eG (MSG) v Les Gravières Rhénanes SARL* [1997] ECR I—911, Rev.crit.dr.int.priv. 1997, 563 (anno. H Gaudemet-Tallon), Nederlandse Jurisprudentie 1998 Nr 565 (anno. P Vlas), Zeitschrift für Zivilprozess International 1997, 161 (anno. P Huber)

2 The questions arose in proceedings between ... [MSG], an inland-waterway transport cooperative based at Würzburg (Germany), and ... [Gravières Rhénanes], whose registered office is in France, concerning compensation for damage caused to an inland-waterway vessel which MSG owned and had chartered to Gravières Rhénanes by a time charter concluded orally between the parties ...

6 It appears from the order of reference that, when the contractual negotiations had been completed, MSG sent Gravières Rhénanes a commercial letter of confirmation containing the following pre-printed statement:

> 'The place of performance is Würzburg and the courts for that place have exclusive jurisdiction.' Moreover, MSG's invoices also mentioned that forum directly and by reference to the conditions of the bill of lading. Gravières Rhénanes did not challenge the commercial letter of confirmation and paid all invoices without objection ...

17 [... t]hat relaxation incorporated in Article 17 by the 1978 Accession Convention does not mean that there is not necessarily any need for consensus between the parties on a jurisdiction clause, since it is still one of the aims of that provision to ensure that there is real consent on the part of the persons concerned ...

20 It must therefore be considered that the fact that one of the parties to the contract did not react or remained silent ... may be deemed to constitute consent to the jurisdiction clause in issue, provided that such conduct is consistent with a practice in force in the area of international trade or commerce in which the parties in question are operating and the parties are or ought to have been aware of that practice.

21 Whilst it is for the national court to determine whether the contract in question comes under the head of international trade or commerce and to find whether there was a practice in the branch of international trade or commerce in which the parties are operating and whether they were aware or are presumed to have been aware of that practice, the Court should nevertheless indicate the objective evidence which is needed in order to make such a determination.

22 [On whether a contract between parties from different Contracting States concerning navigation on the Rhine comes under that head]

23 Next, whether a practice exists must not be determined by reference to the law of one of the Contracting Parties [ie States]. Furthermore, whether such a practice exists should not be determined in relation to international trade or commerce in general, but to the branch of trade or commerce in which the parties to the contract are operating. There is a practice in the branch of trade or commerce in question in particular where a particular course of conduct is generally and regularly followed by operators in that branch when concluding contracts of a particular type ...

As is the case with many national higher courts, the ECJ proceeds slowly, step by step, and is usually mindful not to go any further in its preliminary ruling than the   **16.34** queries posed by the referring national courts strictly require. Two years after *MSG*, the opportunity to expand on that ruling arose. The Corte Suprema di Cassazione (Italian Supreme Court) referred a number of questions regarding the interpretation of the Convention to the Court for a preliminary ruling.

ECJ, 16 March 1999, Case C—159/97 *Trasporti Castelletti Spedizioni Internazionali SpA v Hugo Trumpy SpA* [1999] ECR I—1597, IPRax 2000, 119 (anno. D Girsberger 87), Rev.crit.dr.int.priv. 1999, 559 (anno. H Gaudemet-Tallon), Riv.dir.int.priv.proc. 2000, 184

2 The questions have been raised in proceedings for compensation for damage allegedly caused during the unloading of goods carried under a number of bills of lading from Argentina to Italy, between . . . .('Castelletti'), having its registered office in Milan, Italy, to which the goods were delivered, and . . . ('Trumpy'), having its registered office in Genoa, Italy, in its capacity as agent for the vessel and for the carrier Lauritzen Reefers A/S . . . , whose registered office is in Copenhagen . . . .

3 [Quoting Article 17 the Court points out that the] terminology of the English text was changed by the Convention of 26 May 1989, ie the accession of Spain and Portugal] from 'practices' to 'usages'. The majority of the other language texts use the same terminology (usage, uso, Handelsbrauch . . .). In the translation of the present judgment, the term 'usages' has been adopted [although it did not appear in the text of the convention under consideration] . . . .

5. [. . .] Castelletti brought an action against Trumpy before the Tribunale di Genova (Genoa District Court) seeking an order for payment of compensation.

6 Trumpy, relying on clause 37 of the bills of lading . . . argued that the Genoa court had no jurisdiction.

7 Clause 37, which is drawn up in English as are all the bills of lading in which it is inserted in small, but legible, characters, is the last to appear on the reverse of the printed document. It is worded as follows: 'The contract evidenced by this Bill of Lading shall be governed by English Law and any disputes thereunder shall be determined in England by the High Court of Justice in London according to English Law to the exclusion of the Courts of any other country' . . . .

23 At paragraph 21 of MSG, the Court stated that it is for the national court to determine, first, whether the contract in question is one forming part of international trade or commerce and, second, whether there is a usage in the branch of international trade or commerce in which the parties operate . . .

25 As to the second point, the Court explained in MSG, at paragraph 23, that whether a usage exists is not to be determined by reference to the law of one of the Contracting Parties or in relation to international trade or commerce in general, but in relation to the branch of trade or commerce in which the parties to the contract operate . . .

27 It follows that it is not necessary for such a course of conduct to be established in specific countries or, in particular, in all the Contracting States. The fact that a practice is generally and regularly observed by operators in the countries which play a prominent role in the branch of international trade or commerce in question can be evidence which helps to prove that a usage exists. The determining factor remains, however, whether the course of conduct in question is generally followed by operators in the branch of international trade in which the parties to the contract operate.

28 Since Article 17 of the Convention does not contain any reference to forms of publicity, it must be held … that, although any publicity which might be given in associations or specialised bodies to the standard forms on which a jurisdiction clause appears may help to prove that a practice is generally and regularly followed, such publicity cannot be a requirement for establishing the existence of a usage.

29 A course of conduct satisfying the conditions indicative of a usage does not cease to be a usage because it is challenged before the courts, whatever the extent of the challenges, provided that it still continues to be generally and regularly followed in the trade with which the type of contract in question is concerned. Therefore, the fact that numerous shippers and/or endorsees of bills of lading have challenged the validity of a jurisdiction clause by bringing actions before courts other than those designated would not cause the incorporation of that clause in those documents to cease to constitute a usage, as long as it is established that it amounts to a usage which is generally and regularly followed …

42 Since the validity of the clause under Article 17 must be assessed by reference to the relationship between the original parties, it follows that it is those parties whose awareness of the usage must be assessed, the parties' nationality being irrelevant for the purposes of that investigation.

43 […] it is clear from paragraph 24 of MSG that actual or presumed awareness of a usage on the part of the parties to a contract can be made out, in particular, by showing either that the parties had previously had commercial or trade relations between themselves or with other parties operating in the sector in question, or that, in that sector, a particular course of conduct is sufficiently well known because it is generally and regularly followed when a particular type of contract is concluded, so that it may be regarded as being an established usage.

44 […] given the Convention's silence on the means by which awareness of a usage may be proved, it must be held that, although any publicity which might be given in associations or specialised bodies to the standard forms containing jurisdiction clauses would make it easier to prove awareness, it cannot be essential for this purpose.

Beyond this chapter and in the general context of this book it is interesting to note **16.35** that the ECJ's primary and well-known policy of providing an autonomous framework for the interpretation of Community law leads it to suggest that usages may be international. This would appear to deserve further reflection.[19] It must be borne in mind that the Court looks at the individual branch of trade or commerce concerned. Carriage of goods by sea is obviously a convenient area to demonstrate that such usages do exist and that they are certainly not just 'pan-European' but worldwide. Taken in their entirety the Regulation's solutions for enabling businesses to tailor the jurisdictional bases for dispute resolution to their individual (or industry-wide) needs is impressive.

By comparison, the Member States of the MERCOSUR would appear to be treat- **16.36** ing forum-selection clauses more cautiously. Articles 4 and 5 of the Buenos Aires Protocol on International Jurisdiction in Contractual Matters of 5 August 1994

---

[19] See also para 6.45, above.

in more than one respect reflect earlier case law and statutory provisions in both North America and Europe.

16.37 Similarly, the Hague Convention on Choice of Court Agreements of 30 June 2005, while representing a major break-through at the universal level in recognizing an exclusive selection clause designating the courts of one Contracting State[20] and obliging a court in another Contracting State to suspend or dismiss proceedings to which an exclusive choice of court agreement applies,[21] requires such an agreement to be in writing or equivalent means of communication.[22] The further step to acknowledging that businesses may observe trade usages that reduce the level of formality was obviously too long for a treaty aspiring to be adopted worldwide.

Discretionary limitations of jurisdiction: the doctrine of forum non conveniens

16.38 The doctrine of *forum non conveniens*, first applied in Scotland in the second half of the nineteenth century and over the decades recognized and adopted throughout the common law world,[23] is designed as a tool, to be applied in the court's discretion, to refer a plaintiff to a more appropriate forum. The reasons for such referral may be fairness (vis-à-vis the defendant), the impression that the courts of another country are better equipped or better placed to hear the case, preventing excessive forum shopping in an environment of wide choice of available fora, or simply the desire to conserve scarce judicial resources.

16.39 It has been subject of intense debate whether and, if so, under what circumstances and in which precise form the doctrine of *forum non conveniens* was compatible with the Brussels and the Lugano Conventions, now EC Regulation 44/2001. It is submitted that not only legal certainty but the system of the Regulation which deliberately gives the plaintiff a limited choice of courts would be undermined if the doctrine were to continue to be operational beyond situations addressed in Article 4. From the point of view of its drafters it is incorrect to say that the Convention (now Regulation) is meant to govern only EC-internal procedure; it was their intention to draft a uniform system of rules on jurisdiction for all Member States.

16.40 The debate should have been finally closed by the European Court of Justice's ruling in a case[24] where a British national domiciled in the United Kingdom had suffered a serious accident during a holiday in Jamaica. He brought an action in the

---

[20] Art 5(1).   [21] Art 6.   [22] Art 3 (c)(i).

[23] Where it was not adopted *tout court* similar formulae were developed to achieve those objectives. For English law, cf *The Atlantic Star* [1974] AC 436; *MacShannon v Rockware Glass Ltd* [1978] AC 795; *Spiliada Maritime Corp v Cansulex Ltd* [1987] AC 460; *Lubbe v Cape PLC* [2000] 1 WLR 1545 (HL).

[24] ECJ, 1 March 2005, Case C—281/02 *Owusu v NB Jackson, trading as 'Villa Holidays Bal-Inn Villas' and others.*

UK for breach of contract against the first defendant who was also domiciled there and who had let a beach villa in Mammee Bay (Jamaica) to the claimant and a tort action against several Jamaican companies that were owners and operators of the beaches. The defendants argued that the case had closer links with Jamaica and that the Jamaican courts were a forum in which the case might be tried more suitably. Highlighting the fact that the potentially competing fora, in this case, were a Contracting State and a non-Contracting State, the English Court of Appeal referred the case for a preliminary ruling by the ECJ on the applicability of the doctrine of *forum non conveniens*. While taking all arguments in favour of having the case tried elsewhere into account, the ECJ firmly reiterated its insistence on legal certainty and uniformity of interpretation and application of the Brussels Convention/Regulation as the guiding and paramount principles underlying its rules.

> 43. Moreover, allowing *forum non conveniens* in the context of the Brussels Convention would be likely to affect the uniform application of the rules of jurisdiction contained therein in so far as that doctrine is recognised only in a limited number of Contracting States, whereas the objective of the Brussels Convention is precisely to lay down common rules to the exclusion of derogating national rules.

> 46. In the light of the foregoing considerations, the answer ... must be that the Brussels Convention precludes a court of a Contracting State from declining jurisdiction conferred on it by Article 2 ... on the ground that a court of a non-Contracting State would be a more appropriate forum for the trial of the action even if the the jurisdiction of no other Contracting State is in issue or the proceedings have no connecting factors to any other Contracting State'

On the other hand, a number of cases decided on the basis of the doctrine suggest **16.41** that legal certainty and predictability may not always and in all circumstances be the only and primary objective in transnational commercial law. Moreover, the doctrine ought to be evaluated also in the context of the principle of *lis alibi pendens* to which the EC Regulation[25] and virtually all continental legal systems subscribe. The question has been raised as to whether the 'race to the court house' and 'pre-emptive strike' by one of the parties should be encouraged or discouraged. Non-availability of *forum non conveniens* may be an incentive to strike first in an objectively inappropriate forum. In sum, the issue is in all legal systems the eternal strife between an optimal balance of (abstract) legal certainty and justice to the individual in the case at hand. However, this takes us back to the repeatedly identified imperative for commercial law, namely that the parties' own will and free choices ought to be honoured and must rule supreme. In this perspective it is interesting to note that the 2005 Hague Convention specifically excludes a court chosen by the parties from declining to exercise jurisdiction on the ground that the dispute should be decided by the court of another State.

---

[25] Art 27.

16.42 Another important area for study in relation to cross-border commercial litigation, where traditions based on judicial discretion and others based on pre-defined
grounds for jurisdiction collide, is that of anti-suit injunctions. An anti-suit injunction is a court order obtained, for example, by party A who has brought an action
in London that restrains party B, under sanction of a penalty, from commencing
or continuing legal proceedings in Madrid. The legal analysis, the policies and
objectives both supporting and rejecting the availability of measures of this kind
are illustrated by the ECJ's decision in *Turner v Grovit*.[26]

D. Provisional and Protective Measures

16.43 For merchants and other participants in international trade and finance, time is
frequently of the essence with respect to litigating over their respective rights and
duties arising out of commercial transactions. All legal systems have developed procedural devices that recognize the importance of the time factor. Without them a
court or arbitral tribunal might, for example, reach a conclusion favourable for the
plaintiff after lengthy exchanges of briefs and a hearing only to find out that the
defendant-debtor has taken steps to frustrate any further attempt by or on behalf
of the plaintiff-creditor to obtain what he is entitled to. In international settings
there is an even greater need for rapid action through provisional and protective
measures, because proceedings are longer due to more cumbersome service of process,
greater difficulties in fixing dates for a hearing where people from abroad are to
appear, arranging for the taking of evidence abroad, obtaining expert opinions on
foreign law, linguistic problems and the like.

**Lawrence Collins, 'Provisional and Protective Measures in International Litigation'
(1992) 234 *Recueil des Cours*, 9–238, at 23**

[. . .] The interim protection of rights is no doubt one of those general principles of law
common to all legal systems, and therefore to use the language of Article 38 (1) (c) of the
Statute of the International Court of Justice (now offensive to some), 'the general principles of law recognized by civilized nations'. As President Jiménez de Aréchega put it in
the *Aegean Sea Continental Shelf* case (*Greece v. Turkey*):

> The essential object of provisional measures is to ensure that the execution of a future
> judgment on the merits shall not be frustrated by the actions of one party *pendente*

---

[26] ECJ, 27 April 2004, Case C—159/02 *Gregory Paul Turner v Felix Fareed Ismail Grovit, Harada
Ltd and Changepoint SA* [2004] ECR I-3565. For comments, see A Dickinson, 'A charter for tactical litigation in Europe' [2004] LMCLQ 273; T Kruger, 'The antisuit injunction in the European
Judicial Space: *Turner v Grovit*' (2004) 53 ICLQ 1030, A Mourre, Y Lahlou, 'La construction de l'e-
space judiciaire européen: l'execution des créances incontestées et l'interdiction das anti-suit injunctions' RDAI 2004, 538; A Dutta, C A Heinze, 'Prozessführungsverbote im englischen und
europäischen Zivilverfahrensrecht' ZEuP 2005, 428.

lite ... According to general principles of law recognized in municipal systems, and to the well-established jurisprudence of this Court, the essential justification for the impatience of a tribunal in granting relief before it reached a final decision ... is that the action of one party '*pendente lite*' causes or threatens a damage to the rights of the other, of such a nature that it would be not possible fully to restore those rights, or remedy the infringement thereof, simply by a judgment in its favour.

It is the purpose of the following paragraphs, as it was the purpose of the Hague lectures given by Lord Justice Collins (as he now is), to explore a few issues regarding protective measures in international civil procedure, such as the relevance of whether the court seised would have jurisdiction to decide on the merits, what the prerequisites for granting a measure are, in particular whether *ex parte* measures are available, and, finally, whether protective measures may be, and are in fact, given extraterritorial effect. **16.44**

The emphasis will be, as generally in this book, on transnational commercial law instruments. Tailored to measure for a specific area, Article 43 of the 2001 Cape Town Convention on International Interests in Mobile Equipment[27] is an interesting example of a uniform law provision on jurisdiction and, in connection with Article 13 of the Convention, the content of relief pending final determination of the creditor's claim. However, apart from this highly specific context, it must be borne in mind that not even in an 'internal market for judgments' or a common space for judicial co-operation such as the European Union is there as yet a body of uniform or harmonized rules on protective measures, whether as regards the court's jurisdiction to entertain petitions for such measures or as regards their nature and content. That is why the whole range of prejudgment relief, injunctions, freezing orders, search orders, attachment, *ordonnances sur requête, ordonnances de référé, mesures conservatoires, saisie conservatoire, einstweilige Verfügung, Arrest, provvedimento d'urgenza, sequestro conservativo, kort geding, conservatoir beslag, medidas cautelares*, in particular *embargo preventivo de bienes*, etc., needs to be kept in mind as the background of the analysis. Article 31 of Regulation 44/2001 (Article 24 Brussels and Lugano Conventions) provides that application may be made to the courts of a Member State for such provisional, including protective, measures as may be available under the law of that State, even if the courts of another Member State have jurisdiction as to the substance of the matter. It is to be noted that the court to which the application is made may have jurisdiction according to its own domestic law or on the basis of Articles 2–24 of the Regulation. **16.45**

A survey of devices available under national laws shows that there are basically two types of remedy. Firstly, there are orders ensuring that, pending final determination of the dispute, the status quo will be maintained. In English law, this is achieved by interlocutory injunctions, which may be granted without notice to **16.46**

---

[27] See ch 12.

the defendant, who may, however, on being served with any order apply to have it set aside. Secondly, there are orders designed to secure the ultimate judgment of the court by preventing the defendant from disposing of assets pending final determination of the proceedings. This is the function of what was formerly called the *Mareva* injunction[28] in England, the *Arrest* in Germany and the *saisie* in France and other countries. England being a major centre for international commercial and financial transactions, it would appear particularly interesting to see how this type of protective measure has been developed in the cross-border context before returning to the EC Regulation. A freezing order is an interlocutory injunction restraining a defendant from removing assets out of the jurisdiction pending trial. The claimant has to show that he has a good arguable case on the merits and that there is a real risk that ultimate judgment will be unsatisfied by reason of the disposal of the assets unless the defendant is restrained from disposing of them. In conjunction with such an order the court may grant ancillary orders for discovery and interrogatories to identify where the assets are located.[29]

16.47 The question remained whether the assets to be frozen needed to be in England or whether the English courts would reach beyond the UK's frontiers. In *Babanaft International Co SA v Bassatne*[30] a Panamanian company obtained a judgement in England for $15 million against Lebanese nationals who lived in Switzerland and Greece. They carried on business through companies incorporated in off-shore jurisdictions such as Panama, the Dutch Antilles and Liberia. The court granted a freezing order extending to assets abroad. In *Republic of Haiti v Duvalier*[31] the Republic of Haiti had brought an action in France to recover more than $20 million, funds allegedly embezzled by former President 'Baby Doc' Duvalier. Duvalier's English lawyers held assets on his behalf in various countries. The court granted a worldwide freezing order in aid of the proceedings commenced in France; the English lawyers were ordered to disclose the nature, value and location of Duvalier's funds known to them. The 'worldwide *Mareva* injunction' had been born and continues to flourish.[32]

ECJ, 17 November 1998, Case C—391/95, *Van Uden Maritime BV v Kommanditgesellschaft in Firma Deco-Line and Another* [1998] ECR I— 7091

8 In March 1993 Van Uden and Deco-Line concluded a 'slot/space charter agreement', under which Van Uden undertook to make available to Deco-Line cargo space on board

---

[28] After *Mareva Compania Naviera SA v International Bulkcarriers SA* [1975] 2 Lloyd's Rep 509. The measure is now called a freezing order (Supreme Court Act 1981, s 37(3); CPR r 25.1(f)).

[29] The order operates *in personam* only; it does not confer on the claimant any interest in the frozen assets, which simply remain available to be taken in execution of any judgment the claimant obtains.   [30] [1990] Ch 13 (CA).

[31] [1990] 1 QB 202 (CA).

[32] See also *Crédit Suisse Fides Trust SA v Cuoghi* [1998] QB 818 (CA).

vessels operated by Van Uden ... on a liner service between northern and western parts of Europe and West Africa. In return, Deco-Line was to pay charter hire in accordance with the rates agreed between the parties.

9 Van Uden instituted arbitration proceedings in the Netherlands pursuant to the agreement, on the ground that Deco-Line had failed to pay certain invoices submitted to it by Van Uden.

10 Van Uden also applied to the President of the Rechtbank (District Court), Rotterdam, for interim relief on the grounds that Deco-Line was not displaying the necessary diligence in the appointment of arbitrators and that non-payment of its invoices was disturbing its cash flow. In its application, it sought an order against Deco-Line for payment of DM 837 919.13 to cover four debts due under the agreement.

11 In those proceedings, Deco-Line objected ... that the Netherlands court had no jurisdiction to entertain the claims. Being established in Germany, it could be sued only before the German courts.

12 The President of the Rechtbank dismissed that objection on the ground that an order sought as interim relief must be regarded as provisional measure within the meaning of Article 24 of the Convention [now Article 31 of the Regulation].

13 Referring to Article 126(3) of the Code of Civil Procedure, he decided that, as court of the plaintiff's domicile, he had jurisdiction to entertain an application made a the plaintiff residing in the Netherlands against a defendant with no known residence ... there. He further concluded that the case had the requisite minimum connection with Netherlands law, for two reasons: (i) Deco-Line was engaged in international trade and would thus become a creditor in the Netherlands, so that any judgment against it could be enforced there, and (ii) such a judgment could also be enforced in Germany.

14 Finally, the President of the Rechtbank took the view that his jurisdiction was in no way affected by the fact that the parties had agreed to have their dispute determined by arbitration in the Netherlands since, under Article 1022(2) of the Code of Civil Procedure, an arbitration clause cannot preclude a party's right to seek interim relief.

15 By provisionally enforceable judgment ... the President ... ordered Deco-Line to pay Van Uden the sum of DM 377 625.35 together with interest at the statutory rate.

16 On appeal by Deco-Line, the Gerechtshof te 's-Gravenhage (Regional Court of Appeal, The Hague) quashed that order. In its view, the fact that the case had to have sufficient connection with the Netherlands law meant, in the context of the Convention, that it must be possible for the interim order applied for to be enforced in the Netherlands. The mere fact that Deco-Line could acquire assets there in the future was ... insufficient for that purpose.

17 A further appeal against that decision was brought before the Hoge Raad der Nederlanden, which stayed proceedings and requested a preliminary ruling by the Court on the following questions:

'(1) Where an obligation to pay a sum or sums due under a contract must be performed in a Contracting State—so that, under Article 5, point 1, of the Brussels Convention, the creditor is entitled to sue his defaulting debtor in the courts of that State with a view to obtaining performance, even though the debtor is domiciled in another Contracting State—do the courts of the first-mentioned State (for the same reason) have jurisdiction also to hear and determine a claim brought by the creditor against his debtor in interim [kort geding] proceedings for an order requiring the debtor, by provisionally enforceable judgment, to pay a sum which, in the view of the court hearing the interim application, is very probably due to the creditor, or do additional conditions apply in relation to the jurisdiction of the court hearing the interim application, for example the condition that the relief sought from that court must take effect (or be capable of taking effect) in the Contracting State concerned?

(2) Does it make a difference to the answer to Question 1 whether the contract between the parties contains an arbitration clause and, if so, what the place of arbitration is according to that clause?

(3) If the answer to Question 1 is that, in order for the court hearing the interim application to have jurisdiction, the relief sought from it must also take effect (or be capable of taking effect) in the Contracting State concerned, does that mean that the order applied for must be capable of enforcement in that State, and is it then necessary for this condition to be fulfilled when the interim application is made, or is it sufficient that it can be reasonably expected to be fulfilled in the future?

(4) Does the possibility, provided for in Article 289 et seq. of the Netherlands Code of Civil Procedure, of applying on grounds of pressing urgency to the President of the Arrondissementsrechtbank for a provisionally enforceable judgment constitute a 'provisional' or 'protective' measure within the meaning of Article 24 of the Brussels Convention?

(5) Does it make any difference to the answer to Question 4 whether substantive proceedings on the main issue are, or may become, pending and, if so, is it material that arbitration proceedings had started in the same case?

(6) Does it make any difference to the answer to Question 4 that the interim relief sought is an order requiring performance of an obligation of payment, as referred to in Question 1?

(7) If Question 4 must be answered in the affirmative, and 'the courts of another Contracting State have jurisdiction as to the substance of the matter', must Article 24, and in particular the reference therein to 'such provisional ... measures as may be available under the law of [a Contracting] State', be interpreted as meaning that the court hearing the application for interim measures has (for the same reason) jurisdiction if it has jurisdiction under provisions of its national law, even where those provisions are referred to in the second paragraph of Article 3 of the Brussels Convention, or is its jurisdiction in the latter case conditional on the fulfilment of additional conditions, for example that the interim relief sought from that court must take effect, or be capable of taking effect, in the Contracting State concerned?

(8) If the answer to Question 7 must be that, in order for the court hearing the application for interim relief to have jurisdiction, it is also required that the relief sought from it must take effect (or be capable of taking effect) in the Contracting State concerned, does that mean that the order applied for must be capable of enforcement in that State, and is it then necessary for this condition to be fulfilled when the application for interim relief is made, or is it sufficient that it can reasonably be expected to be fulfilled in the future?'

[...] 22 Thus, the court having jurisdiction as to the substance of a case under ... the Convention also has jurisdiction to order provisional or protective measures, without that jurisdiction being subject to any further conditions, such as mentioned in the ... third question.

23 However, in the present case, the contract ... contains an arbitration clause.

24 Where the parties have validly excluded the jurisdiction of the courts ... and have referred that dispute to arbitration, there are no courts of any State that have jurisdiction as to the substance of the case for the purposes of the Convention. Consequently, a party to such a contract is not in a position to make an application for provisional or protective measures to a court that would have jurisdiction under the Convention as to the substance of the case.

25 In such a case, it is only under Article 24 that a court may be empowered under the Convention to order provisional or protective measures.

26 In that connection, Deco-Line and the German and United Kingdom Governments[33] agreed that, since the parties have agreed to submit their dispute to arbitration, interim proceedings also fall outside the scope of the Convention. The German Government argues in particular that measures sought in interim proceedings, when they are intrinsically bound up with the subject-matter of an arbitration procedure, fall outside the scope of the Convention. In the United Kingdom Government's view, the measures sought in the present case may be regarded as ancillary to the arbitration and are thus excluded from the scope of the Convention.

27 Van Uden and the Commission, however, contend that the existence of an arbitration clause does not have the effect of excluding an application for interim measures from the scope of the Convention. The Commission points out that the subject-matter of the dispute is decisive and that the issue underlying the interim proceedings concerns the performance of a contractual obligation—a matter which falls within the scope of the Convention.

28 It must ... be borne in mind here that Article 24 applies ... provided that the subject-matter falls within the scope ratione materiae of the Convention which covers civil and commercial matters.

29 Thus the mere fact that proceedings have been, or may be, commenced on the substance ... before a court of a Contracting State does not deprive a court of another ... State of its jurisdiction under Article 24 of the Convention.

30 However, Article 24 cannot be relied on to bring within the scope of the Convention provisional measures relating to matters which are excluded from it ....

31 Under Article 1, second paragraph, point 4 ... arbitration is excluded ... By that provision, the Contracting Parties[34] intended to exclude arbitration in its entirety, including proceedings brought before national courts ...

32 The experts' report drawn up on the accession of the Kingdom of Denmark, Ireland and the United Kingdom of Great Britain and Northern Ireland to the Convention (OJ 1979 C 59, p.71, at pp. 92–93) specifies that the Convention does not apply to judgments determining whether an arbitration agreement is valid or not or, because it is invalid, ordering the parties not to continue the arbitration proceedings, or to proceedings and decisions concerning allocations for the revocation, amendment, recognition and enforcement of arbitration awards. Also excluded ... are proceedings ancillary to arbitration

---

[33] Under the rules of procedure, Member States' Governments and the EU Commission may make submissions explaining their views as to the legal issues raised in the case.

[34] That is, the Contracting States of the Convention. For purposes of the Regulation these are the Member States.

proceedings, such as the appointment or dismissal of arbitrators, the fixing of the place of arbitration or the extension of the time-limit for making awards.

33 However, it must be noted in that regard that provisional measures are not in principle ancillary to arbitration proceedings but are ordered in parallel to such proceedings and are intended as measures of support. They concern not arbitration as such but the protection of a wide variety of rights. Their place in the scope of the Convention is thus determined not by their own nature but by the nature of the rights which they serve to protect ...

34 It must therefore be concluded that where, as in the case in the main proceedings, the subject-matter of an application for provisional measures relates to a question falling within the scope ratione materiae of the Convention, the Convention is applicable and Article 24 thereof may confer jurisdiction on the court hearing that application even where proceedings have already been, or may be, commenced on the substance of the case and even where those proceedings are to be conducted before arbitrators.

35 Next, as regards the conditions set out in the Convention for the grant of an application under Article 24, Van Uden submits that no further condition need to be fulfilled for the court hearing such an application to have jurisdiction provided that it has jurisdiction under provisions of its national law even where those provisions are among those listed in the second paragraph of Article 3 ... Deco-Line, however, maintains that the imposition of stricter conditions is clearly justified and that, in any event, the fact that Article 24 refers to national rules on jurisdiction implies that the court in question is free to hold that its jurisdiction is subject to such conditions.

36 In the German Government's view, Article 24 does not authorise a court acting on the basis of one of the rules of jurisdiction listed in ... Article 3 ... to order provisional measures unless the rule of jurisdiction in question is subject to the urgency of the decision or based upon that reasoning and unless the provisional measure, at the time when it is ordered, has a sufficient connecting link with the State of that court. The latter condition is satisfied when the provisional measure can be enforced in that State.

37 In that regard, it must be remembered that the expression 'provisional, including protective, measures' within the meaning of Article 24 ... is to be understood as referring to measures which, in matters within the scope of the Convention, are intended to preserve a factual or legal situation so as to safeguard rights the recognition of which is otherwise sought from the court having jurisdiction as to the substance of the case ...

38 The granting of this type of measure requires particular care on the part of the court in question and detailed knowledge of the actual circumstances in which the measures sought are to take effect. Depending on each case and commercial practices in particular, the court must be able to place a time-limit on its order or, as regards the nature of the assets or goods subject to the measures contemplated, require bank guarantees or nominate a sequestrator and generally make its authorisation subject to all conditions guaranteeing the provisional or protective character of the measure ordered ...

39 In that regard, the Court has held ... that the courts of the place—or, in any event, of the Contracting State—where the assets subject to the measures sought are located are those best placed to assess the circumstances which may lead to the grant or the refusal of the measures sought or to the laying down of procedures and conditions which the plaintiff must observe in order to guarantee the provisional or protective character of the measures authorised.

40 It follows that the granting of provisional or protective measures on the basis of Article 24 is conditional on, inter alia, the existence of a real connecting link between

the subject-matter of the measures sought and the territorial jurisdiction of the Contracting State of the court before which those matters are sought.

41 It further follows that a court ordering measures on the basis of Article 24 must take into consideration the need to impose conditions or stipulations such as to guarantee their provisional or protective character.

42 With regard more particularly to the fact that the national court has in this instance based its jurisdiction on one of the national provisions listed in ... Article 3 ... , it must be borne in mind that, in accordance with the first paragraph of that Article, persons domiciled in a Contracting State may be sued in the courts of another Contracting State only by virtue of the rules set out in Sections 2 to 6 of Title II [now Sections 2 to 7 of the Regulation], that is to say Articles 5 to 18 [now Articles 5 to 24 of the Regulation] .. . Consequently, the prohibition in Article 3 of reliance on rules of exorbitant jurisdiction does not apply to the special regime provided for by Article 24.

43 Finally, with regard to the question whether an interim order requiring payment of a contractual consideration may be classified as a provisional measure within the meaning of Article 24 ... Deco-Line and the Government of the United Kingdom argue that it cannot. The German Government considers that the main proceedings appear to fall outside the definition of provisional or protective measures.

44 Van Uden and the Commission do not share that view. In the Commission's view, provisional measures must be taken to mean those whose validity lapses when the main issue is determined or on the expiry of a specified period. They may comprise positive measures, that is to say an order to perform some act such as the handing-over of property or the payment of a sum of money.

45 Here, it must be noted that it is not possible to rule out in advance, in a general and abstract manner, that interim payment of a contractual consideration, even in an amount corresponding to that sought as principal relief, may be necessary in order to ensure the practical effect of the decision on the substance of the case and may, in certain cases, appear justified with regard to the interests involved ...

46 However, an order for interim payment of a sum of money is, by its very nature, such that it may preempt the decision on the substance of the case. If, moreover, the plaintiff were entitled to secure interim payment of a contractual consideration before the courts of the place where he is himself domiciled, where those courts have no jurisdiction over the substance of the case under Articles 2 to 18 ... , and thereafter to have the order in question recognised and enforced in the defendant's State, the rules of jurisdiction laid down by the Convention could be circumvented.

47 Consequently, interim payment of a contractual consideration does not constitute a provisional measure within the meaning of Article 24 unless, first, repayment to the defendant of the sum awarded is guaranteed if the plaintiff is unsuccessful as regards the substance of his claim and, second, the measure sought relates only to specific assets of the defendant located or to be located within the confines of the territorial jurisdiction of the court to which application is made. [...]

Less than six months later, the Court developed these criteria further in *Hans-Hermann Mietz v Intership Yachting Sneek BV*,[35] where it ruled that decisions

16.48

---

[35] Case C–99/96, [1999] ECR I–2277 (ECJ 27 April 1999).

cannot be the subject of an enforcement order under Title III if (1) they are delivered at the end of proceedings which were not proceedings as to substance but summary proceedings for the granting of interim measures, (2) the defendant was not domiciled in the State of the court of origin and it does not appear from the judgment that, for other reasons, the court had jurisdiction under the Convention as to the substance of the matter, (3) the judgment does not contain any statement of reasons designed to establish the jurisdiction of the court as to the substance of the matter, and (4) the judgment is limited to ordering the payment of a contractual consideration without, on the one hand, repayment to the defendant of the sum being guaranteed if the plaintiff is unsuccessful on the merits or, on the other, the measure sought relating only to specific assets of the defendant located within the territory of the court to which application is made.

16.49 In sum, a court that has Regulation-based jurisdiction as regards the substance of the case may grant injunctions in the sense of 'positive measures' or orders to perform some act without any limitations; enforceability in the State where the measure is granted is immaterial. Conversely, the exercise of jurisdiction based solely on provisions of national law requires that qualified conditions are fulfilled ('real link' between the subject-matter sought and the court's territorial jurisdiction). A measure such as an attachment may be granted only with respect to defined assets of the defendant located within the territorial jurisdiction. Cross-border 'negative measures' or restraining orders without jurisdiction as to the substance would therefore appear to be ruled out. The territorial limitation means that English courts may grant Europe-wide *Mareva* injunctions or freezing orders only where they would have Regulation-based jurisdiction as to the substance of the case.[36]

16.50 The question has been raised whether it is wise to leave these matters to the courts or whether, in particular but not only, in a 'space of judicial co-ordination' time might be ripe to engage in substantive harmonization of the law of provisional and protective measures. The International Law Association has submitted detailed proposals[37] and the ALI/UNIDROIT Principles of Transnational Civil Procedure[38] devote Principle 8 to the issue.

---

[36] But see *Dicey, Morris and Collins on The Conflict of Laws* (14th edn, Sweet & Maxwell, London, 2006), vol 1, r 8-028 discussing *Crédit Suisse Fides Trust SA v Cuoghi* [1998] QB 818 (CA).

[37] International Law Association, 'Principles on Provisional and Protective Measures in International Litigation ("Helsinki Principles")' (1996) 67 ILA Rep 202, 45 Am J Comp L 941 (1997), RabelsZ 62 (1998) 128 with comments by P Nygh at p 115 et seq. For a full discussion N Andrews, 'Juridical Co-operation: Recent Progress, Report to the 1st European Jurists Forum' (Nomos, Baden-Baden, 2001). [38] See below, para 16.62.

E. Conduct of the Proceedings and Judicial Assistance

Service abroad of judicial documents

Service of process as well as other functions which are part of the conduct of cross-   **16.51**
border proceedings (judicial cooperation) is rooted in sharply diverging traditions. Civil law jurisdictions view service of a judicial document as an official act
based on the State's sovereignty which consequently has to be effected by an official of the relevant authority. Common law jurisdictions, on the other hand, are
historically used to the parties, more specifically the claimant, performing these
functions directly or through an agent. Both a significant number of bilateral civil
procedure conventions and the 1965 Hague Convention on the Service Abroad
of Judicial and Extrajudicial Documents in Civil and Commercial Matters provide for institutional mechanisms aimed at bridging this divide. The Convention
provides for three modes of service. First, the authority or judicial officer competent under the law of the State in which the document originates may forward to
a designated Central Authority in the State in which service is required a request
for service of the annexed document.[39] Alternatively, service may be effected
through the traditional channels of transmission, i.e. diplomatic or consular agents.[40]
Finally, the Convention provides for service through the post, judicial officers
(such as the French huissiers), etc., of the State of origin, through the judicial
authorities, etc. of the State of destination, unless the latter State objects to that
mode of service.[41]

The Convention states that it shall apply in 'all cases' where a document has to be   **16.52**
served abroad. There has, in particular in relation to cases originating in the US
courts, been much controversy as to whether the Convention is mandatory,
excluding forms of service abroad not permitted by its provisions.

Volkswagenwerk Aktiengesellschaft v Schlunk 486 US 694, 108 S Ct 2104 (1988)
Justice O'Connor delivered the opinion of the Cour:

I

The parents of respondent Herwig Schlunk were killed in an automobile accident . . .
Schlunk filed a wrongful death action on their behalf in the Circuit Court of Cook
County, Illinois. Schlunk alleged that Volkswagen of America, Inc. (VWoA) had designed
and sold the automobile that his parents were driving, and that defects in the automobile
caused their deaths . . . Schlunk . . . served his complaint on VWoA, and VWoA filed an
answer denying that it had designed or assembled the automobile in question. Schlunk
then amended the complaint to add as a defendant Volkswagen Aktiengesellschaft

---

[39] Arts 2 to 6.   [40] Arts 8 and 9.   [41] Art 10.

(VWAG), which is the petitioner here. VWAG, a corporation established under the laws of the Federal Republic of Germany, has its place of business in that country. VWoA is a wholly-owned subsidiary of VWAG. Schlunk attempted to serve his amended complaint on VWAG by serving VWoA as VWAG's agent.

VWAG filed a special and limited appearance for the purpose of quashing service. VWAG asserted that it could be served only in accordance with the Hague Service Convention, and that Schlunk had not complied with the Convention's requirements. The Cicuit Court denied VWAG's motion. It first observed that VWoA is registered to do business in Illinois and has a registered agent for receipt of process in Illinois. The court then reasoned that VWoA and VWAG are so closely related that VWoA is VWAG's agent for service of process as a matter of law, notwithstanding VWAG's failure or refusal to appoint VWoA formally as an agent. The court relied on the facts that VWoA is a wholly-owned subsidiary of VWAG, that a majority of the members of the board of directors of VWoA are members of the board of directors of VWAG, and that VWoA is ... the exclusive importer and distributor of VWAG products sold in the United States. The court concluded that, because service was accomplished within the United States, the Hague Service Convention did not apply ... [The Illinois Appellate Court affirmed, and the Illinois Supreme Court denied leave to appeal.]

We granted certiorari to address this issue ... which has given rise to disagreement among the lower courts ...

II

[On the nature of the Hague Convention and the United States and Germany being Contracting States]

Article 1 defines the scope of the Convention, which is the subject of controversy in this case. It says: 'The present Convention shall apply in all cases ... where there is occasion to transmit a judicial ... document for service abroad.' ... By virtue of the Supremacy Clause, U.S. Const., Art. VI, the Convention preempts inconsistent methods of service prescribed by state law in all cases to which it applies. Schlunk does not purport to have served his complaint on VWAG in accordance with the Convention. Therefore, if service of process in this case falls within Article 1 of the Convention, the trial court should have granted VWAG's motion to quash ...

The Convention does not specify the circumstances in which there is 'occasion to transmit' a complaint 'for service abroad'. But at least the term 'service of process' has a well-established technical meaning. Service of process refers to the formal delivery of documents that is legally sufficient to charge the defendant with notice of a pending action ... The legal sufficiency of a formal delivery of documents must be measured against some standard. The Convention does not prescribe a standard, so we almost necessarily must refer to the internal law of the forum state. If the internal law of the forum state defines the applicable method of serving process as requiring the transmittal of documents abroad, then the Hague Convention applies ...

VWAG correctly maintains that the Convention also aims to ensure that there will be adequate notice in cases in which there is occasion to serve process abroad. Thus compliance with the Convention is mandatory in all cases to which it applies ... Our interpretation of the Convention does not necessarily advance this particular objective, inasmuch as it makes recourse to the Convention's means of service dependent on the forum's internal law. But we do not think that this country, or any other country, will draft its internal laws deliberately so as to circumvent the Convention in cases in which it would be appropriate to transmit judicial documents for service abroad ...

Furthermore, nothing that we say today prevents compliance with the Convention even when the internal law of the forum does not so require. The Convention provides simple and certain means by which to serve process on a foreign national. Those who eschew its procedures risk discovering that the forum's internal law required transmittal of documents for service abroad, and that the Convention therefore provided the exclusive means of valid service. In addition, parties that comply with the Convention ultimately may find it easier to enforce their judgments abroad ... For these reasons, we anticipate that parties may resort to the Convention voluntarily, even in cases that fall outside the scope of its mandatory application.

III

In this case, the Illinois long-arm statute authorized Schlunk to serve VWAG by substituted service on VWoA, without sending documents to Germany ... VWAG has not petitioned for review of the Illinois Appellate Court's holding that service was proper as a matter of Illinois law. VWAG contends, however, that service on VWAG was not complete until VWoA transmitted the complaint to VWAG in Germany. According to VWAG, this transmission constituted service abroad under the Hague Convention ...

We reject that argument. Where service on a domestic agent is valid and complete under both state law and the Due Process Clause, our inquiry ends and the Convention has no further implications ...

Affirmed.

Justice Brennan concurred in the judgment on different grounds in an opinion **16.53** joined by Justices Marshall and Blackmun. That opinion is interesting in that it cautions against leaving it entirely to contracting States to freely determine that service is 'domestic'. Moreover, it draws on the negotiating history and requirements of uniform interpretation as well as the legislative history of the United States' ratification.

Where a request for service complies with the terms of the Convention, the State **16.54** addressed may refuse to comply only if it deems that compliance would infringe its sovereignty or security.[42] It may not refuse to comply solely on the ground that, under its internal law, it claims exclusive jurisdiction over the subject matter or that its law would not permit the action upon which the application is based.[43]

For Member States of the European Union, except Denmark, the EC Regulation **16.55** on service in Member States[44] replaces the 1965 Hague Convention (or the 1954 Hague Convention on Civil Procedure, as the case may be). The Regulation simplifies and accelerates service procedures. Sovereign interests play, obviously, a significantly reduced role. The ground for refusal previously provided by Article 13 of the Convention[45] has been abolished completely. The Regulation applies where

---

[42] Art 13(1).   [43] Art 13(2).

[44] Council Regulation (EC) No 1348/2000 of 29 May 2000 on the service in the Member States of judicial and extrajudicial documents in civil or commercial matters, (2000) OJ L160/37.

[45] Namely that a State deems that compliance with a request for service would infringe its sovereignty or security.

a document 'has to be transmitted' from one Member State to another for service there.[46] Whether that is the case (or whether fictitious forms of service within the forum State as they are traditionally used in some Member States are sufficient) is for the *lex fori* to decide. The Regulation does, however, make it possible to mitigate the consequences where the law of the addressed State does not provide for such fictions.[47] The justifiable greater degree of informality within the European 'space of judicial co-operation' is particularly evident in the rules regarding the modes of service. While a number of Member States seek to take full advantage of acceleration potential through direct and decentralized transmission at the operational level,[48] others maintain the (Hague Convention) system of transmission through central bodies.[49] Another way of accelerating procedures is to permit transmission 'by any appropriate means', which includes fax and e-mail.[50] In principle, no translation is required,[51] which would appear to be evidence for the cultural background, the pace and the forces driving judicial co-operation in Europe.

Taking of evidence

16.56 The 1970 Hague Convention on the Taking of Evidence Abroad in Civil and Commercial Matters establishes procedures designed to overcome the divide, similar to the one encountered as regards service of process, between, on the one hand, countries where the taking of evidence is viewed as part of the preparation of the trial and, therefore, a responsibility of the parties who may turn to their counsel and, on the other hand, legal systems viewing the obtaining of evidence as a judicial act which may interfere with the sovereignty of the State where the evidence is to be obtained. The United Kingdom's interest in building this multilateral bridge was much weaker than the United States' because the UK has concluded bilateral treaties with many civil-law States that are more liberal than the Hague Convention and provide for efficient handling of the taking of evidence. Under the Convention, there are two avenues. A judicial authority of a Contracting State may, in accordance with the law of that State, request the authority of another Contracting State, by means of a Letter of Request ('LoR'), to obtain evidence, for use in judicial proceedings.[52] The request may be for a variety of forms of evidence, including oral testimony, witness statements, other documentary evidence, and the inspection of property.[53] The LoR is sent to a designated Central Authority in the country where evidence is to be taken.[54] The Convention does not prevent a Contracting State from obtaining evidence by other methods provided for under domestic law of the State in which evidence is sought.[55] The US Supreme Court held that the Convention does not provide a

---

[46] Art 1(1).   [47] Art 19.   [48] Arts 2, 4 to 11.   [49] Art 3.
[50] Arts 2, 4 to 11.
[51] Without a translation the addressee may, however, refuse to accept the document (Art 8).
[52] Art 1.   [53] Art 3.   [54] Art 2.   [55] Art 27.

mandatory or exclusive framework for obtaining evidence abroad. Only considerations of comity vis-à-vis the foreign State which may regard other ways as an
infringement of its sovereignty were held to constitute limits.[56] Others, on both
sides of the Atlantic Ocean, dissented. Since lower courts obviously followed the
Supreme Court's indication, another field where the so-called US-European judicial conflict waged had been created. The revised Federal Rules of Civil Procedure
(FRCP) provide in rule 28(b):

> Depositions may be taken in a foreign country (1) pursuant to any applicable treaty
> or convention, or (2) pursuant to a letter of request ... or (3) on notice before a per-
> son authorized to administer oaths in the place where the examination is held, either
> by the law thereof or by the law of the United States, or (4) before a person commis-
> sioned by the court ...

While Europeans read this as a clear indication that the Convention procedure is **16.57**
considered to take precedence, it may not have changed the US practice fundamentally. A Contracting State may make a reservation to the effect that it will not
execute a LoR issued for the purpose of obtaining pre-trial discovery of documents as known in common law countries.[57] However, parties and witnesses who
are subject to US jurisdiction do have to comply with duties to disclose. Where
the request is unsuccessful because the requested court is unable to force parties to
disclose[58] or because the request would not be attended to in view of a reservation
made under Article 23 a US court may and will compel the production of the documents in the US.

The second mode of obtaining evidence provided for under the Hague Convention **16.58**
is provided for under Articles 15 to 22. A diplomatic officer, or consular agent of
a Contracting State may, in the territory of another Contracting State, take evidence without compulsion of nationals of a State which he represents in aid of
proceedings commenced in the courts of a State which he represents. A Contracting
State may declare that such taking of evidence requires permission by the declaring State.

Again, the Member States of the European Union, mindful of the policy objective **16.59**
to create a common space for judicial proceedings and decisions, are aiming
higher. The EC Regulation on cooperation in the taking of evidence[59] entered
into force on 1 July 2001; it does not apply to Denmark. The words 'swift' and
'swiftest possible means', heavily employed in the text, reflect that policy objective. The basic idea of the Regulation No. 1348/2000 on service of documents,[60]

---

[56] *Société Nationale Industrielle Aérospatiale v US District Court for the Southern District of Iowa*
482 US 522 (1987).   [57] Art 23.

[58] Art 9.

[59] Council Regulation (EC) No. 1206/2001 of 28 May 2001 on cooperation between the courts
of the Member States in the taking of evidence in civil or commercial matters (2001) OJ L 174/1.

[60] Above para 16.55.

i.e. the decentralized and direct communication between the requesting and the requested courts, is also at the heart of the procedure for taking evidence.[61] The central bodies designated by a Member State have only support functions.[62] Chapter II of the Regulation deals in detail with the transmission and execution of requests for the taking of evidence. As far as the former is concerned the salient feature is the use of standardized forms that contemplate almost any conceivable procedural situation and that are annexed to the Regulation. Generally speaking, the requested court executes the request in accordance with its *lex fori*.[63]

F. Recognition and Enforcement of Foreign Judgments

Brussels I Regulation

16.60 As regards *recognition*, Regulation 44/2001[64] has, compared to the Brussels Convention, abolished a few more obstacles. Expeditious processing in the interest of the judgment creditor has been boosted to the detriment of the defendant's protection. Further, under Articles 32 and 33 judgments given in a Member State are recognized in all other Member States without any special procedure being required. Along with the structural and strategic decision to regulate the jurisdiction to adjudicate 'directly', this was the qualitative leap made by the Brussels Convention and its successor instrument. It creates a regional space for the free movement of judgments and the relevant provisions of the Regulation are therefore to be interpreted broadly and in a way favourable to recognition. Reasons justifying *non-recognition* are few and they are all and exclusively identified in the Regulation itself. Firstly, recognition may be refused if it would manifesly conflict with *public policy (ordre public)* in the Member State where the recognition is sought,[65] While there is unanimity that the language ('manifestly') should make sure that its application is an exceedingly rare event, the view is widely held that this 'safety net' is still needed. Moreover, the content of the public policy is thought to be national rather than European. However, it is for the ECJ to see to it that national courts do not overstep the boundaries and thwart the rationale of their duty to recognize. Secondly, where a *default judgment* was given, it may not be recognized if the defendant was not served with the document which instituted the proceedings in sufficient time and in a way that deprived him of a fair chance to arrange for his defence.[66] The Brussels Convention had required that service be done 'properly', opening a whole range of potential inquiries to the detriment of expeditiousness in the judgment creditor's interest. Thirdly, recognition may be refused of a judgment *irreconcilable* with a *judgment* given between the same parties in the Member State where recognition is sought.[67] Lastly, recognition may be

---

[61] Art 2.   [62] Art 3.   [63] Art 10.   [64] Above para 16.24.   [65] Art 34(1).
[66] Art 34(2).   [67] Art 34(3).

refused if the judgment is irreconcilable with an *earlier* judgment given in another Member State or a third State involving the same cause of action and between the same parties, provided the earlier judgment fulfils the conditions for its recognition.[68] Further grounds for refusing recognition are conflicts with selected jurisdiction provisions of the Regulation. Under no circumstances may a foreign judgment be reviewed on its merits.[69]

A judgment given and enforceable in one Member State is enforceable in another Member State when, upon application of any interested party (normally the judgment creditor), it has been *declared enforceable* there.[70] At this stage, only certain formalities have to be complied with and no review under the provisions governing recognition is foreseen. The party against whom enforcement is sought has to appeal the declaration.[71] The appellate court may refuse or revoke a declaration of enforceability only on one of the grounds on which a refusal of recognition can be based.[72] Of the greatest practical importance is that the applicant for a declaration of recognition may avail himself of provisional, including protective, measures under the law of the State where recognition is sought without a declaration of enforceability being required.[73] This again is a tool given to the judgment creditor which considerably strengthens his position and is a disincentive against delaying tactics at this second stage of proceedings to obtain a *European title for execution*. Certain documents which have been formally drawn up (e.g. by a notary public, a governmental agency etc.) or registered as authentic instruments and which are enforceable in one Member State are equally to be declared enforceable in another Member State upon application.[74] The same applies to a settlement which has been approved by a court in the course of proceedings and is enforceable in the Member State in which it was concluded.[75] In light of the significant percentage of cases dispensed with in the form of settlements in certain countries, the practical importance of this provision can hardly be overestimated.

The Las Leñas and Buenos Aires Protocols

The approach taken, for the time being, in the MERCOSUR Member States **16.61** Argentina, Brazil, Paraguay and Uruguay under these two instruments is more conservative than the one introduced by the Brussels Convention. The point of departure is—as it used to be in many European pre-Brussels bilateral treaties on jurisdiction and recognition and enforcement—a provision in Article 20 of the Las Leñas Protocol[76] establishing requirements for the 'extra-territorial effect' of judgments and arbitral awards. Critical for our purposes is the substantive

---

[68] Art 34(4).   [69] Art 36.   [70] Art 38.   [71] Arts 41, 43
[72] Arts 45, 34, 35.   [73] Art 47.   [74] Art 57.   [75] Art 58.
[76] Protocollo de cooperacion y assistencia jurisdiccional en materia civil, comercial, laboral y administrativa of 27 June 1992, MERCOSUR/CMC/DEC No. 05/92.

requirement that judgments are eligible for recognition if rendered 'by a court which, according to the rules on jurisdiction of the State where recognition is sought, was competent'.[77] This is the classic 'indirect' regulation of jurisdiction as we find it in many autonomous national rules on recognition of foreign judgments. The Buenos Aires Protocol on International Jurisdiction in Contractual Matters of 5 August 1994 provides some of those rules. *Recognition and enforcement* is much more cumbersome than in Europe not only because the courts of the State where recognition is sought re-examine the adjudicating forum's decision regarding its jurisdiction, but also for formal and procedural reasons which cannot be discussed in detail here.

G. From International to Transnational Civil Procedure: the ALI/UNIDROIT Principles of Transnational Civil Procedure

Objectives

16.62 The overwhelming majority of rules on civil procedure, whether codified or judge-made, are based on the implicit assumption that both parties are residents of the forum State and, therefore, familiar with the ways civil and, in particular, commercial disputes are resolved in that country's courts. Increasingly, this is not the case as either one or even both parties are foreigners. This may result in an efficiency gap and a fairness gap. International arbitrators are used to this situation and frequently remedy undesirable consequences by modifying and adapting existing rules of procedure or by designing new rules with a view to accommodating the peculiar needs of transnational dispute resolution. Judges do normally not have the freedom to react creatively to this type of peculiarity of a case brought before them. There may be good reasons for giving them some and for providing guidelines how best to use it and to efficiently and fairly address such situations of transnational business disputes where objective needs of the rational administration of justice are to be seen against a multicultural background of parties' expectations. Another source for the desire to fathom the possibilities of harmonizing some basic principles of the law of civil procedure is our experience that the diversity of the 'rules of the game' from one jurisdiction to another leads to enormous potential for a purely tactical approach to the question of where a case should be tried (forum shopping). Moreover, it is reasonable to believe that efforts to universally harmonize the law of jurisdiction and the recognition and enforcement of foreign judgments as well as to put international judicial assistance on more solid foundations will stand a greater chance to succeed if the working of rules of civil

---

[77] Art 20(c).

procedure 'in action'—as opposed to those 'on the books'—and its convergence in many areas is better understood. Finally, the Member States of the European Union, under the Amsterdam Treaty, 'communitarized' a significant area of civil procedure, and it will be important to make sure that bridges between Europe and the rest of the world are available so as to prevent judicial autism. All these considerations constitute the foundations of this instrument. Some are encapsulated in the black letter as well as the comment of the Preamble of the 2004 ALI/UNIDROIT Principles of Transnational Civil Procedure (PTCP).[78] The Preamble reads:

> Scope and Implementation
>
> These Principles are standards for adjudication of transnational commercial disputes. These Principles may be equally appropriate for the resolution of most other kinds of civil disputes and may be the basis for future initiatives in reforming civil procedure.

16.63 Two distinctions appear to be basic. First is the PTCP's focus on transnational disputes; second, the distinction they draw between non-commercial and commercial disputes. There are several reasons for these distinctions, one of them being the historical experience of many jurisdictions with certain branches of the judiciary proceeding according to specific rules of procedure (family matters, labour disputes etc.). Another—politically fundamental—one is obviously that, in the United States, there is no jury involved in the resolution of commercial disputes.

Selected solutions

16.64 At first sight surprisingly (and against some warnings to refrain from doing so), the Working Group for the drawing up of the Principles ventured into the field of *jurisdiction*, distilling a few internationally undisputed grounds for jurisdiction.[79] In that connection, the thorny issues of *lis alibi pendens* and parallel proceedings, one of the reasons for the break down of the Hague Conference's negotiations of a worldwide convention on jurisdiction, are addressed.[80] And, notwithstanding many Europeans' professed awe and hostility vis-à-vis the doctrine of *forum non conveniens*[81]—another stumbling block in The Hague—thorough functional

---

[78] Black letter and Comment are reproduced in (2004) IX Unif L Rev752–809 with contributions on selected issues by R T Nhlapo, C Einstein and A Phipps, H P Glenn, K Kerameus, C Scarpinella Bueno, M Brinkmann and P A Karrer. The official publication is *ALI/UNIDROIT Principles of Transnational Civil Procedure* (CUP, Cambridge, 2006). On previous drafts and the project generally, see 'Harmonising Transnational Civil Procedure: The ALI/UNIDROIT Principles and Rules' Unif LRev 6 (2001), 735–1144 with contributions by H Kronke, G C Hazard, M Storme, P Fouchard, S Goldstein, J Walker, A Gidi, H Schack, L J Priestly, E H Cooper, R Stürner, P Lalive, G Mecarelli, A Kemelmajer de Carlucci, J-P Béraudo, N Andrews, B Beaumont, S H Elsen, V Mikelénas, F Ferrand, T Pfeiffer. Highly important and on the almost finalized draft, is the volume edited by Frédérique Ferrand listed below, under recommended further reading.
[79] Principles 2.1–2.4.   [80] Principle 2.6.   [81] See above, para 16.38.

analysis of Continental case law encouraged the fathers and mothers of the PTCP to accommodate even that device.[82]

16.65 Other key areas covered by the Principles are the *structure of the proceedings* and their endorsing the modern 'main hearing model'[83] as well the *distribution of roles between the court and the parties* where the active, case-managing judge comes to the fore,[84] and *the foreign party and equality of the parties in civil proceedings* which in theory is guaranteed in most jurisdictions but not in respect of many seemingly technical aspects such as language.[85] Few commentators seem to have any doubt, however, that the instrument's most remarkable achievement is Principle 16 where, under the heading 'Access to Information and Evidence', the conceptual and highly politicized issues of discovery, taking of evidence and evaluation of the evidence are addressed in a few lines and the most concise and elegant language. Professor Rolf Stürner, together with Professor Geoffrey C. Hazard Jr. one of the Co-Rapporteurs, writes:

Rolf Stürner, 'The Principles of Transnational Civil Procedure' (2005) 69 Rabels Zeitschrift für ausländisches und internationales Privatrecht 201–54 at 232 ff.

The broad scope of the American pre-trial discovery has often been criticized and is considered as the main obstacle to a multilateral agreement on … procedural harmonization. The … latitude of American discovery is based on two different elements. First, the American civil procedure does not require the assertion of detailed facts and the presentation of individualized means of evidence during the pleading phase. 'Notice pleading' is the rule and 'fact pleading the exception' … An important consequence of notice pleading is that American procedure avoids an early circumscription of fact-finding and evidence taking. This stands in contrast to the continental European legal cultures where strict relevancy requirements limit the scope of fact-finding procedures at a relatively early stage of the dispute. Second, the broad scope of discovery is the result of a more or less unrestricted access to all means of evidence under the control of the opponent or of third parties.

[…] All civil procedure codes of continental tradition have in common the practice of fact pleading which requires the assertion of detailed facts and … exactly specified means of evidence during the pleading phase … The modern English procedure approximates this conception … It requires not only the assertion of reasonably detailed facts in the statement of case but permits also the presentation of specified means of evidence … which is clearly a further step away from the American practice of notice pleading. American civil procedure practiced fact pleading during a long epoch of its early history. The turn toward notice pleading developed in federal civil procedure in the middle of the 20th century, and not all American states have completely followed this development.

Full access to all means of evidence under the control of the opponent or third parties is, in principle, the present modern standard of nearly all procedural cultures of continental tradition … After the most recent reform of the German Code some … authors discuss the question whether the rather reluctant improvement of the access to means of evidence

---

[82] Principle 2.5   [83] Principles 2.1–2.4.   [84] Principles 11, 14 and 22.
[85] Principle 6.

under the opponent's or third parties' control could be considered as a big step towards an adoption of discovery of the American style … If this danger were real, then other European countries such as France, which introduced generous rules on access to means of evidence when reforming its procedure, would have thereby opened their procedure for fishing expeditions of the American style 30 years ago—which in reality never happened …

The Principles recognize the universally accepted, fundamental rule that the court and the parties … should generally have access to all relevant evidence. Insofar as Germany and some other continental or continental-influenced legal systems have not completely put this basic evidentiary conception into effect they have fallen behind the common standard, and a break with this restrictive tradition of disclosure should not be mourned in a provincial manner. Full access to evidence stands also for the right to conduct direct supplemental questioning of another party, witness, or expert who has first been questioned by the judge as is customary in most civil law systems … According to the Principles a party or its lawyer may also conduct a voluntary interview with a potential witness before commencement of proceedings to … facilitate good preparation of the presentation of evidence, always provided that this pe-action contact will not be used for witness coaching. [Restrictions on pre-trial communication with witnesses] may impede full and simplified access to all evidence and often [impairs the parties' assessment of the situation] when preparing legal disputes and calculating their risks. …

On the other hand, the Principles insist that fact pleading is the appropriate instrument for [avoiding] excessively broad discovery. [They] require, therefore, the presentation of the relevant facts in reasonable detail and a description of the available evidence with sufficient specification during the pleading phase. Only when a party shows 'good cause for its inability to provide sufficient specification of relevant facts of evidence' may the court permit very general … contentions or … not exactly specified evidence, e.g., … reference to a class of documents under the control of the opponent, giving 'due regard to the possibility that necessary facts and evidence will develop later in the course of the proceeding'. This formulation [is] a compromise between the American [and] the continental model … In this way the Principles reach a reasonable solution appropriate to avoid the excesses of both traditional legal systems, namely the tendency … towards overbroad discovery on the one hand, and the danger of a too early termination of fact finding in the continental tradition on the other.

Questions

1. Article XXII of the Protocol on Matters Specific to Aircraft Equipment to the 2001 Cape Town Convention on International Interests in Mobile Equipment (see above, ch 12) contains specific provisions regarding jurisdictional immunity. Why were they included in an instrument on secured financing and what are their specific features in light of the general treaties on sovereign immunity?

2. Justice Blackmun, in delivering the US Supreme Court's opinion in *Carnival Cruise* (supra, note 18), notes '[W]e do not adopt the Court of Appeals' determination that a non-negotiated forum selection clause in a … contract is never enforceable simply because it is not the subject of bargaining. Including

a reasonable forum clause in a ... contract ... may be permissible for several reasons ...'. The contract in dispute was a standard form contract. Why would the Justice's reasoning apply even more strongly in an aircraft financing contract? And what, in your view, is the rationale of Article 42 of the Cape Town Convention on International Interests in Mobile Equipment?

3. Comment on the role of practices and usages in international trade and commerce and the respective references to these in Article 9 of the CISG on the one hand, and Article 23 of EC Regulation 44/2001 (Article 17 of the Brussels and Lugano Conventions) as interpreted in ECJ decisions, on the other hand.

4. The defendants in the ECJ case *Owusu v N.B. Jackson and others* (above, note 24) emphasized the adverse consequences that would ensue if the English courts were unable to apply the doctrine of *forum non conveniens* and therefore had to try the case. These included: the expense of the proceedings, the possibility of recovering their costs in England if the claimant's action was dismissed, the logistical difficulties resulting from the geographical distance, the need to assess the merits of the case according to Jamaican standards, the enforceability in Jamaica of a default judgment and the impossibility of enforcing cross-claims against the other defendants. Draft the Advocate-General's advisory opinion on this point.

5. In the preceding chapters, one of the recurring topics was the juxtaposition of 'rule-based' and 'standards-based' transnational commercial-law instruments. Are there parallels as regards potential approaches to drafting uniform instruments on jurisdiction to adjudicate (judicial jurisdiction)? And, if so, are the interests, policies and objectives to be considered by negotiators and legislatures in making their choices comparable?

6. What would be the background analysis and the reasons for counsel of a French or, alternatively, a US party planning to bring a claim against a Dutch party for breach of contract to seek an order (a) in the French (or US) courts, and (b) in the English courts, restraining the defendant from disposing of funds?

7. In your opinion, will an English court normally grant a worldwide injunction in connection with proceedings in England to enforce a foreign judgment or foreign arbitration award?

8. Does the Council Regulation (EC) No 1348/2000 on the Service in the Member States of Judicial and Extrajudicial Documents in Civil and Commercial Matters support the US Supreme Court's view regarding the interpretation and application of the 1965 Hague Convention as expressed in the *Volkswagen* case?

9. Compare Article 16 of the ALI/UNIDROIT Principles of Transnational Civil Procedure as relating to documentary evidence and Article 3 of the 'IBA Rules on the Taking of Evidence in International Commercial Arbitration'.

Further reading

Arroyo, Diego Fernández (ed), 'Derecho internacional privado de los Estados del MERCOSUR' (Zavalia, Buenos Aires, 2003), 135–254, 349–539

Born, Gary, 'International Civil Litigation in the United States' (3rd edn, Kluwer, The Hague, 1996)

Brand, Ronald A, 'Comparative Forum *Non Conveniens* and the Hague Convention on Jurisdiction and Judgments', 37 Texas Intl LJ 467 (2002)

Carbonneau, Thomas, 'International Litigation and Arbitration, Cases and Materials' (Thomson West, St Paul, Minn, 2005)

Dicey, Morris and Collins on The Conflict of Laws, Volume 1 (14th edn, Sweet & Maxwell, London, 2006), chs 8, 11–13

Einstein, Clifford R, Phipps, Alexander 'Trends in International Commercial Litigation in Australia', Praxis des Internationalen Privat- und Verfahrensrechts (IPRax) 2005, 273–9, 365–74

Ferrand, Frédérique (ed), 'La procédure civile mondiale modélisée' (Editions juridiques et techniques: Paris, 2004)

Giardina, Andrea, 'Provisional Measures in Europe: Some Comparative Observations', Etudes en l'Honneur de Pierre Lalive (Helbig und Lichtenhahn, Basel/Frankfurt, 1993), 499

Guinchard, Serge, *et al*, 'Droit processuel—Droit commun et droit comparé du proces' (3rd edn, Dalloz, Paris, 2005)

Hay, Peter, 'Transient Jurisdiction, Especially Over International Defendants: Critical Comments on *Burnham v. Superior Court*' 1990 U Ill LRev 593

Hay, Peter, Weintraub, Russel J, Borchers, Patrick J, 'Conflict of Laws—Cases and Materials' (12th edn, Foundation Press, New York, NY, 2004), 34–211

Hess, Burkhard, 'Die begrenzte Freizügigkeit einstweiliger Massnahmen im Binnenmarkt II—Weitere Klarstellungen des Europäischen Gerichtshofs', Praxis des Internationalen Privat- und Verfahrensrechts (IPRax) 2000, 370

Huber, Peter 'Die englische Forum-non-conveniens Doktrin und ihre Anwendung im Rahmen des EuGVÜ' (Duncker & Humblot, Berlin, 1994)

Kessedjian, Catherine, 'Note on Provisional and Protective Measures in Private International Law and Comparative Law', Hague Conference on Private International Law, Prel. Doc. No 10 (1998)

Kerameus, Konstantinos D, Political Integration and Procedural Convergence in Europe, 45 Am J Comp L 919 (1997)

Kerameus, Konstantinos, 'Enforcement in the International Context', Recueil des Cours 264 (1997), 179–410

Kerameus, Konstantinos, Normand Jacques, 'La necessité de procedures provi-soires dans les litiges transnationaux', in Italo Andolina (ed), 'Trans-National Aspects of Procedural Law' (Giuffrè, Milan, 1998), 1139, 1167

Kohler, Christian, 'Rigueur et souplesse en droit international privé: Les formes prescrites pour une convention attributive de jurisdiction "dans le commerce international" par l'article 17', Diritto del commercio internazionale 1990, 611

Lowenfeld, Andreas F, 'International Litigation and the Quest for Reasonableness', Recueil des Cours 245 (1994), 9–320

Mourre, Alexis, ' Droit judiciaire privé européen des affaires' (Bruylant/FEC, Bruxelles/Paris, 2003)

Schlosser, Peter, 'Jurisdiction and International Judicial and Administrative Co-operation', Recueil des Cours 284 (2000), 9–430

Teitz, Louise Ellen, 'Transnational Litigation' (Michie, Charlottesville, Va 1996; Suppl. Lexis, ibid 1999), 12–23, 31–42, 54–9

17

INTERNATIONAL COMMERCIAL ARBITRATION

A.	**The Nature of International Commercial Arbitration and its Distinguishing Features**			Major arbitration institutions and their rules	17.41
	Arbitration and litigation	17.03		An outline of the UNCITRAL Rules and the ICC Rules	
	Arbitration and expert determination	17.07		Commencing the arbitration	17.43
	Arbitration and adjudication	17.10		Arbitral Tribunal	17.45
	Arbitration and alternative dispute resolution	17.12		Arbitral proceedings	17.50
	When is arbitration 'international'?	17.14		Arbitral awards	17.56
	When is arbitration 'commercial'?	17.19		Costs	17.59
B.	**The Harmonization of the Law of International Commercial Arbitration**	17.23		The principles which underpin the harmonization of international arbitration and the tensions in the modern law	17.60
	The UNCITRAL Model Law	17.27	C.	**Arbitration and the Conflict of Laws**	17.67
	The arbitration agreement	17.28		The law governing the parties' capacity to enter into an arbitration agreement	17.70
	The composition of the arbitral tribunal	17.30		The law governing the arbitration agreement and the performance of that agreement	17.71
	Jurisdiction of the arbitral tribunal	17.31			
	Conduct of arbitral proceedings	17.32			
	Making of award and termination of proceedings	17.33		The law governing the existence and proceedings of the arbitral tribunal— the *lex arbitri*	17.74
	Recourse against the award and the recognition and enforcement of awards	17.34		The 'delocalization' debate	17.79
				The law, or the relevant legal rules, governing the substantive issues in dispute	17.110
	1958 New York Convention on the Recognition and Enforcement of Foreign Arbitral Awards	17.35			
	Rules of arbitration as party-determined framework for dispute settlement through arbitration			The law governing the recognition and enforcement of the award	17.123
			D.	**The Review of Arbitral Awards**	17.124
	Ad hoc arbitration and institutional arbitration	17.39	E.	**Recognition and Enforcement of Arbitral Awards**	17.133

17.01 Arbitration is a widely used alternative to litigation in cross-border commercial disputes and a number of international and regional instruments have been devoted to it.[1] Arbitration has been defined as a 'form of dispute resolution in which the parties agree to submit their differences to a third party or a tribunal for a binding decision'.[2] In many ways, arbitration has proved to be a testing ground for the development of transnational commercial law. It is in the context of international arbitrations that issues such as the meaning and the role of the *lex mercatoria* have had the greatest significance. Similarly, international commercial arbitration has proved to be a vital testing ground for instruments such as the UNIDROIT Principles of International Commercial Contracts (and, to a lesser extent, the Principles of European Contract Law). The greater flexibility which arbitrators enjoy in comparison with that available to judges in State courts has enabled them to make greater use of transnational commercial law in the resolution of commercial disputes.

17.02 In this chapter we shall examine: (i) the nature of international commercial arbitration and its distinguishing features; (ii) the harmonization of the law of international commercial arbitration; (iii) international arbitration and the conflict of laws; (iv) the review of arbitral awards and (v) the recognition and enforcement of arbitral awards.

A. The Nature of International Commercial Arbitration and its Distinguishing Features

Arbitration and litigation

17.03 Many commercial disputes in the modern world are resolved by arbitration rather than litigation. Arbitration can be distinguished from litigation on a number of grounds. First, arbitration is a product of the agreement between the parties, whereas the existence and jurisdiction of state courts is not dependent upon the will of the parties. Second, arbitrators are generally appointed by the parties themselves (or by the arbitral institution to which the parties have agreed to submit their dispute), whereas in state courts judges are appointed by the state and not by the parties. Third, arbitration presupposes the existence of a dispute between the parties, whereas there is no such presupposition in the case of state courts.

17.04 What advantages does arbitration have over litigation as a method of dispute resolution? The relative advantages and disadvantages of arbitration over litigation

---

[1] In addition, many national arbitral laws also cover international commercial arbitrations.
[2] Roy Goode, *Commercial Law* (3rd edn, LexisNexis UK, London, 2004) 1162.

have been assessed in the following passage:

Roy Goode, *Commercial Law* (3rd edn, LexisNexis UK, London, 2004) 1163–4

That arbitration possesses certain advantages for the commercial man is undeniable. The parties can select an arbitrator or arbitrators in whom they have confidence (or respect) and who can be expected to be familiar with the kind of business in which the dispute arises. The proceedings are less formal and more flexible than litigation; the parties have greater control over them; the arbitral tribunal is not bound by rules of evidence or procedure applicable to court proceedings, nor, in a case involving a foreign element, is it obliged to apply English conflict of laws rules; the venue can be fixed by agreement with the arbitrator and (a matter of considerable importance) the hearing is private; and the proceedings and award are relatively confidential. Of particular importance in international commercial arbitration is the availability of enforcement of awards in other jurisdictions under the 1958 New York Convention. Arbitration may also be cheaper and speedier than litigation, but this by no means necessarily follows. The court fees in an action are relatively modest, whereas in an arbitration the parties are responsible for the arbitrator's remuneration and travel and accommodation expenses (which may be particularly heavy if there are several arbitrators coming from different countries), the hire of accommodation for the hearing and the payment of the stenographer if they wish to have a full record of the evidence. In the case of an institutional arbitration the parties also have to pay the administrative charges of the arbitral institution. On the other hand, the arbitrator's greater familiarity with the practices of the industry or market may shorten the proceedings and thus save expense. Arbitration may be faster if the parties cooperate in bringing the case to a swift hearing, but allows more opportunity for delay to the defendant wishing to prolong the proceedings. Moreover, most of the advantages of arbitration, including finality and confidentiality, are lost if an award comes before the court for judicial review. Multi-party proceedings are best suited to litigation, not arbitration. A party cannot be brought before an arbitral tribunal without its prior consent, and procedures such as intervention or joinder of third parties or consolidation of proceedings to avoid multiplicity are not available.

The atmosphere of arbitration is generally considered to be less hostile than that of litigation, and the arbitral award now has a greater degree of finality than a judgment. As against this, the arbitrator's interlocutory powers, though recently reinforced by statute, are still not as extensive as those of a judge, a fact of particular importance if one of the parties wants interim or provisional relief or summary judgment and in multi-party disputes where it may be desirable to bring all parties before the court in a single or consolidated proceeding. Moreover, international commercial arbitration has in some ways become almost as formalized and protracted as litigation, so that over the past decade there has been increasing interest in commercial mediation. Finally, whereas judges are trained to think and act judiciously and to treat the admissibility and weight of evidence with circumspection, some arbitrators without legal qualifications may be inclined to decide a case on their view of what is fair and without sufficient regard to the nature of the evidence or the appropriate rules of law. To this the businessmen will no doubt reply with conviction, and with some justification, that it is only natural for the lawyers to feel happier in their own habitat!

The comparative advantages and disadvantages of arbitration as opposed to litigation have been the subject of substantial discussion in the literature.[3] From the **17.05**

---

[3] See, for example: M Kerr, 'International Arbitration v Litigation' [1980] JBL 164.

extract above it can be seen that the principal advantages of arbitration are said to be flexibility, confidentiality, finality, the enforceability of the award, the ability to choose the arbitrator and the 'neutrality' of the procedure. The disadvantages of arbitration are its cost (although to some extent the high cost of arbitration can be controlled by the parties if they act sensibly) and the limited powers which arbitrators enjoy in comparison with those available to state courts. In relation to the latter point, Redfern and Hunter have pointed out:

> [i]n general . . . the powers accorded to arbitrators, whilst usually adequate for the purpose of resolving the matters in dispute, fall short of those conferred upon a court of law. For example, the power to require the attendance of witnesses under penalty of fine or imprisonment, or to enforce awards by the attachment of a bank account or the sequestration of assets, are powers which form part of the prerogative of the state. They are not powers that any state is likely to delegate to a private arbitral tribunal, however eminent or well-intentioned that arbitral tribunal may be. In practice, if it becomes necessary for an arbitral tribunal to take coercive action in order to deal properly with the case before it, such action must usually be taken indirectly, through the machinery of the local courts, rather than directly, as a judge himself can do.[4]

17.06   It is, however, important to state that the balance of these advantages and disadvantages may be struck differently in different jurisdictions. To take an obvious example, the comparative cost of arbitration will depend upon the cost of litigation within a particular jurisdiction and the cost of litigation varies significantly as between different jurisdictions. A similar point can be made in relation to the confidentiality of arbitral proceedings and of an arbitral award. In some jurisdictions, such as England, the courts have generally affirmed that an obligation of confidence attaches to arbitral proceedings[5] but other jurisdictions, such as Australia, have been more hesitant.[6] It would, perhaps, be fair to state that the issue which divides the various jurisdictions relates to the *scope* of the obligation of confidence rather than its *existence*. While commercial parties may place a high value on confidentiality and on the ability to be able to wash their dirty linen in private, the modern trend in the courts would appear to be in the opposite direction, namely to recognize wider exceptions to the obligation to maintain confidentiality.[7]

Arbitration and expert determination

17.07   Arbitration must also be distinguished from expert determination. While the two have certain elements in common, there are also important differences between

---

   [4] Alan Redfern and Martin Hunter, *Law and Practice of International Commercial Arbitration* (4th edn, Sweet & Maxwell, London, 2004) 1.47.
   [5] See, for example: *Ali Shipping Corp v Shipyard Trogir* [1999] 1 WLR 314 (CA). But the authorities do not reveal unequivocal support for the existence of a duty of confidentiality, particularly in relation to the award itself: *Associated Electric and Gas Insurance Services Ltd v European Reinsurance Company of Zurich* [2003] UKPC 11, [2003] 1 WLR 1041.
   [6] *Esso Australia Resources Ltd v Plowman* (1995) 183 CLR 10 (HC).
   [7] See generally: Andrew Tweeddale and Keren Tweeddale, *Arbitration of Commercial Disputes: International and English Law and Practice* (OUP, Oxford, 2005) [11.09]–[11.28].

them. Expert determination is frequently used in order to decide valuation matters, such as the value of a particular piece of property. In these cases, there need not be a dispute in existence between the parties at the time at which the valuation issue is entrusted to the expert for determination. By contrast, a reference to arbitration presupposes the existence of a dispute between the parties. The essence of expert determination and the fact that it differs in certain respects from arbitration are outlined in the following extract:

Andrew Tweeddale and Keren Tweeddale, *Arbitration of Commercial Disputes:*
International and English Law and Practice **(OUP, Oxford, 2005) [1.40]–[1.41]**

The use of an expert or valuer to determine or assess an issue is a process which has been a feature of commercial and legal practice for centuries. However, as a result of the ever increasing costs associated with arbitration and litigation it is a process which is being called upon more and more often. The use of expert determination is common in resolving valuation disputes such as rent reviews, accountancy, and intellectual property disputes. The process is usually extremely quick and cheap. The expert will conduct its own investigations into the facts and does not need to wait for the parties to provide it with evidence. The expert's decision is often final and binding on the parties and there is no right of appeal. A challenge to the decision will only be permitted in limited circumstances. Enforcement of the expert's decision is by an action for breach of contract.

An expert determination agreement will often include a clause requiring the expert to act 'as an expert and not as an arbitrator'. The expert's determination is not therefore an arbitrator's award nor comparable to a court's judgment. It cannot be enforced under the New York Convention on the Recognition and Enforcement of Foreign Arbitral Awards 1958 . . . In the event that a party fails to comply with the expert's determination then fresh proceedings must be commenced to enforce the decision. A party can generally obtain summary judgment on the determination and thereafter enforcement can take place of the court's judgment.

The extent to which a decision by an expert is amenable to review by a court very **17.08** much depends upon the terms of the particular expert determination clause. It is not uncommon for the contract to state that the decision of the expert shall be 'final and binding'. On the other hand, it is open to contracting parties to provide for a greater degree of review. However, it does not follow from the fact that the clause states that the decision of the expert is 'final and binding' that it is not subject to review by a court. In *Jones v Sherwood Computer Services plc*,[8] a clause provided for the valuation of shares by independent accountants and stated that their determination would be 'conclusive and final and binding for all purposes'. The Court of Appeal held that, in the absence of fraud or collusion, the expert's determination could only be challenged on the ground of mistake if it was clear from the evidence that the expert had departed from his instructions in a material respect. On the

---

[8] [1992] 1 WLR 277 (CA).

facts, the accountants had done precisely what they had been asked to do with the consequence that their determination was not open to challenge.

17.09   In *Veba Oil Supply & Trading GmbH v Petrotrade Inc (The Robin)*,[9] the Court of Appeal distinguished between a departure from instructions by the expert and a mistake made by the expert in the course of carrying out his instructions. In the case of a mistake made by the expert in the course of carrying out his instructions, a mistake can only vitiate the expert's determination if it can be shown that it affected the result. In the case of a departure from instructions, on the other hand, there is no need to show that the departure from instructions affected the result. As Simon Brown LJ acknowledged, 'once a material departure from instructions is established, the court is not concerned with its effect on the result' so that a 'material departure vitiates the determination whether or not it affects the result'.[10]

Arbitration and adjudication

17.10   Arbitration must also be distinguished from adjudication. In the United Kingdom, adjudication is frequently used as a means of dispute resolution in the construction industry. The statutory basis for the adjudication system as it operates in the construction industry in the United Kingdom is to be found in the Housing Grants, Construction and Regeneration Act 1996. Since the Act was brought into force adjudication has gradually replaced litigation as the principal means of dispute resolution in the industry. The aim of adjudication is to provide a cheap and speedy method of dispute resolution. The parties must comply with the decision of the adjudicator but this does not preclude them from subsequently challenging the validity of the decision in court proceedings. The philosophy which underpins adjudication is very much one of 'pay now and litigate later' and the effect of the adjudication scheme has been to improve cash flow in the construction industry. While cases can be found in which the courts have set aside the decision of an adjudicator (for example on the ground that the adjudicator had no jurisdiction to make the decision which he made), these cases have been very much the exception. The courts have been reluctant to interfere with the decisions of adjudicators on the basis that too great a willingness to intervene would undermine the aim of the Act which was 'to introduce a speedy mechanism for settling disputes in construction contracts on a provisional interim basis'.[11]

---

⁹ [2001] EWCA Civ 1832; [2002] 1 All ER 703.

¹⁰ Ibid [28]. This leaves an issue relating to the definition of 'materiality' in the case where the expert departs from his instructions. Simon Brown LJ concluded (at [26]) that any departure from instructions is material 'unless it can truly be characterized as trivial or *de minimis* in the sense of it being obvious that it could make no possible difference to the result'. Dyson LJ stated (at [47]) that the test of materiality is 'whether the parties would reasonably have regarded the departure as sufficient to invalidate the determination'.

¹¹ *Macob Civil Engineering Ltd v Morrison Construction Ltd* [1999] BLR 93 (QBD) 97.

The vital feature of adjudication which distinguishes it from arbitration is that the   **17.11**
decision of the adjudicator is not a final decision but is a provisional, interim decision. This point was made by Lord Gill in *Gillies Ramsay Diamond v PJW Enterprises
Ltd*[12] in the following terms:

> Adjudication has certain superficial similarities to arbitration; but in my opinion it is
> a *sui generis* system of dispute resolution. Whereas arbitration is a form of conclusive
> resolution of disputes, an adjudication is a form of provisional resolution only.
> Adjudication does not oust the jurisdiction of the courts or of an arbiter. Its primary
> purpose is to regulate a dispute *ad interim*, pending a definitive resolution of it by liti-
> gation, arbitration or agreement.[13]

Arbitration and alternative dispute resolution

Finally, arbitration must be distinguished from alternative dispute resolution (such   **17.12**
as mediation, conciliation). The vital distinguishing feature between the two is that
arbitration results in the production of an award which is legally binding on the
parties, whereas mediation does not. The essential point of arbitration is to produce a binding award. Arbitration is not a negotiated settlement of a dispute;
rather, it is a decision reached by an arbitrator by the application of rules of law.[14]
Alternative dispute resolution (ADR), by contrast, does not result in the production of an award which is binding in the same way as an arbitral award. A settlement
reached as a result of ADR may be binding on the parties but only because they
have entered into a binding settlement agreement; that is to say, the settlement may
be enforceable as a contract between the parties. ADR can assume many different
forms but the essence of it is mediation or conciliation by a neutral third party.
However, in the United States, arbitration is regarded as a form of ADR.

Andrew Tweeddale and Keren Tweeddale, *Arbitration of Commercial Disputes:
International and English Law and Practice* **(OUP, Oxford, 2005) 1.12**

The mediation procedure will generally be flexible with a mediator determining how the
process will be conducted. It will be usual for the parties to set out a summary of their
respective cases and any documents on which they wish to rely. Privileged documents can
be shown to the mediator and these will be kept confidential if a party so requests. After
the parties have met and set out their respective cases to the mediator it is usual for the parties to move to separate rooms. The mediator moves between the parties discussing the
issues with each of the parties. This is often referred to as caucuses or breakout sessions. In
this way the mediator can discover where the main issues of contention lie and discuss
these with the parties privately. Once this process has concluded the mediator will then
discuss alternatives to overcome the issues. It is hoped at the end of the process that the
parties will reach a settlement.

---

[12] [2004] BLR 131 (Court of Session (Inner House)).   [13] Ibid 138.
[14] Unless the arbitrator is acting as *amiable compositeur* or is authorized to decide the reference *ex
aequo et bono*, see below, paras 17.116, 17.118.

17.13 As has been noted, that settlement may or may not be contractually binding upon the parties. ADR is now an important feature of commercial disputes. Increasingly, international commercial contracts require contracting parties to attempt to resolve their disputes by mediation before resorting to arbitration or litigation. The courts have generally given effect to these clauses and have stayed court proceedings pending the outcome of the mediation provided that the clause providing for mediation is drafted with sufficient precision.[15]

When is arbitration 'international'?

17.14 It is important to distinguish between domestic and international arbitrations. Many countries have different rules for domestic arbitrations, usually involving greater oversight and involvement of the courts than is the case with international arbitrations.[16] The distinction is important both for legal and for non-legal reasons as the following extract makes clear:

Alan Redfern and Martin Hunter, *Law and Practice of International Commercial Arbitration* (4th edn, Sweet & Maxwell, London, 2004) [1.21]–[1.23]

First, an international arbitration will usually have no connection with the state in which the arbitration takes place, other than the fact that it is taking place on the territory of that state. Secondly, the parties will usually be corporations or state entities, rather than private individuals. Accordingly, the state concerned can afford to take a more relaxed attitude towards such arbitrations. By contrast, domestic arbitrations will usually involve claims by private individuals that may be small in amount, but are of considerable importance to those concerned.

An element of consumer protection is involved. Many years ago, the English appellate court proclaimed that there would be 'no Alsatia in England where the King's Writ does not run'. Its concern was that powerful trade associations would otherwise impose their own 'law' on traders and citizens less powerful than they. For this reason, some control (and even 'supervision') of the arbitral process by the local courts was considered desirable.

By contrast, one of the major features of the Model Law (which was expressly designed to provide for *international* commercial arbitration) is that it imposes strict limits on the extent to which a national court may intervene in the arbitration proceedings. . . .

Another reason for distinguishing between 'international' and 'domestic' arbitrations is that in some states, the state itself (or in some cases, entities of the state) may only enter into an arbitration agreement in respect of international transactions. Accordingly, it is necessary to know how such transactions are defined and whether an arbitration in respect of them would be considered as 'international' by the state concerned.

A further reason, which in practice is perhaps the most significant, is that different nationalities, different legal backgrounds and cultures, different legal systems and different principles

---

[15] *Cable and Wireless plc v IBM United Kingdom Ltd* [2003] EWHC 316 (QBD).

[16] The United Kingdom is an exception. Under the Arbitration Act 1996, domestic and international arbitrations are governed by the same regime. It is only at the enforcement stage that differences arise.

will almost certainly be encountered in international commercial arbitrations. It is important that those concerned, and particularly the members of the arbitral tribunal, should
understand this . . . In order to develop and to work with such a system, it is necessary to
abandon narrow, parochial concepts of how an arbitration should or should not be conducted. This in itself calls for a different and truly 'internationalist' approach to such
arbitrations.

The claims made in the extract above should not all be accepted uncritically. In par-   **17.15**
ticular, the claim that 'an international arbitration will usually have no connection
with the state, other than the fact that it is taking place on its territory' has given rise
to considerable controversy.[17] But the controversy surrounding this claim should
not blind us to the importance differences that exist between international and
domestic arbitrations, in particular the lack of judicial supervision of international
arbitration in comparison with that applicable to domestic arbitration.

Where is the line drawn between an 'international' arbitration and a 'domestic'   **17.16**
arbitration? The best starting point is Article 1(3) and (4) of the UNCITRAL
Model Law on International Commercial Arbitration which provide:

(3) An arbitration is international if
   (a) the parties to an arbitration agreement have, at the time of the conclusion of
      that agreement, their places of business in different States; or
   (b) one of the following places is situated outside the State in which the parties
      have their places of business:
      (i) the place of arbitration if determined in, or pursuant to, the arbitration
         agreement;
      (ii) any place where a substantial part of the obligations of the commercial
         relationship is to be performed or the place with which the subject-matter
         of the dispute is most closely connected; or
   (c) the parties have expressly agreed that the subject-matter of the arbitration
      agreement relates to more than one country.
(4) For the purposes of paragraph (3) of this Article:
   (a) if a party has more than one place of business, the place of business is that
      which has the closest relationship to the arbitration agreement;
   (b) if a party does not have a place of business, reference is to be made to his habit-
      ual residence.

One feature of this definition is that it relies on a mixed approach; that is to say, it   **17.17**
does not focus on one issue to the exclusion of all others. It places significant
emphasis on the place of business of the parties to the arbitration. But it also has
regard to the place of performance of a substantial part of the obligations of the
parties and the place of the arbitration if that is determined in the arbitration

---

[17] The issue is discussed in more detail at paras 17.79–17.109 below.

agreement. Courts called upon to interpret 'international' have generally adopted a broad approach to its interpretation.[18]

17.18   However, this is not the only way in which 'international' can be defined. Article 1 of the ICC Rules of Arbitration states that the function of the ICC International Court of Arbitration is 'to provide for the settlement by arbitration of business disputes of an international character'. Here the emphasis is rather more on the nature of the dispute than the identity of the parties to the dispute.[19] The difference in emphasis between the Model Law and the ICC Rules reflects the fact that there is no universally agreed definition of 'international' in this context with the consequence that national laws can draw the line between 'international' and 'domestic' arbitrations in different places. But the range of factors taken into account in national laws tends to be limited. The principal factors tend to be the nature of the dispute between the parties and the identity of the parties to the dispute. Rather than choose between these two factors, the Model Law adopts a mixed approach and it is suggested that this is the better approach.

When is arbitration 'commercial'?

17.19   Article 1(1) of the UNCITRAL Model Law states that it applies to 'international commercial arbitration, subject to any agreement in force between this State and any other State or States'. What, for this purpose, constitutes a 'commercial' arbitration? A partial answer to this question is provided by a footnote to Article 1(1) which offers some guidance on the approach to be adopted when seeking to ascertain the meaning of the word 'commercial'. The guidance is in the following terms:

> The term 'commercial' should be given a wide interpretation so as to cover matters arising from all relationships of a commercial nature, whether contractual or not. Relationships of a commercial nature include, but are not limited to, the following transactions: any trade transaction for the supply or exchange of goods or services; distribution agreement; commercial representation or agency; factoring; leasing; construction of works; consulting; engineering; licensing; investment; financing; banking; insurance; exploitation agreement or concession; joint venture and other forms of industrial or business co-operation; carriage of goods or passengers by air, sea, rail or road.

17.20   It is clear that the intention behind the footnote is to encourage a broad approach to the interpretation of 'commercial'. Cases can be found in which the courts have accepted the spirit of the footnote and adopted a wide definition of 'commercial'

---

[18] See, for example: *Fung Sang Trading Ltd v Kai Sun Sea Products and Food Co Ltd* [1992] 1 HKLR 40 (HC).

[19] See, for example: ICC Case 5910/1988 involving a sale between two Belgian parties—the arbitration was not considered international under Belgian law, but it was under the ICC rules.

but other cases can be found in which the courts have adopted a more restrictive approach.[20]

The meaning of 'commercial' can also be of significance in other contexts. Thus **17.21** Article 1.3 of the New York Convention on the Recognition and Enforcement of Foreign Arbitral Awards provides that, when signing, ratifying, or acceding to the Convention, a State may declare that:

> it will apply the Convention only to differences arising out of legal relationships, whether contractual or not, which are considered as commercial under the national law of the State making such declaration.

This provision was inserted to reflect the concern of a number of civilian jurisdic- **17.22** tions where arbitration is only permissible for commercial contracts and a considerable proportion of these jurisdictions have made such a declaration. The effect of doing so is to leave to the national law of the State making the declaration the task of drawing a distinction between commercial contracts and other contracts, with only the former being capable of submission to arbitration. Where both contracting parties are acting in the course of a business then it is highly likely that the relationship between them will be characterized as 'commercial'. More difficult cases are those in which one of the parties to the contract is not acting in the course of a business or the transaction is concluded by one party for 'mixed' purposes (that is to say, it relates to his business but includes an element of personal use), the issue relates to a matter between family members, between employer and employee or is related to a boundary dispute between States. The latter are less likely to fall within the definition of 'commercial'.

B. The Harmonization of the Law of International Commercial Arbitration

The process of harmonization of the law of international arbitration has been a **17.23** gradual one. Significant progress was, however, made in the latter half of the twentieth century. The starting point for the modern development of the law is the 1958 New York Convention on the recognition and enforcement of foreign arbitral awards.[21] This is one of the world's most successful international conventions in the field of transnational commercial law (having been ratified by 137 States) and it is also one of the shortest. It deals exclusively with the conditions in which

---

[20] See generally: Andrew Tweeddale and Keren Tweeddale, *Arbitration of Commercial Disputes: International and English Law and Practice* (OUP, Oxford, 2005) [2.44]–[2.58].
[21] The New York Convention was not the first Convention in the field. In 1927, a Convention for the execution of Foreign Arbitral Awards was concluded in Geneva but it is now largely reduced to a historical footnote since the conclusion of the New York Convention.

an award given in one jurisdiction must be recognized and may be enforced in another. A more comprehensive instrument came into being in 1985 when the text of the UNCITRAL Model Law on international commercial arbitration was agreed. The Model Law is devoted to substantive arbitration law and has been widely adopted across the world, albeit with modifications from jurisdiction to jurisdiction. A further development which took place over this period was the development of procedural rules for the conduct of international arbitrations produced by various international organizations. Three sets of rules merit mention at this point, namely the 1976 UNCITRAL Arbitration Rules, the ICC Rules of Arbitration (current edition 1998) and the rules of the International Centre for the Settlement of Investment Disputes (ICSID) established under the 1965 Washington Convention. The first two of these are given effect by incorporation into contracts.[22] The ICSID rules, which are not discussed in any detail in this book, deal with investment disputes between a Contracting State and a national of another Contracting State and apply where the parties have agreed to submit their dispute to ICSID.

17.24   There are also some important regional instruments which have played a role in the development of the law of international commercial arbitration. In 1975, the Organization of American States ('OAS') promulgated the Inter-American Convention on International Commercial Arbitration (also known as the Panama Convention).[23] This convention is designed in particular for disputes between nationals of a State within the OAS and provides for arbitrations to be conducted in accordance with the rules of procedure of the Inter-American Commercial Arbitration Commission (IACAC). Another regional instrument is the 1998 Mercosur Agreement on International Commercial Arbitration which deals with substantive arbitration law and is applicable in Argentina, Brazil, Paraguay and Uruguay.

17.25   It should be noted that these harmonizing instruments take different legal forms, namely international conventions, a Model Law and various contractually incorporated rules. We have already noted the relative advantages and disadvantages of the different legal forms that harmonizing measures can take and the practical consequences which flow from the choice of one form over another.[24] Here it suffices to recall that a Model Law is exactly that; it is a model which States can use as the basis for their national law but they are in no sense bound to follow its exact wording; they can depart from it to a greater or lesser extent. This is obviously not

---

[22] In the case of the UNCITRAL Rules, this may be done either directly by express incorporation into the contract between the parties or because the arbitration rules by which disputes between the parties are governed themselves incorporate the UNCITRAL Rules. Thus, the 1983 Rules of the Iran-US Claims Tribunal adopt the UNCITRAL Arbitration Rules with some modifications.

[23] The Convention has been ratified by seventeen States. For further details, see the Convention's website at: <http://www.wice.oas.org/Disputee.asp>. The text of the Convention is set out in the companion volume to this book.   [24] See ch 5 above.

so in the case of international conventions where the choice of the State is confined to the decision whether or not to ratify and, if the decision is made in favour of ratification, whether or not to make any declarations which the convention permits ratifying States to make. This distinction has important consequences in the field of international commercial arbitration. As one might expect, the UNCITRAL Model Law has not been implemented in a uniform way throughout the world. While it has exerted considerable influence over the development of the law of international commercial arbitration and it has assisted in the gradual convergence of the law, it has not resulted (and was not intended to result) in the complete assimilation of the laws of the various jurisdictions of the world. No such flexibility has been given to States ratifying the New York Convention; they are bound by the text, although, as we shall see, the interpretation of the text has given rise to considerable difficulties and it has not been interpreted in a uniform manner across the jurisdictions.

We shall consider these different instruments in turn. We begin with the Model **17.26** Law before proceeding to the New York Convention and, finally, the UNCITRAL and ICC arbitration rules.

The UNCITRAL Model Law

The 1985 UNCITRAL Model Law is designed to make available to national leg- **17.27** islatures a set of principles and rules that can be adopted to provide or improve national laws governing international commercial arbitration and, in so doing, to bring such laws into closer harmony with each other. The Model Law has been a considerable success and legislation based on it has been enacted in more than forty jurisdictions in the world. The Model Law covers all stages of the arbitral process, from the agreement to arbitrate to recognition and enforcement and the judicial review of arbitral awards. On procedural issues there is considerable overlap between the Model Law and the UNCITRAL Rules of Arbitration, but, as has been noted, the former is given effect by legislation, the latter by agreement of the parties. The Model Law provides a framework for the law relating to international commercial arbitration. A key principle which underpins it is the principle of party autonomy. At a number of points the Model Law gives to the parties the freedom to determine issues and, in so far as it lays down rules, these are frequently default rules; that is to say, the parties are free to contract out of them. Another important feature of the Model Law is the limited supervisory role given to the courts, particularly in relation to the grounds on which an award may be set aside. The principal provisions of the Model Law deal with the following issues.

The arbitration agreement

The starting point for any analysis of international commercial arbitration must **17.28** be the arbitration agreement which has been concluded between the parties.

Arbitration is a 'creature of contract'[25] and it is the arbitration agreement which gives to the arbitrators the jurisdiction to hear and decide the dispute which has been submitted to them by the parties.[26] The Model Law states that an arbitration agreement 'shall be in writing'.[27] Where a dispute between the parties falls within the scope of an arbitration agreement but one of the parties nevertheless attempts to bring the matter before a State court, the court shall, provided that it receives a timely request from the other party, refer the parties to arbitration unless 'it finds that the agreement is null and void, inoperative or incapable of being performed'.[28] In this way courts are required to respect the arbitration agreement agreed by the parties.

17.29 Perhaps rather curiously, the Model Law makes no reference to the concept of 'arbitrability'.[29] Yet it is clearly accepted that not every dispute is suitable for resolution by arbitration. Some disputes clearly fall within the domain of arbitration. The classic example is a contractual dispute between two contracting parties. The issue is of relevance only to the parties to the dispute and there is no objection in principle to them choosing to resolve their dispute by reference to arbitration rather than the local courts. But the greater the element of public interest involved in a dispute, the less likely it is that the issue will be suitable for resolution by arbitration. An obvious example is marriage or divorce; such issues of legal status must be resolved by State courts and not by private arbitration. In the commercial sphere difficulties have arisen in areas such as competition law or antitrust law. The traditional view was that such issues were not arbitrable because of the public interest involved in such cases. But it seems clear that a more relaxed view of the concept of 'arbitrability' is now being adopted and that it cannot be assumed that all competition law issues are incapable of resolution by arbitration.[30] There is a tension here between the wish to reserve matters of public interest to the state courts and the desire to encourage the use of commercial arbitration in the resolution of commercial disputes. Different states may strike the balance between these competing interests in different places and it may be that it was the difficulty in securing agreement on what is arbitrable and what is not that led to the omission of this issue from the Model Law.

The composition of the arbitral tribunal

17.30 In terms of the appointment of arbitrators, the parties are given substantial freedom of choice by the Model Law. It is for them to decide how many arbitrators

---

[25] Andrew Tweeddale and Keren Tweeddale, *Arbitration of Commercial Disputes: International and English Law and Practice* (OUP, Oxford, 2005) [2.04].   [26] See: Art 7 of the Model Law.
[27] Art 7(2), which also contains a definition of 'writing'. This definition has given rise to some difficulties in relation to modern forms of communication, such as electronic communications.
[28] Art 8 (1).
[29] On which see Julian DM Lew, Loukas A Mistelis and Stefan M Kröll, *Comparative International Commercial Arbitration* (Kluwer, The Hague, 2003) ch 9.
[30] See, for example: *Mitsubishi Motors Corp v Soler Chrysler-Plymouth Inc* 473 US 614, 105 S Ct 3346 (1985).

shall be appointed (although if they fail to reach agreement on this, the default position is that the number of arbitrators is three[31]). The parties are also given substantial freedom in relation to the procedure to be adopted for the appointment of arbitrators, although, again, a default procedure is laid down in the event that the parties fail to reach agreement on this matter. The Model Law makes provision for the grounds on which, and the procedure by which, a challenge can be made to the appointment of an arbitrator. It does seek to limit the grounds of challenge and states that an arbitrator may be challenged 'only if circumstances exist that give rise to justifiable doubts as to his impartiality or independence, or if he does not possess qualifications agreed to by the parties'.[32]

Jurisdiction of the arbitral tribunal

The Model Law adopts two already well-established principles of arbitration law **17.31** affecting jurisdiction. The first is that the arbitral tribunal may rule on its own jurisdiction.[33] The second is that an arbitration clause forming part of a contract is to be treated as an independent agreement, with the result that 'a decision by the arbitral tribunal that the contract is null and void does not entail *ipso jure* the invalidity of the arbitration clause'.[34] The tribunal may rule on jurisdiction either in a preliminary award or in an award on the merits. If it rules as a preliminary question that it has jurisdiction a party can apply to a court to decide the matter.[35]

Conduct of arbitral proceedings

Chapter V of the Model law contains provisions for the conduct of the proceed- **17.32** ings. Once again the parties are given considerable freedom in relation to matters such as the place of arbitration,[36] the language or languages to be used in the arbitral proceedings[37] and the procedure to be followed by the tribunal in the conduct of the proceedings.[38] The freedom given to the parties does have its limits, however. In particular, the parties 'shall be treated with equality and each party shall be given a full opportunity of presenting his case.'[39]

Making of award and termination of proceedings

The arbitral tribunal is required to decide the dispute in accordance with such **17.33** 'rules of law' as are chosen by the parties as applicable to the substance of the dispute or, failing such choice, by the law 'determined by the conflict-of-laws rules which it considers applicable'.[40] The reference to 'rules of law' rather than 'law' is an important issue, to which we shall shortly return. The Model Law entitles an arbitral tribunal to decide a dispute *ex aequo et bono* or as an *amiable compositeur*

---

[31] Art 10(2). [32] Art 12(2).

[33] Art 16(1). This is the principle of *Kompetenz-Kompetenz*. [34] Ibid.

[35] Art 16(3). Curiously there is no express provision for recourse to the court if as a preliminary question the tribunal decides it has no jurisdiction. [36] Art 20.

[37] Art 22. [38] Art 19. [39] Art 18. [40] Art 28(1) and (2).

only if the parties have 'expressly authorized it to do so'.[41] The decision of an arbitral tribunal can be made by a majority unless the parties decide otherwise.[42] The arbitral award must be 'made in writing' and must be signed by the arbitrators.[43] The award must state the reasons upon which it is based unless the parties have agreed otherwise.[44]

Recourse against the award and the recognition and enforcement of awards

17.34 A basic objective of the Model Law is to secure the finality of arbitral awards. To that end Article 5 starkly provides that 'in matters governed by this Law, no court shall intervene except where so provided in this Law'. Accordingly, the grounds on which an award may be set aside in the country of origin or refused recognition in another country are limited,[45] and closely follow Article V of the New York Convention,[46] to which we now turn.

1958 New York Convention on the Recognition and Enforcement of Foreign Arbitral Awards

17.35 In comparison with the UNCITRAL Model Law, the New York Convention on the Recognition and Enforcement of Foreign Arbitral Awards is a much more narrowly drawn instrument, concerned as it is only with the recognition and enforcement of foreign arbitral awards. The purpose of the convention is to ensure that courts enforce agreements to arbitrate and to facilitate the recognition and enforcement in a State of arbitral awards made in another State or otherwise constituting non-domestic awards. This facility provides a powerful inducement to use arbitration as a dispute resolution mechanism, since there is no comparable convention for the recognition and enforcement of court judgments.[47]

17.36 The Convention applies to the recognition and enforcement in one State of an arbitral award made in another or, alternatively, to arbitral awards treated by the law of the State of enforcement as non-domestic.[48] So the courts of a State may apply the Convention to the enforcement in that State of an award made in the same State where its arbitration law treats the arbitration as non-domestic, as it might do, for example, if both parties were foreigners.[49]

---

[41] Art 28(3).   [42] Art 29.
[43] Art 31(1). Where there is more than one arbitrator, it will be sufficient for the majority of the members of the arbitral tribunal to sign the award provided that the reason for any omitted signature is given.   [44] Art 31(2).
[45] See: Arts 34–5.
[46] Thus, they do not include such matters as failure to conduct the arbitration in accordance with the procedure agreed by the parties, failure of the award to state reasons, procurement of the award by fraud, corruption or bias on the part of an arbitrator, or wilful disregard of the applicable law.
[47] The Hague Convention on Choice of Court Agreements 2005, which in its early stages had the potential to perform such a role in relation to court judgments, has been progressively narrowed in scope and, in its final form, only covers issues dealing with choice of forum.   [48] Art I(1).
[49] The Convention extends not only to arbitral tribunals appointed for each case but also to permanent arbitral tribunals to whom the parties have submitted.

In order for the Convention to apply, various conditions must be satisfied. First, the **17.37** award must be an arbitral award; it must not be a court judgment, a determination by an expert, an interim adjudication or a non-binding award in a mediation or other form of alternative dispute resolution.[50] Second, the parties must have agreed to refer their differences to arbitration, and these must arise from a defined legal relationship.[51] Third, the arbitration agreement must be in writing,[52] a requirement the meaning of which has given rise to much discussion but is generally taken to include an electronic record capable of being reproduced on a subsequent occasion. Fourth, the subject-matter of the dispute must be capable of settlement by arbitration in the Contracting State where recognition and enforcement are sought.[53] Finally, a Contracting State may declare that it will apply the Convention only on the basis of reciprocity and only to differences arising out of legal relationships considered commercial under its law.[54]

At the request of one of the parties, the court of a Contracting State is obliged to refer **17.38** the parties to arbitration in a dispute falling within the scope of the Convention unless it finds that the agreement to arbitrate is null and void, inoperative or incapable of being performed.[55] Subject to compliance with the requisite formalities[56] the courts of a Contracting State are obliged to recognize and enforce an arbitral award unless the party against whom relief is sought furnishes proof of the existence of one of the grounds of refusal set out in Article V.[57] Though recognition and enforcement may only be refused if one or other of the above grounds exist, the Convention does not preclude enforcement even where such a ground does exist and even where an award has been set aside by a court in the country of origin.[58]

Rules of arbitration as party-determined framework for dispute settlement through arbitration

Ad hoc arbitration and institutional arbitration

There are two principal ways to take a dispute to arbitration: the parties either **17.39** organize the proceedings ad hoc themselves or with minimal outside assistance. Alternatively, they use the services of an institution that specializes in the administration of arbitration proceedings. There is no one-size-fits-all rule where one or the other is more advisable because it is faster, less expensive or 'better' on other accounts. While parties and counsel will have to establish a set of rules governing

---

[50] Art I(1).   [51] Ibid.   [52] Art I(1) and (2).   [53] See further para 17.135 below.
[54] Art I(3), on which see above para 17.21.   [55] Art II(3).   [56] See: Art IV.
[57] See further para 17.135 below.
[58] This follows from the fact that Art V merely restricts the grounds of refusal to enforce, not the grounds of enforcement, and is reinforced by Art VII, which allows the party seeking enforcement to invoke a more generous approach given by the law of the country in which enforcement is sought. In a few countries, the courts have ignored orders of foreign courts setting aside arbitral awards on the ground that, the awards being international and therefore stateless, such orders were of no significance in the country of enforcement, on which see further para 17.81 below.

their ad hoc proceedings, arbitration institutions offer standardized proceedings under their respective rules.

17.40   In 1976, the General Assembly of the United Nations adopted the UNCITRAL Arbitration Rules, a landmark in the modernization of international commercial arbitration. They have become very popular in regulating ad hoc proceedings. Moreover, they acquired bench-mark status for the development of many rules of leading arbitral institutions.

Major arbitration institutions and their rules

17.41   There are a large number of arbitration institutions. Major ones whose published rules may be easily consulted and on whose case load there is accurate statistical information are: American Arbitration Association (AAA), Austrian Federal Economic Chamber, Vienna, China International Economic and Trade Arbitration Commission (CIETAC), Court of International Arbitration of the Chamber of Commerce and Industry of the Russian Federation, Moscow, German Arbitration Institution (DIS), Hong Kong International Arbitration Centre (HKIAC), International Chamber of Commerce (ICC), London Court of International Arbitration (LCIA), Singapore International Arbitration Centre (SIAC) and the Stockholm Chamber of Commerce Arbitration Institute (SCC).

17.42   The International Court of Arbitration of the International Chamber of Commerce (ICC) is the arbitration body attached to the ICC.[59] The Court's members are appointed by the World Council of the ICC. The Court does not itself settle disputes but has the function of ensuring the application of the ICC Rules of Arbitration.[60] The Secretariat of the Court under the direction of its Secretary General is the executive arm of the Court in charge of the actual day-to-day administration of the proceedings.

An outline of the UNCITRAL Rules and the ICC Rules

Commencing the arbitration

17.43   The party initiating recourse to arbitration (the 'claimant'), under the UNCITRAL Rules, gives to the other party (the 'respondent') a 'notice of arbitration',[61] containing information such as the parties' names and contact details, the arbitration agreement, the nature of the contract or other legal relationship giving rise to the dispute, the claim, the relief sought, and particulars concerning the arbitral tribunal.[62] In ICC arbitrations, it is the Secretariat of the institution to whom the 'request for arbitration' is sent and who transmits this request to the respondent[63] for the respondent to reply by an 'answer to the request' which contains similar

---

[59] The ICC is discussed more generally at para 5.32 above.   [60] ICC Rules Art 1(2).
[61] UNCITRAL Rules Art 3(1).   [62] UNCITRAL Rules Art 3(3)–(4).
[63] ICC Rules Art 4(5).

information, comments and, as the case may be, counterclaims.[64] The involvement of the institution's organization in matters such as the setting up of the arbitral tribunal has the consequence that the parties must make advance payments on administrative expenses to the Secretariat.[65]

Where the parties have agreed to submit to arbitration under the ICC Rules[66] and the respondent does not file an answer or a party raises doubts concerning the existence, validity or scope of the arbitration agreement, the Court decides whether to proceed applying a prima facie test, and it is then for the arbitral tribunal to decide whether it has jurisdiction.[67] It may actually have jurisdiction by virtue of a valid arbitration agreement even though the contract as such may be non-existent.[68] A party's refusal or failure to take part in the proceedings does not stop them; the arbitration proceeds.[69]   **17.44**

Arbitral Tribunal

The number of arbitrators—one or three—and who is to serve in the specific case are either agreed upon by the parties or have to be determined in a procedure involving outsiders. Under the UNCITRAL Rules it is the so-called 'appointing authority', an individual or an institution either agreed upon by the parties or designated by the Secretary-General of the Permanent Court of Arbitration at The Hague.[70] Under the ICC Rules it is, in the absence of an agreement, the Court who decides whether a sole arbitrator or a panel of three are to hear a case and who appoints, in the absence of party nominations, the arbitrator(s).[71] Arbitrators nominated by the parties have to be confirmed by the Court or the Secretary General.[72]   **17.45**

A sole arbitrator or the chairman of an arbitral tribunal chosen not by the parties— or, in the case of the chairman, by the arbitrators nominated by the parties—but by the appointing authority (UNCITRAL) or the Court (ICC) will normally be of a nationality other than those of the parties.[73]   **17.46**

Every arbitrator must be and remain independent of the parties involved in the arbitration.[74] A prospective arbitrator must disclose any circumstances likely to give rise to doubts as to his independence or impartiality. The same applies once the arbitrator has been chosen. While the UNCITRAL Rules frame this as a general duty vis-à-vis 'those who approach' the prospective arbitrator or the parties,[75]   **17.47**

---

[64] ICC Rules Art 5.   [65] ICC Rules Arts 4(4)–(5) and 30.
[66] There is a standard clause recommended by the ICC: 'All disputes arising out of or in connection with the present contract shall be finally settled under the Rules of Arbitration of the International Chamber of Commerce by one or more arbitrators appointed in accordance with the said Rules'.
[67] ICC Rules Art 6.   [68] ICC Rules Art 6 (4).   [69] ICC Rules Art 6 (3).
[70] UNCITRAL Rules Arts 6(1)(b), 6(2)–(4), 7(2)–(3) and 8.
[71] ICC Rules Art 8(2)–(4), 9(3)–(6) and 10(2).   [72] ICC Rules Art 9(1)–(2).
[73] UNCITRAL Rules Art 6(4); ICC Rules Art 9(5).   [74] ICC Rules Art 7(1).
[75] UNCITRAL Rules Art 9.

the ICC Rules provide for a formal screening on the basis of declarations of independence submitted by the prospective arbitrator and input from the parties.[76] The Court decides whether to appoint or confirm or replace an arbitrator who has been successfully challenged.[77]

17.48 Both sets of rules provide for a very detailed framework for challenging arbitrators if circumstances exist which give rise to doubts as to their impartiality or independence.[78] While the UNCITRAL Rules envisage that this will primarily be discussed among and decided upon by the parties and the challenged arbitrator and will involve the appointing authority in appropriate cases only as a last resort, in ICC proceedings a challenge is immediately to be submitted to the Secretariat and the Court decides on its admissibility and merits.[79]

17.49 An arbitrator may have to be replaced upon his death, the acceptance of his resignation or a challenge, or in the event of the impossibility of his performing his functions. The ICC Rules confer significant powers—even of an investigative nature—upon the Court.[80] The UNCITRAL Rules apply the provisions regarding appointments fully to replacements.[81] Under the ICC Rules the Court has discretion to decide whether or not to follow the original procedure.[82]

Arbitral proceedings

17.50 Provided that the parties are treated with equality and fairly and that at any stage of the proceedings each party is given a full opportunity of presenting his case,[83] both sets of rules give the parties and the tribunal much leeway for determining the procedure. Where the parties do not agree, under the UNCITRAL Rules the arbitral tribunal will make the necessary decisions.[84] The ICC Rules leave some procedural issues to the ICC Court.[85]

17.51 As to the law or rules of law to be applied by the tribunal to the merits of the dispute, the parties are free to agree upon those rules. In the absence of any such agreement the tribunal applies the law or the rules of law which it determines to be appropriate (ICC) or the law determined by the conflict-of-laws rules which it considers applicable (UNCITRAL).[86] Only if authorized by the parties may the

---

[76] ICC Rules Art 7(2). Arbitrators are also required to immediately inform the Secretariat of circumstances arising during the arbitration: Art 7(3).   [77] ICC Rules Art 7(4).
[78] UNCITRAL Rules Arts 10–12; ICC Rules Art 11. Article 11(1) also indicates other potential grounds for challenge.   [79] ICC Rules Art 11.
[80] ICC Rules Art 12(2)–(3).   [81] UNCITRAL Rules Art 12(2).
[82] ICC Rules Art 12(4).   [83] UNCITRAL Rules Art 15(1); ICC Rules Art 15(1)–(2).
[84] UNCITRAL Rules Art 16 (concerning the place of arbitration) and Art 17 (the language).
[85] ICC Rules Art 14(1) (to fix the place of the arbitration).
[86] UNCITRAL Rules Art 33(1); ICC Rules Art 17(1). This issue is discussed in more detail at paras 17.117–17.121 below.

arbitral tribunal assume the powers of an *amiable compositeur* or decide *ex aequo et bono*.[87]

A distinctive feature of ICC arbitrations is a document ('Terms of Reference') to be **17.52** drawn up by the arbitral tribunal as soon as it receives the file from the Secretariat. In particular, it includes: a summary of the parties' respective claims and the relief sought, a list of the issues to be determined, the place of the arbitration as well as the particulars of the applicable procedural rules, the names and the contact details of the parties and the members of the tribunal.[88] Signed by the parties and the tribunal, the document is submitted to the Court for approval and constitutes a programme and a 'road map' for the proceedings.[89] Moreover, the tribunal has to communicate a provisional timetable to the Court and the parties.[90]

Both the UNCITRAL Rules and the ICC Rules leave it basically to the arbitral tri- **17.53** bunal and the parties how best to establish the facts of the case. Usually a full statement of claim and a full statement of defence state the facts supporting the respective claims, the points at issue, the relief and the remedies sought.[91] Evidence may be submitted in documents, written witness statements and expert reports or by oral testimony.[92] Of its own motion or at the request of either party the tribunal holds a hearing[93] where the parties, witnesses and (tribunal appointed)[94] experts appear to give evidence.

When the arbitral tribunal is satisfied that the parties have had a reasonable oppor- **17.54** tunity to present their cases it declares the proceedings closed.[95]

Both the UNCITRAL Rules and the ICC Rules provide for conservatory and **17.55** interim measures.[96]

Arbitral awards

Normally, an award is given by a majority decision.[97] The ICC Rules provide also **17.56** for an award to be made by the chairman alone if there is no majority.[98] The award must state the reasons upon which it is based.[99]

---

[87] UNCITRAL Rules Art 33(2) (which require also that this is permitted by the law applicable to the procedure); ICC Rules Art 17(3).　　　　　　　　　　　　[88] ICC Rules Art 18.
[89] New claims which fall outside its limits have to be authorized by the tribunal: ICC Rules Art 19. By contrast, Art 20 of the UNCITRAL Rules envisages amendments to the claim and defence as being the rule.　　　　　[90] ICC Rules Art 18(4). Subsequent modifications are also to be communicated.
[91] UNCITRAL Rules Arts 18–19; ICC Rules Art 20.
[92] UNCITRAL Rules Arts 24–25 and 27; ICC Rules Art 20.
[93] UNCITRAL Rules Arts 15(2), 25 and 27(4); ICC Rules Arts 20(2)–(5) and 21.
[94] UNCITRAL Rules Art 27(1); ICC Rules Art 20 (4).
[95] UNCITRAL Rules Art 29; ICC Rules Art 22.
[96] UNCITRAL Rules Art 28; ICC Rules Art 23.
[97] UNCITRAL Rules Art 31(1); ICC Rules Art 25(1).
[98] ICC Rules Art 25(1). The UNCITRAL Rules provide only for the chairman's making decisions on issues of procedure: Art 31(2).　　　　　[99] UNCITRAL Rules Art 32(3); ICC Rules Art 25(2).

17.57 ICC arbitrations are characterized by two additional features. First, there are time limits—fixed by the Rules or the Court—within which the tribunal must render its final award.[100] Second, before signing an award, an ICC tribunal must submit it in draft form to the Court. The Court may lay down modifications as to the form and, without affecting the tribunal's liberty of decision, may also draw its attention to points of substance. No award is rendered until the Court has approved it as to its form.[101]

17.58 Both sets of rules set forth details regarding notification of the award to the parties, deposit, interpretation and correction of the award.[102] The parties undertake to carry out the award without delay.[103]

Costs

17.59 Both sets of rules contain detailed provisions regarding the costs of the arbitration. The arbitral tribunal fixes the costs of the arbitration and decides which of the parties bears them or in what proportion they are borne by the parties.[104] However, the UNCITRAL Rules state that, in principle, the costs shall be borne by the unsuccessful party.[105] While, under the UNCITRAL Rules, it is the tribunal which makes decisions regarding advance payments (deposits) for costs,[106] it is the ICC Court which makes the relevant decisions in arbitrations administered by this institution. [107]

The principles which underpin the harmonization of international arbitration and the tensions in the modern law

17.60 A fundamental principle which underpins the modern law of international commercial arbitration is the importance of the autonomy of the parties. Thus, it has been stated that the 'most fundamental principle' in the UNCITRAL Model Law is the recognition of 'the freedom of the parties'.[108] As has been noted, a similar principle underpins both the UNCITRAL Arbitral Rules and the ICC Arbitration Rules. Thus the arbitrators acquire their jurisdiction from the agreement of the parties as expressed in the arbitration agreement and the parties have considerable freedom in terms of deciding the form which the arbitral proceedings are to assume. As we shall see,[109] the proposition that arbitrators acquire their authority from the consent of the parties has been argued to have far reaching consequences in that it has led to the claim that arbitrators in international arbitrations derive their

---

[100] ICC Rules Art 24.   [101] ICC Rules Art 27.
[102] UNCITRAL Rules Arts 32(6)–(7), 35 and 36; ICC Rules Arts 28–9.
[103] UNCITRAL Rules Art 32(2); ICC Rules Art 28(6).
[104] UNCITRAL Rules Art 38; ICC Rules Art 31(3).   [105] UNCITRAL Rules Art 40(1).
[106] UNCITRAL Rules Art 41.   [107] ICC Rules Art 30.
[108] Gerold Herrmann, 'The role of the courts under the UNCITRAL Model Law' in Julian DM Lew (ed) *Contemporary Problems in International Arbitration* (Martinus Nijhoff, Boston, 1987) 166.
[109] See further para 17.79 below.

authority from the consent of the parties and not from any national legal system. This has been an important thread in the attempt to free international arbitration from what were perceived to be the shackles of various national arbitration laws which were said to be inadequate or unsuitable for international commercial arbitrations.

But there is a competing argument which reflects the quasi-judicial nature of **17.61** arbitration. Arbitration is not a purely private matter in that, provided that certain conditions are met, the award which the arbitrators render is enforceable in state courts. Seen in this way, arbitration can be regarded as a substitute for judicial proceedings and, as a consequence, it is frequently asserted that there are certain minimum standards with which an international arbitration must comply. Chief among these are that the arbitrators must be impartial decision-makers and that the tribunal must afford each party a fair opportunity to present its case. As will be discussed in more detail below, the trend in modern laws relating to challenges to international arbitral awards and the recognition and enforcement of foreign awards is strongly in favour of the recognition and enforcement of awards and against judicial review or challenge, except within narrow limits. This trend makes international commercial arbitration a meaningful substitute for judicial proceedings in the resolution of international commercial disputes and strengthens the quasi-judicial nature of arbitration. The interplay between party autonomy and respect for the minimum requirements of justice is one of the major themes in arbitral jurisprudence. All modern national arbitration laws seek to strike an appropriate balance between these two important principles.[110]

The tension between the demands of party autonomy and the need for some form **17.62** of judicial review of the arbitral process is not the only tension apparent in the modern law of international commercial arbitration: there are a number of other tensions.

The first is the potential conflict between the autonomy of the parties and the laws **17.63** of the state in which the arbitration takes place (often referred to as the conflict between party autonomy and 'territoriality'). The critical question can be stated as follows: how much significance should be attached to the fact that an arbitration is being conducted in a particular jurisdiction? Some commentators take the view that little or no significance should be attached to the claims of the jurisdiction in which the arbitration is being conducted on the basis that the jurisdiction is chosen by the parties for reasons of convenience (or because the jurisdiction is

---

[110] See, for example, section 1 of the Arbitration Act 1996 which sets out the 'principles' upon which the opening Part of the Act is based. These include the principle that 'the object of arbitration is to obtain the fair resolution of disputes by an impartial tribunal without unnecessary delay or expense' and that 'the parties should be free to agree how their disputes are resolved, subject only to such safeguards as are necessary in the public interest'.

regarded by both parties as a neutral venue). In their view, it is the freedom or the autonomy of the parties which has the claim to priority and their freedom should not be impeded by the domestic laws of the jurisdiction in which the arbitration takes place. The claim that an international arbitration can be 'stateless' and that an award can 'float' in the legal stratosphere unconnected with the law of any particular jurisdiction until an attempt is made to enforce it is, as we shall see, a controversial one which requires careful consideration.

17.64 The second tension which occasionally manifests itself in the law of international arbitration is the conflict between the demands of party autonomy and the autonomy of the arbitrators. The appointment of an arbitrator creates a contract between the arbitrator and the parties and their relationship will be governed by the terms of that contract with which both parties are obliged to comply. It can be argued that there is no real tension here in that instruments such as the Model Law and the UNCITRAL and the ICC Arbitral Rules repeatedly emphasize the importance of the autonomy of the parties.[111] The autonomy of the arbitrators thus appears to be subordinate to the autonomy of the parties; that is to say, the arbitrators have freedom in relation to matters in which the parties have not reached agreement. For example, in relation to the procedure to be adopted in the arbitration, the arbitrator's freedom to determine the procedure ends where the parties themselves have agreed on the procedure that is to be adopted; where the parties have reached agreement, it is the duty of the arbitrators to give effect to their agreement. However, this proposition cannot be stated in unqualified terms. What if the parties agree upon a procedure which does not give to each party a full opportunity to present its case? In such a case must the arbitral tribunal give effect to the agreement made by the parties or is it entitled to give priority to the demands of fairness and, in particular, the need to ensure that a fair procedure is adopted? The parties may also find that, while in legal theory their autonomy has priority, there is sometimes little that they can do in the event that the arbitrators disregard their choice and impose their own wishes on the parties. For example, not every departure from the agreed procedure will entitle the parties to challenge the arbitrators' award. As we have noted, the grounds on which a court can review an arbitral award are limited and, while the Model Law states that a court can set aside an award on the ground that 'the arbitral procedure was not in accordance with the agreement of the parties',[112] not every departure from the agreed procedure will lead to a successful challenge to the award. To the extent that the parties are unable to challenge the award, it can be said that the autonomy of the arbitrators can, exceptionally, override the autonomy of the parties.

---

[111] To take one example, see Art 24(1) of the UNCITRAL Model Law which states that 'subject to any contrary agreement by the parties, the arbitral tribunal shall decide whether to hold oral hearings for the presentation of evidence . . .'. [112] Art 34(2)(a)(iv).

The third tension is between the needs of domestic arbitration, on the one hand, **17.65** and international arbitration, on the other hand. We have already noted[113] that there is a greater element of 'consumer protection' in domestic arbitration than in the case of international arbitration. In international arbitrations greater respect is generally given to the autonomy of the parties and the grounds on which national courts can review awards in international arbitrations are often more limited than in the case of domestic arbitrations. This issue is closely connected to the debate about party autonomy and the 'stateless' award. Commentators who argue for the separate treatment of international arbitration often do so because they wish to free international arbitrations from national arbitration laws, in particular the arbitration law of the jurisdiction in which the arbitration took place.

The final tension concerns the relationship between arbitration and litigation. To **17.66** what extent should arbitration resemble litigation? Is an arbitrator bound by the same rules as those that are applicable to a judge in a State court? The answer to the latter question seems obvious, namely that an arbitrator is not bound by the same rules. For example, an arbitrator has greater freedom in terms of the procedure to be adopted at the hearing. An arbitrator is not generally bound by strict rules of evidence and appears to have greater latitude in terms of choosing the law that is applicable to the substance of the dispute between the parties; that is to say, the arbitrator is not necessarily obliged to apply the conflict-of-laws rules of the place in which the arbitration is held.[114] But the freedom given to arbitrators has its limits. Arbitrators are still required to act in accordance with the demands of procedural fairness.[115] While the demands of procedural fairness are not as strict as those applicable to a judge in a State court, there are minimum standards of fairness which are applicable to an arbitrator, though their identification is no easy matter. An analogy can therefore be drawn between a judge and an arbitrator and between litigation and arbitration provided that it is recognized that the standards that are applicable to an arbitrator are more flexible than those applicable to a judge in a State court.

C. Arbitration and the Conflict of Laws

International commercial arbitration can give rise to difficult issues in the conflict **17.67** of laws. The problems here are many. In the first place, there may be more than one applicable law; that is to say, it cannot safely be assumed that all aspects of the arbitration will be governed by the same law. Second, it may be no easy task to identify the law that is applicable to the different stages of the arbitration (particularly in the

---

[113] See para 17.14 above.   [114] On which see further para 17.110 below.
[115] See, for example, Art 18 of the UNCITRAL Model Law.

case where the parties have not made any choice of law). Finally, to the extent that it is open to them to do so, the parties may attempt to free themselves from national law (to a greater or lesser extent) and seek to have their dispute decided in accordance with internationally accepted rules or principles rather than the law of a nation State.

17.68   The range of issues which can give rise to difficulties in the conflict of laws has been set out in the following extract:

> **Alan Redfern and Martin Hunter,** *Law and Practice of International Commercial Arbitration* **(4th edn, Sweet & Maxwell, London, 2004) [2.04]**
>
> International commercial arbitration, unlike its domestic counterpart, usually involves more than one system of law or of legal rules. Indeed it is possible, without undue sophistication, to identify at least five different systems of law which in practice may have a bearing on an international commercial arbitration. These are:
>
> (i) the law governing the parties' capacity to enter into an arbitration agreement;
> (ii) the law governing the arbitration agreement and the performance of that agreement;
> (iii) the law governing the existence and proceedings of the arbitral tribunal—the *lex arbitri*;
> (iv) the law, or the relevant legal rules, governing the substantive issues in dispute— generally described as the 'applicable law', the 'governing law', 'the proper law of the contract', or 'the substantive law';
> (v) the law governing recognition and enforcement of the award (which may, in practice, prove to be not one law, but two or more, if recognition and enforcement is sought in more than one country in which the losing party has, or is thought to have, assets).

17.69   We shall explore these issues in turn.

The law governing the parties' capacity to enter into an arbitration agreement

17.70   Parties to an arbitration agreement must have the capacity to enter into the agreement. Thus Article 5 of the New York Convention on the Recognition and Enforcement of Foreign Arbitral Awards provides that recognition and enforcement of an award may be refused if the parties to the arbitration agreement were 'under some incapacity . . . . under the law to which the parties have subjected it or, failing any indication thereon, under the law of the country where the award was made'. The capacity of a person to enter into a contract is usually determined by reference to the law of the place of domicile or residence of the party concerned. In the case of companies, it is determined by reference to the place of incorporation of the company. In some jurisdictions, State entities are not permitted to refer disputes to which they are a party to arbitration and must litigate their disputes through State courts. As a consequence, a party entering into a contract with a State entity would be well advised to check on the capacity of that entity to enter into an arbitration agreement before entering into it.

The law governing the arbitration agreement and the performance of that agreement

Ideally, the arbitration agreement itself should contain a choice-of-law clause so that the identification of the law governing the agreement becomes a relatively straightforward matter. Where the arbitration agreement takes the form of a submission agreement then it may well not contain a choice-of-law clause. Where the arbitration clause is included as a term in a contract between parties and the parties have chosen a law to govern the contract, the law applicable to the arbitration agreement may well be the law applicable to the contract. In *Union of India Ltd v McDonnell Douglas Corp*,[116] Saville J stated:

> an arbitration clause in a commercial contract like the present one is an agreement inside an agreement . . . The parties may make an express choice of law to govern their commercial bargain and that choice may also be made of the law to govern the agreement to arbitrate. In the present case it is my view that by Art 11 the parties have chosen the law of India not only to govern the rights and obligations arising out of their commercial bargain but also the rights and obligations arising out of their agreement to arbitrate.[117]

However, the inference that the law applicable to the arbitration agreement is the law applicable to the contract is not an inevitable one, particularly given the fact that the arbitration clause is separable from the contract of which it is a part.

Where neither the arbitration submission nor the contract in which the arbitration clause is located contains a choice of law clause, then the law applicable to the arbitration agreement is most likely to be the law of the place of the arbitration.[118] The other alternative is the law applicable to the contract itself. Authority can be found to support either view and commentators are divided on the issue.[119] A further alternative, embodied in Article 1494, paragraph 2, of the French New Code of Civil Procedure, is to leave it to the arbitral tribunal to determine the applicable procedural law.[120]

17.71

17.72

17.73

The law governing the existence and proceedings of the arbitral tribunal—the *lex arbitri*

One of the most controversial issues in the law of international commercial arbitration is the identification of the *lex arbitri* and the debate surrounding its role in

17.74

---

[116] [1993] 2 Lloyd's Rep 48 (QBD).   [117] Ibid 50.

[118] See Art 34(2)(a)(i). See, for example, *Deutsche Schachtbau und Tiefbohrgesellschaft mbH v Shell International Petroleum Co Ltd* [1990] 1 AC 295 (HL) 310 where the contract was held to be governed by general principles of law but the law applicable to the arbitration agreement was held to be Swiss law on the basis that the arbitration agreement provided for ICC arbitration in Geneva.

[119] For a review of the issue, see: Julian DM Lew 'Law Applicable to the Form and Substance of the Arbitration Clause' 9 ICCA Congress 145 (1999).

[120] See Gaillard, Emmanuel and Savage, John (eds) *Fouchard, Gaillard, Goldman on International Commercial Arbitration* (Kluwer Law International, The Hague, 1999) paras 1203–4.

the modern law. In *Paul Smith Ltd v H & S International Holding Inc*,[121] Steyn J described the *lex arbitri* in the following terms:

> What then is the law governing the arbitration? It is . . . a body of rules which sets a standard external to the arbitration agreement, and the wishes of the parties, for the conduct of the arbitration. The law governing the arbitration comprises the rules governing interim measures (eg Court orders for the preservation or storage of goods), the rules empowering the exercise by the Court of supportive measures to assist an arbitration which has run into difficulties (eg filling a vacancy in the composition of the arbitral tribunal if there is no other mechanism) and the rules providing for the exercise by the Court of its supervisory jurisdiction over arbitrations (eg removing an arbitrator for misconduct).[122]

17.75 It can be seen from this description that the *lex arbitri* covers a broad range of issues, many of which concern procedural issues relating to the conduct of the arbitration. In the view of some commentators, the *lex arbitri* is solely concerned with procedural issues. The better view is that it encompasses a broader range of matters, which include the following:

- whether a dispute is capable of being referred to arbitration (that is to say, whether it is 'arbitrable' under the local law);
- time-limits for commencing an arbitration;
- interim measures of protection;
- the conduct of the arbitration, including (possibly) rules concerning the disclosure of documents, the evidence of witnesses and so on;
- the powers of the arbitrators, including any powers to decide as '*amiable compositeurs*';
- the form and validity of the arbitration award; and
- the finality of the award, including any right to challenge it in the courts of the place of arbitration.[123]

Given the breadth of issues which fall within the scope of the *lex arbitri*, it plays a significant role in the law of international commercial arbitration.

17.76 How then do the courts determine the *lex arbitri* in any given case? The answer is that it is generally to be found in the law of the seat of the arbitration. The seat of the arbitration is:

> the juridical seat designated by the parties to the arbitration agreement or by any arbitral or other institution or person vested by the parties with powers in that regard or by the arbitral tribunal if so authorized by the parties. The juridical seat is the place whose law is intended by the parties to govern the arbitral proceedings, not the place where the proceedings are actually held or the award given. The link establishing the seat is therefore legal, not territorial, a sound approach, for the place designated for a

---

[121] [1991] 2 Lloyd's Rep 127 (QBD).   [122] Ibid 130.
[123] Alan Redfern and Martin Hunter, *Law and Practice of International Commercial Arbitration* (4th edn, Sweet & Maxwell, London, 2004) [2-06].

hearing or a pre-hearing may have been chosen for convenience and not because of the relevance of its legal system.[124]

In practice, the seat of the arbitration tends to be the place chosen by the parties for **17.77** the conduct of the arbitration. While it is in theory possible for the parties to choose a *lex arbitri* which is separate from the place chosen by the parties for the conduct of the arbitration, the practical difficulties which may flow from the choice of a different law are such as to persuade a court that in all likelihood the parties intended the *lex arbitri* to be the place in which the arbitration is held. The reason for this was explained by Saville J in the following terms:

> If the parties do not make an express choice of procedural law to govern their arbitration, then the court will consider whether they have made an implicit choice. In this circumstance the fact that the parties have agreed to a place for the arbitration is a very strong pointer that implicitly they must have chosen the law of that place to govern the procedures of the arbitration. The reason for this is essentially one of commonsense. By choosing a country in which to arbitrate the parties have, ex hypothesi, created a close connection between the arbitration and that country and it is reasonable to assume from their choice that they attached some importance to the relevant laws of that country, ie those laws which would be relevant to the arbitration.[125]

There is, however, no requirement that all of the meetings of the arbitrators or that **17.78** all the hearings take place in the jurisdiction of the seat of the arbitration. It is for this reason that the seat is described as a legal or a juridical concept rather than a territorial concept. It is not unusual for a particular meeting, such as a hearing to deal with procedural matters, to be held in another part of the world in order to suit the convenience of the arbitrators or the parties. The fact that a particular hearing is held in another jurisdiction does not alter the seat of the arbitration; it is unaffected by the peripatetic nature of the proceedings.

The 'delocalization' debate

While the *lex arbitri* is important, in the sense that it encompasses a wide range of **17.79** issues, a number of commentators have challenged the need for, and the role of, the *lex arbitri* in the modern law. One of the most contentious debates in the law of international commercial arbitration in recent years has concerned the extent to which it is possible to detach international commercial arbitration from national law, in particular the domestic law of the jurisdiction in which the arbitration takes place. Considerable energy has been devoted to the attempt to free international commercial arbitration from what were perceived to be restrictive, and often inappropriate, domestic rules of law which had the potential to interfere

---

[124] Goode, *Commercial Law* (n 2) 1170. English law now has a statutory definition of the seat of an arbitration, to be found in s 3 of the Arbitration Act 1996.
[125] *McDonnell Douglas* (n 117) 50.

with the arbitral process. The context for this debate is helpfully summarized in the following extract:

Alan Redfern and Martin Hunter, *Law and Practice of International Commercial Arbitration* (4th edn, Sweet & Maxwell, London, 2004) [2.25]–[2.26]

So far as international commercial arbitration is concerned, it would save considerable time, trouble and expense if the laws governing arbitrations were the same throughout the world, so that there was—so to speak—a universal *lex arbitri*. There would then be a 'level playing field' for the conduct of international commercial arbitrations wherever they took place. An arbitral tribunal would not have to enquire whether there were any special provisions governing arbitration which were peculiar to the law of the country which was the seat of the arbitration. On this aspect of the arbitral process, all laws would be the same.

In practice, however, the idea of a universal *lex arbitri* is as illusory as that of universal peace. Each state has its own national characteristics, its own interests to protect and its own concepts of how arbitrations should be conducted on its territory. Even states which adopt the Model Law cannot resist adding their own particular provisions to it. Indeed states with a long history of arbitration and a highly developed law and practice are particularly unlikely to adopt simplified models, which may, in themselves, create fresh problems. Nevertheless, it is inconvenient (to put it no higher) that the regulation of international commercial arbitration should differ from one country to another; and this has led to the search for an escape route.

In this connection, two separate developments are seen. The first (which no doubt should not properly be characterised as an 'escape route') is for the state to loosen considerably the control which it seeks to exercise over international commercial arbitration conducted on its territory. This is the route taken by modern laws of arbitration. These laws take careful note of the theme of the Model Law which is that their courts should not intervene in arbitrations, unless authorised to do so. The role of the courts should be supportive not interventionist.

The second development is to detach an international commercial arbitration from control by the law of the place in which it is held. This is the so-called 'de-localisation' theory, the idea being that instead of a dual system of control, first by the *lex arbitri* and then by the courts of the place of enforcement of the award, there should be only one point of control—that of the place of enforcement. In this way, the whole world (or most of it) would be available for international commercial arbitrations; and international commercial arbitration itself would be 'supra-national', 'a-national', 'transnational', 'de-localised' or even 'expatriate'. More poetically, such an arbitration would be a 'floating' arbitration, resulting in a floating award.

The de-localisation theory took as its starting point the autonomy of the parties—the fact that it was their agreement to arbitrate which brought the proceedings into being—and rested upon two basic (yet frequently confused) arguments. The first assumed that international commercial arbitration was sufficiently regulated by its own rules, which were either adopted by the parties (as an expression of their autonomy) or drawn up by the arbitral tribunal itself. The second assumed that control should only come from the law of the place of enforcement of the award.

17.80 The delocalization theory was most influential in the last quarter of the twentieth century, particularly in France. It owes its origins to a line of cases (mostly, but not exclusively, decided by the French courts) and to the writings of a number of (mostly French) academic writers.[126] We shall examine three of the leading cases and then turn to consider some of the leading academic writings (both those who support and those who are critical of delocalization as a theory).

The first relevant case arose out of a dispute between the Libyan General National Maritime Transport Co ('LGN') and the Swedish shipbuilder Götaverken Arendal AB ('Götaverken').[127] Götaverken agreed to build three tankers for LGN but LGN, having paid three quarters of the purchase price, declined to take delivery of the vessels or to pay the balance of the purchase price on the ground that components of the vessels had been made in Israel in breach of a term in the contract and also in breach of a Libyan law which imposed a boycott on components manufactured in Israel. Further, LGN alleged that the technical specifications for the vessels had not been met. Götaverken insisted that LGN was obliged to take delivery of the vessels and to pay the balance of the price. The resultant dispute between the parties was submitted to ICC arbitration in Paris in accordance with the terms of the contract between the parties. By a majority, the arbitral tribunal issued an award in favour of Götaverken and ordered LGN to pay the unpaid balance of the purchase price and to take delivery of the three vessels. Götaverken then sought to enforce the award in Sweden, while LGN sought to challenge the award in the French courts. Our primary concern is with the proceedings in the French courts. For present purposes it suffices to note that the Swedish Supreme Court held that the award was enforceable, notwithstanding the fact that a challenge had been made against the award in Paris. **17.81**

In the proceedings in Paris LGN sought to have the award set aside on a number of grounds which included its self-contradictory nature, the failure of the arbitrators to give reasoned grounds for aspects of their decision and the fact that the award was alleged to violate French public order in so far as it sought to impose on a Libyan party an obligation to act inconsistently with the terms of the Libyan boycott. The Court of Appeal in Paris dismissed the challenge to the award on the ground that the award issued by the arbitrators could not be considered to be a French award so that the court did not have jurisdiction to set it aside. In reaching this conclusion, the court had regard to the fact that neither party was a French national, the contract was neither signed nor performed in France and Paris had been chosen as the place of arbitration for reasons of neutrality and not because the parties had wished to subject themselves to the *loi procédurale française*. The court also had regard to Article 11 of the (1975) ICC arbitral rules which provided: **17.82**

> The rules governing the proceedings before the arbitrator shall be those resulting from these Rules and, where these Rules are silent, any rules which the parties (or,

---

[126] In particular the work of Professors Goldman, Fouchard and Lalive. See, for example: Berthold Goldman, 'Les Conflits de Lois dans l'Arbitrage International de Droit Privé' (1963) 109 Recueils des Cours 347 and P Fouchard 'La Portée Internationale de l'Annulation de la Sentence Arbitrale dans son Pays d'Origine' [1997] Rev Arb 329.   [127] On which see: (1980) J du Droit Intl 660.

failing them, the arbitrator) may settle, and *whether or not reference is thereby made to a municipal procedural law to be applied to the arbitration.*[128]

17.83   It was the italicized part of Article 11 to which the court attached significance because it differed from the previous version of the same rule where the reference was to the law of the place of the arbitration. The change in wording was held to be important in so far as it recognized the freedom of the parties to 'choose a law without reference to a potential supplementary law'.

17.84   The scope of the decision of the Court of Appeal has been explained in the following terms:

> The judgment of the Paris Court of Appeal did not say in terms that arbitral awards in international arbitration were stateless, merely that on the facts there was no connection with the French legal order. But, since the courts of a state other than that of the seat of the arbitration are unlikely to take jurisdiction in the absence of agreement by the parties, the effect of the *Götaverken* decision, if it were to be applied universally, is that, unless the parties themselves agree to submit to the procedural law of a particular state, the arbitral proceedings are not reviewable by any court other than the court of a state in which enforcement is sought.[129]

17.85   The decision almost immediately generated considerable controversy. Supporters saw in it a clear recognition of the fact that it is possible to detach an international commercial arbitration from the legal system of the country in which the proceedings take place. This can be seen from the following extract:

Jan Paulsson, 'Arbitration Unbound: award detached from the law of its country of origin' (1981) 30 ICLQ 358, 367–71

The decision of the Court of Appeals in Paris constitutes clear acceptance of the detachment phenomenon. Its underlying thesis is that the legal force of transnational arbitration is founded on the parties' creation of a contractual institution; the effect of the proceedings may be left to be controlled by whatever legal system is requested to recognise the award once it is rendered, and that system need not necessarily be that of the place of arbitration . . .

The importance of the Paris decision is *not* its acceptance of the parties' right to agree to rules of conduct for the arbitration . . . Rather, the decision addresses the fundamental issue of whether the legal system of the place of arbitration has imperative authority to rule on the validity of the proceedings as such—and thus on the binding effect of its result: the award.

So when the Court of Paris affirmed that the place of arbitration was chosen only in the interest of geographical neutrality and may not 'be considered an implicit expression of

---

[128]   The current version is Art 15(1) of the 1998 ICC Arbitral Rules. While the current version is not identical to the 1975 version, the differences are immaterial for present purposes.

[129]   Roy Goode, 'The Role of the *Lex Loci Arbitri* in International Commercial Arbitration' in Francis D Rose (ed), *Lex Mercatoria: Essays on International Commercial Law in Honour of Francis Reynolds* (LLP, London, 2000) 245, 253.

the parties' intent to subject themselves, even subsidiarily, to the *loi procédurale française*, this must be understood in the more fundamental sense. Indeed, the decision refers to the fact that the proceedings were not those contemplated by French (arbitration) law, that they had '*no attachment whatsoever to the French legal order*' (in view of the parties' status as foreigners and the lack of connection between their transaction and the territory of France), and that the award was thus not French.

The message seems clear: one is authorised to conclude that the binding force of an international award may be derived from the contractual commitment to arbitrate in and of itself, that is to say without a specific national legal system serving as its foundation. In this sense, an arbitral award may indeed 'drift' but of course it is ultimately subject to the *post facto* control of the execution jurisdiction(s).

In some ways this result is uncontroversial. As was written nearly 20 years ago, 'the doctrine of the autonomy of the parties' will, which is declining everywhere in municipal law, is gaining ground in the international legal order'. . . . the New York Convention of 1958 [has] acknowledged the parties' right to define the workings of their chosen forum. Under the UNCITRAL Rules . . . . arbitral tribunals shall *in all cases* decide in accordance with the terms of the contract and taking into account trade usages applicable to the transaction. To free international contracts from Procustean beds has become commonplace in arbitral awards. Thus, in sum, it is within the power of the parties . . . to establish by contract a procedure whose operations 'must even be deemed to overrule compulsory provisions in the country of arbitration.'

Those who favour the *Götaverken* decision do not necessarily insist on a hands-off attitude; the judge at the place of the arbitration is seen as the best-placed authority to control the award. If he is to assume this role, however, it should be only as an instrument for the control of the conformity of the award to transnational minimum standards such as those embodied in the major international conventions. Unless the parties have agreed otherwise, he has no mission or capacity to apply his own national criteria to the award. This perspective seems to have been that adopted by the French Cour de Cassation in the *Bruynzeel case*, where it was recognised that the parties, having chosen not to refer to a national law to govern the proceedings, had the capacity to leave the arbitrators full discretion to fix their own time limits *because to do so did not violate imperative international norms*. . . .

Unless national courts accept this role as 'transnational' controllers at the seat of arbitration, the detachment principle may be justly criticised on the ground that it leaves no forum where a manifestly deficient award may be set aside.

It can be seen from the latter part of the extract that the aim of Paulsson is not to **17.86** abandon all judicial control over arbitral awards. On the contrary, he expressly concedes that a 'manifestly deficient award' should be set aside. His point is rather to shift attention from the jurisdiction in which the arbitration takes place to the jurisdiction in which enforcement of the award is sought and to lift the horizons of national courts from the details of their domestic arbitration law and to focus rather on 'transnational minimum standards such as those embodied in the major international conventions' (whatever these might be). However, not all commentators have adopted such a favourable view of the decision of the Paris Court of

Appeal. The following extract adopts a more critical approach and suggests that the case may be explained on a more limited basis:

William W Park, *Arbitration of International Business Disputes: studies in law and practice* (OUP, Oxford, 2006) 161

The paradox of a legal obligation independent of a legal order suggests Athena springing full-blown from the head of Zeus: a binding commitment, free from any municipal law, just appears. Grasp of Paulsson's thesis requires a conceptual leap to a document labelled 'obligation' enforced without respect to whether the document constitutes a valid obligation under the legal system normally selected by the enforcement forum's choice of law principles. In other words, the document receives contractual force from the enforcement forum itself regardless of the otherwise governing law.

Götaverken and its progeny lend themselves to a less radical analysis than suggested by Paulsson. An international arbitration, rather than being 'detached from its country of origin,' receives substantially greater autonomy, and is subject to fewer constraints, than a domestic arbitration. The award in *Götaverken* was not annulled. Rather, the French court found the award not subject to a challenge procedure (*appel en nullité*) available only to French awards. Moreover if the facts of *Götaverken* are changed slightly, so that the Swedes deliver cocaine rather than tankers, one wonders whether the French court would exhibit a similar laissez-faire attitude towards alleged public policy violations.

17.87   The second case is *Hilmarton Ltd v Omnium de Traitement et de Valorisation*[130] ('OTV') in which the parties entered into a contract under which Hilmarton agreed to act as a consultant to OTV to advise on tax and economic issues in relation to a bid by OTV to tender for the construction of a drainage system in the city of Algiers and to help OTV obtain the contract. The contract was expressly governed by Swiss law and made provision for ICC arbitration in the event of a dispute, the arbitration to be held in Geneva. After OTV was awarded the Algerian contract, a dispute arose as to the fee to be paid by OTV to Hilmerton. OTV offered to pay approximately half of the fees stipulated in the contract. Hilmarton initiated arbitration proceedings in Geneva. OTV defended the claim on the ground that an Algerian law rendered the contract a nullity because it prohibited the use of intermediaries, such as Hilmerton, in the procurement of such contracts.

17.88   The arbitrator issued an award dismissing Hilmarton's claim. The arbitrator found that the contract was illegal under Algerian law on the basis that the underlying purpose of the contract was to exert influence on Algerian officials and held that enforcing a contract which violated a foreign law was contrary to Swiss public policy. Hilmarton subsequently challenged the award. The challenge was successful. The Swiss Supreme Court, affirming a decision by a Swiss Cantonal Court, annulled the arbitral award on the ground that enforcement of the contract between Hilmarton and OTV was not contrary to Swiss public policy. The court held that, although the

---

[130] On which see generally: (1995) XX Ybk Commercial Arbitration 663 and [1993] Revue de l'arbitrage 317.

contract violated Algerian law, this did not amount to a breach of Swiss law, which was the law applicable to the case.

Once again our interest in the case lies in the response of the French courts to OTV's attempt to secure recognition of the arbitrator's award in France. The Paris *Tribunal de grande instance* recognized the award so that OTV was held not to be liable to pay damages to Hilmarton. The Paris Court of Appeal and the *Cour de Cassation* dismissed Hilmarton's appeal notwithstanding the fact that, in the intervening period, the Swiss courts had set aside the award. The *Cour de Cassation* expressed its conclusion in the following terms:

> Attendu, enfin, que la sentence rendue en Suisse était une sentence internationale qui n'était pas intégrée dans l'ordre juridique de cet Etat, de sorte que son existence demeurait établie malgré son annulation et que sa reconnaissance en France n'était pas contraire à l'ordre public international.[131]

17.89

Unfortunately for the French courts, this was not the end of the matter. Hilmarton, having set aside the arbitrator's award in Switzerland, commenced fresh arbitral proceedings in which it sought to recover its fees. The arbitrator made an award in Hilmarton's favour. Hilmarton then sought to enforce that award in France. While the lower courts were willing to enforce the second award, the *Cour de Cassation* refused to recognize and enforce the second award on the ground that it was precluded from doing so by virtue of its previous decision that the first award was enforceable. Once again the *Cour de Cassation* repeated its view that the award rendered by the arbitrators in Switzerland was an international award which was not integrated into the law of Switzerland so that the award remained in existence and enforceable in France even if it had been set aside in Switzerland. Thus the court chose to follow its own, earlier decision giving effect to the first arbitral award. A different conclusion was, however, reached in England where it was held that there were no public policy objections to the enforcement of the second award.[132] As has been pointed out, the outcome of the litigation on both sides of the Channel was that 'France recognises only the first award, rendered in favour of the French company; England recognises only the second award, rendered in favour of the English company'.[133] This inconsistency of outcome is less than attractive. There is also a possible inconsistency in the approach of the French courts, as Dr Petrochilos has pointed out,

17.90

> The problem with the *Hilmarton* jurisprudence and the upshot of the litigation is that one almost loses one's sense of right and wrong in the procedural technicalities.

---

[131] Lastly, the award rendered in Switzerland is an international award which is not integrated in the legal system of that State, so that it remains in existence even if set aside and its recognition in France is not contrary to international public policy.

[132] *Omnium de Traitement et de Valorisation SA v Hilmarton Ltd* [1999] 2 All ER 146 (QBD).

[133] Pierre Mayer, 'Revisiting *Hilmarton* and *Chromalloy*' in Albert Jan van den Berg (ed), *International Arbitration and National Courts: the never ending story* (Kluwer, The Hague, 2001) 168.

Tempting as it may be to dismiss the case as a classic example of a tough case making bad law, the law did not need to be that bad. The French supreme court seems to be upholding a double standard: an international award cannot be conclusively integrated in the legal order of the state of rendition, but can be so integrated at the state of enforcement. Put bluntly the French position would be that the relative validity of awards is an acceptable concept so long as it is kept out of its backyard. This conclusion is compounded by an exception to the principle of non-integration of arbitral awards (as we may call it) which is not spelt out in the case law but must follow from it. If *res judicata* as amongst French courts must be strictly applied, an award which is international . . . . but made in France cannot be both set aside and effective at the same time; for the judgment setting it aside . . . is *res judicata* in France and cannot be revisited. Practically, the *Hilmarton* rule applies only to awards made abroad . . .[134]

17.91 The final case is *Arab Republic of Egypt v Chromalloy Air Services*. The parties entered into a contract under which Chromalloy agreed to provide equipment, services and technical assistance to the Egyptian Air Force. The contract stated that it was governed by Egyptian law and made provision for any dispute arising out of the contract to be resolved by arbitration in Cairo. The Egyptian authorities subsequently purported to terminate the contract between the parties. Chromalloy brought arbitration proceedings in Egypt and the arbitral tribunal rendered an award in its favour. The Egyptian government appealed to the Cairo Court of Appeal who set aside the award on the ground that the arbitral tribunal had failed to apply Egyptian administrative law which they held to be the law applicable to the contract. Notwithstanding the fact that the award had been annulled by the Egyptian courts, Chromalloy sought to enforce the award both in France and in the United States. The United States District Court for the District of Columbia held that the award was valid and decided to enforce it.[135] In reaching this conclusion, the court emphasized the public policy in favour of the final and binding nature of arbitral awards in international commercial disputes. It should be noted that the approach taken by the United States court in *Chromalloy* was very different from that taken by the French courts, in that the United States court adopted a discretionary standard. It did not dismiss the decision of the Egyptian court out of hand; rather, it did give consideration to the question whether the conclusion that the award was enforceable was not open to them in the light of the principle of *res judicata*. Support for the proposition that enforcement is not an automatic response of the American courts can be gleaned from the fact that other cases can be found in which the American courts have declined to enforce an award which has been set aside in the court where the arbitration took place.[136]

---

[134] Georgios Petrochilos, *Procedural Law in International Arbitration* (OUP, Oxford, 2004) [7.42].
[135] 939 F Supp 907 (DCC 1996).
[136] See, for example: *Baker Marine (Nig) Ltd v Chevron (Nig) Ltd* 191 F 3d 194 (US Ct of Apps (2nd Cir) 1999), where the court refused to enforce a Nigerian award set aside by the courts of Nigeria.

The French courts reached the same conclusion but for different reasons. The **17.92** Paris Court of Appeal concluded:

> La sentence rendue en Egypte étant une sentence internationale qui, par définition, n'était pas intégrée à l'ordre juridique de cet Etat de sorte que son existence est établie malgré son annulation, sa reconnaissance en France n'est pas contraire à l'ordre public international.[137]

It can be seen that this formula very much resembles that adopted by the *Cour de* **17.93** *Cassation* in *Hilmarton*. There is, however, an important difference between the two, which is the addition of the words '*par définition*' in *Chromalloy*. It has been stated that the addition of these words is important in that they have the effect of making the rule:

> a true substantive rule of French private international law (or *règle matérielle*). French law now has a judge-made rule, to the effect that no award rendered in international arbitration is definitively integrated in any legal order; and in consequence the French judge is entitled to examine afresh the regularity of such an award, without being bound by any previous decision of the courts of the place of arbitration, whether confirming or annulling it. That rule would seem to be inflexible, in that it will apply regardless of (and thus upsetting) an agreement of the parties expressly submitting their arbitration to the law of a state which may provide (or permit the parties to agree upon) closer scrutiny of an award or for different remedies than French law.[138]

Not every legal system has followed the French example. Some legal systems, such **17.94** as England, remain opposed to the concept of delocalization. In *Bank Mellat v Helleniki Techniki SA*,[139] Kerr LJ stated that English law 'does not recognize the concept of arbitral procedures floating in the transnational firmament, unconnected with any municipal system of law'.[140] Given these different judicial perceptions of the utility of delocalization, what are the arguments of principle (or of policy) in favour of (and against) the concept?

Jan Paulsson, 'Arbitration Unbound: award detached from the law of its country of origin' (1981) 30 ICLQ 358, 362–3

Academicians defending the notion of an 'internationalised' arbitral process have spoken of 'arbitration escaping the hold of any national law and thus subject directly to international law.' Or, as Berthold Goldman has put it, the search for a source of authority consistent with the nature of international arbitration can lead only to an 'autonomous, non-national' system.

---

[137] 'The award made in Egypt is by definition an international award which, by definition, is not integrated in the legal order of that State so that its existence remains established despite its being annulled and its enforcement in France is not in violation of international public policy.'

[138] Georgios Petrochilos, *Procedural Law in International Arbitration* (OUP, Oxford, 2004) [7.38].

[139] [1984] QB 291 (CA).

[140] Ibid 301. See to similar effect *Star Shipping SA v China National Foreign Trade Transportation Corp (The Star Texas)* [1993] 2 Lloyd's Rep 445. But while under English law the curial law must be that of a municipal system of law, the parties may validly agree that the place of arbitration, and thus by inference the curial law, are to be determined by them at a later date, for example, by one party being given the option to choose between one place and another (*The Star Texas*, above).

In a remarkably concise article which addresses the specific question of choice of law in international arbitration but which has wider implications for the concept of *lex arbitri*, Pierre Lalive reasons as follows in support of the thesis of detachment.

The municipal judge necessarily applies the rules of conflict of the forum, which represent the politico-juridical concepts—particularly as to the territorial limits of legislative power—of the State from which he derives his authority. The international arbitrator is in a fundamentally different position. Whatever one might think of the contractual (as opposed to judicial) source of an arbitral tribunal's authority as a purely internal matter, it is difficult to consider the international arbitrator as a manifestation of the power of a State. His mission, conferred by the parties' consent, is one of a private nature:

> and it would be a rather artificial interpretation to deem his power to be derived, and very indirectly at that, from a tolerance of the State of the place of arbitration.

For Lalive, the notion that the international arbitrator must fit into the mold of the legal system of the place of arbitration records the myth of Procrustes, who seized unsuspecting travellers and made them fit into his bed, cutting off their legs if they were too long, stretching them if they were too short. Parties to international arbitration are indeed sometimes like unsuspecting travellers when the end up in a particular country. Whilst, if their contract had stipulated the jurisdiction of that country's courts, they may have expected the local judge to fit the Procrustean bed of the municipal legal system, which would be his exclusive source of authority, the same need not be true with respect to arbitrators whom the parties, as it were, brought along.

Paulsson returned to this theme in a subsequent article published shortly after the article quoted above. In this article he attempted to justify delocalization as a matter of principle in the following terms:

Jan Paulsson, 'Delocalisation of International Commercial Arbitration: when and why it matters' (1983) 32 ICLQ 53, 54–7

Those who reject the delocalisation process seem to mistake the purpose of permitting parties to unbind arbitrations from the law of the *situs* of proceedings. They wrongly conclude that what is sought is an 'escape' from national jurisdictions.

To seek completely to avoid national jurisdictions would be misguided. Indeed, the international arbitral system would ultimately break down if no national jurisdictions could be called upon to recognise and enforce awards.

The question is rather whether in certain situations international arbitration may be liberated from the local peculiarities of a place of arbitration chosen either fortuitously or for reasons of neutrality having nothing to do with the parties' attachment to local rules of arbitration. . . .

It would appear that the opponents of delocalised arbitration are perplexed, to use Professor Park's image, by the 'paradox' of a legal obligation independent of a legal order springing like Athena 'full-blown from the head of Zeus.' What this critique misses is that the delocalised award is *not* thought to be independent of any legal order. Rather, the point is that a delocalised award may be accepted by the legal order of an enforcement jurisdiction although it is independent from the legal order of its country of origin. This is no stranger than the analysis of a contract signed at Munich airport between a Japanese consortium and an American subcontractor selected to perform engineering services on a project in the Middle-East . . . I submit that it would occur to no-one to complain that the birth of the legal obligation in Munich airport was impermissibly miraculous because it sprang from the brow of the parties and was thus 'independent' of the *German* legal order.

It can be seen from the latter extract that a key part of the argument advanced by those who support delocalization is that, in their view, the place of arbitration is of little or no significance because it is chosen for reasons of 'geographic appropriateness' or for reasons of neutrality and not because its law was thought by the parties to be suitable for international commercial arbitrations. Instead it is the place of enforcement which assumes importance for the proponents of delocalization. It should be for the courts in the state of enforcement to decide whether or not the award is enforceable and, in reaching a decision on this issue, they are not bound by any decision of the court of the place in which the arbitration was held. The emphasis in the delocalization literature is very much on the importance of the autonomy of the parties, the private, consensual nature of arbitration and the fact that arbitrators are not judges in State courts and, consequently, have greater flexibility and freedom than their judicial counterparts.   **17.95**

But the arguments are not all one way. In a recent essay[141] a number of objections have been levelled against declocalization and the concept of a stateless award. The principal objections to it are as follows.   **17.96**

First, there can be no contract without law. Here the point is that an award cannot be binding simply as a consequence of the parties' agreement to be bound because 'a contract depends for its force on recognition by law'.[142] This point was classically made by the late Dr FA Mann in the following passage: **17.97**

> No one has ever or anywhere been able to point to any provision or legal principle which would permit individuals to act outside the confines of a system of municipal law; even the idea of the autonomy of the parties exists only by virtue of a given system of municipal law and in different systems may have different characteristics and effects. Similarly, every arbitration is necessarily subject to the law of a given State. No private person has the right or the power to act on any level other than that of municipal law. Every right or power a private person enjoys is inexorably conferred by or derived from a system of municipal law which may conveniently and in accordance with tradition be called the *lex fori*, though it would be more exact (but less familiar) to speak of the *lex arbitri* or, in French, *la loi d'arbitrage*.[143]

Building on this analysis it has been observed that: **17.98**

> Even the most ardent advocates of party autonomy appear to accept that arbitration must act within some system of law. Their case is that the only relevant system is that

---

[141] Goode, 'The Role of the *Lex Loci Arbitri* in International Commercial Arbitration' (n 129) 245.
[142] Ibid 256.
[143] FA Mann, '*Lex Facit Arbitrum*' in Pieter Sanders (ed), *International Arbitration: liber amicorum for Martin Domke* (Martinus Nijhoff, The Hague, 1967) 160.

of the state of enforcement. But this argument never gets off the ground, for it pre-supposes that the arbitral process works in a complete legal vacuum unless and until application is made to enforce the award as a foreign award. If that were so, then at the time of its rendering the award would have no legal underpinnings at all. It would undoubtedly be the product of the parties' agreement, under which they assented to be bound, but . . . . that assent is no more than an agreement, lacking any legal force unless accepted as binding by the relevant national law; and the only possible law is the *lex loci arbitri*. Moreover, one may ask what, under the autonomy concept, is the status of the arbitral proceedings prior to the award? Do these too rest solely on the will of the parties? Such a contention has only to be stated for its absurdity to become obvious. . . .[144]

17.99   Second, it is argued that the claim, advanced by proponents of declocalization, that the theory of the stateless award respects the autonomy of the parties is used with 'a high degree of selectivity'.[145] That this is so can be demonstrated by refer-ence to the litigation in the French courts in *Hilmarton* where, as we have noted, the French courts found that the award was not integrated into the Swiss legal sys-tem, notwithstanding the fact that the arbitration clause in the contract provided that the arbitration 'shall take place in Geneva under the law of the Canton of Geneva'. A similar outcome can be seen in *Chromalloy* where the French courts concluded that the award was not grounded in Egyptian law despite the fact that the arbitration clause in the contract between the parties provided that 'both par-ties have irrevocably agreed to apply Egypt Laws and to choose Cairo as the seat of the court of arbitration'.

17.100   Third, it is argued that delocalization frustrates the legitimate expectations of the parties to the contract in that it denies effect to their choice of the curial law to govern the arbitration. In this connection, the claim that parties choose the place of arbitration simply for reasons of convenience is disputed. While it is doubtless true that considerations of neutrality feature prominently in the choice of the place of arbitration, it is difficult to believe that parties to international commer-cial arbitrations pay no regard at all to the quality of the law administered in the place in which the arbitration is to be held.

17.101   Fourth, it is claimed that delocalization hinders finality, which is one of the prin-cipal aims of arbitration. As has been pointed out:

> the territorial approach, in insisting that the validity of an arbitral award is governed by the *lex arbitri*, has the great merit of subjecting the question of validity to a single decision of the court of origin. By contrast, denial of the function of a *lex arbitri* may involve litigation in every country in which the respondent has assets, and even within a single country may entail the case being taken up through a two-tier or even a three-tier hierarchical chain and then, where the highest court acts as a court of cas-sation, being sent back again to a new lower court for a fresh determination. One has

---

[144] Goode, 'The Role of the *Lex Loci Arbitri* in International Commercial Arbitration' (n 129) 257–8.   [145] Ibid 259.

only to look at the history of the litigation in some of the cases . . . . to see the disastrous consequences of this . . . . this is not delocalisation, it is multilocalisation.[146]

Fifth, it has been pointed out that delocalization fails to avoid multiple jeopardy **17.102** because:

> the respondent against whom an award is made, having battled successfully through his own courts to have it set aside, is then faced with the prospect of having to relitigate the identical issues before the courts of every country in which he has assets. This can only be described as oppressive.[147]

Sixth, delocalization is said to be inefficient because 'the exposure to a multiplic- **17.103** ity of proceedings in a number of different countries also undermines what should be one of the purposes of international commercial arbitration, namely to promote economic efficiency in the handling of the dispute'.[148]

Seventh, delocalization fails to respect the 'general principle of law that a contract- **17.104** ing party who pursues a particular course of conduct on which the other party reasonably relies cannot subsequently be allowed to follow a course which is inconsistent with the position which he previously took.'[149] As has been observed:

> it is widely accepted that a person who participates in arbitration proceedings and against whom an arbitral award is made cannot in general invoke a ground for attacking the validity of the arbitration agreement or the jurisdiction of the tribunal which he did not advance before the tribunal itself.

> One of the problems of the stateless award is that it fails to respect this well established principle of estoppel. A party against whom an award is made decides to challenge it in the courts of the seat of arbitration. If he is unsuccessful, why should he be allowed a second—or a third or fourth—bite at the cherry in proceedings before a court or courts elsewhere?[150]

Eighth, delocalization gives rise to the 'strong possibility of conflicting decisions **17.105** of different foreign courts',[151] as can be seen in the litigation in both *Hilmarton* and *Chromalloy*.

Ninth, delocalization fails to give proper weight to the privileged status of arbitra- **17.106** tion agreements. These privileges are not derived from the will of the parties but from national law and from international conventions. These privileges assume different forms: a valid agreement to arbitrate invoked by a party against whom court proceedings are instituted effectively halts the proceedings; the parties and their arbitrators have much more freedom in the conduct of the arbitration than national judges; judicial review of an arbitral award is very much more restricted than an appeal against a judgment; an arbitral award can be enforced in the country of the award as if it were a judgment without the need for an action on the

---

[146] Ibid 262. [147] Ibid. [148] Ibid 263. [149] Ibid. [150] Ibid.
[151] Ibid 264.

award; and under the New York Convention and conventions with similar objectives, an award made in one state can be enforced in all other contracting states.

> These privileges derive from national law and international conventions, not from
> contract. How can parties to an arbitration claim the benefit of such laws and con-
> ventions and simultaneously ascribe the binding force of the arbitral award exclusively
> to their mutual will? If it is the case that the agreement to arbitrate is the sole source of
> the binding nature of the award, then let the parties be bound by the consequences
> attaching to any normal contract, namely that the sole method of enforcement is by
> an action on the award and that the resulting judgment will not enjoy the finality of
> an arbitral award or the benefit of the New York Convention.[152]

17.107 Tenth, it has been suggested that delocalization renders Article V of the New York
Convention[153] a 'dead letter' because 'no court would have any regard for the decisions of foreign courts setting aside an award' and 'all courts would take refuge
in their own arbitration law'.[154] Further, it has been stated that delocalization is
'incompatible with the mutual courtesy and respect which each state and its courts
are expected to show to other states and their courts as regards laws and decisions
made by the latter within their respective jurisdictions'.[155]

17.108 Finally, it has been argued that the *raison d'être* for the development of the delocalization theory has disappeared for the following reason:

> the main cause of the reluctance for concern of courts of enforcement states to defer
> to rulings of courts of origin, namely the hostility of local courts in a number of juris-
> dictions to the concept of arbitration and their assertion of excessive jurisdiction over
> arbitral proceedings and awards, has largely (though not entirely) disappeared as state
> after state has departed from its traditional arbitration rules and enacted legislation
> along the lines of the UNCITRAL Model Law. As one authority has rightly com-
> mented, if member states of the European Communities had sufficient confidence in
> each other's courts to ratify the Brussels and Lugano conventions providing for the
> mutual recognition and enforcement of judgments, why should they not have the
> same confidence in judgments of courts of other states setting aside arbitral awards?[156]

17.109 Given these criticisms, it is suggested that the delocalization theory has the potential to cause more problems that it can solve. In particular, the fact that domestic
arbitration laws are increasingly following the outline of the UNCITRAL Model
Law should reduce the incidence of parties being caught out by an 'inconvenient'
local law which is not appropriate for international arbitrations. To this extent, the
need to free international commercial arbitrations from the law of the place in
which the arbitration is held has been reduced and there is less need for the creation of a 'stateless' or a 'floating' award. Difficulties can still arise when an attempt
is made in one State to enforce an award which has already been set aside in the
jurisdiction in which the arbitration was held. As we shall see,[157] difficulties can

---

[152] Ibid 265.   [153] On which see below para 17.135.
[154] Goode, 'The Role of the *Lex Loci Arbitri* in International Commercial Arbitration' (n 129) 265.
[155] Ibid.   [156] Ibid 266–7.   [157] See para 17.138 below.

arise in deciding the extent to which the courts in the state of enforcement should be obliged to respect and give effect to the decision of the court at the place at which the arbitration was held. But it is not necessary to create a theory of delocalization in order to resolve this problem. It can be solved by a careful consideration of the effect in law of the decision of the court at the place of arbitration and the obligation of the courts in the state of enforcement to respect that decision and an examination of the grounds which led that court to set aside (or, as the case may be, not to set aside) the arbitral award.

The law, or the relevant legal rules, governing the substantive issues in dispute

The identification of the law, or legal rules, applicable to the substantive issues in dispute between the parties can give rise to difficulties. To what extent are arbitrators obliged to apply conflict-of-laws rules in order to establish the law applicable to the substance of the dispute? Can they choose the applicable law 'directly', that is to say, without first working through any conflict-of-laws rules? Do arbitrators have a margin of discretion to choose the law that they deem to be the most 'appropriate' to the substance of the dispute (even if that law is not the law that would have been applicable had the arbitrators applied conflict-of-laws rules)? No one answer can be given to these questions. The answer in part depends upon the jurisdiction in which the arbitration is taking place and the extent to which that national law requires arbitrators to apply traditional conflict-of-laws rules in identifying the law applicable to the substance of the dispute between the parties. The gradual drift in the law is in the direction of giving greater flexibility to arbitrators in relation to the identification of the applicable law and, at the same time, giving greater freedom to the parties in relation to the choice of the law or rules of law that are to govern their dispute. **17.110**

The task of identifying the law applicable to the substance of the dispute between the parties is significantly easier in the case where the parties have chosen the law (or rules of law) that are applicable to the dispute. In such a case, the general rule, as we shall see, is that the arbitrators must respect and give effect to the agreement of the parties. Matters are more difficult in the case where the parties have not chosen the applicable law. In such a case it is left to the arbitrators to choose the applicable law. How do they do so? Traditionally, they applied the conflict-of-laws rules at the seat of the arbitration in order to decide how to identify the law applicable to the substance of the dispute. But, as we shall see, the modern approach is to move away from this strict approach and to confer upon arbitrators a greater degree of discretion in terms of the identification of the law that is applicable to the substance of the dispute. **17.111**

This modern approach is reflected in Article 28 of the UNCITRAL Model Law which provides: **17.112**

(1) The arbitral tribunal shall decide the dispute in accordance with such rules of law as are chosen by the parties as applicable to the substance of the dispute. Any designation of

the law or legal system of a given State shall be construed, unless otherwise expressed, as directly referring to the substantive law of that State and not to its conflict of laws rules.

(2) Failing any designation by the parties, the arbitral tribunal shall apply the law determined by the conflict of laws rules which it considers applicable.

(3) The arbitral tribunal shall decide *ex aequo et bono* or as *amiable compositeur* only if the parties have expressly authorized it to do so.

(4) In all cases, the arbitral tribunal shall decide in accordance with the terms of the contract and shall take into account the usages of the trade applicable to the transaction.

17.113 A number of points should be noted about this provision. The first is the importance which Article 28 attaches to party autonomy. The task of the arbitrators is to apply the law (or rules of law) chosen by the parties; they are not entitled to impose a law or rules of law on the parties contrary to their wishes. The parties appear to have complete freedom in relation to the 'law' that is to govern the contract. While in practice the parties will frequently choose the law of one or other of the parties to the contract as the applicable law, they can, if they so wish, choose the law of a neutral state which has no other connection with the parties other than the fact that they have chosen it to be the law applicable to the contract. As we shall see, matters may be slightly more difficult where the parties choose 'rules of law' rather than 'a law' to govern their dispute. This takes us on to the second point, which relates to the use of the phrase 'rules of law' rather than 'law' in Article 28(1). The significance of the phrase 'rules of law' is explained in the Explanatory Note issued by the UNCITRAL Secretariat in the following terms:

> by referring to the choice of 'rules of law' instead of 'law', the Model Law gives the parties a wider range of options as regards the designation of the law applicable to the substance of the dispute in that they may, for example, agree on rules of law that have been elaborated by an international forum but have not yet been incorporated into any national legal system.[158]

17.114 The inclusion of 'rules of law' is important in so far as it enables parties to incorporate 'rules of law' such as the UNIDROIT Principles of International Commercial Contracts or the Principles of European Contract Law as the law applicable to the substance of their dispute. The precise meaning of the phrase 'rules of law' is unclear. While it clearly encompasses the UNIDROIT Principles, does it also include the INCOTERMS, 'general principles of law' or the *lex mercatoria*? The answer is that it probably does. Indeed, it is this type of provision which has breathed life into the UNIDROIT Principles and the *lex mercatoria* and enabled arbitrators to apply them as the law applicable to international contractual disputes.

17.115 Thirdly, it should be noted that Article 28(2) does not give the same freedom to arbitrators. In the case where the parties do not make a choice of law, the arbitrators shall

---

[158] (1985) XVI UNCITRAL Ybk [35].

choose 'the law determined by the conflict of laws rules which it considers applicable'. The use of 'the law' rather than 'rules of law' is vitally important in this context and would appear to deny to arbitrators the ability to select, for example, the UNIDROIT Principles as the law applicable to the contract where it has not been chosen by the parties. In such a case, the arbitrators must choose the law of a nation state. How must the arbitrators choose that law? Article 28(2) provides that it must be determined by the conflict-of-laws rules which it 'considers applicable'. How does an arbitrator decide what is applicable? The Model Law does not provide an answer to that question and so would appear to leave it to the discretion of the arbitrators. So, in choosing the applicable law, the arbitrators are not obliged to apply the conflict-of-laws rules of the seat of the arbitration, but they are obliged to apply the conflict-of-laws rules they consider applicable. They cannot simply choose the applicable law 'directly', that is, without making use of any conflict-of-laws rules.

Fourth, while arbitrators can decide *ex aequo et bono* or as *amiable compositeur*, they can do so only when so authorized by the parties. Once again, we can see the strong commitment to party autonomy which is enshrined in the Model Law. While the parties can authorize the arbitrators to decide *ex aequo et bono*, it is not open to the arbitrators to give to themselves the power so to decide. **17.116**

It is interesting to compare Article 28 of the Model Law with Article 17 of the ICC Rules. The ICC Rules go a step further than the Model Law. The legal nature of the ICC Rules differs from that of the Model Law and, to this extent, the two are not directly comparable. But the ICC Rules are of significance in so far as they may demonstrate the future direction which the law may take. Article 17 is in the following terms: **17.117**

(1) The parties shall be free to agree upon the rules of law to be applied by the Arbitral Tribunal to the merits of the dispute. In the absence of any such agreement, the Arbitral Tribunal shall apply the rules of law which it determines to be appropriate.
(2) In all cases the Arbitral Tribunal shall take account of the provisions of the contract and the relevant trade usages.
(3) The Arbitral Tribunal shall assume the powers of an *amiable compositeur* or decide *ex aequo et bono* only if the parties have agreed to give it such powers.

There are obvious similarities between the ICC Rules and the UNCITRAL Model Law. In both cases the parties are free to agree upon 'rules of law' and the arbitral tribunal can only decide *ex aequo et bono* where the parties have agreed to give it such power. The vital difference between the two instruments concerns the power of the arbitrators in the case where the parties have not chosen the law or the rules of law applicable to their contract. In such a case the ICC Rules do not confine the arbitrators to a choice of 'law' but enable them to choose the 'rules of law' which they determine to be 'appropriate'. This means that arbitrators can choose, for example, the UNIDROIT Principles even in the case where the parties have not chosen it. **17.118**

17.119   How do the arbitrators decide the 'appropriate' rules of law in the case where the parties have not made a choice of law? It would appear that the arbitrators have a broad discretion in making their choice. A number of approaches can be discerned in published ICC awards. These include choice of the conflict-of-laws rules in force at the seat of the arbitration, the cumulative application of the different conflict-of-laws rules of the countries having a connection to the dispute, the application of the 'general principles of the conflict of laws', the application of a conflict-of-law rule directly without reference to a national legal system or systems and, finally, the arbitrator may make a free choice without reference to any system of conflict-of-laws. It is the ability of arbitrators to choose the law directly, without reference to the conflict-of-laws rules of any jurisdiction, that distinguishes the ICC Rules from the Model Law.

17.120   Finally, the ICC Rules can be contrasted with Article 33 of the UNCITRAL Arbitral Rules which, possibly as a result of being drafted earlier in time, adopts a more restrictive stance to the choice of the law applicable to the substance of the dispute. Article 33 provides:

1. The arbitral tribunal shall apply the law designated by the parties as applicable to the substance of the dispute. Failing such designation by the parties, the arbitral tribunal shall apply the law determined by the conflict of laws rules which it considers applicable.

2. The arbitral tribunal shall decide as *amiable compositeur* or *ex aequo et bono* only if the parties have expressly authorized the arbitral tribunal to do so and if the law applicable to the arbitral procedure permits such arbitration.

3. In all cases, the arbitral tribunal shall decide in accordance with the terms of the contract and shall take into account the usages of the trade applicable to the transaction.

17.121   There is no reference in this Article to 'rules of law'; all the references are to 'law' so that both the parties and the arbitrators appear to be confined to the choice of a relevant national law. However 'law' may be interpreted more broadly where the national courts at the seat of the arbitration would adopt such a broad construction. That this is so is confirmed by the following extract:

David D Caron, Lee M Caplan and Matti Pellonpää, *The UNCITRAL Arbitration Rules: a commentary* (OUP, Oxford, 2006) 127–30

Both the text and negotiating history of Article 33(1) suggest that the law designated as applicable should be a definite set of rules, typically the national law of the particular country. While this should not preclude the parties from designating one law to apply, for example, to the modalities and rate of interest, and another to the rest of the merits of the case (*dépecage*), it is doubtful whether the so-called *lex mercatoria* . . . could be designated as the 'law' applicable to the substance of the dispute. There is no straightforward answer to this question. While the principle of party autonomy strongly suggests the acceptance of such a choice, the arbitrators must consider that, by resorting to the evolving concept of *lex mercatoria*, a reaction could be triggered in the place of arbitration, or in the place of the likely enforcement of the award.

If the relevant domestic laws and court practices indicate that the parties' agreement to use *lex mercatoria* or 'general principles of commercial law' as the applicable substantive law is accepted by national courts, an arbitral tribunal operating under the UNCITRAL Rules should respect such a choice . . .

There should be less hesitation to accept public international law as the applicable law than there may be with respect to *lex mercatoria* if the parties have so agreed. Public international law fulfils the criteria of 'law' within the meaning of Article 33(1), regardless of any disagreement surrounding the concept of *lex mercatoria* . . .

The term law, as used in Article 33(1), appears to be limited to legal rules and principles that are in force, thus excluding, for example, Roman law or other ancient laws, except in so far as they form part of an existing legal system. Similarly, it appears that an international convention not yet in force does not qualify as law in the meaning of Article 33(1). In part, it is exactly with the purpose of enabling the tribunal to apply, for example, such a convention that the Model Law employs the words 'rules of law chosen by the parties' instead of simply referring to 'law'. As party autonomy is the overriding principle in the application of the UNCITRAL Rules, the parties' choice of a 'law' not in force should be respected to the extent possible. Accordingly, a convention not in force, but which has been designated as applicable law, should be applied along the same principles and with similar reservations as applicable to *lex mercatoria*.

It would appear that the principle of party autonomy in relation to the choice of **17.122** the law applicable to the substance of the dispute is now firmly enshrined in the law. Less clear is the extent to which, in the case where the parties do not choose a law, it is open to arbitrators to choose the law or 'rules of law' it deems to be appropriate without placing any reliance upon conflict-of-laws rules. This point is discussed in the following extracts:

Emmanuel Gaillard and John Savage (eds), *Fouchard, Gaillard, Goldman on International Commercial Arbitration* **(Kluwer Law International, The Hague, 1999), paras 1550–1553**

1550.—The method which involves the free selection—or even creation—of what appears to be the most suitable choice of law rule is not uncommon in arbitral practice. Where there are serious differences between the various possible choice of law rules, the arbitrators have little option but to adopt a normative approach. The idea will no longer be to look for the convergence of various choice of law systems—whether or not connected with the case—but to determine what appears to be the best or the 'most appropriate' choice of law rule. Of course, it is hard to see how a choice of law rule, which is abstract by nature, could be 'appropriate' for a ;particular case. Nonetheless. in certain legal systems or under certain Rules, the arbitrators are free to select the choice of law rule which, in their opinion, best satisfies the various imperatives of private international law (such as predictability, realism and consistency with other choice of law rules). Moreover, they are not obliged to choose from existing choice of law rules. They are perfectly entitled to invent new ones.

1551.—However, in order to avoid burdening arbitrators with the delicate task of creating a new choice of law rule or with determining the 'appropriate' choice of law rule, certain statues and arbitration rules have abandoned the reference to choice of law rules and adopted what is generally referred to as the '*voie directe*' or direct choice method . . .

1552.—The direct choice method (*voie directe*) involves the arbitrators choosing the applicable law without referring to any choice of law rule, not even a rule they create themselves . . .

The determination made by arbitrators applying the direct choice method may be based on the connections between the case and the chosen law, as in the choice of law method, but it may also be guided by the content of the chosen law. The arbitrators might decide that a particular law, being more modern, is better suited to governing the dispute, or that a law belonging to the continental tradition—or, conversely, the common law tradition— is more suited to the disputed contract given, for example, how the contract is drafted, or the concepts to which it refers. Likewise, the arbitrators may, where the parties have not chosen the applicable law, decide not to apply a law which would lead the contract to be held void. Here, the word 'appropriate', applied to the law governing the merits of the dispute rather than to the choice of law rule, has real meaning.

1553.—It has rightly been observed, however, that the direct choice method often conceals the implicit consideration of a choice of law rule. Awards which are described as illustrating the direct choice method often reveal the existence of connecting factors relied upon by the arbitrators. In such cases, the arbitrators' approach is very similar to the conventional choice of law method . . .

Alan Redfern and Martin Hunter, *Law and Practice of International Commercial Arbitration* (4th edn, Sweet & Maxwell, London, 2004) [2–84]

In reaching its decision on the law to be applied in the absence of any choice by the parties, an arbitral tribunal is entitled (unless otherwise directed by the applicable rules or the *lex arbitri*) to select any of the systems or rules of law upon which the parties themselves might have agreed, if they had chosen to do so.

When it comes to determining how an arbitral tribunal should proceed to its decision, then once again (as so often in the law of international commercial arbitration) no universal rule can be identified. Some systems of law insist that, in making its choice, an arbitral tribunal should follow the rules of conflict of the seat of the arbitration. This attitude looks increasingly anachronistic. The modern tendency is for international conventions and rules of arbitration to give considerable latitude to arbitral tribunals in making their choice of law, whilst still insisting that they do so by way of appropriate or applicable conflict rules. Some national laws (including the French, the Swiss and the Dutch) carry the matter to its logical conclusion: by abandoning the reference to conflict rules altogether they allow an arbitral tribunal to decide for itself what law (or rules of law) it considers appropriate to settle the dispute.

This is an approach to be commended. If an arbitral tribunal can be trusted to decide a dispute, presumably it can be trusted to determine the set of legal rules by which it will be guided in reaching its decision. If the parties do not wish the arbitral tribunal to have such freedom of action, the remedy is in their own hands. They should agree upon the applicable law or set of legal rules, preferably in their contract but, if not, then at any time after the dispute has arisen.

The law governing the recognition and enforcement of the award

17.123 The law governing the recognition and enforcement of the award is discussed at the end of this chapter.

D. The Review of Arbitral Awards

To what extent is it open to national courts to review arbitral awards? What is the **17.124** relationship between arbitral tribunals and national courts? The trend in the modern law is to reduce the grounds on which national courts can review arbitral awards in international (as opposed to domestic) commercial arbitrations. The reason for this is the desire to promote a greater degree of finality and to give effect to the autonomy of the parties in so far as they have chosen arbitration (and not litigation) as the dispute resolution mechanism in their contract. The law has not always taken such a relaxed approach to the review of arbitral awards. In England, prior to 1979, it was relatively easy to appeal an arbitral award to the national courts. While the relatively ready access to the courts made a huge contribution to the development of English contract law (because many of the leading contract cases in English law are appeals from arbitrators' awards), the price of ready access to the courts was that English arbitration law began to fall into disrepute. The advantage of finality was lost as parties could not be confident that the arbitral award would be the last word on the matter; costs were increased as parties had to face the prospect of litigation as well as arbitration and, finally, the advantage of confidentiality was lost in the event that the case was litigated before the national courts. These factors, together with some others, led the English to narrow the right of appeal to the courts in the Arbitration Act 1979. The UNCITRAL Model Law, as we shall see, continues this process by further restricting the ability of national courts to review arbitral awards.

Two principal issues arise in relation to the challenge to an arbitral award. The first **17.125** relates to the identification of the law that is applicable to any challenge to the award. In general it will be the law of the seat of the arbitration which will determine the grounds on which it is possible to challenge an arbitral award. The second relates to the grounds on which challenge is possible. While the precise scope of the grounds of challenge will depend upon the applicable law, the Model Law has had a significant impact in terms of bringing about a greater degree of harmony in relation to the identification of the grounds on which an award should be open to challenge. Article 34 of the Model Law provides:

(1) Recourse to a court against an arbitral award may be made only by an application for setting aside in accordance with paragraphs (2) and (3) of this Article.
(2) An arbitral award may be set aside by the court specified in Article 6 only if:
    (a) the party making the application furnishes proof that:
        (i) a party to the arbitration agreement referred to in Article 7 was under some incapacity; or the said agreement is not valid under the law to which the parties have subjected it or, failing any indication thereon, under the law of this State; or
        (ii) the party making the application was not given proper notice of the appointment of an arbitrator or of the arbitral proceedings or was otherwise unable to present his case; or

       (iii) the award deals with a dispute not contemplated by or not falling within the terms of the submission to arbitration, or contains decisions on matters beyond the scope of the submission to arbitration, provided that, if the decisions on matters submitted to arbitration can be separated from those not so submitted, only that part of the award which contains decisions on matters not submitted to arbitration may be set aside; or

      (iv) the composition of the arbitral tribunal or the arbitral procedure was not in accordance with the agreement of the parties, unless such agreement was in conflict with a provision of this Law from which the parties cannot derogate, or, failing such agreement, was not in accordance with this Law; or

  (b) the court finds that:

     (i) the subject-matter of the dispute is not capable of settlement by arbitration under the law of this State; or

     (ii) the award is in conflict with the public policy of this State.

(3) An application for setting aside may not be made after three months have elapsed from the date on which the party making that application had received the award or, if a request had been made under Article 33, from the date on which that request had been disposed of by the arbitral tribunal.

(4) The court, when asked to set aside an award, may, where appropriate and so requested by a party, suspend the setting aside proceedings for a period of time determined by it in order to give the arbitral tribunal an opportunity to resume the arbitral proceedings or to take such other action as in the arbitral tribunal's opinion will eliminate the grounds for setting aside.

17.126 Before examining the grounds of challenge recognized by Article 34, some general observations may be made:

Alan Redfern and Martin Hunter, *Law and Practice of International Commercial Arbitration* (4th edn, Sweet & Maxwell, London, 2004) [9–18]

Under the Model Law an action for setting aside may only be brought in respect of an award made within the territory of the state concerned. It *must* be brought before the designated court in that state and it may *only* be brought on the grounds set out in the Model Law. These grounds are taken from Article V of the New York Convention.[159] There is a pleasing symmetry here. The New York Convention, in Article V, sets out the grounds on which recognition and enforcement of an international award may be refused. Article 34 of the Model Law sets out the same grounds (with slight differences of language) as the grounds on which such an award may be set aside.

17.127 It should be noted that the grounds set out in Article 34 relate to the capacity of the parties, procedural issues relating to the conduct of the arbitration and the jurisdiction of the arbitral tribunal. The Model Law does not make any provision for the review of the substance of the award, for example on the ground that the arbitrators made a mistake of fact or a mistake of law. This is a point to which we shall return.

---

[159] Discussed below at para 17.135.

The emphasis on procedure in the Model Law can be clearly seen from Article **17.128** 34(a) (ii), (iii) and (iv). Parties are entitled to expect that an international arbitration will be conducted in accordance with certain procedural standards, the aim of which is to ensure that the parties are given adequate notice of the arbitration and sufficient opportunity to present their case. In short, the aim is to ensure that a fair procedure is adopted and natural justice observed. While there is agreement on the general principle that a fair procedure must be adopted, there is no such general agreement on the requirements of a fair procedure in individual cases. The procedure adopted by the arbitrators must also be in accordance with the agreement of the parties. The grounds of challenge also relate to the jurisdiction of the arbitral tribunal; a tribunal which purports to decide an issue which has not been submitted to it is likely to find that its award is open to challenge by the parties.

There are, however, certain respects in which Article 34 extends beyond procedural **17.129** matters. In particular, Article 34(b)(i) provides that an award may be challenged on the ground that the 'subject-matter of the dispute is not capable of settlement by arbitration' under the law of the place of the arbitration. The reference to 'public policy' in Article 34(b)(ii) is more problematic. The difficulty is that different jurisdictions can have widely different conceptions of what 'public policy' requires. Nor is it possible to escape the jurisdiction-specific conceptions of public policy by resort to some international standard because the wording of the provision requires the courts to have regard to the public policy of 'this State'.

Why does the Model Law not entitle a party to challenge an award on the ground **17.130** that the arbitrators have made a mistake of law or fact? The answer probably lies in the need to preserve finality in arbitration, as the following extract makes clear:

Alan Redfern and Martin Hunter, *Law and Practice of International Commercial Arbitration* (4th edn, Sweet & Maxwell, London, 2004) [9.36]–[9.37]

The argument in favour of reviewing arbitral decisions in order to guard against mistakes of law is not difficult to make. There are obvious risks in having a legal system that leaves arbitral decisions free from appeal or judicial review. First, there is the risk of inconsistent decisions as the same or similar points come before different tribunals, each one of which is independent of the other. Such tribunals are generally unaware that the same point of law may already have been decided in a different way by another tribunal. This is likely to be of particular importance where the decision turns upon the correct interpretation of a standard form clause in a widely used contract . . . Secondly, there is the risk that the arbitral tribunal may not do its work as competently or as professionally as it should if its awards are not subject to scrutiny, either by an arbitral institution or by a competent court.

Experience shows, however, that there are serious disadvantages in having a system of arbitration that gives an unrestricted right of appeal from arbitral awards. First, the decisions of national judges may be substituted for the decisions of an arbitral tribunal specifically selected by or on behalf of the parties. Secondly, a party that agreed to arbitration as a private method of resolving disputes may find itself brought unwillingly before national courts that hold their hearings in public. Thirdly, the appeal process may be used simply to postpone the day on which payment is due, so that one of the main purposes of international commercial arbitration—the speedy resolution of disputes—is defeated . . .

It is not easy to strike a balance between the need for finality in the arbitral process and the wider public interest in some measure of judicial control, if only to ensure consistency of decisions and predictability of the operation of the law. Internationally, however, the balance has come down strongly in favour of finality, and against judicial review, except in very limited circumstances. The Model Law sets the tone . . . when it proclaims [in Article 5] that:

'in matters governed by this law, no court shall intervene except where so provided in this Law.'

The extent of court intervention permitted by different states may be viewed as a spectrum. At one end of the spectrum are the states such as France, which exercise a minimum control over international arbitral awards, and Switzerland, which allows non-Swiss parties to 'contract out' of controls altogether. In the middle of the scale, are grouped a considerable number of states that have adopted (either in full or with some modifications) the grounds of recourse laid down in the Model Law. At the other end of the spectrum are countries such as England, which operate a range of controls, including mandatory procedural controls, as well as a limited right of appeal on questions of law that the parties may agree to waive.

17.131   As has been noted, English law is at one end of the spectrum in so far as it recognizes the possibility that an arbitral award can be challenged on the ground that it contains an error of law. The relevant provision is section 69 of the Arbitration Act 1996 which provides:

(1) Unless otherwise agreed by the parties, a party to arbitral proceedings may (upon notice to the other parties and to the tribunal) appeal to the court on a question of law arising out of an award made in the proceedings.

An agreement to dispense with reasons for the tribunal's award shall be considered an agreement to exclude the court's jurisdiction under this section.

(2) An appeal shall not be brought under this section except—
   (a) with the agreement of all the other parties to the proceedings, or
   (b) with the leave of the court.

The right to appeal is also subject to the restrictions in section 70(2) and (3).

(3) Leave to appeal shall be given only if the court is satisfied—
   (a) that the determination of the question will substantially affect the rights of one or more of the parties,
   (b) that the question is one which the tribunal was asked to determine,
   (c) that, on the basis of the findings of fact in the award—
      (i) the decision of the tribunal on the question is obviously wrong, or
      (ii) the question is one of general public importance and the decision of the tribunal is at least open to serious doubt, and
   (d) that, despite the agreement of the parties to resolve the matter by arbitration, it is just and proper in all the circumstances for the court to determine the question.

(4) An application for leave to appeal under this section shall identify the question of law to be determined and state the grounds on which it is alleged that leave to appeal should be granted.

(5) The court shall determine an application for leave to appeal under this section without a hearing unless it appears to the court that a hearing is required.

(6) The leave of the court is required for any appeal from a decision of the court under this section to grant or refuse leave to appeal.

(7) On an appeal under this section the court may by order—

    (a) confirm the award,

    (b) vary the award,

    (c) remit the award to the tribunal, in whole or in part, for reconsideration in the light of the court's determination, or

    (d) set aside the award in whole or in part.

The court shall not exercise its power to set aside an award, in whole or in part, unless it is satisfied that it would be inappropriate to remit the matters in question to the tribunal for reconsideration.

(8) The decision of the court on an appeal under this section shall be treated as a judgment of the court for the purposes of a further appeal. But no such appeal lies without the leave of the court which shall not be given unless the court considers that the question is one of general importance or is one which for some other special reason should be considered by the Court of Appeal.

17.132 The right of appeal enshrined in section 69 is not unrestricted. In the first place, the parties can contract out of the right of appeal.[160] The second is that the right of appeal is confined to questions of English law; it is not available where the mistake of law relates to some other system of law which is applicable to the contract. Third, the right of appeal is only available where the requirements of section 69(3) are satisfied. The criteria found in the subsection attempt to limit the right of appeal to the extreme case where the decision of the arbitral tribunal is 'obviously wrong' or to cases where there is a genuine public interest in establishing the law on a particular point (where the question is one of 'general public importance' and the decision 'is at least open to serious doubt'). While section 69 attempts to strike a balance between finality and the public interest in rectifying mistakes of law, it has been argued by a number of commentators that English law currently strikes the balance in the wrong place. Thus one commentator has asserted that section 69 'ignores modern international arbitration practice and is out of line with the Model Law.'[161] A similar complaint is to be found in the following extract:

> Even with all these restrictions, it remains difficult to predict with any reasonable degree of assurance in what circumstances the court will entertain an appeal that has not been the subject of an exclusion agreement, particularly if the point of law involved is one which interests the court or is felt to require clarification. It is therefore not a sufficient answer that leave to appeal is given in relatively few cases; the problem for parties to arbitration is that they have no means of predicting whether

---

[160] S 69(1).
[161] Stewart Shackleton, 'Challenging Arbitral Awards: Part III—Appeals on Questions of Law' (2002) New LJ 1834, 1835.

their case will be one of the few. There is a case for further restricting the possibility of appeals on points of law.[162]

E. Recognition and Enforcement of Arbitral Awards

17.133 At the outset it is important to distinguish between recognition and enforcement of arbitral awards at the seat of the arbitration and recognition and enforcement of foreign awards, made outside the territory where recognition is sought. Many States treat the recognition of awards made within their boundaries in the same way as domestic arbitral awards and so no particular difficulties surround an attempt to have such an award recognized or enforced. By contrast, the recognition and enforcement of foreign awards tends to give rise to greater difficulty, although here considerable progress has been made as a result of the New York Convention on the Recognition and Enforcement of Foreign Arbitral Awards. Recognition and enforcement of foreign arbitral awards tends to be a more important topic than the recognition and enforcement of court judgments because often court proceedings take place in the country of the defendant's domicile. In arbitral proceedings this will be much rarer as the arbitral proceedings will frequently be held in a neutral jurisdiction.

17.134 Recognition is a defensive process, the aim of which is to obtain recognition of an arbitral award with a view to preventing an attempt to bring new proceedings raising the same issues as those dealt with in the award in respect of which recognition is sought. For example, if an unsuccessful claimant tries to bring court proceedings following an arbitral award which dismissed its claims, a defendant might wish to seek recognition of the arbitral award by the court in which the proceedings have been brought in order to dismiss the claim now brought by the claimant. Enforcement goes a step further than recognition. It is where the successful party seeks the court's assistance in order to ensure that the award is carried out and the claimant obtains the redress to which it is entitled.

17.135 For present purposes our interest lies in the grounds on which recognition or enforcement of an arbitral award can be refused. Here two provisions are of interest. The first provision is Article V of the New York Convention which is in the following terms:

1. Recognition and enforcement of the award may be refused, at the request of the party against whom it is invoked, only if that party furnishes to the competent authority where the recognition and enforcement is sought, proof that:
   (a) The parties to the agreement referred to in Article II were, under the law applicable to them, under some incapacity, or the said agreement is not valid under

---

[162] Goode (n 2) 1194–5.

the law to which the parties have subjected it or, failing any indication thereon, under the law of the country where the award was made; or

(b) The party against whom the award is invoked was not given proper notice of the appointment of the arbitrator or of the arbitration proceedings or was otherwise unable to present his case; or

(c) The award deals with a difference not contemplated by or not falling within the terms of the submission to arbitration, or it contains decisions on matters beyond the scope of the submission to arbitration, provided that, if the decisions on matters submitted to arbitration can be separated from those not so submitted, that part of the award which contains decisions on matters submitted to arbitration may be recognized and enforced; or

(d) The composition of the arbitral authority or the arbitral procedure was not in accordance with the agreement of the parties, or, failing such agreement, was not in accordance with the law of the country where the arbitration took place; or

(e) The award has not yet become binding on the parties, or has been set aside or suspended by a competent authority of the country in which, or under the law of which, that award was made.

2. Recognition and enforcement of an arbitral award may also be refused if the competent authority in the country where recognition and enforcement is sought finds that:

(a) The subject matter of the difference is not capable of settlement by arbitration under the law of that country; or

(b) The recognition or enforcement of the award would be contrary to the public policy of that country.

The second is Article 36 of the UNCITRAL Model Law which provides:

(1) Recognition or enforcement of an arbitral award, irrespective of the country in which it was made, may be refused only:

(a) at the request of the party against whom it is invoked, if that party furnishes to the competent court where recognition or enforcement is sought proof that:

(i) a party to the arbitration agreement referred to in Article 7 was under some incapacity; or the said agreement is not valid under the law to which the parties have subjected it or, failing any indication thereon, under the law of the country where the award was made; or

(ii) the party against whom the award is invoked was not given proper notice of the appointment of an arbitrator or of the arbitral proceedings or was otherwise unable to present his case; or

(iii) the award deals with a dispute not contemplated by or not falling within the terms of the submission to arbitration, or it contains decisions on matters beyond the scope of the submission to arbitration, provided that, if the decisions on matters submitted to arbitration can be separated from those not so submitted, that part of the award which contains decisions on matters submitted to arbitration may be recognized and enforced; or

(iv) the composition of the arbitral tribunal or the arbitral procedure was not in accordance with the agreement of the parties or, failing such agreement, was not in accordance with the law of the country where the arbitration took place; or

(v) the award has not yet become binding on the parties or has been set aside or suspended by a court of the country in which, or under the law of which, that award was made; or

(b) if the court finds that:

(i) the subject-matter of the dispute is not capable of settlement by arbitration under the law of this State; or

(ii) the recognition or enforcement of the award would be contrary to the public policy of this State.

(2) If an application for setting aside or suspension of an award has been made to a court referred to in paragraph (1)(a)(v) of this Article, the court where recognition or enforcement is sought may, if it considers it proper, adjourn its decision and may also, on the application of the party claiming recognition or enforcement of the award, order the other party to provide appropriate security.

17.136 The first thing to notice about these two provisions is that they are substantially similar and that they in turn closely correlate with the grounds on which an award can be challenged, as set out in Article 34 of the Model Law. The decision to replicate the grounds set out in the New York Convention was a policy decision taken by those responsible for drafting the Model Law. The Explanatory Note issued by the UNCITRAL Secretariat puts the matter in the following terms:

> By modelling the recognition and enforcement rules on the relevant provisions of the 1958 New York Convention, the Model Law supplements, without conflicting with, the regime of recognition and enforcement created by that successful Convention . . . . . the grounds on which recognition or enforcement may be refused under the Model Law are identical to those listed in Article V of the New York Convention. Only, under the Model Law, they are relevant not merely to foreign awards but to all awards rendered in international commercial arbitration. While some provisions of that Convention, in particular as regards their drafting, may have called for improvement, only the first ground on the list (i.e. 'the incapacity') was modified since it was viewed as containing an incomplete and potentially misleading conflicts rule. Generally, it was deemed desirable to adopt, for the sake of harmony, the same approach and wording as this important Convention.[163]

17.137 Second, it should be noted that neither the New York Convention nor the Model Law makes provision for the refusal of recognition or enforcement of an award on a ground which is related to the merits of the award. The substantive merits of the award do not, in themselves, constitute a ground on which recognition or enforcement can be refused. Third, the grounds for refusal of recognition or enforcement as set out in both the New York Convention and the Model Law are exhaustive; that is to say, the only grounds on which recognition or enforcement can be refused are those grounds set out in the respective provisions. Fourth, a court is not required to refuse to recognize or enforce an award if one of the itemized grounds is established on the facts. The court 'may' refuse to recognize or enforce the award

---

[163] UNCITRAL Ybk (n 158) [48]–[50].

but it is not mandatory for it to do so.[164] Finally, the intention behind Article V was to narrow the grounds on which a court could refuse to recognize and enforce a foreign award and so the grounds on which it is possible to refuse recognition or enforcement should be restrictively interpreted.

The ground which has given rise to most difficult is, undoubtedly, Article V(1)(e) **17.138** and this takes us back to the heart of the delocalization debate.[165] In what circumstances may a court in the state of enforcement recognize or enforce an award which has already been set aside by a court in the seat of the arbitration? It is tempting to seek to answer this question in an all or nothing way—either the court must always respect the decision of the court at the state of the seat of enforcement to set aside the award or it must never respect that decision. This temptation must be resisted. There is a range of options which must be canvassed, as the following extract makes clear:

Roy Goode, 'The Role of the *Lex Loci Arbitri* in International Commercial Arbitration' in Francis D Rose (ed) Lex Mercatoria: *Essays on International Commercial Law in Honour of Francis Reynolds* (LLP, London, 2000) 245, 250–55

The traditional theory of territoriality is based on the general principle of international law that a state is sovereign within its own borders and that its law and its courts have the exclusive right to determine the legal effect of acts done (and consequently of arbitral awards made) within those borders. The concept of party autonomy in arbitration predicates that the binding authority of an award derives solely from the agreement of the parties, not from national law. However, neither of these two approaches embodies a single, homogeneous concept. The scope of the territoriality principle varies according to the degree of respect the courts of a particular state are willing to accord to the decisions of courts of other states of competent jurisdiction. In fact, territoriality and party autonomy do not represent a sharp dichotomy but together occupy a spectrum, along which we can identify at least six possible, and at least four actual, models, arranged in ascending order of delocalisation.

In the first model the law of the enforcing state *requires* its courts, in the absence of specified conditions, to refuse recognition and enforcement of an arbitral award that has been set aside by a court of competent jurisdiction. In other words, such a law adopts the substance of Article V(1)(e) of the New York Convention but as a mandatory, not a discretionary, provision . . .

In the second model it is recognised that within its own territory a state is sovereign and its courts have the exclusive right to adjudicate on the legality of acts done within that territory. What is said, however, is that laws and court decisions made within the state are not entitled to recognition *erga omnes*—which is clearly correct—but that for policy reasons the decision of a foreign court of competent jurisdiction setting aside an award will usually be respected by courts of the state of enforcement, subject to rights of impeachment in cases such as procedural unfairness or the obtaining of a judgment by fraud. States following this

---

[164] The existence of a discretion is not, however, obvious in the equivalent French text which states: '*La reconnaissance et l'exécution . . . . ne seront refuse . . . que si . . . .*'.

[165] On which see para 17.79 above.

model generally adopt provisions in their arbitration laws which follow those of Article V of the New York Convention, with or without modification, and, like Article V, allow a discretion to enforce notwithstanding the order annulling the award. . . . .

The third model is the same as the first except that under the laws of the enforcing state the grounds for refusal of recognition of a foreign arbitral award are more restricted than those of Article V and in particular do not include the setting aside of the award under the *lex loci arbitri*. The courts of such states are then permitted by Article VII[166] of the New York Convention to recognise the right of the party obtaining the award to benefit from the more generous approach of the domestic law of the state of enforcement and, if the requirements of that law are met, to have the award enforced even though it has been annulled by the court of origin. Nevertheless, though the annulling order is not as such a ground for refusal of recognition, to the extent that it is based on grounds which have a counterpart in the domestic law of the enforcing state the courts of that state may be willing to hold that there is a conclusive, strong or at least *prima facie* presumption that such grounds have been established for the purposes of its domestic law. This approach reflects a traditional principle of the conflict of laws.

In the fourth model the law of the enforcing state, while still recognising the concept of a *lex arbitri*, does not recognise an annulment order in the court of origin either as a ground in itself for refusing recognition of the award or as raising any kind of presumption that such an order establishes facts which would bring the case within an equivalent ground under the law of the enforcing state.

The fifth, and very intense, model is to be found in French legislation and in the jurisprudence of French courts, which have carried the delocalisation principle to the point where an international award—by which is presumably meant an award in an international arbitration—is stateless and derives its force not from the *lex loci arbitri*, or indeed from any other national law, but solely from the will of the parties. This result . . . was reached only in stages [the development of French law from *Götaverken* through to *Hilmarton* is described] . . .

Finally, we come to the most extreme delocalisation model, adopted by the Belgian legislation, to the effect that no court in Belgium could set aside an award unless at least one of the parties was Belgian. As noted later, that law has been modified to allow parties the choice whether to retain or to opt out of judicial review in Belgium. If they do, then the resulting award becomes truly stateless.

17.139 Which of these models is the preferable one? This is an issue on which much academic ink has been spilt.[167] It is suggested that the better view is that the courts in the state of enforcement should generally respect the decision of the courts in the place of the seat of the arbitration. But it is, as the models set out above suggest, a balancing act and the court in the state of enforcement should not be obliged to

---

[166] Art VII is discussed in more detail below at para 17.140.

[167] See, for example: Albert Jan van den Berg 'Residual Discretion and the Validity of the Arbitration Agreement in the Enforcement of Arbitral Awards under the New York Convention of 1958' in Keang Sood Teo, *Current Issues in International Commercial Arbitration* (University of Singapore, Singapore, 1997) 335 and Georgios Petrochilos, 'Enforcing Awards Annulled in their State of Origin under the New York Convention' (1999) 48 ICLQ 856.

follow the decision of the court at the place of the seat of the arbitration in all circumstances. The difficult question relates to the identification of the situations in which a court in the state of enforcement should be free not to follow the decision of the court at the seat of the arbitration. The following rationalization has been suggested:

Georgios Petrochilos, *Procedural Law in International Arbitration* (OUP, Oxford, 2004) [7.86]–[7.88]

Annulment at the place of arbitration or at the country whose law governs the arbitral proceedings is, and should continue to be, in principle dispositive of the fate of the award. This general rule, however, is subject to two exceptions, namely where the setting-aside judgment would in itself fail the test for *res judicata* in and under the law of the enforcement forum; and where the enforcement forum's law applicable to foreign awards would never consider annulment as a circumstance precluding enforcement. Both possibilities . . . always fall within the combined effect of Articles V(1) and VII of the Convention . . .

The premise for the suggestions . . . has been that the New York Convention did not purport to make awards annulled at their state of origin prevail in another forum. At the same time, it did not exclude that possibility. The *travaux préparatoires* show that the issue was not expressly contemplated by the drafters, but that does not mean that it is an issue altogether outside the contemplation of the law. The best position would be that under the Convention this is a question left open to be decided by the courts, which must deal with it by regarding the Convention as made of a single texture and 'not alter the material of which it is woven, but . . . iron out the creases.' Though the New York Convention abolished the prerequisite that an arbitral award must be confirmed at the place of its rendition, which was the solution prevailing under the Geneva Convention, the Convention is built around the notion and presumption of a valid award. The abolition of confirmation at the state of origin was conceived more as an improvement on the speediness of recognition rather than as an outright dismissal of the relevance of the judicial pronouncements at the state of origin.

On the other hand, if the fate of an award in an international arbitration is conclusively and exclusively determined by the courts of the state where it is (or deemed to have been) rendered, it becomes little more than a judgment of the courts of that state, the jurisdiction of which the parties sought to exclude in the first place by agreeing to arbitrate. In fact, it may become something less than that, if the local judiciary is not well predisposed towards awards perceived as prejudicial to the interests of local entities or the local sovereign. The other extreme, where an award annulled at that state travels around the world like an itinerant friar begging for enforcement is equally unattractive. The suggestions made here attempt to remedy the pitfalls of those extreme theses within the framework of the New York Convention.

One final point should be made and that relates to the role of Article VII (1) of the **17.140** New York Convention. It provides:

> 1. The provisions of the present Convention shall not affect the validity of multilateral or bilateral agreements concerning the recognition and enforcement of arbitral awards entered into by the Contracting States nor deprive any interested party of any right he

may have to avail himself of an arbitral award in the manner and to the extent allowed by the law or the treaties of the country where such award is sought to be relied upon.

17.141 This provision is sometimes referred to as the 'more favourable right provision'. In so far as it is intended to resolve conflicts between international conventions, it does not give rise to controversy. It provides that the convention most favourable to enforcement of the award should prevail. More difficult is the reference to 'the law . . . of the country where such award is sought to be relied upon'. The proposition that national law should prevail over the Convention when it comes to enforcement is more controversial in so far as it reverses the traditional position which is that an international convention should normally prevail over domestic law. Contrasting views have been expressed in relation to the merits of Article VII. One view, expressed in the following extract, is that it should be amended:

> A strong case can be made for amending Article VII of the Convention by restricting its scope to treaties entered into by the enforcing state—removing that part of Article VII which enables a party to invoke the more favourable provisions of the law of enforcement—and by leaving courts of enforcing states to rely on the discretion already available to them under Article V, a discretion which itself should be exercised with caution. This should go hand in hand with a self-denying precept of legislatures and courts to the effect that, while the court of enforcement must inevitably have the last word to cater for exceptional cases, in principle judgments of courts of the seat enforcing, suspending or annulling an award should be respected, as should findings of fact by such courts. Obviously there will be such exceptional cases, eg, fraud discovered only after the judgment. But adherence to the general principle is essential if we are to respect party choice, to avoid the cost, inconvenience and risk of inconsistent decisions resulting from a multiplicity of proceedings, and to foster rather than damage mutual respect and co-operation among courts of different states.[168]

17.142 An alternative view is that Article VII should be retained in its present form and, further, that it will become increasingly important as national courts seek to escape from the restrictions of Article V of the New York Convention:

> Article VII of the New York Convention has also been applied in France and other countries to allow more favourable provisions of national law to prevail over the Convention itself. It will undoubtedly apply increasingly often in the future, as the New York Convention becomes more outdated and recent arbitration legislation becomes more favourable to the recognition and enforcement of foreign awards.[169]

17.143 In the event that the latter view does prevail, the better answer would appear to lie in a re-consideration of the Convention itself rather than to leave it to individual

---

[168] Goode, 'The Role of the *Lex Loci Arbitri* in International Commercial Arbitration' (n 129) 267–8.

[169] Emmanuel Gaillard and John Savage (eds), *Fouchard, Gaillard, Golman on International Commercial Arbitration* (Kluwer, The Hague, 1999) [270].

nation States to, in effect, outflank the Convention by enacting more favourable provisions than those to be found in the Convention itself.

Questions

1. 'International commercial arbitration is conducted entirely outside the framework of national legal systems. The parties, and within their terms of reference the arbitrators, enjoy complete autonomy. There is no such thing as a *lex arbitri*.' Discuss.

2. 'No one has ever or anywhere been able to point to any provision or legal principle which would permit individuals to act outside the confines of a system of municipal law; even the idea of the autonomy of the parties exists only by virtue of a given system of municipal law and in different systems may have different characteristics and effects. Similarly, every arbitration is necessarily subject to the law of a given State. No private person has the right or the power to act on any level other than that of municipal law. Every right or power a private person enjoys is inexorably conferred by or derived from a system of municipal law which may conveniently and in accordance with tradition be called the *lex fori*, though it would be more exact (but less familiar) to speak of the *lex arbitri* or, in French, *la loi d'arbitrage*.' (MANN).
   Discuss.

3. In what circumstances may the court of a State which is party to the 1958 New York Convention on the Recognition and Enforcement of Arbitral Awards refuse to recognize or enforce an award made in the territory of another Contracting State?

4. To what extent should an arbitral tribunal be required to apply:
   (1) the conflict-of-laws rules of the seat of the arbitration;
   (2) any conflict-of-laws rules?

5. To what extent is an arbitral tribunal free to apply the *lex mercatoria*:
   (1) in place of the law selected by the parties;
   (2) in place of the applicable law under conflict-of-laws rules where the parties have not selected the law to govern their contract and:
       (a) the tribunal has made a finding as to the applicable law; or
       (b) the tribunal has not sought to determine an applicable law;
   (3) to supplement the applicable law under (1) or (2)?

6. Should an arbitral award made in an international commercial arbitration ever be reviewable by a national court? If so, on what grounds should it be open to review?

7. 'The distinction between litigation and arbitration is purely one of procedure and has no impact on the substantive determination of a dispute.' Discuss.

Further reading

El-Kosheri, A, 'Enforcement of Awards Set Aside in the Country of Origin' in Albert Jan van den Berg (ed), *Improving the Efficiency of Arbitration Agreements and Awards: 40 years of application of the New York Convention* (Kluwer, The Hague, 1999) 544

Gaillard, Emmanuel, 'Enforcement of Awards Set Aside in the Country of Origin: The French Experience' in Albert Jan van den Berg (ed), *Improving the Efficiency of Arbitration Agreements and Awards: 40 years of application of the New York Convention* (Kluwer, The Hague, 1999) 505

Goode, Roy, 'The Role of the *Lex Loci Arbitri* in International Commercial Arbitration' in Francis D Rose (ed), Lex Mercatoria: *essays on international commercial law in honour of Francis Reynolds* (LLP, London, 2000)

Mayer, P, 'Revisiting *Hilmarton* and *Chromalloy*' in Albert Jan van den Berg (ed), *Improving the Efficiency of Arbitration Agreements and Awards: 40 years of application of the New York Convention* (Kluwer, The Hague, 1999) 165

Paulsson, Jan, 'Arbitration Unbound: award detached from the law of its country of origin' (1981) 30 ICLQ 358

Paulsson, Jan, '*May* or *Must* under the New York Convention: an exercise in syntax and linguistics' (1998) 14 Arb Intl 226

Paulsson, Jan, 'Towards Minimum Standards of Enforcement: Feasability of a Model Law' in Albert Jan van den Berg (ed), *Improving the Efficiency of Arbitration Agreements and Awards: 40 years of application of the New York Convention* (Kluwer, The Hague, 1999) 574

Petrochilos, Georgios, 'Enforcing Awards Annulled in their State of Origin under the New York Convention' (1999) 48 ICLQ 856

Petrochilos, Georgios, *Procedural Law in International Arbitration* (OUP, Oxford, 2004) ch 7

Rivkin, D, 'Enforcement of Awards Set Aside in the Country of Origin: The American Experience' in Albert Jan van den Berg (ed), *Improving the Efficiency of Arbitration Agreements and Awards: 40 years of application of the New York Convention* (Kluwer, The Hague, 1999) 528

Rogers, A, 'Enforcement of Awards Set Aside in the Country of Origin' in Albert Jan van den Berg (ed), *Improving the Efficiency of Arbitration Agreements and Awards: 40 years of application of the New York Convention* (Kluwer, The Hague, 1999) 548

Sachs, K, 'Enforcement of Awards Set Aside in the Country of Origin' in Albert Jan van den Berg (ed), *Improving the Efficiency of Arbitration Agreements and Awards: 40 years of application of the New York Convention* (Kluwer, The Hague, 1999) 552

Sampliner, Gary H, 'Enforcement of Nullified Foreign Arbitral Awards. *Chromalloy* Revisited' (1997) 14 J Intl Arb 141

Tweeddale, Andrew, and Tweeddale, Keren, *Arbitration of Commercial Disputes: International and English Law and Practice* (OUP, Oxford, 2005) ch 15

Part VI

RECURRENT ISSUES OF
HARMONIZATION

18

THE SPHERE OF APPLICATION OF A CONVENTION; THE ROLE OF THE CONFLICT OF LAWS; DETERMINING THE CONNECTING FACTOR; CO-EXISTENCE AND CONFLICTS OF INSTRUMENTS

A. Sphere of Application in General	18.01
B. The Role of the Conflict of Laws	18.06
C. The Selection of the Connecting Factor	18.08
D. Co-existence, Concurrence, and Conflicts of Conventions	18.11

A. Sphere of Application in General

In this chapter and chapter 19, certain key issues touched upon in previous chap- **18.01**
ters will be brought together and the threads interwoven and put under a magni-
fying glass. This approach is a first step on the thorny path to distilling and formulating
'general doctrines' of transnational commercial law.[1] By the time of the Diplomatic
Conference for the adoption of the draft UN Sales Convention (CISG), held in
Vienna in 1980, its drafters, the scholars who had been involved in preparing this
text and its predecessors adopted in 1964 in The Hague, and governments, had
experienced difficulties and disappointments flowing from an insufficiently defined
scope of application of uniform law instruments. Past experience and at the same

---

[1] This effort was first undertaken by Jan Kropholler, 'Internationales Einheitsrecht—Allgemeine
Lehren' (Mohr Siebeck, Tübingen, 1975). An interesting recent book that looks at a variety of other
instruments comparing them with the CISG: Marco Torsello, 'Common Features of Uniform
Commercial Law Conventions—A Comparative Study Beyond the 1980 Uniform Sales Law'
(Sellier European Law Publishers, Munich, 2004).

time the presumed or ascertained inability of the delegations to agree on solutions in quite a number of problem areas adjacent to sales contracts prompted them to devote a detailed chapter I, comprising Articles 1 to 6, to the sphere of application. The text is reproduced in volume 2 and reference is made to the comments and materials in chapter 7 above. For the purposes of this chapter, a few additional remarks would, however, appear to be appropriate.

18.02 Article 1(1)(a) of the CISG sets forth the basic principle as regards the determination of *the personal and the territorial sphere of application*: it provides that the Convention applies to contracts between parties whose places of business are in different Contracting States.

18.03 As mentioned previously, exceedingly ambitious projects not infrequently failed because the wider the sphere of application, the stronger the hostile counter-lobby on behalf of vested interests. While not defining a contract of sale, the Convention *excludes certain types of contract* in Articles 2 and 3. These provisions reduce *the substantive sphere of application* significantly. For example, consumer contracts are excluded[2] because some legal systems regulate such contracts heavily with a view to protecting the consumer as the presumably 'weaker party' and because consumer protection law varies greatly from one country to another, depending mainly on the degree of economic development, prevailing social policies etc. Contracts entered into through the very specific mode of sales by auction or by authority of law are also excluded.[3] So too are stocks, shares and other investment securities[4] because they are often acquired and disposed of on exchanges and through intermediaries whose rights and obligations vis-à-vis the investors on whose behalf they carry out such transactions are subject to specific rules of commercial and regulatory law.[5] Money is excluded because the law treats it in some respects as a very distinct phenomenon altogether,[6] negotiable instruments because important aspects governing certain types of them are the subject of specialized uniform law instruments as well as domestic statutes.[7] So-called 'big-ticket items', namely ships, vessels, hovercraft and aircraft[8] and electricity[9] are equally excluded, principally for historical reasons. Article 3 attempts to distinguish a contract for the sale of goods from a contract for services (or a contract for work and materials).

18.04 The reason for excluding from the CISG's sphere of application matters relating to the validity of contracts and the passing of property[10] is, as we have seen, a pragmatic one taken against the backdrop of sharp differences among legal systems in

---

2 Art 2(a).   3 Arts 2(b), (c).   4 Art 2(d).   5 See ch 13 above.

6 See Charles Proctor, *Mann on the Legal Aspects of Money* (6th edn, OUP, Oxford, 2005). A German edition was published in 1960 under the title *Das Recht des Geldes* (Alfred Metzner Verlag, Frankfurt am Main/Berlin, 1960).   7 Art 2(d).

8 Art 2(e).   9 Art 2(f).   10 Art 4.

this regard. Article 5 is the drafters' admission that they had to steer clear of product liability, an area of tort law where the impact of social policies and potential economic consequences of legal rules are evident. Basic policy decisions such as the adoption of the principle of no-fault liability or, even more so, the availability of punitive damages in certain jurisdictions made it imperative for the draftsmen of the CISG to draw a clear line in this regard.

Pragmatism also determined the sphere of application of the 2001 Cape Town **18.05** Convention on International Interests in Mobile Equipment.[11] However, since the subject matter of this instrument is in itself much more specific, fewer and less detailed limits to its the sphere of application were necessary. The only limitation of the *territorial and personal scope of application* considered to be both functionally necessary and acceptable was the debtor's location in a Contracting State.[12] 'Location', in turn, needed to have as extended a catchment area as possible, and that is why it encompasses the debtor's place of business, the place of incorporation or formation, its registered office or statutory seat, and the centre of its administration.[13] The *substantive sphere of application* is circumscribed by Article 2, the provision which creates the legal concept 'international interest' and defines the categories of high-value mobile equipment for which asset-based financing was considered to be potentially the most beneficial. In this connection, it is noteworthy that an early draft of the Convention had provided for seagoing vessels to be included in what is now Article 2(3). However, there were indications that certain maritime circles were confident that their existing instruments were sufficient for their purposes and that the inclusion of ships would trigger an unhelpful counter-lobby.

B. The Role of the Conflict of Laws

Conflict-of-laws rules have different functions in uniform transnational law instru- **18.06** ments. Firstly, they may be used to *widen (or narrow) the territorial and/or personal scope of application*. Thus, Article 1(1) (b) CISG extends, subject to reservations under Article 95, the sphere of application of the Convention so that it applies where the rules of private international law of the forum State lead to the application of the law of a Contracting State. Secondly, the narrower the substantive scope of application of an instrument, the greater the likelihood that issues potentially arising in a transaction between parties and (partly!) covered by the instrument will have to be decided by the applicable law as identified by the forum's

---

[11] See ch 12 above.   [12] Arts 3, 4.

[13] The purpose of this wide range of factors is to give maximum scope to the application of the Convention. See Roy Goode, *Convention on International Interests in Mobile Equipment and Protocol Thereto on Matters Specific to Aircraft Equipment—Official Commentary* (UNIDROIT Rome, 2002), Comment 1 to Art 4.

conflicts rules. Thirdly, the more precisely the crucial provisions are drafted and the more predictable the outcome of disputes on core issues between parties to a transaction, the greater the number of ancillary issues that can be left to the applicable domestic law. Thus, Articles 2 (4), 12, 29 (7), 30, 39, 40 and Articles XI Alternative A (5)(b), (11), Alternative B (2)(b), XVI (2)—to name but a few—of the 2001 Cape Town Convention and the Aircraft Protocol refer to non-unified domestic law.

18.07 Generally speaking, it is easier to find a consensus among States as to which law ought to apply than as to the content of rules of substantive law, because the latter usually touches upon a wider variety of national laws which are, moreover, rooted more deeply in countries' legal traditions. That is why, failing agreement on a substantive uniform rule on any given issue, negotiators in international consultations tend to ask whether at least agreement on a conflicts rule is feasible. In a similar vein, conventions on the conflict-of-laws aspects of a certain type of legal relationship or transaction often precede efforts to reach uniform substantive solutions. A recent example is the adoption of the 2002 Hague Convention on the Law Applicable to Certain Rights in Respect of Securities Held with an Intermediary,[14] which was then followed by negotiations on the draft UNIDROIT Convention on Intermediated Securities dealing with the substantive rights and obligations of parties to transactions involving securities held with an intermediary.

C. The Selection of the Connecting Factor

18.08 Chapter 2 has provided an overview of important connecting factors and their function within the structure of a conflict-of-laws rule. The parties' choice and the closest connection (as indicated, for example, by the place of business of the party that owes the 'characteristic performance') are the most important connecting factors as regards contracts. The place of incorporation or the seat is the connecting factor available to determine the *lex societatis*, that is, the law applicable to matters concerning companies. Connecting factors have different functions. Where a provision in a uniform law instrument leaves it to the 'applicable law' to decide a matter relevant for the interpretation and application of that provision, the court or arbitral tribunal seised will resort to its conflict rules and the connecting factor as determined by those rules. Thus, a court that wishes to determine to which of the three categories of interest mentioned in Article 2(2) of the 2001 Convention on International Interests in Mobile Equipment (Cape Town Convention) a particular interest belongs would look to the law applicable under its own conflict-of-laws rules, applying the connecting factor (the *situs* of the asset, the parties' choice, the entry into a registry, etc.) prescribed by those rules.[15]

---

[14] Discussed in ch 13 above.   [15] Art 2(4).

Uniform law instruments in turn need their own 'connecting factor' to determine **18.09** important aspects of their sphere of application. That connecting factor is sometimes very simple and 'single-tiered' as in Article 3(1) of the Cape Town Convention (debtor situated in a Contracting State).[16] In other cases it may be 'double-tiered' or even more complex.

Franco Ferrari, *International Sale of Goods—Applicability and Applications of the United Nations Convention on Contracts for the International Sale of Goods* (Helbing & Lichtenhahn/Bruylant, Basel/Brussels, 1999) 32–41[16a]

2.   The Internationality of Sales Contracts under the Hague Conventions

At first sight, the most important common feature of the 1980 and the 1964 Conventions appears to be their sphere of application, since the foregoing Conventions all apply solely to sales contracts deemed to be 'international', a choice which has been criticized on the grounds that currently '[the] differences which one time existed between transnational sales and sales of the same goods within one legal system have no reason [to exist].' Despite that apparent commonality, the spheres of application of the aforementioned conventions are fundamentally different. This is due, among others, to the very different criteria adopted by these Conventions in order to determine the internationality of a sales contract (as well as to their relation with the Convention's criteria of applicability. Indeed, the Hague Conventions (as opposed to the Vienna Convention) considered international only those sales which presented two elements of internationality: a subjective *and* an objective one. ... [u]nder the Hague Conventions, unlike under the CISG, the criteria employed to determine the internationality of a contract 'were not only subjective, *i.e.*, referred to the parties, but also objective, that is to say, related to specific aspects of the contractual relationship.' As far as the first element is concerned, the 1964 Conventions required the parties' place of business (or, absent a place of business, their residence) to be located in different States, independent from the parties' citizenship. As for the second element, the objective one, Article 1(1) ULIS[17] required that 'either [the] acts constituting offer and acceptance are effected in different States, or that the goods are sold during international transports or are to be transported internationally, or that the act[s] of offer and acceptance are made in a State other than the State of the place of delivery.' Unlike the 1980 Sales Convention, the Hague Conventions did not require any further element in order to be applicable, that is, no link with a Contracting State's territory or law was required.

But this ... has been criticized for 'having caused the adoption of the so-called *erga omnes approach*,' ... according to which the provisions of the 1964 Conventions had to be applied whenever the contract was considered international, and apparently even in those cases where the contractual relationships developed outside the territory of the Contracting States and independently of the application of private international law rules (which Article 2 ULIS expressly excluded). To most Contracting States this approach, also defined as 'universal' or 'universalist', appeared to be excessive. This is why all Contracting States—except Israel—made reservations in order to limit the scope of the Hague Conventions' application.

---

[16]   However, the Aircraft Protocol has an alternative connecting factor based on the nationality registration of an aircraft in a Contracting State. See Art IV.

[16a]   © Helbing & Lichtenhahn, Basel/Genf/München 1999.

[17]   The reference is to the Uniform Law on the International Sale of Goods of 1 July 1964.

3. The Internationality of Contracts under the CISG

The aforementioned tendency to restrict the Convention's applicability by making reservations along with the ... criticism undoubtedly influenced the decision of the drafters of the CISG to decide against the adoption of the objective criterion of internationality and, more important, the *erga omnes approach* and, thus, simplifying the CISG's approach. ... [T]he sole criterion to determine the internationality of a sales contract corresponds to the subjective criterion of the 1964 Conventions. Thus, under the CISG the internationality of a contract depends merely on the parties having their places of business ... in different States ...

It must be noted, however, that since the CISG did not adopt the approach of the ULIS and ULF according to which the criteria of internationality constituted, at the same time, the only criterion of applicability; the internationality of a sales contract does not suffice to make the CISG applicable. Furthermore, it cannot be argued that the different States in which the parties must have their places of business in order for a sales contract to be international under CISG must also be Contracting States, this being ... a criterion of applicability of the CISG rather than one of internationality. From what has been said thus far ... it also follows that where the 'subjective international prerequisite' is missing, for example, 'where the parties have their places of business in different legal units of the same Contracting State', the Vienna Sales Convention will not be applicable *per se*, even if the contract's execution involves different States, as has recently been confirmed by a German court decision: the court refused to apply the CISG to a case where a German buyer had acquired tickets from a German seller for the 1990 Soccer World Cup final to be handed over in Rome, on the grounds that the contract was not an international one.

On the other hand, the CISG can be applicable even in those cases where the goods do not cross any border and where the parties have the same citizenship, as long as the contract can be considered, from a subjective point of view, an international one.

18.10 Situations or transactions involving more than two parties, more than one contractual relationship, spanning over time or being otherwise 'complex', require particular care in designing the connecting factor(s). An example is the 2001 UN Convention on the Assignment of Receivables.[18] According to its Article 3 this treaty governs, firstly, 'international assignments', i.e. assignments of receivables (assignor's contractual rights to payment) where the assignor and the assignee are located in different States, and secondly, assignments of 'international receivables', i.e. assignment of receivables arising from a contract[19] between an assignor as original creditor and his debtor where the parties to the original contract, at the time of its conclusion, were located in different States. This set up is designed to ensure a comprehensive treatment of trans-border assignments, in particular issues of priority. Under the Convention, the assignor must in any event be located in a Contracting State at the time of the conclusion of the contract of assignment.[20] The rights and obligations of the debtor are only affected if, at the time of conclusion of the original contract, the debtor is (also) located in a Contracting State or the law governing the original contract is the law of a Contracting State.[21]

---

[18] See ch 11 above.   [19] 'Original contract' (Art 5(a)).   [20] Art 1(1)(a).
[21] Art 1(3).

D. Co-existence, Concurrence, and Conflicts of Conventions

Over the first decades of its history, transnational commercial law grew slowly; **18.11** there were very few instruments and those that were concluded addressed very specific areas which were often far apart from each other. As time passed, trans-border commerce and finance evolved and individual transactions became inter-twined, many of them gradually receiving their specific legal regime. The volume of transnational law instruments increased sharply. Businesses more and more often found themselves confronted with a multitude of sources of law that were relevant and needed to be routinely taken into account even in relatively simple transactions. The law of transport and, more specifically, the law of carriage of goods by inland waterways, sea, air, rail and road, is a fascinating area of trans-national commercial law which is too vast to be treated in this book but probably provides the most varied and colourful panorama of the co-existence, the con-currence, and the conflicts of uniform law instruments.

The Convention for the International Carriage of Goods by Road of 19 May **18.12** 1956 (CMR),[22] for example, has to be read, understood, and applied as one elem-ent in a web of international and supranational sources. With a few exceptions the CMR does not itself mention or elaborate on this in any explicit way, let alone give guidance to those called upon to work with it. Article 1(2) CMR refers to the Convention on Road Traffic of 19 September 1949 which, in defining standards for road transportation vehicles, supplements the CMR and contributes to defin-ing the Convention's scope of application. Other treaties establish regulatory rules regarding the conduct of carriers and their employees[23] or labour standards, non-observance of which has implications for the application of the CMR's liability regime. Likewise, non-compliance with treaties regarding the customs regime has consequences for rights and obligations of the parties to a CMR contract.

For two conventions to enter into a conflict with each other their scope of appli- **18.13** cation needs to overlap. This is true for the CMR and the 1980 Rome Convention on the Law Applicable to Contractual Obligations.[24] Both instruments deal with

---

[22] Leading commentaries include: Malcolm A Clarke, *International Carriage of Goods by Road: CMR* (4th edn, Sweet & Maxwell, London, 2003); Jacques Putzeys, Albert Coolen and Claire Bocken, *Le contrat de transport routier de marchandises* (Bruylant, Brussels, 1981); Jürgen Basedow, 'Übereinkommen über den Beförderungsvertrag im Internationalen Strassengüterverkehr (CMR)' in Jürgen Basedow and Karsten Schmidt (eds), *Münchener Kommentar zum Handelsgesetzbuch, Band 7, Transportrecht* (CH Beck, Munich, 1997) 855. A milestone in English case law regarding the interpretation of transnational commercial law is actually a CMR case: *James Buchanan & Co Ltd v Babco Forwarding & Shipping (UK) Ltd* [1978] AC 141 (HL).

[23] See also a number of references in the 2001 Cape Town Convention on International Interests in Mobile Equipment and the Aircraft Protocol to applicable aviation regulations etc.

[24] See ch 2 above.

contracts for the international carriage of goods, even if the Rome Convention does so by determining the substantive domestic law applicable to a set of facts or a claim. Article 21 of the Rome Convention resolves this conflict in giving precedence in principle to the CMR and other important conventions on carriage of goods. To the extent that conflicts arise between the CMR and other private-law instruments (for example, regarding carriage of dangerous goods or carriage of animals), the general rules apply: *lex specialis derogat legi generali, lex posterior derogat legi priori* etc. However, there are also subject-matter-specific conflict rules. For example, a number of treaties in the area of international civil procedure[25] are based on the *lex favorabilior* principle, that is, the principle of maximum efficacy in matters regarding service of documents and other due-process institutions as well as with respect to recognition and enforcement of foreign judgments or arbitral awards. If, as has been suggested by authoritative writers,[26] this could be agreed on as the conflicts rule regarding litigation and arbitration in general, the 1958 UN Convention on Recognition and Enforcement of Foreign Arbitral Awards[27] would prevail over the 1975 Panama Convention and the 1979 Montevideo Convention which deal with the same issue where, in a given case, the 1958 Convention is the more effective one. Equally, the later Conventions could prevail over the UN Convention, even if entering into force in a given country only after the entry into force of the 1958 Convention in that country, if recognition and enforcement of an award were to prove more effective under them than under the 1958 Convention. In other words, conflicts rules may be based on substantive rather than on formal criteria and considerations.

18.14   A special and increasingly frequent situation is the existence of regionally harmonized law and instruments purporting to harmonize transnational law universally. General aspects regarding the driving forces, the methods, institutions involved, and the objectives of regionalism have been briefly discussed in chapter 5 above. As regards conflicts between universal and regional law on the same subject matter, the starting point for reflection may be Article 94 of the CISG and its predecessor, Article II of the Hague Sales Convention. The purpose of the reservation power contained in Article 94 is to enable States which have largely harmonized their domestic sale of goods law to exclude the application of the CISG where the parties to a contract have their places of business in those States. The provision was meant to clear the way for the Nordic States who had already harmonized their sales law. To date, only Denmark, Finland, Norway, and Sweden have made that

---

[25]   See ch 16 above.

[26]   Jan Kleinheisterkamp, 'Conflict of Treaties on International Arbitration in the Southern Cone' in Jan Kleinheisterkamp and Gonzalo Lorenzo Idiarte (eds), *Avances del derecho internacional privado en América Latina: liber amicorum Jürgen Samtleben* (Fundación de Cultura Universitaria, Montevideo, 2002) 687.   [27]   See ch 17 above.

reservation.[28] Another conflicts rule in the CISG is Article 90.[29] It has the same effect as Article 21 of the Rome Convention discussed above in that it states:

> This Convention does not prevail over any international agreement which has already been or may be entered into and which contains provisions concerning the matters governed by this Convention, provided that the parties have their places of business in States parties to such agreement.

Professor Schlechtriem notes in his afore-cited commentary: **18.15**

> 'The provision is of considerable substantive importance, but its precise effect is unclear'.

It is submitted that it is not more than a reference to the general rules upholding the prevalence of the more specific and the later instrument.

Marco Torsello, *Common Features of Uniform Commercial Law Conventions—A Comparative Study Beyond the 1980 Uniform Sales Law* (Sellier European Law Publishers, Munich, 2004), 264–70

Provisions that closely resemble Article 94 CISG have been inserted in the amended version of the Convention on the Limitation Period, in the Agency Convention, in the Factoring Convention and in the Leasing Convention: these are all Conventions that are close in time to the CISG and that closely resemble the latter as far as their unification strategy is concerned. On the contrary, more recent Conventions have rejected that approach and therefore do not contain any provision comparable to Article 94 CISG. It is very difficult to say whether this different approach reflects a different conception of the relationship between global and regional unification. However, what is safe to assert is that, absent a provision like Article 94 CISG and declarations made accordingly, regional laws, even where they are the 'same or closely related' in all the jurisdictions involved, cannot prevail over an international uniform commercial law Convention, unless they are in the form of (regional) supranational uniform laws. [. . .]

[I]n addressing this possible conflict,[30] the CISG [in Article 90] adopts an approach that can be described as "back-stepping" [. . .]. Similar provisions have been reproduced in most subsequent Conventions with only minor changes in the language. None of the Conventions considered here, conversely, sets forth any provision comparable to the one that is found in Article 99 CISG, which 'does not allow a Contracting State to be, at the same time, party' to the CISG and to the 1964 Hague Convention. The rationale of Article 99 CISG seems to reflect the intent of the drafters of the CISG to substitute the new Convention for the 'unsuccessful'[31] Hague Conventions. The substitution of an international instrument for a previous one, however, raises specific problems that must

---

[28] For an assessment of the current position, see Jan Ramberg, 'Unification of Sales Law: a Look at the Scandinavian States' (2003) VIII Unif L Rev 201.

[29] For a detailed analysis, see Peter Schlechtriem' commentary on Art 90, paras 1 et seq, in: Peter Schlechtriem and Ingeborg Schwenzer (eds), *Commentary on the UN Convention on the International Sale of Goods* (2nd (English) edn, OUP, Oxford, 2005).

[30] Here, the author refers to the *general* conflict between Conventions, not the specific situation of *universal v regional* instrument.

[31] The quotation marks are quite appropriate: apart from their intrinsic technical quality, it is too often overlooked that, although the Hague Convention had only a limited number of Contracting States, it covered up to 75 per cent of the total value of their international sales.

be kept separate from those deriving from the occasional conflict of Conventions due to a partial overlap of their scope of application. As far as the latter issue is concerned, the widely accepted 'back-stepping' approach is probably perfectly justified insofar as there are only few international uniform commercial law Conventions likely to be in conflict in view of their different scope of application. [...]

However, as the number of international uniform commercial law Conventions increases, the risk of a conflict of Conventions, due to the partial overlap of their scope of application, increases. Thus, what if two conflicting Conventions both give way to the other one? In such an event, the solution to the problem cannot be found within the text of the conflicting Conventions, but should be based on the general principles of the law of treaties such as that of the *lex posterior*, of the *lex specialis* or of the *lex favorabilior*. The issue ... has emerged as a rather puzzling one in the course of the drafting of the two most recent uniform Conventions, the Assignment Convention and the Cape Town Convention. [...]

The drafters of the Assignment Convention were clearly aware of the possibility of a conflict ... Therefore, in the process of drafting ... the issue of 'conflict of Conventions' was taken into careful consideration. Accordingly, while in the very first versions of the draft text the issue was dealt with in the traditional way (*i.e.*, precedence was given to any other international agreements), a later version introduced the provision according to which the Draft Convention 'prevails over any international convention or other multilateral or bilateral agreement which has been or may be entered into by a Contracting State and which contains provisions concerning matters governed by this Convention'. This 'aggressive' approach has been severely criticized, and, in fact, the provision was deleted in the final text and replaced with the more traditional 'back-stepping' rule. This rule, according to which the Convention 'does not prevail over any [other] international agreement', is however set forth only as a general rule, while a specific exception is provided. Despite the general rule, the Convention 'prevails over the Unidroit Convention on International Factoring'. Although the Assignment Convention assertedly is not intended to entirely displace the Factoring Copnvention, the provision ... closely resembles the CISG's provision on its relationship with the Hague Conventions. The point seems to be that the approach chosen by the Assignment Convention is suitable for adoption in other Conventions only insofar as the drafters are capable of foreseeing the possible conflicts with pre-existing Conventions, whilst in no event can this approach safely prevent a conflict with future Conventions.

Moreover, as the number of international uniform commercial law Conventions constantly increases, foreseeing conflicts of Conventions becomes a much more complicated task. The scope of application of the Cape Town Convention, for instance, includes matters also dealt with ... by the Leasing Convention and by the Assignment Convention ... Given the limited scope of application of the Cape Town Convention *ratione materiae* (the Convention applies only to specific kinds of 'mobile equipment'), it is not surprising that the issue is dealt with in accordance to the *lex specialis* principle. Consistently, the Cape Town Convention prevails over the Assignment Convention 'as it relates to the assignment of receivables which are associated rights related to international interests in aircraft objects, railway rolling stock and space assets'.[32] Furthermore, as to the relationship with the Leasing Convention, the Cape Town Convention leaves it to each Protocol to 'determine the relationship between this Convention and the [Leasing Convention]'. In turn, the Protocol on Matters Specific to Aircraft Equipment clearly states that the Convention

---

[32] The provision referred to is Art 45 *bis* Cape Town Convention.

'shall supersede the UNIDROIT Convention on International Financial Leasing as it relates to aircraft objects'. [...]

The foregoing suggests a distinction between traditional conflicts of Conventions, which are to be dealt with before applying the international instruments and lead to the exclusion of one of the conflicting Conventions, and problems of coordination (or hidden conflicts), which arise when different instruments are all applicable to the same transaction. The increasing possibility of concurrence among the existing Conventions thus makes the need for an overall coherence among the different instruments urgent. In this respect, an effective antidote against ... incoherence may be inferred from the interpretative guideline, common to all uniform Conventions, that imposes to have regard to the international character of the Convention. It has been suggested that this interpretative criterion entails the need to interpret each Convention in the light of other international instruments (and relevant case law) which are based on the same 'autonomous' and 'international' interpretative approach. This conclusion seems to be supported by the role recognized in all the Conventions at hand to other international Conventions: indeed, unlike domestic law, which is set aside as *extrema ratio* for gap-filling purposes, other international Conventions are recognized as having a concurrent position in the context within which interpretation takes place. Evidence of this is provided by the traditional 'back-stepping' rule on conflicts of Conventions: indeed, the possibility of a conflict implies the need for coordination and, in turn, acknowledges the existence of a common international context ... Therefore, the need to interpret an international instrument in accordance to its international character makes cross-reference among international uniform commercial law Conventions admissible and, most likely, even desirable.

The views expressed by Professor Torsello in the concluding paragraph quite naturally attract applause and sympathy. For the sake of argument and better understanding the changing world of transnational commercial law, one might, however, ask whether, although desirable, a 'holistic' approach to interpretation and cross-references is always and under all circumstances admissible.[33] **18.16**

A special situation arises where a regional intergovernmental organization such as the *Organisation pour l'Harmonisation du Droit des Affaires en Afrique (OHADA)* produces uniform law that largely coincides with an instrument adopted for the use at the worldwide level. Of the sixteen OHADA Member States two are also Contracting States of the CISG. However, there does not appear to be a clear provision in the OHADA uniform act, case law, or unanimity of scholarly opinion as to the applicable conflicts rule.[34] The most likely outcome, at least where a court in an OHADA Member State is seised of a dispute, would be the application of the regional instrument on the ground that it is the *lex specialis*.[35] **18.17**

---

[33] More on this in ch 19 below.

[34] See Gaston Kenfack Douajni, 'La vente commerciale OHADA' (2003) VIII Unif L Rev 191; Franco Ferrari, 'Universal and Regional Sales Law: Can They Coexist?' (2003) VIII Unif L Rev 177; as well as the summary of the discussion by Peter Schlechtriem, 'The Sale of Goods: Do Regions Matter?' (2003) VIII Unif L Rev 173.

[35] For details, see the quotation from Professor Basedow's report reproduced in ch 6 (at para 6.45) above.

18.18 Again, the picture is a different one where there is a conflict between a treaty negotiated and adopted at international level and an instrument emanating from a Regional Economic Integration Organization to which its Member States have transferred private-law making powers. Such is the case with the European Community. Under both the Treaty of Rome and ECJ case law the answer is that Community law has precedence over national law, including the international treaties to which Member States may have become parties.[36] No conflict should, in principle, arise where a regional group of States and, in particular, a Regional Economic Integration Organization such as the EC, considers the universally harmonized law as being part of its own pan-regional law. This is the case as regards the CISG which, according to statements made by EU organs, is part of the *quasi-acquis communautaire*.[37]

Questions

1. (a) Outline the reasons for excluding certain types of sales from the CISG's scope of application.
   (b) If you had to draft Articles 2 and 3 of the CISG today, would you provide for the same or for different limits to the scope of application?
2. What are the two different functions that 'connecting factors' established by provisions of uniform law instruments may serve? Give examples from two conventions discussed in this volume.
3. How would you describe the relationship between the tendency to circumscribe the substantive scope of application of more recent instruments on the one hand and, on the other hand transnational commercial law's venturing beyond contract and into areas such as property and insolvency law?
4. Against the background of the critical role of 'internationality' for defining the scope of application of the 2001 United Nations Convention on the Assignment of Receivables in International Trade (see Article 3), is it correct to state that it may even affect domestic assignments of domestic receivables? And if so, what might have been the reasons for this approach?
5. The Cape Town Convention on International Interests was signed on 16 November 2001. The United Nations Convention on the Assignment of Receivables was signed on 12 December 2001. Which has priority in case of conflict? Read Article 45 *bis* of the Cape Town Convention and comment.

---

[36] Again, as regards details, reference is made to Professor Basedow's paper extensively quoted in ch 6 above. [37] See Schlechtriem and Schwenzer (n 29), para 13.

Further reading

Buxbaum, Hannah L, 'Unification of the Law Governing Secured Transactions: progress and prospects for reform' (2003) VIII Unif L Rev 321

Dutoit Bernard, and Majoros, Ferenc, 'Le lacis des conflits de conventions en droit privé et leurs relations possibles' (1984) Revue critique de droit international privé 565

Evans, Malcolm, 'Uniform Law: A Bridge Too Far?' 3 Tul J Intl Comp L 145 (1995)

Putzeys, Jacques, 'Les tendances unificatrices et désunificatrices dans le droit des transports de marchandises: perspectives—Vue d'ensemble' (2003) VIII Unif L Rev 233

Volken, Paul, *Konventionskonflikte im Internationalen Privatrecht* (Schulthess, Zurich, 1977)

19

UNIFORMITY IN TRANSNATIONAL COMMERCIAL LAW

A. The Obstacles to Achieving and Maintaining Uniformity	19.01		E. Reservations and Declarations	19.13
B. Responses (I): Public International Law and its Reception in Domestic Law	19.05		F. Structural Issues and Technical Support Devices for Achieving and Maintaining Uniformity	19.15
C. Responses (II): Devices in Private-Law Instruments	19.07		G. Contract Practice	19.22
D. Uniformity Through Interpretation in a Uniform System?	19.10		H. Do Divergences Matter?	19.23

A. The Obstacles to Achieving and Maintaining Uniformity

19.01 A formidable obstacle to achieving uniformity and a potential source of disruption is insufficient planning and co-ordination among governments and their intergovernmental organizations. It is not unheard of that work on a new instrument gets under way without a full review of possible frictions, inconsistencies or outright conflicts with existing instruments having been carried out and without conscious decisions as to the envisaged solutions of those conflicts having been made. *Mutatis mutandis* the same occasionally happens everywhere at the level of domestic legislation. Fortunately, this is not the main area of concern. Further down the road in the process, there are other obstacles to achieving and maintaining uniformity once an international uniform text has been adopted. In particular, guaranteeing consistent—let alone 'correct', 'just', etc.—interpretation of international instruments by national courts is a daunting challenge. This chapter will focus on both the reasons for this state of affairs and possible remedies.

19.02 If one takes the following provisions from national codifications, the most obvious reasons for the difficulties just mentioned become immediately apparent.

Article 1438 Civil Code of Québec

A clause which is null does not render the contract invalid in other respects, unless it is apparent that the contract may be considered only as an indivisible whole.

The same applies to a clause without effect or deemed unwritten.

Article 242 German Civil Code

The debtor is bound to effect performance according to the requirements of good faith, giving consideration to common usage.

Section 17 English Sale of Goods Act 1979[1]

(1) *Where there is a contract for the sale of specific or ascertained goods the property in them is transferred to the buyer at such time as the parties to the contract intend it to be transferred.*

(2) *For the purposes of ascertaining the intention of the parties regard shall be had to the terms of the contract, the conduct of the parties, and the circumstances of the case.*

19.03 None of these provisions sets objectively identifiable criteria for their 'correct' and consistent interpretation and application. When is it 'apparent' that a contract may be considered only as a whole? What is exactly required of a debtor to be acting in 'good faith' and when is usage 'common'? If a contract for the purchase of 100,000 tonnes of crude oil crossing the ocean does not say a word about the transfer of property, how is one to determine what was the intention of the parties? The problem becomes exacerbated in jurisdictions where a great number of judges and tribunals, each with its own territorial and/or subject-matter competence, interpret and apply the law independently from the others. Over time all legal systems have developed mechanisms to deal with these challenges. One of particular importance in the common law jurisdictions is the doctrine of *stare decisis*, or judicial precedent, by which courts are bound by earlier decisions of higher courts on the same question of law. All systems have their rules or methods of interpretation (*canones*), transmitted from one generation to the next by legal education. Some systems, in particular those with a vast number of adjudicators, not bound by any rule of *stare decisis*, have designed procedural devices to enhance consistency of adjudication, for example by providing that an appellate court that wishes to deviate from the settled case law of its peers should refer the issue to its supreme court with a view to (re-) establishing uniformity. Last but not least, all developed legal systems possess a law reporting system giving participants in the law-making process access to judicial decisions.

19.04 In the absence of both internationally uniform rules of interpretation and the infrastructure supporting uniform interpretation at the transnational level there is a strong inclination to apply national rules or *canones*. For example, in seeking to

---

[1] C 54.

apply a broadly worded and ambiguous provision of a convention 'correctly', an English judge[2] may—consciously or unconsciously— interpret the provision according to rules for the construction of statutes, such as the 'golden rule',[3] the 'mischief rule',[4] the 'literal rule',[5] and the '*eiusdem generis* rule'.[6] On the whole, he would try to be a faithful servant of the legislative text. A German judge may find it quite appropriate to respond to that ambiguity by looking into the *travaux préparatoires* and, having ascertained from these the intention underlying the provision, to interpret it 'teleologically' to bring it into line with that intention.[7] It is evident that, over time and among a potentially great number of jurisdictions parties to that convention and their differing domestic *canones*, uniformity may never actually be achieved or quickly be dissipated. Moreover, *travaux préparatoires* have to be read with a degree of caution, because on particular issues things may take a different turn at the diplomatic Conference. For example, work on the 2002 Hague Securities Convention[8] proceeded on the basis that the Convention would be confined to determination of the law applicable to the proprietary aspects of dealings in indirectly held securities but at the diplomatic Conference the scope was broadened to encompass all rights other than those that are *purely* contractual or otherwise *purely* personal, and various other substantive changes were made. Accordingly in their Explanatory Report on the Convention the rapporteurs cautioned against reliance on the *travaux préparatoires* as a basis for determining the scope of the Convention.[9]

---

[2] This is purposely simplified as English law—like other legal systems—has been and is subject to changes in this regard, some interestingly triggered by the challenges posed by transnational commercial law instruments. See *Fothergill v Monarch Airlines* [1981] AC 251, at 272 *per* Lord Wilberforce; *The Hollandia* [1983] AC 565, at 572 *per* Lord Diplock.

[3] That the literal meaning of a statute should not be adopted where it would lead to an absurd, rather than a sensible, result, unless the words used are so clear as to be incapable of an alternative meaning.

[4] That in interpreting a statute regard should be had to the mischief which the statute was designed to remedy. At the present time the trend is strongly in favour of a purposive interpretation which seeks to give effect to the purpose of the statute.

[5] That a statutory provision should be interpreted according to its plain meaning unless this would produce absurdity.

[6] That where an enumeration of particular things of a particular class is followed by general words, the latter should be interpreted as confined to subjects of the same class (*ejusdem generis*).

[7] However, the same is true of English and American judges in cases where they consider reference to the *travaux préparatoires* helpful. See, for example, the decision of the English Court of Appeal in *Morris v KLM Royal Dutch Airlines* [2002] QB 100 and of the US Supreme Court in *Eastern Airlines Inc v Floyd* 499 US 530 (1991). But the *travaux* are not necessarily a reliable guide. See below, n 9 and p 707.

[8] Convention on the law applicable to certain rights in respect of securities held with an intermediary.

[9] Roy Goode, Hideki Kanda and Karl Kreuzer, assisted by Christophe Bernasconi, *Hague Securities Convention: Explanatory Report* (Koninklijke Brill NV, Leiden, 2005), Int-78. Similar reasoning was applied by the House of Lords in *J I McWilliam Co Inc v Mediterranean Shipping Co SA* [2005] 2 AC 423, *per* Lord Bingham, para 19.

B. Responses (I): Public International Law and its Reception in Domestic Law

19.05 Attempts by international lawmakers as well as national courts and writers to counter the threat of chaos or failure through creeping re-nationalization of transnational texts take different approaches. Public international law[10] is the most obvious source of inspiration and guidance.

F A Mann, 'Uniform Statutes in English Law' (1983) 99 LQR 376

Uniform statutes are provisions enacted or authorised by Parliament and derived from treaties or similar arrangements which a group of nations agrees to incorporate into their respective legal systems with a view to unifying legal rules in a particular field. Even though, as a matter of form, the legislative act itself is, in constitutional law, usually the direct and, indeed, the only source of municipal enforceability, the fact that uniform statutes are the ultimate product of a treaty constitutes their special characteristic. That fact has numerous consequences which it is proposed to examine: Is the interpretation of uniform statutes subject to peculiar rules? In particular, is it possible and perhaps even necessary by some process of interpretation to fill gaps in the uniform text? Do uniform rules really succeed in unifying the law? ...

When some of these questions were examined on a previous occasion, attention was drawn to, and to some extent a distinction was made between, the various methods practised in England with a view to giving effect in English law to the terms of the treaty. The following observations will deal only with the fourth of these methods, *viz.* a statute the schedule to which sets forth the text of the treaty and has the force of law. This may now be described as the most usual method and may well be on a different footing from others ...

The Interpretation of Uniform Statutes

The ultimate object in interpreting uniform statutes is not open to doubt. It is to find answers conforming to the wording, purpose and idea of the treaty and acceptable to all or most of those countries which have ratified it. As Scott L.J. put it, 'the maintenance of uniformity in the interpretation of a rule after its international adoption is just as important as the initial removal of divergence ...' The real question is how this can be achieved.

It has become fashionable to take Lord Macmillan's instruction that the language 'should be construed on broad principles of acceptation.' Today it may be submitted with greater confidence than ever before that such principles are those prevailing in and developed by public international law. For both Lord Diplock and Lord Scarman have recently stated with the fullest possible justification that the interpretation of uniform statutes is governed by the Vienna Convention on the Law of Treaties and has thus become one of the principal points at which public international and private law meet. [there follows the quotation of Articles 31 and 32 of the Convention, reproduced in volume 2]

Admittedly these Articles were designed primarily with a view to texts which are not only concluded under the control of public international law, but also regulate relations between States. But in the law there is no difference between such treaties and those contemplating

---

[10] See ch 3.

relations between private persons: Articles 31 and 32 apply to both types. Moreover, it does not matter that, technically, the Vienna Convention applies only to treaties concluded after January 27, 1980, when it came into effect, for, as again Lord Diplock made clear, it 'does no more than codify already existing public international law.'

If, then, Articles 31 and 32 are taken as a starting point for the interpretation of uniform statutes enacted by Parliament, certain consequences follow.

1. The first and foremost guide to construction should be the ordinary meaning of the words used in the uniform statute. . . . The paramount importance of the literal interpretation has in recent years sometimes become neglected. . . .

Contrary to what is sometimes thought of as continental methods of construction, the predominance of the text has repeatedly been emphasised, for instance, by the Federal Supreme Court of Germany which in a fundamental decision[11] said that a uniform law had to be interpreted 'in good faith in accordance with the ordinary meaning which attaches to its provisions within their context and in the light of its object and purpose.' . . .

It is, however, very clear that notwithstanding its primacy the literal or textual interpretation is liable to be inconclusive. The recent decision of the House of Lords[12] on the words 'other charges incurred in respect of the carriage of goods' is significant. These words occur in Article 23 (4) of the Convention on the Contract for the International Carriage of Goods by Road, the so-called C.M.R., which is scheduled to the Carriage of Goods by Road Act 1965. Was excise duty in respect of stolen whisky paid by the plaintiffs included in those words and therefore recoverable from the defendant carriers? All courts gave an affirmative answer, although the majority in the House of Lords was three to two only. The result is noteworthy, since in ordinary language the word 'charges' may not readily include excise duties.

2. It is now established that for the purpose of ascertaining the ordinary meaning of a uniform statute it is legitimate to refer to a foreign text irrespective of whether it is the only authentic one upon which the English text is based or whether its authenticity is equal with that of the English text. Very frequently, however, this is again a fruitless effort, as it was in the two recent English cases. In particular the French phrase 'frais encourus à l'occasion du transport' gives rise to the same problem as its English counterpart: neither 'charges' nor 'frais' would normally signify excise duty.

What is not yet clear is whether an English court is permitted to look at texts translated into other languages. Thus it would hardly be open to doubt that the German counterpart of the English phrase 'charges incurred in respect of the carriage of goods,' *viz.* the words 'sonstige aus Anlass der Beförderung des Gutes entstandene Kosten' cannot reasonably be understood as including excise duties; the same would probably apply to the Dutch word 'vervoerskosten' which Lord Wilberforce referred to as part of a decision of the Amsterdam court rejecting the carrier's liability for excise duty. It is submitted that a translated text is a permissible and frequently a useful guide to decision, for it is likely to indicate how one of the High Contracting Parties understood the authentic text.

From the point of view of literal interpretation the Dutch court held that excise duty was more of a 'subsequent levy or administrative fine than an item of charges in respect of carriage.' . . .

---

[11] The reference is to the decision of 25 June 1969, in 52 *Entscheidungen des Bundesgerichtshofs in Zivilsachen*, p 216.

[12] The reference is to *James Buchanan & Co Ltd v Babco Forwarding and Shipping (UK) Ltd* [1978] AC 141.

3. The terms of the treaty cannot, however, be read in isolation. Rather they should be construed 'in their context'. This is nothing new. Already in 1961, when construing the words 'due diligence to make the ship seaworthy' in Article III, rule 1 of the Hague Rules scheduled to the Carriage of Goods by Sea Act 1924, the House of Lords held it 'necessary to pay particular regard to their history, origin and context.' Accordingly, the meaning of those words was held to be that which since a decision of 1895 had been attributed to them in England and was in conformity with that prevailing in Canada, New Zealand and the United States of America. Certainly, as Lord Atkin said,[13] the courts should not display any 'predilection' for the local law preceding the Convention, but where the words have been considered and used by courts highly experienced in the subject it is a reasonable inference that the Convention, when using the same word or phrase in connection with the same subject-matter, in all probability does not intend to reject its established meaning; the term may in such circumstances be said to have a special meaning in the sense of Article 31 (4) of the Vienna Convention. ... It is simply common sense that if the Convention adopts a phrase which appears to have been taken from one legal system or from some, where it is used in a specific sense, the international legislators are likely to have had that sense in mind and to intend its introduction into the Convention. History, origin and context, therefore, are peculiarly apt to throw light on the literal meaning. These are elements which are capable of proof. They do not involve guesswork. They are free from the hazards which often bedevil the assessment of a rule's rationale or purpose. Thus when the C.M.R. Convention speaks of 'charges', 'frais', 'Kosten', it is unlikely that in the field of road transport a definite meaning had previously been assigned to any of these terms. ...

4. The next step in the process of interpretation is to look at the treaty 'in the light of its object and purpose'—words which in every language seem to be tautological and the distinction between which has never been explained and, apparently, has not even been discussed. Perhaps the Vienna Convention intends to express two different aspects of interpretation, namely in the first place the object or purpose of unification, which the treaty as a whole undoubtedly pursues, and secondly the object and purpose of the particular provision the terms the terms of which fall to be construed. Irrespective of whether or no such was the intention of the Vienna Convention and whether or no the words used by it are apt to express the two aspects, it should not be open to doubt that for the purpose of interpretation both of them are material and significant. Their effect requires deeper consideration than it has so far received.

(a) As regards the first point, that is, the object or purpose of applying the Convention so that it implements and promotes the unification of the law, this means in practice that the courts should adopt that interpretation which has been or is most likely to be applied by the greatest number of countries. To be even more specific, this means that a judge in England should follow the practice of influential foreign courts even if he himself would not have reached the same result. This is 'subsequent practice in the application of the treaty,' which Article 31 (3) (b) of the Vienna Convention makes an aid to construction, although in a purely English context subsequent practice may be excluded from consideration. What is necessary, therefore, is a comparative approach and a capacity to assess the weight and the probable impact of foreign decisions and, possibly, academic work. ...

---

[13] The reference is to *Stag Line Ltd v Foscolo Mango & Co Ltd* [1939] AC 328, 343.

It is certainly true that, to take a probably extreme case pointed out by Megaw L.J., in six member-States 12 different interpretations of the same words may be produced. But if there are few foreign decisions and if one of them is clearly and persuasively reasoned, as happened in a recent case decided by the House of Lords,[14] the English courts, it is suggested, should follow that case and thus intensify and probably secure a uniform interpretation, albeit that the in the absence of the foreign decision they would have reached the opposite result. In particular, where, as in fact happened, two Law Lords adopted the foreign decision and its reasoning, the majority of three Law Lords would have better served the object and purpose of the Convention, *viz.* the uniformity and harmonisation of the law, if they had refrained from going their own way. As so often, Lord Denning M.R. led the way, when he said in *Corocraft v. Pan American Airways*[15] that even if he disagreed with certain American decisions he 'would follow them in a matter which is of international concern. The courts of all countries should interpret the Convention[16] in the same way.' ...

5. As Article 32 of the Vienna Convention makes clear, a supplementary and, one may add, very much subsidiary means of interpretation is recourse to *travaux préparatoires*. For the purpose of construing an international Convention this is now accepted by English law. ...

The real problem, therefore, is what are relevant *travaux préparatoires* and what weight should in a given case be given to them. These are questions of great general scope, which far exceed the field of treaties, which cannot be comprehensively discussed in the present context and to which it may be necessary to revert. Suffice it to emphasise that the cases in which *travaux préparatoires* can profitably be used must be 'rare,' indeed exceptional. That the minutes of September 27, 1955, which the House of Lords considered[17] and which reproduce a discussion on the meaning of 'damage' were inconclusive is so obvious that no detailed reference is required. But by way of example both Lord Diplock and Lord Fraser referred to another minute of September 20, 1955, where, in relation to a vote taken on a certain amendment, it is stated 'The President stated that, in the event of a negative vote on the proposal, the Conference would be understood as having stated that the word "unreasonable" was not necessary, because it was already implied in Article 19 as at present drafted.' Both Lord Diplock and Lord Fraser seem to have taken the view that a minute of this type could be material and perhaps even helpful. Respectful doubt cannot be suppressed. Suppose the majority or some of the delegates disagreed with the President, but remained silent, not necessarily on account of Macchiavellianism which according to Lord Diplock 'is not extinct at international conferences,' but, for instance, because they were anxious to avoid a long discussion with a foolish President. Is the opinion expressed by the President relevant material? It would be a different matter if the President had not stated his own view, but had purported to summarise the delegates' intentions or had summarised the result of an informal test. But it is submitted that even in the absence of recorded contradiction the President's statement does not carry any weight. It is no more than a personal opinion. It does not imply any legislative intent or authority. ...

---

[14] See the Dutch case mentioned by Lord Wilberforce in *James Buchanan & Co Ltd v Babco Forwarding and Shipping (UK) Ltd* [1978] AC 141, 153–4. [15] [1969] 1 QB 616, 655.

[16] The reference is to the 1929 Warsaw Convention for the Unification of Certain Rules Relating to International Carriage by Air.

[17] In *Fothergill v Monarch Airlines* (note 2). The minutes referred to are those of the diplomatic Conference for the adoption of the 1955 Hague Protocol to Amend the Convention for the Unification of Certain Rules Relating to International Carriage by Air Signed at Warsaw on 12 October 1929.

19.06 While doubts regarding the weight the Vienna Convention should be given in the interpretation of private-law setting treaties continue to be subject of academic discussion in some countries, the formidable examples of its use in achieving and maintaining uniformity provided in particular by British, North American and German as well as other continental European supreme courts in interpreting Conventions on the carriage of goods are evidence of a by now solid *acquis* in this respect.

C. Responses (II): Devices in Private-Law Instruments

19.07 In recent instruments it has become standard for transnational commercial texts to contain provisions specifically designed to enhance the prospects of achieving and maintaining uniformity. Secondly, international legislators employ ever greater care in drafting the preamble. Two examples merit more detailed analysis: the 1980 CISG and the 2001 Cape Town Convention.[18]

1980 United Nations Convention on Contracts for the International Sale of Goods

[Preamble]

The States Parties to this Convention,

bearing in mind the broad objectives in the resolutions adopted by the sixth special session of the General Assembly of the United Nations on the establishment of a New International Economic Order,

considering that the development of international trade on the basis of equality and mutual benefit is an important element in promoting friendly relations among States,

being of the opinion that the adoption of uniform rules which govern contracts for the international sale of goods and take into account the different social, economic and legal systems would contribute to the removal of legal barriers in international trade and promote the development of international trade,

have decreed as follows:

PART I

SPHERE OF APPLICATION AND GENERAL PROVISIONS

[. . .]

Article 7

(1) In the interpretation of this Convention, regard is to be had to its international character and to the need to promote uniformity in its application and the observance of good faith in international trade.

(2) Questions concerning matters governed by this Convention which are not expressly settled in it are to be settled in conformity with the general principles on which it is based or, in the absence of such principles, in conformity with the law applicable by virtue of the rules of private international law.

---

[18] For the full text of both instruments, see vol 2.

2001 Convention on International Interests in Mobile Equipment

PREAMBLE

THE STATES PARTIES TO THIS CONVENTION,

AWARE of the need to acquire and use mobile equipment of high value or particular economic significance and to facilitate the financing of the acquisition and use of such equipment in an efficient manner,

RECOGNISING the advantages of asset-based financing and leasing for this purpose and desiring to facilitate these types of transaction by establishing clear rules to govern them,

MINDFUL of the need to ensure that interests in such equipment are recognised and protected universally,

DESIRING to provide broad and mutual economic benefits for all interested parties,

BELIEVING that such rules must reflect the principles underlying asset-based financing and leasing and promote the autonomy of the parties necessary in these transactions,

CONSCIOUS of the need to establish a legal framework for international interests in such equipment and for that purpose to create an international registration system for their protection,

TAKING INTO CONSIDERATION the objectives and principles enunciated in existing Conventions relating to such equipment,

HAVE AGREED upon the following provisions:

CHAPTER I

SPHERE OF APPLICATION AND GENERAL PROVISIONS

[...]

Article 5—Interpretation and applicable law

1. In the interpretation of this Convention, regard is to be had to its purpose as set forth in the preamble, to its international character and to the need to promote uniformity and predictability in its application.

2. Questions concerning matters governed by this Convention which are not expressly settled in it are to be settled in conformity with the general principles on which it is based or, in the absence of such principles, in conformity with the applicable law.

[...]

The difference between the two preambles could hardly be starker. Whereas the **19.08** CISG makes general statements on macro-economic and development policies and just briefly mentions the objective of achieving uniformity across legal systems, the Cape Town Convention ventures to educate readers and (potential) users of the instrument about the specificities of asset-based financing and the framework necessary to fully develop and protect these techniques at the universal level. With respect to instructions for legislators and judges aimed at achieving uniformity, Article 7 (1) of CISG and Article 5 (1) of the Cape Town Convention share the emphasis on the international character of the provisions and the need to promote uniformity. They seek to secure an autonomous interpretation free from preconceptions of domestic laws. However, the two provisions differ sharply as regards other guiding principles.[19]

Peter Schlechtriem, in Peter Schlechtriem and Ingeborg Schwenzer (eds), *Commentary on the UN Convention on the International Sale of Goods (CISG)* (2nd (English) edn, OUP, Oxford, 2005), Article 7, paras 5 et seq, 10 et seq, 19 et seq

1. Principles of interpretation (paragraph 1)

[...] The reference to the international character of the CISG indicates that the character of its rules must be borne in mind when applying any method of interpretation. It embodies the principle of autonomous interpretation. Unlike domestic legislation, which is adopted in the context of a uniform legal system, usually on the basis of the legislature's clearly recognizable intention and drafting using terms for which standard definitions already exist, the CISG arose out of negotiations between many states which—whether expressly or implicitly—pursued various ideas and aspirations, formulated their proposals on the basis of different legal systems and mostly in a language foreign to them, and made compromises—not as a rule evident from the documents—in order to achieve what they regarded as the minimum required by their particular interests. A convention created in such circumstances must be interpreted with great caution. That is all the more so in view of the fact that it exists in six official languages, all of which are equally authentic (cf. the Convention's signature clause), but are not always consistent in their terminology. ... It certainly excludes any recourse to the meaning of legal terms in the domestic laws of these six languages. ...

Article 7(1) also excludes recourse to methodological theories of interpretation of domestic texts. However, it is not possible to deduce from Article 7 that the CISG should be interpreted in conformity with principles of interpretation of public international law. Those principles are geared primarily to bilateral treaties and to establishing the obligations of states under them and they place too much emphasis on the intentions of the Contracting States. They are therefore not appropriate for the interpretation of civil law rules in Contracting States, where a greater degree of legal certainty is necessary than in international law. That does not preclude individual principles of interpretation under public international law—for example those regarding the interpretation of Conventions drawn up in several languages—also being applied to the CISG. In particular, they are applicable in the interpretation of Part IV of the Convention.

The requirement to promote uniformity is of particular importance in the interpretation of those provisions of the Convention, where the official languages use different terms, thereby inviting different understandings. Notorious examples are paragraphs 1 and 2 of Article 3, where the English and the French versions are inconsistent.[20] 'Promotion of uniformity' in the case of such divergences may require that the clear meaning of words of *one* language must be disregarded, even if draftsmen and representatives at UNCITRAL and at the Vienna conference have used and understood the relevant terms and words during the deliberations on a provision in the precise sense of this, their native language.

---

[19] See below para 19.11.

[20] The author refers to the words 'substantial' as opposed to '*essentielle*' and 'obligations' as opposed to '*obligation*'.

The maxim to have regard to the need to promote uniformity and the policy, advocated here, of taking careful account of decisions of foreign courts ... should not be misunderstood, however, as an exhortation to narrow down the meaning of 'open' terms, deliberately used by the drafters to accommodate the application to the inevitably varying circumstances of individual cases, by following the jurisprudence of another court concretizing such terms. What is reasonable or 'a reasonable period of time' can be determined only on the basis of the circumstances of the particular case. This determination, e.g. of a certain period of time for communicating a notice under Article 39(1), by a court in one case should not be followed as an authority in another case without good and additional reasons speaking for the same length of time. 'Uniform application' as commanded by Article 7(1) does not mean a levelling out of factual differences in the circumstances of particular cases, which must be carefully considered when applying such open terms as 'reasonable' ...

2. Methods of interpretation

Article 7(1) establishes the principle of autonomous interpretation of the Convention. ... This principle also applies to *methods* of interpreting the Convention. Although the CISG does not lay down the methods to be used for its interpretation, it follows from Article 7(2), which requires that interpretation must essentially be based on the Convention, that it is not possible to have recourse to domestic methods of interpretation for that purpose. However, since those systems have now gained experience in such methods, and in the light of the tendency to more objective interpretation even in international law, their methods of interpreting international uniform laws no longer fundamentally differ from each other. They may also help in interpreting the Convention, unless they conflict with the maxims of Article 7(1).

The first step is literal interpretation by having regard to the wording. Only if that does not produce an answer, should recourse be had to the purpose of the provision; when so doing, the *travaux préparatoires* must be used as a guide.

(a) **Literal interpretation**. Literal interpretation can use only the texts of the Convention in English, French, Russian, Arabic, Spanish and Chinese, although translations such as the one into German, prepared by experts on the CISG, may be consulted, too. In case of divergencies in the texts of the official languages, the maxim 'to promote uniformity in ... application' may require that *one* of the versions be neglected. ...

If there is a need to consult the original language versions, then as a rule it will have to be assumed that in the case of discrepancies between the various language versions the English text (and occasionally the French text) express the intention of the Conference better than the other versions. That is because the negotiations were essentially carried out in those languages and English was the language used by the drafting committee.

Legal concepts and principles of the CISG should not, as a rule, be interpreted primarily according to their meaning in the state whose language is used, but by reference to their function in the particular context in which they appear.

(b) *Travaux préparatoires*. Where it is necessary to fall back on the purpose of the CISG, because doubts ... cannot be resolved in any other manner, it is necessary to have regard to the *travaux préparatoires*. Unlike almost all other international conventions, materials on the CISG are extremely accessible. ...

(c) **Comparative law**. When interpreting and applying the Convention, comparative law can be of only limited use. Apart from the practical difficulties posed for courts if they are called upon to consider foreign laws (in theory, the laws of all, or almost all, of the

Contracting States), reliance on the interpretation of particular concepts or principles in other legal systems will, as a rule, not accord with the aim of the Convention. The CISG is a codification, in which terms borrowed from individual legal systems must primarily be interpreted with reference to the purpose of the Convention and the context in which they arise. The meaning of a term under domestic law can be claimed to be relevant only if the other negotiating parties could have recognized it as such during preliminary work on the Convention and intended it to have such a meaning; in such a case, the meaning will be apparent purely from the *travaux préparatoires*.

19.09 There are a few buzzwords that we use in private international law, comparative law and uniform law—as well as, more recently, in European law—as a kind of magic stick. 'Autonomous interpretation' is certainly one of them. There is a strong case to be made that 'un-autonomous', that is, domestically tainted, interpretation leads, immediately or over time, to the re-nationalisation of international uniform rules and that, conversely, autonomous interpretation promotes uniformity. However, experience teaches that 'autonomous' interpretation is not of and by itself a guarantee for achieving and maintaining uniform application of an international instrument. High courts of neighbouring Contracting States of the CISG belonging to the same legal tradition have been known to apply crucial concepts of the Convention not only slightly differently but reaching diametrically opposed results, both claiming in good faith to have conducted an autonomous interpretation of the relevant provisions. Since neither the CISG nor any of the other conventions that enunciate a rule on interpretation such as Article 7 offer any guidance or methodological assistance and since—for quite obvious reasons ('the law must not teach')—this will not change in the medium term, raising the level of consciousness of the difficulties involved is, for the time being, the only thing we can do.

Martin Gebauer, 'Uniform Law, General Principles and Autonomous Interpretation' (2000) V Unif L Rev 68

[...]

II.—UNIFORM APPLICATION AND UNIFORM INTERPRETATION OF UNIFORM LAW

[...]

2. What is autonomous interpretation ?

As mentioned above, an interpretation may be qualified as 'autonomous' if it does not proceed by reference to the meanings and particular concepts of a specific domestic law. However, this is a negative definition. ... The autonomous interpretation of uniform law can also be defined in a positive sense. The Convention's terms and concepts are to be interpreted in the context of the Convention itself. If they are to be regarded as independent terms and concepts, they must be interpreted by reference to the Convention's own system and objectives. Autonomous interpretation, in this sense, may be said to rest on systematic and teleological arguments. This does not mean that in interpreting uniform law other elements, such as literal or historical considerations, are less important, only that they do not constitute the autonomy of the interpretation. If a certain term or concept is well-known in domestic law, and the same term or concept is used in a Convention but with a different meaning, the difference in interpretation is not a literal argument, not a matter of different meanings of the words. If a Convention is drafted in more than one language, autonomous interpretation requires that the literal meaning in all authentic authentic versions is to be taken into account. But the imperative not to focus on one single language with its specific literal meaning does not follow from any literal argument, but is dictated by the need to give an independent interpretation to the Convention. Likewise, if the legislative history history of the uniform law favours a certain interpretative choice that differs from the solutions offered by domestic law, it is not that history that promotes autonomy of interpretation. It is merely an argument in favour of a certain choice of interpretation, not of an independent solution. Thus, autonomous interpretation is not a method of interpretation *in addition* to other methods such as literal, historical, teleological or systematic interpretation. Rather, it would seem to be a *principle* of interpretation that gives preference to a particular kind of teleological and systematic argument in interpreting a legal text.

3. The scope of autonomous interpretation in different Conventions

It is interesting to see how the autonomous interpretation of uniform law can, at least in theory, play different roles in different Conventions. ... [T]he first step [in applying Article 7(2) CISG] is always to seek a solution on the grounds of the Convention, even if there is a gap. Within the ambit of CISG, and in matters governed by the Convention, the domestic law should never be resorted to.... And even for the purpose of gap-filling, recourse to domestic law constitutes an *ultima ratio* ....

By contrast, the interpretation of the Brussels Convention[21] often requires recourse to concepts of national law. Sometimes these concepts are to be determined by virtue of the private international law rules of the forum, sometimes by the internal law of each Contracting State. Yet it is always the Convention that applies; the national law in these cases only serves to determine the concepts, the single terms used by the Convention. This would appear to indicate a difference in the legal structure of the Brussels and the Vienna Conventions. The Vienna Convention is always to be interpreted in favour of an autonomous solution. ... By contrast, national courts applying the Brussels Convention must approach the autonomous interpretation in two steps: (1) they must ask whether or not the concepts of the uniform law (according to the rulings of the European Court of Justice) must be determined by recourse to national law; (2) they must apply the conventional rule by using either the national or the autonomous concept, and establish whether the issue at hand is governed by the Convention. If it is true that autonomous interpretation is a principle of preference for a certain type of argument, then in applying the Brussels Convention this principle is directed in the first place to the Court of Justice ... In a great number of cases, however, the Court of Justice has been able to develop the Convention's autonomous concepts[22]. ....

---

[21] The predecessor of EC Regulation 44/2001. See ch 16.

[22] There follows a detailed discussion of the case law regarding the Brussels Convention's Article 5(1) where both the meaning of certain terms in domestic law (including applicable transnational commercial law) and autonomous interpretation co-exist. In particular, the ECJ's decision in Case C-288/92 *Custom Made Commercial Ltd v Stawa Metallbau GmbH* [1994] ECR-I-2913 which turned on different principles of interpretation and uniformity v. other policies of the Convention is referred to. See above, para 16.27.

4. Comparative law as an instrument of interpretation

Comparative law plays an important part in both autonomous and uniform interpretation. Uniform law without at least some degree of uniform application loses its uniform character, and uniform application of course requires comparative research. However, a distinction must be made between foreign court decisions (and scholarly writing) regarding the interpretation of uniform law on the one hand, and foreign solutions regarding domestic law on the other hand. Foreign court decisions on uniform law must indeed be taken into account. They can serve as arguments to help find the proper solution to an open interpretative question and, as input to the international debate, may also serve as persuasive authority. . . .

In order to give an autonomous interpretation to the Brussels Convention, the European Court of Justice has been known to refer to 'the general principles which stem from the corpus of the national legal systems.' Such comparative research using 'general principles' from the 'common core' of national legal systems would seem to be feasible in Conventions involving a limited number of Contracting States sharing a common legal, economic and cultural basis, such as the Member States of the European Community. . . .

5. Differences between uniform application and autonomous interpretation of uniform law

[...] [U]niformity of result is not the sole objective of interpreting uniform law, nor does it seem to be the supreme goal. The solution must be not just uniform, but right, and whether an interpretative solution seems right or wrong depends on its justification.[23] Interpretation is a matter of well-argued choice between different interpretative alternatives. If a certain interpretative solution and its inherent choice are convincingly argued, the solution appears to be the right one. When uniform law is interpreted autonomously, the justification of a certain interpretative result is based on arguments that consider both the (independent) purposes of the Convention and the need to find solutions acceptable to the other Contracting States. An interpretation that contrasts with the aims of autonomous interpretation, or cannot be justified in its interpretative choice for other reasons, is not convincing. Domestic and foreign decisions that are not convincing in substance cannot constitute a persuasive authority. The relevance of foreign precedents therefore depends on the quality of the decisions. . . .

The flexibility of uniform law is another argument against the binding character of foreign precedents. Many Conventions, especially world-wide ones covering many Contracting States, e.g. the Vienna Sales Convention, are most unlikely to be changed . . . within the next twenty to thirty years. Yet the law needs to be developed. If national courts were prevented from seeking better . . . solutions to a given problem, the application of uniform law would become even more rigid, so defeating its purpose. The interpretation of uniform law stands or falls by the exchange of different ideas in order to develop autonomous solutions.

III.—UNIFORM LAW AND GENERAL PRINCIPLES

1. Different concepts of legal principles

The concept of general principles, as commonly used with regard to uniform law, differs somewhat from the general discussion about principles in legal theory.[24] In legal theory,

---

[23] Sic. It is submitted that the author probably means 'the reasons given' for that solution.

[24] Here the author refers interestingly to a book on secured transactions, a subject matter dealt with in this volume in ch 10 and 12: Jan-Hendrik Röver, *Vergleichende Prinzipien dinglicher Sicherheiten*

the distinction between rules and principles has grown very important in recent decades. A modern approach is to regard this distinction as a matter of quality. Rules are to be either applied or not applied, *i.e.* they are applicable in an all-or-nothing fashion. If a rule is valid, to comply with this rule means doing exactly what the rule says. In case of conflict between two different rules ... the conflict can only be resolved by inserting an exception to one of the conflicting rules, or by declaring one of the conflicting rules invalid or inapplicable. By contrast, the requirements of a principle can be met by adopting a more nuanced approach. Principles require that something be done 'in as much as possible'. They can be weighed against other principles and ... they contain so-called 'commands to optimise' ...

General principles as they are commonly used in the context of uniform law cannot be qualified as principles in the sense just described. If we take the UNIDROIT Principles of International Commercial Contracts or the Principles of European Contract Law, we find that these 'principles'—if we apply the distinction described *supra*—do indeed contain rules, not only principles. Therefore principles in the present context must be understood in a broad, rather than a technical sense, as containing 'rules' and 'principles' as well.

2. Internal and external principles

For the purposes of uniform law and its (autonomous) interpretation, another distinction seems more appropriate in that it is sometimes suggested by the uniform law itself and because it is linked to the autonomy of interpretation and gap-filling. With regard to issues within the scope of uniform law, but not expressly settled by it, *i.e.* in case of a gap, both CISG and the UNIDROIT Principles require that these be settled, respectively

'*in conformity with the general principles on which it* [the CISG] *is based*,'

and

'*in accordance with their* [the UNIDROIT Principles'] *underlying general principles.*'

These 'underlying' principles on which the uniform law 'is based' may be called *internal principles* if they are ... connected with and taken from the uniform law in question, *i.e.* if the relevant arguments can be derived from the system and the *ratio* of the uniform law. *External principles*, by contrast, are requirements and arguments derived from outside the uniform law in question. ... To adopt 'the general principles which stem from the *corpus* of the national legal systems, *e.g.* from the domestic laws of all Contracting States of a Convention, is nothing but the employment of *external* principles, even if these principles are 'underlying' in the sense that they are based on a 'common core' in the different national legal systems.

External principles can also be taken from other uniform law instruments in order to interpret or supplement a Convention's rule. For example, some authors hold the UNIDROIT Principles to be a means of interpreting and supplementing CISG. Such recourse to the external codified rules of another uniform law instrument is a convincing choice where two Conventions can form a coherent body of rules, using the same concepts for similar purposes. ... However, caution is indicated when attempting to embody external concepts, since they should generally be understood in their own context. Also, at times identical words used in a neighbouring Convention turn out to be *faux amis*, conflicting with the aims and fundamental principles of a Convention if transferred to a different context. Many Conventions can be regarded as small legal systems, and to rely on external uniform

---

(C H Beck, Munich, 1999). In the present writers' view there is merit in further studying 'principles' of property law.

solutions may help avoid avoid recourse to national law. However, in case of a conflict between external and internal principles, the latter are to be preferred because they can be based on the system and aims of the uniform law in question.

[There follows a detailed discussion of problems of gap-filling including relevant case law regarding the impact of assignment on the place of performance under Article 571)(a) of the CISG]

7. Grading of arguments revised

[...] [T]his ranking of arguments in the context of uniform law must be understood in a logical rather than a hierarchical sense. The arguments were all 'autonomous' in that they focused on the uniform law and held aloof from specific domestic solutions. Even if the 'first step' to fill a gap is the application by analogy of specific provisions, and the second, recourse to the Convention's general principles, and even if an argument in favour of application by analogy is in sight, this does not mean that the argument in favour of analogy necessarily trumps all other arguments. Arguments 'lower down the scale' can be stronger in single cases. Likewise, the search for arguments should never be suspended just because one argument in favour of a certain solution has been found. In that regard, uniform law does not differ from domestic law. In one as in the other, the different methods of interpretation and gap-filling can be qualified as arguments. Linguistic, systematic, historical and teleological methods of interpretation are collective names for certain kinds of argument, and in general, one kind has no abstract priority over another. The different arguments need to be weighed and, as far as uniform law is concerned, weighed in an autonomous manner.

8. Autonomous interpretation and external principles

[The author now discusses possible conflicts between *internal* and *external* principles against the background of the above-mentioned decision on assignment under the CISG and its relevance for the application of Article 5(1) Brussels Convention—now Regulation EC 44/2001—on the one hand and, on the other hand, the latter's primary rule of jurisdiction *actor sequitur forum rei*, Article 2(1), cf chapter 16 above]

Recourse to external rules and concepts taken from another Convention in order to find a solution for an unsolved question is therefore to be handled with care, but it can be helpful in avoiding recourse to national law, thus promoting autonomous interpretation. In recent years, several State courts and arbitral tribunals have been using the UNIDROIT Principles as a means of interpreting international uniform law, mainly CISG. Some Conventions, such as the Brussels Convention and the Rome Convention,[25] are based on similar principles and form a coherent body of rules. Conventions connected in that way constitute a common legal system, and the autonomous interpretation may even require that allowance be made for the concepts and interpretation of the other. However, in case of conflict between internal principles, *i.e.* the aims and values of the Convention to be interpreted, on the one hand, and external principles on the other hand, autonomous interpretation and gap-filling may require that priority be given to the internal principles. As a consequence, recourse to external rules and principles is only acceptable if they can be shown not to contradict a teleological and systematic interpretation in question.

---

[25] The reference is to the 1980 Rome Convention on the Law Applicable to Contractual Obligations, cf. above, ch 2.

IV.—AUTONOMOUS INTERPRETATION AS A RULE OF PREFERENCE IN FAVOUR OF CERTAIN ARGUMENTS

What, then, is the relationship between autonomous interpretation and the traditional methods of interpretation? Each interpretation may be qualified as argumentation. The activity of interpretation yields an interpretative result and consists of a choice between interpretative alternatives. This choice can only be justified by arguments. The different methods of interpretation such as systematic, literal, historical and teleological interpretation, are merely collective names for certain kinds of argument. Each collective name stands for a wide range of different arguments. The use of comparative law, for example, as a means of interpretation, or the arguments based on the history of a legal problem or on precedents, can be qualified as systematic arguments.

Which role does the autonomous interpretation of uniform law play among the different methods of interpretation? Or, to put it the other way round: do the 'classical' methods of interpretation play any role despite the need to interpret uniform law in an 'autonomous' manner? Are these classical methods excluded when uniform law is to be interpreted? Or is autonomous interpretation merely an additional method amongst others?

The use of the different methods in practice, and the way in which judicial decisions are justified[26] differ considerably from country to country and from one legal culture to another. As a result, the use of domestic techniques and traditions for the purpose of interpreting uniform law is often rejected. Others favour recourse to the traditional '*canones*' of interpretation, but modified to suit the specific purposes of uniform law.

It is certainly true that the interpretation of uniform law by recourse to domestic traditions of argumentation is only acceptable if these interpretative traditions can be shown not to be contrary to the purposes of the uniform law, and that the interpretative result, the solution to the problem, could also be adopted by other legal systems not based on this particular domestic legal tradition. The *common law* tradition for example, which requires statutes to be interpreted restrictively because of their complementary function, cannot be applied in international uniform law. But this is a matter of scope, not of interpretation; it follows from the nature of the uniform law instrument. A Convention such as the CISG does not complement the domestic law, it replaces it. English courts know the difference, and England and other *common law* countries have changed their methods of interpreting uniform law Conventions and Community law over the past decades.

On the other hand, it will never be possible nor is it helpful completely to set aside the reasoning that is peculiar to a given legal culture. There is no reason to exclude any type of argument from the interpretation of uniform law in general. Autonomous interpretation does not require, for example, that certain interpretative methods, such as literal arguments or arguments connected with the legislative history, be avoided. Autonomous interpretation does not exclude arguments in general; rather, it sorts them out. By sorting out different methods of interpretation, autonomous interpretation itself seems to be based on systematic and teleological arguments, in which 'systematic' applies in both a negative and a positive sense. Negative, in that coherence with domestic law should not be a predominant aim of interpretation, and positive, in that accordance with the other rules of the uniform law and with its internal principles should be a predominant aim. Both the negative and the positive systematic aspects are linked to the teleological part of autonomous interpretation: only those arguments pass the test of autonomous interpretation that are

---

[26] See n 23.

in accordance with the aims and purposes of the uniform law and with the need to promote uniformity in its interpretation.

In sorting out other methods of interpretation, autonomous interpretation itself does not seem to be a method of interpretation. The *methods* (or '*canones*') of interpretation can be distinguished from the *rules* of legal interpretation and argumentation. These rules answer the question of how the different arguments are to be used and graded, whether or not priority is to be given to one argument over another. Autonomous interpretation can be qualified as a rule or principle of interpretation giving preference to certain interpretative results and rejecting others. There is no general rule of priority, *e.g.* of literal over systematic arguments. But there may be preference for one argument, for one interpretative choice over another in solving a problem of uniform law. And this preference is due to autonomous interpretation.

D. Uniformity Through Interpretation in a Uniform System?

19.10 The ever-increasing number of transnational commercial law conventions, the likelihood of their impacting concurrently on the same or connected transactions, and the desire either to prevent *ex ante* or at least to iron out *ex post* any conflicts among them have prompted scholars with particular experience in handling uniform law, such as Professors Ulrich Magnus and Franco Ferrari,[27] to explore ways of bringing some coherence into the interpretation and application of the various instruments. As we have seen in chapter 18, there are even calls for inter-conventional *interpretation* and a 'holistic' approach. This assumes (and the idea is very seductive indeed) that there is something like a 'common law of private law conventions'.

19.11 We would strike a note of caution in this respect. Generally speaking, there are only two things transnational commercial law instruments have in common: the instruction given to their users in provisions such as Article 7 of the CISG that regard is to be had to their internationality; and their authors' desire to resist the centrifugal forces of re-nationalization through interpretation under domestic law interpretative rules. It is true that the comparative approach to interpretation should certainly go beyond the analysis of case law and doctrinal writings on the domestic law of Contracting States and take into account other conventions. In applying, for example, the provisions on damages of the Convention on the Carriage of Goods by Road only the most advanced courts and commentators also look to the solutions in the Warsaw Convention on carriage by air.[28] And we would be unable to cite a case where a judge had considered whether the provisions on recoverable damages in the CISG might provide guidance as to what solution should be available under any of the conventions governing the carriage of goods. However, enlightened judicial analysis across all available uniform law

---

[27] See the list of recommended further reading, below.   [28] See chs 1 and 18.

material would come at the price of reduced legal certainty: parties A and B to wholesale contracts for the carriage of goods by any mode of transport can hardly be expected to foresee with which other uniform law instruments Justice X in a Federal District Court in Alabama or Justice Y in New Zealand were familiar and on which they might be inclined to rely in resolving potential disputes arising from those contracts. More specifically, recourse to the 'good faith' yardstick of Article 7 (1) of the CISG in the interpretation of the 2001 Cape Town Convention on International Interests in Mobile Equipment would be plainly against the clear will of that instrument's authors and the Diplomatic Conference that adopted it. The Cape Town Convention being a rule-based instrument—as opposed to standards-based conventions such as the CISG and many other transnational commercial law instruments[29]—its authors deliberately rejected the notion of inserting a provision such as Article 7 (1) of the CISG into the text. Instead, Article 5 (1) Cape Town Convention insists on predictability as the paramount objective and the purpose as set forth in the preamble, that is, fostering the principles underlying asset-based financing and promoting party autonomy. In other words, interpreting the Cape Town Convention in deference to principles established for more general commercial law texts would resemble the attempt to make one step in a line of mathematical reasoning by referring to social-policy dogmata.

19.12 Looked at in the broader perspective, in the background of the discussion of the potential of inter-conventional interpretation there seems to be lingering support by some commentators in favour of the idea of a 'Global Uniform Commercial Code'.[30] As indicated previously and elsewhere, in the opinion of the present writers the materialization of this idea, while firing the imagination, is not yet on the horizon let alone just around the corner.

E. Reservations and Declarations

19.13 Many, if not all, transnational commercial law instruments provide for a wide range of reservations or declarations that limit or otherwise specify the scope of application of the convention or allow in other ways that a State wishing to become a party to the treaty tailors some detail to its specific real or perceived needs.

---

[29] See also chs 12, 13 and 18 above.

[30] See Note by the Secretariat of the International Institute for the Unification of Private Law (UNIDROIT), 'Progressive codification of the law of international trade', (1968–70) I UNCITRAL Ybk 285; Gerold Herrmann, The Role of UNCITRAL, in Ian F Fletcher, Loukas Mistelis and Marise Cremona (eds), *Foundations and Perspectives of International Trade Law* (London, 2001), 28; Ole Lando, 'A Global Commercial Global Code' (2004) 50 Recht der internationalen Wirtschaft, 2004, 161; Michael J Bonell, 'Do We Need a Global Commercial Code', (2000) 5 Unif L Rev 469. Sceptical is H Kronke, 'The UN Sales Convention, the UNIDROIT Contract Principles and the Way Beyond', 25 JL & Comm 451 (2005–6).

Prominent examples are the reservations provided for in Articles 92 to 96 of the CISG, in particular Articles 94 (1) and 95,[31] and Article I (3) of the 1985 New York Convention on the Recognition and Enforcement of Foreign Arbitral Awards.[32]

19.14   In general, reservations—governed by Articles 19 to 23 of the 1969 Vienna Convention on the Law of Treaties—are unilateral; however, a reservation declared by one Contracting State may also be accepted by another Contracting State. Because of their unilateral nature *reservations* are in many cases the source of de-unification or, more precisely, the reason why a treaty never even achieves uniformity in not-insignificant areas of the law it was intended to cover. Conversely, the 2001 Cape Town Convention on International Interests in Mobile Equipment and the 2002 Hague Securities Convention are examples of a new approach to the use of *declarations*. Where the diversity of the factual situations or the legal landscape prior to unification and the policies underlying them are such as to suggest that the only (and more likely) alternative to full-scale unification is no unification at all, but where unification in core areas appears nonetheless desirable and achievable at the price of leaving certain other policy-sensitive areas untouched, a Convention may well respond to those differing policies by providing some flexibility through a system of declarations, a system used extensively in the Cape Town Convention and Aircraft Protocol. This is particularly easy to accept where all potential parties to a transaction affected by any such declaration can access the relevant information in real time, as is the case under the Cape Town Convention by way of the international registry.

F. Structural Issues and Technical Support Devices for Achieving and Maintaining Uniformity

19.15   As we have seen, the Vienna Convention on the Law of Treaties[33] is not only useful but necessary to ascertain the scope and the meaning of a Contracting State's undertakings vis-à-vis other States parties to a commercial law treaty. The various arms of a Contracting State's government are bound by those undertakings. However, problems may obviously arise due to the simple fact that, more often than not, it is not the executive arm itself but the courts that interpret and apply the convention and that this happens in many cases unbeknown to the government. As far as commercial law treaties are concerned, this is the rule. And even in cases where the government is aware of a court's imminent ruling, with the potential not only to imperil international harmony but to breach the State's obligations under public international law, only some legal systems are equipped

---

[31] As to the background and the effects, see ch 7.   [32] See ch 17.
[33] See para 19.05, above; for more details, see ch 3.

with devices that allow the government to intervene in the proceedings, for example as *amicus curiae*.

Much has been written about the desirability of establishing an international tribunal tasked with the interpretation of uniform law and thereby reaching and maintaining uniformity. The European Court of Justice, which has as one of its primary functions the interpretation of Community law, is obviously the model. At the present time there is no such tribunal or other adjudicatory body that would lend itself to maintaining uniformity in the application of worldwide transnational commercial law.[34] Not many remember that the drafters of the 1956 Convention on the Contract for the International Carriage of Goods by Road (CMR) actually provided for the possibility of having the International Court of Justice rule on disputes between Contracting States regarding the interpretation or application of the Convention.[35] Yet this Article was not used once in fifty years of the Convention's (on the whole, successful) history although there were and there still are serious divergences with respect to the interpretation of some provisions. States are not prepared to elevate disputes between private parties to the level of State disputes. There may, however, be alternative routes and future developments.   **19.16**

Indeed, investing international tribunals with jurisdiction over matters regarding the interpretation of private law treaties is not excluded in principle. It has, for example, been suggested that the International Tribunal for the Law of the Sea or the WTO dispute resolution panels should be involved to a greater extent in the resolution of disputes rooted in private law instruments. However, as long as there is no guarantee that such private disputes can reach those tribunals or other bodies[36] and as long as their decisions are not binding, no structural progress towards reliable safeguards for uniformity can be made.   **19.17**

Other tools increasingly available to those involved in interpreting uniform law instruments are the *travaux préparatoires*, including the explanatory reports, official commentaries, etc., of the sponsoring organizations.[37] Acts and proceedings of committees of governmental experts and of diplomatic Conferences, in former times not always readily accessible, are now usually available on the web sites of the sponsoring organizations or are on sale.   **19.18**

International law reporting services, specialized in reporting on the application of uniform law instruments and equivalent to well-established, perfectly run and more or less complete national law reporting systems, are not yet in sight. However,   **19.19**

---

[34] For an interesting hypothesis as to the ECJ's potential as a global judicial service provider, see the last paragraph of the article by Professor Basedow, quoted in ch 6 above.   [35] Art 47.

[36] Either because private parties are given standing to appear before them or because national courts are, in defined circumstances, obliged to refer a case to them.

[37] See, for example, the Official Commentary on the Cape Town Convention, cited in ch 12, and the Explanatory Report of the Hague Securities Convention, cited in ch 13.

there are more than promising beginnings, in particular as regards case law and bibliographical data on the CISG and the UNIDROIT Principles of International Commercial Contracts.[38] Other specialized databases are being created,[39] although their intrinsic technical quality is not matched by the resources that are at the sponsors' disposal, so that the volume of case law and bibliography already processed and available is—and probably will remain—limited.

19.20 Another of the 'general problems' of uniform law which has attracted almost as much attention in academic discussion as the threat of de-unification is 'fossilization' of (possibly still young and developing areas of) commercial law through putting in place hard law conventions. A remedy frequently cited and hoped for in this connection is the inclusion of review clauses and review conferences tasked with keeping a convention in tune with new economic or technical developments of the branch of commerce or finance concerned. Arguably the most advanced provisions in this respect are Article 61 of the 2001 Cape Town Convention and Article XXXVI of the Aircraft Protocol. Under them, the depositary is required to prepare yearly reports as to the manner in which the convention regimen has operated in practice, and at the request of 25 per cent of the Contracting States review conferences must be convened to consider, among other things, the judicial interpretation given to and the application made of the terms of the Convention or Protocol, as the case may be,[40] as well as any amendments to the texts. UNCITRAL's current exploratory review of possible needs for a prudent up-date of the 1958 New York Convention on the recognition of foreign arbitral awards after half a century may also be mentioned in this context.

19.21 However, the present authors would wish to strike a note of caution regarding the likelihood of seeing the Cape Town solution generalized in the future. Firstly, in more general commercial law texts there is not going to be the kind of degree of innovation—including the international registry, the role of the Supervisory Authority, industry's active interest in promoting, testing and, if necessary, pushing for rapid amendment—found in the Cape Town Convention. Secondly, experience tells us that the adoption of a convention is not infrequently followed by a state of exhaustion of all involved. It is unrealistic to assume that the delegates or their successors in the ministries of Contracting States are exceedingly keen—and the governments willing to devote resources—to return to the negotiation room every few years. What status reports and, in exceptional cases, review conferences could usefully do is to collect, analyse and authoritatively bundle and present details of subsequent practice.[41]

---

[38] Unilex, Pace, Freiburg, CLOUT etc. See also para 7.44.

[39] For example, the Unilaw data base accessible at UNIDROIT's web site <www.unidroit.org> currently limited to case law and bibliographic material on the CMR.

[40] Convention, Art 61 (2)(b); Protocol, Art XXXVI (2)(b).

[41] See Vienna Convention on the Law of Treaties, Art 31(3)(b).

G. Contract Practice

There is a substantial volume of literature and even some empirical data[42] on the **19.22**
role played by contract practice, internationally used standard contract terms, 'soft
law instruments' such as the UNIDROIT Principles of International Commercial
Contracts, and the like, on the development of what many have now become used
to calling the *lex mercatoria*.[43] But there has so far been little evidence of how
transactional law 'in action' reacts to the entering into force of a convention that
in turn reflects and casts into 'hard' law pre-existing and highly standardized and
sophisticated contract practices. This may change, albeit, for the time being, only
with respect to a very discrete area, such as secured transactions for the acquisition
or lease of aircraft. Indeed, the Legal Advisory Panel of the Aviation Working
Group, the industry group advising UNIDROIT in the process of elaborating the
Cape Town Convention and the Aircraft Protocol,[44] has just published its analysis and recommendations[45] regarding the inter-relationship between the new
legal framework and contract practice. The Panel, on which a significant number
of the leading specialists in aircraft financing are represented, is planning to also
publish legal opinions drawn up for particular transactions actually or potentially
governed by the Cape Town instruments. It is submitted that these materials will
have a significant impact on the contracts and be the point of departure for any
subsequent interpretation and application of the instruments by the courts.

H. Do Divergences Matter?

Do divergences of interpretation really matter? And will we ever see the day when **19.23**
all courts from the North Cape to the Cape of Good Hope and from the Bering
Strait and Cape Horn to Hokkaido and Fiji will interpret the 1958 New York
Convention on recognition of foreign arbitral awards or the 1999 Montreal
Convention on carriage by air exactly the same way? The answer to the second
question is, obviously, no. Not even core pieces of domestic legislation in a large
European or American country with a great number of courts—possibly complicated by jurisdiction being vested both in federal and state or provincial courts
and exacerbated in systems without a *stare decisis* rule or some procedural requirement to similar effect—are interpreted in all details consistently by those courts.
We know that and we accept it. It would be odd, therefore, if we were to pretend
that consistency with respect to the interpretation of the words 'timely' or 'without

---

[42] Center for Transnational Law, *Transnational Law in Commercial Legal Practice*, Center for
Transnational Law (Quadis, Münster, 1999). [43] See chs 1 and 14, above.
[44] See ch 12.
[45] Legal Advisory Panel of the Aviation Working Group, *Contract Practices Under the Cape Town
Convention*, Cape Town Papers Series, vol 1 (Uniform Law Foundation, The Hague, 2004).

undue delay' in a convention can be reached across continents and regardless of what the local economic and social conditions and, consequently, people's priorities are.

19.24 What we should strive for, on the other hand, is enhanced sensitivity to the fact that there are fundamental divergences on what constitutes a fundamental breach of a sales contract[46] or which additional formalities are acceptable under Article IV of the 1958 New York Convention on the Recognition and Enforcement of Arbitral Awards. Divergences regarding such concepts that persist over time must be identified, analysed and publicized. Judicial independence—to name but one (and the noblest) reason for these—will make it difficult to deliver the message where it belongs and to make sure that mistakes are rectified. However, conducting the discussion and raising awareness is a worthwhile and potentially effective exercise in and by itself. As we should know and recognize by now, the harmonization of commercial law across legal families, cultural contexts and economic abysses is not so much about discrete actions as about long, winding and multilayered processes.

Questions

1. In applying Article 32 of the Vienna Convention on the Law of Treaties to a given problem of interpreting the 2001 Cape Town Convention on International Interests in Mobile Equipment, does it matter whether the *travaux préparatoires* are already public and accessible in all official languages, that they clearly and indisputably point to a definite legislative intention, that the Chairman explicitly indicated that he was summarizing the consensus reached or the view expressed by the majority of delegations? And what weight would a clear contradiction between one of the recitals of the Preamble on the one hand and the Chairman's correct summary of the hall's views on a given point have?

2. Contrary to Dr FA Mann's line of reasoning, Professor Peter Schlechtriem argues that principles of public international law should not govern the CISG (and, perhaps, other transnational commercial law instruments) because:
   (a) those were geared primarily to bilateral treaties between States;
   (b) they placed too much emphasis on the intention of the Contracting States;
   (c) a greater degree of legal certainty was needed in the interpretation of private law rules.

   Comment on each of these three arguments, if possible by including examples of other private law treaties.

---

[46] CISG Arts 25, 72.

3. When the Council Regulation 44/2001 of 22 December 2000 ('Brussels I Regulation') was still the 1968 Brussels Convention on Jurisdiction and the Recognition and Enforcement of Judgments in Civil and Commercial Matters, the European Court of Justice had ruled that the term 'contract' in Article 5(1) was to be construed in an 'autonomous' way, but that the 'place of performance' in the same provision had to be identified under the law governing the obligation in question.

    (a) What does 'autonomous' interpretation mean and which are the objectives it is meant to achieve?

    (b) In your view, what might be the reason for the European Court of Justice's deviating from its general preference for autonomous interpretation with respect to identifying the 'place of performance' of a contractual obligation?

4. Argentina and Brazil are Contracting States of both the 1958 New York Convention on the Recognition and Enforcement of Foreign Arbitral Awards and the 1979 Inter-American Convention on International Commercial Arbitration. Article V of the former and Article 5 of the latter closely resemble one another. Assume you are counsel of Argentine company A who has obtained an award in its favour against Brazilian company B, the recognition of which is being challenged in Brazil under Article 5(1)(b) of the Inter-American Convention. Case law in the Americas on that provision and Article V is not conclusive as regards your precise factual scenario. European cases interpreting Article V of the New York Convention are, and tend to be, supporting your position. Decisions of the European Community Justice interpreting Article 34 of No 2 Council Regulation (EC) No 44/2201 do as well.

    (a) What would be your line of reasoning in the Brazilian court to obtain recognition of the award?

    (b) What might your opponent's counter-arguments be?

5. In one of the quoted texts reference was made to the possibility, advocated by some authoritative writers, to use the UNIDROIT Principles of International Commercial Contracts as a means to interpret the CISG where the latter is silent.

    (a) What are the arguments one may make, in general, in favour and against this proposition?

    (b) More specifically, which questions would you ask and how would you view the relationship between Article 78 of the CISG and Article 7.4.9 of the UPICC bearing in mind that '[t]he rule eventually adopted in Article 78 CISG represents a compromise which bridged irreconcilable differences of opinion in order to prevent the failure of the Conference. There were incompatible basic approaches to the question of interest, based not only on different economic and political approaches but also on philosophical, and even religious views, eg the prohibition of interest in Muslim States.'[47]

6. The Cape Town Convention provides for different types of declaration: opt-in declarations, opt-out declarations, mandatory declarations and other declarations. As regards the creditor's remedies in the case of the debtor's default (Articles 8–15), Article 54(2) provide that a Contracting State *shall* make a declaration whether remedies which under the Convention would be available without leave of the court are to be exercisable only with leave of the court or whether on the other hand such remedies may be exercised without such leave. Discuss the possible background, the reasons why a declaration was provided for and why a declaration on this specific point may be mandatory—in fact the only mandatory one as regards the substance of the Convention.

Further reading

Bariatti, Stefania, *L'interpretazione delle convenzioni internazionali di diritto uniforme* (CEDAM, Padua, 1986)

Basedow, Jürgen, 'Das Konventionsrecht und das Völkerrecht der Staatsverträge' in Leible, Stefan, and Ruffert, Matthias (eds), *Völkerrecht und IPR* (Jenaer Wissenschaftliche Verlagsgesellschaft, Jena, 2006) 153

de Ly, Filip, 'Uniform Interpretation: What is being done? Official Efforts' in Ferrari, Franco (ed), *The 1980 Sales Law: old issues revisited in the light of recent experiences* (Giuffrè, Milan, 2003) 335

Diedrich, Frank, 'Maintaining Uniformity in International Uniform Law via Autonomous Interpretation: software contracts and the CISG' 8 Pace Intl L Rev 303 (1996)

Ferrari, Franco, 'I rapporti tra le convenzioni di diritto materiale uniforme e la necessità di un'interpretazione interconvenzionale' (2000) 3 Rivista di diritto internazionale privato e processuale 669

Ferrari, Franco, 'Gap-Filling and Interpretation of the CISG: overview of international case law' (2003) 2 Intl Bus LJ 221

Kropholler, Jan, *Internationales Einheitsrecht–Allgemeine Lehren* (Mohr Siebeck, Tübingen, 1975)

Magnus, Ulrich, 'Vereinheitlichung von Zivilrecht durch soft law: neuere Erfahrungen' in Basedow, Jürgen, Drobnig, Ulrich and others (eds), *Aufbruch nach Europa—75 Jahre Max-Planck-Institut für Privatrecht* (Mohr Siebeck, Tübingen, 2001) 571

---

[47] Klaus Bacher, in Peter Schlechtriem and Ingeborg Schwenzer (eds), *Commentary on the UN Convention on the International Sale of Goods(CISG)* (2nd (English) edn, OUP, Oxford, 2005) Art 78, para 2.

Sundberg, Jacob WF, 'A Uniform Interpretation of Uniform Law' (1966) 10 Scandanavian Studies in Law 219

Torsello, Marco, *Common Features of Uniform Commercial Law Conventions: a comparative study beyond the 1980 Uniform Sales Law* (Sellier European Law Publishers, Munich, 2004)

Trompenaars, BWM, *Pluriforme unificatie en uniforme interpretatie: in het bijzonder de bijdrage van UNCITRAL aan de internationale unificatie van het privatrecht* (Kluwer, Deventer, 1989)

20

GETTING TO YES: PRACTICAL AND POLITICAL PROBLEMS OF HARMONIZATION

A. Introduction	20.01
B. Organizational Issues	20.04
C. Cultural and Economic Issues	20.18
D. Post-Adoption Stage: Imperatives and Shortcomings	20.21

A. Introduction

Why is it that the treaty collections are littered with conventions that have never **20.01** come into force for want of the required number of ratifications, or have been eschewed by major trading states or targeted developing and law reform countries? As a matter of fact, even if one includes all types of instrument other than regional and supra-national ones, there are scarcely more than nine real, continuing and documented success stories capable of being monitored and not embroiled in constant or periodical divergences regarding their interpretation and application. These are: the Warsaw/Montreal Convention on carriage by air, the CMR on carriage by road, the COTIF on carriage by rail, the New York Convention on arbitral awards, the UNCITRAL Model Law on arbitration, the UNCITRAL Arbitration Rules, the CISG, the UNIDROIT Principles of International Commercial Contracts, the Incoterms and the UCP. A few more, such as the Cape Town Convention and the Hague Securities Convention stand a fair chance to enter transnational commercial law's hall of fame. It should be noted that model laws, legislative or best practice guides, international restatements and even conventions *may* actually have been more influential than we think in that they have served as material influencing domestic legislation even if not explicitly mentioned in it. More generally, it has been said that the framework provided by the international organizations in charge of the harmonization process and, indeed,

729

that very process—in which governments, industry, scholars and legal practitioners come together to discuss problems and conceivable solutions—are arguably at least as productive in inducing law reform and global spread of ideas as finalized and officially adopted texts of transnational commercial law.

20.02 Still, the question why there are so few undisputable success stories is a pertinent one, particularly for those who make proposals for new items to be taken onto the work programmes of the private-law formulating agencies and those who participate in preparing new instruments and administer the process of getting to yes.

20.03 Some of the issues raised and the explanations and remedies offered have been mentioned or alluded to throughout the preceding chapters. What follows is partly a summary and partly an attempt to present them in a more complete, analytical and systematic fashion.

B. Organizational Issues

20.04 The *choice of subject* is the first step in the elaboration process.[1] It is the step where in the past most mistakes have been made and where in all likelihood mistakes will be made in the future. The most obvious one is to tackle problems which the commercial circles involved do not see at all or which are not felt to be really serious. Like all socio-systems, such circles tend to be conservative and to prefer doing things the way they have always been done. 'The shipping industry has its own time-honoured security interests', 'the commodity trade is different', 'the City doesn't like it'—are frequently heard lines and they weigh as heavily as if they were logical arguments. New rules are perceived as disruptive. Adapting the legal structure of a transaction or the organization of a process costs money. Uncertain support from immediately interested quarters should in any event be interpreted by law makers as an orange, if not a red, traffic light. If the result envisaged by the sponsoring governments or organisation is not clearly a win-win situation for both parties to the targeted type of transaction (seller/buyer, carrier/shipper, bank/client, creditor/debtor) and linked transactions (sale/carriage of goods/ insurance/finance), the intensity of the counter-lobby is likely to be significant and the chances of sufficiently wide acceptance of the future instrument recede. Theoreticians, in particular scholars advocating rigorous economic analysis of the *status quo* as well as of conceivable alternatives and improvements in a given field, tend to point to potential gains in terms of greater efficiency of a different rule or an altogether different approach. However, there are usually those who profit from inefficiencies and who will obviously lobby for maintaining the legal environment that generates them and thereby their individual gain at the expense of the collective interest.

---

[1] See ch 6 above.

The *definition of the scope*—in the sense of the substantive, personal, territorial,   **20.05**
etc. field of application—is another source both of difficulties and of opportunities. Looking back over the decades, some adopted instruments and many unfin-
ished projects were either too broadly or too narrowly tailored—more often too
broadly because the ambition of influential government officials or scholars assisting them in the process was excessive or, maybe worse, the subject matter, existing
legal solutions and/or the underlying economics or business concepts, were
poorly understood. In the 1980s and 1990s, for example, a major problem was
that the vast majority of scholars and other experts serving on committees and
governmental delegations, as well as comparatists in general, were experts in the
law of contract with little or no understanding of property law, insolvency, tax law,
or regulatory law affecting those industries for whose bilateral transactional arrangements they sought to provide a new or reformed uniform law. Against that background it happened that, triggered by the success of a new business model[2] in one
country, the United States, a great deal of work and many years were invested in
seeking to bring that success to other parts of the world but were based on the
erroneous analysis that what was involved was essentially the harmonization of
contract law, whereas a closer look would have revealed that in country A the
issues were at bottom issues of intellectual property law, in country B of tax law, in
country C of labour law, in country D of competition law, etc.

Coming back to the pitfall of over-ambition, a good example is the work on a   **20.06**
model law on secured transactions carried out in the 1990s by UNIDROIT. While
it was quite logical to place the—arguably too narrowly framed—1988 Ottawa
Convention on financial leasing in its broader economic context, the time was not
yet ripe for tackling entire 'problem areas' rather than specific types of contract.
Even in countries where financial leasing was advancing quickly, such as Germany,[3]
Italy, France or the Netherlands, courts and legal writers were far from agreeing that
it was, functionally speaking, a secured transaction rather than a simple contract
for hire. Moreover, as was pointed out in previous chapters, property was, on the
whole, still considered a no-go area for the purposes of uniform law.

It was therefore, historically speaking, good fortune that the aviation industry per-   **20.07**
suaded governments and UNIDROIT's governing bodies that it needed an instrument governing secured transactions for the acquisition of aircraft as a matter of
the highest urgency. Work on the model law was suspended and work on a discrete
area, secured transactions for the acquisition of high value, highly mobile equipment, got under way. The chances to make a compelling case for innovative—and

---

[2] For example, franchising. See ch 8 above.
[3] See the acts and proceedings of a symposium aimed at bridging the gap between judges of the
Supreme Court and regional courts of appeal, financial institutions, accountants, commercial
lawyers and tax lawyers with ten contributions, in Archiv für die civilistische Praxis 190 (1990)
204–476.

from the point of view of many legal systems, revolutionary—solutions were good, not least because the universally employed conflict-of-laws rule which pointed to the *lex rei sitae*[4] as the law governing rights *in rem* in assets that continually changed their location was generally agreed to produce utterly unsatisfactory results. The adoption of the 2001 Cape Town Convention in International Interests in Mobile Equipment and its success justified suspension of the work on the wider ranging but at the time unrealistic model law. Today, the situation is different and UNCITRAL will shortly be able to publish if not a model law at least a legislative guide on secured transactions[5] as an educational instrument for legislators, including reasoned recommendations regarding approaches and objectives in this subject-matter area. While there is probably agreement that an instrument with a too broadly tailored scope of application is doomed, things may become even more complicated where negotiating governments and industry clearly disagree as to what kind of scope is (still) feasible and acceptable or, on the contrary, needed as a *condicio sine qua non* for a commercially viable instrument.

20.08   Again, the drafting history of the Cape Town Convention offers a good example. The relevant provisions of the preliminary draft Space Protocol[6] were becoming ever more comprehensive with a view to covering as many assets as possible connected with a satellite subject of the security interest: not merely launch vehicles, transponders, space stations, and the like, but all components of satellites, whether in space or pre-launch. At the time of writing, efforts are being made to reduce the potentially indeterminate number of objects capable of becoming the subject of a registered international interest with a view to avoiding a proliferation of interests in components that cannot sensibly be dealt with separately from the satellite of which they form part. Negotiating governments are also anxious to avoid certain problems such as potential conflicts between the interests of the secured party (manufacturer or financier) and those of government departments using transponder capacity for purposes of communication, navigation, intelligence etc. and demanding, therefore, 'public service exemptions' which would preclude exercise of default remedies by the financier in the event in case of the default of the satellite operator or other debtor. Put quite candidly, what should be done if governments (who negotiate, adopt, and ratify the treaty—or do not!) were eventually to decide to limit the scope of application to the point that the instrument would become worthless in the eyes of industry?

20.09   This brings us to the next ingredient in the process of preparation of an international instrument, one which is not a sufficient but is a necessary condition for

---

[4] See chs 2, 12 and 18.   [5] Document A/CN.9/611/Add 3.

[6] *Convention on International Interests in Mobile Equipment: Preliminary Draft Protocol on Matters Specific to Space Assets*, UNIDROIT 2004, Study LXXIIJ—Doc 13 rev, Rome, February 2004.

the development of successful transnational commercial law instruments: not just the formal but real and deep *involvement of interested business sectors* at the formative stage.[7] There were times—and apparently this still happens in certain intergovernmental organisations—when industry associations were invited to attend the last stage of the intergovernmental negotiations as observers. They took the floor only after the least interested and expert governmental delegation had had the opportunity to paint a detailed and colourful picture of the most exotic domestic situation, and they were not entitled to submit proposals or to be represented on policy shaping bodies or drafting committees. Once the new instrument, designed by government officials (and, in best case scenarios, scholars specializing in the particular field) had been adopted, they were presented with it and asked to take it home and to spread the word among their member businesses: take it or leave it. No wonder that in many instances they chose the latter. Conversely, the most recent and—hopefully—successful instruments are the products of processes where governments and the formulating agencies had approached or been approached by industry, had taken advice flowing from experience in the operational aspects of the commercial transaction in question, listened to industry's concerns, and had found the facts and identified the problems before embarking on detailed drafting.

Who should do what, and how? In other words, which project should be put on **20.10** which organization's work programme so as to give all involved and all interested in a positive result within an acceptable time frame the confidence that the time and the human and other resources to be invested are a good investment? First of all, commercial law-making should be handled by organizations whose institutional mission and expertise are focused on private law. Self-evident as this may seem, it is not always practised. The conventions on the carriage of goods, except for more recent ones on carriage by sea, for example, are negotiated in the framework of organizations whose expertise lies predominantly in the regulatory aspects of those modes of transport: trans-frontier integration of systems and their supervision, technical aspects, safety, navigation, permits and licenses, tariffs, and the like. This does not mean that such organizations have no role to play in private law-making. On the contrary, their involvement may be essential, as in the case of the Cape Town Convention as it affects aircraft objects, where the International Civil Aviation Organization, essentially concerned with the public law regulation of the aviation industry, was nevertheless the only organization which, by virtue of its almost universal membership, was in a position to guarantee universal participation and acceptance. But it is organizations versed in private law—in the case of the Cape Town Convention, UNIDROIT—and the private law experts on whom they are able to call who have to assume the primary responsibility for organization of the project and preparation of the text.

---

[7] See also ch 6.

20.11 Apart from such cases, some decisions and choices are easy to make. It is obvious that a pure conflict-of-laws instrument should be elaborated by the Hague Conference on Private International Law, the specialist body set up to promote uniform conflict-of-laws rules.[8] It is equally obvious that an instrument that is primarily of regional interest should be elaborated within the institutional framework of a regional organization if the region in question has an organization whose statutory remit covers that type of work. As far as the more general question whether, in case regional and universal reform efforts are needed and need to be co-ordinated, the regional process or the worldwide process should take the lead, it is now safe to say that there is no schematic and mechanical answer. The answer will have to be given case by case in function of the operational specificities of the branch of commerce or finance that is to benefit from the future instrument as well as the state of the law in place and the objectives of the reform effort. Projects involving the harmonization of commercial *practice* and the preparation of uniform rules to that end which are effectuated by incorporation into contracts are the province of international non-governmental bodies, of which the most prominent is the International Chamber of Commerce.[9]

20.12 With respect to the division of labour among the principal private law formulating agencies that are active at the worldwide level, UNIDROIT and UNCITRAL, co-ordination is not only desirable but actively pursued. Some criteria are recorded in the article by José Angelo Estrella Faria, Senior Legal Officer at UNCITRAL, quoted in chapter 5 above. He mentions the relatively loosely knit regulation of procedure at UNIDROIT. In principle, an instrument aimed at the specific needs of a great number of African countries under UNIDROIT rules could be discussed among those target countries, industry and guided by a few expert scholars or practitioners and with relatively little involvement on the part of Europe, the Americas and the developed Asian economic powers. Generally speaking, UNCITRAL, a commission of the UN General Assembly, is the right choice where universal acceptance is essential: the CISG and the Model Law on Arbitration are the examples illustrating this thesis. On the other hand, UNIDROIT would currently appear the ideal institutional framework to elaborate instruments based solely on commercial considerations and not in need of universal acceptability. Both the Cape Town Convention and the draft Convention on intermediated securities fall into this category.

20.13 The organizations and their secretariats are merely, or mainly, administrators of processes where the participating governments (or in the case of the International Chamber of Commerce, banking and business interests) are the real actors. What would be the ideal scenario as regards the situation backstage in the ministries and agencies of those governments? There would be a unit in the relevant ministry

---

[8] See ch 5.   [9] For further details, see chs 5 and 6.

(mostly Justice, Trade and Industry, and/or Foreign Affairs) exclusively in charge of the particular government's involvement in transnational commercial law and conflict-of-laws projects undertaken by intergovernmental organizations. In the Member States of the European Union that unit ought to be connected with the unit where EU legislation on private law is handled. Secondly, greater continuity is desirable. It is by no means uncommon to see an official who has driven and co-ordinated his government's work on a highly technical project (for example, on custody, clearing and settlement of investment securities) leave his unit between the last session of the committee of governmental experts and the Diplomatic Conference for the adoption of the instrument to take over medical malpractice law just because three-year terms in any unit is the time-honoured rule in that department. On the other hand, gestation periods for projects should be shortened. Thirdly, a government official should enjoy the freedom to negotiate a *private* law convention as such, focusing on its technical and legal aspects and its potential for enhancing legal certainty or efficiency, rather than under instructions to defend, or expectations of defending, his or her own domestic solution as though it were a matter of national dignity and cultural identity.

With respect to the *working methods* employed—or, more to the point, the **20.14** re-definition of transnational commercial law's objectives—the importance of what is now commonly referred to as the 'commercial approach'[10] can hardly be overestimated. The idea is simple and revolutionary at the same time. The drafters concern is less the process of getting to yes than the result. The focus is on the meeting of legitimate commercial concerns and objectives. Thus the Cape Town Convention and Aircraft Protocol were driven by the need to provide a legal regime and institutional structure for aviation financing agreements that would enhance the legal security of transactions, prescribe effective interim and final default remedies and provide an international registration system to secure the perfection and priority of international interests. The overall objective was to make credit available, or to reduce the cost of credit, in countries where the inadequacy of the legal regime either deterred potential financiers from extending credit at all or led to high credit charges.

Where the commercially most viable solution originates is immaterial. Anything **20.15** in the process preparing a good landing is good. Anything taking the process astray is tolerable only within a certain margin. Compromise, however negotiated and crafted, is not a success but a failure if its effect is to undermine the utility of the project.

---

[10] Jeffrey Wool, 'Rethinking the notion of uniformity in the drafting of international commercial law: a preliminary proposal for the development of a policy-based unification model', (1997) II Unif L Rev 46; 'The case for a commercial orientation to the proposed UNIDROIT Convention as applied to aircraft equipment' (1999) IV Unif L Rev 289.

20.16 This commercial approach is, of course, designed primarily for instruments in the fields of private commercial and financial law. Outside these areas other factors may play a more dominant role, for example, consumer protection, safety and security of the public, the protection of State interests or cultural values.

20.17 As has been repeatedly pointed out, apart from notoriously under-funded and under-staffed secretariats in charge of structuring and administering the work process, the most visible and constant shortcomings in the harmonization process are insufficiently committed governments and short-term-oriented business interests. Governments which may have devoted significant resources to a project for an international convention all too often walk away from the convention after it has been concluded, while even sophisticated industries tend to shy away from investing in, say, asset-based finance rules for the financing of space assets or railway rolling stock as long as the demand for space assets is low and venture financing sufficient or as long as railway infrastructure is still viewed as a sector to be funded from tax revenues. Clearer time lines and shorter gestation periods would, in general, be capable of reducing the number of drop-outs and no-shows. On the other hand, governments, business and the general public must understand and accept that producing good law is fundamentally different from making sausages[11] or manufacturing computer chips. While it is true that between sessions of Committees of governmental experts the process not infrequently grinds to a halt, that time is not always lost. Efficient process management may either encourage inter-sessional work by a few enlightened leaders—a procedure with its own inherent risks—or, alternatively, organize visits by a core-group of trusted and didactically gifted intellectual leaders and practitioners to the slow, difficult, or recalcitrant participants to win them over on their home turf. Both approaches are currently being tried out.

C. Cultural and Economic Issues

20.18 Oliver Wendell Holmes, Jr once remarked that 'the life of the law has not been logic: it has been experience'.[12] In the same vein, one might say that an instrument of transnational commercial law results from an encounter of cultures rather than from a purely technical debate on a piece of domestic legislation in a chamber of parliament.

20.19 First of all, there is the issue of language. Even today, only a minority of delegates are capable of discussing effectively highly technical concepts and possible solutions in any language other than their mother tongue. Yet most have no choice as

---

[11] But they may have some things in common. The German Chancellor Otto von Bismarck (1815–98) famously remarked that 'laws are like sausages; it's better not to see them being made'.

[12] *The Common Law* (Little Brown, Boston, 1881) 1.

the working languages of the small agencies in our field are only English and French. In UNCITRAL meetings (though not in its drafting committees) delegates may also express themselves in the other UN languages—Arabic, Chinese, Russian and Spanish. Native speakers—and in particular bilinguals from the Canadian province of Quebec—obviously have a significant advantage over others and one has to make allowance for that. However, language is by no means only a source of difficulty, delays, discrimination and cost. It is also a medium for conveying legal concepts and their cultural underpinnings. It is generally accepted that drafts improve if the issues are contemporaneously discussed in more than one language. Only recently did intergovernmental organisations become aware of a quite different linguistic obstacle at the other end of the process, namely the fact that certain languages do not have any means at all to express modern commercial law concepts. For example, the Government of Indonesia advised that, for its parliament to ratify the Cape Town Convention on International Interests in Mobile Equipment legislators, not surprisingly, needed a text in Bahasa Indonesia, the country's official language. Local legal terminology, however, apparently did not evolve in this area after de-colonization, and the Dutch Civil Code of 1838 did not make provision for modern forms of secured transaction. Turkey and the Arab-speaking countries seem to be experiencing similar difficulties.

Finally, law is obviously a tool to strengthen a country's economic power and to **20.20** enhance its businesses' opportunities abroad. At the same time, it is an exceedingly effective vehicle for the transfer of a country's economic, cultural and social values and aspirations. Some governments are keenly aware of this and use the stage of international negotiations to make a sales pitch for their domestic solutions. Others are not. For some, the adjective 'aggressive' has a positive connotation, and they will approach the negotiation process accordingly; for others aggressiveness, or even assertiveness, is simply an expression of bad manners. Good heads of delegations and experienced conference officers know this, anticipate tensions and know how to deal with them so as to avoid a situation in which participants are offended and the negotiations suffer.

D. Post-Adoption Stage: Imperatives and Shortcomings

On this count probably all private law formulating agencies except the Hague **20.21** Conference on Private International Law are sinners and, like their masters the member States, behave irrationally. Relentless and focused post-adoption promotion would be normal given that the expenses of all delegations for years of negotiation taken together—and without even considering the overheads and budgets of the sponsoring agency—may reach significant amounts. Yet the resources put at their disposal in the annual budget for promotion of concluded international instruments are wholly inadequate.

20.22 Another area where a much greater effort is needed to guarantee a return on the investment of producing conventions is the inducement of political will and an effective legislative machinery. Suffice it, again, to look at the Cape Town Convention. While the economic benefits both for States whose companies tend to be security providers (debtors) and home States of manufacturers and financiers (creditors) are substantial, the supposed lack of parliamentary time and political bickering between certain governments on matters wholly unrelated to the Convention has denied a group of States the ability to ratify the Convention and enjoy its benefits.

Questions

1. Describe some of the problems confronting those involved in preparing the Space Protocol to the Cape Town Convention.
2. 'The problem of language is a serious obstacle to international law-making.' Discuss.
3. You are asked to recommend measures by which work leading to the conclusion of international commercial law instruments could be expedited and the quality of the instruments improved.
   Summarize your recommendations.
4. Why do many international conventions never come into force? And what steps can be taken to facilitate the adoption of an international convention?

Further reading

Estrella Faria, José Angelo, 'The Relationship Between Formulating Agencies in International Legal Harmonization: competition, cooperation, or peaceful coexistence?' 51 Loy L Rev 253 (2005)

Goode, Roy, 'International Restatements of Contract and English Contract Law' (1997) II Unif L Rev 231

Goode, Roy, 'Rule, Practice, and Pragmatism in Transnational Commercial Law' (2005) 54 ICLQ 539

Kronke, Herbert, 'Which Type of Activity for Which Organisation? Reflections on UNIDROIT's Triennial Work Programme 2006–2008 in its Context' (2006) XI Unif L Rev 135

Kronke, Herbert, 'The Takeover Directive and the "Commercial Approach" to Harmonization of Private Law' in Berger, Klaus Peter, Borges, Georg and others (eds), *Zivil und Wirtschaftsrecht in Europäischen und Globalen Kontext—Private and Commercial Law in a European and Global Context, Festschrift für Norbert Horn zum 70. Geburtstag* (De Gruyter Recht, Berlin, 2006) 445

Wool, Jeffrey, 'Economic Analysis and Harmonised Modernisation of Private Law' (2003) VIII Unif L Rev 389

INDEX

administration
centre of main interests 15.27 *see also* **centre of main interests (COMI)**
principal place of company's 2.42
adjudication 17.10
ADR *see* **alternative dispute resolution (ADR)**
agency *see also* **franchising, UNIDROIT Agency in the International Sale of Goods Convention 1983, UNIDROIT Principles of International Commercial Contracts**
agency costs 8.01
Commercial Agents Directive 8.03, 8.09–8.16
direct and indirect representation 8.28
external aspects of agency 8.03, 8.05
First Company Law Directive 8.06–8.08
German law 8.02
Hague Agency Convention 2.36, 2.53
harmonization 8.03
ICC Agency Model Contract 8.04
internal aspects of agency 8.03, 8.05
Principles of European Contract Law 8.05, 8.28
relationships 8.01
standard terms 8.04
UNIDROIT Agency Convention 1983 8.17–8.27
UNIDROIT Principles of International Commercial Contracts 8.03, 8.05, 8.28, 14.57
air transport *see also* **Aircraft Protocol to Cape Town Convention, Warsaw Convention on International Carriage by Air 1929**
EC law, liability regime in 6.45
Geneva Convention on the International Recognition of Rights in Aircraft 1948 2.39
International Air Transport Association (IATA) 6.03, 12.08
International Civil Aviation Organization (ICAO) 3.68, 5.17, 6.03, 12.08, 12.10, 12.37, 20.10
Aircraft Protocol to Cape Town Convention 10.28, 12.08, 12.11–12.19
Aircraft Protocol Group 12.13

Aviation Working Group 12.06–12.08, 12.13
choice of law 12.16, 12.25
commercial approach 20.14
conflict of laws 18.06
connecting factors 12.32
Consolidated Text 12.18
contract practice 19.22
declarations 12.51, 19.14
definitions 3.38, 12.24
de-registration 12.16, 12.36
diplomatic protection 12.34
entry into force 3.43
export 12.16, 12.36
immunities 3.67–3.68
insolvency 12.16
interim relief 3.66, 12.34
International Civil Aviation Organization (ICAO) 20.10
International Registry 12.37
jurisdiction 3.66
key features 12.16
outright sales 12.27
priority 12.47
registration 12.37, 12.40
remedies 12.16, 12.36
searches and search certificates 12.42
ALI/UNIDROIT Principles of Transnational Civil Procedure 16.62–16.65
access to information and evidence 16.65
commercial and non-commercial disputes, distinction between 16.62
discovery 16.65
jurisdiction 16.64
alternative dispute resolution (ADR)
awards 17.12
mediation or conciliation 17.12–17.13
United States 17.12
Amalfitan Tables 1.16
American Law Institute (ALI)
ALI/UNIDROIT Principles of Transnational Civil Procedure 16.62–16.65
restatements 1.58, 14.04
anti-suit injunctions 16.42
APEC (Asia Pacific Economic Cooperation) 5.17

741

applicable law *see also* **choice of law, conflict of laws**
  advance designation of , proposal for 15.10
  arbitration 17.110–17.113
  connecting factors 18.08
  fall-back rules 13.23
  Hague Securities Convention 2002
    13.19–13.25
  insolvency 15.10, 15.29–15.30
  Insolvency Regulation 15.29–15.30
  primary rules 13.22
arbitration *see* **ICC Arbitration Rules, international**
    commercial arbitration, conflict of laws
    and, international commercial
    arbitration, harmonization of,
    UNCITRAL Arbitration Rules,
    UNCITRAL Model Arbitration Law
Asia Pacific Economic Cooperation (APEC) 5.17
assignment *see* **Cape Town Convention on**
    International Interests in Mobile
    Equipment, UN Convention on
    Assignment of Receivables in
    International Trade, UNIDROIT
    International Factoring Convention
Association of South East Asian Nations (ASEAN)
    5.17
Austin, John 4.04
autonomous transnational commercial law
    1.29–1.30, 1.38–1.51, 1.64, 1.67, 2.03
autonomy *see* **autonomous transnational**
    commercial law, party autonomy
awards *see* **international commercial arbitration**
    awards

bailment 10.06
bank payment undertakings 9.01–9.58 *see also*
    Uniform Customs and Practices for
    Documentary Credits (UCP), Uniform
    Rules for Demand Guarantees (URDG)
    (ICC)
  bank, interests of 9.08
  beneficiaries, interests of 9.08
  bills of lading 9.02
  bonds 9.07, 9.54–9.58
  demand guarantees 9.05, 9.07–9.08, 9.11
  direct pay standby credits 9.06, 9.07
  fraud 9.10
  International Chamber of Commerce 9.09–9.11,
    9.54–9.58
  International Standby Practices (ISP98)
    9.46–9.50
  letters of credit *see also* **letters of credit**
    autonomy principle 9.11
    conformity 9.13
    contracts of sale as central contracts 9.13

    demand guarantees compared with 9.11
    rejection 9.13
  principal, interests of 9.08
  role of banks in financing international trade
    9.01–9.06
  rules of banking practice 9.09
  standby credits 9.08, 9.11, 9.46–9.54
  suretyship guarantees 9.07
  terminological problems 9.07
  UN Convention on Independent Guarantees and
    Standby Letters of Credit 1995 9.11,
    9.51–9.54
  Uniform Rules for Contract Bonds (ICC)
    9.54–9.58
Bartolus of Sassoferrato 2.15
Bentham, Jeremy 4.04
bills of exchange 1.15, 1.18
bills of lading 1.06, 9.02
Black Book of the Admiralty 1.16
bonds 9.07, 9.54–9.58
Brussels Convention on Jurisdiction and
    Enforcement of Judgments in Civil and
    Commercial Matters 1968
  Brussels I Regulation 16.07, 16.17, 16.24–16.29,
    16.60
  civil procedure 16.06, 16.07
  enforcement and recognition of foreign judgments
    16.60
  forum non conveniens 16.39–16.40
  interpretation by European Court of Justice
    16.24
  jurisdiction 16.17, 16.24–16.29
  service 16.17
Brussels I Regulation on jurisdiction and the
    recognition and enforcement of
    judgments in civil and commercial
    matters
  autonomous domestic rules of jurisdiction 16.24,
    16.33–16.35
  branch, agency or other establishments, disputes
    arising out of operation of 16.28
  Brussels Convention 1968 16.07, 16.24–16.29,
    16.60
  characterization 16.26–16.27
  civil procedure 16.07, 16.60
  contract, matters relating to a 16.25
  default judgments 16.60
  delivery, place of 16.25
  foreign judgments, enforcement and recognition
    of 16.60
  forum non conveniens 16.39–16.41
  forum selection clauses 16.29, 16.32–16.34
  groups of companies 16.28
  judgments, enforcement and recognition of 16.60

party autonomy 16.29
place of performance of obligation in question
    16.25, 16.27
prorogation 16.29
provisional and protective measures 16.45
recognition and enforcement of foreign
    judgments 16.60
settlements 16.60
Bustamante Code 5.06, 15.04

Caemarrer, Ernst von 1.11
Cape Town Convention on International Interests
    in Mobile Equipment 2001
    10.28–10.31, 12.01–12.52 *see also*
    Aircraft Protocol to Cape Town
    Convention, Luxembourg Protocol to
    Cape Town Convention
Assignment of Receivables in International Trade
    Convention 2001 (UN), priority over
    3.44
associated rights 11.04, 12.48
autonomy 12.35
Aviation Working Group 12.06, 12.17
breach of obligations by state 3.31
characterization or classification of causes of
    action 2.40
choice of law 12.25
conditional sales agreements 12.05, 12.29,
    12.33
conflict of laws 2.62, 3.16, 12.02, 18.07–18.09
connecting factors 2.40, 12.32, 18.08–18.09
Consolidated Text 12.18
consumer agreements, exclusion of 3.38
declarations 3.46, 12.35, 12.50–12.52, 19.14
default remedies 12.33–12.36
definitions 3.38, 12.24
developing countries 10.29
domestic law, relationship with 12.26
entry into force 3.42, 3.44
exclusions 12.05, 18.05
formalities 12.31
forum selection clauses 16.31–16.32
good faith 3.53
immunities 3.67–3.68
insolvency 12.07, 12.22, 12.49
interim relief 3.66, 12.34
International Air Transport Association (IATA)
    12.08
International Civil Aviation Organization (ICAO)
    3.68, 12.08, 12.10, 12.37
international interests, concept of 12.27–12.32,
    18.05
International Registry 3.43, 12.22, 12.37–12.45
internationality 12.27

interpretation 3.53, 3.56–3.57, 12.25, 19.11,
    19.20–19.21
jurisdiction 3.66, 12.45, 16.31–16.32
key features 12.14–12.16
leasing agreements 12.05
location of debtor 18.05
priority rules 11.15, 12.26, 12.31, 12.46–12.48
private party, enforcement by 3.65–3.68
privileges and immunities 3.67–3.68, 12.22
provisional and protective measures 16.45
Rail Protocol 12.09, 12.17
receivables financing 11.04
registration system 12.30–12.52
  asset-based 12.05
  assignment 12.40
  connecting factors 12.32
  document filing 12.37
  duration of 12.43
  electronic system 12.14, 12.39
  International Civil Aviation Organization
    (ICAO) 12.37
  International Registry 2.43, 12.22,
    12.37–12.45
  jurisdiction 12.45
  liability of registrar 12.44
  meaning of registration 12.37
  notice registration 12.37
  preparatory work 12.07
  priority 12.46–12.48
  prospective interests 12.40
  Registration Working Group 12.07
  search and search certificates 12.42
  Supervisory Authority 12.37
  what is registrable 12.40–12.41
remedies 12.33–12.36, 12.51
reservation of title 12.27, 12.30
search and search certificates 12.42
ships, exclusion of 12.05, 18.05
space protocol 12.08, 12.17, 20.08
sphere of application 12.21–12.26, 18.05
state responsibility 3.65–3.68
subrogation 12.48
Supervisory Authority 3.28, 3.67–3.68
  privileges and immunities 3.67–3.68
  provisional 3.43
two-instrument approach 12.17–12.20
underlying principles 12.12–12.13
centre of main interests (COMI) 15.09, 15.25,
    15.27–15.28, 15.31, 15.34
certificates, law of place of 13.08
characteristic performance 2.35, 18.08
characterization
  Brussels I Regulation 16.26–16.27
  Cape Town Convention 2001 2.40

characterization (*cont.*)

conflict of laws 2.45–2.46, 16.26, 16.28

contract 2.45, 16.26

governing law 2.45–2.46

Hague Securities Convention 2002
13.17–13.18

investors' rights 13.17

state immunity 16.10

substantive law, court's own 2.46

tort 2.45

choice of law 2.29, 2.32–2.34 *see also* **forum
selection clauses**

absent parties' choice 2.34

Aircraft Protocol to Cape Town Convention
12.16, 12.25

arbitration 17.110–17.114, 17.116, 17.118,
17.120–17.121

Cape Town Convention 2001 12.25

conflict of laws 2.13, 2.34, 17.110–17.112

connecting factors 2.23, 2.26–2.34, 2.37–2.38

consent as to choice 2.33

ICC Arbitration Rules 17.118–17.120

Inter-American Convention on International
Contracts 2.29, 2.32–2.33, 14.20–14.22,
14.24

lex mercatoria 1.40

party autonomy 2.13, 2.23, 2.26–2.30

Principles of European Contract Law 2.31,
14.20–14.27

property 2.37–2.38

restatements 2.19

Rome Convention 1980 2.28, 2.31, 2.33,
14.20–14.21

UNCITRAL Model Arbitration Law
17.113–17.114, 17.116, 17.118,
17.120–17.121

UNIDROIT Principles of International
Commercial Contracts 2.31,
14.20–14.27

United States 2.33, 16.30, 16.32

CISG *see* **UN Sales Convention (CISG)**

civil law 1.10–1.13 *see also* **civil law and common
law, comparison between**

classification of legal systems 4.07, 4.12–4.16

commercial codes 1.10–1.11

company law 1.12

definition 1.10

French Civil Code 1.10

French Commercial Code 1.10, 1.13

German Commercial Code 1.10, 1.13

good faith 14.45

harmonization 6.12

objective/subjective dichotomy 1.10, 1.13

receivables financing 11.03

UN Sales Convention (CISG) 7.105

Uniform Commercial Code (United States) 1.11

civil law and common law, comparison between
4.12–4.16

English language, importance of 4.16

exportability 4.13, 4.67

freedom of parties 4.15–4.16

French Civil Code 4.13

good faith 8.12, 14.45

interpretation of uniform laws 4.43

judicial decisions 4.14

specific performance 7.73, 7.105

UN Sales Convention (CISG) 7.105

UNIDROIT Agency Convention 8.18–8.19,
8.22

classification of legal systems

American law 4.09

civil law systems 4.07, 4.12–4.16

common law family 4.07–4.08, 4.12–4.16

comparative law 4.07–4.17

financial laws 4.10

French law 4.07–4.09

Germanic family 4.07–4.09

Hindu family 4.07

hybrid systems 4.07

Islamic family 4.07, 4.17

issue-based classification systems 4.11

legal style 4.07

limitations of classification 4.08

Romanist family 4.07–4.09

Scandinavian countries 4.07

socialist countries 4.07

South Africa 4.09

Clearstream 13.10, 13.34

CMI *see* **Comité Maritime International**

CMR Convention

co-existence with other conventions 18.12

conflict between conventions 18.12–18.13

interpretation 19.11, 19.16

Rome Convention 1980 18.13

sources of 18.12

codes

bills of exchange 1.15

commercial codes 1.10–1.11, 1.14

comparative law 4.67–4.68

customary law 1.60

early and medieval codes 1.15–1.19

economies in transition 1.14

European Civil Code project 1.58

European Contract Code, proposal for 4.38

French Civil Code 1.10, 4.13, 4.67, 16.14–16.16

French Commercial Code 1.10, 1.13

French New Code of Civil Procedure 17.73

German Commercial Code 1.10, 1.13

Global Uniform Commercial Code, proposal for
    19.12
harmonization 5.14
history of commercial law 1.15–1.19
nationalization of commercial law 1.24
proposal for an international code 1.26–1.27
Québec Civil Code 19.02
Uniform Commercial Code (United States) 1.11
uniformity 19.02
Collateral Directive 13.32–13.33
Comité Maritime International (CMI) 6.03
comity 2.16, 3.23
commentaries and reports 3.50, 7.24, 7.25
Commercial Agents Directive 8.03, 8.09–8.16
    commission 8.14, 8.16
    common law 8.09–8.10, 8.12
    compensation 8.14–8.16
    good faith 8.12
    indemnities 8.14–8.16
    interpretation 8.09
    principal/agent relationship 8.09–8.16
    remuneration 8.13–8.14, 8.16
    scope of application 8.11
    termination 8.14–8.15
commercial codes 1.10–1.11, 1.14
Commission on European Contract Law *see*
    Principles of European Contract Law
common law *see also* **civil law and common law,**
    comparison between
    agency 8.01–8.02
    classification of legal systems 4.07–4.08,
        4.12–4.16
    Commercial Agents Directive 8.09–8.10, 8.12
    comparative law 4.67
    dominant position in commercial law world 4.16
    exportability 4.67
    good faith 14.45
    receivables financing 11.03
    suppletive rules of 1.35
    UNIDROIT Principles of International
        Commercial Contracts 14.38, 14.40
company law 1.12
comparative law 4.01–4.74
    aims of 4.18–4.49
    classification of legal systems 4.07–4.17
    common solution or best solution approach
        4.54–4.55
    European Union 4.37–4.39
    functional approach 4.50–4.53, 4.59, 4.72
    harmonization 4.04, 4.33, 4.35, 4.47, 4.54, 4.56,
        4.72, 6.10–6.12
    history 4.04–4.06, 4.19
    International Academy of Comparative Law 4.06
    Islamic law 4.17

Israel 4.27
language 4.44–4.45, 4.62, 4.71
methodology 4.50–4.58
nature 4.01–4.03
practical uses 4.23–4.48, 4.72–4.74
Principles of European Contract Law
    (UNIDROIT) 4.33, 4.58
problems 4.59–4.64
restatements 4.33, 4.38
similarities and differences 4.63–4.64
sociological perspective 4.19
transplants and comparative law, legal 4.63–4.71,
    4.74
UNCITRAL 4.03
UNIDROIT 4.03, 4.33, 4.38
unification of international commercial law,
    proposal for 4.35–4.37
uniform laws 4.42–4.46, 4.72, 19.09, 19.11
university law schools 4.04
conciliation 9.58, 17.12
conditional sales agreements 12.05, 12.29, 12.33
conflict of laws 2.01–2.62, 18.06–18.07 *see also*
    connecting factors, conflict of laws and,
    international commercial arbitration,
    conflict of laws and, securities
    transactions, conflict of laws and
    Aircraft Protocol to Cape Town Convention
        2.13, 18.06
    arbitration 1.40, 17.30
    Assignment of Receivables in International Trade
        Convention 2001 2.62, 11.30,
        11.39–11.40
    Cape Town Convention 2001 2.62, 3.16, 12.02,
        18.07
    characterization 2.45–2.47, 16.27–16.28
    choice of law 2.13
    Collateral Directive 13.32–13.33
    comity 2.16
    connecting factor *see* **connecting factors, conflict**
        of laws
    contract 2.13, 2.23–2.36, 2.48–2.56, 14.09
    definition 2.01–2.03
    EC law 3.16, 3.18, 14.03
    foreign element, meaning of 2.02
    future need for conflict of laws 2.61–2.62
    Hague Securities Convention 2002 13.11–13.27,
        13.36, 18.07
    Hague Uniform Sales Laws 2.12, 2.61
    harmonization 5.01, 5.06, 14.01–14.03, 18.14,
        20.11
    ICC Arbitration Rules 17.51
    Insolvency Regulation 3.16
    jurisdiction 2.14
    lex mercatoria 1.40, 2.12, 2.61–2.62

conflict of laws (*cont.*)
  mandatory rules in the law of contracts
      2.51–2.56
  multilateralist rule 2.21, 2.22
  national rules 2.03
  nature of 2.01–2.06
  neo-statutist theory 2.57
  OHADA 18.17
  origins 2.03
  property 2.37–2.41
  public policy (*ordre public*) 2.48–2.50
  regionalism 18.14–18.18
  renvoi 2.58–2.60
  restatements 2.18–2.20
  role in international commercial law 2.07–2.13
  Rome Convention 1980 2.05
  rules versus approaches 2.15–2.21
  treaties 2.01, 2.12, 2.61–2.62, 3.72–3.73, 6.45,
      18.11–18.18
  UN Sales Convention (CISG) 2.12, 2.61, 7.12,
      7.19–7.29, 18.06, 18.14–18.16, 18.18
  UN Convention on Assignment of Receivables in
      International Trade 2001
  vested rights, enforcement of 2.18
  Warsaw Convention 1929 2.10–2.12, 2.62
connecting factors, conflict of laws and 2.22–2.44,
      18.08–18.10
  administration, place of 2.42
  agency 8.21
  Aircraft Protocol to Cape Town Convention
      12.32
  applicable law 18.08
  Assignment of Receivables in International Trade
      Convention 2001 18.10
  Cape Town Convention 2001 12.32,
      18.08–18.09
  characteristic performance 18.08
  companies 2.42, 18.08
    administration, place of 2.42
    EC law 2.42
    place of incorporation 2.42
  contract 2.23–2.36, 18.08
  domicile 2.22
  EC law 2.42
  factoring 2.42, 11.17
  financial leasing 10.13
  habitual residence 2.22
  incorporation, place of 18.08
  insolvency 2.43
  intellectual property 2.43
  jurisdiction 16.13, 16.17, 16.19
  labour law 2.43
  nationality 2.22
  neo-statutist theory 2.57

place of the wrong 2.22
property 2.37–2.41
securities transactions, conflict of laws and
      13.08–13.10
tort 2.22
UN Sales Convention 7.14–7.29, 18.09
UNCITRAL Assignment of Receivables in
      International Trade Convention
      2001 18.10
UNIDROIT Agency Convention 8.21
UNIDROIT International Factoring Convention
      2.42, 11.17
UNIDROIT International Financial Leasing
      Convention 1988 10.13
connecting factors, contract and
  absent parties' choice 2.34
  characteristic performance 2.35–2.36
  choice of law 2.23, 2.26–2.34
  conflict of laws 2.23–2.36
  consent as to choice 2.33
  domicile 2.34
  general principles of international commercial
      law 2.32
  Hague Agency Convention 1978 2.36
  Hague Securities Interests Convention 2002 2.30
  Inter-American Convention on the Law
      Applicable to International Contracts
      1994 2.29, 2.32–2.33
  interpretation 2.23–2.36
  nationality 2.34
  non-national body of rules of law, choice of 2.31
  objective connecting factors 2.34
  party autonomy 2.23, 2.26–2.30
  performance, mode of 2.23–2.36
  place of contract, law of 2.33
  Principles of European Contract Law 2.31
  Rome Convention 1980 2.28, 2.31, 2.33
  significant relationship with the transaction, law
      of the state with the most 2.34–2.35
  social function of contracts 2.35
  subjective connecting factors 2.34
  UNIDROIT Principles of International
      Commercial Contracts 2.31
  United States 2.33, 2.35
  validity 2.23–2.36
connecting factors, property and
  Cape Town Convention 2001 2.40
  choice of law 2.37–2.38
  conflict of laws 2.37–2.41
  Geneva Convention on the International
      Recognition of Rights in Aircraft 1948
      2.39
  goods in transit 2.38
  Hague Securities Interests Convention 2002 2.41

in rem rights or immovables 2.38
Maritime Liens and Mortgages Convention 1926
    2.39
movables 2.38–2.41
party autonomy 2.41
place where property is situated, law of 2.38
security interests 2.38–2.41
conservatory and interim measures 17.55 *see also*
        provisional and protective measures
Consulate of the Sea 1.16, 1.19
contract *see also* **Principles of European Contract**
        Law, UNIDROIT Principles of
        International Commercial Contracts,
        restatements of contract law
agency 8.04
arbitration 17.64
characterization 2.45, 16.26
conflict of laws 2.23–2.36, 2.51–2.56, 18.08
domestic commercial law, sources of 1.33
European Contract Code, proposal for 4.38
express terms 1.33
harmonization 14.01–14.03, 17.64
ICC Agency Model Contract 8.04
implied terms 1.33
Incoterms, incorporation into contracts of 1.56,
    7.35, 7.67
Inter-American Convention on the Law
        Applicable to International Contracts
        1994 2.29, 2.32–2.33, 2.50, 2.60, 14.01,
        14.03
international organizations, incorporation of rules
        of 5.11–5.14
interpretation 19.22
lex mercatoria 1.43–1.51
mandatory rules 2.51–2.56
OHADA 7.12
party autonomy 1.33
usage 1.33
validity of contracts 1.43–1.51, 2.23–2.36, 7.30,
    18.04
conventions *see* **treaties and conventions**
co-operation and coordination
harmonization 20.12
insolvency 15.01–15.12, 15.22–15.23,
    15.35
political problems 20.12
UNCITRAL 5.28, 5.34, 15.21, 20.12
UNCITRAL Model Law on Cross Border
        Insolvency 1997 15.21
UNIDROIT 20.12
costs 17.05–17.06, 17.55, 17.59
cultural and economic issues 4.40, 20.18–20.20
Currie, Brainerd 2.20
customary international law 3.05, 3.21–3.25

application of 1.03
chronological paradox 3.23
codification 1.60
comity 3.23
declarations 3.24
domestic law 3.08
early and medieval codes 1.16
harmonization 5.12
international organizations, rules of 5.12
interpretation of treaties and conventions 3.59
lex mercatoria 1.60
maritime law 1.16
opinio juris 3.21, 3.23
state practice 3.21, 3.23–3.24
trade usage 1.34, 1.64, 3.21–3.23, 3.25, 7.69
treaties 3.02, 3.05, 3.24, 3.30
custody 13.04, 13.07

David, René 1.21, 1.25, 2.12, 6.27
declarations *see* **reservations and declarations in**
        treaties
definition of commercial law 1.02
definition of transnational commercial law
international economic law, distinguished
        from 1.03
sources of law 1.03
three concepts of 1.03
uniform law 1.03
delivery, place of 16.25
delocalization debate, international arbitration
        law and
arbitration agreements 17.106
awards, recognition and enforcement of
        arbitration 17.138–17.139
change of position 17.104
conflicting decisions, risk of 17.105
finality 17.101
France 17.80–17.96
legitimate expectations 17.100
multiple jeopardy 17.102
New York Arbitration Convention 1958
        17.138–17.139
party autonomy 17.98–17.99
setting aside awards 17.107
UNCITRAL Model Law 17.109
demand guarantees 9.05, 9.07–9.08, 9.11
        see also **Uniform Rules for Demand**
        Guarantees (URDG) (ICC)
dematerialized securities 13.06, 13.08–13.10
Denning, Lord 4.29
depositaries 3.02, 3.45–3.46
developing countries
Cape Town Convention 2001 10.29
franchising 8.29

developing countries (*cont.*)
　international development and loan bodies, role of
　　4.39
　leasing 10.28–10.31
　UNIDROIT International Financial Leasing
　　Convention 1988 10.27
Dicey, A.V. 2.18
diplomatic conferences or sessions
　Cape Town Convention 2001 6.20, 6.22,
　　12.08–12.09, 12.18
　Committee (Commission) of the Whole 6.21–6.23
　drafting committees 6.21–6.22, 6.24
　explanatory reports 6.19, 6.24
　Final Act, signature of 6.23
　Hague Conferences 5.20, 6.19, 6.42
　harmonization 6.19–6.24, 6.40
　organization 6.20
　treaties 6.19–6.24
　UN Sales Convention (CISG) 7.07, 18.01
　UNCITRAL 5.30, 6.19
　UNIDROIT 5.25–5.26, 6.19
diplomatic or consular officials
　Hague Service Convention 1965 16.58
　Hague Taking of Evidence Abroad Convention
　　1970 16.58
diplomatic protection 3.63
directives, preambles to 3.34–3.35
disclosure, pre-contractual duty of 4.51–4.52, 4.59
discovery 16.65
dispute resolution *see also* international commercial
　　arbitration
　adjudication 17.10
　alternative dispute resolution (ADR)
　　17.12–17.13
　comparative law 4.41
　conciliation 9.58, 17.12
　expert determination 17.06–17.09
　lex mercatoria 1.21
　mediation 17.12–17.13
　Principles of European Contract Law 14.13,
　　14.26–14.27
　state entity, where one party is 3.02
　treaties and conventions 3.02
　UNIDROIT Principles of International
　　Commercial Contracts 14.13,
　　14.26–14.27
documentary credits *see* letters of credit, Uniform
　　Customs and Practices for Documentary
　　Credits (UCP)
domestic law
　autonomous domestic rules of jurisdiction
　　16.13–16.19, 16.24, 16.33–16.35
　conflict of laws 2.01–2.06
　customary international law 3.08

EC law 3.15
international law
　relationship with 3.05, 3.07–3.10
　interpretation of treaties and conventions 3.47,
　　19.05–19.06
　sources of commercial law 1.32–1.36
domicile 2.22, 2.34, 16.24, 16.28
drafting committees 6.21–6.22, 6.24
dualism 3.07–3.08

early and medieval codes 1.15–1.19
EC law 1.31, 3.15–3.18 *see also* Brussels
　　Convention on Jurisdiction and
　　Enforcement of Judgments in Civil and
　　Commercial Matters 1968, Brussels I
　　Regulation on jurisdiction and the
　　recognition and enforcement of
　　judgments in civil and commercial
　　matters, Insolvency Regulation
　air transport liability regime 6.45
　Cape Town Convention 2001 3.15–3.16
　civil procedure 16.07, 16.60, 16.62
　Collateral Directive 13.32–13.33, 13.36
　Commercial Agents Directive 8.03, 8.09–8.16
　competence 3.15–3.16
　connecting factors 2.42
　Consumer Sales and Associated Guarantees
　　Directive 7.13
　direct effect 3.17–3.19
　directives, preamble to 3.34–3.35
　European Contract Code, proposal for 4.38
　First Company Law Directive 8.06–8.08
　harmonization 5.17, 6.44–6.45, 13.02, 14.03
　Insolvency Proceedings Convention 15.04,
　　15.24
　interpretation 19.16
　Principles of European Contract Law 4.38,
　　14.11–14.12
　provisional and protective measures 16.46–16.48
　service 16.55, 16.59
　supremacy of EC law 6.44, 6.45, 18.18
　takeover bids 13.02
　treaties and conventions 3.15–3.18, 5.19
　　direct effect of 3.17–3.18
　　Treaty of Amsterdam 5.17, 6.44–6.45
ECE (UN Economic Commission for Europe)
　　5.17, 6.44
economies in transition
　Cape Town Convention 2001 10.29
　commercial codes 1.14
　franchising 8.29
　leasing 10.28–10.31
　Legal Transition Programme of the EBRD 1.14
　legislation, reforms of 1.14

electronic systems
Cape Town Convention 2001 12.14, 12.39
International Standby Practices (ISP98) 9.47
Uniform Customs and Practices for Documentary
Credits (UCP) 9.26–9.28
enforcement of arbitration awards *see* **recognition
and enforcement of arbitral awards**
enforcement of judgments *see* **recognition and
enforcement of judgments**
England
Chair of commercial law 1.26
law merchant 1.22
Euroclear 13.10, 13.34
European Civil Code project 1.58
European Contract Code, proposal for 4.38
European Union *see* **EC law**
evidence
EC law 16.59
Hague Taking of Evidence Abroad Convention
1970 16.06, 16.56–16.59
ICC Arbitration Rules 17.53
Principles of European Contract Law 14.49
UNCITRAL Arbitration Rules 17.53
UNIDROIT Principles of International
Commercial Contracts 14.49
expert determination 17.06–17.09
experts
civil procedure 16.06, 16.56–16.59
comparative law 4.73
harmonization 6.18
International Chamber of Commerce (ICC) 5.32
transport 20.10
explanatory reports 6.19, 6.24–6.25

factoring 11.05–11.10
accounts, maintenance of 11.07
characterization of transactions 11.07
collection of debts 11.07
definition 11.05–11.10
direct export factoring 11.09
direct import factoring 11.09
facultative sales agreements 11.08
finance, provision of 11.07
full-service or old-line factoring 11.07
import factor 11.09
invoice discounting 11.07
maturity factoring 11.07
non-notification factoring (invoice discounting)
11.07
receivables financing 11.01, 11.05
sales agreements, alternative forms of 11.08
transfer of risk of default 11.07
whole turnover sales agreements 11.08
fair dealing *see* **good faith and fair dealing**

fairs 1.17, 1.18
finance *see also* **receivables financing**
factoring 11.07
harmonization 6.39, 20.11
First Company Law Directive 8.06–8.08
force majeure 7.97–7.100, 7.105
frustration 7.98
Principles of European Contract Law 7.100
UNIDROIT Principles of International
Commercial Contracts 7.100
forum non conveniens
anti-suit injunctions 16.42
Brussels Convention 1968 16.39–16.40
Brussels I Regulation 16.39–16.41
Hague Choice of Court Agreements Convention
2005 16.41
jurisdiction 16.38–16.42
legal certainty 16.41
lis alibi pendens 16.41
Lugano Convention 1988 16.39
meaning 16.38
predictability 16.41
forum selection clauses
arbitration 17.71–17.73
Brussels I Regulation 16.29, 16.32–16.34
Hague Choice of Court Agreements Convention
2005 16.37, 16.41
jurisdiction 16.30–16.37
MERCOSUR 16.36
trade usage 16.37
treaties and conventions 3.10
United States 16.30–16.32
France
arbitration 17.73
Civil Code 1.10, 4.13, 4.67, 16.14–16.16
exportability 4.67
civil law and common law, comparison between 4.13
classification of legal systems 4.07–4.09
Commercial Code 1.10, 1.13
delocalization debate, international commercial
arbitration and 17.80–17.86
great medieval fairs 1.17
jurisdiction 16.14–16.16
New Code of Civil Procedure 17.73
renvoi 2.58–2.60
franchising *see* **UNIDROIT Model Franchise
Disclosure Law**
developing countries 8.29
distribution 8.29
economies in transition 8.29
ICC International Franchising Model Contract 8.30
know-how 8.29
UNIDROIT *Guide to International Master
Franchise Arrangements* 8.30

fraud 9.10, 9.19, 9.22–9.23, 15.03
freezing injunctions 16.46–16.48
  criteria 16.46–16.48
  good arguable case 16.46
  worldwide 16.46–16.48
frustration 7.98

general average 1.15
general principles of international law 1.59, 3.20
  connecting factors 2.32
  contract 2.32
  lex mercatoria 1.04, 1.66–1.67
  sources of transnational commercial law 1.59, 1.67
  trade usage 1.53, 1.66
  UN Sales Convention 7.55–7.65
  UNIDROIT Principles of International
    Commercial Contracts 7.64–7.65
Geneva Convention on the International
    Recognition of Rights in Aircraft
    1948 2.39
Germanic family of legal systems 4.07–4.09
Germany
  agency 8.02
  Code of Civil Procedure 16.16, 16.18–16.19
  Collateral Directive 13.36
  Commercial Code 1.10, 1.13
  in rem actions 16.18
  securities transactions, conflict of laws and
    13.35–13.36
  Settlement Finality Directive 13.35–13.36
Goldman, Berthold 1.29
good faith and fair dealing
  abuse of rights 14.46–14.47
  Cape Town Convention 2001 3.67–3.68
  civil law 14.45
  Commercial Agents Directive 8.12
  common law 14.44–14.45
    civil law systems and 8.12, 14.45
  interpretation of treaties and conventions 3.48,
    3.53–3.54
  Principles of European Contract Law 14.42,
    14.44–14.48
  UN Sales Convention 7.46–7.65, 14.44
  UNIDROIT Agency Convention 8.23
  UNIDROIT Principles of International
    Commercial Contracts 14.38, 14.40,
    14.42, 14.44–14.48
  Uniform Customs and Practices for Documentary
    Credits (UCP) 9.22
great medieval fairs 1.17, 1.18
groups of companies 15.03, 15.35, 16.28
guarantees *see also* Uniform Rules for Demand
    Guarantees (URDG) (ICC)
  demand guarantees 9.05, 9.07–9.08, 9.11

suretyship guarantees 9.07
UNCITRAL Independent Guarantees and
    Standby Letters of Credit Convention
    1995 9.11, 9.51–9.54
Uniform Rules for Contract Guarantees
    1978 9.29
Gutteridge, Harold 2.12, 4.05, 6.01, 6.06

habitual residence 2.22
Hague Agency Convention 2.36, 2.53
Hague Choice of Court Agreements Convention
    2005 16.37
Hague Conference on Private International Law
    5.06, 5.19–5.21, 5.33
  civil procedure 16.62
  Council 5.20
  diplomatic sessions 5.20, 6.13, 6.19
  drafting committees 6.42
  European Community 5.19, 6.44
  Hague Securities Convention 2002 13.11
  Hague Uniform Sales Laws 2.12, 2.61
  instrument, types of 6.15
  mandate 5.19
  members 5.19
  ordinary sessions 5.20
  Permanent Bureau 5.20
  regional harmonization 5.33, 6.44
  Secretary-General 5.20
  Special Commissions 5.20, 6.14, 6.17
  treaties 5.19–5.21
  working methods 5.21
Hague Convention on the Law Applicable to
    Certain Rights in Respect of Securities
    Held with an Intermediary 2002 *see*
    Hague Securities Convention 2002
Hague Securities Convention 2002
  account holders' rights 13.20
  applicable laws 13.19–13.25
    fall-back rules 13.23
    primary rule 13.22
  characterization 13.17–13.18
  Collateral Directive 13.32–13.33, 13.36
  conflict of laws 13.11–13.27, 13.36, 18.07
  connecting factors 2.30
  contract 2.30, 2.56, 13.17–13.18
  dematerialized securities 13.17
  exclusions 13.16–13.18
  fungible pool or omnibus account, securities held
    in 13.12
  Germany 13.36
  Hague Conference 13.11
  insolvency 13.24
  internationality 13.19
  interpretation 19.04

party autonomy 2.41

personal rights 13.17–13.18

PRIMA approach (place of the relevant intermediary approach) 13.14, 13.20

public policy 2.50, 13.25

qualifying office test 13.32–13.33

scope of Convention 13.15–13.16

Settlement Finality Directive 13.31

transferor's law and transferee's law, relationship between 13.26–13.27

travaux préparatoires 19.04

Hague Service Convention 1965 16.06, 16.51–16.55

abroad, service 16.06, 16.51–16.55

civil law 16.51

common law 16.51

diplomatic or consular agents 16.51

judicial authority, service through 16.51

judicial officers, authority of 16.51

mandatory, whether Convention is 16.52

refusal of requests 16.54

types 16.51

United States 16.52–16.53

Hague Taking of Evidence Abroad Convention 1970 16.06, 16.56–16.59

diplomatic or consular officials 16.58

judicial authorities 16.56–16.57

letters of request 16.56–16.57

United States 16.56–16.57

Hague Uniform Law on the Formation of Contracts for the International Sale of Goods 1964 7.03–7.07

Hague Uniform Sales Laws 2.12, 2.61, 7.03–7.07, 18.14

Hammurbai, Code of 1.15, 4.04

harmonization of commercial law 5.01–5.34 *see also* **political problems of harmonization**

advantages of 1.28

agency 8.03

approval of projects by relevant organs of agencies 6.13

Asia Pacific Economic Cooperation (APEC) 5.17

Association of South East Asian Nations (ASEAN) 5.17

Bustamante Code 5.06

Cape Town Convention 2001 5.05, 6.20, 6.22

civil law 6.12

codifications 5.14

collaboration between bodies 6.03, 6.08

Comité Maritime International (CMI) 6.03

committee of governmental experts 6.18

common law 6.12

comparative law 4.04, 4.33, 4.35, 4.47, 4.54, 4.56, 4.72, 6.10–6.12

concepts, differences in legal 6.36

conflict of laws 5.01, 5.06, 14.01–14.03, 18.14

contract law 14.01–14.03

cultural issues 20.18–20.20

delay 6.39–6.42

drafting 6.21–6.22, 6.24, 6.37

draft texts

consideration of, problems with 6.39–6.40

distribution 6.16

duplication 6.09

economic issues 20.18–20.20

establishing the existence of a problem 6.06–6.07

European Union 5.17, 6.44–6.45, 13.02, 14.03

experts 6.18

explanatory reports 6.19, 6.24–6.25

facultative instruments 5.08

finance 6.39

formulatory stage 6.01

guides 5.15

Incoterms 5.12

industry organizations 5.33

insolvency 15.01–15.12

Insolvency Regulation 15.12

instruments of international harmonization 5.07–5.16, 6.15, 6.26

Inter-American Convention on the Law Applicable to International Contracts 14.03

international organizations

best practice guides 5.15

codifications and restatements 5.14

contractually incorporated non-binding rules of 5.11–5.14

custom and usage, rules codifying 5.12

model contracts 5.13

model general conditions of contract 5.13

process of harmonization 6.03

role of 5.33

internationalism 1.28

interpreters 6.38, 6.39

language 6.37–6.39, 20.18

League of Nations 5.04

legally binding, instruments intended to be 5.07

legislative activities, co-ordination of 5.34

MERCOSUR/MERCOSUL 5.17, 6.45

model contracts 5.13

model general conditions of contract 5.13

model laws 5.08–5.10, 6.15

official commentaries 6.25

OHADA 5.17, 6.44, 6.45

Organization of American States (OAS) 5.17, 6.44

organizational problems 6.39–6.42

over-ambition 6.30–6.32

harmonization of commercial law (*cont.*)
  problems of harmonization 6.27–6.42,
      20.01–20.22
  professional and industry organizations 5.33
  regionalism 1.31, 6.43–6.45, 18.14
  restatements 5.14, 5.16
  secretariats
    explanatory reports 6.25
    ideas from 6.04
    importance of 6.04
  securities, transactions in 13.01–13.02
  soft law 14.01
  state immunity 1.55
  study groups, establishment of 6.14
  subjects, choice of 6.28
  timetable 6.42
  trade usage 4.47
  treaties *see* **treaties and conventions**
  Treaties of Montevideo 5.06
Hindu family of legal systems 4.07
hire-purchase 10.06
history of commercial law 1.15–1.31
  bills of lading 1.06
  characteristics of medieval law merchant 1.20–1.23
  codes, early and medieval 1.15–1.19
  comparative law 4.06–4.09, 4.19
  great medieval fairs 1.17, 1.18
  growth of transnational commercial law 1.25–1.30
  internationalism 1.25–1.30
  Middle Ages, nature of commercial law in the 1.06
  maritime law 1.15–1.16
  nationalization of commercial law 1.24
  regionalism, growth of 1.31
human rights 3.14, 3.20
Huvelin, Paul 1.17

ICC *see* **International Chamber of Commerce (ICC)**
ICC Arbitration Rules 17.42–17.59
  arbitrators 17.45–17.49
    appointment 17.45–17.46
    challenging 17.48
    independence or impartiality 17.47–17.48
    replacement of 17.49
  awards 17.56–17.58
    draft 17.57
    reasons 17.56
    time limits 17.57
  choice of law 17.118–17.120
  commencement of arbitration 17.43–17.44
  conflict of laws 17.51, 17.117–17.120
  conservatory and interim measures 17.55
  costs 17.59
  definition of international arbitration 17.18
  evidence 17.53

  harmonization 17.42–17.59
  International Court of Arbitration 5.32, 17.42
  jurisdiction 17.44
  party autonomy 17.60, 17.64
  procedure 17.50–17.55
  requests, transmission of 17.43
  terms of reference, contents of 17.52
  timetable 17.52
immunities *see also* **state immunity**
  Aircraft Protocol to Cape Town Convention
      3.67–3.68
  Cape Town Convention 2001 3.67–3.68, 12.22
  civil procedure 16.09–16.12
  International Civil Aviation Organization (ICAO)
      3.68
in rem **rights** *see* **property**
incorporation, place of 13.13, 13.23, 18.08
Incoterms 1.56, 5.12, 7.35, 7.67
industry organizations 5.33
injunctions
  anti-suit injunctions 16.42
  forum non conveniens 16.42
  freezing injunctions 16.46–16.48
  interlocutory 16.46
  worldwide 16.46–16.48
insolvency *see also* **Insolvency Regulation,**
      UNCITRAL Model Law on Cross
      Border Insolvency 1997
  advance designation of applicable law, forum and
      insolvency regime, proposal for 15.10
  Aircraft Protocol to Cape Town Convention 12.16
  bilateral treaties 15.04
  Bustamente Code 15.04
  Cape Town Convention 2001 12.07, 12.22, 12.49
  Collateral Directive 13.32
  concurrent proceedings, judicial co-operation in
      15.22–15.23
  connecting factors 2.43
  co-operation 15.01–15.12, 15.22–15.23
  EU Insolvency Proceedings Convention 15.04
  factoring 11.27
  financial leasing 10.24–10.25
  groups, fraud within 15.03
  Hague Securities Convention 2002 13.24
  harmonization 15.01–15.12
  hotch-pot rule 15.11
  Insolvency Working Group 12.07
  judicial co-operation in concurrent proceedings
      15.22–15.23
  jurisdiction 15.01, 15.04, 15.06–15.12
  non-discrimination against foreign creditors 15.11
  parallel proceedings 15.02, 15.06–15.07
  protocols for co-operation 15.22–15.23
  ranking 13.24

reorganization and restructuring 15.02
rescue culture 15.02
Settlement Finality Directive 13.28, 13.30
UNIDROIT International Factoring Convention
    11.27
UNIDROIT International Financial Leasing
    Convention 1988 10.24–10.25
unity or plurality of proceedings principle 15.02,
    15.06–15.07
universalism 15.06–15.09
Insolvency Regulation 3.16, 15.04, 15.24–15.35
amendments 15.24
applicable law 15.29–15.30
background 15.24
centre of main interests (COMI) 15.25,
    15.27–15.28, 15.31, 15.34
commencement of proceedings 15.33–15.34
conflict of laws 3.16
co-operation 15.35
enforcement of judgments 15.31–15.34
groups 15.35
harmonization 15.12
Insolvency Proceedings Convention (EU) 15.24
interpretation 15.24
judgments, recognition and enforcement of
    15.31–15.34
jurisdiction 15.31
liquidators as commencement of proceedings,
    appointment of 15.33
lis alibi pendens 15.35
main proceedings 15.26
pre-insolvency rules of law, balance between
    insolvency rules and 15.29–15.30
property rights 15.29–15.30
ranking 15.29–15.30
recognition, principle of 15.31–15.34
reorganization or restructuring 15.25, 15.26,
    15.35
reservation of title 15.30
scope 15.25
substantive law 15.12
territorial proceedings 15.26
types of insolvency proceedings 15.26
Virgós-Schmit Report 15.24
winding up 15.25
institutions *see also* particular institutions
    (eg UNCITRAL, UNIDROIT)
arbitration 17.39–17.42
harmonization, principal institutions involved in
    5.17–5.34
institutional law 1.02
intellectual property 2.43
**Inter-American Commercial Arbitration
    Commission, rules of** 17.24

Inter-American Convention on International
    Arbitration (Panama Convention) 17.24
**Inter-American Convention on the Law Applicable
    to International Contracts 1994**
choice of law 2.29, 2.32–2.33, 14.20–14.22,
    14.24
connecting factors 2.29, 2.32–2.33
general principles of international commercial law
    2.32
harmonization 14.03
public policy 2.50
renvoi 2.60
restatements 14.01
interest 7.61, 7.64, 7.88–7.96
domestic law 7.95
Eastern Europe 7.90
general principle 7.94–7.96
Islamic law 7.90
LIBOR 7.94
Principles of European Contract Law 7.95–7.96
rate 7.91–7.96
UNIDROIT Principles of International
    Commercial Contracts 7.95–7.96
**International Centre for the Settlement of
    Investment Disputes (ICSID)
    Arbitration Rules** 17.23
International Court of Arbitration (ICC) 5.32, 17.42
interim relief *see* provisional and protective measures
International Academy of Comparative Law 4.06
International Air Transport Association (IATA)
    6.03, 12.08
international and regional instruments *see also*
    particular instruments (eg Rome
    Convention on the Law Applicable to
    Contractual Obligations 1980)
European Union 1.54
facilitative instruments 1.54
legally binding, instruments intended to become
    1.54
model laws and rules 1.54
international bank payment undertakings *see* bank
    payment undertakings
International Chamber of Commerce (ICC)
    see also ICC Arbitration Rules, Incoterms,
    Uniform Customs and Practices for
    Documentary Credits (UCP), Uniform
    Rules for Demand Guarantees (URDG)
    (ICC)
Agency Model Contract 8.04
aims 1.56
arbitration 5.32, 9.58, 17.42
bank payment undertakings 9.09–9.11,
    9.54–9.58
bonds 9.54–9.58

International Chamber of Commerce (ICC) (*cont.*)
  commissions 6.13, 6.17, 9.11
  Conciliation and Arbitration Rules 9.58
  franchising 8.30
  guarantees 9.29
  International Court of Arbitration 5.32, 17.42
  International Franchising Model Contract 8.30
  lex mercatoria, creeping codification of 5.32
  members 5.32, 9.11
  role 6.08–6.09, 9.11
  special status of 9.11
  task forces 6.14
  Uniform Rules for Contract Bonds 9.54–9.58
  Uniform Rules for Contract Guarantees
    1978 9.29
  working groups 6.14
International Civil Aviation Organization (ICAO)
  Aircraft Protocol to Cape Town Convention
    20.10
  Cape Town Convention 2001 3.68, 12.08,
    12.10, 12.37
  harmonization 5.17, 6.03
  privileges and immunities 3.68
  United Nations 3.68
international civil procedure 16.01–16.65
  ALI/UNIDROIT Principles of Transnational
    Civil Procedure 16.62–16.65
  access to information and evidence 16.65
  discovery 16.65
  commercial and non-commercial disputes,
    distinction between 16.62
  jurisdiction 16.64
  Brussels Convention 1968 16.06, 16.07
  Brussels I Regulation 16.07, 16.60
  enforcement of decisions abroad 16.04
  European Union 16.07, 16.60, 16.62
  evidence 16.06, 16.56–16.59
  expeditiousness 16.04
  fairness 16.04
  Hague Service Convention 1965 16.06,
    16.51–16.55
  Hague Taking of Evidence Abroad Convention
    1970 16.06, 16.56–16.59
  harmonization 16.62
  independence and impartiality 16.04
  jurisdiction 16.02–16.04, 16.08, 16.62
    adjudicate, to 16.13–16.42
    ALI/UNIDROIT Principles of Transnational
      Civil Procedure 16.64
    autonomous domestic rules on jurisdiction
      16.08, 16.13–16.42
    immunities 16.09–16.12
  legitimate expectations 16.04
  Lugano Convention 1988 16.06

MERCOSUR Las Leñas and Buenos Aires
    Protocols 16.61
  personal capacity of parties 16.02
  predictability of structure of proceedings and
    administration 16.04
  present one's case fully, guarantee to 16.04
  provisional and protective measures 16.43–16.51
  regional economic integration organizations
    16.07
  service 16.51–16.55
  seven pillars systems should be based on 16.04
  sources of law 16.06–16.08
  state immunity 16.09–16.12
  trade usage 16.04
  treaties 16.06–16.07
international commercial arbitration 3.10,
    17.01–17.143 *see also* **ICC Arbitration**
    Rules, international commercial
    arbitration, conflict of laws and,
    international commercial arbitration,
    harmonization of, UNCITRAL
    Arbitration Rules, UNCITRAL Model
    Arbitration Law
  adjudication
    construction industry 17.10
    distinguished from 17.10–17.11
    provisional decisions 17.11
    review by courts 17.10
  advantages and disadvantages 17.04–17.05
  alternative dispute resolution
    awards 17.12
    distinguished from 17.12–17.13
    mediation or conciliation 17.12–17.13
    United States 17.12
  arbitrators
    appointment of 1.46, 17.03
    powers of 1.29, 17.05
  commercial arbitration, meaning of 17.19–17.22
  conciliation 17.12
  confidentiality 17.06
  costs 17.05–17.06
  definition 17.01
  determination in accordance with the law 1.47
  domestic arbitration, distinguished from
    17.14–17.18
  expert determination
    distinguished from 17.06–17.09
    review by courts 17.08–17.09
  ICC Arbitration Rules
  ICC International Court of Arbitration 5.32
  Inter-American Commercial Arbitration
    Commission, rules of 17.24
  Inter-American Convention on International
    Arbitration (Panama Convention) 17.24

International Centre for the Settlement of
    Investment Disputes (ICSID) Arbitration
    Rules 17.23
lex mercatoria 14.31, 14.35
litigation, compared with 17.03–17.06
mediation 17.12–17.13
MERCOSUR International Commercial
    Arbitration Agreement 17.24
nature of 17.03–17.22
New York Convention 1958 1.29, 17.21–17.22
Principles of European Contract Law
    14.26–14.27, 14.29, 14.31–14.32,
    14.35–14.36, 17.01
UNCITRAL Arbitration Rules 17.40, 17.43–17.59
UNCITRAL Model Arbitration Law 17.23,
    17.27–17.34
UNIDROIT Principles of International
    Commercial Contracts 14.26–14.32,
    14.35–14.36, 14.40–14.41, 17.01
international commercial arbitration awards
    see also **recognition and enforcement of
    arbitral awards, UNCITRAL Arbitration
    Rules, UNCITRAL Model
    Arbitration Law**
appeals 17.124, 17.132
binding awards 17.12
confidentiality 17.124
conflict of laws
    delocalization debate 17.79–17.109
    finality 17.101
    judicial control over awards 17.80–17.86
    jurisdiction 17.86
    lex mercatoria 1.40
    setting aside awards 17.107
    stateless awards 17.63, 17.65, 17.79–17.109,
        17.138
ICC Arbitration Rules 17.56–17.58
internationalism 1.29
lex mercatoria 1.40, 1.51
New York Arbitration Convention 1958 17.137
public policy 17.129
review by national courts of 17.124–17.133
    UNCITRAL Model Law 17.125–17.130
stateless awards 17.63, 17.65, 17.79–17.109,
    17.138
time limits 17.57
UNCITRAL Arbitration Rules 17.56–17.58
UNCITRAL Model Law 17.34, 17.125–17.131
**international commercial arbitration, conflict of
    laws and** 17.67–17.123
International Court of Justice 3.04, 3.19–3.20, 3.59
**international development and loan bodies,
    role of** 4.39
international economic law 1.03

International Institute for the Unification of Private
    Law *see* UNIDROIT (International
    Institute for the Unification of
    Private Law)
international law *see also* interpretation of treaties
    and conventions
    applications of 3.10
    arbitration 3.10
    complexity of international law-making process,
        impact of 3.12
    customary law 3.05
    diplomatic protection 3.63
    domestic law
        priority over 3.10
        relationship with 3.05, 3.07–3.10
    EC law 3.15–3.18
    general principles of law 3.20
    human rights 3.14, 3.20
    individual, enhanced role of 3.14
    influences on 3.11–3.14
    International Court of Justice 3.04, 3.19–3.20
    investment treaties 3.10, 3.13
    law, as 3.04
    law-making organizations, impact of specialized
        and sophisticated 3.11
    New York Arbitration Convention 1958 3.10
    norms 3.04
    soft law, relationship with 3.05–3.06
    sources of international law 3.19–3.20
    state immunity 3.10
    trade, impact of bodies financing of 3.13
    trade usage 3.05
International Law Commission Draft Articles
    3.61–3.62
international legal practice 4.74
International Maritime Organization (IMO) 5.17,
    6.03
International Monetary Fund (IMF) 5.17
international organizations
    accountability 3.29
    arbitration 17.23
    best practice guides 5.15
    codifications and restatements 5.14
    contractually incorporated non-binding rules of
        5.11–5.14
    custom and usage, rules codifying 5.12
    Hague Conference on Private International Law
        5.33
    harmonization 5.11–5.14, 5.33, 6.03, 20.01,
        20.09–20.11
    model contracts 5.13
    role of 5.33
    rules and trade terms as sources of law 1.56
    treaties and conventions 3.28–3.29

international organizations (*cont.*)
UNCITRAL 5.33
UNIDROIT 5.33
International Standby Practices (ISP98) 9.46–9.50
definition of standby credits 9.49
electronic presentation 9.47
extend or pay demands 9.47
letters of credit, distinguished from 9.50
international trade usage, *see* **trade usage**
international tribunal, proposal for 19.16–19.17
internationalism 1.25–1.30 *see also* **internationality**
arbitration 1.29
code, proposal for an international 1.26–1.27
conflict of laws 1.25
forum shopping 1.25
growth of transnational commercial law
1.25–1.30
harmonization 1.25–1.28
unification of private international law 1.25
uniformity 1.25–1.28
internationality *see also* **internationalism**
Hague Securities Convention 2002 13.19
UN Sales Convention 7.12–7.13, 19.11
UN Assignment of Receivables Convention
2001 11.33
UNIDROIT Agency Convention 8.21
UNIDROIT International Financial Leasing
Convention 1988 10.12
interpretation *see also* **interpretation of treaties and**
conventions, uniformity, interpretation
and
Cape Town Convention 2001 3.53, 12.25
Commercial Agents Directive 8.09
connecting factors 2.23–2.36
factoring 3.52–3.54, 11.19–11.20
foreign decisions 4.43
Hague Securities Convention 2002 19.04
Insolvency Regulation 15.24
Islamic law 4.17
language 4.44–4.45
Principles of European Contract Law 14.50
supplemental material 4.43
transport 4.44–4.45
UN Assignment of Receivables Convention
2001 11.30
UNIDROIT International Factoring Convention
3.52–3.54, 11.19–11.20
UNIDROIT Principles of International
Commercial Contracts 14.49
interpretation of treaties and conventions 3.10,
3.47–3.59
agreement or practice, subsequent 3.50
autonomous interpretation 3.47
commentaries and reports 3.50

comparative law 4.26, 4.42–4.45
context 3.48
customary international law 3.59
declarations 3.69
domestic law 3.47
errors in a convention 3.55–3.58
foreign decisions 4.43
good faith 3.48, 3.53–3.54
International Court of Justice 3.59
language 4.44–4.45
materials 3.50
objects and purpose 3.48
private law conventions 4.46
purposive interpretation 3.58
supplemental material 4.43
teleological approach 3.53
travaux préparatoires 3.49, 3.57
uniform laws 4.42–4.46
Vienna Convention on Treaties 1969 3.47–3.49,
3.52, 3.56, 3.59
invoice discounting 11.07
Islamic law 4.07, 4.17, 7.90
Israel 4.27
Italy 1.18

Jhering, Rudolf von 4.21, 4.23
journals 4.04
judgments *see also* **recognition and enforcement of**
judgments
default judgments 16.60
irreconcilable judgments 16.60
jurisdiction
Aircraft Protocol to Cape Town Convention 3.66
ALI/UNIDROIT Principles of Transnational
Civil Procedure 16.64
arbitration 17.63, 17.86, 17.110
autonomous domestic rules 16.08,
16.13–16.42
Brussels Convention 1968 16.17, 16.24
Brussels I Regulation 16.24–16.29, 16.33–16.35
Cape Town Convention 2001 3.66, 12.45,
16.31–16.32
centre of main interests 15.09
civil procedure 16.02–16.04, 16.08–16.42,
16.62, 16.64
conflict of laws 2.14
connecting factors 16.13, 16.17, 16.19
demand guarantees 9.44
domestic systems, traditional autonomous rules in
16.13–16.19
fairness tests 16.20–16.22
forum non conveniens 16.38–16.42
forum selection clauses 16.30–16.37
French Civil Code 16.14–16.15

German Code of Civil Procedure 16.16, 16.18–16.19
ICC Arbitration Rules 17.44
immunities 16.09–16.12
in personam rights 16.13, 16.19
in rem actions 16.18–16.19, 16.22
insolvency 15.01, 15.04, 15.06–15.12, 16.31
Insolvency Regulation 15.31
Lugano Convention 1988 16.24
MERCOSUR 16.36
minimum contacts test 16.20–16.22
nationality discrimination 16.13
service 16.17
UNCITRAL Model Arbitration Law 17.31
Uniform Rules for Contract Bonds (ICC) 9.57–9.58
Uniform Rules for Demand Guarantees (URDG) (ICC) 9.44
United States
    choice of law 16.30, 16.32
    fairness tests 16.20–16.22
    forum selection clauses 16.30–16.32
    minimum contacts test 16.20–16.23
    modernization 16.20–16.21
    restatements 16.18, 16.22
Warsaw Convention 1929 2.10
jus cogens 1.43

labour law 2.43
Lambert, Edouard 4.04
land *see* property
language
    Cape Town Convention 2001 20.19
    civil law and common law, comparison between 4.13, 4.67
    comparative law 4.44–4.45, 4.62, 4.71
    English language, importance of 4.16
    harmonization 6.37–6.39, 20.20
    interpretation 4.44–4.45
    interpreters 6.38, 6.39
    UNCITRAL 20.19
law reporting 19.03, 19.19
Laws of Oléron *see* Rolls of Oléron
Laws of Wisby 1.16, 1.19
League of Nations 5.04
leasing *see also* UNIDROIT International Financial Leasing Convention 1988
    Cape Town Convention 2001 12.05
    developing countries 10.28–10.31
    economies in transition 10.28–10.31
    model law 10.28–10.31
    secured transactions 20.06–20.07
legal education 4.24–4.25, 4.48
Legal Transition Programme of the EBRD 1.14

letters of credit *see also* Uniform Customs and Practices for Documentary Credits (UCP) 9.03–9.04, 9.11
    autonomy principle 9.11
    conformity 9.13
    contracts of sale as central contracts 9.13
    demand guarantees compared with 9.11
    International Standby Practices (ISP98), distinguished from 9.50
    rejection 9.13
    UNCITRAL Independent Guarantees and Standby Letters of Credit Convention 1995 9.51–9.53
    Uniform Rules for Demand Guarantees (URDG) (ICC) 9.31–9.32
letters of request 16.56–16.57
Levi, Leone 1.26–1.27
Lex Mercatoria (treatise) 1.04
lex mercatoria
    arbitration 1.40, 1.51, 14.31, 14.35
    autonomous 1.29–1.30, 1.38–1.51, 1.64, 1.67
    characteristics of 1.20–1.23
    choice of law 1.40
    conflict of laws 1.39–1.51, 2.12, 2.61–2.62
    contract 1.43–1.51
    customary rules 1.04, 1.21, 1.60, 1.67
    definition 1.04
    dispute resolution 1.21
    England 1.22
    general principles of law 1.04, 1.66–1.67
    interpretation 19.22
    jus cogens 1.43
    legal system, status as 1.40
    nationalization of commercial law 1.24
    norms, legal 1.47–1.51
      standard terms as 1.49–1.51
      usage 1.61–1.64
    Principles of European Contract Law 14.25, 14.29, 14.31–14.35
    Rome Convention 1980 1.40
    sources of 1.53, 1.60
    standard terms 1.49–1.51
    trade usage 1.04, 1.53, 1.60–1.67
    transnational commercial law, as equated with 1.04
    UNIDROIT Principles of International Commercial Contracts 14.25, 14.29, 14.31–14.35
    uniformity 19.22
lis alibi pendens 15.35, 16.41
litigation compared with arbitration 17.03–17.06, 17.66
loans 1.07, 4.39
local authority swaps 1.09

Lugano Convention on Jurisdiction and Enforcement of Judgments in Civil and Commercial Matters 1988 16.06, 16.24, 16.38
Luxembourg Protocol to the Cape Town Convention 12.09

mandatory rules in the law of contracts 2.51–2.56, 14.58–14.62
  definition of mandatory rules 2.54
  party autonomy 2.51
  public policy 2.52, 2.56
  third countries, mandatory rules of 2.53
  treaties 2.52–2.56
maritime law
  Amalfitan Tables 1.16
  codes, early and medieval 1.15–1.16
  customary law 1.16
  general average 1.15
  Maritime Liens and Mortgages Convention 1926 2.39
  Rhodian law 1.15
  Rolls of Oléron 1.16, 1.19, 4.04
mediation 17.12–17.13
medieval law merchant, characteristics of 1.20–1.23
Mercanzia court in Florence 1.18
MERCOSUR
  arbitration 17.24
  Buenos Aires Protocol on International Jurisdiction in Contractual Matters 1994 16.36, 16.61
  civil procedure 16.61
  foreign judgments, enforcement and recognition of 16.61
  forum selection clauses 16.36
  harmonization 5.17, 6.45
  Las Leñas Protocol 16.61
  recognition and enforcement of foreign judgments 16.61
mistake
  arbitration awards 17.130–17.132
  comparative law 4.32
  interpretation of treaties and conventions 3.55–3.59
    correction, procedure for 3.56
    depositaries, authorization of correction by 3.56
    uncorrected errors 3.57–3.58
  money paid under mistake of law 4.32
  treaties and conventions, errors in text of 3.46, 3.55–3.59
mobile equipment *see* **Cape Town Convention on International Interests in Mobile Equipment 2001**

model contracts
  general conditions of contract 5.13
  harmonization 5.13
  international organizations 5.13
  Uniform Rules for Demand Guarantees (URDG) (ICC) 9.29
model laws *see also* **UNCITRAL Model Arbitration Law, UNCITRAL Model Law on Cross Border Insolvency 1997**
  arbitration 17.25
  Cape Town Convention 2001 10.28–10.31
  franchising 8.31
  harmonization 5.08–5.10, 6.15, 20.01, 20.06–20.07
  international and regional instruments 1.54
  leasing 10.28–10.31
  political problems 20.01, 20.06–20.07
  secured transactions 20.06–20.07
  UNIDROIT Model Franchise Disclosure Law 8.31
money paid under mistake of law 4.32
monism 3.07–3.08
Montesquieu, Charles de Secondat, Baron de 4.04

nationality 2.22, 2.34, 16.13
nationalization of commercial law 1.24
nature of commercial law 1.01–1.14
  civil law 1.10–1.13
  courts upholding transactions 1.09
  definitions 1.02–1.05
  drivers of commercial law 1.05–1.09
  economies in transition 1.14
  Middle Ages 1.06
neo-statutist theory 2.57
New York Convention on the Recognition and Enforcement of Foreign Arbitral Awards 1958 1.29, 3.10, 17.21–17.22, 17.133
  arbitration agreements 17.37–17.38
  conditions for application 17.37
  conflict between conventions 18.13
  conflict of laws 17.70, 18.13
  delocalization debate 17.138–17.139
  domestic law, conventions prevailing over 17.140–17.143
  harmonization 17.23, 17.35–17.38
  interpretation 19.20, 19.24
  meaning of commercial arbitration 17.21–17.22
  merits of awards 17.137
  most favourable right provision 17.140–17.143
  reciprocity 17.37
  refusal of recognition and enforcement 17.38, 17.135–17.138
  review clauses and review conferences 19.20
  stateless awards 17.138
novation 9.25, 11.35, 14.56

official commentaries 6.25
OHADA (Organization for the Harmonization of
    Business Law in Africa)
  conflict of laws 18.17
  harmonization 5.17, 6.44, 6.45
  sales contracts, law for commercial 7.12
  UN Sales Convention 18.17
  UNIDROIT 4.33
opinio juris 3.21, 3.23
Oléron *see* Rolls of Oléron
ordre public see public policy (*ordre public*)
Organization of American States (OAS) 5.17,
  6.44

pacta sunt servanda 14.43 *see also* party autonomy
party autonomy
  arbitration 17.61–17.65, 17.113, 17.116
  Brussels I Regulation 16.29
  choice of law 2.13, 2.23, 2.26–2.30
  connecting factors 2.23, 2.26–2.30, 2.41
  contract 1.33, 2.51
  delocalization debate, international commercial
    arbitration and 17.98–17.99
  Hague Securities Convention 2.41
  ICC Arbitration Rules 17.60, 17.64
  interpretation 19.11
  property 2.41
  Rome Convention 1980 14.21
  UNCITRAL Model Arbitration Law 17.27,
    17.60, 17.64, 17.116
passing of property and risk 7.30, 7.101–7.103,
  18.04
PECL *see* Principles of European Contract Law
place of administration of companies, principal
  2.42
place of business 7.12, 7.16–7.29, 17.17
place of certificates, law of 13.08
place of contract, law of 2.33
place of delivery 16.25
place of incorporation 13.13, 13.23, 18.08
place of performance 16.25, 16.27, 17.17
place of the wrong 2.22
place where property is situated 2.38
place where the register is kept 13.13
place where the transaction took place, law of 13.08
Plato's *Laws* 4.04
political problems of harmonization 20.01–20.22
  best practice guides 20.01
  business sectors, involvement of 20.09
  Cape Town Convention 2001 20.08–20.10,
    20.14, 20.22
  commercial approach 20.14–20.16
  commercial practice, harmonization of 20.11
  comparative law 4.70

conflict of laws 20.11
co-ordination between agencies 20.12
drafting 20.09
gestation periods for projects 20.13, 20.17
governments
  involvement of 20.13, 20.17
  ministries and agencies of, involvement of 20.13
Hague Conference on Private International Law
  20.11, 20.21
international organizations 20.01, 20.09–20.11
knowledge, gaps in 20.05
model laws 20.01, 20.06–20.07
organizational issues 20.04–20.17
over-ambition, problem of 20.06–20.07
post-adoption stage 20.21–20.22
preparation of international instruments
  20.09–20.11
private law organizations, projects handled by
  20.10–20.13
promotion, finance for 20.21
regional organizations 20.11
restatements 20.01
scope, definition of the 20.05
secured transactions 20.06–20.08
subjects, choice of 20.04
success stories 20.01–20.02
treaties 20.01
UNCITRAL, co-ordination between agencies and
  20.12
UNIDROIT, co-ordination between agencies and
  20.12
working methods 20.14
preambles
  Cape Town Convention 2001 20.10
  directives 3.34–3.35
  EC law 3.34–3.35
  examples 3.33–3.35
  importance of 3.33, 3.35
  Principles of European Contract Law 14.11
  treaties and conventions 3.33–3.35
  UN Sales Convention 3.33
  UNIDROIT International Financial Leasing
    Convention 1988 3.33
  UNIDROIT Principles of International
    Commercial Contracts 14.10, 14.40
precedent 19.03, 19.23
Principles of European Contract Law 1.58, 14.01,
  14.05–14.62
  agency 8.05, 8.28
  arbitration 14.26–14.27, 14.29, 14.31–14.32,
    14.35–14.36, 17.01
  assignment 14.56
  change of circumstances 14.34, 14.40,
    14.54–14.55

Principles of European Contract Law (*cont.*)
characteristic performance 2.35
choice of law 2.31, 14.20–14.27
conflict of laws 14.09
contract, incorporation into 14.09, 14.18–14.19,
    14.26, 14.58
cure default, opportunity to 14.53
customary law 14.35
dispute resolution 14.13, 14.26–14.27
drafting 14.06, 14.13
European Union 4.38, 14.11–14.21
force majeure 7.100
freedom of contract 14.42
good faith and fair dealing 14.42, 14.44–14.48
governing law, as 14.18–14.22
interest 7.95–7.96
interpretation 14.50
Lando Commission 14.05, 14.07–14.08,
    14.11–14.12
legally binding, not intended to be 14.06–14.07,
    14.09
lex mercatoria 14.25, 14.29, 14.31–14.35
mandatory rules 14.58–14.62
nature 14.07–14.09
novation 14.56
pacta sunt servanda 14.43
performance, adequate assurances of 14.50
price, reduction in 14.53
purposes of 14.10–14.14
Rome Convention 1980 14.19–14.24
scope of 14.15–14.16
specific performance 7.74, 14.51–14.52
sphere of application 14.17–14.40
trade usage 14.35, 14.39
UN Sales Convention 7.74, 7.95–7.96, 7.100,
    14.06, 14.51, 14.55
Principles of International Commercial Contracts
    see **UNIDROIT Principles of**
    International Commercial Contracts
private international law *see* **conflict of laws**
privileges and immunities 3.67–3.68, 12.22
professional organizations, harmonization and 5.33
property
connecting factors 2.37–2.41
German Code of Civil Procedure 16.18
Insolvency Regulation 15.29–15.30
jurisdiction 16.13, 16.18–16.19, 16.22
UN Assignment of Receivables Convention
    2001 11.30, 11.39–11.40, 18.10
provisional and protective measures 16.43–16.51
Aircraft Protocol to Cape Town Convention
    3.66, 12.34
Brussels I Regulation 16.45
Cape Town Convention 2001 3.66, 12.34, 16.45

EC law 16.45
freezing injunctions 16.46–16.48
    criteria 16.46–16.48
    good arguable case 16.46
    worldwide 16.46–16.48
harmonization 16.50
ICC Arbitration Rules 17.55
injunctions (restraining orders) 16.46–16.49
public law 1.02
public policy (*ordre public*) 2.48–2.50
arbitration awards 17.129
Brussels I Regulation 16.60
conflict of laws 2.48–2.50
contract, mandatory rules in the law of
    2.52, 2.56
enforcement of judgments 15.32, 16.60
foreign law, application of 2.48–2.49
Hague Securities Convention 2002 2.50, 13.25
Inter-American Convention on the Law
    Applicable to Certain Contracts
    1994 2.50
recognition and enforcement of foreign judgments
    16.60
Rome Convention 1980 2.50
substantive law, court's own 2.48–2.49
UNCITRAL Model Arbitration Law 17.129

questionnaires 4.56–4.57, 6.07, 12.03

Rail Protocol to the Cape Town Convention, *see*
    Luxembourg Protocol to the Cape Town
    Convention
rail transport 12.09, 12.17
receivables financing 11.01–11.04 *see also* **UN**
    Assignment of Receivables in
    International Trade Convention 2001,
    UNIDROIT International Factoring
    Convention 1998
Cape Town Convention 2001 11.04
asset-based finance, as 11.02
assignment 11.01
civil law 11.03
common law 11.03
factoring 11.01, 11.05
international regime, need for 11.03–11.04
nature of 11.01–11.02
non-recourse finance 11.02
receivables, meaning of 11.01
securitization 11.02
special purpose vehicles, use of 11.02
transfer 11.01
UN Assignment of Receivables in International
    Trade Convention 2001 11.04
recitals 13.32

recognition and enforcement of arbitral awards
17.61, 17.133–17.143
conflict of laws 17.79–17.109
defensive process, recognition as 17.134
delocalization debate 17.138–17.139
harmonization 17.61
merits of awards 17.137
New York Arbitration Convention 1958 17.38,
17.135–17.138
refusal 17.38, 17.135–17.143
stateless awards 17.138–17.139
UNCITRAL Model Arbitration Law 17.34,
17.135–17.137
recognition and enforcement of judgments
Brussels Convention 1968 16.60
Brussels I Regulation 16.60
foreign judgments 16.04, 16.60–16.61
Insolvency Regulation 15.31–15.34
MERCOSUR 16.61
public policy 15.32
regions
arbitration 17.24
civil procedure 16.07
conflict of laws 18.14–18.16
development banks 5.17
European Union 1.31
growth of regionalism 1.31
Hague Conference on Private International Law
6.44
harmonization 1.31, 5.17, 6.43–6.45, 18.14
regional economic integration organizations
16.07
regional instruments 1.54
sources of transnational commercial law, regional
instruments as 1.55
renvoi see conflict of laws
research 4.56–4.57
reservation of title 12.27, 12.30, 15.30
reservations and declarations in treaties 3.69,
19.14
Aircraft Protocol 12.51, 19.14
Cape Town Convention 2001 19.14
Hague Securities Convention 19.14
interpretation 19.13–19.14
UN Sales Convention 7.16–7.29, 18.14
Vienna Convention on the Law of Treaties 19.14
restatements *see also* restatements of contract law
American Restatements 2.18, 2.35, 16.18,
16.22
choice of law 2.19
conflict of laws 2.18–2.20, 16.18
harmonization 5.14, 5.16, 20.01
international organizations 5.14
sources 1.55, 1.58, 5.16

restatements of contract law 14.04–14.62 *see also*
Principles of European Contract Law,
UNIDROIT Principles of International
Commercial Contracts
American Law Institute 1.58, 14.04
comparative law 4.33, 4.38
European Civil Code project 1.58
Inter-American Convention on the Law
Applicable to International Contracts
14.01, 14.20–14.22, 14.24
soft law 1.58, 14.01
restraining orders 16.49
Rhodian law 1.15
road transport 18.12–18.13, 19.11, 19.16
Rolls of Oléron 1.16, 1.19, 4.04
Roman law 1.18, 4.04, 4.07–4.09
Rome Convention on the Law Applicable to
Contractual Obligations 1980
choice of law 14.20–14.21
CMR Convention 18.13
conflict between conventions 18.13
conflict of laws 2.05, 18.13
harmonization 14.01, 14.03
lex mercatoria 1.40
mandatory rules 2.51, 2.53
party autonomy 14.22
public policy 2.50
renvoi 2.60
UNIDROIT Principles of International
Commercial Contracts 14.20–14.24
Rome I Regulation on the law applicable to
contractual obligations, proposal for
harmonization 14.03
mandatory rules 2.54–2.55

Saleilles, Raymond 4.24
Savigny, Friedrich Carl von 2.12, 2.15, 2.17, 4.49
Scandinavian legal systems 4.07
Schmitthoff, Clive 2.12
secretariats
explanatory reports 6.25
harmonization 6.04, 6.25
ideas from 6.04
importance of 6.04
UNCITRAL 5.30
UNIDROIT 5.24, 5.25
secured transactions
harmonization, political problems of
20.06–20.08
leasing 20.06
Legal Transition Programme of the EBRD 1.14
model law 20.06–20.07
UNCITRAL 20.07
UNIDROIT 20.06–20.07

securities, transactions in 13.01–13.41 *see also*
    Hague Securities Interests Convention
    2002, securities transactions, conflict of
    laws and
  UN Assignment of Receivables Convention
    2001 11.34
  UNIDROIT draft Harmonized Rules Regarding
    Intermediated Securities Convention
    13.40–13.41, 18.07
securities transactions, conflict of laws and, *and see*
    Hague Securities Convention 2002
  Clearstream 13.10, 13.34
  Collateral Directive 13.32–13.33, 13.36
  Euroclear 13.10, 13.34
  Settlement Finality Directive *see* Settlement
    Finality Directive
service
  Brussels Convention 1968 16.17
  civil procedure 16.51–16.55
  EC law 16.55, 16.59
  Hague Service Convention 1965 16.06,
    16.56–16.59
Settlement Finality Directive 13.28–13.31
  aims 13.28, 13.30
  Collateral Directive 13.32
  Germany 13.35–13.36
  Hague Securities Convention 2002 13.31
  insolvency 13.28, 13.30
  scope 13.29
  securities, transactions in 13.28–13.31, 13.35
  systemic risks 13.28
ships, Cape Town Convention 2001 and 12.05,
  18.05
socialist legal systems 4.07
soft law
  advantages of 3.06
  customary law 3.06
  definition 3.06
  forms of 3.06
  harmonization 14.01
  international law, relationship with 3.05–3.06
  norms or principles, as 3.06
  restatements 1.58, 14.01
  treaties, alternatives to 3.06
sources of international law 3.19–3.20
sources of national commercial law 1.32–1.36
  common law, suppletive rules of 1.35
  contract 1.33
  course of dealing 1.33
  restatements 5.16
  usage 1.34
sources of transnational commercial law 1.03,
  1.37, 1.52–1.59
  autonomous transnational commercial law 1.38

civil procedure 16.06–16.08
general principles of international law 1.59, 1.67
international and regional instruments 1.54
judicial or legislative parallelism, conscious or
  unconscious 1.55
lex mercatoria 1.53, 1.60
positivism 1.42
restatements of scholars 1.58
rules and trade terms of international
  organizations 1.56
standard terms 1.50
treaties 3.26–3.31, 5.16
South Africa 4.09
sovereign immunity *see* state immunity
Space Protocol of Cape Town Convention 2001
  12.08, 12.17, 20.08
special commissions 6.14, 6.17
special purpose vehicles 1.08, 11.02
specific performance 7.73–7.74, 7.105,
  14.51–14.52
standard forms
  agency 8.04
  battle of the forms 7.71
  distribution 8.04
  general conditions of contract 5.13
  harmonization 5.13
  ICC Agency Model Contract 8.04
  international organizations 5.13
  lex mercatoria 1.49–1.51
  sources of transnational commercial law 1.50
  UN Sales Convention 7.71
  UNIDROIT International Financial Leasing
    Convention 1988 1.50
standby credits 9.08, 9.11, 9.29, 9.46–9.54
stare decisis 19.03, 19.23
state immunity
  characterization 16.10
  civil procedure 16.09–16.12
  commercial activities 3.03
  comparative law 4.29–4.30
  enforcement 3.03
  execution, immunity from 16.12
  harmonization 1.55
  international law 3.10
  restrictive 3.03, 16.10
  treaties 3.03, 16.09–16.10
  waiver 16.10
state practice 3.21, 3.23–3.24
state responsibility
  Cape Town Convention 2001 3.65–3.68
  corporations 3.63–3.68
  diplomatic protection 3.63–3.68
  International Law Commission Draft Articles
    3.61–3.62

investment treaties 3.63, 3.65
treaties 3.60–3.68
Washington Convention on the Settlement of
    Investment Disputes between States and
    Nationals of Other States 1965 3.65
wrongful acts, for 3.60–3.68
stateless arbitration awards 17.63, 17.65,
    17.79–17.109, 17.138–17.139
Story, Joseph 2.12, 2.15–2.16
study groups 4.72–4.73, 5.25, 6.14, 6.18
substantive law
characterization or classification of causes of
    action 2.46
conflict of laws 2.04–2.05, 18.06–18.07
court's own 2.46
harmonization 5.06, 14.01, 15.12
Insolvency Regulation 15.12
Principles of European Contract Law 14.35, 14.39
public policy 2.48–2.49
securities, transactions in 13.37
treaties and conventions 3.39–3.40
UN Assignment of Receivables Convention 2001
    11.30, 11.40
suretyship guarantees 9.07, 9.33

takeover bids 13.02
tort
characterization or classification of causes of
    action 2.45
connecting factors 2.22
place of the wrong 2.22
trade usage 1.13
binding, becoming 1.61–1.64
comparative law 4.47
consistency of determination of 4.47
contract 1.33
customary international law 3.21–3.23, 3.25,
    7.69
    distinguished from 1.34, 1.64
external validation 1.63
general principles of international law 1.53, 1.66
Hague Choice of Court Agreements Convention
    2005 16.37
harmonization 4.47, 5.12
Incoterms 7.67
international law 3.05
international organizations, rules of 5.12
judicial decisions 1.64
lex mercatoria 1.04, 1.53, 1.60–1.67
meaning 1.34, 7.69
normative force of 1.61–1.64
self-validating, as 1.62
treaties and conventions 1.65, 3.02, 3.05
UN Sales Convention 7.66–7.69

UNCITRAL Independent Guarantees and
    Standby Letters of Credit Convention
    1995 9.53
UNIDROIT Principles of International
    Commercial Contracts 14.35, 14.39
Uniform Customs and Practice for Documentary
    Credits 1.64, 9.14, 9.20
unwritten 1.34, 1.64
Vienna Sales Convention 1.64, 1.65
transnational commercial law
nature and sources 1.03, 1.37
transport *see also* **air transport, Cape Town**
    Convention on International Interests in
    Mobile Equipment 2001
carriage of goods, passing of risk and
    7.101–7.103
CMR Convention 18.12–18.13, 19.12, 19.16
EC law, air transport liability regime in 6.45
expertise of law-makers 20.10
Geneva Convention on the International
    Recognition of Rights in Aircraft 1948
    2.39
International Maritime Organization (IMO)
    5.17, 6.03
interpretation 4.44–4.45
maritime law 1.15–1.16, 1.19, 4.04
Maritime Liens and Mortgages Convention
    1926 2.39
rail transport 12.09, 12.17
road transport 18.12–18.13, 19.11, 19.16
treaties and conventions 1.03, 18.11–18.13
travaux préparatoires 3.49, 3.57, 19.04, 19.18
treaties and conventions *see also* **interpretation of**
    treaties and conventions, particular
    conventions (eg Warsaw Convention on
    International Carriage by Air 1929)
accession 3.30
binding parties only 3.30
co-existence of conventions 18.12–18.13
concurrence of treaties 18.12–18.13
conflicts between conventions 3.72–3.73,
    18.11–18.18
constitutional law 3.02, 3.08
corporations, standing of 3.01
customary international law *see* **customary**
    international law
declarations 2.58–2.60, 19.14
denunciation 3.70–3.71
depositary, functions of 3.02, 3.45
domestic courts, jurisdiction of 3.10
domestic law 3.07–3.08, 17.140–17.143
EC law 3.15–3.18, 5.19
enforcement of private rights against states 3.03,
    3.05, 3.60–3.68

treaties and conventions (*cont.*)
  entry into force 3.42
  errors in the text 3.46
  explanatory reports 6.19, 6.24
  final clauses 3.41–3.46
  Hague Conference on Private International Law
    5.19–5.21
  investment treaties 3.10, 3.13, 3.63, 3.65
  nature of 3.01–3.18
  organizations, creation of 3.02
  preamble 3.33–3.35
    importance of 3.33, 3.35
  private parties, enforcement by 3.63–3.68
  ratification 3.08, 3.30
  reservations 3.69, 19.14
  sources of Treaty law 3.26–3.31
  sphere of application 3.37–3.38
  standing 3.01
  state immunity 3.03, 16.09–16.10
  state responsibility 3.60–3.68
  state sovereignty 3.09
  states
    dispute resolution 3.02
    duties imposed by private law conventions on
      3.02
    enforcement 3.03, 3.05, 3.60–3.68
  successive treaties, conflict between 3.73
  third states bound by treaties 3.30
  treaty, meaning of 3.27
  typical structure of private law conventions
    3.32–3.46
  United Kingdom 3.08
  United States, self-executing treaties in 3.08
  Vienna Convention on the Law of Treaties 1969
    3.26, 3.30, 3.45–3.46, 3.69, 19.06,
    19.14–19.15
  withdrawal 3.70–3.71
tribunal, proposal for international 19.16–19.17
Twelve Tables of Roman Law 4.04

UCP *see* **Uniform Customs and Practices for**
    Documentary Credits (UCP)
UN Commission on International Trade Law *see*
    UNCITRAL
UN Convention on Assignment of Receivables in
    International Trade 2001 11.04,
    11.29–11.40
  Cape Town Convention 2001 3.44
  conflict of laws 2.62, 11.30, 11.39–11.40, 18.10
  connecting factors 18.10
  debtor provisions 11.38
  effectiveness of assignments 11.36
  exclusions 11.32, 11.33, 11.35
  international assignments 18.10

  international receivables 18.10
  internationality 11.33
  interpretation 11.30
  negotiable instruments 11.35
  non-market assignments 11.32
  notice of assignment 11.38
  novation 11.35
  property 11.30, 11.39–11.40, 18.10
  registration 11.39–11.40
  relations between assignor and assignee 11.37
  security, assignments by way of 11.34
  set-off 11.38
  sphere of application 11.31–11.35
UN Convention on Independent Guarantees and
    Standby Letters of Credit 1995 9.51–9.53
  features of 9.51–9.52
  rules, recognition of international 9.53
  Uniform Customs and Practice 9.51–9.53
  Uniform Rules for Demand Guarantees (URDG)
    9.52–9.53
  usage, recognition of 9.53
UN Economic Commission for Europe (ECE)
    5.17, 6.44
UN Sales Convention (CISG) 7.01–7.106
  application, sphere of 7.09–7.13, 7.39,
    18.01–18.06
  autonomous 7.38–7.45
  avoidance 7.78, 7.85–7.87
  battle of the forms 7.71
  buyers
    duties 7.77
    remedies 7.75–7.76
  carriage of goods, passing of risk and
    7.101–7.103
  civil law 7.105
  CLOUT database 7.44
  commentaries 7.24, 7.45
  common law and civil law principles, bringing
    together 7.105
  conflict of laws 2.21, 2.61, 7.12, 7.19–7.29,
    18.05, 18.14–18.16, 18.18
  connecting factors 7.14–7.19, 18.09
    both parties in contracting states 7.15
    rules of private international law leading to law
      of contracting state 7.16–7.26
  consumer sales, exclusion of 7.11, 18.03
  contracting out 7.32–7.35, 7.68
  contracts of sale covered, types of 7.11
  death or personal injury, exclusion of liability for
    7.31
  drafting 18.01
  exclusions 7.30–7.35, 7.104, 18.03–18.04
    consumer sales 7.11, 18.03
    implied 7.33–7.34

passing of property 7.30, 18.04
validity of contracts 18.30, 18.04
exemptions for non-performance 7.97–7.100
faux amis, problem of 7.39–7.40
force majeure 7.97–7.100, 7.105, 14.55
  frustration 7.98
  Principles of European Contract Law 7.100
  UNIDROIT Principles of International
    Commercial Contracts 7.100
formation of contracts of sale 7.70–7.71
frustration 7.98
fundamental breach 7.77–7.87
genesis of convention 7.02–7.08
general principles 7.55–7.65
good faith 7.46–7.65, 14.44
Hague Uniform Law on the Formation of
    Contracts for the International Sale of
    Goods 1964 7.03–7.07
Hague Uniform Law on the International Sale of
    Goods 1964 7.03–7.07, 18.14
Incoterms 7.35, 7.67
interest 7.61, 7.64, 7.88–7.96
  Principles of European Contract Law
    7.95–7.96
  UNIDROIT Principles of International
    Commercial Contracts 7.95–7.96
International Sales Convention Advisory Council
    (CISG-AC) 7.45
internationality requirement 7.12–7.13, 19.11
interpretation 3.47, 7.36–7.45, 7.106,
    19.07–19.09, 19.11
law reporting 19.19
manufacture or production, contracts for 7.11
non-performance, exemptions for 7.97–7.100
OHADA 18.17
origins 7.07
passing of property, exclusion relating to 7.30,
    18.04
passing of risk 7.101–7.103
personal injury, exclusion of liability for 7.31
place of business of parties 7.12, 7.16–7.29
remedies
  buyers 7.75–7.76
  sellers 7.77
renvoi 7.28
reservations 7.16–7.29, 18.14
rights of parties 7.73–7.77
risk, passing of 7.101–7.103
rules of private international law leading to law of
    contracting state 7.16–7.26
sellers
  duties of 7.75–7.76
  remedies 7.77
services, contracts for 7.11

specific performance 7.73–7.74
sphere of application 7.09–7.13, 7.39,
    18.01–18.06
trade usage 1.64, 1.65
UNCITRAL 7.07, 10.20
UNIDROIT 7.03
  Principles of International Commercial
    Contracts 7.64–7.65, 7.73, 7.95–7.96,
    7.100, 14.06, 14.37, 14.40, 14.51, 14.55
Unilex database 7.44
United Kingdom 7.08
United States 7.16–7.17, 7.20–7.23
validity of contract, exclusion relating to 7.30,
    18.04
UNCITRAL *see also* **UNCITRAL Arbitration**
    Rules, UN Assignment of Receivables in
    International Trade Convention 2001,
    UNCITRAL Model Arbitration Law,
    UNCITRAL Model Law on Cross
    Border Insolvency 1997
co-ordination with other organizations 5.28,
    5.34, 20.12
database infrastructure, provision of 5.31
General Assembly 5.29, 5.30
harmonization 5.04, 5.28–5.31, 5.33
  approval of text 6.17
  Commission 6.17
  instruments, types of 6.15
  legislative activities, co-ordination of 5.34
  process 6.03, 6.08
  UNIDROIT, overlap with 6.08
Independent Guarantees and Standby Letters of
    Credit Convention 1995 9.51–9.53
languages 20.19
mandate 5.28
members 5.29
Secretariat 5.30
secured transactions 20.07
sources, providing access to 5.31
UN Sales Convention 7.07
UNIDROIT 6.13
working groups 5.30
UNCITRAL Arbitration Rules 17.40,
    17.43–17.59
arbitrators 17.45–17.49
  appointment 17.45–17.46
  challenging 17.48
  independence or impartiality 17.47–17.48
  replacement of 17.49
awards 17.56–17.58
choice of law 17.120
commencement of arbitration 17.43–17.44
conflict of laws 17.51
conservatory and interim measures 17.55

UNCITRAL Arbitration Rules (*cont.*)
costs 17.59
evidence 17.53
harmonization 5.09, 17.40, 17.43–17.59
notice of arbitration 17.43
party autonomy 17.64
procedure 17.50–17.55
UNCITRAL Model Arbitration Law 1.29, 17.23,
 17.27–17.34
arbitrability, concept of 17.29
arbitration agreement 17.28, 17.32
arbitrators
 appointment of 17.30
 challenging 17.30
 composition of 17.30
 impartiality 17.30
awards 17.34, 17.125–17.130
 fair procedure 17.128
 mistake of law or fact 17.130–17.131
 public policy 17.129
 recognition and enforcement of 7.135–7.136
choice of law 17.113–17.114, 17.116, 17.118,
 17.120–17.121
commercial arbitration, meaning of 17.19–17.20
conduct of proceedings 17.32
conflict of laws 17.30, 17.108–17.109,
 17.113–17.114
 choice of law 17.113–17.114, 17.116, 17.118,
  17.120–17.121
 party autonomy 17.116
 rules of law, meaning of 17.113–17.114,
  17.118, 17.121
courts, supervisory role of 17.27
definition of international arbitration 17.16–17.18
delocalization debate 17.109
flexibility 17.25
harmonization 5.09, 17.23, 17.27–17.34
ICC Arbitration Rules 17.18
jurisdiction 17.31
mistake of law or fact 17.130–17.131
party autonomy 17.27, 17.60, 17.116
public policy 17.129
recognition of foreign awards 17.34
recourse against award 17.34
rules of law chosen by parties 17.30,
 17.113–17.114, 17.118, 17.121
termination of proceedings 17.33
UNCITRAL Arbitration Rules 17.27
UNCITRAL Model Law on Cross Border
 Insolvency 1997 15.02, 15.12–15.21
aims 15.15
automatic stay 15.20
binding force, having no 15.15
collective proceedings 15.17

co-operation with foreign courts and foreign
 representatives 15.21
foreign courts 15.16, 15.21
foreign proceedings 15.16–15.17
foreign representatives
 access by 15.18–15.19
 co-operation with 15.21
 relief, forms of 15.19
Guide to Enactment 15.13
harmonization 15.12
nature and purpose 15.14–15.15
recognition of foreign proceedings 15.18–15.19
relief, forms of 15.19
reorganization 15.17
sphere of application 15.16–15.17
standing 15.18
stay 15.20
substantive law 15.12
winding up 15.17
UNCTAD (UN Conference on Trade and
 Development) 6.03
UNESCO (UN Educational, Scientific, and
 Cultural Organization) 6.03
UNIDROIT
agency, convention on 8.17–8.27
ALI/UNIDROIT Principles of Transnational
 Civil Procedure 16.62–16.65
 access to information and evidence 16.65
 discovery 16.65
 commercial and non-commercial disputes,
  distinction between 16.62
 jurisdiction 16.64
Cape Town Convention, *see* **Cape Town**
 Convention on International Interests in
 Mobile Equipment
committees of government experts 5.26
comparative law 4.03, 4.33, 4.38
diplomatic conferences 5.25–5.26, 6.19
EC law 6.44–6.45
franchising 8.30
General Assembly 5.24
Governing Council 5.24, 5.25, 6.13, 6.17, 6.18
Guide to International Master Franchise
 Arrangements 8.30
harmonization 5.03–5.04, 5.07, 5.22–5.27, 5.33
 UNCITRAL, overlap with 6.08
 working groups 6.13
instruments, types of 6.15
Intermediated Securities Convention (draft) 18.07
League of Nations 5.04
library 5.27
members 5.22–5.23
OHADA 4.33
publications 5.27

Secretariat 5.24, 5.25
secured transactions 20.06–20.07
securities, transactions in 13.40–13.41
statute 5.23
structure 5.24
study groups 5.25, 6.18
UN Sales Convention 7.03
UNCITRAL 6.08
Uniform Law Review 5.27
UNILEX 7.44
working methods 5.25, 6.13
UNIDROIT Agency in the International Sale of
Goods Convention 1983 8.17–8.27
assessment of Convention 8.25–8.27
authority 8.22–8.23
commission 8.18
common law and civil law 8.18–8.19, 8.22
connecting factor 8.21
direct and indirect representation 8.18
disclosed agency 8.18
external aspects of agency 8.19, 8.21
good faith 8.23
internationality 8.21
legal effect of acts of agent 8.22–8.23
principal/agent relationship 8.24
sphere of application 8.21
termination 8.24
UN Sales Convention, relationship with 8.20
undisclosed agency 8.18
UNIDROIT International Factoring Convention
1988 11.04, 11.11–11.28
assignment 11.14–11.16, 11.21–11.23,
11.25–11.26
barriers to acquisition of receivables, removal of
11.21–11.25
conflict of laws 11.12, 11.16–11.17
connecting factors 11.17
defences 11.26
derogation 11.18
entry into force 11.11
evaluation 11.28
exclusions 11.18
general principles 11.20
general provisions 3.37
genesis of Convention 11.11–11.12
insolvency 11.27
interpretation 3.52–3.54, 11.19–11.20
no-assignment clauses 11.23
place of business in different states 11.16
Principles of European Contract Law 11.23,
11.25–11.26
priority rules 11.15
set-off 11.26
sphere of application 3.37, 11.13–11.18

transfer 11.22
types of transaction 11.14
UNIDROIT Leasing Convention 1988, conflict
with 3.72
UNIDROIT Principles of International
Commercial Contracts 11.25–11.26
Uniform Commercial Code (United States)
11.22, 11.24–11.25
unjust enrichment 11.27
UNIDROIT International Financial Leasing
Convention 1988 1.50, 3.33, 3.72,
10.01–10.27
accounting rules, capitalization of future rentals in
10.02
background 10.02–10.06
characteristics of transactions 10.03–10.06,
10.08–10.10
conflict of laws 2.61
connecting factors 10.13
damages 10.22, 10.26
default remedies of lessor 10.26
developing countries 10.27
exclusions 10.14
governing law of contracting states 10.13
hire-purchase 10.06
insolvency, protection against 10.24–10.25
internationality principle 10.12
personal, family or household purposes,
equipment not used for 10.11
place of business
contracting states, in 10.13
different states, lessor and lessee having place of
business in 10.12
purpose of Convention 10.15
remedies of lessor, default 10.26
removal of responsibility from lessor to supplier
10.16–10.22
sale and lease back 10.01
security agreements, finance leases as 10.06
sphere of application 10.07–10.13
suppliers
conferment of rights against the supplier
10.19–10.20
exculpation of lessor from liability under the
leasing agreement 10.21–10.22
removal of responsibility from lessor to supplier
10.16–10.22
tax 10.04
third parties, liability to 10.23
title finance 10.01
UNIDROIT International Interests in Mobile
Equipment Convention 2001 *see* **Cape**
Town Convention on International
Interests in Mobile Equipment 2001

UNIDROIT Model Franchise Disclosure Law
  8.30–8.35
  agency 8.03
  contract law 8.31
  disclosure documents, delivery of 8.33–8.34
  information 8.33
  misrepresentation 8.34
  Principles of European Contract Law 8.31
  scope of application 8.32
  UNIDROIT Principles of International
    Commercial Contracts 8.31
  waiver 8.35
UNIDROIT Principles of International
    Commercial Contracts 1.58, 8.28,
    14.01, 14.05–14.62
  agency 8.03, 8.28, 14.57
    external aspects 8.03, 8.05
    internal aspects 8.03, 8.05
  arbitration 14.26–14.32, 14.35–14.36,
    14.40–14.41, 17.01
  assignment 14.56
  choice of law 2.31, 14.20–14.27
  common law 14.38, 14.40
  conflict of laws 2.13, 14.09
  connecting factors 2.31
  contract, incorporation into 14.09, 14.18–14.19,
    14.26, 14.58
  cure default, opportunity to 14.53
  customary law 14.35
  dispute resolution 14.13, 14.26–14.27
  domestic law, supplementing or interpreting
    14.38
  drafting 14.06, 14.13
  duplication 14.11–14.14
  editions 14.06
  evidence, range of 14.49
  exclusions 14.61–14.62
  force majeure 7.100
  general principles of law 7.64–7.65,
    14.29–14.30
  good faith and fair dealing 14.38, 14.40, 14.42,
    14.44–14.48
  governing law, as 14.18–14.22
  hardship 14.34, 14.40, 14.54–14.55
  harmonization 14.01
  interest 7.95–7.96
  interpretation 14.49, 19.19, 19.22
  law reporting 19.19
  legally binding, not intended to be 14.06–14.07,
    14.09
  lex mercatoria 14.25, 14.29, 14.31–14.35
  mandatory rules 14.58–14.62
  Model Franchise Disclosure Law 8.31
  nature of principles 14.07–14.09

  novation 14.56
  pacta sunt servanda 14.43
  performance, adequate assurances of 14.50
  price, reduction in 14.53
  Principles of European Contract Law
    14.11–14.16, 14.33
  purposes of 14.10–14.14
  remedies 14.53
  Rome Convention 1980 14.20–14.24
  specific performance 7.73, 14.51–14.52
  sphere of application 14.17–14.40
  supplement to other international instruments, as
    14.37, 14.40
  trade usage 14.35, 14.39
  UN Sales Convention 7.64–7.65, 7.73,
    7.95–7.96, 7.100, 14.06, 14.37, 14.40,
    14.51, 14.55
  UNIDROIT International Factoring Convention
    11.25–11.26
unification of international commercial law,
    proposal for 4.35–4.37
Uniform Commercial Code (United States) 1.11,
    4.67, 11.22, 11.24–11.25, 13.34
Uniform Customs and Practices for Documentary
    Credits (UCP) 9.14–9.28
  acceptance 9.17
  advising bank 9.16
  apparent good order of documents 9.22
  autonomy principle 9.19, 9.22
  classification of credits by payment method
    9.17
  conformity 9.21, 9.24
  contracts
    incorporation into 9.11–9.12, 9.14
    theory of 9.20
  course of dealing 9.14
  deferred payment 9.17
  documentary character of the credit 9.21
  documents to be presented 9.15
  drafts 9.11
  eUCP 9.26–9.28
  fraud 9.19, 9.22–9.23
  good faith 9.22
  harmonization 5.12
  irrevocable credits 9.20
  issue, taking effect upon 9.20
  negotiation 9.17
  novation 9.25
  opening of a credit 9.16
  principals not agents, banks dealing as 9.23
  principles of documentary credits law
    9.18–9.25
  revisions 9.11
  sight payment 9.17

standby credits 9.46
trade usage 1.64, 9.14, 9.20
transfer 9.25
UCP 500 9.14, 9.46
UCP 600 9.14, 9.46
UN Independent Guarantees and Stand-by
    Letters of Credit Convention 1995
    9.51–9.53
Uniform Rules for Contract Bonds (ICC)
    9.54–9.58
contracts
    applicable law 9.58
    incorporation into 9.55
default 9.56
governing law 9.57–9.58
ICC Rules of Conciliation and Arbitration 9.58
jurisdiction 9.57–9.58
Uniform Rules for Demand Guarantees 9.54
Uniform Rules for Demand Guarantees (URDG)
    (ICC) 9.29–9.45
advantages 9.36
breach, statements of 9.41–9.42
conformity 9.40
counter-guarantees, law governing 9.44–9.45
demand for payment 9.40–9.41
direct and indirect guarantees, application
    to 9.35
extend or pay demands 9.42
fundamental principles 9.37–9.38
governing law 9.44
guarantee structures 9.35
independent character 9.34, 9.38
international character 9.34
irrevocability 9.39
jurisdiction 9.44
letters of credit, distinguished from 9.31–9.32
Model Forms for Issuing Demand Guarantees 9.29
purpose of 9.29
standby credits 9.29, 9.46
statements of breach 9.41–9.42
success 9.30
suretyship guarantees, distinguished from 9.33
termination 9.43
UNCITRAL Independent Guarantees and
    Standby Letters of Credit Convention
    1995 9.52–9.53
Uniform Rules for Contract Bonds 9.54
Uniform Rules for Contract Guarantees
    1978 9.29
uniformity, interpretation and 19.01–19.24
Aircraft Protocol
    contract practice 19.22
    review clauses and review conferences 19.20
autonomous interpretation 19.09

civil law and common law, comparison
    between 4.43
codes 19.02
consistency in interpretation 4.42–4.46,
    19.01–19.03
divergences, importance of 19.23–19.24
domestic courts, interpretation by 19.01–19.09,
    19.11, 19.15, 19.23
European Court of Justice 19.16
Global Uniform Commercial Code 19.12
international tribunal, desirability of
    19.16–19.17
internationalism 1.25–1.28
law reporting 19.03, 19.19
lex mercatoria 19.22
New York Convention 1958 19.20, 19.24
obstacles 19.01–19.04
party autonomy 19.11
precedent (*stare decisis*) 19.03, 19.23
Québec Civil Code 19.02
reservations and declarations 19.13–19.14
travaux préparatoires 19.04, 19.18
UN Sales Convention 19.07–19.09, 19.11,
    19.19
UNIDROIT Principles of International
    Commercial Contracts 19.19, 19.22
uniform system of interpretation 19.10–19.12
Vienna Convention on the Law of Treaties 19.06,
    19.15
United Nations Convention on International Trade
    Law *see* **UNCITRAL**
United States
alternative dispute resolution 17.12
choice of law 16.18, 16.30, 16.32
conflict of laws 2.18–2.21, 16.18
jurisdiction 16.20–16.23, 16.30–16.32
minimum contacts test 16.20–16.23
modernization 16.20–16.21
restatements 2.18, 16.18, 16.22
treaties, self-executing 3.08
Uniform Commercial Code 1.11, 4.67, 11.22,
    11.24–11.25
universalism
comparative law 4.05
home country 15.07
insolvency 15.06–15.09
modified 15.08
qualified 15.09
university law schools 4.04
usage *see* **trade usage**

Vienna Convention on Contracts for the
    International Sale of Goods 1980 (CISG)
    see **UN Sales Convention (CISG)**

Vienna Convention on Treaties 1969 3.26, 3.30,
    3.45–3.49, 3.52, 3.56, 3.59, 3.69, 19.06,
    19.14–19.15

Warsaw Convention on International Carriage by
    Air 1929
  conflict of laws 2.10–2.12, 2.62
  entry into force 2.12
  interpretation 4.44–4.45
  jurisdiction 2.10

Montreal Convention 1999 2.12
Washington Convention on the Settlement of
    Investment Disputes between States and
    Nationals of Other States 1965 3.65
working groups 5.30, 6.13–6.14
World Bank 5.17
World Intellectual Property Organization (WIPO)
    5.17

Zweigert, Konrad 4.21, 4.23, 4.50